macromedia
COLDFUSION® MX

Web Application Construction Kit

Ben Forta and Nate Weiss
with Leon Chalnick and Angela Buraglia

Macromedia ColdFusion MX Web Application Construction Kit, Fifth Edition

Ben Forta and Nate Weiss
with Leon Chalnick and Angela Buraglia

Published by Macromedia Press, in association with Peachpit Press,
a divison of Pearson Education

Macromedia Press
1249 Eighth Street, Berkeley, CA 94710
510/524-2178 • Fax: 510/524-2221

Find us on the World Wide Web at:
http://www.peachpit.com
http://www.macromedia.com

To report errors, please send a note to errata@peachpit.com

Editor: Angela Kozlowski
Production Coordinator: Connie Jeung-Mills
Copyeditors: Hon Walker, Gail Nelson-Bonebrake, Christine McGeever
Technical Editors: Jim Schley, Chris Hiester
Composition: Happenstance Type-O-Rama
Indexer: Joy Dean Lee
Cover Design: Happenstance Type-O-Rama

ISBN 0-321-12516-9

9 8 7

Printed and bound in the United States of America

Dedication

What is there to say or do, Jon? Naomi? Dolores? Stan Sr.? —Nate Weiss

I would like to dedicate my contribution to this book to the excellent staff at Advanta Solutions, Inc. for their outstanding efforts in keeping our clients happy while I was busy working on this book.—Leon Chalnick

For my son Gaetano, with all my love.
—Angela C. Buraglia

CONTENTS AT A GLANCE

CONTENTS

ABOUT THE AUTHORS

Ben Forta is Macromedia Inc.'s Senior Product Evangelist, and has two decades of experience in the computer industry in product development, support, training, and marketing. Ben is the author of the best-selling *ColdFusion Web Application Construction Kit* and its sequel *Advanced ColdFusion Application Development*, as well as books on SQL, JavaServer Pages, WAP, Windows development, and more. Over 1 million Ben Forta books have been printed in a dozen languages worldwide. Ben co-authored the official Macromedia ColdFusion training material, as well as the certification tests and Macromedia Press study guides for those tests, and is now working on several new titles dedicated to Macromedia's new MX platform. He writes regular columns on ColdFusion and Internet development, and now spends a considerable amount of time lecturing and speaking on application development worldwide. Ben welcomes your e-mail at ben@forta.com and invites you to visit his web site at http://www.forta.com/.

Nate Weiss has been building web applications for many years, most of them with ColdFusion. Along the way, he became an active member of the ColdFusion developer community as a member of what is now the Team Macromedia peer-to-peer support program, and by contributing popular custom tags and other free, reusable code at his website, `nateweiss.com`. He has spoken on various topics at many of Macromedia's ColdFusion developer conferences, has written articles for the developer's section of the Macromedia website, and put together the WDDX SDK at openwddx.org. Nate lives in Brooklyn with Stephanie, his foxy and charming lady-friend, loves the city and especially its fabulous Public Library, writes fiction on the fire escape when he's not working with ColdFusion, and is trying to write some music too. He is pleased and proud to help shape another edition in Ben Forta's distinctive series on ColdFusion development. Nate can be reached at nate@nateweiss.com.

Leon Chalnick is president of Advanta Solutions, Inc., a boutique software consulting firm headquartered in Los Angeles. Advanta specializes in streamlining complex business processes by developing Web-enabled applications. Advanta is a Macromedia Alliance Consulting Partner.

Since 1992, Mr. Chalnick has authored or co-authored several books and articles on programming and database design and has co-authored all but one edition of the ColdFusion Web Application Construction Kit.

Mr. Chalnick's technical expertise and entrepreneurial success fill his speaking venues at technical conferences. He is a founder of the Southern California ColdFusion User Group and has served as its president since 1998. Mr. Chalnick received his MBA from Northwestern University's Kellogg (Graduate) School of Management. Please visit: www.advantasolutions.com.

After six years as an independent film makeup artist, **Angela C. Buraglia** realized she wanted a career that would allow her to start a family and stay home with her husband and child. In an effort to give back to the Macromedia Dreamweaver newsgroup community that helped and encouraged her in her new career, she founded DreamweaverFAQ.com. Although she only intended to be a web developer, life's path has led her to become that and more. In addition to her contribution to this book, Angela is the Lead Technical Editor for the Dreamweaver MX Bible (Wiley Publishing, formerly Hungry Minds) and Contributing Author to Dreamweaver MX Magic (New Riders). Currently, she is also a Team Macromedia volunteer for Dreamweaver. Angela's future plans are to continue developing DreamweaverFAQ.com, to build and sell Dreamweaver extensions, to give presentations at conferences, and perhaps to become involved in new book projects. Long gone are the days of applying makeup; now Angela applies Behaviors and CSS to Web sites—and most importantly—is home with her little boy.

ACKNOWLEDGMENTS

Thanks to my co-authors, Nate Weiss, Leon Chalnick, and Angela Baraglia for their outstanding contributions—although this book is now affectionately known by thousands as “the Ben Forta book”, it is, in truth, as much theirs as it is mine. Thanks to my new Macromedia Press family for making me feel so welcome, and for granting me the creative freedom needed to create titles like these. Thanks to the thousands of you who write to me with comments, suggestions, and criticism (thankfully not too much of the latter)—I do read each and every message (and even attempt to reply to them all, eventually) and all are appreciated. A very special thank you to my acquisitions editor, Angela Kozlowski, who has been my advisor, slave-driver, partner, scheduling department, and muse since I published my first book way back when. And last, but by no means least, a heartfelt thank you to my wife Marcy for so many years of love, support, and encouragement – her tireless and selfless work make it possible for me to do what I do, it is she who deserves the real credit for all I have accomplished, and I would not be where I am today without her.—*Ben Forta*

Showers of thanks to my writing companions and sources of inspiration, specifically Stephanie Hawkins, Ben Forta, Jeanmarie Williams, and the Clinton Four (Matthew Gershoff, Jenny Lee Turner, and Stanley Williams). Influences include Sleater-Kinney, the Cocteau Twins, Patience, Fortitude, and the majestic Rose Reading Room at the Forty-Second Street Public Library in New York City, capital of the world. A *huge* shout out and general mad, frenzied thanks to Angela Kozlowski and everyone else at Peachpit who helped us deliver this book. Also, big ups to John “Giant Sandwich” Scott and Melissa “Press Nine” Caruso for giving me a home for a while there. Of course, I’ve just gotta name-check everyone at Macromedia that helped contribute to the quality of this edition, either directly or indirectly (especially, but of course not limited to, Jeremy Allaire, Camille Batarekh, Tim Buntel, Ray Camden, Damon Cooper, John Fisher, Tom Harwood, Peter Muzilla, Sim Simeonov, Edwin Smith, Peter Watson, and Spike Washburn). Finally, thanks to Mom, Dad, Liz, Ken, Carrie, Gigi, Don, Judith, Robin, and Cousin Sarah, and yes, there will be a quiz.—*Nate Weiss*

I would like to acknowledge the contribution of Muliadi Jeo, a senior consultant at Advanta Solutions, Inc. to the chapter on Development Methodologies. Muliadi wrote much of the code in the Fusebox example application presented in this chapter.—*Leon Chalnick*

If anyone were to tell me a year ago that I would be an author, I'd think they were crazy! One thing I know for sure is if it weren't for all the great people I've worked with over the last year, I wouldn't be writing this today. Certainly, if it were not for the help and encouragement of Wojciech Miskiweicz in my earliest days with Dreamweaver, I'd probably have given up and found another career. Thank you Wojciech! Daniel Short, Massimo Foti, Danilo Celic, Brad Halstead, Ray West, Paul R. Boon, Murray R. Summers, Trent Pastrana, Jay A. Grantham and Joseph Lowery, you've helped and inspired me more than you'll ever know and I am eternally thankful. There are too many DreamweaverFAQ.com tutorial authors to name you all , but I do want you to know I appreciate each and every one of you. To my wonderful husband Ambrogio, thank you for your incredible patience, understanding and for taking care of our adorable little Gaetano as I work on all my projects. I love you honey! Mom and Dad, if it weren't for your constant help and support I don't know what I'd do or where I'd be. Thank you for everything.—*Angela C. Buraglia*

IN THIS INTRODUCTION

Introduction

Who Should Use This Book

This book is written for anyone who wants to create cutting-edge Web-based applications.

If you are a Webmaster or Web page designer and want to create dynamic, data-driven Web pages, this book is for you. If you are an experienced database administrator who wants to take advantage of the Web to publish or collect data, this book is for you, too. If you are starting to create your Web presence but know you want to serve more than just static information, this book will help get you there. If you have used ColdFusion before and want to learn what's new in Macromedia ColdFusion MX, this book is also for you. Even if you are an experienced ColdFusion user, this book provides you with invaluable tips and tricks and also serves as the definitive ColdFusion developer's reference.

This book teaches you how to create real-world applications that solve real-world problems. Along the way, you acquire all the skills you need to design, implement, test, and roll out world-class applications.

How to Use This Book

This book is designed to serve two different, but complementary, purposes.

First, it is a complete tutorial of everything you need to know to harness ColdFusion's power. As such, the book is divided into four sections, each of which introduces new topics building on what has been discussed in prior sections. Ideally, you will work through these sections in order, starting with ColdFusion basics and then moving on to advanced topics.

Second, this book is an invaluable desktop reference tool. The appendixes and accompanying CD-ROM contain reference chapters that will be of use to you while developing ColdFusion applications. The reference chapters are cross-referenced to the appropriate tutorial sections, so that step-by-step information is always readily available.

NOTE

Now in its sixth major release, ColdFusion has matured into a massive application, and a single volume could not do justice to all its features. As such, this book is being released in conjunction with a second book, *Advanced ColdFusion MX Application Development* (Macromedia Press, ISBN: 0-321-12710-2).

Part I—Getting Started

Part I of this book introduces ColdFusion and explains what exactly it is that ColdFusion enables you to accomplish. Internet fundamentals are also introduced; a thorough understanding of these is a prerequisite to ColdFusion application development. This part also includes coverage of databases, SQL, Macromedia Dreamweaver MX, and everything else you need to know to get up and running quickly.

In Chapter 1, "Introducing ColdFusion," the core technologies upon which ColdFusion is built are introduced. The Internet and how it works are explained, as are DNS servers and URLs, Web servers and browsers, HTML, and Web server extensions. A good understanding of these technologies is a vital part of creating Web-based applications. This chapter also teaches you how ColdFusion works and explains its various components.

Chapter 2, "Building the Databases," provides a complete overview of databases and related terms. Databases are an integral part of almost every ColdFusion application, so database concepts and technologies must be well understood. Databases are mechanisms for storing and retrieving information, and almost every Web-based application you build will sit on top of a database of some kind. Key database concepts, such as tables, rows, columns, data types, keys, and indexes, are taught, as are the basics of the relational database model. You also learn the differences between client-server– and shared-file–based databases, as well as the pros and cons of each.

Chapter 3, "Accessing the ColdFusion Administrator," introduces the ColdFusion Administrator. This Web-based program, written in ColdFusion itself, manages and maintains every aspect of your ColdFusion Application Server.

To whet your appetite, Chapter 4, "Previewing ColdFusion," walks you through creating two real working applications using Macromedia Dreamweaver MX code generation, and manually, too.

In Chapter 5, "Introducing SQL," you learn the basics of the SQL language. SQL is a standard language for interacting with database applications, and all ColdFusion database manipulation is performed using SQL statements. The link between ColdFusion and your database itself is via database drivers, so this chapter introduces the technology and walks you through the process of creating data sources. This chapter also teaches you how to use the SQL `SELECT` statement.

Chapter 6, "SQL Data Manipulation," introduces three other important SQL statements: `INSERT`, `UPDATE`, and `DELETE`.

Chapter 7, "Introducing Macromedia Dreamweaver MX," introduces this brand-new ColdFusion development environment. Dreamweaver MX is a powerful HTML and CFML editor, as well as a mature and trusted page layout and design tool. You learn how to use the editor, how to work with sites, and how to configure the environment to work the way you do.

Part II—Using ColdFusion

With the introductions taken care of, Part II quickly moves on to real development. Starting with language basics and progressing to database-driven applications and more, the chapters here will make you productive using ColdFusion faster than you thought possible.

Chapter 8, "Using ColdFusion," introduces ColdFusion templates and explains how they are created and used. Variables are explained (including complex variable types, such as arrays and structures), as are CFML functions and the `<CFSET>` and `<CFOUTPUT>` tags.

Chapter 9, "CFML Basics," teaches all the major CFML program flow language elements. From if statements (using `<CFIF>`) to loops (using `<CFLOOP>`) to switch statements (using `<CFSWITCH>` and `<CFCASE>`) to template reuse (using `<CFINCLUDE>`), almost every tag that ColdFusion developers use regularly is explained here, all with real, usable examples.

Chapter 10, "Creating Data-Driven Pages," is where you create your first data-driven ColdFusion application, albeit a very simple one. You also learn how to use `<CFQUERY>` to create queries that extract live data from your databases and how to display query results using `<CFOUTPUT>`. Various formatting techniques, including the use of tables and lists, are taught as well. One method of displaying data on the Web is data drill-down (which has become very popular); this approach to data interaction is also taught.

In Chapter 11, "ColdFusion Forms," you learn how to collect user-supplied data via HTML forms. This data can be used to build dynamic SQL statements that provide you with infinite flexibility in creating dynamic database queries. This chapter also teaches you how to create search screens that enable visitors to search on as many different fields as you allow.

Continuing with the topic of collecting data from users, Chapter 12, "Form Data Validation," explains the various techniques and options available for data validation. ColdFusion can generate JavaScript client-side validation code automatically, without your having to learn JavaScript. You learn how to use this feature and how to provide your own validation rules.

Chapter 13, "Using Forms to Add or Change Data," teaches you how to use forms to add, update, and delete data in database tables. The ColdFusion tags `<CFINSERT>` and `<CFUPDATE>` are introduced, and you learn how `<CFQUERY>` can be used to insert, update, and delete data.

Chapter 14, "Debugging and Troubleshooting," teaches you the types of things that can go wrong in ColdFusion application development and what you can do to rectify them. You learn how to use ColdFusion's debugging and logging features and how to trace your own code; most importantly, you learn tips and techniques that can help you avoid problems in the first place.

Part III—Building ColdFusion Applications

Part II concentrates on ColdFusion coding. In Part III, all the ideas and concepts are brought together in the creation of complete applications.

Experienced developers know that it takes careful planning to write good code. Chapter 15, "Planning an Application," teaches important design and planning techniques you can leverage within your own development.

In Chapter 16, "Introducing the Web Application Framework," you learn how to take advantage of the ColdFusion Web application framework to facilitate the use of persistent variables, sophisticated parameter and variable manipulation, and customized error-message handling. You also learn how to use the application template to establish application-wide settings and options and how to use the `APPLICATION` scope.

Chapter 17, "Working with Sessions," teaches you all you need to know about `CLIENT` and `SESSION` variables, as well as HTTP cookies. These special data types play an important part in creating a complete application that can track a client's state.

Chapter 18, "Securing Your Applications," introduces important security concepts and explains which you should worry about and why. You learn how to create login screens, access control, and more.

Chapter 19, "Building User-Defined Functions, " introduces the `<CFFUNCTION>` tag and explains how it can (and should) be used to extend the CFML language.

Chapter 20, "Building Reusable Components," explains two other code reuse options: custom tags and ColdFusion Components. Both are extremely important application building blocks, so you learn exactly what they are, when to use them, and how to do so.

Chapter 21, "Improving the User Experience," helps you create applications that really get used. You learn important user interface concepts, how to build sophisticated browse screens, and much more.

Developers are always looking for ways to tweak their code, squeezing out a bit more performance wherever possible. Chapter 22, "Improving Performance," provides tips, tricks, and techniques you can use to create applications that will always be snappy and responsive.

Macromedia Flash is fast becoming the tool of choice for the creation of rich, highly interactive, portable, and lightweight user interfaces. Chapter 23, "Integrating with Macromedia Flash MX," introduces Flash from a ColdFusion developer's perspective and explains how the two can be used together using new Flash remoting capabilities.

In Chapter 24, "Enhancing Forms with Client-Side Java," you learn how to take advantage of the ColdFusion-supplied Java form controls. These controls include a Windows Explorer–style tree control, an editable grid control, a slider control, and a highly configurable text-input control. You also learn how to embed your own Java applets using the `<CFAPPLET>` tag.

Chapter 25, "Graphing," introduces ColdFusion's new high-performance graphing engine. You learn how to use the `<CFCHART>` tag (and related child tags) to create all sorts of business graphics (including bar charts, pie charts, and more) for use within your applications.

Chapter 26, "Interacting with Email," introduces ColdFusion's email capabilities. ColdFusion enables you to create SMTP-based email messages using its `<CFMAIL>` tag. You learn how to send email messages containing user-submitted form fields, how to email the results of a database query, and how to do mass mailings to addresses derived from database tables. Additionally, you learn how to retrieve mail from POP mailboxes using the `<CFPOP>` tag.

Chapter 27, "Online Commerce," teaches you how to perform real-time electronic commerce, including credit card authorization. You build an entire working shopping-cart application—one you can use as a stepping-stone when writing your own shopping applications.

Part IV—Advanced ColdFusion

Part IV teaches you advanced ColdFusion capabilities and techniques. The chapters in this section have been written with the assumption that you are familiar with basic SQL syntax and are very comfortable creating ColdFusion templates.

Chapter 28, "ColdFusion Server Configuration," revisits the ColdFusion Administrator, this time explaining every option and feature, while providing tips, tricks, and hints you can use to tweak your ColdFusion server.

Chapter 29, "More on SQL and Queries," teaches you how to create powerful SQL statements using subqueries, joins, unions, scalar functions, and more. You also learn how to calculate averages, totals, and counts and how to use the `EXISTS`, `NOT EXISTS`, and `DISTINCT` keywords.

Chapter 30, "Working with Stored Procedures," takes advanced SQL one step further by teaching you how to create stored procedures and how to integrate them into your ColdFusion applications.

Chapter 31, "Error Handling," teaches you how to create applications that can both report errors and handle error conditions gracefully. You learn how to use the `<CFTRY>` and `<CFCATCH>` tags (and their supporting tags) and how they can be used as part of a complete error-handling strategy.

ColdFusion is used primarily to generate Web content, but that is not all it can do. In Chapter 32, "Generating Non-HTML Content," you learn how to use `<CFCONTENT>` to generate content for popular applications (such as Microsoft Word and Microsoft Excel), as well as mobile technologies such as WAP.

Chapter 33, "Interacting with the Operating System," introduces the powerful and flexible Cold-Fusion `<CFFILE>` and `<CFDIRECTORY>` tags. You learn how to create, read, write, and append local files; manipulate directories; and even add file-uploading features to your forms. You also learn how to spawn external applications when necessary.

Chapter 34, "Full-Text Searching," introduces the Verity search engine. Verity provides a mechanism that performs full-text searches against all types of data. The Verity engines (yes, there are two of them) are bundled with the ColdFusion Application Server, and the `<CFINDEX>` and `<CFSEARCH>` tags provide full access to Verity indexes from within your applications.

Chapter 35, "Event Scheduling," teaches you to create tasks that execute automatically and at timed intervals. You also learn how to dynamically generate static HTML pages using ColdFusion's scheduling technology.

In Chapter 36, "Managing Your Code," you learn about coding standards, documentation, version control, and more, as well as why these are all so important.

Continuing with the topic of coding standards, Chapter 37, "Development Methodologies," introduces several popular independent development methodologies designed specifically for ColdFusion development.

Part V—Appendixes

Appendix A, “Installing ColdFusion MX and Dreamweaver MX,” goes over system, hardware, and operating-system prerequisites and walks you through the entire process of installing Macromedia ColdFusion MX and Macromedia Dreamweaver MX. Various installation options are explained, as is the installation of ColdFusion MX on top of J2EE servers. The sample applications used in this book are also installed here.

Appendix B, “ColdFusion Tag Reference,” is an alphabetical listing of all CMFL tags and descriptions, complete with examples for each and extensive cross-referencing.

Appendix C, “ColdFusion Function Reference,” is a complete listing of every CFML function organized by category, complete with examples for each and extensive cross-referencing.

Appendix D, “Special ColdFusion Variables and Result Codes,” lists every special variable, prefix, and tag result code available within your applications.

Appendix E, “Verity Search Language Reference,” is a complete guide to the Verity search language. Using the information provided here, you will be able to perform incredibly complex searches with minimal effort.

Appendix F, “ColdFusion MX Directory Structure,” explains the directories and files that make up ColdFusion MX, providing lots of useful tips and tricks in the process.

Appendix G, “Sample Application Data Files,” lists the format of the database tables used in the sample applications throughout this book.

The CD-ROM

The accompanying CD-ROM contains everything you need to start writing ColdFusion applications, including

- Evaluation and developer editions of ColdFusion MX
- Evaluation edition of Macromedia Dreamweaver MX
- Evaluation edition of Macromedia Flash MX
- Source code and databases for all the examples in this book
- Electronic versions of some chapters

So, turn the page and start reading. In no time, you’ll be creating powerful applications powered by ColdFusion MX.

PART 1

Getting Started

IN THIS PART

CHAPTER 1

Introducing ColdFusion MX

IN THIS CHAPTER

The Basics

If you're embarking on learning ColdFusion then you undoubtedly have an interest in applications that are Web (shorthand for *World Wide Web*) based. ColdFusion is built on top of the Internet (and the Web), so before getting started, a good understanding of the Internet and related technologies is a must.

There is no need to introduce you to the Internet and the Web. The fact that you're reading this book is evidence enough that these are important to you (as they should be). The Web is everywhere—and Web site addresses appear on everything from toothpaste commercials to movie trailers to cereal boxes to car showrooms. In August 1981, 213 hosts (computers) were connected to the Internet. By the turn of the millennium that number had grown to about 100 million! And most of them are accessing the Web.

What has made the World Wide Web so popular? That, of course, depends on whom you ask. But most will agree that these are the two primary reasons:

- **Ease of use.** Publishing information on the Web and browsing for information are relatively easy tasks.
- **Quantity of content.** With millions of Web pages from which to choose and thousands more being created each day, there are sites and pages to cater to almost every surfer's tastes.

A massive potential audience awaits your Web site and the services it offers. Of course, massive competition awaits you too. Most Web sites still primarily consist of static information, sometimes dubbed *brochureware*. That's rather sad, the Web is a powerful medium and is capable of so much more. You could, and should, be offering much more than just static text and images. You need features like:

- Dynamic, data-driven Web pages
- Database connectivity
- Intelligent, user-customized pages
- Sophisticated data collection and processing
- Email interaction
- Rich and engaging user interfaces

ColdFusion enables you to do all this—and more.

But you need to take a step back before starting ColdFusion development. As I mentioned, ColdFusion takes advantage of existing Internet technologies. As such, a prerequisite to ColdFusion development is a good understanding of the Internet, the World Wide Web, Web servers and browsers, and how all these pieces fit together.

The Internet

Much ambiguity and confusion surround the Internet, so we'll start with a definition. Simply put, the Internet is the world's largest network.

The networks found in most offices today are *local area networks (LANs)*, comprised of a group of computers in relatively close proximity to each other and linked by special hardware and cabling (see Figure 1.1). Some computers are clients (more commonly known as *workstations*); others are servers (also known as *file servers*). All these computers can communicate with each other to share information.

Now imagine a bigger network—one that spans multiple geographical locations. This type of network is typically used by larger companies with offices in multiple locations. Each location has its own LAN, which links the local computers together. All these LANs in turn are linked to each other via some communications medium. The linking can be anything from simple dial-up modems to high-speed T1 or T3 connections and fiber-optic links. The complete group of interconnected LANs, as shown in Figure 1.2, is called a *wide area network (WAN)*.

Figure 1.1
A LAN is a group of computers in close proximity linked by special cabling.

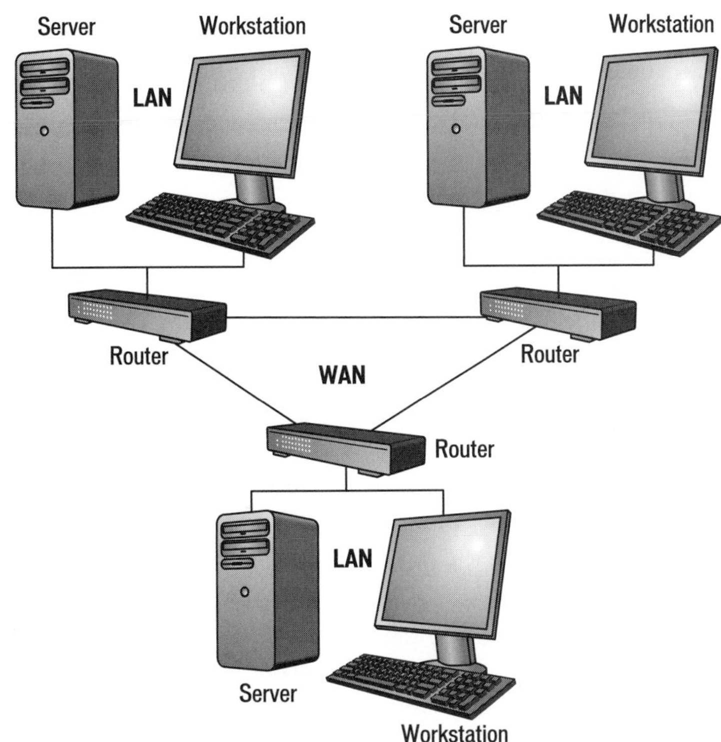

Figure 1.2
A WAN is made up of multiple, interconnected LANs.

WANs are used to link multiple locations within a single company. Suppose you need to create a massive network that links every computer everywhere. How would you do this?

You'd start by running high-speed *backbones*, connections capable of moving large amounts of data at once, between strategic locations—perhaps large cities or different countries. These backbones would be similar to high-speed, multilane, interstate highways connecting various locations.

You'd build in fault tolerance to make these backbones fully redundant so that if any connection broke, at least one other way to reach a specific destination would be available.

You'd then create thousands of local links that would connect every city to the backbones over slower connections—like state highways or city streets. You'd allow corporate WANs, LANs, and even individual users with dial-up modems to connect to these local access points. Some would stay connected at all times, whereas others would connect as needed.

You'd create a common communications language so that every computer connected to this network could communicate with every other computer.

Finally, you'd devise a scheme to uniquely identify every computer connected to the network. This would ensure that information sent to a given computer actually reached the correct destination.

Congratulations, you've just created the Internet!

Even though this is an oversimplification, it is exactly how the Internet works.

The high-speed backbones do exist. Many are owned and operated by the large telecommunications companies.

The local access points, more commonly known as *points of presence (POPs)*, are run by phone companies, online services, cable companies, and local Internet service providers (also known as ISPs).

The common language is IP, the Internet protocol, except that the term *language* is a misnomer. A *protocol* is a set of rules governing behavior in certain situations. Foreign diplomats learn local protocol to ensure that they behave correctly in another country. The protocols ensure that no communication breakdowns or serious misunderstandings occur. Computers also need protocols to ensure that they can communicate with each other correctly and that data is exchanged correctly. IP is the protocol used to communicate across the Internet, so every computer connected to the Internet must be running a copy of IP.

The unique identifiers are *IP addresses*. Every computer, or host, connected to the Internet has a unique IP address. These addresses are made up of four sets of numbers separated by periods—`208.193.16.100`, for example. Some hosts have *fixed* (or *static*) IP addresses, whereas others have dynamically assigned addresses (assigned from a pool each time a connection is made). Regardless of how an IP address is obtained, no two hosts connected to the Internet can use the same IP address at any given time. That would be like two homes having the same phone number or street address. Information would end up in the wrong place all the time.

Internet Applications

The Internet itself is simply a massive communications network and offers very little to most users, which is why it took 20 years for the Internet to become the phenomenon is it today.

The Internet has been dubbed the Information Superhighway, and that analogy is quite accurate. Highways themselves are not nearly as exciting as the places you can get to by traveling them—and the same is true of the Internet. What makes the Internet so exciting are the applications that run over it and what you can accomplish with them.

The most popular application now is the World Wide Web. It is the Web that single-handedly transformed the Internet into a household word. In fact, many people mistakenly think that the World Wide Web is the Internet. This is definitely not the case, and Table 1.1 lists some of the more popular Internet-based applications.

All these various applications—and many others—use IP to communicate across the Internet. The information transmitted by these applications is broken into *packets*, small blocks of data, which are sent to a destination IP address. The application at the receiving end processes the received information.

Table 1.1 Some Internet-Based Applications

APPLICATION	DESCRIPTION
Email	Simple Mail Transfer Protocol (SMTP) is the most popular email transmission mechanism, and the Post Office Protocol (POP) is the most used mail access interface.
FTP	File Transfer Protocol is used to transfer files between hosts.
Gopher	This menu-driven document retrieval system was very popular before the creation of the World Wide Web.
IRC	Internet Relay Chat enables real-time, text-based conferencing over the Internet.
NFS	Network File System is used to share files among various hosts.
Newsgroups	Newsgroups are threaded discussion lists, of which thousands exist (accessed via NNTP).
Telnet	Telnet is used to log on to a host from a remote location.
VPN	Virtual Private Networks facilitate the secure access of private networks over the Internet.
WWW	The World Wide Web.

DNS

IP addresses are the only way to uniquely specify a host. When you want to communicate with a host—a Web server, for example—you must specify the IP address of the Web server you are trying to contact.

As you know from browsing the Web, you rarely specify IP addresses directly. You do, however, specify a hostname, such as `www.forta.com` (my Web site). If hosts are identified by IP addresses, how does your browser know which Web server to contact if you specify a hostname?

The answer is the Domain Name Service (DNS). DNS is a mechanism that maps hostnames to IP addresses. When you specify the destination address `www.forta.com`, your browser sends an address resolution request to a DNS server asking for the IP address of that host. The DNS server returns an actual IP address, in this case `208.193.16.100`. Your browser can then use this address to communicate with the host directly.

If you've ever mistyped a hostname, you've seen error messages similar to the one seen in Figure 1.3, which tell you the host could not be found, or that no DNS entry was found for the specified host. These error messages mean the DNS server was unable to resolve the specified hostname.

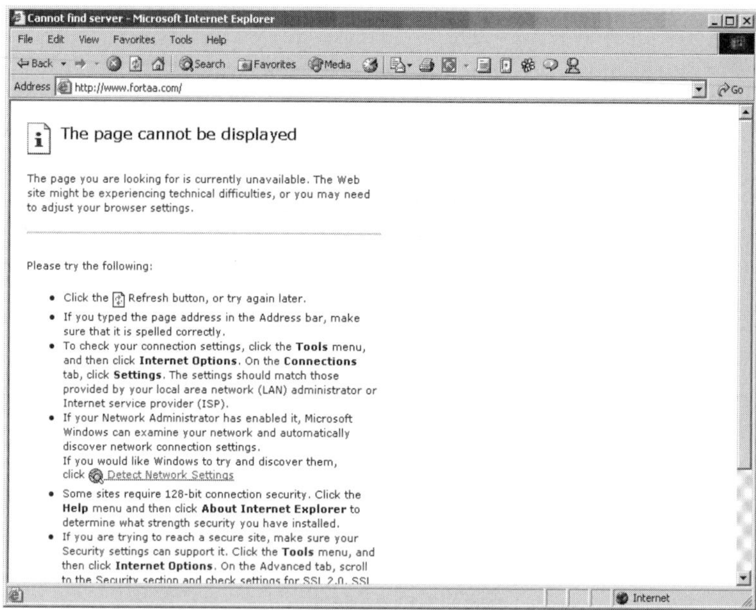

Figure 1.3

Mistyping a URL often causes DNS errors.

DNS is never actually needed (well, usually, there is an exception that I'll get to in a moment). Users can always specify the name of a destination host by its IP address to connect to the host. There are, however, some very good reasons not to:

- **IP addresses are hard to remember and easy to mistype.** Users are more likely to find `www.forta.com` than they are `208.193.16.100`.
- **IP addresses are subject to change.** For example, if you switch service providers, you might be forced to use a new set of IP addresses for your hosts. If users identified your site only by its IP address, they'd never be able to reach your host if the IP address changed. Your DNS name, however, stays the same even if your IP address switches. You need to change only the mapping so the hostname maps to the new, correct IP address (the new service provider usually handles that).
- **IP addresses must be unique, as already explained, but DNS names need not.** Multiple hosts, each with a unique IP address, can all share the same DNS name. This enables load balancing between servers, as well as the establishment of redundant servers (so that if a server goes down, another server will still process requests).
- **A single host, with a single IP address, can have multiple DNS names.** This enables you to create aliases if needed. For example, `ftp.forta.com`, `www.forta.com`, and even just plain `forta.com` might point to the same IP address, and thus the same server.

DNS servers are special software programs. Your ISP will often host your DNS entries, so you don't need to install and maintain your own DNS server software.

You can host your own DNS server and gain more control over the domain mappings, but in doing so, you inherit the responsibility of maintaining the server. If your DNS server is down, there won't be any way of resolving the hostname to an IP address, and no one will be able to find your site.

Intranets and Extranets

Intranets and Extranets were the big buzzwords a few years back, and while some of the hype has worn off, Intranets and Extranets are still in use and still of value. It was not too long ago that most people thought *intranet* was a typo; but in a very short period of time, intranets and extranets became recognized as legitimate and powerful new business tools.

An *intranet* is nothing more than a private Internet. In other words, it is a private network, usually a LAN or WAN, that enables the use of Internet-based applications in a secure and private environment. As on the public Internet, intranets can host Web servers, FTP servers, and any other IP-based services. Companies have been using private networks for years to share information. Traditionally, office networks have not been information friendly. Old private networks did not have consistent interfaces, standard ways to publish information, or client applications that were capable of accessing diverse data stores. The popularity in the public Internet has spawned a whole new generation of inexpensive and easy-to-use client applications. These applications are now making their way back into the private networks. The reason intranets are now getting so much attention is that they are a new solution to an old problem.

Extranets take this new communication mechanism one step further. *Extranets* are intranet-style networks that link multiple sites or organizations using intranet-related technologies. Many extranets actually use the public Internet as their backbones and employ encryption techniques to ensure the security of the data being moved over the network.

The two things that distinguish intranets and extranets from the Internet is who can access them and from where they can be accessed. Don't be confused by hype surrounding applications that claim to be intranet ready. If an application can be used over the public Internet, it will work on private intranets and extranets, too.

Web Servers

As mentioned earlier, the most commonly used Internet-based application is now the World Wide Web. The recent growth of interest in the Internet is the result of growing interest in the World Wide Web.

The World Wide Web is built on a protocol called the Hypertext Transport Protocol (HTTP). HTTP is designed to be a small, fast protocol that is well suited for distributed, multimedia information systems and hypertext jumps between sites.

The Web consists of pages of information on hosts running Web-server software. The host is often referred to as the Web server, which is technically inaccurate. The Web server is software, not the computer itself. Versions of Web server software can run on almost all computers. There is nothing intrinsically special about a computer that hosts a Web server, and no rules dictate what hardware is appropriate for running a Web server.

The original World Wide Web development was all performed under various flavors of Unix. The majority of Web servers still run on Unix boxes, but this is changing. Now Web server versions are available for almost every major operating system. Web servers hosted on high-performance operating systems, such as Windows 2000 and Windows XP, are becoming more and more popular. This is because Unix is still more expensive to run than Windows and is also more difficult for the average user to use. Windows XP (built on top of Windows NT) has proven itself to be an efficient, reliable, and cost-effective platform for hosting Web servers. As a result, Windows' slice in the Web server operating system pie is growing. At the same time, Linux (a flavor of Unix) is growing in popularity as a Web platform thanks to its low cost, its robustness, and the fact that it is slowly becoming more usable to less technical users.

What exactly is a Web server? A *Web server* is a program that serves Web pages upon request. Web servers typically don't know or care what they are serving. When a user at a specific IP address requests a specific file, the Web server tries to retrieve that file and send it back to the user. The requested file might be a Web page's HTML source code, a GIF image, a Flash file, a XML document, or an AVI file. It is the Web browser that determines what should be requested, not the Web server. The server simply processes that request, as shown in Figure 1.4.

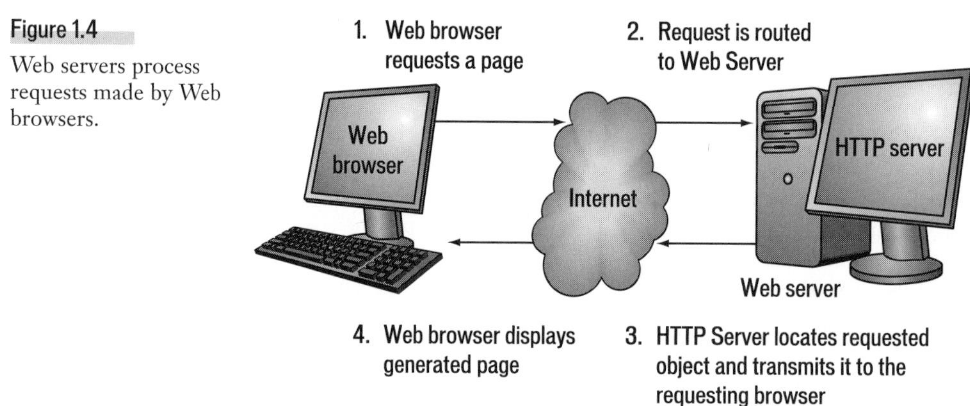
1. Web browser requests a page
2. Request is routed to Web Server
Web browser
Internet
HTTP server
Web server
4. Web browser displays generated page
3. HTTP Server locates requested object and transmits it to the requesting browser

Figure 1.4

Web servers process requests made by Web browsers.

It is important to note that Web servers typically do not care about the contents of these files. HTML code in a Web page, for example, is markup that the Web browser—not the Web server—will process. The Web server returns the requested page as is, regardless of what the page is and what it contains. If HTML syntax errors exist in the file, those errors will be returned along with the rest of the page.

Connections to Web servers are made on an as-needed basis. If you request a page from a Web server, an IP connection is made over the Internet between your host and the host running the Web server. The requested Web page is sent over that connection, and the connection is broken as soon as the page is received. If the received page contains references to additional information to be downloaded (for example, GIF or JPG images), each would be retrieved using a new connection. Therefore, it takes at least six requests, or *hits*, to retrieve all of a Web page with five pictures in it.

NOTE

This is why the number of hits is such a misleading measure of Web server activity. When you learn of Web servers that receive millions of hits in one day, it might not mean that there were millions of visitors. Hits do not equal the number of visitors or pages viewed. In fact, hits are a useful measure only of changes in server activity.

Web servers often are not the only IP-based applications running on a single host. In fact, aside from performance issues, there is no reason a single host cannot run multiple services. For example, a Web server, an FTP server, a DNS server, and an SMTP POP3 mail server can run at the same time. Each server is assigned a port address to ensure that each server application responds only to requests and communications from appropriate clients. If IP addresses are like street addresses, ports can be thought of as apartment or suite numbers. A total of 65,536 ports are available on every host—ports `0–1023` are the *Well Known Ports*, ports reserved for special applications and protocols (such as HTTP). Vendor-specific applications that communicate over the Internet (such as America Online's Instant Messenger, Microsoft SQL Server, and the Real Media player) typically use ports `1024–49151`. No two applications can share a port at the same time.

Most servers use a standard set of port mappings, and some of the more common ports are listed in Table 1.2.

Table 1.2 Common IP Port Numbers

PORT	USE
20	FTP
21	FTP
23	Telnet
25	SMTP
43	Whois
53	DNS
70	Gopher
79	Finger
80	HTTP
107	Remote Telnet service
109	POP2
110	POP3
119	NNTP
143	IMAP4, Interactive Mail Access Protocol version 4 (previously used by IMAP2)
194	IRC
220	IMAP3
389	LDAP, Lightweight Directory Access Protocol
443	HTTPS, HTTP running over secure sockets
540	UUCP, Unix to Unix Copy
1723	PPTP (used by VPN's, Virtual Private Networks)

Most Web servers use port `80`, but you can change that. If desired, Web servers can be installed on nonstandard ports to *hide* Web servers, as well as host multiple Web servers on a single computer by mapping each one to a different port. Remember that if you do use a nonstandard port mapping, users will need to know the new port number.

NOTE

This discussion of port numbers is very important in ColdFusion MX, we'll come back to it in a few pages.

Web Pages

Information on the World Wide Web is stored in *pages*. A page can contain any of the following:

- Text
- Headers
- Lists
- Menus
- Tables
- Forms
- Graphics
- Scripts
- Style sheets
- Multimedia

Web pages are constructed using a series of client-side technologies that are processed and displayed by Web browsers.

Web Browsers

Web browsers are client programs used to access Web sites and pages. The Web browser has the job of processing received Web pages and displaying them to the user. The browser attempts to display graphics, tables, forms, formatted text, or whatever the page contains.

The most popular Web browsers now in use are Netscape Navigator and Microsoft Internet Explorer. Other lesser-used browsers exist too, for example Mozilla and Opera.

Web page designers have to pay close attention to the differences between browsers because different Web browsers support different HTML tags. Unfortunately, no one single browser supports every tag currently in use. Furthermore, the same Web page often looks different on two different browsers; every browser renders and displays Web page objects differently. Even the same browser running on different operating systems will often behave differently.

For this reason, most Web page designers use multiple Web browsers and test their pages in every one to ensure that the final output appears as intended. Without this testing, some Web site visitors will not see the pages you published correctly.

TIP

Dreamweaver MX, used to create Web pages, has its own built in browser that is neither Microsoft Internet Explorer, nor Netscape Navigator, nor any other browser. To help you test your Web pages in as many browsers as possible, Dreamweaver MX allows you to define external browsers that may be launched to view your creations.

HTML

Web pages are plain text files constructed via Hypertext Markup Language (HTML). HTML is implemented as a series of easy-to-learn tags. Web page authors use these tags to mark up a page of text. Browsers then use these tags to render and display the information for viewing.

HTML is constantly being enhanced with new features and tags. To ensure backward compatibility, browsers must ignore tags they do not understand. For example, if you use the `<MARQUEE>` tag in an effort to create a scrolling text marquee, browsers that do not support this tag display the marquee text but do not scroll the text.

Web pages also can contain *hypertext jumps*, which are links to other pages or Web sites. Users can click links to jump to either other pages on the same site or any page on any site.

Pages on a Web server are stored in various directories. When requesting a Web page, a user might provide a full path (directory and filename) to specify a particular document.

You can specify a *default* Web page, a page that is sent back to the user when only a directory is specified, with a Web server. These default pages are often called `index.html` or `default.htm` (or `index.cfm` for ColdFusion pages). If no default Web page exists in a particular directory, you see either an error message or a list of all the available files, depending on how the server is set up.

JavaScript

HTML is a page markup language. It enables the creation and layout of pages and forms but not much else. Building intuitive and sophisticated user interfaces requires more than straight HTML—client-side scripting is necessary, too. Scripting enables you to write code (small programs) that runs within Web browsers.

The most popular client-side scripting language is JavaScript, which is supported (more or less) by almost every browser out there. Using JavaScript you can

- Perform form field validation
- Pop open windows
- Animate text and images
- Create drop-down menus or navigation controls
- Perform rudimentary text and numeric processing
- ...and much more

NOTE

The other major client-side scripting language is VBScript (modeled in Visual Basic). But VBScript is supported only in Microsoft Internet Explorer and is thus generally used less than JavaScript.

Scripting enables developers to trap and process *events*—things that occur within the browser. For example, a page being loaded, a form being submitted, and the mouse pointer moving over an image are all events, and scripts can be automatically executed by the Web browser when these occur. It is this that facilitates the types of features I just listed.

Script code is either embedded in the HTML file or stored in an external file and linked within the HTML code. Either way, the script is retrieved and processed by the Web browser.

CAUTION

Writing client-side scripts is more difficult than writing simple HTML. Not only are scripting languages harder to learn than HTML, there is an additional complexity in that various browsers support various levels of scripting. Writing portable scripts is possible, but it is not trivial.

Other Client Technologies

Most new browsers also enable the use of add-on technologies that are supported either directly or via plug-in modules. Some of the most significant ones are

- **CSS (Cascading Style Sheets).** Provide a means of separating presentation from content so that both can be more readily reused and managed.
- **DHTML (Dynamic HTML).** A combination of HTML, scripting, and CSS that, when used together, provide extremely rich and powerful user-interface options.
- **Java applets.** Small programs that run within the Web browser (actually, they run within a Java Virtual Machine, but we'll not worry about that just yet). Applets were popular in the late '90s but are seldom used now because they are difficult to write; slow to download; and tend to be terribly incompatible with all the computers, operating systems, and browsers in use.
- **Macromedia Flash.** A technology that is now embedded in over 98% of all browsers in use. Flash provides a mechanism for creating rich and portable interactive user interfaces (complete with audio, video, and animation, if needed), and Flash is being ported to all sorts of new platforms and devices.

URLs

So, now you know what Web servers, Web browsers, and Web pages are. The piece that links them all together is the URL.

Every Web page on the World Wide Web has an address. This is what you type into your browser to instruct it to load a particular Web page.

These addresses are called *Uniform Resource Locators (URLs)*. URLs are not just used to identify World Wide Web pages or objects. Files on an FTP server, for example, also have URL identifiers.

World Wide Web URLs consist of up to six parts (see Figure 1.5) as explained in Table 1.3.

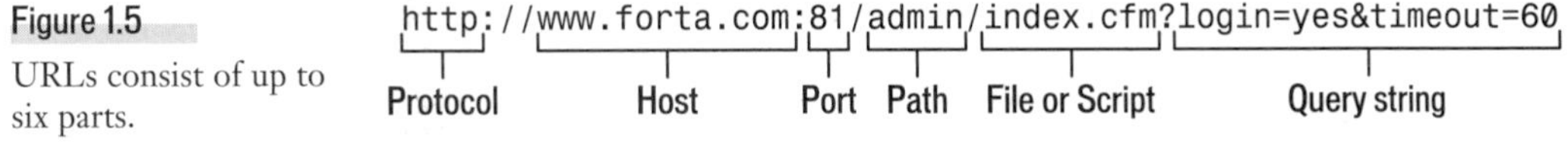

Figure 1.5
URLs consist of up to six parts.

Table 1.3 Anatomy of a URL

PART	DESCRIPTION
Protocol	The protocol to retrieve the object. This is usually `http` for objects on the World Wide Web. If the protocol is specified then it must be followed by `://` (which separates the protocol from the host name).
Host	The Web server from which to retrieve the object. This is specified as a DNS name or an IP address.
Port	The host machine port on which the Web server is running. If omitted, the specified protocol's default port is used; for Web servers, this is port `80`. If specified, the port must be preceded by a colon (`:`).
Path	Path to file to retrieve or script to execute.
File	The file to retrieve or the script to execute.
Query String	Optional script parameters. If a query string is specified, it must be preceded by a question mark (`?`).

Look at some sample URLs:

- `http://www.forta.com`. This URL points to a Web page on the host `www.forta.com`. Because no document or path was specified, the default document in the root directory is served.
- `http://www.forta.com/`. This URL is the same as the previous example and is actually the correct way to specify the default document in the root directory (although most Web browsers accept the previous example and insert the trailing slash automatically).
- `http://www.forta.com/books/`. This URL also points to a Web page on the host `www.forta.com`, but this time the directory `/books/` is specified. Because no page name was provided, the default page in the `/books/` directory is served.
- `http://208.193.16.100/books/`. This URL points to the same file as the previous example, but this time the IP address is used instead of the DNS name.
- `http://www.forta.com/books/topten.html`. Once again, this URL points to a Web page on the `www.forta.com` host. Both a directory and a filename are specified this time. This retrieves the file `topten.html` from the `/books/` directory, instead of the default file.

- `http://www.forta.com:81/administration/index.html`. This is an example of a URL that points to a page on a Web server assigned to a nonstandard port. Because port `81` is not the standard port for Web servers, the port number must be provided.
- `http://www.forta.com/cf/tips/syndhowto.cfm`. This URL points to a specific page on a Web server, but not an HTML page. CFM files are ColdFusion templates, which are discussed later in this chapter.
- `http://www.forta.com/cf/tips/browse.cfm?search=mx`. This URL points to another ColdFusion file, but this time a parameter is passed to it. A `?` is always used to separate the URL itself (including the script to execute) from any parameter.
- `http://www.forta.com/cf/tips/browse.cfm?search=mx&s=1`. This URL is the same as the previous example, with one additional parameter. Multiple parameters are separated by ampersands (the `&` character).
- `ftp://ftp.forta.com/pub/catalog.zip`. This is an example of a URL that points to an object other than a Web page or script. The protocol `ftp` indicates that the object referred to is a file to be retrieved from an FTP server using the File Transfer Protocol. This file is `catalog.zip` in the `/pub/` directory.

Links in Web pages are references to other URLs. When a user clicks a link, the browser processes whatever URL it references.

Hosts and Virtual Hosts

As already explained, the term *host* refers to a computer connected to the Internet. The *host name* is the DNS name by which that machine may be referred to.

A Web site is hosted on a host (which, if you think about it, makes perfect sense). So host `www.forta.com` (which has an IP address of `208.193.16.100`) hosts my Web site. But that host also hosts many other Web sites (some mine and some belonging to other people). If a request arrives at a host that hosts multiple Web sites, how does the host know which Web site to route it to?

There are actually several ways that this can be accomplished:

- Earlier I explained that IP address must be unique, that is, no two hosts may share the same IP address. But what I did not explain is that a single host may have more than one IP address (assuming the operating system allows this, and most in fact do). If a host has multiple IP addresses, each may be mapped in the Web server software to *virtual hosts* (which are exactly that, virtual hosts). Each virtual host is has an associated *Web root* (the base directory for any and all content), and depending on the IP address that the request came in on, the Web server can route the request to the appropriate virtual host and directory structure.
- Some Web servers allow multiple virtual hosts using the same IP address. How do they do this? By looking at the DNS name that was specified. You will recall that I earlier explained that multiple DNS names can resolve to the same IP address, and so Web

servers may allow the mapping of virtual hosts by DNS name (rather than IP address). This is the instance I was referring to earlier when I said that there is a scenario in which DNS names *must* be used.

In both of these configurations, all of the hosts (including virtual hosts) are processed by the same Web server. There is another way to support multiple hosts without using different DNS names or IP addresses:

- Depending on the Web server software being used, it may be possible to run multiple Web servers on the same computer. In this configuration each and every instance of the Web server must be running on a different port (you will recall that no two applications may share a port at the same time). When requests are made the port must be specified in the URL (or else, as previously explained, the request will default to port `80`). Each Web server has its own Web root which is then the root for a specific virtual host.

In this configuration multiple Web servers are used, one per host.

The difference may seem subtle, but it is very important, as you will soon see.

Understanding ColdFusion

Millions of Web sites exist that attract millions of visitors daily. Many Web sites are being used as electronic replacements for newspapers, magazines, brochures, and bulletin boards. The Web offers ways to enhance these publications using audio, images, animation, multimedia, and even virtual reality.

No one will dispute that these sites add value to the Net because information is knowledge, and knowledge is power. All this information is available at your fingertips—literally. Web sites, however, are capable of being much more than electronic versions of paper publications because of the underlying technology that makes the Web tick. Users can interact with you and your company, collect and process mission-critical information in real-time (allowing you to provide new levels of user support), and much more.

The Web is not merely the electronic equivalent of a newspaper or magazine—it is a communication medium that is limited only by the lack of innovation and creativity of Web site designers.

The Dynamic Page Advantage

Dynamic pages (containing dynamic content) are what bring the Web to life. Linking your Web site to live data is a tremendous advantage, but the benefits of database interaction go beyond extending your site's capabilities.

Dynamic Web pages are becoming the norm for good reason. Consider the following:

- **Static Web pages.** Static Web pages are made up of text, images, and HTML formatting tags. These pages are manually created and maintained so that when information changes, so must the page. This usually involves loading the page into an editor, making the changes, reformatting text if needed, and then saving the file. Of course, not everyone in the organization can make these changes. The Webmaster or Web design team is responsible for maintaining the site and implementing all changes and enhancements. This often means that by the time information finally makes it onto the Web site, it's out of date.

- **Dynamic Web pages.** Dynamic Web pages contain very little text. Instead, they pull needed information from other applications. Dynamic Web pages communicate with databases to extract employee directory information, spreadsheets to display accounting figures, client-server database management systems to interact with order processing applications, and more. A database already exists. Why re-create it for Web page publication?

Creating dynamic pages enables you to create powerful applications that can include features such as these:

- Querying existing database applications for data
- Creating dynamic queries facilitating more flexible data retrieval
- Executing stored procedures (in databases that support them)
- Executing conditional code on-the-fly to customize responses for specific situations
- Enhancing the standard HTML form capabilities with data validation functions
- Dynamically populating form elements
- Customizing the display of dates, times, and currency values with formatting functions
- Easing the creation of data entry and data drill-down applications with wizards
- Generating email automatically (perhaps in response to form submissions)
- Shopping carts and e-commerce sites
- Data syndication and affiliate programs
- ...and much more

Understanding Web Applications

As was explained earlier, Web servers do just that: They serve. Web browsers make requests, and Web servers fulfill those requests—they serve back the requested information to the browser. These are usually HTML files, as well as the other file types discussed previously.

And that's really all Web servers do. In the grand scheme of things, Web servers are actually pretty simple applications—they sit and wait for requests that they attempt to fulfill as soon as they arrive. Web servers do not let you interact with a database; they don't let you personalize Web pages; they don't let you process the results of a user's form submission; they do none of that. All they do is serve pages.

So how do you extend your Web server to do all the things just listed? That's where Web application servers come into play. A *Web application server* is a piece of software that extends the Web server, enabling it to do things it could not do by itself—kind of like teaching an old dog new tricks.

Here's how it all works. When a Web server receives a request from a Web browser, it looks at that request to determine whether it is a simple Web page or a page that needs processing by a Web application server. It does this by looking at the MIME type (or file extension). If the MIME type indicates that the file is a simple Web page (for example, it has an `HTM` extension) then the Web server fulfills the request and sends the file to the requesting browser as is. But if the MIME type indicates that the requested file is a page that needs processing by a Web application server (for example, it has a `CFM` extension), the Web server passes it to the appropriate Web application server and returns the results it gets back rather than the actual page itself. Figure 1.6 illustrates this concept (in contrast to simple HTTP processing seen previously in Figure 1.4).

Figure 1.6

Web servers pass requests to Web application servers, which in turn pass results back to the Web server for transmission to the requesting browser.

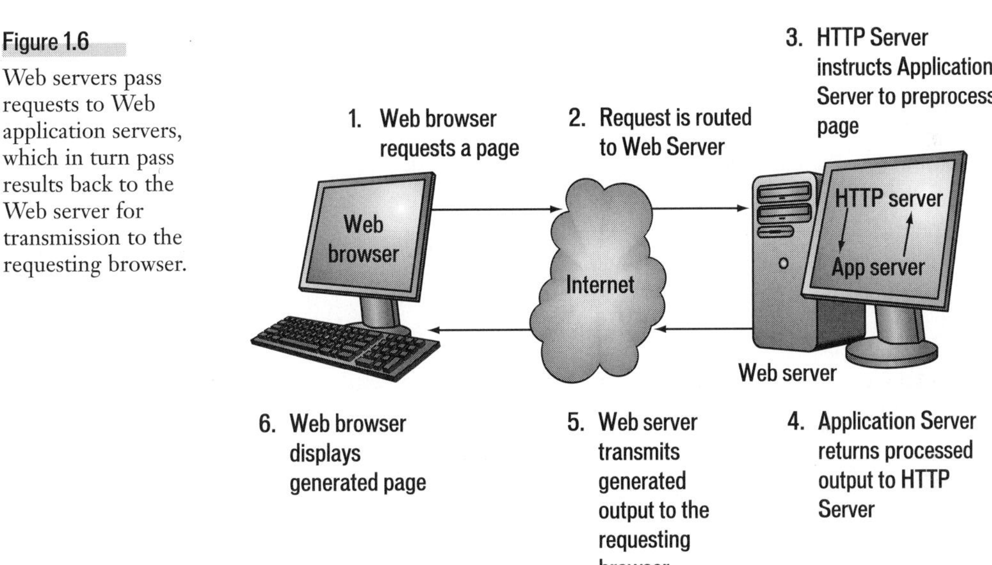
1. Web browser requests a page
2. Request is routed to Web Server
3. HTTP Server instructs Application Server to preprocess page
Web browser
Internet
HTTP server
App server
Web server
6. Web browser displays generated page
5. Web server transmits generated output to the requesting browser
4. Application Server returns processed output to HTTP Server

In other words, Web application servers are page preprocessors. They process the requested page before it is sent back to the client (the browser), and in doing so they open the door to developers to do all sorts of interesting things on the server, things such as

- Creating guest books
- Conducting surveys
- Changing your pages on the fly based on date, time, first visit, and whatever else you can think of
- Personalizing pages for your visitors
- In fact, all the features listed previously

What Is ColdFusion?

Initially, developing highly interactive and data-rich sites was a difficult process. Writing custom Web-based applications was a job for experienced programmers only. A good working knowledge of Unix was a prerequisite, and experience with traditional development or scripting languages was a must.

But all that has changed. Macromedia's ColdFusion enables you to create sites every bit as powerful and capable as those listed earlier, without a long and painful learning curve. In fact, rather than being painful, the process is actually fun!

So, what exactly is ColdFusion? Simply put, ColdFusion is an application server—one of the very best out there (as well as the very first one out there; ColdFusion actually created the Application Server category back in 1995).

ColdFusion does not require coding in traditional programming languages, although traditional programming constructs and techniques are fully supported. Instead, you create applications by extending your standard HTML files with high-level formatting functions, conditional operators, and database commands. These commands are instructions to the ColdFusion processor and form the building blocks on which to build industrial-strength applications.

This method of creating Web applications has significant advantages over conventional application development. Advantages include

- ColdFusion applications can be developed rapidly because no coding, other than use of simple HTML style tags, is required.
- ColdFusion applications are easy to test and roll out.
- The ColdFusion language contains all the processing and formatting functions you'll need (and the capability to create your own functions if you really run into a dead end).
- ColdFusion applications are easy to maintain because no compilation or linking step is required (files actually are compiled, but that happens transparently as I'll explain shortly). The files you create are the files used by ColdFusion.
- ColdFusion provides all the tools you need to troubleshoot and debug applications, including a powerful development environment and debugger.
- ColdFusion comes with all the hooks necessary to link to almost any database application and any other external system.
- ColdFusion is fast, thanks to its scalable, multithreaded, service-based architecture.
- ColdFusion is built on industry standard Java architecture, and supports all major standards and initiatives.

ColdFusion and Your Intranet or Extranet

Although we've been discussing Internet sites, the benefits of ColdFusion apply to intranets and extranets, too.

Most companies have masses of information stored in various systems. Users often don't know what information is available or even how to access it.

ColdFusion bridges the gap between existing and legacy applications and your employees. It empowers employees with the tools to work more efficiently.

ColdFusion Explained

You're now ready to take a look at ColdFusion so you can understand what it is and how it works its magic.

And if you're wondering why you went through all this discussion about the Internet and Web servers, here's where it will all fit together.

The ColdFusion Application Server

ColdFusion is an application server—a piece of software that (usually) resides on the same computer as your Web server, enabling the Web server to do things it would not normally know how to do.

ColdFusion is actually made up of several pieces of software (applications on Windows; and daemons on Linux, Solaris, and HP-UX). The ColdFusion Application Server is the program that actually parses (reads and compiles) and processes any supplied instructions.

Instructions are passed to ColdFusion using templates. A *template* looks much like any HTML file, with one big difference. Unlike HTML files, ColdFusion templates can contain special tags that instruct ColdFusion to perform specific operations. This is a sample ColdFusion template; it is one that you'll use later in this book.

```
<!--- Get movies sorted by release date --->
<CFQUERY DATASOURCE="ows" NAME="movies">
 SELECT MovieTitle, DateInTheaters
 FROM Films
 ORDER BY DateInTheaters
</CFQUERY>

<!--- Create HTML page --->
<HTML>
<HEAD>
<TITLE>Movies by Release Date</TITLE>
</HEAD>

<BODY>

<H1>Movies by Release Date</H1>

<!--- Display movies in list format --->
<UL>
<CFOUTPUT QUERY="movies">
 <LI><B>#Trim(MovieTitle)#</B> - #DateFormat(DateInTheaters)#</LI>
</CFOUTPUT>
</UL>

</BODY>

</HTML>
```

Earlier in this chapter, it was stated that Web servers typically return the contents of a Web page without paying any attention to the file contents.

That's exactly what ColdFusion does not do. When ColdFusion receives a request, it parses through the template looking for special ColdFusion tags (they all begin with `CF`) or ColdFusion variables and functions (always surrounded by pound signs). Any HTML or plain text is left alone and is output to the Web server untouched. Any ColdFusion instructions are processed, and any existing results are sent to the Web server (just like in Figure 1.6 above). The Web server can then send the entire output back to the requester's browser. As explained earlier, the request file type tells the Web server that a request is to be handled by an application server. All ColdFusion files have an extension of `.cfm` or `.cfml`, like this:

```
http://www.forta.com/books/index.cfm
```

When ColdFusion is installed, it configures your Web server so it knows that any file with an extension of `.cfm` (or `.cfml`) is a ColdFusion file. Then, whenever a ColdFusion file is requested, the Web server knows to pass the file to ColdFusion for processing rather than return it.

TIP

As ColdFusion is bound to a Web server, ColdFusion can be used to process any and all requests sent to a Web server, regardless of which host or virtual host it is sent to. But, ColdFusion is only ever bound to a single Web server, and so if you have multiple Web servers installed only one of them will be usable with ColdFusion (unless you plan to do lots of tweaking, a process not recommended at all). So, if you need to support multiple hosts, use a single Web server with IP or DNS based virtual hosts rather than multiple Web servers.

It is worth noting that ColdFusion MX actually does not need a Web server because it has one built in. So as not to conflict with any other installed Web servers (like Apache and Microsoft IIS) the internal Web server runs on port `8500` (instead of the default port `80`). During ColdFusion MX installation you'll be asked whether you want to run ColdFusion in standalone mode (bound to the integrated Web server) or using an existing Web server. If you opt to use the internal Web server you'll need to specify the port number in all URLs.

NOTE

The examples in this book use the internal Web server, and thus include the port number. If you are using an external Web server just drop the port number from the URL's.

TIP

Macromedia does not recommend that the internal Web server (standalone mode) be used on production boxes. ColdFusion MX's integrated HTTP server is intended for use on development boxes only.

The ColdFusion Markup Language

Earlier it was stated that ColdFusion is an application server, which is true, but that is not all ColdFusion is. In fact, ColdFusion is two distinct technologies:

- The ColdFusion Application Server
- The CFML language

And although the ColdFusion Application Server itself is important, ColdFusion's power comes from its capable and flexible language. ColdFusion Markup Language (CFML) is modeled after HTML, which makes it very easy to learn.

CFML extends HTML by adding tags with the following capabilities:

- Read data from, and update data to, databases and tables
- Create dynamic data-driven pages
- Perform conditional processing
- Populate forms with live data
- Process form submissions
- Generate and retrieve email messages
- Interact with local files
- Perform HTTP and FTP operations
- Perform credit-card verification and authorization
- Read and write client-side cookies

And that's not even the complete list.

The majority of this book discusses ColdFusion pages (often called *templates*) and the use of CFML.

Linking to External Applications

One of ColdFusion's most powerful features is its capability to connect to data created and maintained in other applications. You can use ColdFusion to retrieve or update data in many applications, including the following:

- Corporate databases
- Client/server database systems (such as Microsoft SQL Server and Oracle)
- Spreadsheets
- XML data
- Contact-management software
- ASCII-delimited files
- Java beans, JSP tag libraries, and EJBs
- Web Services

ColdFusion accesses these applications via database drivers (JDBC and ODBC).

➜ Database drivers are explained in detail in Chapter 5, "Introducing SQL."

Extending ColdFusion

As installed, ColdFusion will probably do most of what you need, interacting with most of the applications and technologies you'll be using. But in the event that you need something more, ColdFusion provides all the hooks and support necessary to communicate with just about any application or service in existence. Integration is made possible via:

- C and C++
- Java
- COM
- CORBA
- Web Services

These technologies and their uses are beyond the scope of this book and are covered in detail in the sequel *Advanced ColdFusion MX Application Development* (Macromedia Press, ISBN: 0321127102).

Beyond the Web

As was explained earlier, the Web and the Internet are not one and the same. The Web is an application that runs on top of the Internet, one of many applications. Others do exist, and you can use and take advantage of many of them.

One of the most exciting new technologies is Wireless Application Protocol (WAP), which can be used to power applications accessed via wireless devices (such as phones and PDAs).

As explained earlier, Web servers (and thus application servers) send content back to requesters without paying attention to what that content is. The requester (known as the *client* or *user agent*) is typically a Web browser, but it need not be. In fact, WAP browsers (the Internet browsers built into WAP devices) can also make requests to Web servers.

➜ WAP and generating WAP content using ColdFusion are discussed in Chapter 32, "Generating Non-HTML Content."

In other words, although ColdFusion is primarily used to generate Web content, it is not limited to doing so in any way, shape, or form. As seen in Figure 1.7, the same server can generate content for the Web, WAP, email, and more.

Inside ColdFusion MX

ColdFusion MX is the most remarkable ColdFusion to date, and is the first completely redesigned and rebuilt ColdFusion since the product was first created back in 1995. While understanding the inner workings of ColdFusion MX are not a prerequisite to using the product, understanding what ColdFusion is doing under the hood will help you to better leverage this remarkable product.

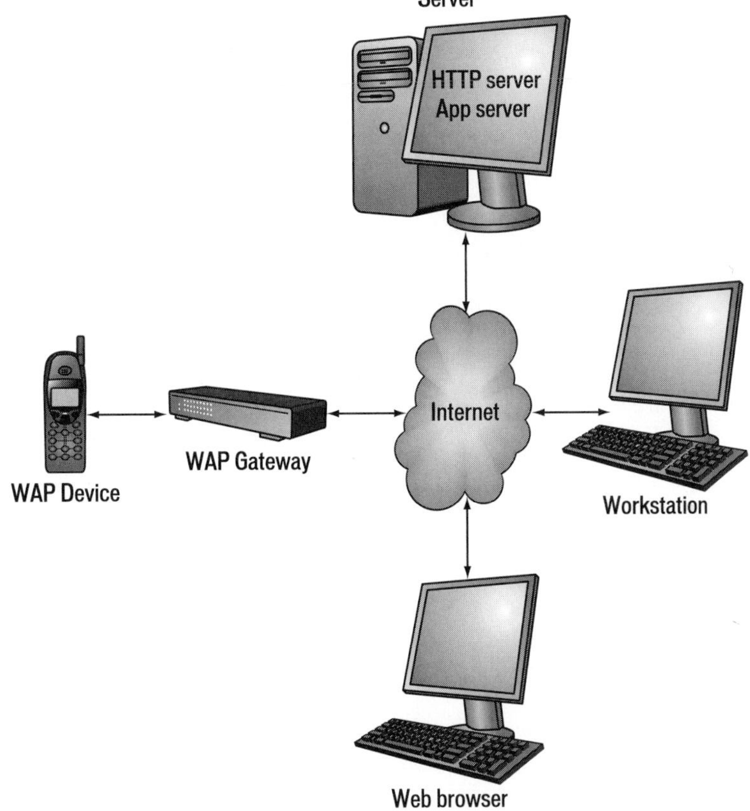

Figure 1.7

ColdFusion is client independent and can generate content for many types of clients, not just Web browsers.

As already explained, ColdFusion is a page preprocessor—it processes pages and returns the results as opposed to the page itself. To do this ColdFusion has to read each file, check and validate the contents, and then perform the desired operations. But there is actually much more to it than that—in fact, within ColdFusion is a complete J2EE (Java 2 Enterprise Edition) server that provides the processing power ColdFusion needs.

NOTE

Don't worry, you need know no Java at all to use ColdFusion.

First, a clarification. When people talk about Java they generally mean two very different things:

- The Java language is just that, a programming language. It is powerful and not at all easy to learn or use.
- The Java platform, a complete set of building blocks and technologies to build rich and powerful applications.

Of the two, the former is of no interest (well, maybe little interest) to ColdFusion developers. After all, why write complex code in Java to do what CFML can do in a single tag? But Java the platform, now that is compelling. The Java platform provides the wherewithal to:

- Access all sorts of databases
- Interact with legacy systems
- Support mobile devices
- Use directory services
- Create multilingual and internationalized applications
- Leverage transactions, queuing, and messaging
- Create robust and highly scalable applications

In the past you'd have had to write Java code in order to leverage the Java platform, but not anymore. ColdFusion MX runs on top of the Java platform, providing the power of underlying Java made accessible via the simplicity of CFML.

NOTE

By default, the Java engine running ColdFusion MX is Macromedia's own award-winning J2EE server, JRun. ColdFusion MX can also be run on top of third party J2EE servers like IBM's WebSphere and BEA's WebLogic. See Appendix A, "Installing ColdFusion MX and Dreamweaver MX" for more information.

But don't let the CFML (and CFM files) fool you—when you create a ColdFusion application you are actually creating a Java application. In fact, when ColdFusion MX processes your CFM pages it actually creates Java source code and compiles it into Java bytecode for you, all in the background.

This behavior is new to ColdFusion MX, and is part of why this is the most important new ColdFusion to date. Using ColdFusion MX you can truly have the best of both worlds—the power of Java, and the simplicity of ColdFusion, and all without having to make any sacrifices at all.

➜ Appendix F, "ColdFusion MX Directory Structure", explains many of the Java files used in ColdFusion MX.

Powered by ColdFusion

You were probably planning to use ColdFusion to solve a particular problem or fill a specific need. Although this book helps you do just that, I hope that your mind is now racing and beginning to envision just what else ColdFusion can do for your Web site.

In its relatively short life, ColdFusion has proven itself to be a solid, reliable, and scalable development platform. ColdFusion MX is the eighth major release of this product, and with each release it becomes an even better and more useful tool. It is easy to learn, fun to use, and powerful enough to create real-world, Web-based applications. With a minimal investment of your time, your Web site can be powered by ColdFusion MX.

CHAPTER 2

Building the Databases

IN THIS CHAPTER

Database Fundamentals

You have just been assigned a project. You must create and maintain a list of all the movies produced by your employer—Orange Whip Studios.

What do you use to maintain this list? Your first thought might be to use a word processor. You could create the list, one movie per line, and manually insert each movie's name so the list is alphabetical and usable. Your word processor provides you with sophisticated document-editing capabilities, so adding, removing, or updating movies is no more complicated than editing any other document.

Initially, you might think you have found the perfect solution—that is, until someone asks you to sort the list by release date and then alphabetically for each date. Now you must re-create the entire list, again sorting the movies manually and inserting them in the correct sequence. You end up with two lists to maintain. You must add new movies to both lists and possibly remove movies from both lists as well. You also discover that correcting mistakes or simply making changes to your list has become more complicated because you must make every change twice. Still, the list is manageable. You have only the two word-processed documents to be concerned with, and you can even open them both at the same time and make edits simultaneously.

Okay, the word processor is not the perfect solution, but it is still a manageable solution—that is, until someone else asks for the list sorted by director. As you fire up your word processor yet again, you review the entire list-management process in your mind. New movies must now be added to three lists. Likewise, any deletions must be made to all three lists. If a movie tag line changes, you must change just the multiple lists.

And then, just as you think you have the entire process worked out, your face pales and you freeze. What if someone else wants the list sorted by rating? And then, what if yet another department needs the list sorted in some other way? You panic, break out in a sweat, and tell yourself, "There must be a better way!"

This example is a bit extreme, but the truth is that a better way really does exist. You need to use a database.

Databases: A Definition

Let's start with a definition. A *database* is simply a structured collection of similar data. The important words here are *structured* and *similar*, and the movie list is a perfect example of both.

Imagine the movie list as a two-dimensional grid or table, similar to that shown in Figure 2.1. Each horizontal row in the table contains information about a single movie. The rows are broken up by vertical columns. Each column contains a single part of the movie record. The `Movie Title` column contains movie titles, and so on.

The movie list contains similar data for all movies. Every movie record, or row, contains the same type of information. Each has a title, tag line, budget amount, and so on. The data is also structured in that the data can be broken into logical columns, or fields, that contain a single part of the movie record.

Here's the rule of thumb: Any list of information that can be broken into similar records of structured fields should probably be maintained in a database. Product prices, phone directories, invoices, invoice line items, vacation schedules, and lists of actors and directors are all database candidates.

Figure 2.1

Databases display data in an imaginary two-dimensional grid.

Movies

Movie Title	Rating	Budget
Being Unbearably Light	5	300000
Charlie's Devils	1	750000
Closet Encounters of the Odd Kind	5	350000
Four Bar-Mitzvahs and a Circumcision	1	175000

Where Are Databases Used?

You probably use databases all the time, often without knowing it. If you use a software-based accounting program, you are using a database. All accounts payable, accounts receivable, vendor, and customer information is stored in databases. Scheduling programs use databases to store appointments and to-do lists. Even email programs use databases for directory lists and folders.

These databases are designed to be hidden from you, the end user. You never add accounts receivable invoice records into a database yourself. Rather, you enter information into your accounting program, and it adds records to the database.

Clarification of Database-Related Terms

Now that you understand what a database is, I must clarify some important database terms for you. In the SQL world (you learn about SQL in depth in Chapter 5, "Introduction to SQL"), this collection of data is called a *table*. The individual records in a table are called *rows*, and the fields that make up the rows are called *columns*. A collection of tables is called a *database*.

Picture a filing cabinet. The cabinet houses drawers, each of which contains groups of data. The cabinet is a means of keeping related but dissimilar information in one place. Each cabinet drawer contains a set of records. One drawer might contain employee records, whereas another drawer might contain sales records. The individual records within each drawer are different, but they all contain the same type of data, in fields.

The filing cabinet shown in Figure 2.2 is the database—a collection of drawers or tables containing related but dissimilar information. Each drawer contains one or more records, or rows, made up of different fields, or columns.

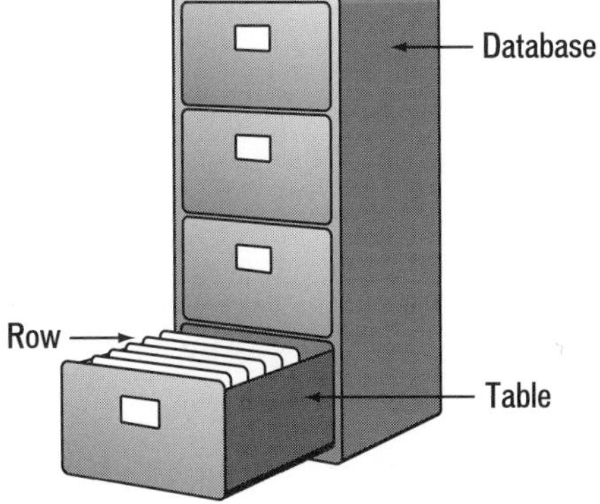

Figure 2.2

Databases store information in tables, columns, and rows, similarly to how records are filed in a filing cabinet.

Data Types

Each row in a database table is made up of one or more columns. Each column contains a single piece of data, part of the complete record stored in the row. When a table is created, each of its columns needs to be defined. Defining columns involves specifying the column's name, size, and data type. The data type specifies what data can be stored in a column.

Data types specify the characteristics of a column and instruct the database as to what kind of data can be entered into it. Some data types allow the entry of free-form alphanumeric data. Others restrict data entry to specific data, such as numbers, dates, or true or false flags. A list of common data types is shown in Table 2.1.

Table 2.1 Common Database Data Types and How They Are Used

DATA TYPE	RESTRICTIONS	TYPICAL USE
Character	Upper and lowercase text, numbers, symbols	Names, addresses, descriptions
Numeric	Positive and negative numbers, decimal points	Quantities, numbers
Date	Dates, times	Dates, times
Money	Positive and negative numbers, decimal points	Prices, billing amounts, invoice line items
Boolean	`Yes` and `No` or `True` and `False`	On/off flags, switches
Binary	Non-text data	Pictures, sound, and video data

Most database applications provide a graphic interface to database creation, enabling you to select data types from a list. Microsoft Access uses a drop-down list box, as shown in Figure 2.3, and provides a description of each data type.

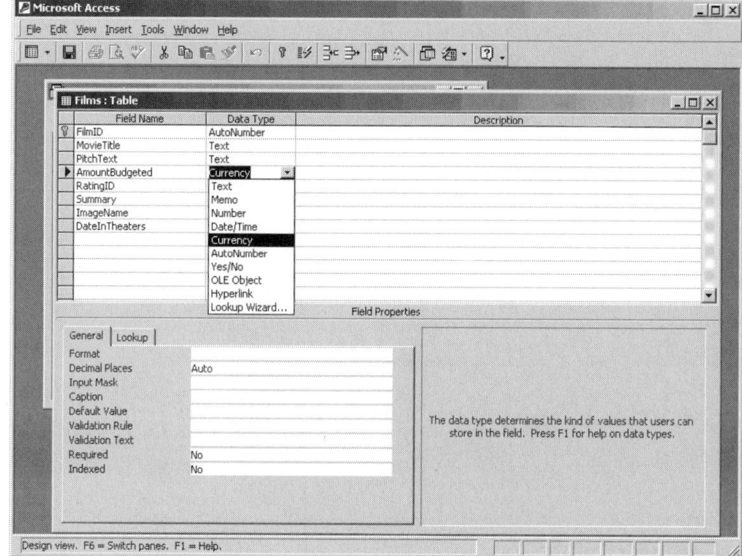

Figure 2.3

Microsoft Access uses a drop-down list box to enable you to select data types easily.

You use data types for several reasons, instead of just entering all data into simple text fields. One of the main reasons is to control or restrict the data a user can enter into that field. A field that has to contain a person's age, for example, could be specified as a numeric field. This way, the user cannot enter characters into it—only the digits `0`–`9` would be allowed. This restriction helps ensure that no invalid data is entered into your database.

Various data types are also used to control how data is sorted. Data entered in a text field is sorted one character at a time, as if it were left-justified. The digit `0` comes before `1`, which comes before `9`, which comes before `a`, and so on. Because each character is evaluated individually, a `text` field containing the number `10` is listed after `1` but before `2` because `10` is greater than `1` but less than `2`, just as a `0` is greater than `a` but less than `b`. If the value being stored in this column is a person's age, correctly sorting the table by that column would be impossible. Data entered into a numeric field, however, is evaluated by looking at the complete value rather than a character at a time; `10` is considered greater than `2` instead of less than `2`. Figure 2.4 shows how data is sorted if numbers are entered into a text field.

The same is true for date fields. Dates in these fields are evaluated one character at a time, from left to right. The date `02/05/01` is considered less than the date `10/12/99` because the first character of the date `02/05/01`—the digit `0`—is less than the first character of the date `10/12/99`—the digit `1`. If the same data is entered in a date field, the database evaluates the date as a complete entity and therefore sorts the dates correctly.

Figure 2.4

Unless you use the correct data type, data might not be sorted the way you want.

1000
2
248
39
7

The final reason for using various data types is the storage space that plain-text fields take up. A text field that is large enough to accommodate up to 10 characters takes up 10 bytes of storage. Even if only 2 characters are entered into the field, 10 bytes are still stored. The extra space is reserved for possible future updates to that field. Some types of data can be stored more efficiently when not treated as text. For example, a 4-byte numeric field can store numeric values from 0 to over 4,000,000,000! Storing 4,000,000,000 in a text field requires 10 bytes of storage. Similarly, a 4-byte date/time field can store the date and time with accuracy to the minute. Storing that same information in a text field would take a minimum of 14 bytes or as many as 20 bytes, depending on how the data is formatted.

TIP

In addition to all that has already been said about picking the appropriate data types, it is also important to note that picking the wrong type can have a significant impact on performance.

NOTE

Different database applications use different terms to describe the same data type. For example, Microsoft Access uses the term *text* to describe a data type that allows the entry of all alphanumeric data. Microsoft SQL Server calls this same data type char and uses text to describe variable-length text fields. After you determine the type of data you want a column to contain, refer to your database application's manuals to ensure that you use the correct term when making data type selections.

When you're designing a database, you should give careful consideration to data types. You usually cannot easily change the type of a field after the table is created. If you do have to change the type, you might have to create a new table and write routines to convert the data from one table to the new one.

Planning the size of fields is equally important. With most databases, you can't change the size of a field after the table is created. Getting the size right the first time and allowing some room for growth can save you much aggravation later.

CAUTION

When you're determining the size of data fields, always try to anticipate future growth. If you're defining a field for phone numbers, for example, realize that not all phone numbers follow the three-digit area code plus seven-digit phone number convention used in the United States and Canada. Paris, France, for example, has eight-digit phone numbers, and area codes in small towns in England can contain four or five digits.

Using a Database

Back to the example. At this point, you have determined that a database will make your job easier and might even help preserve your sanity. You create a table with columns for movie title, tag line (or pitch text), release date, and the rest of the required data. You enter your movie list into the table, one row at a time, and are careful to put the correct data in each column.

Next, you instruct the database application to sort the list by movie title. The list is sorted in a second or less, and you print it out. Impressed, you try additional sorts—by rating and by budgeted amount. The results of these sorts are shown in Figures 2.5, 2.6, and 2.7.

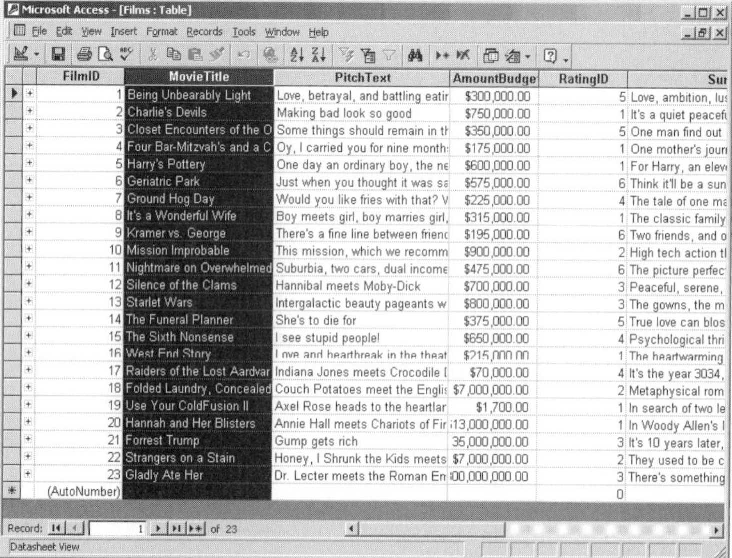

Microsoft Access - [Films : Table]

FilmID	MovieTitle	PitchText	AmountBudge	RatingID	Sur
1	Being Unbearably Light	Love, betrayal, and battling eatir	$300,000.00	5	Love, ambition, lus
2	Charlie's Devils	Making bad look so good	$750,000.00	1	It's a quiet peacefu
3	Closet Encounters of the O	Some things should remain in tł	$350,000.00	5	One man find out
4	Four Bar-Mitzvah's and a C	Oy, I carried you for nine month:	$175,000.00	1	One mother's journ
5	Harry's Pottery	One day an ordinary boy, the ne	$600,000.00	1	For Harry, an elev
6	Geriatric Park	Just when you thought it was sa	$575,000.00	6	Think it'll be a sun
7	Ground Hog Day	Would you like fries with that? V	$225,000.00	4	The tale of one ma
8	It's a Wonderful Wife	Boy meets girl, boy marries girl,	$315,000.00	1	The classic family
9	Kramer vs. George	There's a fine line between frienc	$195,000.00	6	Two friends, and o
10	Mission Improbable	This mission, which we recomm	$900,000.00	2	High tech action tl
11	Nightmare on Overwhelmed	Suburbia, two cars, dual income	$475,000.00	6	The picture perfec
12	Silence of the Clams	Hannibal meets Moby-Dick	$700,000.00	3	Peaceful, serene,
13	Starlet Wars	Intergalactic beauty pageants w	$800,000.00	3	The gowns, the m
14	The Funeral Planner	She's to die for	$375,000.00	5	True love can blos
15	The Sixth Nonsense	I see stupid people!	$650,000.00	4	Psychological thri
16	West End Story	Love and heartbreak in the theat	$215,000.00	1	The heartwarming
17	Raiders of the Lost Aardvar	Indiana Jones meets Crocodile [	$70,000.00	4	It's the year 3034,
18	Folded Laundry, Concealed	Couch Potatoes meet the Englis	$7,000,000.00	2	Metaphysical rom
19	Use Your ColdFusion II	Axel Rose heads to the heartlar	$1,700.00	1	In search of two le
20	Hannah and Her Blisters	Annie Hall meets Chariots of Fir	13,000,000.00	1	In Woody Allen's I
21	Forrest Trump	Gump gets rich	35,000,000.00	3	It's 10 years later,
22	Strangers on a Stain	Honey, I Shrunk the Kids meets	$7,000,000.00	2	They used to be c
23	Gladly Ate Her	Dr. Lecter meets the Roman Em	00,000,000.00	3	There's something
(AutoNumber)				0	

Record: 1 of 23

Datasheet View

Figure 2.5

Data entered once in a Microsoft Access table can be sorted any way you want.

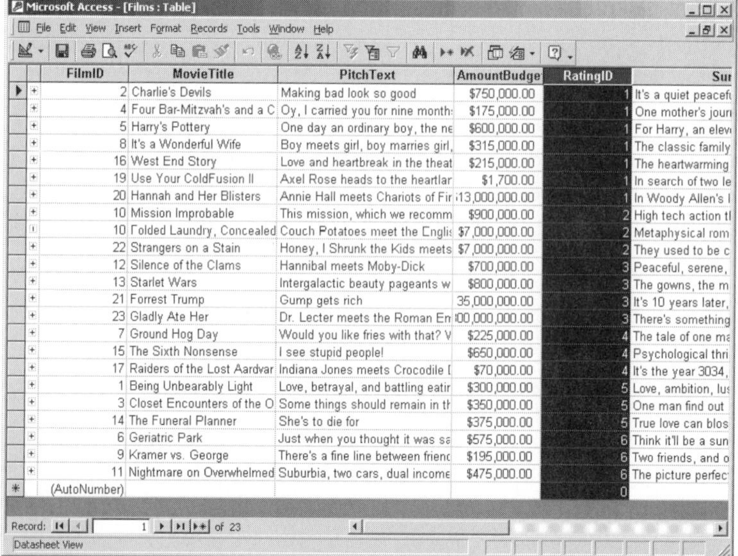

Microsoft Access - [Films : Table]

FilmID	MovieTitle	PitchText	AmountBudge	RatingID	Sur
2	Charlie's Devils	Making bad look so good	$750,000.00	1	It's a quiet peacefu
4	Four Bar-Mitzvah's and a C	Oy, I carried you for nine month:	$175,000.00	1	One mother's journ
5	Harry's Pottery	One day an ordinary boy, the ne	$600,000.00	1	For Harry, an elev
8	It's a Wonderful Wife	Boy meets girl, boy marries girl,	$315,000.00	1	The classic family
16	West End Story	Love and heartbreak in the theat	$215,000.00	1	The heartwarming
19	Use Your ColdFusion II	Axel Rose heads to the heartlar	$1,700.00	1	In search of two le
20	Hannah and Her Blisters	Annie Hall meets Chariots of Fir	13,000,000.00	1	In Woody Allen's I
10	Mission Improbable	This mission, which we recomm	$900,000.00	2	High tech action tl
10	Folded Laundry, Concealed	Couch Potatoes meet the Englis	$7,000,000.00	2	Metaphysical rom
22	Strangers on a Stain	Honey, I Shrunk the Kids meets	$7,000,000.00	2	They used to be c
12	Silence of the Clams	Hannibal meets Moby-Dick	$700,000.00	3	Peaceful, serene,
13	Starlet Wars	Intergalactic beauty pageants w	$800,000.00	3	The gowns, the m
21	Forrest Trump	Gump gets rich	35,000,000.00	3	It's 10 years later,
23	Gladly Ate Her	Dr. Lecter meets the Roman Em	00,000,000.00	3	There's something
7	Ground Hog Day	Would you like fries with that? V	$225,000.00	4	The tale of one ma
15	The Sixth Nonsense	I see stupid people!	$650,000.00	4	Psychological thri
17	Raiders of the Lost Aardvar	Indiana Jones meets Crocodile [	$70,000.00	4	It's the year 3034,
1	Being Unbearably Light	Love, betrayal, and battling eatir	$300,000.00	5	Love, ambition, lus
3	Closet Encounters of the O	Some things should remain in tł	$350,000.00	5	One man find out
14	The Funeral Planner	She's to die for	$375,000.00	5	True love can blos
6	Geriatric Park	Just when you thought it was sa	$575,000.00	6	Think it'll be a sun
9	Kramer vs. George	There's a fine line between frienc	$195,000.00	6	Two friends, and o
11	Nightmare on Overwhelmed	Suburbia, two cars, dual income	$475,000.00	6	The picture perfec
(AutoNumber)				0	

Record: 1 of 23

Datasheet View

Figure 2.6

Data sorted by rating.

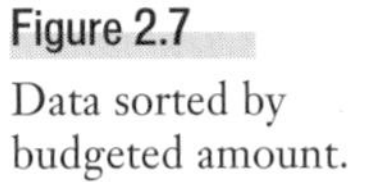

Figure 2.7

Data sorted by budgeted amount.

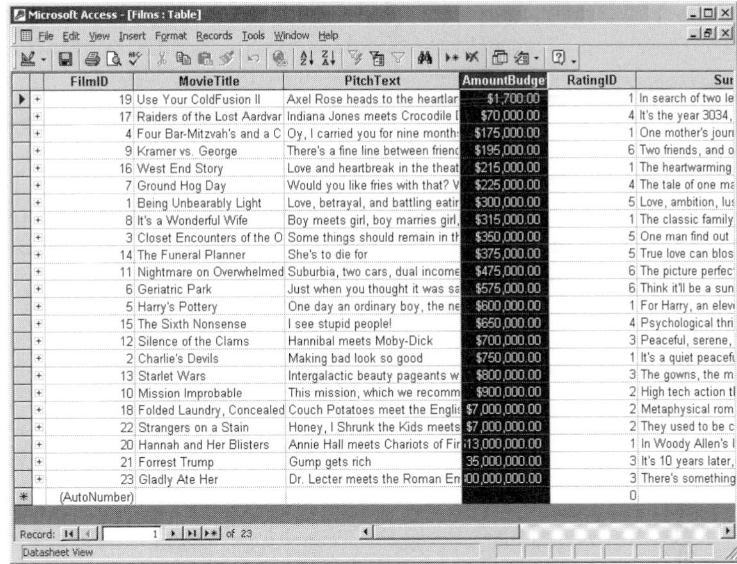

Microsoft Access - [Films : Table]

FilmID	MovieTitle	PitchText	AmountBudge	RatingID	Sur
19	Use Your ColdFusion II	Axel Rose heads to the heartlar	$1,700.00	1	In search of two le
17	Raiders of the Lost Aardvar	Indiana Jones meets Crocodile [	$70,000.00	4	It's the year 3034,
4	Four Bar-Mitzvah's and a C	Oy, I carried you for nine month:	$175,000.00	1	One mother's jour
9	Kramer vs. George	There's a fine line between frienc	$195,000.00	6	Two friends, and o
16	West End Story	Love and heartbreak in the theat	$215,000.00	1	The heartwarming
7	Ground Hog Day	Would you like fries with that? V	$225,000.00	4	The tale of one ma
1	Being Unbearably Light	Love, betrayal, and battling eatir	$300,000.00	5	Love, ambition, lus
8	It's a Wonderful Wife	Boy meets girl, boy marries girl,	$315,000.00	1	The classic family
3	Closet Encounters of the O	Some things should remain in th	$350,000.00	5	One man find out
14	The Funeral Planner	She's to die for	$375,000.00	5	True love can blos
11	Nightmare on Overwhelmed	Suburbia, two cars, dual income	$475,000.00	6	The picture perfec
6	Geriatric Park	Just when you thought it was sa	$575,000.00	6	Think it'll be a sun
5	Harry's Pottery	One day an ordinary boy, the ne	$600,000.00	1	For Harry, an elev
15	The Sixth Nonsense	I see stupid people!	$650,000.00	4	Psychological thri
12	Silence of the Clams	Hannibal meets Moby-Dick	$700,000.00	3	Peaceful, serene,
2	Charlie's Devils	Making bad look so good	$750,000.00	1	It's a quiet peacef
13	Starlet Wars	Intergalactic beauty pageants w	$800,000.00	3	The gowns, the m
10	Mission Improbable	This mission, which we recomm	$900,000.00	2	High tech action tl
18	Folded Laundry, Concealed	Couch Potatoes meet the Englis	$7,000,000.00	2	Metaphysical rom
22	Strangers on a Stain	Honey, I Shrunk the Kids meets	$7,000,000.00	2	They used to be c
20	Hannah and Her Blisters	Annie Hall meets Chariots of Fir	13,000,000.00	1	In Woody Allen's I
21	Forrest Trump	Gump gets rich	35,000,000.00	3	It's 10 years later,
23	Gladly Ate Her	Dr. Lecter meets the Roman En	00,000,000.00	3	There's something
(AutoNumber)				0	

Record: 1 of 23

Datasheet View

You now have two or more lists, but you had to enter the information only once; because you were careful to break the records into multiple columns, you can sort or search the list in any way necessary. You just need to reprint the lists whenever your records are added, edited, or deleted. And the new or changed data is automatically sorted for you.

"Yes," you think to yourself, "this really is a better way."

A Database Primer

You have just seen a practical use for a database. The movie list is a simple database that involves a single table and a small set of columns. Most well designed database applications require many tables and ways to link them. You'll revisit the movie list when relational databases are introduced.

Your first table was a hit. You have been able to accommodate any list request, sorted any way anyone could need. But just as you are beginning to wonder what you're going to do with all your newfound spare time, your boss informs you that he'll need reports sorted by the director name.

"No problem," you say. You open your database application and modify your table. You add two new columns, one for the director's first name and one for the last name. Now, every movie record can contain the name of the director, and you even create a report of all movies including director information. Once again, you and your database have saved the day, and all is well.

Or so you think. Just when things are looking good, you receive a memo asking you to include movie expenses in your database so as to be able to run reports containing this information.

You think for a few moments and come up with two solutions to this new problem. The first solution is simply to add lots more columns to the table, three for each expenses item (date, description, and amount).

This, you realize, is not a long-term solution at all. How many expenses should you allow space for? Every movie can, and likely will, have a different set of expenses, and you have no way of knowing how many expenses you should accommodate for. Inevitably, whatever number you pick will not be enough at some point. In addition, adding all these extra columns, which will not be used by most records, is a tremendous waste of disk space. Furthermore, data manipulation becomes extremely complicated if data is stored in more than one column. If you need to search for specific expenses, you'd have to search multiple columns. This situation greatly increases the chance of incorrect results. It also makes sorting data impossible because databases sort data one column at a time, and you have data that must be sorted together spread over multiple columns.

NOTE

An important rule in database design is that if columns are seldom used by most rows, they probably don't belong in the table.

Your second solution is to create additional rows in the table, one for each expense for each movie. With this solution, you can add as many expenses as necessary without creating extra columns.

This solution, though, is not workable. Although it does indeed solve the problem of handling more than a predetermined number of expenses, doing so introduces a far greater problem. Adding additional rows requires repeating the basic movie information—things such as title and tag line—over and over, for each new row.

Not only does reentering this information waste storage space, it also greatly increases the likelihood of your being faced with conflicting data. If a movie title changes, for example, you must be sure to change every row that contains that movie's data. Failing to update all rows would result in queries and searches returning conflicting results. If you do a search for a movie and find two rows, both of which have different ratings, how would you know which is correct?

This problem is probably not overly serious if the conflicting data is the spelling of a name—but imagine that the data is customer-billing information. If you reenter a customer's address with each order and then the customer moves, you could end up shipping orders to an incorrect address.

You should avoid maintaining multiple live copies of the same data whenever possible.

NOTE

Another important rule in database design is that data should never be repeated unnecessarily. As you multiply the number of copies you have of the same data, the chance of data-entry errors also multiplies.

TIP

One point worth mentioning here is that the "never duplicate data" rule does not apply to backups of your data. Backing up data is incredibly important, and you can never have too many backup plans. The rule of never duplicating data applies only to *live data*–data to be used in a production environment on an ongoing basis.

And while you are thinking about it, you realize that even your earlier solution for including director names is dangerous. After all, what will happen when a movie has two directors? You've allocated room for only one name.

Understanding Relational Databases

The solution to your problem is to break the movie list into multiple tables. Let's start with the movie expenses.

The first table, the movie list, remains just that—a movie list. To link movies to other records, you add one new column to the list, a column containing a unique identifier for each movie. It might be an assigned movie number or a sequential value that is incremented as each new movie is added to the list. The important thing is that no two movies have the same ID.

TIP

Never reusing record-unique identifiers is generally a good idea. If the movie with ID number 105 is deleted, for example, that number should never be reassigned to a new movie. This policy guarantees that there is no chance of the new movie record getting linked to data that belonged to the old movie.

Next, you create a new table with several columns: movie ID, expense date, expense description, and expense amount. As long as a movie has no associated expenses, the second table—the expenses table—remains empty. When an expense is incurred, a row is added to the expenses table. The row contains the movie that uniquely identifies this specific movie and the expense information.

The point here is that no movie information is stored in the expenses table except for that movie ID, which is the same movie ID assigned in the movie list table. How do you know which movie the record is referring to when expenses are reported? The movie information is retrieved from the movie list table. When displaying rows from the expenses table, the database relates the row back to the movie list table and grabs the movie information from there. This relationship is shown later in this chapter, in Figure 2.8.

This database design is called a *relational database*. With it you can store data in various tables and then define *links*, or *relationships*, to find associated data stored in other tables in the database. In this example, a movie with two expenses would have two rows in the expenses table. Both of these rows contain the same movie ID, and therefore both refer to the same movie record in the movie table.

NOTE

The process of breaking up data into multiple tables to ensure that data is never duplicated is called *normalization*.

Primary and Foreign Keys

Primary key is the database term for the column(s) that contains values that uniquely identify each row. A primary key is usually a single column, but doesn't have to be.

There are only two requirements for primary keys:

- *Every row must have a value in the primary key*—Empty fields, sometimes called *null fields*, *are not allowed.*
- *Primary key values can never be duplicated*—If two movies were to have the same ID, all relationships would fail. In fact, most database applications prevent you from entering duplicate values in primary key fields.

When you are asked for a list of all expenses sorted by movie, you can instruct the database to build the relationship and retrieve the required data. The movie table is scanned in alphabetical order, and as each movie is retrieved, the database application checks the expenses table for any rows that have a movie ID matching the current primary key. You can even instruct the database to ignore the movies that have no associated expenses and retrieve only those that have related rows in the expenses table.

TIP

Many database applications support a feature that can be used to auto-generate primary key values. Microsoft Access refers to this as an Auto Number field, SQL Server uses the term Identity, and other databases use other terms (for essentially the same thing). Using this feature, a correct and safe primary key is automatically generated every time a new row is added to the table.

NOTE

Not all data types can be used as primary keys. You cannot use columns with data types for storing binary data, such as sounds, images, variable-length records, or OLE links, as primary keys.

The movie ID column in the expenses table is not a primary key. The values in that column are not unique if any movie has more than one expense listed. All records of a specific movie's expenses contain the same movie ID. The movie ID is a primary key in a different table—the movie table. This is a *foreign key*. A foreign key is a nonunique key whose values are contained within a primary key in another table.

To see how the foreign key is used, assume that you have been asked to run a report to see which movies incurred expenses on a specific date. To do so, you instruct the database application to scan the expenses table for all rows with expenses listed on that date. The database application uses the value in the expenses table's movie ID foreign key field to find the name of the movie; it does so by using the movie table's primary key. This relationship is shown in Figure 2.8.

The relational database model helps overcome scalability problems. A database that can handle an ever-increasing amount of data without having to be redesigned is said to *scale well*. You should always take scalability into consideration when designing databases.

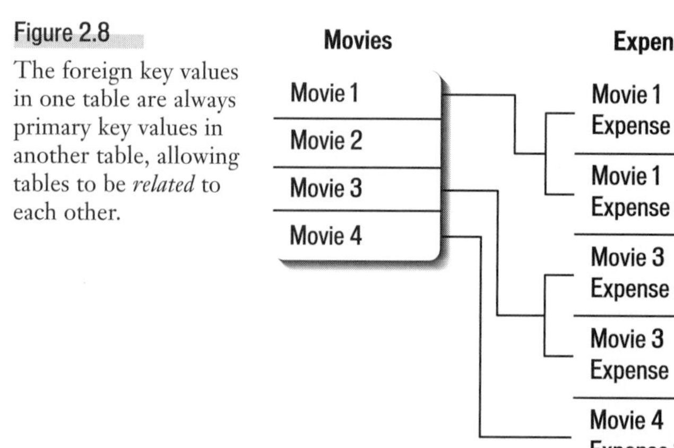

Figure 2.8

The foreign key values in one table are always primary key values in another table, allowing tables to be *related* to each other.

Now you've made a significant change to your original database, but what you've created is a manageable and scalable solution. Your boss is happy once again, and your database management skills save the day.

Different Kinds of Relationships

The type of relationship discussed up to this point is called a *one-to-many* relationship. This kind of relationship allows an association between a single row in one table and multiple rows in another table. In the example, a single row in the movie list table can be associated with many rows in the expenses table. The one-to-many relationship is the most common type of relationship in a relational database.

Two other types of relational database relationships exist: the *one-to-one* relationship and the *many-to-many* relationship.

The one-to-one relationship allows a single row in one table to be associated with no more than one row in another table. This type of relationship is used infrequently. In practice, if you run into a situation in which a one-to-one relationship is called for, you should probably revisit the design. Most tables that are linked with one-to-one relationships can simply be combined into one large table.

The many-to-many relationship is also used infrequently. The many-to-many relationship allows one or more rows in one table to be associated with one or more rows in another table. This type of relationship is usually the result of bad design. Most many-to-many relationships can be more efficiently managed with multiple one-to-many relationships.

Multitable Relationships

Now that you understand relational databases, let's look at the directors problem again. You will recall that the initial solution was to add the directors directly into the movie table, but that was not a viable solution because it would not allow for multiple directors in a single movie.

Actually, an even bigger problem exists with the suggested solution. As I said earlier, relational database design dictates that data never be repeated. If the director's name was listed with the movie, any director who directed more than one movie would be listed more than once.

In other words, unlike the expenses—which are always associated with a single movie—directors can be associated with multiple movies, and movies can be associated with multiple directors. Two tables will not help here.

The solution to this type of relationship problem is to use three database tables:

- Movies are listed in their own table, and each movie has a unique ID.
- Directors are listed in their own table, and each director has a unique ID.
- A new third table is added, which relates the two previous tables.

For example, if movie number `105` was directed by director number `3`, a single row would be added to the third table. It would contain two foreign keys, the primary keys of each of the movie and director tables. To find out who directed movie number `105`, all you'd have to do is look at that third table for movie number `105` and you'd find that director `3` was the director. Then, you'd look at the directors table to find out who director `3` is.

That might sound overly complex for a simple mapping, but bear with me—this is all about to make a lot of sense.

If movie number `105` had a second director (perhaps director ID `5`), all you would need to do is add a second row to that third table. This new row would also contain `105` in the movie ID column, but it would contain a different director ID in the director column. Now you can associate two, three, or more directors with each movie. Each director is associated with a movie by simply adding one more record to that third table.

And if you wanted to find all movies directed by a specific director, you could do that too. First, you'd find the ID of the director in the directors table. Then, you'd search that third table for all movie IDs associated with the director. And then you'd scan the movies table for the names of those movies.

This type of multitable relationship frequently is necessary in larger applications, and you'll be using it later in this chapter. Figure 2.9 summarizes the relationships used.

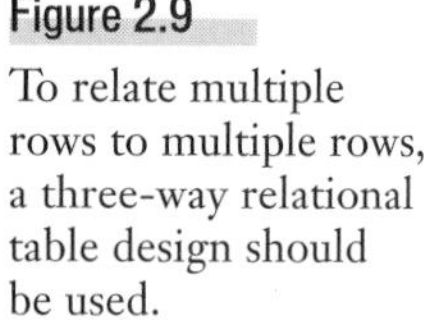

Figure 2.9

To relate multiple rows to multiple rows, a three-way relational table design should be used.

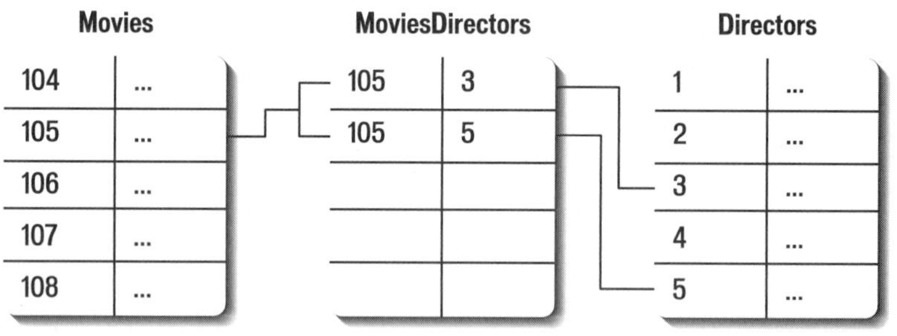

To summarize, two tables are used if the rows in one table might be related to multiple rows in a second table and when rows in the second table are only related to single rows in the first table. If, however, rows in both tables might be related to multiple rows, three tables must be used.

Indexes

Database applications make extensive use of a table's primary key whenever relationships are used. It is therefore vital that accessing a specific row by primary key value be a fast operation. When data is added to a table, you have no guarantee that the rows are stored in any specific order. A row with a higher primary key value could be stored before a row with a lower value. You should make no assumptions about the actual physical location of any rows within your table.

Now take another look at the relationship between the movie list table and the expenses table. You have the database scan the expenses table to learn which movies have incurred expenses on specific dates; only rows containing that date are selected. This operation, however, returns only the movie IDs—the foreign key values. To determine to which movies these rows are referring, you have the database check the movie list table. Specific rows are selected—the rows that have this movie ID as their primary key values.

To find a specific row by primary key value, you could have the database application sequentially read through the entire table. If the first row stored is the one needed, the sequential read is terminated. If not, the next row is read, and then the next, until the desired primary key value is retrieved.

This process might work for small sets of data. Sequentially scanning hundreds, or even thousands, of rows is a relatively fast operation, particularly for a fast computer with plenty of available system memory. As the number of rows increases, however, so does the time it takes to find a specific row.

The problem of finding specific data quickly in an unsorted list is not limited to databases. Suppose you're reading a book on mammals and are looking for information on cats. You could start on the first page of the book and read everything, looking for the word *cat*. This approach might work if you have just a few pages to search through, but as the number of pages grows, so does the difficulty of locating specific words and the likelihood that you will make mistakes and miss references.

To solve this problem, books have indexes. An index allows rapid access to specific words or topics spread throughout the book. Although the words or topics referred to in the index are not in any sorted order, the index itself is. *Cat* is guaranteed to appear in the index somewhere after *bison*, but before *cow*. To find all references to *cat*, you would first search the index. Searching the index is a quick process because the list is sorted. You don't have to read as far as *dog* if the word you're looking for is *cat*. When you find *cat* in the index list, you also find the page numbers where cats are discussed.

Databases use indexes in much the same way. Database indexes serve the same purpose as book indexes—allowing rapid access to unsorted data. Just as book indexes list words or topics alphabetically to facilitate the rapid location of data, so do database table indexes list the values indexed in a sorted order. Just as book indexes list page numbers for each index listing, database table indexes list the physical location of the matching rows, as shown in Figure 2.10. After the database application knows the physical location of a specific row, it can retrieve that row without having to scan every row in the table.

However, two important differences exist between an index at the back of a book and an index to a database table. First, an index to a database table is *dynamic*. This means that every time a row is added to a table, the index is automatically modified to reflect this change. Likewise, if a row is updated or deleted, the index is updated to reflect this change. As a result, the index is always up-to-date and always useful. Second, unlike a book index, the table index is never explicitly browsed by the end user. Instead, when the database application is instructed to retrieve data, it uses the index to determine how to complete the request quickly and efficiently.

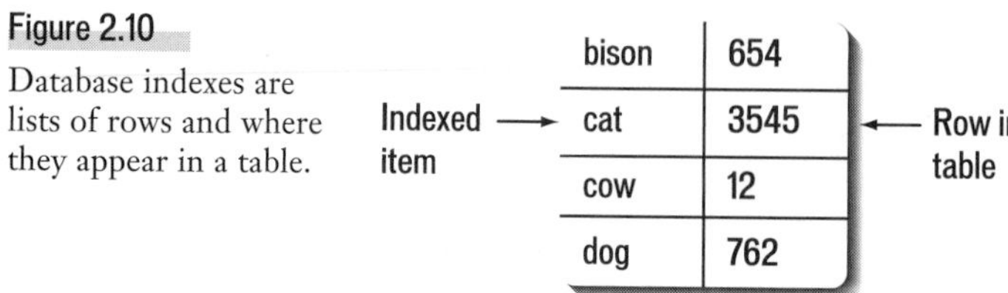

Figure 2.10

Database indexes are lists of rows and where they appear in a table.

The index is maintained by the database application and is used only by the database application. You never actually see the index in your database, and in fact, most modern database applications hide the actual physical storage location of the index altogether.

When you create a primary key for a table, it is automatically indexed. The database assumes the primary key will be used constantly for lookups and relationships and therefore does you the favor of creating that first index automatically.

When you run a report against the expenses table to find particular entries, the following process occurs. First, the database application scans the expenses table to find any rows that match the desired date. This process returns the IDs of any matching expenses. Next, the database application retrieves the matching movie for each expense row it has retrieved. It searches the primary key index to find the matching movie record in the movie list table. The index contains all movie IDs in order and, for each ID, lists the physical location of the required row. After the database application finds the correct index value, it obtains a row location from the index and then jumps directly to that location in the table. Although this process might look involved on paper, it actually happens very quickly and in less time than any sequential search would take.

Using Indexes

Now revisit your movies database. Movie production is up, and the number of movies in your movies table has grown, too. Lately, you've noticed that operations are taking longer than they used to. The alphabetical movie list report takes considerably longer to run, and the performance drops even further as more movies are added to the table. The database design was supposed to be a scalable solution, so why is the additional data bringing the system to its knees?

The solution here is the introduction of additional indexes. The database application automatically creates an index for the primary key. Any additional indexes have to be explicitly defined. To improve sorting and searching by rating, you just need an index on the rating column. With this index, the database application can instantly find the rows it is looking for without having to sequentially read through the entire table.

The maximum number of indexes a table can have varies from one database application to another. Some databases have no limit at all and allow every column to be indexed. That way, all searches or sorts can benefit from the faster response time.

CAUTION

Some database applications limit the number of indexes any table can have. Before you create dozens of indexes, check to see whether you should be aware of any limitations.

Before you run off and create indexes for every column in your table, you have to realize the trade-off. As explained earlier, unlike an index at the end of a book, a database table index is dynamic. As data changes, so do the indexes, and updating indexes takes time. The more indexes a table has, the longer write operations take. Furthermore, each index takes up additional storage space, so unnecessary indexes waste valuable disk space.

When, then, should you create an index? The answer is entirely up to you. Adding indexes to a table makes read operations faster and write operations slower. You have to decide the number of indexes to create and which columns to index for each application. Applications that are used primarily for data entry have less need for indexes. Applications that are used heavily for searching and reporting can definitely benefit from additional indexes.

For example, you should probably index the movie list table by rating because you often will be sorting and searching by movie rating. You will seldom need to sort by movie summary, so you don't have any justification for indexing the summary column. You still can search or sort by summary if the need arises, but the search will take longer than a rating search. Likewise, the release date column might be a candidate for indexing. Whether you add indexes is up to you and your determination of how the application will be used.

TIP

With many database applications, you can create and drop indexes as needed. You might decide that you want to create additional temporary indexes before running a batch of infrequently used reports. They enable you to run your reports more quickly. You can drop the new indexes after you finish running the reports, which restores the table to its previous state. The only downside to doing so is that write operations are slower while the additional indexes are present. This slowdown might or might not be a problem; again, the decision is entirely up to you.

Indexing on More than One Column

Often, you might find yourself sorting data on more than one column; an example is indexing on last name plus first name. Your directors table might have more than one director with the same last name. To correctly display the names, you need to sort on last name plus first name. This way, Jack Smith always appears before Jane Smith, who always appears before John Smith.

Indexing on two columns—such as last name plus first name—is not the same as creating two separate indexes (one for last name and one for first name). You have not created an index for the first name column itself. The index is of use only when you're searching or sorting the last name column, or both the last name and first name.

As with all indexes, indexing more than one column often can be beneficial, but this benefit comes with a cost. Indexes that span multiple columns take longer to maintain and take up more disk space. Here, too, you should be careful to create only indexes that are necessary and justifiable.

Understanding the Various Types of Database Applications

All the information described to this point applies equally to all databases. The basic fundamentals of databases, tables, keys, and indexes are supported by all database applications. At some point, however, databases start to differ. They can differ in price, performance, features, security, scalability, and more.

One decision you should make very early in the process is whether to use a *shared-file–based* database, such as Microsoft Access, or a *client/server* database application, such as Microsoft SQL Server and Oracle. Each has advantages and disadvantages, and the key to determining which will work best for you is understanding the difference between shared-file–based applications and client/server systems.

Shared-File-Based Databases

Databases such as Microsoft Access and Visual FoxPro and Borland dBASE are shared-file–based databases. They store their data in data files that are shared by multiple users. These data files usually are stored on network drives so they are easily accessible to all users who need them, as shown in Figure 2.11.

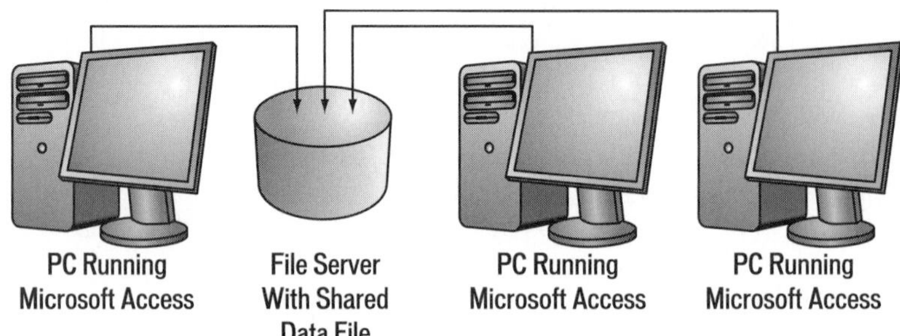

Figure 2.11
The data files in a shared-file–based database are accessed by all users directly.

When you access data from a Microsoft Access table, for example, that data file is opened on your computer. Any data you read is also read by Microsoft Access running on your computer. Likewise, any data changes are made locally by the copy of Access running on your computer.

Considering this point is important when you're evaluating shared-file–based database applications. The fact that every running copy of Microsoft Access has the data files open locally has serious implications:

- *Shared data files are susceptible to data corruption*—Each user accessing the tables has the data files open locally. If the user fails to terminate the application correctly or the computer hangs, those files don't close gracefully. Abruptly closing data files like this can corrupt the file or cause garbage data to be written to it.
- *Shared data files create a great deal of unnecessary network traffic*—If you perform a search for specific expenses, the search takes place on your own computer. The database application running on your computer has to determine which rows it wants and which it does not. The application has to know of all the records—including those it will discard for this particular query—for this determination to occur. Those discarded records have to travel to your computer over a network connection. Because the data is discarded anyway, unnecessary network traffic is created.
- *Shared data files are insecure*—Because users have to open the actual data files with which they intend to work, they must have full access to those files. This also means that users can delete, either intentionally or accidentally, the entire data file with all its tables.

This is not to say that you should never use shared-file–based databases. The following are some reasons to use this type of database:

- Shared-file–based databases are inexpensive. The software itself costs far less than client/server database software. Furthermore, unlike client/server software, shared-file–based databases do not require dedicated hardware for database servers.
- Shared-file–based databases are easier to use and easier to learn than client/server–based databases.

Client/Server-Based Databases

Databases such as Microsoft SQL Server and Oracle are client/server–based databases. Client/server applications are split into two distinct parts. The *server* portion is a piece of software that is responsible for all data access and manipulation. This software runs on a computer called the *database server*. In the case of Microsoft SQL Server, it is a computer running Windows NT (or XP) and the SQL Server software.

Only the server software interacts with the data files. All requests for data, data additions and deletions, and data updates are funneled through the server software. These requests or changes come from computers running client software. The *client* is the piece of software with which the user interacts. If you request a list of movies sorted by rating, for example, the client software submits that request over the network to the server software. The server software processes the request; filters, discards, and sorts data as necessary; and sends the results back to your client software. This process is illustrated in Figure 2.12.

All this action occurs transparently to you, the user. The fact that data is stored elsewhere or that a database server is even performing all this processing for you is hidden. You never need to access the data files directly. In fact, most networks are set up so that users have no access to the data, or even the drives on which it is stored.

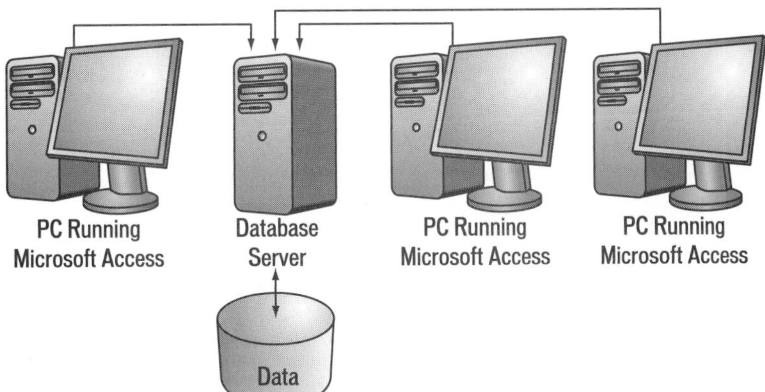

Figure 2.12

Client/server databases enable clients to perform database operations that are processed by the server software.

Client/server–based database servers overcome the limitations of shared-file–based database applications in the following ways:

- *Client/server–based data files are less susceptible to data corruption caused by incorrect application termination*—If a user fails to exit a program gracefully, or if her computer locks up, the data files do not get damaged. That is because the files are never actually open on that user's computer.
- *Client/server–based database servers use less network bandwidth*—Because all data filtering occurs on the server side, all unnecessary data is discarded before the results are sent back to the client software. Only the necessary data is transmitted over the network.
- *End users in a client/server database environment need never have access to the actual physical data files*—This lack of access helps ensure that the files are not deleted or tampered with.
- *Client/server databases offer greater performance*—This is true of the actual database server itself. In addition, client/server databases often have features not available in shared-file based databases that can provide even greater performance.

As you can see, client/server databases are more secure and more robust than shared-file databases—but all this extra power and security comes with a price:

- *Running client/server databases is expensive*—The software itself is far more expensive than shared-file database applications. In addition, you need a database server to run a client/server database. It must be a high-powered computer that is often dedicated for just this purpose.
- *Client/server databases are more difficult to set up, configure, and administer*—Many companies hire full-time database administrators to do this job.

Which Database Product to Use

Now that you have learned the various types of database systems you can use, how do you determine which is right for your application?

Unfortunately, this question has no simple answer. You really need to review your application needs, the investment you are willing to make in the system, and which systems you already have in place.

To get started, try to answer as many of the following questions as possible:

- Do you have an existing database system in place? If yes, is it current technology that is still supported by the vendor? Do you need to link to data in this system, or are you embarking on a new project that can stand on its own feet?
- Do you have any database expertise or experience? If yes, with which database systems are you familiar?

- Do you have database programmers or administrators in-house? If yes, with which systems are they familiar?
- How many users do you anticipate will use the system concurrently?
- How many records do you anticipate your tables will contain?
- How important is database uptime? What is the cost associated with your database being down for any amount of time?
- Do you have existing hardware that can be used for a database server?

These questions are not easy to answer, but the effort is well worth your time. The more planning you do up front, the better chance you have of making the right decision. Getting the job done right the first time will save you time, money, and aggravation later.

Of course, there is no way you can anticipate all future needs. At some point you might, in fact, need to switch databases. If you ever do have to migrate from one database to another, contact the database vendor to determine which migration tools are available. As long as you select known and established solutions from reputable vendors, you should be safe.

TIP

As a rule, shared-file-based databases should never be used on production servers.

Most developers opt to use client/server databases for production applications because of the added security and scalability. Shared file databases, however, often are used on development and testing machines because they are cheaper and easier to use.

This is a good compromise, and one that is highly recommended if it is not possible to run client/server databases on all machines–client/server on production machines, shared-file on development machines (if necessary).

Building the OWS Database Tables

Now that you've reviewed the important database fundamentals, let's walk through the tables used in the Orange Whip Studios application (the database you'll be using throughout this book).

ON THE CD

For your convenience, the created and populated Access MDB file is on the accompanying CD-ROM.

The database is made up of 12 tables, all of which are related. These relationships are graphically shown in Figure 2.13.

NOTE

What follows is not a complete definition of the tables; it is a summary intended to provide a quick reference that will be of use to you when building the applications. You might want to bookmark this page for future reference.

➜ See Appendix G, "Sample Application Data Files," for a more thorough description of the tables used.

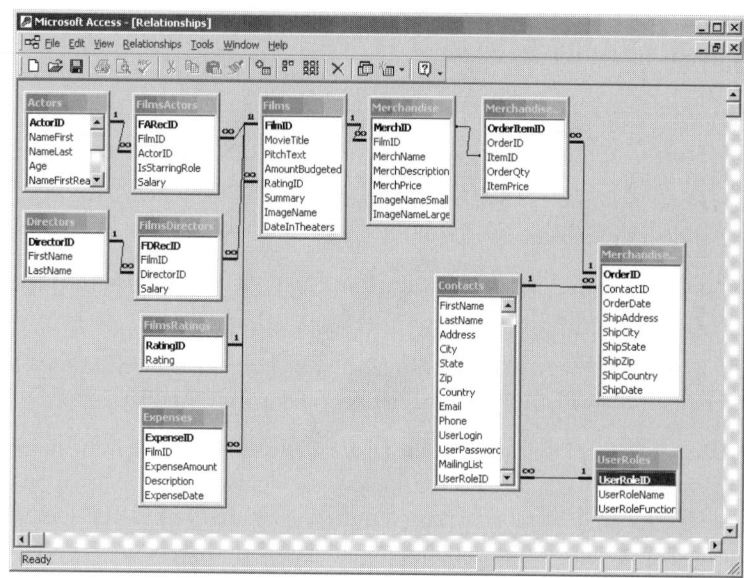

Figure 2.13

Many database applications allow relationships to be defined and viewed graphically.

The `Films` Table

The `Films` table contains the movies list.

The primary key for this table is the `FilmID` column.

This table contains a single foreign key:

- The `RatingID` column is related to the primary key of the `FilmsRatings` table.

Table 2.2 The `Films` Table

COLUMN	DATA TYPE	DESCRIPTION AND SIZE
`FilmID`	Numeric	Unique ID for each movie; can be populated manually when rows are inserted or automatically (if defined as an Auto Number field)
`MovieTitle`	Text	Movie title
`PitchText`	Text	Movie pitch text; the tag line
`AmountBudgeted`	Numeric, currency	Amount budgeted for movie (may not be equal to the actual cost plus expenses)
`RatingID`	Numeric	ID of associated rating in the `FilmRatings` table
`Summary`	Memo or long text	Full movie summary stored in a variable-length text field (to enable longer summaries)
`ImageName`	Text	Filename of associated image (if there is one)
`DateInTheaters`	Date	Expected movie release date

The Expenses Table

The Expenses table contains the expenses associated with any movies listed in the Films table.

Table 2.3 The Expenses Table

COLUMN	DATA TYPE	DESCRIPTION AND SIZE
ExpenseID	Numeric	Unique ID for each expense; can be populated manually when rows are inserted or automatically (if defined as an Auto Number field)
FilmID	Numeric	ID of associated movie
ExpenseAmount	Numeric, or currency	Expense amount
Description	Text	Expense description
ExpenseDate	Date	Expense date

The primary key for this table is the ExpenseID column.

This table contains a single foreign key:

- The FilmID column is related to the primary key of the Films table.

The Directors Table

The Directors table contains the list of directors. This table is related to the Films table via the FilmsDirectors table.

Table 2.4 The Directors Table

COLUMN	DATA TYPE	DESCRIPTION AND SIZE
DirectorID	Numeric	Unique ID for each director; can be populated manually when rows are inserted or automatically (if defined as an Auto Number field)
FirstName	Text	Director's first name
LastName	Text	Director's last name

The primary key for this table is the DirectorID column.

This table contains no foreign keys.

The FilmsDirectors Table

The FilmsDirectors table is used to relate the Films and Directors tables (so as to associate directors with their movies).

Table 2.5 The `FilmsDirectors` Table

COLUMN	DATA TYPE	DESCRIPTION AND SIZE
`FDRecID`	Numeric	Unique ID for each row; can be populated manually when rows are inserted or automatically (if defined as an Auto Number field)
`FilmID`	Numeric	ID of associated movie
`DirectorID`	Numeric	ID of associated director
`Salary`	Numeric, or currency	Actor's salary

The primary key for this table is the `FDRecID` column.

This table contains two foreign keys:

- The `FilmID` column is related to the primary key of the `Films` table.
- The `DirectorID` column is related to the primary key of the `Directors` table.

The `Actors` Table

The `Actors` table contains the list of actors. This table is related to the `Films` table via the `FilmsActors` table.

Table 2.6 The `Actors` Table

COLUMN	DATA TYPE	DESCRIPTION AND SIZE
`ActorID`	Numeric	Unique ID for each actor; can be populated manually when rows are inserted or automatically (if defined as an Auto Number field)
`NameFirst`	Text	Actor's first name
`NameLast`	Text	Actor's last name
`Age`	Numeric	Actor's age
`NameFirstReal`	Text	Actor's real first name
`NameLastReal`	Text	Actor's real last name
`AgeReal`	Numeric	Actor's real age (this one actually increases each year)
`IsEgomaniac`	Bit or Yes/No	Flag specifying whether actor is an egomaniac
`IsTotalBabe`	Bit or Yes/No	Flag specifying whether actor is a total babe
`Gender`	Text	Actor's gender (`M` or `F`)

The primary key for this table is the `ActorID` column.

This table contains no foreign keys.

The `FilmsActors` Table

The `FilmsActors` table is used to relate the `Films` and `Actors` tables (so as to associate actors with their movies).

Table 2.7 The `FilmsActors` Table

COLUMN	DATA TYPE	DESCRIPTION AND SIZE
`FARecID`	Numeric	Unique ID for each row; can be populated manually when rows are inserted or automatically (if defined as an Auto Number field)
`FilmID`	Numeric	ID of associated movie
`ActorID`	Numeric	ID of associated actor
`IsStarringRole`	Bit or Yes/No	Flag specifying whether this is a starring role
`Salary`	Numeric or currency	Actor's salary

The primary key for this table is the `FARecID` column.

This table contains two foreign keys:

- The `FilmID` column is related to the primary key of the `Films` table.
- The `ActorID` column is related to the primary key of the `Actors` table.

The `FilmsRatings` Table

The `FilmsRatings` table contains a list of film ratings used in the `Films` table (which is related to this table).

Table 2.8 The `FilmsRatings` Table

COLUMN	DATA TYPE	DESCRIPTION AND SIZE
`RatingID`	Numeric	Unique ID for each rating; can be populated manually when rows are inserted or automatically (if defined as an Auto Number field)
`Rating`	Text	Rating description

The primary key for this table is the `RatingID` column.

This table contains no foreign keys.

The `UserRoles` Table

The `UserRoles` table defines user security roles used by secures applications. This table is not related to any of the other tables.

Table 2.9 The `UserRoles` Table

COLUMN	DATA TYPE	DESCRIPTION AND SIZE
`UserRoleID`	Numeric	Unique ID of user roles; can be populated manually when rows are inserted or automatically (if defined as an Auto Number field)
`UserRoleName`	Text	User role name (title)
`UserRoleFunction`	Text	User role description

The primary key for this table is the `UserRoleID` column.

This table contains no foreign keys.

The `Contacts` Table

The `Contacts` table contains a list of all contacts (including customers).

Table 2.10 The `Contacts` Table

COLUMN	DATA TYPE	DESCRIPTION AND SIZE
`ContactID`	Numeric	Unique ID for each contact; can be populated manually when rows are inserted or automatically (if defined as an Auto Number field)
`FirstName`	Text	Contact first name
`LastName`	Text	Contact last name
`Address`	Text	Contact address
`City`	Text	Contact city
`State`	Text	Contact state (or province)
`Zip`	Text	Contact ZIP code (or postal code)
`Country`	Text	Contact country
`Email`	Text	Contact email address
`Phone`	Text	Contact phone number
`UserLogin`	Text	Contact login name
`UserPassword`	Text	Contact login password
`MailingList`	Bit or Yes/No	Flag specifying whether this contact is on the mailing list
`UserRoleID`	Numeric	ID of associated security level

The primary key for this table is the `ContactID` column.

This table contains a single foreign key:

- The `UserRoleID` column is related to the primary key of the `UserRoles` table.

The `Merchandise` Table

The `Merchandise` table contains a list of merchandise for sale. Merchandise is associated with movies, so this table is related to the `Films` table.

Table 2.11 The `Merchandise` Table

COLUMN	DATA TYPE	DESCRIPTION AND SIZE
`MerchID`	Numeric	Unique ID for each item of merchandise; can be populated manually when rows are inserted or automatically (if defined as an Auto Number field)
`FilmID`	Numeric	ID of associated movie
`MerchName`	Text	Item name
`MerchDescription`	Text	Item description
`MerchPrice`	Numeric or currency	Item price
`ImageNameSmall`	Text	Filename of small image of item (if present)
`ImageNameLarge`	Text	Filename of large image of item (if present)

The primary key for this table is the `MerchID` column.

This table contains a single foreign key:

- The `FilmID` column is related to the primary key of the `Films` table.

The `MerchandiseOrders` Table

The `MerchandiseOrders` table contains the orders for movie merchandise. Orders are associated with contacts (the buyer), so this table is related to the `Contacts` table.

Table 2.12 The `MerchandiseOrders` Table

COLUMN	DATA TYPE	DESCRIPTION AND SIZE
`OrderID`	Numeric	Unique ID of order (order number); can be populated manually when rows are inserted or automatically (if defined as an Auto Number field)
`ContactID`	Numeric	ID of associated contact
`OrderDate`	Date	Order date
`ShipAddress`	Text	Order ship to address
`ShipCity`	Text	Order ship to city
`ShipState`	Text	Order ship to state (or province)
`ShipZip`	Text	Order ship to ZIP code (or postal code)
`ShipCountry`	Text	Order ship to country
`ShipDate`	Date	Order ship date (when shipped)

The primary key for this table is the `OrderID` column.

This table contains a single foreign key:

- The `ContactID` column is related to the primary key of the `Contacts` table.

The `MerchandiseOrdersItems` Table

The `MerchandiseOrdersItems` table contains the individual items within an order. Order items are associated with an order and the merchandise being ordered, so this table is related to both the `MerchandiseOrders` and `Merchandise` tables.

Table 2.13 The `MerchandiseOrdersItems` Table

COLUMN	DATA TYPE	DESCRIPTION AND SIZE
`OrderItemID`	Numeric	Unique ID of order items; can be populated manually when rows are inserted or automatically (if defined as an Auto Number field)
`OrderID`	Numeric	ID of associated order
`ItemID`	Numeric	ID of item ordered
`OrderQty`	Numeric	Item quantity
`ItemPrice`	Numeric or currency	Per-item price

The primary key for this table is the `OrderItemID` column.

This table contains two foreign keys:

- The `OrderID` column is related to the primary key of the `MerchandiseOrders` table.
- The `ItemID` column is related to the primary key of the `Merchandise` table.

TIP

Many database applications, including Microsoft Access and Microsoft SQL Server, provide interfaces to map relationships graphically. If your database application supports this feature, you might want to use it and then print the output for immediate reference.

Accessing the ColdFusion Administrator

IN THIS CHAPTER

The ColdFusion server is a piece of software—an application. And as explained in Chapter 1, "Introducing ColdFusion," the software usually runs on a computer running Web server software. Production servers (servers that run finished and deployed applications) usually are connected to the Internet with a high-speed always-on connection. Development machines (used during the application development phase) often are standalone computers or workstations on a network and usually run locally installed Web server software and ColdFusion.

The ColdFusion Application Server software (I'll just call it ColdFusion for readability's sake) has all sorts of configuration and management options. Some must be configured before features will work (for example, connections to databases), whereas others are configured only if necessary (for example, the extensibility options). Yet others are purely management and monitoring related (for example, log file analysis).

All these configuration options are managed via a special program—the ColdFusion Administrator. The ColdFusion Administrator is a Web-based application; you access it using any Web browser, from any computer with an Internet connection. This is important because

- Local access to the computer running ColdFusion often is impossible (especially if hosting with an ISP or in an IT department).
- ColdFusion servers can be managed easily, without needing to install special client software.
- ColdFusion can be managed from any Web browser, even those running on platforms not directly supported by ColdFusion, and even on browsers not running on PCs.

Of course, such a powerful Web application needs to be secure (otherwise, anyone would be able to reconfigure your ColdFusion server!). At install time, you were prompted for a password with which to secure the ColdFusion Administrator—and without that password, you will not be able to access the program.

TIP

Many ColdFusion developers abbreviate ColdFusion Administrator to CF Admin. So, if you hear people talking about "CF Admin," you'll know what they are referring to.

Logging In to (and Out of) the ColdFusion Administrator

When ColdFusion is installed, a program group named Macromedia ColdFusion MX is created. Within that group is an option named Administrator that, when selected, launches the ColdFusion Administrator.

It is important to note that this menu option is just a shortcut, and you can access the ColdFusion Administrator by specifying the appropriate URL directly. This is especially important if Cold-Fusion is not installed locally, or if you simply want to bookmark the administrator directly.

TIP

As a rule, if you are serious about ColdFusion development, you should install a server locally. Although you can learn ColdFusion and write code against a remote server, not having access to the server will complicate both your learning and your ongoing development.

The URL for the local ColdFusion Administrator is

```
http://localhost/CFIDE/administrator/index.cfm
```

As explained in Chapter 1, ColdFusion MX has an integrated (standalone) Web server that may be used for development. That server is on port `8500` (instead of the default Web port of `80`) and so any URL's referring to the integrated Web server must specify that port. As such, the URL for the local ColdFusion Administrator (when using the integrated Web server) is:

```
http://localhost:8500/CFIDE/administrator/index.cfm
```

TIP

If, for some reason, `localhost` does not work, the IP address `127.0.0.1` can be used instead:

```
http://127.0.0.1/CFIDE/administrator/index.cfm
```

NOTE

To access the ColdFusion Administrator on a remote server, use the same URL but replace `localhost` with the DNS name (or IP address) of that remote host.

So, using the Program Group option or any of the URLs listed previously, start your ColdFusion Administrator. You should see a login screen similar to the one shown in Figure 3.1.

Enter your password, and then click the Password button. Assuming your password is correct (you'll know if it is not), you'll see the Administrator Home Page, as shown in Figure 3.2.

NOTE

The ColdFusion Administrator password is initially set during ColdFusion installation.

The Home Page is divided into several regions:

- The upper-left section contains a Home button (use this to get back to the home page if you find yourself lost) and a Logout button.
- To the right of the Home and Logout buttons is a toolbar with links to Documentation, and other important information.

- The left side of the screen contains menus with all the administrative and configuration options.
- To the right of the menus is the main Administrator screen, which varies based on the menu options selected. When at the home page, this screen contains links to documentation, online support, training, product registration, community sites, the Security Zone, and much more.

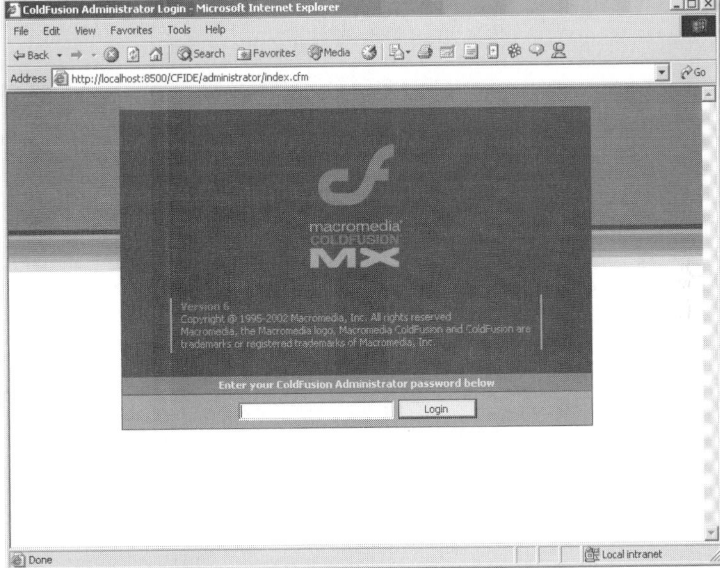

Figure 3.1

To prevent unauthorized use, access to the Cold-Fusion Administrator is password-protected.

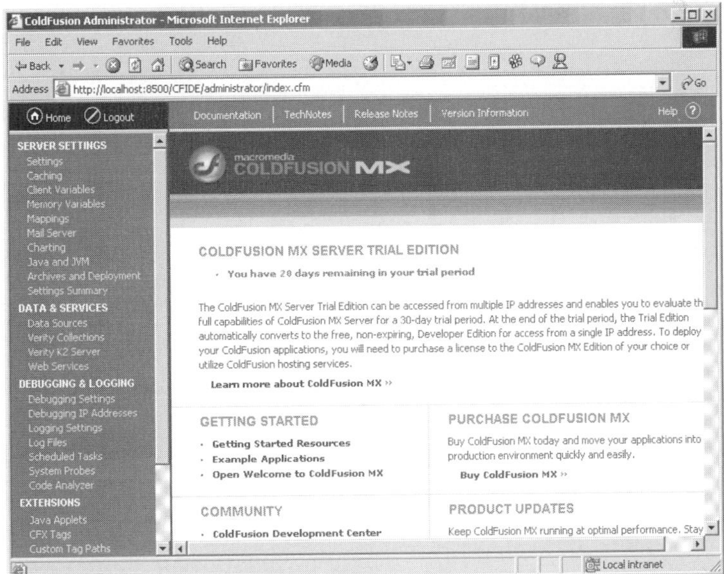

Figure 3.2

The ColdFusion Administrator Home Page provides instant access to help, documentation, and other important resources.

At the top right of the screen is a Help option. This link is always available, and additional help options are available as necessary.

Try logging out of the administrator (use the Logout button) and then log in again. You should get in the habit of always logging out of the administrator when you are finished using it.

TIP

If you are logged into the administrator, your login will timeout after a period of inactivity (forcing you to log in again), but don't rely on this. If you leave your desk or work in an environment in which others can access your computer, always explicitly log out of the ColdFusion Administrator when finished (or when you leave).

Using the ColdFusion Administrator

Let's take a brief look at the administrator and then configure the few options needed so that you can begin development. If you have logged out of the ColdFusion Administrator (or if you have yet to log in), log in now.

→ This chapter does not provide full coverage of the ColdFusion Administrator. In fact, later in this book is an entire chapter (Chapter 28, "ColdFusion Server Configuration") that covers every Administrator option in detail.

Creating a Data Source

In Chapter 5, "Introducing SQL," you'll learn about SQL and data sources, so don't worry if these terms are not familiar to you yet. For now, it is sufficient to know that for ColdFusion to interact with a database, a connection to that database must be defined – and that connection is defined by creating a data source.

The Orange Whip Studios applications use a database that you will be using extensively as you work through this book, so let's create a data source for this database now.

NOTE

If you have not yet installed the sample file and databases, refer to the end of Appendix A, "Installing ColdFusion MX and Dreamweaver MX."

Here are the steps to perform:

1. In the ColdFusion Administrator, select the Data Sources menu option (it's in the section labeled Data& Services); you'll see a screen similar to the one shown in Figure 3.3. Of course, the list of available data sources on your computer will likely differ from the figure.
2. All defined data sources are listed in this screen, and data sources can be added and edited here as well. At the top of the screen enter `ows` as the name for the new data source and set the driver type to `Microsoft Access` (as shown in Figure 3.4); then click the Add button.
3. The Data Source definition screen, shown in Figure 3.5, prompts for any information necessary to define the data source. The only field necessary for a Microsoft Access data

source is Database File, so provide the full path to the `ows.mdb` file in this field (it usually is `\ows\data\ows.mdb` under the Web root). You also can click the Browse Server button to display a tree control (created using a Java applet) that can be used to browse the server's hard drive to locate the file interactively (as shown in Figure 3.6).

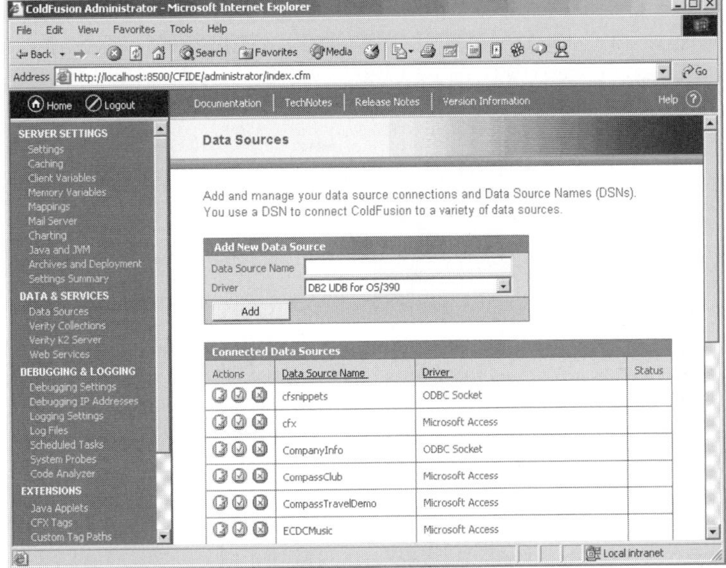

Figure 3.3

The Data Sources screen lists all defined data sources.

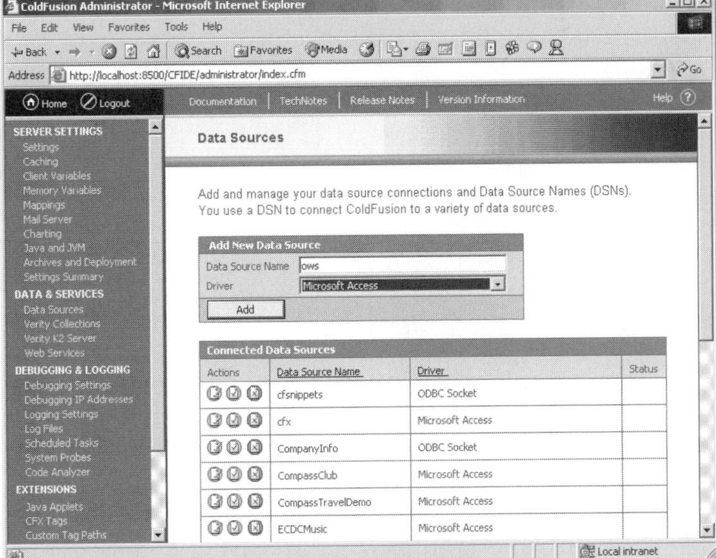

Figure 3.4

Data sources can be defined (and edited) from within the Data Sources screen.

4. When you have filled in any required fields, click the Create button to create the new data source. The list of data sources will be redisplayed, and the new `ows` data source will be listed with a Status of OK and the screen will report that the data source was successfully updated (as shown in Figure 3.7). If the Status is error and an error message is returned (as shown in Figure 3.8), click `ows` to make any necessary corrections.

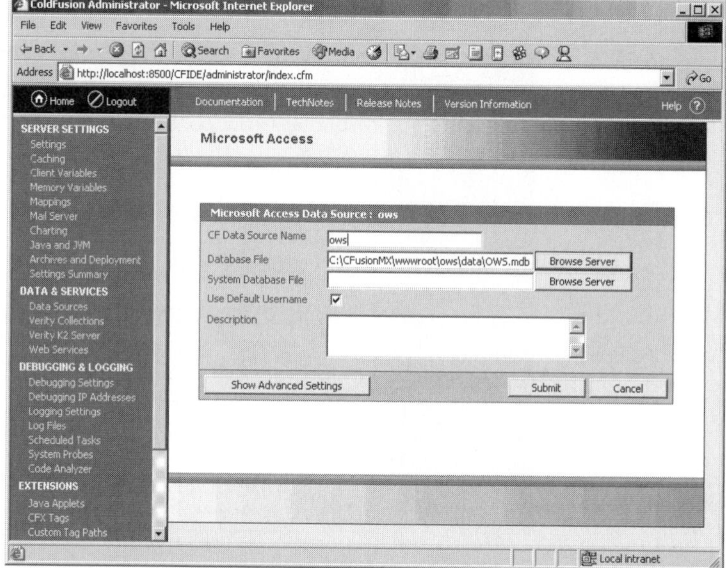

Figure 3.5

The Data Source screen varies based on the driver selected.

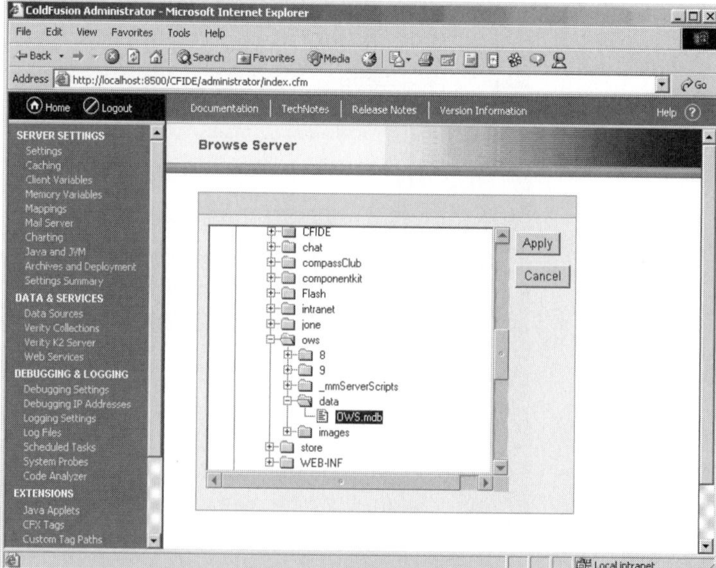

Figure 3.6

Files can be located interactively using the tree control driver browser.

You've now created a data source! You'll start using it in the next chapter.

NOTE

The options required in a data source definitions vary based on the driver used. As such, the screen used to create and edit data sources varies based on the driver used.

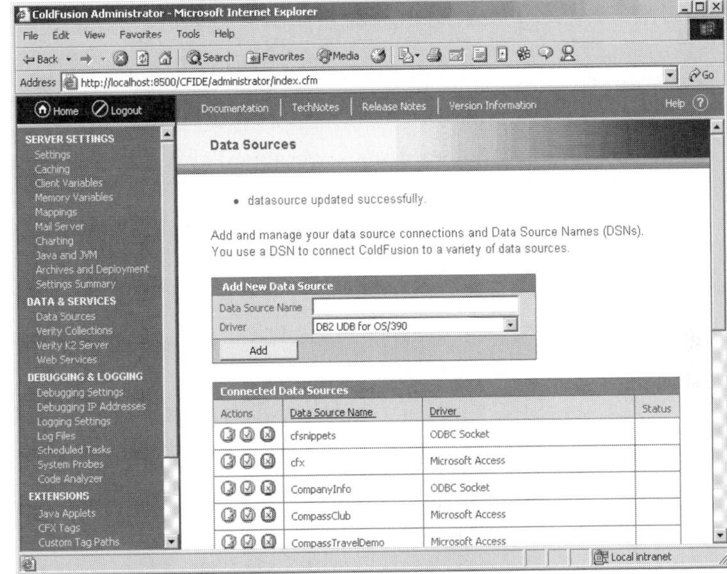

Figure 3.7
Newly created data sources are automatically verified, and the verification status is displayed.

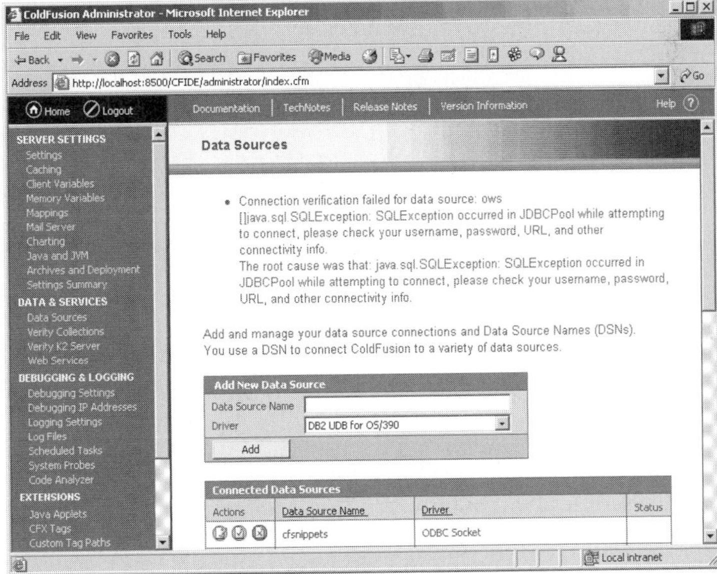

Figure 3.8
If a data source can't be used, the status indicates the failure.

Defining a Mail Server

Later in the book (in Chapter 26, "Interacting with Email"), you learn how to generate email messages with ColdFusion. ColdFusion does not include a mail server; therefore, to generate email the name of a mail server (an SMTP server) must be provided.

NOTE

> If you do not have access to a mail server or do not know the mail server name, don't worry. You won't be using this feature for a while, and omitting this setting now will not preclude you from following along in the next lessons.

To set up your SMTP mail server, do the following:

1. In the ColdFusion Administrator, select the Mail Server menu option (it's in the section labeled Server Settings); you'll see a screen similar to the one shown in Figure 3.9.

Figure 3.9

The Mail Server Settings screen is used to define the default SMTP mail server and other mail-related options.

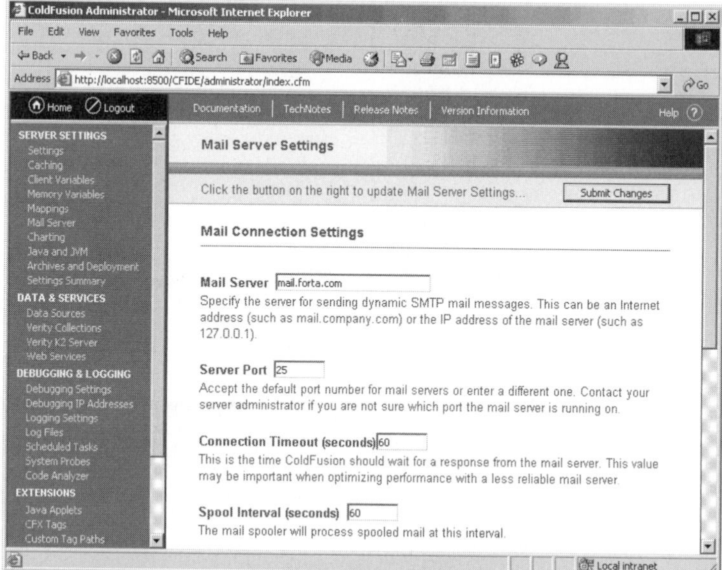

2. The first field (titled Mail Server) prompts for the mail server host (either the DNS name or IP address). Provide this information as requested.
3. Before you submit the form, you always should ensure that the specified mail server is valid (and accessible). To do this, check the Verify Mail Server Connection checkbox (lower down the page).
4. Click the Submit Changes button (there is one at both the top and the bottom of the screen). Assuming the mail server was accessible, you'll see a success message at the top of the screen as shown in Figure 3.10. (You'll see an error message if the specified server could not be accessed.)

You have now configured your mail server and can use ColdFusion to generate SMTP email.

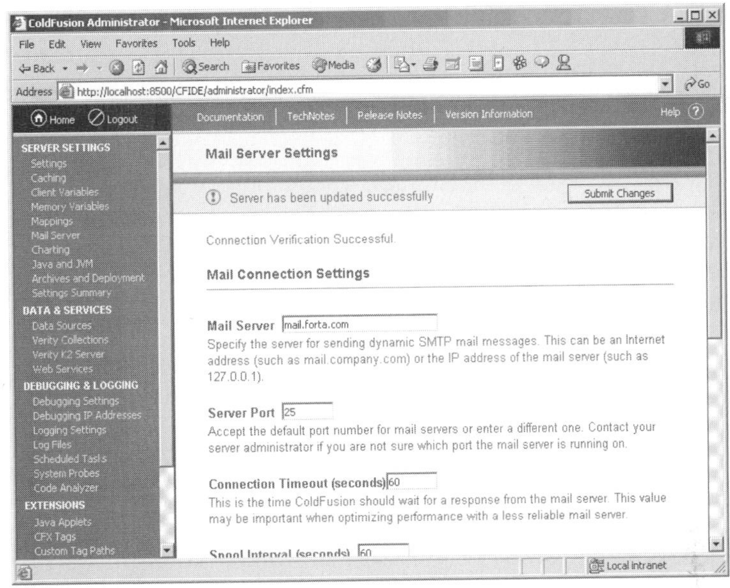

Figure 3.10

The Mail Server Settings screen optionally reports the mail server verification status.

Enabling Debugging

Another important set of screens that you should be familiar with are the debugging screens, starting with the Debugging Settings screen, shown in Figure 3.11. To access this screen, select Debugging Settings (it's in the section labeled Debugging & Logging).

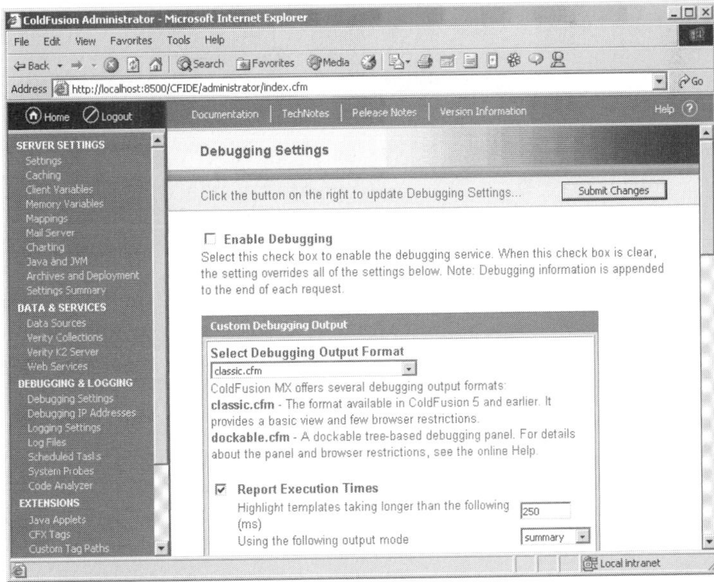

Figure 3.11

The Debugging Settings screen is used to enable and display debug output.

I do not want you to turn on any of these options now, but I do want you to know where these options are (and how to get to them) so that you'll be ready to use them in Chapter 10, "Creating Data-Driven Pages."

NOTE

When you do turn on debugging, you should turn on all the options on this page except for the first. That one is used for performance monitoring and, in truth, is not a debug option at all.

Now go to the Debugging IP Address screen (shown in Figure 3.12). To get to it, select the Debugging IP Addresses option (it's also in the section labeled Debugging & Logging). This screen is used to define the IP addresses of clients who will receive debug output (this will make more sense in later chapters, I promise). Ensure that the address `127.0.0.1` is listed; if it is not, add it. If you don't have a locally installed ColdFusion (and are accessing a remote ColdFusion server), add your own IP address, too (type it and click the Add button).

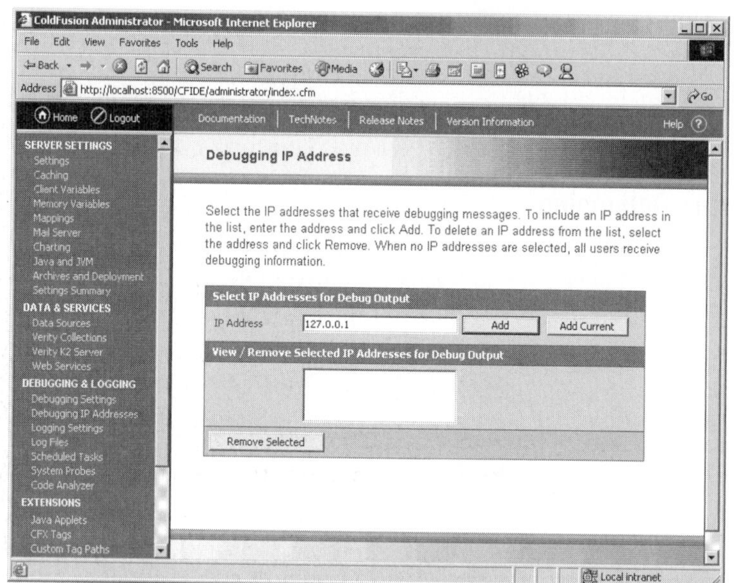

Figure 3.12

The Debugging IP Address screen is used to define the IP address that will receive generated debug output.

TIP

You may click the Add Current button to add your own IP address. If you are accessing the ColdFusion Administrator using `localhost` or `127.0.0.1` then IP address `127.0.0.1` will be added, otherwise your actual IP address will be added.

Debugging and the generated debug output are an important part of application development, as you'll see later in the book.

→ Chapter 14, "Debugging and Troubleshooting," covers the debugging options in detail.

Viewing Settings

The final screen I'd like to show you is the Settings Summary screen, which, as its name implies, reports all ColdFusion settings (included all defined data sources). To access this screen select the Settings Summary menu option (it's in the Server Setting section). ColdFusion Administrator will read all settings and will then generate a complete report like the one shown in Figure 3.13. Settings are also linked allowing quick access to the appropriate screens if changes are to be made.

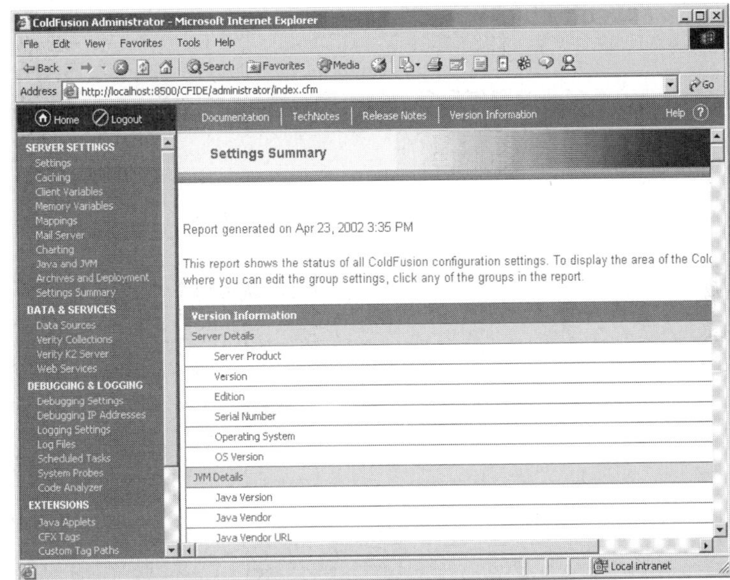

Figure 3.13

The Settings Summary is a report of all ColdFusion Administrator settings.

TIP

It is a good idea to keep a copy of this screen so that you'll have all the settings readily available if you ever have to restore them.

For now, though, you are finished with the ColdFusion Administrator. So log out and proceed to the next chapter.

TIP

To log out of the ColdFusion Administrator click on the Logout button in the top right box.

NOTE

Feel free to browse through the other administrator screens, but resist the urge to make changes to settings until you have studied Chapter 28.

CHAPTER 4

Previewing ColdFusion

IN THIS CHAPTER

Preparing to Learn ColdFusion

You're just about ready to go. But before you do, you need to know a little about the sample applications you'll be using and how to use them.

Orange Whip Studio is a low-budget movie studio waiting for its first big break. To help it get there, you need to create a series of Web applications. These include:

- A public Web site that will allow viewers to learn about the movies
- Intranet screens for movie management (budgets, actors, directors, and more)
- A public e-commerce site allowing fans to purchase movie goodies and memorabilia
- And more

Your job throughout this book is to build these applications.

TIP

Most of the applications created in this book share common resources (images and data, for example) but are actually stand-alone, meaning they don't require components or code created elsewhere. Although this is not typical of real-world application development, in this book it is deliberate and by design.

Here are a few things you must know about how to manage code and resources:

- You'll create and store the Orange Whip Studio applications in a folder named `ows` beneath the Web root.
- `ows` contains a folder named `images`, which—this should come as no surprise—contains images used in many of the applications.
- A folder named `data` in the `ows` folder contains the database used by the applications.

- Web applications are usually organized into a directory structure that maps to application features or sections. However, you won't do that here. To simplify the learning process, you'll create a folder beneath `ows` for each chapter in the book: `4` for Chapter 4, `5` for Chapter 5, and so on. The files you create in each chapter should go in the appropriate folders.

ON THE CD

The files and directories on the accompanying CD follow the same organization and naming conventions as described here.

Assuming you are running ColdFusion locally (this is advised), and assuming you installed the files in the default locations, the URL to access the `ows` folder will be `http://localhost:8500/ows/` if you're using the integrated HTTP server, or `http://localhost/ows/` if you're using an external HTTP server. You would then access folders beneath `ows`, such as the folder for this chapter, as `http://localhost:8500/ows/4/` or `http://localhost/ows/4/` (again, depending on whether you're using ColdFusion's integrated HTTP server).

TIP

If you have problems resolving host `localhost`, try using IP address `127.0.0.1` instead. `127.0.0.1` is a special IP address that always refers to your own host, and `localhost` is the host name that should always resolve to `127.0.0.1`.

NOTE

If you have yet to install the sample files, or have not yet configured the `ows` datasource as explained in Chapter 3, "Accessing the ColdFusion Administrator," you should do so now, as you'll need these to complete this chapter (as well as all future chapters).

Macromedia Dreamweaver MX is a development environment for creating Web sites and applications. Built by combining the feature sets of Macromedia Dreamweaver (a tool primarily for page designers), Macromedia Dreamweaver UltraDev (used for rapid application prototyping and basic application development), and Macromedia ColdFusion Studio (a professional-strength editing and coding environment), this new integrated development environment is the one development tool designers and developers alike can use.

As a ColdFusion developer you'll be using Dreamweaver MX extensively, and so I'll dedicate an entire chapter to this product shortly (see Chapter 7, "Introducing Macromedia Dreamweaver MX"). For now, to give you a sneak peak at what ColdFusion is all about, you'll use Dreamweaver to build two applications:

- A movie browser that displays a list of movies and contains links for moving from one page of the listing to another
- An age calculator that asks for your date of birth and calculates your age

You'll set up both of these applications using Dreamweaver MX, but you'll create each very differently. The former will use Dreamweaver features that require no coding at all, and you'll code the latter manually.

And now you're *really* ready to go.

Using Dreamweaver MX Code Generation

The first thing you'll need to do is start Dreamweaver MX. If you are using Windows, you'll see an option for this in the Macromedia programs group. The first time you start Dreamweaver MX, you'll be prompted for the Workspace to use (as seen in Figure 4.1), and you'll have two options:

- **Dreamweaver MX Workspace.** This option is intended for developers (an additional selection allows HomeSite style coding; HomeSite and ColdFusion Studio users will want to check this box).
- **Dreamweaver 4 Workspace.** This makes Dreamweaver MX look and feel like the prior version of the program; this option is intended for designers (or anyone with prior Dreamweaver experience).

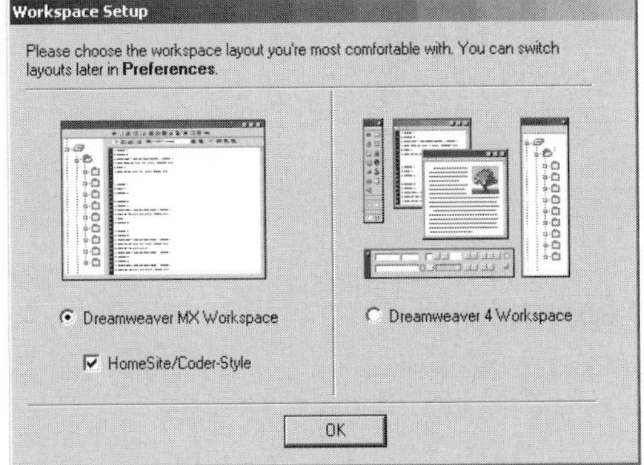

Figure 4.1

Dreamweaver MX supports two different workspaces, and you can switch between them as needed.

As a ColdFusion developer you'll want to use the Dreamweaver MX Workspace, and all examples in this book assume that you are using this option.

TIP

Not using the Dreamweaver MX Workspace? You can switch to it easily. Select Preferences from the Edit menu (or press Ctrl-U) to display the Preferences dialog, select the General category, and then click the Change Workspace button to display the Workspace Setup screen shown in Figure 4.1. Select the left option (and the checkbox) to switch to the Dreamweaver MX Workspace, and then click OK.

Your Dreamweaver screen should look something like the one shown in Figure 4.2, although you may have different panels open. You may expand and collapse panels as needed by clicking the little arrow to the left of the panel name; when the arrow points downward, the panel is expanded; when the arrow points right, the panel is collapsed.

The most important panel for developers is the Files panel, which provides access to all your code, so make sure you have Files expanded and ready for use.

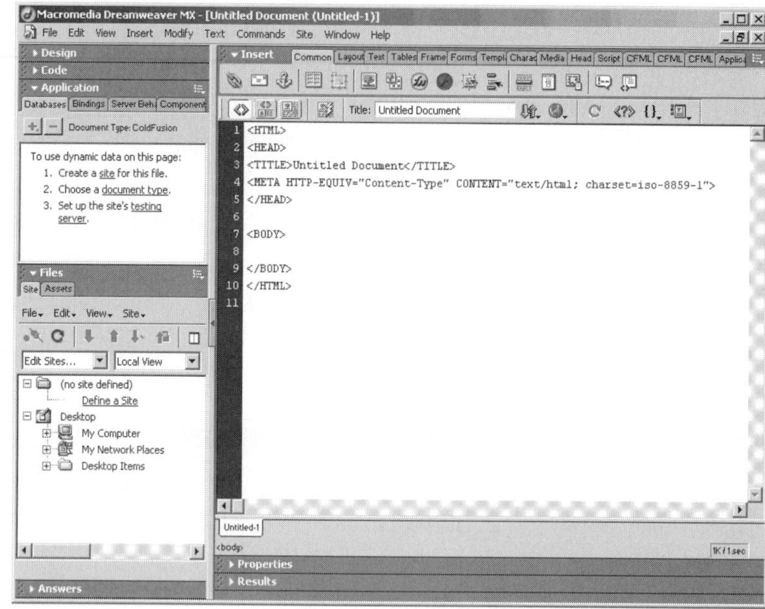

Figure 4.2

In the Dreamweaver MX workspace, Dreamweaver features a large editor window and many surrounding panels.

Preparing to Create an Application

You're now ready to create a ColdFusion application using Dreamweaver MX. Here are the steps you'll need to complete:

- Create the application root directory.
- Define a site in Dreamweaver MX.
- Verify that the application directory is set up properly and ready to use.

Creating the Application Root

Every application should go in its own directory structure, and as explained earlier the Orange Whip Studio applications reside in a directory named `ows` beneath the Web root.

If you are using the integrated HTTP server and you installed ColdFusion MX in the default location, then the Web root will be `c:\cfusionmx\wwwroot`, and the application root for the Orange Whip Studio application will be `c:\cfusionmx\wwwroot\ows`. If you are using an external HTTP server, the paths will vary accordingly. For example, if you are using Microsoft IIS, the Web root will be `c:\inetpub\wwwroot`, and the application root should be `c:\inetpub\wwwroot\ows`.

So, the first order of business is to create that application root. You can use your operating system's file utilities (for example, Windows Explorer), or you can do this directly within ColdFusion MX using the Files panel.

TIP

To create a new folder, within the Dreamweaver File panel, right-click any folder and select New Folder.

You don't have to put anything in the new ows folder to make it accessible. The fact that ows is beneath the Web root makes that happen automatically.

Creating the Site

Next you need a *site*. Every application you create in Dreamweaver MX requires a site containing all the files that make up the application, along with settings and configuration options pertaining to servers and deployment. I am not going to cover sites in any detail just now, but you will go through the basics of setting up a site. For now it will suffice to know that you must create a site for each application as follows:

1. To start the Site Definition process, click Define A Site in the Site tab of the Files panel (you may also select New Site from the Site menu). This will display the Site Definition window as seen in Figure 4.3. If your screen does not look like this, make sure you've selected the Basic tab at the top (not the Advanced one).

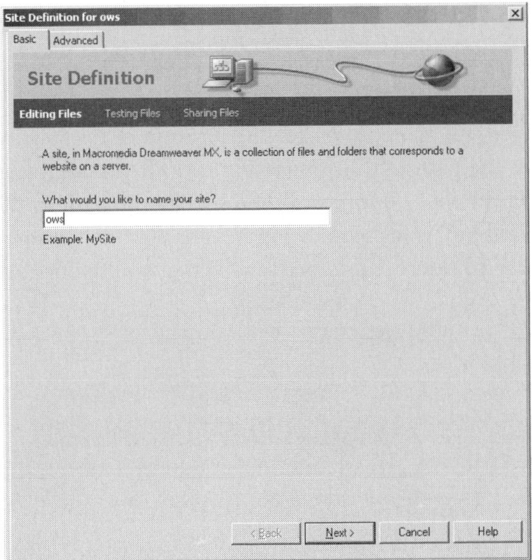

Figure 4.3
The Site Definition window is used to create and edit sites.

2. Every site must have a name, so name this one ows (as seen in Figure 4.3), then click the Next button.
3. You can use Dreamweaver MX to create static sites (ones that do not use server-side processing), as well as dynamic sites powered by several different server-side technologies. You're creating a ColdFusion site, so check the "Yes, I want to use server technology" option, and make sure you've selected ColdFusion as the server technology to use.

If ColdFusion is installed locally (it should be), Dreamweaver will detect and state its presence as seen in Figure 4.4. When you have made your selections, click the Next button.

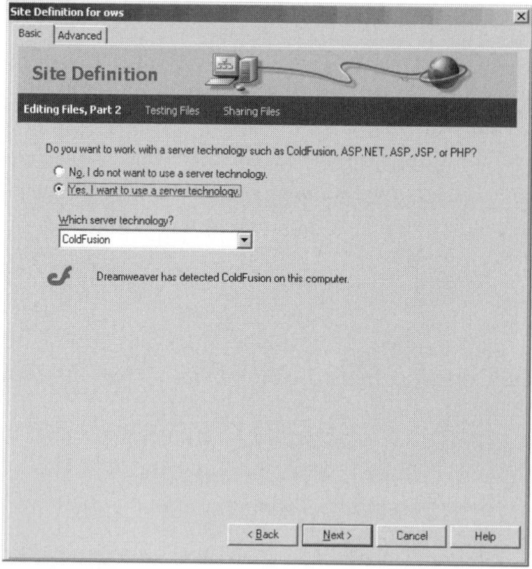

Figure 4.4

Dreamweaver MX sites can be used for both dynamic and static content.

4. Next, Dreamweaver will prompt you for the location of the hosting server (local or remote), as well as the path to the application root. If you are using a locally installed ColdFusion, select the first option, and then specify the path to the newly created `ows` directory in the field below (as seen in Figure 4.5). You may either type the path, or click the little folder icon to select it interactively. When you're done, click the Next button.

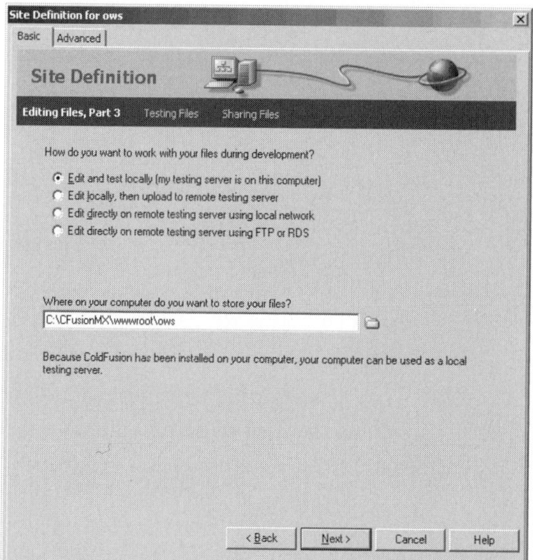

Figure 4.5

When creating a site, you must specify the application root.

TIP

If you are not using a locally installed ColdFusion, you should generally choose the second option. As a rule, you should not use the last two options (the ones that use direct editing against remote files).

5. Dreamweaver needs to be able to communicate with the application server you're using (ColdFusion), so it needs to know the application root's URL. Generally Dreamweaver MX autodetects the correct URL (as seen in Figure 4.6), so check the URL (and correct it if needed), then click the Next button.

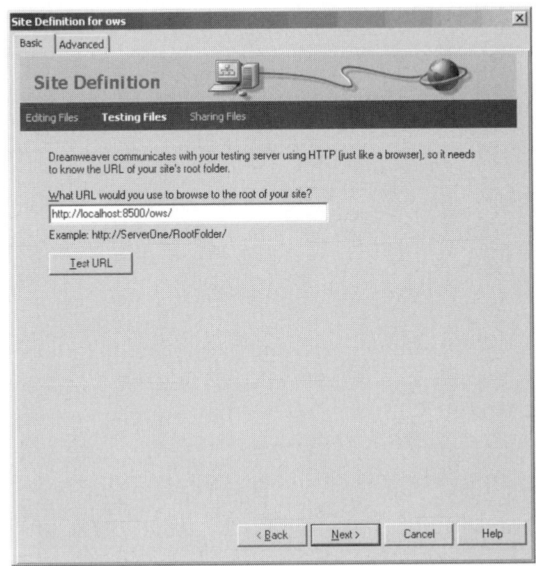

Figure 4.6

To process your code correctly, Dreamweaver requires a complete, valid URL to the application root.

TIP

To check that the URL is valid, click the Test URL button. If all is well, you'll see a verification message like the one shown in Figure 4.7.

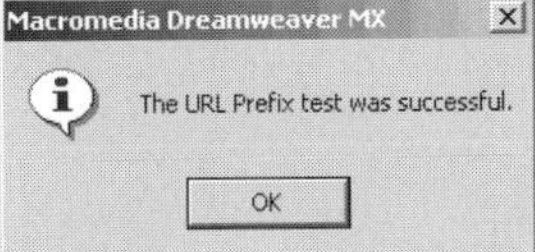

Figure 4.7

It is advisable to test the specified URL before proceeding.

6. Sites defined in Dreamweaver MX can point to up three servers: a local server (for development), a testing server, and a production server. You won't be using any remote servers for the ows application, so select No as shown in Figure 4.8, and then click the Next button.

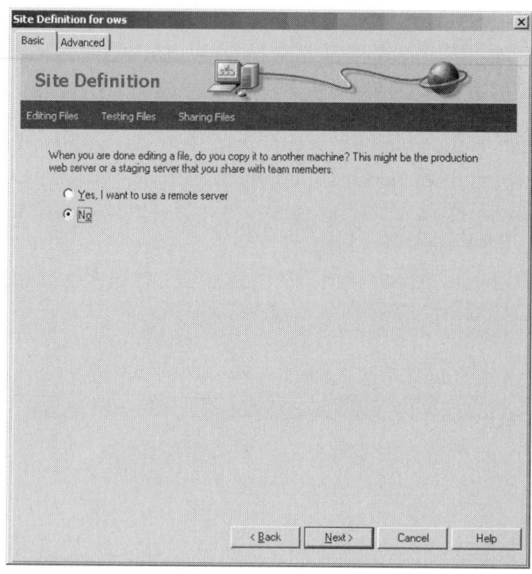

Figure 4.8

If you're using remote servers for testing or deployment, you may specify them as part of the Site Definition.

7. Dreamweaver MX will display a summary screen as seen in Figure 4.9. Check that all the information is correct, and then click Next to create the site.

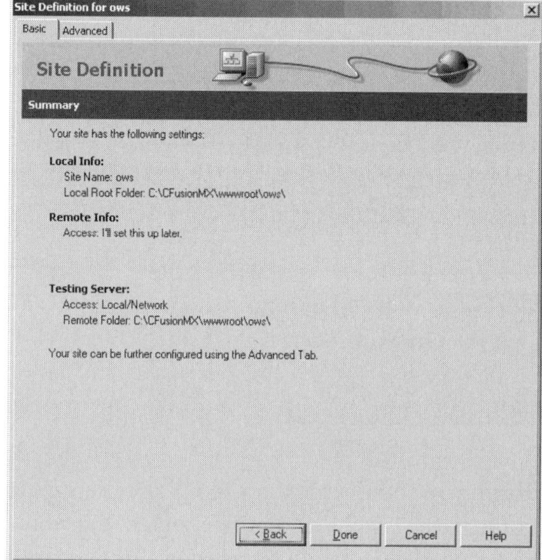

Figure 4.9

Before creating the new site, Dreamweaver MX displays a summary of all the specifies settings and options.

8. You've now created a site, and Dreamweaver MX automatically opens it, ready for use (as seen in Figure 4.10).

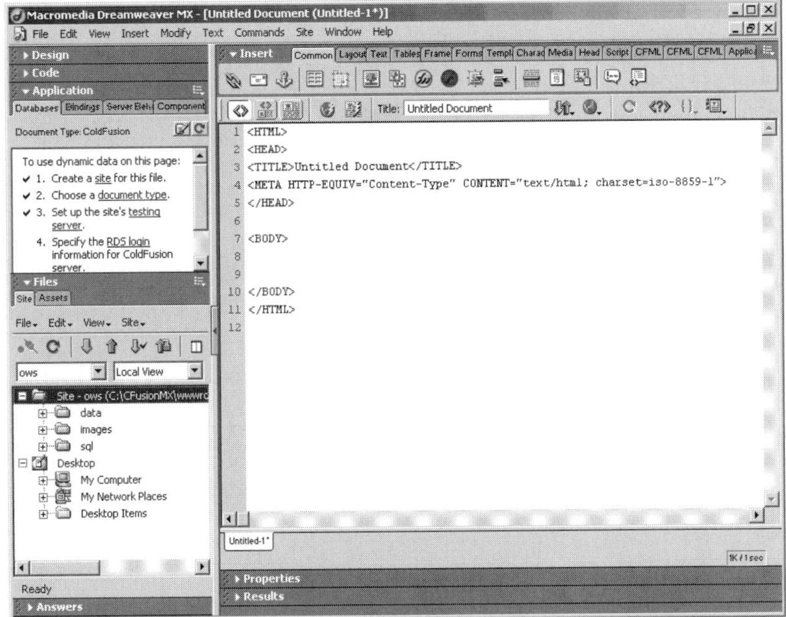

Figure 4.10

Once a site has been created, Dreamweaver MX opens it for immediate use.

NOTE

In the future you can open the site by selecting it from the drop-down list at the top of the Site tab in the Files panel.

9. If you are using ColdFusion as the server-side technology to power your site, then you must perform one additional step. In order for Dreamweaver MX to access server information (for example, databases and their contents), it needs the RDS password (specified during ColdFusion installation). The Application panel (shown in Figure 4.10) indicates that the RDS password is needed, so click the RDS log-in link in that panel to display the password prompt dialog shown in Figure 4.11. Enter the password and click OK. If all is well, you'll see a list of available datasources in the Application panel's Databases tab, as seen in Figure 4.12 (of course, your own list of datasources will likely differ, but the `ows` datasource created in Chapter 3 should be present).

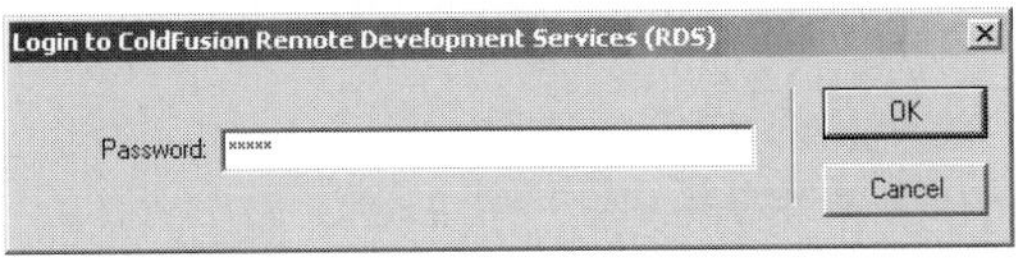

Figure 4.11

You must provide the RDS password, which protects ColdFusion resources, in order for Dreamweaver MX to access them.

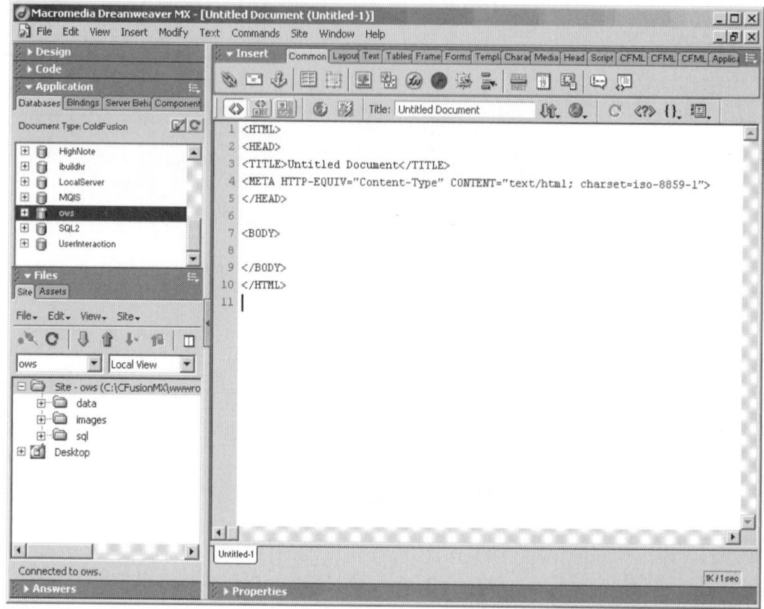

Figure 4.12

If Dreamweaver MX can connect to the ColdFusion server properly, the Databases tab will list available server datasources.

TIP

Not seeing any databases? Try clicking the little refresh button on the right side of the panel header to force a refresh.

NOTE

You may edit site settings as needed, and the Advanced tab in the Site Definition window provides access to additional configuration options.

You now have a working Dreamweaver MX site. Let's create a file in it.

➜ Sites are explained in greater detail in Chapter 7, "Introducing Macromedia Dreamweaver MX"

Creating a Work Directory and File

As I explained earlier, to simplify organizing the code created in this book, each chapter's code goes in its own directory.

To create a directory for this chapter, do the following:

1. Right-click the site name in the Site tab in the Files panel.
2. Select New Folder.
3. Name the folder `4` (for Chapter 4), and then press Enter.

TIP

Remember these steps, as you'll need to repeat them for most of the chapters in this book.

Now you'll create a file to display a list of movies. The file will go in the new `4` directory, and will be named `movies.cfm`.

1. Right-click the `4` directory in the Site tab in the Files panel.
2. Select New File.
3. Name the file `movies.cfm`, and then press Enter.
4. Double-click the new file to open it in the editor.

TIP

You can also create files by selecting New from the File menu, or by pressing Ctrl-N.

Let's name the file right away (with an HTML name, the one that appears in the Browser title bar). Above the editor window is a toolbar, and one of the options is a field for the HTML title. By default it will be `Untitled Document`, so change it to `Movie List` by typing that text in the field. Press Enter to update the title; the HTML below will reflect the change as seen in Figure 4.13.

Saving, Closing, and Opening Files

Before you go any further, you need to know how to save, close, and open files.

To save a file, do one of the following:

- Press Ctrl-S.
- Select Save from the File menu.
- Right-click the file name tab (beneath the editor) and select Save.

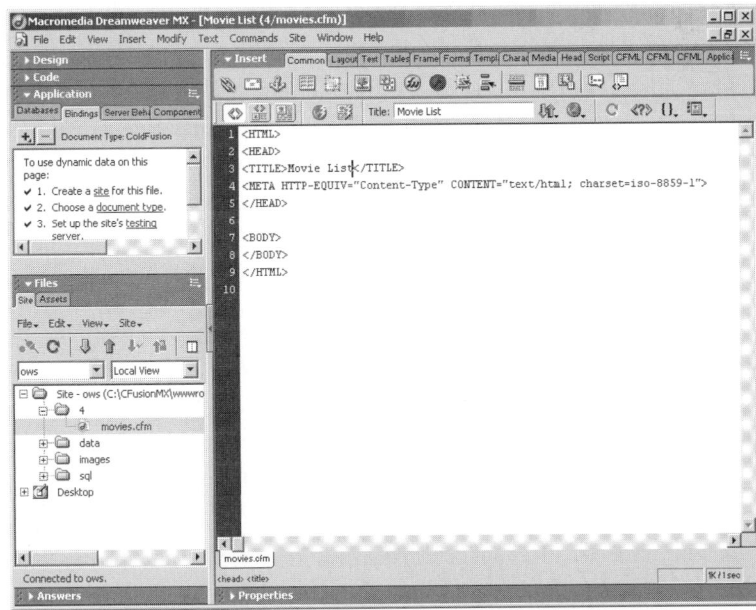

Figure 4.13

The editor window contains your code and reflects any changes made using toolbars or menu options.

TIP

If a file has changed since the last save and therefore needs saving again, an asterisk will appear after its name in the file tab.

To close a file, do one of the following:

- Press Ctrl-W.
- Select Close from the File menu.
- Right-click the file tab and select Close.

TIP

Windows users can press Ctrl-F4 to close an open file.

To open a file, do one of the following:

- Press Ctrl-O.
- Select Open from the File menu.
- Double-click the file in the site list.

As you changed `movies.cfm` (you added the HTML title), save the file.

Testing the Page

Now that you have created a page, you should make sure it is accessible via a Web browser. Open your browser and enter the URL to the page. If you are using the integrated HTTP server, the URL will be:

```
http://localhost:8500/ows/4/movies.cfm
```

If you are using a local external Web server, the URL will probably be:

```
http://localhost/ows/4/movies.cfm
```

The file displayed will be empty (you've put nothing in it), but as long as you do not receive a browser error, and the browser title bar reflects the specified title, you'll know it's working properly. You can now create ColdFusion pages in Dreamweaver MX and access them via ColdFusion using your browser.

TIP

Windows users can launch a browser directly from within Dreamweaver MX by pressing F12.

Creating an Application in Dreamweaver MX

Most of this book teaches ColdFusion coding, so you won't be using Dreamweaver's code-generation (*codegen* for short) features very much. However, to create the movie-listing application quickly (without writing any code at all), you'll let Dreamweaver MX do the work.

The application is rather simple; it displays a list of movies and their tag lines. As this list could include lots of movies, the application displays just ten at a time, so you'll need navigation options to move from page to page (as well as to the start and end of the list).

As you won't be coding manually right now, you'll switch Dreamweaver from Code View to Code and Design View (you could use Design view, but it's kind of fun to see Dreamweaver writing the code for you). To do so, click the Show Code and Design Views button on the toolbar above the editor window (it's the second button from the left).

TIP

If you are having a hard time finding the buttons to switch views, just select the desired view from the View menu.

Dreamweaver MX will display a split screen, as seen in Figure 4.14, with the code at the top and a design window beneath it. As you add design elements and features at the bottom, Dreamweaver MX will update the code above.

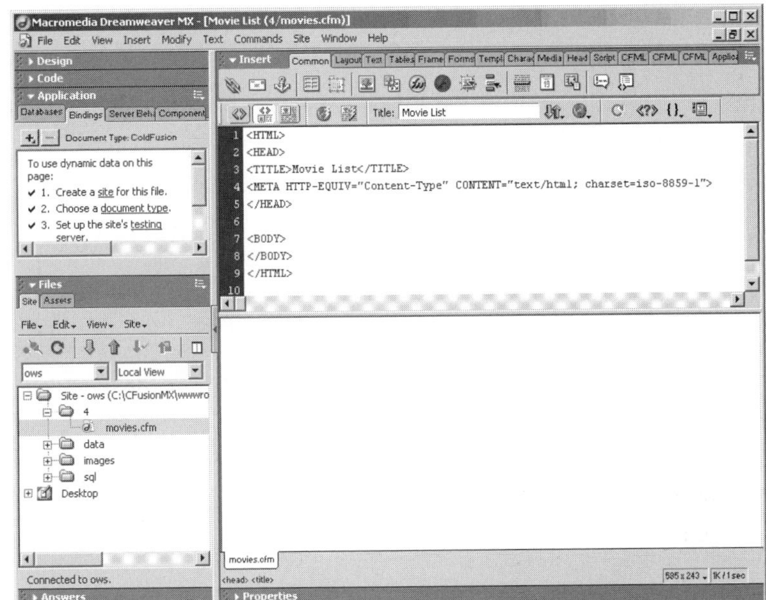

Figure 4.14

Dreamweaver MX features a Code View, a Design View, or a Code and Design View in split-screen mode.

Creating a Recordset

The Orange Whip Studios movies are stored in a database, and so the first thing you need to do is to tell Dreamweaver MX how to get that data. In Dreamweaver this is done by creating a Recordset.

➜ Chapter 5, "Introducing SQL," and Chapter 6, "SQL Data Manipulation," cover databases, recordsets, SQL, and more in detail.

You'll now create a recordset that retrieves all movies sorted alphabetically by title:

1. In the Application panel, select the Bindings tab. This tab displays any defined bindings (there are none yet), and allows you to define bindings of your own. Click the plus (+) button and select Recordset (query) to display the Recordset window seen in Figure 4.15.

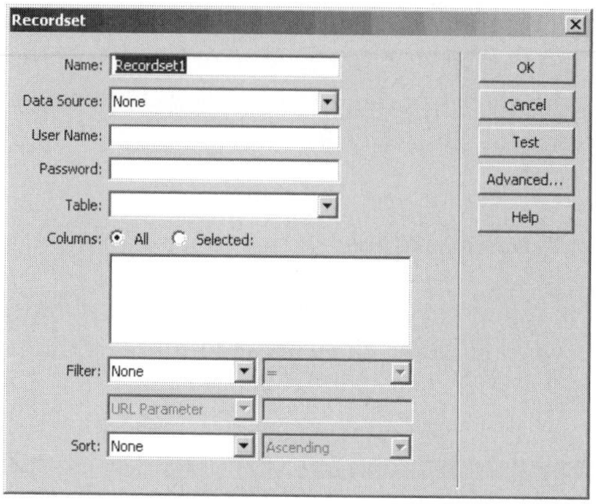

Figure 4.15

To define recordsets, you must provide database and selection information.

2. Name the records `films` (as that it the name of the database table that the data will be retrieve data from), and then select `ows` from the list of available datasources. This will populate a list of available tables as seen in Figure 4.16.

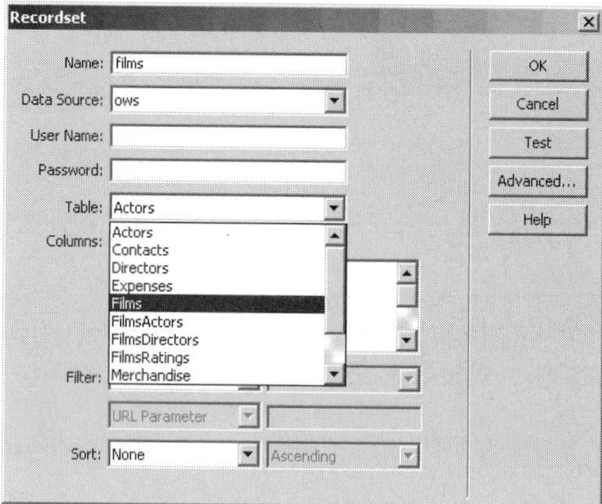

Figure 4.16

Recordsets are built interactively, and the options and selections available will vary based on prior selections.

3. Select the `Films` table. Additional options allow you to specify the columns to retrieve and filter information; leave those as is for now.

4. In the Sort field, select `MovieTitle` to sort the returned data by movie title.

5. The selections you just made built a SQL query (I'll explain that in Chapters 5 and 6). To test that the query is working properly, click the Test button to execute it. You should see a display like the one shown in Figure 4.17. If it looks correct, click OK to return to the Recordset window.

TIP

For access to the generated SQL and additional options, click the Advanced button in the Recordset window.

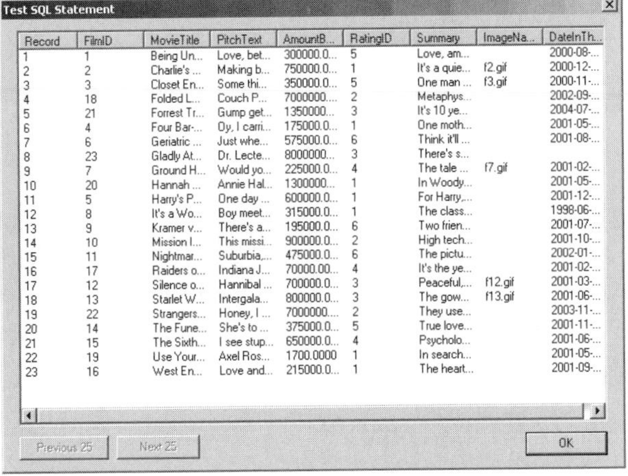

Record	FilmID	MovieTitle	PitchText	AmountB...	RatingID	Summary	ImageNa...	DateInTh...
1	1	Being Un...	Love, bet...	300000.0...	5	Love, am...		2000-08-...
2	2	Charlie's ...	Making b...	750000.0...	1	It's a quie...	f2.gif	2000-12-...
3	3	Closet En...	Some thi...	350000.0...	5	One man ...	f3.gif	2000-11-...
4	18	Folded L...	Couch P...	7000000....	2	Metaphys...		2002-09-...
5	21	Forrest Tr...	Gump get...	1350000...	3	It's 10 ye...		2004-07-...
6	4	Four Bar-...	Oy, I carri...	175000.0...	1	One moth...		2001-05-...
7	6	Geriatric ...	Just whe...	575000.0...	6	Think it'll ...		2001-08-...
8	23	Gladly At...	Dr. Lecte...	8000000...	3	There's s...		
9	7	Ground H...	Would yo...	225000.0...	4	The tale ...	f7.gif	2001-02-...
10	20	Hannah ...	Annie Hal...	1300000...	1	In Woody...		2001-05-...
11	5	Harry's P...	One day ...	600000.0...	1	For Harry,...		2001-12-...
12	8	It's a Wo...	Boy meet...	315000.0...	1	The class...		1998-06-...
13	9	Kramer v...	There's a...	195000.0...	6	Two frien...		2001-07-...
14	10	Mission I...	This missi...	900000.0...	2	High tech...		2001-10-...
15	11	Nightmar...	Suburbia,...	475000.0...	6	The pictu...		2002-01-...
16	17	Raiders o...	Indiana J...	70000.00...	4	It's the ye...		2001-02-...
17	12	Silence o...	Hannibal ...	700000.0...	3	Peaceful,...	f12.gif	2001-03-...
18	13	Starlet W...	Intergala...	800000.0...	3	The gow...	f13.gif	2001-06-...
19	22	Strangers...	Honey, I ...	7000000....	2	They use...		2003-11-...
20	14	The Fune...	She's to ...	375000.0...	5	True love...		2001-11-...
21	15	The Sixth...	I see stup...	650000.0...	4	Psycholo...		2001-06-...
22	19	Use Your...	Axel Ros...	1700.0000	1	In search...		2001-05-...
23	16	West En...	Love and...	215000.0...	1	The heart...		2001-09-...

Figure 4.17

The Test button executes SQL queries and displays returned results.

6: Click OK to save the recordset. You'll notice that Dreamweaver has inserted the database query into the code at the top of the editor.

This ColdFusion page will not display any data yet, but it now knows how to obtain a movie list from the database.

Displaying Dynamic Data

Next, you want to display the data. You'll use an HTML table with a header above each column, and you'll let Dreamweaver create that table for you:

1. Click in the Design window.
2. Select the Tables tab in the Insert toolbar above the editor window, and click the Insert Table button (the one on the left) to display the Insert Table dialog. You want `2` rows, `2` columns, and no border, so enter those settings (as seen in Figure 4.18) and then click OK to insert the table.

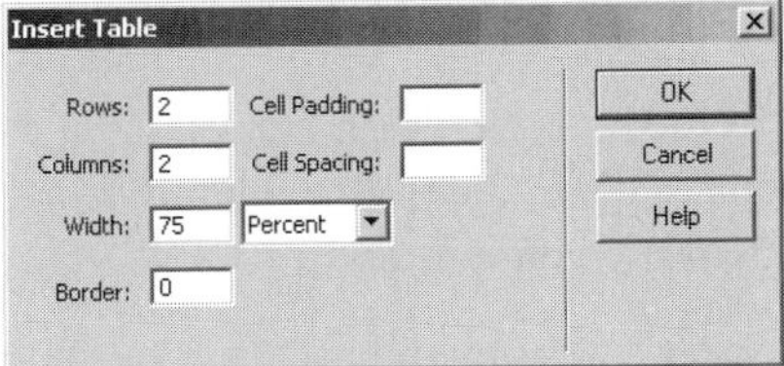

Figure 4.18

The Insert Table dialog prompts for table information, and then generates the complete HTML table.

3. The Design window will display the inserted table, and the generated HTML code will appear above, as seen in Figure 4.19.

NOTE

If you select any code in the code window, that highlights the corresponding design element in the design window. Similarly, selecting any design element in the design window highlights its code in the code window.

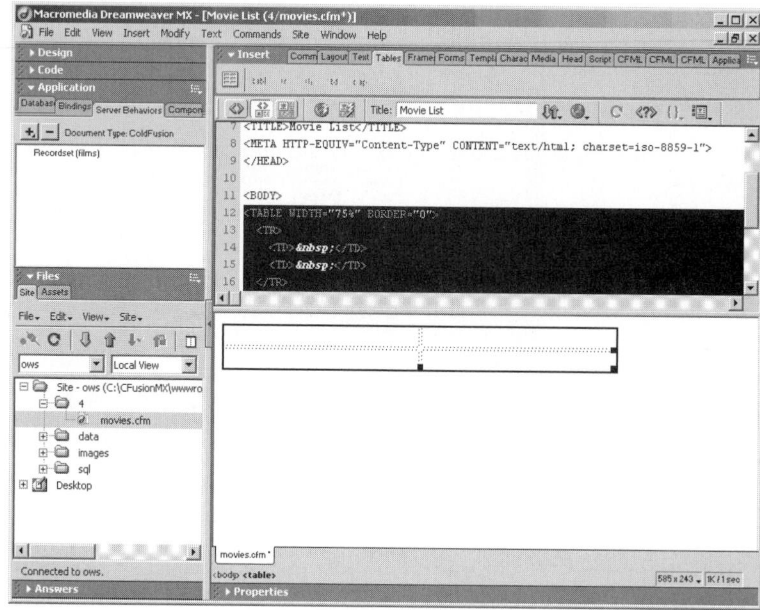

Figure 4.19
Dreamweaver automatically syncs highlighted code in the code window with design elements in the design window.

Next you'll add the titles and database columns to the HTML table:

1. Type `Movie` in the top left table cell and type `Tag Line` in the top right table cell. These will be the headers.
2. You need to make the headers centered and bold. Open the Properties panel (it's beneath the editor window) and highlight the text `Movie`, then click the bold button (the one with a big B) and the center button (top row in the Properties panel, third from the right). Repeat this for the text `Tag Line`. You now have table headers like those in Figure 4.20. When you're done, collapse the Properties panel.
3. Next you'll add the database columns (the ones you retrieved in the recordset earlier). The Bindings tab in the Application panel contains the films recordset. Click the + sign to the left of the recordset to expand it and display its columns .
4. Click the `MovieTitle` column in the recordset, then drag it to the design window, dropping it in the bottom left cell in your HTML table. The column name will appear in curly braces (so that you know it's dynamic content, not text).
5. Repeat the last step, this time dragging column `PitchText` to the bottom right cell. Your page should now look like the one in Figure 4.21.

Save your changes, and reload the page in your browser (refer to the "Testing the Page" section earlier in this chapter if you need help). You should see output similar to that in Figure 4.22—a single movie listed beneath the specified headers.

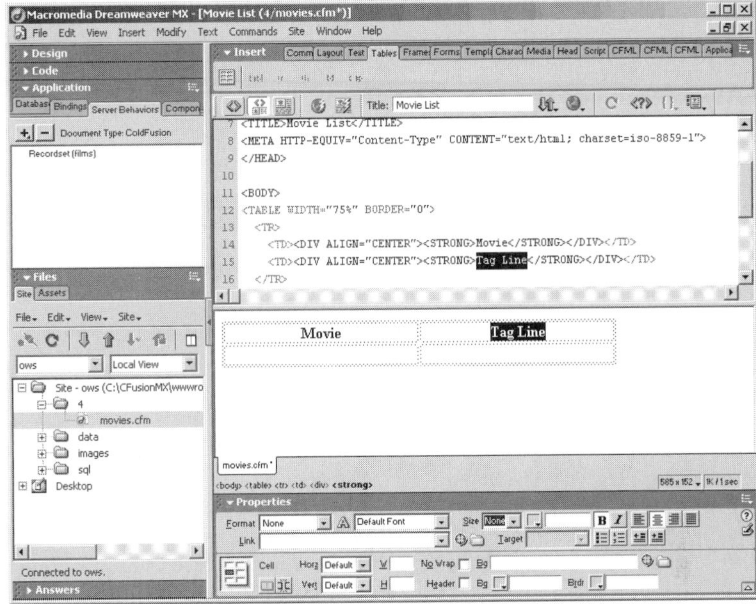

Figure 4.20

The Properties panel provides access to formatting and other options.

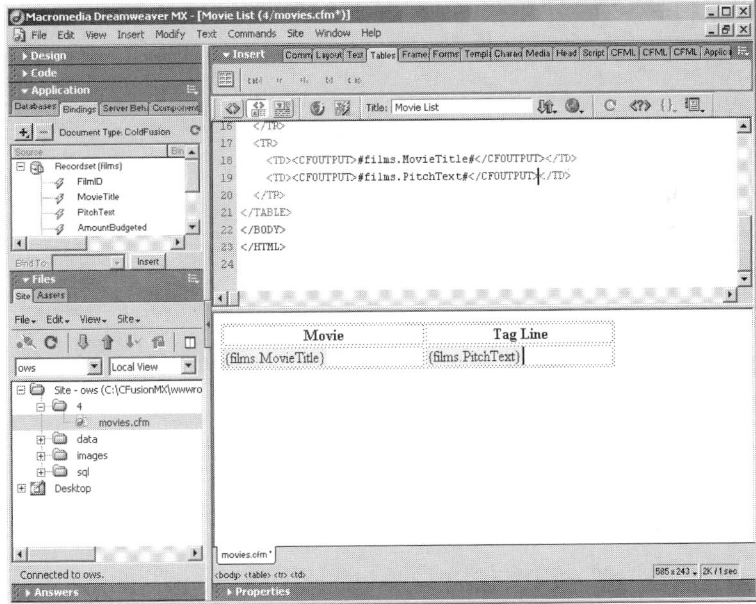

Figure 4.21

In design view, dynamic data is highlighted and surrounded by curly braces.

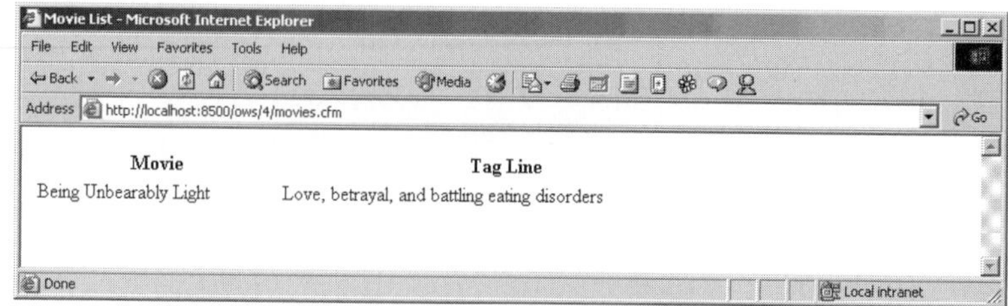

Figure 4.22

When building dynamic content, keep checking the results in a browser as you work.

Displaying Multiple Rows

So far, so good—but the page displayed just the first movie, and as Figure 4.17 shows, the database actually contains 23 movies. So why did only the first movie display? Because you didn't tell Dreamweaver to show more.

So your next task is to define a Repeat Region, a block of code or design that will repeat once per row retrieved. Here are the steps:

1. Select the Server Behaviors tab in the Application panel. You'll see the recordset listed along with the two dynamic elements, the database columns you dragged into the page as seen in Figure 4.23.
2. Before you can create a Repeat Region, you need to specify exactly what it is you want to repeat. Select the entire second row of the HTML table, as that is what you'd like to repeat for each movie.

TIP

If you place the pointer just to the left of the table row, it will turn into a left-facing arrow, allowing you to click-select the entire row.

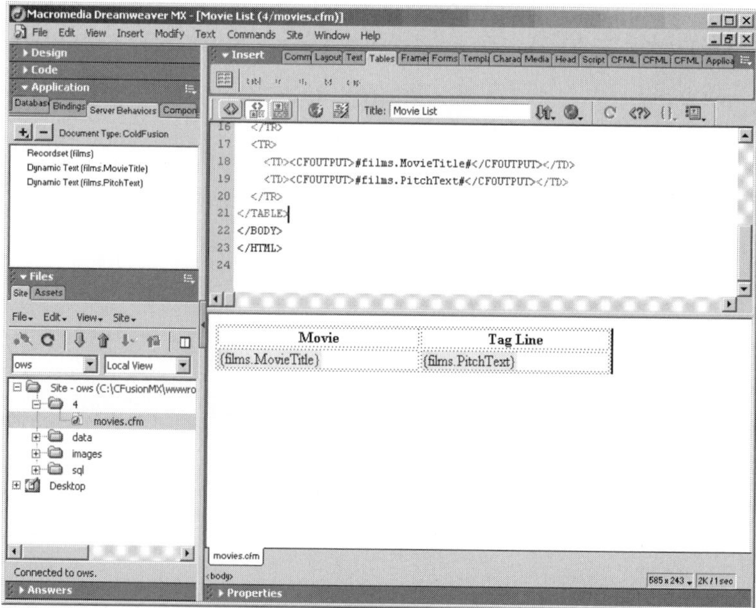

Figure 4.23

The Server Behaviors tab lists the server-side dynamic elements in your page.

3. Now that you've selected the second row, click the + button in the Server Behaviors tab to display the Repeat Region dialog seen in Figure 4.24. The correct recordset will be listed (as that is the only one defined right now), and the default value of "show 10 records at a time" will work, so click OK to create the Repeat Region.

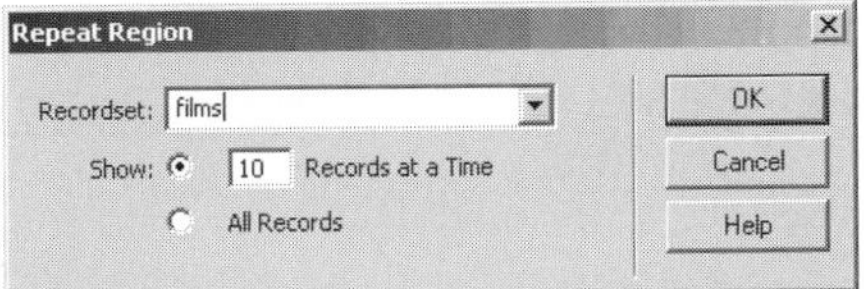

Figure 4.24

A Repeat Region is a block of code or design that is repeated once per database record.

Save your changes and refresh the browser to test your new code. You'll now see the first ten rows as seen in Figure 4.25.

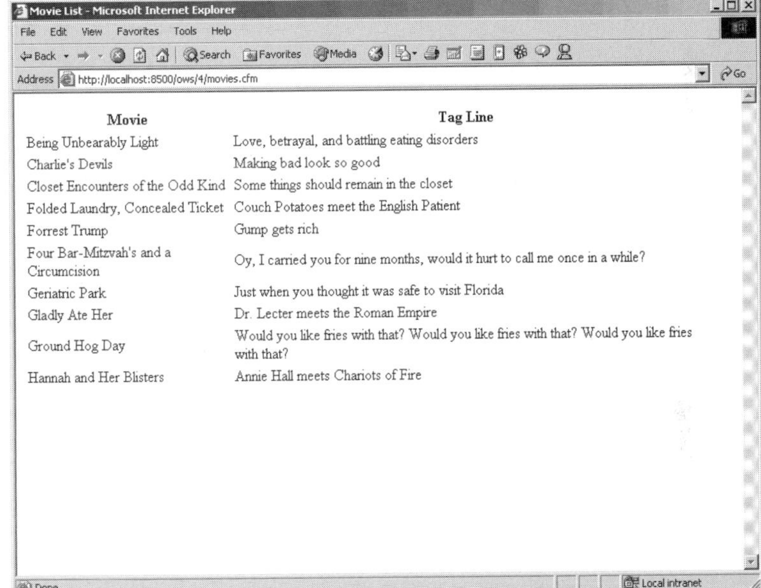

Figure 4.25

Refresh your browser anytime you want to test changes you've made to the code.

Implementing Page Navigation

This new version is much better, but now you need a way to get to the next page or any other page. Dreamweaver MX can generate the code for this too, using Recordset Paging behaviors. Here are the steps:

1. First of all, you need the text that the user will click, so insert a line above the table (just press Enter) and type the following:

```
[<< First] [< Previous] [Next >] [Last >>]
```

2. When the user clicks `<< First`, the list should jump to the first page of movies. So highlight that text without the square brackets as seen in Figure 4.26.

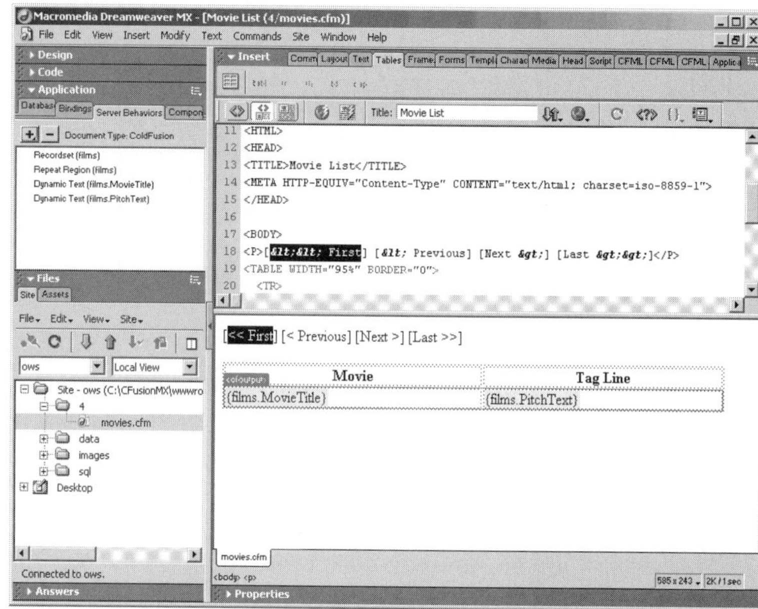

Figure 4.26

Recordset Paging, like many other Dreamweaver Server Behaviors, requires that you first select the text to which you're applying the behavior.

3 Click the + button in the Server Behaviors tab (in the Application panel), and select Recordset Paging, then Move to First Page. Verify your selections in the dialog box (seen in Figure 4.27), then click OK to create the behavior.

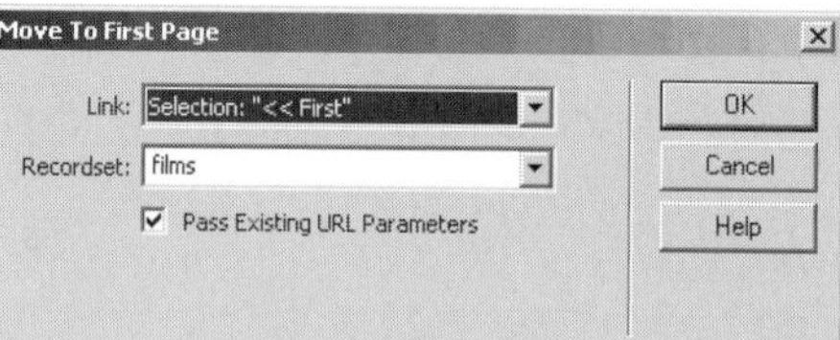

Figure 4.27

When creating Recordset Paging, you verify each behavior before applying it.

4. Highlight `< Previous` to create the previous page link (this one will take the user to the previous page), click the + button in the Server Behaviors tab, and select Recordset Paging, then Move to Previous Page. When the dialog box appears, click OK to apply the behavior.

5. Now create the next page link (this one will go to the next page). Highlight `Next >` and apply the Move to Next Page behavior to it.

6. Finally, create the last page link (it will go to the last page). Highlight `Last >>` and apply the Move to Last Page behavior to it.

Now save the page and test it once again in your browser. As seen in Figure 4.28, the page displays the first ten movies, and navigation links allow you to move between pages and jump to the first or last page.

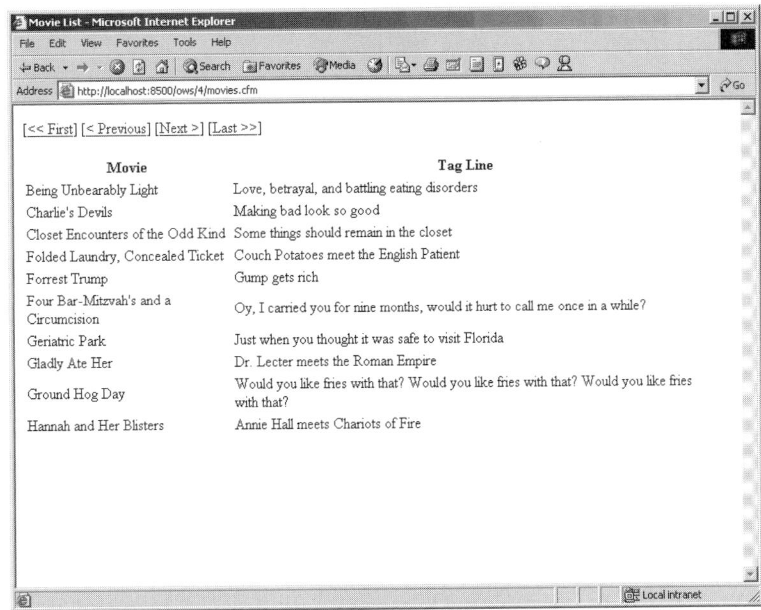

Figure 4.28

Always test all options and links in your application.

And there you have it—your very first ColdFusion application. If you look at the code window, you'll see that the entire application is about 40 lines of code, not bad at all for this much functionality (and even better considering that you didn't have to write any of the code yourself).

Trying It Yourself

Codegen is OK for some tasks (and is wonderful for rapid prototyping), but more often than not it won't be enough. This is why the majority of this book discusses coding. To give you a taste of what's to come, try this small (and very simple) application. I won't go into the details of the code itself at this point; for now, concentrate on creating and executing CFM files so they work (if you can get all these to function, you'll have a much easier time working through the book).

The `bday` application is really simple; it prompts you for your name and date of birth and calculates your age (using simple date arithmetic). The application is made up of two files:

- `bday1.cfm` (shown in Listing 4.1) is the form that prompts for the name and date of birth.
- `bday2.cfm` (shown in Listing 4.2) processes the form and displays the results.

Using Dreamweaver MX, create these two new files, saving them both in the `4` directory. Then enter the code below in each file (exactly as it appears here—your files should contain this code and nothing else):

Listing 4.1 `bday1.cfm`

```
<HTML>
<BODY>
<FORM ACTION="bday2.cfm" METHOD="post">
Name: <INPUT TYPE="text" NAME="name">
<BR>
Date of birth: <INPUT TYPE="text" NAME="dob">
<BR>
<INPUT TYPE="submit" VALUE="Calculate">
</FORM>
</BODY>
</HTML>
```

The code in `bday1.cfm` is simple HTML—there's no ColdFusion code at all (in fact, you could have named the file with an HTML extension and it would have worked properly). `bday1.cfm` contains an HTML form with two form fields—`name` for the user name and `dob` for the date of birth.

Listing 4.2 `bday2.cfm`

```
<HTML>
<BODY>
<CFOUTPUT>
Hello #FORM.name#,
you are #DateDiff("YYYY", FORM.dob, Now())#.
</CFOUTPUT>
</BODY>
</HTML>
```

The code in `bday2.cfm` is a mixture of HTML and CFML. The `name` form field displays the Hello message, and the `dob` field calculates the age.

To try the application, open a browser and go to the following URL:

```
http://localhost:8500/ows/4/bday1.cfm
```

NOTE

If you are not using the integrated HTTP server, adjust the URL accordingly.

Another form, similar to the one in Figure 4.29, will prompt you for your name and date of birth. Fill in the two fields, and then click the form submission button to display your age (see Figure 4.30).

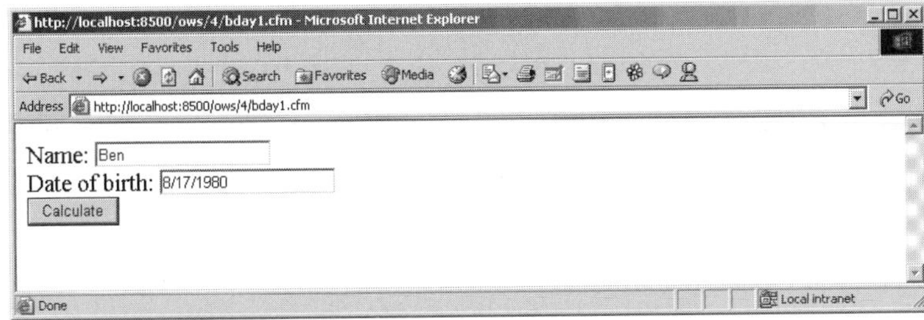

Figure 4.29

ColdFusion forms are created using standard HTML tags.

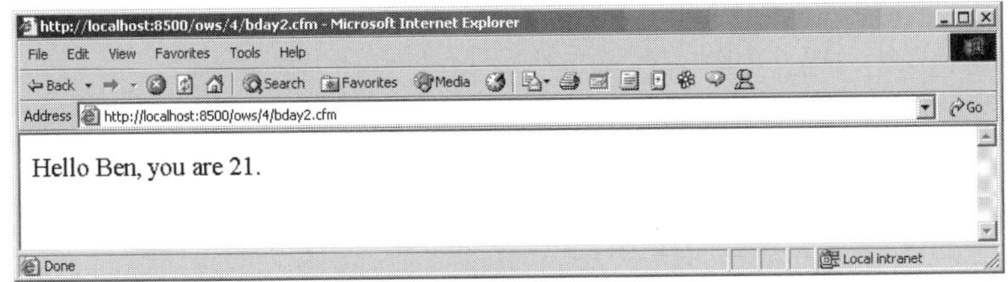

Figure 4.30

ColdFusion generates output displayed in a browser.

Was that a little anticlimactic after the Dreamweaver MX–generated application? Perhaps. But you've now learned all you need to know about creating, saving, and executing ColdFusion applications. And now the fun starts.

CHAPTER 5

Introducing SQL

IN THIS CHAPTER

SQL, pronounced `sequel` or `S-Q-L`, is an acronym for Structured Query Language. SQL is a language you use to access and manipulate data in a relational database. It is designed to be both easy to learn and extremely powerful, and its mass acceptance by so many database vendors proves that it has succeeded in both.

In 1970, Dr. E. F. Codd, the man credited with being the father of the relational database, described a universal language for data access. In 1974, engineers at IBM's San Jose Research Center created the Structured English Query Language, or SEQUEL, built on Codd's ideas. This language was incorporated into System R, IBM's pioneering relational database system.

Toward the end of the 1980s, two of the most important standards bodies, the American National Standards Institute (ANSI) and the International Standards Organization (ISO), published SQL standards, opening the door to mass acceptance. With these standards in place, SQL was poised to become the de-facto standard used by every major database vendor.

Although SQL has evolved a great deal since its early SEQUEL days, the basic language concepts and its founding premises have remained the same. The beauty of SQL is its simplicity. But don't let that simplicity deceive you. SQL is a powerful language, and it encourages you to be creative in your problem solving. You can almost always find more than one way to perform a complex query or to extract desired data. Each solution has pros and cons, and no solution is explicitly right or wrong.

Before you panic at the thought of learning a new language, let me reassure you that SQL really is easy to learn. In fact, you need to learn only four statements to be able to perform almost all the data manipulation you will need on a regular basis. Table 5.1 lists these statements.

Table 5.1 SQL-Based Data Manipulation Statements

STATEMENT	DESCRIPTION
SELECT	Queries a table for specific data.
INSERT	Adds new data to a table.
UPDATE	Updates existing data in a table.
DELETE	Removes data from a table.

Each of these statements takes one or more keywords as parameters. By combining various statements and keywords, you can manipulate your data in as many ways as you can imagine.

ColdFusion provides you with all the tools you need to add Web-based interaction to your databases. ColdFusion itself, though, has no built-in database. Instead, it communicates with whatever database you select, passing updates and requests and returning query results.

TIP

This chapter (and the next) is by no means a complete SQL tutorial, so a good book on SQL is a must for ColdFusion developers. If you want a crash course on all the major SQL language elements, you might want to pick a copy of my "Sams Teach Yourself SQL in 10 Minutes" *(ISBN: 0672321289).*

Understanding Data Sources

Back in Chapter 3, "Accessing the ColdFusion Administrator," you created a data source which you'll now use to experiment with SQL. But before doing so, it is worth taking a moment to understand data sources, databases, and how the relate to each.

As explained in Chapter 2, "Building the Databases," a database is a collection of tables that store related data. Databases are generally used in one of two ways:

- Directly within a DBMS application, for example, Microsoft Access or SQL Server's Enterprise Manager. These applications tend to be very database specific (they are usually designed by the database vendor for use with specific databases).
- Via third party applications, commercial or custom, that know how to interact with existing external databases.

ColdFusion MX is the latter. ColdFusion is not a database product. It does, however, let you write applications that will interact with any and all databases.

How do third party applications interact with databases (usually created by other vendors)? That's where data sources come in to the picture, but first we need to look at the *database driver*. Almost every databases out there has available database drivers—special bits of software that provide access to the databases. Each database product requires its own driver (the Oracle driver, for example, will not work for SQL Server), although a single driver can support multiple databases (the same SQL Server driver can access many different SQL Server installations).

There are two primary standards for databases drivers:

- ODBC has been around for a long time, and is one of the most widely used database driver standards. ODBC is primarily used on Windows, although other platforms are supported too.
- JDBC is Java's database driver implementation, and is supported on all platforms and environments running Java.

NOTE

ColdFusion 5 and earlier used ODBC database drivers. ColdFusion MX, which is Java based, uses JDBC instead.

Regardless of the database driver or standard used, the purpose of the driver remains the same—database drivers conceal databases differences providing simplified access to databases. For example, the internal workings of Microsoft Access and Oracle are very different, but when accessed via a database driver they look the same (or at least more alike). This allows the same application to interact with all sorts of databases, without needing to be customized or modified for each. Database drivers are very database specific, and in being so access to databases need not be database specific at all.

Of course, different database drivers need different information—for example, the Microsoft Access driver simply needs to know the name and location of the MDB file to use, whereas the Oracle and SQL Server database drivers need to know server information and well as an account login and password.

This driver specific information could be provided each time it is needed, or a data source could be created. A data source is simply a driver plus any related information stored for future use. Client applications, like ColdFusion, use data sources to interact with databases.

Preparing to Write SQL Queries

Now that you have a data source, all you need is a client application with which to access the data. Ultimately, the client you will use is ColdFusion via CFML code; after all, that is why you're reading this book. But to start learning SQL, we'll use something simpler, a SQL Query Tool (written in ColdFusion). The tool is named `sql.cfm` and is in a directory named `sql` under the `ows` directory, and so the path to it (if using the integrated Web server) will be:

```
http://localhost:8500/ows/sql/sql.cfm
```

The SQL Query Tool, shown in Figure 5.1, allows you to enter SQL statements in the box provided which are executed when the Execute button is clicked. Results, if there are any, are displayed in the bottom half of the screen.

CAUTION

The SQL Query Tool is intended for use on development computers and should not be installed on live (production) servers.

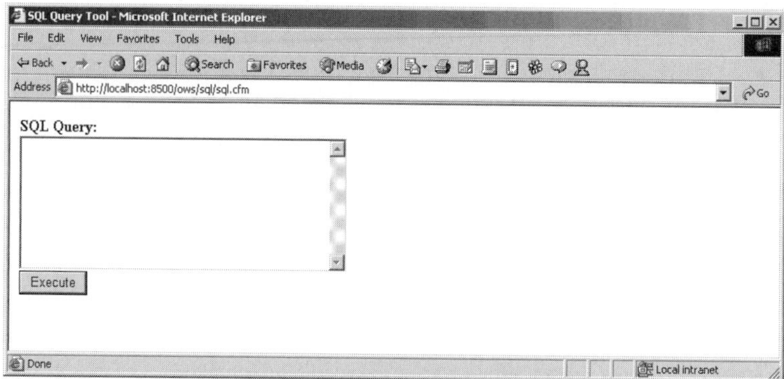

Figure 5.1
The SQL Query Tool allows SQL statements to be entered manually and then executed.

NOTE

The SQL Query Tool allows SQL statements to be executed against databases. As a rule, this type of tool is dangerous as it could be used to delete or change data (accidentally or maliciously). To help prevent this from occurring SQL Query Tool has several built in security measures; by default it only allows `SELECT` statements, it has a hardcoded data source, and it only allows SQL statements to be executed locally (local IP address only). To use SQL Query Tool remotely you must explicitly allow your own IP address access to the tool by modifying the `Application.cfm` file specifying the address in the `ip_restrict` variable.

NOTE

Readers of prior editions of this book will note that in the past tools like MS-Query were used in these SQL chapters. As ColdFusion MX is Java based, and thus uses JDBC, data sources created using the ColdFusion Administrator will not be accessible via MS-Query or any other ODBC based tool. As such, a ColdFusion based SQL Query Tool is being used instead.

Creating Queries

With all the preliminaries taken care of, you can roll up your sleeves and start writing SQL. The SQL statement you will use most is the `SELECT` statement. You use `SELECT`, as its name implies, to select data from a table.

Most `SELECT` statements require at least the following two parameters:

- What data you want to select, known as the select list. If you specify more than one item, you must separate each with a comma.
- The table (or tables) from which to select the data, specified with the `FROM` keyword.

The first SQL `SELECT` you will create is a query for a list of movies in the `Films` table. Type the code in Listing 5.1 as seen in Figure 5.2, and then execute the statement by clicking the Execute button.

Listing 5.1 Simple `SELECT` Statement

```
SELECT
MovieTitle
FROM Films
```

That's it! You've written your first SQL statement. The results will be shown as seen in Figure 5.3.

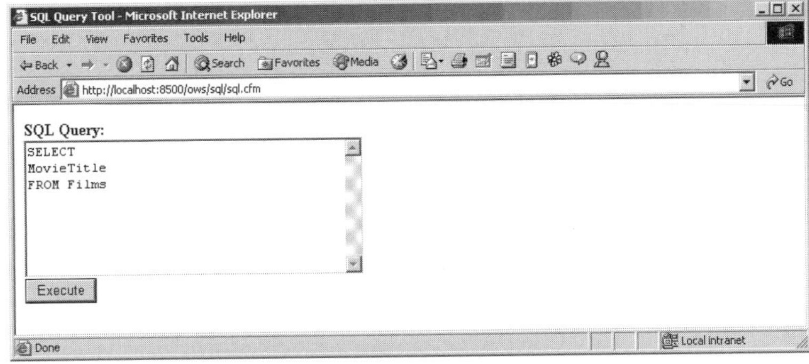

Figure 5.2

SQL statements are entered in the SQL Query Tool's SQL Query field.

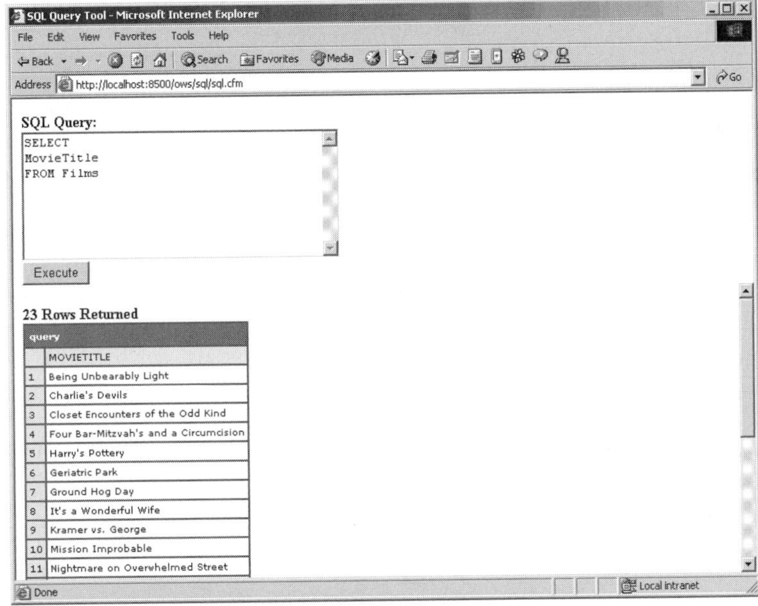

Figure 5.3

The SQL Query Tool displays query results in the bottom half of the screen.

TIP

You can enter SQL statements on one long line or break them up over multiple lines. All whitespace characters (spaces, tabs, newline characters) are ignored when the command is processed. If you break a statement into multiple lines and indent parameters, you make the statement easier to read and debug.

Here is another example. Type the code in Listing 5.2 and then click the Execute button to display two columns as seen in Figure 5.4.

Listing 5.2 Multi-column `SELECT` Statement

```
SELECT
MovieTitle, PitchText
FROM Films
```

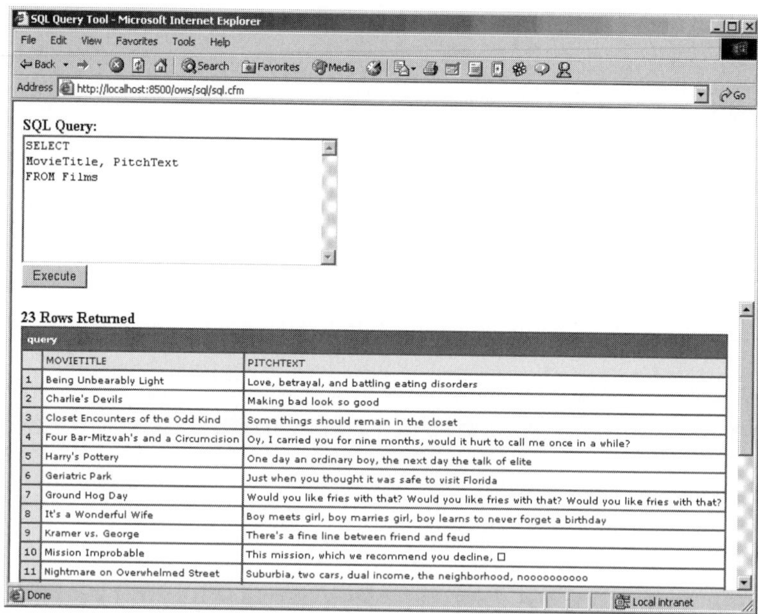

Figure 5.4

The SQL Query Tool displays the results of all specified columns.

Before you go any further, take a closer look at the SQL code in Listing 5.2. The first parameter you pass to the `SELECT` statement is a list of the two columns you want to see. A column is specified by its name (for example, `MovieTitle`) or as `table.column` (such as `Films.MovieTitle`, where `Films` is the table name and `MovieTitle` is the column name).

Because you want to specify two columns, you must separate them with commas. No comma appears after the last column name, so if you have only one column in your select list, you don't need a comma.

Right after the select list, you specify the table on which you want to perform the query. You always precede the table name with the keyword `FROM`. The table is specified by name, in this case `Films`.

NOTE

> SQL statements are not case sensitive; that is, you can specify the `SELECT` statement as `SELECT`, `select`, `Select`, or however you want. Common practice, however, is to enter all SQL keywords in uppercase and parameters in lowercase or mixed case. This way, you can read the SQL code and spot typos more easily.

Now modify the `SELECT` statement so it looks like the code in Listing 5.3; then execute it.

Listing 5.3 `SELECT` All Columns

```
SELECT
*
FROM Films
```

This time, instead of specifying explicit columns to select, you use an asterisk (*). The asterisk is a special select list option that represents all columns. The data pane now shows all the columns in the table in the order in which they are returned by the database table itself.

CAUTION

Generally, you should not use an asterisk in the select list unless you really need every column. Each column you select requires its own processing, and retrieving unnecessary columns can dramatically affect retrieval times as your tables get larger.

Sorting Query Results

When you use the `SELECT` statement, the results are returned to you in the order in which they appear in the table. This is usually the order in which the rows were added to the table, typically not a sort order that is of much use to you. More often than not, when you retrieve data using a `SELECT` statement, you want to sort the query results. To sort rows, you need to add the `ORDER BY` clause. `ORDER BY` always comes after the table name; if you try to use it before, you generate a SQL error.

Now click the SQL button, enter the SQL code shown in Listing 5.4, and then click OK.

Listing 5.4 `SELECT` with Sorted Output

```
SELECT MovieTitle, PitchText, Summary
FROM Films
ORDER BY MovieTitle
```

Your output is then sorted by the `MovieTitle` column, as shown in Figure 5.5.

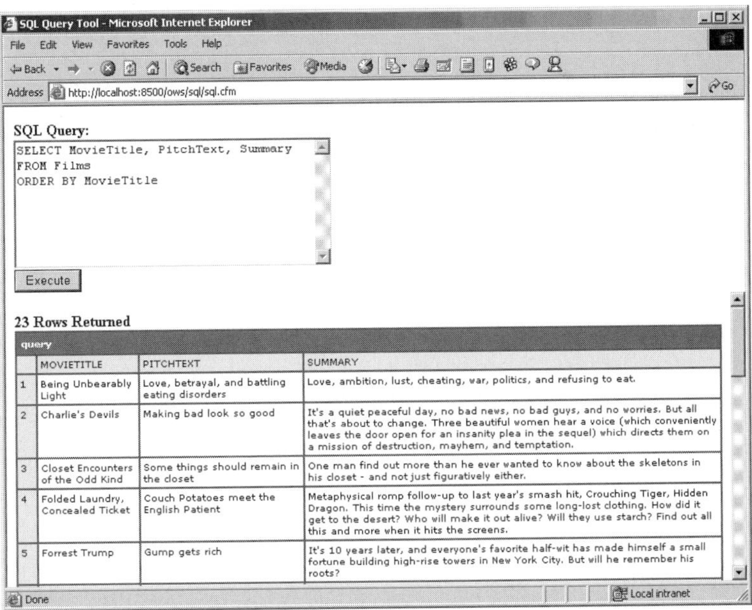

Figure 5.5

You use the `ORDER BY` clause to sort `SELECT` output.

What if you need to sort by more than one column? No problem. You can pass multiple columns to the ORDER BY clause. Once again, if you have multiple columns listed, you must separate them with commas. The SQL code in Listing 5.5 demonstrates how to sort on more than one column by sorting by RatingID, and then by MovieTitle within each RatingID. The sorted output is shown in Figure 5.6.

Listing 5.5 SELECT with Output Sorted on More Than One Column

```
SELECT RatingID, MovieTitle, Summary
FROM Films
ORDER BY RatingID, MovieTitle
```

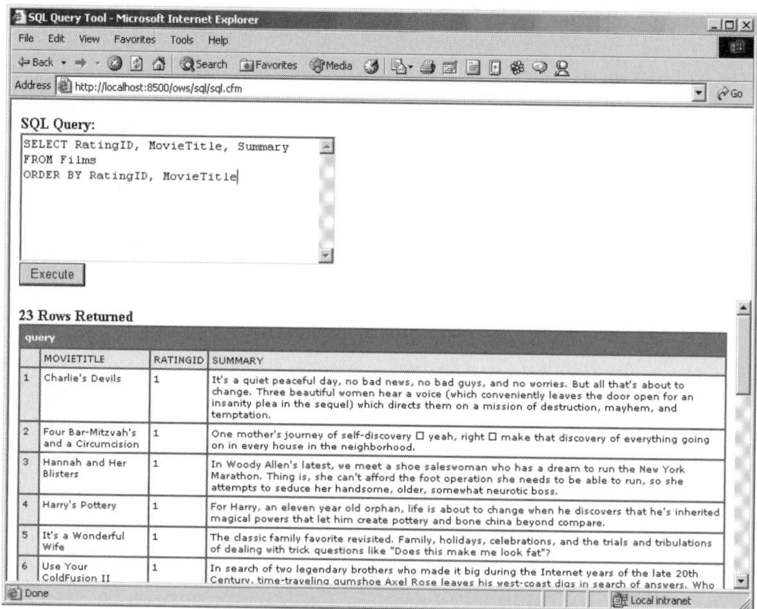

Figure 5.6

You can sort output by more than one column via the ORDER BY clause.

You also can use ORDER BY to sort data in descending order (Z–A). To sort a column in descending order, just use the DESC (short for descending) parameter. Listing 5.6 retrieves all the movies and sorts them by title in reverse order. Figure 5.7 shows the output that this SQL SELECT statement generates.

Listing 5.6 SELECT with Output Sorted in Reverse Order

```
SELECT MovieTitle, PitchText, Summary
FROM Films
ORDER BY MovieTitle DESC
```

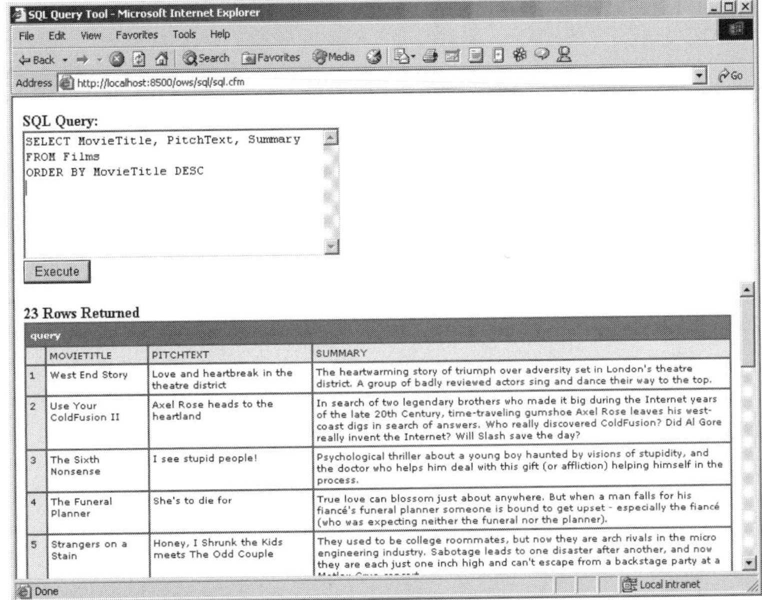

Figure 5.7

Using the `ORDER BY` clause, you can sort data in a descending sort sequence.

Filtering Data

So far, all your queries have retrieved all the rows in the table. You also can use the `SELECT` statement to retrieve only data that matches specific search criteria. To do so, you must use the `WHERE` clause and provide a restricting condition. If a `WHERE` clause is present, when the SQL `SELECT` statement is processed, every row is evaluated against the condition. Only rows that pass the restriction are selected.

If you use a `WHERE` clause, it must appear after the table name. If you use both the `ORDER BY` and `WHERE` clauses, the `WHERE` clause must appear after the table name but before the `ORDER BY` clause.

Filtering on a Single Column

To demonstrate filtering, modify the `SELECT` statement to retrieve only movies with a RatingID of 1. Listing 5.7 contains the `SELECT` statement, and the resulting output is shown in Figure 5.8.

Listing 5.7 `SELECT` with `WHERE` Clause

```
SELECT MovieTitle, PitchText, Summary
FROM Films
WHERE RatingID=1
ORDER BY MovieTitle DESC
```

Figure 5.8

Using the `WHERE` clause, you can restrict the scope of a `SELECT` search.

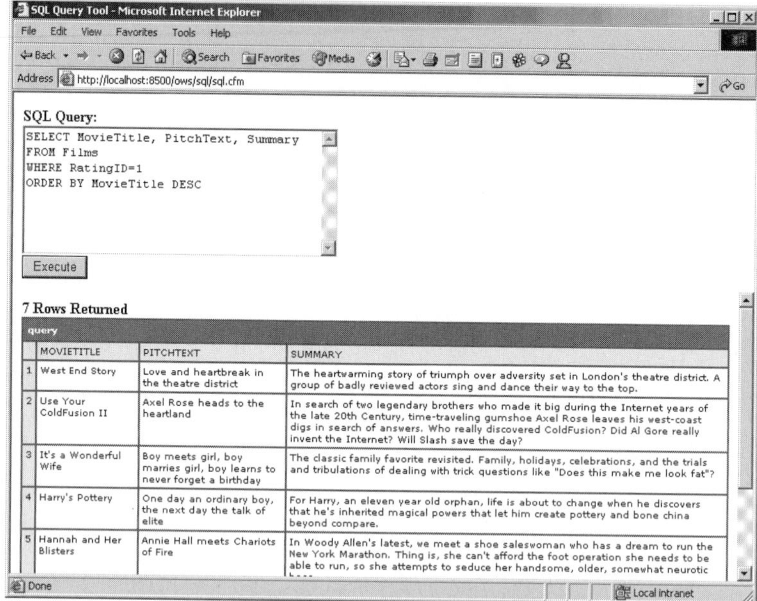

Filtering on Multiple Columns

The `WHERE` clause also can take multiple conditions. To search for `Ben Forta`, you can specify a search condition in which the first name is `Ben` and the last name is `Forta`, as shown in Listing 5.8. As Figure 5.9 shows, only `Ben Forta` is retrieved.

Listing 5.8 `SELECT` with Multiple `WHERE` Clauses

```
SELECT FirstName, LastName, Email
FROM Contacts
WHERE FirstName='Ben' AND LastName='Forta'
```

Figure 5.9

You can narrow your search with multiple `WHERE` clauses.

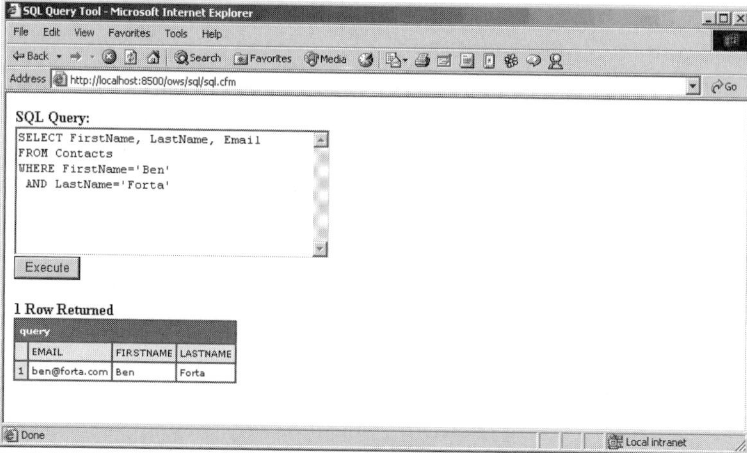

CAUTION

Text passed to a SQL query must be enclosed within quotation marks. If you omit the quotation marks, the SQL parser thinks that the text you specified is the name of a column, and you receive an error because that column does not exist. Pure SQL allows strings to be enclosed within single quotation marks ('like this') or within double quotation marks ("like this"). But when passing text in a SQL statement to an ODBC or JDBC driver, you *must* use single quotation marks. If you use double quotation marks, the parser treats the first double quotation mark as a statement terminator, ignoring all text after it.

The AND and OR Operators

Multiple `WHERE` clauses can be evaluated as `AND` conditions or `OR` conditions. The example in Listing 5.8 is an `AND` condition. Only rows in which both the last name is `Forta` and the first name is `Ben` will be retrieved. If you change the clause to the following, contacts with a first name of `Ben` will be retrieved (regardless of last name) and contacts with a last name of `Forta` will be retrieved (regardless of first name):

```
WHERE FirstName='Ben' OR LastName='Forta'
```

You can combine the `AND` and `OR` operators to create any search condition you need. Listing 5.9 shows a `WHERE` clauses that can be used to retrieve only `Ben Forta` and `Rick Richards`.

Listing 5.9 Combining `WHERE` Clauses with `AND` and `OR` Operators

```
SELECT NameFirst, NameLast, Email
FROM Contacts
WHERE FirstName='Ben' AND LastName='Forta'
 OR FirstName='Rick' AND LastName='Richards'
```

Evaluation Precedence

When a `WHERE` clause is processed, the operators are evaluated in the following order of precedence:

- Parentheses have the highest precedence.
- The `AND` operator has the next level of precedence.
- The `OR` operator has the lowest level of precedence.

What does this mean? Well, look at the `WHERE` clause in Listing 5.9. The clause reads `WHERE FirstName='Ben' AND LastName='Forta' OR FirstName='Rick' AND LastName='Richards'`. `AND` is evaluated before `OR` so this statement looks for `Ben Forta` and `Rick Richards`, which is what we wanted.

But what would a `WHERE` clause of `WHERE FirstName='Rick' OR FirstName='Ben' AND LastName='Forta'` return? Does that statement mean *anyone whose first name is either Rick or Ben, and whose last name is Forta*, or does it mean *anyone whose first name is Rick, and also Ben Forta*? The difference is subtle, but if the former is true then only contacts with a last name of `Forta` will be retrieved, whereas if the latter is true then any `Rick` will be retrieved, regardless of last name.

So which is it? Because `AND` is evaluated first, the clause means *anyone whose first name is Rick, and also Ben Forta*, which might be what you want. And then again, it might not.

To prevent the ambiguity created by mixing AND and OR statements, parentheses are used to group related statements. Parentheses have a higher order of evaluation than both AND and OR, so they can be used to explicitly match related clauses. Consider the following WHERE clauses:

```
WHERE (FirstName='Rick' OR FirstName='Ben') AND (LastName='Forta')
```

This clause means *anyone whose first name is either Rick or Ben, and whose last name is Forta.*

```
WHERE (FirstName='Rick') OR (FirstName='Ben' AND LastName='Forta')
```

This clause means *anyone whose first name is Rick, and also Ben Forta.*

As you can see, the exact same set of WHERE clauses can mean very different things depending on where parentheses are used.

TIP

Always using parentheses whenever you have more than one WHERE clause is good practice. They make the SQL statement easier to read and easier to debug.

WHERE Conditions

For the examples to this point, you have used only the = (equal) operator. You filtered rows based on their being equal to a specific value. Many other operators and conditions can be used with the WHERE clause; they're listed in Table 5.2.

Table 5.2 WHERE Clause Search Conditions

CONDITION	DESCRIPTION
=	Equal to. Tests for equality.
<>	Not equal to. Tests for inequality.
<	Less than. Tests that the value on the left is less than the value on the right.
<=	Less than or equal to. Tests that the value on the left is less than or equal to the value on the right.
>	Greater than. Tests that the value on the left is greater than the value on the right.
>=	Greater than or equal to. Tests that the value on the left is greater than or equal to the value on the right.
BETWEEN	Tests that a value is in the range between two values; the range is inclusive.
EXISTS	Tests for the existence of rows returned by a subquery.
IN	Tests to see whether a value is contained within a list of values.
IS NULL	Tests to see whether a column contains a NULL value.
IS NOT NULL	Tests to see whether a column contains a non-NULL value.
LIKE	Tests to see whether a value matches a specified pattern.
NOT	Negates any test.

Feel free to experiment with different `SELECT` statements using any of the `WHERE` clauses listed here. The SQL Query tool is safe, it will not update or modify data (by default) and so there is no harm in using it to experiment to with statements and clauses.

Testing for Equality: =

You use the = operator to test for value inequality. The following example retrieves only contacts whose last name is `Smith`:

```
WHERE LastName = 'Smith'
```

Testing for Inequality: <>

You use the <> operator to test for value inequality. The following example retrieves only contacts whose first name is not `Kim`:

```
WHERE FirstName <> 'Kim'
```

Testing for Less Than: <

By using the < operator, you can test that the value on the left is less than the value on the right. The following example retrieves only contacts whose last name is less than `C`, meaning that their last name begins with an `A` or a `B`:

```
WHERE LastName < 'C'
```

Testing for Less Than or Equal To: <=

By using the <= operator, you can test that the value on the left is less than or equal to the value on the right. The following example retrieves actors aged `21` or less:

```
WHERE Age <= 21
```

Testing for Greater Than: >

You use the > operator to test that the value on the left is greater than the value on the right. The following example retrieves only movies with a rating of `3` or higher (greater than `2`):

```
WHERE RatingID > 2
```

Testing for Greater Than or Equal To: >=

You use the >= operator to test that the value on the right is greater than or equal to the value on the left. The following example retrieves only contacts whose first name begins with the letter `J` or higher:

```
WHERE FirstName >= 'J'
```

BETWEEN

Using the BETWEEN condition, you can test whether a value falls into the range between two other values. The following example retrieves only actors aged 20 to 30. Because the test is inclusive, ages 20 and 30 are also retrieved:

```
WHERE Age BETWEEN 20 AND 30
```

The BETWEEN condition is actually nothing more than a convenient way of combining the >= and <= conditions. You also could specify the preceding example as follows:

```
WHERE Age >= 20 AND Age <= 30
```

The advantage of using the BETWEEN condition is that it makes the statement easier to read.

EXISTS

Using the EXISTS condition, you can check whether a subquery returns any rows.

➜ Subqueries are explained in Chapter 29, "More About SQL and Queries."

IN

You can use the IN condition to test whether a value is part of a specific set. The set of values must be surrounded by parentheses and separated by commas. The following example retrieves contacts whose last name is Black, Jones, or Smith:

```
WHERE LastName IN ('Black', 'Jones', 'Smith')
```

The preceding example is actually the same as the following:

```
WHERE LastName = 'Black' OR LastName = 'Jones' OR LastName = 'Smith'
```

Using the IN condition does provide two advantages. First, it makes the statement easier to read. Second, and more importantly, you can use the IN condition to test whether a value is within the results of another SELECT statement.

IS NULL and IS NOT NULL

A NULL value is the value of a column that is empty. The IS NULL condition tests for rows that have a NULL value; that is, the rows have no value at all in the specified column. IS NOT NULL tests for rows that have a value in a specified column.

The following example retrieves all contacts whose Email column is left empty:

```
WHERE Email IS NULL
```

To retrieve only the contacts who do have an email address, use the following example:

```
WHERE Email IS NOT NULL
```

LIKE

Using the LIKE condition, you can test for string pattern matches using wildcards. Two wildcard types are supported. The % character means that anything from that position on is considered a match. You also can use [] to create a wildcard for a specific character.

The following example retrieves actors whose last name begins with the letter S. To match the pattern, a last name must have an S as the first character, and anything at all after it:

```
WHERE LastName LIKE 'S%'
```

To retrieve actors with an S anywhere in their last names, you can use the following:

```
WHERE LastName LIKE '%S%'
```

You also can retrieve just actors whose last name ends with S, as follows:

```
WHERE LastName LIKE '%S'
```

The `LIKE` condition can be negated with the `NOT` operator. The following example retrieves only actors whose last name does not begin with S:

```
WHERE LastName NOT LIKE 'S%'
```

Using the `LIKE` condition, you also can specify a wildcard on a single character. If you want to find all actors named `Smith` but are not sure whether the one you want spells his or her name `Smyth`, you can use the following:

```
WHERE LastName LIKE 'Sm[iy]th'
```

This example retrieves only names that start with `Sm`, then have an `i` or a `y`, and then a final `th`. With this example, as long as the first two characters are `Sm` and the last two are `th`, and as long as the middle character is `i` or `y`, the name is considered a match.

TIP

Using the powerful `LIKE` condition, you can retrieve data in many ways. But everything comes with a price, and the price here is performance. Generally, `LIKE` conditions take far longer to process than other search conditions, especially if you use wildcards at the beginning of the pattern. As a rule, use `LIKE` and wildcards only when absolutely necessary.

For even more powerful searching, `LIKE` may be combined with other clauses using `AND` and `OR`. And you may even include multiple `LIKE` clauses in a single `WHERE` clause.

SQL Data Manipulation

IN THIS CHAPTER

Chapter 5, "Introducing SQL," introduced data drivers, data sources, SQL, and data retrieval (using the SELECT statement). You'll probably find that you spend far more time retrieving data than you do inserting, updating, or deleting data (which is why we concentrated on SELECT first).

NOTE

As in the last chapter, the SQL Query Tool in the ows/sql directory will be used to execute the SQL statements. For security's sake (to prevent accidental data changes) the SQL Query Tool defaults to on allowing execution of SELECT statements (and no other SQL statements).

To change this behavior edit the Application.cfm file in the ows/sql directory. You will see a series of variables that are set, one of which is select_only which is a flag that is set to yes (the default setting) instructing the utility to only execute SELECT statements. Change this value to no before proceeding (and save the updated Application.cfm) with the examples in this chapter (or an error will be thrown).

And you might want to set the flag back to yes when done, just to be safe.

Adding Data

You will need to insert data into tables at some point, so now let's take a look at data inserting using the INSERT statement.

NOTE

In this chapter, you will add, update, and delete rows from tables in the ows data source. The reason you delete any added rows is to ensure that any example code and screenshots later in the book actually look like you'd expect them to.

Feel free to add more rows if you'd like, but realize that if you do not clean up when you're finished, your screens will look different from the ones shown in the figures. This is not a problem, and you are welcome to do so; just keep it in mind so you know why things don't look the same.

Using the `INSERT` Statement

You use the `INSERT` statement to add data to a table. `INSERT` is usually made up of three parts:

- The table into which you want to insert data, specified with the `INTO` keyword.
- The column(s) into which you want to insert values. If you specify more than one item, each must be separated by a comma.
- The values to insert, which are specified with the `VALUES` keyword.

The `Directors` table contains the list of movie directors working with (or for) Orange Whip Studios. Directors cannot be assigned projects (associated with movies) if they are not listed in this table, so any new directors must be added immediately.

➜ See Appendix G, "Sample Application Data Files" for an explanation of each of the data files and their contents.

Now you're ready to add the new director. The following code contains the SQL `INSERT` statement:

```
INSERT INTO Directors(FirstName, LastName)
VALUES('Benjamin', 'FORTA')
```

Enter this statement into the SQL Query field as seen in Figure 6.1. Feel free to replace my name with your own. When you're finished, click the Execute button to insert the new row. Assuming no problems occur, you should see a confirmation screen similar to the one shown in Figure 6.2.

TIP

So how can you tell if an `INSERT` succeeds or fails? Well, no news is good news - if no error is returned then the `INSERT` has succeeded, but if an error occurs then it will be displayed.

Understanding `INSERT`

Now that you've successfully inserted a row using the SQL `INSERT` statement, take a minute to look at the statement's syntax.

The first line of your statement reads as follows:

```
INSERT INTO Directors(FirstName, LastName)
```

The text immediately following the `INTO` keyword is the name of the table into which the new row is being inserted. In this case, it is the `Directors` table.

Next, the columns being added are specified. The columns are listed within parentheses, and if multiple columns are specified, each must be separated by a comma. A row in the `Directors` table requires both a `FirstName` and a `LastName`, so the `INSERT` statement specifies both columns.

NOTE

When you insert a row into a table, you can provide values for as many (or as few) columns as you prefer. The only restriction is that any columns defined as `NOT NULL` columns–meaning they can't be left empty–must have values specified. If you do not set a value for a `NOT NULL` column, the database driver returns an error message and the row is not inserted.

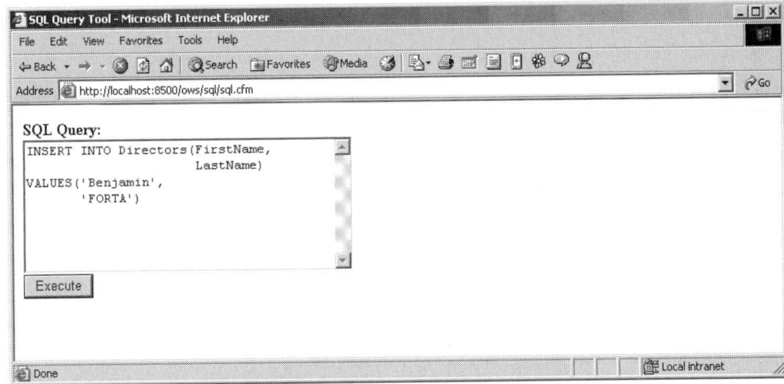

Figure 6.1

Type the statement into the SQL Query field, and then click Execute.

Figure 6.2

As `INSERT` statements do not return data, no results will be returned.

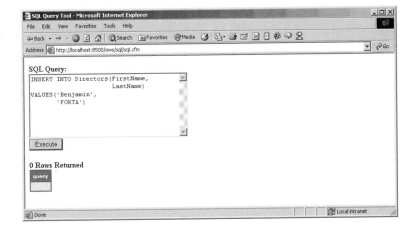

The next line reads as follows:

```
VALUES('Benjamin', 'FORTA')
```

A value must be specified for every column listed whenever you insert a row. Values are passed to the `VALUES` keyword; all values are contained within parentheses, just like their column names. Two columns are specified, so two values are passed to the `VALUES` keyword.

NOTE

When inserting rows into a table, columns can be specified in any order. But be sure that the order of the values in the `VALUES` keyword exactly matches the order of the columns after the table name or you'll insert the wrong data into the columns.

To verify that the new director was added to the table, retrieve the complete list of directors using the following SQL statement:

```
SELECT * FROM Directors
```

As explained in Chapter 5, `SELECT *` means select all columns. As you can see in Figure 6.3, the new row was added to the table. Make a note of the `DirectorID`, which you'll need later to update or delete this row.

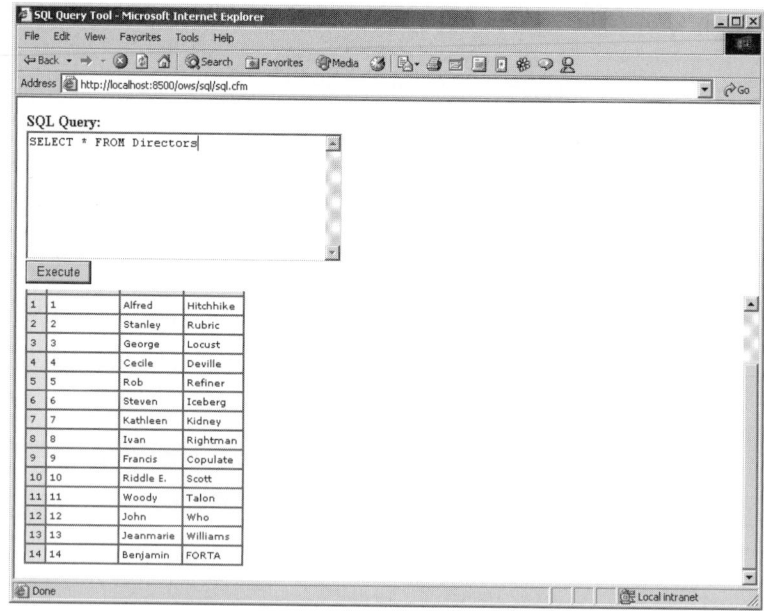

Figure 6.3

Use `SELECT` statements to verify that `INSERT` operations were successful.

NOTE

In the previous `INSERT` statement, no value was provided for the `DirectorID` column. So, where did that value come from? The `Directors` table was set up to automatically assign primary key values every time a new row is inserted. This is a feature supported by many databases–Access calls these AutoNumber columns, SQL Server uses the term Identity, and other databases have other names for the same feature. The end result is that you don't have to worry about creating unique values because the database does that for you.

TIP

`INSERT` can insert only one row at a time, unless the data being inserted is being retrieved from another table. In that case, a special form of the `INSERT` statement (called `INSERT SELECT`) can be used to insert all retrieved rows in a single operation.

Modifying Data

You use the SQL `UPDATE` statement to update one or more columns. This usually involves specifying the following:

- The table containing the data you want to update.
- The column or columns you want to update, preceded by the `SET` keyword. If you specify more than one item, each must be separated by a comma.
- An optional `WHERE` clause to specify which rows to update. If no `WHERE` clause is provided, all rows are updated.

Try updating a row. Enter the following SQL statement (ensuring that the ID number used in the `WHERE` clause is the `DirectorID` you noted earlier).

```
UPDATE Directors
SET FirstName='Ben'
WHERE DirectorID = 14
```

Your code should look similar to the example shown in Figure 6.4 (although the `DirectorID` might be different). Click Execute to perform the update. Again, no results will be displayed as `UPDATE` does not return data.

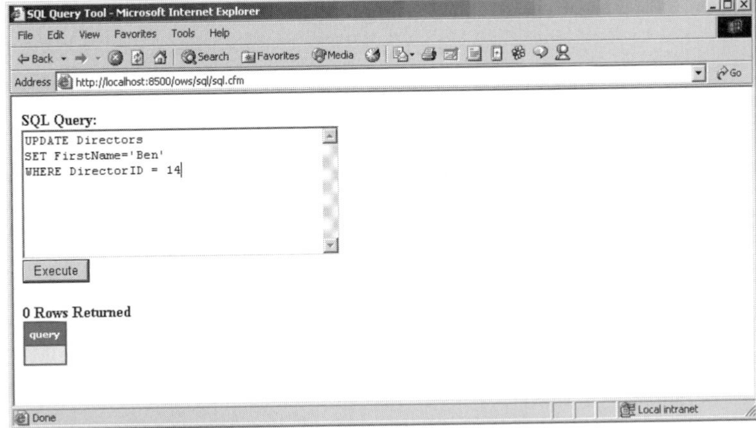

Figure 6.4

Update statements can be entered manually and entered on one line or broken over many lines.

If you now select the contents of the `Directors` table, you see that the new director's first name has been changed.

Understanding UPDATE

Now, take a closer look at the SQL statement you just used. The first line issued the `UPDATE` statement and specified the name of the table to update. As with the `INSERT` and `DELETE` statements, the table name is required.

You next specified the column you wanted to change and its new value:

```
SET FirstName='Ben'
```

This is an instruction to update the `FirstName` column with the text `Ben`. The `SET` keyword is required for an `UPDATE` operation because updating rows without specifying what to update makes little sense.

The `SET` keyword can be used only once in an `UPDATE` statement. If you are updating multiple rows—for example, to change `Benjamin` to `Ben` and to set the `LastName` to `Forta` in one operation—the `SET` keyword would look like this:

```
SET FirstName='Ben', LastName='Forta'
```

When updating multiple columns, each column must be separated by a comma. The complete (revised) `UPDATE` statement would then look like this:

```
UPDATE Directors
SET FirstName='Ben', LastName='Forta'
WHERE DirectorID = 14
```

The last line of the code listing specifies a `WHERE` clause. The `WHERE` clause is optional in an `UPDATE` statement. Without it, all rows will be updated. The following code uses the primary key column to ensure that only a single row gets updated:

```
WHERE DirectorID = 14
```

To verify that the updates worked, try retrieving all the data from the `Directors` table. The results should be similar to those seen in Figure 6.5 (showing the updated final row).

CAUTION

Be sure to provide a `WHERE` clause when using the SQL `UPDATE` statement; otherwise, all rows will be updated.

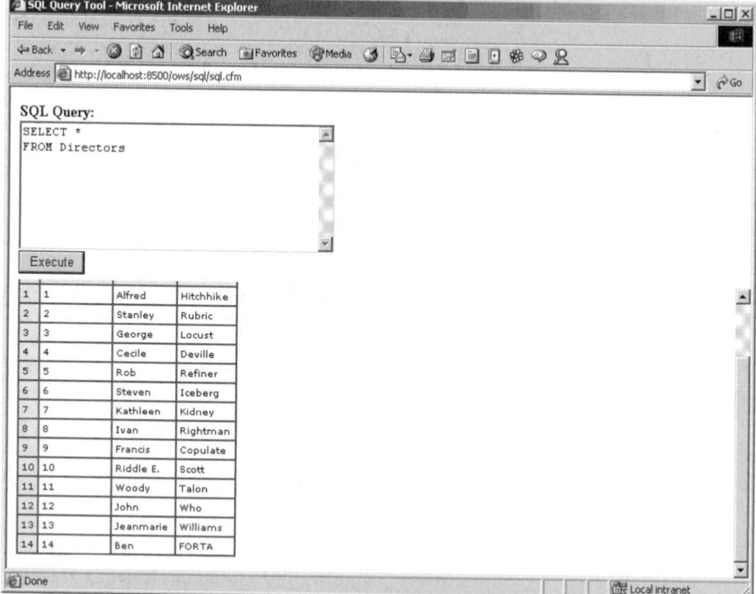

Figure 6.5

When experimenting with updates, it is a good idea to retrieve the table contents to check that the update worked properly.

Making Global Updates

You occasionally will want to update all rows in a table. To do this, you use `UPDATE`, too—you'd just omit the `WHERE` clause or specify a `WHERE` clause that matches multiple rows.

When updating multiple rows using a `WHERE` clause, always be sure to test that `WHERE` clause with a simple `SELECT` statement before executing the `UPDATE`. If the `SELECT` returns the correct data (the data you want updated), you'll know that it is safe to use with `UPDATE`. Failure to do this can result in you updating the wrong data!

TIP

Before executing `INSERT`, `UPDATE`, or `DELETE` operations that contain complex statements or `WHERE` conditions, you should test the statement or condition by using it in a `SELECT` statement. If `SELECT` returns incorrect statement results or an incorrect subset of data filtered by the `WHERE` clause, you'll know that the statement or condition is incorrect. The `SELECT` statement never changes any data, unlike `INSERT`, `UPDATE`, and `DELETE`. So, if an error exists in the statement or condition, you'll find out about it before any damage is done.

Deleting Data

Deleting data from a table is even easier than adding or updating data—perhaps too easy.

You use the SQL `DELETE` statement to delete data. The statement takes only two parameters—one required and one optional:

- The name of the table from which to delete the data must be specified immediately following the words `DELETE FROM`.
- An optional `WHERE` clause can be used to restrict the scope of the deletion process.

The `DELETE` statement is dangerously easy to use. Look at the following line of code (but don't execute it):

```
DELETE FROM Directors
```

This statement removes all directors from the `Directors` table without any warnings or confirmation.

TIP

Some databases, client/server databases (such as Microsoft SQL Server and Oracle) in particular, offer safeguards against accidental (or malicious) deletions. There generally are two approaches to preventing mass deletion.

One is to create a *trigger* (a piece of code that runs on the server when specific operations occur) that verifies every `DELETE` statement and blocks any `DELETE` without a `WHERE` clause.

Another popular option is to restrict the use of `DELETE` without a `WHERE` clause based on login name. Only certain users, usually those with administrative rights, are granted permission to execute `DELETE` without a `WHERE` clause. Any other user attempting a mass `DELETE` will receive an error message, and the operation will abort.

Not all database systems support these techniques. Consult the database administrator's manuals to ascertain which safeguards are available to you.

The `DELETE` statement is most often used with a `WHERE` clause. For example, the following SQL statement deletes a single director from the `Directors` table (the one you just added):

```
DELETE FROM Directors
WHERE DirectorID=14
```

To verify that the row was deleted, retrieve all the `Directors` one last time (as seen in Figure 6.6).

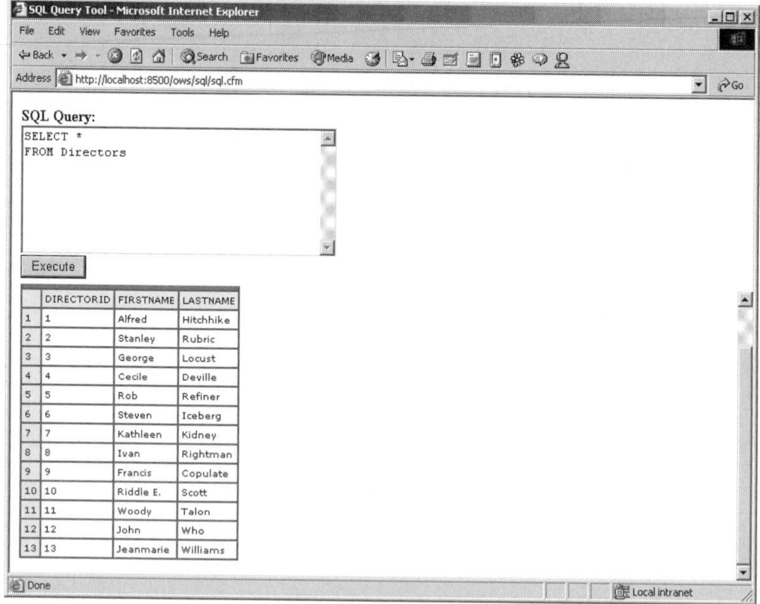

Figure 6.6

Most databases delete rows immediately (as opposed to flagging them for deletion), and this will be reflected when listing the table contents.

As with all `WHERE` clauses, the `DELETE` statement's `WHERE` clause can be a `SELECT` statement that retrieves the list of rows to delete. If you do use a `SELECT` statement for a `WHERE` clause, be careful to test the `SELECT` statement first to ensure that it retrieves all the values you want, and only those values you want.

TIP

Feel free to `INSERT`, `UPDATE`, and `DELETE` rows as necessary, but when you're finished either clean up the changes or just copy overwrite the data file with the original (to restore it to its original state).

NOTE

Primary key values are never reused. If you `INSERT` rows after you have performed delete operations, the new rows will be assigned brand new IDs, and the old (deleted) IDs will not be reused. This behavior is a required part of how relational databases work as was explained in Chapter 2, "Building the Databases."

CHAPTER 7

Introducing Macromedia Dreamweaver MX

IN THIS CHAPTER

Dreamweaver MX Overview

A single chapter cannot possibly cover all areas of a program as feature-rich as Macromedia Dreamweaver MX. After all, there are entire books devoted to the subject. Therefore, I'll give you a brief tour of the program—what you need to know to develop ColdFusion applications using Dreamweaver. I'll discuss the features you're most likely to use more specifically.

Dreamweaver is a tool for designers and developers alike. As of the latest version, Dreamweaver MX, it is far more than just a visual HTML editor. Dreamweaver is a feature-rich set of tools that enable you to develop a Web site visually—through an approximation of the design—while allowing you to jump into the code and get your feet wet. If you're strictly a hand-coder, you can turn off Design view and work in Code view. If you prefer, you can even work in both the Code and Design views simultaneously! Dreamweaver makes mundane, common tasks quick and easy, so you can focus on more important things.

NOTE

Dreamweaver is not a WYSIWYG HTML generator. Sure, you'll see an estimation in Design view of what you can expect to see in a browser, but by no means should you expect exactitude. In fact there is no such thing as a WYSIWYG HTML generator; there are far too many possible renditions of a page in the various available browsers for Dreamweaver to match any of them precisely.

- Dreamweaver MX offers the following features and more:
- A customizable workspace with floating panels, which can be docked with other panels in panel groups
- Various viewing options—Code view to get under the hood of the page, Design view to simplify the creation of many HTML elements (such as tables, layers, and forms), Code and Design view for those who want both, as well as Live Data view and Server Debug view

- Menus, toolbars, and the Insert bar, all of which provide shortcuts to common elements and commands
- Code Coloring and Code Hints for HTML, CFML, and other languages that may be customized in Preferences
- Templates, library items, and snippets
- Drag-and-drop editing and context-sensitive right-click (Ctrl-click) options
- The Tag Editor dialog box for common HTML and CFML tags, which contains context-sensitive reference material
- Context-sensitive Reference panel containing reference guides for HTML, CFML, CSS, JavaScript, and other languages
- Built-in HTML and XHTML validation
- The Behaviors panel and Server Behaviors panel for fast generation of robust client and server-side scripts.
- Ability to upload and download files over an Internet connection (using FTP, RDS, SourceSafe Database, or WebDAV)
- The Check in/Check out version-control system
- Integration with other Macromedia Web development products, such as HomeSite, Fireworks, Flash, and more
- Flexibility of having the option to develop in ASP, ASP.Net, JSP, and PHP, as well as ColdFusion

If you're looking for a versatile tool that will improve your productivity, Dreamweaver is exactly what you need. Its tight integration with other Macromedia products, such as Fireworks and Flash, means you are sure to see improved speed in your workflow.

NOTE

When a keyboard shortcut is given the Macintosh equivalent is given in parenthesis. If a shortcut does not appear in parenthesis, it can be assumed that the given shortcut is the same for both Windows and Macintosh users.

Getting Help

Never fear—help is always near in Dreamweaver. More often than not, when you need additional information about a panel or dialog, Dreamweaver's help system will take you right to the information you want automatically. You can gather context-sensitive help in the following ways:

- Select Help > Using Dreamweaver or press F1 (Figure 7.1).
- Choose Help from the Options menu or context menu.
- Select the Help button if it's available in the current dialog box.

- You can access assistance with code-specific issues from the Reference panel (see "The Reference Panel" section later in this chapter) by choosing Help > Reference or pressing the Shift-F1 keyboard shortcut.

Should you require the ColdFusion MX–specific help documentation, which includes a complete CFML reference (as does the Reference panel), select Help > Using ColdFusion or press Ctrl-F1 (Command-F1).

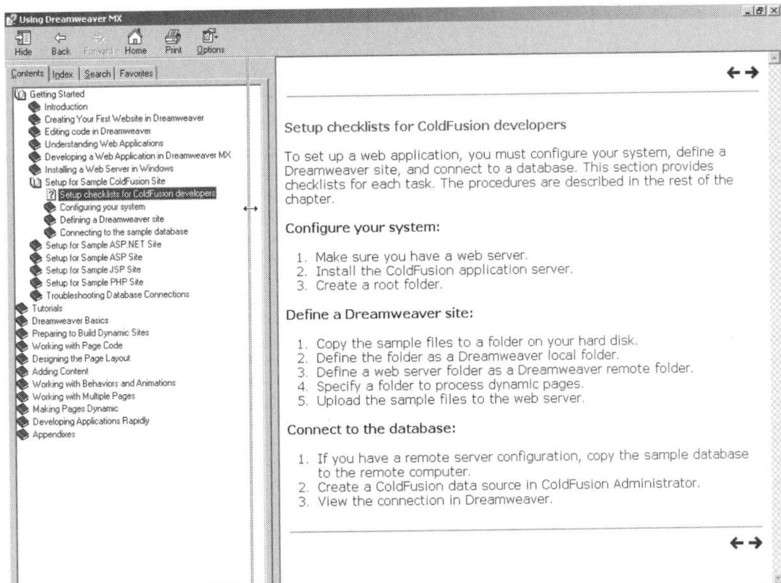

Figure 7.1

The Using Dreamweaver help system is a fast and simple way to obtain the answers you seek. You can adjust the width of the two areas by clicking and dragging the bar between them.

When viewing the Using Dreamweaver or Using ColdFusion help system, you will notice several categories available for selection:

- **Contents.** The Contents section presents you with all the major topics and subtopics, just as in a printed manual. As you click each topic or subtopic, the area on the right updates to show the corresponding information.

- **Index.** As in most manuals, the Index section makes available an alphabetical listing of keywords and phrases. Type a keyword and press Enter (Return), or select one from the list and then choose the Display button to view the results on the right.

- **Search.** The search facility is a very quick way to find help. First type a keyword or phrase, then choose List Topics to obtain the results of your search term. Choose the result you wish to see, then select the Display button to view the information on the right.

TIP

To narrow your search, use a phrase enclosed in quotations, as in "Tag inspector"–this will return results for the exact phrase only, instead of all the results for the words *Tag* and *inspector.*

- **Favorites.** Once you have found helpful material that you may need to view again later, you can store the page in your list of favorites to save time. You may place the currently listed topic in your list of favorites by clicking the Add button. To view a favorite item, highlight it in the list and then choose Display. To remove the item permanently from your favorites, first highlight it in the list and then click the Remove button.

The Answers Panel

The Answers panel provides a means to connect directly to Macromedia's Web site to obtain all the latest product information, including TechNotes and Dreamweaver extensions (Figure 7.2). You may access the Answers panel by choosing Window > Answers or by pressing Alt-F1 (Option-F1). The first time you use the panel, click the Update button so a list menu will appear with options. Use the Settings option in the list to choose whether to display the results in the panel or in the browser when performing searches in categories such as TechNotes or Extensions.

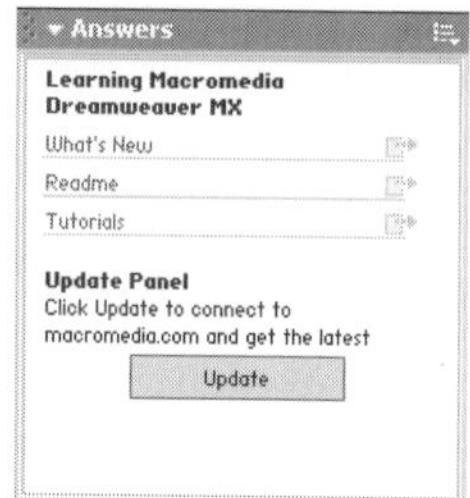

Figure 7.2

Get all the latest product information from the Answers Panel.

TIP

The Macromedia forums offer some of the best help you can possibly find for using Dreamweaver. Visit `www.macromedia.com/support/forums/` or point your newsreader to `news://forums.macromedia.com`.

The Dreamweaver Workspace

How you maintain your workspace is up to you. Dreamweaver is very flexible in this regard. As you learned in chapter 4, the first time you start Dreamweaver (Windows only) you will be asked which workspace you'd like to use -. Here is a little bit about what you can expect from each workspace option:

NOTE

Macintosh users do not have the option to choose a workspace, though the environment for the Macintosh platform most closely resembles the Dreamweaver 4 workspace. You will notice that all figures are shown in the HomeSite/Coder-Style workspace.

- **Dreamweaver MX Workspace.** Panel groups are arranged to the right of the Document window. The Insert bar is located above the Document window, and the Property inspector below. Code and Design view are enabled simultaneously, with code on top and design below. A blank document is open, but not maximized.

- **Dreamweaver MX Workspace: HomeSite/Coder-Style.** Enabling this option arranges the workspace in a pattern similar to Macromedia HomeSite's environment. A blank document is maximized—thus displaying the new MDI (multiple document interface)—in Code view. The workspace is optimized for hand-coders, but as you will see, it is not very different from the default Dreamweaver MX Workspace. The difference is just a matter of which panels you enable and where they are placed.
- **Dreamweaver 4 Workspace.** This option is similar to Dreamweaver 4/UltraDev 4. Choose it if you prefer floating panels and inspectors. In this workspace, the MDI is not available; multiple documents are displayed as individual floating windows.

If you've previously used ColdFusion Studio or HomeSite, you may be most comfortable in the HomeSite/Coder-Style workspace (see Figure 7.3). Feel free to change your workspace and try each option until you find what works best for you. To change your workspace option, select Edit > Preferences or press the Ctrl-U (Command-U) keyboard shortcut. Select the General category on the left and then choose the Change Workspace button. You will be alerted that the change will not happen until you have restarted Dreamweaver.

NOTE

If you switch between workspaces, your panel layouts are not saved for when you return to that workspace. With each switch, the original default for that workspace is presented.

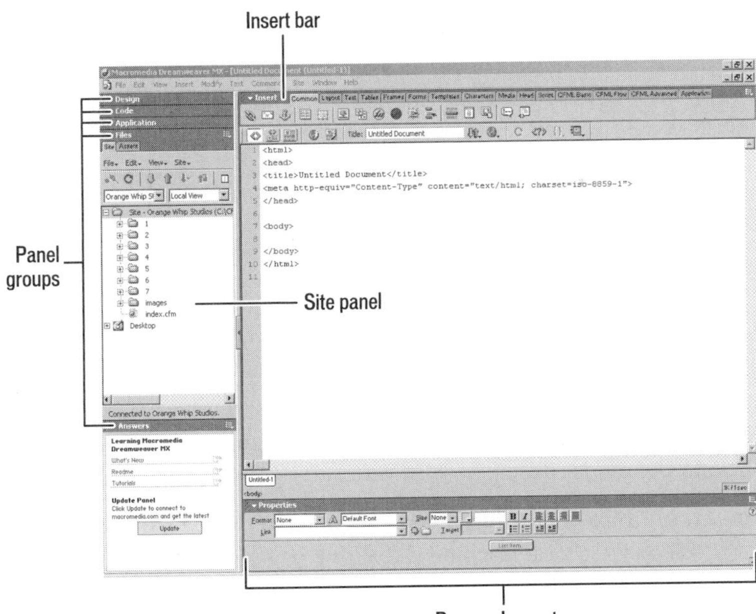

Figure 7.3

Throughout this book, the Dreamweaver MX HomeSite/Coder Style workspace is used.

Site Definitions

Nearly all site operations depend on having a site defined. This is especially important for ensuring that paths to images and other files are created and maintained properly. Template and library items depend on knowing which files are located in your site so that updates to templates can propagate to dependent files. Communication with remote and testing servers requires that a site be defined so that getting and putting files, as well as synchronizing files and the Check in/Check out system, may be used. Perhaps most important, if you do not define a site, Dreamweaver cannot communicate with the database, cannot create or use record sets, and will not allow the use of the Server Behaviors panel and various other operations.

You learned about the Basic category in Chapter 4, "Previewing ColdFusion," when creating the ows site definition. You may wish to set up additional options in the Advanced section of the Site Definition dialog (Figure 7.4). Select Site > Edit Sites from the Dreamweaver menu, or double-click the site name in the list menu located in the Site panel.

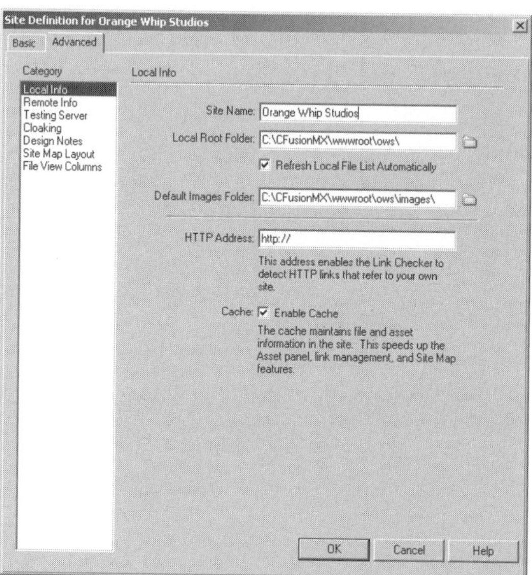

Figure 7.4

Use the Advanced category to set up additional site definition options.

The following describes what you'll find in the categories listed on the left in the Advanced section of the Site Definitions dialog:

- **Local Info.** The information contained in this category pertains to the location of the site on your local machine and allows you to enable and disable the site's cache, which helps manage links and other site operations.
- **Remote Info.** This section holds the data needed to connect to the remote server via FTP, Local/Network, RDS, SourceSafe, or WebDAV.
- **Testing Server.** This section stores the facts relating to the server used for testing your application.

- **Cloaking.** This section specifies file types that should not be included in site operations such as uploading using Dreamweaver's cloaking feature (see "The Site Panel" section later in this chapter). Items such as original source files for graphics and Flash usually do not need to be uploaded to the server, and therefore the .png and .fla file extensions are already listed for you to include as cloaked file types. To add other file types to the list, just type a space, followed by the file extension, at the end of the list.

TIP

Two common file types that you may wish to cloak are Dreamweaver templates (.dwt) and library items (.lbi). If these are listed, Dreamweaver knows not to include the files in operations such as uploading. Though cloaked files are usually excluded from the Assets panel, Dreamweaver is smart and knows to include templates and library items in those operations.

- **Design Notes.** Design Notes allow developers to share file status, comments, and other information. You may choose whether to Maintain Design Notes, Clean Up Design Notes (remove existing ones that do not have a file association), or disable Design Note sharing via uploading.
- **Site Map Layout.** The settings in this section determine the appearance of the Site Map used in the Site panel. After leaving the Site Definition dialog, you may view the Site Map by selecting Site > Site Map from the Dreamweaver menu or pressing the Alt-F8 (Option-F8) keyboard shortcut.
- **File View Columns.** This category enables you to customize the order of the columns within the Site panel and include your own additional columns if desired.

TIP

If at any time while using the Site definitions dialog you need more information to make the appropriate selections or entries, choose the Help button, and you will be shown the information available for the particular category you are viewing.

Once you have modified the site definition to suit your desires, click OK. The dialog will close, and you will return to the workspace.

The Site Panel

The Site panel helps you manage all files associated with your Web application (Figure 7.5). To toggle the display of the Site panel, select Window > Site or press the F8 key.

NOTE

The Site panel is always a floating window (not tabbed) for Macintosh users and Dreamweaver 4 Workspace users. In the lower left corner of the Site panel is a small arrow that you can use to collapse the panel to display the width of the local site files.

The Site panel displays files using a Windows Explorer–like interface with hierarchical file trees. Clicking the plus (+) or minus (–) symbol (Windows) or the disclosure triangles (Macintosh) to the left of folders will expand or contract the directory to reveal or hide its contents.

You can easily build the site's structure from within the Site panel. To create files and folders within the Site panel, right-click (Control-click-) on the folder where you would like to create the new file or folder. When the context menu appears, choose New File or New Folder.

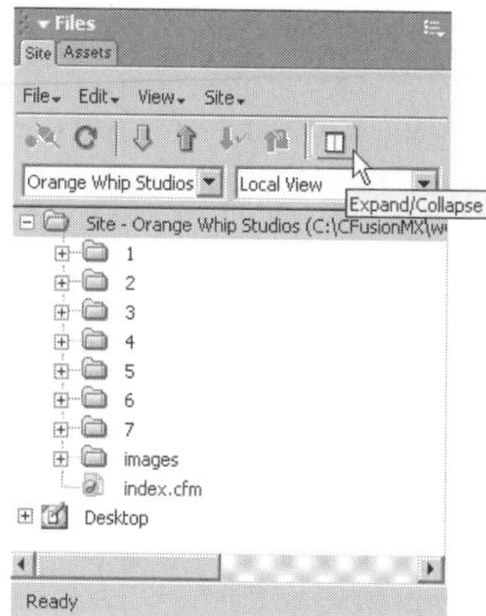

Figure 7.5

The Site panel is the central location for all site file management; you can toggle between tabbed panel size and full size by clicking the Expand/ Collapse button.

TIP

Make it a habit to right-click (Control-click) documents, panels, or toolbars to view additional options available to you in the context-sensitive menu that appears.

To open a file in Dreamweaver from the Site panel, you may either double-click it or select Open from the context menu. Select Open With from the context menu if you would like to open the file with a listed editor or browse to the editor of your choosing. Various standard file and folder options such as Cut, Copy, Paste, Delete, Duplicate, and Rename are also available from the Site panel's context menu.

Cloaking a folder excludes the folder and its entire contents from site operations such as uploading and synchronizing (Figure 7.6). Individual files cannot be cloaked. If you would like to cloak an individual file, you must cloak the folder containing it, which in turn cloaks all files within that folder. You may enable cloaking from the Site panel by selecting Cloaking > Enable Cloaking from the context menu. To cloak a folder, right-click (Control-click) and select Cloaking > Cloak from the menu.

If cloaking is enabled, a checkmark appears beside the Enable Cloaking option in the Cloaking submenu. Use the Cloaking > Enable Cloaking option to disable all cloaked items temporarily so that site operations can include them. Choose this menu option again to cloak them once more.

From the context menu, select Cloaking > Uncloak to remove cloaking from the selected folder and its contents. Cloaking> Uncloak All removes cloaking from all files and folders in the entire site and cannot be undone, so use this option carefully. Uncloaking all files will disable the specified files in the Cloaking section of the Site Definition dialog. Right-click (Control-click) any file or folder in the Site panel and choose Cloaking > Settings to return to the Site Definition dialog to adjust the options.

You can conduct site operations, such as getting and putting files and folders to the remote server, from the context menu, although you may find the buttons easier to use, when available. Some of these same options also appear as buttons -at the top of the Site panel. To the left of the list of sites are three buttons used to control which view is shown in the Site panel. You can obtain more information about these operations by selecting Help from the Options menu (Dreamweaver MX workspace only) or pressing F1.

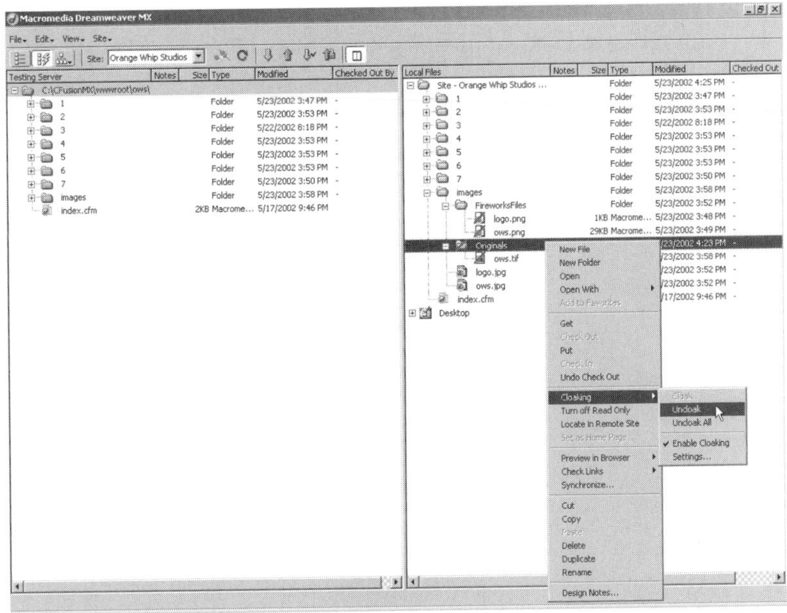

Figure 7.6

The icons of cloaked file types and cloaked folders—and all files and folders within them—are marked by a red slash in the Site panel.

A very powerful Dreamweaver feature is the ability to track file paths. If you ever choose to move a file or folder, you should always do so through the Site panel via dragging and dropping. Dreamweaver will prompt you to update all files that depend on the location of the folder or file you're moving. When you agree, Dreamweaver will modify all paths affected by the change so that you aren't left with broken images or links.

NOTE

Dreamweaver can't find and update paths located within scripts unless it has generated those scripts. Take care to update those paths manually.

The Document Window

In Dreamweaver MX, you will build your ColdFusion application in the document window, which can display five types of views for developing ColdFusion applications (Figure 7.7):

- **Code.** This view displays the code used to create your page.
- **Code and Design.** This view divides and displays both the code and the visual environment.
- **Design.** This view provides an environment in which you can visually develop ColdFusion applications.
- **Server Debug.** Exclusive to ColdFusion pages, this view allows you to preview your application in a browser from within Dreamweaver and displays debugging information within the Server Debug panel.

- **Live Data.** This view displays the page with processed server-side code in Design view, all the while remaining fully editable so that you can see changes instantly.

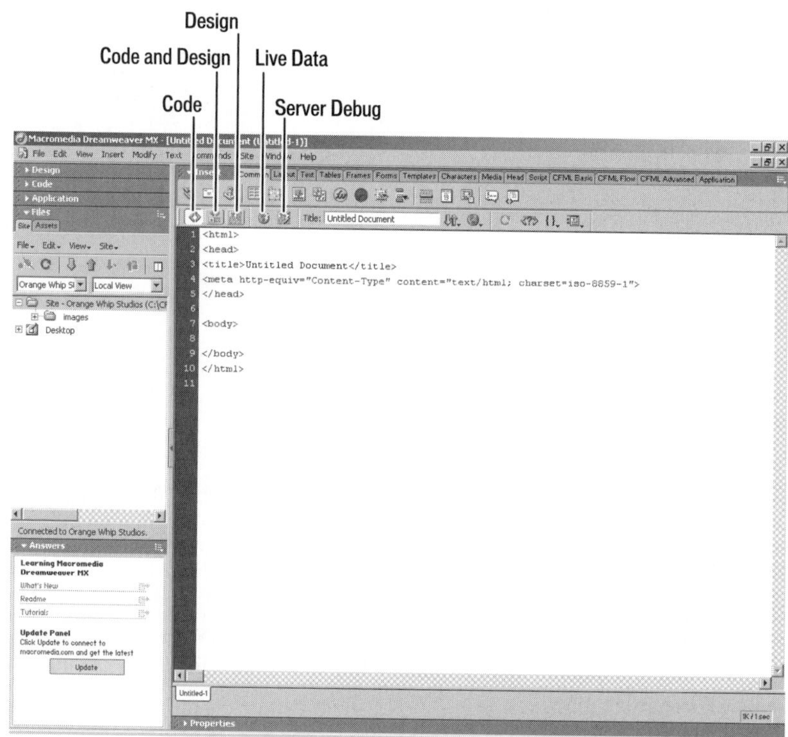

Figure 7.7

Dreamweaver offers several viewing options for ColdFusion application development. Shown here is a document open in Code view.

Along the lower left of the Document window, you will find the tag selector. As you work, you will notice that a chain of tags appears, depending on where you've positioned the pointer within the document. You use the tag selector to ensure that a specific tag is entirely selected in the code so that you can apply CSS or Behaviors to it (Figure 7.8). The tag selector has many other uses. Right-click (Control-click) any tag listed in the tag selector to view its options.

Working with Files

In chapter 4, you learned a about creating, saving, closing and opening files using Dreamweaver. Now let's focus a little bit on how to work with those files in the Dreamweaver environment.

TIP

The Standard toolbar, which can be enabled from the View menu in the Toolbar submenu, contains buttons for creating, opening, closing, and saving files.

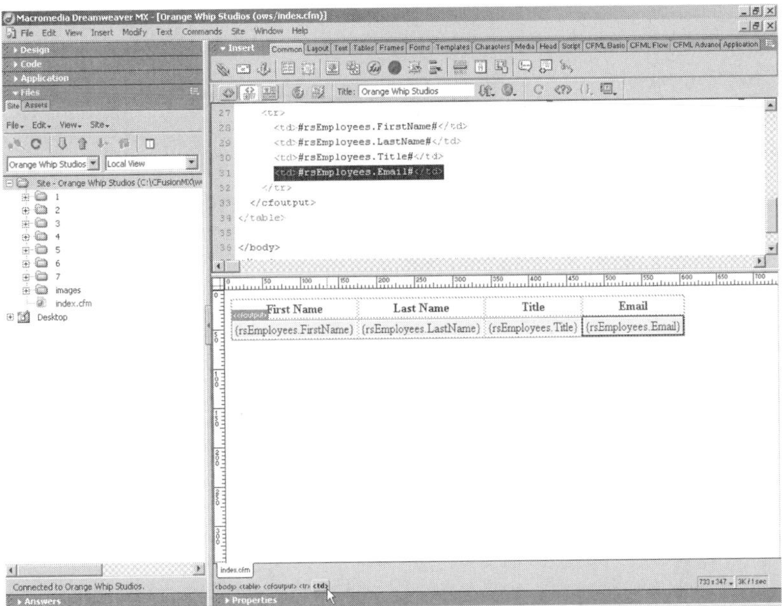

Figure 7.8

Use the tag selector to select individual tags in their entirety.

The Dreamweaver title bar shows the name of the currently active document. You may open as many documents as your system resources allow. Several commands in the Window menu (Windows only) will help you quickly arrange open documents:

- **Cascade.** Each document window beginning from the upper left of the Dreamweaver MX Workspace is tiled, placing them on top of each other with a slight top and left offset.
- **Tile Horizontally.** Each document window takes up the available screen width and is placed above the next, without overlapping. Once four or more documents are open, tiling occurs in a horizontal order that is optimal for the available screen space.
- **Tile Vertically.** Each document window takes up the available screen height and is placed above the next, without overlapping. Once four or more documents are open, tiling occurs in a vertical order that is optimal for the available screen space.

Users of the Dreamweaver MX or HomeSite/Coder-Style workspace may also take advantage of the new MDI by choosing the Maximize control at the far right of the title bar. You can then easily switch between documents by selecting the filename tabs at the bottom of the document (Figure 7.9).

To use individual windows instead of the MDI, choose any of the Window menu options mentioned earlier. You may also use the controls located in the upper right, just below the Dreamweaver window controls.

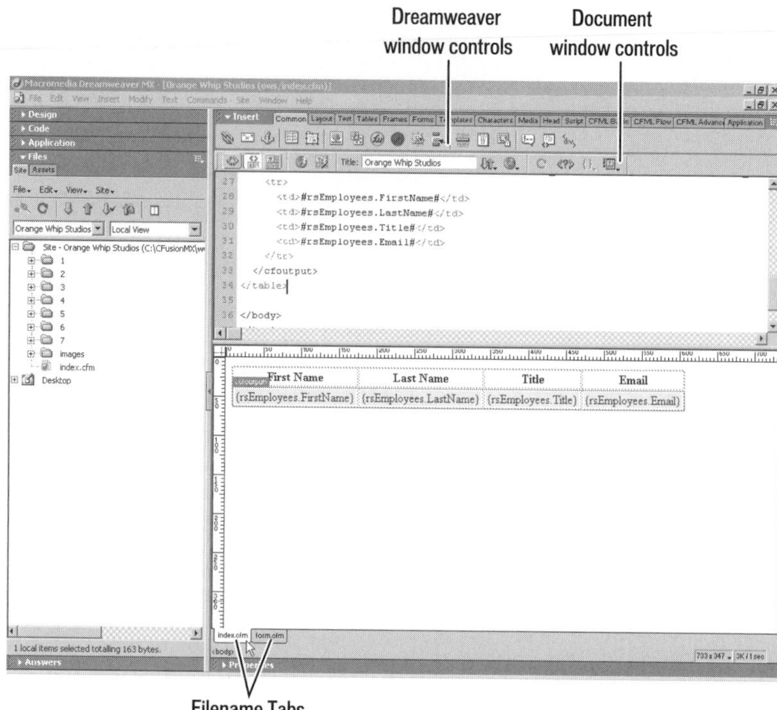

Figure 7.9

You can switch between documents quickly using the filename tabs.

Managing Panels

The most common way to customize Dreamweaver is to arrange the various panels in such a way that is comfortable for you in your workflow. In the Dreamweaver 4 Workspace and on Macintosh, the panels are located in a floating dock area. The Dreamweaver MX and HomeSite/Coder-Style workspaces have a dock area attached to the Dreamweaver workspace. Panels are arranged in what are known as a panel group. The name of the panel group is located to the right of the gripper—the set of five dots. If a panel is grouped with other panels, a tab indicating the panel name is shown.

Between the gripper and the panel group's name is an expander arrow that indicates whether the panels are hidden (when pointing right) or exposed (when pointing down). Single-click the arrow or panel group name to expand and collapse the panels.

To move a panel group, click and drag the group by the gripper to the new location (Figure 7.10). As you drag the panel group, you will notice that it is only an outline. When you have positioned the group in an allowed location, a darker outline appears; or, if you are moving the panel group's position within the dock area, a dark line will appear where you will be placing the panel. Once you have properly positioned the panel group, release the gripper and it will snap into place. If you have not positioned the panel correctly and do not see the dark line, when you release the panel group, it will float over the workspace.

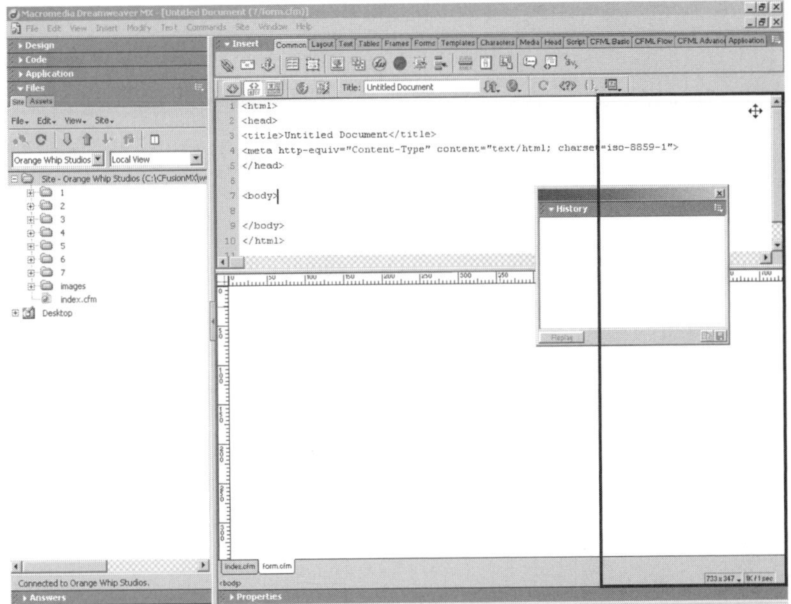

Figure 7.10

Use the gripper to click and drag the panel to a new position.

To arrange a panel with another panel, simply choose Group *panel* with > *panel group* from the Options menu – where *panel* is the name of the current panel and *panel group* is the name of the target panel group (Figure 7.11). The panel is then moved to the last position within the panel group.

NOTE

The Properties inspector and Insert bar may not be grouped with any other panels. Though the grouping option appears to be available at first glance in the Options menu, you will see that the list of panel groups is unavailable.

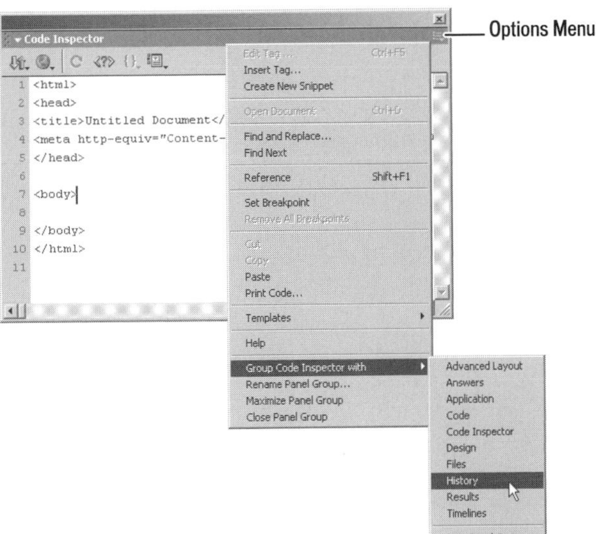

Figure 7.11

Using the Options menu, you may move panels to existing panel groups or to create a new panel group for the panel.

Each panel has its own Options menu, located in the top right corner of the panel group, that when clicked upon offers a unique list of choices for the current panel. Common to all Options menus are the choices to group with another panel group, rename, maximize, or close the panel group and contextual help regarding the currently selected panel's usage.

NOTE

When a panel group is collapsed, the Options menu is not visible.

TIP

If you'd like to be able to view two portions of code at the same time, as is possible with HomeSite or ColdFusion Studio, move the Code inspector to the Code panel group or along the left or right side of the document window with another established panel group. Essentially, you will be left with Code-Code view. You may wish to turn on Word Wrapping as shown in Figure 7.12 so that the code is fully visible in the panel without requiring that you scroll.

You can dock panels to the left and right of the Document window and collapse them using the Expand/Collapse button (Dreamweaver MX Workspace only). Use the F4 key to quickly show and hide all panels. To widen or narrow the dock area of the panel groups, click and drag the divider. You may also adjust the height of an expanded docked panel by clicking and dragging its bottom or top edge.

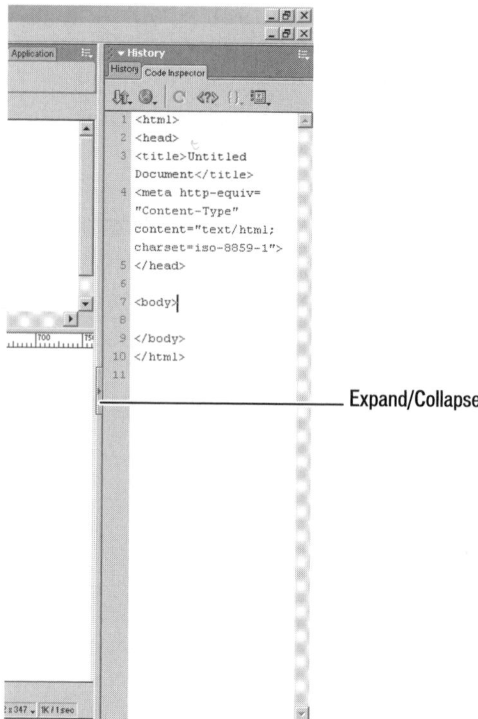

Figure 7.12

In the Dreamweaver MX workspace, you can show or hide all panel groups using the expander arrow.

Code Editing

Dreamweaver is built in such a way that developers can usually accomplish tasks in several ways. Though having so many options may be intimidating at first—or perhaps even a bit confusing—you will soon find the method that is most comfortable for you. That is the beauty of Dreamweaver: You can work however you like. Some people prefer pure Code view, while others prefer to avoid manually editing code by using dialog boxes and panels, and the rest fall somewhere in between the two extremes. Whatever your preference is in terms of code editing, Dreamweaver can help you get the job done.

Code Hints and Tag Completion

To most developers, the thought of typing in every bit of code manually isn't very appealing. The more you have to type yourself, the greater the chances are that you'll make a typo or forget to close a tag. Code hints and tag completion make the job of hand-coding so much easier.

TIP

You can control Code Hints and tag completion settings from the Code Hints category of Edit > Preferences. For more information, see the "Preferences" section later in this chapter.

Here's how Code Hints and Tag Completion work in Code view:

1. To add a new tag, type an opening angle bracket (<).
2. A list of tags will appear. Type the first letter of the tag you wish to insert. For example, if you would like to add a `<select>` tag to the document, type the letter `s`.

   The list will jump to the first tag that begins with the letter you typed. In this case, it jumps to the `<samp>` tag. You will need to type the next letter in the tag, `e`.

   Depending which tag you are trying to choose, you may need to type additional letters (Figure 7.13). Alternatively, you could use the pointer to scroll to the correct tag and select it, or you may use the down-arrow key to scroll to the tag.
3. Now that the tag is highlighted in the list, press Enter (Return). The highlighted text in the list is inserted into the document.

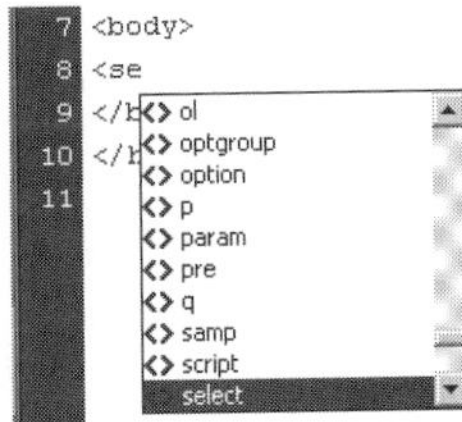

Figure 7.13

Type the first letter of the tag, then additional letters as needed, until the tag you require is highlighted.

4. If you wish to add attributes to the tag, press the spacebar. If there are attributes known for the current tag, a list is displayed for you (Figure 7.14). As described in step 2, you can choose the attribute from the list by typing the first letter then additional letters as needed or by scrolling to the attribute.

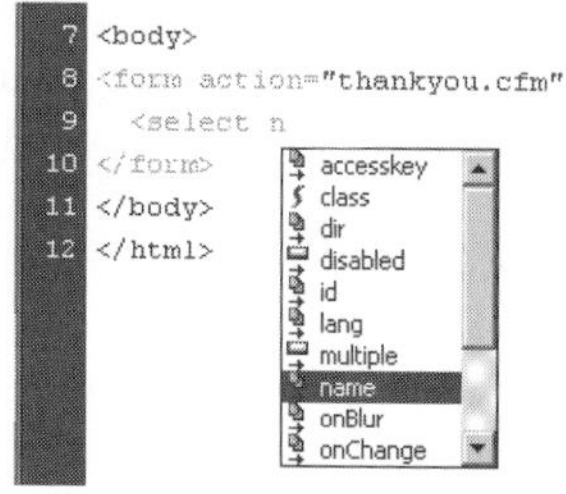

Figure 7.14

If attributes are known for the current tag, they too are available as code hints.

TIP

If you make a mistake and use the backspace to correct your error, the code hint menu will disappear. To bring it back into view, press Ctrl-Space (Command-Space).

5. Once you've highlighted the attribute in the list, press Enter (Return). The attribute, followed by an equal sign (=), is added to the code. Your cursor is placed conveniently between a pair of quotes so that you may add the attribute's value if a hint menu appears or by typing the shortcut manually.

   If the attribute has possible default text values available, they are listed in another code hint menu and may be chosen in the same way as tags and attributes. If the attribute's value is a color, the color picker appears. If the attribute's value can be a file path or file name, the browse option appears so that you may locate the file; Dreamweaver will add the path accordingly.

6. After adding the attribute's value, you need to move past the closing quotation mark by either pressing the right-arrow key or clicking after the quote mark. You can add more attributes by repeating step 4 through 6 as needed.

7. When you are ready, finish off the opening tag by typing the closing angle bracket (>). The closing tag will be added following your cursor so that you may enter additional tags, text, or other contents within the newly entered tag.

NOTE

Dreamweaver will only add a closing HTML tag if it is optional or required. In other words, Dreamweaver will not attempt to add closing HTML tags to "empty tags" such as `<br>`, `<meta>`, `<hr>`, and so forth.

TIP

Select Edit > Tag Libraries to create your own tag libraries, or import existing ones-such as the JSP tag library-using Dreamweaver's Tag Library Editor (Figure 7.15). The Tag Library Editor also offers a multitude of options that determine how Dreamweaver formats code. Custom tags and attributes that you add to the Tag Library Editor are available as Code Hints. For more information about tag libraries and how to import them or create your own, click the Help button on the Tag Library Editor dialog.

➜ Custom tags are discussed in chapter 20, "Building Reusable Components" and are ideal for adding to your tag library.

➜ For more information on Extending ColdFusion with Java, see chapter 26, "Extending ColdFusion with Java", in our companion book, "Advanced ColdFusion MX Application Development" (Macromedia Press, 0-321-12710-2).

The Code Panel Group

Bundled together in the Code panel group are three of the most useful panels that deal strictly with using code. With a little bit of code know-how, you can insert code quickly using the Snippets panel and the Tag Inspector panel. The Reference panel offers context-sensitive information that is much easier to search through than a huge stack of books.

The Tag Inspector panel

Split into two very useful sections, the upper portion of the Tag Inspector panel presents the entire structure of the document in a familiar hierarchal tree menu structure, while the lower half displays the property sheet for selected tags. Here you can add, edit, and remove tags without going into Code view, and add, edit, or remove attributes from the selected tag in the property sheet. To display the Tag inspector, select Window > Tag Inspector or press F9.

Managing this panel is very similar to how the Site panel is used. Expand and collapse the structure by clicking the + or – symbol (Windows) or the disclosure triangles (Macintosh). Use the context menu or the Options menu to add, edit, or remove tags. As you select tags in the Tag inspector, Dreamweaver selects the corresponding code in Code view.

As you would expect, the options for New Tag Before, New Tag Inside, and New Tag After respectively place the new tag before, inside, or after the currently selected tag. The difference between the submenu options, New Tag and New Empty Tag, may not be as apparent.

NOTE
Dreamweaver automatically adds the opening and closing angle brackets. For example, to add an image tag, you would type `img`, not `<img>`. Typing < > would leave an extra pair of angle brackets: `<<img>>`.

- **New Tag.** This option adds the tag with its closing tag to the document. Dreamweaver won't add a closing HTML tag if you attempt to add a tag known to have a forbidden closing tag, such as `<meta>`, `<hr>`, `<br>`, and so on.
- **New Empty Tag.** Empty tags are those that do not require a closing tag. Examples of tags that are never closed with a corresponding closing tag are `<img>`, `<hr>`, and `<meta>`. Tags that have optional closing tags, such as `<td>` and `<p>`, may be added using New Empty Tag.

NOTE
It is a good practice to always close tags that have an optional closing tag. Remember, XHTML requires that all tags have a closing tag and that empty tags close with a forward slash. For example, `<br>` would be `<br />` in XHTML. The Tag inspector will recognize if the document is XHTML and insert the slash when needed. For more about XHTML, visit www.w3.org/TR/xhtml1.

If a selected tag has known possible attributes, they are listed in the property sheet. In the column to the right of the attribute you'd like added to the tag, you may manually enter the value or use the options presented via their respective icons (Figure 7.15). For example, if you have chosen to add a background color to a table, when you click inside or tab to the field to the right of `bgcolor`, the familiar color-swatch icon will appear so that you can use Dreamweaver's color picker to select a color for the attribute. If the attribute is one that would require a path to a file, a folder icon and the point-to-file icon (more about that in "The Property Inspector" section of this chapter) appears so that you may browse to or point to that file. Another feature of the property sheet is similar to code hints: If values are known for the attribute, a down arrow appears; when clicked, it presents a list of possible values. Perhaps one of the most useful aspects of adding values through the property sheet is that you can make any value dynamic by choosing the lightning-bolt icon. When the data source dialog appears, simply choose the appropriate data source field in the tree menu that contains the value for the attribute.

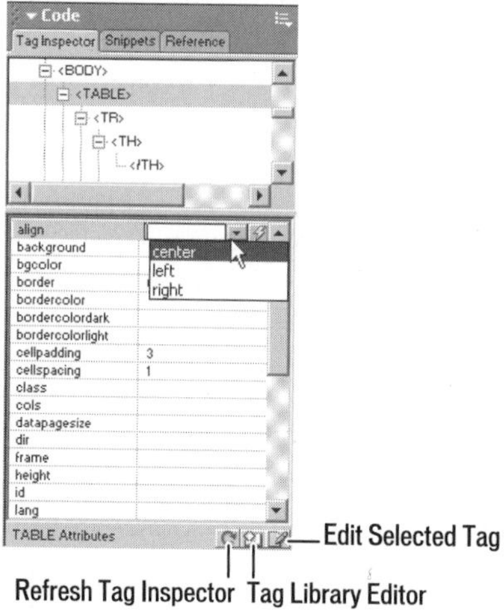

Figure 7.15
The Tag inspector is great for adding attributes to a tag all at once.

Along the bottom of the Tag inspector are three icons:

- **Refresh Tag Inspector.** In most cases, the Tag inspector will refresh to reflect changes you have made to the document when it is given focus. In the event that it does not update automatically—as may happen with XML documents—you can update the panel manually with this button.
- **Tag Library Editor.** This icon opens the same Tag Library Editor that is available in the menu under Edit >Tag Libraries. You may use the Tag Library Editor to create, modify, or remove tags and their attributes.
- **Edit Selected Tag.** The Tag Editor dialog box is displayed for the selected tag. Most Tag Editor dialogs present a category on the left. Select the category on the left and then fill in the values on the right. Some Tag Editor dialogs simply present a dialog with various fields to complete. Choose the Tag Info button to reveal the reference book entry for helpful information.

The Snippets Panel

Often you will find that you can easily reuse some pieces of code—that is, if you don't have to go out of your way to find them. Many developers store their reusable code in plain text files, but spend too much of their time hunting through the file(s) for the piece they need. The Snippets panel makes storing and reusing code pieces a breeze (Figure 7.16). The kinds of code you may store as a snippet are limitless: HTML, CFML, JavaScript, CSS, or any other type you fancy. You may even drag and drop the snippets and folders within the Snippets panel to reorganize them. To display the Snippets panel, select Window > Snippets or press Shift-F9.

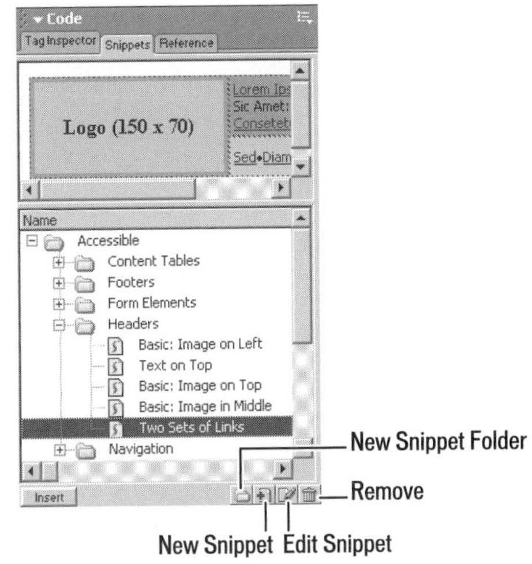

Figure 7.16

The Snippets panel stores pieces of reusable code that you can insert into the document whenever you need them.

To create a new folder:

1. Position your cursor in the structure where you wish the new folder to be added, just as you would if you were adding a new folder in the Site panel.
2. Choose one of the following options:
   - Click the New Folder icon located along the bottom of the panel.
   - Select Options > New Folder.
   - Right-click (Control-click) and choose New Folder.
3. Once the folder appears with the default name highlighted beside it, give the folder a meaningful name so you can easily locate your snippet later.
4. Press Enter (Return) or click elsewhere to make the folder name change complete.

To add a new snippet:

1. If the code is already located in the current document, select it.
2. Position your cursor in the structure where you wish to add the new snippet, just as you would if you were adding a new file in the Site panel.
3. Choose one of the following options:
   - Click the New Snippet icon located along the bottom of the panel.
   - Use the Options menu to choose New Snippet.
   - Right-click (Control-click) and choose New Snippet.
4. When the Snippets dialog box appears, if you had selected some code, it will appear in the dialog (Figure 7.17). Complete the fields and select the proper options:
   - **Name.** Use this field to assign a descriptive title to the snippet that will appear in the panel.
   - **Description.** This field provides a place for you to enter a description or other notations pertinent to the snippet code.
   - **Snippet Type.** If Wrap Selection is chosen, Dreamweaver will place the code listed in the Insert Before field prior to the selection in the document, and the code listed in the Insert After field following the current selection. Choose Insert Block if the piece of code should be inserted where your cursor is positioned.
   - **Insert Before.** This field is shown when the Wrap Selection option is chosen. The code in this field will be inserted prior to the cursor position or selected code.
   - **Insert After.** This field is shown when the Wrap Selection option is chosen. The code in this field will be inserted following the cursor position or selected code.
   - **Insert Code.** This field is shown when the Insert Block option is chosen. The contents of this field are inserted prior to the cursor position or selected code.
   - **Preview Type.** The choice of displaying the snippet either as code or as a preview of the design in the top portion of the Snippets panel is given as Code and Design, respectively. If Dreamweaver is unable to render a design for the snippet, the code is displayed instead.

TIP

Hundreds of snippets of virtually all types are available for download at the Snippets Exchange located at `www.dwfaq.com/Snippets/`.

Figure 7.17

The Snippets dialog is used for both creating and editing snippets.

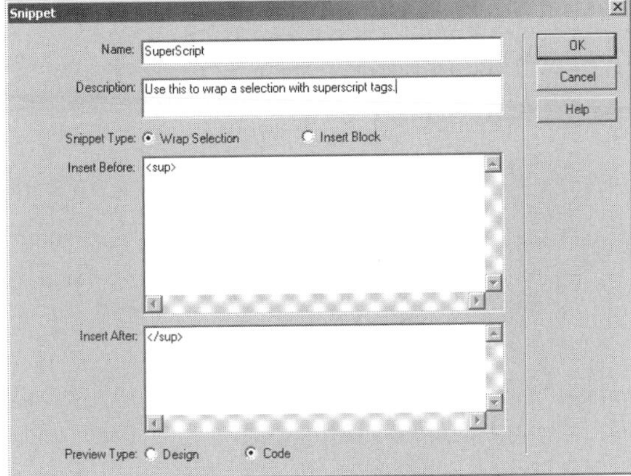

To edit a snippet:

1. Locate, then select the snippet you wish to modify.
2. Choose one of the following options:
   - Click the Edit Snippet icon located along the bottom of the panel.
   - Use the Options menu to choose Edit.
   - Right-click (Control-click) and choose Edit.
3. The same dialog appears that is used to create snippets. Make the necessary changes, then click OK.

To insert a snippet:

1. Position your cursor in the code or make a selection of code.
2. Locate, then select the snippet you would like to insert.
3. Choose one of the following options:
   - Click the Insert button located at the bottom left of the panel
   - Use the Options menu to choose Insert.
   - Right-click (Control-click) and choose Insert.
   - Click and drag the snippet into the document.

TIP

When inserting a snippet, it is best to do so in Code view -or at least with Code and Design view both open-so that you are certain the code will be placed in the proper location. Using snippets in Code view is especially important if you are attempting to insert a snippet that wraps the selection.

To delete a snippet or folder:

1. Locate, then select the folder or snippet you wish to eliminate permanently.
2. Choose one of the following options:
   - Click the Remove button located at the bottom left of the panel.
   - Use the Options menu to choose Remove.
   - Right-click (Control-click) and choose Remove.

NOTE

Due to a new file format, the snippets created in Dreamweaver MX are not compatible with other Macromedia programs that also use snippets. If you have snippets in HomeSite or ColdFusion Studio that you would like to make available in Dreamweaver, use the Snippets Converter extension by Massimo Foti, available for download at `www.dwfaq.com/Snippets/converter.asp`.

The Reference panel

To help you with your coding, Macromedia provides several helpful reference books within the Reference panel (Figure 7.18). To display the Reference panel, select Window > Reference or press Shift-F1.

TIP

The Reference panel is context sensitive. If your cursor is positioned in a recognized element, when you choose to display the Reference panel it will open to the pertinent information.

The basic premise for each reference book is the same. To use the Macromedia CFML Reference, select it from the list of Books. Choose the CFML tag from the list on the left to view a description of the tag. Choose the attribute in the Description list menu, if available, to display information regarding the attribute for the specific tag. You may change the font size used in this panel by choosing a large, medium, or small font from the Options menu.

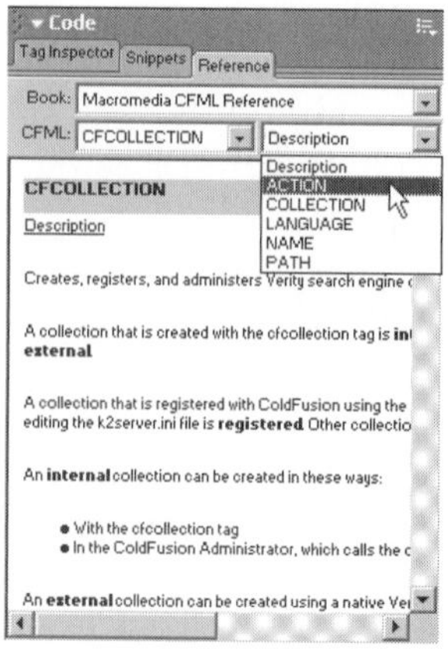

Figure 7.18

The Reference panel holds several useful reference books that will help you with coding questions. Shown here is the Macromedia ColdFusion Reference.

The Application Panel Group

Within the Application panel group, you will find four of the most useful panels for ColdFusion application development. The panels help you connect to your database to retrieve records, allow you to format the data on the page, and more. You can add code to the page manually through Code view, or use Design view to get the job done using the dialogs provided. However you choose to work, these panels are truly indispensable and can save you loads of time.

The Databases panel

Dreamweaver's Databases panel functions as the window to your database (Figure 7.19). To display the Databases panel, choose Window > Databases or press Ctrl-Shift-F10 (Command-Shift-F10).

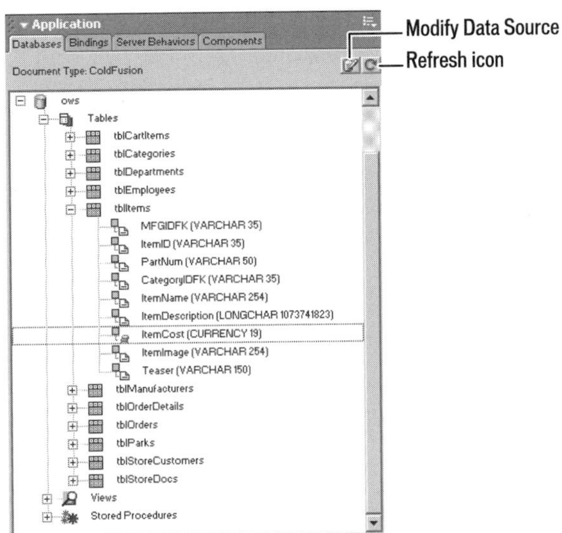

Figure 7.19 Dreamweaver displays known data sources in the Databases panel.

All available data sources are displayed in this panel. If you need to establish the data source, click the Modify Data Sources button. This will launch your browser and take you to the Data Sources page in ColdFusion Administrator (after logging in), where you can set up a new connection to a data source or modify an existing listing. Click the Refresh button to update the Databases panel.

Clicking the + or – symbol (Windows) or the disclosure triangles (Macintosh) to the left of the icons in the list will expand or contract the database and tables to reveal or hide the contents. You may drag and drop any listed item into Code view for hand-coding. For example, if you were to click and drag the `ows` database listed in the Databases panel onto your page, Dreamweaver would insert the following code:

```
<CFQUERY NAME="" DATASOURCE="ows"></CFQUERY>
```

Drag and drop a listed table or field into place in Code view to insert its name. This is an especially handy method if you prefer to hand-code, but have difficulty remembering the names of tables and fields, or wish to avoid introducing errors.

Dragging and dropping any listed database, table, or field into Design view will initiate the Recordset dialog box. See the Bindings panel section for more information.

The Bindings panel

Using the Bindings panel, you can define and call recordsets and stored procedures without writing a single line of SQL (Figure 7.20).The Bindings panel helps you to automate the process of inserting and calling variables in your code, such as CGI, URL, form, and session variables and so on. When you create a record set, Dreamweaver inserts the `<cfquery>` tag that connects to your database to pull specified records. This panel makes it easy to insert a Stored Procedure or a `<cfparam>` tag. To display the Databases panel, select Window > Databases or press Ctrl-F10 (Command-F10).

NOTE

Chapter 4, "Previewing ColdFusion," describes recordset creation.

You may drag and drop a data source into Code or Design view or first select it and then choose the Insert button. The Bindings panel displays three columns, though you can't see the second two without scrolling unless you widen the panel:

- **Source.** The first column indicates the source of the data (that is, the record set, stored procedure, session variable, and so on). Choose the Add (+) button to supply the Bindings panel with more data sources. Use the Remove (–) button to delete the selected data source from the panel and the document code.
- **Binding.** Data may be bound to attributes of certain visual tag types, such as form elements, links, and images. With the element selected in Code or Design view, choose the attribute listed in the Bind To field and then select the Bind button. If a data source is bound to the selected element already, then the Bind To field will be dimmed and you may choose the Unbind button to remove the bond.
- **Format.** You may add server-side formatting (date formats, currency formats, change selection to uppercase or lowercase text, and so forth) when a listed data source is selected in the document. Apply formats to fields only where appropriate to avoid errors. For instance, do not apply Date formatting if the data source is not specifically set up to handle dates.

The Server Behaviors panel

Dreamweaver's server behaviors add dynamic functionality to your Web pages. The server behaviors that ship with Dreamweaver can fulfill many of the most common needs of a dynamic page. The Server Behaviors panel even allows you to create your own server behaviors easily with the Server Behavior Builder. To display the Server Behaviors panel, select Window > Server Behaviors or press Ctrl-F9 (Command-F9).

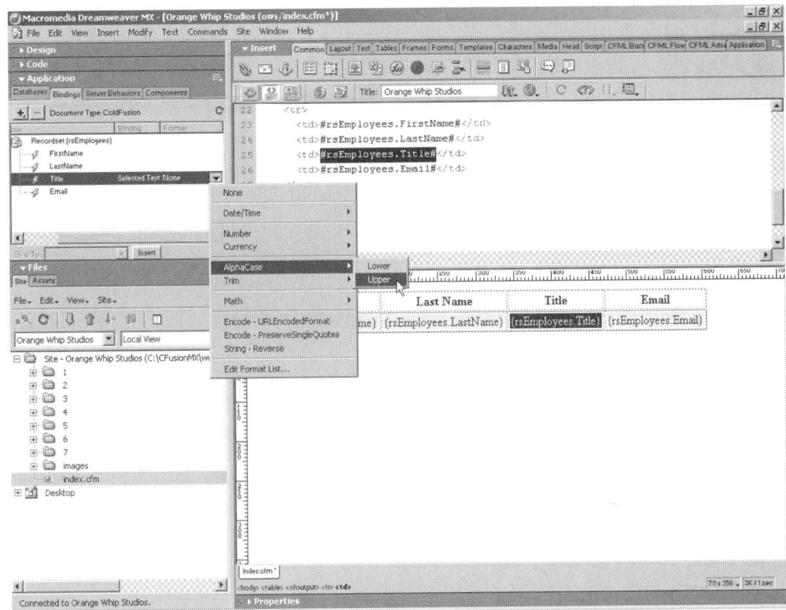

Figure 7.20
Use the Bindings panel to call, insert, and format data sources.

The Repeat Region server behavior will insert the <cfoutput> tag pair into the document (Figure 7.21). Repeat Region uses the current selection and repeats it according to the specifications made in the dialog. After you've used the Repeat Region server behavior, you may find yourself needing to move through many returned records. The Recordset Paging server behavior allows you to create a link to the first, next, previous, or last record.

Show Region implements the <cfif> tag and creates a conditional region. This versatile tag lets you choose to show any selection based on a recordset.

Within the list of available server behaviors, you will find Insert Record, Update Record, and Delete Record. As you may have already guessed, Insert Record creates a form on the page that, when viewed online, allows you to insert new records into the database. Update Record allows you to modify existing records with a similar form. Delete Record allows you to remove a record from the database.

Use the Dynamic Text option to initiate the Dynamic Text dialog, where you may select a record from the tree menu, then choose a format to apply to that record. Dynamic Form Elements specify specific records that will appear within the form element as its value, as the factor for which a checkbox or radio button is selected, and more.

As long as you have a recordset established, you may choose one of the options in the submenu for the Show Region server behavior. Select whatever code you wish to show based on the criteria of whether the record is empty, first, or last, and choose the respective Show Region server behavior. If you are using Design view, a tab labeled <cfif> will appear in the upper left of a rectangular area that surrounds the conditional region.

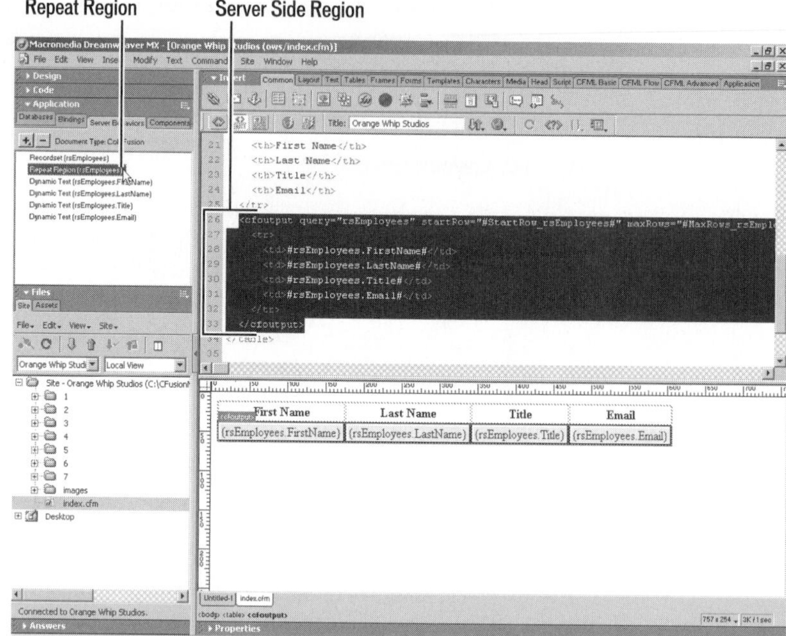

Figure 7.21

To help you recognize where server side code appears in the document while in Design view, Dreamweaver uses a tab with the appropriate label. In this case, a Repeat Region is shown.

The Components panel

The Components panel lists all ColdFusion Components (CFCs) and Web Services detected on the testing server (Figure 7.22). For more information about ColdFusion Components, see Chapter 20, "Building Reusable Components."

Dreamweaver MX automatically finds any CFCs on your server (using the server information provided when you created your site). You may right-click any listed components to learn more about them, and you may drag them into your code to instantiate them.

To use a component, expand the first two levels of the tree to reveal the CF Component icon(s), then click the `Insert code to invoke a function` button. If you prefer, you can drag and drop the component into Code view.

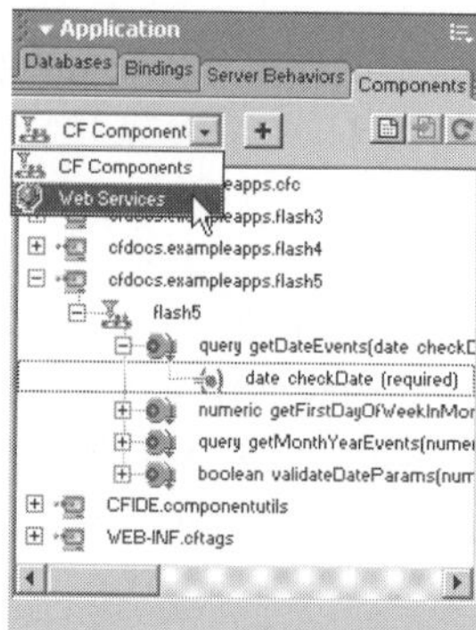

Figure 7.22

Installed ColdFusion Components are readily available in the Components panel.

Double-click a listed component to have Dreamweaver open it for editing in the Document window. Alternatively, you may select the Options menu in the panel group and choose `Edit the code` from the list.

To create a new ColdFusion Component using the Create Component dialog box click the Add (+) button or select `Create new CFC` from the Options menu.

If details are available about your selection in the Components panel, the Get details icon is enabled. Choose the icon, or select `Get details` from the Options menu. An alert message will appear with any available details about your selection.

Also available in the Options menu is the `Get description` option, which will open a browser window to the detailed information page for the selected component within ColdFusion Administrator. As always, you must be logged in to view the page.

You can also use this panel to introspect and use Web Services. The drop-down list box at the top allows you to toggle between components and Web Services. When displaying Web Services, click the + button to add a new service (specifying its WSDL URL), and Dreamweaver will display its methods for you to use.

Design Tools

During development, at times you will want to see how the page is taking shape. Design view displays an approximation of how the browser will display your code, while maintaining your ability to modify the page contents as necessary. Design view is great for applying Cascading Style Sheets (CSS), drawing layers, viewing and even drawing tables, and creating framesets, and is required for use when previewing Live Data.

The CSS Panel

Perhaps the most useful design tool is the CSS Styles panel (Figure 7.23). To display the CSS Styles panel, select Window > CSS Styles or press Shift-F11. Applying and editing CSS are available as two separate modes controlled by the radio buttons labeled Apply Styles and Edit Styles, respectively. You may attach style sheets, create new styles, and edit and delete styles using either the context menu, the Options menu, or the buttons located along the bottom of the panel.

You can add new styles to the current document only, or store them in an external style sheet. Creation of CSS styles takes place within the Style Definitions dialog box. Choose the category on the left and select or enter the options for that category on the right. When you are satisfied, click OK.

If you are using dynamic style sheets or have absolute paths to your CSS files in your code, Dreamweaver cannot display their contents in the CSS panel. However, Dreamweaver has a very useful feature known as Design Time Style Sheets that allows you to take advantage of CSS during development without adding any code to the document. Access the Design Time Style Sheets dialog box by selecting Design Time Style Sheets from either the Options menu or the context menu. Use the Add (+) or Remove (–) buttons to list CSS files to include or exclude during design time.

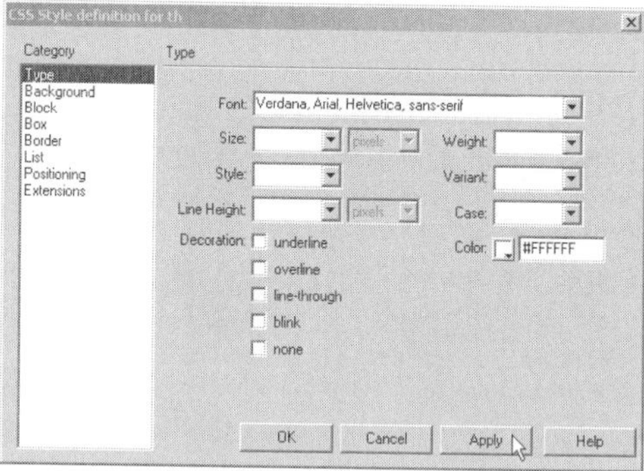

Figure 7.23

In the Style Definitions dialog, you create and edit CSS code.

The Insert Bar

Using objects found in the Insert bar is a great way to insert elements quickly into the page while working in Design view. The Insert bar is home to well over 200 objects, from tables to forms to layers to CFML code, and so much more. To display the Insert bar, select Window > Insert or press Ctrl-F2 (Command-F2). The Insert bar consists of 12 categories—despite the current document's file type—and additional categories if the current document is a dynamic page. ColdFusion pages—that is, those saved with the .cfm or .cfml file extension—will invoke 3 additional categories specific to ColdFusion for a total of 15 categories (see Figure 7.24).

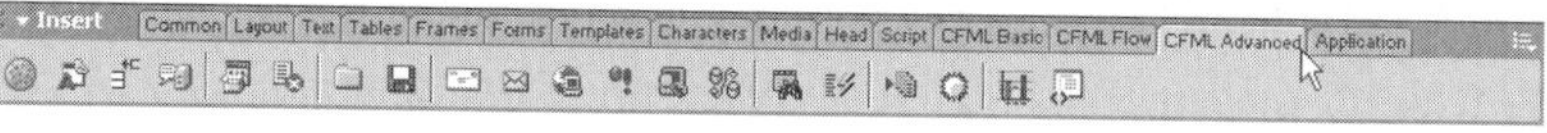

Figure 7.24

The Insert bar displays 12 categories common to all documents, and 3 additional categories just for ColdFusion files.

Some objects are not available in Code view but are available in Design view, and vice versa. Unavailable objects are dimmed, but become active again when you give focus to the opposite view by either clicking inside the document or by selecting View > Switch Views. Additionally, some objects function differently based on whether you're in Code or Design view. You are encouraged to explore and find differences between working with objects in each view and to choose the method that works best for you.

If you are in the Dreamweaver 4 Workspace, the Insert bar does not have a tabbed appearance. Instead, the Insert bar is a vertical panel that you can drag by the title bar and resize by clicking and dragging the lower right or left corner (Figure 7.25). Macintosh users may also choose to use the vertical-style Insert bar by selecting the Vertical/Horizontal Insert bar toggle button. You may also choose to drag and drop a panel group over the Insert bar's title bar to attach it below the panel group. Select the downward-pointing triangle in the upper right corner of the vertical-style Insert bar, and you will be presented with a list, from which you may choose the appropriate category.

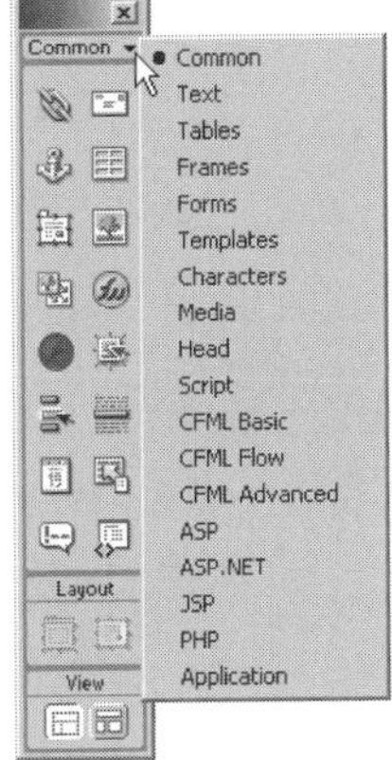

Figure 7.25

When you display the Insert bar as a vertical floating panel, you can select its categories from a list in the pop-up menu.

TIP

You can easily identify an object by its tool tip, which appears when you place the pointer over it. However, if you find this cumbersome, you may want to change the Insert Panel preference to Icons and Text in the General category of Edit > Preferences.

The following offers a brief explanation of the types of objects found in the 15 categories available when editing a ColdFusion document:

- **Common.** The most standard objects used in creating Web pages, such as links, tables, layers, images, and rollovers, are grouped in this category.

TIP

- The Tag Chooser object (it's the last one in this category) brings up a dialog that holds a listing of tags available to several languages (Figure 7.26). Once you have located the tag you want, if it has a Tag Editor dialog, this will be made available for adding the appropriate attributes to the tag. From either dialog, you may choose the Tag Info button to gain a description that may help you with your decision.

- **Layout.** While in Design view, switch from Standard view to Layout view to use the Draw Table and Draw Table cell objects. This approach to table design works similarly to slicing an image in a graphics program. You can switch between views using the options in the Table Views submenu of the View menu. You may also find the keyboard shortcuts Ctrl-Shift-F6 (Command-Shift-F6 on Mac) and Ctrl-F6 (Command-F6) useful for switching views.

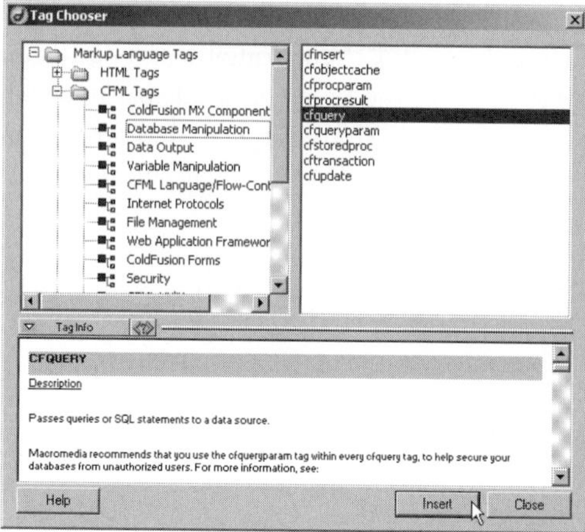

Figure 7.26

Use the Tag Chooser to insert tags from different languages, including HTML and CFML.

NOTE

Layout view limits your design options. For instance, Drawing Layers is unavailable, and there's no option for background images in the Property inspector. If you encounter a situation that leaves you without an option, simply switch back to Standard view using one of the methods described above.

NOTE

Layout view may create empty table cells in your code if you drag the table to resize it and possibly in other situations. Empty table cells are known to cause problems in Netscape 4. You should always verify the code that Layout view creates to be sure it is to your satisfaction.

- **Text.** Various text-formatting objects are offered in this category, including bold, italics, strong, emphasis, ordered lists, unordered lists, headings, and more. In Design view, these objects work much the same way as their equivalents in the Property inspector. However, in Code view, the objects wrap the current selection with the appropriate tag or place the tag pair in the code with your cursor positioned between them.
- **Tables.** Only the Insert Table object is available in Design view for this category. This is the same Insert Table object found in the Common and Layout categories of the Insert bar, but is available here for convenience while working in Code view. The remaining table objects are available in Code view and allow you to build your table structure quickly without having to type the code manually.
- **Frames.** This category groups 13 preconfigured objects for creating framesets, for use in either Design or Code view. When in Code view, you may choose to insert the remaining frame-related tags objects into the code.

TIP

Right-click (Control-click) within the angle brackets of the opening or closing tag in Code view, then choose Edit Tag or press Ctrl-F5 (Command-F5) to display the corresponding Tag Editor so you may add attributes through its interface.

- **Forms.** All objects related to form creation are stored in the Forms category—from the initial form tag to the fields, checkboxes, radio buttons, and form buttons.

TIP

You can click and drag many of the objects onto the page where you would like them to appear. This ability comes in especially handy when placing form fields on the page in Design view.

- **Templates.** Dreamweaver uses a very powerful template system for which these objects were created. You may use the objects in the Templates category to insert the various types of editable regions in Dreamweaver templates. When used to their full potential, templates can even mimic dynamic pages in some ways. For more information regarding Dreamweaver templates, select Help > Using Dreamweaver and search for Templates.
- **Characters.** You can insert code for the most commonly used special characters, such as the copyright symbol, from the objects shown in the Characters category. The final icon in this category is the Other Characters object. The Other Character dialog allows you to choose any of 99 special characters.

TIP

The first character shown is the Line Break object, which adds a `<br>` tag to the document when selected. However, you may find the keyboard shortcut Shift-Enter (Shift-Return) more convenient. Likewise, you may find the shortcut Ctrl-Shift-Space (Command-Shift-Space on Mac) for the Non-Breaking Space object, which inserts ` `, equally convenient.

- **Media.** You may insert applets, Shockwave, Plugins, Active X controls, and Flash using the objects found in this category. Dreamweaver offers two special types of Flash insertion objects: Flash Button and Flash Text. The Flash Button object allows you to choose from a list of different button styles and add your own text and links to them. The Flash Text object allows you to use any font installed on your system for your chosen text and even choose the colors needed to create a Flash rollover.
- **Head.** Use these objects to insert the various `<meta>` tags, such as keywords and descriptions, as well as the `<link>` tag that belongs in the `<head>` of a document.
- **Scripts.** Three handy objects are displayed in the Scripts category: Scripts, noscript and Server-Side Includes. The Script object allows you to insert either JavaScript or VBScript within a `<script>` tag and gives you an option to include `<noscript>` content. In the event that you've already inserted your script and you'd like to include `<noscript>` information, you may choose the noscript object. You may insert server-side includes with the Server-Side object, and then modify them in the Property inspector or Code view.
- **CFML Basic.** The most frequently used CFML tags are available on this tab, including `<CFQUERY>` (the button with the yellow cylinder representing a database), `<CFOUTPUT>` (the OUT button), and `<CFINCLUDE>` (the picture of a disk that's included in a page).

TIP

A very useful button is the one with two number signs (#) on it; click this to surround any highlighted text with number signs.

- **CFML Flow.** CFML flow control tags, such as `<CFIF>` and `<CFLOOP>`, are accessible on this tab, as are the error-handling tags `<CFTRY>` and `<CFCATCH>`.

- **CFML Advanced.** Although this tab is named Advanced, it actually contains many frequently used tags, including `<CFMAIL>` (used to send email) and `<CFCOOKIE>` (used to set client-side cookies).

NOTE

The rightmost button on this tab provides access to the Tag Chooser, which lists every CFM tag, as well as tags used by other languages (including HTML).

- **Application.** These objects will interact with your data source very much like the some of the options found in the Server Behaviors panel. However, these objects will actually generate the entire form, whereas the server behaviors require that you set up your form first manually. For instance, if you need to create a form that will add records to your database, you can use the Record Insertion Form object (second from the right). The dialog will let you choose which fields in your data source to include in the form, the label that appears prior to the form element, and will also let you choose a default value for each form element. All HTML and CFML code is generated for you and saving you an enormous amount of time. Instead of having to insert a table then apply the Repeat Region server behavior, you can complete both tasks in one shot by using the Dynamic Table object (third from left). As you can see, these objects can be enormous time-savers.

TIP

When you're installing additional objects via the Extension Manager while Dreamweaver is running, you will be prompted to restart Dreamweaver to make them active. Instead of restarting, Ctrl-Click (Command-Click) either the Options menu or the category arrow if the panel is vertically oriented, and choose Reload Extensions from the list. This works in most cases, so it is always worth a try so that you can avoid restarting unnecessarily.

The Property Inspector

When you're working in Design view, the Property inspector is quite practical for modifying the underlying code of your page (Figure 7.27). As you select various elements and tags or position your cursor within them, the Property inspector for that specific item appears. For instance, if you select a layer, the Layer Property inspector displays the various attributes of the layer within form fields. Placing your cursor within a table cell in Design view—as long as you haven't selected another element—will show the attributes of the `<td>` tag. You may add, edit, or remove the values presented, and Design view will update to reflect the code changes.

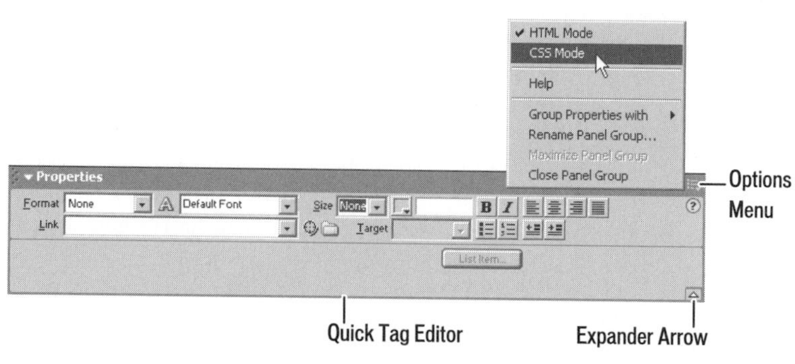

Figure 7.27

The Property inspector provides an interface to view and edit various aspects of the current element.

You can activate the Property inspector by selecting Window > Properties or by using the keyboard shortcut Ctrl-F3 (Command-F3). To display a specific Property inspector for an element, either select the item in Design view, or place your cursor appropriately in code view.

TIP

Additional properties may be available in the lower half of the Property inspector, so keep the Property inspector fully visible until you are familiar with the different inspectors. Once you are comfortable, use the expander arrow located in the lower right of the panel to decrease the Property inspector's height to half size.

Though many options are available for modifying an element's properties from within the Property inspector, sometimes a quick hand-tweaking of the code is necessary. Use the Quick Tag editor to modify the tag of the current element without having to switch to Code view.

The default text Property inspector is the one you're likely to use most often. Use it to apply HTML formatting such as paragraphs, headings, bold, italics, and other types to the selection in the document. The Property inspector does not limit you to HTML for text formatting; you also have CSS Mode as an option. Use the Options menu to switch to CSS Mode, or click the A icon to the left of the field that lists the font options. When CSS Mode is activated, the A icon is replaced with a CSS icon, and the formatting options not pertinent to CSS are removed. The list that once held all the possible font choices now contains a list of available classes, if any, and the option to add a new style, edit a style, and attach a style sheet.

Though you may be inclined to choose the folder icon to browse for files, Dreamweaver offers a handy alternative known as the point-to-file icon. Click and drag from the point-to-file icon to the file listed in the site panel, to another open document, or to a named anchor on the page. This will add the file path to the field adjacent to the icon.

Customizing Dreamweaver

Macromedia engineered Dreamweaver so as to give the user maximum control over the program's environment and tools. Customization is much more than being able to drag and drop panels and panel groups into various locations. This section will briefly discuss the following:

- **Commands.** You can give steps saved from the History panel a name and make them available in the Commands menu.
- **Keyboard Shortcuts.** You can modify, create, or remove the current set's keyboard shortcuts. You may create entirely new shortcut sets, or choose from the list of sets available.
- **Extensions.** Additional functionality can be added to Dreamweaver through the use of third party extensions.
- **Preferences.** You can set your preferences for everything from tag case to code coloring to code formatting and more.

NOTE

Dreamweaver 's powerful extensibility layer allows users to customize their environment and workflow completely. If Dreamweaver lacks a feature, you can build an extension to do the job. Building extensions is beyond the scope of this book, however. You may wish to look at the documentation provided under Help > Extending Dreamweaver.

Commands

If you are JavaScript savvy, you can certainly write your own commands. However, Dreamweaver engineers have built a simple-to-use method of creating commands into the History panel (Figure 7.28). To access the History panel, select Window > Others > History or press Shift-F10. The History panel is disabled in Code view, and only steps created in Design view or steps not marked by a red X can be saved as commands. Select the step or multiple steps by Ctrl-clicking each step. Then choose the "Save selected steps as a command" button or select Save As Command from either the context menu or the Options menu.

TIP

Choose the Replay steps button first to be sure the command yields the results you expect. Then you can select and save only the Replay Steps entry in the History panel.

Figure 7.28

Use the History panel to save steps as a command. Custom commands may be simple text as shown here, or more complicated steps, as long as the steps are not marked by a red X.

You will be prompted to enter a name for the command, which will appear near the bottom of the Commands menu.

Keyboard Shortcuts

Using keyboard shortcuts for commonly used commands can tremendously improve your workflow. Some people find memorizing preassigned shortcuts difficult. Macromedia recognized that users would benefit from being able to assign their own keyboard shortcuts, so the company developed an easy-to-use keyboard shortcut editor (Figure 7.29). You can choose from the various presets, or create your own based on an existing set.

To create and modify your own keyboard-shortcut set:

1. From the Dreamweaver menu, select Edit > Keyboard Shortcuts.

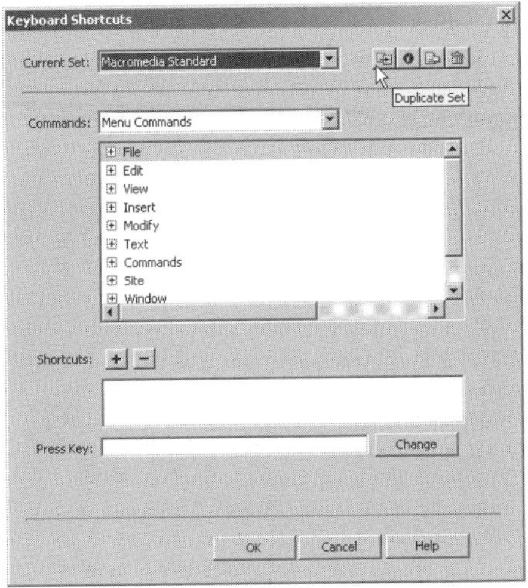

Figure 7.29

The keyboard shortcut dialog offers an interface that allows you to add, edit, modify, or remove keyboard shortcuts.

2. The dialog will take a few moments to initialize. Once the Keyboard Shortcuts dialog becomes available, select the Duplicate Set button.
3. In the Duplicate Set dialog box, enter a name for the new set.
4. From the Commands Options menu, choose the type of command you wish to modify.
5. Locate, then select the command listed in the tree menu for which you wish to edit or create a new keyboard shortcut.
6. If a keyboard shortcut does not exist already in the Shortcuts text field, you may skip this step. You can have up to two shortcuts for each command. To add a second shortcut, you must first select the Add (+) button. This will create a blank space below the first shortcut.
7. Position your cursor in the Press Key field, then press the keyboard shortcut you would like assigned to the command. If the shortcut is already in use, a warning message will appear.
8. If another command is already using the shortcut but you would like to use it anyway, choose Change. If the shortcut is in use, you will receive an alert to let you know that the keyboard shortcut is taken. You may wish to disregard the message and make the change by choosing OK, which will remove the keyboard shortcut from the previous command and reassign it. Naturally, if the keyboard shortcut were not already in use, choosing Change would immediately update the dialog.

You can change the name of a keyboard-shortcut set with the `Rename Set` button. Use the Export Set as HTML button to save an HTML listing of all keyboard shortcuts that you can preview in the browser and then print for handy reference. You may permanently discard a keyboard-shortcut set by selecting the set in the Current Set list, then choosing the Delete Set button.

Extensions

The depths to which Dreamweaver can go to include new functionality are truly amazing. Extensions can be as basic as an object that inserts a simple line of code, or as advanced as complete integration of a server model. Extension developers provide the Dreamweaver community with hundreds of useful extensions via the Macromedia Exchange for Dreamweaver. To launch your browser window and visit the Macromedia Exchange, choose Help > Dreamweaver Exchange.

The Dreamweaver installation includes an additional program known as the Extension Manager (Figure 7.30). Browse to the Extension Manager on your computer and launch it as you would any other program, or choose Help > Manage Extensions.

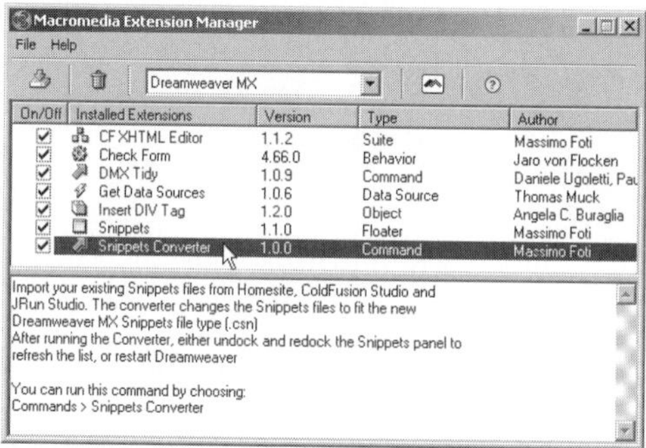

Figure 7.30
The Extension Manager installs and displays information about the extension, such as version, author, description and access info.

To install an extension, make sure Dreamweaver MX is selected in the list and then choose one of the following options:

- Select File > Install Extension
- Click the Install New Extension button.
- Press Ctrl-I (Command-I).

You will need to browse to the extension file (.mxp) that you have downloaded to your computer and accept the Macromedia Extensions Disclaimer. You'll then be prompted with the outcome of the installation, to which you should click OK.

Select the installed extension from the list to view the description and user interface access information in the area below. You may disable an extension by removing the checkmark beside it or permanently remove it by first highlighting the extension and then choosing the Delete Extension button.

NOTE

The Extension Manager supports multiuser configurations. For more information, select Help > Using the Macromedia Extension Manager from the Extension Manager menu or press F1 and search for the phrase "Installing and managing extensions in multi-user environments".

Preferences

Nearly everything imaginable is customizable in Dreamweaver's Edit Preferences dialog. To edit your preferences, select Edit > Preferences or use the Ctrl-U (Command-U) keyboard shortcut. As in other Dreamweaver dialogs you have encountered, the categories appear on the left, and when one is selected, that category's options are on the right (Figure 7.31).

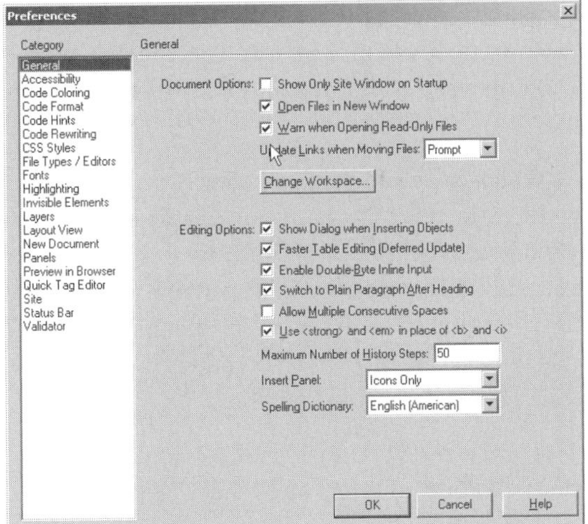

Figure 7.31

Select one of the categories listed on the left to view and modify your preferences on the right.

Describing every preference entirely is beyond the scope of this book. However, here are some of the most common preferences you may want to modify within each category:

- **General.** As mentioned earlier, this category offers the option to change your workspace (Windows Only), as well as add text labels to the objects in the Insert bar. You may also disable the dialogs shown when inserting objects so that their default values are inserted. If you're working in a document that's in a different language, Dreamweaver makes available the choice of 14 other dictionaries you can use with Text > Check Spelling or the Shift-F7 keyboard shortcut.
- **Accessibility.** To accommodate additional code attributes needed for user friendliness, Dreamweaver prompts special accessibility dialogs, which appear when you insert the appropriate item into the page—usually through the Insert bar, Site panel, or Assets panel.
- **Code Coloring.** You can customize practically every bit of code within Code view to appear in not only the color you prefer, but also against a desired background color and in italic, bold, underlined, or normal text. Highlight the Document Type listed, then choose the Edit Coloring Scheme button. You may also set the overall background color of Code view.

- **Code Format.** Formatting your code exactly as you like it has never been easier. Options to use lowercase or uppercase for tags or attributes as well as indentation and line breaks can all be specified here. Use the Tag Library Editor link to access the dialog for additional formatting options.
- **Code Hints.** You may disable code hints or tag completion if desired and determine how quickly they become visible. Code hints can appear for tag names, tag attributes, attribute values, function arguments, object methods and variables, and HTML entities. You can enable or disable each of the code hint menus. Use the Tag Library Editor link to access the dialog so that you may add additional tags and attributes to include in code hints as you edit documents.
- **Code Rewriting.** Dreamweaver can help you correct coding errors such as invalid nesting of tags and missing or extra closing tags. If you enable rewriting, when you create links through dialogs or the Property inspector, Dreamweaver can encode special characters so the browser will read the URL correctly and display the page. Encoding of special characters is not limited to links, but includes all file paths, including those to images. You may also specify which files may never be rewritten by adding their extension type to the "Never Rewrite Code In Files With Extension" text box.
- **CSS Styles.** This category gives you various options for the use of shorthand when developing style sheets. When editing a style sheet, you have the option to use shorthand if it was originally written using shorthand, or to always use the specified setting.
- **File Types/Editors.** You may specify which files open automatically in Code view by adding their file extensions to the list. You may specify an external editor for modifying code-based documents. The editor will then be listed in the Edit menu or the context menu when the file is selected in the Site panel. Additional options allow you to specify external editors for various other file extensions.
- **Fonts.** The text sizes used for documents of various encoding are easily modified in the Fonts category. You may also choose the system font and size to use for Code view and the Tag inspector.
- **Highlighting.** Dreamweaver uses highlighting within the Design view of a document to help you distinguish regions of code. You may specify the colors used by Dreamweaver template regions, library items, and third-party tags. Live Data, such as record set–dependent code, will use the untranslated color as its background color when you are editing the document. While you're viewing the document using Live Data preview, the data is pulled into Design view and uses the translated color as its background.
- **Invisible Elements.** While editing in Design view, it's often important to be aware of certain underlying code such as line breaks, layers, server-side code, and other elements. Invisible elements listed in this category show the icon—also known as a third-party tag—that denotes the invisible element in Design view. Server-Side Include rendering is also controlled in the Invisible Elements category, and when "Show Contents of Include" is disabled, Dreamweaver's performance will improve when working in Design view.

TIP

You may move the code associated with invisible element markers by dragging and dropping them into position within the Design view.

- **Layers.** The default values for layers added through Insert > Layer is determined by the entries in the Layers category. When a browser is resized using Netscape 4, layers lose their correct positioning. The Netscape Resize Fix adds a piece of JavaScript code that forces the page to reload when resized.
- **Layout View.** The Layout view category lets you specify a transparent GIF file for use as a spacer image that is inserted into tables created in Layout view. The coloring of the table and cell outline, cell highlighting and table background color are determined by the values listed in this category.

NOTE

The table background color serves as a visual reminder of which areas have not been specifically drawn. The color is not the actual attribute of the `<table>` tag; you must specifically choose the background color for each drawn table.

- **New Document.** You can specify the new document file type to use if the New File Dialog is disabled, as long as the site definition has not declared a server model. You can also choose the default encoding used in the `<meta>` tag of new documents and whether you'd like the document to be XHTML compliant.
- **Panels.** When panels are not docked with all other panels in the dock area or when you are using the Dreamweaver 4 Workspace or Macintosh, panels will float above the workspace as long as the appropriate box is checked. If the panel is not marked to be Always on Top, it is hidden from view when other areas of the document window are given focus. Other than minimizing or moving other windows and panels, the only ways to bring the panel back are via its menu entry or keyboard shortcut, or by choosing the appropriate panel icon in the launcher. The panels that ship with Dreamweaver have corresponding icons that represent them. You may enable these icons to show up in the tab and the document status bar so that you can quickly toggle on and off the panels you need.
- **Preview in Browser.** Dreamweaver's design view offers an approximation of what the page will look like when viewed in a browser. However, there is no substitute for the real thing. You can establish up to 20 different browsers to list in the File > Preview in Browser submenu. A temporary file is created and used to preview the file unless you've marked the option Preview Using Temporary File.

NOTE

You may install as many versions of Netscape as you like on your computer. However, you can't install multiple versions of Internet Explorer (Windows only).

- **Quick Tag Editor.** Changes made to the code in the Quick Tag Editor may be applied during or after editing, depending on the first checkbox listed in the Quick Tag Editor category. This category also controls whether to allow code hints and how fast they appear within the Quick Tag Editor.

- **Site.** The Site category allows you to determine which side to view the local files on in the expanded Site panel. From this category, you may also specify whether you would like to be prompted to include dependent files when uploading and downloading files. Firewall information is stored in this category, since it is unlikely to change between sites. You can save files before uploading, and you may choose the Edit button to modify your list of defined sites using the Site Definition dialog.
- **Status Bar.** The Status bar appears in the lower right portion of the Document window. The options in the Status bar category let you determine window sizes and connection speeds so you can approximate what your page will look like in a browser at the chosen size while in Design view and how quickly it would download at the chosen speed.
- **Validator.** Dreamweaver offers a built-in code validator, called from File > Check File > Validate Markup or by using the Shift-F6 keyboard shortcut. The settings for validation are determined by a listing of various document specifications, marked by a checkbox if enabled. The Options button displays the Validation Options dialog, used to determine how and which types of results appear in the Validation panel.

I encourage you to change preferences as much as you like and explore the various options. Information about each category is only a Help button away.

PART 2
Using ColdFusion

IN THIS PART

CHAPTER 8 Using ColdFusion

IN THIS CHAPTER

Working with Templates

Back in Chapter 4, "Previewing ColdFusion," I walked you through creating several simple applications. ColdFusion applications are made up of one or more files, each with a `.CFM` extension. These files often are referred to as *templates*; you'll see the terms *templates*, *files*, and even *pages* used somewhat interchangeably—just so you know, they all refer to the same thing. (I'll explain why the term *templates* is used in a few moments.)

NOTE

As explained in Chapter 3, "Accessing the ColdFusion Administrator", the URL used with ColdFusion will vary based on whether or not an external Web server is being used. For the sake of simplicity, all URL's used in this (and future) chapters assume that ColdFusion is being used in conjunction with the integrated Web server ("standalone" mode). As such, you'll see the port address `:8500` specified in all URLs (both in the content and the figures). If you are not using the standalone Web server simply omit the `:8500` from any URLs.

Creating Templates

As already explained, ColdFusion templates are plain text files. As such, they may be created using many different programs. Obviously, the best choice for ColdFusion developers, as already seen, is Macromedia Dreamweaver MX. So that's what you'll use here (and throughout the rest of this book).

To create a new ColdFusion file (or template; as I said, the terms are used interchangeably), simply start Dreamweaver MX. The editor will be ready for you to start typing code, and what you save is the ColdFusion file (as long as you save it with a `.CFM` extension, that is).

The code shown below is the contents of a simple ColdFusion file named `hello1.cfm`. Actually, at this point no ColdFusion code exists in the listing—it is all straight HTML and text, but we'll change that soon. Launch Dreamweaver MX (if it is not already open), and type the code as shown next (see Listing 8.1).

Listing 8.1 `hello1.cfm`

```
<HTML>
<HEAD>
   <TITLE>Hello 1</TITLE>
</HEAD>

<BODY>

Hello, and welcome to ColdFusion!

</BODY>
</HTML>
```

TIP

Tag case is not important, so `<BODY>` or `<body>` or `<Body>` can be used–it's your choice.

Saving Templates

Before ColdFusion can process pages, they must be saved onto the ColdFusion server. If you are developing against a local server (ColdFusion running on your own computer) then you can save the files locally; if you are developing against a remote server then you must save your code on that server.

Where you save your code is extremely important—the URL used to access the page is based on where files are saved (and how directories and paths are configured on the server).

All the files you create throughout this book will go in directories beneath the `ows` directory under the Web root (as discussed in Chapter 4). To save the code you just typed, create a new directory named `8` under `ows` and then save the code as `hello1.cfm`. To save the file do one of the following:

- Select Save from the File menu.
- Right click on the file tab, and select Save.
- Press Ctrl-S.

TIP

Forgotten how to create directories in Dreamweaver MX? Here's a reminder: In the Files window select the directory in which the new directory is to be created, right-click in the file pane below, and select New Folder.

Executing Templates

Now, let's test the code. There are several ways to do this. The simplest is to right click on the file in the Files window and select Preview in Browser (selecting your browser off the list).

You may also execute the page directly yourself, simply open your Web browser and go to this URL:

```
http://localhost:8500/ows/8/hello1.cfm
```

TIP

Not using the integrated Web server? See the note at the start of this chapter.

You should see a page similar to the one shown in Figure 8.1. Okay, so I admit that this is somewhat anticlimactic, but wait; it'll get better soon enough.

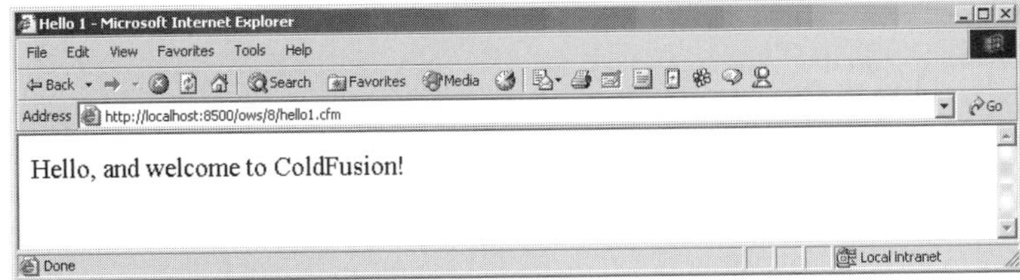

Figure 8.1
ColdFusion-generated output usually is viewed in any Web browser.

There's another way to browse the code you write. Assuming it is a page that can be executed directly (meaning it is not one that needs to be processed after another page—for example, a page that expects to be processed after a form is submitted), you can browse it directly in Dreamweaver MX by switching to Design View and activating Live Data View as seen in Figure 8.2.

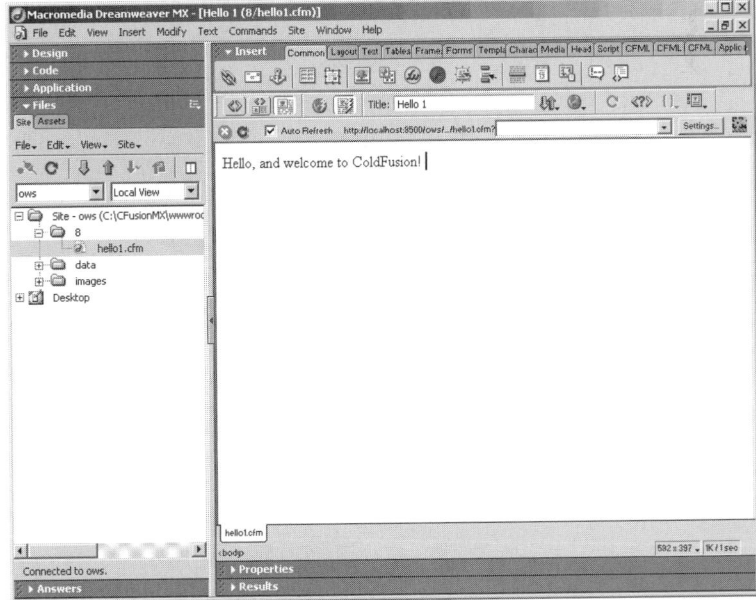

Figure 8.2
If configured correctly, you'll be able to browse much of your ColdFusion code within Dreamweaver MX itself.

➜ For Live Data View to work your site must be configured so that Dreamweaver knows how to pass the page to ColdFusion for processing. Sites, and how to define them, are explained in Chapter 7, "Introducing Macromedia Dreamweaver MX;" refer to that chapter if necessary.

Templates Explained

I promised to explain why ColdFusion files are often referred to as templates. Chapter 1, "Introducing ColdFusion," explains that ColdFusion pages are processed differently from Web pages—when requested, Web pages are sent to the client (the browser) as is, whereas ColdFusion files are processed and the generated results are returned to the client instead.

In other words, ColdFusion files are never sent to the client, but what they create is. And depending on what a ColdFusion file contains, it likely will generate multiple different outputs all from that same single `.CFM` file. And thus the term *template*.

Using Functions

And this is where it starts to get interesting. CFML (the ColdFusion Markup Language) is made up of two primary language elements:

- *Tags*—Perform operations, such as accessing a database, evaluating a condition, and flagging text for processing.
- *Functions*—Return (and possibly process) data and do things such as getting the current date and time, converting text to uppercase, and rounding a number to its nearest integer.

Writing ColdFusion code requires the use of both tags and functions. The best way to understand this is to see it in action. Here is a revised hello page. Type Listing 8.2 in a new page, and save it as `hello2.cfm` in the `ows/8` directory.

Listing 8.2 `hello2.cfm`

```
<HTML>
<HEAD>
   <TITLE>Hello 2</TITLE>
</HEAD>

<BODY>

Hello, and welcome to ColdFusion!
<BR>
<CFOUTPUT>
It is now #Now()#
</CFOUTPUT>

</BODY>
</HTML>
```

After you have saved the page, try it by browsing it either in a Web browser or right within Dreamweaver MX (if using a Web browser the URL will be `http://localhost:8500/ows/8/hello2.cfm`). The output should look similar to Figure 8.3 (of course, your date and time will probably be different).

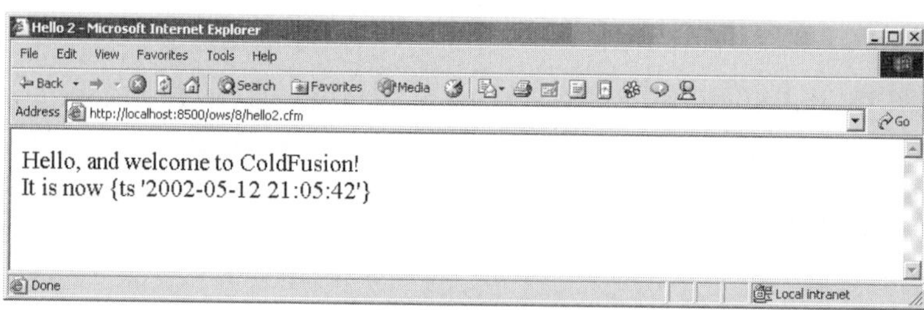

Figure 8.3

ColdFusion code can contain functions, including one that returns the current date and time.

Now, before we go any further, let's take a look at Listing 8.2. You will recall that when ColdFusion processes a .CFM file, it looks for CFML code to be processed and returns any other code to the client as is. So, the first line of code is

```
<HTML>
```

That is not CFML code—it's plain HTML. Therefore, ColdFusion ignores it and sends it on its way (to the client browser). The next few lines are also HTML code:

```
   <TITLE>Hello 2</TITLE>
</HEAD>

<BODY>

Hello, and welcome to ColdFusion!
<BR>
```

No ColdFusion language elements exist there, so ColdFusion ignores the code and sends it to the client as is.

But the next three lines of code are not HTML:

```
<CFOUTPUT>
It is now #Now()#
</CFOUTPUT>
```

<CFOUTPUT> is a ColdFusion tag (all ColdFusion tags begin with CF). <CFOUTPUT> is used to mark a block of code to be processed by ColdFusion. All text between the <CFOUTPUT> and </CFOUTPUT> tags is parsed, character by character, and any special instructions within that block are processed.

In the example, the following line was between the <CFOUTPUT> and </CFOUTPUT> tags:

```
It is now #Now()#
```

The text `It is now` is not an instruction, so it is sent to the client as is. But the text #Now()# *is* a ColdFusion instruction—within strings of text instructions are delimited by pound signs (the # character). #Now()# is an instruction telling ColdFusion to execute a function named Now()—a function that returns the current date and time. Thus the output in Figure 8.3 is generated.

The entire block of text from <CFOUTPUT> until </CFOUTPUT> is referred to as a "<CFOUTPUT> block". Not all the text in a <CFOUTPUT> block need be CFML functions. In the previous example, literal text was used, too, and that text was sent to the client untouched. As such, you also could have entered the code like this:

```
It is now <CFOUTPUT>#Now()#</CFOUTPUT>
```

Only the #Now()# expression needs ColdFusion processing, so only it really needs to be within the <CFOUTPUT> block. But what if you had not placed the expression within a <CFOUTPUT> block? Try it—remove the <CFOUTPUT> tags, save the page, and execute it. You'll see output similar to that in Figure 8.4—obviously not what you want. Because any content not within a <CFOUTPUT> block is sent to the client as is, using Now() outside a <CFOUTPUT> block causes the text Now() to be sent to the client instead of the data returned by Now(). Why? Because if it is outside a <CFOUTPUT> block, ColdFusion will never process it.

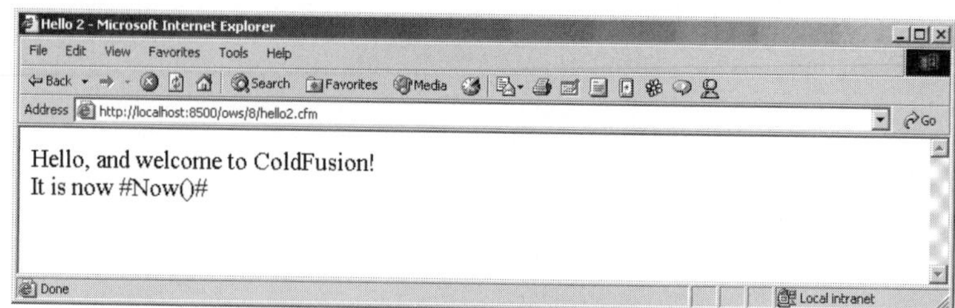

Figure 8.4

If expressions are sent to the browser, it usually means you have omitted the `<CFOUTPUT>` tags.

Omitting the pound signs has a similar effect. Put the `<CFOUTPUT>` tags back where they belong, but change `#Now()#` to `Now()` (removing the pound signs from before and after it). Then save the page, and execute it. The output will look similar to Figure 8.5. Why? Because all `<CFOUTPUT>` does is flag a block of text as needing processing by ColdFusion. However, ColdFusion does not process *all* text between the tags—instead, it looks for expressions delimited by pound signs, and any text *not* within pound signs is assumed to be literal text that is to be sent to the client as is.

➜ `<CFOUTPUT>` has another important use when working with database-driven content. More information about that can be found in Chapter 10, "Creating Data-Driven Pages."

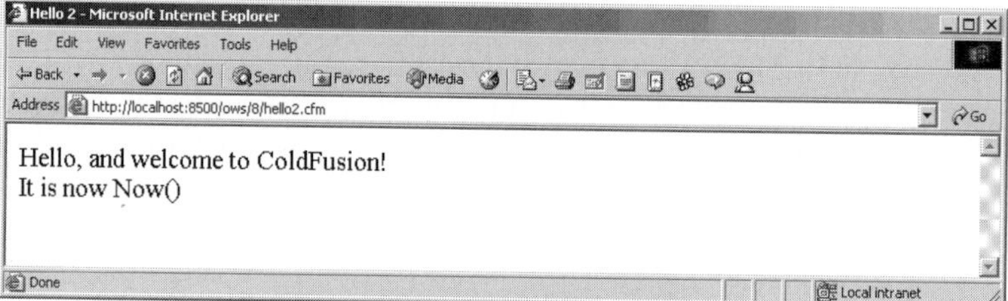

Figure 8.5

signs are needed around all expressions; otherwise, the expression is sent to the client instead of being processed.

`Now()` is a function, one of many functions supported in CFML. `Now()` is used to retrieve information from the system (the date and time), but the format of that date is not entirely readable. Another function, `DateFormat()`, can help here. `DateFormat()` is one of ColdFusion's output formatting functions, and its job is to format dates so they are readable (in all types of formats). Here is a revision of the code you just used (see Listing 8.3); save it as `hello3.cfm` and browse the file to see output similar to what is shown in Figure 8.6.

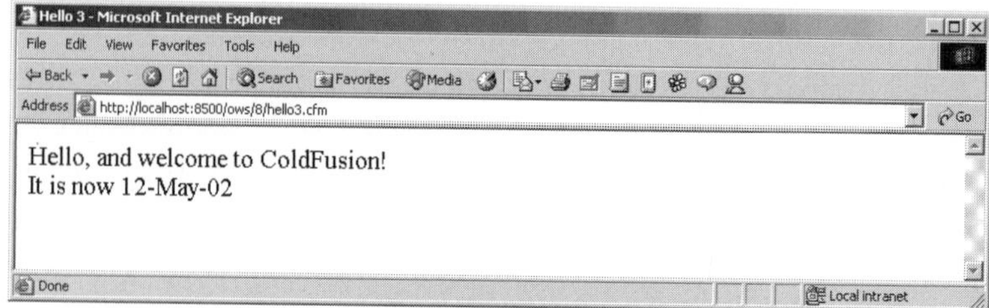

Figure 8.6

ColdFusion features a selection of output formatting functions that can be used to better control generated output.

Listing 8.3 `hello3.cfm`

```
<HTML>
<HEAD>
   <TITLE>Hello 3</TITLE>
</HEAD>

<BODY>

Hello, and welcome to ColdFusion!
<BR>
<CFOUTPUT>
It is now #DateFormat(Now())#
</CFOUTPUT>

</BODY>
</HTML>
```

`DateFormat()` is an example of a function that accepts (and requires) that data must be passed to it—after all, it needs to know which date you want to format for display. `DateFormat()` can accept dates as hard-coded strings (as in `#DateFormat("12/13/02")#`), as well as dates returned by other expressions, such as the `Now()` function. `#DateFormat(Now())#` tells ColdFusion to format the date returned by the `Now()` function.

NOTE

Passing a function as a parameter to another function is referred to as *nesting*. In this chapter's example, the `Now()` function is said to be *nested* in the `DateFormat()` function.

`DateFormat()` takes a second optional attribute, too: a format mask used to describe the output format. Try replacing the `#DateFormat(Now())#` in your code with any of the following (and try each to see what they do):

- `#DateFormat(Now(), "MMMM-DD-YYYY")#`
- `#DateFormat(Now(), "MM/DD/YY")#`
- `#DateFormat(Now(), "DDD, MMMM DD, YYYY")#`

Parameters passed to a function are always separated by commas. Commas are not used if a single parameter is passed, but when two or more parameters exist, every parameter must be separated by a comma.

You've now seen a function that takes no parameters, a function that takes a required parameter, and a function that takes both required and optional parameters. All ColdFusion functions, and you'll be using many of them, work the same way—some take parameters, and some do not. But all functions, regardless of parameters, return a value.

NOTE

It is important to remember that # is not part of the function–the functions you used here were `DateFormat()` and `Now()`. The pound signs were used to delimit (mark) the expressions, but they are not part of the expression itself.

I know I have already said this, but it is worth repeating—CFML code is processed on the server, not on the client. The CFML code you write is *never* sent to the Web browser. What is sent to the browser? Most browsers feature a View Source option that displays code as received. If you view the source of for page `hello3.cfm` you'll see something like this:

```
<HTML>
<HEAD>
   <TITLE>Hello 3</TITLE>
</HEAD>

<BODY>

Hello, and welcome to ColdFusion!
<BR>

It is now 15-Apr-02


</BODY>
</HTML>
```

As you can see, there is no CFML code here at all. The `<CFOUTPUT>` tags, the functions, the pound signs—all have been stripped out by the ColdFusion Server, and what was sent to the client is the output that they generated.

TIP

Viewing the generated source is an invaluable debugging trick. If you ever find that output is not being generated as expected, viewing the source can help you understand exactly what was generated and why.

Using Variables

Now that you've had the chance to use some basic functions, it's time to introduce variables. Variables are an important part of just about every programming language, and CFML is no exception. A *variable* is a container that stores information in memory on the server. Variables are named, and the contents of the container are accessed via that name. Let's look at a simple example. Type the code in Listing 8.4 into a new file, save it as `hello4.cfm`, and browse it. You should see a display similar to the one shown in Figure 8.7.

Listing 8.4 `hello4.cfm`

```
<HTML>
<HEAD>
   <TITLE>Hello 4</TITLE>
</HEAD>

<BODY>

<CFSET FirstName="Ben">
<CFOUTPUT>
Hello #FirstName#, and welcome to ColdFusion!
</CFOUTPUT>

</BODY>
</HTML>
```

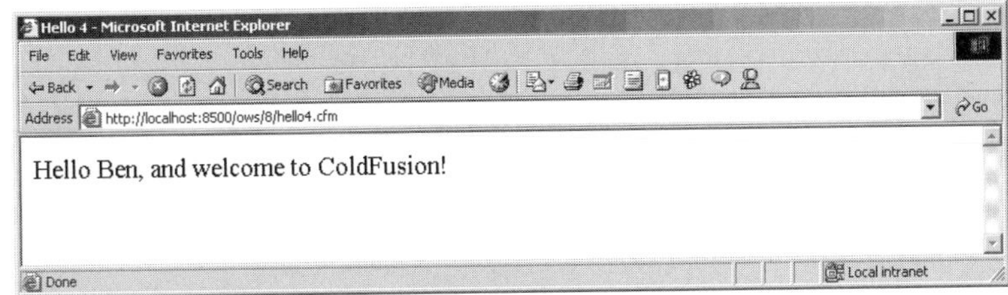

Figure 8.7
Variables are replaced by their contents when content is generated.

This code is similar to the previous code listings. It starts with plain HTML that is sent to the client as is. Then a new tag is used, `<CFSET>`:

```
<CFSET FirstName="Ben">
```

`<CFSET>` is used to set variables. Here, a variable named `FirstName` is created, and a value of `"Ben"` is stored in it. After it's created, that variable will exist until the page has finished processing and can be used as seen in the next line of code:

```
Hello #FirstName#, and welcome to ColdFusion!
```

This line of code was placed in a `<CFOUTPUT>` block so ColdFusion would know to replace `#FirstName#` with the contents of `FirstName`. The generated output is then:

```
Hello Ben, and welcome to ColdFusion!
```

Variables can be used as many times as necessary, as long as they exist. Try moving the `<CFSET>` statement after the `<CFOUTPUT>` block, or delete it altogether. Executing the page now will generate an error, similar to the one seen in Figure 8.8. This error message is telling you that you referred to (tried to access) a variable that does not exist. The error message tells you the name of the variable that caused the problem, as well as the line and column in your code (to help you find and fix the problem easily). More often than not, this error is caused by typos.

Figure 8.8
ColdFusion produces an error if a referenced variable does not exist.

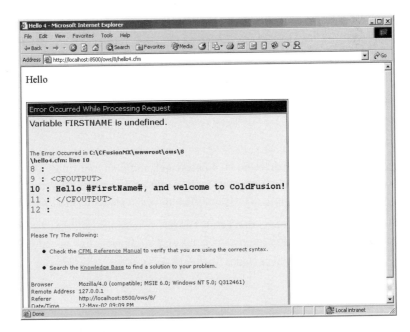

Hello 4 - Microsoft Internet Explorer
Address http://localhost:8500/ows/8/hello4.cfm

Hello

Error Occurred While Processing Request

Variable FIRSTNAME is undefined.

The Error Occurred in C:\CFusionMX\wwwroot\ows\8\hello4.cfm: line 10

```
8 :
9 : <CFOUTPUT>
10 : Hello #FirstName#, and welcome to ColdFusion!
11 : </CFOUTPUT>
12 :
```

Please Try The Following:

- Check the CFML Reference Manual to verify that you are using the correct syntax.
- Search the Knowledge Base to find a solution to your problem.

Browser Mozilla/4.0 (compatible; MSIE 6.0; Windows NT 5.0; Q312461)
Remote Address 127.0.0.1
Referer http://localhost:8500/ows/8/
Date/Time 12-May-02 09:09 PM

➜ Regular variables exist only in the page that creates them. If you define a variable named `FirstName` in one page, you can't use it in another page unless you explicitly pass it to that page (see Chapter 10). An exception to this rule does exist. In Chapter 17, "Working with Sessions," you learn how to create and use variables that persist across requests (each page access is known as a *request*).

Here is a new version of the code, this time using the variable `FirstName` five times. Save Listing 8.5 as `hello5.cfm`, and then try this listing for yourself (feel free to replace my name with your own). The output is shown in Figure 8.9.

Listing 8.5 `hello5.cfm`

```
<HTML>
<HEAD>
   <TITLE>Hello 5</TITLE>
</HEAD>

<BODY>

<CFSET FirstName="Ben">
<CFOUTPUT>
Hello #FirstName#, and welcome to ColdFusion!<P>
Your name in uppercase: #UCase(FirstName)#<BR>
Your name in lowercase: #LCase(FirstName)#<BR>
Your name in reverse: #Reverse(FirstName)#<BR>
Characters in your name: #Len(FirstName)#<BR>
</CFOUTPUT>

</BODY>
</HTML>
```

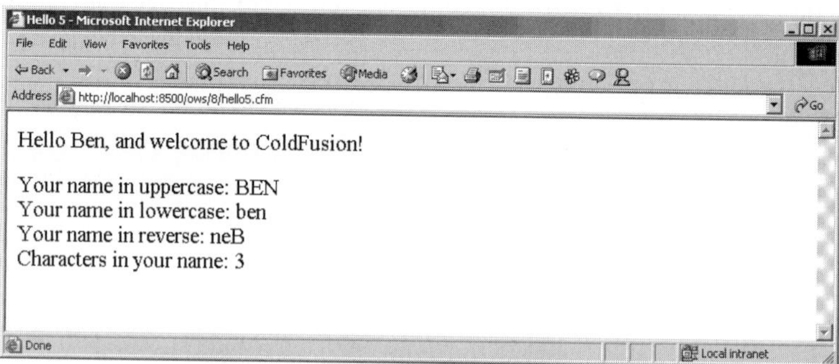

Figure 8.9

There is no limit to the number of functions that can be used in one page, which enables you to render content as you see fit.

Let's take a look at the above code. A `<CFSET>` is used to create a variable named `FirstName`. That variable is used once by itself (the Hello message), and then four times with functions. `UCase()` converts a string to uppercase, `LCase()` converts a string to lowercase, `Reverse()` reverses the string, and `Len()` returns the length of a string (the number of characters in it).

But functions such as `UCase()` don't truly convert strings; instead, they return converted strings. The difference is subtle but important. Look at the following line of code:

```
Your name in uppercase: #UCase(FirstName)#
```

`UCase()` returns `FirstName` converted to uppercase, but the contents of `FirstName` itself are intact and are not converted to anything at all. `FirstName` was not modified; a copy was made and modified instead, and that copy was returned. To save the uppercase `FirstName` to a variable, you must do something like this:

```
<CFSET UpperFirstName=UCase(FirstName)>
```

Here a new variable, `UpperFirstName`, is created. `UpperFirstName` is assigned the value that is returned by `UCase(FirstName)`, the uppercase `FirstName`. And this new variable can be used like any other variable, and as often as necessary. Listing 8.6 is a modified version of the Listing 8.5. Try it for yourself—the output will be exactly the same as in Figure 8.9.

Listing 8.6 `hello6.cfm`

```
<HTML>
<HEAD>
   <TITLE>Hello 6</TITLE>
</HEAD>

<BODY>

<CFSET FirstName="Ben">
<CFSET UpperFirstName=UCase(FirstName)>
<CFSET LowerFirstName=LCase(FirstName)>
<CFSET ReverseFirstName=Reverse(FirstName)>
<CFSET LenFirstName=Len(FirstName)>

<CFOUTPUT>
Hello #FirstName#, and welcome to ColdFusion!<P>
Your name in uppercase: #UpperFirstName#<BR>
Your name in lowercase: #LowerFirstName#<BR>
Your name in reverse: #ReverseFirstName#<BR>
Characters in your name: #LenFirstName#<BR>
</CFOUTPUT>

</BODY>
</HTML>
```

This code deserves a look. Five `<CFSET>` tags now exist, and five variables are created. The first creates the `FirstName` variable, just like in the previous examples. The next creates a new variable named `UpperFirstName`, which contains the uppercase version of `FirstName`. And then `LowerFirstName`, `ReverseFirstName`, and `LenFirstName` are each created with additional `<CFSET>` statements.

The `<CFOUTPUT>` block here contains no functions at all. Rather, it just displays the contents of the variables that were just created. In this particular listing there is actually little value in doing this, aside from the fact that the code is a little more organized this way. The real benefit in saving function output to variables is realized when a function is used many times in a single page. Then, instead of using the same function over and over, you can use it once, save the output to a variable, and just use that variable instead.

One important point to note here is that variables can be overwritten. Look at the following code snippet:

```
<CFSET FirstName="Ben">
<CFSET FirstName="Nate">
```

Here, `FirstName` is set to `Ben` and then set again to `Nate`. Variables can be overwritten as often as necessary, and whatever the current value is when accessed (displayed, or passed to other functions), that's the value that will be used.

Knowing that, what do you think the following line of code does?

```
<CFSET FirstName=UCase(FirstName)>
```

This is an example of variable overwriting, but here the variable being overwritten is the variable itself. I mentioned earlier that functions such as `UCase()` do not convert text; they return a converted copy. So how could you really convert text? By using code such as the line just shown. `<CFSET FirstName=UCase(FirstName)>` sets `FirstName` to the uppercase version of `FirstName`, effectively overwriting itself with the converted value.

Variable Naming

This would be a good place to discuss variable naming. When you create a variable you get to name it, and the choice of names is up to you. However, you need to know a few rules about variable naming:

- Variable names can contain alphanumeric characters but can't begin with a number (so `result12` is okay, but `4thresult` is not).
- Variable names can't contain spaces. If you need to separate words, use underscores (for example, `monthly_sales_figures` instead of `monthly sales figures`).
- Aside from the underscore, non-alphanumeric characters can't be used in variable names (so `Sales!`, `SSN#`, and `first-name` are all invalid).
- Variable names are case insensitive (`FirstName` is the same as `FIRSTNAME` which is the same as `firstname`).

Other than that, you can be as creative as necessary with your names. Pick any variable name you want; just be careful not to overwrite existing variables by mistake.

TIP

Avoid the use of abbreviated variable names, such as `fn` or `c`. Although these are valid names, what they stand for is not apparent just by looking at them. Yes, `fn` is less keystrokes than `FirstName`, but the first time you (or someone else) has to stare at the code trying to figure out what a variable is for, you'll regret saving that little bit of time. As a rule, make variable names descriptive.

Using Prefixes

ColdFusion supports many variable types, and you'll become very familiar with them as you work through this book. For example, local variables (the type you just created) are a variable type. Submitted form fields are a variable type, as are many others.

ColdFusion variables can be referenced in two ways:

- The variable name itself.
- The variable name with the type as a prefix.

For example, the variable `FirstName` that you used a little earlier is a local variable (type `VARIABLES`). So, that variable can be referred to as `FirstName` (as you did previously) and as `VARIABLES.FirstName`. Both are valid, and both will work (you can try editing file `hello6.cfm` to use the `VARIABLES` prefix to try this).

So, should you use prefixes? Well, there are pros and cons. Here are the pros:

- Using prefixes improves performance. ColdFusion will have less work to do finding the variable you are referring to if you explicitly provide the full name (including the prefix).
- If multiple variables exist with the same name but are of different types, the only way to be 100% sure that you'll get the variable you want is to use the prefix.

As for the cons, there is just one:

- If you omit the prefix then multiple variable types will be accessible (perhaps form fields and URL parameters, which are discussed in the following chapters). If you provide the type prefix, you restrict access to the specified type, and although this does prevent ambiguity (as just explained), it does make your code a little less reusable.

The choice is yours, and there is no real right or wrong. You can use prefixes if you see fit, and not use them if not. If you don't specify the prefix, ColdFusion will find the variable for you. And if multiple variables of the same name do exist (with differing types) then a predefined order of precedence is used (don't worry if these types are not familiar yet, they will become familiar soon enough, and you can refer to this list when necessary):

- Query results
- Local variables (`VARIABLES`)
- `CGI` variables
- `FILE` variables
- `URL` parameters
- `FORM` fields
- `COOKIE` values
- `CLIENT` variables

In other words, if you refer to `#FirstName#` (without specifying a prefix) and that variable exists both as a local variable (`VARIABLES.FirstName`) and as a `FORM` field (`FORM.FirstName`), `VARIABLES.FirstName` will be used automatically.

NOTE

An exception to this does exist. Some ColdFusion variable types must *always* be accessed with an explicit prefix; these are covered in later chapters.

Working with Expressions

I've used the term *expressions* a few times in this chapter. What is an expression? The official ColdFusion documentation explains that expressions are "language constructs that allow you to create sophisticated applications." A better way to understand it is that expressions are strings of text made up of one or more of the following:

- Literal text (strings), numbers, dates, times, and other values
- Variables
- Operators (+ for addition, & for concatenation, and so on)
- Functions

So, `UCase(FirstName)` is an expression, as are `"Hello, my name is Ben"`, `12+4`, and `DateFormat(Now())`. And even though many people find it hard to articulate exactly what an expression is, realize that expressions are an important part of the ColdFusion language.

Building Expressions

Expressions are typed where necessary. Expressions can be passed to a `<CFSET>` statement as part of an assignment, used when displaying text, and passed to almost every single CFML tag (except for the few that take no attributes).

Simple expressions can be used, such as those discussed previously (variables, functions, and combinations thereof). But more complex expressions can be used, too, and expressions can include arithmetic, string, and decision operators (you'll use these in the next few chapters).

When using expressions, pound signs are used to delimit ColdFusion functions and variables within a block of text. So, how would you display the # itself? Look at the following code snippet:

```
<CFOUTPUT>
#1: #FirstName#
</CFOUTOUT>
```

You can try this yourself if you so feel inclined; you'll see that ColdFusion generates an error when it processes the code (see Figure 8.10).

What causes this error? Well, when ColdFusion encounters the # at the start of the line, it assumes you are delimiting a variable or a function and tries to find the matching # (which of course does not exist, as this is not a variable reference at all). The solution is to *escape* the pound sign (flag it as being a real pound sign), as follows:

```
<CFOUTPUT>
##1: #FirstName#
</CFOUTOUT>
```

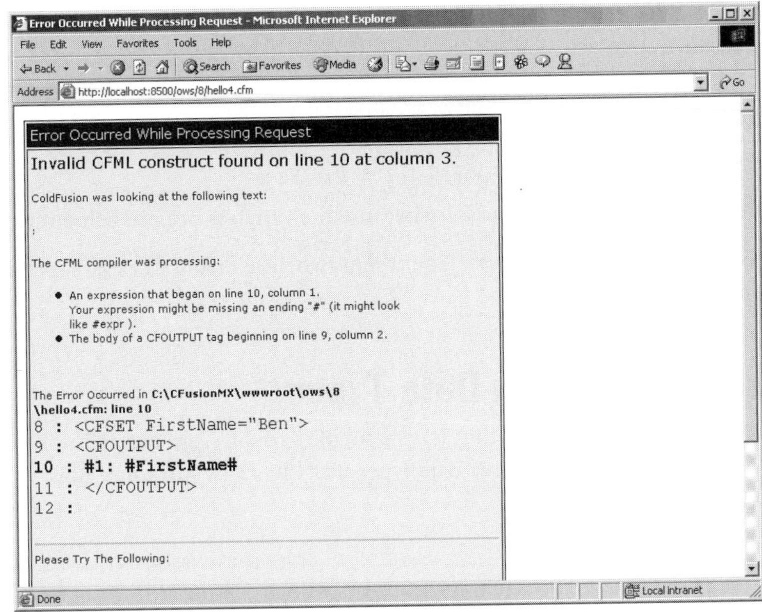

Figure 8.10

Pound signs in text must be escaped; otherwise, ColdFusion produces an error.

When ColdFusion encounters `##`, it knows that `#` is not delimiting a variable or function. Instead, it correctly displays a single `#`.

When To Use #, and When Not To

Before we go any further, let's clarify exactly when pound signs are needed and when they're not.

Simply put, pound signs are needed to flag functions and variables within a string of text.

So, in this first example, the pound signs are obviously needed:

```
Hello #VARIABLES.FirstName#
```

But what about when a variable is used within a tag, like this?

```
<CFSET UpperFirstName=UCase(FirstName)>
```

Here pound signs are not necessary because ColdFusion assumes that anything passed to a tag is a function or variable unless explicitly defined as a string. So, the following is incorrect:

```
<CFSET #UpperFirstName#=#UCase(FirstName)#>
```

This code will actually work (ColdFusion is very forgiving), but it is still incorrect and should not be used.

This next example declares a variable and assigns a value that is a string, so no pound signs are needed here:

```
<CFSET FirstName="Ben">
```

But if the string contains variables, pound signs would be necessary. Look at this next example: `FullName` is assigned a string, but the string contains two variables (`FirstName` and `LastName`) and those variables must be enclosed within pound signs (otherwise ColdFusion will assign the text, not the variable values):

```
<CFSET FullName="#FirstName# #LastName#">
```

Incidentally, the previous line of code is functionally equivalent to the following:

```
<CFSET FullName=FirstName & " " & LastName>
```

Here pound signs are not necessary because the variables are not being referred to within a string.

Again, the rule is this—only use pound signs when referring to variables and functions within a block of text. Simple as that.

Using ColdFusion Data Types

The variables you have used thus far are simple variables, are defined, and contain a value. ColdFusion supports three advanced data types that I'll briefly introduce now.

NOTE

This is just an introduction to lists, arrays, and structures. All three are used repeatedly throughout the rest of this book, so don't worry if you do not fully understand them by the time you are done reading this chapter. Right now, the intent is to ensure that you know these exist and what they are. You'll have lots of opportunities to use them soon enough.

Lists

Lists are used to group together related information. Lists are actually strings (plain text)—what makes them lists is that a delimiter is used to separate items within the string. For example, the following is a comma-delimited list of five U.S. states:

```
California,Florida,Michigan,Massachusetts,New York
```

The next example is also a list. Even though it might not look like a list, a sentence is a list delimited by spaces:

```
This is a ColdFusion list
```

Lists are created just like any other variables. For example, this next line of code uses the `<CFSET>` tag to create a variable named `fruit` that contains a list of six fruits:

```
<CFSET fruit="apple,banana,cherry,grape,mango,orange">
```

The code in Listing 8.7 demonstrates the use of lists. Type the code and save it as `list.cfm` in the `8` directory; then execute it. You should see an output similar to the one shown in Figure 8.11.

Listing 8.7 `list.cfm`

```
<HTML>
<HEAD>
   <TITLE>List Example</TITLE>
</HEAD>

<BODY>

<CFSET fruit="apple,banana,cherry,grape,mango,orange">
```

Listing 8.7 (continued)

```
<CFOUTPUT>
Complete list: #fruit#<BR>
Number of fruit in list: #ListLen(fruit)#<BR>
First fruit: #ListFirst(fruit)#<BR>
Last fruit: #ListLast(fruit)#<BR>
<CFSET fruit=ListAppend(fruit, "pineapple")>
Complete list: #fruit#<BR>
Number of fruit in list: #ListLen(fruit)#<BR>
First fruit: #ListFirst(fruit)#<BR>
Last fruit: #ListLast(fruit)#<BR>
</CFOUTPUT>

</BODY>
</HTML>
```

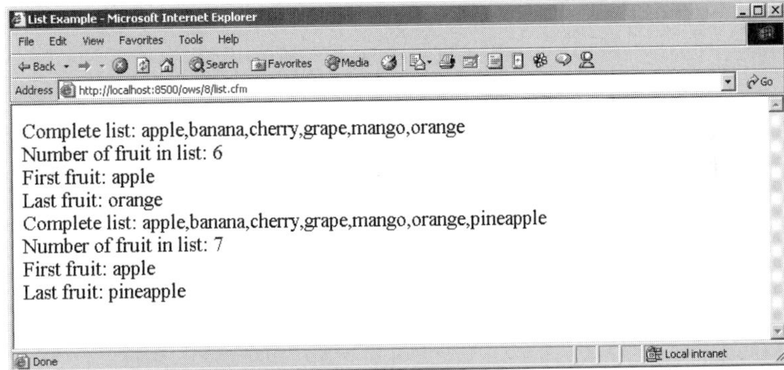

Figure 8.11

Lists are useful for grouping related data into simple sets.

Let's walk through the code in Listing 8.7. A `<CFSET>` is used to create a list, which is simply a string. Therefore, a simple variable assignment can be used.

Next comes the `<CFOUTPUT>` block, starting with displaying `#fruit#` (the complete list). The next line of code uses the `ListLen()` function to return the number of items in the list (there are `6` of them). Individual list members can be retrieved using `ListFirst()` (used here to get the first list element), `ListLast()` (used here to get the last list element), and `ListGetAt()` (used to retrieve any list element, but not used in this example).

Then another `<CFSET>` tag is used, as follows:

```
<CFSET fruit=ListAppend(fruit, "pineapple")>
```

This code uses the `ListAppend()` function to add an element to the list. You will recall that functions return copies of modified variables, not modified variables themselves. So the `<CFSET>` tag assigns the value returned by `ListAppend()` to `fruit`, effectively overwriting the list with the new revised list.

Then the number of items, as well as the first and last items, are displayed again. This time `7` items are in the list, and the last item has changed to `pineapple`.

As you can see, lists are very easy to use and provide a simple mechanism for grouping related data.

NOTE

I mentioned earlier that a sentence is a list delimited by spaces. The default list delimiter is indeed a comma. Actually, though, *any* character can be used as a list delimiter, and every list function takes an optional delimiter attribute if necessary.

Arrays

Arrays, like lists, store multiple values in a single variable. But unlike lists, arrays can contain far more complex data (including lists and even other arrays).

Unlike lists, arrays support multiple dimensions. A single dimensional array is actually quite similar to a list: It's a linear collection. A two-dimensional array is more like a grid (imagine a spreadsheet), and data is stored in rows and columns. ColdFusion also supports three-dimensional arrays, which can be envisioned as cubes of data.

If this all sounds somewhat complex, well, it is. Arrays are not as easy to use as lists are, but they are far more powerful (and far quicker). Here is a simple block of code that creates an array and displays part of it; the output is shown in Figure 8.12. To try it out, type the code in Listing 8.8 and save it as `array.cfm`.

Listing 8.8 `array.cfm`

```
<HTML>
<HEAD>
   <TITLE>Array Example</TITLE>
</HEAD>

<BODY>

<CFSET names=ArrayNew(2)>
<CFSET names[1][1]="Ben">
<CFSET names[1][2]="Forta">
<CFSET names[2][1]="Nate">
<CFSET names[2][2]="Weiss">

<CFOUTPUT>
The first name in the array #names[1][1]# #names[1][2]#
</CFOUTPUT>

</BODY>
</HTML>
```

Figure 8.12

Arrays treat data as if it were in a one-, two-, or three-dimensional grid.

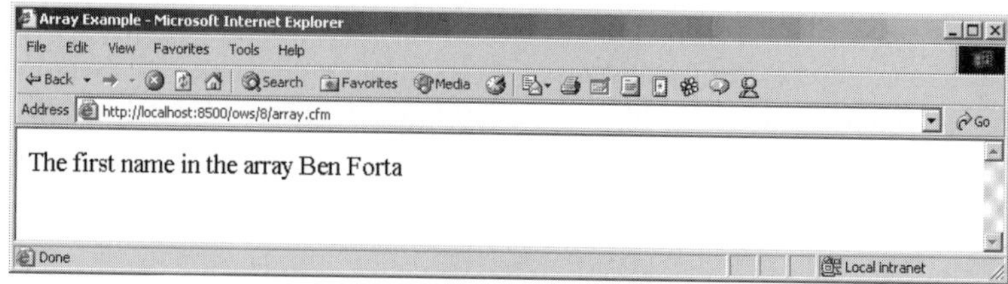

Arrays are created using the `ArrayNew()` function. `ArrayNew()` requires that the desired dimension be passed as a parameter, so the following code creates a two-dimensional array named `names`:

```
<CFSET names=ArrayNew(2)>
```

Array elements are set using `<CFSET>`, just like any other variables. But unlike other variables, when array elements are set the element number must be specified using an index (a relative position starting at 1). So, in a single dimensional array, `names[1]` would refer to the first element and `names[6]` would refer to the sixth. In two-dimensional arrays, both dimensions must be specified, as seen in these next four lines (taken from the previous code listing):

```
<CFSET names[1][1]="Ben">
<CFSET names[1][2]="Forta">
<CFSET names[2][1]="Nate">
<CFSET names[2][2]="Weiss">
```

`names[1][1]` refers to the first element in the first dimension—think of it as the first column of the first row in a grid. `names[1][2]` refers to the second column in that first row, and so on.

When accessed, even for display, the indexes must be used. Therefore, the following line of code

```
The first name in the array #names[1][1]# #names[1][2]#
```

generates this output:

```
The first name in the array Ben Forta
```

As you can see, although they're not as easy to use as lists, arrays are a very flexible and powerful language feature.

Structures

Structures are the most powerful and flexible data type within ColdFusion, so powerful in fact that many internal variables (including ones listed in Appendix C, "Special ColdFusion Variables and Result Codes") are structures internally.

Simply put, structures provide a way to store data within data. Unlike arrays, structures have no special dimensions and are not like grids. Rather, they can be thought of as top-level folders that can store data, or other folders, which in turn can store data, or other folders, and so on. Structures can contain lists, arrays, and even other structures.

To give you a sneak peek at what structures look like, here is some code. Give it a try yourself; save the file as `structure.cfm` (see Listing 8.9), and you should see output as shown in Figure 8.13.

Listing 8.9 `structure.cfm`

```
<HTML>
<HEAD>
   <TITLE>Structure Example</TITLE>
</HEAD>

<BODY>

<CFSET contact=StructNew()>
<CFSET contact.FirstName="Ben">
```

Listing 8.9 (continued)

```
<CFSET contact.LastName="Forta">
<CFSET contact.EMail="ben@forta.com">

<CFOUTPUT>
E-Mail:
<A HREF="mailto:#contact.EMail#">#contact.FirstName# #contact.LastName#</A>
</CFOUTPUT>

</BODY>
</HTML>
```

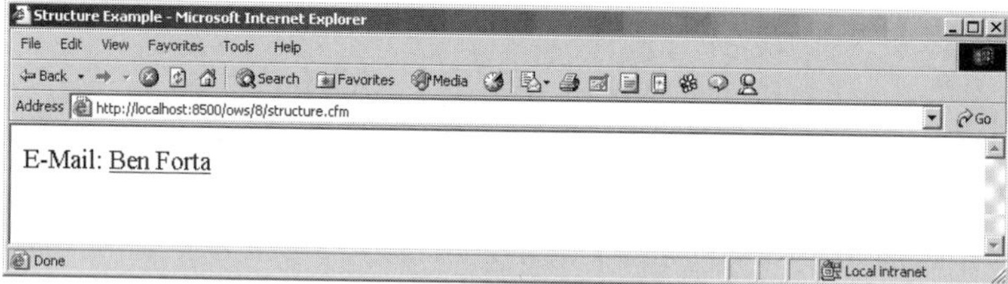

Figure 8.13

Structures are the most powerful data type in ColdFusion and are used internally extensively.

Structures are created using `StructNew()`, which—unlike `ArrayNew()`—takes no parameters. After a structure is created, variables can be set inside it. The following three lines of code all set variables with the `contact structure`:

```
<CFSET contact.FirstName="Ben">
<CFSET contact.LastName="Forta">
<CFSET contact.EMail="ben@forta.com">
```

To access structure members, simply refer to them by name. `#contact.FirstName#` accesses the `FirstName` member of the `contact structure`. Therefore, the code

```
<A HREF="mailto:#contact.EMail#">#contact.FirstName# #contact.LastName#</A>
```

generates this output:

```
<A HREF="mailto:ben@forta.com">Ben Forta</A>
```

And that's just scratching the surface. Structures are incredibly powerful, and you'll use them extensively as you work through this book.

For simplicity's sake, I have described only the absolute basic form of structure use. ColdFusion features an entire set of structure manipulation functions that can be used to better take advantage of structures—you use some of them in the next chapter, "CFML Basics."

"Dumping" Expressions

While talking about expressions and introducing all these data types I would remiss if I did not point out the `<CFDUMP>` tag. This invaluable tag is never used in live applications, but it is an invaluable testing and debugging tool. `<CFDUMP>` lets you display any expression in a cleanly formatted table. To show you what I mean, try this example. Type the following code into a new document (see Listing 8.10), save it as `cfdump.cfm`, and then execute it in your browser. The output is shown in Figure 8.14.

Listing 8.10 `cfdump.cfm`

```
<HTML>
<HEAD>
   <TITLE>CFDUMP Example</TITLE>
</HEAD>

<BODY>

<CFSET contact=StructNew()>
<CFSET contact.FirstName="Ben">
<CFSET contact.LastName="Forta">
<CFSET contact.EMail="ben@forta.com">

<CFDUMP var="#contact#">

</BODY>
</HTML>
```

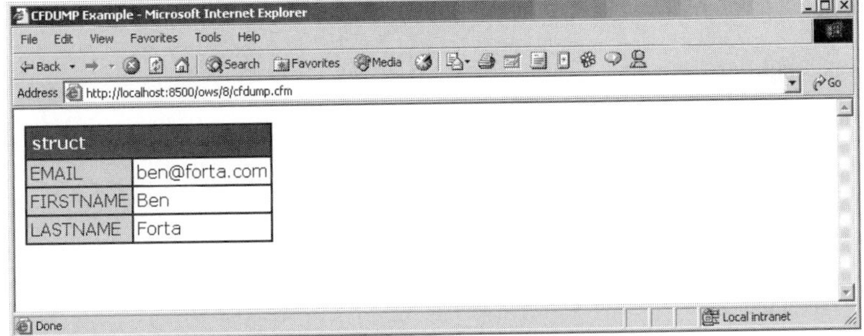

Figure 8.14

<CFDUMP> is an invaluable diagnostics and debugging tool capable of displaying all sorts of data in a clean and easy to read format.

In this listing we've removed the `<CFOUTPUT>` block. Instead, a `<CFDUMP>` tag is being used to dump (display) the contents of the `contact` structure. As you can see in Figure 8.14, `<CFDUMP>` creates a nicely formatted table containing the data contained within the structure. Our structure was pretty simple (three members, and no nested data types) but as the variables and data types you work with grow in complexity you'll find `<CFDUMP>` to be an invaluable utility tag.

TIP

`<CFDUMP>` actually does more than just paint an HTML table. Try clicking on any of the boxes with colored backgrounds—you'll be able to collapse and expand them as needed. When working with very large complex expressions this feature is incredibly useful, and to make it work ColdFusion automatically generates DHTML code (with supporting JavaScript) all automatically. To appreciate just how much work this little tag does, View Source in your Web browser.

Commenting Your Code

The last introductory topic I want to mention is commenting your code. Many books leave this to the very end, but I believe it is so important that I am introducing the concept right here—before you start real coding.

The code you have worked with thus far has been short, simple, and rather self-explanatory. But as you start building bigger and more complex applications, your code will become more involved and more complex. And then comments become vital. The reasons to comment your code include

- If you make code as self-descriptive as possible, when you revisit it at a later date you'll remember what you did, and why.
- This is even truer if others have to work on your code. The more detailed and accurate comments are, the easier (and safer) it will be to make changes or corrections when necessary.
- Commented code is much easier to debug than uncommented code.
- Commented code tends to be better organized, too.

And that's just the start of it.

Listing 8.11 is a revised version of `hello6.cfm`; all that has changed is the inclusion of comments. And as you can see from Figure 8.15, this has no impact on generated output whatsoever.

Listing 8.11 `hello7.cfm`

```
<!---
Name:        hello7.cfm
Author:      Ben Forta (ben@forta.com)
Description: Demonstrate use of comments
Created:     3/27/02
--->

<HTML>
<HEAD>
   <TITLE>Hello 7</TITLE>
</HEAD>

<BODY>

<!--- Save name --->
<CFSET FirstName="Ben">

<!--- Save converted versions of name --->
<CFSET UpperFirstName=UCase(FirstName)>
<CFSET LowerFirstName=LCase(FirstName)>
<CFSET ReverseFirstName=Reverse(FirstName)>

<!--- Save name length --->
<CFSET LenFirstName=Len(FirstName)>

<!--- Display output --->
<CFOUTPUT>
Hello #FirstName#, and welcome to ColdFusion!<P>
Your name in uppercase: #UpperFirstName#<BR>
Your name in lowercase: #LowerFirstName#<BR>
Your name in reverse: #ReverseFirstName#<BR>
Characters in your name: #LenFirstName#<BR>
</CFOUTPUT>

</BODY>
</HTML>
```

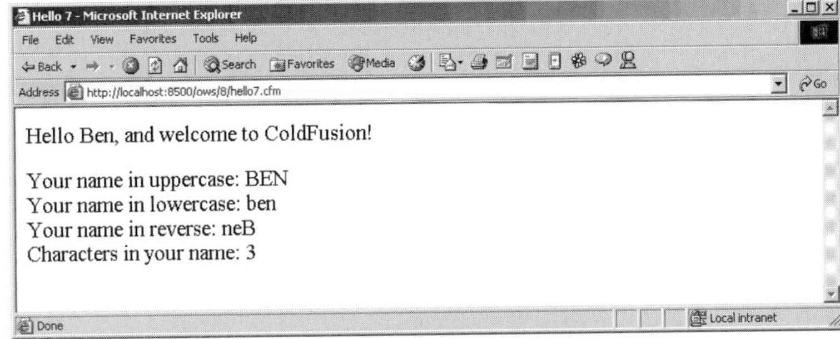

Figure 8.15

ColdFusion comments in your code are never sent to the client browser.

Comments are typed between `<!---` and `--->` tags. Comments should never be nested and should never be mismatched (such as having a starting tag without an end tag, or vice versa).

NOTE

ColdFusion uses `<!---` and `--->` to delimit comments. HTML uses `<!--` and `-->` (two hyphens instead of three). Within ColdFusion code, always use ColdFusion comments and not HTML comments. The latter will be sent to the client (they won't be displayed, but they will still be sent), whereas the former won't.

CAUTION

Be sure not to mix comment styles, using two hyphens on one end of the comment and three on the other. Doing so could cause your code to not be executed as expected.

TIP

Commenting code is a useful debugging technique. When you are testing code and need to eliminate specific lines, you can ***comment them out*** temporarily by wrapping them within `<!---` and `--->` tags.

CHAPTER 9

CFML Basics

IN THIS CHAPTER

Working with Conditional Processing

Chapter 8, "Using ColdFusion," introduced two ColdFusion tags (`<CFOUTPUT>` and `<CFSET>`), functions, and variables. This chapter takes CFML one big step further, adding conditional and programmatic processing—the stuff that starts to add real power to your code.

The code you wrote in the last chapter was linear—ColdFusion started at the top of the page and processed every line in order. And although that works for simple applications, more often than not you'll need to write code that does various things based on conditions, such as the following:

- Displaying different messages based on the time of day or day of week
- Personalizing content based on user login
- Informing users of the status of searches or other operations
- Displaying (or hiding) options based on security level

All these require intelligence within your code to facilitate decision making. Conditional processing is the mechanism by which this is done, and ColdFusion supports two forms of conditional processing:

- If statements, created using `<CFIF>` and related tags
- Switch statements, created using `<CFSWITCH>` and `<CFCASE>`

Let's start by taking a look at these in detail.

If Statements

If statements are a fundamental part of most development languages, and even though the syntax varies from one language to the next, the basic concepts and options are the same. If statements are used to create conditions that are evaluated, enabling you to perform actions based on the result.

The conditions passed to if statements always evaluate to `TRUE` or `FALSE`, and any condition that can be expressed as a `TRUE` / `FALSE` (or `YES` / `NO`) question is valid. Here are some examples of valid conditions:

- Is today Monday?
- Does variable `FirstName` exist?
- Were any rows retrieved from a database?
- Does variable one equal variable two?
- Is a specific word in a sentence?

More complex conditions (multiple conditions) are allowed, too:

- Is today Sunday or Saturday?
- Was a credit card number provided, and if yes, has it been validated?
- Does the currently logged-in user have a first name of `Ben` and a last name of `Forta`, or a first name of `Nate` and a last name of `Weiss`?

The common denominator here is that all these conditions can be answered with `TRUE` or `FALSE`, so they are all valid conditions.

NOTE

In ColdFusion the words `TRUE` and `FALSE` can be used when evaluating conditions. In addition, `YES` can be used in lieu of `TRUE`, and `NO` can be used in lieu of `FALSE`. It is also worth noting that *all numbers are either* `TRUE` or `FALSE`: `0` is `FALSE`, and any other number (positive or negative) is `TRUE`.

Basic If Statements

ColdFusion if statements are created using the `<CFIF>` tag. `<CFIF>` takes no attributes; instead, it takes a condition. For example, the following `<CFIF>` statement checks to see whether a variable named `FirstName` contains the value `Ben`:

```
<CFIF FirstName IS "Ben">
```

The keyword `IS` is an operator used to test for equality. Other operators are supported, too, as listed in Table 9.1.

As seen in Table 9.1, most CFML operators have shortcuts equivalents that you may use. The `IS` operator used in the previous code example is actually a shortcut for `EQUAL`, and that condition is actually

```
<CFIF FirstName EQUAL "Ben">
```

To test whether `FirstName` is not `Ben`, you could use the following code:

```
<CFIF FirstName IS NOT "Ben">
```

or

```
<CFIF FirstName NEQ "Ben">
```

or

```
<CFIF FirstName NOT EQUAL "Ben">
```

or even

```
<CFIF NOT FirstName IS "Ben">
```

In this last snippet, the `NOT` operator is used to negate a condition.

Table 9.1 CFML Evaluation Operators

OPERATOR	SHORTCUT	DESCRIPTION
`EQUAL`	`IS, EQ`	Tests for equality
`NOT EQUAL`	`IS NOT, NEQ`	Tests for nonequality
`GREATER THAN`	`GT`	Tests for greater than
`GREATER THAN OR EQUAL TO`	`GTE`	Tests for greater than or equal to
`LESS THAN`	`LT`	Tests for less than
`LESS THAN OR EQUAL TO`	`LTE`	Tests for less than or equal to
`CONTAINS`		Tests whether a value is contained within a second value
`DOES NOT CONTAIN`		Tests whether a value is not contained within a second value

Ready to try `<CFIF>` yourself? What follows is a simple application that checks to see whether it is the weekend (see Figure 9.1). Save the file as `if1.cfm`, and execute in from within Dreamweaver MX or your Web browser (if the latter then the URL to use will be `http://localhost:8500/ows/9/if1.cfm` if the integrated Web server is being used):

TIP

Don't forget to create the `9` directory under `ows`; all the code created in this chapter should go in that directory.

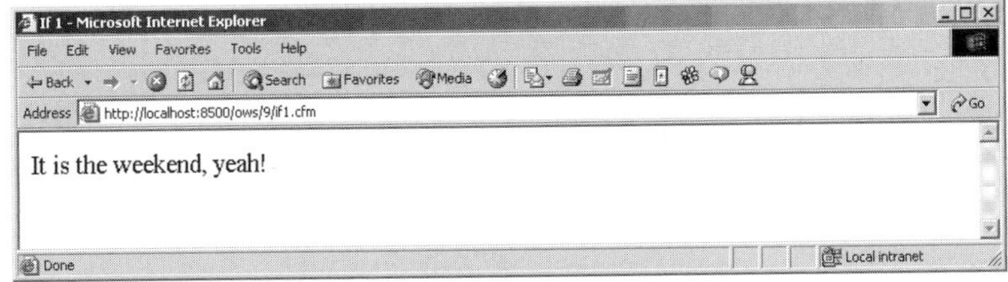

Figure 9.1

`<CFIF>` statements can be used to display output conditionally.

Listing 9.1 `if1.cfm`

```
<!---
Name:        if1.cfm
Author:      Ben Forta (ben@forta.com)
Description: Demonstrate use of <CFIF>
Created:     3/27/02
--->

<HTML>
<HEAD>
   <TITLE>If 1</TITLE>
</HEAD>

<BODY>

<!--- Is it the weekend? --->
<CFIF DayOfWeek(Now()) IS 1>
   <!--- Yes it is, great! --->
   It is the weekend, yeah!
</CFIF>

</BODY>
</HTML>
```

The code in Listing 9.1 should be pretty self-explanatory. A comment header describes the code, and then the standard HTML `<HEAD>` and `<BODY>` tags are used to create the page. Then comes the `<CFIF>` statement:

```
<CFIF DayOfWeek(Now()) IS 1>
```

As you already have seen, `Now()` is a function that returns the current system date and time. `DayOfWeek()` is a function that returns the day of the week for a specified date (a variable, a literal, or another function). `DayOfWeek(Now())` returns the current day of the week: `1` for Sunday, `2` for Monday, `3` for Tuesday, and so on. The condition `DayOfWeek(Now()) IS 1` then simply checks to see whether it is Sunday—if it is Sunday then the condition evaluates to `TRUE`, and if not, it evaluates to `FALSE`.

If the condition is `TRUE`, the text between the `<CFIF>` and `</CFIF>` tags is displayed. It's as simple as that.

Multicondition If Statements

A couple of problems exist with the code in Listing 9.1, the most important of which is that weekends are made up of both Sundays and Saturdays. Therefore, the code to check whether it is the weekend needs to check for both days.

Here is a revised version of the code (see Listing 9.2); save this file as `if2.cfm`, and then execute it.

TIP

So as not to have to retype all the code as you make changes, use Dreamweaver MX's File, Save As menu option to save the file with the new name, and then edit the newly saved file.

Listing 9.2 `if2.cfm`

```
<!---
Name:        if2.cfm
Author:      Ben Forta (ben@forta.com)
Description: Demonstrate use of multiple conditions
Created:     3/27/02
--->

<HTML>
<HEAD>
   <TITLE>If 2</TITLE>
</HEAD>

<BODY>

<!--- Is it the weekend? --->
<CFIF (DayOfWeek(Now()) IS 1) OR (DayOfWeek(Now()) IS 7)>
   <!--- Yes it is, great! --->
   It is the weekend, yeah!
</CFIF>

</BODY>
</HTML>
```

The code is the same as Listing 9.1, except for the `<CFIF>` statement itself:

```
<CFIF (DayOfWeek(Now()) IS 1) OR (DayOfWeek(Now()) IS 7)>
```

This statement contains two conditions, one that checks whether the day of the week is `1` (Sunday), and one that checks whether it is `7` (Saturday). If it is Sunday or Saturday, the message is displayed correctly—problem solved.

To tell ColdFusion to test for either condition, the `OR` operator is used. By using `OR` if either of the specified conditions is `TRUE`, the condition returns `TRUE`. `FALSE` is returned only if *neither* condition is `TRUE`. This is in contrast to the `AND` operator, which requires that *both* conditions are `TRUE` and returns `FALSE` if only one or no conditions are `TRUE`. Look at the following code snippet:

```
<CFIF (FirstName IS "Ben") AND (LastName IS "Forta")>
```

For this condition to be `TRUE`, the `FirstName` must be `Ben` and the `LastName` must be `Forta`. `Ben` with any other `LastName` or `Forta` with any other `FirstName` fails the test.

`AND` and `OR` are logical operators (sometimes called *Boolean* operators). These two are the most frequently used logical operators, but others are supported, too, as listed in Table 9.2.

TIP

You probably noticed that when multiple conditions (either **AND** or **OR**) were used, each condition was enclosed within parentheses. This is not required but is generally good practice. Not only does it make the code cleaner and easier to read, but it also prevents bugs from being introduced by expressions being evaluated in ways other than you expected. For example, if both **AND** and **OR** are used in a condition, **AND** is always evaluated before **OR**, which might or might not be what you want. Parentheses are evaluated before **AND**, so by using parentheses you can explicitly manage the order of evaluation.

Table 9.2 CFML Logical Operators

OPERATOR	DESCRIPTION
AND	Returns TRUE only if both conditions are TRUE
OR	Returns TRUE if at least one condition is TRUE
XOR	Returns TRUE if either condition is TRUE, but not if both or neither are TRUE
EQV	Tests for equivalence and returns TRUE if both conditions are the same (either both TRUE or both FALSE, but not if one is TRUE and one is FALSE)
IMP	Tests for implication; returns FALSE only when the first condition is TRUE and the second is FALSE
NOT	Negates any other logical operator

If and Else

The code in Listing 9.2 is logically correct: If it is Sunday or Saturday then it is indeed the weekend, and the weekend message is displayed. But what if it is not Sunday or Saturday? Right now, nothing is displayed at all—that must be fixed.

Listing 9.3 contains the revised code, capable of displaying a non-weekend message if necessary (see Figure 9.2). Save this code as `if3.cfm`, and then execute it.

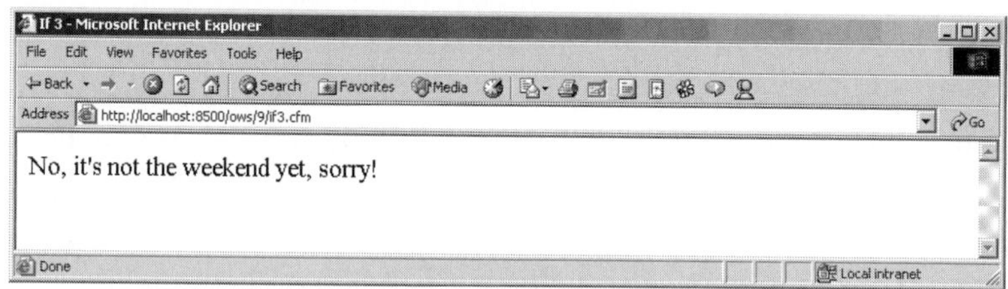

Figure 9.2

<CFELSE> enables the creation of code to be executed when a <CFIF> test fails.

Listing 9.3 `if3.cfm`

```
<!---
Name:        if3.cfm
Author:      Ben Forta (ben@forta.com)
Description: Demonstrate use of <CFIF> and <CFELSE>
Created:     3/27/02
--->

<HTML>
<HEAD>
   <TITLE>If 3</TITLE>
</HEAD>

<BODY>

<!--- Is it the weekend? --->
<CFIF (DayOfWeek(Now()) IS 1) OR (DayOfWeek(Now()) IS 7)>
   <!--- Yes it is, great! --->
```

Listing 9.3 (continued)

```
    It is the weekend, yeah!
<CFELSE>
    <!--- No it is not :-( --->
    No, it's not the weekend yet, sorry!
</CFIF>

</BODY>
</HTML>
```

The only real difference between Listings 9.2 and 9.3 is the introduction of a new tag—`<CFELSE>`. `<CFIF>` is used to define code to be executed when a condition is `TRUE`, and `<CFELSE>` defines code to be executed when a condition is `FALSE`. `<CFELSE>` takes no attributes and can be used only between `<CFIF>` and `</CFIF>` tags. The new code will now display `It is the weekend, yeah!` if it is Sunday or Saturday and `No, it's not the weekend yet, sorry!` if not. Much better.

But before you move on, Listing 9.4 contains one more refinement—a cleaner `<CFIF>` statement. Save Listing 9.4 as `if4.cfm`, and then execute it (it should do exactly what Listing 9.3 did).

Listing 9.4 `if4.cfm`

```
<!---
Name:        if4.cfm
Author:      Ben Forta (ben@forta.com)
Description: Demonstrate use of <CFIF> and <CFELSE>
Created:     3/27/02
--->

<HTML>
<HEAD>
    <TITLE>If 4</TITLE>
</HEAD>

<BODY>

<!--- Is it the weekend? --->
<CFSET weekend=(DayOfWeek(Now()) IS 1) OR (DayOfWeek(Now()) IS 7)>

<!--- Let the user know --->
<CFIF weekend>
    <!--- Yes it is, great! --->
    It is the weekend, yeah!
<CFELSE>
    <!--- No it is not :-( --->
    No, it's not the weekend yet, sorry!
</CFIF>

</BODY>
</HTML>
```

The more complex conditions become, the harder they are to read. So, many developers prefer to save the results of executed conditions to variables for later use. Look at this line of code (from Listing 9.4):

```
<CFSET weekend=(DayOfWeek(Now()) IS 1) OR (DayOfWeek(Now()) IS 7)>
```

Here, <CFSET> is used to create a variable named weekend. The value stored in this variable is whatever the condition returns. So, if it is a weekend (Sunday or Saturday), weekend will be TRUE, and if it is not a weekend then weekend will be FALSE.

→ See Chapter 8, "Using ColdFusion," for detailed coverage of the <CFSET> tag.

After weekend is set, it can be used in the <CFIF> statement:

```
<CFIF weekend>
```

If weekend is TRUE then the first block of text is displayed; otherwise, the <CFELSE> text is displayed.

But what is weekend being compared to? In every condition thus far, you have used an operator (such as IS) to test a condition. Here, however, no operator is used; so what is weekend being tested against?

Actually, weekend is indeed being tested; it is being compared to TRUE. Within a <CFIF> the comparison is optional, and if it's omitted, a comparison to TRUE is assumed. So, <CFIF weekend> is functionally the same as

```
<CFIF weekend IS TRUE>
```

The weekend variable contains either TRUE or FALSE. If it's TRUE, the condition is effectively

```
<CFIF TRUE IS TRUE>
```

which obviously evaluates to TRUE. But if weekend is FALSE, the condition is

```
<CFIF FALSE IS TRUE>
```

which obviously is FALSE.

I said that weekend contained either TRUE or FALSE, but feel free to test that for yourself. If you add the following line to your code, you'll be able to display the contents of weekend:

```
<CFOUTPUT>#weekend#</CFOUTPUT>
```

As you can see, you have a lot of flexibility when it comes to writing <CFIF> statements.

Multiple If Statements

There's one more feature of <CFIF> that you need to look at—support for multiple independent conditions (as opposed to one condition made up of multiple conditions).

The best way to explain this is with an example. In the previous listings you displayed a message on weekends. But what if you wanted to display different messages on Sunday and Saturday? You could create multiple <CFIF> </CFIF> blocks, but there is a better way.

Listing 9.5 contains yet another version of the code; this time the filename should be if5.cfm.

Listing 9.5 if5.cfm

```
<!---
Name:        if5.cfm
Author:      Ben Forta (ben@forta.com)
Description: Demonstrate use of <CFIF>
Created:     3/27/02
--->
```

Listing 9.5 (continued)

```
<HTML>
<HEAD>
   <TITLE>If 5</TITLE>
</HEAD>

<BODY>

<!--- Get day of week --->
<CFSET dow=DayOfWeek(Now())>

<!--- Let the user know --->
<CFIF dow IS 1>
   <!--- It's Sunday --->
   It is the weekend! But make the most of it, tomorrow it's back to work.
<CFELSEIF dow IS 7>
   <!--- It's Saturday --->
   It is the weekend! And even better, tomorrow is the weekend too!
<CFELSE>
   <!--- No it is not :-( --->
   No, it's not the weekend yet, sorry!
</CFIF>

</BODY>
</HTML>
```

Let's take a look at the previous code. A `<CFSET>` is used to create a variable named `dow`, which contains the day of the week (the value returned by `DayOfWeek(Now())`, a number from `1` to `7`).

The `<CFIF>` statement checks to see whether `dow is 1`, and if `TRUE`, displays the Sunday message (see Figure 9.3). Then a `<CFELSEIF>` is used to provide an alternative `<CFIF>` statement:

```
<CFELSEIF dow IS 7>
```

The `<CFELSEIF>` checks to see whether `dow is 7`, and if `TRUE`, displays the Saturday message (see Figure 9.4). And then finally, `<CFELSE>` is used to display text if neither the `<CFIF>` nor the `<CFELSEIF>` are `TRUE`.

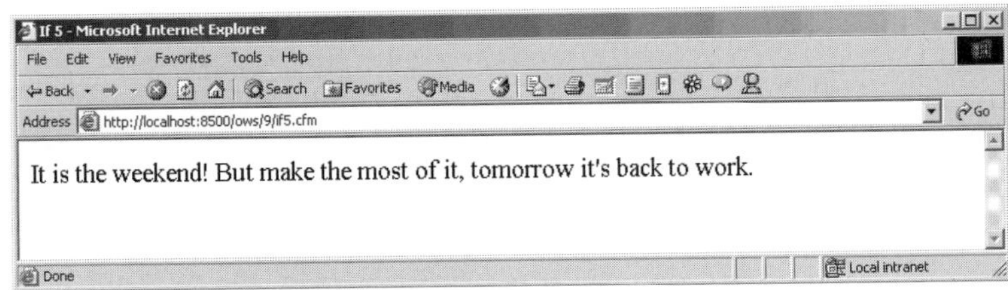

Figure 9.3

If `dow` is `1`, the Sunday message is displayed.

`<CFELSEIF>` is essentially a combined `<CFELSE>` and `<CFIF>`, and thus its name.

Aside from being more readable, there is another benefit in saving conditions' results to variables (as you did here with the `dow` variable and previously with `weekend`). As a rule, you should avoid repeating code—with the exact same expressions (getting the day of the week) used in multiple places, you run the risk that one day you'll update the code and not make all the changes in all the required locations. If just a single expression must be changed, that potential problem is avoided.

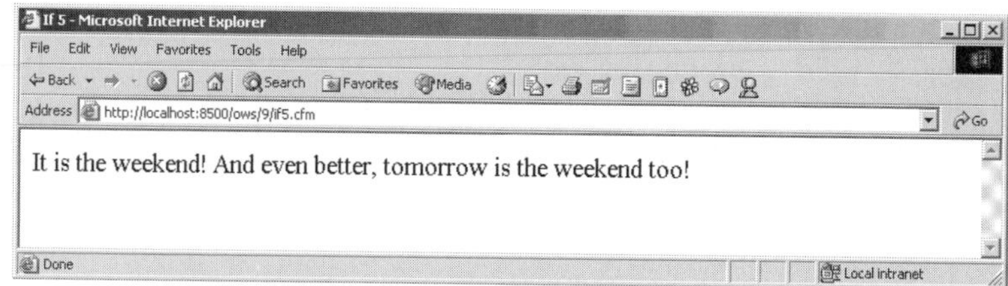

Figure 9.4
If `dow` is `7`, the Saturday message is displayed.

No limit exists to the number of `<CFELSEIF>` statements you use within a `<CFIF>` tag, but you can never use more than one `<CFIF>` or `<CFELSE>`.

NOTE

Use of `<CFELSEIF>` and `<CFELSE>` are optional. However, if `<CFELSE>` is used, it must always be the last tag before the `</CFIF>`.

Putting It All Together

`<CFIF>` is one of the most frequently used tags in CFML. So before we move on to the next subject, let's walk through one more example—a slightly more complex one.

Guess the Number is a simple game, similar to *I'm thinking of a number between 1 and 10, guess what number I am thinking of.* ColdFusion selects a random number, you guess a number, and ColdFusion will tell you whether you guessed the correct number.

Listing 9.6 contains the code for `guess1.cfm`. Save it in the `9` directory, but do not execute it from within Dreamweaver MX. Instead, use this URL to execute it:

```
http://localhost:8500/ows/9/guess1.cfm?guess=n
```

Replace `n` with a number from `1` to `10`. For example, if you guess `5`, use this URL:

```
http://localhost:8500/ows/9/guess1.cfm?guess=5
```

You'll see an output similar to the ones shown in Figures 9.5 and 9.6 (actually, if you reload the page often enough, you'll see both figures).

Figure 9.5 `URL.guess` matched the number ColdFusion picked.

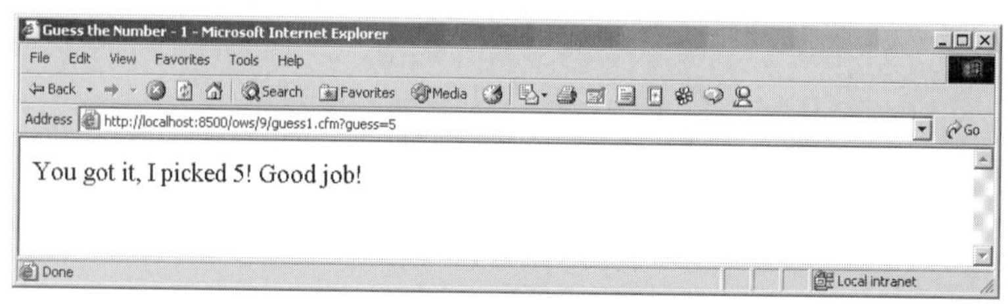

Figure 9.5
`URL.guess` matched the number Cold-Fusion picked.

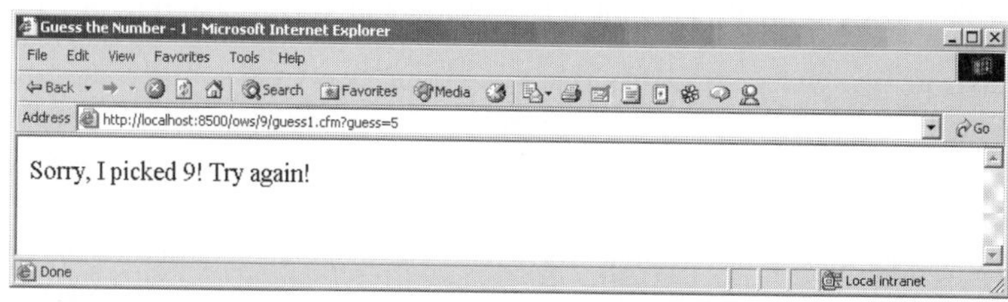

Figure 9.6
`URL.guess` did not match the number ColdFusion picked.

Listing 9.6 guess1.cfm

```
<!---
Name:        guess1.cfm
Author:      Ben Forta (ben@forta.com)
Description: Demonstrate use of multiple if statements
Created:     3/27/02
--->

<HTML>
<HEAD>
   <TITLE>Guess the Number - 1</TITLE>
</HEAD>

<BODY>

<!--- Pick a random number --->
<CFSET RandomNumber=RandRange(1, 10)>

<!--- Check if matched --->
<CFIF RandomNumber IS URL.guess>
   <!--- It matched --->
   <CFOUTPUT>
   You got it, I picked #RandomNumber#! Good job!
   </CFOUTPUT>
<CFELSE>
   <!--- No match --->
   <CFOUTPUT>
   Sorry, I picked #RandomNumber#! Try again!
   </CFOUTPUT>
</CFIF>

</BODY>
</HTML>
```

The first thing the code does is pick a random number. To do this, the `RandRange()` function is used—`RandRange()` takes two parameters (the range) and returns a random number within that range. The following line of code thus returns a random number from `1` to `10` (inclusive) and saves it in a variable named `RandomNumber`:

```
<CFSET RandomNumber=RandRange(1, 10)>
```

Next, the randomly generated number is compared to the guessed number (which was passed as a URL parameter) using the following `<CFIF>` statement:

```
<CFIF RandomNumber IS URL.guess>
```

`URL.guess` is the variable containing the `guess value provided in the URL`. If the two match then the first message is displayed, and if they don't then the second message is displayed.

➔ URL variables, and how they are used, are covered in detail in Chapter 10, "Creating Data-Driven Pages." For now, though, it is sufficient to know that variables passed as parameters to a URL are accessible via the URL scope.

But what if no guess parameter was specified? You will recall from Chapter 8 that referring to a variable that does not exist generates an error. Therefore, you should modify the code to check that URL.guess exists before using it. Listing 9.7 contains the modified version of the code; save this file as guess2.cfm.

NOTE

This is why I said not to try guess1.cfm from within Dreamweaver, as the code would have been executed without allowing you to pass the necessary URL parameter, and an error would have been generated.

Listing 9.7 guess2.cfm

```
<!---
Name:        guess2.cfm
Author:      Ben Forta (ben@forta.com)
Description: Demonstrate use of multiple if statements
Created:     3/27/02
--->

<HTML>
<HEAD>
   <TITLE>Guess the Number - 2</TITLE>
</HEAD>

<BODY>

<!--- Pick a random number --->
<CFSET RandomNumber=RandRange(1, 10)>

<!--- Check if number was passed --->
<CFIF IsDefined("URL.guess")>

   <!--- Yes it was, did it match? --->
   <CFIF RandomNumber IS URL.guess>
      <!--- It matched --->
      <CFOUTPUT>
      You got it, I picked #RandomNumber#! Good job!
      </CFOUTPUT>
   <CFELSE>
      <!--- No match --->
       <CFOUTPUT>
       Sorry, I picked #RandomNumber#! Try again!
       </CFOUTPUT>
   </CFIF>

<CFELSE>

   <!--- No guess specified, give instructions --->
   You did not guess a number.<BR>
   To guess a number, reload this page adding
   <B>?guess=n</B> (where n is the guess, for
   example, ?guess=5). Number should be between
   1 and 10.

</CFIF>

</BODY>
</HTML>
```

Listing 9.7 introduces a new concept in `<CFIF>` statements—nested `<CFIF>` tags. Let's take a look at the code. The first `<CFIF>` statement is

```
<CFIF IsDefined("URL.guess")>
```

`IsDefined()` is a CFML function that checks whether a variable exists. `IsDefined("URL.guess")` returns `TRUE` if `guess` was passed on the `URL` and `FALSE` if not. Using this function, you can process the guess only if it actually exists. So, the entire code block (complete with `<CFIF>` and `<CFELSE>` tags) is within the `TRUE` block of the outer `<CFIF>` and the original `<CFIF>` block is now nested—it is a `<CFIF>` within a `<CFIF>`.

This then also enables you to add another `<CFELSE>` block—on the outer `<CFIF>`. Remember, the outer `<CFIF>` checks whether `URL.guess` exists, so `<CFELSE>` can be used to display a message if it does not. Therefore, not only will the code no longer generate an error if `guess` was not specified, it will also provide help and instruct the user appropriately (see Figure 9.7).

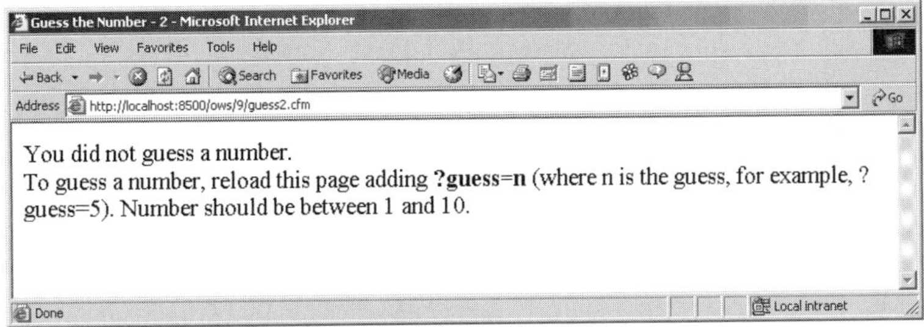

Figure 9.7

By checking for the existence of expected variables, your applications are capable of providing assistance and instructions if necessary.

NOTE

The code in Listing 9.7 clearly demonstrates the value of indenting your code. The code within each `<CFIF>` block is indented, and the deeper the nesting, the further the indentation. This type of formatting is extremely popular among professional developers because it makes finding matching code blocks (or mismatched code blocks) much easier.

As a rule, nesting should be avoided unless absolutely necessary. Nesting really isn't necessary in this game. Listing 9.8 takes the game code one step further, this time using `<CFELSEIF>` and multiple clause conditions to create tighter (and better performing) code. Save Listing 9.8 as `guess3.cfm`.

Listing 9.8 `guess3.cfm`

```
<!---
Name:        guess3.cfm
Author:      Ben Forta (ben@forta.com)
Description: Demonstrate use of multiple if statements
Created:     3/27/02
--->

<HTML>
<HEAD>
   <TITLE>Guess the Number - 3</TITLE>
</HEAD>

<BODY>

<!--- Pick a random number --->
```

Listing 9.8 (CONTINUED)

```
<CFSET RandomNumber=RandRange(1, 10)>

<!--- Check if number was passed --->
<CFIF IsDefined("URL.guess") AND (RandomNumber IS URL.guess)>
   <!--- It matched --->
   <CFOUTPUT>
   You got it, I picked #RandomNumber#! Good job!
   </CFOUTPUT>
<CFELSEIF IsDefined("URL.guess") AND (RandomNumber IS NOT URL.guess)>
   <!--- Did not match --->
   <CFOUTPUT>
    Sorry, I picked #RandomNumber#! Try again!
   </CFOUTPUT>
<CFELSE>
   <!--- No guess specified, give instructions --->
   You did not guess a number.<BR>
   To guess a number, reload this page adding
   <B>?guess=n</B> (where n is the guess, for
   example, ?guess=5). Number should be between
   1 and 10.
</CFIF>

</BODY>
</HTML>
```

Again, the code starts with the random number generation. Then this `<CFIF>` statement is used:

```
<CFIF IsDefined("URL.guess") AND (RandomNumber IS URL.guess)>
```

As explained earlier, `AND` requires that both conditions be `TRUE`. Therefore, the first message is displayed only if `URL.guess` exists and if the numbers match. The second condition is in a `<CFELSEIF>` statement:

```
<CFELSEIF IsDefined("URL.guess") AND (RandomNumber IS NOT URL.guess)>
```

Here, too, `IsDefined()` is used to check that `URL.guess` exists. The second condition is `TRUE` only when the numbers do not match, in which case the second message is displayed.

The `<CFELSE>` here is evaluated only if `<CFIF>` and `<CFELSEIF>` are both not evaluated, in which case it would be clear that `URL.guess` was not defined.

The same result occurs, but this time without nesting.

CAUTION

As a rule, don't nest unless you really have to. Although nesting is legal within your code, nested code tends to be easier to make mistakes in, harder to debug, and slower to execute.

Take a look at this line of code again:

```
<CFIF IsDefined("URL.guess") AND (RandomNumber IS URL.guess)>
```

You might be wondering why an error would not be generated if `URL.guess` did not exist. After all, if the `IsDefined()` returns `FALSE`, should the next condition cause an error because `URL.guess` is being referred to?

The answer is no, because ColdFusion supports *short-circuit evaluation*. What this means is that conditions that do not affect a result are never evaluated. In an AND condition, if the first condition returns FALSE then the result will always be FALSE, regardless of whether the second condition returns TRUE or FALSE. Similarly, in an OR condition, if the first condition is TRUE then the result will always be TRUE, regardless of whether the second condition is TRUE or FALSE. With short-circuit evaluation, conditions that do not affect the final result are not executed (to save processing time). So, in the previous example, if IsDefined("URL.guess") returns FALSE, RandomNumber IS URL.guess is never even evaluated.

Let's finish this game application with one last revision. Listing 9.9 should be saved as file guess4.cfm.

Listing 9.9 guess4.cfm

```
<!---
Name:        guess4.cfm
Author:      Ben Forta (ben@forta.com)
Description: Demonstrate use of multiple if statements
Created:     3/27/02
--->

<HTML>
<HEAD>
   <TITLE>Guess the Number - 4</TITLE>
</HEAD>

<BODY>

<!--- Set range --->
<CFSET GuessLow=1>
<CFSET GuessHigh=10>

<!--- Pick a random number --->
<CFSET RandomNumber=RandRange(GuessLow, GuessHigh)>

<!--- Was a guess specified? --->
<CFSET HaveGuess=IsDefined("URL.guess")>

<!--- If specified, did it match? --->
<CFSET Match=(HaveGuess) AND (RandomNumber IS URL.guess)>

<!--- Feedback --->
<CFOUTPUT>
<CFIF Match>
   <!--- It matched --->
   You got it, I picked #RandomNumber#! Good job!
<CFELSEIF HaveGuess>
   <!--- Did not match --->
   Sorry, I picked #RandomNumber#! Try again!
<CFELSE>
   <!--- No guess specified, give instructions --->
   You did not guess a number.<BR>
   To guess a number, reload this page adding
   <B>?guess=n</B> (where n is the guess, for
```

Listing 9.9 (continued)

```
    example, ?guess=5). Number should be between
    #GuessLow# and #GuessHigh#.
</CFIF>
</CFOUTPUT>

</BODY>
</HTML>
```

Quite a few changes were made in Listing 9.9. First, the range high and low values are now variables, defined as follows:

```
<!--- Set range --->
<CFSET GuessLow=1>
<CFSET GuessHigh=10>
```

By saving these to variables, changing the range (perhaps to allow numbers `1–20`) will be easier. These variables are passed to the `RandRange()` function and are used in the final output (when instructions are given if no `guess` was specified), so the allowed range is included in the instructions.

Next, the simple assignment `<CFSET HaveGuess=IsDefined("URL.guess")>` sets variable `HaveGuess` to either `TRUE` (if `guess` was specified) or `FALSE`. The next assignment sets a variable named `Match` to `TRUE` if the numbers match (and `guess` was specified) or to `FALSE`. In other words, two simple `<CFSET>` statements contain all the necessary intelligence and decision making, and because the results are saved to variables, using this information is very easy indeed.

This makes the display code much cleaner. `<CFIF Match>` displays the first message if the correct `guess` was provided. `<CFELSEIF HaveGuess>` is executed only if the `<CFIF>` failed, which must mean the `guess` was wrong. In addition, the `<CFELSE>` displays the instructions (with the correct range included automatically).

It does not get much cleaner than that.

NOTE

Listing 9.9 demonstrates a coding technique whereby logic (or intelligence) and presentation are separated. This is a practice that should be adopted whenever possible, as the resulting code will be both cleaner and more reusable.

Switch Statements

All the conditional processing used thus far has involved `<CFIF>` statements. But, as I stated at the beginning of this chapter, ColdFusion also supports another form of conditional processing–switch statements.

The best way to understand switch statements is to see them used. Listing 9.10 should be saved as file `switch.cfm`.

If you have executed Listing 9.10 (you should have), you'd have noticed that it does exactly what Listing 9.5 (file `if5.cfm`) does. But the code here is very different.

Listing 9.10 switch.cfm

```
<!---
Name:        switch.cfm
Author:      Ben Forta (ben@forta.com)
Description: Demonstrate use of <CFSWITCH> and <CFCASE>
Created:     3/27/02
--->

<HTML>
<HEAD>
   <TITLE>Switch</TITLE>
</HEAD>

<BODY>

<!--- Get day of week --->
<CFSET dow=DayOfWeek(Now())>

<!--- Let the user know --->
<CFSWITCH EXPRESSION="#dow#">

   <!--- Is it Sunday? --->
   <CFCASE VALUE="1">
   It is the weekend! But make the most of it, tomorrow it's back to work.
   </CFCASE>

   <!--- Is it Saturday? --->
   <CFCASE VALUE="7">
   It is the weekend! And even better, tomorrow is the weekend too!
   </CFCASE>

   <!--- If code reaches here it's not the weekend --->
   <CFDEFAULTCASE>
   No, it's not the weekend yet, sorry!
   </CFDEFAULTCASE>
</CFSWITCH>

</BODY>
</HTML>
```

First the day of the week is saved to variable dow (as you did earlier), but then that variable is passed to a <CFSWITCH> statement:

```
<CFSWITCH EXPRESSION="#dow#">
```

<CFSWITCH> takes an EXPRESSION to evaluate; here, the value in dow is used. The EXPRESSION is a string, so pound signs are needed around dow (otherwise, the text dow will be evaluated instead of the value of that variable).

<CFSWITCH> statements include <CFCASE> statements, which each match a specific value that EXPRESSION could return. The first <CFCASE> is executed if EXPRESSION is 1 (Sunday) because 1 is specified as the VALUE in <CFCASE VALUE="1">. Similarly, the second <CFCASE> is executed if EXPRESSION is 7 (Saturday). Whichever <CFCASE> matches the EXPRESSION is the one that is processed, and in this example, the text between the <CFCASE> and </CFCASE> tags is displayed.

If no <CFCASE> matches the EXPRESSION, the optional <CFDEFAULTCASE> block is executed—<CFDEFAULTCASE> is similar to <CFELSE> in a <CFIF> statement.

As already stated, the end result is exactly the same as in the example using <CFIF>. So, why would you use <CFSWITCH> over <CFIF>? There are two reasons:

- <CFSWITCH> usually executes more quickly than <CFIF>.
- <CFSWITCH> code tends to be neater and more manageable.

But you can't always use <CFSWITCH>. Unlike <CFIF>, <CFSWITCH> can be used only if all conditions are checking against the same EXPRESSION—the conditions are all the same, just the values being compared against differ. If you need to check a set of entirely different conditions, <CFSWITCH> would not be an option (which is why you could not use it in the game example).

TIP

Although the example here uses <CFSWITCH> to display text, that is not all this tag can do. In fact, just about any code you can imagine can be placed between <CFCASE> and </CFCASE>.

<CFCASE> tags are evaluated in order, so placing the values that you expect to match more frequently before those that will match much less frequently makes sense. Doing so can improve application performance slightly because ColdFusion will not have to evaluate values unnecessarily.

This is also true of sets of <CFIF> and <CFELSEIF> statements: Conditions that are expected to match more frequently should be moved higher up the list.

Using Looping

Loops are another fundamental language element supported by most development platforms. *Loops* do just that—they loop. Loops provide a mechanism with which to repeat tasks, and ColdFusion supports several types of loops, all via the <CFLOOP> tag:

- Index loops, used to repeat a set number of times
- Conditional loops, used to repeat until a specified condition becomes FALSE
- Query loops, used to iterate through database query results
- List loops, used to iterate through a specified list
- Collection loops, used to loop through structures

You won't use all these loop types here, but to acquaint you with <CFLOOP>, let's look at a few examples.

The Index Loop

One of the most frequently used loops is the index loop, used to loop a set number of times (from a specified value to another specified value). To learn about this loop, you'll generate a simple list (see Figure 9.8). Type the code in Listing 9.11, and save it in 9 as loop1.cfm.

Listing 9.11 loop1.cfm

```
<!---
Name:        loop1.cfm
Author:      Ben Forta (ben@forta.com)
Description: Demonstrate use of <CFLOOP FROM TO>
Created:     3/27/02
--->

<HTML>
<HEAD>
   <TITLE>Loop 1</TITLE>
</HEAD>

<BODY>

<!--- Create list --->
<UL>

<!--- Loop from 1 to 10 --->
<CFLOOP FROM="1" TO="10" INDEX="i">
   <!--- Write item --->
   <CFOUTPUT><LI>Item #i#</LI></CFOUTPUT>
</CFLOOP>

<!--- End list --->
</UL>

</BODY>
</HTML>
```

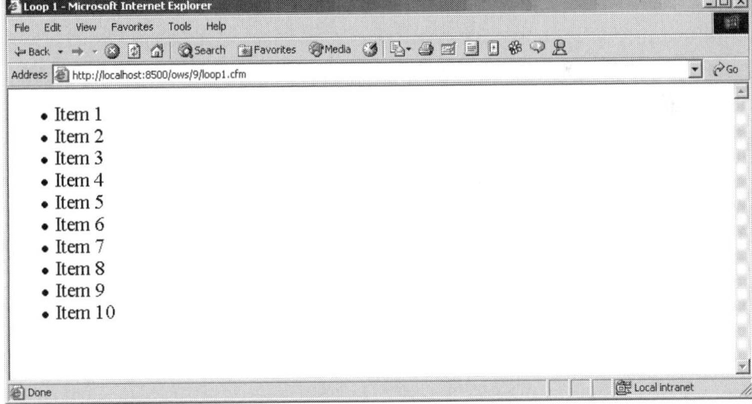

Figure 9.8

Loops can build lists and other display elements automatically.

`<CFLOOP>` is used to create a block of code to be executed over and over. The code in Listing 9.11 creates a simple loop that displays a list of numbers (in an HTML unordered list) from `1` to `10`. The HTML unordered list is started before the `<CFLOOP>` (you wouldn't want to start it in the loop, because you'd be starting a new list on each iteration) and ends after the `</CFLOOP>`. The loop itself is created using the following code:

```
<CFLOOP FROM="1" TO="10" INDEX="i">
```

In an index loop the FROM and TO values must be specified and the code between <CFLOOP> and </CFLOOP> is repeated that many times. Here, FROM="1" and TO="10", so the loop repeats 10 times. Within the loop itself, a variable named in the INDEX attribute contains the current increment, so i will be 1 the first time around, 2 the second time, and so on.

Within the loop, the value of i is displayed in a list item using the following code:

```
<CFOUTPUT><LI>Item #i#</LI></CFOUTPUT>
```

The first time around, when i is 1, the generated output will be

```
<LI>Item 1</LI>
```

and on the second loop it will be

```
<LI>Item 2</LI>
```

and so on.

TIP

Want to loop backwards? You can. Use the STEP attribute to specify how to count from the FROM value to the TO value. STEP="-1" makes the count go backward, one number at a time.

The List Loop

List loops are designed to make working with ColdFusion lists simple and error-free. Whether it is lists created by form submissions, manual lists, lists derived from database queries (regardless of the origin), any list (with any delimiter) can be iterated over using <CFLOOP>.

➜ For information about lists, see Chapter 8.

The following example uses the lists created in Chapter 8 and loops through the list displaying one element at a time (see Figure 9.9). Save Listing 9.12 as loop2.cfm.

Listing 9.12 loop2.cfm

```
<!---
Name:        loop2.cfm
Author:      Ben Forta (ben@forta.com)
Description: Demonstrate use of <CFLOOP LIST>
Created:     3/27/02
--->

<HTML>
<HEAD>
   <TITLE>Loop 2</TITLE>
</HEAD>

<BODY>

<!--- Create list --->
<CFSET fruit="apple,banana,cherry,grape,mango,orange,pineapple">

<!--- Loop through list --->
<CFLOOP LIST="#fruit#" INDEX="i">
   <!--- Write item --->
   <CFOUTPUT>#i#<BR></CFOUTPUT>
```

Listing 9.12 (continued)

```
</CFLOOP>

</BODY>
</HTML>
```

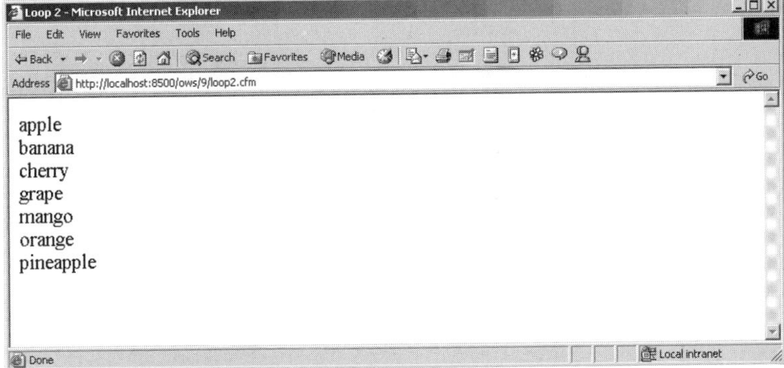

Figure 9.9

Any lists, with any delimiter, can be iterated using `<CFLOOP>`.

`<CFSET>` is used to create the list (a comma-delimited list of fruit). `<CFLOOP>` takes the list to be processed in the `LIST` attribute, and because `LIST` accepts a string, pound signs must be used around the variable name `fruit`.

`<CFLOOP>` repeats the loop once for every element in the list. In addition, within the loop, it makes the current element available in the variable specified in the `INDEX` attribute—in this example, `i`. So, `i` is `apple` on the first iteration, `banana` on the second iteration, and so on.

NOTE

Lists also can be looped over using index loops. `FROM="1" TO="#ListLen(fruit)#"` sets the `TO` and `FROM` properly. Within the loop, `ListGetAt()` can be used to obtain the element.

Nested Loops

Similar to the `<CFIF>` and `<CFSWITCH>` statements, loops can be nested. Nesting loops enables the creation of extremely powerful code, as long as you are very careful in constructing the loops. Listing 9.13 contains a practical example of nested loops, using three loops to display a table of Web browser-safe colors (seen in Figure 9.10). Save the code as `loop3.cfm`.

Listing 9.13 `loop3.cfm`

```
<!---
Name:        loop3.cfm
Author:      Ben Forta (ben@forta.com)
Description: Demonstrate use of nested loops
Created:     3/27/02
--->

<HTML>
<HEAD>
   <TITLE>Loop 3</TITLE>
```

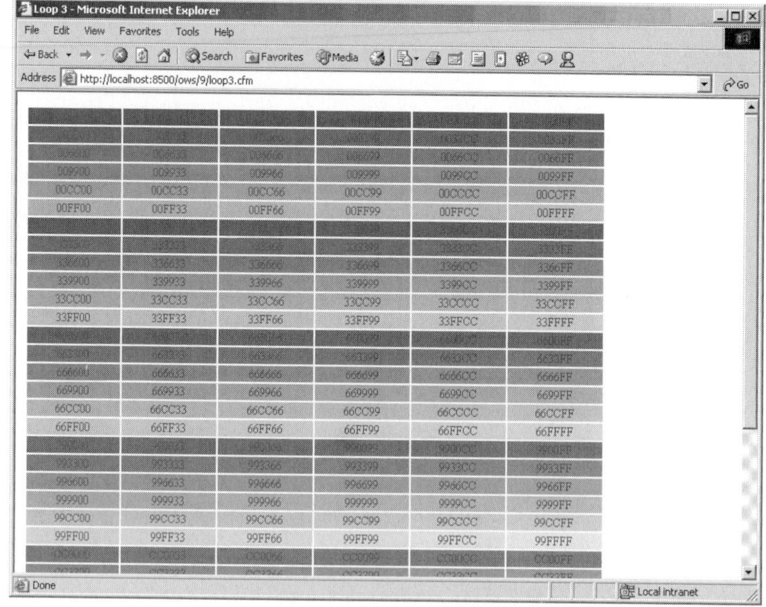

Figure 9.10 Displaying the Web browser-safe color palette requires the use of three nested loops.

Listing 9.13 (continued)

```
</HEAD>

<BODY>

<!--- Hex value list --->
<CFSET hex="00,33,66,99,CC,FF">

<!--- Create table --->
<TABLE>

<!--- Start RR loop --->
<CFLOOP INDEX="red" LIST="#hex#">
   <!--- Start GG loop --->
   <CFLOOP INDEX="green" LIST="#hex#">
      <TR>
      <!--- Start BB loop --->
      <CFLOOP INDEX="blue" LIST="#hex#">
         <!--- Build RGB value --->
         <CFSET rgb=red&green&blue>
         <!--- And display it --->
         <CFOUTPUT>
         <TD BGCOLOR="#rgb#" WIDTH="100" ALIGN="center">#rgb#</TD>
         </CFOUTPUT>
      </CFLOOP>
      </TR>
   </CFLOOP>
</CFLOOP>

</TABLE>

</BODY>
</HTML>
```

Listing 9.13 warrants explanation. Colors in Web pages are expressed as RGB values (as in red, green, blue). The idea is that by adjusting the amount of red, green, and blue within a color, every possible color can be created. RGB values are specified using hexadecimal notation, and don't panic if you have forgotten base-n arithmetic—it's quite simple, actually. The amount of color is specified as a number, from `0` (none) to `255` (all). But instead of `0–255`, the hexadecimal equivalents (`00–FF`) are used. So, pure red is all red and no green or blue, or `FF0000`; yellow is all red and green and no blue, or `FFFF00`.

Still confused? Execute the code and you'll see a complete list of colors and the RGB value for each.

To list all the colors, the code must loop through all possible combinations—list all shades of red, and within each shade of red list each shade of green, and within each shade of green list each shade of blue. In the innermost loop, a variable named `rgb is created as follows:`

```
<CFSET rgb=red&green&blue>
```

On the very first iteration red, green, and blue are all `00`, so `rgb` is `000000`. On the next iteration red and green are still `00`, but blue is `33`, so `rgb` is `000033`. By the time all the loops have been processed, a total of 216 colors has been generated (6 to the power of 3 for you mathematicians out there, because each color has six possible shades as defined in variable `hex`).

And although the exact mechanics of RGB value generation are not that important here, the key is that loops can be nested quite easily and within each loop the counters and variables created at an outer loop are visible and usable.

Reusing Code

All developers write code (or should write code) with reuse in mind. The many reasons this is a good idea include:

- *Saving time*—If it is written once, don't write it again.
- *Easier maintenance*—Make a change in one place and any code that uses it gets that change automatically.
- *Easier debugging*—Fewer copies exist out there that will need to be fixed.
- *Group development*—Developers can share code more easily.

Most of the code reuse in this book involves ColdFusion code, but to demonstrate basic reuse, let's look at a simple example.

Orange Whip Studios is building a Web site, slowly. Figure 9.11 shows a home page (still being worked on), and Figure 9.12 shows a contact us page (also being worked on). Both pages have a lot in common—both have the same header, the same logo, and the same copyright notice. If you were writing plain HTML, you'd have no choice but to copy all the code that creates those page components into every page you were creating.

But you're using ColdFusion, and ColdFusion makes code reuse incredibly simple. The CFML `<CFINCLUDE>` tag is used to include one page in another. `<CFINCLUDE>` specifies the name of a file to include, and at runtime, when ColdFusion encounters a `<CFINCLUDE>` tag, it reads the contents of the specified file and processes it as if it were part of the same file.

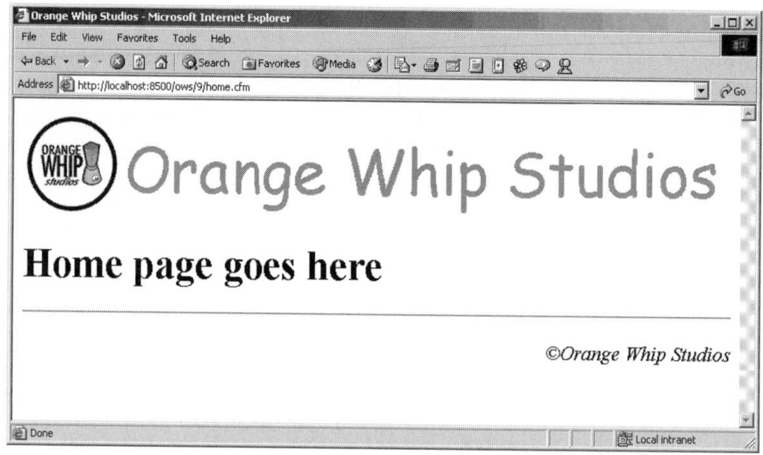

Figure 9.11 The home page contains basic logos and branding.

To demonstrate this, look at Listings 9.14 and 9.15. The former is `ows_header.cfm`, and the latter is `ows_footer.cfm`. Between the two files, all the formatting for the Orange Whip Studios pages is present.

Listing 9.14 `ows_header.cfm`

```
<HTML>
<HEAD>
   <TITLE>Orange Whip Studios</TITLE>
</HEAD>

<BODY>

<!--- Header --->
<TABLE WIDTH="100%">
<TR>
<TD>
   <IMG SRC="../images/logo_c.gif" WIDTH="101" HEIGHT="101" ALT="" BORDER="0">
</TD>
<TD>
   <FONT FACE="Comic Sans MS" SIZE="7" COLOR="#FF8000">Orange Whip Studios</FONT>
</TD>
</TR>
</TABLE>
<P>
```

Listing 9.15 `ows_footer.cfm`

```
<P>
<HR>
<P ALIGN="right">
<I>&copy;Orange Whip Studios</I>
</P>

</BODY>
</HTML>
```

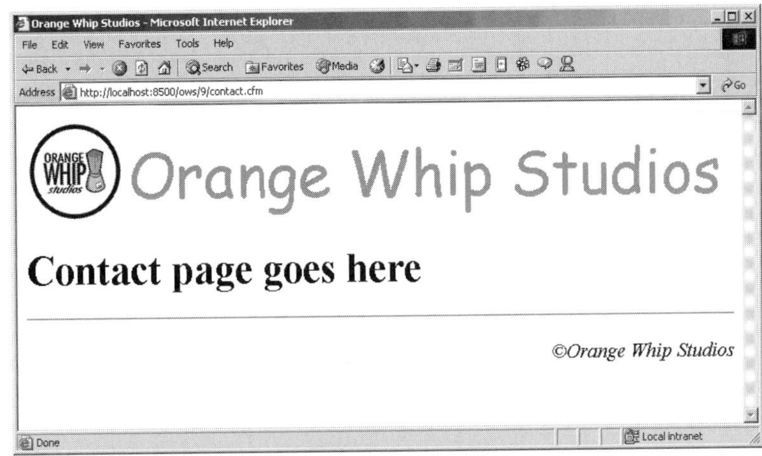

Figure 9.12

The Contact page contains the same elements as the home page.

Now that the page header and footer have been created, `<CFINCLUDE>` can be used to include them in the pages. Listing 9.16 is `home.cfm`, and Listing 9.17 is `contact.cfm`.

Listing 9.16 `home.cfm`

```
<!---
Name:        home.cfm
Author:      Ben Forta (ben@forta.com)
Description: Demonstrate use of <CFINCLUDE>
Created:     3/27/02
--->

<!--- Include page header --->
<CFINCLUDE TEMPLATE="ows_header.cfm">

<H1>Home page goes here</H1>

<!--- Include page footer --->
<CFINCLUDE TEMPLATE="ows_footer.cfm">
```

Listing 9.17 `contact.cfm`

```
<!---
Name:        contact.cfm
Author:      Ben Forta (ben@forta.com)
Description: Demonstrate use of <CFINCLUDE>
Created:     3/27/02
--->

<!--- Include page header --->
<CFINCLUDE TEMPLATE="ows_header.cfm">

<H1>Contact page goes here</H1>

<!--- Include page footer --->
<CFINCLUDE TEMPLATE="ows_footer.cfm">
```

As you can see, very little code exists in Listings 9.16 and 9.17. Each listing contains two `<CFINCLUDE>` statements: The first includes file `ows_header.cfm` (Listing 9.14), and the second includes file `ows_footer.cfm` (Listing 9.15). ColdFusion includes those two files and generates the output seen previously in Figures 9.11 and 9.12. The content that is unique to each page can be placed between the two `<CFINCLUDE>` tags.

To see the real value here, modify `ows_header.cfm` (change colors, text, or anything else) and then reload `home.cfm` and `contact.cfm` to see your changes automatically applied to both.

➜ ColdFusion supports another form of code reuse–custom tags. This subject is covered in detail in Chapter 20, "Building Reusable Components."

Revisiting Variables

The last tag this chapter discusses is `<CFPARAM>`. You won't use this tag here, but in preparation for the next chapters, I'll explain what this tag is and how it is used.

Earlier in this chapter, you used a function named `IsDefined()`, which is used to check whether a variable exists. You used `IsDefined()` to simply check for a variable's existence, but what if you wanted to create a variable with a default value if it did not exist? You could do something similar to this:

```
<CFIF NOT IsDefined("FirstName")>
   <CFSET FirstName="Ben">
</CFIF>
```

Why would you want to do this? Well, as a rule, you should not include data validation code in the middle of your core code. This is bad practice for several reasons, the most important of which are that it helps create unreliable code, makes debugging difficult, and makes code reuse very difficult. So, best practices dictate that all variable validation occur before your core code. If required variables are missing, throw an error, redirect the user to another page, or do something else. If optional variables are missing, define them and assign default values. Either way, by the time you get to your core code, you should have no need for variable checking of any kind—that should all have been done already.

And thus the type of code I just showed you.

`<CFPARAM>` has several uses, but the most common use is simply a way to shortcut the previous code. Look at the following:

```
<CFPARAM NAME="FirstName" DEFAULT="Ben">
```

When ColdFusion processes this line, it checks to see whether a variable named `FirstName` exists. If it does then the tag is ignored and processing continues. If, however, the variable does not exist, it will be created right then and there and assigned the value specified in `DEFAULT`. So, by using `<CFPARAM>` you can ensure that after that tag has been processed, one way or another the variable referred to exists. And that makes writing clean code that much easier.

TIP

`<CFPARAM>` can be used to check for (and create) variables in specific scopes, including `URL` and `FORM`. This can greatly simplify the processing of passed values, as you will see in the coming chapters.

CHAPTER 10

Creating Data-Driven Pages

IN THIS CHAPTER

Accessing Databases

In the past few chapters, you created and executed ColdFusion templates. You worked with different variable types, conditional processing, code reuse, and more.

But this chapter is where it starts to get really interesting—now it's time to learn how to connect to databases to create complete dynamic and data-driven pages.

NOTE

> The examples in this chapter, and indeed all the chapters that follow, use the data in the `ows` data sources and database. These must be present before continuing.
>
> And I'll remind you just this once, all the files created in this chapter need to go in a directory named `10` under the application root (the `ows` directory under the Web root).

For your first application, you will create a page that lists all movies in the `Films` table.

Static Web Pages

Before you create your first data-driven ColdFusion template, let's take a look at how *not* to create this page.

Listing 10.1 contains the HTML code for the movie list Web page. The HTML code is relatively simple; it contains header information and then a list of movies, one per line, separated by line breaks (the HTML `<BR>` tag).

Listing 10.1 `movies.htm`—HTML Code for Movie List

```
<HTML>
<HEAD>
    <TITLE>Orange Whip Studios - Movie List</TITLE>
</HEAD>

<BODY>

<H1>Movie List</H1>

Being Unbearably Light<BR>
Charlie's Devils<BR>
Closet Encounters of the Odd Kind<BR>
Folded Laundry, Concealed Ticket<BR>
Forrest Trump<BR>
Four Bar-Mitzvahs and a Circumcision<BR>
Geriatric Park<BR>
Gladly Ate Her<BR>
Ground Hog Day<BR>
Hannah and Her Blisters<BR>
Harry's Pottery<BR>
It's a Wonderful Wife<BR>
Kramer vs. George<BR>
Mission Improbable<BR>
Nightmare on Overwhelmed Street<BR>
Raiders of the Lost Aardvark<BR>
Silence of the Clams<BR>
Starlet Wars<BR>
Strangers on a Stain<BR>
The Funeral Planner<BR>
The Sixth Nonsense<BR>
Use Your ColdFusion II<BR>
West End Story<BR>

</BODY>
</HTML>
```

Figure 10.1 shows the output this code listing generates.

Dynamic Web Pages

Why is a static HTML file not the way to create the Web page? What would you have to do when a new movie is created, or when a movie is dropped? What would you do if a movie title or tag line changed?

You could directly modify the HTML code to reflect these changes, but you already have all this information in a database. Why would you want to have to enter it all again? You'd run the risk of making mistakes—information being misspelled, entries out of order, and possibly missing movies altogether. As the number of movies in the list grows, so will the potential for errors occurring. In addition, visitors will be looking at inaccurate information during the period between updating the table and updating the Web page.

A much easier and more reliable solution is to have the Web page display the contents of your `Films` table; this way any table changes are immediately available to all viewers. The Web page would be dynamically built based on the contents of the `Films` table.

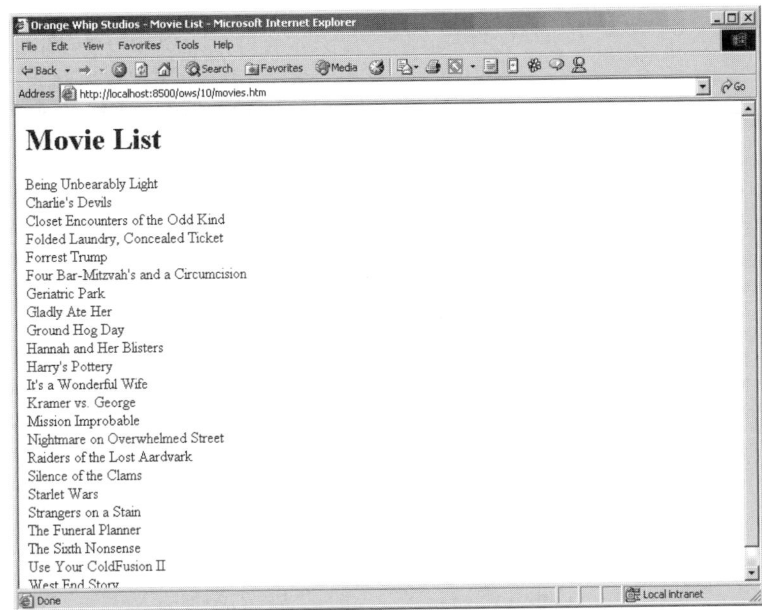

Figure 10.1

You can create the movie list page as a static HTML file.

To create your first data-driven ColdFusion template, enter the code as it appears in Listing 10.2 and save it in the `10` directory as `movies1.cfm`. (Don't worry if the ColdFusion code does not make much sense yet; I will explain it in detail in just a moment.)

Listing 10.2 `movies1.cfm`—The Basic Movie List

```
<!---
Name:        movies1.cfm
Author:      Ben Forta (ben@forta.com)
Description: First data-driven Web page
Created:     4/1/02
--->

<!--- Get movie list from database --->
<CFQUERY NAME="movies" DATASOURCE="ows">
SELECT MovieTitle
FROM Films
ORDER BY MovieTitle
</CFQUERY>

<!--- Create HTML page --->
<HTML>
<HEAD>
    <TITLE>Orange Whip Studios - Movie List</TITLE>
</HEAD>

<BODY>

<H1>Movie List</H1>
```

Listing 10.2 (continued)

```
<!--- Display movie list --->
<CFOUTPUT QUERY="movies">
#MovieTitle#<BR>
</CFOUTPUT>

</BODY>
</HTML>
```

Now, execute this page in your browser as

```
http://localhost:8500/ows/10/movies1.cfm
```

TIP

As a reminder, the port number (`8500` in the above URL) is only needed if you are using the integrated HTTP server. If you are ColdFusion with an external HTTP server then do not specify the port.

The results are shown in Figure 10.2.

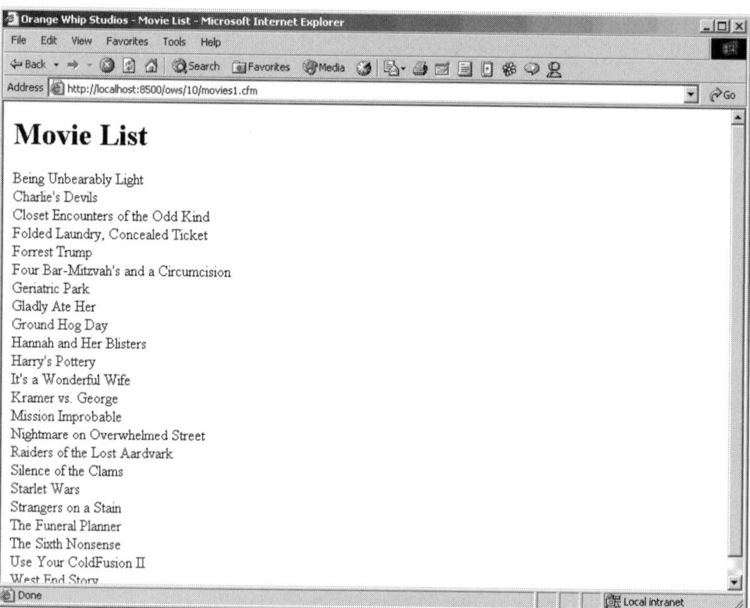

Figure 10.2

Ideally, the movie list page should be generated dynamically, based on live data.

TIP

You could also browse the page right from within Dreamweaver MX as seen in Figure 10.3. As a reminder, to do this switch to Design View (click the Show Design View button, or select Design from the View menu) and turn on Live Data View (click the Live Data View button, select Live Data from the View menu, or press Ctrl-Shift-R).

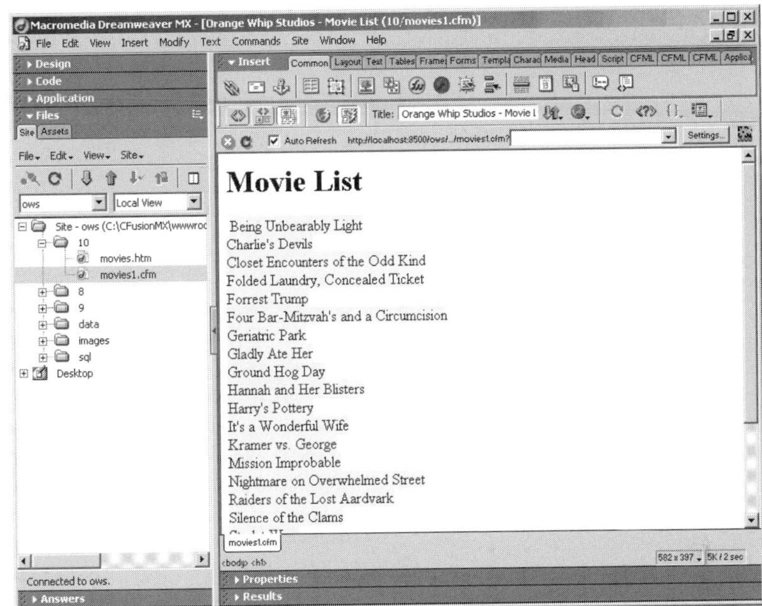

Figure 10.3

ColdFusion pages may be browsed directly within Dreamweaver MX by switching to Design View with Live Data View enabled.

Understanding Data-Driven Templates

Now compare Figure 10.1 to Figure 10.2. Can you see the difference between them? Look carefully.

Give up? The truth is that there is no difference at all (well, other than the URL that is). The screen shots are identical, and if you looked at the HTML source that generated Figure 10.2, you'd see that aside from a lot of extra whitespace, the dynamically generated code is exactly the same as the static code you entered in Listing 10.1 and nothing like the (much shorter) dynamic code you entered in Listing 10.2.

How did the code in Listing 10.2 become the HTML source code that generated Figure 10.1? Let's review the code listing carefully.

The <CFQUERY> Tag

Listing 10.2 starts off with a comment block (as should all the code you write). Then comes a ColdFusion tag called `<CFQUERY>` which submits a SQL statement to a specified data source. The SQL statement is usually a SQL `SELECT` statement, but it could also be an `INSERT`, an `UPDATE`, a `DELETE`, a stored procedure call, or any other SQL statement.

➜ See Chapter 3, "Accessing the ColdFusion Administrator," for information on how to create data sources.

➜ See Chapter 5, "Introducing SQL," for an overview of SQL and SQL statements.

The <CFQUERY> tag has several attributes, or parameters, that are passed to it when used. The <CFQUERY> in Listing 10.2 uses only two attributes:

- NAME—This attribute is used to name the query and any returned data.
- DATASOURCE—This attribute contains the name of the data source to be used.

The query NAME you specified is Movies. This name will be used later when you process the results generated by the query.

CAUTION

Do not use reserved words (words that have special meaning to ColdFusion) as your query name. For example. Do not name a query URL and URL is a reserved prefix.

NOTE

Query names passed to <CFQUERY> need not be unique to each query within your page. If you do reuse query names, subsequent <CFQUERY> calls will overwrite the results retrieved by the earlier query.

You specified ows for the DATASOURCE attribute, which is the name of the data source you created in Chapter 3. DATASOURCE is required; without it ColdFusion would not know which database to execute the SQL statement against.

The SQL statement to be executed is specified between the <CFQUERY> and </CFQUERY> tags. The following SQL statement was used, which retrieves all movie titles sorted alphabetically:

```
SELECT MovieTitle
FROM Films
ORDER BY MovieTitle
```

TIP

The SQL statement in Listing 10.2 is broken up over many lines to make the code more readable. Although it is perfectly legal to write a long SQL statement that is wider than the width of your editor, these generally should be broken up over as many lines as needed.

ColdFusion pays no attention to the actual text between the <CFQUERY> and </CFQUERY> tags (unless you include CFML tags or functions, which we'll get to later in this chapter). Whatever is between those tags gets sent to the data source for processing.

When ColdFusion encounters a <CFQUERY> tag, it creates a query request and submits it to the specified data source. The results, if any, are stored in a temporary buffer and are identified by the name specified in the NAME attribute. All this happens before ColdFusion processes the next line in the template.

NOTE

You will recall that ColdFusion tags (including the <CFQUERY> tag) are never sent to the Web server for transmission to the browser. Unlike HTML tags, which are browser instructions, CFML tags are ColdFusion instructions.

NOTE

ColdFusion does not validate the SQL code you specify. If syntax errors exist in the SQL code, ColdFusion will not let you know because that's not its job. The data source will return error messages if appropriate, and ColdFusion will display those to you. But it is the data source (and the database or database driver) that returns those error messages, not ColdFusion.

It is important to note that, at this point, no data has been displayed. <CFQUERY> retrieves data from a database table, but it does not display that data. Actually, it does nothing at all with the data—that's your job. All it does is execute a specified SQL statement when the </CFQUERY> tag is reached. <CFQUERY> has no impact on generated content at all, and retrieved data is never sent to the client (unless you send it).

The next lines in the template are standard HTML tags, headers, title, and headings. Because these are not ColdFusion tags, they are sent to the Web server and then on to the client browser.

Using <CFOUTPUT> to Display <CFQUERY> Data

Next, the query results are displayed, one row per line. To loop through the query results, the <CFOUTPUT> tag is used.

<CFOUTPUT> is the same ColdFusion output tag you used earlier (in Chapter 8, "Using ColdFusion"). This time, however, you use it to create a code block that is used to output the results of a <CFQUERY>. For ColdFusion to know which query results to output, the query name is passed to <CFOUTPUT> in the QUERY attribute. The name provided is the same that was assigned to the <CFQUERY> tag's NAME attribute. In this case, the NAME is Movies.

CAUTION

The query NAME passed to <CFQUERY> must be a valid (existing) query; otherwise, ColdFusion will generate an error.

The code between <CFOUTPUT QUERY="Movies"> and </CFOUTPUT> is the output code block. ColdFusion uses this code once for every row retrieved. Because 23 rows are currently in the Films table, the <CFOUTPUT> code is looped through 23 times. And any HTML or CFML tags within that block are repeated as well—once for each row.

NOTE

So what is the minimum number of times a <CFOUTPUT> code block will be processed? Well, that depends on whether you are using the QUERY attribute. Without a QUERY, the code block is processed once. However, with a QUERY block, it is processed once if a single row exists in the query, and not at all if the query returned no results.

TIP

You'll notice that I put the SQL query at the very top of the page instead of right where it was needed (in the middle of the output). This is the recommended way to write your code–queries should be organized at the top of the page, all together. This will help you write cleaner code and will also simplify any testing and debugging if (or rather, when) the need arises.

Using Table Columns

As explained in Chapter 8, ColdFusion uses # to delimit expressions and variables. ColdFusion expressions also can be columns retrieved by a <CFQUERY>. Whatever column name is specified is used; ColdFusion replaces the column name with the column's actual value. When ColdFusion processed the output block, it replaced #MovieTitle# with the contents of the MovieTitle column that was retrieved in the Movies query. Each time the output code block is used, that row's MovieTitle value is inserted into the HTML code.

ColdFusion-generated content can be treated as any other content in an HTML document; any of the HTML formatting tags can be applied to them. In this example, the query results must be separated by a line break (the `<BR>` tag).

Look at the following line of code:

```
#MovieTitle#<BR>
```

That code becomes the following for the movie `Being Unbearably Light`:

```
Being Unbearably Light<BR>
```

Figure 10.2 shows the browser display this template creates. It is exactly the same result as Figure 10.1, but without any actual data in the code. The output of Listing 10.2 is dynamically generated—each time the page is refreshed, the database query is executed and the output is generated.

NOTE

Want to prove this for yourself? Open the database and make a change to any of the movie titles and then refresh the Web page–you'll see that the output will reflect the changes as soon as they are made.

TIP

If you are thinking that constantly rereading the database tables seems unnecessary and likely to impact performance, you're right. Chapter 22, "Improving Performance," teaches tips and techniques to optimize the performance of data-driven sites.

The Dynamic Advantage

To see the real power of data-driven pages, take a look at Listing 10.3. This is the same code as in Listing 10.2, but a column has been added to the SQL statement (retrieving `PitchText` as well now) and the output has been modified so that it displays both the `MovieTitle` and `PitchText` columns. Save this file as `movies2.cfm` (you can edit `movies1.cfm` and use the Save As option (in the File menu) to save it as `movies2.cfm`, if you find that easier). Now, execute this page in your browser as follows:

```
http://localhost:8500/ows/10/movies2.cfm
```

TIP

Again, drop the port if not using the internal HTTP server.

Figure 10.4 shows the output generated by the revised code.

Listing 10.3 `movies2.cfm`—The Extended Movie List

```
<!---
Name:        movies2.cfm
Author:      Ben Forta (ben@forta.com)
Description: Retrieving multiple database columns
Created:     4/1/02
--->

<!--- Get movie list from database --->
<CFQUERY NAME="movies" DATASOURCE="ows">
SELECT MovieTitle, PitchText
FROM Films
```

Listing 10.3 (continued)

```
ORDER BY MovieTitle
</CFQUERY>

<!--- Create HTML page --->
<HTML>
<HEAD>
    <TITLE>Orange Whip Studios - Movie List</TITLE>
</HEAD>

<BODY>

<H1>Movie List</H1>

<!--- Display movie list --->
<CFOUTPUT QUERY="movies">
<B>#MovieTitle#</B><BR>#PitchText#<P>
</CFOUTPUT>

</BODY>
</HTML>
```

So what changed in Listing 10.3? Two things. First, the SQL statement passed to `<CFQUERY>` now retrieves two columns:

```
SELECT MovieTitle, PitchText
FROM Films
ORDER BY MovieTitle
```

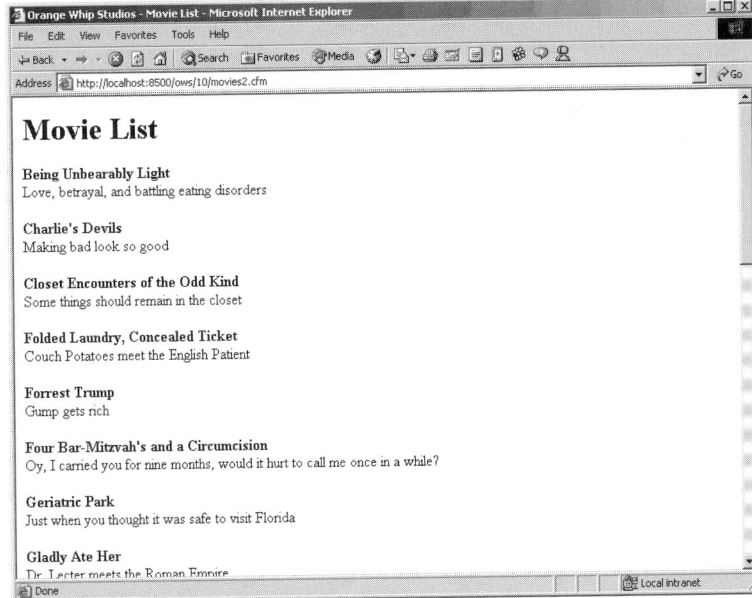

Figure 10.4

Data-driven pages are easy to modify because only the template needs changing, not every single row.

And second, the code within the <CFOUTPUT> block now reads

```
<CFOUTPUT QUERY="movies">
<B>#MovieTitle#</B><BR>#PitchText#<P>
</CFOUTPUT>
```

As you can see, two table columns are now used, each delimited by pound signs. The `MovieTitle` is displayed in bold (using <B> and </B> tags) and is followed by a line break; on the next line `PitchText` is displayed followed by a paragraph break. So, for the first row displayed, the previous code becomes

```
<B>Being Unbearably Light</B><BR>
Love, betrayal, and battling eating disorders<P>
```

Compare that to what you'd have had to change in `movies.htm` to update a static page to look like Figure 10.4, and you'll start to appreciate the dynamic page advantage.

Excited? You should be. Welcome to ColdFusion and the wonderful world of dynamic data-driven Web pages!

Displaying Database Query Results

Listings 10.2 and 10.3 displayed data in simple line-by-line outputs. But that is not all you can do with ColdFusion—in fact, there is no type of output that *can't* be generated with ColdFusion. ColdFusion has absolutely nothing to do with formatting and generating output; as long as you can write what you want (in HTML, JavaScript, Flash, DHTML, or any other client technology), ColdFusion generates the output dynamically.

To better understand this, let's take a look at some alternative output options.

Displaying Data Using Lists

HTML features support for two list types—ordered lists (in which each list item is automatically numbered) and unordered lists (in which list items are preceded by bullets). Creating HTML lists is very simple:

1. Start the list with <UL> (for an unordered list) or <OL> (for an ordered list).
2. End the list with a matching end tag (</UL> or </OL>).
3. Between the list's start and end tags, specify the list members (called *list items*) between <LI> and </LI> tags.

For example, the following is a simple bulleted (unordered) list containing two names:

```
<UL>
    <LI>Ben Forta</LI>
    <LI>Nate Weiss</LI>
</UL>
```

The numbered (ordered) equivalent of this list would be:

```
<OL>
    <LI>Ben Forta</LI>
    <LI>Nate Weiss</LI>
</OL>
```

So, how would you display the movie list in an unordered list? Listing 10.4 contains the code, which you should save as `movies3.cfm`. Execute the code in your browser (or in Dreamweaver, whichever you prefer); the output should look similar to Figure 10.5.

Listing 10.4 `movies3.cfm`—The Movie List in an Unordered List

```
<!---
Name:        movies3.cfm
Author:      Ben Forta (ben@forta.com)
Description: Data-driven HTML list
Created:     4/1/02
--->

<!--- Get movie list from database --->
<CFQUERY NAME="movies" DATASOURCE="ows">
SELECT MovieTitle, PitchText
FROM Films
ORDER BY MovieTitle
</CFQUERY>

<!--- Create HTML page --->
<HTML>
<HEAD>
    <TITLE>Orange Whip Studios - Movie List</TITLE>
</HEAD>

<BODY>

<H1>Movie List</H1>

<!--- Display movie list --->
<UL>
<CFOUTPUT QUERY="movies">
<LI><B>#MovieTitle#</B> - #PitchText#</LI>
</CFOUTPUT>
</UL>

</BODY>
</HTML>
```

Let's review Listing 10.4 together. It should look familiar because it is essentially the same code as Listing 10.3 (`movies2.cfm`), only the actual data output has changed. The new output code is:

```
<UL>
<CFOUTPUT QUERY="movies">
<LI><B>#MovieTitle#</B> - #PitchText#</LI>
</CFOUTPUT>
</UL>
```

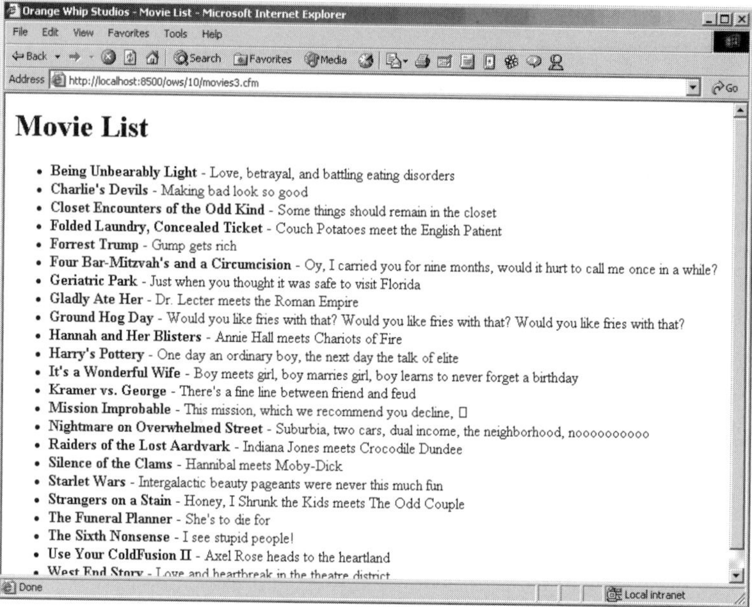

Figure 10.5

HTML unordered lists are a simple way to display data-driven output.

As you can see, the list is started before the `<CFOUTPUT>` tag, and it is ended after the `</CFOUTPUT>` tag. This is important—everything within the output block is repeated once for every row retrieved. Therefore, if the list was started inside the output block, 23 lists would be generated, with each containing a single movie—instead of a single list containing 23 movies. Only the data to be repeated should be placed inside the output block.

The output code itself is simple. For the first row, the code

```
<LI><B>#MovieTitle#</B> - #PitchText#</LI>
```

becomes

```
<LI><B>Being Unbearably Light</B> - Love, betrayal, and battling eating
disorders</LI>
```

which is a valid list item with the movie title in bold (using `<B>` and `</B>`) is followed by the tag line.

NOTE

As you can see, changing output formatting affects (or should affect) only an isolated portion of your code. As such, many developers first test whether their code works using simple output (line breaks or lists) before they write complex user interfaces. This can make development much easier (debugging core code and the user interface at the same time is not fun).

CAUTION

Be careful when placing code within an output block. Only code that is to be repeated for each row should be placed between `<CFOUTPUT>` and `</CFOUTPUT>`. Any other code should go outside the tags.

Displaying Data Using Tables

Probably the layout feature most frequently used (and most useful) is tables. HTML tables enable you to create grids that can contain text, graphics, and more. Tables are used to facilitate a more controlled page layout, including placing content side by side, in columns, and wrapped around images.

Creating tables involves three sets of tags:

- `<TABLE>` and `</TABLE>`—Used to create the table
- `<TR>` and `</TR>`—Used to create rows in the table
- `<TD>` and `</TD>`—Used to insert cells within a table row (`<TH>` and `</TH>` also can be used for header cells—essentially data cells formatted a little differently, usually centered and in bold)

So, a simple table with a header row, two columns, and two rows of data (as seen in Figure 10.6) might look like this:

```
<TABLE>
    <TR>
        <TH>First Name</TH>
        <TH>Last Name</TH>
    </TR>
    <TR>
        <TD>Ben</TD>
        <TD>Forta</TD>
    </TR>
    <TR>
        <TD>Nate</TD>
        <TD>Weiss</TD>
    </TR>
</TABLE>
```

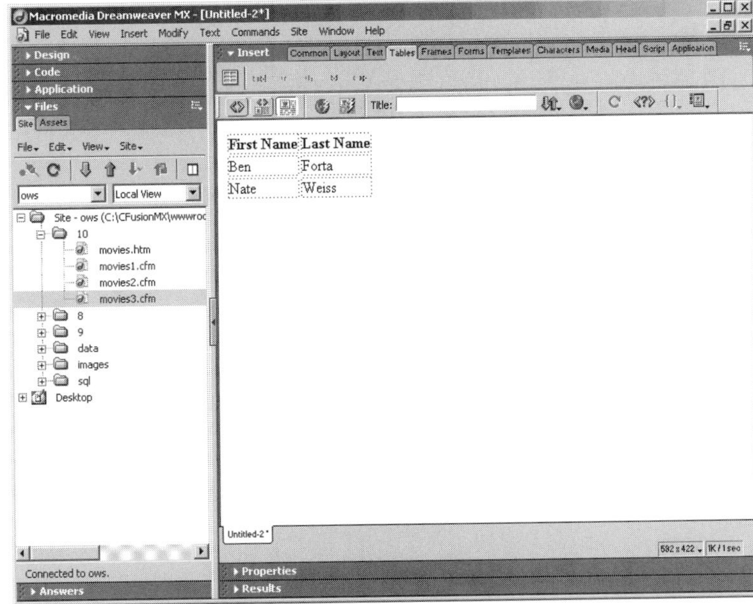

Figure 10.6

HTML tables are constructed using tags to create the table, rows, and individual cells.

TIP

The Dreamweaver MX Tables toolbar contains buttons and shortcuts to simplify table creation and manipulation.

So, with that brief intro to HTML tables, let's modify the movie listing to display the list in an HTML table. Listing 10.5 contains a modified version of the code (again, you can use Save As to create a copy of the previous version for editing). Save the file as `movies4.cfm`, and then execute it to display an output similar to that shown in Figure 10.7.

Listing 10.5 `movies4.cfm`—The Movie List in an HTML Table

```
<!---
Name:        movies4.cfm
Author:      Ben Forta (ben@forta.com)
Description: Data-driven HTML table
Created:     4/1/02
--->

<!--- Get movie list from database --->
<CFQUERY NAME="movies" DATASOURCE="ows">
SELECT MovieTitle, PitchText
FROM Films
ORDER BY MovieTitle
</CFQUERY>

<!--- Create HTML page --->
<HTML>
<HEAD>
    <TITLE>Orange Whip Studios - Movie List</TITLE>
</HEAD>

<BODY>

<H1>Movie List</H1>

<!--- Display movie list --->
<TABLE BORDER="1">
<CFOUTPUT QUERY="movies">
<TR>
 <TD>#MovieTitle#</TD>
 <TD>#PitchText#</TD>
</TR>
</CFOUTPUT>
</TABLE>

</BODY>
</HTML>
```

Once again, the code in Listing 10.5 is similar to the previous examples, and once again, it is only the output block that has changed.

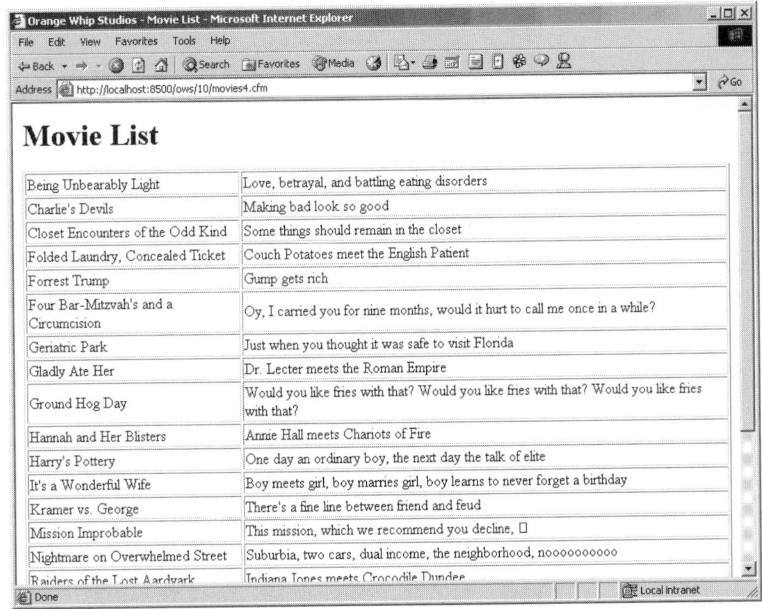

Figure 10.7

Tables provide a convenient mechanism to display data in a grid-like format.

The table is created using the code `<TABLE BORDER="1">`—a table with a border. The `<TABLE>` and `</TABLE>` tags are placed *outside* the output block (you want a single table, not a table for each row).

The table needs a new table row for each row in the query. So, the `<TR>` and `</TR>` tags are within the output loop, and within them are two cells (containing `MovieTitle` and `PitchText`).

As you can see in Figure 10.7, this code creates a single table with as many rows as there are query rows (23 in this example).

TIP

Viewing the source code generated by ColdFusion is useful when debugging template problems. When you view the source, you are looking at the complete output as it was sent to your browser. If you ever need to ascertain why a Web page does not look the way you intended it to look, a good place to start is comparing your template with the source code it generated.

You'll probably find yourself using tables extensively, so, to ensure that dynamic HTML table creation is properly understood, another example is in order.

This time the table will contain two rows for each query row. The first will contain two cells—one for the title and tag line and one for the release date. The second row will contain the movie summary (and because the summary can be lengthy, its cell spans both columns). The output generated can be seen in Figure 10.8.

Listing 10.6 contains the revised code; this time save the file as `movies5.cfm` and execute it in your browser.

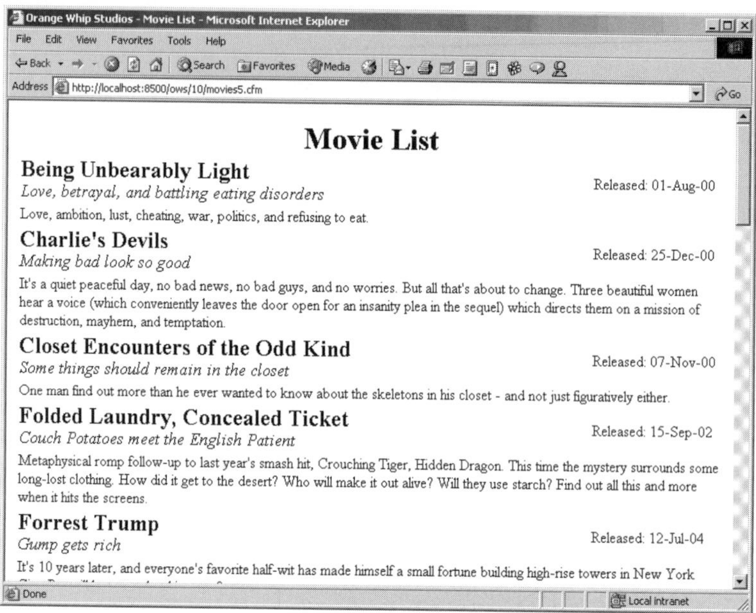

Figure 10.8 For greater control, HTML tables can contain cells that span two or more columns (and rows).

Listing 10.6 `movies5.cfm`—The Movie List in an HTML Table

```
<!---
Name:        movies5.cfm
Author:      Ben Forta (ben@forta.com)
Description: Data-driven HTML table
Created:     4/1/01
--->

<!--- Get movie list from database --->
<CFQUERY NAME="movies" DATASOURCE="ows">
SELECT MovieTitle, PitchText, Summary, DateInTheaters
FROM Films
ORDER BY MovieTitle
</CFQUERY>

<!--- Create HTML page --->
<HTML>
<HEAD>
    <TITLE>Orange Whip Studios - Movie List</TITLE>
</HEAD>

<BODY>

<!--- Display movie list --->
<TABLE>
<TR>
 <TH COLSPAN="2"><FONT SIZE="+3">Movie List</FONT></TH>
</TR>
<CFOUTPUT QUERY="movies">
<TR>
```

Listing 10.6 (continued)

```
  <TD>
   <FONT SIZE="+2"><B>#MovieTitle#</B></FONT><BR>
   <FONT SIZE="+1"><I>#PitchText#</I></FONT>
  </TD>
  <TD>Released: #DateFormat(DateInTheaters)#</TD>
 </TR>
 <TR>
  <TD COLSPAN="2">#Summary#</TD>
 </TR>
 </CFOUTPUT>
 </TABLE>

 </BODY>
 </HTML>
```

A few changes have been made in Listing 10.6. First, the `<CFQUERY> SELECT` statement has been modified to retrieve two additional columns—`Summary` contains the movie summary, and `DateInTheaters` contains the movie's public release date.

In addition, a new row has been added *before* the `<CFOUTPUT>` tag containing the following line of code:

```
<TH COLSPAN="2"><FONT SIZE="+3">Movie List</FONT></TH>
```

This creates a header cell (header contents usually are centered and displayed in bold) containing the text `Movie List` as a table title. Because the table is two columns wide, the title must span both columns, so the optional attribute `COLSPAN="2"` is specified.

The output block itself creates two rows (two sets of `<TR>` and `</TR>` tags). The first contains two cells—one with the `MovieTitle` and `PitchText` (with a line break between them) and the other with the release date formatted for display using the `DateFormat()` function. The second row contains a single cell spanning both columns and displaying `Summary`.

➜ The `DateFormat()` function was introduced in Chapter 8.

TIP

Pay close attention to which code you place within and without the `<CFOUTPUT>` block. Misplacing a `<TR>` or `</TD>` tag could result in a badly formatted HTML table, and some browsers might opt to not even display that table.

As you can see, as long as you know the basic HTML syntax and know what needs to be repeated for each database row and what doesn't, creating dynamic data-driven output is quick and painless.

TIP

ColdFusion features a tag named `<CFTABLE>` that can be used to automate the entire process of creating data-driven HTML tables. Although this tag works, I recommend against using it. HTML tables are not difficult to learn and create, and doing so is well worth the effort because you'll find that you have far more control over the exact format and output.

CAUTION

I know I have said it several times already, but because this is one of the most common beginners' mistakes (and a very aggravating one to debug at that), I'll say it one last time.

When creating dynamic output, pay special attention to what needs to be repeated and what does not. Anything that needs to be displayed once per row (either before or after the row) must go in the output block; anything else must not.

NOTE

HTML tables are a useful way to format data, but a cost is associated with using tables. For a browser to correctly display a table, it cannot display any part of that table until it has received the entire table from the Web server. This is because any row, even one near the end of the table, can affect the width of columns and how the table will be formatted. Therefore, if you display data in a table, the user will see no data at all until all the data is present. If you were to use another type of display–a list, for example–the data would be displayed as it was received. The reality of it is that the page likely will take as long to fully load with or without tables. The disadvantage of using tables is that it takes longer for any data to appear. Actual ColdFusion processing time is identical regardless of whether tables are used, but the user perception could be one of a slower application if you create large HTML tables.

Using Query Variables

So far, you have displayed data retrieved using database queries. But sometimes you'll need access to data about queries (and not just data within queries). For example, if you wanted to display the number of movies retrieved, where would you get that count from?

To simplify this type of operation, ColdFusion includes special variables in every query. Table 10.1 lists these variables, and as you can see, `RecordCount` can provide the number of rows retrieved.

Table 10.1 Query Variables

VARIABLE	DESCRIPTION
`ColumnList`	Names of columns in query results (comma-delimited list)
`ExecutionTime`	Query execution time (in milliseconds)
`RecordCount`	Number of rows in a query

To demonstrate using these special variables, create the file `movies6.cfm`, as shown in Listing 10.7. This code, which is based on `movies5.cfm`, generates the output seen in Figure 10.9. Save the code, and execute it in your browser.

Listing 10.7 `movies6.cfm`—Using Query Variables

```
<!---
Name:        movies6.cfm
Author:      Ben Forta (ben@forta.com)
Description: Using query variables
Created:     4/1/02
--->

<!--- Get movie list from database --->
<CFQUERY NAME="movies" DATASOURCE="ows">
SELECT MovieTitle, PitchText, Summary, DateInTheaters
FROM Films
ORDER BY MovieTitle
</CFQUERY>
```

Listing 10.7 (continued)

```
<!--- Create HTML page --->
<HTML>
<HEAD>
    <TITLE>Orange Whip Studios - Movie List</TITLE>
</HEAD>

<BODY>

<!--- Display movie list --->
<TABLE>
<TR>
 <CFOUTPUT>
 <TH COLSPAN="2">
  <FONT SIZE="+3">Movie List (#Movies.RecordCount# movies)</FONT>
 </TH>
 </CFOUTPUT>
</TR>
<CFOUTPUT QUERY="movies">
<TR>
 <TD>
  <FONT SIZE="+2"><B>#CurrentRow#: #MovieTitle#</B></FONT><BR>
  <FONT SIZE="+1"><I>#PitchText#</I></FONT>
 </TD>
 <TD>Released: #DateFormat(DateInTheaters)#</TD>
</TR>
<TR>
 <TD COLSPAN="2">#Summary#</TD>
</TR>
</CFOUTPUT>
</TABLE>

</BODY>
</HTML>
```

So, what changed here? Only two modifications were made to this code. The title (above the output block) now reads as follows:

```
Movie List (#Movies.RecordCount# movies)
```

`#Movies.RecordCount#` returns the number of rows retrieved—in this case, `23`. Like any other expression, the text `Movies.RecordCount` must be enclosed within pound signs and must be between `<CFOUTPUT>` and `</CFOUTPUT>` tags. But unlike many other expressions, here the prefix `Movies` is required. Why? Because this code is not within a query-driven `<CFOUTPUT>` (there is no `QUERY` attribute). Therefore, for ColdFusion to know which query's count you want, you must specify it.

TIP

Here the query name prefix is required because the query was not specified in the `<CFOUTPUT>` loop. Within an output loop, the query name is not required, but it can be used to prevent ambiguity (for example, if there were variables with the same names as table columns).

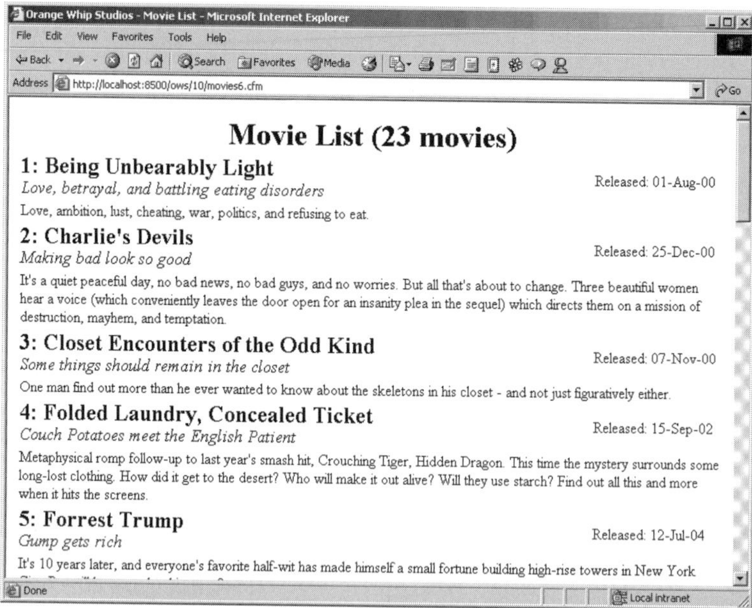

Figure 10.9

`RecordCount` can be accessed to obtain the number of rows in a query.

Here you use `RecordCount` purely for display purposes. But as you will see later in this chapter, it can be used in other ways, too (for example, checking to see whether a query returned any data at all).

Incidentally, why is `Movies.RecordCount` not in a `<CFOUTPUT QUERY="Movies">` block? I'll not answer that one because the last time I explained it, I said it would be the last time I'd do so. (That was your hint.)

The other line of code that changed is the movie title display, which now has `#CurrentRow#:` in front of it. `CurrentRow` is another special variable, but this time it's in `<CFOUTPUT>` instead of `<CFQUERY>`. Within an output loop, `CurrentRow` keeps a tally of the iterations—it contains `1` when the first row is processed, `2` when the second row is processed, and so on. In this example, it's used to number the movies (as seen in Figure 10.9).

`CurrentRow` can also be used it to implement fancy formatting, for example, alternating the background color for every other row (a "green paper" effect) as seen in Figure 10.10. Listing 10.8 is `movies7.cfm`, a modified version of `movies4.cfm` (I used that older version as it is simpler and looks better for this example).

The big change in Listing 10.8 is the `<CFIF>` statement right inside the `<CFOUTPUT>` loop. As you will recall, `<CFIF>` is used to evaluate if statements (conditions), and here the following `<CFIF>` statement is used:

```
<CFIF CurrentRow MOD 2 IS 1>
```

➜ <CFIF> was introduced back in Chapter 9, "CFML Basics".

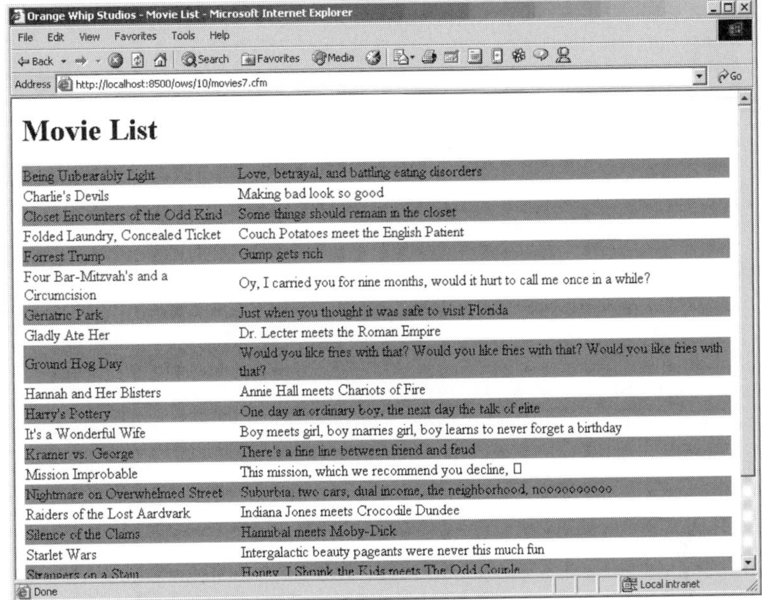

Figure 10.10

`RecordCount` can be used to alternate output colors.

Listing 10.8 `movies7.cfm`—Implementing Alternating Colors

```
<!---
Name:        movies7.cfm
Author:      Ben Forta (ben@forta.com)
Description: Implementing alternating colors
Created:     4/1/02
--->

<!--- Get movie list from database --->
<CFQUERY NAME="movies" DATASOURCE="ows">
SELECT MovieTitle, PitchText
FROM Films
ORDER BY MovieTitle
</CFQUERY>

<!--- Create HTML page --->
<HTML>
<HEAD>
    <TITLE>Orange Whip Studios - Movie List</TITLE>
</HEAD>

<BODY>

<H1>Movie List</H1>

<!--- Display movie list --->
<TABLE CELLSPACING="0">
<CFOUTPUT QUERY="movies">
<!--- What color should this row be? --->
```

Listing 10.8 (continued)

```
  <CFIF CurrentRow MOD 2 IS 1>
      <CFSET bgcolor="lime">
 <CFELSE>
      <CFSET bgcolor="white">
 </CFIF>
 <TR BGCOLOR="#bgcolor#">
  <TD>#MovieTitle#</TD>
  <TD>#PitchText#</TD>
 </TR>
 </CFOUTPUT>
 </TABLE>

 </BODY>
 </HTML>
```

`CurrentRow` contains the current loop counter as previously explained. `MOD` is an arithmetic operator which returns the reminder of an equation, and so testing for `MOD 2` is a way to check for odd or even numbers (divide a number by `2`, if the remainder is `1` the number is odd otherwise the number is even). So checking `MOD 2 IS 1` is effectively checking that *the number is odd*.

Within the `<CFIF>` statement one of two `<CFSET>` tags will be called; if the `CurrentRow` is odd then the first is called (setting a variable named `bgcolor` to `lime`), and if even then the second if called (setting `bgcolor` to `white`). Once the `</CFIF>` is reached a variable named `bgcolor` will exist and will contain a color (`lime` or `white`, depending on whether `CurrentRow` is odd or even). As the `<CFIF>` code is within the `<CFOUTPUT>` block it is processed once for every row, and so `bgcolor` is reset on each row.

➜ Refer to Chapter 8, "Using ColdFusion", for an introduction to the <CFSET> tag.

Then `bgcolor` is then passed to the `<TR>` tag's `BGCOLOR` attribute (`BGCOLOR` specifies the background color) so that on odd rows the `<TR>` tag becomes:

```
<TR BGCOLOR="lime>
```

and on even rows it becomes:

```
<TR BGCOLOR="white">
```

The result is shown in Figure 10.10.

TIP

You'll notice that I named the variable in Listing 10.8 `bgcolor`, the same as the HTML attribute with which it was used. This is not required (you may name variables as you wish) but doing so makes the code clearer as the variable's use is then blatantly obvious.

NOTE

The value in `CurrentRow` is not the row's unique ID (primary key). In fact, the number has nothing to do with the table data at all. It is merely a loop counter and should never be relied on as anything else.

Grouping Result Output

Before a new level of complexity is introduced, let's review how ColdFusion processes queries.

In ColdFusion, data queries are created using the `<CFQUERY>` tag. `<CFQUERY>` performs a SQL operation and retrieves results if any exist. Results are stored temporarily by ColdFusion and remain only for the duration of the processing of the template that contained the query.

The `<CFOUTPUT>` tag is used to output query results. `<CFOUTPUT>` takes a query name as an attribute and then loops through all the rows that were retrieved by the query. The code block between `<CFOUTPUT>` and `</CFOUTPUT>` is repeated once for each and every row retrieved.

All the examples created until now displayed results in a single list or single table.

What would you do if you wanted to process the results in subsets? For example, suppose you wanted to list movies by rating. You could change the SQL statement in the `<CFQUERY>` to retrieve the rating ID and set the sort order to be `RatingID` and then by `MovieTitle`.

This would retrieve the data in the correct order, but how would you display it? If you used `<CFOUTPUT>` as you have until now, every row created by the `<CFOUTPUT>` block would have to be the same. If one had the rating displayed, all would have to because every row that is processed is processed with the same block of code.

Look at Figure 10.11. As you can see, the screen contains nested lists. The top-level list contains the rating IDs, and within each rating ID is a second list containing all the movies with that rating. How would you create an output like this?

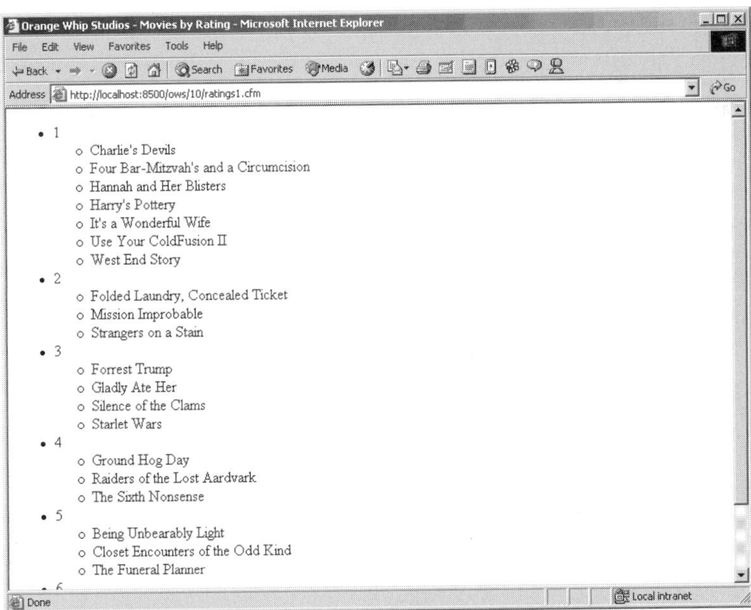

Figure 10.11

Grouping provides a means with which to display data grouped into logical sets.

Listing 10.9 contains the code for a new page; save this as `ratings1.cfm` and execute it in your browser.

Listing 10.9 `ratings1.cfm`—Grouping Query Output

```
<!---
Name:        ratings1.cfm
Author:      Ben Forta (ben@forta.com)
Description: Query output grouping
Created:     4/1/02
--->

<!--- Get movie list from database --->
<CFQUERY NAME="movies" DATASOURCE="ows">
SELECT MovieTitle, RatingID
FROM Films
ORDER BY RatingID, MovieTitle
</CFQUERY>

<!--- Create HTML page --->
<HTML>
<HEAD>
    <TITLE>Orange Whip Studios - Movies by Rating</TITLE>
</HEAD>

<BODY>

<!--- Display movie list --->
<UL>
<!--- Loop through ratings --->
<CFOUTPUT QUERY="movies" GROUP="RatingID">
<LI>#RatingID#</LI>
 <UL>
 <!--- For each rating, list movies --->
 <CFOUTPUT>
  <LI>#MovieTitle#</LI>
 </CFOUTPUT>
 </UL>
</CFOUTPUT>
</UL>

</BODY>
</HTML>
```

Listing 10.9 starts with the comment block, followed by a `<CFQUERY>` that retrieves all the movies (title and rating only) sorted by `RatingID` and `MovieTitle` (by `RatingID` and within each `RatingID` by `MovieTitle`).

The display section of the code starts by creating an unordered list—this is the outer list, which contains the ratings.

Then, `<CFOUTPUT>` is used again to create an output block, but this time the `GROUP` attribute has been added. `GROUP="RatingID"` tells the output block to loop through the outer loop only when `RatingID` changes. In other words, the outer loop is processed once per group value. So, in this example, it's processed once per `RatingID` value—regardless of the number of movies with that `RatingID`.

Then the `RatingID` is displayed, and a second unordered list is started—this is for the inner list within each `RatingID`.

Next, comes a second `<CFOUTPUT>` block that displays the `MovieTitle`. No `QUERY` is specified here; ColdFusion does not need one. Why? Because `GROUP` is being used, ColdFusion knows which query is being used and loops through the inner `<CFOUTPUT>` only as long as `RatingID` does not change.

As soon as `RatingID` changes, the inner `<CFOUTPUT>` loop stops and the inner list is terminated with a `</UL>`.

This repeats until all rows have been processed, at which time the outer `<CFOUTPUT>` terminates and the final `</UL>` is generated.

So, how many times is each `<CFOUTPUT>` processed? The movie list contains 23 rows with a total of 6 ratings. So the outer loop is processed 6 times, and the inner loop is processed 23 times. This outer list contains 6 items (each `RatingID` value), and each item contains a sublist containing the movies with that `RatingID`.

NOTE

For grouping to work, groups must be created in the exact same order as the sort order (the `ORDER BY` clause) in the SQL statement itself.

Listing 10.10 contains a modified version of Listing 10.9, this time displaying the results in an HTML table (as seen in Figure 10.12). Save Listing 10.10 as `ratings2.cfm`, and then execute it in your browser.

Listing 10.10 `ratings2.cfm`—Grouping Query Output

```
<!---
Name:        ratings2.cfm
Author:      Ben Forta (ben@forta.com)
Description: Query output grouping
Created:     4/1/02
--->

<!--- Get movie list from database --->
<CFQUERY NAME="movies" DATASOURCE="ows">
SELECT MovieTitle, RatingID
FROM Films
ORDER BY RatingID, MovieTitle
</CFQUERY>

<!--- Create HTML page --->
<HTML>
<HEAD>
    <TITLE>Orange Whip Studios - Movies by Rating</TITLE>
</HEAD>

<BODY>

<!--- Display movie list --->
<TABLE>
<!--- Loop through ratings --->
```

Listing 10.10 (CONTINUED)

```
<CFOUTPUT QUERY="movies" GROUP="RatingID">
 <TR VALIGN="top">
  <TH>
   #RatingID#
  </TH>
  <TD>
   <!--- For each rating, list movies --->
   <CFOUTPUT>
    #MovieTitle#<BR>
   </CFOUTPUT>
  </TD>
 </TR>
</CFOUTPUT>
</TABLE>

</BODY>
</HTML>
```

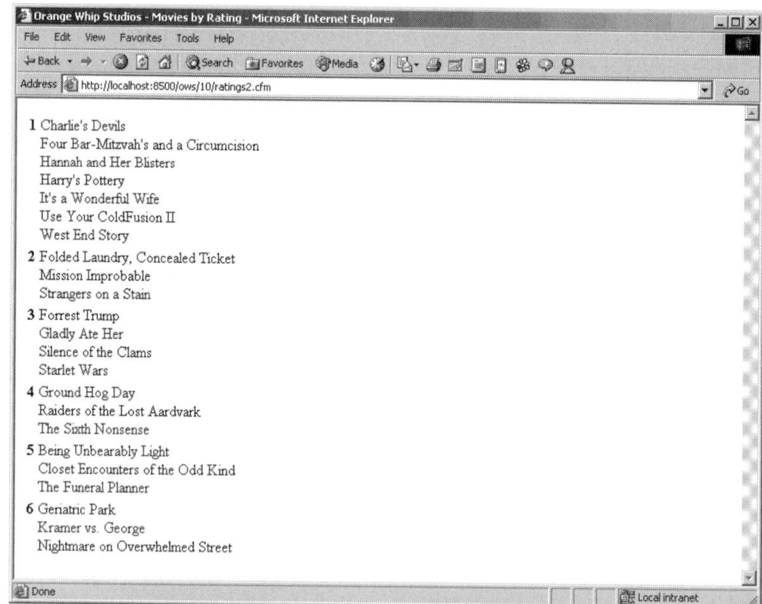

Figure 10.12

Grouped data can be used in lists, tables, and any other form of data presentation.

The only thing that has changed in Listing 10.10 is the output code. Again, the `<CFOUTPUT>` tags are nested—the outer loops through `RatingID` and the inner loops through the movies.

The HTML table is created before any looping occurs (you want only one table). Then, for each `RatingID` a new table row is created containing two cells. The left cell contains the `RatingID`, and the right cell contains the movies.

To do this, the inner `<CFOUTPUT>` loop is used in that right cell (between the `<TD>` and `</TD>` tags) so that, for each `RatingID` listed on the left, all the appropriate movies are listed on the right.

TIP

A single level of grouping is used here, but there is no limit to the number of levels in which data can be grouped. To group multiple levels (groups within groups), you simply need an additional `<CFOUTPUT>` per group (and of course, the SQL statement must sort the data appropriately).

Using Data Drill-Down

Now that you've learned almost everything you need to know about the `<CFOUTPUT>` tag, let's put it all together in a complete application.

Data drill-down is a popular form of user interface within Web applications because it enables the progressive and gradual selection of desired data. Data drill-down applications usually are made up of three levels of interface:

- A search screen
- A results screen (displaying the results of any searches)
- A details screen (displaying the details for any row selected in the results screen)

You won't create the search screen here (forms are introduced in the next chapter), but you will create the latter two screens. Your application will display a list of movies (similar to the screens created earlier in this chapter) and will allow visitors to click any movie to see detailed information about it.

Implementing Data Drill-Down Interfaces

The first screen you need to create is the details page—the one that will be displayed when a movie is selected. Figure 10.13 shows the details for one movie.

Listing 10.11 contains the code for the file `details1.cfm`. Save the code, and then execute it in your browser with this URL:

```
http://localhost:8500/ows/10/details1.cfm?FilmID=2
```

You should see a screen similar to the one shown in Figure 10.13.

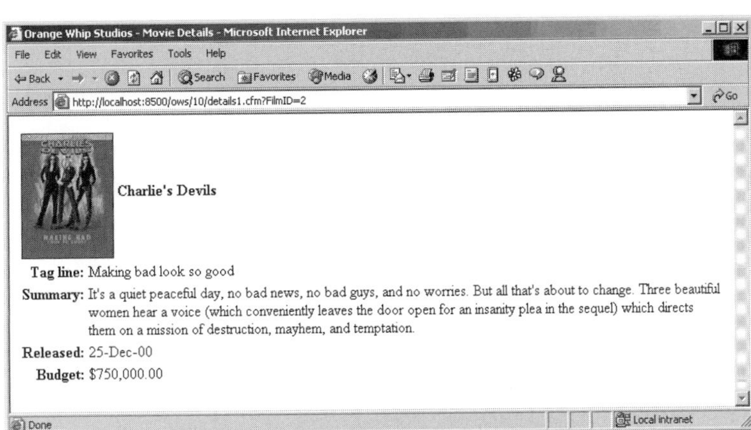

Figure 10.13

In data drill-down applications, the details page displays all the details for a specific record.

Listing 10.11 `details1.cfm`—Data Drill-Down Details

```
<!---
Name:        details1.cfm
Author:      Ben Forta (ben@forta.com)
Description: Data drill-down details
Created:     4/1/02
--->

<!--- Get a movie from database --->
<CFQUERY NAME="movie" DATASOURCE="ows">
SELECT FilmID, MovieTitle, PitchText,
       Summary, DateInTheaters, AmountBudgeted
FROM Films
WHERE FilmID=#URL.FilmID#
</CFQUERY>

<!--- Create HTML page --->
<HTML>
<HEAD>
    <TITLE>Orange Whip Studios - Movie Details</TITLE>
</HEAD>

<BODY>

<!--- Display movie details --->
<CFOUTPUT QUERY="movie">
 <TABLE>
  <TR>
   <TD COLSPAN="2">
    <IMG SRC="../images/f#FilmID#.gif" ALT="#MovieTitle#" ALIGN="MIDDLE">
    <B>#MovieTitle#</B>
   </TD>
  </TR>
  <TR VALIGN="top">
   <TH ALIGN="right">Tag line:</TH>
   <TD>#PitchText#</TD>
  </TR>
  <TR VALIGN="top">
   <TH ALIGN="right">Summary:</TH>
   <TD>#Summary#</TD>
  </TR>
  <TR VALIGN="top">
   <TH ALIGN="right">Released:</TH>
   <TD>#DateFormat(DateInTheaters)#</TD>
  </TR>
  <TR VALIGN="top">
   <TH ALIGN="right">Budget:</TH>
   <TD>#DollarFormat(AmountBudgeted)#</TD>
  </TR>
 </TABLE>
</CFOUTPUT>

</BODY>
</HTML>
```

There are several important things to point out in Listing 10.11. Let's start with the SQL statement:

```
SELECT FilmID, MovieTitle, PitchText,
       Summary, DateInTheaters, AmountBudgeted
FROM Films
WHERE FilmID=#URL.FilmID#
```

The `WHERE` clause here is used to select a specific movie by its primary key (`FilmID`). But instead of comparing it to a real number, a ColdFusion variable is used—`#URL.FilmID#`.

➜ See Chapter 5, "Introducing SQL", for a detailed explanation of the `SELECT` statement and its `WHERE` clause.

Earlier I said that ColdFusion paid no attention to the text between `<CFQUERY>` and `</CFQUERY>`, but that is not entirely true. When ColdFusion prepares the `SELECT` statement to be sent to the database driver, it checks for any CFML (tags, functions, or expressions). When it encounters `#URL.FilmID#`, it replaces that expression with whatever the value of the `URL` parameter `FilmID` is. So, if the `URL` parameter `FilmID` had a value of `2`, the generated SQL would look like this:

```
SELECT FilmID, MovieTitle, PitchText,
       Summary, DateInTheaters, AmountBudgeted
FROM Films
WHERE FilmID=2
```

This is why I had you append `?FilmID=2` to the URL when you executed this page. Without a `FilmID` parameter, this code would have failed, but we'll get to that in a moment.

The beauty of this technique is that it allows the same details page to be used for an unlimited number of database records—each `FilmID` specified generates a different page. If `FilmID` were `10`, the SQL statement would have a `WHERE` clause of `FilmID=10`, and so on.

➜ URL variables were briefly introduced in Chapter 9, "CFML Basics."

The rest of the code in Listing 10.11 is rather self-explanatory. The details are displayed in an HTML table with the title spanning two columns. Dates are formatted using the `DateFormat()` function, and monetary amounts are formatted using the `DollarFormat()` function (which, as its name suggests, formats numbers as dollar amounts).

NOTE

Support for other currencies also are available via the locale functions.

One interesting line of code, though, is the `<IMG>` tag (used to display the movie poster image):

```
<IMG SRC="../images/f#FilmID#.gif" ALT="#MovieTitle#" ALIGN="MIDDLE">
```

Binary data, like images, can be stored in databases just like any other data, but accessing these images requires special processing that is beyond the scope of this chapter. And so in this application images are stored in a directory and named using the primary key values. Therefore, in this example, the image for `FilmID 2` is `f2.gif`, and that image is stored in the `images` directory under the application root. By using `#FilmID#` in the filename, images can be referred to dynamically. In this example, for `FilmID 2` the `<IMG>` tag becomes

```
<IMG SRC="../images/f2.gif" ALT="Charlie's Devils" ALIGN="MIDDLE">
```

Try executing Listing 10.11 again, but this time do not pass the `FilmID` parameter. What happens when you execute the code? You probably received an error message similar to the one in Figure 10.14 telling you that you were referring to a variable that does not exist. You can't use `URL.FilmID` in your SQL statement if no `URL` parameter named `FilmID` exists.

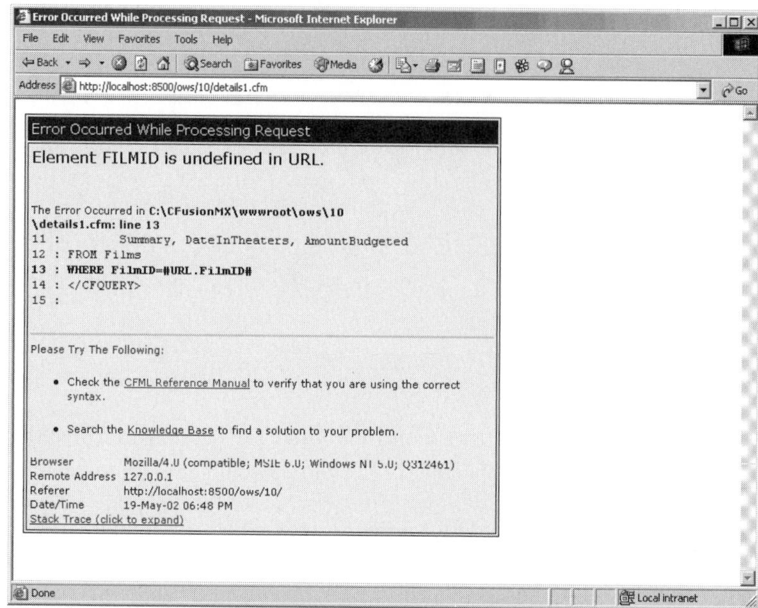

Figure 10.14

Do not refer to a variable that does not exist or an error message will be generated.

The solution (which you looked at briefly in Chapter 9) is to check that the variable exists before using it. Listing 10.12 contains an updated version of the code; save it as `details2.cfm` and execute it. What happens now if no `FilmID` is specified?

Listing 10.12 `details2.cfm`—Data Drill-Down Details

```
<!---
Name:        details2.cfm
Author:      Ben Forta (ben@forta.com)
Description: Data drill-down details with basic validation
Created:     4/1/02
--->

<!--- Make sure FilmID was passed --->
<CFIF NOT IsDefined("URL.FilmID")>
 <!--- It wasn't, send to movie list --->
 <CFLOCATION URL="movies6.cfm">
</CFIF>

<!--- Get a movie from database --->
<CFQUERY NAME="movie" DATASOURCE="ows">
SELECT FilmID, MovieTitle, PitchText,
       Summary, DateInTheaters, AmountBudgeted
FROM Films
```

Listing 10.12 (continued)

```
WHERE FilmID=#URL.FilmID#
</CFQUERY>

<!--- Create HTML page --->
<HTML>
<HEAD>
    <TITLE>Orange Whip Studios - Movie Details</TITLE>
</HEAD>

<BODY>

<!--- Display movie details --->
<CFOUTPUT QUERY="movie">
 <TABLE>
  <TR>
   <TD COLSPAN="2">
    <IMG SRC="../images/f#FilmID#.gif" ALT="#MovieTitle#" ALIGN="MIDDLE">
    <B>#MovieTitle#</B>
   </TD>
  </TR>
  <TR VALIGN="top">
   <TH ALIGN="right">Tag line:</TH>
   <TD>#PitchText#</TD>
  </TR>
  <TR VALIGN="top">
   <TH ALIGN="right">Summary:</TH>
   <TD>#Summary#</TD>
  </TR>
  <TR VALIGN="top">
   <TH ALIGN="right">Released:</TH>
   <TD>#DateFormat(DateInTheaters)#</TD>
  </TR>
  <TR VALIGN="top">
   <TH ALIGN="right">Budget:</TH>
   <TD>#DollarFormat(AmountBudgeted)#</TD>
  </TR>
 </TABLE>
</CFOUTPUT>

</BODY>
</HTML>
```

The only thing that has changed in Listing 10.12 is the inclusion of the following code *before* the `<CFQUERY>` tag:

```
<!--- Make sure FilmID was passed --->
<CFIF NOT IsDefined("URL.FilmID")>
 <!--- It wasn't, send to movie list --->
 <CFLOCATION URL="movies6.cfm">
</CFIF>
```

If `FilmID` was not passed then the user should never have gotten to this page, so why not send her where she belongs? `<CFLOCATION>` is a ColdFusion tag that redirects users to other pages (or even other sites). So, the `<CFIF>` statement checks to see whether `URL.FilmID` exists (using the `IsDefined()`

function). If it does not, the user is sent to the `movies6.cfm` page automatically. Now the SQL code can't execute without a `FilmID`. Therefore, if no `FilmID` exists, the `<CFQUERY>` tag is never even reached.

➜ The `IsDefined()` function was introduced in Chapter 9.

So far so good, but you're not there yet. Two other possible trouble spots still exist. Try executing the following URL:

```
http://localhost:8500/ows/10/details2.cfm?FilmID=1
```

`1` is a valid `FilmID`, so the movie details are displayed. But `FilmID 1` does not have a movie image, which means the `<IMG>` tag is pointing to a nonexistent image, causing a browser error (as seen in Figure 10.15).

In addition, try this URL:

```
http://localhost:8500/ows/10/details2.cfm?FilmID=1000
```

No movie with a `FilmID` of `1000` exists, so no movie is displayed, but no error message is displayed either.

Neither of these problems is critical, but they should be addressed anyway. Listing 10.13 contains a final version of the details page; save this file as `details3.cfm`.

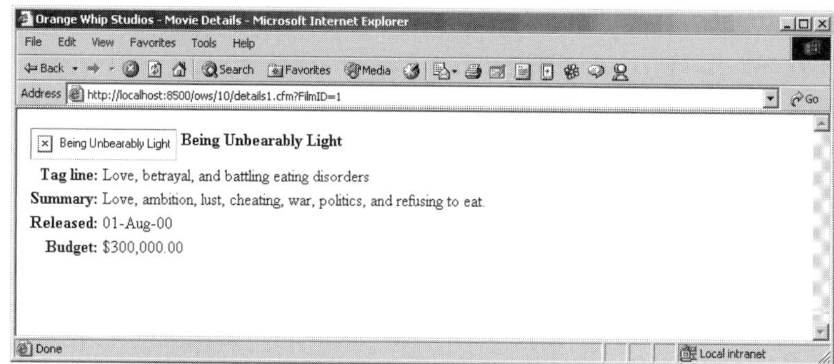

Figure 10.15

When referring to images dynamically, care must be taken to ensure that the image actually exists.

Listing 10.13 `details3.cfm`—Data Drill-Down Details

```
<!---
Name:        details3.cfm
Author:      Ben Forta (ben@forta.com)
Description: Data drill-down details with complete validation
Created:     4/1/02
--->

<!--- Movie list page --->
<CFSET list_page="movies8.cfm">

<!--- Make sure FilmID was passed --->
<CFIF NOT IsDefined("URL.FilmID")>
 <!--- It wasn't, send to movie list --->
 <CFLOCATION URL="#list_page#">
</CFIF>
```

Listing 10.13 (continued)

```
<!--- Get a movie from database --->
<CFQUERY NAME="movie" DATASOURCE="ows">
SELECT FilmID, MovieTitle, PitchText,
       Summary, DateInTheaters, AmountBudgeted
FROM Films
WHERE FilmID=#URL.FilmID#
</CFQUERY>

<!--- Make sure valid FilmID was passed --->
<CFIF movie.RecordCount IS 0>
 <!--- It wasn't, send to movie list --->
 <CFLOCATION URL="#list_page#">
</CFIF>

<!--- Build image paths --->
<CFSET image_src="../images/f#movie.FilmID#.gif">
<CFSET image_path=ExpandPath(image_src)>

<!--- Create HTML page --->
<HTML>
<HEAD>
    <TITLE>Orange Whip Studios - Movie Details</TITLE>
</HEAD>

<BODY>

<!--- Display movie details --->
<CFOUTPUT QUERY="movie">
 <TABLE>
  <TR>
   <TD COLSPAN="2">
    <!--- Check of image file exists --->
    <CFIF FileExists(image_path)>
     <!--- If it does, display it --->
     <IMG SRC="#image_src#" ALT="#MovieTitle#" ALIGN="MIDDLE">
    </CFIF>
     <B>#MovieTitle#</B>
   </TD>
  </TR>
  <TR VALIGN="top">
   <TH ALIGN="right">Tag line:</TH>
   <TD>#PitchText#</TD>
  </TR>
  <TR VALIGN="top">
   <TH ALIGN="right">Summary:</TH>
   <TD>#Summary#</TD>
  </TR>
  <TR VALIGN="top">
   <TH ALIGN="right">Released:</TH>
   <TD>#DateFormat(DateInTheaters)#</TD>
  </TR>
  <TR VALIGN="top">
   <TH ALIGN="right">Budget:</TH>
   <TD>#DollarFormat(AmountBudgeted)#</TD>
  </TR>
```

Listing 10.13 (continued)

```
  </TABLE>
</CFOUTPUT>

<P>

<!--- Link back to movie list --->
<CFOUTPUT><A HREF="#list_page#">[Movie list]</A></CFOUTPUT>

</BODY>
</HTML>
```

A lot has changed here, so let's walk through the code together.

The first line of code is a `<CFSET>` statement that sets a variable named `list_page` to `movies8.cfm`. You'll see why this was done in a moment.

Next comes the check for the `URL` parameter `FilmID`. If it is not present, `<CFLOCATION>` is used to redirect the user to the page referred to in variable `list_page` (the movie list, same as before).

Then comes the query itself—same as before; no changes there.

After the query comes a new `<CFIF>` statement that checks to see whether `Movie.RecordCount IS 0`. You will recall that `RecordCount` lets you know how many rows were retrieved by a query, so if `RecordCount IS 0`, you know that no rows were retrieved. The only way this could happen is if an invalid `FilmID` were specified, in which case `<CFLOCATION>` would be used to send the user back to the movie list page—one problem solved. (Earlier I said that I'd show you an alternative use for `RecordCount`; well, I just did.)

Next comes a set of two `<CFSET>` statements:

```
<!--- Build image paths --->
<CFSET image_src="../images/f#movie.FilmID#.gif">
<CFSET image_path=ExpandPath(image_src)>
```

The goal here is to check that the movie image exists before the `<IMG>` tag is used to insert it. ColdFusion provides a function named `FileExists()` that can be used to check for the existence of files, but there is a catch.

Images always have at least two paths by which they are referred—the actual path on disk and the URL (usually a relative URL). So, in this example, the image for `FilmID` 2 would have a path on disk that might look similar to `c:\cfusionmx\wwwroot\ows\images\f2.gif` and a URL that might look similar to `..\images\f2.gif`. Usually, you care about only the URL—the actual physical location of a file is not important within the browser. But to check for a file's existence, you do need the actual path (that is what you must pass to `FileExists()`). And the code you used to build the path (using `#FilmID#` in the `SRC`) was a relative path.

Enter the two `<CFSET>` statements. The first simply creates a variable named `image_src` that contains the dynamically generated relative filename (in the case of `FilmID` 2, it would be `..\images\f2.gif`), the same technique used in the `<IMG>` tag in the previous versions of this code. The second uses a ColdFusion function named `ExpandPath()` that converts relative paths to complete physical paths (here saving that path to `image_path`).

At this point, no determination has been made as to whether to display the image. All you have done is created two variables, each containing a path—one physical, suitable for using with `FileExists()`, and one relative, suitable for use in an `<IMG>` tag.

Next comes the details display, which is the same as it was before, except now the `<IMG>` tag is enclosed within a `<CFIF>` statement that checks whether `FileExists(image_path)`. If the image exists, `FileExists()` returns `TRUE` and the `<IMG>` tag is inserted using `image_src` as the `SRC`. If `FileExists()` returns `FALSE` (meaning the movie had no image), the `<IMG>` tag is not generated—problem two solved.

NOTE

Of course, the two variables `image_path` and `image_src` are not actually necessary, and the code would have worked if the processing was all done inline. But, the approach used here is cleaner, more intuitive, easier to read and will help you write better code.

At the very bottom of the page is a new link that enables users to get back to the movie list page. This link also uses the `list_page` variable. And by now, I hope the reason that a variable for the movie link URL is used is blatantly obvious. The code now has three locations that refer to the movie list file. Had they all been hard-coded, making changes would involve more work and would be more error-prone (the likelihood of you missing one occurrence grows with the number of occurrences). By using a variable, all that needs to change is the variable assignment at the top of the page—the rest all works as is.

The last thing to do is to update the movie listing page so it contains links to the new `details3.cfm` page. Listing 10.14 contains the revised movie listing code (based on `movies6.cfm`). Save it as `movies8.cfm`, and then execute it to see a page similar to the one shown in Figure 10.16.

Listing 10.14 `movies8.cfm`—Data Drill-Down Results Page

```
<!---
Name:        movies8.cfm
Author:      Ben Forta (ben@forta.com)
Description: Data drill-down
Created:     4/1/02
--->

<!--- Get movie list from database --->
<CFQUERY NAME="movies" DATASOURCE="ows">
SELECT FilmID, MovieTitle, PitchText, Summary, DateInTheaters
FROM Films
ORDER BY MovieTitle
</CFQUERY>

<!--- Create HTML page --->
<HTML>
<HEAD>
    <TITLE>Orange Whip Studios - Movie List</TITLE>
</HEAD>

<BODY>

<!--- Display movie list --->
<TABLE>
<TR>
```

Listing 10.14 (continued)

```
<CFOUTPUT>
 <TH COLSPAN="2">
  <FONT SIZE="+3">Movie List (#Movies.RecordCount# movies)</FONT>
 </TH>
</CFOUTPUT>
</TR>
<CFOUTPUT QUERY="movies">
<TR>
 <TD>
  <FONT SIZE="+2">
  <B>#CurrentRow#: <A HREF="details3.cfm?FilmID=#URLEncodedFormat(Trim(FilmID))#">
#MovieTitle#</A></B>
  </FONT>
  <BR>
  <FONT SIZE="+1">
  <I>#PitchText#</I>
  </FONT>
 </TD>
 <TD>Released: #DateFormat(DateInTheaters)#</TD>
</TR>
<TR>
 <TD COLSPAN="2">#Summary#</TD>
</TR>
</CFOUTPUT>
</TABLE>

</BODY>
</HTML>
```

Just two changes have been made in Listing 10.14. The `SELECT` statement in the `<CFQUERY>` now also retrieves the `FilmID` column—you need that to pass to the details page. (You will recall that the details page needs the `FilmID` passed as a `URL` parameter.)

The display of `MovieTitle` has been changed to read

```
<A HREF="details3.cfm?FilmID=#URLEncodedFormat(Trim(FilmID))#">#MovieTitle#</A>
```

The HTML `<A HREF>` tag is used to create links to other pages. The text between the `<A>` and `</A>` tags is clickable, and when it's clicked, the user is taken to the URL specified in the `HREF` attribute. So, the tag `<A HREF="details3.cfm">Click here</A>` displays the text `Click here`, which, if clicked, takes the user to page `details3.cfm`.

But you need `FilmID` to be passed to the details page, so for `FilmID 1` the `HREF` needed would read

```
<A HREF="details3.cfm?FilmID=1>Being Unbearably Light</A>
```

And for `FilmID 2` it would have to be

```
<A HREF="details3.cfm?FilmID=2>Charlie's Devils</A>
```

The links are created using the `FilmID` column so that the URL parameter `FilmID` is correctly populated with the appropriate value for each movie. As ColdFusion loops through the movies, it creates a link for each one of them. The links all point to the same page—`details3.cfm`. The only thing that differs is the value passed to the `FilmID` parameter, and this value is then used in `details3.cfm` to display the correct movie. So, for the movie with `FilmID` of `1`, the URL correctly becomes

```
<A HREF="details3.cfm?FilmID=1>Being Unbearably Light</A>
```

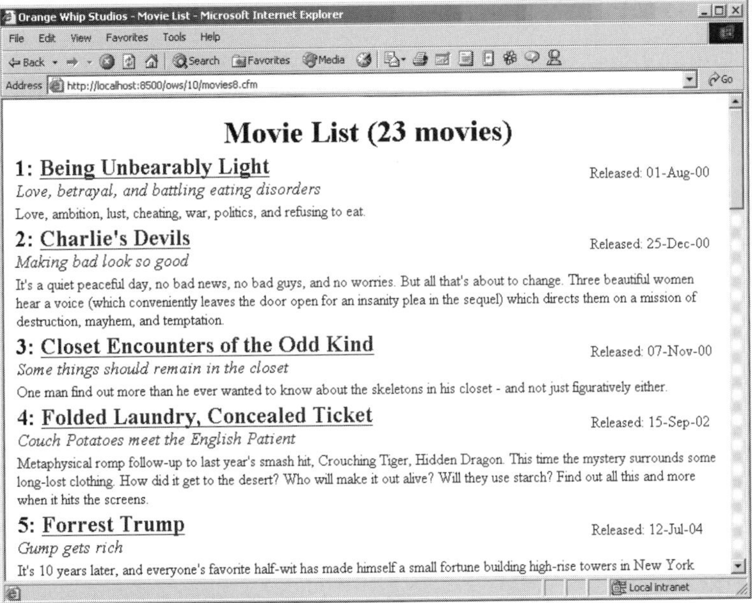

Figure 10.16

Dynamically generated URLs make creating data drill-down interfaces easy.

Try it out; you should be able to click any movie to see the details and then click the link at the bottom of the details page to get back.

Pretty impressive for just two files containing less than 150 lines of ColdFusion code (including all HTML and comments).

NOTE

You probably noticed that when constructing URLs for an `HREF`, two functions were used, `Trim()` and `URLEncodedFormat()`, instead of just referring to the column directly.

`Trim()` was used to get rid of any extra spaces (if any existed). URLs have size limitations, and care should be taken to not waste URL space.

The `URLEncodedFormat()` function is even more important. As you already know, **?** is used to separate the URL from any parameters passed to it, = is used to assign parameter values, and **&** is used to separate parameters. Of course, this means that these characters can't be used within URL parameter values; many others can't be used, either (spaces, periods, and so on).

So, how are these values passed? They're passed using a special format in which characters are replaced by a set of numbers that represent them. On the receiving end, the numbers can be converted back to the original characters (and ColdFusion does this for you automatically).

The `URLEncodedFormat()` function takes a string and returns a version of it that is URL safe.

When you populate a URL from a variable (any variable, including a database column), you run the risk that the values used might contain these illegal characters–characters that need to be converted. Therefore, you always should use `URLEncodedFormat()` (as was done in the previous example) so that if any invalid characters exist, they will be converted automatically and transparently. (Even in this chapter's example, in which you know `FilmID` contains only numbers that are safe, it still pays to encode the values in case someone changes something someday.)

Displaying Data Using Frames

Another form of data drill-down, albeit a less popular one, involves the use of HTML *frames*. Frames enable you to split your browser window in two or more windows and control what gets displayed within each. ColdFusion templates are very well suited for use within frames.

Creating frames involves creating multiple templates (or HTML pages). Each window in a frame typically displays a different template; you need two templates if you have two windows. In addition, one more page is always used to lay out and create the frames.

When the frames are created, each window is titled with a unique name. In a non-framed window, the new page is opened in the same window every time you select a hyperlink, replacing whatever contents were there previously. In a framed window, you can use the window name to control the destination for any output.

Figure 10.17 shows a frames-based version of the movie listing application. As you can see, movies are listed on the left, and when a movie is selected its details are displayed on the right.

Now that you know how frames work, the first thing you need to do is create the template to define and create the frames. The code for template `frame.cfm` is shown in Listing 10.15.

This template first defines the frames. `<FRAMESET COLS="250,*">` creates two columns (or windows)—one 250 pixels wide and the other as wide as the remaining space allows.

TIP

Sizes also can be specified as percentages, so `<FRAMESET COLS="50%,50%">` would create two windows, each `50%` of the width of the browser.

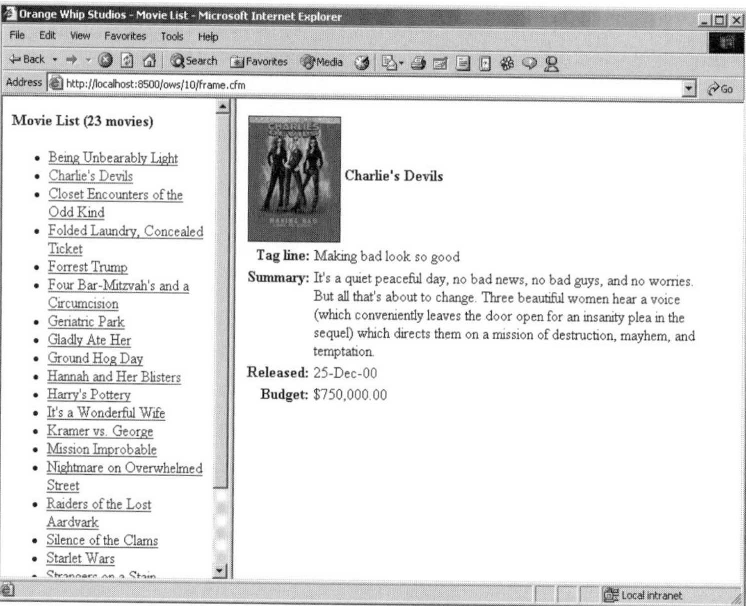

Figure 10.17

Frames-based interfaces are effective for data drill-down applications.

Listing 10.15 `frame.cfm`—ColdFusion-Powered Frames

```
<!---
Name:        frame.cfm
Author:      Ben Forta (ben@forta.com)
Description: Frames for frames-based data drill-down
Created:     4/1/02
--->

<HTML>
<HEAD>
    <TITLE>Orange Whip Studios - Movie List</TITLE>
</HEAD>

<!-- frames -->
<FRAMESET COLS="250,*">
    <FRAME NAME="left" SRC="frame_movies.cfm">
    <FRAME NAME="right" SRC="frame_blank.cfm">
</FRAMESET>
```

The two columns are then defined: `<FRAME NAME="left" SRC="frame_movies.cfm">` creates the left frame; the `NAME` attribute names the window; and the `SRC` attribute specifies the name of the template to initially display within the window when the frame is first displayed. Listing 10.16 contains the code for the file `movies.cfm`.

Listing 10.16 `frame_movies.cfm`—Movie List for Left Frame

```
<!---
Name:        frame_movies.cfm
Author:      Ben Forta (ben@forta.com)
Description: Left frame for data drill-down
Created:     4/1/02
--->

<!--- Get movie list from database --->
<CFQUERY NAME="movies" DATASOURCE="ows">
SELECT FilmID, MovieTitle
FROM Films
ORDER BY MovieTitle
</CFQUERY>

<BODY>

<CFOUTPUT>
<B>Movie List (#Movies.RecordCount# movies)</B>
</CFOUTPUT>

<!--- Movie list --->
<UL>
 <CFOUTPUT QUERY="movies">
  <LI><A HREF="frame_details.cfm?FilmID=#URLEncodedFormat(Trim(FilmID))#"
TARGET="right">#MovieTitle#</A>
 </CFOUTPUT>
</UL>

</BODY>
```

No movie is selected when the frame is first displayed, and therefore no information exists to display in the details window (the right frame). You obviously can't display movie information in that frame before the user selects the movie to view, so instead you display an empty page. `SRC="frame_blank.cfm"` loads a blank page in the frame named `right`, the source for which is shown in Listing 10.17.

Listing 10.17 `frame_blank.cfm`—Initial Blank Right Frame

```
<!---
Name:        frame_blank.cfm
Author:      Ben Forta (ben@forta.com)
Description: Blank initial frame content
Created:     4/1/02
--->

<BODY>
</BODY>
```

Listing 10.16 (`frame_movies.cfm`) contains code similar to the code used in previous listings in this chapter. The only difference is the link itself. The `<A>` tag now contains a new attribute: `TARGET="right"`. `TARGET` specifies the name of the target window in which to open the URL. Because you named the right window `right` (you named the left window `left`), when a link is clicked in the left window, the appropriate URL is opened in the right window.

TIP

Frames can be named with any names you want, but be careful not to reuse frame names unless you want to reuse the same frame. To open links in a new window (effectively creating a frame as needed), use the target of `_new`.

The link itself is a file named `frame_details.cfm` (a modified version of the details files created earlier). Listing 10.18 contains the source for this file.

Listing 10.18 `frame_details.cfm`—Movie Details for Right Frame

```
<!---
Name:        frame_details.cfm
Author:      Ben Forta (ben@forta.com)
Description: Detail for frames-based data drill-down
Created:     4/1/02
--->

<!--- Make sure FilmID was passed --->
<CFIF NOT IsDefined("URL.FilmID")>
 <!--- This should never happen --->
 <CFLOCATION URL="frame_blank.cfm">
</CFIF>

<!--- Get a movie from database --->
<CFQUERY NAME="movie" DATASOURCE="ows">
SELECT FilmID, MovieTitle, PitchText,
       Summary, DateInTheaters, AmountBudgeted
FROM Films
WHERE FilmID=#URL.FilmID#
```

Listing 10.18 (continued)

```
</CFQUERY>

<!--- Make sure valid FilmID was passed --->
<CFIF movie.RecordCount IS 0>
 <!--- This should never happen --->
 <CFLOCATION URL="frame_blank.cfm">
</CFIF>

<!--- Build image paths --->
<CFSET image_src="../images/f#movie.FilmID#.gif">
<CFSET image_path=ExpandPath(image_src)>

<!--- Create HTML page --->
<BODY>

<!--- Display movie details --->
<CFOUTPUT QUERY="movie">
 <TABLE>
  <TR>
   <TD COLSPAN="2">
    <!--- Check if image file exists --->
    <CFIF FileExists(image_path)>
     <!--- If it does, display it --->
     <IMG SRC="#image_src#" ALT="#MovieTitle#" ALIGN="MIDDLE">
    </CFIF>
    <B>#MovieTitle#</B>
   </TD>
  </TR>
  <TR VALIGN="top">
   <TH ALIGN="right">Tag line:</TH>
   <TD>#PitchText#</TD>
  </TR>
  <TR VALIGN="top">
   <TH ALIGN="right">Summary:</TH>
   <TD>#Summary#</TD>
  </TR>
  <TR VALIGN="top">
   <TH ALIGN="right">Released:</TH>
   <TD>#DateFormat(DateInTheaters)#</TD>
  </TR>
  <TR VALIGN="top">
   <TH ALIGN="right">Budget:</TH>
   <TD>#DollarFormat(AmountBudgeted)#</TD>
  </TR>
 </TABLE>
</CFOUTPUT>

<P>

</BODY>
```

Listing 10.18 should be self-explanatory by this point. The only real change here is that if no `FilmID` is passed, or if `FilmID` is invalid (neither condition should ever actually occur, but it pays to be safe), file `blank.cfm` is loaded. You could change this to display an appropriate error message if you want.

After you have created all four files (`frame.cfm`, `frame_blank.cfm`, `frame_movies.cfm`, and `frame_details.cfm`), execute the application in your browser by going to the following URL:

```
http://localhost:8500/ows/10/frame.cfm
```

You should see a screen similar to the one shown previously in Figure 10.17. Try clicking any link on the left; the appropriate movie will be displayed on the right.

And there you have it—two simple tags, `<CFQUERY>` and `<CFOUTPUT>`, generating any output you can imagine.

Debugging Dynamic Database Queries

Before we finish this chapter, there is something you should be aware of. Look at the following code:

```
<!--- Get a movie from database --->
<CFQUERY NAME="movie" DATASOURCE="ows">
SELECT FilmID, MovieTitle, PitchText,
       Summary, DateInTheaters, AmountBudgeted
FROM Films
WHERE FilmID=#URL.FilmID#
</CFQUERY>
```

As you now know, this code builds a dynamic SQL statement—the expression `#URL.FilmID#` is replaced by the contents of that variable to construct a complete SQL `SELECT` statement at runtime.

This particular example is a simple one, a single expression is used in a simple `WHERE` clause. But as the complexity of the expressions (or the number of them) increases, so does the chance that you'll introduce problems in your SQL. And to find these problems, you'll need to know exactly what SQL was generated by ColdFusion—taking into account all dynamic processing.

Fortunately, ColdFusion enables you to do this. In Chapter 3, "Accessing the ColdFusion Administrator," I mentioned the debugging screens (and told you that we'd use them in this chapter). The debugging screens can be used to append debug output to the bottom of generated pages, as seen in Figure 10.18.

As you can see, the appended output contains database query information (including the SQL, number of rows retrieved, and execution time), page execution time, passed parameters, CGI variables, and much more.

To try this for yourself, see Chapter 3 for instructions on turning on debug output. Once enabled, execute any page in your browser and the debug output will be appended automatically.

NOTE

If you are browsing files within Dreamweaver MX the debug output will be displayed in the results window beneath the editor.

TIP

Most ColdFusion developers find that the tags you have learned thus far, `<CFQUERY>`, `<CFOUTPUT>`, `<CFSET>`, `<CFIF>`, and `<CFLOCATION>`, account for almost all the CFML code they ever write. As such, it is highly recommended that you try every example in this chapter before proceeding.

Figure 10.18

Debug output can be used to discover the dynamic SQL generated by ColdFusion.

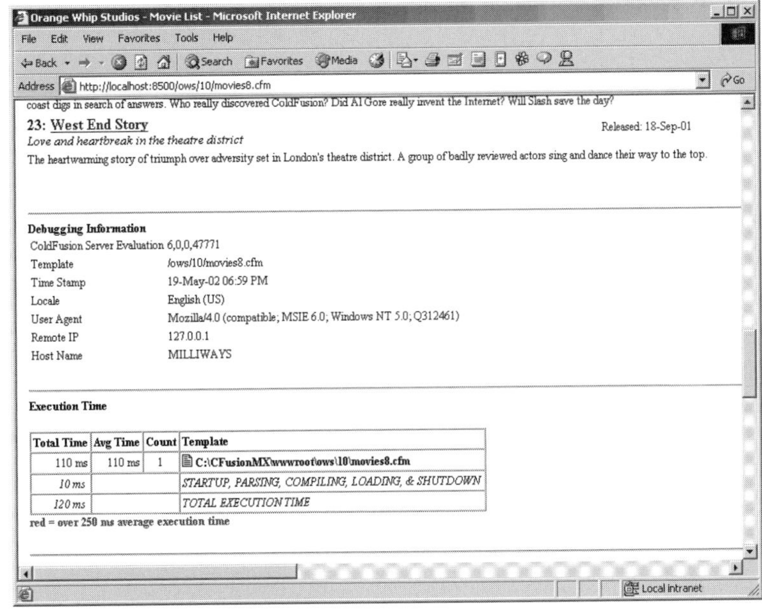

CHAPTER 11

ColdFusion Forms

IN THIS CHAPTER

Using Forms

In Chapter 10, "Creating Data-Driven Pages," you learned how to create ColdFusion templates that dynamically display data retrieved from databases. The `Films` table has just 23 rows, so the data fit easily within a Web browser window and required only minimal scrolling.

What do you do if you have hundreds or thousands of rows? Displaying all that data in one long list is impractical. Scrolling through lists of movies to find the one you want just doesn't work well. The solution is to enable users to search for what they want by specifying what they are looking for. You can allow them to enter a title, actors, or part of the tag-line, and then you can display only the movies that meet the search criteria.

To accomplish this solution, you need to do two things. First, you must create your search form using the HTML `<FORM>` tags. Second, you must create a template that builds SQL `SELECT` statements dynamically based on the data collected and submitted by the form.

➜ See Chapter 5, "Introducing SQL," for an explanation of the SELECT statement.

Creating Forms

Before you can create a search form, you need to learn how ColdFusion interacts with HTML forms. Listing 11.1 contains the code for a sample form that prompts for a first and last name. Create this template, and then save it in a new folder named `11` (under the application root) as `form1.cfm`.

TIP

Just a reminder, the files created in this chapter are in directory `11`, so use that in your URLs too.

Listing 11.1 `form1.cfm`—HTML Forms can be Used to Collect and Submit Data to ColdFusion for Processing

```
<!---
Name:        forms.cfm
Author:      Ben Forta (ben@forta.com)
Description: Introduction to forms
Created:     4/15/02
--->

<HTML>
<HEAD>
    <TITLE>Learning ColdFusion Forms 1</TITLE>
</HEAD>

<BODY>

<!--- Movie search form --->
<FORM ACTION="form1_action.cfm" METHOD="POST">

Please enter the movie name and then click
<B>Process</B>.
<P>
Movie:
<INPUT TYPE="text" NAME="MovieTitle">
<BR>
<INPUT TYPE="submit" VALUE="Process">

</FORM>

</BODY>
</HTML>
```

Execute this code to display the form, as shown in Figure 11.1.

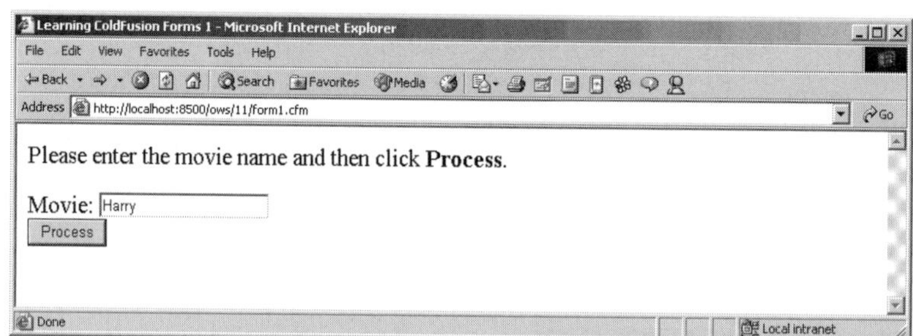

Figure 11.1

You can use HTML forms to collect data to be submitted to ColdFusion.

This form is simple, with a single data entry field and a submit button, but it helps clearly demonstrate how forms are used to submit data to ColdFusion.

Using HTML Form Tags

You create HTML forms by using the `<FORM>` tag. `<FORM>` usually takes two parameters passed as tag attributes. The `ACTION` attribute specifies the name of the script or program the Web server should execute in response to the form's submission. To submit a form to ColdFusion, you specify the name of the ColdFusion template that will process the form. The following example specifies that the template `form1_action.cfm` should process the submitted form:

```
ACTION="form1_action.cfm"
```

The `METHOD` attribute specifies how data is sent back to the Web server. As a rule, all ColdFusion forms should be submitted as type `POST`.

CAUTION

The default submission type is not `POST`; it is usually `GET`. If you omit the `METHOD="POST"` attribute from your form tag, you run the risk of losing form data–particularly in long forms or forms with `TEXTAREA` controls.

Your form has only a single data entry field: `<INPUT TYPE="text" NAME="MovieTitle">`. This is a simple text field. The `NAME` attribute in the `<INPUT>` tag specifies the name of the field, and ColdFusion uses this name to refer to the field when it is processed.

Each field in a form usually is given a unique name. If two fields have the same name, both sets of values are returned to be processed and are separated by a comma. You usually want to be able to validate and manipulate each field individually, so each field should have its own name. The notable exceptions are the check box and radio button input types, which will be described shortly.

The last item in the form is an `<INPUT>` of type `submit`. The submit `<INPUT>` type creates a button that, when clicked, submits the form contents to the Web server for processing. Almost every form has a submit button (or a graphic image that acts like a submit button). The `VALUE` attribute specifies the text to display within the button, so `<INPUT TYPE="submit" VALUE="Process">` creates a submit button with the text `Process` in it.

TIP

When you're using an `INPUT` type of submit, you always should specify button text by using the `VALUE` attribute. If you don't, the default text `Submit Query` (or something similar) is displayed, and this text is likely to confuse your users.

Form Submission Error Messages

If you enter a movie title into the field and submit the form right now, you will receive a ColdFusion error message similar to the one shown in Figure 11.2. This error says that file `form1_action.cfm` cannot be found.

This error message, of course, is perfectly valid. You submitted a form to be passed to ColdFusion and processed it with a template, but you have not created that template yet. Your next task, then, is to create a template to process the form submission.

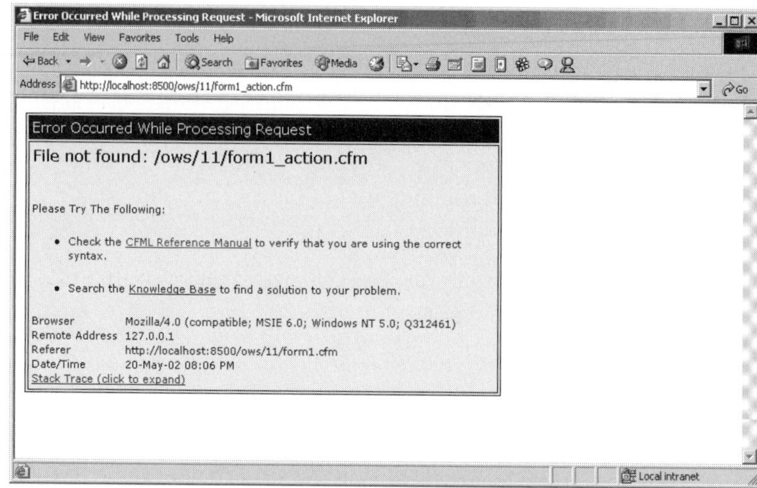

Figure 11.2

ColdFusion returns an error message when it cannot process your request.

Processing Form Submissions

To demonstrate how to process returned forms, you must create a simple template that echoes the movie title you entered. The template is shown in Listing 11.2.

Listing 11.2 `form1_action.cfm`—Processing Form Fields

```
<!---
Name:        form1_action.cfm
Author:      Ben Forta (ben@forta.com)
Description: Introduction to forms
Created:     4/15/02
--->

<HTML>
<HEAD>
    <TITLE>Learning ColdFusion Forms 1</TITLE>
</HEAD>

<BODY>

<!--- Display search text --->
<CFOUTPUT>
<B>Movie title:</B> #FORM.MovieTitle#
</CFOUTPUT>

</BODY>
</HTML>
```

Processing Text Submissions

By now the `<CFOUTPUT>` tag should be familiar to you; you use it to mark a block of code that ColdFusion should parse and process. The line `<B>Movie title:</B> #FORM.MovieTitle#` is processed by ColdFusion. `#FORM.MovieTitle#` is replaced with the value you entered in the `MovieTitle` form field.

NOTE

Use of the prefix **FORM** is optional. Using it prevents ambiguity and improves performance, but it also makes the code less reusable.

➜ See Chapter 8, "Using ColdFusion," for a detailed discussion of the ColdFusion `<CFOUTPUT>` tag.

Create a template called `form1_action.cfm` that contains the code in Listing 11.2 and save it. Then resubmit your name by clicking the form's submit button again. This time you should see a browser display similar to the one shown in Figure 11.3. Whatever name you enter in the Movie field in the form is displayed.

As you can see, `FORM` fields are used in ColdFusion like any other variable type.

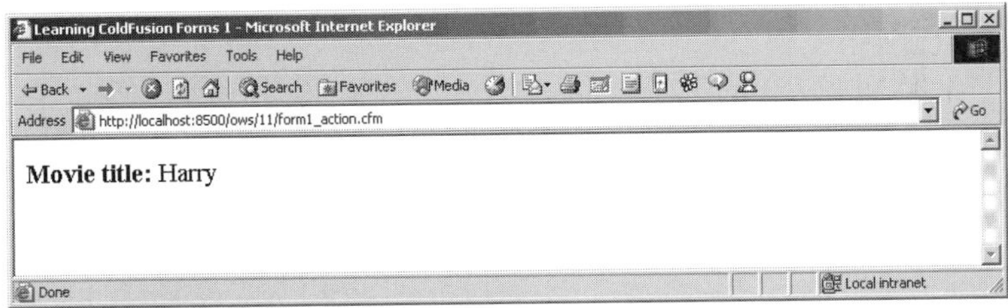

Figure 11.3

Submitted form fields can be displayed simply by referring to the field name.

Processing Check Boxes and Radio Buttons

Other input types you will frequently use are check boxes and radio buttons.

- *Check boxes* are used to select options that have one of two states: on or off, yes or no, and true or false. To ask a visitor whether he wants to be added to a mailing list, for example, you would create a check box field. If the user selects the box, his name is added to the mailing list; if the user does not select the box, his name is not added.
- *Radio buttons* are used to select one of at least two mutually exclusive options. You can implement a field prompting for payment type with options such as Cash, Check, Credit card, or P.O.

The code example in Listing 11.3 creates a form that uses both option buttons and check box fields.

Listing 11.3 `form2.cfm`—Using Check Boxes and Radio Buttons

```
<!---
Name:        form2.cfm
Author:      Ben Forta (ben@forta.com)
Description: Introduction to forms
Created:     4/15/02
--->

<HTML>

<HEAD>
    <TITLE>Learning ColdFusion Forms 2</TITLE>
</HEAD>

<BODY>

<!--- Payment and mailing list form --->
<FORM ACTION="form2_action.cfm" METHOD="POST">

Please fill in this form and then click <B>Process</B>.
<P>
<!--- Payment type radio buttons --->
Payment type:<BR>
<INPUT TYPE="radio" NAME="PaymentType" VALUE="Cash">Cash<BR>
<INPUT TYPE="radio" NAME="PaymentType" VALUE="Check">Check<BR>
<INPUT TYPE="radio" NAME="PaymentType" VALUE="Credit card">Credit card<BR>
<INPUT TYPE="radio" NAME="PaymentType" VALUE="P.O.">P.O.
<P>
<!--- Mailing list checkbox --->
Would you like to be added to our mailing list?
<INPUT TYPE="checkbox" NAME="MailingList" VALUE="Yes">
<P>
<INPUT TYPE="submit" VALUE="Process">

</FORM>

</BODY>

</HTML>
```

Figure 11.4 shows how this form appears in your browser.

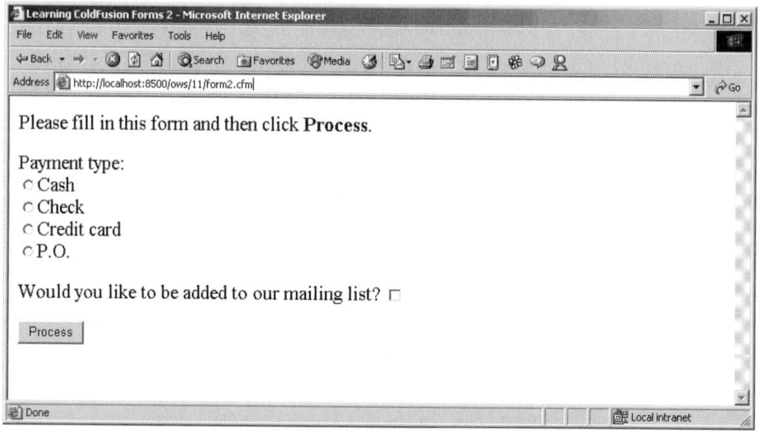

Figure 11.4

You can use input types of option buttons and check boxes to facilitate the selection of options.

Before you create `form2_action.cfm` to process this form, you should note a couple of important points. First, look at the four lines of code that make up the Payment Type radio button selection:

```
<INPUT TYPE="radio" NAME="PaymentType" VALUE="Cash">Cash<BR>
<INPUT TYPE="radio" NAME="PaymentType" VALUE="Check">Check<BR>
<INPUT TYPE="radio" NAME="PaymentType" VALUE="Credit card">Credit card<BR>
<INPUT TYPE="radio" NAME="PaymentType" VALUE="P.O.">P.O.
```

Each one contains the exact same `NAME` attribute—`NAME="PaymentType"`. The four `<INPUT>` fields have the same name so your browser knows they are part of the same set. If each radio button had a separate name, the browser would not know that these buttons are mutually exclusive and thus would allow the selection of more than one button.

Another important point is that, unlike `<INPUT>` type text, radio buttons do not prompt the user for any textual input. Therefore, you must use the `VALUE` attribute for the browser to associate a particular value with each radio button. The code `VALUE="Cash"` instructs the browser to return the value `Cash` in the `PaymentType` field if that radio button is selected.

Now that you understand radio button and check box fields, you're ready to create a template to process them. Create a template called `form2_action.cfm` using the template code in Listing 11.4.

Listing 11.4 `form2_action.cfm`—Processing Option Buttons and Check Boxes

```
<!---
Name:        form2_action.cfm
Author:      Ben Forta (ben@forta.com)
Description: Introduction to forms
Created:     4/15/02
--->

<HTML>

<HEAD>
   <TITLE>Learning ColdFusion Forms 2</TITLE>
</HEAD>

<BODY>

<!--- Display feedback to user --->
<CFOUTPUT>

<!--- Payment type --->
Hello,<BR>
You selected <B>#FORM.PaymentType#</B> as your payment type.<BR>

<!--- Mailing list --->
<CFIF MailingList IS "Yes">
 You will be added to our mailing list.
<CFELSE>
 You will not be added to our mailing list.
</CFIF>

</CFOUTPUT>

</BODY>

</HTML>
```

The form processing code in Listing 11.4 displays the payment type the user selects. The field `PaymentType` is fully qualified with the `FORM` field type to prevent name collisions.

When the check box is selected, the value specified in the `VALUE` attribute is returned; in this case, the value is `Yes`. If the `VALUE` attribute is omitted, the default value of `on` is returned.

➜ See Chapter 9, "CFML Basics," for details on using the `<CFIF>` tag.

Now, execute `form2.cfm` in your browser, select a payment option, and then select the mailing list check box. Click the Process button. Your browser display should look similar to the one shown in Figure 11.5.

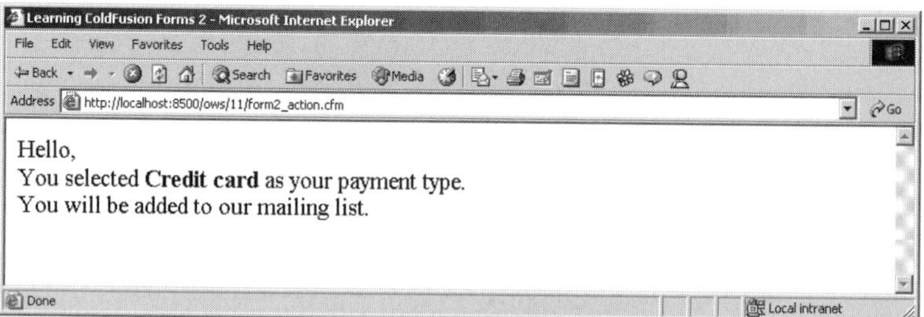

Figure 11.5

You can use ColdFusion templates to process user-selected options.

That worked exactly as intended, so now get ready to complicate things a little. Reload template `form2.cfm` and submit it without selecting a payment type or with the `MailingList` check box not selected. ColdFusion generates an error message, as shown in Figure 11.6. As you can see, the field you do not select generates a `variable is undefined` error.

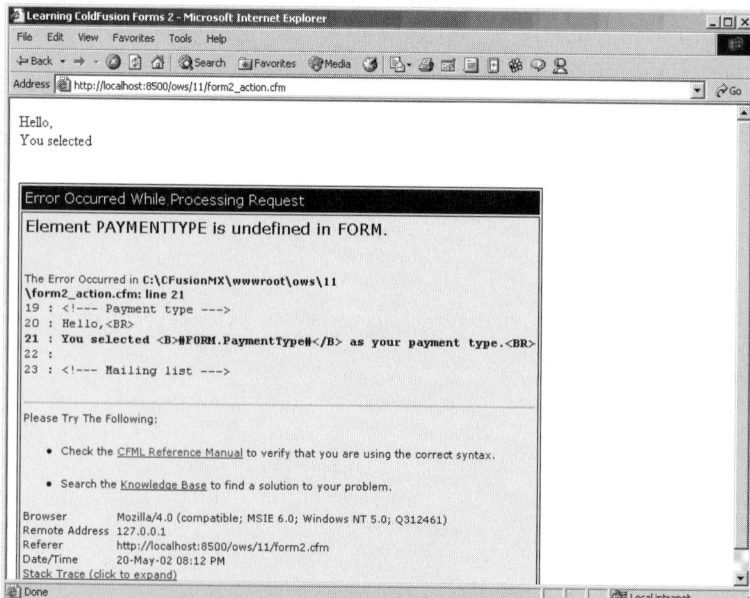

Figure 11.6

Option buttons or check boxes that are submitted with no value generate a ColdFusion error.

Check the code in Listing 11.3 to verify that the form fields do in fact exist. Why does ColdFusion report that the form field does not exist? That is one of the quirks of HTML forms. If you select a check box, the `on` value is submitted; however, *nothing* is submitted if you do not select the check box—not even an empty field. The same is true of radio buttons: If you make no selection, the field is not submitted at all. (This behavior is the exact opposite of the text `<INPUT>` type, which returns empty fields as opposed to no field.)

How do you work around this limitation? You can choose from a couple of solutions.

The first: Modify your form processing script to check which fields exist by using the `#IsDefined()#` function and, if the field exists, process it.

The second: The simpler solution is to prevent the browser from omitting fields that are not selected. You can modify the radio button field so that one radio button is pre-selected. This way, users will have to make a selection or use the pre-selected option. To pre-select a radio button, just add the attribute `CHECKED` to it.

Check boxes are trickier because by their nature they must be able to be turned off. Check boxes are used for on/off states, and, when the check box is off, there is no value to submit. The solution here is to set a default value in the `ACTION` template. As you have already learned, this can be done easily using the `<CFPARAM>` tag. Look at this code:

```
<CFPARAM NAME="FORM.MailingList" DEFAULT="No">
```

When ColdFusion encounters this line, it checks to see whether a variable named `FORM.MailingList` exists. If it does, processing continues. If it does not exist, though, ColdFusion creates the variable and sets the value to whatever is specified in the `DEFAULT` attribute. The key here is that either way—whether the variable exists or not—the variable does exist after the `<CFPARAM>` tag is processed. It is therefore safe to refer to that variable further down the template code.

The updated form is shown in Listing 11.5. The first option button in the `PaymentType` field is modified to read `<INPUT TYPE="radio" NAME="PaymentType" VALUE="Cash" CHECKED>`. The `CHECKED` attribute ensures that a button is checked. The `MailingList` check box has a `VALUE` of `Yes` when it is checked, and the `<CFPARAM>` in the action page ensures that if `MailingList` is not checked, the value automatically is set to `No`.

Listing 11.5 `form3.cfm`—Pre-Selecting Form Field Values

```
<!---
Name:        form3.cfm
Author:      Ben Forta (ben@forta.com)
Description: Introduction to forms
Created:     4/15/02
--->

<HTML>

<HEAD>
    <TITLE>Learning ColdFusion Forms 3</TITLE>
</HEAD>

<BODY>
```

Listing 11.5 (continued)

```
<!--- Payment and mailing list form --->
<FORM ACTION="form3_action.cfm" METHOD="POST">

Please fill in this form and then click <B>Process</B>.
<P>
<!--- Payment type radio buttons --->
Payment type:<BR>
<INPUT TYPE="radio" NAME="PaymentType" VALUE="Cash" CHECKED>Cash<BR>
<INPUT TYPE="radio" NAME="PaymentType" VALUE="Check">Check<BR>
<INPUT TYPE="radio" NAME="PaymentType" VALUE="Credit card">Credit card<BR>
<INPUT TYPE="radio" NAME="PaymentType" VALUE="P.O.">P.O.
<P>
<!--- Mailing list checkbox --->
Would you like to be added to our mailing list?
<INPUT TYPE="checkbox" NAME="MailingList" VALUE="Yes">
<P>
<INPUT TYPE="submit" VALUE="Process">

</FORM>

</BODY>

</HTML>
```

Create and save this template as `form3.cfm`. Then create a new file named `form3_action.cfm` containing the code in `form2_action.cfm`, and add the following code to the top of the page (right below the comments).:

```
<!--- Initialize variables --->
<CFPARAM NAME="MailingList" DEFAULT="No">
```

Try using it and experiment with the two fields. You'll find that this form is reliable and robust, and it does not generate ColdFusion error messages, no matter which options are selected (or not).

Processing List Boxes

Another field type you will frequently use is the list box. Using list boxes is an efficient way to enable users to select one or more options. If a list box is created to accept only a single selection, you can be guaranteed that a value is always returned. If you don't set one of the options to be preselected, the first one in the list is selected. An option always has to be selected.

List boxes that allow multiple selections also allow no selections at all. If you use a multiple-selection list box, you once again have to find a way to ensure that ColdFusion does not generate `variable is undefined` errors.

Listing 11.6 contains the same data-entry form you just created, but it replaces the option buttons with a list box. Save this template as `form4.cfm`, and then test it with your browser.

Listing 11.6 `form4.cfm`—Using a `<SELECT>` List Box for Options

```
<!---
Name:        form4.cfm
Author:      Ben Forta (ben@forta.com)
Description: Introduction to forms
Created:     4/15/02
--->

<HTML>

<HEAD>
    <TITLE>Learning ColdFusion Forms 4</TITLE>
</HEAD>

<BODY>

<!--- Payment and mailing list form --->
<FORM ACTION="form3_action.cfm" METHOD="POST">

Please fill in this form and then click <B>Process</B>.
<P>
<!--- Payment type select list --->
Payment type:<BR>
<SELECT NAME="PaymentType">
    <OPTION VALUE="Cash">Cash</OPTION>
    <OPTION VALUE="Check">Check</OPTION>
    <OPTION VALUE="Credit card">Credit card</OPTION>
    <OPTION VALUE="P.O.">P.O.</OPTION>
</SELECT>
<P>
<!--- Mailing list checkbox --->
Would you like to be added to our mailing list?
<INPUT TYPE="checkbox" NAME="MailingList" VALUE="Yes">
<P>
<INPUT TYPE="submit" VALUE="Process">

</FORM>

</BODY>

</HTML>
```

For this particular form, the browser display shown in Figure 11.7 is probably a better user interface. The choice of whether to use radio buttons or list boxes is yours, and no hard and fast rules exist as to when to use one versus the other. The following guidelines, however, might help you determine which to use:

- If you need to allow the selection of multiple items or of no items at all, use a list box.
- List boxes take up less screen space. With a list box, 100 options take up no more precious real estate than a single option.
- Radio buttons present all the options to the users without requiring mouse clicks (and statistically, users more often than not select options that are readily visible).

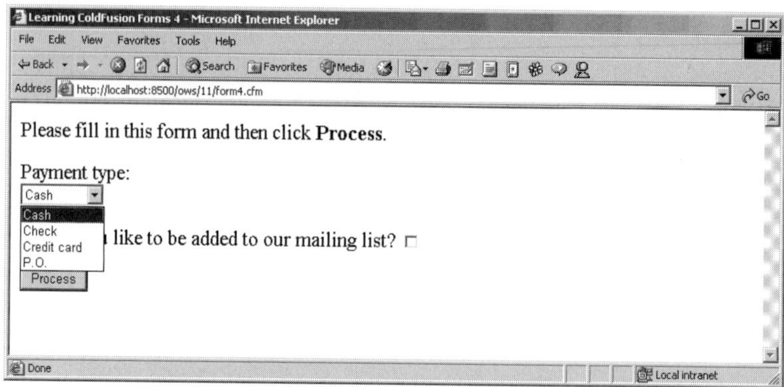

Figure 11.7

You can use HTML list boxes to select one or more options.

Processing Text Areas

Text area fields are boxes in which the users can enter free-form text. When you create a text area field, you specify the number of rows and columns of screen space it should occupy. This area, however, does not restrict the amount of text users can enter. The field scrolls both horizontally and vertically to enable the users to enter more text.

Listing 11.7 creates an HTML form with a text area field for user comments. The field's width is specified as a number of characters that can be typed on a single line; the height is the number of lines that are displayed without scrolling.

TIP

The `<TEXTAREA>` `COLS` attribute is specified as a number of characters that can fit on a single line. This setting is dependent on the font in which the text is displayed, and the font is browser specific. Be sure you test any `<TEXTAREA>` fields in more than one browser because a field that fits nicely in one might not fit at all in another.

Listing 11.7 `form5.cfm`—Using a Text Area Field

```
<!---
Name:        form5.cfm
Author:      Ben Forta (ben@forta.com)
Description: Introduction to forms
Created:     4/15/02
--->

<HTML>

<HEAD>
    <TITLE>Learning ColdFusion Forms 5</TITLE>
</HEAD>

<BODY>

<!--- Comments form --->
<FORM ACTION="form5_action.cfm" METHOD="POST">
```

Listing 11.7 (continued)

```
Please enter your comments in the box provided, and then click <B>Send</B>.
<P>
<TEXTAREA NAME="Comments" ROWS="6" COLS="40"></TEXTAREA>
<P>
<INPUT TYPE="submit" VALUE="Send">

</FORM>

</BODY>

</HTML>
```

Listing 11.8 contains ColdFusion code that displays the contents of a `<TEXTAREA>` field.

Listing 11.8 `form5_action.cfm`—Processing Free-Form Text Area Fields

```
<!---
Name:        form5_action.cfm
Author:      Ben Forta (ben@forta.com)
Description: Introduction to forms
Created:     4/15/02
--->

<HTML>

<HEAD>
    <TITLE>Learning ColdFusion Forms 5</TITLE>
</HEAD>

<BODY>

<!--- Display feedback to user --->
<CFOUTPUT>

Thank you for your comments. You entered:
<P>
<B>#FORM.comments#</B>

</CFOUTPUT>

</BODY>

</HTML>
```

Figure 11.8 shows the `<TEXTAREA>` field you created, and Figure 11.9 shows how ColdFusion displays the field.

Try entering line breaks (by pressing the Enter key) in the text field and then submit it. What happens to the line breaks? Line break characters are considered whitespace characters (just like spaces) by your browser, and all whitespace is ignored by browsers. `WHITESPACE IS IGNORED` is displayed no differently than `WHITESPACE    IS    IGNORED`.

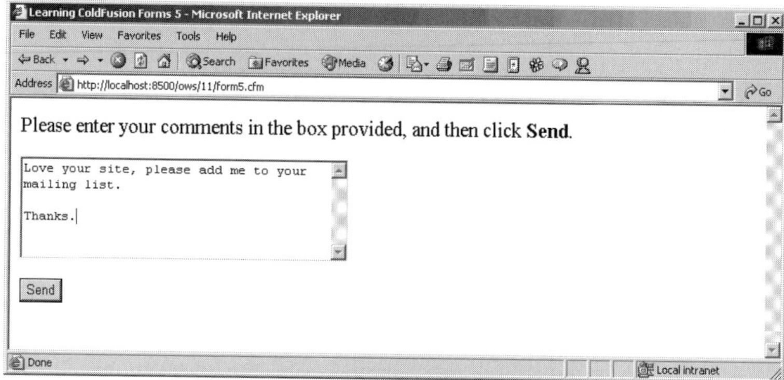

Figure 11.8

The HTML <TEXTAREA> field is a means by which you can accept free-form text input from users.

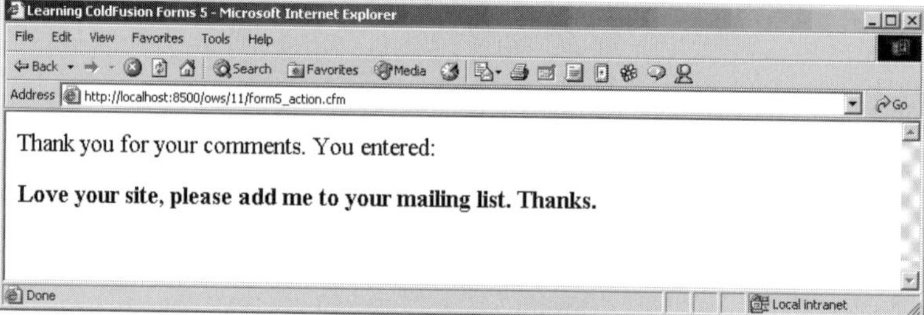

Figure 11.9

Without ColdFusion output functions, <TEXTAREA> fields are not displayed with line breaks preserved.

The only way to display line breaks is to replace the line break with an HTML paragraph tag: `<P>`. You therefore have to parse through the entire field text and insert `<P>` tags wherever necessary. Fortunately, ColdFusion makes this task a simple one. The ColdFusion `#ParagraphFormat()#` function automatically replaces every double line break with a `<P>` tag. (Single line breaks are not replaced because ColdFusion has no way of knowing whether the next line is a new paragraph or part of the previous one.)

TIP

The ColdFusion `Replace()` and `ReplaceList()` functions can be used instead of `ParagraphFormat()` to have greater control over the paragraph formatting. These functions are explained in Appendix C, "ColdFusion Function Reference."

The code in Listing 11.9 contains the same comments form as the one in Listing 11.7, with two differences. First, default field text is provided. Unlike other `<INPUT>` types, `<TEXTAREA>` default text is specified between `<TEXTAREA>` and `</TEXTAREA>` tags—not in a `VALUE` attribute.

Second, you use the `WRAP` attribute to wrap text entered into the field automatically. `WRAP="VIRTUAL"` instructs the browser to wrap to the next line automatically, just as most word processors and editors do.

NOTE

Some older browsers do not support the `<TEXTAREA>` `WRAP` attribute. These browsers ignore the attribute and require the users to enter line breaks manually. Because the attribute is ignored when not supported, you can safely use this option when necessary; your forms do not become incompatible with older browsers.

Listing 11.9 `form6.cfm`—The HTML `<TEXTAREA>` Field with Wrapping Enabled

```
<!---
Name:        form6.cfm
Author:      Ben Forta (ben@forta.com)
Description: Introduction to forms
Created:     4/15/02
--->

<HTML>

<HEAD>
    <TITLE>Learning ColdFusion Forms 6</TITLE>
</HEAD>

<BODY>

<!--- Comments form --->
<FORM ACTION="form6_action.cfm" METHOD="POST">

Please enter your comments in the box provided, and then click <B>Send</B>.
<P>
<TEXTAREA NAME="Comments" ROWS="6" COLS="40" WRAP="virtual">
Enter your comments here ...
</TEXTAREA>
<P>
<INPUT TYPE="submit" VALUE="Send">

</FORM>

</BODY>

</HTML>
```

Listing 11.10 shows the template to display the user-supplied comments. The Comments field code is changed to `#ParagraphFormat(FORM.Comments)#`, ensuring that multiple line breaks are maintained and displayed correctly, as shown in Figure 11.10.

Listing 11.10 `form6_action.cfm`—Using the `ParagraphFormat()` Function to Preserve Line Breaks

```
<!---
Name:        form6_action.cfm
Author:      Ben Forta (ben@forta.com)
Description: Introduction to forms
Created:     4/15/02
--->

<HTML>

<HEAD>
    <TITLE>Learning ColdFusion Forms 6</TITLE>
</HEAD>

<BODY>

<!--- Display feedback to user --->
<CFOUTPUT>
```

Listing 11.10 (continued)

```
Thank you for your comments. You entered:
<P>
<B>#ParagraphFormat(FORM.comments)#</B>

</CFOUTPUT>

</BODY>

</HTML>
```

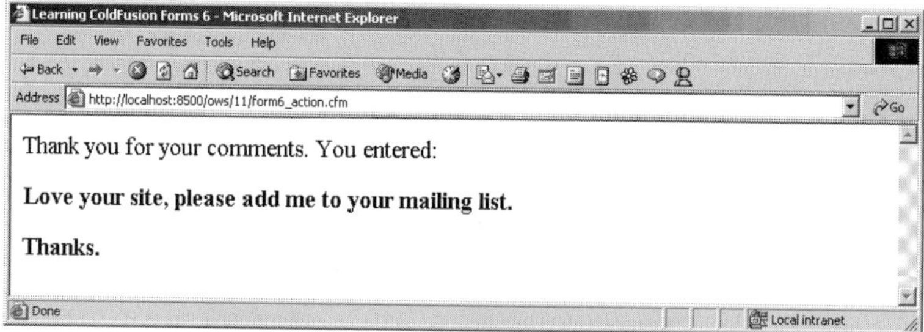

Figure 11.10 You should use the ColdFusion `ParagraphFormat()` function to display `<TEXTAREA>` fields with their line breaks preserved.

Processing Buttons

The HTML forms specification supports only two types of buttons. Almost all forms, including all the forms you create in this chapter, have a submit button. Submit, as its name implies, instructs the browser to submit the form fields to a Web server.

TIP

Most newer browsers actually require no submit button at all and force a submit if the Enter key is pressed.

The second supported button type is reset. *Reset* clears all form entries and restores default values if any existed. Any text entered into `<INPUT TYPE="text">` or `<TEXTAREA>` fields is cleared, as are any check box, list box, and option button selections. Many forms have reset buttons, but you never need more than one.

On the other hand, you might want more than one submit button. For example, if you're using a form to modify a record, you could have two submit buttons: one for Update and one for Delete. (Of course, you also could use two forms to accomplish this task.) If you create multiple submit buttons, you must name the button with the `NAME` attribute and be sure to assign a different `VALUE` attribute for each. The code in Listing 11.11 contains a reset button and two submit buttons.

Listing 11.11 `form7.cfm`—Template with a Reset Button and Multiple Submit Buttons

```
<!---
Name:        form7.cfm
Author:      Ben Forta (ben@forta.com)
Description: Introduction to forms
Created:     4/15/02
--->

<HTML>
```

Listing 11.11 (CONTINUED)

```
<HEAD>
    <TITLE>Learning ColdFusion Forms 7</TITLE>
</HEAD>

<BODY>

<!--- Update/delete form --->
<FORM ACTION="form7_action.cfm" METHOD="POST">

<P>

Movie:
<INPUT TYPE="text" NAME="MovieTitle">

<P>
<!--- Submit buttons --->
<INPUT TYPE="submit" NAME="Operation" VALUE="Update">
<INPUT TYPE="submit" NAME="Operation" VALUE="Delete">
<!--- Reset button --->
<INPUT TYPE="reset" VALUE="Clear">

</FORM>

</BODY>

</HTML>
```

The result of this code is shown in Figure 11.11.

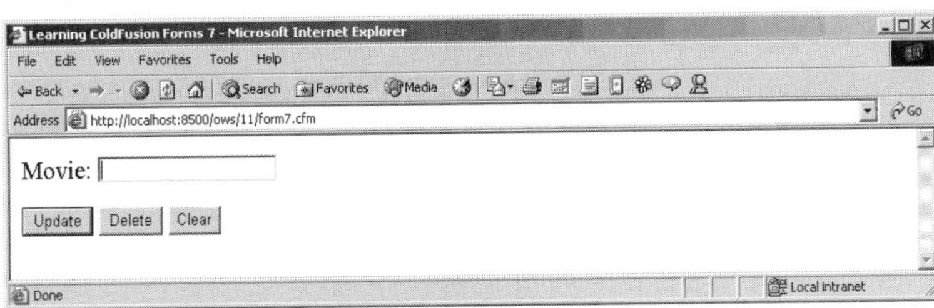

Figure 11.11

When you're using multiple submit buttons, you must assign a different value to each button.

When you name submit buttons, you treat them as any other form field. Listing 11.12 demonstrates how to determine which submit button was clicked. The code `<CFIF FORM.Operation IS "Update">` checks whether the Update button was clicked, and `<CFELSEIF FORM.Operation IS "Delete">` checks whether Delete was clicked, but only if Update was not clicked.

Listing 11.12 `form7_action.cfm`—ColdFusion Example of Multiple Submit Button Processing

```
<!---
Name:        form7_action.cfm
Author:      Ben Forta (ben@forta.com)
Description: Introduction to forms
Created:     4/15/01
--->
```

Listing 11.12 (continued)

```
<HTML>

<HEAD>
    <TITLE>Learning ColdFusion Forms 7</TITLE>
</HEAD>

<BODY>

<!--- User feedback --->
<CFOUTPUT>

<CFIF FORM.Operation IS "Update">
    <!--- Update button clicked --->
    You opted to <B>update</B> #MovieTitle#
<CFELSEIF FORM.Operation IS "Delete">
    <!--- Delete button clicked --->
    You opted to <B>delete</B> #MovieTitle#
</CFIF>

</CFOUTPUT>

</BODY>

</HTML>
```

Creating Dynamic SQL Statements

Now that you're familiar with forms and how ColdFusion processes them, you can return to creating a movie search screen. The first screen enables visitors to search for a movie by title. Because this requires text input, you will need an `<INPUT>` field of type text. The field name can be anything you want, but using the same name as the table column to which you're comparing the value is generally a good idea.

TIP

When you're creating search screens, you can name your form fields with any descriptive name you want. When you're creating insert and update forms, however, the field name must match the table column names so ColdFusion knows which field to save with each column. For this reason, you should get into the habit of always naming form fields with the appropriate table column name.

The code in Listing 11.13 contains a simple HTML form, not unlike the test forms you created earlier in this chapter. The form contains a single text field called `MovieTitle` and a submit button.

Listing 11.13 `search1.cfm`—Code Listing for Movie Search Screen

```
<!---
Name:        search1.cfm
Author:      Ben Forta (ben@forta.com)
Description: Creating search screens
Created:     4/15/02
--->
```

Listing 11.13 (continued)

```
<HTML>

<HEAD>
    <TITLE>Orange Whip Studios - Movies</TITLE>
</HEAD>

<BODY>

<!--- Page header --->
<CFINCLUDE TEMPLATE="header.cfm">

<!--- Search form --->
<FORM ACTION="results1.cfm" METHOD="POST">

<TABLE ALIGN="center" BORDER="1">
    <TR>
        <TD>
            Movie:
        </TD>
        <TD>
            <INPUT TYPE="text" NAME="MovieTitle">
        </TD>
    </TR>
    <TR>
        <TD COLSPAN="2" ALIGN="center">
            <INPUT TYPE="submit" VALUE="Search">
        </TD>
    </TR>
</TABLE>

</FORM>

</BODY>

</HTML>
```

Save this form as `search1.cfm`, and then execute it to display a screen similar to the one shown in Figure 11.12.

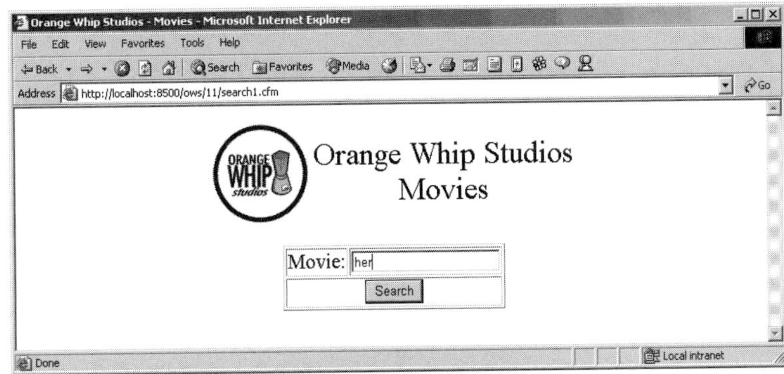

Figure 11.12

The movie search screen enables users to search by movie title.

Listing 11.13 starts off with a comment block, followed by the standard HTML headers and `<BODY>` tag. Then a `<CFINCLUDE>` tag is used to include a common header, file `header.cfm` (which puts the logo and title at the top of the page).

➜ See Chapter 9 for information on using the `<CFINCLUDE>` tag.

The form itself is placed inside an HTML table—this is a very popular technique that can be used to better control form field placement. The form contains a single field, `MovieTitle`, and a submit button.

The `<FORM>` `ACTION` attribute specifies which ColdFusion template should be used to process this search. The code `ACTION="results1.cfm"` instructs ColdFusion to use the template `results1.cfm`, which is shown in Listing 11.14. Create this template and save it as `results1.cfm`.

Listing 11.14 `results1.cfm`—Using a Passed Form Field in a SQL `WHERE` Clause

```
<!---
Name:        results1.cfm
Author:      Ben Forta (ben@forta.com)
Description: Creating search screens
Created:     4/15/02
--->

<!--- Get movie list from database --->
<CFQUERY NAME="movies" DATASOURCE="ows">
SELECT MovieTitle, PitchText, Summary, DateInTheaters
FROM Films
WHERE MovieTitle LIKE '%#FORM.MovieTitle#%'
ORDER BY MovieTitle
</CFQUERY>

<!--- Create HTML page --->
<HTML>
<HEAD>
    <TITLE>Orange Whip Studios - Movies</TITLE>
</HEAD>

<BODY>

<!--- Page header --->
<CFINCLUDE TEMPLATE="header.cfm">

<!--- Display movie list --->
<TABLE>
<TR>
 <CFOUTPUT>
 <TH COLSPAN="2">
  <FONT SIZE="+3">Movie List (#Movies.RecordCount# movies)</FONT>
 </TH>
 </CFOUTPUT>
</TR>
<CFOUTPUT QUERY="movies">
<TR>
 <TD>
```

Listing 11.14 (continued)

```
   <FONT SIZE="+2"><B>#CurrentRow#: #MovieTitle#</B></FONT><BR>
   <FONT SIZE="+1"><I>#PitchText#</I></FONT>
  </TD>
  <TD>Released: #DateFormat(DateInTheaters)#</TD>
 </TR>
 <TR>
  <TD COLSPAN="2">#Summary#</TD>
 </TR>
 </CFOUTPUT>
 </TABLE>

 </BODY>
 </HTML>
```

The code in Listing 11.14 is based on the movie lists created in the last chapter, so most of the code should be very familiar. The only big change here is in the `<CFQUERY>` tag.

The `WHERE` clause in Listing 11.14 contains a ColdFusion field rather than a static value. You will recall that when ColdFusion parses templates, it replaces field names with the values contained within the field. So, look at the following `WHERE` clause:

```
WHERE MovieTitle LIKE '%#FORM.MovieTitle#%'
```

`#FORM.MovieTitle#` is replaced with whatever was entered in the `MovieTitle` form field. If the word `her` was entered then the `WHERE` clause becomes

```
WHERE MovieTitle LIKE '%her%'
```

which will find all movies with the text `her` anywhere in the `MovieTitle`. If you search for all movies containing `C`, the code `WHERE MovieTitle LIKE '%#FORM.MovieTitle#%'` would become `WHERE MovieTitle LIKE '%C%'`. And so on. You can do this with any clauses, not just the `LIKE` operator.

NOTE

If no search text is specified at all, the clause becomes `WHERE MovieTitle LIKE '%%'`–a wildcard search that finds all records.

➜ See Chapter 10 for an introduction to the `<CFQUERY>` tag.

➜ See Chapter 5 for an explanation of the `LIKE` operator.

You use a `LIKE` clause to enable users to enter partial text. The clause `WHERE MovieTitle = 'her'` finds only movies with a title of `her`; movies with `her` in the name along with other text are not retrieved. Using a wildcard, as in `WHERE MovieTitle LIKE '%her%'`, enables users to also search on partial names.

Try experimenting with different search strings. The sample output should look similar to the output shown in Figure 11.13. Of course, depending on the search criteria you specify, you'll see different search results.

Figure 11.13

By building `WHERE` clauses dynamically, you can create different search conditions on-the-fly.

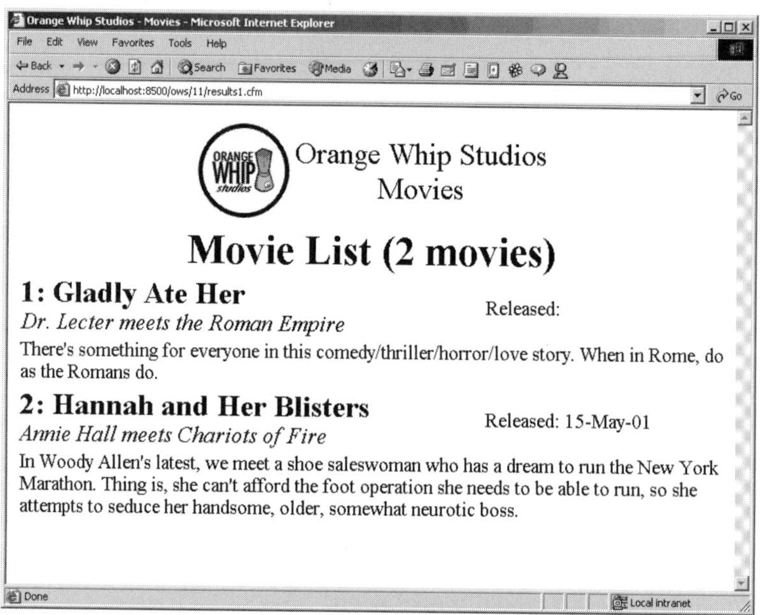

To complete the application, try copying the movie detail page (created in Chapter 10) and modify `results1.cfm` so that it enables the drill-down of the displayed search results. You'll then have a complete drill-down application.

Building Truly Dynamic Statements

When you roll out your movie search screen, you are immediately inundated with requests. "Searching by title is great, but what about by tag-line or rating?" your users ask. Now that you have introduced the ability to search for data, your users want to be able to search on several fields.

Adding fields to your search screen is simple enough. Add two fields: one for tag-line and one for rating. The code for the updated search screen is shown in Listing 11.15.

Listing 11.15 `search2.cfm`—Movie Search Screen

```
<!---
Name:        search2.cfm
Author:      Ben Forta (ben@forta.com)
Description: Creating search screens
Created:     4/15/02
--->

<HTML>

<HEAD>
```

Listing 11.15 (continued)

```
      <TITLE>Orange Whip Studios - Movies</TITLE>
   </HEAD>

   <BODY>

   <!--- Page header --->
   <CFINCLUDE TEMPLATE="header.cfm">

   <!--- Search form --->
   <FORM ACTION="results2.cfm" METHOD="POST">

   <TABLE ALIGN="center" BORDER="1">
      <TR>
         <TD>
            Movie:
         </TD>
         <TD>
            <INPUT TYPE="text" NAME="MovieTitle">
         </TD>
      </TR>
      <TR>
         <TD>
            Tag line:
         </TD>
         <TD>
            <INPUT TYPE="text" NAME="PitchText">
         </TD>
      </TR>
      <TR>
         <TD>
            Rating:
         </TD>
         <TD>
            <INPUT TYPE="text" NAME="RatingID"> (1-6)
         </TD>
      </TR>
      <TR>
         <TD COLSPAN="2" ALIGN="center">
            <INPUT TYPE="submit" VALUE="Search">
         </TD>
      </TR>
   </TABLE>

   </FORM>

   </BODY>

   </HTML>
```

This form enables the users to specify text in one of three fields, as shown in Figure 11.14.

You must create a search template before you can actually perform a search. The complete search code is shown in Listing 11.16; save this file as `results2.cfm`.

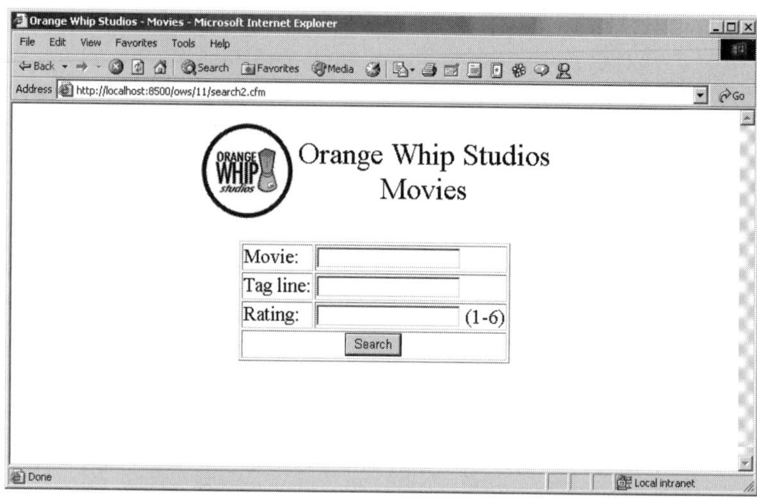

Figure 11.14 The movie search screen now allows searching by three fields.

Listing 11.16 `results2.cfm`—Building SQL Statements Dynamically

```
<!---
Name:        results2.cfm
Author:      Ben Forta (ben@forta.com)
Description: Creating search screens
Created:     4/15/02
--->

<!--- Get movie list from database --->
<CFQUERY NAME="movies" DATASOURCE="ows">
SELECT MovieTitle, PitchText, Summary, DateInTheaters
FROM Films
<!--- Search by movie title --->
<CFIF FORM.MovieTitle IS NOT "">
    WHERE MovieTitle LIKE '%#FORM.MovieTitle#%'
</CFIF>
<!--- Search by tag line --->
<CFIF FORM.PitchText IS NOT "">
    WHERE PitchText LIKE '%#FORM.PitchText#%'
</CFIF>
<!--- Search by rating --->
<CFIF FORM.RatingID IS NOT "">
    WHERE RatingID = #FORM.RatingID#
</CFIF>
ORDER BY MovieTitle
</CFQUERY>

<!--- Create HTML page --->
<HTML>
<HEAD>
    <TITLE>Orange Whip Studios - Movies</TITLE>
</HEAD>

<BODY>
```

Listing 11.16 (continued)

```
<!--- Page header --->
<CFINCLUDE TEMPLATE="header.cfm">

<!--- Display movie list --->
<TABLE>
<TR>
 <CFOUTPUT>
 <TH COLSPAN="2">
  <FONT SIZE="+3">Movie List (#Movies.RecordCount# movies)</FONT>
 </TH>
 </CFOUTPUT>
</TR>
<CFOUTPUT QUERY="movies">
<TR>
 <TD>
  <FONT SIZE="+2"><B>#CurrentRow#: #MovieTitle#</B></FONT><BR>
  <FONT SIZE="+1"><I>#PitchText#</I></FONT>
 </TD>
 <TD>Released: #DateFormat(DateInTheaters)#</TD>
</TR>
<TR>
 <TD COLSPAN="2">#Summary#</TD>
</TR>
</CFOUTPUT>
</TABLE>

</BODY>
</HTML>
```

Understanding Dynamic SQL

Before you actually perform a search, take a closer look at the template in Listing 11.16. The `<CFQUERY>` tag is similar to the one you used in the previous search template, but in this one the SQL `SELECT` statement in the SQL attribute is incomplete. It does not specify a `WHERE` clause with which to perform a search, nor does it specify a search order. No `WHERE` clause is specified because the search screen has to support not one, but four search types, as follows:

- If none of the three search fields is specified, no `WHERE` clause should be used so that all movies can be retrieved.
- If a movie title is specified, the `WHERE` clause must filter data to find only movies containing the specified title text. For example, if `the` is specified as the search text, the `WHERE` clause has to be `WHERE MovieTitle LIKE '%the%'`.
- If tag-line text is specified, the `WHERE` clause needs to filter data to find only movies containing the specified text. For example, if `bad` is specified as the search text, the `WHERE` clause must be `WHERE PitchText LIKE '%bad%'`.
- If you're searching by rating and specify `2` as the search text, a `WHERE` clause of `WHERE RatingID = 2` is necessary.

How can a single search template handle all these search conditions? The answer is dynamic SQL.

When you're creating dynamic SQL statements, you break the statement into separate common SQL and specific SQL. The common SQL is the part of the SQL statement you always want. The sample SQL statement has two common parts:

```
SELECT MovieTitle, PitchText, Summary, DateInTheaters
FROM Films
```

and

```
ORDER BY MovieTitle
```

The common text is all the SQL statement you need if no search criteria is provided. If, however, search text is specified, the number of possible `WHERE` clauses is endless.

Take another look at Listing 11.16 to understand the process of creating dynamic SQL statements. The code `<CFIF FORM.MovieTitle IS NOT "">` checks to see that the `MovieTitle` form field is not empty. This condition fails if no text is entered into the `MovieTitle` field in the search form, in which case any code until the `</CFIF>` is ignored.

➜ See Chapter 9 for details on using `<CFIF>`.

If a value does appear in the `MovieTitle` field, the code `WHERE MovieTitle LIKE '#FORM.MovieTitle#%'` is processed and appended to the SQL statement. `#FORM.MovieTitle#` is a field and is replaced with whatever text is entered in the `MovieTitle` field. If `the` is specified as the text for which to search, this statement translates to `WHERE MovieTitle LIKE '%the%'`. This text is appended to the previous SQL statement, which now becomes the following:

```
SELECT MovieTitle, PitchText, Summary, DateInTheaters
FROM Films
WHERE MovieTitle LIKE '%the%'
```

All you need now is the `ORDER BY` clause. Even though `ORDER BY` is fixed and does not change with different searches, it must be built dynamically because the `ORDER BY` clause must come after the `WHERE` clause (if one exists). After ColdFusion processes the code `ORDER BY MovieTitle`, the finished SQL statement reads as follows:

```
SELECT MovieTitle, PitchText, Summary, DateInTheaters
FROM Films
WHERE MovieTitle LIKE '%the%'
ORDER BY MovieTitle
```

NOTE

You may not use double quotation marks in a SQL statement. When ColdFusion encounters a double quotation mark, it thinks it has reached the end of the SQL statement. It then generates an error message because extra text appears where ColdFusion thinks there should be none. To include text strings with the SQL statement, use only single quotation marks.

Similarly, if a `RatingID` is specified (for example, the value `2`) as the search text, the complete SQL statement reads as follows:

```
SELECT MovieTitle, PitchText, Summary, DateInTheaters
FROM Films
WHERE RatingID = 2
ORDER BY MovieTitle
```

The code `<CFIF FORM.MovieTitle IS NOT "">` evaluates to `FALSE` because `FORM.MovieTitle` is actually empty; ColdFusion therefore checks the next condition, which is also `FALSE`, and so on. Because `RatingID` was specified, the third `<CFIF>` condition is `TRUE` and the previous `SELECT` statement is generated.

NOTE

You might have noticed that there are single quotation marks around `FORM.MovieTitle` and `FORM.PitchText` but not `FORM.RatingID`. Why? Because `MovieTitle` and `PitchText` have text data types in the database table, whereas `RatingID` is numeric. SQL is not `typeless`, and it will require that you specify quotes where needed to create strings if that is what is expected.

So, one template is capable of generating four different sets of SQL `SELECT` statements, of which the values can be dynamic. Try performing various searches, but for now, use only one form field at a time.

Concatenating SQL Clauses

Now try entering text in two search fields, or all three of them. What happens? You probably generated an error similar to the one shown in Figure 11.15.

Why did this happen? Well, what if `the` was specified as the `MovieTitle` and `2` as the `RatingID`. Walk through the `<CFIF>` statements to work out what the generated SQL would look like. The first condition will be `TRUE`, the second will be `FALSE`, and the third will be `TRUE`. The `SELECT` statement would therefore look like this:

```
SELECT MovieTitle, PitchText, Summary, DateInTheaters
FROM Films
WHERE MovieTitle LIKE '%the%'
WHERE RatingID = 2
ORDER BY MovieTitle
```

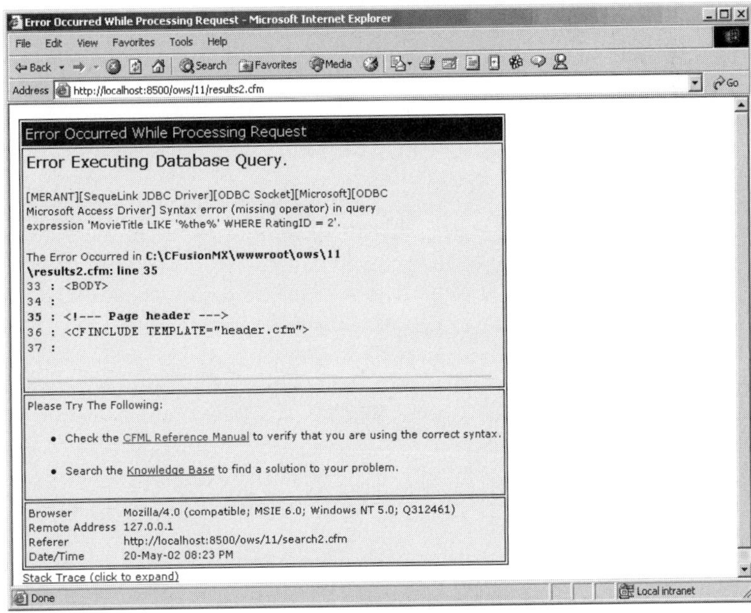

Figure 11.15

Dynamic SQL must be generated carefully to avoid building invalid SQL.

Obviously, this is not a valid `SELECT` statement—only one `WHERE` clause is allowed. The correct syntax for this statement is

```
SELECT MovieTitle, PitchText, Summary, DateInTheaters
FROM Films
WHERE MovieTitle LIKE '%the%'
 AND RatingID = 2
ORDER BY MovieTitle
```

So, how would you generate this code? You could not hard-code any condition with a `WHERE` or an `AND` because you wouldn't know whether it was the first clause. Yes, the `MovieTitle` clause, if used, will always be the first, but it might not always be used.

One obvious solution (which I suggest you avoid at all costs) is to use embedded `<CFIF>` statements to intelligently include `WHERE` or `AND` as necessary. However, this type of code is very complex and error-prone.

A better solution would be to never need `WHERE` at all—only use `AND`. How can you do this? Look at the following SQL statement:

```
SELECT MovieTitle, PitchText, Summary, DateInTheaters
FROM Films
WHERE 0=0
 AND MovieTitle LIKE '%the%'
 AND RatingID = 2
ORDER BY MovieTitle
```

`WHERE 0=0` is a dummy clause. Obviously `0` is equal to `0`, so `WHERE 0=0` retrieves every row in the table. For each row the database checks to see whether `0` is `0`, which of course it always is. This is a legal `WHERE` clause, but it does nothing because it is always `TRUE`.

So why use it? Simple. Now that there is a `WHERE` clause, you can safely use `AND` for every dynamic condition. If no other condition exists then only the `WHERE 0=0` will be evaluated; however, if additional conditions do exist, no matter how many, they can all be appended using `AND`.

NOTE

There is nothing magical about `WHERE 0=0`; you can use any condition that will always be `TRUE`: `WHERE 'A'='A'`, `WHERE primary key = primary key` (using the table's primary key), and just about anything else you want.

Listing 11.17 contains a revised search page (this time using a drop-down list box for the rating); save it as `search3.cfm`. Figure 11.16 shows the new and improved search screen.

Listing 11.18 contains the revised results page; save it as `results3.cfm`.

Listing 11.17 `search3.cfm`—Revised Movie Search Screen

```
<!---
Name:        search3.cfm
Author:      Ben Forta (ben@forta.com)
Description: Creating search screens
Created:     4/15/02
--->

<HTML>
```

Listing 11.17 (continued)

```
<HEAD>
    <TITLE>Orange Whip Studios - Movies</TITLE>
</HEAD>

<BODY>

<!--- Page header --->
<CFINCLUDE TEMPLATE="header.cfm">

<!--- Search form --->
<FORM ACTION="results3.cfm" METHOD="POST">

<TABLE ALIGN="center" BORDER="1">
    <TR>
        <TD>
            Movie:
        </TD>
        <TD>
            <INPUT TYPE="text" NAME="MovieTitle">
        </TD>
    </TR>
    <TR>
        <TD>
            Tag line:
        </TD>
        <TD>
            <INPUT TYPE="text" NAME="PitchText">
        </TD>
    </TR>
    <TR>
        <TD>
            Rating:
        </TD>
        <TD>
            <SELECT NAME="RatingID">
                <OPTION VALUE=""></OPTION>
                <OPTION VALUE="1">General</OPTION>
                <OPTION VALUE="2">Kids</OPTION>
                <OPTION VALUE="3">Accompanied Minors</OPTION>
                <OPTION VALUE="4">Teens</OPTION>
                <OPTION VALUE="5">Adults</OPTION>
                <OPTION VALUE="6">Mature Audiences</OPTION>
            </SELECT>
        </TD>
    </TR>
    <TR>
        <TD COLSPAN="2" ALIGN="center">
            <INPUT TYPE="submit" VALUE="Search">
        </TD>
    </TR>
</TABLE>

</FORM>

</BODY>

</HTML>
```

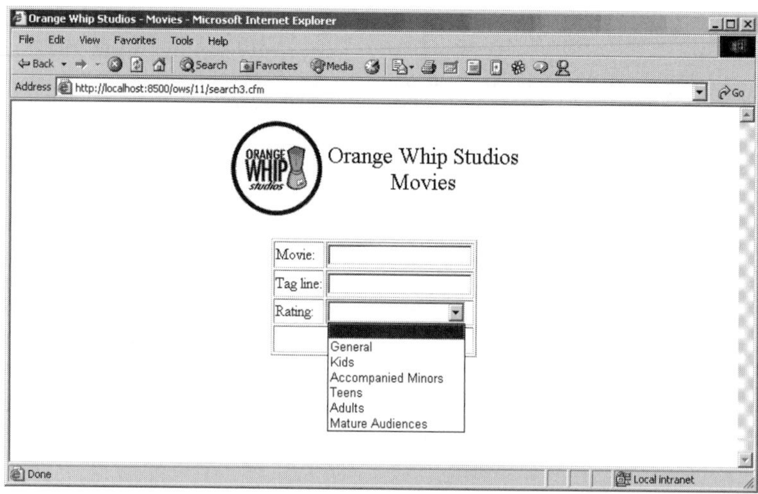

Figure 11.16

Drop-down list boxes are well suited for selections of one of a set of finite options.

The only change in Listing 11.17 is the drop-down list box for the `RatingID`. Manually entering `1` to `6` is not intuitive and is highly error-prone. For finite lists such as this drop-down list, boxes are a better option. This does not change the form field processing, though—either way, `RatingID` is sent to the `ACTION` page, shown in Listing 11.18.

Listing 11.18 `results3.cfm`—Concatenating SQL Clauses

```
<!---
Name:        results3.cfm
Author:      Ben Forta (ben@forta.com)
Description: Creating search screens
Created:     4/15/02
--->

<!--- Get movie list from database --->
<CFQUERY NAME="movies" DATASOURCE="ows">
SELECT MovieTitle, PitchText, Summary, DateInTheaters
FROM Films
WHERE 0=0
<!--- Search by movie title --->
<CFIF FORM.MovieTitle IS NOT "">
    AND MovieTitle LIKE '%#FORM.MovieTitle#%'
</CFIF>
<!--- Search by tag line --->
<CFIF FORM.PitchText IS NOT "">
    AND PitchText LIKE '%#FORM.PitchText#%'
</CFIF>
<!--- Search by rating --->
<CFIF FORM.RatingID IS NOT "">
    AND RatingID = #FORM.RatingID#
</CFIF>
ORDER BY MovieTitle
</CFQUERY>

<!--- Create HTML page --->
```

Listing 11.18 (CONTINUED)

```
<HTML>
<HEAD>
    <TITLE>Orange Whip Studios - Movies</TITLE>
</HEAD>

<BODY>

<!--- Page header --->
<CFINCLUDE TEMPLATE="header.cfm">

<!--- Display movie list --->
<TABLE>
<TR>
 <CFOUTPUT>
 <TH COLSPAN="2">
  <FONT SIZE="+3">Movie List (#Movies.RecordCount# movies)</FONT>
 </TH>
 </CFOUTPUT>
</TR>
<CFOUTPUT QUERY="movies">
<TR>
 <TD>
  <FONT SIZE="+2"><B>#CurrentRow#: #MovieTitle#</B></FONT><BR>
  <FONT SIZE="+1"><I>#PitchText#</I></FONT>
 </TD>
 <TD>Released: #DateFormat(DateInTheaters)#</TD>
</TR>
<TR>
 <TD COLSPAN="2">#Summary#</TD>
</TR>
</CFOUTPUT>
</TABLE>

</BODY>
</HTML>
```

The <CFQUERY> in Listing 11.18 now contains a dummy clause and then three optional AND clauses, each within a <CFIF> statement. So, what will this do?

- If no form fields are filled in then only the dummy WHERE clause will be used.
- If any single form field is filled in then the WHERE clause will contain the dummy and a single real clause appended using AND.
- If any two form fields are filled in then the WHERE clause will have three clauses, one dummy and two real.
- If all three clauses are filled in then the WHERE clause will contain four clauses, one dummy and three real.

In other words, a single template can now generate eight different combinations of WHERE clauses, and each can have an unlimited number of values. All that in less than 20 lines of code—it doesn't get much more powerful than that.

After you create the template, use your browser to perform various combinations of searches. You'll find that this new search template is both powerful and flexible. Indeed, this technique for creating truly dynamic SQL `SELECT` statements will likely be the basis for some sophisticated database interaction in real-world applications.

Creating Dynamic Search Screens

There is one final improvement to be made to your application. The list of ratings used in the search form have been hard-coded (refer to Listing 11.17). Remember that you're creating data-driven applications. Everything in your application should be data-driven. You don't want to have to manually enter data, not even in list boxes. Rather, you want the list box to be driven by the data in the `FilmsRatings` table. This way, you can acquire changes automatically when ratings are added or when a rating name changes.

Listing 11.19 is identical to Listing 11.17, with the exception of the addition of a new `<CFQUERY>` and a `<CFOUTPUT>` block to process its contents.

Listing 11.19 `search4.cfm`—Data-Driven Forms

```
<!---
Name:        search4.cfm
Author:      Ben Forta (ben@forta.com)
Description: Creating search screens
Created:     4/15/02
--->

<!--- Get ratings --->
<CFQUERY DATASOURCE="ows" NAME="ratings">
SELECT RatingID, Rating
FROM FilmsRatings
ORDER BY RatingID
</CFQUERY>

<HTML>

<HEAD>
    <TITLE>Orange Whip Studios - Movies</TITLE>
</HEAD>

<BODY>

<!--- Page header --->
<CFINCLUDE TEMPLATE="header.cfm">

<!--- Search form --->
<FORM ACTION="results3.cfm" METHOD="POST">

<TABLE ALIGN="center" BORDER="1">
    <TR>
        <TD>
            Movie:
        </TD>
```

Listing 11.19 (continued)

```
            <TD>
                <INPUT TYPE="text" NAME="MovieTitle">
            </TD>
        </TR>
        <TR>
            <TD>
                Tag line:
            </TD>
            <TD>
                <INPUT TYPE="text" NAME="PitchText">
            </TD>
        </TR>
        <TR>
            <TD>
                Rating:
            </TD>
            <TD>
                <SELECT NAME="RatingID">
                    <OPTION VALUE=""></OPTION>
                    <CFOUTPUT QUERY="ratings">
                        <OPTION VALUE="#RatingID#">#Rating#</OPTION>
                 </CFOUTPUT>
             </SELECT>
            </TD>
        </TR>
        <TR>
            <TD COLSPAN="2" ALIGN="center">
                <INPUT TYPE="submit" VALUE="Search">
            </TD>
        </TR>
    </TABLE>

    </FORM>

    </BODY>

    </HTML>
```

The code in Listing 11.19 demonstrates a data-driven form. The `<CFQUERY>` at the top of the template should be familiar to you by now. It creates a result set called `ratings`, which contains the ID and name of each rating in the database.

The drop-down list box also has been changed. The `<SELECT>` tag creates the list box, and it is terminated with the `</SELECT>` tag, as before. The individual entries in the list box are specified with the `<OPTION>` tag, but here that tag is within a `<CFOUTPUT>` block. This block is executed once for each row retrieved by the `<CFQUERY>`, creating an `<OPTION>` entry for each one.

As it loops through the `ratings` resultset, the `<CFQUERY>` block creates the individual options, using the `RatingID` field as the `VALUE` and `Rating` as the description. So, when ColdFusion processes `RatingID 1 (General)`, the code generated is

```
<OPTION VALUE="1">General</OPTION>
```

The end result is exactly the same as the screen shown previously in Figure 11.16, but this time it is populated by a database query (instead of being hard-coded).

Also notice that a blank `<OPTION>` line is included in the list box. Remember that list boxes always must have a selection, so if you want to allow your users to not select any option, you need to give them a *no option* option (the blank option).

And there you have it—dynamic data-driven forms used to perform dynamic data-driven searches using dynamic data-driven SQL.

CHAPTER 12

Form Data Validation

IN THIS CHAPTER

Understanding Form Validation

HTML forms are used to collect data from users by using several field types. Forms are used for data entry, as front-end search engines, for filling out orders, for signing guest books, providing user names and passwords to secure applications, and much more. Although forms have become one of the most important features in HTML, these forms provide almost no data validation tools.

This becomes a real problem when developing Web-based applications. As a developer, you need to be able to control what data users can enter into what fields. Without that, your programs will constantly be breaking due to mismatched or unanticipated data. And thus far, you have used forms only as search front ends—when forms are used to insert or update database tables (as you'll see in Chapter 13, "Using Forms to Add or Change Data"), this becomes even more critical.

Thankfully, ColdFusion provides a complete and robust set of tools with which to implement form data validation, both client-side and server-side.

Since its inception, HTML has always provided Web page developers with a variety of ways to format and display data. With each revision to the HTML specification, additional data display mechanisms have been made available. As a result, HTML is a powerful data-publishing tool.

Although its data presentation options continue to improve, HTML's data collection capabilities leave much to be desired. In fact, they have barely changed at all since the language's very early days.

HTML data collection is performed using forms. HTML forms support the following field types:

- Free-form text fields
- Select box (or drop-down list boxes)
- Radio buttons
- Check boxes

- Multi-line text boxes
- Password (hidden input) boxes

➜ See Chapter 11, "ColdFusion Forms," for more information about HTML forms and using them with ColdFusion.

So what's wrong with this list? Actually, nothing at all. These field types are all the standard fields you would expect to be available to you in any development language. What is wrong, however, is that these fields have extremely limited capabilities. There are two primary limitations:

- Inability to mark fields as required
- Inability to define data types or filters—only accepting digits, a ZIP code, or a phone number, for instance

What this means is that there is no simple way to tell HTML to disallow form submission if certain fields are left empty. Similarly, HTML cannot be instructed to accept only certain values or types of data in specific fields.

HTML itself has exactly one validation option, the `MAXLENGTH` attribute, which can be used to specify the maximum number of characters that can be entered in a text field. But that's it. No other validation options are available.

To work around these limitations, HTML developers have typically adopted two forms of validation options:

- Server-side validation
- Client-side validation

Comparing Server-Side and Client-Side Validation

Server-side validation involves checking for required fields or invalid values after a form has been submitted. The script on the server first validates the form and then continues processing only if all validation requirements are met. Typically, an error message is sent back to the user's browser if validation fails; the user then makes the corrections and resubmits the form. Of course, the form submission must be validated again upon resubmission, and the process must be repeated if the validation fails again.

Client-side scripting enables the developer to embed instructions to the browser within the HTML code. Because HTML itself provides no mechanism for doing this, developers have resorted to using scripting languages, such as JavaScript (supported by both Netscape Navigator and Microsoft Internet Explorer) or VBScript (supported by Microsoft Internet Explorer only). These interpreted languages support basic data manipulation and user feedback and are thus well suited for form validation. To validate a form, the page author would create a function to be executed as soon as a Submit button is clicked. This function would perform any necessary validation and allow the submission to proceed only if the validation check was successful. The advantage of this approach is that the user does not have to submit a form to find out an error occurred in it. Notification of any errors occurs prior to form submission.

Understanding the Pros and Cons of Each Option

Neither of these options is perfect, and they are thus often used together, complementing each other. Table 12.1 lists the pros and cons of each option.

Table 12.1 The Pros and Cons of Client and Server Form Validation

VALIDATION TYPE	PROS	CONS
Server-side	Most flexible; validation is browser independent; supports non-HTML clients	User must submit form before validation occurs; any errors require resubmission
Client-side	Validation occurs prior to submission allowing for a more intuitive and less aggravating user experience	Not supported by all browsers; scripting languages have a lengthy learning curve; may be possible to disable script execution in the browser

From a user's perspective, client-side validation is preferable. Obviously, users want to know what is wrong with the data they entered *before* they submit the form for processing. From a developer's perspective, however, server-side validation is simpler to code, guaranteed to always work regardless of the browser used, and less likely to fall victim to browser incompatibilities.

TIP

Form field validation should never be considered optional, and you should get in the habit of always using some type of validation in each and every form you create. Failure to do so will inevitably cause errors and broken applications later.

Using Server-Side Validation

As mentioned earlier, server-side validation involves adding code to your application that performs form field validation after the form is submitted. In ColdFusion this usually is achieved with a series of `<CFIF>` statements that check each field's value and data types. If any validation steps fail, processing can be terminated with the `<CFABORT>` function, or the user can be redirected to another page (maybe the form itself) using `<CFLOCATION>`.

Two ways to perform server-side validation are available in ColdFusion. Let's look at basic server-side validation first, and then you'll use embedded validation codes to automate the validation where possible.

Using Basic Server-Side Validation

The code shown in Listing 12.1 is a simple login prompt used to gain access to an intranet site. The file, which should be saved as `login1.cfm` (in a new directory named `12`), prompts for a user ID and password. HTML's only validation rule, `MAXLENGTH`, is used in both form fields to restrict the number of characters that can be entered. The form itself is shown in Figure 12.1.

Listing 12.1 `login1.cfm`—Login Screen Shown in Figure 12.1

```
<!---
Name:        login1.cfm
Author:      Ben Forta (ben@forta.com)
Description: Form field validation demo
Created:     4/15/02
--->

<HTML>

<HEAD>
    <TITLE>Orange Whip Studios - Intranet</TITLE>
</HEAD>

<BODY>

<!--- Page header --->
<CFINCLUDE TEMPLATE="header.cfm">

<!--- Login form --->
<FORM ACTION="process.cfm" METHOD="POST">

<TABLE ALIGN="center" BGCOLOR="orange">
    <TR>
        <TD ALIGN="right">
            ID:
        </TD>
        <TD>
            <INPUT TYPE="text" NAME="LoginID" MAXLENGTH="5">
        </TD>
    </TR>
    <TR>
        <TD ALIGN="right">
            Password:
        </TD>
        <TD>
            <INPUT TYPE="password" NAME="LoginPassword" MAXLENGTH="20">
        </TD>
    </TR>
    <TR>
        <TD COLSPAN="2" ALIGN="center">
            <INPUT TYPE="submit" VALUE="Login">
        </TD>
    </TR>
</TABLE>

</FORM>

</BODY>

</HTML>
```

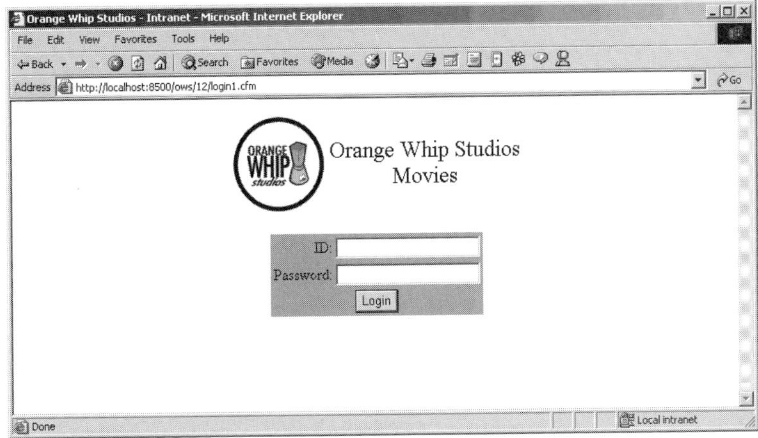

Figure 12.1
HTML forms support basic field types, such as text and password boxes.

This particular form gets submitted to a template named `process.cfm` (specified in the `ACTION` attribute). That template is responsible for validating the user input and processing the login only if all the validation rules passed. The validation rules necessary here are

- Login ID is required.
- Login ID must be numeric.
- Login password is required.

To perform this validation, three `<CFIF>` statements are used, as shown in Listing 12.2.

Listing 12.2 `process.cfm`—Basic Server-Side Validation Code

```
<!---
Name:        process.cfm
Author:      Ben Forta (ben@forta.com)
Description: Form field validation demo
Created:     4/15/02
--->

<HTML>

<HEAD>
    <TITLE>Orange Whip Studios - Intranet</TITLE>
</HEAD>

<BODY>

<!--- Page header --->
<CFINCLUDE TEMPLATE="header.cfm">

<!--- Make sure LoginID is not empty --->
<CFIF Len(Trim(LoginID)) IS 0>
 <H1>ERROR! ID cannot be left blank!</H1>
 <CFABORT>
</CFIF>
```

Listing 12.2 (continued)

```
<!--- Make sure LoginID is a number --->
<CFIF IsNumeric(LoginID) IS "No">
 <H1>ERROR! Invalid ID specified!</H1>
 <CFABORT>
</CFIF>

<!--- Make sure LoginPassword is not empty --->
<CFIF Len(Trim(LoginPassword)) IS 0>
 <H1>ERROR! Password cannot be left blank!</H1>
 <CFABORT>
</CFIF>

<CENTER>
<H1>Intranet</H1>
</CENTER>

Intranet would go here.

</BODY>

</HTML>
```

The first `<CFIF>` checks the length of `LoginID` after trimming it with the `Trim()` function. The `Trim()` function is necessary to trap space characters that are technically valid characters in a text field but are not valid here. If the `Len()` function returns `0`, an error message is displayed, and the `<CFABORT>` statements halts further processing.

TIP

Checking the length of the trimmed string (to determine whether it is empty) is functionally the same as doing a comparison against an empty string, like this:

```
<CFIF Trim(LoginID) IS "">
```

The reason I used `Len()` to get the string length (instead of comparing it to `""`) is that numeric comparisons are processed more quickly than string comparisons. For even greater performance, I could have eliminated the comparison value and used the following:

```
<CFIF NOT Len(Trim(LoginID))>
```

The second `<CFIF>` statement checks the data type. The `IsNumeric()` function returns `TRUE` if the passed value was numeric (contained only digits, for example) or `FALSE` if not. Once again, if the `<CFIF>` check fails, an error is displayed and `<CFABORT>` halts further processing, as shown in Figure 12.2. The third `<CFIF>` checks that a password was specified (and that that the field was not left blank).

This form of validation is the most powerful and flexible of all the validation options available to you. There is no limit to the number of `<CFIF>` statements you can use, and there is no limit to the number of functions or tags you can use within them. You can even perform database operations (perhaps to check that a password matches) and use the results in comparisons.

→ See Appendix C, "ColdFusion Function Reference," for a complete list of functions that can be used for form field validation. Most of the decision functions begin with `is` (for example, `IsDefined()` and `IsDate()`).

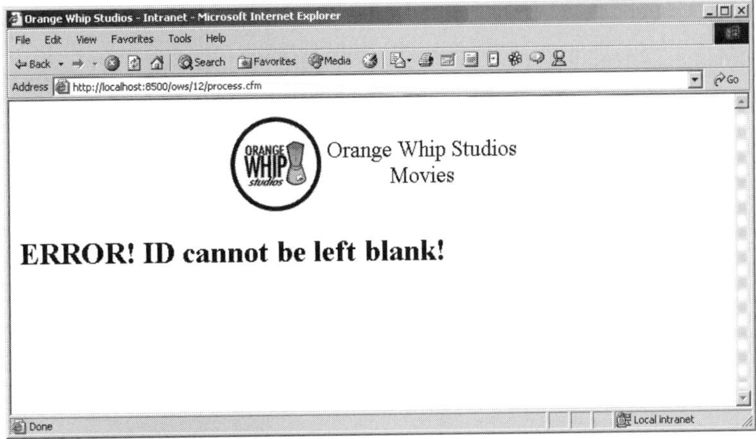

Figure 12.2

<CFIF> statements can be used to perform validation checks and then display error messages if the checks fail.

TIP

<CFIF> statements can be combined using AND and OR operators if necessary. For example, the first two <CFIF> statements shown in Listing 12.1 could be combined to read

```
<CFIF (Len(Trim(LoginID)) IS 0) OR (NOT IsNumeric(LoginID))>
```

The big downside here, however, is that this type of validation code is neither clean nor manageable. If you were to add or rename a field, for example, you'd have to remember to update the destination form (the form to which the fields get submitted, as specified in the <FORM> ACTION attribute), as well as the form itself. As your forms grow in complexity, so does the likelihood of your forms and their validation rules getting out of sync.

Using ColdFusion Embedded Form Validation

To work around this problem, ColdFusion enables developers to embed basic form validation instructions within an HTML form. These instructions are embedded as hidden form fields. They get sent to the user's browser along with the rest of the form fields, but they are not displayed to the user. Nonetheless, when the user submits the form back to the Web server, those hidden fields are submitted too. ColdFusion can then use them to perform automatic field validation.

To add a validation rule, you must add a hidden field to the form—you will need to add one hidden field for each validation rule necessary. The field name must be the name of the field to validate, followed by the validation rule—for example, `_required` (an underscore followed by the word `required`) to flag a field as required. The field's `VALUE` attribute can be used to specify the error message to be displayed if the validation fails. This next line of code tells ColdFusion that the `LoginID` field is required and that the error message `ID is required!` should be displayed if it's not present:

```
<INPUT TYPE="hidden" NAME="LoginID_required" VALUE="ID is required!">
```

ColdFusion supports seven basic validation rules, as listed in Table 12.2. It is important to remember that even though the validation rules are being sent to the browser as hidden form fields, the actual validation still occurs on the server after the form has been submitted.

Table 12.2 Form Field Validation Rule Suffixes

SUFFIX	DESCRIPTION
`_date`	Date in most common date formats, such as MM/DD/YY and MM/DD/YYYY (year is optional, and will default to the current year if omitted)
`_eurodate`	Same as `_date`, but with day before month (European format)
`_float`	Numeric data, decimal point allowed
`_integer`	Numeric data, decimal point not allowed
`_range`	Range of values; the minimum and maximum values (or just one of them) must be specified in the `VALUE` attribute as `MIN=` and `MAX=`—for example, `MIN=5 MAX=10`
`_required`	Field is required and can't be left blank
`_time`	Time in most common time formats

NOTE

There is no limit to the number of validation rules you can embed in a form. The only restriction is that every validation rule must be embedded as a separate hidden field. So, to flag a field as required and numeric, you'd need two embedded rules, as shown in Listing 12.3.

To demonstrate using these validation rules, update the login prompt screen created earlier. Listing 12.3 shows the updated form to which three lines of code have been added. Save this file as `login2.cfm`.

Listing 12.3 `login2.cfm`— Login Prompt Screen with Embedded Field Validation Rules

```
<!---
Name:        login2.cfm
Author:      Ben Forta (ben@forta.com)
Description: Form field validation demo
Created:     4/15/02
--->

<HTML>

<HEAD>
    <TITLE>Orange Whip Studios - Intranet</TITLE>
</HEAD>

<BODY>

<!--- Page header --->
<CFINCLUDE TEMPLATE="header.cfm">

<!--- Login form --->
<FORM ACTION="process.cfm" METHOD="POST">

<TABLE ALIGN="center" BGCOLOR="orange">
    <TR>
        <TD ALIGN="right">
            ID:
        </TD>
        <TD>
```

Listing 12.3 (continued)

```
                <INPUT TYPE="text"
                       NAME="LoginID"
                       MAXLENGTH="5">
                <INPUT TYPE="hidden"
                       NAME="LoginID_required"
                       VALUE="ID is required!">
                <INPUT TYPE="hidden"
                       NAME="LoginID_integer"
                       VALUE="Invalid ID specified!">
            </TD>
        </TR>
        <TR>
            <TD ALIGN="right">
                Password:
            </TD>
            <TD>
                <INPUT TYPE="password"
                       NAME="LoginPassword"
                       MAXLENGTH="20">
                <INPUT TYPE="hidden"
                       NAME="LoginPassword_required"
                       VALUE="Password is required!">
            </TD>
        </TR>
        <TR>
            <TD COLSPAN="2" ALIGN="center">
                <INPUT TYPE="submit" VALUE="Login">
            </TD>
        </TR>
    </TABLE>

    </FORM>

    </BODY>

    </HTML>
```

The first rule specifies that the `LoginID` field is a required field. The second rule further specifies that only numeric data can be entered into the `LoginID` field. And finally, the third rule flags the `LoginPassword` field as required, too.

So, what happens if the validation rules fail? The screen shown in Figure 12.3 is what gets displayed if non-numeric data was entered into the login field and the password field was left blank.

NOTE

The screen shown in Figure 12.3 is the default validation error screen. This screen can be changed using the `<CFERROR>` tag.

➜ See Chapter 16, "Introducing the Web Application Framework," for information about using `<CFERROR>`.

As you can see, the ColdFusion validation rules are both simple and effective. And best of all, because the validation rules are embedded into the form itself, your forms and their rules are less likely to get out of sync.

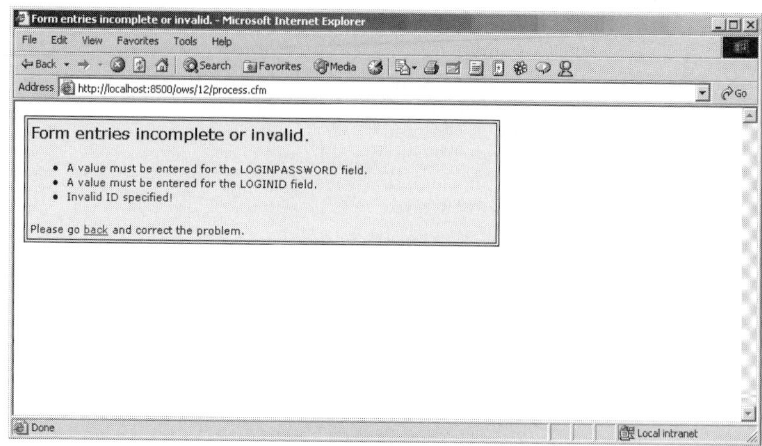

Figure 12.3

When using embedded form field validation, ColdFusion automatically displays an error message listing which checks failed.

TIP

Validation rules can be embedded anywhere in your form, either before or after the field being validated. To make maintaining your code easier, you should establish guidelines governing rule placement. Two popular standards are grouping all the rules together at the very top of the form, and listing validation rules right after the field they validate (as you did in Listing 12.3).

Of course, when validation errors occur the user will still have to go back to the form to make any corrections. The benefits of embedded validation rules are really only developer benefits—embedded validation does nothing to improve the user experience. For that you need client-side validation.

Using Client-Side Validation

The biggest drawback in using server-side validation is that the validation occurs after form submission. This means that if any validation rules fail, the user must go back to the form, make the corrections, and resubmit it to the server. To make matters worse, many browsers lose the data in the form fields when the Back button is clicked, forcing the user to reenter all the data.

Obviously, this is not a user-friendly interface. Too many good Web sites have lost visitors because their forms were too aggravating to work with.

Fortunately, an alternative is available: client-side validation.

Understanding Client-Side Validation

To perform client-side validation, you add a series of browser instructions to your Web page. The browser interprets these instructions and executes them right on the client (the user's computer) before the form ever gets submitted to the server.

These instructions are written in scripting languages, such as JavaScript (supported by both Netscape Navigator and Microsoft Internet Explorer, as well as some lesser used browsers such as Opera and Mozilla) or VBScript (based on Visual Basic and supported by Microsoft Internet Explorer only). These are interpreted languages that enable you to control browser behavior.

NOTE

Don't confuse JavaScript with Java. Java is a true compiled object-oriented application development language, one that can be used to write entire programs. JavaScript (including JScript, which is a variant of JavaScript) is an interpreted language designed to control Web browsers. Unlike Java, JavaScript cannot access anything on your computer other than your Web browser.

To validate a form, you write a script that will trap the form submission and allow it to proceed only if a series of validation checks have passed. If any checks fail, you would display an error message and prevent the form from being submitted.

Of course, to do this, you'd have to learn JavaScript (or VBScript).

Using <CFFORM>

To simplify the process of embedding client-side validation scripting code into your forms, ColdFusion includes a tag called `<CFFORM>`. `<CFFORM>` is an extremely powerful tag that actually has several distinct functions. The function you are most interested in here is its support for client-side JavaScript.

➜ See Chapter 24, "Enhancing Forms with Client-Side Java," for more information about `<CFFORM>` and how to use its Java applets to extend your forms.

So, what can `<CFFORM>` do for you here? Simply put, `<CFFORM>` can *automatically* generate JavaScript code to handle most forms of data validation. And the best part of it is that you don't even have to know or learn JavaScript.

To see `<CFFORM>` in action, once again modify your login screen.

The code in Listing 12.4 is essentially the same code as your original form (refer to Listing 12.1). The only thing you've changed is replacing `<FORM>` with `<CFFORM>` and `</FORM>` with `</CFFORM>`. Make these changes and save the file as `login3.cfm`.

Listing 12.4 `login3.cfm`—Code for `<CFFORM>` Driven Login Form

```
<!---
Name:        login3.cfm
Author:      Ben Forta (ben@forta.com)
Description: Form field validation demo
Created:     4/15/02
--->

<HTML>

<HEAD>
    <TITLE>Orange Whip Studios - Intranet</TITLE>
</HEAD>

<BODY>

<!--- Page header --->
<CFINCLUDE TEMPLATE="header.cfm">

<!--- Login form --->
```

Listing 12.4 (continued)

```
<CFFORM ACTION="process.cfm">

<TABLE ALIGN="center" BGCOLOR="orange">
    <TR>
        <TD ALIGN="right">
            ID:
        </TD>
        <TD>
            <INPUT TYPE="text"
                   NAME="LoginID"
                   MAXLENGTH="5">
        </TD>
    </TR>
    <TR>
        <TD ALIGN="right">
            Password:
        </TD>
        <TD>
            <INPUT TYPE="password"
                   NAME="LoginPassword"
                   MAXLENGTH="20">
        </TD>
    </TR>
    <TR>
        <TD COLSPAN="2" ALIGN="center">
            <INPUT TYPE="submit" VALUE="Login">
        </TD>
   </TR>
</TABLE>

</CFFORM>

</BODY>

</HTML>
```

So, what happens when ColdFusion processes this form? The best way to understand it is to look at the code this template generates. You can do this by selecting the View Source option in your browser. The code you see should look similar to this:

```
<HTML>

<HEAD>
    <TITLE>Orange Whip Studios - Intranet</TITLE>

<SCRIPT LANGUAGE="JavaScript"
        TYPE="text/javascript" SRC="/CFIDE/scripts/cfform.js">
</SCRIPT>

<SCRIPT LANGUAGE="JavaScript" TYPE="text/javascript">
<!--

function  _CF_checkCFForm_1(_CF_this)
{
    return true;
}
```

```
//-->
</SCRIPT>

</HEAD>

<BODY>

<TABLE ALIGN="center">
 <TR>
  <TD>
   <IMG SRC="../images/logo_c.gif" ALT="Orange Whip Studios">
  </TD>
  <TD ALIGN="center">
   <FONT SIZE="+2">Orange Whip Studios<BR>Movies</FONT>
  </TD>
 </TR>
</TABLE>


<FORM NAME="CFForm_1"
      ACTION="process.cfm"
      METHOD="POST"
      onSubmit="return _CF_checkCFForm_1(this)">

<TABLE ALIGN="center" BGCOLOR="orange">
    <TR>
        <TD ALIGN="right">
            ID:
        </TD>
        <TD>
            <INPUT TYPE="text"
                   NAME="LoginID"
                   MAXLENGTH="5">
        </TD>
    </TR>
    <TR>
        <TD ALIGN="right">
            Password:
        </TD>
        <TD>
            <INPUT TYPE="password"
                   NAME="LoginPassword"
                   MAXLENGTH="20">
        </TD>
    </TR>
    <TR>
        <TD COLSPAN="2" ALIGN="center">
            <INPUT TYPE="submit" VALUE="Login">
        </TD>
    </TR>
</TABLE>

</FORM>

</BODY>

</HTML>
```

The first thing you'll notice is that a JavaScript function has been added to the top of the page. The function currently always returns `true` because no validation rules have been set up yet. As you add validation rules to `<CFFORM>`, this function will automatically be expanded.

NOTE

Unlike CFML, JavaScript is case sensitive, so `true` and `false` can't be replaced with `TRUE` and `FALSE`.

The `<CFFORM>` and `</CFFORM>` tags in your code (refer to Listing 12.4) have been replaced with standard HTML `<FORM>` and `</FORM>` tags.

The `<FORM>` tag itself now has a `NAME` attribute with a unique value that was assigned by ColdFusion.

CAUTION

`<CFFORM>` enables you to provide a name yourself, in which case ColdFusion would use your own name instead of generating one for you. If you do specify your own name, be sure that each form on your page is uniquely named.

And finally, an `onSubmit` attribute was added. This is the JavaScript instruction to your browser that tells it to execute the JavaScript function specified prior to submitting the form to the server. If the specified function returns `true`, the form submission will continue. If the function returns `false`, the submission will be canceled.

NOTE

Actually, I lied. There was one other change in Listing 12.4. If you look carefully, you'll notice that I omitted the `METHOD` from the form–something I previously said you should never do. Why did I do this? Take a look at the generated code again; you'll see that ColdFusion automatically put the `METHOD="POST"` in there for me. That's another useful `<CFFORM>` feature.

Using `<CFINPUT>`

`<CFFORM>` creates the foundation on which to build JavaScript validation. To specify the validation rules themselves, you have to use the `<CFINPUT>` tag. `<CFINPUT>` does the same thing as the standard HTML `<INPUT>` tag and takes the same attributes as parameters. But it also takes additional optional attributes, attributes you can use to specify validation rules.

Look at this code sample:

```
<CFINPUT TYPE="text" NAME="LoginID" SIZE="5" MAXLENGTH="5" REQUIRED="Yes">
```

It looks just like a standard `<INPUT>` tag. The only differences are `<CFINPUT>` instead of `<INPUT>` and the extra `REQUIRED` attribute which has a value of `Yes`.

And yet this code does so much more than `<INPUT>`. This `<CFINPUT>` tag instructs ColdFusion to generate the JavaScript code required to flag this field as required.

So, update your login screen once again.

Listing 12.5 is yet another updated version of your login screen (this is file `login4.cfm`). This time the `LoginID` field's `<INPUT>` tag has been replaced with a `<CFINPUT>` tag.

Listing 12.5 login4.cfm—Login Prompt Screen with <CFINPUT> Used to Flag Required Field

```
<!---
Name:        login4.cfm
Author:      Ben Forta (ben@forta.com)
Description: Form field validation demo
Created:     4/15/02
--->

<HTML>

<HEAD>
    <TITLE>Orange Whip Studios - Intranet</TITLE>
</HEAD>

<BODY>

<!--- Page header --->
<CFINCLUDE TEMPLATE="header.cfm">

<!--- Login form --->
<CFFORM ACTION="process.cfm">

<TABLE ALIGN="center" BGCOLOR="orange">
    <TR>
        <TD ALIGN="right">
            ID:
        </TD>
        <TD>
            <CFINPUT TYPE="text"
                     NAME="LoginID"
                     MAXLENGTH="5"
                     REQUIRED="Yes">
        </TD>
    </TR>
    <TR>
        <TD ALIGN="right">
            Password:
        </TD>
        <TD>
            <INPUT TYPE="password"
                   NAME="LoginPassword"
                   MAXLENGTH="20">
        </TD>
    </TR>
    <TR>
        <TD COLSPAN="2" ALIGN="center">
            <INPUT TYPE="submit" VALUE="Login">
        </TD>
    </TR>
</TABLE>

</CFFORM>

</BODY>

</HTML>
```

When ColdFusion processes this new form, it embeds complete JavaScript validation code (as shown here), and all automatically:

```
<HTML>

<HEAD>
    <TITLE>Orange Whip Studios - Intranet</TITLE>

<SCRIPT LANGUAGE="JavaScript"
        TYPE="text/javascript"
        SRC="/CFIDE/scripts/cfform.js">
</SCRIPT>

<SCRIPT LANGUAGE="JavaScript"
        TYPE="text/javascript">
<!--

function  _CF_checkCFForm_1(_CF_this)
{
    if  (!_CF_hasValue(_CF_this.LoginID, "TEXT" ))
    {
        if  (!_CF_onError(_CF_this, _CF_this.LoginID, _CF_this.LoginID.value, "Error
in LoginID text."))
        {
            return false;
        }
    }

    return true;
}

//-->
</SCRIPT>

</HEAD>

<BODY>

<TABLE ALIGN="center">
 <TR>
  <TD>
   <IMG SRC="../images/logo_c.gif" ALT="Orange Whip Studios">
  </TD>
  <TD ALIGN="center">
   <FONT SIZE="+2">Orange Whip Studios<BR>Movies</FONT>
  </TD>
 </TR>
</TABLE>

<FORM NAME="CFForm_1"
      ACTION="process.cfm"
      METHOD="POST"
      onSubmit="return _CF_checkCFForm_1(this)">

<TABLE ALIGN="center" BGCOLOR="orange">
    <TR>
        <TD ALIGN="right">
            ID:
```

```
            </TD>
            <TD>
                <INPUT TYPE="text" NAME="LoginID" MAXLENGTH="5">
            </TD>
        </TR>
        <TR>
            <TD ALIGN="right">
                Password:
            </TD>
            <TD>
                <INPUT TYPE="password"
                       NAME="LoginPassword"
                       MAXLENGTH="20">
            </TD>
        </TR>
        <TR>
            <TD COLSPAN="2" ALIGN="center">
                <INPUT TYPE="submit" VALUE="Login">
            </TD>
        </TR>
    </TABLE>

    </FORM>

    </BODY>

    </HTML>
```

NOTE

The actual JavaScript validation code is in a file named `cfform.js` in the `cfide/scripts` directory beneath the Web root. This file is included dynamically using a `<SCRIPT>` tag whenever any validation is used.

As you can see, the `<CFINPUT>` tag has been replaced by a standard HTML `<INPUT>` tag. In fact, the generated tag looks exactly the same as the `<INPUT>` tag looked before you added the `<CFINPUT> REQUIRED` attribute. That attribute was used by ColdFusion to generate the JavaScript code, which ensures that a blank `LoginID` field cannot be submitted. If the user tries to submit the form, the JavaScript will pop up an error message box, as shown in Figure 12.4.

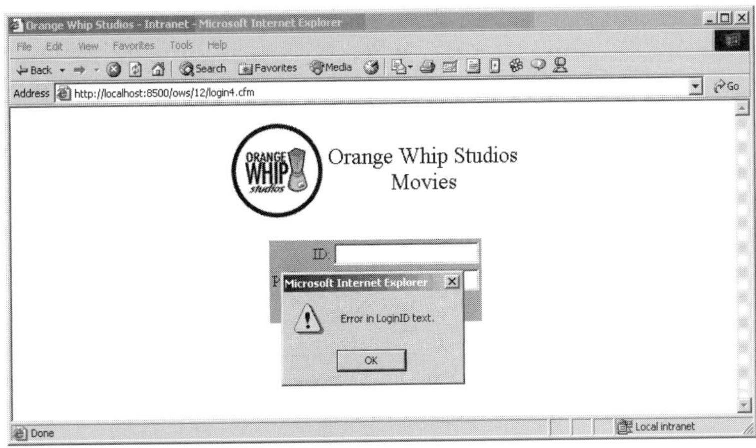

Figure 12.4

Unless otherwise specified, a default error message is used when JavaScript validation rules fail.

NOTE

The pop-up error box is a standard browser dialog box that varies from browser to browser, and there is no way to change what it looks like. The only thing you can change is the actual error message itself.

Using `<CFINPUT>` Validation Options

So far, you have used `<CFINPUT>` to flag fields as required. And if you were impressed with that, wait, there's more. `<CFINPUT>` also lets you specify data type validation rules, as well as customized error messages.

To provide these capabilities, `<CFINPUT>` supports all the attributes supported by HTML `<INPUT>`, as well as some additional ones. These are listed in Table 12.3.

Table 12.3 `<CFINPUT>` Attributes

ATTRIBUTE	DESCRIPTION
`MESSAGE`	Error message text to pop up if this field's validation fails.
`ONERROR`	The name of a JavaScript function to execute if a validation rule fails, overriding the default error function.
`ONVALIDATE`	To override the default JavaScript validation code, and to use your own JavaScript, specify the JavaScript function name here.
`PATTERN`	Regular expression pattern, required if `VALIDATE` is `regular_expression`.
`RANGE`	Range of valid values (for numeric data only) specified as `minimum,maximum`.
`REQUIRED`	Set to `Yes` to flag field as required, default is `No`.
`VALIDATE`	One of the nine supported data validation types, as listed in Table 12.4.

The `<CFINPUT>` `VALIDATE` attribute takes a data type as a value. The supported data types are listed in Table 12.4.

Table 12.4 `<CFINPUT>` Data Validation Types

ATTRIBUTE	DESCRIPTION
`creditcard`	Blanks and dashes are stripped, and the number is verified using the mod10 algorithm.
`date`	Verifies U.S. date entry in the form mm/dd/yyyy.
`eurodate`	Verifies valid European date entry in the form dd/mm/yyyy.
`float`	Verifies a floating-point entry.
`integer`	Verifies an integer entry.
`regular_expression`	Verifies against any provided regular expression.
`social_security_number`	Social Security number in the form ###-##-#### (the hyphen separator can be replaced with a blank).

Table 12.4 (continued)

`telephone`	Verifies a telephone entry; telephone data must be entered as ###-###-#### (the hyphen separator can be replaced with a blank); the area code and exchange must begin with a digit between 1 and 9.
`time`	Verifies a time entry in the form hh:mm:ss.
`zipcode`	(U.S. formats only) Number can be a 5-digit or 9-digit ZIP in the form #####-#### (the hyphen separator can be replaced with a blank).

Now that you've seen what `<CFINPUT>` can do, update your login screen one final time. The code shown in Listing 12.6 uses `<CFINPUT>` tags for both input fields and flags both of them as required fields. In addition, the `LoginID` field has a validation type of `integer`, which prevents the user from entering non-numeric data in it. And finally, both fields have custom error messages specified using the `MESSAGE` attribute. If validation fails, the specified error message is displayed, as shown in Figure 12.5.

Listing 12.6 `login5.cfm`—The Completed Prompt Form, with JavaScript Validation

```
<!---
Name:        login5.cfm
Author:      Ben Forta (ben@forta.com)
Description: Form field validation demo
Created:     4/15/02
--->

<HTML>

<HEAD>
    <TITLE>Orange Whip Studios - Intranet</TITLE>
</HEAD>

<BODY>

<!--- Page header --->
<CFINCLUDE TEMPLATE="header.cfm">

<!--- Login form --->
<CFFORM ACTION="process.cfm">

<TABLE ALIGN="center" BGCOLOR="orange">
    <TR>
        <TD ALIGN="right">
            ID:
        </TD>
        <TD>
            <CFINPUT TYPE="text"
                     NAME="LoginID"
                     MESSAGE="Valid numeric ID is required!"
                     VALIDATE="integer"
                     REQUIRED="Yes"
                     MAXLENGTH="5">
        </TD>
    </TR>
```

Listing 12.6 (continued)

```
        <TR>
            <TD ALIGN="right">
                Password:
            </TD>
            <TD>
                <CFINPUT TYPE="password"
                         NAME="LoginPassword"
                         MESSAGE="Password is required!"
                         REQUIRED="Yes"
                         MAXLENGTH="20">
            </TD>
        </TR>
        <TR>
            <TD COLSPAN="2" ALIGN="center">
                <INPUT TYPE="submit" VALUE="Login">
            </TD>
       </TR>
    </TABLE>

    </CFFORM>

    </BODY>

    </HTML>
```

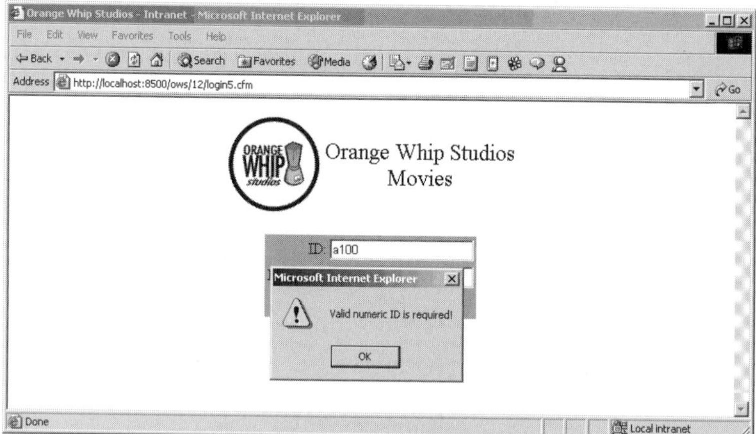

Figure 12.5

The <CFINPUT> MESSAGE attribute can be used to customize the displayed error message.

Extending <CFINPUT> Validation Options

You cannot add your own validation types to <CFINPUT>, but you can extend the validation by providing *regular expressions*. A regular expression is a search pattern used to match strings. Full coverage of regular expressions is beyond the scope of this book, but here are some examples to help explain the concept.

Colors used in Web pages are often specified as RGB values (colors specified in amounts of red, green and blue). RGB values are 6 characters long—3 sets of two hexadecimal values (`00` to `FF`). To obtain a set of RGB values in a form you could use three `<CFINPUT>` tags like this:

```
Red:
<CFINPUT TYPE="text"
         NAME="color_r"
         VALIDATE="regular_expression"
         PATTERN="[A-Fa-f0-9]{2,}"
         MESSAGE="RGB value must be 00-FF"
         SIZE="2"
         MAXLENGTH="2">
<BR>
Green:
<CFINPUT TYPE="text"
         NAME="color_g"
         VALIDATE="regular_expression"
         PATTERN="[A-Fa-f0-9]{2,}"
         MESSAGE="RGB value must be 00-FF"
         SIZE="2"
         MAXLENGTH="2">
<BR>
Blue
<CFINPUT TYPE="text"
         NAME="color_b"
         VALIDATE="regular_expression"
         PATTERN="[A-Fa-f0-9]{2,}"
         MESSAGE="RGB value must be 00-FF"
         SIZE="2"
         MAXLENGTH="2">
<BR>
```

`VALIDATE="regular_expression"` specifies that regular expressions are to be used for validation. The regular expression itself is passed to the `PATTERN` attribute. `[A-Fa-f0-9]` matches a single character of `A` through `F` (upper or lower case) or `0` through `9`. The `{2,}` instructs the browser to only accept a minimum of `2` instances of the previous expression. That coupled with `MAXLENGTH="2"` provides the exact validation rule needed to accept RGB values.

Here's another example, one that we probably all wish was a built in rule—it validates that an e-mail address is formed correctly:

```
<CFINPUT TYPE="text"
         NAME="email"
         VALIDATE="regular_expression"
         PATTERN="[A-Za-z0-9_]+@[A-Za-z0-9_]+\.[A-Za-z]+"
         MESSAGE="Please enter a valid E-Mail address">
```

Here the Regular Expression matches one of more alphanumeric characters (or an underscore), followed by an `@` sign, followed by one or more alphanumeric characters (again allowing underscores), followed by a period, and then followed by one or more alphanumeric characters. This won't actually check that a specified e-mail address is a valid working address, but it will at least prevent completely invalid addresses from being entered.

As you can see, with minimal work you can write Regular Expressions to validate all sorts of things.

NOTE

The Regular Expressions used here are not the same as those used in the CFML `RE` functions. The Regular Expressions passed to `<CFINPUT>` are those supported by JavaScript.

As you can see, with `<CFINPUT>`, implementing client-side validation is a clean and simple process—ColdFusion does it for you.

Putting It All Together

Before you run off and plug `<CFFORM>` and `<CFINPUT>` into all your templates, there are some other details that you should know:

- *Not all browsers support JavaScript*—Also, those that don't will generally ignore it, enabling your forms to be submitted without being validated.
- *You should combine the use of JavaScript validation with server-side validation using embedded fields*—These will never fail validation if the browser does support JavaScript, and if the browser does not, at least you have some form of validation.
- *Older browsers (including some versions of Netscape 3) might have trouble with some of the generated JavaScript*—So, be sure you test your forms in as many different browsers as possible.
- *The JavaScript code can be quite lengthy*—This will increase the size of your Web page and thus the time it takes to download it from your Web server.

Other Form Validation Options

Other form validation options are possible too. Here are two additional options to consider, both of which are highly usable and very intuitive, and both of which are beyond the scope of this chapter. Still, it is worth mentioning them so that you'll know what options are available to you when you need them.

Form Redisplay

One form of form processing that is gaining popularity is server-side validation with a twist. Instead of aborting processing and displaying validation errors, you can redisplay the original form (containing all the information entered by the user), flagging the fields that need correction with an indicator and a message.

To create this type of interface, you must create your form with the capability to display existing values (as explained in the last chapter), as well as with all the conditional logic necessary to display messages where and when needed. One way to accomplish this is to create a form that submits to itself, the flow would go something like this:

1. First define all the form fields as variables—initially these will be empty (or will contain default values), when redisplaying the form these will contain the user input.

2. Create an array of form field names, along with a status (validated or not) and error message for each.
3. If processing a form submission (you can determine this by checking for the presence of `FORM` variables) validate each field setting its status appropriately.
4. If validated, redirect to another CFM page to continue processing.
5. If not validated, render the form, and for each field check the validation status to be able to display the field as needed.

This is not trivial code to write, but keep the idea in mind. When you are ready to tackle it, it's definitely an interface worthy of consideration for your applications.

Flash

One final alternative is the use of Flash to create your forms. Flash MX comes with pre-built components for form controls and is thus an ideal solution for creating very intuitive data entry screens.

Using Flash you'll be able to:

- Create forms that contain all sorts of form fields.
- Implement tab dialogs and other sophisticated interfaces.
- Perform powerful data validation, even using server-side validation internally if needed (via Flash remoting).
- Manage focus, and enable or disable form fields as needed.
- Create a data entry experience not possible using HTML itself.

➜ Chapter 23, "Integrating with Macromedia Flash MX", covers the basics of ColdFusion Flash integration.

CHAPTER 13

Using Forms to Add or Change Data

IN THIS CHAPTER

Adding Data with ColdFusion

Now that you have learned all about forms and form data validation (in the previous two chapters), it's time to combine the two so as to be able to add and update database table data.

→ See Chapter 11, "ColdFusion Forms," to learn about HTML forms and how to use them within your ColdFusion applications.

→ See Chapter 12, "Form Data Validation," for coverage of form field validation techniques and options.

When you created the movie search forms in Chapter 11, you had to create two templates for each search. One created the user search screen that contains the search form, and the other performs the actual search using the ColdFusion `<CFQUERY>` tag. ColdFusion developers usually refer to these as the `<FORM>` and `ACTION` pages (because one contains the form and the other is the file specified as the `<FORM> ACTION`).

Breaking an operation into more than one template is typical of ColdFusion, as well as all Web-based data interaction. As explained in Chapter 1, "Introduction to ColdFusion," a browser's connection to a Web server is made and broken as necessary. An HTTP connection is made to a Web server whenever a Web page is retrieved. That connection is broken as soon as that page is retrieved. Any subsequent pages are retrieved with a new connection that is used just to retrieve that page.

There is no real way to keep a connection alive for the duration of a complete process—when searching for data, for example. Therefore, the process must be broken up into steps, and as shown in Chapter 11, each step is a separate template.

Adding data via your Web browser is no different. You generally need at least two templates to perform the insertion. One displays the form you use to collect the data, and the other processes the data and inserts the record.

Adding data to a table involves the following steps:

1. Display a form to collect the data. The names of any input fields should match the names of the columns in the destination table.
2. Submit the form to ColdFusion for processing. ColdFusion adds the row via the data source using a SQL statement.

Creating an Add Record Form

Forms used to add data are no different from the forms you created to search for data. As seen in Listing 13.1, the form is created using form tags, with a form control for each row table column to be inserted. Save this file as `insert1.cfm` (in the `13` directory under `ows`). You'll be able to execute the page to display the form, but don't submit it yet (you've yet to create the `ACTION` page).

Listing 13.1 `insert1.cfm`—New Movie Form

```
<!---
Name:        insert1.cfm
Author:      Ben Forta (ben@forta.com)
Description: Table row insertion demo
Created:     4/20/02
--->

<!--- Get ratings --->
<CFQUERY DATASOURCE="ows" NAME="ratings">
SELECT RatingID, Rating
FROM FilmsRatings
ORDER BY RatingID
</CFQUERY>

<!--- Page header --->
<CFINCLUDE TEMPLATE="header.cfm">

<!--- New movie form --->
<FORM ACTION="insert2.cfm" METHOD="post">

<TABLE ALIGN="center" BGCOLOR="orange">
    <TR>
        <TH COLSPAN="2">
            <FONT SIZE="+1">Add a Movie</FONT>
        </TH>
    </TR>
    <TR>
        <TD>
            Movie:
        </TD>
        <TD>
            <INPUT TYPE="Text"
                   NAME="MovieTitle"
                   SIZE="50"
                   MAXLENGTH="100">
        </TD>
    </TR>
    <TR>
```

Listing 13.1 (continued)

```
            <TD>
                Tag line:
            </TD>
            <TD>
                <INPUT TYPE="Text"
                       NAME="PitchText"
                       SIZE="50"
                       MAXLENGTH="100">
            </TD>
        </TR>
        <TR>
            <TD>
                Rating:
            </TD>
            <TD>
                <!--- Ratings list --->
                <SELECT NAME="RatingID">
                    <CFOUTPUT QUERY="ratings">
                        <OPTION VALUE="#RatingID#">#Rating#</OPTION>
                    </CFOUTPUT>
                </SELECT>
            </TD>
        </TR>
        <TR>
            <TD>
                Summary:
            </TD>
            <TD>
                <TEXTAREA NAME="summary"
                          COLS="40"
                          ROWS="5"
                          WRAP="virtual"></TEXTAREA>
            </TD>
        </TR>
        <TR>
            <TD>
                Budget:
            </TD>
            <TD>
                <INPUT TYPE="Text"
                       NAME="AmountBudgeted"
                       SIZE="10"
                       MAXLENGTH="10">
            </TD>
        </TR>
        <TR>
            <TD>
                Release Date:
            </TD>
            <TD>
                <INPUT TYPE="Text"
                       NAME="DateInTheaters"
                       SIZE="10"
                       MAXLENGTH="10">
            </TD>
```

Listing 13.1 (continued)

```
        </TR>
        <TR>
            <TD>
                Image File:
            </TD>
            <TD>
                <INPUT TYPE="Text"
                         NAME="ImageName"
                         SIZE="20"
                         MAXLENGTH="50">
            </TD>
        </TR>
        <TR>
            <TD COLSPAN="2" ALIGN="center">
                <INPUT TYPE="submit" VALUE="Insert">
            </TD>
       </TR>
    </TABLE>

    </FORM>

    <!--- Page footer --->
    <CFINCLUDE TEMPLATE="footer.cfm">
```

NOTE

Listing 13.1 contains a form, not unlike all the forms created in Chapters 11 and 12. This form uses form techniques and validation options described in both of those chapters; refer to them if necessary.

The file `insert1.cfm` (and indeed all the files in this chapter) includes common header and footer files (`header.cfm` and `footer.cfm`, respectively). These files contain the HTML page layout code, including any logos. They are included in each file (using `<CFINCLUDE>` tags) to facilitate code reuse (and to keep code listings shorter and more manageable). Listings 13.2 and 13.3 contain the code for these two files.

➔ `<CFINCLUDE>` and code reuse are introduced in Chapter 9, "CFML Basics."

Listing 13.2 `header.cfm`—Movie Form Page Header

```
<!---
Name:        header.cfm
Author:      Ben Forta (ben@forta.com)
Description: Page header
Created:     4/20/02
--->

<HTML>

<HEAD>
    <TITLE>Orange Whip Studios - Intranet</TITLE>
</HEAD>

<BODY>
```

Listing 13.2 (continued)

```
<TABLE ALIGN="center">
 <TR>
  <TD>
   <IMG SRC="../images/logo_c.gif" ALT="Orange Whip Studios">
  </TD>
  <TD ALIGN="center">
   <FONT SIZE="+2">Orange Whip Studios<BR>Movie Maintenance</FONT>
  </TD>
 </TR>
</TABLE>
```

Listing 13.3 `footer.cfm`—Movie Form Page Footer

```
<!---
Name:        footer.cfm
Author:      Ben Forta (ben@forta.com)
Description: Page footer
Created:     4/20/02
--->

</BODY>

</HTML>
```

The `<FORM>` `ACTION` attribute specifies the name of the template to be used to process the insertion; in this case it's `insert2.cfm`.

Each `<INPUT>` (or `<CFINPUT>`, if used) field has a field name specified in the `NAME` attribute. These names correspond to the names of the appropriate columns in the `Films` table.

TIP

Dreamweaver MX users can take advantage of the built-in drag-and-drop features when using table and column names within your code. Simply open the Database tab in the Application panel, expand the data source, and then expand the tables item to display the list of tables within the data source. You can then drag the table name into your source code. Similarly, expanding the table name displays a list of the fields within that table, and those too can be dragged into your source code.

You also specified the `SIZE` and `MAXLENGTH` attributes in each of the text fields. `SIZE` is used to specify the size of the text box within the browser window. Without the `SIZE` attribute, the browser uses its default size, which varies from one browser to the next.

The `SIZE` attribute does not restrict the number of characters that can entered into the field. `SIZE="50"` creates a text field that occupies the space of `50` characters, but the text scrolls within the field if you enter more than `50` characters. To restrict the number of characters that can be entered, you must use the `MAXLENGTH` attribute. `MAXLENGTH="100"` instructs the browser to allow no more than `100` characters in the field.

The `SIZE` attribute primarily is used for aesthetics and the control of screen appearance. `MAXLENGTH` is used to ensure that only data that can be handled is entered into a field. Without `MAXLENGTH`, users could enter more data than would fit in a field, and that data would be truncated upon database insertion (or might even generate database errors).

➜ You should always use both the `SIZE` and `MAXLENGTH` attributes for maximum control over form appearance and data entry. Without them, the browser will use its defaults–and there are no rules governing what these defaults should be.

The `RatingID` field is a drop-down list box populated with a `<CFQUERY>` (just as you did in the last chapter).

The Add a Movie form is shown in Figure 13.1.

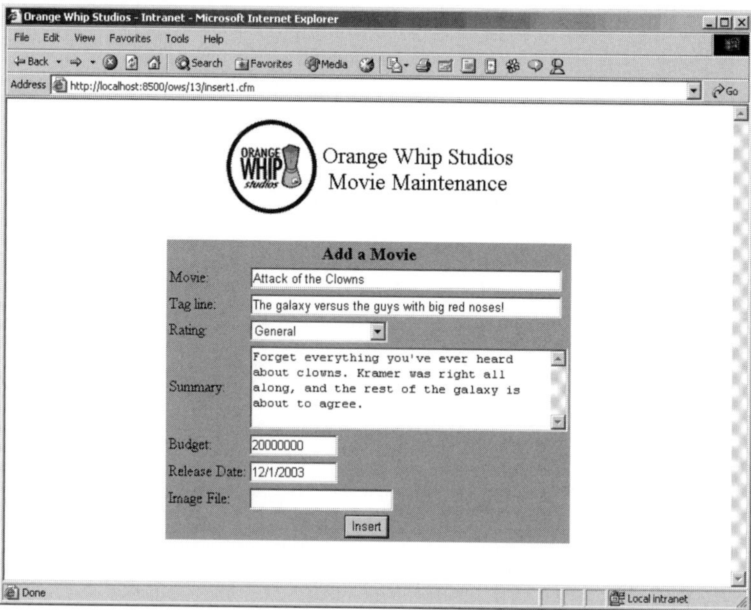

Figure 13.1

HTML forms can be used as a front end for data insertion.

Processing Additions

The next thing you need is a template to process the actual data insertion—the `ACTION` page mentioned earlier. In this page use the SQL `INSERT` statement to add the new row to the `Films` table.

➜ See Chapter 6, "SQL Data Manipulation," for an explanation of the `INSERT` statement.

As shown in Listing 13.4, the `<CFQUERY>` tag can be used to pass any SQL statement—not just `SELECT` statements. The SQL statement here is `INSERT`, which adds a row to the `Films` table and sets the values in seven columns to the form values passed by the browser.

Listing 13.4 `insert2.cfm`—Adding Data with the SQL `INSERT` Statement

```
<!---
Name:        insert2.cfm
Author:      Ben Forta (ben@forta.com)
Description: Table row insertion demo
Created:     4/20/02
--->
```

Listing 13.4 (continued)

```
<!--- Insert movie --->
<CFQUERY DATASOURCE="ows">
INSERT INTO Films(MovieTitle,
                  PitchText,
                  AmountBudgeted,
                  RatingID,
                  Summary,
                  ImageName,
                  DateInTheaters)
VALUES('#Trim(FORM.MovieTitle)#',
       '#Trim(FORM.PitchText)#',
       #FORM.AmountBudgeted#,
       #FORM.RatingID#,
       '#Trim(FORM.Summary)#',
       '#Trim(FORM.ImageName)#',
       #CreateODBCDate(FORM.DateInTheaters)#)
</CFQUERY>

<!--- Page header --->
<CFINCLUDE TEMPLATE="header.cfm">

<!--- Feedback --->
<CFOUTPUT>
<H1>New movie #FORM.MovieTitle# added</H1>
</CFOUTPUT>

<!--- Page footer --->
<CFINCLUDE TEMPLATE="footer.cfm">
```

Listing 13.4 is pretty self-explanatory. The `<CFQUERY>` tag performs the actual `INSERT` operation. The list of columns into which values are to be assigned is specified, as is the matching `VALUES` list (these two lists must match exactly, both the columns and their order).

Each of the values used is from a `FORM` field, but some differences do exist in how the fields are used:

- All string fields have their values enclosed within single quotation marks.
- The two numeric fields (`AmountBudgeted` and `RatingID`) have no single quotation marks around them.
- The date field (`DateInTheaters`) is formatted as a date using the `CreateODBCDate()` function.

It is important to remember that SQL is not typeless, so it is your job to use quotation marks where necessary to explicitly type variables.

TIP

ColdFusion MX is very good at handling dates, and can correctly process dates in all sorts of formats. But occasionally a date may be specified in a format that ColdFusion cannot parse properly in which case it will be your responsibility to format the date so that ColdFusion understands it. You can do this using the `DateFormat()` function or the ODBC date function `CreateODBCDate()` (or the `CreateODBCTime()` and `CreateODBCDateTime()` functions). Even though ColdFusion MX uses JDBC database drivers, the ODBC format generated by the ODBC functions is understood by ColdFusion and will be processed correctly. Listing 13.4 demonstrates the use of the `CreateODBCDate()` function.

NOTE

Notice that the `<CFQUERY>` in Listing 13.4 has no `NAME` attribute. `NAME` is an optional attribute and is necessary only if you need to manipulate the data returned by `<CFQUERY>`. Because the operation here is an `INSERT`, no data is returned; the `NAME` attribute is therefore unnecessary.

Save Listing 13.4 as `insert2.cfm`, and then try submitting a new movie using the form in `insert1.cfm`. You should see a screen similar to the one shown in Figure 13.2.

NOTE

You can verify that the movie was added by browsing the table using any of the search templates you created in Chapter 11.

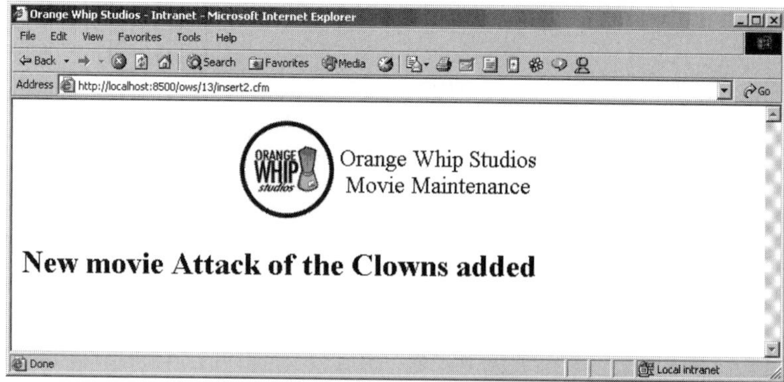

Figure 13.2

Data can be added via ColdFusion using the SQL `INSERT` statement.

Introducing `<CFINSERT>`

The example in Listing 13.4 demonstrates how to add data to a table using the standard SQL `INSERT` command. This works very well if you have to provide data for only a few columns, and if those columns are always provided. If the number of columns can vary, using SQL `INSERT` gets rather complicated.

For example, assume you have two or more data-entry forms for similar data. One might collect a minimal number of fields, whereas another collects a more complete record. How would you create a SQL `INSERT` statement to handle both sets of data?

You could create two separate templates, with a different SQL `INSERT` statement in each, but that's a situation you should always try to avoid. As a rule, you should try to avoid having more than one template perform a given operation. That way you don't run the risk of future changes and revisions being applied incorrectly. If a table name or column name changes, for example, you won't have to worry about forgetting one of the templates that references the changed column.

TIP

As a rule, you should never create more than one template to perform a specific operation. This helps prevent introducing errors into your templates when updates or revisions are made. You are almost always better off creating one template with conditional code than creating two separate templates.

Another solution is to use dynamic SQL. You could write a basic INSERT statement and then gradually construct a complete statement by using a series of <CFIF> statements.

Even though this might be a workable solution, it is not a very efficient one. The conditional SQL INSERT code is far more complex than conditional SQL SELECT. The INSERT statement requires that both the list of columns and the values be dynamic. In addition, the INSERT syntax requires that you separate all column names and values by commas. This means that every column name and value must be followed by a comma—except the last one in the list. Your conditional SQL has to accommodate these syntactical requirements when the statement is constructed.

A better solution is to use <CFINSERT>, which is a special ColdFusion tag that hides the complexity of building dynamic SQL INSERT statements. <CFINSERT> takes the following parameters as attributes:

- DATASOURCE—The name of the data source that contains the table to which the data is to be inserted.
- TABLENAME—The name of the destination table.
- FORMFIELDS—An optional comma-separated list of fields to be inserted. If this attribute is not provided, all the fields in the submitted form are used.

Look at the following ColdFusion tag:

```
<CFINSERT DATASOURCE="ows" TABLENAME="Films">
```

This code does exactly the same thing as the <CFQUERY> tag in Listing 13.4. When ColdFusion processes a <CFINSERT> tag, it builds a dynamic SQL INSERT statement under the hood. If a FORMFIELDS attribute is provided, the specified field names are used. No FORMFIELDS attribute was specified in this example, so ColdFusion automatically uses the form fields that were submitted, building the list of columns and the values dynamically. <CFINSERT> even automatically handles the inclusion of single quotation marks where necessary.

CAUTION

If you are using Windows 98 or ME and are using Microsoft Access, you will not be able to use the <CFINSERT> tag due to limitations with the Access database drivers on these platforms. You can still insert data using <CFQUERY> and INSERT, and <CFINSERT> will function correctly if you are using Access on Windows 2000 or Windows XP.

And while we are it, the form created in insert1.cfm did not perform any data validation which could cause database errors to be thrown (try inserting text in a numeric field and see what happens).

Listing 13.5 contains a revised form (a modified version of insert1.cfm); save this file as insert3.cfm. Listing 13.6 contains a revised action page (a modified version of insert2.cfm); save this file as insert4.cfm.

Listing 13.5 insert3.cfm—Using <CFFORM> For Field Validation

```
<!---
Name:        insert3.cfm
Author:      Ben Forta (ben@forta.com)
Description: Table row insertion demo
```

Listing 13.5 (continued)

```
Created:     4/20/02
--->

<!--- Get ratings --->
<CFQUERY DATASOURCE="ows" NAME="ratings">
SELECT RatingID, Rating
FROM FilmsRatings
ORDER BY RatingID
</CFQUERY>

<!--- Page header --->
<CFINCLUDE TEMPLATE="header.cfm">

<!--- New movie form --->
<CFFORM ACTION="insert4.cfm">

<TABLE ALIGN="center" BGCOLOR="orange">
    <TR>
        <TH COLSPAN="2">
            <FONT SIZE="+1">Add a Movie</FONT>
        </TH>
    </TR>
    <TR>
        <TD>
            Movie:
        </TD>
        <TD>
            <CFINPUT TYPE="Text"
                     NAME="MovieTitle"
                     MESSAGE="MOVIE TITLE is required!"
                     REQUIRED="Yes"
                     SIZE="50"
                     MAXLENGTH="100">
        </TD>
    </TR>
    <TR>
        <TD>
            Tag line:
        </TD>
        <TD>
            <CFINPUT TYPE="Text"
                     NAME="PitchText"
                     MESSAGE="TAG LINE is required!"
                     REQUIRED="Yes"
                     SIZE="50"
                     MAXLENGTH="100">
        </TD>
    </TR>
    <TR>
        <TD>
            Rating:
        </TD>
        <TD>
            <!--- Ratings list --->
            <SELECT NAME="RatingID">
```

Listing 13.5 (continued)

```
                <CFOUTPUT QUERY="ratings">
                    <OPTION VALUE="#RatingID#">#Rating#</OPTION>
                </CFOUTPUT>
            </SELECT>
        </TD>
    </TR>
    <TR>
        <TD>
            Summary:
        </TD>
        <TD>
            <TEXTAREA NAME="summary"
                      COLS="40"
                      ROWS="5"
                      WRAP="virtual"></TEXTAREA>
        </TD>
    </TR>
    <TR>
        <TD>
            Budget:
        </TD>
        <TD>
            <CFINPUT TYPE="Text"
                     NAME="AmountBudgeted"
                     MESSAGE="BUDGET must be a valid numeric amount!"
                     VALIDATE="integer"
                     REQUIRED="NO"
                     SIZE="10"
                     MAXLENGTH="10">
        </TD>
    </TR>
    <TR>
        <TD>
            Release Date:
        </TD>
        <TD>
            <CFINPUT TYPE="Text"
                     NAME="DateInTheaters"
                     MESSAGE="RELEASE DATE must be a valid date!"
                     VALIDATE="date"
                     REQUIRED="NO"
                     SIZE="10"
                     MAXLENGTH="10">
        </TD>
    </TR>
    <TR>
        <TD>
            Image File:
        </TD>
        <TD>
            <CFINPUT TYPE="Text"
                     NAME="ImageName"
                     REQUIRED="NO"
                     SIZE="20"
                     MAXLENGTH="50">
```

Listing 13.5 (continued)

```
            </TD>
        </TR>
        <TR>
            <TD COLSPAN="2" ALIGN="center">
                <INPUT TYPE="submit" VALUE="Insert">
            </TD>
        </TR>
    </TABLE>

    </CFFORM>

    <!--- Page footer --->
    <CFINCLUDE TEMPLATE="footer.cfm">
```

Listing 13.6 is the same form as used previously, except that `<INPUT>` has been replaced with `<CFINPUT>` so as to validate submitted data.

Listing 13.6 `insert4.cfm`—Adding Data with the `<CFINSERT>` Tag

```
<!---
Name:        insert4.cfm
Author:      Ben Forta (ben@forta.com)
Description: Table row insertion demo
Created:     4/20/02
--->

<!--- Insert movie --->
<CFINSERT DATASOURCE="ows" TABLENAME="Films">

<!--- Page header --->
<CFINCLUDE TEMPLATE="header.cfm">

<!--- Feedback --->
<CFOUTPUT>
<H1>New movie #FORM.MovieTitle# added</H1>
</CFOUTPUT>

<!--- Page footer --->
<CFINCLUDE TEMPLATE="footer.cfm">
```

Try adding a movie with these new templates. You'll see that the database inserting code in Listing 13.6 does exactly the same thing as the code in Listing 13.4, but with a much simpler syntax and interface.

Controlling `<CFINSERT>` Form Fields

`<CFINSERT>` instructs ColdFusion to build SQL `INSERT` statements dynamically. ColdFusion automatically uses all submitted form fields when building this statement.

Sometimes you might want ColdFusion to not include certain fields. For example, you might have hidden fields in your form that are not table columns, such as the hidden field shown in Listing 13.7.

That field might be there as part of a security system you have implemented; it is not a column in the table. If you try to pass this field to `<CFINSERT>`, ColdFusion passes the hidden `Login` field as a column to the database. Obviously, this generates an database error, as seen in Figure 13.3, because no `Login` column exists in the `Films` table.

Listing 13.7 `insert5.cfm`—Template That Adds a Movie

```
<!---
Name:        insert5.cfm
Author:      Ben Forta (ben@forta.com)
Description: Table row insertion demo
Created:     4/20/02
--->

<!--- Get ratings --->
<CFQUERY DATASOURCE="ows" NAME="ratings">
SELECT RatingID, Rating
FROM FilmsRatings
ORDER BY RatingID
</CFQUERY>

<!--- Page header --->
<CFINCLUDE TEMPLATE="header.cfm">

<!--- New movie form --->
<CFFORM ACTION="insert6.cfm">

<!--- Login field --->
<INPUT TYPE="hidden" NAME="Login" VALUE="Ben">

<TABLE ALIGN="center" BGCOLOR="orange">
    <TR>
        <TH COLSPAN="2">
            <FONT SIZE="+1">Add a Movie</FONT>
        </TH>
    </TR>
    <TR>
        <TD>
            Movie:
        </TD>
        <TD>
            <CFINPUT TYPE="Text"
                     NAME="MovieTitle"
                     MESSAGE="MOVIE TITLE is required!"
                     REQUIRED="Yes"
                     SIZE="50"
                     MAXLENGTH="100">
        </TD>
    </TR>
    <TR>
        <TD>
            Tag line:
        </TD>
        <TD>
```

Listing 13.7 (continued)

```
        <CFINPUT TYPE="Text"
                 NAME="PitchText"
                 MESSAGE="TAG LINE is required!"
                 REQUIRED="Yes"
                 SIZE="50"
                 MAXLENGTH="100">
    </TD>
</TR>
<TR>
    <TD>
        Rating:
    </TD>
    <TD>
        <!--- Ratings list --->
        <SELECT NAME="RatingID">
            <CFOUTPUT QUERY="ratings">
                <OPTION VALUE="#RatingID#">#Rating#</OPTION>
            </CFOUTPUT>
        </SELECT>
    </TD>
</TR>
<TR>
    <TD>
        Summary:
    </TD>
    <TD>
        <TEXTAREA NAME="summary"
                  COLS="40"
                  ROWS="5"
                  WRAP="virtual"></TEXTAREA>
    </TD>
</TR>
<TR>
    <TD>
        Budget:
    </TD>
    <TD>
        <CFINPUT TYPE="Text"
                 NAME="AmountBudgeted"
                 MESSAGE="BUDGET must be a valid numeric amount!"
                 VALIDATE="integer"
                 REQUIRED="NO"
                 SIZE="10"
                 MAXLENGTH="10">
    </TD>
</TR>
<TR>
    <TD>
        Release Date:
    </TD>
    <TD>
        <CFINPUT TYPE="Text"
                 NAME="DateInTheaters"
                 MESSAGE="RELEASE DATE must be a valid date!"
                 VALIDATE="date"
```

Listing 13.7 (continued)

```
                    REQUIRED="NO"
                    SIZE="10"
                    MAXLENGTH="10">
        </TD>
    </TR>
    <TR>
        <TD>
            Image File:
        </TD>
        <TD>
            <CFINPUT TYPE="Text"
                    NAME="ImageName"
                    REQUIRED="NO"
                    SIZE="20"
                    MAXLENGTH="50">
        </TD>
    </TR>
    <TR>
        <TD COLSPAN="2" ALIGN="center">
            <INPUT TYPE="submit" VALUE="Insert">
        </TD>
    </TR>
</TABLE>

</CFFORM>

<!--- Page footer --->
<CFINCLUDE TEMPLATE="footer.cfm">
```

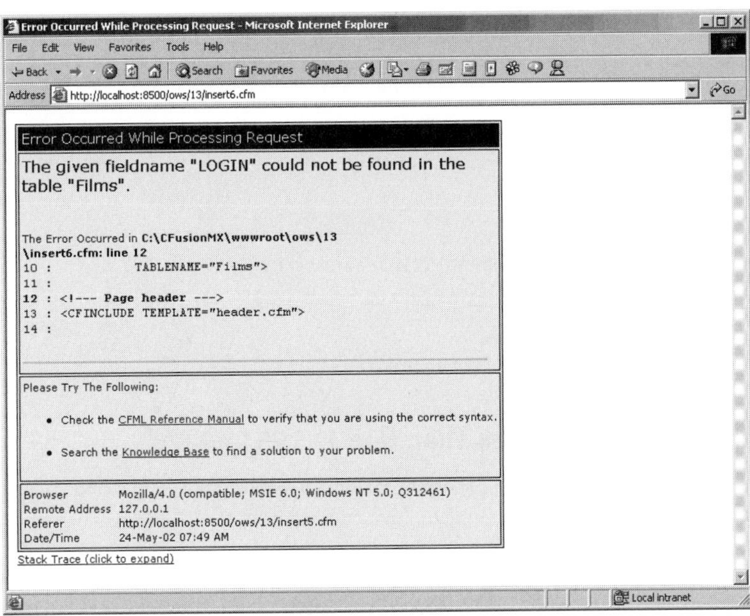

Figure 13.3

An error message is generated if ColdFusion tries to insert fields that are not table columns.

To solve this problem, you must use the FORMFIELDS attribute. FORMFIELDS instructs ColdFusion to process only form fields that are in the list. Any other fields are ignored.

It is important to note that FORMFIELDS is not used to specify which fields ColdFusion should process. Rather, it specifies which fields should *not* be processed. The difference is subtle. Not all fields listed in the FORMFIELDS value need be present. They are processed *if* they are present; if they are not present, they are not processed (so no error will be generated). Any fields not listed in the FORMFIELDS list are completely ignored.

Listing 13.8 contains an updated data insertion template. The <CFINSERT> tag now has a FORMFIELDS attribute, so now ColdFusion knows to ignore the hidden Login field.

Listing 13.8 insert6.cfm—Using the <CFINSERT> FORMFIELDS Attribute to Specify Which Fields to Avoid Processing

```
<!---
Name:        insert6.cfm
Author:      Ben Forta (ben@forta.com)
Description: Table row insertion demo
Created:     4/20/02
--->

<!--- Insert movie --->
<CFINSERT DATASOURCE="ows"
          TABLENAME="Films"
          FORMFIELDS="MovieTitle,
                      PitchText,
                      AmountBudgeted,
                      RatingID,
                      Summary,
                      ImageName,
                      DateInTheaters">

<!--- Page header --->
<CFINCLUDE TEMPLATE="header.cfm">

<!--- Feedback --->
<CFOUTPUT>
<H1>New movie #FORM.MovieTitle# added</H1>
</CFOUTPUT>

<!--- Page footer --->
<CFINCLUDE TEMPLATE="footer.cfm">
```

Collecting Data for More Than One INSERT

Another situation in which <CFINSERT> FORMFIELDS can be used is when a form collects data that needs to be added to more than one table. You can create a template that has two or more <CFINSERT> statements by using FORMFIELDS.

As long as each <CFINSERT> statement has a FORMFIELDS attribute that specifies which fields are to be used with each INSERT, ColdFusion correctly executes each <CFINSERT> with its appropriate fields.

<CFINSERT> Versus SQL INSERT

Adding data to tables using the ColdFusion <CFINSERT> tag is simpler and helps prevent the creation of multiple similar templates.

Why would you ever avoid using <CFINSERT>? Is there ever a reason to use SQL INSERT instead of <CFINSERT>?

The truth is that both are needed. <CFINSERT> can be used only for simple data insertion to a single table. If you want to insert the results of a SELECT statement, you could not use <CFINSERT>. Similarly, if you want to insert values other than FORM fields—perhaps variables or URL parameters—you'd be unable to use <CFINSERT>.

Here are some guidelines to help you decide when to use each method:

- For simple operations (single table and no complex processing) use <CFINSERT> to add data.
- If you find that you need to add specific form fields—and not all that were submitted—use the <CFINSERT> tag with the FORMFIELDS attribute.
- If <CFINSERT> cannot be used because you need a complex INSERT statement or are using fields that are not form fields, use SQL INSERT.

TIP

I have seen many documents and articles attempt to dissuade the use of <CFINSERT> (and <CFUPDATE> discussed below) primarily because of the limitations already mentioned. In my opinion there is nothing wrong with using these tags at all, recognizing their limitations of course. In fact, I'd even argue that their use is preferable as they are dynamic (if the form changes they may not need changing) and are type aware (the handle type conversions automatically). So don't let the naysayers get you down-CFML is all about making your development life easier, if these tags make coding easier then use them.

Updating Data with ColdFusion

Updating data with ColdFusion is similar to inserting data. You generally need two templates to update a row—a data-entry form template and a data update template. The big difference between a form used for data addition and one used for data modification is that the latter needs to be populated with existing values, similar to the screen shown in Figure 13.4.

Building a Data Update Form

Populating an HTML form is a simple process. First, you must retrieve the row to be updated from the table. You do this with a standard <CFQUERY>; the retrieved values are then passed as attributes to the HTML form.

Listing 13.9 contains the code for update1.cfm, a template that updates a movie. Save it as update1.cfm, and then execute it. Be sure to append the FilmID—for example, ?FilmID=13—as a URL parameter. Your screen should look similar to the one shown in Figure 13.4.

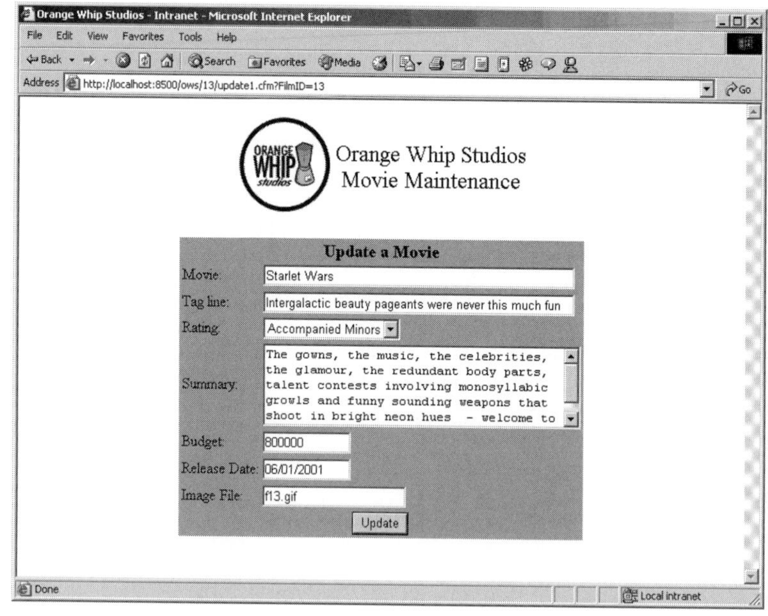

Figure 13.4 When using forms to update data, the form fields usually need to populated with existing values.

Listing 13.9 `update1.cfm`—Movie Update Form

```
<!---
Name:        update1.cfm
Author:      Ben Forta (ben@forta.com)
Description: Table row update demo
Created:     4/20/02
--->

<!--- Check that FilmID was provided --->
<CFIF NOT IsDefined("URL.FilmID")>
 <H1>You did not specify the FilmID</H1>
 <CFABORT>
</CFIF>

<!--- Get the film record --->
<CFQUERY DATASOURCE="ows" NAME="film">
SELECT FilmID, MovieTitle, PitchText,
       AmountBudgeted, RatingID,
       Summary, ImageName, DateInTheaters
FROM Films
WHERE FilmID=#URL.FilmID#
</CFQUERY>

<!--- Get ratings --->
<CFQUERY DATASOURCE="ows" NAME="ratings">
SELECT RatingID, Rating
FROM FilmsRatings
ORDER BY RatingID
</CFQUERY>
```

Listing 13.9 (continued)

```
<!--- Page header --->
<CFINCLUDE TEMPLATE="header.cfm">

<!--- Update movie form --->
<CFFORM ACTION="update2.cfm">

<!--- Embed primary key as a hidden field --->
<CFOUTPUT>
<INPUT TYPE="hidden" NAME="FilmID" VALUE="#Film.FilmID#">
</CFOUTPUT>

<TABLE ALIGN="center" BGCOLOR="orange">
    <TR>
        <TH COLSPAN="2">
            <FONT SIZE="+1">Update a Movie</FONT>
        </TH>
    </TR>
    <TR>
        <TD>
            Movie:
        </TD>
        <TD>
            <CFINPUT TYPE="Text"
                     NAME="MovieTitle"
                     VALUE="#Trim(film.MovieTitle)#"
                     MESSAGE="MOVIE TITLE is required!"
                     REQUIRED="Yes"
                     SIZE="50"
                     MAXLENGTH="100">
        </TD>
    </TR>
    <TR>
        <TD>
            Tag line:
        </TD>
        <TD>
            <CFINPUT TYPE="Text"
                     NAME="PitchText"
                     VALUE="#Trim(film.PitchText)#"
                     MESSAGE="TAG LINE is required!"
                     REQUIRED="Yes"
                     SIZE="50"
                     MAXLENGTH="100">
        </TD>
    </TR>
    <TR>
        <TD>
            Rating:
        </TD>
        <TD>
            <!--- Ratings list --->
            <SELECT NAME="RatingID">
                <CFOUTPUT QUERY="ratings">
                    <OPTION VALUE="#RatingID#" <CFIF ratings.RatingID IS
                    ➥film.RatingID>SELECTED</CFIF>>#Rating#</OPTION>
```

Listing 13.9 (continued)

```
                </CFOUTPUT>
            </SELECT>
        </TD>
    </TR>
    <TR>
        <TD>
            Summary:
        </TD>
        <TD>
            <CFOUTPUT>
            <TEXTAREA NAME="summary"
                      COLS="40"
                      ROWS="5"
                      WRAP="virtual">#Trim(Film.Summary)#</TEXTAREA>
            </CFOUTPUT>
        </TD>
    </TR>
    <TR>
        <TD>
            Budget:
        </TD>
        <TD>
            <CFINPUT TYPE="Text"
                     NAME="AmountBudgeted"
                     VALUE="#Int(film.AmountBudgeted)#"
                     MESSAGE="BUDGET must be a valid numeric amount!"
                     VALIDATE="integer"
                     REQUIRED="NO"
                     SIZE="10"
                     MAXLENGTH="10">
        </TD>
    </TR>
    <TR>
        <TD>
            Release Date:
        </TD>
        <TD>
            <CFINPUT TYPE="Text"
                     NAME="DateInTheaters"
                     VALUE="#DateFormat(film.DateInTheaters, "MM/DD/YYYY")#"
                     MESSAGE="RELEASE DATE must be a valid date!"
                     VALIDATE="date"
                     REQUIRED="NO"
                     SIZE="10"
                     MAXLENGTH="10">
        </TD>
    </TR>
    <TR>
        <TD>
            Image File:
        </TD>
        <TD>
            <CFINPUT TYPE="Text"
                     NAME="ImageName"
                     VALUE="#Trim(film.ImageName)#"
```

Listing 13.9 (continued)

```
                          REQUIRED="NO"
                          SIZE="20"
                          MAXLENGTH="50">
            </TD>
        </TR>
        <TR>
            <TD COLSPAN="2" ALIGN="center">
                <INPUT TYPE="submit" VALUE="Update">
            </TD>
        </TR>
    </TABLE>

    </CFFORM>

    <!--- Page footer --->
    <CFINCLUDE TEMPLATE="footer.cfm">
```

There is a lot to look at in Listing 13.9. And don't submit the form yet; you have yet to create the `ACTION` page.

To populate a form with data to be updated, you must first retrieve that row from the table. Therefore, you must specify a `FilmID` to use this template. Without it, ColdFusion would not know which row to retrieve. To ensure that the `FilmID` is passed, the first thing you do is check for the existence of the `FilmID` parameter. The following code returns `TRUE` only if `FilmID` was not passed, in which case an error message is sent back to the user and template processing is halted with the `<CFABORT>` tag:

```
<CFIF NOT IsDefined("URL.FilmID")>
```

Without the `<CFABORT>` tag, ColdFusion continues processing the template. An error message is generated when the `<CFQUERY>` statement is processed because the `WHERE` clause `WHERE FilmID = #URL.FilmID#` references a nonexistent field.

The first `<CFQUERY>` tag retrieves the row to be edited, and the passed URL is used in the `WHERE` clause to retrieve the appropriate row. The second `<CFQUERY>` retrieves the list of ratings for the `<SELECT>` control. To populate the data-entry fields, the current field value is passed to the `<INPUT>` (or `<CFINPUT>`) `VALUE` attribute. Whatever is passed to `VALUE` is displayed in the field, so `VALUE="#Film.MovieTitle#"` displays the `MovieTitle` table column.

NOTE

The query name is necessary here as a prefix because it is not being used within a `<CFOUTPUT>` associated with a query.

`<CFINPUT>` is a ColdFusion tag, so you can pass variables and columns to it without needing to use `<CFOUTPUT>`. If you were using `<INPUT>` instead of `<CFINPUT>` then the `<INPUT>` tags would need to be within a `<CFOUTPUT>` block.

This is actually another benefit of using `<CFINPUT>` instead of `<INPUT>`–`<CFINPUT>` makes populating form fields with dynamic data much easier.

To ensure that no blank spaces exist after the retrieved value, the fields are trimmed with the ColdFusion `Trim()` function before they are displayed. Why would you do this? Some databases, such as Microsoft SQL Server, pad text fields with spaces so they take up the full column width in the table. The `MovieTitle` field is a 255-character–wide column, so a movie title could have a lot of spaces after it. The extra space can be very annoying when you try to edit the field. To append text to a field, you'd first have to backspace or delete all those extra characters.

➜ When populating forms with table column values, you always should trim the field first. Unlike standard browser output, spaces in form fields are not ignored. Removing them allows easier editing. The ColdFusion `Trim()` function removes spaces at the beginning and end of the value. If you want to trim only trailing spaces, you could use the `RTrim()` function instead. See Appendix C, "ColdFusion Function Reference," for a complete explanation of the ColdFusion `Trim()` functions.

Dates and numbers are also being formatted specially. By default, dates are displayed in a rather unusable format (and a format that will not be accepted upon form submission). Therefore, `DateFormat()` is used to format the date in a usable format.

The `AmountBudgeted` column allows numbers with decimal points; to display the number within the trailing decimal point and zeros, the `Int()` function can be used to round the number to an integer. You also could have used `NumberFormat()` for more precise number formatting.

One hidden field exists in the `FORM`. The following code creates a hidden field called `FilmID`, which contains the ID of the movie being updated:

```
<INPUT TYPE="hidden" NAME="FilmID" VALUE="#Film.FilmID#">
```

This hidden field must be present. Without it, ColdFusion has no idea which row you were updating when the form was actually submitted. Also, because it is an `<INPUT>` field (not `<CFINPUT>`), it must be enclosed within `<CFOUTPUT>` tags.

Remember that HTTP sessions are created and broken as necessary, and every session stands on its own two feet. ColdFusion might retrieve a specific row of data for you in one session, but it does not know that in the next session. Therefore, when you update a row, you must specify the primary key so ColdFusion knows which row to update. Hidden fields are one way of doing this because they are sent to the browser as part of the form, but they are never displayed and thus cannot be edited. However, they are still form fields, and they are submitted along with all other form fields intact upon form submission.

Processing Updates

Just as with adding data, there are two ways to update rows in a table. The code in Listing 13.10 demonstrates a row update using the SQL `UPDATE` statement.

➜ See Chapter 6 for an explanation of the `UPDATE` statement.

Listing 13.10 `update2.cfm`—Updating a Table with the SQL `UPDATE` Statement

```
<!---
Name:        update2.cfm
Author:      Ben Forta (ben@forta.com)
Description: Table row update demo
Created:     4/20/02
--->

<!--- Update movie --->
<CFQUERY DATASOURCE="ows">
UPDATE Films
```

Listing 13.10 (continued)

```
SET MovieTitle='#Trim(FORM.MovieTitle)#',
    PitchText='#Trim(FORM.PitchText)#',
    AmountBudgeted=#FORM.AmountBudgeted#,
    RatingID=#FORM.RatingID#,
    Summary='#Trim(FORM.Summary)#',
    ImageName='#Trim(FORM.ImageName)#',
    DateInTheaters=#CreateODBCDate(FORM.DateInTheaters)#
WHERE FilmID=#FORM.FilmID#
</CFQUERY>

<!--- Page header --->
<CFINCLUDE TEMPLATE="header.cfm">

<!--- Feedback --->
<CFOUTPUT>
<H1>Movie #FORM.MovieTitle# updated</H1>
</CFOUTPUT>

<!--- Page footer --->
<CFINCLUDE TEMPLATE="footer.cfm">
```

This SQL statement updates the seven specified rows for the movie whose ID is the passed `FORM.FilmID`.

To test this update template, try executing template `update1.cfm` with different `FilmID` values (passed as URL parameters), and then submit your changes.

Introducing <CFUPDATE>

Just as you saw earlier in regards to inserting data, hard-coded SQL statements are neither flexible nor easy to maintain. ColdFusion provides a simpler way to update rows in database tables.

CAUTION

If you are using Windows 98 or ME and are using Microsoft Access, you will not be able to use the `<CFUPDATE>` tag due to limitations with the Access database drivers on these platforms. You can still insert data using `<CFQUERY>` and `UPDATE`, and `<CFUPDATE>` will function correctly if you are using Access on Windows 2000 or Windows XP.

The `<CFUPDATE>` tag is similar to the `<CFINSERT>` tag discussed earlier in this chapter. `<CFUPDATE>` requires just two attributes: the data source and the name of the table to update, and supports an optional `FORMFIELDS` too.

- `DATASOURCE`—The name of the data source that contains the table to which the data is to be updated.
- `TABLENAME`—The name of the destination table.
- `FORMFIELDS`—An optional comma-separated list of fields to be updated. If this attribute is not provided, all the fields in the submitted form are used.

When using <CFUPDATE>, ColdFusion automatically locates the row you want to update by looking at the table to ascertain its primary key. All you have to do is ensure that the primary key value is passed, as you did in Listing 13.9 using a hidden field.

The code in Listing 13.11 performs the same update as that in Listing 13.10, but it uses the <CFUPDATE> tag rather than the SQL UPDATE tag. Obviously, this code is more readable, reusable, and accommodating of form-field changes you might make in the future.

Listing 13.11 update3.cfm—Updating Data with the <CFUPDATE> Tag

```
<!---
Name:        update3.cfm
Author:      Ben Forta (ben@forta.com)
Description: Table row update demo
Created:     4/20/02
--->

<!--- Update movie --->
<CFUPDATE DATASOURCE="ows" TABLENAME="Films">

<!--- Page header --->
<CFINCLUDE TEMPLATE="header.cfm">

<!--- Feedback --->
<CFOUTPUT>
<H1>Movie #FORM.MovieTitle# updated</H1>
</CFOUTPUT>

<!--- Page footer --->
<CFINCLUDE TEMPLATE="footer.cfm">
```

To use this code, you must change the <FORM> ACTION attribute in update1.cfm so that it points to update3.cfm. Make this change, and try updating several movies.

<CFUPDATE> Versus SQL UPDATE

Just as with adding data, the choice to use <CFUPDATE> or SQL UPDATE is yours. The guidelines as to when to use each option are similar as well.

The following are some guidelines that help you decide when to use each method:

- Whenever appropriate, use <CFUPDATE> to update data.
- If you find that you need to update specific form fields—not all that were submitted—use the <CFUPDATE> tag with the FORMFIELDS attribute.
- If <CFUPDATE> can't be used because you need a complex UPDATE statement or you are using fields that are not form fields, use SQL UPDATE.
- If you ever need to update multiple (or all) rows in a table, you must use SQL UPDATE.

Deleting Data with ColdFusion

Unlike adding and updating data, ColdFusion provides no efficient way to delete data. DELETE is always a dangerous operation, and the ColdFusion developers didn't want to make it too easy to get rid of the wrong data.

To delete data in a ColdFusion template, you must use the SQL DELETE statement, as shown in Listing 13.12. The code first checks to ensure that a FilmID was passed; it terminates if the URL.FilmID field is not present. If a FilmID is passed, a <CFQUERY> is used to pass a SQL DELETE statement to the data source.

➜ See Chapter 6 for an explanation of the DELETE statement.

Listing 13.12 delete1.cfm—Deleting Table Data with the SQL DELETE Statement

```
<!---
Name:        delete1.cfm
Author:      Ben Forta (ben@forta.com)
Description: Table row delete demo
Created:     4/20/02
--->

<!--- Check that FilmID was provided --->
<CFIF NOT IsDefined("FilmID")>
 <H1>You did not specify the FilmID</H1>
 <CFABORT>
</CFIF>

<!--- Delete a movie --->
<CFQUERY DATASOURCE="ows">
DELETE FROM Films
WHERE FilmID=#FilmID#
</CFQUERY>

<!--- Page header --->
<CFINCLUDE TEMPLATE="header.cfm">

<!--- Feedback --->
<H1>Movie deleted</H1>

<!--- Page footer --->
<CFINCLUDE TEMPLATE="footer.cfm">
```

No <CFDELETE> tag exists in ColdFusion. The only way to delete rows is using a SQL DELETE.

Reusing Forms

You can now add to as well as update and delete from your Films table. But what if you need to change the form? What if you needed to add a field, or change validation, or update colors? Any changed needed to be made to the Add form also must be made to the Update form.

With all the effort you have gone to in the past few chapters to prevent any duplication of effort, this seems counterproductive.

Indeed it is.

The big difference between an Add and an Update form is whether the fields are prefilled to show current values. Using ColdFusion conditional expressions, you can create a single form that can be used for both adding and updating data.

To do this, all you need is a way to conditionally include the `VALUE` attribute in `<INPUT>`. After all, look at the following two `<INPUT>` statements:

```
<INPUT TYPE="text" NAME="MovieTitle"><INPUT TYPE="text" NAME="MovieTitle"
VALUE="#MovieTitle#">
```

The first `<INPUT>` is used for new data; there is no prefilled `VALUE`. The second is for editing, and thus the field is populated with an initial `VALUE`.

It would therefore not be difficult to create `<INPUT>` fields with `<CFIF>` statements embedded in them, conditionally including the `VALUE`. Look at the following code:

```
<INPUT TYPE="text" NAME="MovieTitle"
    <CFIF IsDefined("URL.FilmID")>
        VALUE="#MovieTitle#"
    </CFIF>
>
```

This `<INPUT>` field includes the `VALUE` attribute only if the `FilmID` was passed (meaning that this is an edit operation as opposed to an add operation). Using this technique, a single form field can be used for both adds and edits.

This is perfectly valid code, and this technique is quite popular. The only problem with it is that the code can get very difficult to read. All those embedded `<CFIF>` statements, one for every row, make the code quite complex. There is a better solution.

`VALUE` can be empty: The attribute `VALUE=""` is perfectly legal and valid. So why not *always* use `VALUE`, but conditionally populate it? The best way to demonstrate this is to try it, so Listing 13.13 contains the code for `edit1.cfm`—a new dual purpose form.

Listing 13.13 `edit1.cfm`—Combination Insert and Update Form

```
<!---
Name:        edit1.cfm
Author:      Ben Forta (ben@forta.com)
Description: Dual purpose form demo
Created:     4/20/02
--->

<!--- Check that FilmID was provided --->
<!--- If yes, edit, else add --->
<CFSET EditMode=IsDefined("URL.FilmID")>

<!--- If edit mode then get row to edit --->
<CFIF EditMode>
```

Listing 13.13 (continued)

```
    <!--- Get the film record --->
    <CFQUERY DATASOURCE="ows" NAME="film">
    SELECT FilmID, MovieTitle, PitchText,
           AmountBudgeted, RatingID,
           Summary, ImageName, DateInTheaters
    FROM Films
    WHERE FilmID=#URL.FilmID#
    </CFQUERY>

    <!--- Save to variables --->
    <CFSET MovieTitle=Trim(film.MovieTitle)>
    <CFSET PitchText=Trim(film.PitchText)>
    <CFSET AmountBudgeted=Int(film.AmountBudgeted)>
    <CFSET RatingID=film.RatingID>
    <CFSET Summary=Trim(film.Summary)>
    <CFSET ImageName=Trim(film.ImageName)>
    <CFSET DateInTheaters=DateFormat(film.DateInTheaters, "MM/DD/YYYY")>

    <!--- Form text --->
    <CFSET FormTitle="Update a Movie">
    <CFSET ButtonText="Update">

<CFELSE>

    <!--- Save to variables --->
    <CFSET MovieTitle="">
    <CFSET PitchText="">
    <CFSET AmountBudgeted="">
    <CFSET RatingID="">
    <CFSET Summary="">
    <CFSET ImageName="">
    <CFSET DateInTheaters="">

    <!--- Form text --->
    <CFSET FormTitle="Add a Movie">
    <CFSET ButtonText="Insert">

</CFIF>

<!--- Get ratings --->
<CFQUERY DATASOURCE="ows" NAME="ratings">
SELECT RatingID, Rating
FROM FilmsRatings
ORDER BY RatingID
</CFQUERY>

<!--- Page header --->
<CFINCLUDE TEMPLATE="header.cfm">

<!--- Add/update movie form --->
<CFFORM ACTION="edit2.cfm">

<CFIF EditMode>
    <!--- Embed primary key as a hidden field --->
    <CFOUTPUT>
```

Listing 13.13 (continued)

```
        <INPUT TYPE="hidden" NAME="FilmID" VALUE="#Film.FilmID#">
        </CFOUTPUT>
    </CFIF>

    <TABLE ALIGN="center" BGCOLOR="orange">
        <TR>
            <TH COLSPAN="2">
                <CFOUTPUT>
                <FONT SIZE="+1">#FormTitle#</FONT>
                </CFOUTPUT>
            </TH>
        </TR>
        <TR>
            <TD>
                Movie:
            </TD>
            <TD>
                <CFINPUT TYPE="Text"
                         NAME="MovieTitle"
                         VALUE="#MovieTitle#"
                         MESSAGE="MOVIE TITLE is required!"
                         REQUIRED="Yes"
                         SIZE="50"
                         MAXLENGTH="100">
            </TD>
        </TR>
        <TR>
            <TD>
                Tag line:
            </TD>
            <TD>
                <CFINPUT TYPE="Text"
                         NAME="PitchText"
                         VALUE="#PitchText#"
                         MESSAGE="TAG LINE is required!"
                         REQUIRED="Yes"
                         SIZE="50"
                         MAXLENGTH="100">
            </TD>
        </TR>
        <TR>
            <TD>
                Rating:
            </TD>
            <TD>
                <!--- Ratings list --->
                <SELECT NAME="RatingID">
                    <CFOUTPUT QUERY="ratings">
                        <OPTION VALUE="#RatingID#" CFIF ratings.RatingID IS
                        ➥<VARIABLES.RatingID>SELECTED</CFIF>>#Rating#</OPTION>
                    </CFOUTPUT>
                </SELECT>
            </TD>
        </TR>
        <TR>
```

Listing 13.13 (continued)

```
        <TD>
            Summary:
        </TD>
        <TD>
            <CFOUTPUT>
            <TEXTAREA NAME="summary"
                      COLS="40"
                      ROWS="5"
                      WRAP="virtual">#Summary#</TEXTAREA>
            </CFOUTPUT>
        </TD>
    </TR>
    <TR>
        <TD>
            Budget:
        </TD>
        <TD>
            <CFINPUT TYPE="Text"
                     NAME="AmountBudgeted"
                     VALUE="#AmountBudgeted#"
                     MESSAGE="BUDGET must be a valid numeric amount!"
                     VALIDATE="integer"
                     REQUIRED="NO"
                     SIZE="10"
                     MAXLENGTH="10">
        </TD>
    </TR>
    <TR>
        <TD>
            Release Date:
        </TD>
        <TD>
            <CFINPUT TYPE="Text"
                     NAME="DateInTheaters"
                     VALUE="#DateInTheaters#"
                     MESSAGE="RELEASE DATE must be a valid date!"
                     VALIDATE="date"
                     REQUIRED="NO"
                     SIZE="10"
                     MAXLENGTH="10">
        </TD>
    </TR>
    <TR>
        <TD>
            Image File:
        </TD>
        <TD>
            <CFINPUT TYPE="Text"
                     NAME="ImageName"
                     VALUE="#ImageName#"
                     REQUIRED="NO"
                     SIZE="20"
                     MAXLENGTH="50">
        </TD>
    </TR>
```

Listing 13.13 (continued)

```
      <TR>
          <TD COLSPAN="2" ALIGN="center">
              <CFOUTPUT>
              <INPUT TYPE="submit" VALUE="#ButtonText#">
              </CFOUTPUT>
          </TD>
     </TR>
</TABLE>

</CFFORM>

<!--- Page footer --->
<CFINCLUDE TEMPLATE="footer.cfm">
```

The code first determines whether the form will be used for an Add or an Update. How can it know this? The difference between how the two are called is in the URL—whether `FilmID` is passed. The code `<CFSET EditMode=IsDefined("URL.FilmID")>` created a variable named `EditMode`, which will be `TRUE` if `URL.FilmID` exists and `FALSE` if not. This variable can now be used as necessary throughout the page.

Next comes a `<CFIF>` statement. If editing (`EditMode is TRUE`) then a `<CFQUERY>` is used to retrieve the current values. The fields retrieved by that `<CFQUERY>` are saved in local variables using multiple `<CFSET>` tags. No `<CFQUERY>` is used if it is an insert operation, but `<CFSET>` is used to create empty variables.

By the time the `</CFIF>` has been reached, a set of variables have been created. They'll either contain values (from the `Films` table) or be empty. But either way, they are usable as `VALUE` attributes in `<INPUT>` and `<CFINPUT>` tags.

Look at the `<CFINPUT>` fields themselves. You'll notice that no conditional code exists within them as did before. Instead, every `<INPUT>` tag has a `VALUE` attribute regardless of whether this is an insert or an update. The value in the `VALUE` attribute is a ColdFusion variable—a variable that is set at the top of the template, not a database field.

The rest of the code in the template uses these variables, without needing any conditional processing. Even the page title and Submit button text can be initialized in variables this way, so `<CFIF>` tags are not necessary for them, either.

The primary key, embedded as a hidden field, is necessary only if a movie is being edited, so the code to embed that field is enclosed within a `<CFIF>` statement:

```
<CFIF EditMode>
    <!--- Embed primary key as a hidden field --->
    <CFOUTPUT>
    <INPUT TYPE="hidden" NAME="FilmID" VALUE="#Film.FilmID#">
    </CFOUTPUT>
</CFIF>
```

Even the form header (at the top of the page) and the text of the Submit button are populated using variables. This way the `<FORM>` is completely reusable:

```
<INPUT TYPE="submit" VALUE="#ButtonText#">
```

This form is submitted to the same `ACTION` page regardless of whether data is being added or updated. Therefore, the `ACTION` page also must support both additions and updates. Listing 13.14 contains the new `ACTION` template, `edit2.cfm`.

Listing 13.14 `edit2.cfm`—Combination Insert and Update Page

```
<!---
Name:        edit2.cfm
Author:      Ben Forta (ben@forta.com)
Description: Dual purpose form demo
Created:     4/20/02
--->

<!--- Insert or update? --->
<CFSET EditMode=IsDefined("FORM.FilmID")>

<CFIF EditMode>
    <!--- Update movie --->
    <CFUPDATE DATASOURCE="ows" TABLENAME="Films">
    <CFSET action="updated">
<CFELSE>
    <!--- Add movie --->
    <CFINSERT DATASOURCE="ows" TABLENAME="Films">
    <CFSET action="added">
</CFIF>

<!--- Page header --->
<CFINCLUDE TEMPLATE="header.cfm">

<!--- Feedback --->
<CFOUTPUT>
<H1>Movie #FORM.MovieTitle# #action#</H1>
</CFOUTPUT>

<!--- Page footer --->
<CFINCLUDE TEMPLATE="footer.cfm">
```

This code also first determines the `EditMode`—this time by checking for a `FORM` field named `FilmID` (the hidden form field). If `EditMode` is `TRUE`, a `<CFUPDATE>` is used to update the row; otherwise, a `<CFINSERT>` is used to insert it. The same `<CFIF>` statements also is used to set a variable that is used later in the page when providing user feedback.

It's clean, simple, and reusable.

Creating a Complete Application

Now that you've created add, modify, and delete templates, let's put it all together and create a finished application.

The following templates are a combination of all you have learned in this and previous chapters.

The template shown in Listing 13.15 is the main movie maintenance page. It displays all the movies in the `Films` table and provides links to edit and delete them (using the data drill-down techniques discussed in previous chapters); it also has a link to add a new movie. The administration page is shown in Figure 13.5.

Listing 13.15 `movies.cfm`—Movie List Maintenance Page

```
<!---
Name:        movies.cfm
Author:      Ben Forta (ben@forta.com)
Description: Movie maintenance application
Created:     4/20/02
--->

<!--- Get all movies --->
<CFQUERY DATASOURCE="ows" NAME="movies">
SELECT FilmID, MovieTitle
FROM Films
ORDER BY MovieTitle
</CFQUERY>

<!--- Page header --->
<CFINCLUDE TEMPLATE="header.cfm">

<TABLE ALIGN="center" BGCOLOR="orange">

    <!--- Loop through movies --->
    <CFOUTPUT QUERY="movies">
        <TR>
            <!--- Movie name --->
            <TD><B>#MovieTitle#</B></TD>
            <!--- Edit link --->
            <TD>
             <A HREF="movie_edit.cfm?FilmID=#FilmID#">
            </TD>
            <!--- Delete link --->
            <TD>
             <A HREF="movie_delete.cfm?FilmID=#FilmID#">[Delete]</A>
            </TD>
        </TR>
    </CFOUTPUT>

    <TR>
        <TD></TD>
        <!--- Add movie link --->
        <TD COLSPAN="2" ALIGN="center">
         <A HREF="movie_edit.cfm">[Add]</A>
        </TD>
    </TR>

</TABLE>

<!--- Page footer --->
<CFINCLUDE TEMPLATE="footer.cfm">
```

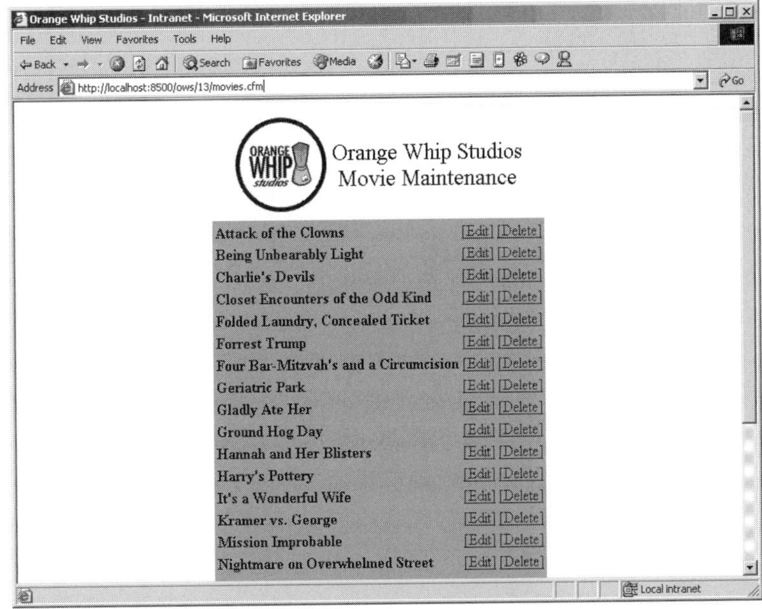

Figure 13.5

The movie administration page is used to add, edit, and delete movies.

Listing 13.15 has two links for each movie, an edit link (that links to `movie_edit.cfm` passing the `FilmID`) and a delete link (`movie_delete.cfm`, also passing the `FilmID`). The add link at the bottom of the page also points to `movie_edit.cfm` but does not pass a `FilmID` (so the form will be used as an add form).

➜ Dynamic links and data drill down were covered in Chapter 11, "ColdFusion Forms".

Listing 13.16 is essentially the same reusable add and update form you created earlier, but with another useful shortcut.

Listing 13.16 `movie_edit.cfm`—Movie Add and Update Form

```
<!---
Name:        movie_edit.cfm
Author:      Ben Forta (ben@forta.com)
Description: Dual purpose movie edit form
Created:     4/20/02
--->

<!--- Check that FilmID was provided --->
<!--- If yes, edit, else add --->
<CFSET EditMode=IsDefined("URL.FilmID")>

<!--- If edit mode then get row to edit --->
<CFIF EditMode>

    <!--- Get the film record --->
    <CFQUERY DATASOURCE="ows" NAME="film">
    SELECT FilmID, MovieTitle, PitchText,
```

Listing 13.16 (continued)

```
               AmountBudgeted, RatingID,
               Summary, ImageName, DateInTheaters
        FROM Films
        WHERE FilmID=#URL.FilmID#
        </CFQUERY>

        <!--- Save to variables --->
        <CFSET MovieTitle=Trim(film.MovieTitle)>
        <CFSET PitchText=Trim(film.PitchText)>
        <CFSET AmountBudgeted=Int(film.AmountBudgeted)>
        <CFSET RatingID=film.RatingID>
        <CFSET Summary=Trim(film.Summary)>
        <CFSET ImageName=Trim(film.ImageName)>
        <CFSET DateInTheaters=DateFormat(film.DateInTheaters, "MM/DD/YYYY")>

        <!--- Form text --->
        <CFSET FormTitle="Update a Movie">
        <CFSET ButtonText="Update">

    <CFELSE>

        <!--- Save to variables --->
        <CFSET MovieTitle="">
        <CFSET PitchText="">
        <CFSET AmountBudgeted="">
        <CFSET RatingID="">
        <CFSET Summary="">
        <CFSET ImageName="">
        <CFSET DateInTheaters="">

        <!--- Form text --->
        <CFSET FormTitle="Add a Movie">
        <CFSET ButtonText="Insert">

    </CFIF>

    <!--- Get ratings --->
    <CFQUERY DATASOURCE="ows" NAME="ratings">
    SELECT RatingID, Rating
    FROM FilmsRatings
    ORDER BY RatingID
    </CFQUERY>

    <!--- Page header --->
    <CFINCLUDE TEMPLATE="header.cfm">

    <!--- Add/update movie form --->
    <CFFORM ACTION="movie_process.cfm">

    <CFIF EditMode>
        <!--- Embed primary key as a hidden field --->
        <CFOUTPUT>
        <INPUT TYPE="hidden" NAME="FilmID" VALUE="#Film.FilmID#">
        </CFOUTPUT>
    </CFIF>
```

Listing 13.16 (CONTINUED)

```
<TABLE ALIGN="center" BGCOLOR="orange">
    <TR>
        <TH COLSPAN="2">
            <CFOUTPUT>
            <FONT SIZE="+1">#FormTitle#</FONT>
            </CFOUTPUT>
        </TH>
    </TR>
    <TR>
        <TD>
            Movie:
        </TD>
        <TD>
            <CFINPUT TYPE="Text"
                     NAME="MovieTitle"
                     VALUE="#MovieTitle#"
                     MESSAGE="MOVIE TITLE is required!"
                     REQUIRED="Yes"
                     SIZE="50"
                     MAXLENGTH="100">
        </TD>
    </TR>
    <TR>
        <TD>
            Tag line:
        </TD>
        <TD>
            <CFINPUT TYPE="Text"
                     NAME="PitchText"
                     VALUE="#PitchText#"
                     MESSAGE="TAG LINE is required!"
                     REQUIRED="Yes"
                     SIZE="50"
                     MAXLENGTH="100">
        </TD>
    </TR>
    <TR>
        <TD>
            Rating:
        </TD>
        <TD>
            <!--- Ratings list --->
            <CFSELECT NAME="RatingID"
                      QUERY="ratings"
                      VALUE="RatingID"
                      DISPLAY="Rating"
                      SELECTED="#VARIABLES.RatingID#">
            </CFSELECT>
        </TD>
    </TR>
    <TR>
        <TD>
            Summary:
        </TD>
        <TD>
```

Listing 13.16 (continued)

```
            <CFOUTPUT>
            <TEXTAREA NAME="summary"
                      COLS="40"
                      ROWS="5"
                      WRAP="virtual">#Summary#</TEXTAREA>
            </CFOUTPUT>
        </TD>
    </TR>
    <TR>
        <TD>
            Budget:
        </TD>
        <TD>
            <CFINPUT TYPE="Text"
                     NAME="AmountBudgeted"
                     VALUE="#AmountBudgeted#"
                     MESSAGE="BUDGET must be a valid numeric amount!"
                     VALIDATE="integer"
                     REQUIRED="NO"
                     SIZE="10"
                     MAXLENGTH="10">
        </TD>
    </TR>
    <TR>
        <TD>
            Release Date:
        </TD>
        <TD>
            <CFINPUT TYPE="Text"
                     NAME="DateInTheaters"
                     VALUE="#DateInTheaters#"
                     MESSAGE="RELEASE DATE must be a valid date!"
                     VALIDATE="date"
                     REQUIRED="NO"
                     SIZE="10"
                     MAXLENGTH="10">
        </TD>
    </TR>
    <TR>
        <TD>
            Image File:
        </TD>
        <TD>
            <CFINPUT TYPE="Text"
                     NAME="ImageName"
                     VALUE="#ImageName#"
                     REQUIRED="NO"
                     SIZE="20"
                     MAXLENGTH="50">
        </TD>
    </TR>
    <TR>
        <TD COLSPAN="2" ALIGN="center">
            <CFOUTPUT>
            <INPUT TYPE="submit" VALUE="#ButtonText#">
```

Listing 13.16 (CONTINUED)

```
                </CFOUTPUT>
            </TD>
        </TR>
    </TABLE>

    </CFFORM>

    <!--- Page footer --->
    <CFINCLUDE TEMPLATE="footer.cfm">
```

There are only two changes in Listing 13.16. The `ACTION` has been changed to point to a new file—`movie_process.cfm`. In addition, look at the `RatingID` field. It uses a new tag named `<CFSELECT>`. This tag, which can be used only within `<CFFORM>` and `</CFFORM>` tags, simplifies the creation of dynamic data-driven `<SELECT>` controls. The code

```
<CFSELECT NAME="RatingID"
          QUERY="ratings"
          VALUE="RatingID"
          DISPLAY="Rating"
          SELECTED="#VARIABLES.RatingID#">
</CFSELECT>
```

is functionally the same as

```
<SELECT NAME="RatingID">
    <CFOUTPUT QUERY="ratings">
        <OPTION VALUE="#RatingID#" <CFIF ratings.RatingID
IS VARIABLES.RatingID>SELECTED</CFIF>>#Rating#</OPTION>
    </CFOUTPUT>
</SELECT>
```

Obviously, the `<CFSELECT>` is much cleaner and simpler. It creates a `<SELECT>` control named `RatingID` that is populated with the `ratings` query, using the `RatingID` column as the value and displaying the `Rating` column. Whatever value is in the variable `RatingID` will be used to pre-select the selected option in the control.

Listings 13.17 and 13.18 perform the actual data insertions, updates, and deletions. The big change in these templates is that they themselves provide no user feedback at all. Instead, they return to the administration screen using the `<CFLOCATION>` tag as soon as they finish processing the database changes. `<CFLOCATION>` is used to switch from the current template being processed to any other URL, including another ColdFusion template. The following sample code instructs ColdFusion to switch to the `movies.cfm` template:

```
<CFLOCATION URL="movies.cfm">
```

This way, the updated movie list is displayed, ready for further processing, as soon as any change is completed.

Listing 13.17 `movie_process.cfm`—Movie Insert and Update Processing

```
<!---
Name:        movie_process.cfm
Author:      Ben Forta (ben@forta.com)
Description: Dual purpose edit page
Created:     4/20/02
--->

<!--- Edit or update? --->
<CFIF IsDefined("FORM.FilmID")>
    <!--- Update movie --->
    <CFUPDATE DATASOURCE="ows" TABLENAME="Films">
<CFELSE>
    <!--- Add movie --->
    <CFINSERT DATASOURCE="ows" TABLENAME="Films">
</CFIF>

<!--- When done go back to movie list --->
<CFLOCATION URL="movies.cfm">
```

Listing 13.18 `movie_delete.cfm`—Movie Delete Processing

```
<!---
Name:        movie_delete.cfm
Author:      Ben Forta (ben@forta.com)
Description: Delete a movie
Created:     4/20/02
--->

<!--- Check that FilmID was provided --->
<CFIF NOT IsDefined("FilmID")>
 <H1>You did not specify the FilmID</H1>
 <CFABORT>
</CFIF>

<!--- Delete a movie --->
<CFQUERY DATASOURCE="ows">
DELETE FROM Films
WHERE FilmID=#FilmID#
</CFQUERY>

<!--- When done go back to movie list --->
<CFLOCATION URL="movies.cfm">
```

And there you have it—a complete application featuring data display, edit and delete using data-drill down, reusable data-driven add and edit forms, all in under 300 lines of code (including comments). Extremely powerful, and not complicated at all.

CHAPTER 14

Debugging and Troubleshooting

IN THIS CHAPTER

Troubleshooting ColdFusion Applications

As with any development tool, sooner or later you're going to find yourself debugging or troubleshooting a ColdFusion problem. Many applications and interfaces have to work seamlessly for a ColdFusion application to function correctly. The key to quickly isolating and correcting problems is a thorough understanding of ColdFusion, data sources, SQL syntax, URL syntax, and your Web server—and more importantly, how they all work with each other.

If the prospect of debugging an application sounds daunting, don't panic. Thankfully, ColdFusion has powerful built-in debugging and error-reporting features. These capabilities, coupled with logical and systematic evaluation of trouble spots, enable you to diagnose and correct all sorts of problems.

This chapter teaches you how to use the ColdFusion debugging tools and introduces techniques that help you quickly locate the source of a problem. More importantly, because an ounce of prevention is worth a pound of cure, guidelines and techniques that will help prevent common errors from occurring in the first place are introduced.

Understanding What Can Go Wrong

As an application developer, sooner or later you are going to have to diagnose, or *debug*, a ColdFusion application problem. Because ColdFusion relies on so many other software components to work its magic, there are a lot of places where things can go wrong.

As you are reading this chapter, the following assumptions are made:

- You are familiar with basic ColdFusion concepts.
- You understand how ColdFusion uses datasources for all database interaction.
- You are familiar with basic SQL syntax and use.

- You know how to use the ColdFusion Administrator.
- You are comfortable using Macromedia Dreamweaver MX

If you are not familiar with any of these topics, it is strongly recommended that you read the chapters about them before proceeding.

➜ See Chapter 1, "Introducing ColdFusion," for more information on how ColdFusion works and how all the pieces fit together to create a complete application.

➜ See Chapter 3, "Accessing the ColdFusion Administrator," to learn how to enable debugging options using the ColdFusion Administrator.

➜ See Chapter 2, "Building the Databases," for a detailed explanation of databases, tables, rows, columns, keys, and other database-related terms.

➜ See Chapter 5, "Introducing SQL," for more information about data sources and how ColdFusion uses them for all database interaction.

Almost all ColdFusion problems fall into one of the following categories:

- Web server configuration problems
- Database driver errors
- SQL statement syntax or logic errors
- ColdFusion syntax errors
- URL and path problems
- Logic problems within your code

Let's look at each of these potential problem areas to learn what can go wrong in each.

Debugging Web Server Configuration Problems

You should almost never encounter problems caused by Web server misconfiguration during routine, day-to-day operations. These types of problems almost always occur either during the initial ColdFusion setup or while testing ColdFusion for the first time. After ColdFusion in installed and configured correctly, it will stay that way.

The only exception to this is the possibility of you receiving an error telling you that ColdFusion is not running. This error will only occur if using an external HTTP server (not ColdFusion's integrated server), and will be generated when the Web server ColdFusion extensions cannot communicate with the ColdFusion Application Server.

Obviously, the Application Server must be running for ColdFusion to process templates. Steps to verifying that the server is running, and starting it if it is not, differ based on your operating system:

- If you are running ColdFusion on a Windows 2000 or Windows XP machine, you should run the Services applet. It will display whether the service is running and will enable you to start it if is not.

- If you are running Windows 9x/ME, you'll see the ColdFusion icon on the taskbar (near the clock) when the Application Server is running. If it is not running, select ColdFusion from the ColdFusion program groups under your Start button menu.
- If you are running ColdFusion on Unix/Linux, use the `ps` command (or `ps -ef|grep cfusion`) to list running processes to see whether ColdFusion is running.

TIP

Windows 2000 and Windows XP services can be started automatically every time the server is restarted. The service Startup option must be set to Automatic for a service to start automatically. Windows 9x users can automatically start ColdFusion by ensuring that the ColdFusion Application Server is in the Programs, Startup group. This setting is turned on by the ColdFusion installation procedure and typically should be left on at all times. However, if the service does not automatically start, check these options.

TIP

If your operating system features a mechanism by which to automatically restart services or daemons upon shutdown, use it.

One other situation worth noting is when you are prompted to save a file every time you request a ColdFusion page. If this is the case then one of two things is happening:

- ColdFusion is not installed on the server correctly (if not using the integrated HTTP server).
- You are accessing URLs locally (using the browser File, Open option) instead of via the Web server.

Debugging Data Driver Errors

ColdFusion relies on database drivers (JDBC or ODBC) for all its database interaction. You will receive data driver error messages when ColdFusion can't communicate with the appropriate driver or when the driver can't communicate with the database.

Database driver error messages always are generated by the driver, not by ColdFusion. ColdFusion merely displays whatever error message it has received from the database driver, and unfortunately these error messages tend to often be cryptic or even misleading.

Database driver error messages always contain an error number, which in and of itself is pretty useless. A text message that describes the problem follows the error number, however. The text of these messages varies from driver to driver, so it would be pointless to list all the possible error messages here. Instead, the more common symptoms and how to fix the problems that cause them are listed.

TIP

You can use the ColdFusion Administrator to verify that a datasource is correctly set up and attached to the appropriate data file.

Receiving the Error Message `Data Source Not Found`

ColdFusion communicates with databases via database drivers. These drivers access data sources—external data files. If the database driver reports that the data source could not be found, check the following:

- Make sure you have created the datasource.

- Verify that the datasource name is spelled correctly. Datasource names are not case sensitive, so don't worry about that.
- If you are using ODBC drivers, note that under Windows NT and Windows 2000, ODBC data sources are *user login specific*. This means if you create a data source from within the ODBC Control Panel applet while logged in as a user without administrator privileges, only that user will have access to that ODBC data source.

Receiving the Error Message `File Not Found`

You might get the error message `File not found` when trying to use a datasource you have created. This error message applies only to datasources that access data files directly (such as Microsoft Access, Microsoft Excel, and Borland dBASE), and not to client/server database systems (such as Microsoft SQL Server and Oracle).

`File not found` simply means that the database driver could not locate the data file in the location it was expecting to find it. To diagnose this problem, perform the following steps:

1. Data files must be created before datasources can use them. If you have not yet created the data file, you must do so before proceeding.
2. Check the datasource settings, verify that the file name is spelled correctly, and ensure that the file exists.
3. If you have moved the location of a data file, you must manually update any datasources that reference it.

Receiving Login or Permission Errors When Trying to Access a Data Store

Some database systems, such as Microsoft SQL Server, Sybase, and Oracle, require that you log on to a database before you can access it. When setting up a datasource to this type of database, you must specify the login name and password the driver should use to gain access.

The following steps help you locate the source of this problem:

1. Verify that the login name and password are spelled correctly. (You will not be able to see the password—only asterisks are displayed in the password field.)
2. On some database systems, passwords are case sensitive. Ensure that you have not left the Caps Lock key on by mistake.
3. Verify that the name and password you are using does indeed have access to the database to which you are trying to connect. You can do this using a client application that came with your database system.
4. Verify that the login being used actually has rights to the specific tables and views you are using and to the specific statements (`SELECT`, `INSERT`, and so on). Many better DBMSs enable administrators to grant or deny rights to specific objects and specific operations on specific objects.

TIP

When you are testing security- and rights-related problems, be sure you test using the same login and password as the ones used in the data source definition.

Receiving the Error Message `Unknown Table`

After verifying that the data source name and table names are correct, you might still get `unknown table` errors. A very common problem, especially with client/server databases such as Microsoft SQL Server, is forgetting to provide a fully qualified table name. You can do this in two ways:

- *Explicitly provide the fully qualified table name whenever it is passed to a SQL statement*—Fully qualified table names are usually made up of three parts, separated by periods. The first is the name of the database containing the table; the second is the owner name (usually specified as `dbo`); the third is the actual table name itself.
- *Some database drivers, such as the Microsoft SQL Server driver, enable you to specify a default database to be used if none is explicitly provided*—If this option is set, its value is used whenever a fully qualified name is not provided.

TIP

If your database driver allows you to specify a default database name, use that feature. This enables you to write fewer and simpler hard-coded SQL statements.

Debugging SQL Statement or Logic Errors

Debugging SQL statements is one of the two types of troubleshooting you'll spend most of your debugging time doing (the other is debugging ColdFusion syntax errors, which we'll get to next). You will find yourself debugging SQL statements if you run into either of these situations:

- ColdFusion reports SQL syntax errors. Figure 14.1, for example, is an error caused by misspelling a table name in a SQL statement.
- No syntax errors are reported, but the specified SQL statement did not achieve the expected results.

Obviously, a prerequisite to debugging SQL statements is a good working knowledge of the SQL language. I'm assuming you are already familiar with the basic SQL statements and are comfortable using them.

➜ See Chapter 6, "SQL Data Manipulation," for information about basic SQL statements and examples of their uses.

TIP

The Debug Options screen in the ColdFusion Administrator contains a checkbox labeled Database Activity. During development, turn on this option so that the full SQL statement and datasource name is displayed in any database-related error messages.

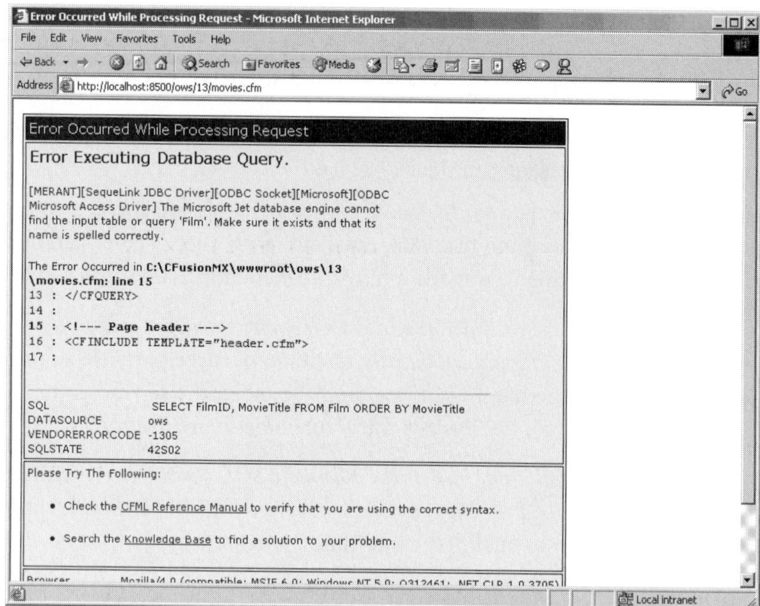

Figure 14.1

ColdFusion displays SQL error messages as reported by the database driver.

The keys to successfully debugging SQL statements are as follows:

1. Isolate the problem. Debugging SQL statements inside ColdFusion templates can be tricky, especially when creating dynamic SQL statements. Try executing the same statement from within another database client replacing dynamic parameters with fixed values if appropriate.

2. The big difference between ColdFusion SQL statements and statements entered into any other database client is the use of ColdFusion fields. If you are using ColdFusion fields within your statement, verify that you are enclosing them within quotation marks when necessary. If the value is a string, it must be enclosed in single quotation marks. If it is a number, it must not be enclosed in quotation marks. (And be sure double quotation marks are never used within SQL statements because this will terminate the statement prematurely.)

3. Look at the bigger picture. Dynamic SQL statements are one of ColdFusion's most powerful features, but this power comes with a price. When you create a dynamic SQL statement, you are effectively relinquishing direct control over the statement itself and are allowing it to be changed based on other conditions. This means that the code for a single ColdFusion query can be used to generate an infinite number of queries. Because some of these queries might work—and others might not—debugging dynamic SQL requires that you be able to determine exactly what the dynamically created SQL statement looks like. Thankfully, ColdFusion makes this an easy task, as you will see later in the section "Using the ColdFusion Debugging Options."

4. Break complex SQL statements into smaller, simpler statements. If you are debugging a query that contains subqueries, verify that the subqueries properly work independently of the outer query.

CAUTION

Be careful to not omit pound signs from around variable names in your SQL code. Consider the following SQL statement:

```
DELETE Actors
WHERE ActorID=ActorID
```

What the code is supposed to do is delete a specific actor, the one whose ID is specified in `ActorID`. But because pound signs were omitted, instead of passing the actor ID, the name of the actor ID column is passed. The result? Every row in the `Actors` table is deleted instead of just the one–all because of missing pound signs. The correct statement should have looked like this:

```
DELETE Actors
WHERE ActorID=#ActorID#
```

Incidentally, this is why you should always test `WHERE` clauses in a `SELECT` before using them in a `DELETE` or `UPDATE`.

Whenever a SQL syntax error occurs, ColdFusion displays the SQL statement it submitted. The fully constructed statement is displayed if your SQL statement was constructed dynamically. The field names are displayed as submitted if the error occurred during an `INSERT` or `UPDATE` operation, but the values are replaced with question marks (except for `NULL` values, which are displayed as `NULL`).

NOTE

If you ever encounter strange database driver error messages about mismatched data types or incorrect numbers of parameters, the first thing you should check is that you have not mistyped any table or column names and that you have single quotation marks where necessary. More often than not, that is what causes that error.

TIP

If you are using Dreamweaver MX (and you should be), you can completely avoid typos in table and column names by using the database drag-and-drop support. To do this, open the Application panel and select the Database tab, select the desired datasource, and expand the tables to find the table and column you need. You can then click the table or column name and just drag it to the editor window, where it will be inserted when you release the mouse key.

Debugging ColdFusion Syntax Errors

Debugging ColdFusion syntax errors is the other type of troubleshooting you'll find yourself doing. Thankfully, and largely as a result of the superb ColdFusion error-reporting and debugging capabilities, these are usually the easiest bugs to find.

ColdFusion syntax errors are usually one of the following:

- Mismatched pound signs or quotation marks
- Mismatched begin and end tags; a `<CFIF>` without a matching `</CFIF>`, for example
- Incorrectly nested tags
- A tag with a missing or incorrectly spelled attribute
- Missing quotation marks around tag attributes

- Using double quotation marks instead of single to delimit strings when building SQL statements
- Illegal use of tags

If any of these errors occur, ColdFusion generates a descriptive error message, as shown in Figure 14.2. The error message lists the problematic code (and a few lines before and after it) and identifies exactly what the problem is.

CAUTION

If your template contains HTML forms, frames, or tables, you might have trouble viewing generated error messages. If an error occurs in the middle of a table, for example, that table will never be terminated, and there is no way to know how the browser will attempt to render the partial table. If the table is not rendered and displayed properly, you will not see the error message.

TIP

If you think an error has occurred but no error message is displayed, you can view the source in the browser. The generated source will contain any error messages that were included in the Web page but not displayed.

One of the most common ColdFusion errors is missing or mismatched tags. Indenting your code, as shown in the following, is a good way to ensure that all tags are correctly matched:

```
<CFIF some condition here>
   <CFOUTPUT>
      Output code here
      <CFIF another condition>
         Some other output code here
      </CFIF>
   </CFOUTPUT>
<CFELSE>
   Some action here
</CFIF>
```

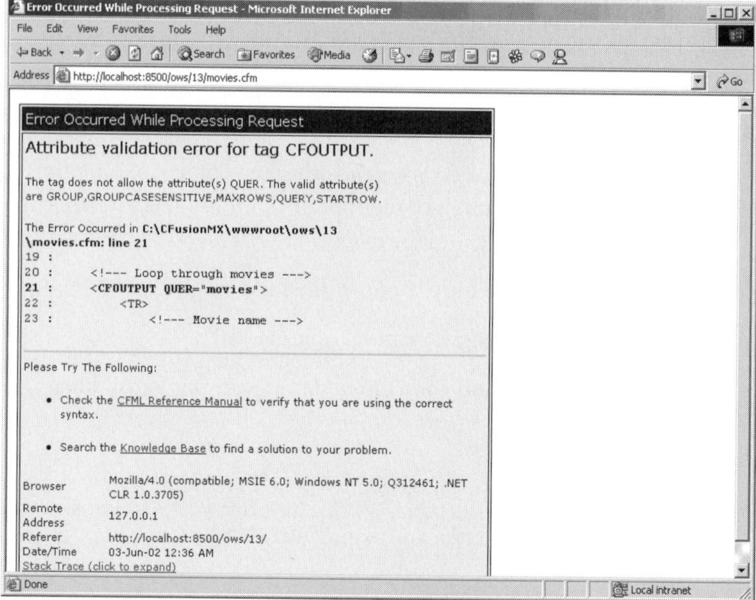

Figure 14.2

ColdFusion generates descriptive error messages when syntax errors occur.

Dreamweaver MX users should take advantage of the available features designed to help avoid common mismatching problems. Color coding is one of these (if the code is not colored correctly you've done something wrong), as is right mouse click support for Tag Editors.

➜ See Chapter 7 for more information about Macromedia Dreamweaver MX.

Inspecting Variable Contents

Sometimes problems throw no errors at all—this occurs when your code is syntactically valid but a logic problem exists somewhere. Aside from using the interactive debugger (which is discussed shortly), the primary means to locating this type of bug is to inspect variable contents during processing. Two ways to do this are available:

- Embed variable display code as necessary in your page, dumping the contents of variables to the screen (or to HTML comments you can view using View Source in your browser).
- The `<CFDUMP>` tag can display the contents of any variable, even complex variables, and can be used to aid debugging when necessary.

➜ `<CFDUMP>` was introduced in Chapter 8, "Using ColdFusion".

By displaying variable contents, you usually can determine what various code blocks are doing at any given point during page processing.

TIP

You can use `<CFABORT>` anywhere in the middle of your template to force ColdFusion to halt further processing. You can move the `<CFABORT>` tag farther down the template as you verify that lines of code work.

TIP

During development, when you find yourself alternating between needing debugging information and not needing it, you can enclose debug code in `<CFIF IsDebugMode()>` and `</CFIF>`. This way your debug output will be processed only if debugging is enabled.

Using the Document Validator

To help you catch syntax errors before your site goes live, Dreamweaver MX has an integrated validation engine. The validation engine can be used to check for mismatched tags, unknown variables, missing pound signs, and other common errors (and not just CFML errors either).

To use the validator, open the file to be checked in Dreamweaver MX and then open the Results panel and select the Validation tab. Click the Validate button (the green arrow at the top left of the panel) and select what it is you'd like to validate (the first option is the one you should use to validate the current document). Dreamweaver MX that validates your code and lists any errors in a results window at the bottom of the screen, as seen in Figure 14.3.

To quickly jump to the problematic code, just click on any error message in the Results panel. As seen in Figure 14.4, Dreamweaver goes to the appropriate line of code and even highlights the trouble spot for you. This enables you to fix errors before you roll out your application.

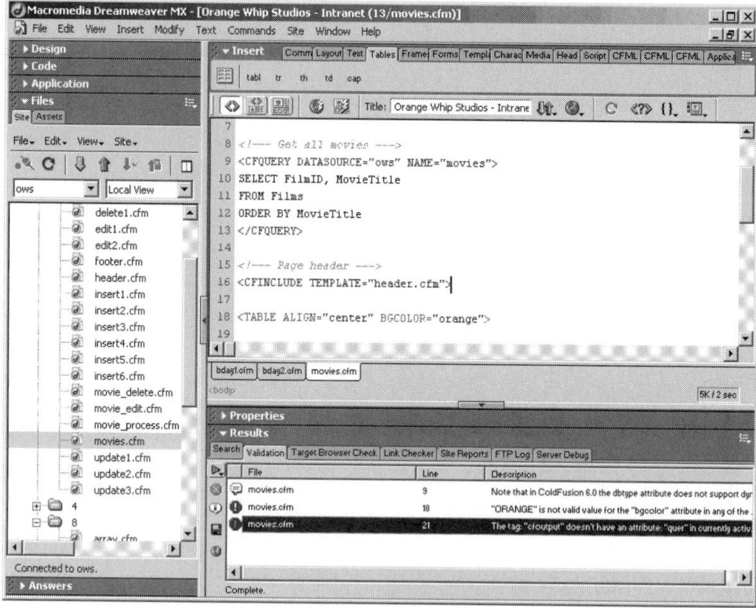

Figure 14.3

The Dreamweaver MX validation engine lists any errors in the Results panel.

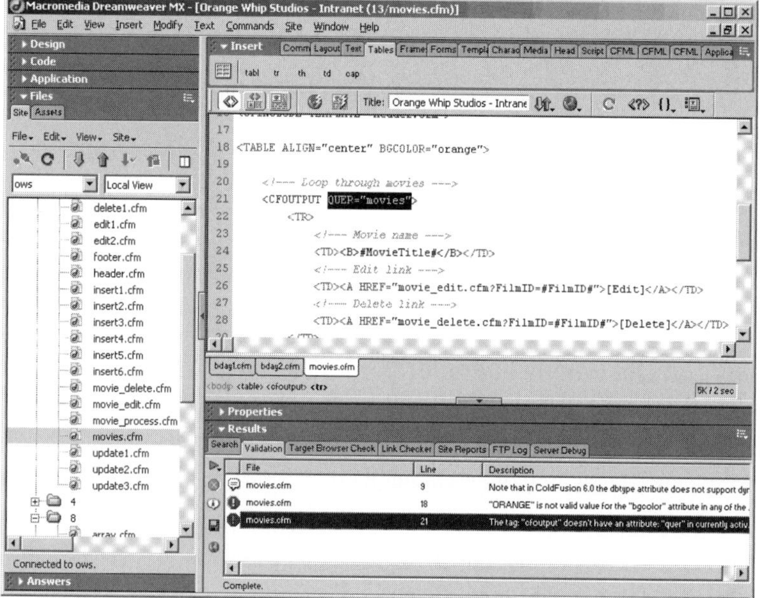

Figure 14.4

The Dreamweaver MX validation engine can flag problem code for you.

TIP

Ctrl-Shift-F7 is a shortcut that takes you directly to the Validation tab.

NOTE

You can customize the behavior of the validation engine, including specifying what gets validated and which tags to validate. To do this, open the Preferences screen, and then select the Validator tab.

Debugging URL and Path Problems

URL- and path-related problems are some of the easiest to diagnose and resolve because they tend to be rather binary in nature—they either work consistently or they fail consistently.

Images Are Not Displayed

If image files (and other files) are not always displayed when you reference them from within ColdFusion then the problem might be path related. If you are using relative paths (and you generally should be), ensure that the path as it is sent to the browser is valid. Having too many or too few periods and slashes in the path is a common culprit.

TIP

Most browsers let you check image paths (constructing full URLs from relative paths in your code) by right-clicking the image and viewing the properties.

Passing Parameters That Are Not Processed

Parameters you pass to a URL can't be processed by ColdFusion, even though you see them present in the URL. URLs are finicky little beasts, and you have to abide by the following rules:

- URLs can have only one question mark character in them—The question mark separates the URL itself from the query.
- Each parameter must be separated by an ampersand (`&`) to pass multiple parameters in the URL query section.
- URLs must not have spaces in them—If you are generating URLs dynamically based on table column data, you must be sure to trim any spaces from those values. If you must use spaces, replace them with plus signs. ColdFusion correctly converts the plus signs to spaces when used. Use the ColdFusion `URLEncodedFormat()` function to convert text to URL-safe text.

TIP

ColdFusion debug output, discussed in the following section, lists all passed URL parameters. This is an invaluable debugging tool.

Debugging Form Problems

If a form is submitted without data, it can cause an error. Web browsers submit data to Web servers in two ways. These ways are called `GET` and `POST`, and the submission method for use is specified in the `FORM METHOD` attribute.

As a rule, forms being submitted to ColdFusion always should be submitted using the `POST` method. The default method is `GET`, so if you omit or misspell `METHOD="POST"`, ColdFusion may be incapable of processing your forms correctly.

You occasionally might get a `variable is undefined` error message when referring to form fields in the action template. Radio buttons, check boxes, and list boxes are not submitted if no option was selected. It is important to remember this when referring to form fields in an action template. If you refer to a check box without first checking for its existence (and then selecting it), you'll generate an error message.

The solution is to always check for the existence of any fields or variables before using them. Alternatively, you can use the `<CFPARAM>` tag to assign default values to fields, thereby ensuring that they always exist.

➜ See Chapter 11, "ColdFusion Forms," for more information about working with form fields and working with specific form controls.

How can you check which form fields were actually submitted and what their values are? Enable ColdFusion debugging—any time you submit a form, its action page contains a debugging section that describes the submitted form. This is shown in Figure 14.5. A field named `FORM.FORMFIELDS` contains a comma-delimited list of all the submitted fields, as well as a list of the submitted fields and their values.

Here are some other things to look for:

- Ensure all form fields have names.
- Ensure related check boxes or radio buttons have the same name.
- Ensure form field names are specified within double quotation marks.
- Ensure form field names have no spaces or other special characters in them.
- Ensure that all quotation marks around attribute values match.

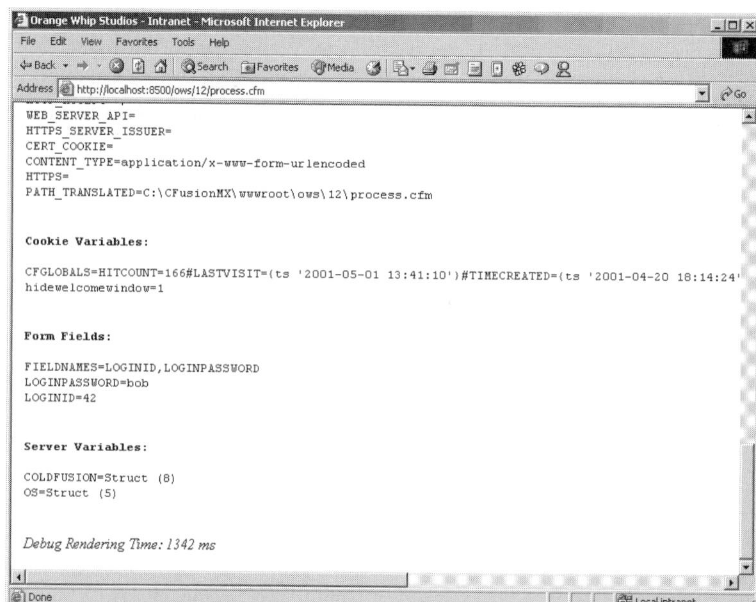

Figure 14.5

ColdFusion displays form-specific debugging information if debugging is enabled.

All these are HTML related, not ColdFusion related. But every one of them can complicate working with forms, and HTML itself will not generate errors upon form generation.

Using the ColdFusion Debugging Options

The ColdFusion debugging options are enabled or disabled via the ColdFusion Administrator, as explained in Chapter 3, "Accessing the ColdFusion Administrator."

TIP

You can restrict the display of debugging information to specific IP addresses. If you enable debugging, you should use this feature to prevent debugging screens from being displayed to your site's visitors.

CAUTION

At a minimum, the local host IP address (`127.0.0.1`) should be specified. If no IP address is in the list, debugging information will be sent to anyone who browses any ColdFusion page.

ColdFusion MX supports three different debugging modes (all of which provide the same basic functionality, but with different interfaces.

Classic Debugging

The *classic* debugging interface appends debugging information to the end of any generated Web pages, as shown in Figure 14.6. The advantage of this format is that it does not use any complex client-side technology, and is therefore safer to use on a wide variety of browsers.

To select this option, select `classic.cfm` as the debug format in the ColdFusion Administrator.

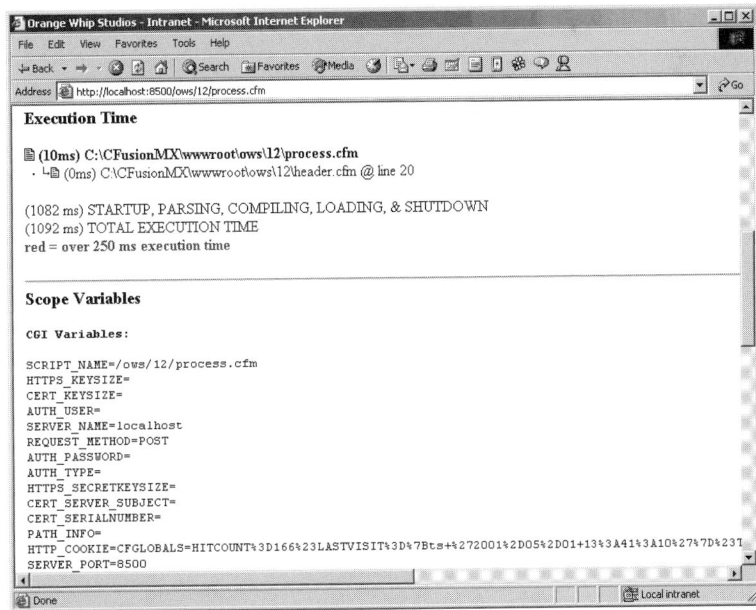

Figure 14.6

ColdFusion can append debugging information to any generated Web page.

NOTE

This is known as the classic format as this is the format supported in ColdFusion ever since the very first versions of the product.

Dockable Debugging

New to ColdFusion MX is a powerful new DHTML based debugging interface. As seen in Figure 14.7, debug information is displayed in a tree control in a separate popup window, or docked to the output itself as seen in Figure 14.8. The advantage of this format (aside from a much cleaner and easier to use interface) is that the debug output does not interfere with the page itself.

To select this option, select `dockable.cfm` as the debug format in the ColdFusion Administrator.

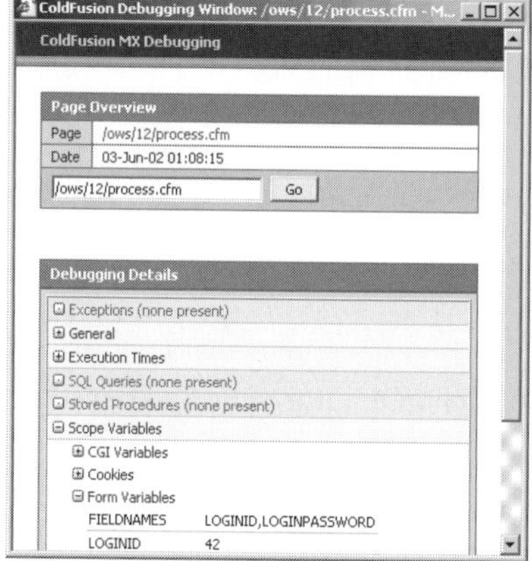

Figure 14.7

ColdFusion debug output can be displayed in a popup DHTML based window.

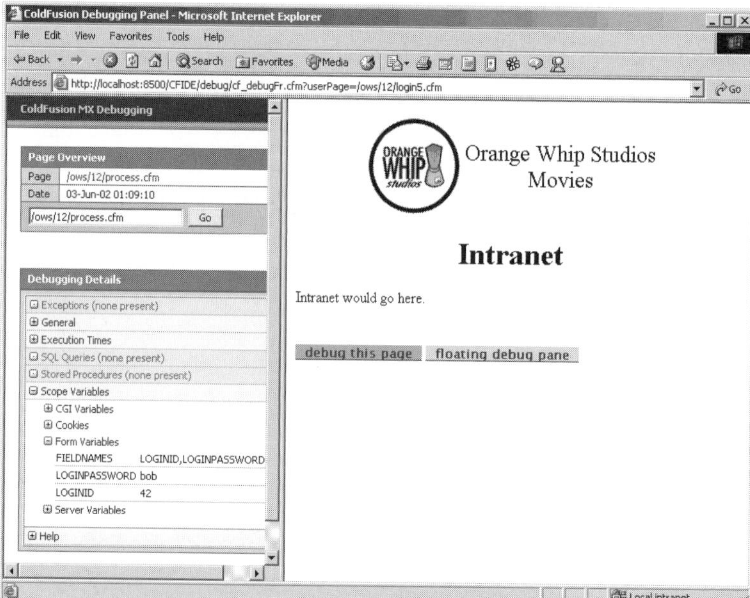

Figure 14.8

Debug output may be "docked" to the page if preferred.

Dreamweaver MX Debugging

Debug output is also accessible from within Dreamweaver MX itself, as seen in Figure 14.9. Any ColdFusion MX page may be debugged from within Dreamweaver MX by clicking the Server Debug button on top of the Dreamweaver editor window. Debug output is displayed in the Results panel below in a tree format.

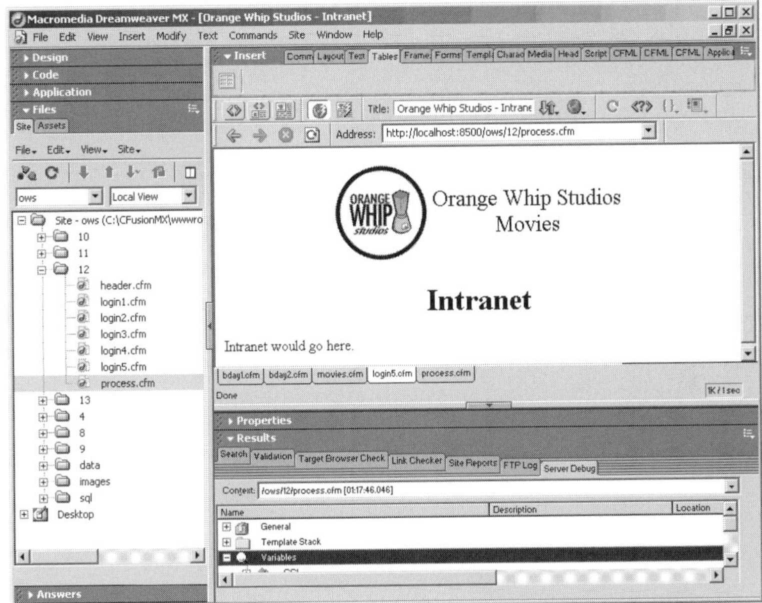

Figure 14.9

Within Dreamweaver MX ColdFusion debug output is displayed in the Results panel.

Using Debugging Options

Regardless of how the debugging information is access (any of the options just listed) you'll have access to the same information:

- Execution time so as to be able to locate poorly performing code.
- Database activity so as to be able to determine exactly what was passed to the database drivers (post any dynamic processing) and what was returned.
- Tracing information (explained below).
- Variables and their values.

As you move from page to page within your application, the debug output will provide insight into what is actually going on within your code.

NOTE

The exact information displayed in debug output is managed by options in the ColdFusion Administrator.

Using Tracing

In addition to all the invaluable information provided by the debugger, you may on occasion want to generate your own debug output too. For example, you may want to:

- Check the values of variables within a loop.
- Determine which code path or branch (perhaps in a series of `<CFIF>` statements) is being followed.
- Inspect `SESSION` or other variables.
- Check for the presence of expected `URL` parameters or `FORM` fields.
- Display the number of rows retrieved by a query.

This kind of information is useful in debugging logic problems – those annoying situations where code is valid syntactically, but some logic flaw (or unexpected situation) is preventing code from functioning correctly.

To insert your own information in debug output use the `<CFTRACE>` tag which embeds trace information. `<CFTRACE>` takes a series of attributes (all optional) that allow you to dump variable contents, display text (dynamic or static), abort processing, and more. As seen in Figure 14.10, the generated trace output is included with the standard debug output (if that option is enabled in the ColdFusion Administrator).

NOTE

`<CFTRACE>` is new to ColdFusion MX.

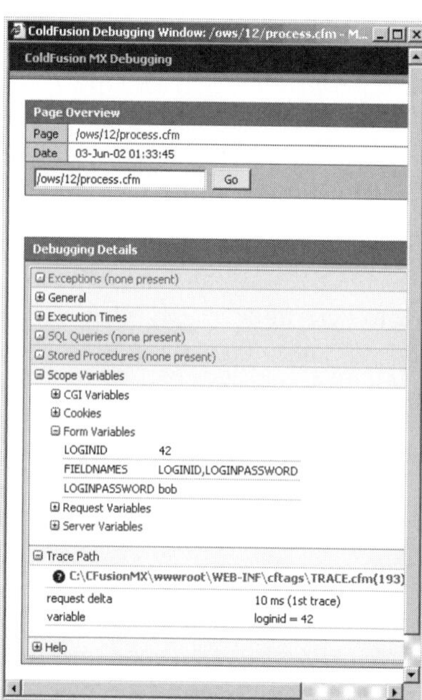

Figure 14.10 Trace output (generated using `<CFTRACE>`) is included with debug output.

Using the ColdFusion Log Files

ColdFusion logs all warnings and errors to log files, which aids you and Macromedia Technical Support in troubleshooting problems. ColdFusion log files are created when the ColdFusion service starts. You can delete these log files if they get too large or move them to another directory for processing. If you do move or delete the log files, ColdFusion creates new ones automatically.

All the ColdFusion log files are plain-text, comma-delimited files. You can import these files into a database or spreadsheet application of your choice for analysis. The ColdFusion Administrator includes a sophisticated log file viewer that enables you to browse, search, and analyze log file data as necessary.

ColdFusion creates several log files. Some of the important ones are

- `application.log`—Contains generated CFML errors, syntax errors, and other runtime error conditions and messages.
- `cftrace.log`—Contains entries made using the `<CFTRACE>` tag.
- `exception.log`—Contains Java exceptions thrown when errors occur.
- `server.log`—Contains information about the ColdFusion Application Server itself, including server stop and start times.
- `schedule.log`—Logs scheduled event execution.

In addition to the standard log files, specific operations (such as restoring an archive) can create their own log files, too.

As a rule you should monitor and browse log files regularly, as these often contain the first indication of problems occurring. For added convenience, the log file viewer in the ColdFusion Administrator allows filtering, sorting, downloading for further analysis, and archiving.

TIP

Some errors are browser related. If you are having a hard time reproducing reported error messages, try to determine which version of which browser the user was running and on which platform. You might find that you have run into browser bugs (yes, some versions of popular browsers are very buggy). To help you find these problems, the log files list any identification information provided by a browser, along with the error message.

Preventing Problems

As mentioned earlier, the best approach to troubleshooting ColdFusion problems (and indeed any development problems) is to prevent them from ever occurring in the first place.

Bugs are inevitable. As the size of an application grows, so does the likelihood of a bug being introduced. As an application developer, you need to have two goals in mind:

1. Develop 100% bug-free code.
2. In the event that your code is not 100% bug-free, make sure that it is easy to debug.

As an application developer myself, I know that these are lofty goals. The reality of it is that application development almost always takes longer than planned, and sacrifices have to be made if release dates are to be met. Code quality is usually the first thing that gets sacrificed.

Of course, sooner or later these sacrifices come back to haunt you. Then come the long debugging sessions, rapid code fixes, software upgrades, and possibly even data conversion. Then, because the rapidly patched code often introduces bugs of its own, the whole cycle starts again.

Although there is no sure-fire way of preventing all bugs, some guidelines and coding practices can both help prevent many of them and make finding them easier when they do occur. Here are my 10 Commandments of ColdFusion development:

I. **Plan Before You Code.** We've all done it, and probably more than once. ColdFusion makes it so easy to start coding that you're often tempted to start projects by firing up an editor and creating CFM files. That's a bad thing indeed. Nothing is more harmful to your development efforts than failing to plan properly, and you should be spending more time planning that coding, not less. And I don't mean planning your IPO. Planning involves thinking through every aspect of your application, from database design to UI considerations, from resource management to schedules and deliverables, and from feature lists with implementation details to language and presentation. You'd never build a house without detailed blueprints (well, you might try, but you'd never get the necessary permission to begin work), and building an application is no different. I am constantly amazed by the number of applications I am asked to look at that have no supporting documentation. And these aren't just from small development shops—I am talking about some of the largest and most respected corporations, too. Scalability problems? I would not doubt it. I'd actually be amazed if such an application ever did scale. You can't expect an application that grew in spite of its developers to scale. Nor can you expect it to be bug-free, manageable, or delivered on time. Yes, I know that detailed planning takes time, time none of us have. But in the long run you'll come out ahead.

II. **Organize Your Application.** An extension of planning your application is organizing it (along with any other applications). Applications are made up of lots of little bits and pieces, and keeping them organized is imperative. This includes directory structures and determining where common files should go, moving images to their own directory (or server), breaking long files into smaller, more manageable (and more reusable) ones, and even ensuring consistent organization among different applications. And going back to the prior commandment, Plan Before You Code, all organization should be documented in detail as part of that plan.

III. **Set Coding Standards.** This is an interesting one, and one I get asked about often. Macromedia has not published formal recommendations on coding standards, nor in my opinion should they. Macromedia's job is to create killer tools and products for developers, and our job is to use them however works best for us. I don't believe that a single set of coding standards would work for all developers, but at the same time, I don't believe any developer should be writing code that does not adhere to a standard—any standard. Coding standards include everything from file naming and directory-naming conventions, to variable-naming conventions, to code organization and ordering within your source, to error-handling, to componentization, and much more. For example, if all variables that contain dates begin with `dt`, for example, then references to a variable named `dtOrderDate` become self-explanatory. The purpose of coding standards is to ensure some level of consistency in your code. Whether it is to allow other developers to understand and work with your code or simply so that you'll know what the heck you did (and why) six months down the line, coding standards provide a mechanism to create code that describes and explains itself. There is no right or wrong coding standard, as long as it is used. The only thing wrong about coding standards is not using one.

IV. **Comment Your Code.** This is an obvious one, but apparently few of us have the time to pay attention to the obvious. So, I'll say it once again: All code must be commented. (For the record, I'd fire an employee on the spot for turning in code that is not commented; that's how serious an offense I believe this one to be.) Every source code file needs a descriptive header listing a description, the author information, the creation date, a chronological list of changes, any dependencies and assumptions, and any other relevant information. In addition, every conditional statement, every loop, every set of variable assignments, and every include or component reference must be commented with a simple statement explaining what is being done and why. It's a pain, I know. But the next time you (or anyone else) has to work with the code, you'll appreciate the effort immeasurably. And you might even be able to safely make code changes without breaking things in the process.

V. **Never Make Changes on a Live Server.** This is another obvious one, but one worth stating anyway. All development and testing must occur on servers established for just that purpose. Yes, this means you'll need additional hardware, but the cost of a new box is nothing compared to the cost of bringing down your application because that little change was not as little as you expected. Write your code, test it, debug it as necessary, deploy it to a testing server, test it some more, and test it some more, and then finally deploy it to your live production server. And don't repeat this process too often. Instead of uploading slightly changed versions of your application every day, collect the changes, test them some more, and deploy them monthly, or weekly, or whenever works best for you. The key here is that your production server is sacred; don't touch it at all unless you have to—and the less frequently, the better. And never, ever, make changes on live servers, even minor ones. Nothing is ever as minor and as isolated as it seems, and there is no change that is worth crashing a server over.

VI. **Functionality First, Then Features.** This is yet another obvious one, and a common beginner's mistake. Yes, writing fancy DHTML menu-generation code is far more fun that writing data-entry validation routines, but the latter is far more important to the success of your application. Concentrate on creating a complete working application; then pretty it up as necessary. Do so and increase the chance that you'll finish on schedule for a change. The final result might not be as cool as you'd like, but there is something to be said for an application that actually works, even an uncool one. Furthermore, (as explained in the next commandment) debugging logic problems is difficult when the code is cluttered with fancy formatting and features.

VII. **Build and Test Incrementally.** Testing and debugging complete applications is difficult. The bigger an application is, the more components that are used, and the more developers working on a project, all make debugging and testing anything but trivial. When you develop core components of your application, test them. Write little test routines, hard-code, or smoke-and-mirror as necessary, but however you do it, do it. Obviously, you'll have to test your complete application when you're finished and some problems won't come to light until then, but the more you can test code blocks in isolation, the better.

VIII. **Never Reinvent the Wheel, and Plan Not To.** This is one I have written about extensively. Write code with reuse in mind, and reuse code whenever possible. When designing your code, put the extra time in up front to ensure it is not hard-coded or highly task specific unless it absolutely has to be. The benefits? Being able to reuse existing code shortens your development time. You also stand a far greater chance of creating bug-free code when you use components that have already been used and tested. Plus, if you do make subsequent fixes and corrections, all code that uses the improved components benefit. This has a lot of benefits and no downside whatsoever.

IX. **Use All the Tools at Your Disposal, Not Just ColdFusion.** ColdFusion applications are usually not standalone entities. They rely on database servers, mail servers, and much more. In addition, ColdFusion can leverage Web Services, Java, COM, CORBA, C/C++ code, and more. Use these tools, as many as necessary, and always attempt to select the best one for a specific job. The best ColdFusion applications are not the ones written purely in ColdFusion; they are the ones that leverage the best technologies for the job, all held together by ColdFusion.

X. **Implement Version Control and Source Code Tracking.** Source code changes, and changes are dangerous. As your applications grow, so does the need for tracking changes and source code control. Select a version control package that works for you, and use it. Key features to look for are the ability to lock files (so no one else edits a file while you edit it—if that does happen, someone's changes will be lost), the ability to view change history (what changed, by whom, and when), the ability to roll back complete applications (so that when the latest upgrade bombs you can easily roll back an entire application to a prior known state), the ability to create and check file dependencies (so you'll know what other code is affected by changes you make), and reporting. In addition, if you can integrate the product with Macromedia Dreamweaver MX, that's even better. The bottom line: I don't care which product you use, just use one.

➜ Chapter 20, "Building Reusable Components," teaches the basics of code reuse and creating your own components.

➜ Chapter 37, "Development Methodologies," introduces several independent coding methodologies and standards, including the most popular one: Fusebox.

PART 3

Building ColdFusion Applications

IN THIS PART

CHAPTER 15

Planning an Application

IN THIS CHAPTER

Getting Started on Your Application

When many developers get a new project to work on, their first instinct is usually to start coding right away. It's easy to understand why. Those first few hours or days of coding can be a lot of fun. The "inner geek" in each of us gets a special thrill from sinking its teeth into a new project, watching an application take shape, and carving something unique and useful out of thin air. Plus, there's often a deadline looming, so it seems like the best idea is to just start writing code as soon as humanly possible.

The problem is that even the simplest applications have a way of becoming much more complicated than they seemed at first. Nine times out of ten, if you take the time to plan your application and development process right from the start, you will do a better job in less time. Of course, people say that about almost everything in life. But in Web application development, it really is true.

Admit it! Your inner geek is already telling you to skip this chapter and get on with the coding. Resist the geek, if you can. The advice in this chapter will mean a bit more work for you up front. You might find that you even need to write a few documents. But you probably will end up doing more cool stuff and less tedious work if you know exactly where your application is headed at all times. Really. Seriously. Honest. Your inner geek might even buy you a drink when you're done.

Defining the Project

The first thing to do is to ensure that the project is as completely defined as possible. You need to know exactly what type of application to build, and that usually means doing some research and asking lots of questions.

In a perfect world, you would already have a written description of the application that defines its every aspect. You would know exactly what the expectations are for the project, and who will be testing it, using it, and benefiting from it. You would have complete understanding of every aspect of the project, from what technologies should be used to how the database should look.

In reality, you might have only a short description, such as "we want to personalize our online store," or "we need an accounting section in the company intranet." Sounds great, but you can't exactly start working yet.

The Importance of Being Inspired

If you can, try to have a "vision" about the project early on. Make it ambitious. Figure out how people are thinking about the project, and try to come up with some twist or feature that takes it to a whole new level—something an end user would be happy to see, and that you would be proud to implement. Why? Because it's important for you to be as interested in the project as you can be. If you're having fun during the development process, the application will most likely turn out better. If at first the application sounds like something you've done or seen a million times before, try to think of something to add to make it unique. Even if the project already sounds difficult or daunting, think of some way to make it even more of a challenge.

Then, after you've gotten yourself excited about the project, try to get everyone else excited about it, too. Come up with a trademark-like name or code name for the project (perhaps from a favorite movie or a play on words based on the name of your competition). Talk about the project as if it were the cure for all diseases, as if it were going to save the world. Sell the thing. Even if it's filled with irony, your enthusiasm will bubble over onto the next desk or into the next room. At the very least, the project will be a little bit more fun. And how can that not be a good thing?

Understanding the Project

Now that you're enthused about the project, you need to get yourself educated as well. Before going further, be sure you know the answers to these questions:

- **Internet, Intranet, or Extranet?** Most projects will fall into one of these categories. Be sure you know which one yours falls into, and why. It is usually obvious that a project is an Internet project because it targets end users. Sometimes the difference between intranets and extranets can be more subtle, especially if the application is meant to be used by your company's business partners as well as in house. Even though it's just a word, be sure you and your client or boss agree on the word.
- **Totally new or "Version 2.0?"** You should know whether you are replacing an existing Web application. If so, why? What exactly is wrong with the current one? To what extent should you be using the existing application as a guide? Is the original just showing its age, or was it a total disaster from its very conception?
- **New process or existing process?** You should know whether your application is creating something totally new ("we have never had anything in place to do this"), or a modification of a current process ("we have always done this, but it was partly on paper and partly in a spreadsheet").

- **Integrating with existing site?** You should know whether your application is going to sit within the context of a larger Web site. If so, how will people get to your part of the site? How will they get back? Do you need to keep the navigation consistent?
- **Integrating with other systems?** Does any back-end or legacy integration need to be done? Perhaps your application needs to receive periodic updates from some type of batch process that occurs within the organization. If so, learn as much about the existing systems as you can. Also, find out if the project calls for the use of any Web Services that are currently available or are in the progress of being built. ColdFusion MX makes it easy to use ("consume") functionality provided by Web Services.
- **Existing database schemas?** Frequently, there is some type of existing database that at least part of your application will need to be aware of. Perhaps a table of customers and their IDs already exists somewhere within the organization. Find out whether your application can add tables and columns to this database or whether it should have its own database. Remember that ColdFusion generally has no problem dealing with information from multiple databases.

Conducting a Few Interviews

We recommend that you conduct a few informal interviews amongst the people who might actually be using your application when it's completed. Depending on the project, that might mean people within the company or a few potential end users you find out on the street. Ask these people what they would like to see in the application. How could it be even more useful to them?

NOTE

A fun question to ask is, "If there were only a single button to click in this new application, what should it be?" At first, you might get sarcastic answers, such as, "It should find me a better husband," or "It should do my job for me," but you'll also get serious answers that can be quite telling.

These potential users will likely tell you more about how your application will actually be used than your normal contacts within the company can. They often are more likely to be able to describe what they need in ordinary terms. You might find that you think about the project differently after a couple of these short interviews, and you might end up reevaluating the importance of various features.

TIP

If your application is meant to replace or improve a process these people perform manually or with an existing application, you might want to observe them doing their jobs for a short amount of time. You might find that users spend most of their time doing task "X," while you intended the application to assist primarily with task "Y."

This interview process serves another, more subtle purpose as well. It associates a real person—a face, or several faces—with the project for you. When you reach a stumbling block later, or when you design a form, you can have these people in mind (hmmm, what would that cute accountant like to see here?). Perhaps without totally realizing it, you will actually be creating the application *for* these people. When it's finished, you are likely to have improved their day-to-day work experiences or somehow made things more fun or easier for people using your application at home. You'll find it more rewarding, and your application will have much more perceived value.

Setting Expectations

This is perhaps the most important thing to nail down as early as possible. Even the most savvy people have a way of expecting things from an application that they never told you about. Setting appropriate expectations is perhaps the most important thing to nail down as early as possible in the process.

Discussing a few of the finer points of the project with your boss or client can go a long way toward establishing reasonable expectations. Keep in mind that many of these items are matters of give and take. You might frame the discussion by clearly defining the choices: "the upside of doing this would be X, but the downside would be Y." Consider:

- **Modem users.** If you're lucky, you're building an intranet that will never be used outside the local network. If not, you probably have to consider the poor folks connecting at 56K. Try to define an expected level of service for modem users (perhaps the first page must come up in 15 seconds or less and all other pages in 10 seconds or less). Depending on to whom you are talking, talking in terms of image size (no more than 50KB of images per page) might be easier than talking in terms of download time. It's often best to talk in terms of file size with graphic artists and in terms of download time with everyone else.
- **Screen resolution and color depth.** Most developers and graphic artists have great computer monitors that display lots of pixels at a time. But many people use monitors that have only 800-by-600 (or even 640-by-480) screen resolution. If those people are important to you, but the current design calls for a luxurious, cinematic layout that uses a lot of horizontal space, it's helpful to point out that some people are going to have to use the scroll bar at the bottom of the browser window to see all elements on the page.
- **The importance of security.** You should know to what extent your application needs to be secure. Many applications need some level of security (based on a password of some kind, as discussed in Chapter 18, "Securing Your Applications"), but do they need more? Should the pages be further secured using HTTPS and SSL, or restricted according to IP address? Or should it be secured even further, using client certificates? Where will the application reside in relation to the company's firewall, assuming the company has one?
- **Concurrent Users.** If your client is thinking about the application getting a million hits per minute, but you have only an old 486 computer to use to host the thing, that could be a problem. Of course, ColdFusion's multiple deployment options make it inherently scalable, and you could always use a cluster of better servers later, but it can't hurt to ensure that you and your boss or client agree on load expectations.
- **Browser compatibility.** Does the application need to be capable of looking great with every browser ever made, from the first beta of Netscape Navigator to the latest service pack for Internet Explorer? Probably not. But you do need to determine exactly

what the expectations are. Point out that if you are using client-side features, such as JavaScript or Dynamic HTML, the more browsers you need to support, and the more testing you might need to do. Note that using Macromedia Flash in place of DHTML can go a long way toward avoiding browser compatibility issues.

- **Platform.** Unfortunately, today's Web browsers often display the same page differently on Macs and Windows machines. If you need to support only one platform (you're building an intranet for a strictly Linux shop, for example), your job might be a lot easier. Again, just be sure you and your boss or client agree on what's expected.

Knowing the Players

Unless you are producing every aspect of the application on your own—including artwork, testing, and deployment—you need to know who is going to be working on the various aspects of the project. Depending on the circumstances, you might need to assemble a team on your own.

Commonly, a team consists of the following basic positions. Even if one person is performing more than one function, be sure you know who is who:

- **ColdFusion Coders.** How many people will program the application? Just you, or a team of 20? Are the coders all under your control, or do they have their own chains of command or other responsibilities?
- **Graphic Artists.** Who will provide graphics, banners, and buttons? Who will design the overall look and feel of the application? Who will design the site's navigation and structure?
- **Database People.** Who will determine the new database structure or make changes to any existing databases? Does that person see herself as a developer (designing tables for applications and so on), or more of a database administrator (tuning the database, adjusting indexes, scheduling maintenance, and the like)?
- **Project Managers.** Who will ensure that the various elements of the project are completed on time and meeting all requirements? Who will keep an eye on everyone's schedules? Who will that person report to within the company? Who will report to that person within your team?

Fact Finding

Next, it's time to do a bit of research. This might sound like a lot of work, but the truth is you can often do the research suggested here in a couple of hours. It is almost always time well spent.

Looking at Similar Sites

Spend some time searching the Internet for sites that are similar to your project. Even if you can't find a Web site that does the exact same thing as the application you're building, at least try to find a few sites that are in the same conceptual space or that have pages that present the same type of information that your application will presents.

For example, say one of your pages is going to be an "Advanced Search" page, and another will present data in rows and columns. Find the best examples you can of such pages. What do you like about them? What don't you like? How does the use of color or spacing affect your opinion of the existing pages? When do the best sites use a button instead of a link, and why? When do graphics help, and when do they just get in the way?

Decide Which Technologies to Use

You also should research and decide which technologies you will use. Most likely, ColdFusion will give you most of the functionality you need, but you still need to answer a few questions:

- **What's the database?** Assuming your application requires a database of some kind, you need to decide which type of relational database system (RDBMS) you will use. Many smaller Web applications are built using Access (.mdb) tables or delimited text files as their information stores, and there is nothing wrong with this for smaller applications. Most people will advise you to consider a server-based database product (such as Oracle, MySQL, or Microsoft's SQLServer) for larger-scale applications.
- **Any scripting or Dynamic HTML?** ColdFusion makes all its decisions on the server side, just before a page is delivered to the browser. Sometimes, your application will benefit from some type of client-side scripting using JavaScript or perhaps Dynamic HTML. If so, decide where you will use scripting, and to what end.
- **Any Flash, video, or other multimedia?** Depending on the project, you might need to include dynamic, interactive content such as Macromedia Flash movies, Shockwave presentations, or 3D worlds in your pages. These days, most computers are already equipped with the Flash player; with the Flash 6 player you can also deliver sound and video without an additional plug-in. Other types of multimedia content may require a plug-in installed on each user's browser. Such plug-ins generally can be installed automatically for Internet Explorer users (especially under Windows) but usually they must be downloaded and installed manually for other browsers and platforms. Keep these issues in mind as you discuss the project.
- **Any custom tags?** You should decide whether you will build reusable custom tags while you construct your application. If you will, you might want to sketch out what each custom tag will do and what each tag's attributes might be. (CFML custom tags are discussed in Chapter 20, "Building Reusable Components.")
- **Any custom-built extensions?** Depending on the situation, you might want (or need) to code certain parts of your application using a different programming language, such as C++, Java, or Visual Basic. For example, you might compile a CFX tag to use within your ColdFusion templates. Or, you might create a COM object, servlet, or Java class, which you can also invoke within your ColdFusion template code. These subjects are not discussed in this book, but they are discussed in great detail in our companion book, *Advanced ColdFusion MX Application Development* (Macromedia Press, ISBN: 0-321-12710-2).

Investigating Existing Custom Tags

The ColdFusion Developer's Exchange site is a great place to look for existing Custom Tags or ColdFusion Components that might help you build your application more quickly. Using these prebuilt extensions to ColdFusion often enables you to get your application finished more easily. Why reinvent the wheel if someone else has already done the work and is willing to share it with you for free (or for a nominal charge)?

The Developer's Exchange is located at `http://devex.macromedia.com`.

Searching the ColdFusion Forums

Another good place to go during the planning phase is the Online Support Forums for ColdFusion, where users discuss problems and answer questions for each other. Support engineers from Macromedia also participate in the forum discussions.

Try running searches for the type of application you are building or for specific features you might not have fully formed in your mind yet. It's likely you'll find message threads that discuss various approaches of displaying the type of information you need to present, as well as any pitfalls or gotchas to keep in mind. You'll probably find code snippets and examples you can adapt as well.

The ColdFusion Support Forums are located at `http://webforums.macromedia.com/coldfusion`.

Investigating Standard or Third-Party Extensions

As mentioned, ColdFusion can invoke and communicate with Java classes and ActiveX objects. ColdFusion can also invoke and communicate with Web Services. You don't have to write Java, C++, or Visual Basic code to use these items; instead, you use them through CFML's `CreateObject()` function or through the `<CFOBJECT>` tag. The basic idea is the same as when using Custom Tags: Why reinvent the wheel when someone has already done the work for you?

Therefore, it is worth a quick look on the Internet to see whether third-party Web Services, Java classes, or ActiveX controls are available to help with some part of the functionality your application is meant to provide:

- **Java classes.** It is also worth checking for Java classes that could provide specific chunks of functionality you need. For example, if you need a platform-agnostic way to deal with reading the public keys associated with a server's SSL certificate, you could take a look at the classes provided by the `java.security.cert` package in the standard Java Development Kit (JDK) from `www.javasoft.com`. Of course, you could look beyond the JDK as well; a great number of third-party products can be invoked through Java, which generally means you can invoke them via ColdFusion.
- **Third-party ActiveX Controls.** With only a few exceptions, any nonvisual ActiveX control (also known as a COM Object) can be used with ColdFusion. A good way to look for these items is to consult the components sections of the various Active Server Pages sites out there—just about any COM/ActiveX object marketed to ASP developers can

be used in your ColdFusion templates. Of course, these components can be used only if you are using ColdFusion under Windows. For more on this topic, check out `www.cfcomet.com`.

- **Third-party Web Services.** As of this writing, Web Services are really coming into their own as another way of integrating other people's work into your own application. Instead of installing something on your ColdFusion server, you simply access the information exposed by the Web Service over the Internet. Nearly all Web Services can be used via a simple call to the `<CFINVOKE>` tag or the `CreateObject()` function.

➜ A real discussion of how to use these objects in your ColdFusion templates is beyond the scope of this book. See *Advanced ColdFusion MX Application Development* (Macromedia Press, ISBN: 0-321-12710-2) for complete explanations and examples. Also see Appendix B, "ColdFusion Tag Reference," to learn more about the `<CFOBJECT>` and `<CFINVOKE>` tag, and Appendix C, "ColdFusion Function Reference," to learn about the `CreateObject()` function.

Planning the Process

By now, you have probably met with your client or boss a few times and have done your initial research. You have a pretty good idea about what your application is going to be about. You probably also are beginning to have a strong sense about how it will be laid out. In other words, you should be able to see the application in your mind. Time to get that down on paper. Then you can start doing the real work!

Design Documents

Even the most accomplished developers sometimes jump in without writing anything down on paper first. Those same developers will tell you that in most instances, working this way turns out to be a mistake. Sooner or later you realize you forgot some feature your boss or client was expecting. Without documents, whether you really forgot the feature—or whether your client simply didn't mention it—can't be proven. In short, it simply can't hurt to put things down on paper.

Specification Document

At the very least, you should have some type of project specifications document that describes the application in plain English (or whatever) and lists all the critical elements or features. This document should also include approximations of how long you think each item will take to complete.

The document should have a big picture or executive summary portion that, if read by an outsider, will provide an explanation of the project. It should also have a detailed portion that is as specific as possible about individual features.

You also might want the document to prioritize the various elements or features; it could be that a shopping cart and an events calendar are both required elements, but that the events calendar is to be your primary focus. Most importantly, the specifications document should include the expectations that you have agreed upon for the project (see the section "Setting Expectations," earlier in this chapter).

Flowcharts and Storyboards

Depending on the project and your client, you might want to put together some visual aids, such as flowcharts or storyboards, that visually explain the various pages that will make up your application and what elements will be visible on each.

If you own a copy of the software product called Visio, you could use it to lay out flowcharts or storyboards. You could also use just about any other drawing program (such as PowerPoint) or just plain old paper or whiteboards. These flowcharts might be *logical* (mapping out the flow of decisions a template will make or the flow of choices your users might make) or *physical* (representing the pages in your application and the sequence or links from one to the other).

You might even end up with sketches of each page. In any case, be sure the important elements and features from your specification document are represented.

Milestones Document

Just as most analysts stress the importance of setting boundaries in your personal life, most developers recommend establishing *milestones* during the development of an application. Milestones are like checkpoints along the way to an application's completion. You might try to set five milestones, say, each representing approximately 20 percent of the application's features or pages. After each milestone, your client or boss should take a look, give you preliminary feedback, and generally let you know that you are on the right track.

Milestones are good for everyone involved. Your boss or client gets a positive feeling of progress whenever a milestone is reached. You also get a positive feeling of accomplishment, but more importantly, you are ensuring that your boss or client is reasonably satisfied with the development at a number of junctures. This involvement protects you a bit—if your boss or client has reviewed your progress as you reach these milestones, you know there's little chance of her disliking the whole project at the end because of some misunderstanding.

Planning the Testing Phase

You should now have a good roadmap for the development of your project, in the form of your specifications and milestones documents (see the previous section). Next, you should put together a similar type of roadmap for the testing phase. No matter how great a coder you are, at least one bug is bound to be in your application the first time around. It's important that you and your client or boss expect and leave time for some type of beta or testing phase.

Who Can Help with Q.A.?

Somebody should be assigned the job of overseeing quality assurance (Q.A.) for your application. In other words, someone should put the application through its paces to ensure that everything works as intended. Do all the links work? What if certain form fields are left out? What if a user submits a form more than once?

The Q.A. folks also can be the ones ensuring that your application meets all the expectations agreed upon earlier (see the section "Setting Expectations," earlier in this chapter). If you agreed on a maximum download time for modem users, trying some of the pages using a modem can be part of the Q.A. process. If you agreed on IE and Netscape compatibility, someone should view the application using each relevant browser.

You also might want to make a list of all the items in your application that should be tested whenever you update the code. That way, your Q.A. team (which might be just you) has a checklist of links, mouse clicks, and form submissions, for example, that must function properly before an iteration of the application can be said to be complete.

Beta Testing

In addition to internal Q.A. work, it's often a good idea to have some kind of semi-public beta test in which real users get to put the application through its paces. Everyday users have a way of finding even the most obscure problems. Navigation elements that seem intuitive to you might be completely baffling to average folks. They might consistently overlook the most important button on the page, for instance.

Depending on the application, the appropriate beta testers can be select people within the company (perhaps the same folks you interviewed while you were defining the project, as discussed earlier in this chapter). They might be a group of the company's customers, or you might decide to open the beta site to the general public. There are also a variety of automated load-testing tools available that can test how your application will perform when used by many users at once.

Tracking Bug Reports

You might want to set up a way for people to report bugs in the application so that a list of unresolved issues exists in a central place. Doing so will also keep your client or boss off your back as you complete the project. Let's face it: People like to see progress. Anyone who can report bugs through some type of official channel—and see that the bug has been fixed a few days later—will be impressed with your professionalism.

You can approach bug tracking in many ways. Various commercial project-management applications include bug-tracking functionality. Check out Macromedia's SiteSpring product, or use ColdFusion to put together your own Web-based bug-tracker that your Q.A. people and beta users can use whenever they find a bug. Just be sure the bug tracker doesn't have any bugs of its own!

NOTE

If you do create a Web-based bug tracker, you could include a link to it whenever a ColdFusion error message gets displayed for whatever reason. See "Customizing Error Messages" in Chapter 16, "Introducing the Web Application Framework," for details.

Separate Development Environment

Plan to have a separate development environment (server or set of servers) that will be used only by you (and the rest of your development team, if there is one). While your Q.A. people are checking out the application and finding bugs, you can be working on those bugs without worrying whether the Q.A. people can still work while you're making changes. Many people achieve this by installing a private copy of the ColdFusion server and database server on their own workstations. Performance might not be optimal, but it is usually fine for development.

Staging/Production

Most developers recommend having separate staging and production environments. The *staging* environment is a server or set of servers your boss or client visits to review your progress. It's also the server your Q.A. or beta users visit. The *production* server is where the final code goes after everyone is satisfied with it, and it is the server your actual end users visit. Any updates to the code are made first to staging tested there, and then moved to production.

Ideally, the staging and production environments should be as identical as possible (same hardware, same software versions, and so on), so no surprise incompatibilities or other issues occur.

While You Are Working

The last thing to plan out before you start coding is how you will continue to document the project as you go along. After all, if you've worked to create all those great flowcharts and other design documents, it would be silly to not keep them up to date while you work.

Charting Page Flow

One of the most valuable things to have at any time is an up-to-date list of important pages and the links between them. Dreamweaver MX can help you with this by letting you organize your application files maintaining links between all the templates in your project (see Chapter 7, "Introducing Macromedia Dreamweaver MX"). But sometimes there's just no replacement for a proper paper document (perhaps a Visio drawing) that you can keep pegged to your wall for reference.

If you keep your page-flow document up to date throughout, you'll have that much more to refer to if you need to make adjustments to the application a year from now. And let's not forget that clients and bosses always like to see documents with recent dates on them, no matter what's actually in the documents.

Include Files and Custom Tags

Another handy document to keep current while you work is a list of include files and custom tags. You learned about include files in Chapter 9, "CFML Basics," and you will learn about custom tags in Chapter 19, "Building User-Defined Functions." Although both types of files are handy because they enable you to isolate and reuse your code, it can sometimes be easy to forget which files rely on which other files. Therefore, a simple spreadsheet or document that keeps track of these interdependencies can really help.

Commenting Style

Throughout this book, we encourage you to comment your code as much as possible. Any code, ColdFusion or otherwise, is a hundred times more valuable if it is thoroughly commented. And it becomes a *thousand* times more valuable if all the code for an application is commented in a consistent style.

You should decide ahead of time how you will comment your code, and stick to it while you work. For instance, you might make resolutions like these:

- Each .cfm file should have a header comment that explains the purpose of the file, when it was first written, and the original author's name.
- When anyone makes a significant change to the file, the header comment should be amended, explaining which portions were added or changed. Over time, you'll develop a detailed revision history for each file.
- The header comment should list the variables used within the template and what they are for. If the file is a custom tag, perhaps each attribute should be listed and explained.
- Each significant change or addition to a file should be noted in place with an explanation, date, and the developer's initials.
- There should be at least one line of comment before each CFML tag—perhaps a few exceptions can be made for self-explanatory tags such as `<CFOUTPUT>`, however.

Naming Conventions

Some developers are strict about naming conventions—for very good reason. We're not going to suggest any specific sets of naming conventions here because different people have different ideas about what makes sense. It's something you and your team should decide for yourselves.

That said, here are a few ideas:

- Because short variable names can result in cryptic-looking code, you might require that every variable name consist of at least two words, with the first letter of each word in uppercase. So instead of variable names such as `tot` and `fn`, you would have names such as `CurrentTotal` and `FirstName`.
- Many coders like to use the first letter of each variable's name to suggest the type of information the variable will hold. For example, you could use `sFirstName` and `sShipAddress` instead of `FirstName` and `ShipAddress` to instantly see that the actual values will be strings. Similarly, you might use `dFirstVisit` for dates and `nCurrentPrice` or `iProductsOrdered` for numbers. You also could use similar naming conventions for the columns in your database tables.
- Similarly, some people find that having the names of their database tables start with a `t` or `tbl`, such as `tCustomers` or `tblCustomers`, is useful. Sometimes people also choose to come up with a convention to indicate the relationship between related tables, such as calling a table `tCustomers_Orders` or `rCustomers2Orders` if the table relates rows from the `tCustomers` and `tOrders` tables.
- Some developers like to put all forms into a separate include file and start the filename with `frm`, as in `frmNewUser.cfm` or perhaps `frm_NewUser.cfm`. Other people do something similar with each `<CFQUERY>` tag, ending up with files with names such as `qryGetDirectors` and so on. See Chapter 37, "Development Methodologies," for more information.

Keeping the Directory Structure in Mind

There are no hard and fast rules about how to organize your ColdFusion templates and other files into folders, but you should put some real thought into it and come up with a scheme that makes sense to you.

Here are some things to keep in mind:

- Make every effort to keep the directory structure of your application as organized as possible. For instance, it often makes sense to have a folder that corresponds to each high-level section of the site (the sections that appear on your main navigation bar, or the sections accessible from the application's home page).
- Folders are like friends. Unless they are too full of themselves, the more you have, the better. It is almost always better to have lots of directories with relatively few files in them, rather than a few directories with hundreds of files in each.
- Decide where your images and other media files will be kept. For instance, this book calls for keeping them all in a single folder named `images`. You might decide to maintain a number of subfolders within images. Of course, you could also decide to use an entirely different strategy, perhaps keeping your image files in the same folders as the templates that use them. Just choose a method and stick with it.
- In general, it is most convenient to use long, descriptive filenames—However, if you will be displaying a link to a particular template many, many times on a page (for each record in a database, say), a long filename might add to the size of the final HTML code your template generates. Try to use somewhat shorter filenames for templates that will be linked to extremely often. The same goes for images that will be included in pages frequently.

TIP

The Yahoo! site is a good place to look for an example of a site that exposes a very sensible, hierarchical URL structure, but where each portion of the URL is kept very short (often just a letter or two).

Moving Targets and Feature Creep

Unless you are particularly blessed by the gods of application development, you will deal with the twin evils of *Moving Targets* and *Feature Creep*. These scorned, ugly creatures are sometimes so filthy and wretched as to be barely distinguishable from one another. Moving Targets, of course, are those aspects of an application that your client or boss keeps changing her mind about from one day to the next. Feature Creep is what happens if little extra features keep getting piled onto the application while you work. Either one will keep you from getting your project done on time.

On the other hand, it's only natural that the best suggestions and most exciting "eureka!" moments will come while the application is being built. Development is a creative process, and you or others might stumble upon a really brilliant idea that must be in there. Therefore, you should plan on making a few concessions or adjustments during the development process. Have some type of agreement in place about how to deal with incoming ideas.

CHAPTER 16

Introducing the Web Application Framework

IN THIS CHAPTER

ColdFusion provides a small but very important set of features for building sophisticated Web applications. The features all have to do with making all your ColdFusion templates for a particular site or project behave as if they were related to one another—that is, to make them behave as a single application. These features are referred to collectively as the Web application framework.

The Web application framework is designed to help you with the following:

- **Consistent Look and Feel.** The application framework enables you to easily include a consistent header or footer at the top and bottom of every page in your application. It also lets you apply the same look and feel to error messages that might need to be displayed to the user. You can also use it to keep things like fonts and headings consistent from page to page.
- **Sharing Variables Between Pages.** So far, the variables you have worked with in this book all "die" when each page request has been processed. The Web application framework gives you a variety of ways to maintain the values of variables between page requests. The variables can be maintained on a per-user, per-session, or application-wide basis.
- **Before and After Processing.** The application framework gives you an easy way to execute custom code you want just *before* each page request. A common use for this capability is to provide password security for your application. You can also execute custom code just *after* the request.

Considered together, it's the Web application framework that really lets you present a Web experience to your users. Without these features, your individual templates would always stand on their own, acting as little miniprograms. The framework is the force that binds your templates together. Use The Force, Luke.

Using Application.cfm

To get started with the Web application framework, you first must create a special file called `Application.cfm`. In most respects, this file is just an ordinary ColdFusion template. Only two things make `Application.cfm` special:

- The code in your `Application.cfm` file will be automatically included just before any of your application pages. The behavior is just as if you included the file using an ordinary `<CFINCLUDE>` tag at the very top of each of your regular .cfm files.
- You can't visit an `Application.cfm` page directly. If you attempt to visit an `Application.cfm` page with a browser, you will receive an error message from ColdFusion.

The `Application.cfm` file is sometimes referred to as the application template. It might not sound all that special so far, but you will find that the two special properties actually go a long way toward making your applications more cohesive and easier to develop.

TIP

Even though you can put any CFML code in the template that you want, you should generally not do so. `Application.cfm` has special uses, as you will see.

NOTE

On Unix/Linux systems, filenames are case sensitive. The `Application.cfm` file must be spelled exactly as shown here, using a capital A. Even if you are doing your development with Windows systems in mind, pay attention to the case so ColdFusion will be capable of finding the file if you decide to move your application to a Linux or Unix server later.

Placement of `Application.cfm`

As stated previously, the code in your `Application.cfm` file is automatically executed just before each of the pages that make up your application. You might be wondering how exactly ColdFusion does this. How will it know which files make up your application and which ones do not?

The answer is quite simple: Whenever a user visits a .cfm page, ColdFusion looks to see whether a file named `Application.cfm` exists in the same directory as the requested page. If so, ColdFusion automatically includes it, just as if you had put a `<CFINCLUDE>` tag at the top of the requested template.

If no `Application.cfm` exists in the same folder as the requested page, ColdFusion looks in that folder's parent folder. If no `Application.cfm` file exists there, it looks in *that* parent's folder, and so on, until there are no more parent folders to look in.

All this means is that you should do something you were probably already going to do anyway. Namely, you should put all the ColdFusion templates for a particular application within a single folder, somewhere within your Web server's document root. Let's call that directory your application folder. Within the application folder, you can organize your ColdFusion templates in any manner you choose, using any number of subfolders, sub-subfolders, and so on. If you put an `Application.cfm` file in the application folder, all of its code will automatically be included in all your application's templates. It's that simple.

For instance, consider the fictional folder structure shown in Figure 16.1. Here, the application folder is the folder named `MyApp`, which is sitting within the Web server's document root. Some basic Web pages are located in there, such as the company's home page (`Index. cfm`), a How To Contact Us page (`ContactUs.cfm`), and a Company Info page (`Company.cfm`). There is also a `SiteHeader.cfm` template there, which we intend to include at the top of each page.

Because a file called `Application.cfm` also exists in this folder, it is automatically included every time a user visits `Index.cfm` or `ContactUs.cfm`. It also is included whenever a user visits any of the ColdFusion templates stored in the Intranet or Store folders, or any of the subfolders of the Intranet folder. No matter how deep the subfolder structure gets, the `Application.cfm` file in the `OrangeWhip` folder will be automatically included.

NOTE

Don't worry about re-creating this folder structure yourself. None of the actual code examples for this chapter rely on it. We're just trying to clarify where your Application.cfm template might go in a real-world application.

A Basic `Application.cfm` Template

Take a look at Listing 16.1, a simple `Application.cfm` file. Because the two `<CFSET>` tags are executed before each page request, the `DataSource` and `CompanyName` variables can be referred to within any of the application's ColdFusion templates. For instance, the value of the `DataSource` variable will always be `ows`.

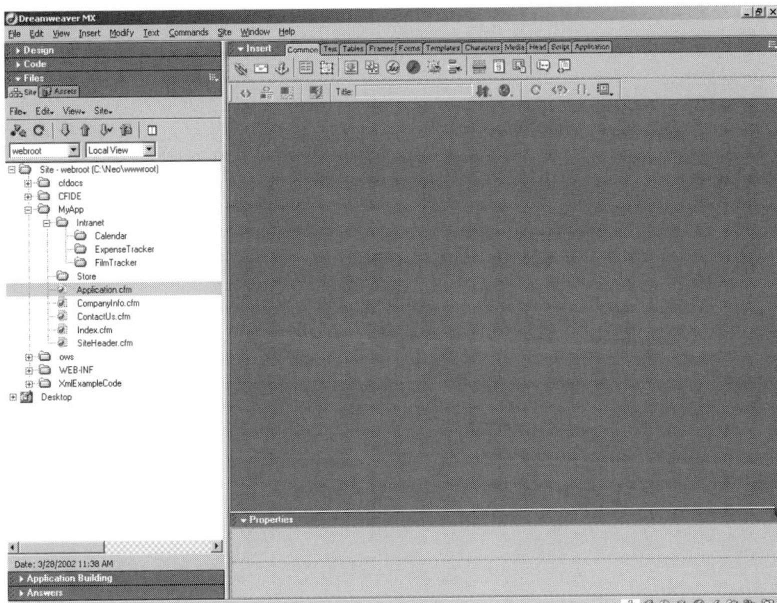

Figure 16.1

The `Application.cfm` file gets included before any of your application's templates.

If you save this listing, be sure to save it as `Application.cfm`, not `Application1.cfm`.

Listing 16.1 `Application1.cfm`—A Simple Application Template

```
<!---
  Filename:      Application.cfm (The "Application Template")
  Created by:    Nate Weiss (NMW)
  Please Note:   All code here gets executed with every page request!!
  Purpose:       Sets "constant" variables and includes consistent header
--->

<!--- Any variables set here can be used by all our pages --->
<CFSET DataSource  = "ows">
<CFSET CompanyName = "Orange Whip Studios">

<!--- Display our Site Header at top of every page --->
<CFINCLUDE TEMPLATE="SiteHeader.cfm">
```

NOTE

Later, you can refer to this variable as the `DATASOURCE` attribute for all the `<CFQUERY>` tags in the application, as in `DATASOURCE="#CompanyName#"`. That way, if the data source name changes later, for whatever reason, you will need to update your code in only one place, rather than in each individual `<CFQUERY>` tag.

In addition, the `<CFINCLUDE>` tag in Listing 16.1 ensures that the company's standard page header will be shown at the top of each page. Listing 16.2 shows the `SiteHeader.cfm` template itself. Note that it can use the `CompanyName` variable that gets set by `Application.cfm`.

If this were your application, you would no longer have to put that `<CFINCLUDE>` tag at the top of the `Index.cfm` or `CompanyInfo.cfm` pages (see Figure 16.1), and you wouldn't have to remember to include it in any new templates. ColdFusion would now be taking care of that for you.

Listing 16.2 `SiteHeader.cfm`—Simple Header That Is Included on Each Page by Application.cfm

```
<!---
  Filename:      SiteHeader.cfm
  Created by:    Nate Weiss (NMW)
  Please Note:   Included in every page by Application.cfm
--->

<HTML>
<HEAD>
  <TITLE><CFOUTPUT>#CompanyName#</CFOUTPUT></TITLE>
</HEAD>

<BODY>
<FONT FACE="sans-serif" SIZE="2">

<!--- Company Logo --->
<IMG SRC="../images/logo_c.gif" WIDTH="101" HEIGHT="101" ALT="" ALIGN="absmiddle"
BORDER="0">
<CFOUTPUT><FONT SIZE="4">#CompanyName#</FONT></CFOUTPUT><BR CLEAR="left">
```

Using OnRequestEnd.cfm

The Web application framework also reserves the special `OnRequestEnd.cfm` filename, which is included automatically at the very end of every page request, rather than at the beginning. Like the `Application.cfm` file, this file cannot be visited directly using a Web browser.

ColdFusion looks for `OnRequestEnd.cfm` in the same folder in which it finds `Application.cfm`. So, for `OnRequestEnd.cfm` to be executed, just place it in the same location in which your `Application.cfm` file is sitting (your application folder).

Listing 16.3 demonstrates one common use for `OnRequestEnd.cfm`. It has just one line of code, a simple `<CFINCLUDE>` tag to include the `SiteFooter.cfm` template at the bottom of every page. Listing 16.4 shows the `SiteFooter.cfm` file itself, which displays a copyright notice. The net effect is that the copyright notice is displayed at the bottom of every page in the application, as shown in Figure 16.2.

Of course, there are other ways to get this effect. You could forget about this `OnRequestEnd.cfm` business and just put the `<CFINCLUDE>` tag at the bottom of every page in your application. But that might be tedious, and you might forget to do it sometimes. Or, you could just put the copyright notice in the `OnRequestEnd.cfm` file and get rid of the `SiteFooter.cfm` file altogether. That would be fine, but leaving them in separate files can keep things more manageable if the footer becomes more complicated in the future.

Listing 16.3 `OnRequestEnd.cfm`—Including a Site Footer at the Bottom of Every Page

```
<!---
  Filename:     OnRequestEnd.cfm
  Created by:   Nate Weiss (NMW)
  Please Note:  All code here gets executed with every page request!!
--->

<!--- Display our Site Footer at bottom of every page --->
<CFINCLUDE TEMPLATE="SiteFooter.cfm">
```

NOTE

Again, remember that filenames are case sensitive on Unix/Linux systems. The `OnRequestEnd.cfm` file must be spelled exactly as shown here. Even if you are doing your development with Windows systems in mind, pay attention to the case so ColdFusion will be capable of finding the file if you decide to move your application to a Linux or Unix server later.

Listing 16.4 `SiteFooter.cfm`—Simple Footer That Gets Included by `OnRequestEnd.cfm`

```
<!---
  Filename:     SiteFooter.cfm
  Created by:   Nate Weiss (NMW)
  Please Note:  Included in every page by OnRequestEnd.cfm
--->

<!--- Display copyright notice at bottom of every page --->
<CFOUTPUT>
  <FONT SIZE="1" FACE="sans-serif" COLOR="Silver ">
  <P>(c) #Year(Now())# #CompanyName#. All rights reserved.<BR>
</CFOUTPUT>

</BODY>
</HTML>
```

TIP

The expression `#Year(Now())#` is a simple way to display the current year. You also could use `#DateFormat(Now(),"yyyy")#` to get the same effect. You can find out more about the `DateFormat`, `Year`, and `Now` functions in Appendix C, "ColdFusion Function Reference."

Listing 16.5 provides preliminary code for Orange Whip Studio's home page. As you can see, it is just a simple message that welcomes the user to the site. Of course, in practice, this is where you would provide links to all the interesting parts of the application. The point of this template is to demonstrate that the site header and footer are now going to be automatically included at the top and bottom of all ordinary ColdFusion templates in this folder (or its subfolders), as shown in Figure 16.2. Note that this template is also able to use the `CompanyName` variable that was set in the `Application.cfm` file.

Listing 16.5 `Index1.cfm`—A Basic Home Page for Orange Whip Studios

```
<!---
  Filename:      Index.cfm
  Created by:    Nate Weiss (NMW)
  Date Created: 2/18/2001
  Please Note:   Header and Footer are automatically provided
--->

<CFOUTPUT>
  <BLOCKQUOTE>
  <P>Hello, and welcome to the home of
  #CompanyName# on the web!  We certainly
  hope you enjoy your visit.  We take pride in
  producing movies that are almost as good
  as the ones they are copied from.  We've
  been doing it for years.  On this site, you'll
  be able to find out about all our classic films
  from the golden age of Orange Whip Studios,
  as well as our latest and greatest new releases.
  Have fun!<BR>
  </BLOCKQUOTE>
</CFOUTPUT>
```

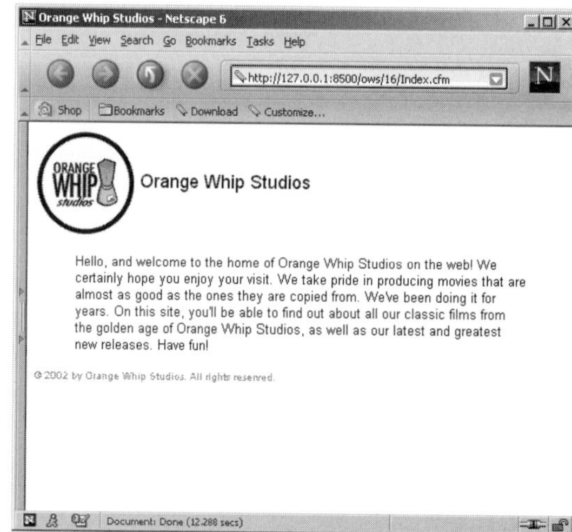

Figure 16.2

The application framework makes it easy to keep things consistent throughout your site.

Customizing the Look of Error Messages

The Web application framework provides a simple way to customize the look of error messages that can occur while users are accessing your pages. As you know, error messages might appear because of syntax problems in your code, because of database connection problems, or just because the user has left out one or more required fields while he is filling out a form.

The application framework enables you to customize any of these error messages. You can even hide them from the user's view entirely if you want. This enables you to maintain a consistent look and feel throughout your application, even when those dreaded error messages occur.

Introducing the `<CFERROR>` Tag

You use the `<CFERROR>` tag to specify how error messages should be displayed. Customizing the error messages that appear throughout your application is generally a two-step process:

1. First, you create an *error display template*, which displays the error message along with whatever graphics or other formatting you consider appropriate.
2. Next, you include a `<CFERROR>` tag that tells ColdFusion to display errors using the error display template you just created. In general, you place the `<CFERROR>` tag in your `Application.cfm` file.

Table 16.1 shows the attributes supported by the `<CFERROR>` tag.

The next two sections discuss how to customize the error messages displayed for *exception errors* (syntax errors, database errors, and so on) and *validation errors* (when the user fails to fill out a form correctly).

Table 16.1 `<CFERROR>` Tag Attributes

ATTRIBUTE	DESCRIPTION
`TYPE`	The type of error you want to catch and display using your customized error display template. The allowable values are `Request`, `Validation`, `Monitor`, and `Exception`. The first two types are covered in this chapter; the latter two are discussed in Chapter 31, "Error Handling." If you don't supply this attribute, it is assumed to be `Request`, but it is best to always supply it.
`TEMPLATE`	Required. The relative path and filename of your customized error display template. You specify the filename in the same way as you would specify an include file with the `<CFINCLUDE>` tag.

Table 16.1 (CONTINUED)

ATTRIBUTE	DESCRIPTION
`MAILTO`	Optional. An email address for a site administrator that the user could use to send some type of notification that the error occurred. The only purpose of this attribute is to pass an appropriate email address to your error display template. *It does not actually send any email messages on its own.*
`EXCEPTION`	Optional. The specific exception that you want to catch and display using your customized error display template. The default value is `Any`, which is appropriate for most circumstances. See Chapter 31 for a discussion of the other values you can supply here.

Request Versus Exception Error Templates

If you want to customize the way error messages are displayed, you first must create an error display template. This template is displayed to the user whenever a page request cannot be completed because of some type of uncaught error condition.

ColdFusion actually allows you to create two types of error display templates:

- **Request Error Display Templates.** The simplest way to show a customized error message. You can include whatever images or formatting you want so that the error matches your site's look and feel. However, CFML tags, such as `<CFOUTPUT>`, `<CFSET>`, or `<CFINCLUDE>`, are not allowed. CFML functions and variables also are not allowed.
- **Exception Error Display Templates.** These are more flexible. You can use whatever CFML tags you want. For instance, you might want to have ColdFusion automatically send an email to the Webmaster when certain types of errors occur. The main caveat is that ColdFusion cannot display such a template for certain serious errors.

In general, the best practice is to create one template of each type. Then, the exception template is displayed most often, unless the error is so serious that ColdFusion cannot safely continue interpreting CFML tags, in which case the request template is displayed. The request template also kicks in if the exception template *itself* causes an error or cannot be found.

NOTE

If you don't care about being able to use CFML tags in these error display templates, you can just create the request template and skip creating the exception one.

NOTE

For those history buffs out there, the request type of error display template is somewhat of a holdover from earlier versions of ColdFusion. At one time, you could never respond intelligently to any type of error. Thankfully, those days are over.

Creating a Customized Request Error Page

To create the request display template, do the following:

1. Create a new ColdFusion template called `ErrorRequest.cfm`, located in the same directory as your `Application.cfm` file. Include whatever images or formatting you want, using whatever `<IMG>` or other tags you would normally. Remember to *not* put any CFML tags in this template.
2. Include the special `ERROR.Diagnostics` variable wherever you want the actual error message to appear, if you want it to appear at all. Contrary to what you are used to, the variable should not be between `<CFOUTPUT>` tags.
3. If you want, you can include the special `ERROR.MailTo` variable to display the email address of your site's Webmaster or some other appropriate person. You also can use any of the other variables shown in Table 16.2.
4. Include a `<CFERROR>` tag in your `Application.cfm` file, with the `TYPE` attribute set to `Request` and the `TEMPLATE` attribute set to `ErrorRequest.cfm`. This is what associates your error display template with your application.

Table 16.2 Special `ERROR` Variables Available in an Error Display Template

ATTRIBUTE	DESCRIPTION
`ERROR.Browser`	The browser that was used when the error occurred, as reported by the browser itself. This is the same value that is normally available to you as the `#CGI.HTTP_USER_AGENT#` variable, which generally includes the browser version number and operating system.
`ERROR.DateTime`	The date and time that the error occurred, in the form MM/DD/YY HH:MM:SS. You can use the `DateFormat()` function to format the date differently in an exception template, but not in a request template.
`ERROR.Diagnostics`	The actual error message. In general, this is the most important thing to include (or to decide not to include) in an error display template. Please note that the exact text of this message can be affected by the settings currently enabled in the Debugging Settings page of the ColdFusion Administrator. See Chapter 14, "Debugging and Troubleshooting," for details.
`ERROR.GeneratedContent`	The actual HTML that had been generated by the requested ColdFusion template (and any included templates and so on) up until the moment that the error occurred. You could use this to display the part of the page that had been successfully generated. This variable is not available in the request type of error display template.
`ERROR.HTTPReferer`	The page the user was coming from when the error occurred, assuming that the user got to the problem page via a link or form submission. This value is reported by the browser and can sometimes be blank (especially if the user visited the page directly by typing its URL). Note the incorrect spelling of the word *referrer*.

Table 16.2 (continued)

ATTRIBUTE	DESCRIPTION
ERROR.MailTo	An email address, presumably for a site administrator or Webmaster, as provided to the <CFERROR> tag. See the following examples to see how this actually should be used.
ERROR.QueryString	The query string provided to the template in which the error occurred. In other words, everything after the ? sign in the page's URL. This is the same value that is normally available to you as the #CGI.QUERY_STRING# variable.
ERROR.RemoteAddress	The IP address of the user's machine.
ERROR.Template	Filename of the ColdFusion template (.cfm file) in which the error occurred.

Listing 16.6 is a good example of a request error display template. Note that no <CFOUTPUT> or other CFML tags are present. Also note that the only variables used are the special ERROR variables mentioned previously.

Listing 16.6 ErrorRequest.cfm—Customizing the Display of Error Messages

```
<!---
  Filename:      ErrorRequest.cfm
  Created by:    Nate Weiss (NMW)
  Please Note:   Included via <CFERROR> in Application.cfm
--->

<HTML>
<HEAD><TITLE>Error</TITLE></HEAD>
<BODY>

<!--- Display sarcastic message to poor user --->
<h2>Who Knew?</h2>
<P>We are very sorry, but a technical problem prevents us from
showing you what you are looking for.  Unfortunately, these things
happen from time to time, even though we have only the most
top-notch people on our technical staff.  Perhaps all of
our programmers need a raise, or more vacation time. As always,
there is also the very real possibility that SPACE ALIENS
(or our rivals at Miramax Studios) have sabotaged our website.<BR>
<P>That said, we will naturally try to correct this problem
as soon as we possibly can.  Please try again shortly.

<!--- Provide "mailto" link so user can send email --->
<P>If you want, you can
<A HREF="mailto:#ERROR.MailTo#">send the webmaster an email</A>.
<P>Thank you.<BR>

<!--- Maybe the company logo will make them feel better --->
<IMG SRC="../images/logo_b.gif" WIDTH="73" HEIGHT="73" ALT="" BORDER="0">

<!--- Display the actual error message --->
<BLOCKQUOTE>
```

Listing 16.6 (continued)

```
  <HR><FONT SIZE="-1" COLOR="Gray">#ERROR.Diagnostics#</FONT>
</BLOCKQUOTE>

</BODY>
</HTML>
```

NOTE

ColdFusion also provides the `<CFTRY>` and `<CFCATCH>` tags, which enable you to trap specific errors and respond to or recover from them as appropriate. See Chapter 31, "Error Handling," for details.

Listing 16.7 shows how to use the `<CFERROR>` tag in your `Application.cfm` file. Note that the email address `webmaster@orangewhipstudios.com` is being provided as the tag's `MAILTO` attribute, which means that the Webmaster's email address will be inserted in place of the `ERROR.MailTo` reference in Listing 16.8. Figure 16.3 shows how an error message would now be shown if you were to make a coding error in one of your templates.

To test this listing, save it as `Application.cfm`, not `Application2.cfm`.

Listing 16.7 `Application2.cfm`—Use of the `<CFERROR>` Tag in `Application.cfm`

```
<!---
  Filename:     Application.cfm (The "Application Template")
  Created by:   Nate Weiss (NMW)
  Please Note:  All code here gets executed with every page request!!
--->

<!--- Any variables set here can be used by all our pages --->
<CFSET DataSource  = "ows">
<CFSET CompanyName = "Orange Whip Studios">
<CFSET ErrorEmail  = "webmaster@orangewhipstudios.com">

<!--- Display Custom Message for "Request" Errors --->
<CFERROR
  TYPE="Request"
  TEMPLATE="ErrorRequest.cfm"
  MAILTO="#ErrorE-mail#">

<!--- Display our Site Header at top of every page --->
<CFINCLUDE TEMPLATE="SiteHeader.cfm">
```

Additional ERROR Variables

In Listing 16.6, you saw how the `ERROR.Diagnostics` variable can be used to show the user which specific error actually occurred. A number of additional variables can be used in the same way. You will see a several of these used in Listing 16.8 in the next section.

NOTE

Note that the `ERROR.GeneratedContent` variable is not available in request error display templates.

Figure 16.3

Customized error pages help maintain your application's look and feel.

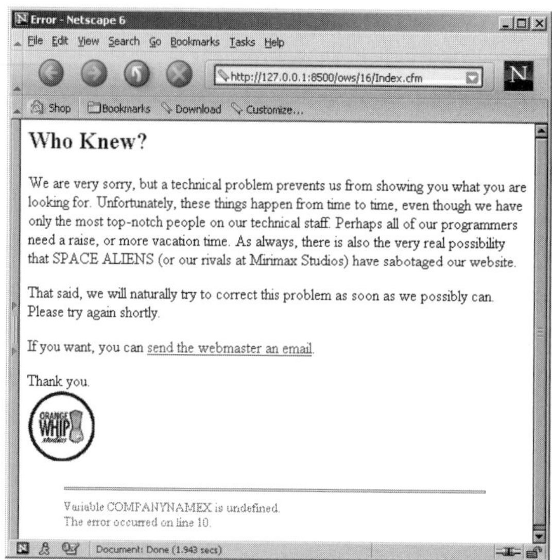

TIP

These are the only variables you can use in *request* error display templates. You can use all types of ColdFusion variables in exception error display templates, discussed next.

Creating a Customized Exception Error Page

You already have seen how to create a request error display template, in which you are prevented from using any CFML tags or functions. Now you can create an exception error template, in which you *can* use whatever CFML tags and functions you want.

For instance, Listing 16.8 is similar to Listing 16.6, but it does not display the `ERROR.Diagnostics` message to the user. This means that the user will not know which type of error actually occurred. After all, your users might not care about the specifics, and you might not want them to see the actual error message in the first place. In addition, instead of allowing the user to send an email message to the Webmaster, this template has ColdFusion send an email message to the Webmaster automatically, via the `<CFMAIL>` tag.

Now all you have to do is add a second `<CFERROR>` tag to your `Application.cfm` file, this time specifying `TYPE="Exception"`. You should put this `<CFERROR>` tag right after the first one, so the first one can execute if some problem occurs with your exception error display template. Listing 16.9 (in the next section) shows how this would look in your `Application. cfm` file.

Listing 16.8 `ErrorException.cfm`—Sending an Email When an Error Occurs

```
<!---
  Filename:     ErrorException.cfm
  Created by:   Nate Weiss (NMW)
  Please Note:  Included via <CFERROR> in Application.cfm
--->
```

Listing 16.8 (continued)

```
<HTML>
<HEAD><TITLE>Error</TITLE></HEAD>
<BODY>

<!--- Display sarcastic message to poor user --->
<h2>Who Knew?</h2>
<P>We are very sorry, but a technical problem prevents us from
showing you what you are looking for.  Unfortunately, these things
happen from time to time, even though we have only the most
top-notch people on our technical staff.  Perhaps all of
our programmers need a raise, or more vacation time. As always,
there is also the very real possibility that SPACE ALIENS
(or our rivals at Miramax Studios) have sabotaged our website.<BR>
<P>That said, we will naturally try to correct this problem
as soon as we possibly can.  Please try again shortly.
Thank you.<BR>

<!--- Maybe the company logo will make them feel better --->
<IMG SRC="../images/logo_b.gif" WIDTH="73" HEIGHT="73" ALT="" BORDER="0">

<!--- Send an email message to site administrator --->
<!--- (or whatever address provided to <CFERROR>) --->
<CFIF ERROR.MailTo NEQ "">
  <CFMAIL
    TO="#ERROR.MailTo#"
    FROM="errorsender@orangewhipstudios.com"
    SUBJECT="Error on Page #ERROR.Template#">
    Error Date/Time: #ERROR.DateTime#
    User's Browser:  #ERROR.Browser#
    URL Parameters:  #ERROR.QueryString#
    Previous Page:   #ERROR.HTTPReferer#
    ------------------------------------
    #ERROR.Diagnostics#
  </CFMAIL>
</CFIF>
```

NOTE

Because sending automated error emails is a great way to show how exception templates can be used, the `<CFMAIL>` tag has been introduced a bit ahead of time here. Its use in Listing 16.8 should be fairly self-explanatory: The ColdFusion server sends a simple email message to the Webmaster. The email will contain the error message, date, browser version, and so on because of the `ERROR` variables referred to between the opening and closing `<CFMAIL>` tags.

➜ See Chapter 26, "Interacting with Email," for details.

TIP

The Webmaster could also look in ColdFusion's logs to see any errors that might be occurring throughout the application.

➜ See Chapter 14, "Debugging and Troubleshooting," for details.

Creating a Customized Validation Error Page

Now, your application responds in a friendly and consistent manner, even when problems occur in your code. The Web application framework also enables you to customize the page that appears if a user's form input doesn't comply with the validation rules you have set up using the hidden form fields technique (as described in Chapter 12, "Form Data Validation").

To create your own validation error display template, follow the same steps you performed to create your request template (see the section "Creating a Customized Request Error Page," earlier in this chapter). The only differences are that you use the special `ERROR` variables listed in Table 16.3 instead of those in Table 16.2, and that you should specify `TYPE="Validation"` in the `<CFERROR>` tag you include in your `Application.cfm` file.

Table 16.3 Special `ERROR` Variables Available in an Validation Display Template

ATTRIBUTE	DESCRIPTION
`ERROR.InvalidFields`	The actual problems with the way the user has filled out the form. The text is preformatted as a bulleted list (the text includes `<UL>` and `<LI>` tags). In general, you would always want to include this in your error display template; otherwise, the user wouldn't have any indication of what she did wrong.
`ERROR.ValidationHeader`	The default text that normally appears above the bulleted list of problems when you are not using a customized error message. The message reads, "Form Entries Incomplete or Invalid. One or more problems exist with the data you have entered." You can include this variable in your template if you want this wording to appear. Otherwise, you can just provide your own text.
`ERROR.ValidationFooter`	The default text that normally appears above the bulleted list of problems when you are not using a customized error message. The message reads, "Use the Back button on your Web browser to return to the previous page and correct the listed problems."

Listing 16.9 shows a completed validation error display template. Figure 16.4 shows how it would look to the end user, if he were to submit a form without filling it out correctly.

Listing 16.10 shows how your `Application.cfm` file would look at this point. Note that it now contains three `<CFERROR>` tags: one for each type of error display template you've learned to create in this chapter.

Listing 16.9 `ErrorValidation.cfm`—Customizing the Display of Form Validation Messages

```
<!---
  Filename:     ErrorValidation.cfm
  Created by:   Nate Weiss (NMW)
  Please Note:  Included via <CFERROR> in Application.cfm
--->

<HTML>
<HEAD><TITLE>Form Fields Missing or Incomplete</TITLE></HEAD>
```

Listing 16.9 (continued)

```
<BODY>

<!--- Introductory Message --->
<IMG SRC="../images/logo_b.gif" WIDTH="73" HEIGHT="73" ALT="" ALIGN="absmiddle"
➥BORDER="0">
<FONT SIZE= "4">Please take a moment...</FONT><BR CLEAR="all">
Maybe it's because we are in the entertainment business and thus have lost
touch with the kinds of problems that ordinary people have, but we can't
quite figure out how to deal with the information you just provided.
Here are the "problems" that we need you to correct:

<!--- Display actual form-field problems --->
#ERROR.InvalidFields#

<!--- Link back to previous page --->
<P>Please
<A HREF="javascript:history.back()">return to the form</A>
and correct these minor problems.<BR>
Or, just use your browser's Back button.<BR>
</BODY>
</HTML>
```

Listing 16.10 `Application3.cfm`—Using Request, Exception, and Validation Templates Together

```
<!---
  Filename:     Application.cfm (The "Application Template")
  Created by:   Nate Weiss (NMW)
  Please Note:  All code here gets executed with every page request!!
--->

<!--- Any variables set here can be used by all our pages --->
<CFSET DataSource  = "ows">
<CFSET CompanyName = "Orange Whip Studios">
<CFSET ErrorEmail  = "webmaster@orangewhipstudios.com">

<!--- Display Custom Message for "Request" Errors --->
<CFERROR
  TYPE="Request"
  TEMPLATE="ErrorRequest.cfm"
  MAILTO="#ErrorEmail#">

<!--- Display Custom Message for "Exception" Errors --->
<CFERROR
  TYPE="Exception"
  EXCEPTION="Any"
  TEMPLATE="ErrorException.cfm"
  MAILTO="#ErrorEmail#">

<!--- Display Custom Message for "Validation" Errors --->
<CFERROR
  TYPE="Validation"
  TEMPLATE="ErrorValidation.cfm ">

<!--- Display our Site Header at top of every page --->
<CFINCLUDE TEMPLATE="SiteHeader.cfm">
```

NOTE

ColdFusion also provides the <CFTRY> and <CFCATCH> tags, which allow you to trap specific errors and respond to or recover from them as appropriate. See Chapter 31, "Error Handling," for details.

Figure 16.4

A customized display template makes it less jarring for users who fail to fill out a form correctly.

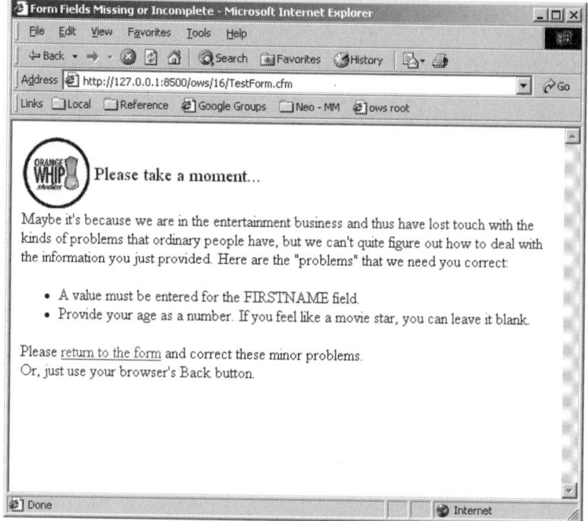

Using Application Variables

So far in this chapter, you have seen how ColdFusion's Web application framework features help you maintain a consistent look and feel throughout your application. You also have seen how easy it is to set up "before and after" processing with the special application templates (`Application.cfm` and `OnRequestEnd.cfm`). In other words, your pages are starting to look and behave cohesively.

Next, you learn how your application's templates can start sharing variables between page requests. Basically, this is the part where your application gets a piece of the server's memory in which to store values. This is where it gets a brain.

What Are Application Variables?

Pretend it's Oscar season. Orange Whip Studios feels that all of its films are contenders. Tensions are high, and the president is demanding to see a "featured movie" box on the studio's home page to help create more "buzz" than Miramax can create. The featured movie should be different each time the home page is viewed, shamelessly rotating through all of the studio's movies. It's your job to get this project done, pronto.

Hmmm. You could retrieve all the movies from the database for each page request and somehow pick one at random, but that wouldn't guarantee that the same movie didn't get picked three or four times in a row. What you want is some way to remember your current spot in the list of movies, so they all get shown evenly, in order. You consider making a table to remember which movies have been shown and then deleting all rows from the table when it's time to rotate through them again, but that seems like overkill. You wish there was some kind of variable that would persist between page requests, instead of dying at the bottom of each page like the ColdFusion variables you're used to.

That's exactly what application variables are for. Instead of setting a variable called `LastMovieID`, you could call it `APPLICATION.LastMovieID`. After you set this variable value to `5`, say, it remains set at `5` until you change it again (or until the server is restarted). In essence, application variables enable you to set aside a little piece of ColdFusion's memory, which your application can use for its own purposes.

When to Use Application Variables

Generally, you can use application variables whenever you need a variable to be shared among all pages and all visitors to your application. The variable is kept in ColdFusion's memory, and any page in your application can access or change its value. If some code on one of your pages changes the value of an application variable, the next hit to any of your application's pages will reflect the new value.

NOTE

This means you should *not* use application variables if you want a separate copy of the variable to exist for each visitor to your site. In other words, application variables should not be used for anything personalized because they do not attempt to distinguish between your site's visitors.

➜ Chapter 17, "Working with Sessions," explains how to create variables that are maintained separately for each visitor.

Consider application variables for:

- Rotating banner ads evenly, so that all ads get shown the same number of times
- Rotating other types of content, such as the featured movie problem mentioned previously, or products that might be on sale
- Keeping counters of various types of events, such as the number of people currently online or the number of hits since the server was started
- Maintaining some type of information that changes only occasionally or perhaps doesn't change at all, but can take a bit of time to compute or retrieve

Do not use application variables for per-user tasks, such as these:

- Maintaining a shopping cart
- Remembering a user's email address or username from visit to visit
- Keeping a history of the pages a user has visited while he has been on your site

Introducing the `<CFAPPLICATION>` Tag

As a part of the Web application framework, ColdFusion provides a tag called `<CFAPPLICATION>`, which is used primarily for enabling various types of persistent variables. Application variables are one type of persistent variable; you will learn about two other types—client and session variables—in Chapter 17.

Application variables can be used only after a `<CFAPPLICATION>` tag has been encountered. This tag tells ColdFusion where to store the variables in its memory. Because you generally want to share the variables throughout your application, it is almost always best to put the `<CFAPPLICATION>` tag in your `Application.cfm` file.

The tag takes a number of attributes, most of which are relevant only for session and client variables, discussed in the next chapter. For now, only two attributes are important, as shown in Table 16.4.

Table 16.4 `<CFAPPLICATION>` Tag Attributes Relevant to Application Variables

ATTRIBUTE	DESCRIPTION
`NAME`	A name for your application. The name can be anything you want, up to 64 characters long. ColdFusion uses this name internally to store and look up your application variables for you. It should be unique per application. This attribute is required to enable the use of application variables.
`APPLICATIONTIMEOUT`	Optional. How long you want your application variables to live in the server's memory. If you don't provide this value, it defaults to whatever is set up in the Variables page of the ColdFusion Administrator. See the section "Application Variable Timeouts," later in this chapter.

Enabling Application Variables

Listing 16.11 shows how your `Application.cfm` page is continuing to evolve. The `<CFAPPLICATION>` tag is now present, in addition to the `<CFERROR>` and other tags you learned about earlier in this chapter. Therefore, you can start using application variables in any ColdFusion templates in the same folder (or subfolders) as `Application.cfm`.

Listing 16.11 `Application4.cfm`—Using `<CFAPPLICATION>` to Enable Application Variables

```
<!---
  Filename:     Application.cfm (The "Application Template")
  Created by:   Nate Weiss (NMW)
  Please Note:  All code here gets executed with every page request!!
--->

<!--- Name our application, and enable Application variables --->
<CFAPPLICATION
  NAME="OrangeWhipSite">

<!--- Any variables set here can be used by all our pages --->
<CFSET DataSource  = "ows">
<CFSET CompanyName = "Orange Whip Studios">
<CFSET ErrorEmail  = "webmaster@orangewhipstudios.com">

<!--- Display Custom Message for "Request" Errors --->
```

Listing 16.11 (continued)

```
<CFERROR
  TYPE="Request"
  TEMPLATE="ErrorRequest.cfm"
  MAILTO="#ErrorEmail#">

<!--- Display Custom Message for "Exception" Errors --->
<CFERROR
  TYPE="Exception"
  EXCEPTION="Any"
  TEMPLATE="ErrorException.cfm"
  MAILTO="#ErrorEmail#">

<!--- Display Custom Message for "Validation" Errors --->
<CFERROR
  TYPE="Validation"
  TEMPLATE="ErrorValidation.cfm">

<!--- Display our Site Header at top of every page --->
<CFINCLUDE TEMPLATE="SiteHeader.cfm">
```

NOTE

ColdFusion maintains your application variables based on the `<CFAPPLICATION>` tag's `NAME` attribute. Therefore, it is important that no other applications on the same ColdFusion server use the same `NAME`. If they do, ColdFusion will consider them to be the same application and will share the variables among all the combined pages. Changing a variable in one also changes it in the other, and so on. It's conceivable to find yourself in a situation where this is actually what you want (if for some reason all the pages in your application simply can't be nested within a single folder); otherwise, make sure that each `<CFAPPLICATION>` tag gets its own `NAME`.

Using Application Variables

Now that application variables have been enabled, using them is quite simple. Basically, you create or set an application variable the same way you would set a normal variable, generally using the `<CFSET>` tag. The only difference is the presence of the word `APPLICATION`, followed by a dot. For instance, the following line would set the `APPLICATION.OurHitCount` variable to `0`. The variable would then be available to all pages in the application and would hold the value of `0` until it was changed:

```
<CFSET APPLICATION.OurHitCount = 0>
```

You can use application variables in any of the same places you would use ordinary ones. For instance, the following code adds one to an application variable and then outputs the new value, rounded to the nearest thousandth:

```
<CFSET APPLICATION.OurHitCount = APPLICATION.OurHitCount + 1>
<CFOUTPUT>#Round(APPLICATION.OurHitCount / 1000)># thousand</CFOUTPUT>
```

You also can use application variables with ColdFusion tags, such as `<CFIF>`, `<CFPARAM>`, and `<CFOUTPUT>`. See Chapter 8, "Using ColdFusion," and Chapter 9, "CFML Basics," if you want to review the use of variables in general.

NOTE

In general, there is no reason to place a variable in the `APPLICATION` scope unless its value will be changing as the application runs. If the value will always be the same, then you are essentially using it as what other programming environments would call a "constant." In such a case, you should just set normal, local variables in `Application.cfm` (like the `DataSource` variable that gets set in the `Application.cfm` examples in this chapter).

Putting Application Variables to Work

Application variables can make it relatively easy to get the little featured movie widget up and running. Again, the idea is for a callout-style box, which cycles through each of Orange Whip Studio's films, to display on the site's home page. The box should change each time the page is accessed, rotating through all the movies evenly.

Listing 16.12 shows one simple way to get this done, using application variables. Note that the template is broken into two separate parts. The first half is the interesting part, in which an application variable called `MovieList` is used to rotate the featured movie correctly. The second half simply outputs the name and description to the page, as shown in Figure 16.5.

NOTE

Before using application variables in your own code, please make sure to read the next section, "Using Locks to Protect Against Race Conditions," as well. It's important.

Listing 16.12 `FeaturedMovie.cfm`—Using Application Variables to Track Content Rotation

```
<!---
  Filename:     FeaturedMovie.cfm
  Created by:   Nate Weiss (NMW)
  Purpose:      Displays a single movie on the page, on a rotating basis
  Please Note:  Application variables must be enabled
--->

<!--- List of movies to show (list starts out empty) --->
<CFPARAM NAME="APPLICATION.MovieList" TYPE="string" DEFAULT="">

<!--- If this is the first time we're running this,  --->
<!--- Or we have run out of movies to rotate through --->
<CFIF ListLen(APPLICATION.MovieList) EQ 0>
  <!--- Get all current FilmIDs from the database --->
  <CFQUERY NAME="GetFilmIDs" DATASOURCE="#DataSource#">
    SELECT FilmID FROM Films
    ORDER BY MovieTitle
  </CFQUERY>

  <!--- Turn FilmIDs into a simple comma-separated list --->
  <CFSET APPLICATION.MovieList = ValueList(GetFilmIDs.FilmID)>
</CFIF>

<!--- Pick the first movie in the list to show right now --->
<CFSET ThisMovieID = ListGetAt(APPLICATION.MovieList, 1)>
<!--- Re-save the list, as all movies *except* the first --->
<CFSET APPLICATION.MovieList = ListDeleteAt(APPLICATION.MovieList, 1)>
```

Listing 16.12 (CONTINUED)

```
<!--- Now that we have chosen the film to "Feature", --->
<!--- Get all important info about it from database. --->
<CFQUERY NAME="GetFilm" DATASOURCE="#DataSource#">
  SELECT
    MovieTitle, Summary, Rating,
    AmountBudgeted, DateInTheaters
  FROM Films f, FilmsRatings r
  WHERE FilmID = #ThisMovieID#
  AND f.RatingID = r.RatingID
</CFQUERY>

<!--- Now Display Our Featured Movie --->
<CFOUTPUT>
  <!--- Define formatting for our "feature" display --->
  <STYLE TYPE="text/css">
    TH.fm {background:RoyalBlue;color:white;text-align:left;
           font-family:sans-serif;font-size:10px}
    TD.fm {background:LightSteelBlue;
           font-family:sans-serif;font-size:12px}
  </STYLE>

  <!--- Show info about featured movie in HTML Table --->
  <TABLE WIDTH="150" ALIGN="right" BORDER="0" CELLSPACING="0">
    <TR><TH CLASS="fm">
      Featured Film
    </TH></TR>
    <!--- Movie Title, Summary, Rating --->
    <TR><TD CLASS="fm">
      <B>#GetFilm.MovieTitle#</B><BR>
      #GetFilm.Summary#<BR>
      <P ALIGN="right">Rated: #GetFilm.Rating#</P>
    </TD></TR>
    <!--- Cost (rounded to millions), release date --->
    <TR><TH CLASS="fm">
      Production Cost $#Round(GetFilm.AmountBudgeted / 1000000)# Million<BR>
      In Theaters #DateFormat(GetFilm.DateInTheaters, "mmmm d")#<BR>
    </TH></TR>
  </TABLE>
  <BR CLEAR="all">
</CFOUTPUT>
```

As you can see, the top half of the template is pretty simple. The idea is to use an application variable called `MovieList` to hold a list of available movies. If 20 movies are in the database, the list holds 20 movie IDs at first. The first time the home page is visited, the first movie is featured and then removed from the list, leaving 19 movies in the list. The next time, the second movie is featured (leaving 18), and so on until all the movies have been featured. Then the process begins again.

Looking at the code line by line, you can see how this actually happens:

1. The `<CFPARAM>` tag is used to set the `APPLICATION.MovieList` variable to an empty string if it doesn't exist already. Because the variable will essentially live forever once set, this line has an effect only the first time this template runs (until the server is restarted).

2. The <CFIF> tag is used to test whether the MovieList variable is currently empty. It is empty if this is the first time the template has run or if all the available movies have been featured in rotation already. If the list is empty, it is filled with the list of current movie IDs. Getting the current list is a simple two-step process of querying the database and then using the ValueList function to create the list from the query results.

3. The ListGetAt() function is used to get the first movie's ID from the list. The value is placed in the ThisMovieID variable. This is the movie to feature on the page.

4. Finally, the ListDeleteAt() function is used to chop off the first movie ID from the APPLICATION.MovieList variable. The variable now holds one fewer movie. Eventually, its length will dwindle to zero, in which case step 2 will occur again, repeating the cycle.

TIP

Because you are interested in the first element in the list, you could use ListFirst() in place of the ListGetAt() function shown in Listing 16.11, if that reads more clearly for you. You also could use ListRest() instead of the ListDeleteAt() function.

➜ See Appendix B for details.

Now that the movie to feature has been picked (it's in the ThisMovieID variable), actually displaying the movie's name and other information is straightforward. The <CFQUERY> in the second half of Listing 16.12 selects the necessary information from the database, and then a simple HTML table is used to display the movie in a nicely formatted box.

At this point, Listing 16.12 can be visited on its own, but it really was meant to show the featured movie on Orange Whip's home page. Simply include the template using the <CFINCLUDE> tag, as shown in Listing 16.13.

Figure 16.5 shows the results.

Listing 16.13 Index2.cfm—Including the Featured Movie in the Company's Home Page

```
<!---
  Filename:     Index.cfm
  Created by:   Nate Weiss (NMW)
  Please Note:  Header and Footer are automatically provided
--->

<CFOUTPUT>
  <P>Hello, and welcome to the home of
  #CompanyName# on the web!  We certainly
  hope you enjoy your visit.  We take pride in
  producing movies that are almost as good
  as the ones they are copied from.  We've
  been doing it for years.  On this site, you'll
  be able to find out about all our classic films
  from the golden age of Orange Whip Studios,
  as well as our latest and greatest new releases.
  Have fun!<BR>
</CFOUTPUT>

<!--- Show a "Featured Movie" --->
<CFINCLUDE TEMPLATE="FeaturedMovie.cfm">
```

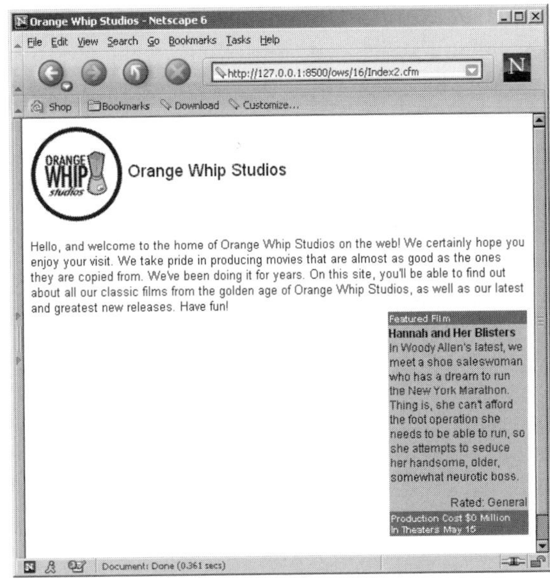

Figure 16.5

Application variables enable the featured movie to be rotated evenly among all page requests.

Using Locks to Protect Against Race Conditions

ColdFusion is a *multithreaded* application, meaning that the server can process more than one page request at a time. Generally speaking, this is a wonderful feature. Because the server can in effect do more than one thing at a time, it can tend to two or three (or 50) simultaneous visitors to your application.

As wonderful as multithreading is, it also means that you need to think carefully about situations where more than one person is accessing a particular page at the same time. Unless you take steps to prevent it, the two page requests can be reading or changing the same application variable at the very same moment. If you are using Application variables to track any type of data that changes over time, and the integrity of the data is "critical" to your application (such as any type of counter, total, statistic, or the like), then you must tell ColdFusion what to do when two page requests are trying to execute the same "shared data changing" code at the same time.

NOTE

This isn't something that only ColdFusion programmers have to deal with. In one fashion or another, you'll run into these issues in any multithreaded programming environment. ColdFusion just makes the issue really easy to deal with.

Of course, ColdFusion provides solutions to help you deal with concurrent page requests quite easily. Either of the following can be used to control what happens when several page requests are trying to read or change information in the application scope:

- You can use the `<CFLOCK>` tag to mark the areas of your code that set, change, access, or display application variables. The `<CFLOCK>` tag ensures that those potentially problematic parts of your code don't execute at the same time as other potentially problematic parts.

As you will learn in this section, your locking instructions will cause one page to wait a moment while the other does its work, thus avoiding any potential problems. In other words, you keep your code tread-safe yourself.

- In the Server Settings page of the ColdFusion Administrator, you can set the Limit Simultaneous Requests To value to `1`. Doing so guarantees that your whole application will be thread-safe because only one page request will be processed at once. Therefore, you can use application variables freely without having to worry about locking them. Unless your application is used only occasionally or by just a few users, you probably don't want to do this because you will be thus giving up the benefits of multithreading. See Chapter 28, "ColdFusion Server Configuration," for details.

NOTE

This discussion assumes you are developing applications for ColdFusion MX. Previous versions of ColdFusion required you to use locks far more frequently, even when there wasn't a race condition issue at hand. Basically, you needed to lock every line of code that used application or session variables. This is no longer the case. Beginning in ColdFusion MX, you need only lock application or session variables if you are concerned about race condition issues, as explained in the next section.

What Is A `Race Condition`?

It's time to pause for just a moment of theory. You need to understand the concept of a *race condition* and how such conditions can occur in your ColdFusion applications. Simply put, a race condition is any situation where two different page requests can change the same information at the very same moment in time. In many situations, race conditions can lead to undesired results. In other situations, you may not care about them at all.

NOTE

Seriously, we really recommend taking a few moments to really visualize and understand this stuff, in particular if you are going to be using application variables to hold values that change over time (especially values that increment numerically as your application does its work).

Here's an example that should make this all really easy to understand. Imagine an application variable called Application.HitCount. The purpose of this variable is to track the number of individual page views that an application has responded to since the ColdFusion server was started. Simple code like the following is used to advance the counter by one every time a user visits a page:

```
<CFSET APPLICATION.HitCount = APPLICATION.HitCount + 1>
```

So far, so good. The code seems to do what it's supposed to. Every time a page is viewed, the variable's value is increased by one. You can output it at any time to display the current number of hits. No problem.

But what happens if two people visit a page at the same time? We know that ColdFusion doesn't process the pages one after another; it processes them at the very same time. Keeping that in mind, consider what ColdFusion has to do to execute the `<CFSET>` tag shown above. Three basic mini-steps are required to complete it. First, ColdFusion gets the current value of `APPLICATION.HitCount`. Next, it adds one to the value. The third mini-step is to set `the APPLICATION.HitCount` to the new, incremented value.

The big problem is that another page request may have changed the value of the variable betwen steps one and two, or between steps two and three. Just for fun, let's say the hit count variable is currently holding a value of 100. Now two users, Bob and Jane, both type in your application's URL at the same time. For whatever reason, Jane's request gets to the server just a split moment after Bob's. Bob's request performs the first mini-step (getting the value of 100). Now, while Bob's request is performing the second mini-step (the addition), Jane's request is doing its first step: finding out what ColdFusion has for the current value of the application variable (uh oh, still 100). While Bob's request performs the *third* mini-step (updating the counter to 101), Jane's request is still doing its *second* step (adding one to 100). Jane's request now finishes its third step, which sets the application variable to, you guessed it, 101. That is, when both requests are finished, the hit count has only increased by one, even though two requests have come through since hit number 100. A bit of information has been lost.

Granted, for a simple hit counter like this, a teensy bit of information loss is probably not all that important. You probably don't care that the hit count is off by one or two every once in a while. But what if the application variable in question was something more like `APPLICATION.TotalSalesToDate`? If a similar kind of "mistake" occurred in something like a sales total, you might have a real problem on your hands.

NOTE

Again, it is important to note that this is not a problem specific to ColdFusion. It's a simple, logical problem that would present itself in almost any real-world situation where several different "people" (here, the people are web users) are trying to look at and/or change the same information at the same time.

NOTE

Almost by definition, the chances of a race condition problem actually occurring in an application will increase as the number of people using the application increases. That is, these kinds of problems tend to be "stealth" problems that are difficult to catch until an application is battle-tested.

The solution is to use `<CFLOCK>` tags to make make sure that two requests don't execute the `<CFSET>` tag (or whatever problematic code) at the same exact moment. For example, `<CFLOCK>` tags would cause Jane's request to wait for Bob's request to be finished with that `<CFSET>` before it started working on the `<CFSET>` itself.

NOTE

Does all this "two related things happening at the same moment in different parts of the world" stuff sound like something out of a Kieslowski film? Or remind you of bad song lyrics, perhaps something cut from The Police's "Synchronicity" album? Perhaps. But this kind of freak coincidence really can and will happen sooner or later. So, no, I can't promise that the lovely Irene Jacob, Julie Delpy, or Juliette Binoche will just happen to show up at your doorstep one day, any more than I can promise you tea in the Sahara. But I can assure you that some kind of unexpected results will occur someday if this kind of race condition is allowed to occur, unchecked, in your code. How's that for fatalism?

`<CFLOCK>` Tag Syntax

Now that you know what race conditions are and how they can potentially lead to unpredictable results, it's time to learn how to use locking to avoid them. We'll get into some of the nuances shortly, but the basic idea is to place opening and closing `<CFLOCK>` tags around any part of your code that changes application variables (or session variables, which are discussed in the next chapter) or any other type of information that might be shared or changed by concurrent page requests. Table 16.5 takes a closer look at the tag's syntax.

Table 16.5 <CFLOCK> Tag Syntax

ATTRIBUTE	DESCRIPTION
TYPE	Optional. The type, or strength, of the lock. Allowable values are `Exclusive` and `ReadOnly`. You should use Exclusive to indicate blocks of code that change the values of shared variables. Use ReadOnly to indicate blocks of code that aren't going to be changing any shared values, but that always need to be reading or outputting the most recent version of the information. If you don't provide a `TYPE`, the default of `Exclusive` is assumed.
SCOPE	The type of persistent variables you are using between the `<CFLOCK>` tags. Allowable values are `Application`, `Session`, and `Server`. You would use a `<CFLOCK>` with `SCOPE="Application"` around any code that uses application variables. You would set this value to `Session` around code that uses session variables, which are discussed in the next chapter. The use of server variables is not discussed in this book and is generally discouraged.
NAME	Optional. You can provide a `NAME` attribute instead of `SCOPE` to get finer-grained control over your locks. This is discussed in the "Using Named Locks" section, later in this chapter. You must always provide a `NAME` or a `SCOPE`, but you can't provide both.
TIMEOUT	Required. The length of time, in seconds, that ColdFusion will wait to obtain the lock. If another visitor's request has a similar `<CFLOCK>` on it, ColdFusion will wait for this many seconds for the locked part of the other request to finish before proceeding. Generally, `10` is a sensible value to use here.
THROWONTIMEOUT	Optional. The default is `Yes`, which means an error message will be displayed if ColdFusion cannot obtain the lock within the `TIMEOUT` period you specified. (You can catch this error using `<CFCATCH>` to deal with the situation differently. See Chapter 31, "Error Handling," for details.

Using Exclusive Locks

As Table 16.5 shows, there are two types of locks: Exclusive and Read-Only. Let's start off simple, and talk about `<CFLOCK>` tags of `TYPE="Exclusive"`. If you want, you can solve your race condition problems using only exclusive locks.

Exclusive locks work like this. When your template gets to an opening `<CFLOCK>` tag in your code, it requests the corresponding lock from the server. There is only one available lock for each scope (`Application` or `Session`), which is why it's called "exclusive." Once this exclusive lock has been bestowed upon your template, it stays there until the closing `</CFLOCK>` tag in your code, at which point the lock is released and returned to the server. While your template has the lock (that is, while the code between the `<CFLOCK>` tags is running), all other templates that want an application-level lock must wait in line. ColdFusion pauses the other templates (right at their opening `<CFLOCK>` tags) until your template releases the lock.

The code shown in Listing 16.14 shows how to place exclusive locks in your code. This listing is similar to the previous version of the Featured Movie template (Listing 16.12). The only important difference is the pair of `<CFLOCK>` tags at the top of the code. Note that the `<CFLOCK>` tags surround the entire portion of the template that is capable of changing the current value of the `APPLICATION.MovieList` variable.

Listing 16.14 `FeaturedMovie2.cfm`—Using Exclusive Locks to Safely Update Application Data

```
<!---
  Filename:     FeaturedMovie.cfm
  Created by:   Nate Weiss (NMW)
  Purpose:      Displays a single movie on the page, on a rotating basis
  Please Note:  Application variables must be enabled
--->

<!--- Need to lock when accessing shared data --->
<CFLOCK SCOPE="APPLICATION" TYPE="Exclusive" TIMEOUT="10">

  <!--- List of movies to show (list starts out empty) --->
  <CFPARAM NAME="APPLICATION.MovieList" TYPE="string" DEFAULT="">

  <!--- If this is the first time we're running this,  --->
  <!--- Or we have run out of movies to rotate through --->
  <CFIF ListLen(APPLICATION.MovieList) EQ 0>
    <!--- Get all current FilmIDs from the database --->
    <CFQUERY NAME="GetFilmIDs" DATASOURCE="#DataSource#">
      SELECT FilmID FROM Films
      ORDER BY MovieTitle
    </CFQUERY>

    <!--- Turn FilmIDs into a simple comma-separated list --->
    <CFSET APPLICATION.MovieList = ValueList(GetFilmIDs.FilmID)>
  </CFIF>

  <!--- Pick the first movie in the list to show right now --->
  <CFSET ThisMovieID = ListGetAt(APPLICATION.MovieList, 1)>
  <!--- Re-save the list, as all movies *except* the first --->
  <CFSET APPLICATION.MovieList = ListDeleteAt(APPLICATION.MovieList, 1)>
</CFLOCK>



<!--- Now that we have chosen the film to "Feature", --->
<!--- Get all important info about it from database. --->
<CFQUERY NAME="GetFilm" DATASOURCE="#DataSource#">
  SELECT
    MovieTitle, Summary, Rating,
    AmountBudgeted, DateInTheaters
  FROM Films f, FilmsRatings r
  WHERE FilmID = #ThisMovieID#
  AND f.RatingID = r.RatingID
</CFQUERY>

<!--- Now Display Our Featured Movie --->
<CFOUTPUT>
  <!--- Define formatting for our "feature" display --->
  <STYLE TYPE="text/css">
```

Listing 16.14 (continued)

```
    TH.fm {background:RoyalBlue;color:white;text-align:left;
           font-family:sans-serif;font-size:10px}
    TD.fm {background:LightSteelBlue;
           font-family:sans-serif;font-size:12px}
  </STYLE>

  <!--- Show info about featured movie in HTML Table --->
  <TABLE WIDTH="150" ALIGN="right" BORDER="0" CELLSPACING="0">
    <TR><TH CLASS="fm">
      Featured Film
    </TH></TR>
    <!--- Movie Title, Summary, Rating --->
    <TR><TD CLASS="fm">
      <B>#GetFilm.MovieTitle#</B><BR>
      #GetFilm.Summary#<BR>
      <P ALIGN="right">Rated: #GetFilm.Rating#</P>
    </TD></TR>
    <!--- Cost (rounded to millions), release date --->
    <TR><TH CLASS="fm">
      Production Cost $#Round(GetFilm.AmountBudgeted / 1000000)# Million<BR>
      In Theaters #DateFormat(GetFilm.DateInTheaters, "mmmm d")#<BR>
    </TH></TR>
  </TABLE>
  <BR CLEAR="all">
</CFOUTPUT>
```

The purpose of the `<CFLOCK>` tag in Listing 16.14 is to ensure that only one "instance" of the block is ever allowed to occur at the very same moment in time. For instance, consider what happens if two different users request the page just a moment after one another. If, by chance, the second page request gets to the start of the block before the first one has exited it, the second request will be forced to wait until the first instance of the block has completed its work. This guarantees that funny race condition behavior doesn't take place (like one of the movies getting "skipped" or shown twice).

TIP

If it helps, think of locks as being similar to hall passes back in grade school. If you wanted to go to the bathroom, you needed to get a pass from the teacher. Nobody else would be able to go to the bathroom until you came back and returned the pass. This was to protect the students (and the bathroom) from becoming, um, corrupted, right?

Using Read-Only Locks

Okay, you've seen how Exclusive locks work. They simply make sure that no two blocks of the same `SCOPE` are allowed to execute at once. If two requests need the same lock at the same time, the first one blocks the second one. In some situations, this can be overkill, and can lead to more waiting around than is really necessary.

ColdFusion also provides *Read-Only* locks, which are less extreme. Read-only locks don't block each other. They only get blocked by Exclusive locks. In plain English, a read-only lock means "If the variables in this block are being changed somewhere else, wait until the changes are finished before running this block." Use a read-only lock if you have some code that definitely needs to read the correct, current value of an application variable, but isn't going to change it at all. Then just double-check that all code that *does* change the variable is between Exclusive locks. This way, you are guaranteed to always be reading or displaying the correct, most current value of the variable, but without the unwanted side-effect of forcing other page requests to wait in line.

Do this whenever you are going to be reading the value of a variable a lot, but changing its value only occaisonally.

NOTE

In other words, Read-Only locks don't have any effect on their own. They only have an effect when some other page request has an Exclusive lock.

To demonstrate how much sense this all makes, let's adapt the featured movie example a bit. So far, the featured movie has rotated with every page request. What if you still wanted the movies to rotate evenly and in order, but instead of rotating with every page request, you want the featured movie to change once every five minutes (or 10 minutes, or once an hour)?

Here is an adapted version of the featured movie template that gets this job done (see Listing 16.15). The code is a bit more complicated than the last version. For the moment, don't worry about the code itself. Just note that the portion of the code that makes changes in the `APPLICATION` scope is in an exclusive lock. The portion of the code that grabs the current feature movie from the `APPLICATION` scope (which is also really short and quick) is inside a read-only lock.

Listing 16.15 `FeaturedMovie3.cfm`—Using Exclusive and Read-Only Locks

```
<!---
  Filename:      FeaturedMovie.cfm
  Created by:    Nate Weiss (NMW)
  Purpose:       Displays a single movie on the page, on a rotating basis
  Please Note:   Application variables must be enabled
--->


<!--- We want to obtain an exclusive lock if this --->
<!--- is the first time this template has executed, --->
<!--- or the time for this featured movie has expired --->
<CFIF (NOT IsDefined("APPLICATION.MovieRotation"))
  OR (DateCompare(APPLICATION.MovieRotation.CurrentUntil, Now()) EQ -1)>

  <!--- Make sure all requests wait for this block --->
  <!--- to finish before displaying the featured movie --->
  <CFLOCK SCOPE="APPLICATION" TYPE="Exclusive" TIMEOUT="10">

    <!--- If this is the first time the template has executed... --->
    <CFIF NOT (IsDefined("APPLICATION.MovieRotation"))>

      <!--- Get all current FilmIDs from the database --->
      <CFQUERY NAME="GetFilmIDs" DATASOURCE="#DataSource#">
        SELECT FilmID FROM Films
        ORDER BY MovieTitle
      </CFQUERY>

      <!--- Create structure for rotating featured movies --->
      <CFSET st = StructNew()>
```

Listing 16.15 (continued)

```
        <CFSET st.MovieList = ValueList(GetFilmIDs.FilmID)>
        <CFSET st.CurrentPos = 1>

        <!--- Place structure into APPLICATION scope --->
        <CFSET APPLICATION.MovieRotation = st>

      <!--- ...otherwise, the time for the featured movie has expired --->
      <CFELSE>
        <!--- Shorthand name for structure in application scope --->
        <CFSET st = APPLICATION.MovieRotation>

        <!--- If we haven't gotten to the last movie yet --->
        <CFIF st.CurrentPos LT ListLen(st.MovieList)>
          <CFSET st.CurrentPos = st.CurrentPos + 1>
        <!--- if already at last movie, start over at beginning --->
        <CFELSE>
          <CFSET st.CurrentPos = 1>
        </CFIF>

      </CFIF>

      <!--- In any case, choose the movie at the current position in list --->
      <CFSET st.CurrentMovie = ListGetAt(st.MovieList, st.CurrentPos)>
      <!--- This featured movie should "expire" a short time from now --->
      <CFSET st.CurrentUntil = DateAdd("s", 5, Now())>
    </CFLOCK>
  </CFIF>


  <!--- Use a read-only lock to grab current movie from application scope... --->
  <!--- If the exclusive block above is current executing in another thread, --->
  <!--- then ColdFusion will 'wait' before executing the code in this block. --->
  <CFLOCK SCOPE="APPLICATION" TYPE="ReadOnly" TIMEOUT="10">
    <CFSET ThisMovieID = APPLICATION.MovieRotation.CurrentMovie>
  </CFLOCK>



  <!--- Now that we have chosen the film to "Feature", --->
  <!--- Get all important info about it from database. --->
  <CFQUERY NAME="GetFilm" DATASOURCE="#DataSource#">
    SELECT
      MovieTitle, Summary, Rating,
      AmountBudgeted, DateInTheaters
    FROM Films f, FilmsRatings r
    WHERE FilmID = #ThisMovieID#
    AND f.RatingID = r.RatingID
  </CFQUERY>

  <!--- Now Display Our Featured Movie --->
  <CFOUTPUT>
    <!--- Define formatting for our "feature" display --->
    <STYLE TYPE="text/css">
      TH.fm {background:RoyalBlue;color:white;text-align:left;
             font-family:sans-serif;font-size:10px}
```

Listing 16.15 (continued)

```
    TD.fm {background:LightSteelBlue;
           font-family:sans-serif;font-size:12px}
  </STYLE>

  <!--- Show info about featured movie in HTML Table --->
  <TABLE WIDTH="150" ALIGN="right" BORDER="0" CELLSPACING="0">
    <TR><TH CLASS="fm">
      Featured Film
    </TH></TR>
    <!--- Movie Title, Summary, Rating --->
    <TR><TD CLASS="fm">
      <B>#GetFilm.MovieTitle#</B><BR>
      #GetFilm.Summary#<BR>
      <P ALIGN="right">Rated: #GetFilm.Rating#</P>
    </TD></TR>
    <!--- Cost (rounded to millions), release date --->
    <TR><TH CLASS="fm">
      Production Cost $#Round(Val(GetFilm.AmountBudgeted) / 1000000)# Million<BR>
      In Theaters #DateFormat(GetFilm.DateInTheaters, "mmmm d")#<BR>
    </TH></TR>
  </TABLE>
  <BR CLEAR="all">
</CFOUTPUT>
```

The first thing this template does is check whether changes need to be made in the `APPLICATION` scope. Changes will be made if the template hasn't been run before, or if it's time to rotate the featured movie (remember, it's rotating based on time now). If changes are called for, an `Exclusive` lock is opened. Within the lock, if the template hasn't been run before, a list of movies is retrieved from the database and stored as a value called `MovieList`, just as before. In addition, a value called `CurrentPos` is set to `1` (to indicate the first movie). This value will increase as the movies are cycled through. Execution then proceeds to the bottom of the `<CFLOCK>` block, where the current movie id is plucked from the list, and a value called `CurrentUntil` is set to a moment in time a few seconds in the future.

On the other hand, if the lock was opened because the `CurrentUntil` value has passed (we're still inside the Exclusive lock block), then it's time to pick the next movie from the list. As long as the end of the list hasn't already been reached, the only thing required is to advance `CurrentPos` by one. If the last movie *has* already been reached, the `CurrentPos` is reset to the beginning of the list.

NOTE

At any rate, the entire Exclusive lock block at the top of the template executes only once in a while, when the movie needs to change. If you are rotating movies every 10 minutes and have a fair amount of visitors, the lock is needed only in the vast minority of page requests.

Underneath, a second `<CFLOCK>` block of `TYPE="ReadOnly"` uses a `<CFSET>` to read the current featured movie from the `APPLICATION` scope into a local variable. The Read-Only lock ensures that if the featured movie is currently being changed in some other page request, the `<CFSET>` will wait until the change is complete. Since the change occurs only once in a while, the page is usually able to execute without having to wait at all.

TIP

Think of read-only locks as a way of optimizing the performance of code that needs some kind of locking to remain correct. For instance, this template could have been written using only exclusive locks, and doing so would have made sure that the results were always correct (no race conditions). The introduction of the read-only lock is a way of making sure that the locks have as little impact on performance as possible.

NOTE

You'll encounter the notion of explicitly locking potentially concurrent actions in database products as well. Conceptually, database products use the SQL keywords `BEGIN TRANSACTION` and `COMMIT TRANSACTION` in a way that's analagous to ColdFusion's interpretation of beginning and ending `<CFLOCK>` tags.

➜ See Chapter 29, "More About SQL and Queries" for details about database transactions.

Using Named Locks instead of SCOPE

You've seen why locks are sometimes needed to avoid race conditions. You've seen the simplest way to implement them–with Exclusive locks. You've seen how to avoid potential bottlenecks by using a mix of Exclusive and Read-Only locks. Hopefully, you've noticed a pattern emerging: when you're worried about race conditions, your goal should be to protect your data with `<CFLOCK>`, but to do so in the least obtrusive way possible. That is, you want your code to be "smart" about when page requests wait for each other.

So far, all of the `<CFLOCK>` tags in this chapter have been *scoped locks*. Each of them have used a a `SCOPE="Application"` attribute to say "this lock should block or be blocked by all other locks in the application." As you have seen, scoped locks are really simple to implement once you "get" the conceptual issue at hand. The problem with scoped locks is that they often end up locking too much.

There's no problem when you are using only application variables to represent a single concept. For instance, the various versions of the "featured movie" template track a few different variables, but they are all related to the same concept of a featured movie that rotates over time.

Consider what happens, though, if you need to add a rotating "featured actor" widget to your application. Such a widget would be similar to the featured movie but it would rotate at a different rate or according to some other logic. Just for the heck of it, pretend there's also a "featured director" widget, plus a couple of hit counters that also maintain data at the application level, and so on. Assume for the moment that these various widgets appear on different pages, rather than all on the same page.

Using the techniques you've learned so far, whenever one of these mini-applications needs to change the data it keeps in the `APPLICATION` scope, it will use a `<CFLOCK>` with `SCOPE="Application"` to protect itself against race conditions. The problem is that the `SCOPE="Application"` lock is not only going to block or be blocked by instances of that same widget in other page requests. It's going to block or be blocked by all locks in the entire application. If all of your widgets are only touching their own application variables, this approach is overkill. If the featured actor widget doesn't touch the same variables that the featured movie widget uses, then there's no possibility of a race condition. Therefore, allowing reads and writes by the two widgets to block one another is a waste of time, but `SCOPE="Application"` doesn't know that.

ColdFusion allows you to gain further control for this kind of problem by supporting named locks. To add named locks to your code, you use a NAME attribute in your <CFLOCK> tags, instead of a SCOPE attribute. Named lock blocks will block or wait for only other lock blocks that have the same NAME.

For instance, instead of using a scoped lock, like this:

```
<CFLOCK
  SCOPE="Application"
  TYPE="Exclusive"
  TIMEOUT="10">
```

you could use a named lock, like this:

```
<CFLOCK
  NAME="OrangeWhipMovieRotation"
  TYPE="Exclusive"
  TIMEOUT="10">
```

This way, you can feel comfortable manipulating the variables used by the featured movie widget, knowing that the exclusive lock you've asked for will affect only those pieces of code that are also dealing with the same variables. Page requests that need to display the featured movie or featured director widgets won't be blocked needlessly.

The name of the lock is considered globally for the entire server, not just for your application, so you need to make sure that the name of the lock isn't used in other applications. The easiest way to do this is to always incorporate the application's name (or something similar) as a part of the lock name. That's why the <CFLOCK> tag shown above includes OrangeWhip at the start of the NAME attribute. Another way to get the same effect would be to use the automatic APPLICATION.ApplicationName variable as a part of the NAME, like so:

```
<CFLOCK
  Name="#APPLICATION.ApplicationName#MovieRotation"
  TYPE="Exclusive"
  TIMEOUT="10">
```

The CD-ROM for this book includes a FeauturedMovie4.cfm template, which is almost the same as FeaturedMovie3.cfm, shown in Listing 16.15. The only difference is that it uses NAME="OrangeWhip-MovieRotation" (as shown above) instead of SCOPE="Application" in each of the <CFLOCK> tags.

NOTE

So, it turns out that the SCOPE="Application" attribute is really just a shortcut. Its effect is equivalent to writing a named lock that uses the name of your application (or some other identifier that is unique to your application) as the NAME.

Nested Locks and Deadlocks

It's usually okay to nest named locks within one another, as long as the NAME for each lock block is different. However, if they aren't nested in the same order in all parts of your code, it is possible that your application could encounter *deadlocks* while it runs. Deadlocks are situations where it's impossible for two page requests to move forward because they are each requesting a lock that the other already has. Consider a template with an Exclusive lock named LockA, with another <CFLOCK> named LockB nested within it. Now consider another template, which nests LockA within LockB. If both templates execute at the same time, the first page request might be granted an exclusive lock for LockA, and the second could get an exclusive lock for LockB. Now neither template can move forward: this is deadlock. Both locks will time out and throw errors.

Entire books have been written about various ways to solve this kind of puzzle; there's no way we can tell you how to handle every possible situation. Our advice is this: if you need to nest named locks, go ahead as long as they will be nested in the same combination and order in all of your templates. If the combination or order needs to be different in different places, use scoped locks instead. The overhead and aggravation you might encounter in trying to manage and debug potential deadlocks is probably not worth the added cost introduced by the SCOPE shorthand.

Don't confuse this discussion (nesting locks with different names) with nesting locks that have the same NAME or SCOPE. In general, you should never nest <CFLOCK> tags that have the same SCOPE or NAME. A read-only lock that is nested within an exclusive lock with the same SCOPE or NAME has no additional benefit (it's always safe to read if already have an exclusive lock). And if the exclusive lock is nested within a read-only lock, then the exclusive lock can never be obtained (because it needs to wait for all read-only locks to end first), and thus will always time out and throw an error.

Locking with ColdFusion 5 and Earlier

The advice about when and how to use locks given in this chapter applies only to ColdFusion MX and later. Previous versions of ColdFusion approached locking differently within the guts of the server. The result was that *every* read or write of any shared variable needed to be locked, regardless of whether there was a possibility of a logical race condition. Without the locks, ColdFusion's internal memory space would eventually become corrupted, and the server would crash or begin to exhibit strange and unstable behavior. In other words, locks were needed not only to protect the logical integrity of shared data, but also to protect the ColdFusion server from itself. Thankfully, this shortcoming has gone away as of ColdFusion MX, because shared variables end up being synchronized internally by the new Java-based runtime engine.

This means that if you are writing an application that you want to be backward-compatible with ColdFusion 5 and earlier, you must lock every single reference to any Application, Session, or Server variable, even if you are just outputting its value. Even IsDefined() tests and <CFPARAM> tags must be locked under ColdFusion 5 and earlier.

Application Variable Timeouts

By default, application variables are kept on the server almost indefinitely. They die only if two whole days pass without any visits to any of the application's pages. After two days of inactivity, ColdFusion considers the APPLICATION scope to have expired, and all associated application variables are flushed from its memory.

If one of your applications uses a large number of application variables but is used very rarely, you could consider decreasing the amount of time that the APPLICATION scope takes to expire. Doing so would enable ColdFusion to reuse the memory taken up by the application variables. In practice, there might be few situations in which this flexibility is useful, but you should still know what your options are if you want to think about ways to tweak the way your applications behave.

Two ways are available to adjust the application timeout period from its two-day default value. You can use the ColdFusion Administrator or the `APPLICATIONTIMEOUT` attribute of the `<CFAPPLICATION>` tag.

Adjusting Timeouts Using APPLICATIONTIMEOUT

As shown in Table 16.4, the `<CFAPPLICATION>` tag takes an optional `APPLICATIONTIMEOUT` attribute. You can use this to explicitly specify how long an unused `APPLICATION` scope will remain in memory before it expires.

The `APPLICATIONTIMEOUT` attribute expects a ColdFusion *time span* value, which is a special type of numeric information used to describe a period of time in terms of days, hours, minutes, and seconds. All this means is that you must specify the application timeout using the `CreateTimeSpan()` function, which takes four numeric arguments to represent the desired number of days, hours, minutes, and seconds, respectively (for more information about the `CreateTimeSpan()` function, see Appendix C).

For instance, to specify that an application should time out after two hours of inactivity, you would use code such as this:

```
<CFAPPLICATION
  NAME="OrangeWhipSite"
  APPLICATIONTIMEOUT="#CreateTimeSpan(0,2,0,0)#">
```

NOTE

If you do not specify an `APPLICATIONTIMEOUT` attribute, the Default Timeout value in the Variables page of the ColdFusion Administrator is used. See the next section, "Adjusting Timeouts Using the ColdFusion Administrator," for details.

NOTE

If you specify an `APPLICATIONTIMEOUT` that exceeds the Maximum Timeout value in the Variables page of the ColdFusion Administrator, the Maximum Timeout in the Administrator is used instead. See the next section, "Adjusting Timeouts Using the ColdFusion Administrator," for details.

Adjusting Timeouts Using the ColdFusion Administrator

To adjust the amount of time that each application's `APPLICATION` scope should live before it expires, follow these steps:

1. Navigate to the Variables page of the ColdFusion Administrator.
2. Under Default Timeout, fill in the days, hours, minutes, and seconds fields for application variables, as shown in Figure 16.6.
3. If you want, you also can adjust the Maximum Timeout for application variables here. If any developers attempt to use a longer timeout with the `APPLICATIONTIMEOUT` attribute of the `<CFAPPLICATION>` tag, this value will be used instead (no error message is displayed).
4. Click Apply.

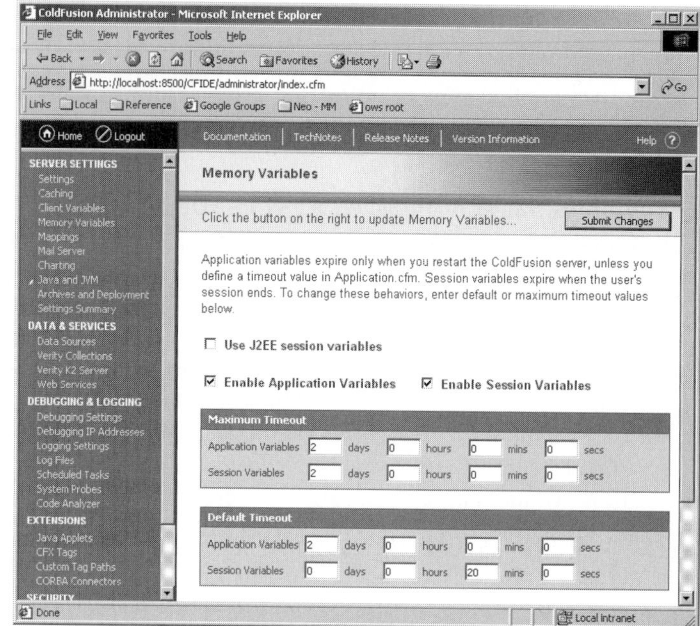

Figure 16.6

You can adjust when an application expires using the Variables page of the ColdFusion Administrator.

CHAPTER 17 Working with Sessions

IN THIS CHAPTER

In the last chapter, "Introducing the Web Application Framework," you learned about *application variables*, which live in your ColdFusion server's memory between page requests. You also learned that application variables are shared between all pages in your application. There are plenty of uses for application variables, but because they are not maintained separately for each user, they don't go far in helping you create a personalized site experience.

This chapter continues the discussion of the Web application framework, focusing on the features that let you track variables on a per-user basis. This opens up all kinds of opportunities for keeping track of what each user needs, wants, has seen, or is interacting with. And in true ColdFusion style, it's all very easy to learn and use.

Addressing the Web's Statelessness

The basic building blocks of the Web—that is, TCP/IP, HTTP, and HTML—don't directly address any notion of a "session" on the Web. Users don't log in to the Web. Nor do they ever log out. So, without some additional work, each page visit stands alone, in its own context. Content is requested by the browser, the server responds, and that's the end of it. No connection is maintained, and the server is not notified when the user leaves the site altogether.

Out of the box, HTTP and HTML don't even provide a way to know who the user is or where he is. As a user moves from page to page in your site—perhaps interacting with things along the way—there's no way to track his progress or choices along the way. As far as each page request is concerned, there's only the current moment, with no future and no past. The Web is thus said to be stateless because it doesn't provide any built-in infrastructure to track the *state* (or status or condition) of what a user is doing.

What does the Web's statelessness mean to you as a Web developer? It means that without some type of server-side mechanism to simulate the notion of a session, you would have no way to remember that a user has put something into a shopping cart, say, or to remember the fact that the user has logged in to your site. So, essentially, the problem is that the Web itself provides no short-term memory for remembering the contents of shopping carts and other types of choices users make during a visit. You need something to provide that short-term memory for you. That's exactly what you learn about in this chapter.

The Problem of Maintaining State

The fact that HTTP and HTML are stateless is certainly no accident. A main reason the Web is so wildly popular is the fact that it is so simple. The Web probably wouldn't have gotten to be so big so fast if a whole infrastructure had needed to be in place for logging in and out of each Web server, or if it assumed that one needed to maintain a constant connection to a server to keep one's current session open.

The simplicity of the sessionless approach also enables the tremendous scalability from which Web applications—and the Web as a whole—benefit. It's what makes Web applications so thin and lightweight and what allows Web servers to serve so many people simultaneously. So, the Web's statelessness is by design, and most people should be glad that it is.

Except for us Web developers. Our lives would probably be a lot easier if some kind of universal user ID existed, issued by, um, the United Nations or something. That couldn't be faked. And that could identify who the user was, no matter what computer he was sitting at. Until that happens, we need another way to track a user's movements as he moves through our own little pieces of the Web.

Solutions Provided by ColdFusion

Expanding on the Web application framework—which already sets aside part of the server's brain to deal with each application—ColdFusion provides three types of variables that help you maintain the state of a user's visit from page to page and between visits.

Similar to application variables (which you learned about in the last chapter), all three of these are persistent variables because they stay alive between page requests. However, they are different from application variables because they are maintained separately for each browser that visits your site. It's almost as if ColdFusion had a tiny little part of its memory set aside for each visitor.

Cookies

Cookies are a simple mechanism for asking a browser to remember something, such as a user's favorite color or perhaps some type of ID number. The information is stored in the client machine's memory (or on one of its drives). You can store only a small amount of information using cookies, and users generally have a way to turn off cookies in their browsers' settings. Unfortunately, cookies have gotten a lot of bad press in the past few years, so many users do choose to turn them off at the browser level.

Client Variables

Client variables are similar to cookies, except that the information is stored on the server, rather than on the client machine. The values are physically stored in the server's Windows Registry or in a database. Client variables are designed to hold semipermanent data, such as preferences that should live for weeks or months between a user's visits.

Session Variables

Similar to client variables, *session variables* are stored on the server. However, instead of being stored physically, they are simply maintained in the server's RAM. Session variables are designed to hold temporary data, such as items in a shopping cart or steps in some type of wizard-style data-entry mechanism that takes the user several pages to complete.

Choosing Which Type of Variables to Use

With three types of per-visitor variables from which to choose, developers sometimes have a hard time figuring out the best type to use for a particular task. We certainly recommend that you look through this whole chapter before you start using any of them in your own application. However, in the future, you might want to refresh your memory about which type to use. Table 17.1 lists the major pros and cons of cookies, client variables, and session variables. In addition, Figure 17.1 is a simple decision tree to help guide you through the process of choosing the type of variable to use.

Table 17.1 Pros and Cons of Cookies, Client Variables, and Session Variables

VARIABLE TYPE	PROS	CONS
`COOKIE`	Not ColdFusion specific, so are familiar to most developers. Simple values only (no arrays, structures or queries)	Can persist for same visit only, or until a specific date/time. Limited storage capacity. User can turn them off. Have a bad reputation.
`CLIENT`	Much larger storage capacity. Values never leave the server. Persist between server restarts. Cookies not needed to retain values during single visit. Stored in server's registry or in any SQL database.	Can persist for months. Cookies required to remember values between visits. Simple values only (no arrays, structures, and so on), but see `<CFWDDX>` note in this chapter.
`SESSION`	High performance; stored in ColdFusion server's RAM only. Complex values allowed (arrays, structures, and so on). Can be used without cookies.	Values do not persist between server restarts.

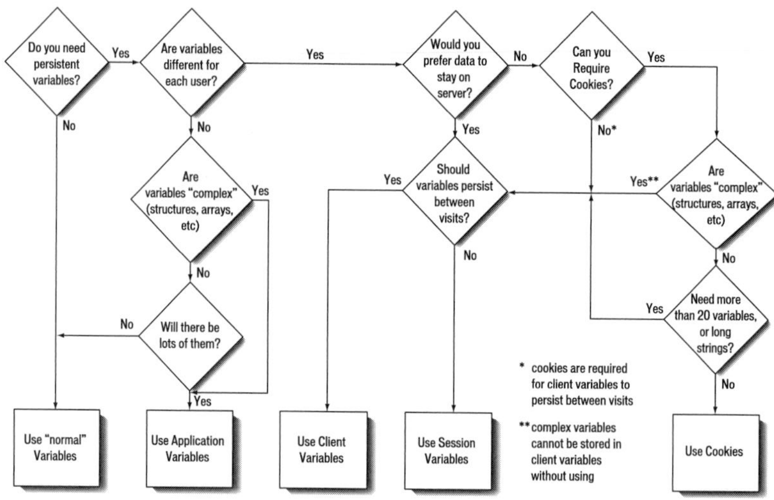

Figure 17.1

Choosing whether to use cookies, client variables, or session variables.

Using Cookies to Remember Preferences

Cookies are simple variables that can be stored on a client machine. Basically, the server asks the browser to remember a variable with such-and-such a name and such-and-such a value. The browser returns the variable to the server as it requests successive pages from that same server. In other words, after the server sets the value on the browser, the browser continues to remind the server about it as the user moves from page to page. The net effect is that each site essentially has a small portion of the browser's memory in which to store little bits of information.

NOTE

Cookies first appeared in early versions of Netscape Navigator and have since been adopted by nearly all browser software. As of this writing, the original specification document for cookies is still available at `www.netscape.com/newsref/std/cookie_spec.html`. It is somewhat of an interesting read, if only because it underscores how important Netscape's early innovations have become to today's Web. No substantive changes have been made to the cookies since.

Introducing the `COOKIE` Scope

Cookies are not something specific to ColdFusion. Any server-side scripting programming environment can set them (they can even be set by client-side languages such as JavaScript). Of course, depending on the language, the actual code necessary to set or retrieve a cookie varies a bit. The best implementations keep coders from having to understand the details of the actual communication between the browser and server. It's best if the coder can just concentrate on the task at hand.

In ColdFusion, the notion of cookies is exposed to you via the simple, elegant `COOKIE` scope. Similar to the `APPLICATION` scope you learned about in the previous chapter, the `COOKIE` scope is automatically maintained by ColdFusion. Setting a variable within the `COOKIE` scope instructs the browser to remember the cookie. Referring to a variable within the `COOKIE` scope returns the value of the cookie on the browser's machine.

For instance, the following line asks the user's browser to remember a cookie variable called `MyMessage`. The value of the cookie is `"Hello, World!"`:

```
<CFSET COOKIE.MyMessage = "Hello, World!">
```

From that point on, you could output the value of `#COOKIE.MyMessage#` in your CFML code, between `<CFOUTPUT>` tags. The `"Hello, World"` message would be output in place of the variable.

Simple Exercise

Here is a simple exercise that will help illustrate what's going on when you use cookies. First, temporarily change your browser's preferences so that you will receive notice whenever a cookie is being set.

To be notified when a cookie is set on your browser, follow these guidelines:

- If you are using a Netscape 4 browser, select Preferences from the Edit menu; then check the Warn Me Before Accepting a Cookie box on the Advanced page of the Preferences dialog box. With Netscape 6, this check box is called Warn Me Before Storing a Cookie, on the Cookies page (under Privacy and Security) in the Preferences dialog box.
- If you are using Internet Explorer (version 5 or later), select Internet Options from the Tools menu, and then select the Security tab. Make sure the appropriate zone is selected; then select Custom Level and check the Prompt options for both Allow Cookies That Are Stored on Your Computer and Allow Per-Session Cookies.
- If you are using some other browser or version, the steps you take might be slightly different, but you should have some way to turn on some type of notification when cookies are set.

Now, use your browser to visit the `CookieSet.cfm` template shown in Listing 17.1. You should see a prompt similar to the one shown in Figure 17.2. The prompt might look different depending on browser and version, but it generally will show you the name and value of the cookie being set. Note that you can even refuse to allow the cookie to be set. Go ahead and let the browser store the cookie by clicking OK.

If you now visit the `CookieShow.cfm` template shown in Listing 17.2, you will see the message `you started your visit at`, followed by the exact time you visited the code in Listing 17.1. Click your browser's Reload button a few times, so you can see that the value does not change. The value persists between page requests. If you go back to Listing 17.1, the cookie will be reset to a new value.

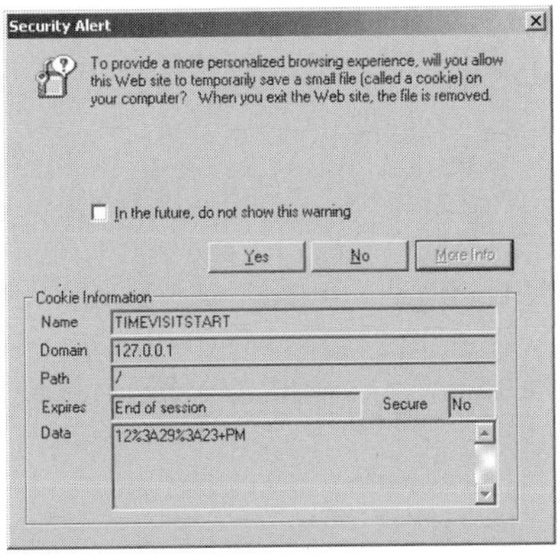

Figure 17.2

Click OK to let the browser store the cookie.

Close your browser, reopen it, and visit the `CookieShow.cfm` template again. You will see an error message from ColdFusion, telling you that the `COOKIE.TimeVisitStart` variable does not exist. By default, cookies expire when the browser is closed. Therefore, the variable is no longer passed to the server with each page request and is unknown to ColdFusion.

Listing 17.1 `CookieSet.cfm`—Setting a Cookie

```
<!---
  Filename:     CookieSet.cfm
  Created by:   Nate Weiss (NMW)
  Purpose:      Sets a cookie to remember time of this page request
--->

<HTML>
<HEAD><TITLE>Cookie Demonstration</TITLE></HEAD>
<BODY>

<!--- Set a cookie to remember the time right now --->
<CFSET COOKIE.TimeVisitStart = TimeFormat(Now(), "h:mm:ss tt")>

The cookie has been set.

</BODY>
</HTML>
```

Listing 17.2 `CookieShow.cfm`—Displaying a Cookie's Value

```
<!---
  Filename:     CookieShow.cfm
  Created by:   Nate Weiss (NMW)
  Please Note:  Displays the value of the TimeVisitStart cookie,
                which gets set by CookieSet.cfm
--->

<HTML>
<HEAD><TITLE>Cookie Demonstration</TITLE></HEAD>
<BODY>

<CFOUTPUT>
  You started your visit at:
  #COOKIE.TimeVisitStart#<BR>
</CFOUTPUT>

</BODY>
</HTML>
```

Using Cookies

You easily can build on the last example to make it a more useful real-world example. For instance, you wouldn't want the Time Started value to be reset every time the user visited the first page; rather, you probably want the value to be recorded only the first time. So, it would probably make sense to first test for the cookie's existence and only set the cookie if it doesn't already exist. Also, it would probably be sensible to remember the full date/time value of the user's first visit, rather than just the time.

So, instead of

```
<CFSET COOKIE.TimeVisitStart = TimeFormat(Now(), "h:mm:ss tt")>
```

you could use

```
<CFIF IsDefined("COOKIE.VisitStart") EQ "No">
  <CFSET COOKIE.VisitStart = Now()>
</CFIF>
```

In fact, the `IsDefined` test and the `<CFSET>` tag can be replaced with a single `<CFPARAM>` tag:

```
<CFPARAM NAME="COOKIE.VisitStart" TYPE="date" DEFAULT="#Now()#">
```

This `<CFPARAM>` tag can be placed in your `Application.cfm` file so it is encountered before each page request is processed. You can now be assured that ColdFusion will set the cookie the first time the user hits your application, no matter what page she starts on, and that you will never get a `parameter doesn't exist` error message, because the cookie is guaranteed to always be defined. As discussed previously, the cookie will be reset if the user closes and reopens her browser.

→ If you need a quick reminder on the difference between `<CFSET>` and `<CFPARAM>`, see Chapter 8, "Using ColdFusion," and Chapter 9, "CFML Basics."

You could then output the time elapsed in your application by outputting the difference between the cookie's value and the current time. You could put this code wherever you wanted in your application, perhaps as part of some type of header or footer message. For instance, the following code would display the number of minutes that the user has been using the application:

```
<CFOUTPUT>
  Minutes Elapsed: #DateDiff("n", COOKIE.VisitStart, Now())#
</CFOUTPUT>
```

The next two listings bring these lines together. Listing 17.3 is an `Application.cfm` file that includes the `<CFPARAM>` tag shown previously. Listing 17.4 is a file called `ShowTimeElapsed.cfm`, which can be used to display the elapsed time in any of the current application's pages by using `<CFINCLUDE>`. You also can visit Listing 17.4 on its own—Figure 17.3 shows what the results would look like.

Be sure to save Listing 17.3 as `Application.cfm`, not `Application1.cfm`.

Listing 17.3 `Application1.cfm`—Defining a Cookie Variable in `Application.cfm`

```
<!---
  Filename:     Application.cfm
  Created by:   Nate Weiss (NMW)
  Please Note:  Executes for each page request
--->

<!--- If no "VisitStart" cookie exists, create it --->
<!--- Its value will be the current date and time --->
<CFPARAM NAME="COOKIE.VisitStart" TYPE="date" DEFAULT="#Now()#">
```

Listing 17.4 `ShowTimeElapsed.cfm`—Performing Calculations Based on Cookies

```
<!---
  Filename:     ShowTimeElapsed.cfm
  Created by:   Nate Weiss (NMW)
  Please Note:  Can be <CFINCLUDED> in any page in your application
--->

<!--- Find number of seconds passed since visit started  --->
<!--- (difference between cookie value and current time) --->
<CFSET SecsSinceStart = DateDiff("s", COOKIE.VisitStart, Now())>
```

Listing 17.4 (continued)

```
<!--- Break it down into numbers of minutes and seconds --->
<CFSET MinutesElapsed = Int(SecsSinceStart / 60)>
<CFSET SecondsElapsed = SecsSinceStart MOD 60>

<!--- Display the minutes/seconds elapsed --->
<CFOUTPUT>
  Minutes Elapsed:
  #MinutesElapsed#:#NumberFormat(SecondsElapsed, "00")#
</CFOUTPUT>
```

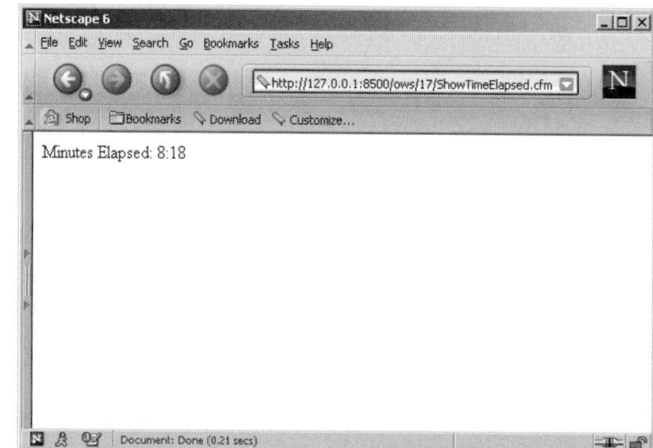

Figure 17.3
Cookies can be used to track users, preferences, or—in this case—elapsed times.

Because `COOKIE.VisitStart` always is a ColdFusion date/time value, getting the raw number of seconds since the visit started is easy—you use the `DateDiff` function. If the difference in seconds between the cookie value and the present moment (the value returned by the `Now` function) is 206, you know that 206 seconds have passed since the cookie was set.

Because most people would be more comfortable seeing time expressed in minutes and seconds, Listing 17.4 does some simple math on the raw number of seconds elapsed. First, it calculates the number of whole minutes that have elapsed, by dividing `SecsSinceStart` by 60 and rounding down to the nearest integer. Next, it calculates the number of seconds to display after the number of minutes by finding the modulus (which is the remainder left when `SecsSinceStart` is divided by 60).

➜ See Appendix C, "ColdFusion Function Reference," for explanations of the `DateDiff`, `Int`, and `Now` functions.

Gaining More Control with <CFCOOKIE>

You already have learned how to set cookies using the `<CFSET>` tag and the special `COOKIE` scope (Listings 17.1–17.3). Using that technique, setting cookies is as simple as setting normal variables. However, sometimes you will want to have more control over how cookies get set.

Introducing the <CFCOOKIE> Tag

To provide you with additional control, ColdFusion provides the `<CFCOOKIE>` tag, which is an alternative syntax for setting cookie variables. Once set, you can access or display the cookies as you have learned so far, by referring to them in the special `COOKIE` scope.

Table 17.2 introduces the attributes available when using `<CFCOOKIE>`.

Table 17.2 `<CFCOOKIE>` Tag Syntax

ATTRIBUTE	PURPOSE
`NAME`	Required. The name of the cookie variable. If you use `NAME="VisitStart"`, the cookie will thereafter become known as `COOKIE.VisitStart`.
`VALUE`	Required. The value of the cookie. To set the cookie's value to the current date and time, use `VALUE="#Now()#"`.
`EXPIRES`	Optional. When the cookie should expire. You can provide any of the following: A specific expiration date (such as 3/18/2002) or a date/time value. The number of days you want the cookie to exist before expiring, such as 10 or 90. The word `NEVER`, which is a shortcut for setting the expiration date far into the future, such that it effectively will never expire. The word `NOW`, which is a shortcut for setting the expiration date in the recent past, such that it is already considered expired. This is how you delete a cookie. If you do not specify an `EXPIRES` attribute, the cookie will do what it does normally, which is to expire when the user closes her browser. See "Controlling Cookie Expiration" in the next section.
`DOMAIN`	Optional. You can use this attribute to share the cookie with other servers within your own Internet domain. By default, the cookie is visible only to the server that set it. See the section "Controlling How Cookies Are Shared," later in this chapter.
`PATH`	Optional. You can use this attribute to specify which pages on your server should be able to use this cookie. By default, the cookie can be accessed by all pages on the server once set. See the section "Controlling How Cookies Are Shared," later in this chapter.
`SECURE`	Optional. You can use this attribute to specify whether the cookie should be sent back to the server if a secure connection is being used. The default is No. See the section "Controlling How Cookies Are Shared," later in this chapter.

Controlling Cookie Expiration

The most common reason for using `<CFCOOKIE>` instead of a simple `<CFSET>` is to control how long the cookie will exist before it expires. For instance, looking back at the `Application.cfm` file shown in Listing 17.3, what if you didn't want the Elapsed Time counter to start over each time the user closed her browser?

Say you wanted the elapsed time to keep counting for up to a week. You would replace the <CFPARAM> line in Listing 17.3 with the following:

```
<!--- If no "VisitStart" cookie exists, create it --->
<CFIF IsDefined("COOKIE.VisitStart") EQ "No">
  <CFCOOKIE
    NAME="VisitStart"
    VALUE="#Now()#"
    EXPIRES="7">
</CFIF>
```

Controlling How Cookies Are Shared

Netscape's original cookie specification defines three additional concepts that have not yet been discussed. All three of them have to do with giving you more granular control over which pages your cookies are visible to:

- **A domain can be specified as each cookie is set.** The basic idea is that a cookie should always be visible only to the server that set the cookie originally. This is to protect users' privacy. However, if a company is running several Web servers, it is considered fair that a cookie set on one server be visible to the others. Specifying a domain for a cookie makes it visible to all servers within that domain.
- **In addition, a path can be specified as each cookie is set.** This enables you to control whether the cookie should be visible to the entire Web server (or Web servers), or just part. For instance, if a cookie will be used only by the pages within the ows folder in the Web server's root, it might make sense for the browser to not return the cookie to any other pages, even those on the same server. The path could be set to /ows, which would ensure that the cookie is visible only to the pages within the ows folder. This way, two applications on the same server can each set cookies with the same name without overwriting one another, as long as the applications use different paths when setting the cookies.
- **A cookie can be marked as secure.** This means that it should be returned to the server only when a secure connection is being used (that is, if the page's URL starts with `https://` instead of `http://`). If the browser is asked to visit an ordinary (nonsecure) page on the server, the cookie is not sent and thus is not visible to the server. Please note that this does not mean that the cookie will be stored on the user's computer in a more secure fashion; it just means that it won't be transmitted back to the server unless SSL encryption is being used.

As a ColdFusion developer, you have access to these three concepts by way of the `DOMAIN`, `PATH`, and `SECURE` attributes of the `<CFCOOKIE>` tag. As Table 17.2 showed, all three attributes are optional.

Let's say you have three servers, named `one.orangewhip.com`, `two.orangewhip.com`, and `three.orangewhip.com`. To set a cookie that would be shared among the three servers, take the portion of the domain names they share, including the first dot. The following code would set a cookie visible to all three servers (and any other servers whose host names end in .orangewhip.com):

```
<!--- Share cookie over our whole domain --->
<CFCOOKIE
  NAME="VisitStart"
  VALUE="#Now()#"
  DOMAIN=".orangewhip.com">
```

The next example uses the PATH attribute to share the cookie among all pages that have a /ows at the beginning of the path portion of their URLs (the part after the host name). For instance, the following would set a cookie that would be visible to a page with a path of /ows/Home.cfm and /ows/store/checkout.cfm, but not /owintra/login.cfm:

```
<!--- Only share cookie within ows folder --->
<CFCOOKIE
  NAME="VisitStart"
  VALUE="#Now()#"
  PATH="/ows">
```

And finally, this example uses the SECURE attribute to tell the browser to make the cookie visible only to pages that are at secure (https://) URLs. In addition, the cookie will expire in 30 days and will be shared among the servers in the orangewhip.com domain, but only within the /ows portion of each server:

```
<!--- This cookie is shared but confidential --->
<CFCOOKIE
  NAME="VisitStart"
  VALUE="#Now()#"
  EXPIRES="30"
  DOMAIN=".orangewhip.com"
  PATH="/ows"
  SECURE="Yes">
```

NOTE

You can specify that you want to share cookies only within a particular subdomain. For instance, DOMAIN=".intranet.orangewhip.com" shares the cookie within all servers that have .intranet.orangewhip.com at the end of their host names. However, there must always be a leading dot at the beginning of the DOMAIN attribute.

You cannot share cookies based on IP addresses. To share cookies between servers, the servers must have Internet domain names.

The DOMAIN attribute is commonly misunderstood. Sometimes, people assume that you can use it to specify other domains with which to share the cookies. DOMAIN, however, can be used only to specify whether to share the cookies with other servers in the same domain.

Sharing Cookies with Other Applications

Because cookies are not a ColdFusion-specific feature, cookies set with, say, Active Server Pages are visible in ColdFusion's COOKIE scope, and cookies set with <CFCOOKIE> are visible to other applications, such as PHP, Perl, or JavaServer Pages. The browser doesn't know which language is powering which pages. All it cares about is whether the requirements for the domain, path, security, and expiration have been met. If so, it makes the cookie available to the server.

TIP

If you find that cookies set in another language don't seem to be visible to ColdFusion, the problem might be the path part of the cookie. For instance, whereas ColdFusion sets the path to `/` by default so that the cookie is visible to all pages on the server, JavaScript sets the path to match that of the current page by default. Try setting the path part of the cookie to `/` so that it will behave more like one set with ColdFusion. The syntax to do this varies from language to language.

Cookie Limitations

There are some pretty serious restrictions on what you can store in cookies:

- **Only simple strings can be stored.** Because dates and numbers can be expressed as strings, you can store them as cookies. But no ColdFusion-specific data types, such as arrays and structures, can be specified as the value for a cookie.
- **The cookie specification establishes that a maximum of 20 cookies can be set within any one domain.** This prevents cookies from eventually taking up a lot of hard drive space. Browsers might or might not choose to enforce this limit.
- **Each cookie can be a maximum of only 4 Kbytes in length.** The name of the cookie is considered part of its length.
- **According to the original specification, the browser is not obligated to store more than 300 cookies** (total, considering all cookies set by all the world's servers together). The browser can delete the least recently used cookie when the 300-cookie limit has been reached. That said, many modern browsers choose not to enforce this limit.

Using Client Variables

Client variables are similar to cookies, except that they are stored on the server, rather than on the client (browser) machine. In many situations, you can use the two almost interchangeably. So, because you're already familiar with cookies, learning how to use client variables will be a snap. Instead of using the `COOKIE` prefix before a variable name, you simply use the `CLIENT` prefix.

Okay, there's a little bit more to it than that. But not much.

NOTE

Before you can use the `CLIENT` prefix, you must enable ColdFusion's Client Management feature. See the section "Enabling Client Variables," later in this chapter.

NOTE

This might be a bit confusing at this point, but it's worth noting that client variables can also be configured so that they are stored on the browser machine, if you take special steps in the ColdFusion Administrator. They then become essentially equivalent to cookies. See the section "Adjusting How Client Variables Are Stored," later in this chapter.

How Do Client Variables Work?

Client variables work like this:

1. The first time a particular user visits your site, ColdFusion generates a unique ID number to identify the user's browser.
2. ColdFusion sets this ID number as a cookie called `CFID` on the user's browser. From that point on, the browser identifies itself to ColdFusion by presenting this ID.
3. When you set a client variable in your code, ColdFusion stores the value for you on the server side, without sending anything to the browser machine. It stores the `CFID` number along with the variable, to keep them associated internally.
4. Later, when you access or output the variable, ColdFusion simply retrieves the value based on the variable name and the `CFID` number.

For the most part, this process is hidden to you as a developer. You simply use the `CLIENT` scope prefix in your code; ColdFusion takes care of the rest.

Enabling Client Variables

Before you can use client variables in your code, you must enable them using the `<CFAPPLICATION>` tag. In the last chapter, you learned how to use this tag to enable application variables. `<CFAPPLICATION>` takes several additional attributes that are relevant to client variables, as shown in Table 17.3.

Table 17.3 Additional `<CFAPPLICATION>` Attributes Relevant to Client Variables

ATTRIBUTE	DESCRIPTION
`NAME`	Optional. A name for your application. For more information about the `NAME` attribute, see the section "Enabling Application Variables" in the last chapter, "Introducing the Web Application Framework."
`CLIENTMANAGEMENT`	Yes or No. Setting this value to Yes enables client variables for the rest of the page request. Assuming that the `<CFAPPLICATION>` tag is placed in your Application.cfm file, client variables will be enabled for all pages in your application.
`CLIENTSTORAGE`	Optional. You can set this attribute to the word Registry, which means the actual client variables will be stored in the Registry (on Windows servers). You can also provide a data source name, which will cause the variables to be stored in a database. If you omit this attribute, it defaults to Registry unless you have changed the default in the ColdFusion Administrator. For details, see "Adjusting How Client Variables Are Stored," later in this chapter.

Table 17.3 (continued)

ATTRIBUTE	DESCRIPTION
SETCLIENTCOOKIES	Optional. The default is Yes, which allows ColdFusion to automatically set the CFID cookie on each browser, which it uses to track client variables properly for each browser. You can set this value to No if you don't want the cookies to be set. But if you do so, you will need to do a bit of extra work. For details, see "Adjusting How Client Variables Are Stored," later in this chapter.
SETDOMAINCOOKIES	Optional. The default is No, which tells ColdFusion to set the CFID cookie so that it is visible only to the current server. If you have several ColdFusion servers operating in a cluster together, you can set this to Yes to share client variables between all your ColdFusion servers. For details, see "Adjusting How Client Variables Are Stored," later in this chapter.

For now, just concentrate on the CLIENTMANAGEMENT attribute (the others are discussed later). Listing 17.5 shows how easy it is to enable client variables for your application. After you save this code in the Application.cfm file for your application, you can start using client variables. (Be sure to save Listing 17.5 as Application.cfm, not Application2.cfm.)

NOTE

If you attempt to use client variables without enabling them first, an error message will be displayed.

Listing 17.5 Application2.cfm—Enabling Client Variables in Application.cfm

```
<!---
  Filename:     Application.cfm
  Created by:   Nate Weiss (NMW)
  Please Note:  Executes for each page request
--->

<!--- Any variables set here can be used by all our pages --->
<CFSET DataSource  = "ows">
<CFSET CompanyName = "Orange Whip Studios">

<!--- Name our application, and enable Client and Application variables --->
<CFAPPLICATION
  NAME="OrangeWhipSite"
  CLIENTMANAGEMENT="Yes">
```

Using Client Variables

Client variables are ideal for storing things such as user preferences, recent form entries, and other types of values that you don't want to force your users to provide over and over again.

Remembering Values for Next Time

For instance, consider a typical search form, in which the user types what he is looking for and then submits the form to see the search results. It might be nice if the form could remember what the user's last search was.

The code in Listing 17.6 lets it do just that. The basic idea is that the form's search criteria field will already be filled in, using the value of a variable called `SearchPreFill`. The value of this variable is set at the top of the page and will be set to the last search the user ran, if available. If no last search information exists (if this is the first time the user has used this page), it will be blank.

Listing 17.6 `SearchForm1.cfm`—Using Client Variables to Remember the User's Last Search

```
<!---
  Filename:     SearchForm.cfm
  Created by:   Nate Weiss (NMW)
  Please Note:  Maintains "last" search via Client variables
--->

<!--- Determine value for "Search Prefill" feature --->
<!--- When user submits form, save search criteria in client variable --->
<CFIF IsDefined("Form.SearchCriteria")>
  <CFSET CLIENT.LastSearch = Form.SearchCriteria>
  <CFSET SearchPreFill     = Form.SearchCriteria>

<!--- If not submitting yet, get prior search word (if possible) --->
<CFELSEIF IsDefined("CLIENT.LastSearch")>
  <CFSET SearchPreFill = CLIENT.LastSearch>

<!--- If no prior search criteria exists, just show empty string --->
<CFELSE>
  <CFSET SearchPreFill = "">
</CFIF>


<HTML>
<HEAD><TITLE>Search Orange Whip</TITLE></HEAD>
<BODY>
  <H2>Search Orange Whip</H2>

  <!--- Simple search form, which submits back to this page --->
  <CFFORM ACTION="#CGI.SCRIPT_NAME#" METHOD="Post">

    <!--- "Search Criteria" field --->
    Search For:
    <CFINPUT NAME="SearchCriteria" VALUE="#SearchPreFill#"
      REQUIRED="Yes"
      MESSAGE="You must type something to search for!">

    <!--- Submit button --->
    <INPUT TYPE="Submit" VALUE="Search"><BR>

  </CFFORM>

</BODY>
</HTML>
```

The first part of this template (the `<CFIF>` part) does most of the work because it's in charge of setting the `SearchPreFill` variable that provides the "last search" memory for the user. There are three different conditions to deal with. If the user currently is submitting the form to run his search, his search criteria should be saved in a client variable called `_CLIENT.LastSearch`. If the user is not currently submitting the form but has run a search in the past, his last search criteria should be retrieved from the `LastSearch` client variable. If no last search is available, the `IsDefined("CLIENT.LastSearch")` test will fail, and `SearchPreFill` should just be set to an empty string.

The rest of the code is an ordinary form. Note, though, that the value of the `SearchPreFill` variable is passed to the `<CFINPUT>` tag, which presents the user with the search field.

If you visit this page in your browser for the first time, the search field will be blank. To test the use of client variables, type a word or two to search for and submit the form. Of course, no actual search takes place because no database code yet exists in the example, but the form should correctly remember the search criteria you typed. You can close the browser and reopen it, and the value should still be there.

NOTE

In fact, assuming that you haven't changed anything in the ColdFusion Administrator to the contrary, the value of `CLIENT.LastSearch` will continue to be remembered until the user is away from the site for 90 days.

Using Several Client Variables Together

No limit is set on the number of client variables you can use. Listing 17.7 builds on the search form from Listing 17.6, this time allowing the user to specify the number of records the search should return. A second client variable, called `LastMaxRows`, remembers the value, using the same simple `<CFIF>` logic shown in the previous listing.

Listing 17.7 `SearchForm2.cfm`—Using Several Client Variables to Remember Search Preferences

```
<!---
  Filename:     SearchForm.cfm
  Created by:   Nate Weiss (NMW)
  Please Note:  Maintains "last" search via Client variables
--->

<!--- When user submits form, save search criteria in Client variable --->
<CFIF IsDefined("Form.SearchCriteria")>
  <CFSET CLIENT.LastSearch  = Form.SearchCriteria>
  <CFSET CLIENT.LastMaxRows = Form.SearchMaxRows>
<!--- If not submitting yet, get prior search word (if possible) --->
<CFELSEIF IsDefined("CLIENT.LastSearch") AND IsDefined("CLIENT.LastMaxRows")>
  <CFSET SearchCriteria = CLIENT.LastSearch>
  <CFSET SearchMaxRows  = CLIENT.LastMaxRows>
<!--- If no prior search criteria exists, just show empty string --->
<CFELSE>
  <CFSET SearchCriteria = "">
  <CFSET SearchMaxRows  = 10>
</CFIF>



<HTML>
<HEAD><TITLE>Search Orange Whip</TITLE></HEAD>
<BODY>
  <H2>Search Orange Whip</H2>
```

Listing 17.7 (continued)

```
<!--- Simple search form, which submits back to this page --->
<CFFORM ACTION="#CGI.SCRIPT_NAME#" METHOD="Post">

  <!--- "Search Criteria" field --->
  Search For:
  <CFINPUT NAME="SearchCriteria" VALUE="#SearchCriteria#"
    REQUIRED="Yes"
    MESSAGE="You must type something to search for!">

  <!--- Submit button --->
  <INPUT TYPE="Submit" VALUE="Search"><BR>

  <!--- "Max Matches" field --->
  <I>show up to
  <CFINPUT NAME="SearchMaxRows" VALUE="#SearchMaxRows#" SIZE="2"
    REQUIRED="Yes" VALIDATE="integer" RANGE="1,500"
    MESSAGE="Provide a number from 1-500 for search maximum.">
  matches</I><BR>
</CFFORM>

<!--- If we have something to search for, do it now --->
<CFIF SearchCriteria NEQ "">
  <!--- Get matching film entries from database --->
  <CFQUERY NAME="GetMatches" DATASOURCE="#DataSource#">
    SELECT FilmID, MovieTitle, Summary
    FROM Films
    WHERE MovieTitle LIKE '%#SearchCriteria#%'
       OR Summary    LIKE '%#SearchCriteria#%'
    ORDER BY MovieTitle
  </CFQUERY>

  <!--- Show number of matches --->
  <CFOUTPUT>
    <HR><I>#GetMatches.RecordCount# records found for
    "#SearchCriteria#"</I><BR>
  </CFOUTPUT>

  <!--- Show matches, up to maximum number of rows --->
  <CFOUTPUT QUERY="GetMatches" MAXROWS="#SearchMaxRows#">
    <P><B>#MovieTitle#</B><BR>
    #Summary#<BR>
  </CFOUTPUT>
</CFIF>
</BODY>
</HTML>
```

Next, the actual search is performed, using simple `LIKE` code in a `<CFQUERY>` tag. When the results are output, the user's maximum records preference is provided to the `<CFOUTPUT>` tag's `MAXROWS` attribute. Any rows beyond the preferred maximum are not shown. (If you want to brush up on the `<CFQUERY>` and `<CFOUTPUT>` code used here, see Chapter 10, "Creating Data-Driven Pages.")

Not only does this version of the template remember the user's last search criteria, but it also actually reruns the user's last query before she even submits the form. This means the user's last search results will be redisplayed each time she visits the page, making the search results appear to be persistent. The results are shown in Figure 17.4.

You easily could change this behavior by changing the second `<CFIF>` test to `IsDefined("Form.SearchCriteria")`. The last search would still appear prefilled in the search form, but the search itself wouldn't be rerun until the user clicked the Search button. Use client variables in whatever way makes sense for your application.

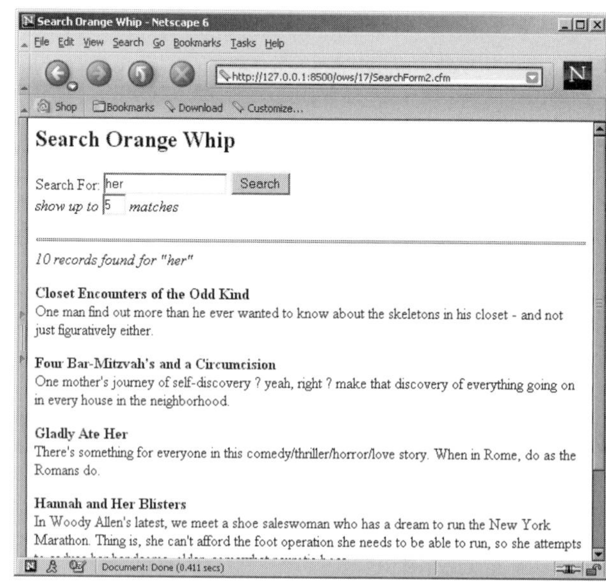

Figure 17.4

Client variables make maintaining the state of a user's recent activity easy.

TIP

To improve performance, you could add a `CACHEDWITHIN` or `CACHEDAFTER` attribute to the `<CFQUERY>` tag, which enables ColdFusion to deliver any repeat searches directly from the server's RAM memory.

➜ For details, see Chapter 22, "Improving Performance."

TIP

Say 15 matching records exist in the database, but the user has typed `10` in the Show Up To field. This template will show only the first 10 matches, but the records-found message will reflect the full 15. Therefore, the user will know that there are more records to be seen. You could consider adding a `MAXROWS` attribute to the `<CFQUERY>` tag as well, which would cause only 10 records to be retrieved from the database in the first place. The records-found message would then show 10 instead of 15.

Deleting Client Variables

Once set, client variables are stored semipermanently. Client variables are deleted only if a user's browser doesn't return to your site for 90 days. In the next section, you learn how to adjust the number of days that the variables are kept, but sometimes you still will need to delete a client variable programmatically.

NOTE

It is important to understand that a client does not have its own expiration date. Client variables do not expire individually; the whole client record is what expires. So, it's not that a client variable is deleted 90 days after it is set. Rather, the client variable (and all other client variables assigned to the user's machine) is deleted after the user lets 90 days pass before revisiting any pages in the application. For more information about tweaking the expiration system, see "Adjusting How Long Client Variables Are Kept," in the next section.

ColdFusion provides a `DeleteClientVariable()` function, which enables you to delete individual client variables by name. The function takes one argument: the name of the client variable you want to delete (the name is not case sensitive). Another handy housekeeping feature is the `GetClientVariablesList()` function, which returns a comma-separated list of the client-variable names that have been set for the current browser.

Listing 17.8 shows how these two functions can be used together to delete all client variables that have been set for a user's browser. You could use code such as this on some start-over type of page, or if the user has chosen to log out of a special area.

Listing 17.8 `DeleteClientVars.cfm`—Deleting All Client Variables That Have Been Set for the Current Browser

```
<!---
  Filename:     DeleteClientVars.cfm
  Created by:   Nate Weiss (NMW)
  Purpose:      Deletes all client variables associated with browser
--->

<HTML>
<HEAD><TITLE>Clearing Your Preferences</TITLE></HEAD>
<BODY>

<H2>Clearing Your Preferences</H2>

<!--- For each client-variable set for this browser... --->
<CFLOOP LIST="#GetClientVariablesList()#" INDEX="ThisVarName">
  <!--- Go ahead and delete the client variable! --->
  <CFSET DeleteClientVariable(ThisVarName)>

  <CFOUTPUT>#ThisVarName# deleted.<BR></CFOUTPUT>
</CFLOOP>

<P>Your preferences have been cleared.

</BODY>
</HTML>
```

Adjusting How Client Variables Are Stored

Out of the box, ColdFusion stores client variables in the server's Registry and will delete all client variables for any visitors who don't return to your site for 90 or more days. You can, of course, tweak these behaviors to suit your needs. This section discusses the client-variable storage options available.

Adjusting How Long Client Variables Are Kept

Normally, client variables are maintained on what amounts to a permanent basis for users who visit your site at least once every 90 days. If a user actually lets 90 days pass without visiting your site (shame on her!), all of her client variables are purged by ColdFusion. This helps keep the client-variable store from becoming ridiculously large.

To adjust this value from the default of 90 days, do the following:

1. Open the ColdFusion Administrator.
2. Navigate to the Client Variables page.
3. Under Storage Name, click the Registry link.
4. Change the Purge Data for Clients That Remain Unvisited For value to the number of days you want; then click Submit Changes.

NOTE

It's important to understand that there isn't a separate time-out for each client variable. The only time client variables are automatically purged is if the client browser hasn't visited the server at all for 90 days (or whatever the purge-data setting has been set to).

Storing Client Variables in a Database

ColdFusion can store your client variables in a database instead of in the Registry. This will appeal to people who just don't like the idea of the Registry being used for storage, or who find that they must make the Registry very large to accommodate the number of client variables they need to maintain. The ability to store client variables in a SQL database is particularly important if you are running several servers in a cluster. You can have all the servers in the cluster keep your application's client variables in the same database, thereby giving you a way to keep variables persistent between pages without worrying about what will happen if the user ends up at a different server in the cluster on her next visit. See the section "Sharing Client Variables Between Servers," later in this chapter.

NOTE

When using the term *Registry*, we are referring to the Windows Registry, assuming that ColdFusion Server is installed on a Windows machine. On other platforms, ColdFusion ships with a simple Registry replacement for storage of client variables. So, Linux and Unix users can still use the default client storage mechanism of the Registry. However, the Registry replacement is not a high-performance beast, and is not recommended for applications that receive a high volume of traffic.

To store your client variables in a database, follow these steps:

1. Create a new database to hold the client variables. You don't need to create any tables in the database; ColdFusion will do that on its own. If you want, you can use an existing database, but we recommend that you use a fresh, dedicated database for storing client variables.
2. Use the ColdFusion Administrator to create a new data source for your new database. See Chapter 5, "Introducing SQL," for details.

3. Navigate to the Client Variables page of the ColdFusion Administrator.
4. Select your new data source from the drop-down list, and then click the Add Client Variable Store button. The Add/Edit Client Store page appears, as shown in Figure 17.5.
5. Adjust the Purge Data for Clients That Remain Unvisited For value as desired. This value is described previously in the section "Adjusting How Long Client Variables Are Kept." As the page in the Administrator notes, if you are using the client variable database in a cluster situation, this option should be enabled for only one server in the cluster. If you are not using a cluster, you should keep this option enabled.
6. Check the Disable Global Client Variable Updates check box unless you are particularly interested in the accuracy of the `HITCOUNT` and `LASTVISIT` properties (see Appendix D, "Special ColdFusion Variables and Result Codes"). In general, we recommend that you check this option, because it can greatly lessen the strain on the database. The only side effect is that client variables will be purged based on the last time a client variable was set or changed, rather than the last time the user visited your site.
7. Leave the Create Client Database Tables option checked, unless you have already gone through that process for this database in the past.
8. Click the Submit Changes button.

You now can supply the new data source name to the `CLIENTSTORAGE` attribute of the `<CFAPPLICATION>` tag (refer to Table 17.3). All of your application's client variables now will be stored in the database instead of in the Registry.

TIP

If you go back to the Client Variables page of the ColdFusion Administrator and change the Default Storage Mechanism for Client Sessions value to the data source you just created, it will be used for all applications that don't specify a `CLIENTSTORAGE` attribute (refer to Table 17.3).

Sharing Client Variables Between Servers

As explained at the beginning of this section, ColdFusion tracks each browser by setting its own client-tracking cookie called `CFID`. Normally, it sets this cookie so that it is sent back only to the server that set it. If you have three ColdFusion servers, each visitor will be given a different `CFID` number for each server, which in turn means that client variables will be maintained separately for each server.

In many situations, especially if you are operating several servers in a cluster, you will want client variables to be shared between the servers, so that a `CLIENT.LastSearch` variable set by one server will be visible to the others.

To share client variables between servers, do the following:

1. Have ColdFusion store your application's client variables in a database, rather than in the Registry. Be sure to do this on all servers in question. For instructions, see the section "Storing Client Variables in a Database," earlier in this chapter.

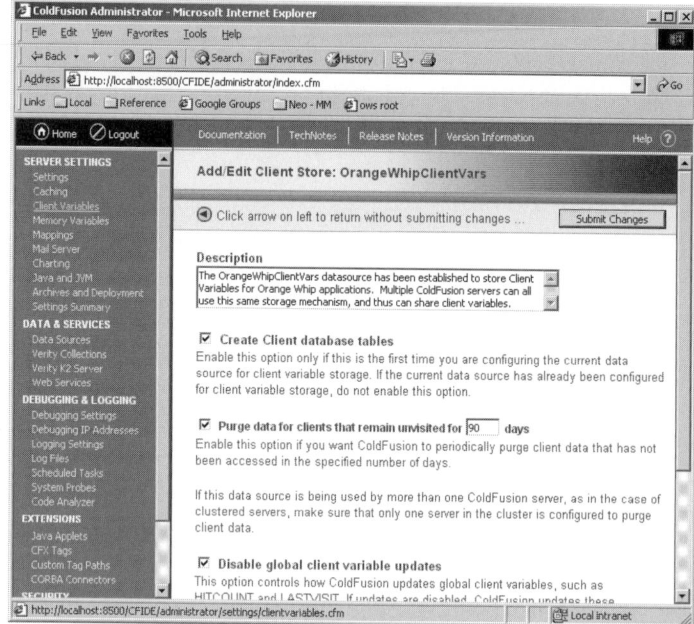

Figure 17.5

You can have ColdFusion store your application's client variables in a database, rather than in the Registry.

2. Add a `SETDOMAINCOOKIES="Yes"` attribute to your application's `<CFAPPLICATION>` tag. This causes ColdFusion to set the `CFID` cookie in such a way that it will be shared among all servers in the same Internet domain. This is the rough equivalent of using the `DOMAIN` attribute in a `<CFCOOKIE>` tag.

Now you can use client variables in your code as you normally would. No matter which server a user visits, ColdFusion will store all client variables in the common database you set up.

NOTE

For cookies to be shared between servers, they all must be members of the same top-level Internet domain (for instance, `orangewhip.com`).

→ For more information about using client variables in a clustered environment, see the "Managing Session State in Clusters" chapter in the companion volume, *Advanced ColdFusion MX Application Development* (ISBN 0-321-12710-2; Macromedia Press).

Backing Up Your Server's Client Variables

If you are keeping client variables in a database, you can back up all client variables by simply backing up the database itself. If it's an Access or some other file-based database, that entails making a backup copy of the database (.mdb) file itself. Otherwise, you must use whatever backup facility is provided with your database software.

If you are using a Windows server and are keeping client variables in the Registry, you can make a copy of the appropriate portion of the Registry. Just follow these steps:

1. Open the Registry Editor by selecting Run from the Windows Start menu and then typing `regedit` in the Run dialog box.

2. Navigate to the following Registry branch (folder):
   `HKEY_LOCAL_MACHINE\SOFTWARE\Allaire\ColdFusion\CurrentVersion\Clients`

3. Select Export Registry File from the Registry menu, then save the file wherever you want. Be sure to leave the Selected Branch option enabled.

Storing Client Variables As a Cookie

You can, somewhat paradoxically, tell ColdFusion to store your application's client variables in cookies on the user's machine, rather than on the server side. You do this by setting the `CLIENTSTORAGE` attribute of the `<CFAPPLICATION>` tag to `Cookie`. This basically enables you to continue using the `CLIENT` prefix even if you want the variables to essentially be stored as cookies.

This might be useful, for instance, in situations in which you are selling your code as a third-party application and want your licensees to have the option of using a server-side or client-side data store. Unfortunately, the size limitations for cookies will apply (see the section "Cookie Limitations," earlier in this chapter). Because this is a somewhat esoteric subject, it isn't discussed in full here. Please consult the ColdFusion documentation for more information about this feature.

NOTE

The cookie storage mechanism for client variables can be useful in a clustered environment or a site that gets an extremely large number of discrete visitors.

➜ For more information about using client variables in a clustered environment, see the "Managing Session State in Clusters" chapter in our companion volume, *Advanced ColdFusion MX Application Development* (ISBN 0-321-12710-2; Macromedia Press).

Using Client Variables Without Requiring Cookies

Earlier in this chapter, you learned that ColdFusion maintains the association between a browser and its client variables by storing a `CFID` cookie on the browser machine. That would seem to imply that client variables will not work if a browser doesn't support cookies or has had them disabled. Don't worry; all is not completely lost.

Actually, ColdFusion normally sets two cookies with which to track client variables: the `CFID` value already mentioned and a randomly generated `CFTOKEN` value. Think of `CFID` and `CFTOKEN` as being similar to a user name and password, respectively. Only if the `CFID` and `CFTOKEN` are both valid will ColdFusion be capable of successfully looking up the appropriate client variables. If the browser does not provide the values for whatever reason (perhaps because the user has configured the browser not to use cookies or because a firewall between the user and your server is stripping cookies out of each page request), ColdFusion will not be capable of looking up the browser's client variables. In fact, ColdFusion will be forced to consider the browser to be a new, first-time visitor, and it will generate a new `CFID` and `CFTOKEN` for the browser—which, of course, means that all client variables that might have been set during previous page visits will be lost.

You can still use client variables without requiring cookies, but you must do a bit more work. Basically, you need to make the `CFID` and `CFTOKEN` available to ColdFusion yourself, by passing the values manually in the URL to every single page in your application.

So, if you want your client variables to work for browsers that don't (or won't) support cookies, you must include the `CFID` and `CFTOKEN` as URL parameters. So, a link such as

```
<A HREF="MyPage.cfm">Click Here</A>
```

would be changed to the following, which would need to be placed between `<CFOUTPUT>` tags:

```
<A HREF="MyPage.cfm?CFID=#CLIENT.CFID#&CFTOKEN=#CLIENT.CFTOKEN#">Click Here</A>
```

ColdFusion provides a shortcut property you can use to make this task a bit less tedious. Instead of providing the `CFID` and `CFTOKEN` in the URL, you can just pass the special `CLIENT.URLTOKEN` property, which always holds the current `CFID` and `CFTOKEN` name/value pairs together in one string, including the `&` and `=` signs. This means the previous line of code can be shortened to the following, which would still need to be placed between `<CFOUTPUT>` tags:

```
<A HREF="MyPage.cfm?#CLIENT.URLTOKEN#">Click Here</A>
```

TIP

It is recommended that you always use the `URLTOKEN` variable as shown here, rather than passing `CFID` and `CFTOKEN` separately. This way you will have fewer changes to make if ColdFusion's method of tracking clients is changed in the future.

You must be sure to pass `CLIENT.URLTOKEN` in every URL, not just in links. For instance, if you are using a `<FORM>` (or `<CFFORM>`) tag, you must pass the token value in the form's `ACTION`, such as this:

```
<FORM ACTION="MyPage.cfm?#CLIENT.URLTOKEN#" METHOD="Post">
```

If you are using frames, you must pass the token value in the `SRC` attribute, such as this:

```
<FRAME SRC="MyPage.cfm?#CLIENT.URLTOKEN#">
```

And so on. Basically, you must look through your code and ensure that whenever you see one of your .cfm templates in a URL of any type, you correctly pass the token value.

NOTE

Remember that the token value must always be placed between `<CFOUTPUT>` tags, unless the URL is being passed as an attribute to a CFML tag (any tag that starts with `CF`, such as `<CFFORM>`).

TIP

If users bookmark one of your pages, the `CFID` and `CFTOKEN` information should be part of the bookmarked URL, so that their client variables are not lost even if their browsers don't support cookies. However, if they just type your site's URL into their browsers directly, it's unlikely that they will include the `CFID` and `CFTOKEN`. Therefore, ColdFusion will be forced to consider them as new visitors, which in turn means that the prior visit's client variables will be lost. ColdFusion will eventually purge the lost session (see the section "Adjusting How Long Client Variables Are Kept," earlier in this chapter).

NOTE

In addition to the `CFID`, `CFTOKEN`, and `URLTOKEN` properties mentioned here, several other automatically maintained properties of the `CLIENT` scope are available, including `HITCOUNT`, `LASTVISIT`, and `TIMECREATED`.

➜ See Appendix D, "Special ColdFusion Variables and Result Codes."

Storing Complex Data Types in Client Variables

As mentioned earlier, you can store only simple values (strings, numbers, dates, and Boolean values) in the CLIENT scope. If you attempt to store one of ColdFusion's complex data types (structures, arrays, queries, and object references) as a client variable, you get an error message.

You can, however, use the <CFWDDX> tag to transform a complex value into an XML-based string. In this serialized form, the value can be stored as a client variable. Later, when you want to use the variable, you can use <CFWDDX> again to transform it from the string format back into its complex form.

There isn't space here to discuss the <CFWDDX> tag fully, but the following code snippets will be enough to get you started. For more information about <CFWDDX>, see Appendix B. For more information about the WDDX technology in general and how it can be used to do much more than this, consult our companion volume, *Advanced ColdFusion MX Development*, or visit www.openwddx.org.

Assuming, for instance, that MyStruct is a structure, the following would store it in the CLIENT scope:

```
<CFWDDX
  ACTION="CFML2WDDX"
  INPUT="#MyStruct#"
  OUTPUT="Client.MyStructAsWddx">
```

Later, to retrieve the value, you could use the following:

```
<CFWDDX
  ACTION="WDDX2CFML"
  INPUT="#Client.MyStructAsWddx#"
  OUTPUT="MyStruct">
```

You then could refer to the values in MyStruct normally in your code. If you made any changes to the structure, you would need to store it anew using the first snippet.

NOTE

You can use the IsSimpleValue() function to test whether a value can be stored in the CLIENT scope without using this WDDX technique.

NOTE

You can use the IsWDDX() function to test whether a client variable actually contains a valid WDDX value.

➜ See Appendix C for details on functions

Using Session Variables

This chapter already has covered a lot of ground. You have learned about cookies and client variables and how they can be used to make an application aware of its individual users and what they are doing. ColdFusion's Web application framework provides one more type of persistent variable to discuss: session variables.

What Are Session Variables?

Session variables are similar to client variables in that they are stored on the server rather than in the browser's memory. Unlike client variables, however, session variables persist only for a user's current session. Later you'll learn exactly how a session is defined, but for now, think of it as being a synonym for a user's visit to your site. Session variables, then, should be thought of as per-visit variables, whereas client variables are per-user variables intended to persist between each user's visits.

Session variables are not stored physically in a database or the server's Registry. Instead, they are stored in the server's RAM. This makes sense, considering the fact that they are intended to persist for only a short time. Also, because ColdFusion doesn't need to physically store and retrieve the variables, you can expect session variables to work a bit more quickly than client variables.

Enabling Session Variables

As with client variables, you must enable session variables using the `<CFAPPLICATION>` tag before you can use them in your code. Table 17.4 lists the additional attributes relevant to session variables. In general, all you need to do is specify a `NAME` and then set `SESSIONMANAGEMENT="Yes"`.

Table 17.4 `<CFAPPLICATION>` Attributes Relevant to Session Variables

ATTRIBUTE	PURPOSE
`NAME`	A name for your application. For more information about the `NAME` attribute, see the section "Enabling Application Variables," in Chapter 16.
`SESSIONMANAGEMENT`	Yes or No. Set to Yes to enable the use of session variables. If you attempt to use session variables in your code without setting this attribute to Yes, an error message will be displayed when the code is executed.
`SESSIONTIMEOUT`	Optional. How long you want your session variables to live in the server's memory. If you don't provide this value, it defaults to whatever is set up in the Variables page of the ColdFusion Administrator. See the section "When Does a Session End?" later in this chapter.

For example, to enable session management, you might use something such as this in your `Application.cfm` file:

```
<!--- Name application and enable Session and Application variables --->
<CFAPPLICATION
  NAME="OrangeWhipSite"
  SESSIONMANAGMENT="Yes">
```

NOTE

Session variables can be disabled globally (for the entire server) in the ColdFusion Administrator. If the Enable Session Variables option on the Memory Variables page of the Administrator has been unchecked, you will not be able to use session variables, regardless of what you set the `SESSIONMANAGEMENT` attribute to.

The CD-ROM for this book includes an `Application3.cfm` template, which enables session management. It is identical to the `Application2.cfm` template used earlier to enable client variables (Listing 17.5), except that `SESSIONMANAGEMENT` is set to `Yes`, rather than to `CLIENTMANAGEMENT`.

Using Session Variables

After you have enabled session variables using `<CFAPPLICATION>`, you can start using them in your code. ColdFusion provides a special `SESSION` variable scope, which works similarly to the `CLIENT` and `COOKIE` scopes you are already familiar with. You can set and use session variables by simply using the `SESSION` prefix in front of a variable's name.

For instance, instead of the `CLIENT.LastSearch` used in the `SearchForm.cfm` examples earlier in this chapter, you could call the variable `SESSION.LastSearch`. The examples would still work in essentially the same way. The only difference in behavior would be that the memory interval of each user's last search would be short (until the end of the session), rather than long (90 days, by default).

And, for something such as search results, the shorter memory provided by the use of session variables might feel more intuitive for the user. That is, a user might expect the search page to remember her last search phrase during the same visit, but she might be surprised or irritated if it remembered search criteria from weeks or months in the past.

You will often find yourself using session and client variables together in the same application. Generally, things that should be remembered for only the current visit belong in session variables, whereas things that should be remembered between visits should be kept in client variables.

Using Session Variables for Multiple-Page Data Entry

Session variables can be especially handy for data-entry processes that require the user to fill out a number of pages. For instance, say you have been asked to put together a data-entry interface for Orange Whip Studios' intranet. The idea is for your users to be able to add new film records to the studio's database. A number of pieces of information will need to be supplied by the user (title, director, actors, and so on).

The most obvious solution would be to just create one long, complex form. However, suppose further that you have been specifically asked not to do this because it might confuse the interns the company hires to do its data-entry tasks.

Carefully considering your options, you decide to present the data-entry screens in a familiar wizard format, with Next and Back buttons the users can use to navigate between steps. However, it is important that nothing actually be entered into the database until the user has finished all the steps. This means the wizard must remember everything the user has entered, even though she will be able to freely move back and forth between steps.

Hmm. You could pass everything from step to step as hidden form fields, but that sounds like a lot of work, and it feels wrong to put the burden of remembering all that data on the client. You'd like to keep the information on the server side. You could create some type of temporary tables in your database, and keep updating the temporary values until the user is finished, but that also sounds like a lot of work. Plus, how would you keep the values separate for each user? And what if the user abandons the wizard partway through?

The answer, of course, is to use session variables, which are perfect for this type of situation. You need to track the information for only a short time, so session variables are appropriate in that respect. Also, session variables aren't kept permanently on the server, so you won't be storing any excess data if the user doesn't finish the wizard.

Maintaining Structures in the `SESSION` Scope

For instance, the following code snippet creates a new structure called `SESSION.MovWiz`. The structure contains several pieces of information, most of which start out blank (set to an empty string). Because the variable is in the `SESSION` scope, a separate version of the structure is kept for each user, but only for the user's current visit. The `StepNum` value is in charge of tracking which step of the data-entry wizard each user is currently on:

```
<CFIF NOT IsDefined("SESSION.MovWiz")>
  <!--- If structure is undefined, create/initialize it --->
  <CFSET SESSION.MovWiz = StructNew()>
  <!--- Represents current wizard step; start at one --->
  <CFSET SESSION.MovWiz.StepNum = 1>
  <!--- We will collect these from user; start blank --->
  <CFSET SESSION.MovWiz.MovieTitle  = "">
  <CFSET SESSION.MovWiz.PitchText   = "">
  <CFSET SESSION.MovWiz.DirectorID  = "">
  <CFSET SESSION.MovWiz.RatingID    = "">
  <CFSET SESSION.MovWiz.ActorIDs    = "">
  <CFSET SESSION.MovWiz.StarActorID = "">
</CFIF>
```

Updating the values in the `SESSION.MovWiz` structure is simple enough. Assume for the moment that the wizard contains Back and Next buttons named `GoBack` and `GoNext`, respectively. The following snippet would increment the `StepNum` part of the structure by 1 when the user clicks the Next button, and decrement it by 1 if the user clicks Back:

```
<!--- If user clicked Back button, go back a step --->
<CFIF IsDefined("Form.GoBack")>
  <CFSET SESSION.MovWiz.StepNum = SESSION.MovWiz.StepNum - 1>
<!--- If user clicked Next button, go forward one --->
<CFELSEIF IsDefined("Form.GoNext")>
  <CFSET SESSION.MovWiz.StepNum = SESSION.MovWiz.StepNum + 1>
</CFIF>
```

The other values in the `MovWiz` structure can be accessed and updated in a similar way. For instance, to present the user with a text-entry field for the new movie's title, you could use something such as this:

```
<CFINPUT
  NAME="MovieTitle"
  VALUE="#SESSION.MovWiz.MovieTitle#">
```

The input field will be prefilled with the current value of the `MovieTitle` part of the `MovWiz` structure. If the previous snippet was in a form and submitted to the server, the value the user typed could be saved back into the `MovWiz` structure using the following line:

```
<CFSET SESSION.MovWiz.MovieTitle = Form.MovieTitle>
```

Putting It All Together

The code in Listing 17.9 combines all the previous snippets into a simple, intuitive wizard interface that users will find familiar and easy to use. The listing is a bit longer than usual, but each part is easy to understand.

The idea here is to create a self-submitting form page that changes depending on which step of the wizard the user is on. The first time the user comes to the page, he sees Step 1 of the wizard. He submits the form, which calls the template again, he sees Step 2, and so on.

This data-entry wizard will collect information from the user in five steps, as follows:

1. The film's title, a one-line description, and the rating, which eventually will be placed in the `Films` table
2. The film's director (the user can list only one), which is inserted in the `FilmsDirectors` table
3. The actors in the movie (the user can list any number), which will be inserted in the `FilmsActors` table
4. Which of the film's actors gets top billing, which sets the `IsStarringRole` column of the `FilmsActors` table to true
5. A final confirmation screen, with a Finish button

The following examples use variables in the `SESSION` scope without locking the accesses by way of the `<CFLOCK>` tag. While extremely unlikely, it is theoretically possible that simultaneous visits to this template *from the same browser* could cause the wizard to collect information in an inconsistent manner. See the section "Locking Revisited," later in this chapter.

Listing 17.9 `NewMovieWizard.cfm`—Using Session Variables to Guide a User Through a Multistep Process

```
<!---
  Filename:     NewMovieWizard.cfm
  Created by:   Nate Weiss (NMW)
  Please Note:  Session variables must be enabled
--->

<!--- Total Number of Steps in the Wizard --->
<CFSET NumberOfSteps = 5>

<!--- The SESSION.MovWiz structure holds users' entries --->
<!--- as they move through wizard. Make sure it exists! --->
<CFIF NOT IsDefined("SESSION.MovWiz")>
  <!--- If structure undefined, create/initialize it --->
  <CFSET SESSION.MovWiz = StructNew()>
  <!--- Represents current wizard step; start at one --->
  <CFSET SESSION.MovWiz.StepNum = 1>
  <!--- We will collect these from user; start blank --->
  <CFSET SESSION.MovWiz.MovieTitle  = "">
  <CFSET SESSION.MovWiz.PitchText   = "">
  <CFSET SESSION.MovWiz.DirectorID  = "">
  <CFSET SESSION.MovWiz.RatingID    = "">
```

Listing 17.9 (continued)

```
    <CFSET SESSION.MovWiz.ActorIDs     = "">
    <CFSET SESSION.MovWiz.StarActorID = "">
  </CFIF>


  <!--- If user just submitted MovieTitle, remember it --->
  <!--- Do same for the DirectorID, Actors, and so on. --->
  <CFIF IsDefined("FORM.MovieTitle")>
    <CFSET SESSION.MovWiz.MovieTitle = FORM.MovieTitle>
    <CFSET SESSION.MovWiz.PitchText  = FORM.PitchText>
    <CFSET SESSION.MovWiz.RatingID   = FORM.RatingID>
  <CFELSEIF IsDefined("FORM.DirectorID")>
    <CFSET SESSION.MovWiz.DirectorID = FORM.DirectorID>
  <CFELSEIF IsDefined("FORM.ActorID")>
    <CFSET SESSION.MovWiz.ActorIDs = FORM.ActorID>
  <CFELSEIF IsDefined("FORM.StarActorID")>
    <CFSET SESSION.MovWiz.StarActorID = FORM.StarActorID>
  </CFIF>


  <!--- If user clicked "Back" button, go back a step --->
  <CFIF IsDefined("FORM.GoBack")>
    <CFSET SESSION.MovWiz.StepNum = URL.StepNum - 1>
  <!--- If user clicked "Next" button, go forward one --->
  <CFELSEIF IsDefined("FORM.GoNext")>
    <CFSET SESSION.MovWiz.StepNum = URL.StepNum + 1>
  <!--- If user clicked "Finished" button, we're done --->
  <CFELSEIF IsDefined("FORM.GoDone")>
    <CFLOCATION URL="NewMovieCommit.cfm">
  </CFIF>


  <HTML>
  <HEAD><TITLE>New Movie Wizard</TITLE></HEAD>
  <BODY>

  <!--- Show title and current step --->
  <CFOUTPUT>
    <B>New Movie Wizard</B><BR>
    Step #SESSION.MovWiz.StepNum# of #NumberOfSteps#<BR>
  </CFOUTPUT>


  <!--- Data Entry Form, which submits back to itself --->
  <CFFORM
    ACTION="NewMovieWizard.cfm?StepNum=#SESSION.MovWiz.StepNum#"
    METHOD="POST">

    <!--- Display the appropriate wizard step --->
    <CFSWITCH EXPRESSION="#SESSION.MovWiz.StepNum#">
      <!--- Step One: Movie Title --->
      <CFCASE VALUE="1">
        <!--- Get potential film ratings from database --->
        <CFQUERY NAME="GetRatings" DATASOURCE="#DataSource#">
          SELECT RatingID, Rating
          FROM FilmsRatings
```

Listing 17.9 (continued)

```
    ORDER BY RatingID
  </CFQUERY>

  <!--- Show text entry field for title --->
  What is the title of the movie?<BR>
  <CFINPUT
    NAME="MovieTitle"
    SIZE="50"
    VALUE="#SESSION.MovWiz.MovieTitle#">

  <!--- Show text entry field for short description --->
  <P>What is the "pitch" or "one-liner" for the movie?<BR>
  <CFINPUT
    NAME="PitchText"
    SIZE="50"
    VALUE="#SESSION.MovWiz.PitchText#">

  <!--- Series of radio buttons for movie rating --->
  <P>Please select the rating:<BR>
  <CFLOOP QUERY="GetRatings">
    <!--- Re-select this rating if it was previously selected --->
    <CFSET IsChecked = RatingID EQ SESSION.MovWiz.RatingID>
    <!--- Display radio button --->
    <CFINPUT
      TYPE="Radio"
      NAME="RatingID"
      CHECKED="#IsChecked#"
      VALUE="#RatingID#"><CFOUTPUT>#Rating#<BR></CFOUTPUT>
  </CFLOOP>
</CFCASE>

<!--- Step Two: Pick Director --->
<CFCASE VALUE="2">
  <!--- Get list of directors from database --->
  <CFQUERY NAME="GetDirectors" DATASOURCE="#DataSource#">
    SELECT DirectorID, FirstName+' '+LastName As FullName
    FROM Directors
    ORDER BY LastName
  </CFQUERY>

  <!--- Show all Directors in SELECT list --->
  <!--- Pre-select if user has chosen one --->
  Who will be directing the movie?<BR>
  <CFSELECT
    SIZE="#GetDirectors.RecordCount#"
    QUERY="GetDirectors"
    NAME="DirectorID"
    DISPLAY="FullName"
    VALUE="DirectorID"
    SELECTED="#SESSION.MovWiz.DirectorID#"/>
</CFCASE>

<!--- Step Three: Pick Actors --->
<CFCASE VALUE="3">
  <!--- Get list of actors from database --->
  <CFQUERY NAME="GetActors" DATASOURCE="#DataSource#">
```

Listing 17.9 (continued)

```
      SELECT * FROM Actors
      ORDER BY NameLast
    </CFQUERY>

    What actors will be in the movie?<BR>
    <!--- For each actor, display checkbox --->
    <CFLOOP QUERY="GetActors">
      <!--- Should checkbox be pre-checked? --->
      <CFSET IsChecked = ListFind(SESSION.MovWiz.ActorIDs, ActorID)>
      <!--- Checkbox itself --->
      <CFINPUT
        TYPE="Checkbox"
        NAME="ActorID"
        VALUE="#ActorID#"
        CHECKED="#IsChecked#">
      <!--- Actor name --->
      <CFOUTPUT>#NameFirst# #NameLast#</CFOUTPUT><BR>
    </CFLOOP>
  </CFCASE>

  <!--- Step Four: Who is the star? --->
  <CFCASE VALUE="4">
    <CFIF SESSION.MovWiz.ActorIDs EQ "">
      Please go back to the last step and choose at least one
      actor or actress to be in the movie.
    <CFELSE>
      <!--- Get actors who are in the film --->
      <CFQUERY NAME="GetActors" DATASOURCE="#DataSource#">
        SELECT * FROM Actors
        WHERE ActorID IN (#SESSION.MovWiz.ActorIDs#)
        ORDER BY NameLast
      </CFQUERY>

      Which one of the actors will get top billing?<BR>
      <!--- For each actor, display radio button --->
      <CFLOOP QUERY="GetActors">
        <!--- Should radio be pre-checked? --->
        <CFSET IsChecked = SESSION.MovWiz.StarActorID EQ ActorID>
        <!--- Radio button itself --->
        <CFINPUT
          TYPE="Radio"
          NAME="StarActorID"
          VALUE="#ActorID#"
          CHECKED="#IsChecked#">
        <!--- Actor name --->
        <CFOUTPUT>#NameFirst# #NameLast#</CFOUTPUT><BR>
      </CFLOOP>
    </CFIF>
  </CFCASE>

  <!--- Step Five: Final Confirmation --->
  <CFCASE VALUE="5">
    You have successfully finished the New Movie Wizard.<BR>
    Click the Finish button to add the movie to the database.<BR>
    Click Back if you need to change anything.<BR>
```

Listing 17.9 (continued)

```
    </CFCASE>
  </CFSWITCH>


  <P>
  <!--- Show Back button, unless at first step --->
  <CFIF SESSION.MovWiz.StepNum GT 1>
    <INPUT TYPE="Submit" NAME="GoBack" VALUE="&lt;&lt; Back">
  </CFIF>
  <!--- Show Next button, unless at last step --->
  <!--- If at last step, show "Finish" button --->
  <CFIF SESSION.MovWiz.StepNum LT NumberOfSteps>
    <INPUT TYPE="Submit" NAME="GoNext" VALUE="Next &gt;&gt;">
  <CFELSE>
    <INPUT TYPE="Submit" NAME="GoDone" VALUE="Finish">
  </CFIF>
</CFFORM>

</BODY>
</HTML>
```

NOTE

To help keep this code as clear as possible, Listing 17.9 does not prevent the user from leaving various form fields blank. See Listing 17.11 for a version that validates the user's entries, using the techniques introduced in Chapter 12, "Form Data Validation."

First, a variable called `NumberOfSteps` is defined, set to `5`. This keeps the `5` from needing to be hard-coded throughout the rest of the template. Next, the `SESSION.MovWiz` structure is defined, using the syntax shown in the first code snippet that appeared before this listing. The structure contains a default value for each piece of information that will be collected from the user.

Next, a `<CFIF>` / `<CFELSEIF>` block is used to determine whether the step the user just completed contains a form element named `MovieTitle`. If so, the corresponding value in the `SESSION.MovWiz` structure is updated with the form's value, thus remembering the user's entry for later. The other possible form fields are also tested for this block of code in the same manner.

Next, the code checks to see whether a form field named `GoBack` was submitted. If so, it means the user clicked the Back button in the wizard interface (see Figure 17.6). Therefore, the `StepNum` value in the `MovWiz` structure should be decremented by 1, effectively moving the user back a step. An equivalent test is performed for fields named `GoNext` and `GoFinish`. If the user clicks `GoFinish`, he is redirected to another template called `NewMovieCommit.cfm`, which actually takes care of inserting the records in the database.

The rest of the code displays the correct form to the user, depending on which step he is on. If he is on step 1, the first `CFCASE` tag kicks in, displaying form fields for the movie's title and short description. Each of the form fields is prefilled with the current value of the corresponding value from `SESSION.MovWiz`. That means the fields will be blank when the user begins, but if he later clicks the Back button to return to the first step, he will see the value that he previously entered. That is, a session variable is being used to maintain the state of the various steps of the wizard.

The other <CFCASE> sections are similar to the first. Each presents form fields to the user (check boxes, radio buttons, and so on), always prefilled or preselected with the current values from `SESSION.MovWiz`. As the user clicks Next or Back to submit the values for a particular step, his entries are stored in the `SESSION.MovWiz` structure by the code near the top of the template.

The last bit of code simply decides whether to show Next, Back, and Finish buttons for each step of the wizard. As would be expected, the Finish button is shown only on the last step, the Next button for all steps except the last, and the Back button for all steps except the first.

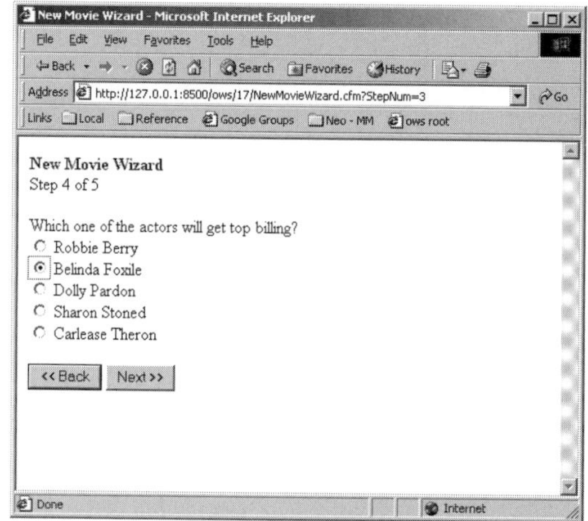

Figure 17.6

Session variables are perfect for creating wizard-style interfaces.

Deleting Session Variables

Unlike the `CLIENT` scope, the `SESSION` variable scope is actually just a ColdFusion structure. So, rather than using some specific function to delete a session variable (perhaps called `DeleteSessionVariable()`), you use the same `StructDelete()` function that removes a value from any other structure.

For instance, to delete the `SESSION.MovWiz` variable, you could use the following line:

```
<CFSET StructDelete(SESSION, "MovWiz")>
```

TIP

Do not use the `StructClear()` function on the `SESSION` scope itself, as in `StructClear(SESSION)`. This erases the session itself, rather than all session variables, which can lead to undesirable results.

➜ If you need to delete all variables from the `SESSION` scope at once, see the section "Expiring a Session Programmatically," later in this chapter.

Listing 17.10 is the `NewMovieCommit.cfm` template, which is called when the user clicks the Finish button on the last step of the New Movie Wizard (refer to Listing 17.9). Most of this listing is made up of ordinary <CFQUERY> code, simply inserting the values from the `SESSION.MovWiz` structure into the correct tables in the database.

After all of the records are inserted, the `MovWiz` variable is removed from the `SESSION` structure, using the syntax shown previously. At that point, the user can be directed back to the `NewMovieWizard.cfm` template, where he can enter information for another movie. The wizard code will see that the `MovWiz` structure no longer exists for the user, and therefore will create a new structure, with blank initial values for the movie title and other information.

Listing 17.10 `NewMovieCommit.cfm`—Session Variables Can Be Deleted When No Longer Necessary

```
<!---
  Filename:    NewMovieCommit.cfm
  Created by:  Nate Weiss (NMW)
  Purpose:     Inserts new movie and associated records into
               database. Gets called by NewMovieWizard.cfm
--->


<!--- Insert film record --->
<CFQUERY DATASOURCE="#DataSource#">
  INSERT INTO Films(
    MovieTitle,
    PitchText,
    RatingID)
  VALUES (
    '#SESSION.MovWiz.MovieTitle#',
    '#SESSION.MovWiz.PitchText#',
    #SESSION.MovWiz.RatingID# )
</CFQUERY>
<!--- Get ID number of just-inserted film --->
<CFQUERY DATASOURCE="#DataSource#" NAME="GetNew">
  SELECT Max(FilmID) As NewID FROM Films
</CFQUERY>
<!--- Insert director record --->
<CFQUERY DATASOURCE="#DataSource#">
  INSERT INTO FilmsDirectors(FilmID, DirectorID, Salary)
  VALUES (#GetNew.NewID#, #SESSION.MovWiz.DirectorID#, 0)
</CFQUERY>
<!--- Insert actor records --->
<CFLOOP LIST="#SESSION.MovWiz.ActorIDs#" INDEX="ThisActor">
  <CFSET IsStar = IIF(ThisActor EQ SESSION.MovWiz.StarActorID, 1, 0)>
  <CFQUERY DATASOURCE="#DataSource#">
    INSERT INTO FilmsActors(FilmID, ActorID, Salary, IsStarringRole)
    VALUES (#GetNew.NewID#, #ThisActor#, 0, #IsStar#)
  </CFQUERY>
</CFLOOP>


<!--- Remove MovWiz variable from SESSION structure --->
<!--- User will be started over on return to wizard --->
<CFSET StructDelete(SESSION, "MovWiz")>


<!--- Display message to user --->
<HTML>
<HEAD><TITLE>Movie Added</TITLE></HEAD>
<BODY>
```

Listing 17.10 (continued)

```
  <H2>Movie Added</H2>
  <P>The movie has been added to the database.

  <!--- Link to go through the wizard again --->
  <P><A HREF="NewMovieWizard.cfm">Enter Another Movie</A>
 </BODY>
 </HTML>
```

One interesting thing about the wizard metaphor is that users expect wizards to adapt themselves based on the choices they make along the way. For instance, the last step of this wizard (in which the user indicates which of the movie's stars gets top billing) looks different depending on the previous step (in which the user lists any number of stars in the movie). You also could decide to skip certain steps based on the film's budget, add more steps if the director and actors have worked together before, and so on. This would be relatively hard to do if you were collecting all the information in one long form.

As you can see in Listing 17.10, this version of the wizard doesn't collect salary information to be inserted into the `FilmsActors` and `FilmsDirectors` tables.Nor does it perform any data validation. For instance, the user can leave the movie title field blank without getting an error message. If you want, take a look at the `NewMovieWizard2.cfm` and `NewMovieCommit2.cfm` templates (Listings 17.11 and 17.12). This slightly expanded version of the wizard adds some data validation for the form elements and adds another step in which the user enters financial information.

The following examples use variables in the `SESSION` scope without locking the accesses with the `<CFLOCK>` tag. This is an acceptable practice here; however, in other situations it would be advisable to add locks to prevent undesired concurrent requests. See the section "Locking Revisited," later in this chapter.

Listing 17.11 `NewMovieWizard2.cfm`—Expanded Version of New Movie Wizard, with Budgeting Step and Form Validation

```
<!---
  Filename:      NewMovieWizard2.cfm
  Created by:    Nate Weiss (NMW)
  Please Note:   Session variables must be enabled
--->

<!--- Total Number of Steps in the Wizard --->
<CFSET NumberOfSteps = 6>

<!--- The SESSION.MovWiz structure holds users' entries --->
<!--- as they move through wizard. Make sure it exists! --->
<CFIF (NOT IsDefined("SESSION.MovWiz")) OR (NOT IsDefined("URL.StepNum"))>
  <!--- If structure undefined, create/initialize it --->
  <CFSET SESSION.MovWiz = StructNew()>
  <!--- Represents current wizard step; start at one --->
  <CFSET SESSION.MovWiz.StepNum = 1>
  <!--- We will collect these from user; start blank --->
  <CFSET SESSION.MovWiz.MovieTitle  = "">
  <CFSET SESSION.MovWiz.PitchText   = "">
  <CFSET SESSION.MovWiz.DirectorID  = "">
```

Listing 17.11 (continued)

```
    <CFSET SESSION.MovWiz.DirectorSal = "">
    <CFSET SESSION.MovWiz.RatingID    = "">
    <CFSET SESSION.MovWiz.ActorIDs    = "">
    <CFSET SESSION.MovWiz.StarActorID = "">
    <CFSET SESSION.MovWiz.MiscExpense = "">
    <CFSET SESSION.MovWiz.ActorSals   = StructNew()>
  </CFIF>


  <!--- If user just submitted MovieTitle, remember it --->
  <!--- Do same for the DirectorID, Actors, and so on. --->
  <CFIF IsDefined("Form.MovieTitle")>
    <CFSET SESSION.MovWiz.MovieTitle = Form.MovieTitle>
    <CFSET SESSION.MovWiz.PitchText  = Form.PitchText>
    <CFSET SESSION.MovWiz.RatingID   = FORM.RatingID>
  <CFELSEIF IsDefined("Form.DirectorID")>
    <CFSET SESSION.MovWiz.DirectorID = Form.DirectorID>
  <CFELSEIF IsDefined("Form.ActorID")>
    <CFSET SESSION.MovWiz.ActorIDs = Form.ActorID>
  <CFELSEIF IsDefined("Form.StarActorID")>
    <CFSET SESSION.MovWiz.StarActorID = Form.StarActorID>
  <CFELSEIF IsDefined("Form.DirectorSal")>
    <CFSET SESSION.MovWiz.DirectorSal = Form.DirectorSal>
    <CFSET SESSION.MovWiz.MiscExpense = Form.MiscExpense>
    <!--- For each actor now in the movie, save their salary --->
    <CFLOOP LIST="#SESSION.MovWiz.ActorIDs#" INDEX="ThisActor">
      <CFSET SESSION.MovWiz.ActorSals[ThisActor] = Form["ActorSal#ThisActor#"]>
    </CFLOOP>
  </CFIF>


  <!--- If user clicked "Back" button, go back a step --->
  <CFIF IsDefined("Form.GoBack")>
    <CFSET SESSION.MovWiz.StepNum = URL.StepNum - 1>
  <!--- If user clicked "Next" button, go forward one --->
  <CFELSEIF IsDefined("Form.GoNext")>
    <CFSET SESSION.MovWiz.StepNum = URL.StepNum + 1>
  <!--- If user clicked "Finished" button, we're done --->
  <CFELSEIF IsDefined("Form.GoDone")>
    <CFLOCATION URL="NewMovieCommit2.cfm">
  </CFIF>


  <HTML>
  <HEAD><TITLE>New Movie Wizard</TITLE></HEAD>
  <BODY>

  <!--- Show title and current step --->
  <CFOUTPUT>
    <B>New Movie Wizard</B><BR>
    Step #SESSION.MovWiz.StepNum# of #NumberOfSteps#<BR>
  </CFOUTPUT>


  <!--- Data Entry Form, which submits back to itself --->
```

Listing 17.11 (continued)

```
<CFFORM
  ACTION="NewMovieWizard2.cfm?StepNum=#SESSION.MovWiz.StepNum#"
  METHOD="POST">

  <!--- Display the appropriate wizard step --->
  <CFSWITCH EXPRESSION="#SESSION.MovWiz.StepNum#">
    <!--- Step One: Movie Title --->
    <CFCASE VALUE="1">
      <!--- Get potential film ratings from database --->
      <CFQUERY NAME="GetRatings" DATASOURCE="#DataSource#">
        SELECT RatingID, Rating
        FROM FilmsRatings
        ORDER BY RatingID
      </CFQUERY>

      <!--- Show text entry field for title --->
      What is the title of the movie?<BR>
      <CFINPUT
        NAME="MovieTitle"
        SIZE="50"
        REQUIRED="Yes"
        MESSAGE="Please don't leave the movie title blank."
        VALUE="#SESSION.MovWiz.MovieTitle#">

      <!--- Show text entry field for title --->
      <P>What is the "pitch" or "one-liner" for the movie?<BR>
      <CFINPUT
        NAME="PitchText"
        SIZE="50"
        REQUIRED="Yes"
        MESSAGE="Please provide the pitch text first."
        VALUE="#SESSION.MovWiz.PitchText#">

      <!--- Series of radio buttons for movie rating --->
      <P>Please select the rating:<BR>
      <CFLOOP QUERY="GetRatings">
        <!--- Re-select this rating if it was previously selected --->
        <CFSET IsChecked = RatingID EQ SESSION.MovWiz.RatingID>
        <!--- Display radio button --->
        <CFINPUT
          TYPE="Radio"
          NAME="RatingID"
          CHECKED="#IsChecked#"
          VALUE="#RatingID#"><CFOUTPUT>#Rating#<BR></CFOUTPUT>
      </CFLOOP>
    </CFCASE>

    <!--- Step Two: Pick Director --->
    <CFCASE VALUE="2">
      <!--- Get list of directors from database --->
      <CFQUERY NAME="GetDirectors" DATASOURCE="#DataSource#">
        SELECT DirectorID, FirstName+' '+LastName As FullName
        FROM Directors
        ORDER BY LastName
      </CFQUERY>
```

Listing 17.11 (continued)

```
    <!--- Show all Directors in SELECT list --->
    <!--- Pre-select if user has chosen one --->
    Who will be directing the movie?<BR>
    <CFSELECT
      SIZE="#GetDirectors.RecordCount#"
      QUERY="GetDirectors"
      NAME="DirectorID"
      DISPLAY="FullName"
      VALUE="DirectorID"
      REQUIRED="Yes"
      MESSAGE="You must choose a director first."
      SELECTED="#SESSION.MovWiz.DirectorID#"/>
  </CFCASE>

  <!--- Step Three: Pick Actors --->
  <CFCASE VALUE="3">
    <!--- Get list of actors from database --->
    <CFQUERY NAME="GetActors" DATASOURCE="#DataSource#">
      SELECT * FROM Actors
      ORDER BY NameLast
    </CFQUERY>

    What actors will be in the movie?<BR>
    <!--- For each actor, display checkbox --->
    <CFLOOP QUERY="GetActors">
      <!--- Should checkbox be pre-checked? --->
      <CFSET IsChecked = ListFind(SESSION.MovWiz.ActorIDs, ActorID)>
      <!--- Checkbox itself --->
      <CFINPUT
        TYPE="Checkbox"
        NAME="ActorID"
        VALUE="#ActorID#"
        REQUIRED="Yes"
        MESSAGE="You must choose at least one actor first."
        CHECKED="#IsChecked#">
      <!--- Actor name --->
      <CFOUTPUT>#NameFirst# #NameLast#</CFOUTPUT><BR>
    </CFLOOP>
  </CFCASE>


  <!--- Step Four: Who is the star? --->
  <CFCASE VALUE="4">
    <CFIF SESSION.MovWiz.ActorIDs EQ "">
      Please go back to the last step and choose at least one
      actor or actress to be in the movie.
    <CFELSE>
      <!--- Get actors who are in the film --->
      <CFQUERY NAME="GetActors" DATASOURCE="#DataSource#">
        SELECT * FROM Actors
        WHERE ActorID IN (#SESSION.MovWiz.ActorIDs#)
        ORDER BY NameLast
      </CFQUERY>

      Which one of the actors will get top billing?<BR>
```

Listing 17.11 (continued)

```
      <!--- For each actor, display radio button --->
      <CFLOOP QUERY="GetActors">
        <!--- Should radio be pre-checked? --->
        <CFSET IsChecked = SESSION.MovWiz.StarActorID EQ ActorID>
        <!--- Radio button itself --->
        <CFINPUT
          TYPE="Radio"
          NAME="StarActorID"
          VALUE="#ActorID#"
          REQUIRED="Yes"
          MESSAGE="Please select the starring actor first."
          CHECKED="#IsChecked#">
        <!--- Actor name --->
        <CFOUTPUT>#NameFirst# #NameLast#</CFOUTPUT><BR>
      </CFLOOP>
    </CFIF>
  </CFCASE>


  <!--- Step Five: Expenses and Salaries --->
  <CFCASE VALUE="5">
    <!--- Get actors who are in the film --->
    <CFQUERY NAME="GetActors" DATASOURCE="#DataSource#">
      SELECT * FROM Actors
      WHERE ActorID IN (#SESSION.MovWiz.ActorIDs#)
      ORDER BY NameLast
    </CFQUERY>

    <!--- Director's Salary --->
    <P>How much will we pay the Director?<BR>
    <CFINPUT
      TYPE="Text"
      SIZE="10"
      NAME="DirectorSal"
      REQUIRED="Yes"
      VALIDATE="float"
      MESSAGE="Please provide a number for the director's salary."
      VALUE="#SESSION.MovWiz.DirectorSal#">

    <!--- Salary for each actor --->
    <P>How much will we pay the Actors?<BR>
    <CFLOOP QUERY="GetActors">
      <!--- Grab actors's salary from ActorSals structure --->
      <!--- Initialize to "" if no salary for actor yet --->
      <CFIF NOT StructKeyExists(SESSION.MovWiz.ActorSals, ActorID)>
        <CFSET SESSION.MovWiz.ActorSals[ActorID] = "">
      </CFIF>
      <!--- Text field for actor's salary --->
      <CFINPUT
        TYPE="Text"
        SIZE="10"
        NAME="ActorSal#ActorID#"
        REQUIRED="Yes"
        VALIDATE="float"
        MESSAGE="Please provide a number for each actor's salary."
```

Listing 17.11 (continued)

```
        VALUE="#SESSION.MovWiz.ActorSals[ActorID]#">
      <!--- Actor's name --->
      <CFOUTPUT>for #NameFirst# #NameLast#<BR></CFOUTPUT>
    </CFLOOP>

    <!--- Additional Expenses --->
    <P>How much other money will be needed for the budget?<BR>
    <CFINPUT
      TYPE="Text"
      NAME="MiscExpense"
      REQUIRED="Yes"
      VALIDATE="float"
      MESSAGE="Please provide a number for additional expenses."
      SIZE="10"
      VALUE="#SESSION.MovWiz.MiscExpense#">
  </CFCASE>


  <!--- Step Six: Final Confirmation --->
  <CFCASE VALUE="6">
    You have successfully finished the New Movie Wizard.<BR>
    Click the Finish button to add the movie to the database.<BR>
    Click Back if you need to change anything.<BR>
  </CFCASE>
 </CFSWITCH>


 <P>
 <!--- Show Back button, unless at first step --->
 <CFIF SESSION.MovWiz.StepNum GT 1>
   <INPUT TYPE="Submit" NAME="GoBack" VALUE="&lt;&lt; Back">
 </CFIF>
 <!--- Show Next button, unless at last step --->
 <!--- If at last step, show "Finish" button --->
 <CFIF SESSION.MovWiz.StepNum LT NumberOfSteps>
   <INPUT TYPE="Submit" NAME="GoNext" VALUE="Next &gt;&gt;">
 <CFELSE>
   <INPUT TYPE="Submit" NAME="GoDone" VALUE="Finish">
 </CFIF>
</CFFORM>

</BODY>
</HTML>
```

Listing 17.12 NewMovieCommit2.cfm—Expanded Version of Wizard Commit Code

```
<!---
  Filename:     NewMovieCommit2.cfm
  Created by:   Nate Weiss (NMW)
  Date Created: 2/18/2001
--->

<!--- Compute Total Budget --->
<!--- First, add the director's salary and miscellaneous expenses --->
<CFSET TotalBudget = SESSION.MovWiz.MiscExpense + SESSION.MovWiz.DirectorSal>
```

Listing 17.12 (continued)

```
<!--- Now add the salary for each actor in the movie --->
<CFLOOP LIST="#SESSION.MovWiz.ActorIDs#" INDEX="ThisActor">
  <CFSET ThisSal = SESSION.MovWiz.ActorSals[ThisActor]>
  <CFSET TotalBudget = TotalBudget + ThisSal>
</CFLOOP>

<!--- Insert Film Record --->
<CFQUERY DATASOURCE="#DataSource#">
  INSERT INTO Films(
    MovieTitle,
    PitchText,
    RatingID,
    AmountBudgeted)
  VALUES (
    '#SESSION.MovWiz.MovieTitle#',
    '#SESSION.MovWiz.PitchText#',
    #SESSION.MovWiz.RatingID#,
    #TotalBudget#)
</CFQUERY>
<!--- Get ID number of just-inserted film --->
<CFQUERY DATASOURCE="#DataSource#" NAME="GetNew">
  SELECT Max(FilmID) As NewID FROM Films
</CFQUERY>
<!--- Insert director record --->
<CFQUERY DATASOURCE="#DataSource#">
  INSERT INTO FilmsDirectors(FilmID, DirectorID, Salary)
  VALUES (#GetNew.NewID#, #SESSION.MovWiz.DirectorID#, #SESSION.MovWiz.DirectorSal#)
</CFQUERY>
<!--- Insert actor records --->
<CFLOOP LIST="#SESSION.MovWiz.ActorIDs#" INDEX="ThisActor">
  <CFSET IsStar  = IIF(ThisActor EQ SESSION.MovWiz.StarActorID, 1, 0)>
  <CFQUERY DATASOURCE="#DataSource#">
    INSERT INTO FilmsActors(FilmID, ActorID, Salary, IsStarringRole)
    VALUES (#GetNew.NewID#, #ThisActor#, #SESSION.MovWiz.ActorSals[ThisActor]#,
#IsStar#)
  </CFQUERY>
</CFLOOP>

<!--- Remove MovWiz variable from SESSION structure --->
<!--- User will be started over on return to wizard --->
<CFSET StructDelete(SESSION, "MovWiz")>


<!--- Display message to user --->
<HTML>
<HEAD><TITLE>Movie Added</TITLE></HEAD>
<BODY>
 <H2>Movie Added</H2>
 <P>The movie has been added to the database.

 <!--- Link to go through the wizard again --->
 <P><A HREF="NewMovieWizard2.cfm">Enter Another Movie</A>
</BODY>
</HTML>
```

One item of note in these slightly expanded versions is that the new `ActorSals` part of the `SESSION.MovWiz` structure is itself a structure. The fact that you can use complex data types such as structures and arrays is one important advantage that session variables have over client variables and cookies.

➜ See the "Other Examples of Session Variables" section at the end of this chapter for a list of other listings in this book that use session variables.

When Does a Session End?

Developers often wonder when exactly a session ends. The simple answer is that, by default, ColdFusion's Session Management feature is based on time. A particular session is considered to be expired if more than 20 minutes pass without another request from the same client. At that point, the `SESSION` scope associated with that browser is freed from the server's memory.

That said, ColdFusion MX provides a few options that you can use to subtly change the definition of a session, and to control more precisely when a particular session ends.

J2EE Session Variables and ColdFusion MX

ColdFusion MX includes a new option that allows you to use J2EE session variables. This new option is different from the "classic" ColdFusion implementation of session variables, which have been available in previous versions.

The traditional implementation uses ColdFusion-specific `CFID` and `CFTOKEN` cookies to identify the the client (that is, the browser). Whenever a client visits pages in your application within a certain period of time, those page requests are considered to be part of the same session. By default, this time period is 20 minutes. If more than 20 minutes pass without another page request from the client, the session "times out" and the session information is discarded from the server's memory. If the user closes her browser, then reopens it and visits your page again, the same session will still be in effect. That is, ColdFusion's classic strategy is to uniqely identify the machine, then define the concept of "session" solely in terms of time.

The J2EE session variables option causes ColdFusion to define a session somewhat differently. Instead of using `CFID` and `CFTOKEN` cookies, which persist between sessions, to track the user's *machine*, it uses a different cookie, called `JSESSIONID`. This cookie is not persistent, and thus expires when a user closes her browser. Therefore, if the user reopens her browser and visits your page again, it is an entirely new session.

To enable the J2EE session variables feature, select the Use J2EE Session Variables check box on the ColdFusion Administrator's Memory Variables page.

Once you enable this option, sessions will expire whenever the user closes their browser, or when the session timeout period elapses between requests (whichever comes first).

NOTE

The use of the JSESSIONID cookie is part of the Java J2EE specification. Using J2EE session variables makes it easy to share session variables with other J2EE code that may be working alongside your ColdFusion templates, such as Java Servlets, Enterprise JavaBeans, JSPs, and so on. In other words, telling ColdFusion MX to use J2EE session variables is a great way to integrate your ColdFusion code with other J2EE technologies so they can all behave as a single application. The assumption here is that the closing of a browser should be interpreted as a desire to end a session.

Default Behavior

Again, by default, a session does not automatically end when the user closes her browser. You can see this yourself by visiting one of the session examples discussed in this book, such as the New Movie Wizard (refer to Listing 17.9). Fill out the wizard partway, and then close your browser. Now reopen it. Nothing has happened to your session's copy of the `SESSION` scope, so you still are on the same step of the wizard that you were before you closed your browser. As far as ColdFusion is concerned, you just reloaded the page.

Adjusting the Session Time-out Period

You can adjust the session time-out period for your session variables by following the same basic steps you take to adjust the time-out period for application variables. That is, you can adjust the default time-out of 20 minutes using the ColdFusion Administrator, or you can use the `SESSIONTIMEOUT` attribute of the `<CFAPPLICATION>` tag to set a specific session time-out for your application.

For specific instructions, see the section "Application Variable Time-outs" in Chapter 16.

Expiring a Session Programmatically

If you want a session in your code to expire, you can use a `<CFAPPLICATION>` tag such as the one in your `Application.cfm` file, except with a `SESSIONTIMEOUT` length of 0 seconds. For instance, if you wanted to give your users some type of log-out link, you could include a `SessionLogout.cfm` template containing something such as the following:

```
<!--- Expire the session --->
<CFAPPLICATION
  NAME="OrangeWhipSite"
  SESSIONMANAGEMENT="Yes"
  SESSIONTIMEOUT="#CreateTimeSpan(0,0,0,0)#">
```

Ending the Session when the Browser Closes

The simplest way to make session variables expire when the user closes his browser is by telling ColdFusion to use J2EE session variables, as explained earlier in the "J2EE Session Variables and ColdFusion MX" section. When in this mode, the ColdFusion server sets a nonpersistent cookie to track the session (as opposed to the traditional session-variable mode, in which persistent cookies are set). Thus, when the browser is closed, the session-tracking cookie is lost, which means that a new session will be created if the user reopens his browser and comes back to your application.

Assuming that you are not using J2EE session variables, one option is to set the `SETCLIENTCOOKIES` attribute of `<CFAPPLICATION>` to `No`, which means that the `CFID` and `CFTOKEN` cookies ColdFusion normally uses to track each browser's session (and client) variables will not be maintained as persistent cookies on each client machine. If you are not using client variables, or don't need your client variables to persist after the user closes his browser, this can be a viable option.

If you do decide to set `SETCLIENTCOOKIE="No"`, you must manually pass the `CFID` and `CFTOKEN` in the URL for every page request, as if the user's browser did not support cookies at all. See the section "Using Client Variables Without Requiring Cookies," earlier in this chapter, for specific instructions.

If you want to use `SETCLIENTCOOKIE="No"` but don't want to pass the `CFID` and `CFTOKEN` in every URL, you could set the `CFID` and `CFTOKEN` on your own, as nonpersistent cookies. This means the values would be stored as cookies on the user's browser, but the cookies would expire when the user closes his browser. The most straightforward way to get this effect is to use two `<CFSET>` tags in your `Application.cfm` file, just after your `<CFAPPLICATION>` tag, as follows:

```
<!--- Name application, and enable Session and Application variables --->
<CFAPPLICATION
  NAME="OrangeWhipSite"
  SESSIONMANAGEMENT="Yes"
  SETCLIENTCOOKIES="No">

<!--- Preserve Session/Client variables only until browser closes --->
<CFSET Cookie.CFID    = SESSION.CFID>
<CFSET Cookie.CFTOKEN = SESSION.CFTOKEN>
```

This technique essentially causes ColdFusion to lose all memory of the client machine when the user closes his browser. When the user returns next time, no `CFID` will be presented to the server, and ColdFusion will be forced to issue a new `CFID` value, effectively abandoning any session and client variables that were associated with the browser in the past. The expiration behavior will be very similar to that of J2EE session variables.

NOTE

Please note that by setting the `CFID` and `CFTOKEN` cookies yourself in this way, you will lose all session *and* client variables for your application when the user closes his browser. If you are using both client and session variables, and want the client variables to persist between sessions but the session variables to expire when the user closes his browser, then you should use either the technique shown next or J2EE session variables as discussed earlier.

A completely different technique is to set your own nonpersistent cookie, perhaps called `Cookie.BrowserOpen`. If a user closes the browser, the cookie no longer exists. Therefore, you can use the cookie's nonexistence as a cue for the session to expire programmatically, as discussed in the previous section. In your `Application.cfm` file you could use code such as the following:

```
<!--- If our BrowserOpen cookie is not sent --->
<CFIF NOT IsDefined("Cookie.BrowserOpen")>
  <!--- Expire the session, if any --->
  <CFAPPLICATION
    NAME="OrangeWhipSite"
    SESSIONMANAGEMENT="Yes"
    SESSIONTIMEOUT="#CreateTimeSpan(0,0,0,0)#">

  <!--- Set cookie, to expire when browser closes --->
```

```
  <CFSET Cookie.BrowserOpen = "Yes">
</CFIF>

<!--- Name application, and enable Session and Application variables --->
<CFAPPLICATION
  NAME="OrangeWhipSite"
  SESSIONMANAGEMENT="Yes">
```

Unfortunately, there is a downside to this technique. If the browser doesn't support cookiesor has had them disabled, the session will expire with every page request. However, as long as you know that cookies will be supported (for instance, in an intranet application), it will serve you well.

Using Session Variables Without Requiring Cookies

Unless you take special steps, the browser must accept a cookie or two in order for session variables to work correctly in ColdFusion. If your application needs to work even with browsers that don't (or won't) accept cookies, you need to pass the value of the special `SESSION.URLToken` variable in each URL, just as you need to pass `CLIENT.URLToken` to allow client variables to work without using cookies. This will ensure that the appropriate `CFID`, `CFTOKEN`, or `JSESSIONID` values are available for each page request, even if the browser can't provide the value as a cookie. See "Using Client Variables Without Requiring Cookies," earlier in this chapter, for specific instructions; just pass `SESSION.URLToken` instead of `CLIENT.URLToken`.

TIP

If you are using both client *and* session variables in your application, you can just pass either `SESSION.URLToken` or `CLIENT.URLToken`. You don't need to worry about passing both values in the URL. If you do pass them both, that's fine too.

Other Examples of Session Variables

A number of other examples in this book use session variables. You might want to skim through the code listings outlined here to see some other uses for session variables:

- In Chapter 18, "Securing Your Applications," session variables are used to track the logged-in status of users.
- In Chapter 26, "Interacting with Email," session variables are used to help users check their email messages from a ColdFusion template.
- The Ad Server examples in Chapter 32, "Generating Non-HTML Content," use session variables to track which ads have been shown on which pages on a per-visit basis.

Locking Revisited

Like application variables, session variables are kept in the server's RAM. This means that the same types of race-condition problems can occur if session variables are being read and accessed by two different page requests at the same time. (See the section "Using Locks to Protect Against Race Conditions" in Chapter 16.)

➜ If you haven't yet read "Preventing Memory Corruption with Locking" in Chapter 16, please take a look at that section before you continue.

Sessions and the `<CFLOCK>` Tag

Just as it's possible to run into race conditions with application variables, it's also possible for race conditions to crop up when using session variables. In general, it's much less likely that race conditions will occur at the session level than at the application level, as there is usually only one page request coming from each session at any given time. Even though it's unlikely in the grand scheme of things, it still is quite possible that more than one request could be processed from a session at the same time. Here are some examples:

- Pages that use frames can allow a browser to make more than one page request at the same time. If, say, a frameset contains three individual frame pages, most browsers will issue all three follow-up requests at once.
- If for whatever reason (perhaps network congestion or a heavy load on your ColdFusion server) a particular page is taking a long time to come up, many users tend to click their browser's Reload or Refresh button a few times. Or they might submit a form multiple times. In either case, it's quite possible that a second or third request might get to the server before the first request does.
- If you are using `<CFCONTENT>` to serve up images, as in the Ad Server examples in Chapter 32, "Generating Non-HTML Content," and there are three or four such images on a page, most browsers will make the requests for the images concurrently.

In other words, although race conditions are probably less likely to occur with session variables than they are with application variables, it is still possible to encounter them. Therefore, if the nature of your session variables is such that concurrent access would be a bad thing, you need to use the `<CFLOCK>` tag. In general, you will use `<CFLOCK>` just as it was shown in Chapter 16, except you use `SCOPE="Session"` instead of `SCOPE="Application"`.

NOTE

Locks of `SCOPE="Session"` will affect only those locks that have been issued to the same session, which is of course what you want. In plain English, a `<CFLOCK>` with `SCOPE="Session"` means "don't let other page requests from this session interfere with the code in this block."

Exclusive vs. Read-Only Locks

In Chapter 16, you learned that there are two types of locks: exclusive and read-only. The main reason to use a read-only lock is to reduce the amount of time your application pages need to sit around waiting for locks to be released and granted.

You should use the same basic strategy with session variables. That is, use exclusive locks when making changes, and use read-only locks when just retrieving or outputting the value of a session variable. Since it is less likely for you to get concurrent page requests at the session level than at the application level, using both types of locks is less likely to make a huge difference in overall system performance. But it's still the best practice, since it guarantees that you won't encounter race conditions in your code.

Scoped vs. Named Locks

In Chapter 16, you also learned that you can use `SCOPE` or `NAME` to identify a lock. The main purpose for using `NAME` is to be able to lock with more precision so that one widget's locks don't affect another's. Because concurrent page accesses are relatively unlikely to occur at the session level, you probably don't need to worry about getting so specific. Therefore, locking monolithically at the session level is probably sufficient. The only likely scenario where you would benefit from using named locks around session variables would be a frameset page that loaded three or four individual frame pages, all of them needing to change and access different session variables. In such a situation, you could make your locks finely grained by creating names for the different "widgets" that store information at the session level.

Remember that lock names are considered globally, across the whole server, so you will need to make sure that the lock names include something that uniquely identifies the session. The best way to do this is to use the automatic `#SESSION.SessionID#` variable as a part of the lock name. For instance, a lock like the following might be used around reads or writes to shopping cart information being maintained at the session level:

```
<CFLOCK
  NAME="OrangeWhipShoppingCart#SESSION.SessionID#"
  TYPE="Exclusive"
  TIMEOUT="10">
```

➜ See Chapter 27, "Online Commerce," for examples that use locks in this way.

CHAPTER 18

Securing Your Applications

IN THIS CHAPTER

At this point, you have learned how to create interactive, data-driven pages for your users and have started to see how your applications can really come alive using the various persistent scopes (particularly client and session variables) provided by Macromedia ColdFusion's Web application framework. Now is a good time to learn how to lock down your application pages so they require a user name and password and show only the right information to the right people.

Options for Securing Your Application

This section briefly outlines four topics to consider if you need to secure access to your ColdFusion templates:

- SSL encryption
- HTTP basic authentication
- Session-based security
- ColdFusion MX's new `<CFLOGIN>` framework
- ColdFusion resource ("sandbox") security

You can use more than one of these options at the same time if you want. The third and fourth items are the primary focus of this chapter.

SSL Encryption

Most of today's Web servers allow you to make a connection between the browser and the server more secure by using encryption. After encryption has been enabled, your ColdFusion templates and related files become available at URLs that begin with `https://` instead of `http://`. The HTML code your templates generate is scrambled on its way out of the Web server. Provided that everything has been set up correctly, browsers can unscramble the HTML and use it normally. The framework that makes all of this possible is called the Secure Sockets Layer (SSL).

Browsers generally show a small key or lock icon in their status bar to indicate that a page is encrypted. You probably have encountered many such sites yourself, especially on pages where you are asked to provide a credit card number.

This topic is not discussed in detail here because encryption is enabled at the Web-server level and doesn't affect the ColdFusion Application Server directly. You don't need to do anything special in your ColdFusion templates for it to work properly. The encryption and decryption are taken care of by your Web server and each user's browser.

You might want to look into turning on your Web server's encryption options for sections of your applications that need to display or collect valuable pieces of information. For instance, most users hesitate to enter a credit card number on a page that is not secure, so you should think about using encryption during any type of checkout process in your applications.

TIP

If you are working on a company intranet project, you might consider enabling SSL for the entire application, especially if employees will access it from outside your local network.

The steps you take to enable encryption differ depending on which Web server software you are using (Apache, Netscape/iPlanet, Microsoft IIS, and so on). You will need to consult your Web server's documentation for details. Along the way, you will learn a bit about public and private keys, and you probably will need to purchase an SSL certificate on an annual basis from a company such as VeriSign. VeriSign's Web site is also a good place to look if you want to find out more about SSL and HTTPS technology in general. Visit the company at `www.verisign.com`.

TIP

If you want your code to be capable of detecting whether a page is being accessed with an `https://` URL, you can use one of the variables in the `CGI` scope to make this determination. The variables might have slightly different names from server to server, but they generally start with `HTTPS`. For instance, on a Microsoft IIS server, the value of `CGI.HTTPS` is `on` or `off`, depending on whether the page is being accessed in an encrypted context. Another way to perform the test is by looking at the value of `CGI.SERVER_PORT`; under most circumstances, it will hold a value of `443` if encryption is being used, and a value of `80` if not. We recommend that you turn on the Show Variables debugging option in the ColdFusion Administrator to see which HTTPS-related variables are made available by your Web server software.

HTTP Basic Authentication

Nearly all Web servers provide support for something called HTTP basic authentication. *Basic authentication* is a method for password-protecting your Web documents and images and usually is used to protect static files, such as straight HTML files. However, you can certainly use basic authentication to password-protect your ColdFusion templates. Users will be prompted for their user names and passwords via a dialog box presented by the browser, as shown in Figure 18.1. You will not have control over the look or wording of the dialog box, which varies from browser to browser.

Basic authentication is not the focus of this chapter. However, it is a quick, easy way to put a password on a particular folder, individual files, or an entire Web site. It is usually best for situations in which you want to give the same type of access to everyone who has a password. With basic authentication, you don't need to write any ColdFusion code to control which users are allowed to see what. Depending on the Web server software you are using, the user names and passwords for each user might be kept in a text file, an LDAP server, an ODBC database, or some type of proprietary format.

Figure 18.1

Basic authentication prompts the user to log in using a standard dialog box.

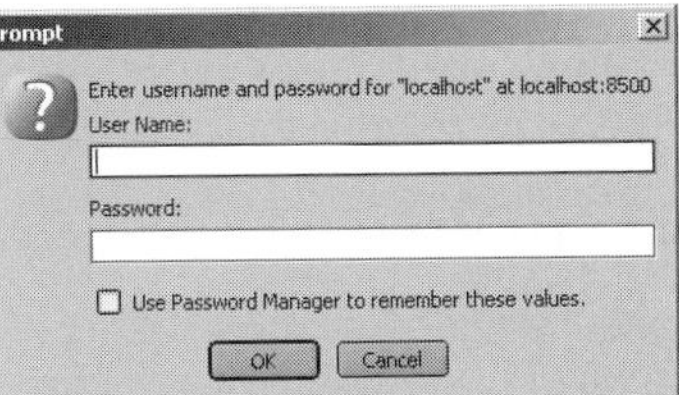

To find out how to enable basic authentication, see your Web server's documentation.

NOTE

One of the shortcomings of HTTP Basic Authentication is that the user's entries for username and password are sent to the server with every page request, and the password is not scrambled strongly. Therefore you may want to consider enabling SSL Encryption (discussed in the previous section) when using HTTP Basic Authentication, which will cause all communications between server and browser to be scrambled.

TIP

When basic authentication is used, you should be able to find out which user name was provided by examining either the `#CGI.AUTH_USER#` variable or the `#CGI.REMOTE_USER#` variable. The variable name depends on the Web server software you are using.

NOTE

Microsoft's Web servers and browsers extend the idea of basic authentication by providing a proprietary option called Integrated Windows Authentication (also referred to as *NTLM* or *Challenge/Response Authentication*), which enables people to access a Web server using their Windows user names and passwords. For purposes of this section, consider Windows Authentication to be in the same general category as basic authentication. That is, it is not covered specifically in this book and is enabled at the Web-server level.

Session-Based Security

The term *application-based security* is used here to cover any situation in which you give users an ordinary Web-based form with which to log in. Most often, this means using the same HTML form techniques you already know to present that form to the user, then using a database query to verify that the user name and password he typed was valid.

This method of security gives you the most control over the user experience, such as what the login page looks like, when it is presented, how long users remain logged in, and what they have access to. In other words, by creating a homegrown security or login process, you get to make it work however you need it to. The downside, of course, is that you must do a bit of extra work to figure out exactly what you need and how to get it done. That's what a large portion of this chapter is all about.

ColdFusion MX's New <CFLOGIN> Framework

ColdFusion MX provides a new set of tags and functions for creating login pages and generally enforcing rules about which of your application's pages can be used by whom. The new tags are `<CFLOGIN>`, `<CFLOGINUSER>`, and `<CFLOGOUT>`. For basic web applications, the new framework provides the same kind of user experience as Session-Based security. The main purpose of the new framework is to make it easier to secure more advanced applications that make use of ColdFusion Components and Flash Remoting.

➜ For details and examples, see the "Using ColdFusion's New <CFLOGIN> Framework," later in this chapter.

ColdFusion Resource Security

ColdFusion MX also provides a new set of features called Resource Security (also called Sandbox Security), which takes the place of the Advanced Security system present in previous versions of ColdFusion. Advanced Security attempted to provide a unified system that could be used internally by CFML developers in their applications, and also by hosting companies needing to be able to turn off certain parts of ColdFusion for individual developers. It included the `<CFAUTHENTICATE>` and `<CFIMPERSONATE>` tags, and a number of specialized CFML functions. Many people complained that this system, while very powerful, was too complex.

Aimed mostly at Internet Service Providers and hosting companies, the new Resource Security system in ColdFusion MX is simpler, while still remaining flexible and powerful. It is now possible to use the ColdFusion Administrator to designate which data sources, CFML tags, and other server resources can be used by which applications. For instance, if a single ColdFusion server is being used by several different developers, they can each feel confident that the other developers will not be able to access the data in their data sources. Also, if an ISP doesn't want developers to be able to create or read files on the server itself via the `<CFFILE>` tag (discussed in Chapter 33, "Interacting with the Operating System"), it's easy for the ISP to disallow the use of `<CFFILE>` while still allowing developers to use the rest of CFML's functionality.

➜ Because it is designed primarily for ISPs and hosting companies that administer ColdFusion servers, Resource Security is not covered in detail in this book. If you have an interest in what the Resource Security system can allow and disallow, please refer to the ColdFusion MX documentation, the online help for the Sandbox Security page in the ColdFusion Administrator, or our companion volume, *Advanced ColdFusion MX Application Development* (Macromedia Press, ISBN 0-321-12710-2).

Using ColdFusion to Control Access

The remainder of this chapter discusses how to build your own form-based security mechanism. In general, putting such a mechanism in place requires three basic steps:

- Deciding which pages or information should be password-protected
- Creating a login page and verifying the user name and password
- Restricting access to pages or information based on who the user is, either using a homegrown Session-Based mechanism, or with the new `<CFLOGIN>` framework.

Deciding What to Protect

Your first step is to decide exactly what it is you are trying to protect with your security measures. Of course, this step doesn't involve writing any code, but we strongly recommend that you think about this as thoroughly as possible. You should spend some time just working through what type of security measures your applications need and how users will gain access.

Be sure you have answers to these questions:

- Does the whole application need to be secured, or just a portion of it? For company intranets, you usually want to secure the whole application. For Internet sites available to the general public, you usually want to secure only certain sections (Members Only or Registered Users areas, for instance).
- What granularity of access do you need? Some applications need to lock only certain people out of particular folders or pages. Others need to lock people out at a more precise, data-aware level. For instance, if you are creating some type of Manage Your Account page, you aren't trying to keep a registered user out of the page. Instead, you need to ensure that the users see and change only their own account information.
- When should the user be asked for her user name and password? When she first enters your application, or only when she tries to get something that requires it? The former might make the security seem more cohesive to the user, whereas the latter might be more user friendly.

We also recommend that you put some thought into the following questions. These have to do with how passwords will be maintained, rather than what they will protect:

- Should user names and passwords become invalid after a period of time? For instance, if a user has purchased a 30-day membership to your site, what happens on the 31st day?
- Does the user need the option of voluntarily changing her password? What about her user name?
- Should some users be able to log in only from certain IP addresses? Or during certain times of the day, or days of the week?
- How will user names and passwords be managed? Do you need to implement some form of user groups, such as users in an operating system? Do you need to be able to grant rights to view certain items on a group level? What about on an individual user level?

The answers to these questions will help you create whatever database tables or other validation mechanics will be necessary to implement the security policies you have envisioned. You will learn where and when to refer to any such custom tables as you work through the code examples in this chapter.

Using Session Variables for Authentication

An effective and straightforward method for handling the mechanics of user logins is outlined in the following section. Basically, the strategy is to turn on ColdFusion's session-management features, which you learned about in Chapter 17, "Working with Sessions," and use session variables to track whether each user has logged in. There are many ways to go about this, but it can be as simple as setting a single variable in the SESSION scope after a user logs in.

NOTE

Before you can use the SESSION scope in your applications, you need to enable it using the <CFAPPLICATION> tag. See Chapter 17 for details.

Checking and Maintaining Login Status

For instance, assume for the moment that the user has just filled out a user name/password form (more on that later), and you have verified that the user name and password are correct. You could then use a line such as the following to remember that the user is logged in:

```
<CFSET SESSION.IsLoggedIn = "Yes">
```

As you learned in the last chapter, the IsLoggedIn variable is tracked for the rest of the user's visit (until his session times out). From this point forward, if you wanted to ensure that the user was logged in before he was shown something, all you would need to do would be to check for the presence of the variable:

```
<CFIF NOT IsDefined("SESSION.IsLoggedIn")>
  Sorry, you don't have permission to look at that.
  <CFABORT>
</CFIF>
```

And with that, you have modest security. Clearly, this isn't final code yet, but that really is the basic idea. A user will not be able to get past the second snippet unless his session has already encountered the first. The rest of the examples in this chapter are just expanded variations on these two code snippets.

So, all you have to do is put these two lines in the correct places. The first line must be wrapped within whatever code validates a user's password (probably by checking in some type of database table), and the second line must be put on whatever pages you need to protect.

Restricting Access to Your Application

Assume for the moment that you want to require your users to log in as soon as they enter your application. You could put a login form on your application's front page or home page, but what if a user doesn't go through that page for whatever reason? For instance, if he uses a bookmark or types the URL for some other page, he would bypass your login screen. So, you need to figure out a way to ensure that the user gets prompted for a password on the first page request for each session, regardless of which page he actually is asking for.

A great solution is to use the special Application.cfm file set aside by ColdFusion's Web application framework, which you learned about in Chapter 16, "Introducing the Web Application Framework." You will recall that if you create a template called Application.cfm, it automatically is included before each page request. This means you could put some code in Application.cfm to see whether the SESSION scope is holding an IsLoggedIn value, as discussed previously. If it's not holding a value, the user must be presented with a login form. If it is holding a value, the user has already logged in during the current session.

With that in mind, take a look at the Application.cfm file shown in Listing 18.1. Make sure to save this listing as Application.cfm, not Application1.cfm.

Listing 18.1 Application1.cfm—Sending a User to a Login Page if Not Logged In

```
<!---
  Filename:     Application.cfm
  Created by:   Nate Weiss (NMW)
  Please Note:  Executes for every page request
--->

<!--- Any variables set here can be used by all our pages --->
<CFSET DataSource  = "ows">
<CFSET CompanyName = "Orange Whip Studios">

<!--- Name our app, and enable Session variables --->
<CFAPPLICATION
  NAME="OrangeWhipSite"
  SESSIONMANAGEMENT="Yes">

<!--- If user is not logged in, force them to now --->
<CFIF NOT IsDefined("SESSION.Auth.IsLoggedIn")>
  <!--- If the user is now submitting "Login" form, --->
  <!--- Include "Login Check" code to validate user --->
  <CFIF IsDefined("Form.UserLogin")>
    <CFINCLUDE TEMPLATE="LoginCheck.cfm">
  </CFIF>

  <CFINCLUDE TEMPLATE="LoginForm.cfm">
  <CFABORT>
</CFIF>
```

First, session variables are enabled using the <CFAPPLICATION> tag. Then, an IsDefined() test is used to check whether the IsLoggedIn value is present. If it's not, a <CFINCLUDE> tag is used to include the template called LoginForm.cfm, which presents a login screen to the user. Note that a <CFABORT> tag is placed directly after the <CFINCLUDE> so that nothing further is presented.

The net effect is that all pages in your application have now been locked down and will never appear until you create code that sets the SESSION.Auth.IsLoggedIn value.

NOTE

Soon, you will see how the Auth structure can be used to hold other values relevant to the user's login status. If you do not need to track any additional information along with the login status, you could use a variable named SESSION.IsLoggedIn instead of SESSION.Auth.IsLoggedIn. However, it's not much extra work to add the Auth structure, and it gives you some extra flexibility.

Creating a Login Page

The next step is to create a login page, where the user can enter her user name and password. The code in Listing 18.1 is a simple example. Of course, this code still doesn't actually do anything when submitted, but it's helpful to see that most login pages are built with ordinary <FORM> or <CFFORM> code. Nearly all login pages are some variation of this skeleton.

Figure 18.2 shows what the form will look like to a user.

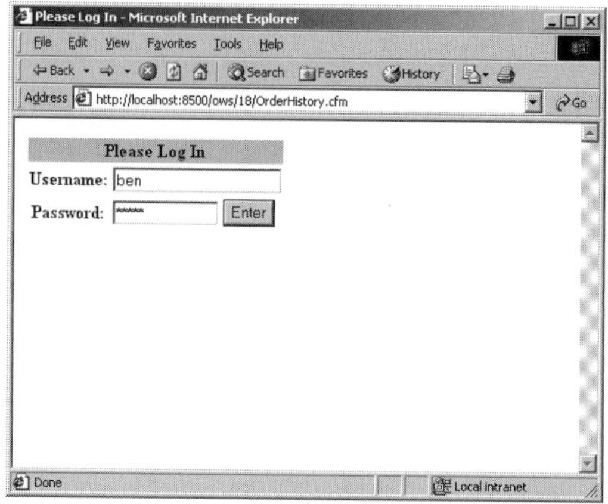

Figure 18.2

Users are forced to log in before they can access sensitive information in this application.

NOTE

Use `TYPE="Password"` wherever you ask your users to type a password, as shown in Listing 18.2. That way, as the user types, her password will be masked so that someone looking over her shoulder can't see her password.

Listing 18.2 `LoginForm.cfm`—A Basic Login Page

```
<!---
  Filename:     LoginForm.cfm
  Created by:   Nate Weiss (NMW)
  Purpose:      Presented whenever a user has not logged in yet
  Please Note:  Included by Application.cfm
--->

<!--- If the user is now submitting "Login" form, --->
<!--- Include "Login Check" code to validate user --->
<CFIF IsDefined("Form.UserLogin")>
  <CFINCLUDE TEMPLATE="LoginCheck.cfm">
</CFIF>



<HTML>
<HEAD>
  <TITLE>Please Log In</TITLE>
</HEAD>

<!--- Place cursor in "User Name" field when page loads--->
<BODY onLoad="document.LoginForm.UserLogin.focus();">

<!--- Start our Login Form --->
<CFFORM ACTION="#CGI.SCRIPT_NAME#" NAME="LoginForm" METHOD="POST">
  <!--- Make the UserLogin and UserPassword fields required --->
  <INPUT TYPE="Hidden" NAME="UserLogin_required">
  <INPUT TYPE="Hidden" NAME="UserPassword_required">
```

Listing 18.2 (continued)

```
<!--- Use an HTML table for simple formatting --->
<TABLE BORDER="0">
  <TR><TH COLSPAN="2" BGCOLOR="Silver">Please Log In</TH></TR>
  <TR>
    <TH>Username:</TH>
    <TD>

    <!--- Text field for "User Name" --->
    <CFINPUT
      TYPE="Text"
      NAME="UserLogin"
      SIZE="20"
      VALUE=""
      MAXLENGTH="100"
      REQUIRED="Yes"
      MESSAGE="Please type your Username first.">

    </TD>
  </TR><TR>
    <TH>Password:</TH>
    <TD>

    <!--- Text field for Password --->
    <CFINPUT
      TYPE="Password"
      NAME="UserPassword"
      SIZE="12"
      VALUE=""
      MAXLENGTH="100"
      REQUIRED="Yes"
      MESSAGE="Please type your Password first.">

    <!--- Submit Button that reads "Enter" --->
    <INPUT TYPE="Submit" VALUE="Enter">

    </TD>
  </TR>
</TABLE>

</CFFORM>

</BODY>
</HTML>
```

NOTE

In general, users will not be visiting `LoginForm.cfm` directly. Instead, the code in Listing 18.2 is included by the `<CFIF>` test performed in the `Application.cfm` page (Listing 18.1) the first time the user accesses some other page in the application (such as the `OrderHistory.cfm` template shown in Listing 18.4).

Please note that this form's `ACTION` attribute is set to `#CGI.SCRIPT_NAME#`. The special `CGI.SCRIPT_NAME` variable always holds the relative URL to the currently executing ColdFusion template. So, for example, if the user is being presented with the login form after requesting a template called `HomePage.cfm`, this form will rerequest that same page when submitted. In other words, this form always submits back to the URL of the page on which it is appearing.

TIP

Using `CGI.SCRIPT_NAME` can come in handyanytime your code needs to be capable of reloading or resubmitting the currently executing template.

➜ See Appendix D, "Special ColdFusion Variables and Result Codes," for details.

When the form is actually submitted, the `Form.UserLogin` value will exist, indicating that the user has typed a user name and password that should be checked for accuracy. As a result, the `<CFINCLUDE>` tag fires, and includes the password-validation code in the `LoginCheck.cfm` template (see Listing 18.3).

The Text and Password fields on this form use the `REQUIRED` and `MESSAGE` client-side validation attributes provided by `<CFINPUT>` and `<CFFORM>`. The two `Hidden` fields add server-side validation. See Chapter 12, "Form Data Validation," if you need to review these form field validation techniques.

NOTE

This template's `<BODY>` tag has JavaScript code in its `onLoad` attribute, which causes the cursor to be placed in the `UserLogin` field when the page loads. You must consult a different reference for a full discussion of JavaScript, but you can use this same basic technique to cause any form element to have focus when a page first loads.

TIP

JavaScript is case sensitive, so the `onLoad` code must be capitalized correctly; otherwise, scripting-error messages will pop up in the browser. Of course, you can just leave out the `onLoad` code altogether if you want.

Verifying the Login Name and Password

Listing 18.3 provides simple code for your `LoginCheck.cfm` template. This is the template that will be included when the user attempts to gain access by submitting the login form from Listing 18.2.

The most important line in this template is the `<CFSET>` line that sets the `SESSION.Auth.IsLoggedIn` variable to `Yes`. After this value is set for the session, the `IsDefined()` test in the `Application.cfm` file (refer to Listing 18.1) will succeed and the user will be able to view pages normally.

Listing 18.3 `LoginCheck.cfm`—Granting Access When the User Name and Password Are Correct

```
<!---
  Filename:     LoginCheck.cfm
  Created by:   Nate Weiss (NMW)
  Purpose:      Validates a user's password entries
  Please Note:  Included by LoginForm.cfm
--->


<!--- Make sure we have Login name and Password --->
<CFPARAM NAME="Form.UserLogin" TYPE="string">
<CFPARAM NAME="Form.UserPassword" TYPE="string">

<!--- Find record with this Username/Password --->
<!--- If no rows returned, password not valid --->
<CFQUERY NAME="GetUser" DATASOURCE="#DataSource#">
```

Listing 18.3 (continued)

```
    SELECT ContactID, FirstName
     FROM Contacts
     WHERE UserLogin    = '#Form.UserLogin#'
       AND UserPassword = '#Form.UserPassword#'
  </CFQUERY>

  <!--- If the username and password are correct --->
  <CFIF GetUser.RecordCount EQ 1>
    <!--- Remember user's logged-in status, plus --->
    <!--- ContactID and First Name, in structure --->
    <CFSET SESSION.Auth = StructNew()>
    <CFSET SESSION.Auth.IsLoggedIn = "Yes">
    <CFSET SESSION.Auth.ContactID  = GetUser.ContactID>
    <CFSET SESSION.Auth.FirstName  = GetUser.FirstName>

    <!--- Now that user is logged in, send them --->
    <!--- to whatever page makes sense to start --->
    <CFLOCATION URL="#CGI.SCRIPT_NAME#">
  </CFIF>
```

TIP

The query in this template can be adapted or replaced with any type of database or lookup procedure you need. For instance, rather than looking in a database table, you could query an LDAP server to get the user's first name.

→ For more information about LDAP, see the `<CFLDAP>` tag in Appendix B, or consult our companion volume, *Advanced ColdFusion MX Application Development*.

First, the two `<CFPARAM>` tags ensure that the login name and password are indeed available as form fields, which they should be unless a user has somehow been directed to this page in error. Next, a simple `<CFQUERY>` tag attempts to retrieve a record from the `Contacts` table where the `UserLogin` and `UserPassword` columns match the user name and password that were entered in the login form. If this query returns a record, the user has, by definition, entered a valid user name and password and thus should be considered logged in.

Assume for the moment that the user name and password are correct. The value of `GetUser.RecordCount` is therefore `1`, so the code inside the `<CFIF>` block executes. A new structure called `Auth` is created in the `SESSION` scope, and three values are placed within the new structure. The most important of the three is the `IsLoggedIn` value, which is used here basically in the same way that was outlined in the original code snippets near the beginning of this chapter.

The user's unique ID number (his `ContactID`) is also placed in the `SESSION.Auth` structure, as is his first name. The idea here is to populate the `SESSION.Auth` structure with whatever information is pertinent to the fact that the user has indeed been authenticated. Therefore, any little bits of information that might be helpful to have later in the user's session can be saved in the `Auth` structure now.

TIP

By keeping the `SESSION.Auth.FirstName` value, for instance, you will be able to display the user's first name on any page, which will give your application a friendly, personalized feel. And, by keeping the `SESSION.Auth.ContactID` value, you will be able to run queries against the database based on the user's authenticated ID number.

Finally, the `<CFLOCATION>` tag is used to redirect the user to the current value of `CGI.SCRIPT_NAME`. Because `CGI.SCRIPT_NAME` also was used for the `ACTION` of the login form, this value will still reflect the page for which the user was originally looking, before the login form appeared. The browser will respond by rerequesting the original page. This time, the `SESSION.Auth.IsLoggedIn` test in `Application.cfm` (refer to Listing 18.1) will not `<CFINCLUDE>` the login form, and the user will thus be allowed to see the content he originally was looking for.

NOTE

The underlying assumption here is that no two users can have the same `UserLogin` and `UserPassword`. You must ensure that this rule is enforced in your application. For instance, when a user first chooses (or is assigned) his user name and password, there needs to be a check in place to ensure that nobody else already has them.

Personalizing Based on Login

After Listings 18.1–18.3 are in place, the `SESSION.Auth` structure is guaranteed to exist for all your application's pages. What's more, the user's unique ID and first name will be available as `SESSION.Auth.ContactID` and `SESSION.Auth.FirstName`, respectively. This makes providing users with personalized pages, such as Manage My Account or My Order History, easy.

Listing 18.4 shows a template called `OrderHistory.cfm`, which enables a user to review the merchandise orders she has placed in the past. Because the authenticated `ContactID` is readily available, getting this done in a reasonably secure fashion is easy. In most respects, this is just a data-display template, the likes of which you learned about in Chapter 10, "Creating Data-Driven Pages." The only new concept here is the notion of using authenticated identification information from the `SESSION` scope (in this case, the `ContactID`).

Listing 18.4 `OrderHistory.cfm`—Personalizing Content Based on Login

```
<!---
  Filename:     OrderHistory.cfm
  Created by:   Nate Weiss (NMW)
  Purpose:      Displays a user's order history
--->

<!--- Retrieve user's orders, based on ContactID --->
<CFQUERY NAME="GetOrders" DATASOURCE="#DataSource#">
  SELECT OrderID, OrderDate,
    (SELECT Count(*)
     FROM MerchandiseOrdersItems oi
     WHERE oi.OrderID = o.OrderID) AS ItemCount
  FROM MerchandiseOrders o
  WHERE ContactID = #SESSION.Auth.ContactID#
  ORDER BY OrderDate DESC
</CFQUERY>

<HTML>
<HEAD>
  <TITLE>Your Order History</TITLE>
</HEAD>
<BODY>
```

Listing 18.4 (continued)

```
<!--- Personalized message at top of page--->
<CFOUTPUT>
  <h2>Your Order History</h2>
  <P><B>Welcome back, #SESSION.Auth.FirstName#</B>!<BR>
  You have placed <B>#GetOrders.RecordCount#</B>
  orders with us to date.</P>
</CFOUTPUT>


<!--- Display orders in a simple HTML table --->
<TABLE BORDER="1" WIDTH="300" CELLPADDING="5" CELLSPACING="2">
  <!--- Column headers --->
  <TR>
    <TH>Date Ordered</TH>
    <TH>Items</TH>
  </TR>

  <!--- Display each order as a table row --->
  <CFOUTPUT QUERY="GetOrders">
    <TR>
      <TD>
        <A HREF="OrderHistory.cfm?OrderID=#OrderID#">
          #DateFormat(OrderDate, "mmmm d, yyyy")#
        </A>
      </TD>
      <TD>
        <B>#ItemCount#</B>
      </TD>
    </TR>
  </CFOUTPUT>
</TABLE>

</BODY>
</HTML>
```

First, a fairly ordinary `<CFQUERY>` tag is used to retrieve information about the orders the user has placed. Because the user's authenticated `ContactID` is being used in the `WHERE` clause, you can be certain that you will be retrieving the order information appropriate only for this user.

Next, a personalized message is displayed to the user, including her first name. Then the order records are displayed using an ordinary `<CFOUTPUT QUERY>` block. The order records are displayed in a simple tabular format using simple HTML table formatting. Figure 18.3 shows what the results will look like for the end user.

Being Careful with Passed Parameters

When you are dealing with sensitive information, such as account or purchase histories, you need to be more careful when passing parameters from page to page. It's easy to let yourself feel that your work is done after you force your users to log in. Of course, forcing them to log in is an important step, but your code still needs to check things internally before it exposes sensitive data.

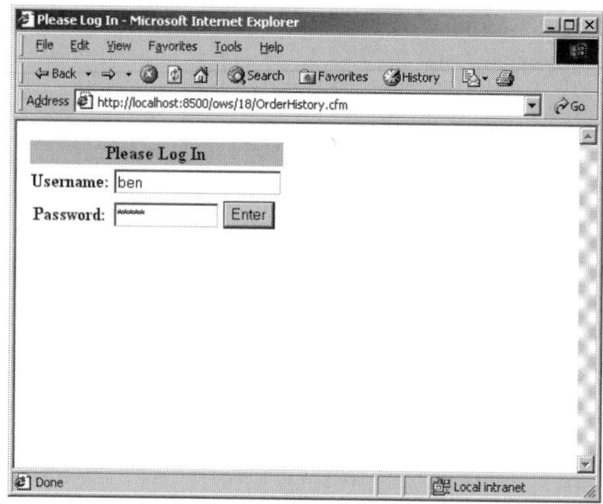

Figure 18.3

After a user's identification information is authenticated, providing a personalized experience is easy.

Recognizing the Problem

Here's a scenario that illustrates a potential vulnerability. After putting together the `OrderHistory.cfm` template shown in Listing 18.4, you realize that people will need to be able to see the details of each order, such as the individual items purchased. You decide to allow the user to click in each order's Order Date column to see the details of that order. You decide, sensibly, to turn each order's date into a link that passes the desired order's ID number as a URL parameter.

So, you decide to change this:

```
#DateFormat(OrderDate, "mmmm d, yyyy")#
```

to this:

```
<A HREF="OrderHistory.cfm?OrderID=#OrderID#">
  #DateFormat(OrderDate, "mmmm d, yyyy")#
</A>
```

This is fine. When the user clicks the link, the same template is executed—this time with the desired order number available as `URL.OrderID`. You just need to add an `IsDefined()` check to see whether the URL parameter exists, and if so, run a second query to obtain the detail records (item name, price, and quantity) for the desired order. After a bit of thought, you come up with the following:

```
<CFIF IsDefined("URL.OrderID")>
  <CFQUERY NAME="GetDetail" DATASOURCE="#DataSource#">
    SELECT m.MerchName, oi.ItemPrice, oi.OrderQty
    FROM Merchandise m, MerchandiseOrdersItems oi
    WHERE m.MerchID = oi.ItemID
    AND oi.OrderID  = #URL.OrderID#
  </CFQUERY>
</CFIF>
```

The problem with this code is that it doesn't ensure that the order number passed in the URL indeed belongs to the user. After the user notices that the order number is being passed in the URL, he might try to play around with the passed parameters just to, ahem, see what happens. And, indeed, if the user changes the `?OrderID=5` part of the URL to, say, `?OrderID=10`, he will be able to see the details of some other person's order. Depending on what type of application you are building, this kind of vulnerability could be a huge problem.

Checking Passed Parameters

The problem is relatively easy to address. You just need to ensure that, whenever you retrieve sensitive information based on a URL or FORM parameter, you somehow verify that the parameter is one the user has the right to request. In this case, you must ensure that the URL.OrderID value is associated with the user's ID number, SESSION.Auth.ContactID.

In this application, the easiest policy to enforce is probably ensuring that each query involves the SESSION.Auth.ContactID value somewhere in its WHERE clause. Therefore, to turn the unsafe query shown previously into a safe one, you would add another subquery or inner join to the query, so the Orders table is directly involved. After the Orders table is involved, the query can include a check against its ContactID column.

A safe version of the snippet shown previously would be the following, which adds a subquery at the end to ensure the OrderID is a legitimate one for the current user:

```
<CFIF IsDefined("URL.OrderID")>
  <CFQUERY NAME="GetDetail" DATASOURCE="#DataSource#">
    SELECT m.MerchName, oi.ItemPrice, oi.OrderQty
    FROM Merchandise m, MerchandiseOrdersItems oi
    WHERE m.MerchID = oi.ItemID
    AND oi.OrderID  = #URL.OrderID#
    AND oi.OrderID IN
      (SELECT o.OrderID FROM MerchandiseOrders o
       WHERE o.ContactID = #SESSION.Auth.ContactID#)
  </CFQUERY>
</CFIF>
```

Another way to phrase the query, using an additional join, would be

```
<CFIF IsDefined("URL.OrderID")>
  <CFQUERY NAME="GetDetail" DATASOURCE="#DataSource#">
    SELECT
      m.MerchName, m.MerchPrice,
      oi.ItemPrice, oi.OrderQty
    FROM
    (Merchandise m INNER JOIN
    MerchandiseOrdersItems oi
      ON m.MerchID = oi.ItemID) INNER JOIN
    MerchandiseOrders o
      ON o.OrderID = oi.OrderID
    WHERE o.ContactID = #SESSION.Auth.ContactID#
      AND oi.OrderID  = #URL.OrderID#
  </CFQUERY>
</CFIF>
```

With either of these snippets, it doesn't matter if the user alters the OrderID in the URL. Because the ContactID is now part of the query's WHERE criteria, it will return zero records if the requested OrderID is not consistent with the session's authenticated ContactID. Thus, the user will never be able to view any orders but his own.

Putting It Together and Getting Interactive

The `OrderHistory2.cfm` template shown in Listing 18.5 builds on the previous version (refer to Listing 18.4) by adding the ability for the user to view details about each order. The code is a bit longer, but there really aren't any big surprises here. The main additions display the detail information. Some formatting has also been applied to make the template look nicer when displayed to the user.

Listing 18.5 `OrderHistory2.cfm`—Safely Providing Details About a User's Orders

```
<!---
  Filename:     OrderHistory2.cfm
  Created by:   Nate Weiss (NMW)
  Purpose:      Displays a user's order history
--->

<!--- Retrieve user's orders, based on ContactID --->
<CFQUERY NAME="GetOrders" DATASOURCE="#DataSource#">
  SELECT OrderID, OrderDate,
    (SELECT Count(*)
     FROM MerchandiseOrdersItems oi
     WHERE oi.OrderID = o.OrderID) AS ItemCount
  FROM MerchandiseOrders o
  WHERE ContactID = #SESSION.Auth.ContactID#
  ORDER BY OrderDate DESC
</CFQUERY>

<!--- Determine if a numeric OrderID was passed in URL --->
<CFSET ShowDetail = IsDefined("URL.OrderID") AND IsNumeric(URL.OrderID)>

<!--- If an OrderID was passed, get details for the order --->
<!--- Query must check against ContactID for security --->
<CFIF ShowDetail>
  <CFQUERY NAME="GetDetail" DATASOURCE="#DataSource#">
    SELECT m.MerchName, oi.ItemPrice, oi.OrderQty
    FROM Merchandise m, MerchandiseOrdersItems oi
    WHERE m.MerchID = oi.ItemID
    AND oi.OrderID  = #URL.OrderID#
    AND oi.OrderID IN
      (SELECT o.OrderID FROM MerchandiseOrders o
       WHERE o.ContactID = #SESSION.Auth.ContactID#)
  </CFQUERY>

  <!--- If no Detail records, don't show detail --->
  <!--- User may be trying to "hack" URL parameters --->
  <CFIF GetDetail.RecordCount EQ 0>
    <CFSET ShowDetail = False>
  </CFIF>
</CFIF>


<HTML>
<HEAD>
  <TITLE>Your Order History</TITLE>

  <!--- Apply some simple CSS style formatting --->
  <STYLE TYPE="text/css">
```

Listing 18.5 (continued)

```
    BODY {font-family:sans-serif;font-size:12px;color:navy}
    H2   {font-size:20px}
    TH   {font-family:sans-serif;font-size:12px;color:white;
          background:MediumBlue;text-align:left}
    TD   {font-family:sans-serif;font-size:12px}
  </STYLE>
</HEAD>
<BODY>

<!--- Personalized message at top of page--->
<CFOUTPUT>
  <h2>Your Order History</h2>
  <P><B>Welcome back, #SESSION.Auth.FirstName#</B>!<BR>
  You have placed <B>#GetOrders.RecordCount#</B>
  orders with us to date.</P>
</CFOUTPUT>


<!--- Display orders in a simple HTML table --->
<TABLE BORDER="1" WIDTH="300" CELLPADDING="5" CELLSPACING="2">
  <!--- Column headers --->
  <TR>
    <TH>Date Ordered</TH>
    <TH>Items</TH>
  </TR>

  <!--- Display each order as a table row --->
  <CFOUTPUT QUERY="GetOrders">
    <!--- Determine whether to show details for this order --->
    <!--- Show Down arrow if expanded, otherwise Right --->
    <CFSET IsExpanded = ShowDetail AND (GetOrders.OrderID EQ URL.OrderID)>
    <CFSET ArrowIcon  = IIF(IsExpanded, "'ArrowDown.gif'", "'ArrowRight.gif'")>

    <TR>
      <TD>
        <!--- Link to show order details, with arrow icon --->
        <A HREF="OrderHistory2.cfm?OrderID=#OrderID#">
          <IMG SRC="../images/#ArrowIcon#" WIDTH="16" HEIGHT="16" BORDER="0">
          #DateFormat(OrderDate, "mmmm d, yyyy")#
        </A>
      </TD>
      <TD>
        <B>#ItemCount#</B>
      </TD>
    </TR>

    <!--- Show details for this order, if appropriate --->
    <CFIF IsExpanded>
      <CFSET OrderTotal = 0>
      <TR>
        <TD COLSPAN="2">

          <!--- Show details within nested table --->
          <TABLE WIDTH="100%" CELLSPACING="0" BORDER="0">
            <!--- Nested table's column headers --->
```

Listing 18.5 (continued)

```
          <TR>
            <TH>Item</TH><TH>Qty</TH><TH>Price</TH>
          </TR>

          <!--- Show each ordered item as a table row --->
          <CFLOOP QUERY="GetDetail">
            <CFSET OrderTotal = OrderTotal + ItemPrice>
            <TR>
              <TD>#MerchName#</TD>
              <TD>#OrderQty#</TD>
              <TD>#DollarFormat(ItemPrice)#</TD>
            </TR>
          </CFLOOP>

          <!--- Last row in nested table for total --->
          <TR>
            <TD COLSPAN="2"><B>Total:</B></TD>
            <TD><B>#DollarFormat(OrderTotal)#</B></TD>
          </TR>
        </TABLE>
      </TD>
    </TR>
  </CFIF>
 </CFOUTPUT>
</TABLE>

</BODY>
</HTML>
```

The first `<CFQUERY>` is unchanged from Listing 18.4. Next, a Boolean variable called `ShowDetail` is created. Its value is `True` if a number is passed as `URL.OrderID`. In that case, the second `<CFQUERY>` (which was shown in the code snippet before the listing) executes and returns only detail records for the session's `ContactID`. The `<CFIF>` test after the query resets `ShowDetail` to `False` if the second query fails to return any records. The remainder of the code can rely on `ShowDetail` being `True` only if a legitimate `OrderID` was passed in the URL.

Two `<CFSET>` tags have been added at the top of the main `<CFOUTPUT>` block to determine whether the `OrderID` of the order currently being output is the same as the `OrderID` passed in the URL. If so, the `IsExpanded` variable is set to `True`. Additionally, an `ArrowIcon` variable is created, which is used to display an open or closed icon to indicate whether each order record is expanded. If the current order is the one the user has asked for details about, `IsExpanded` is `True` and `ArrowIcon` is set to show the `ArrowDown.gif` image. If not, the `ArrowRight.gif` image is shown instead. The appropriate arrow is displayed using an `<IMG>` tag a few lines later.

At the end of the template is a large `<CFIF>` block, which causes order details to be shown if `IsExpanded` is `True`. If so, an additional row is added to the main HTML table, with a `COLSPAN` of `2` so that the new row has just one cell spanning the `Date Ordered` and `Items` columns. Within the new cell, another, nested `<TABLE>` is added, which shows one row for each record in the `GetDetail` query via a `<CFLOOP>` block. As each detail row is output, the `OrderTotal` variable is incremented by the price of each item. Therefore, by the time the `<CFLOOP>` is finished, `OrderTotal` will indeed contain the total amount the customer paid. The total is displayed as the last row of the nested table.

The result is a pleasant-looking interface in which the user can quickly see the details for each order. At first, only the order dates and item counts are displayed (as shown previously in Figure 18.3), with an arrow pointing to the right to indicate that the order is not expanded. If the user clicks the arrow or the order date, the page is reloaded, now with the arrow pointing down and the order details nested under the date. Figure 18.4 shows the results.

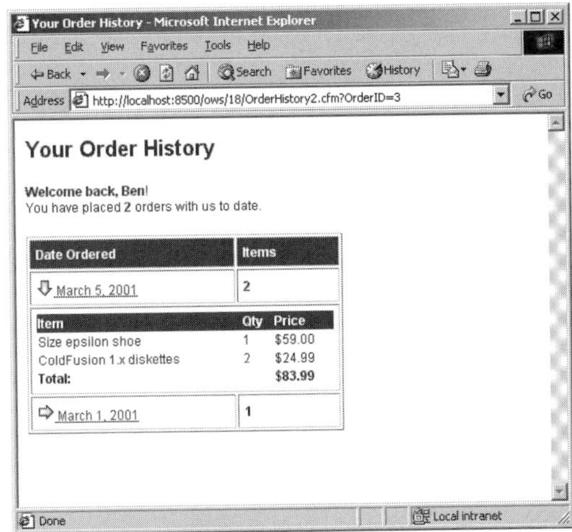

Figure 18.4
With a little bit of caution, you can safely provide an interactive interface for sensitive information.

NOTE

A `<STYLE>` block is included in the `<HEAD>` section of this listing to apply some CSS-based formatting. All type on the page will be shown in a blue, sans serif font (usually Arial or Helvetica, depending on the operating system), except for `<TH>` cells, which will be shown with white type on a blue background. Consult a CSS reference for details.

Other Scenarios

This chapter has outlined a usable way to force a user to log in to your application and to show her only the appropriate information. Of course, your actual needs are likely to vary somewhat from what has been discussed here. Here are a couple of other scenarios that are commonly encountered, with suggestions about how to tackle them.

Delaying the Login Until Necessary

The examples in this chapter assume that the entire application needs to be secured and that each user should be forced to log in when she first visits any of your application's pages. If, however, only a few pages need to be secured here and there, you might want to delay the login step until the user actually requests something of a sensitive nature. For instance, it might be that the user doesn't need to log in unless she tries to visit pages such as Manage My Account or My Order History. For all other pages, no security measures are necessary.

To get this effect, you could move the `IsDefined("SESSION.Auth.IsLoggedIn")` check from `Application.cfm` (refer to Listing 18.1) to a new template called `ForceLogin.cfm`. Then, at the top of any page that requires a password, you could put a `<CFINCLUDE>` tag with a `TEMPLATE="ForceLogin.cfm"` attribute. This is a simple but effective way to enforce application security only where it's needed.

Implementing Different Access Levels

This chapter has focused on the problems of forcing users to log in and using the login information to safely provide sensitive information. Once logged in, each user is treated equally in this chapter's examples. Each user simply has the right to see his own data.

If you are building a complex application that needs to allow certain users to do more than others, you might need to create some type of access right or permission or user level. This need is most commonly encountered in intranet applications, in which executives need to be able to view report pages that most employees cannot see, or in which only certain high-level managers can review the performance files of other employees.

It might be that all you need is to add another column somewhere to tell you which type of user each person is. For the Orange Whip Studios example, this might mean adding a new Yes/No column called `IsPrivileged` to the `Contacts` table. The idea is that if this column is set to `true`, the user should get access to certain special things that others do not have. Then, in `LoginCheck.cfm` (refer to Listing 18.3), select this new column along with the `ContactID` and `FirstName` columns in the `<CFQUERY>`, and add a line that saves the `IsPrivileged` value in the `SESSION.Auth` structure, such as this:

```
<CFSET SESSION.Auth.IsPrivileged = GetUser.IsPrivileged>
```

TIP

For an intranet application, you might use a column called `IsSupervisor` or `IsAdministrator` instead of `IsPrivileged`.

Now, whenever you need to determine whether something that requires special privileges should be shown, you could use a simple `<CFIF>` test, such as

```
<CFIF SESSION.Auth.IsPrivileged>
  <A HREF="SalesData.cfm">Sacred Sales Data</A>
</CFIF>
```

Or, instead of a simple Yes/No column, you might have a numeric column named `UserLevel` and save it in the `SESSION.Auth` structure in `LoginCheck.cfm`. This would give you an easy way to set up various access levels, where `1` might be used for normal employees, `2` for supervisors, `3` for managers, `4` for executives, and `100` for developers. So, if only security level `3` and above should be able to view a page, you could use something similar to this:

```
<CFIF SESSION.Auth.UserLevel LT 3>
  Access denied!
  <CFABORT>
</CFIF>
```

Access Rights, Users, and Groups

Depending on the application, you might need something more sophisticated than what is suggested in the previous code snippets. If so, you may want to consider creating database tables to represent some notion of access rights, users, and groups. A typical implementation would establish a many-to-many relationship between users and groups, so that a user can be in more than one group, each group with any number of users. In addition, a one-to-many relationship generally would exist between groups and access rights. Tables with names such as `GroupsUsers` and `GroupsRights` would maintain the relationships.

After the tables were in place, you could adapt the code examples in this chapter to enforce the rules established by the tables. For instance, assuming that you had a table called `Rights`, which had columns named `RightID` and `RightName`, you might put a query similar to the following after the `GetUser` query in `LoginCheck.cfm` (refer to Listing 18.3):

```
<!--- Find what rights user has from group membership --->
<CFQUERY NAME="GetRights" DATASOURCE="#DataSource#">
  SELECT r.RightName
  FROM Rights r, GroupsContacts gu, GroupsRights gr
  WHERE r.RightID    = gr.RightID
    AND gu.GroupID   = gr.GroupID
    AND gu.ContactID = #SESSION.Auth.ContactID#
</CFQUERY>

<!--- Save comma-separated list of rights in SESSION --->
<CFSET SESSION.Auth.RightsList = ValueList(GetRights.RightName)>
```

Now, `SESSION.Auth.RightsList` would be a list of string values that represented the rights the user should be granted. The user is being granted these rights because the rights have been granted to the groups she is in.

After the previous code is in place, code such as the following could be used to find out whether a particular user is allowed to do something, based on the rights she has actually been granted:

```
<CFIF ListFind(SESSION.Auth.RightsList, "SalesAdmin">
  <A HREF="SalesData.cfm">Sacred Sales Data</A>
</CFIF>
```

or

```
<CFIF NOT ListFind(SESSION.Auth.RightsList, "SellCompany">
  Access denied.
  <CFABORT>
</CFIF>
```

NOTE

The `<CFLOGIN>` framework discussed in the next section provides the `IsUserInRole()` function, which is a similar way to implement security based on groups or rights. In particular, the `OrderHistory4.cfm` template shown in Listing 18.9 uses this function to provide different levels of access to different users.

Using ColdFusion's New <CFLOGIN> Framework

So far, this chapter has presented a simple session-based method for securing and personalizing an application, built on user names and passwords. Using the preceding examples as a foundation, you can easily create your own custom security framework. For the purposes of this section, let's call this type of security a *homegrown* security framework.

With ColdFusion MX, you also have the option of using a new security framework that ships as part of the CFML language itself. This new framework includes a few new tags; most important is the <CFLOGIN> tag, which you will learn about in this section. The ColdFusion MX documentation refers to the new framework as *user security*. For clarity, let's call it the <CFLOGIN> framework.

Because the new <CFLOGIN> framework can boast tight integration with the rest of the CFML language, you may want to use it to provide security for some applications. That said, you may want to stick to a homegrown approach for flexibility. In either case, you will probably end up writing approximately the same amount of code.

Table 18.1 shows some of the advantages and disadvantages of the <CFLOGIN> framework versus a homegrown framework.

NOTE

Note that one key advantage of the <CFLOGIN> framework is its integration with the ColdFusion Components (CFC) system, which is something you haven't learned about yet.

→ CFCs are covered in Chapter 20, "Building Reusable Components."

Table 18.1 Comparing the <CFLOGIN> framework with homegrown approaches

STRATEGY	ADVANTAGES	DISADVANTAGES
Homegrown Framework	Since you're writing it yourself, you know it will do what you need it to.	Easy to implement based on examples in this chapter. Not immediately recognizable by other developers. Not automatically recognized and enforced by CFCs.
<CFLOGIN> Framework	Part of ColdFusion itself, so other developers will understand the code and are likely to recognize it as a best practice. Tightly integrated with CFCs: You just tell the component which user groups (roles) may access each method.	While open and flexible, it is possible that it won't suit your particular needs. Still requires approximately the same amount of careful coding as the homegrown approach does.

Tags and Functions Provided by the <CFLOGIN> Framework

The <CFLOGIN> framework currently includes five CFML tags and functions, as shown in Table 18.2. You will see how these tags work together in a moment. For now, all you need is a quick sense of the tags and functions involved.

Table 18.2 CFLOGIN> and related tags and functions

TAG OR FUNCTION	PURPOSE
`<CFLOGIN>`	Indicates that a page requires users to log in before proceeding. This tag is always used in a pair. Between the opening and closing tags, you place whatever code is needed to determine whether the user should be able to proceed. In most situations, this means checking the validity of the user name and password being presented. You will often place this tag in `Application.cfm`.
`<CFLOGINUSER>`	Once the user has provided a valid user name and password, you use the `<CFLOGINUSER>` tag to tell ColdFusion that the user should now be considered logged in. This tag always appears within a pair of `<CFLOGIN>` tags. Like `<CFLOGIN>`, this tag will typically get called by `Application.cfm`.
`GetAuthUser()`	Once the user has logged in, you can use this function to retrieve or display the user's name, ID, or other identifying information.
`IsUserInRole()`	If you want different users to have different rights or privileges, you can use this function to determine whether they should be allowed to access a particular page or piece of information.
`<CFLOGOUT>`	If you want to provide a way for users to explicitly log out, just use the `<CFLOGOUT>` tag. Otherwise, users will be logged out when their sessions expire (or when they close their browser, if you are using J2EE sessions as discussed in Chapter 17).

Using <CFLOGIN> and <CFLOGINUSER>

The first thing you need to do is add the `<CFLOGIN>` and `<CFLOGINUSER>` tags to whatever parts of your application you want to protect. To keep things nice and clean, the examples in this chapter keep the `<CFLOGIN>` and `<CFLOGINUSER>` code in a separate ColdFusion template called `ForceUserLogin.cfm` (Listing 18.6).

Once a template like this is in place, you just need to include it via `<CFINCLUDE>` from any ColdFusion page that you want to password-protect. Of course, to protect an entire application, just place the `<CFINCLUDE>` into your `Application.cfm` template. Since it automatically executes for every page request, the `<CFLOGIN>` and related tags will be automatically protecting all of your application's pages.

Listing 18.6 `ForceUserLogin.cfm`—Using the `<CFLOGIN>` Framework

```
<!---
  Filename:      ForceUserLogin.cfm
  Created by:    Nate Weiss (NMW)
  Purpose:       Requires each user to log in
  Please Note:   Included by Application.cfm
--->


<!--- Force the user to log in --->
```

Listing 18.6 (continued)

```
<!--- *** This code only executes if the user has not logged in yet! *** --->
<!--- Once the user is logged in via <CFLOGINUSER>, this code is skipped --->
<CFLOGIN>

  <!--- If the user hasn't gotten the login form yet, display it --->
  <CFIF NOT (IsDefined("FORM.UserLogin") AND IsDefined("FORM.UserPassword"))>
    <CFINCLUDE TEMPLATE="UserLoginForm.cfm">
    <CFABORT>

  <!--- Otherwise, the user is submitting the login form --->
  <!--- This code decides whether the username and password are valid --->
  <CFELSE>

    <!--- Find record with this Username/Password --->
    <!--- If no rows returned, password not valid --->
    <CFQUERY NAME="GetUser" DATASOURCE="#DataSource#">
      SELECT ContactID, FirstName, UserRoleName
      FROM Contacts LEFT OUTER JOIN UserRoles
        ON Contacts.UserRoleID = UserRoles.UserRoleID
      WHERE UserLogin    = '#Form.UserLogin#'
        AND UserPassword = '#Form.UserPassword#'
    </CFQUERY>

    <!--- If the username and password are correct... --->
    <CFIF GetUser.RecordCount EQ 1>
      <!--- Tell ColdFusion to consider the user "logged in" --->
      <!--- For the NAME attribute, we will provide the user's --->
      <!--- ContactID number and first name, separated by commas --->
      <!--- Later, we can access the NAME value via GetAuthUser() --->
      <CFLOGINUSER
        NAME="#GetUser.ContactID#,#GetUser.FirstName#"
        PASSWORD="#FORM.UserPassword#"
        ROLES="#GetUser.UserRoleName#">

    <!--- Otherwise, re-prompt for a valid username and password --->
    <CFELSE>
      Sorry, that username and password are not recognized.
      Please try again.
      <CFINCLUDE TEMPLATE="UserLoginForm.cfm">
      <CFABORT>
    </CFIF>


  </CFIF>
</CFLOGIN>
```

NOTE

Note that this template is very similar conceptually to the homegrown `LoginCheck.cfm` template discussed earlier (see Listing 18.3). The logic still centers around the `GetUser` query, which checks the user name and password that have been provided. It just remembers each user's login status using `<CFLOGIN>` and `<CFLOGINUSER>`, rather than the homegrown `SESSION.Auth` structure.

NOTE

Whenever Listing 18.6 needs to display a login form to the user, it does so by including `UserLoginForm.cfm` with a `<CFINCLUDE>` tag. This login form is nearly identical to the one shown earlier in Listing 18.2; the main difference is that it takes advantage of two user-defined functions to preserve any `URL` and `FORM` variables that might be provided before the login form is encountered. The actual code for this version of the login form is included on the CD-ROM for this book; it is also discussed in Chapter 19, "Building User-Defined Functions."

The first thing to note is the pair of `<CFLOGIN>` tags. In most cases, the `<CFLOGIN>` tag can be used with no attributes to simply declare that a login is necessary (see the notes before Table 18.3 for information about `<CFLOGIN>`'s optional attributes). It is up to the code inside the `<CFLOGIN>` tag to do the work of collecting a user name and password, or forcing the user to log in. If she has already logged in, the code within the `<CFLOGIN>` block is skipped completely. The `<CFLOGIN>` code executes only if the user has yet to log in.

At the top of the `<CFLOGIN>` block, a simple `<CFIF>` test sees whether form fields named `UserLogin` and `UserPassword` have been provided. In other words, has the user been presented with a login form? If not, the login form is presented via a `<CFINCLUDE>` tag. Note that the `<CFABORT>` tag is needed to make sure that execution stops once the form is displayed.

Therefore, the code beginning with `<CFELSE>` executes only if the user has not yet successfully logged in and is currently attempting to log in with the login form. First, a simple `<CFQUERY>` tag is used to validate the user name and password. This is almost the same as the query used in Listing 18.3. The only difference is that this query also retrieves the name of the user's security role from the `UserRoles` table.

NOTE

For this example application, the security role is conceptually similar to that of a user group in an operating system; you can use the role to determine which users have access to what. For instance, those in the `Admin` security role might be able to do things other users cannot. You'll see how this works in the `OrderHistory4.cfm` template, later in this chapter.

TIP

You don't have to use database queries to validate users' credentials and retrieve their information. For instance, if you are storing this type of user information in an LDAP data store (such as one of the iPlanet server products, or Microsoft's Windows 2000, XP, or .NET systems), you could use the `<CFLDAP>` tag instead of `<CFQUERY>` to validate the user's security data. The ColdFusion MX documentation includes an example of using `<CFLDAP>` together with `<CFLOGIN>` and `<CFLOGINUSER>` in such a way.

If the user name and password are valid, the `<CFLOGINUSER>` tag tells ColdFusion that the user should now be considered logged in. If not, the login form is redisplayed. Table 18.3 shows the attributes `<CFLOGINUSER> supports.`

Take a look at how `<CFLOGINUSER>` is used in Listing 18.6. The purpose of the `NAME` attribute is to pass a value to ColdFusion that identifies the user in some way. The actual value of `NAME` can be whatever you want; ColdFusion retains the value for as long as the user is logged in. At any time, you can use the `GetAuthUser()` function to retrieve the value you passed to `NAME`. Because the various pages in the application need to have the user's `ContactID` and first name handy, they are passed to `NAME` as a simple comma-separated list.

NOTE

Behind the scenes, the <CFLOGIN> framework sets a cookie on the browser machine to remember that a user has been logged in. The cookie's name will start with CFAUTHORIZATION; the <CFLOGIN> tag supports two optional attributes that control how that cookie is set. The COOKIEDOMAIN attribute allows you to share the authorization cookie between servers in the same domain; it works like the DOMAIN attribute of the <CFCOOKIE> tag (as discussed in Chapter 17). The APPLICATIONTOKEN attribute can be used to share a user's login state among several applications; normally, this attribute defaults to the current application's name (which means that all pages that use the same NAME in their <CFAPPLICATION> tag will share login information), but if you provide a different value, then all <CFLOGIN> blocks that use the same APPLICATIONTOKEN will share the login information (creating a "single sign on" effect). See Appendix B for a complete list of <CFLOGIN> attributes.

TIP

The <CFLOGIN> tag supports an optional IDLETIMEOUT attribute which you can use to control how long a user remains logged in between page requests. The default value is 1800 seconds (30 minutes). If you want users to be considered logged out after just 5 minutes of inactivity, use IDLETIMEOUT="300". See Appendix B for a complete list of <CFLOGIN> attributes.

Table 18.3 CFLOGINUSER> Tag Attributes

ATTRIBUTE	PURPOSE
NAME	Required. Some kind of identifying string that should be remembered for as long as the user remains logged in. Whatever value you provide here will be available later via the GetAuthUser() function. It is important to note that the value you provide here does not actually need to be the user's name. It can contain any simple string information that you would like to be able to refer to later in the user's session, like an ID number.
PASSWORD	Required. The password that the user logs in with. This is used internally by ColdFusion to track the user's login status.
ROLES	Optional. The role or roles that you want the user to be considered a part of. Later, you will be able to use the IsUserInRole() function to find out whether the user is a member of a particular role.

The other values passed to <CFLOGINUSER> are straightforward. The password that the user entered is supplied to the PASSWORD attribute, and the name of the role to which the user is assigned is passed as the ROLE. Later, any page in the application will be able to test whether the currently logged-in user is a member of a particular role with the IsUserInRole() function.

NOTE

It is up to you to ensure that each possible combination of NAME and PASSWORD is unique (this is almost always the case anyway; an application should never allow two users to have the same user name and password). The best practice would be to make sure that some kind of unique identifier (such as the ContactID) be used as part of the NAME, just to make sure that ColdFusion understands how to distinguish your users from one another.

NOTE

The way the Orange Whip Studios example database is designed, each user will always have only one role (or associated group). That is, they can be assigned to the Admin role or the Marketing role, but not both. If your application needed to let users be in multiple roles or groups, you would likely have an additional database table with a row for each combination of ContactID and UserRoleID. Then, before your <CFLOGINUSER> tag, you might have a query called GetUserRoles that retrieved the appropriate list of role names from the database. You would then use the ValueList() function to supply this query's records to the NAME attribute as a comma-separated list; for instance: NAME="#ValueList(GetUserRoles.UserRoleName)#".

Now that the code to force the user to log in is in place, it just needs to be pressed into service via `<CFINCLUDE>`. You could either place the `<CFINCLUDE>` at the top of each ColdFusion page that you wanted to protect, or you can just place it in `Application.cfm` to protect all your application's templates. Listing 18.7 shows such an `Application.cfm` file.

Listing 18.7 `Application2.cfm`—Forcing Users to Log In with the `<CFLOGIN>` Framework

```
<!---
  Filename:     Application.cfm
  Created by:   Nate Weiss (NMW)
  Please Note:  Executes for every page request
--->

<!--- Any variables set here can be used by all our pages --->
<CFSET DataSource  = "ows">
<CFSET CompanyName = "Orange Whip Studios">

<!--- Name our app and enable session variables --->
<CFAPPLICATION
  NAME="OrangeWhipSite"
  SESSIONMANAGEMENT="Yes">

<!--- Force the user to log in --->
<CFINCLUDE TEMPLATE="ForceUserLogin.cfm">
```

Using `GetAuthUser()` in Your Application Pages

Once you save Listing 18.7 as a file named `Application.cfm`, users will be forced to log in whenever they visit any of the pages in that folder (or its subfolders). However, the order history pages that were created earlier in this chapter will no longer work, since they rely on the `SESSION.Auth` variables populated by the homegrown login framework. A few changes must be made to allow the order history pages with the `<CFLOGIN>` framework. Basically, this just means referring to the value returned by `GetAuthUser()` to get the user's ID and first name, rather than using `SESSION.Auth.ContactID` and `SESSION.Auth.FirstName`. Listing 18.8 shows the new version of the order history template.

Listing 18.8 `OrderHistory3.cfm`—Using `GetAuthUser()` to Provide Personlized Content

```
<!---
  Filename:     OrderHistory3.cfm
  Created by:   Nate Weiss (NMW)
  Purpose:      Displays a user's order history
--->

<HTML>
<HEAD>
  <TITLE>Order History</TITLE>

  <!--- Apply some simple CSS style formatting --->
  <STYLE TYPE="text/css">
    BODY {font-family:sans-serif;font-size:12px;color:navy}
    H2   {font-size:20px}
    TH   {font-family:sans-serif;font-size:12px;color:white;
          background:MediumBlue;text-align:left}
    TD   {font-family:sans-serif;font-size:12px}
  </STYLE>
```

Listing 18.8 (continued)

```
</HEAD>
<BODY>

<!--- GetAuthUser() returns whatever was supplied to the NAME --->
<!--- attribute of the <CFLOGIN> tag when the user logged in. --->
<!--- We provided user's ID and first name, separated by  --->
<!--- commas; we can use list functions to get them back. --->
<CFSET ContactID = ListFirst(GetAuthUser())>
<CFSET ContactName = ListRest(GetAuthUser())>


<!--- Personalized message at top of page--->
<CFOUTPUT>
  <h2>YourOrder History</h2>
  <P><B>Welcome back, #ContactName#</B>!<BR>
</CFOUTPUT>



<!--- Retrieve user's orders, based on ContactID --->
<CFQUERY NAME="GetOrders" DATASOURCE="#DataSource#">
  SELECT OrderID, OrderDate,
    (SELECT Count(*)
     FROM MerchandiseOrdersItems oi
     WHERE oi.OrderID = o.OrderID) AS ItemCount
  FROM MerchandiseOrders o
  WHERE ContactID = #ContactID#
  ORDER BY OrderDate DESC
</CFQUERY>



<!--- Determine if a numeric OrderID was passed in URL --->
<CFSET ShowDetail = IsDefined("URL.OrderID") AND IsNumeric(URL.OrderID)>

<!--- If an OrderID was passed, get details for the order --->
<!--- Query must check against ContactID for security --->
<CFIF ShowDetail>
  <CFQUERY NAME="GetDetail" DATASOURCE="#DataSource#">
    SELECT m.MerchName, oi.ItemPrice, oi.OrderQty
    FROM Merchandise m, MerchandiseOrdersItems oi
    WHERE m.MerchID = oi.ItemID
    AND oi.OrderID  = #URL.OrderID#
    AND oi.OrderID IN
      (SELECT o.OrderID FROM MerchandiseOrders o
       WHERE o.ContactID = #ContactID#)
  </CFQUERY>

  <!--- If no Detail records, don't show detail --->
  <!--- User may be trying to "hack" URL parameters --->
  <CFIF GetDetail.RecordCount EQ 0>
    <CFSET ShowDetail = False>
  </CFIF>
</CFIF>
```

Listing 18.8 (continued)

```
<CFIF GetOrders.RecordCount EQ 0>
  <P>No orders placed to date.<BR>
<CFELSE>
  <CFOUTPUT>
    <P>Orders placed to date:
    <B>#GetOrders.RecordCount#</B><BR>
  </CFOUTPUT>

  <!--- Display orders in a simple HTML table --->
  <TABLE BORDER="1" WIDTH="300" CELLPADDING="5" CELLSPACING="2">
    <!--- Column headers --->
    <TR>
      <TH>Date Ordered</TH>
      <TH>Items</TH>
    </TR>

    <!--- Display each order as a table row --->
    <CFOUTPUT QUERY="GetOrders">
      <!--- Determine whether to show details for this order --->
      <!--- Show Down arrow if expanded, otherwise Right --->
      <CFSET IsExpanded = ShowDetail AND (GetOrders.OrderID EQ URL.OrderID)>
      <CFSET ArrowIcon  = IIF(IsExpanded, "'ArrowDown.gif'", "'ArrowRight.gif'")>

      <TR>
        <TD>
          <!--- Link to show order details, with arrow icon --->
          <A HREF="OrderHistory3.cfm?OrderID=#OrderID#">
            <IMG SRC="../images/#ArrowIcon#" WIDTH="16" HEIGHT="16" BORDER="0">
            #DateFormat(OrderDate, "mmmm d, yyyy")#
          </A>
        </TD>
        <TD>
          <B>#ItemCount#</B>
        </TD>
      </TR>

      <!--- Show details for this order, if appropriate --->
      <CFIF IsExpanded>
        <CFSET OrderTotal = 0>
        <TR>
          <TD COLSPAN="2">

            <!--- Show details within nested table --->
            <TABLE WIDTH="100%" CELLSPACING="0" BORDER="0">
              <!--- Nested table's column headers --->
              <TR>
                <TH>Item</TH><TH>Qty</TH><TH>Price</TH>
              </TR>

              <!--- Show each ordered item as a table row --->
              <CFLOOP QUERY="GetDetail">
                <CFSET OrderTotal = OrderTotal + ItemPrice>
                <TR>
                  <TD>#MerchName#</TD>
                  <TD>#OrderQty#</TD>
                  <TD>#DollarFormat(ItemPrice)#</TD>
                </TR>
```

Listing 18.8 (continued)

```
                    </CFLOOP>

                    <!--- Last row in nested table for total --->
                    <TR>
                      <TD COLSPAN="2"><B>Total:</B></TD>
                      <TD><B>#DollarFormat(OrderTotal)#</B></TD>
                    </TR>
                  </TABLE>
                </TD>
              </TR>
            </CFIF>
          </CFOUTPUT>
        </TABLE>
      </CFIF>

      </BODY>
      </HTML>
```

As noted earlier, `GetAuthUser()` always returns whatever value was provided to the `NAME` attribute of the `<CFLOGINUSER>` tag at the time of login. The examples in this chapter provide the user's ID and first name to `NAME` as a comma-separated list. Therefore, the current user's ID and name can easily be retrieved with the `ListFirst()` and `ListRest()` functions, respectively. Two `<CFSET>` tags near the top of Listing 18.8 use these functions to set two simple variables called `ContactID` and `ContactName`. The rest of the code is essentially identical to the previous version of the template (refer to Listing 18.5). The only change is the fact that `ContactID` is used instead of `SESSION.Auth.ContactID`, and `ContactName` is used instead of `SESSION.Auth.FirstName`.

Using Roles to Dynamically Restrict Functionality

So far, the examples in this chapter provide the same level of access for each person. That is, each user is allowed access to the same type of information. ColdFusion MX's new `<CFLOGIN>` framework also provides a simple way for you to create applications in which different people have different levels of access. The idea is for your code to make decisions about what to show each user based on the person's *role* (or roles) in the application.

NOTE

For the purposes of this discussion, consider the word *role* to be synonymous with *group*, *right*, or *privilege*. How exactly you view a role is up to you. The example application for this book thinks of roles as groups. That is, each contact is a member of a role called `Admin` or `User` or the like. Those role names sound a lot like group names. Other ColdFusion applications might have role names that sound more like privileges; for instance, `MayReviewAccountHistory` or `MayCancelOrders`. Use the concept of a role in whatever way makes sense for your application.

Back in Listing 18.6, the name of the role assigned to the current user was supplied to the `ROLES` attribute of the `<CFLOGINUSER>` tag. As a result, ColdFusion always knows which users belong to which roles. Elsewhere, the `IsUserInRole()` function can be used to determine whether the user is a member of a particular role.

For instance, if you want to display some kind of link, option, or information for members of the Admin role but not for other users, the following <CFIF> test would do the trick:

```
<CFIF IsUserInRole("Admin")>
  <!--- special information or options here --->
</CFIF>
```

Listing 18.9 is one more version of the order history template. This version uses the IsUserInRole() function to determine whether the user is a member of the Admin role. If so, the user is given the ability to view any customer's order history, via a drop-down list. If the user is an ordinary visitor (not a member of Admin), then she has access to only her own order history.

Listing 18.9 OrderHistory4.cfm—Using IsUserInRole() to Restrict Access on the Fly

```
<!---
  Filename:     OrderHistory4.cfm
  Created by:   Nate Weiss (NMW)
  Purpose:      Displays a user's order history
--->

<HTML>
<HEAD>
  <TITLE>Order History</TITLE>

  <!--- Apply some simple CSS style formatting --->
  <STYLE TYPE="text/css">
    BODY {font-family:sans-serif;font-size:12px;color:navy}
    H2   {font-size:20px}
    TH   {font-family:sans-serif;font-size:12px;color:white;
          background:MediumBlue;text-align:left}
    TD   {font-family:sans-serif;font-size:12px}
  </STYLE>
</HEAD>
<BODY>

<!--- GetAuthUser() returns whatever was supplied to the NAME --->
<!--- attribute of the <CFLOGIN> tag when the user logged in. --->
<!--- We provided user's ID and first name, separated by  --->
<!--- commas; we can use list functions to get them back. --->
<CFSET ContactID = ListFirst(GetAuthUser())>
<CFSET ContactName = ListRest(GetAuthUser())>


<!--- If current user is an administrator, allow user --->
<!--- to choose which contact to show order history for --->
<CFIF IsUserInRole("Admin")>
  <!--- This session variable tracks which contact to show history for --->
  <!--- By default, assume the user should be viewing her own records --->
  <CFPARAM NAME="SESSION.OrderHistorySelectedUser" DEFAULT="#ContactID#">

  <!--- If user is currently choosing a different contact from list --->
  <CFIF IsDefined("FORM.SelectedUser")>
    <CFSET SESSION.OrderHistorySelectedUser = FORM.SelectedUser>
  </CFIF>
```

Listing 18.9 (continued)

```
    <!--- For rest of template, use selected contact's ID in queries --->
    <CFSET ShowHistoryForContactID = SESSION.OrderHistorySelectedUser>


    <!--- Simple HTML form, to allow user to choose --->
    <!--- which contact to show order history for --->
    <CFFORM
      ACTION="#CGI.SCRIPT_NAME#?#SESSION.URLToken#"
      METHOD="POST">

      <h2>Order History</h2>
      Customer:

      <!--- Get a list of all contacts, for display in drop-down list --->
      <CFQUERY DATASOURCE="#DataSource#" NAME="GetUsers">
        SELECT ContactID, LastName + ', ' + FirstName AS FullName
        FROM Contacts
        ORDER BY LastName, FirstName
      </CFQUERY>

      <!--- Drop-down list of contacts --->
      <CFSELECT
        NAME="SelectedUser"
        SELECTED="#ContactID#"
        QUERY="GetUsers"
        DISPLAY="FullName"
        VALUE="ContactID"></CFSELECT>

      <!--- Submit button, for user to choose a different contact --->
      <INPUT TYPE="Submit" VALUE="Go">

    </CFFORM>


  <!--- Normal users can view only their own order history --->
  <CFELSE>
    <CFSET ShowHistoryForContactID = ContactID>

    <!--- Personalized message at top of page--->
    <CFOUTPUT>
      <h2>YourOrder History</h2>
      <P><B>Welcome back, #ContactName#</B>!<BR>
    </CFOUTPUT>

  </CFIF>



  <!--- Retrieve user's orders, based on ContactID --->
  <CFQUERY NAME="GetOrders" DATASOURCE="#DataSource#">
    SELECT OrderID, OrderDate,
      (SELECT Count(*)
       FROM MerchandiseOrdersItems oi
       WHERE oi.OrderID = o.OrderID) AS ItemCount
    FROM MerchandiseOrders o
    WHERE ContactID = #ShowHistoryForContactID#
```

Listing 18.9 (CONTINUED)

```
  ORDER BY OrderDate DESC
</CFQUERY>



<!--- Determine if a numeric OrderID was passed in URL --->
<CFSET ShowDetail = IsDefined("URL.OrderID") AND IsNumeric(URL.OrderID)>

<!--- If an OrderID was passed, get details for the order --->
<!--- Query must check against ContactID for security --->
<CFIF ShowDetail>
  <CFQUERY NAME="GetDetail" DATASOURCE="#DataSource#">
    SELECT m.MerchName, oi.ItemPrice, oi.OrderQty
    FROM Merchandise m, MerchandiseOrdersItems oi
    WHERE m.MerchID = oi.ItemID
    AND oi.OrderID  = #URL.OrderID#
    AND oi.OrderID IN
      (SELECT o.OrderID FROM MerchandiseOrders o
       WHERE o.ContactID = #ShowHistoryForContactID#)
  </CFQUERY>

  <!--- If no Detail records, don't show detail --->
  <!--- User may be trying to "hack" URL parameters --->
  <CFIF GetDetail.RecordCount EQ 0>
    <CFSET ShowDetail = False>
  </CFIF>
</CFIF>



<CFIF GetOrders.RecordCount EQ 0>
  <P>No orders placed to date.<BR>
<CFELSE>
  <CFOUTPUT>
    <P>Orders placed to date:
    <B>#GetOrders.RecordCount#</B><BR>
  </CFOUTPUT>

  <!--- Display orders in a simple HTML table --->
  <TABLE BORDER="1" WIDTH="300" CELLPADDING="5" CELLSPACING="2">
    <!--- Column headers --->
    <TR>
      <TH>Date Ordered</TH>
      <TH>Items</TH>
    </TR>

    <!--- Display each order as a table row --->
    <CFOUTPUT QUERY="GetOrders">
      <!--- Determine whether to show details for this order --->
      <!--- Show Down arrow if expanded, otherwise Right --->
      <CFSET IsExpanded = ShowDetail AND (GetOrders.OrderID EQ URL.OrderID)>
      <CFSET ArrowIcon  = IIF(IsExpanded, "'ArrowDown.gif'", "'ArrowRight.gif'")>

      <TR>
        <TD>
          <!--- Link to show order details, with arrow icon --->
```

Listing 18.9 (continued)

```
          <A HREF="OrderHistory3.cfm?OrderID=#OrderID#">
            <IMG SRC="../images/#ArrowIcon#" WIDTH="16" HEIGHT="16" BORDER="0">
            #DateFormat(OrderDate, "mmmm d, yyyy")#
          </A>
        </TD>
        <TD>
          <B>#ItemCount#</B>
        </TD>
      </TR>

      <!--- Show details for this order, if appropriate --->
      <CFIF IsExpanded>
        <CFSET OrderTotal = 0>
        <TR>
          <TD COLSPAN="2">

            <!--- Show details within nested table --->
            <TABLE WIDTH="100%" CELLSPACING="0" BORDER="0">
              <!--- Nested table's column headers --->
              <TR>
                <TH>Item</TH><TH>Qty</TH><TH>Price</TH>
              </TR>

              <!--- Show each ordered item as a table row --->
              <CFLOOP QUERY="GetDetail">
                <CFSET OrderTotal = OrderTotal + ItemPrice>
                <TR>
                  <TD>#MerchName#</TD>
                  <TD>#OrderQty#</TD>
                  <TD>#DollarFormat(ItemPrice)#</TD>
                </TR>
              </CFLOOP>

              <!--- Last row in nested table for total --->
              <TR>
                <TD COLSPAN="2"><B>Total:</B></TD>
                <TD><B>#DollarFormat(OrderTotal)#</B></TD>
              </TR>
            </TABLE>
          </TD>
        </TR>
      </CFIF>
    </CFOUTPUT>
  </TABLE>
</CFIF>

</BODY>
</HTML>
```

As you can see, the `IsUserInRole()` function is used to determine whether the user is an administrator. If so, the `<CFSELECT>` tag is used to provide the user with a drop-down list of everyone from the `Contacts` table. The `SESSION.OrderHistorySelectedUser` variable is used to track the user's current drop-down selection; this is very similar conceptully to the way the `CLIENT.LastSearch` variable was used in the `SearchForm.cfm` examples in Chapter 17. Another variable, called `ShowHistoryForContactID`, is created to hold the current value of `SESSION.OrderHistorySelectedUser`.

If, on the other hand, the user is not an administrator, the value of `ShowHistoryForContactID` is simply set to her own contact ID number. In other words, after the large `<CFIF>` block at the top of this listing is finished, `ShowHistoryForContactID` always holds the appropriate ID number with which to retrieve the order history. The rest of the code is very similar to that in the earlier versions of the template in this chapter; it just uses `ShowHistoryForContactID` in the `WHERE` parts of its queries to make sure the user sees the appropriate order history records.

Figure 18.5 shows the results for users who log in as administrators (you can log in with username `Ben` and password `Forta` to see these results). All other users will continue to see the interface shown in Figure 18.4.

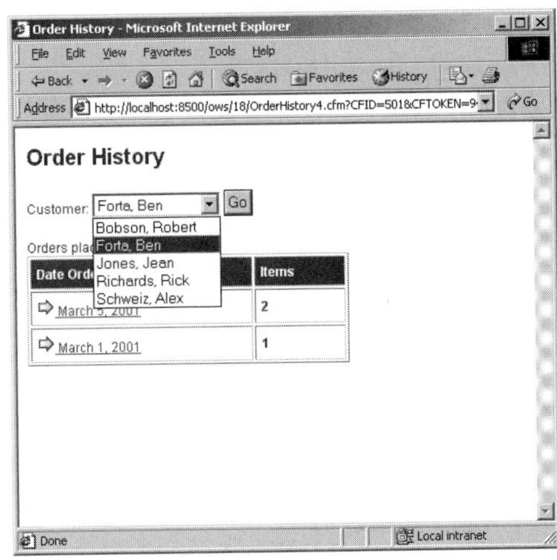

Figure 18.5
The concept of user roles can be used to expose whatever functionality is appropriate for each

CHAPTER 19

Building User-Defined Functions

IN THIS CHAPTER

This chapter will introduce you the brave new world of user-defined functions (UDFs), a feature that has received a complete overhaul in ColdFusion MX. You can now create your own functions to do just about anything you can think of. User-defined functions are easy to write and even easier to use. You use them just like ColdFusion's built-in functions.

Thinking About Extending CFML

Throughout this book, you have been learning how to use CFML's built-in tags and functions to produce dynamic Web pages. You have used tags like `<CFQUERY>` and `<CFOUTPUT>` to display information stored in databases, and you have used functions like `UCase()` and `DateFormat()` to further tweak your work.

For the next few chapters, you will be exploring how to *extend* the CFML language by creating your own tags, functions, and components. Once you see how easy it is to do so, you will find that you can make your application code much more elegant and maintainable. It's a very exciting topic indeed. It's even fun.

There are four basic ways in which you can extend ColdFusion:

- **User-Defined Functions.** As the name implies, UDFs are functions that you create yourself. If you feel that some function is missing from ColdFusion's list of built-in ones, or that a particular function would come in really handy for an application you're building, you can just make the function yourself. UDFs are what this chapter is all about.
- **Custom Tags.** While UDFs allow you to make your own functions, Custom Tags allow you to create your own CFML tags. Of all the extensibility methods listed here, Custom Tags remain the most flexible and powerful. For more information, see Chapter 20, "Building Reusable Components."

- **ColdFusion Components (CFCs).** CFCs are similar conceptually to Custom Tags, but imply a more structured, object-oriented manner of programming. CFCs are also at the heart of ColdFusion MX's new Flash and Web Services integration. See Chapter 20 for details.
- **CFX Tags.** It is also possible to write your own CFX tags. You can write the code to make the tag do its work in either Java or C++. For more information about writing CFX tags, see the ColdFusion MX documentation or consult our companion book, *Advanced ColdFusion MX Application Development* (Macromedia Press, 0-321-12710-2).

NOTE

If you wish, you can also extend ColdFusion MX by writing JSP tag libraries, COM/ActiveX controls, Java classes or JavaBeans, and more. The list above is simply meant to summarize the extensibility methods specific to ColdFusion.

In this chapter, I will concentrate on the first option, user-defined functions. I recommend that you also make yourself familiar with Chapter 20 so you know the extensibility options available to you. In many cases, you can get a particular task done by creating a tag or a function, so it will be helpful if you have an understanding of both.

Functions Turn Input into Output

Think about a few of the CFML functions you already know. Almost all of them accept at least one piece of information, do something with the information internally, and then return some kind of result. For instance, ColdFusion's `UCase()` function accepts one piece of information (a string), performs an action (converts it to uppercase), then returns a result (Figure 19.1).

Figure 19.1

UCase() function process

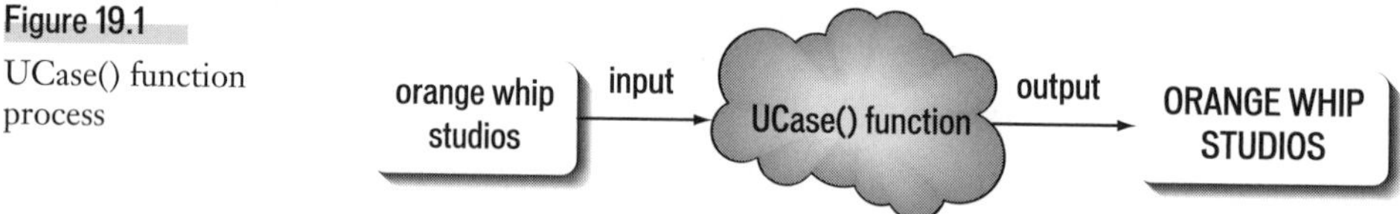

So you can think of most functions as being like little engines, or mechanisms on an assembly line. Some functions accept more than one piece of information (more than one argument), but the point is still the same: Almost all functions are about accepting input and creating some kind of corresponding output. A function's *arguments* provide the input, and its output is passed back as the function's *return value*.

As the designer of your own functions, you get to specify the input by declaring one or more arguments. You also get to pass back whatever return value you wish.

Building Your First UDF

Let's say that as a ColdFusion developer for Orange Whip Studios, you often need to display movie titles. Of course, it's easy enough to write a `<CFQUERY>` tag that retrieves the title for a particular movie based on its ID, but even that can get a bit repetitive if you need to do it on many different pages. Also, you must keep the database's design in mind at all times, instead of just concentrating on the task at hand.

You find yourself wishing you had a function called `GetFilmTitle()` that would return the title of whatever `FilmID` you passed to it. So, for example, if you wanted to display the title of film number 8, you could just use this:

```
<CFOUTPUT>#GetFilmTitle(8)#</CFOUTPUT>
```

Well, it turns out that ColdFusion MX makes it remarkably easy to create this function. And you get to create it using the good old `<CFQUERY>` tag you already know and love. All you need to do is to surround the `<CFQUERY>` with a few extra tags, and voilà!

Let's take a look at what it will take to put this new function into place.

Basic Steps

To create a user-defined function, you follow four basic steps:

1. Start with a pair of `<CFFUNCTION>` tags. You will insert all the code needed to make the function do its work between the opening and closing `<CFFUNCTION>` tags.
2. Add a `<CFARGUMENT>` tag for each argument your function will be using as input. If you wish, you can specify some arguments as required and others as optional.
3. After the `<CFARGUMENT>` tags, add whatever CFML code is needed to make your function do its work. Feel free to use whatever tags and functions you want in this section.
4. The last step is to use the `<CFRETURN>` tag to return the result of whatever computations or processing your function does. In other words, you use `<CFRETURN>` to specify what your function's output should be.

NOTE

The `<CFFUNCTION>` and related tags discussed in this chapter are new for ColdFusion MX. In previous versions of ColdFusion, the only way to create UDFs was with the less powerful `<CFSCRIPT>` tag, which is not discussed specifically in this book. If you come across a UDF that was created using `<CFSCRIPT>`, you can use it in your code just like the ones discussed in this chapter. For creating new UDFs, we strongly recommend using `<CFFUNCTION>` rather than the older, script-based method.

Normally, I would formally introduce the syntax and attributes for each of these new tags, but in this case it's going to be easier if we just jump right in so you can see how the tags work together.

Here is the code needed to create the `GetFilmTitle()` user-defined function:

```
<CFFUNCTION NAME="GetFilmTitle">
  <CFARGUMENT NAME="FilmID" TYPE="numeric" REQUIRED="Yes">

  <!--- Get the film's title --->
  <CFQUERY NAME="GetFilm" DATASOURCE="#Datasource#"
    CACHEDWITHIN="#CreateTimespan(0,1,0,0)#">
    SELECT MovieTitle FROM Films
    WHERE FilmID = #ARGUMENTS.FilmID#
  </CFQUERY>
```

```
    <!--- Return the film's title --->
    <CFRETURN GetFilm.MovieTitle>
  </CFFUNCTION>
```

As you can see, all three UDF-related tags are used here. First, a pair of <CFFUNCTION> tags surrounds the code for the whole function. Next, a <CFARGUMENT> tag at the top of the function defines what its input should be. Finally, a <CFRETURN> tag at the end returns the function's output. Nearly all UDFs are constructed using this basic pattern.

Everything else between the <CFFUNCTION> tags is the actual CFML code that will be executed each time the function is actually used. In this simple example, the only processing that needs to occur to generate the function's output is a simple database query.

As you can see, a special ARGUMENTS scope will contain the value of each argument when the function is actually used. So, if the number 8 is passed to the function's FilmID argument, then the value of the ARGUMENTS.FilmID variable will be 8. In this case, ARGUMENTS.FilmID dynamically creates the SQL that will retrieve the appropriate film title from the database. All that's left to do is to return the title as the function's output, using the <CFRETURN> tag.

Wow, that was easy.

Using the Function

Once you've written a UDF, you can use it just like any other function. For instance, after the <CFFUNCTION> code shown above, you can use the function to display the title for a film, like this:

```
<CFOUTPUT>#GetFilmTitle(8)#</CFOUTPUT>
```

When ColdFusion encounters the function, it will run the code between the corresponding <CFFUNCTION> tags. For the GetFilmTitle() function, this means running the <CFQUERY> tag and returning the film title that gets retrieved from the database.

Of course, you can provide input to the function's arguments dynamically, just as with any other function. For instance, if you have a form field named ShowFilmID, then you could use code like the following to display the title corresponding to the ID number that the user provides on the form:

```
<CFOUTPUT>#GetFilmTitle(FORM.ShowFilmID)#</CFOUTPUT>
```

You can also use UDFs in <CFSET> tags or any other place where you would use a CFML expression. For instance, the following <CFSET> tag would create a variable called MyFilmInUpperCase, which is the uppercase version of the selected film's title:

```
<CFSET MyFilmInUpperCase = UCase(GetFilmTitle(FORM.ShowFilmID))>
```

UDF Tag Syntax

Now that you have seen a simple example of how the code for a user-defined function is structured, let's take a closer look at the attributes supported by each of the tags involved: <CFFUNCTION>, <CFARGUMENT>, and <CFRETURN>. Tables 19.1, 19.2, and 19.3 show the syntax supported by these three important tags.

Table 19.1 <CFFUNCTION> Tag Syntax

ATTRIBUTE	PURPOSE
NAME	The name of the new function. To actually use the function, you will call it using the name you provide here. The name needs to be a valid CFML identifier, which means it can contain only letters, numbers, and underscores, and the first character must be a letter.
RETURNTYPE	Optional. If you want, you can use this attribute to indicate the type of information that the function will return, such as string, numeric, date, and so on. See Appendix B, "ColdFusion Tag Reference," for the complete list of data types. This attribute isn't really important except when used with ColdFusion Components, as discussed in Chapter 20. That said, you are always free to specify a RETURNTYPE to make your functions more self-documenting.

NOTE

The <CFFUNCTION> tag actually supports several more attributes, which are relevant only when the tag is used within the context of a ColdFusion Component. You will learn about the other <CFFUNCTION> attributes in Chapter 20.

Table 19.2 <CFARGUMENT> Tag Syntax

ATTRIBUTE	PURPOSE
NAME	The name of the argument. Within the function, a variable will be created in the ARGUMENTS scope that contains the value passed to the argument when the function is actually used.
TYPE	Optional. The data type that should be supplied to the argument when the function is actually used. If you supply a TYPE, then ColdFusion will display an error message if someone tries to use the function with the wrong kind of input.
REQUIRED	Optional. Whether the argument is required for the function to be able to do its work. The default is No (not required).
DEFAULT	Optional. For optional arguments (that is, when REQUIRED="No"), this determines what the value of the argument should be if a value is not passed to the function when it is actually used.

One of the neatest things about the UDF framework is how easy it is to create functions that have required arguments, optional arguments, or both:

- If a <CFARGUMENT> tag uses REQUIRED="Yes", then the argument must be provided when the function is actually used. If the argument is not provided at run time, ColdFusion will display an error message.
- If REQUIRED="No" and a DEFAULT attribute have been specified, then the function can be called either with or without the argument at run time. Just go ahead and use the ARGUMENTS scope to refer to the value of the argument. If a value is provided when the function is actually used, that value will be what is present in the ARGUMENTS scope. If not, the DEFAULT value will be what is in the ARGUMENTS scope.

- If `REQUIRED="No"` and the `DEFAULT` attribute have *not* been specified, the argument is still considered optional. If the function is called without the argument, then there will be no corresponding value in the `ARGUMENTS` scope. You can use the `IsDefined()` function to determine whether the argument was provided at runtime. For instance, you would use `IsDefined("ARGUMENTS.FilmID")` within a function's code to determine if an optional `FilmID` argument was provided.

You will see optional arguments at work in Listing 19.4.

NOTE

By "run time," I just mean "at the time when the function is actually used." Programmers often use this term to refer to the actual moment of execution for a piece of code.

Table 19.3 `<CFRETURN>` Tag Syntax

RETURN VALUE	PURPOSE
(any expression)	The `<CFRETURN>` tag doesn't have any attributes per se. Instead, you simply place whatever string, number, date, variable, or other expression you want directly within the `<CFRETURN>` tag.

For instance, if you wanted your function to always return the letter *A*, you would use:

```
<CFRETURN "A">
```

If you wanted your function to return the current time, you would use:

```
<CFRETURN TimeFormat(Now())>
```

You can use complex expressions as well, like this:

```
<CFRETURN "The current time is: " & TimeFormat(Now())>
```

Using Local Variables

To get its work done, a UDF often needs to use `<CFSET>` or other tags that create variables. Most of the time, you don't want these variables to be visible to pages that use the function.

Why Local Variables Are Important

Consider the `GetFilmTitle()` function, which you have already seen. The code for this function runs a query named `GetFilm` within the body of the function (that is, between the `<CFFUNCTION>` tags). That query returns only one column, `MovieTitle`. You probably don't want that query object to continue existing after the function is called. After all, what if someone already has a `<CFQUERY>` called `GetFilm` that selects *all* columns from the Films table, then calls the UDF? That's right—after the UDF runs, the function's version of the `GetFilm` query (which has only one column) will overwrite the one that the page created before calling the function, and any subsequent code that refers to `GetFilms` probably won't work as expected.

NOTE

Developers often refer to this type of situation as a "variable collision" or a "namespace collision." Whatever the name, such a situation can be bad news because it can lead to unpredictable or surprising results, especially if you are using a UDF that someone else wrote.

What you need is some way to tell ColdFusion that a particular variable should be visible only within the context of the `<CFFUNCTION>` block. Such a variable is called a *local variable*.

How to Declare a Local Variable

It's really easy to create local variables in a UDF. All you need to do is *declare* the variable as a local variable, using the `<CFSET>` tag and the new `var` keyword, like this:

```
<CFSET var MyLocalVariable = "Hello">
```

The `var` keyword tells ColdFusion that the variable should cease to exist when the `<CFFUNCTION>` block ends, and that it shouldn't interfere at all with any other variables elsewhere that have the same name. You almost always want to declare all variables you create within a `<CFFUNCTION>` block as local with the `var` keyword.

NOTE

To put it another way, you usually don't want a function to have any "side effects" other than producing the correct return value. That way, you know it is always safe to call a function without having to worry about its overwriting any variables you might already have defined.

Here are some rules and regulations about local variables:

- You can declare as many local variables as you want. Just use a separate `<CFSET>` for each one, using the `var` keyword each time.
- The `<CFSET>` tags needed to declare local variables must be at the very top of the `<CFFUNCTION>` block, right after any `<CFARGUMENT>` tags. If ColdFusion encounters the `var` keyword after any line of code that does anything else, it will display an error message.
- It is not possible to declare a local variable without giving it a value. That is, `<CFSET var MyLocalVariable>` alone is not valid. There has to be an equals sign (=) in there, with an initial value for the variable. You can always change the value later in the function's code, so just set the variable to an empty string if you're not ready to give it its real value yet.

To make the `GetFilmTitle()` function work correctly so that the `GetFilm` query object is discarded after the function does its work, you just need to add a `<CFSET>` tag at the top of the function body, declaring the `GetFilm` variable as a local variable, like so:

```
<CFFUNCTION NAME="GetFilmTitle">
  <CFARGUMENT NAME="FilmID" TYPE="numeric" REQUIRED="Yes">

  <!--- This variable is for this function's use only --->
  <CFSET var GetFilm = "">

  <!--- Get the film's title --->
  <CFQUERY NAME="GetFilm" DATASOURCE="#Datasource#"
```

```
        CACHEDWITHIN="#CreateTimespan(0,1,0,0)#">
        SELECT MovieTitle FROM Films
        WHERE FilmID = #ARGUMENTS.FilmID#
      </CFQUERY>

      <!--- Return the film's title --->
      <CFRETURN GetFilm.MovieTitle>
    </CFFUNCTION>
```

Because the <CFSET> uses the var keyword, ColdFusion now understands that it should discard the GetFilm variable after the function executes, and that it should not interfere with any variables elsewhere that have the same name.

NOTE

This <CFSET> sets the GetFilm variable to an empty string. It doesn't really matter what this initial value is, since the variable will be set to the results of <CFQUERY> on the next line. In other languages, you might use an initial value of null, but CFML doesn't support the notion of a null value. Every variable always has some kind of value.

Where to Save Your UDFs

Now that you have seen what a completed <CFFUNCTION> block looks like, you may be wondering where exactly you are supposed to place it. The answer is simple: You can place your <CFFUNCTION> blocks anywhere you want, in any ColdFusion template. Your code can make use of the function anywhere after it encounters the <CFFUNCTION> block.

Creating and Using a UDF in the Same File

For instance, Listing 19.1 is a template that uses the <CFFUNCTION> block shown earlier to create the GetFilmTitle() function, then uses the function to display a list of films (Figure 19.2).

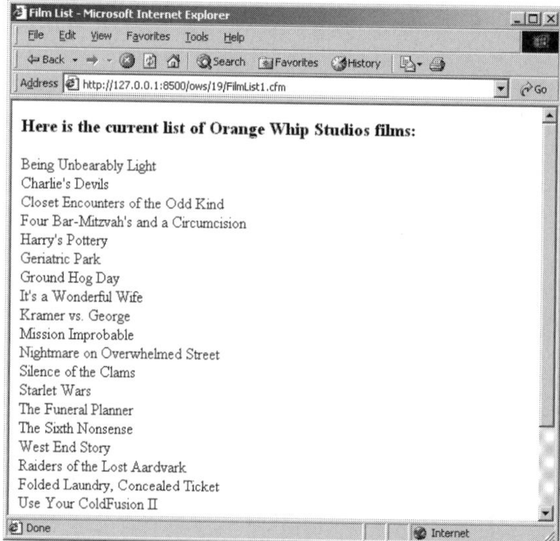

Figure 19.2

The GetFilmTitle() function makes it easy to display film titles.

Listing 19.1 `FilmList1.cfm`—Creating and using a UDF

```
<!---
  Filename:     FilmList.cfm
  Created by:   Nate Weiss (NMW)
  Please Note  Displays a list of films
--->

<!--- ****** BEGIN FUNCTION DEFINITIONS ******  --->
<!--- Function: GetFilmTitle() --->
<!--- Returns the title of a film, based on FilmID --->
<CFFUNCTION NAME="GetFilmTitle">
  <!--- One argument: FilmID --->
  <CFARGUMENT NAME="FilmID" TYPE="numeric" REQUIRED="Yes">

  <!--- This variable is for this function's use only --->
  <CFSET var GetFilm = "">

  <!--- Get the film's title --->
  <CFQUERY NAME="GetFilm" DATASOURCE="#Datasource#"
    CACHEDWITHIN="#CreateTimespan(0,1,0,0)#">
    SELECT MovieTitle FROM Films
    WHERE FilmID = #Arguments.FilmID#
  </CFQUERY>

  <!--- Return the film's title --->
  <CFRETURN GetFilm.MovieTitle>
</CFFUNCTION>
<!--- ****** END FUNCTION DEFINITIONS ******  --->

<!--- Get a list of all FilmIDs --->
<CFQUERY NAME="GetFilms" DATASOURCE="#Datasource#">
  SELECT FilmID
  FROM Films
</CFQUERY>

<HTML>
<HEAD><TITLE>Film List</TITLE></HEAD>
<BODY>
  <H3>Here is the current list of Orange Whip Studios films:</H3>

  <!--- Now it is extremely easy to display a list of film links --->
  <CFOUTPUT QUERY="GetFilms">
    #GetFilmTitle(FilmID)#<BR>
  </CFOUTPUT>

</BODY>
</HTML>
```

Saving UDFs in Separate Files for Easy Reuse

In Listing 19.1, you saw how to create and use a user-defined function, all in the same ColdFusion template. While the function works just fine, it doesn't really make anything any easier. You wouldn't want to have to retype that function every time you wanted to display a movie's title.

Most of the time, you'll want to keep your UDFs in separate files to make them easy to reuse in your various ColdFusion pages. For instance, it would probably be a good idea to create a file named `FilmFunctions.cfm` that contains the `GetFilmTitle()` function.

Later, as you create other film-related functions, you could put them in the same file. Once you have this file in place, you can simply `<CFINCLUDE>` it to use the function it contains.

Listing 19.2 shows how to create such a file. As you can see, this is the same `<CFFUNCTION>` block shown in Listing 19.1; here it's simply dropped into its own template.

Listing 19.2 `FilmFunctions1.cfm`—Placing a UDF in a separate file

```
<!---
  Filename:    FilmFunctions1.cfm
  Created by: Nate Weiss (NMW)
  Purpose:     Creates a library of user-defined functions
               related to films
--->

<!--- Function: GetFilmTitle() --->
<!--- Returns the title of a film, based on FilmID --->
<CFFUNCTION NAME="GetFilmTitle">
  <!--- One argument: FilmID --->
  <CFARGUMENT NAME="FilmID" TYPE="numeric" REQUIRED="Yes">

  <!--- This variable is for this function's use only --->
  <CFSET var GetFilm = "">

  <!--- Get the film's title --->
  <CFQUERY NAME="GetFilm" DATASOURCE="#Datasource#"
    CACHEDWITHIN="#CreateTimespan(0,1,0,0)#">
    SELECT MovieTitle FROM Films
    WHERE FilmID = #ARGUMENTS.FilmID#
  </CFQUERY>

  <!--- Return the film's title --->
  <CFRETURN GetFilm.MovieTitle>
</CFFUNCTION>
```

Once you have a file like this in place, you just need to include the file via a simple `<CFINCLUDE>` tag to be able to use the function(s) it contains. For instance, Listing 19.3 is a revised version of the Film List template from Listing 19.1. The results in the browser are exactly the same (Figure 19.2), but the code is much cleaner.

Listing 19.3 `FilmList2.cfm`—Using UDFs stored in a separate file

```
<!--- Include the set of film-related user-defined functions --->
<CFINCLUDE TEMPLATE="FilmFunctions1.cfm">

<!--- Get a list of all FilmIDs --->
<CFQUERY NAME="GetFilms" DATASOURCE="#Datasource#">
  SELECT FilmID
  FROM Films
  ORDER BY MovieTitle
```

Listing 19.3 (continued)

```
</CFQUERY>

<HTML>
<HEAD><TITLE>Film List</TITLE></HEAD>
<BODY>
  <H3>Here is the current list of Orange Whip Studios films:</H3>

  <!--- Now it is extremely easy to display a list of film links --->
  <CFOUTPUT QUERY="GetFilms">
    #GetFilmTitle(FilmID)#<BR>
  </CFOUTPUT>
</BODY>
</HTML>
```

Reusing Code Saves Time and Effort

The `<CFINCLUDE>` tag at the top of Listing 19.3 allows you to use the `GetFilmTitle()` function later in the same template. You could use this same `<CFINCLUDE>` tag in any other templates that need to use the function.

In other words, once you have created a user-defined function, it is incredibly easy to reuse it wherever you need. This makes your work easier and more efficient. And if you ever have to make a correction in the `GetFilmTitle()` function, you only need to do so in one place. This makes your project much easier to maintain over time.

TIP

If you want to be able to use the functions in a particular file throughout your entire application, you can just move the `<CFINCLUDE>` tag to your `Application.cfm` file. You're then free to use the functions wherever you wish.

Creating Libraries of Related UDFs

ColdFusion developers often refer to a file of conceptually related UDFs as a *UDF library*. Actually, there are no specific rules about what kinds of UDFs you can collect into a library, but it just makes common sense to group your UDFs into different files according to some kind of common concept.

In fact, you have already seen a small UDF library: the `FilmFunctions1.cfm` file shown in Listing 19.2. It contains only one function, but you can still think of it as a library that you could expand to include other film-related functions in the future.

Designing the UDF Library

Let's say your team needs some more film-related functions added to the FilmFunctions library. Sounds like fun! You decide to create a new version of the library file, called `FilmFunctions2.cfm`. You sit down with the other members of your team, and come up with the list of functions shown in Table 19.4.

Table 19.4 Functions in the `FilmFunctions` UDF Library

FUNCTION	PURPOSE
`GetFilmsQuery()`	This function returns a query object that contains information about films in the database. It supports one argument called `FilmID`, which is optional. If the function is called without `FilmID`, the function simply executes a `<CFQUERY>` that gets information about all films from the database and returns the query object. If a `FilmID` is provided, however, the query object will only contain one row, corresponding to the specified film.
`GetFilmTitle()`	This behaves in the same way as the `GetFilmTitle()` function created in the first version of the library file. It takes one argument, `FilmID`, which is the ID of the film to get the title for. Internally, this function can make use of the `GetFilmsQuery()` function.
`GetFilmURL()`	This function is similar to `GetFilmTitle()`. It takes one argument, `FilmID`. Instead of returning the film's title, however, it returns a standardized URL to a page called `ShowFilm.cfm` containing details about the film. The function includes the film's ID number in the URL so the `ShowFilm.cfm` template can display information about the correct film.
`MakeFilmPopupLink()`	This function also accepts a `FilmID` argument. It returns the HTML code needed to display a link for the selected film. When the link is clicked, a pop-up window appears with some basic information about the selected film. Internally, this function calls a general-purpose UDF function called `JavaScriptPopupLink()`, discussed later in this section.

Listing 19.4 shows the code for the new `FilmFunctions2.cfm` UDF library.

Listing 19.4 `FilmFunctions2.cfm` —A UDF function library

```
<!---
  Filename:   FilmFunctions2.cfm
  Created by: Nate Weiss (NMW)
  Purpose:    Creates a library of user-defined functions
              related to films
--->


<!--- Function: GetFilmsQuery() --->
<!--- Returns a query object from the Films table in the database --->
<CFFUNCTION NAME="GetFilmsQuery" RETURNTYPE="query">
  <!--- Optional argument: FilmID --->
  <CFARGUMENT NAME="FilmID" TYPE="numeric" REQUIRED="No">

  <!--- This variable is for this function's use only --->
  <CFSET var FilmsQuery = "">

  <!--- Query the database for information about all films --->
  <!--- The query is cached to improve performance --->
  <CFQUERY NAME="FilmsQuery" DATASOURCE="#Datasource#">
    SELECT * FROM Films
```

Listing 19.4 (continued)

```
    <!--- If a FilmID argument was provided, select that film only --->
    <CFIF IsDefined("ARGUMENTS.FilmID")>
      WHERE FilmID = #ARGUMENTS.FilmID#
    <!--- Otherwise, get information for all films, in alphabetical order --->
    <CFELSE>
      ORDER BY MovieTitle
    </CFIF>
  </CFQUERY>

  <!--- Return the query --->
  <CFRETURN FilmsQuery>
</CFFUNCTION>


<!--- Function: GetFilmTitle() --->
<!--- Returns the title of a film, based on FilmID --->
<CFFUNCTION NAME="GetFilmTitle">
  <!--- One argument: FilmID --->
  <CFARGUMENT NAME="FilmID" TYPE="numeric" REQUIRED="Yes">

  <!--- This variable is for this function's use only --->
  <CFSET var GetFilm = "">

  <!--- Get a query object of all films in the database --->
  <CFSET GetFilm = GetFilmsQuery(ARGUMENTS.FilmID)>

  <!--- Return the film's title --->
  <CFRETURN GetFilm.MovieTitle>
</CFFUNCTION>



<!--- Function: GetFilmURL() --->
<!--- Returns the URL to a film's detail page, based on FilmID --->
<CFFUNCTION NAME="GetFilmURL">
  <!--- One argument: FilmID --->
  <CFARGUMENT NAME="FilmID" TYPE="numeric" REQUIRED="Yes">

  <!--- Return the appropriate URL --->
  <CFRETURN "ShowFilm.cfm?FilmID=#ARGUMENTS.FilmID#">
</CFFUNCTION>


<!--- Include another UDF function library --->
<!--- This one creates the JavaScriptPopupLink() function --->
<CFINCLUDE TEMPLATE="SimpleJavaScriptFunctions.cfm">


<!--- Function: MakeFilmPopupLink() --->
<!--- Returns an HTML link for a film, based on FilmID --->
<CFFUNCTION NAME="MakeFilmPopupLink">
  <!--- One argument: FilmID --->
  <CFARGUMENT NAME="FilmID" TYPE="numeric" REQUIRED="Yes">

  <!--- Return a link for the film --->
  <CFRETURN JavaScriptPopupLink(GetFilmURL(FilmID), GetFilmTitle(FilmID))>
</CFFUNCTION>
```

Each of the `<CFFUNCTION>` blocks in Listing 19.4 is fairly simple. One of the interesting things to note here is that UDFs can call other UDFs in the same file. They can even call functions in other files, as long as the `<CFINCLUDE>` tag has been used to include the other files.

NOTE

In fact, UDF A can always call UDF B, as long as you've included UDF B in one of the ColdFusion files involved in the page request. It doesn't matter if some of the files are turn included by other files, or deeply the files are included within each other. The order of inclusion doesn't matter either.

Let's take a closer look at each one of these new UDFs individually:

- For the `GetFilmsQuery()`, note that the `<CFARGUMENT>` tag includes a `REQUIRED="No"` attribute, which means the argument is optional. The first thing this function does is execute a `<CFQUERY>` tag film information from the database. Within the query, a simple `IsDefined("ARGUMENTS.FilmID")` test is used to find out whether the optional `FilmID` argument has been provided when the function is actually used. If so, a `WHERE` clause is dynamically included in the SQL statement (so the query retrieves just the information about the specified film).
- The `GetFilmTitle()` function has been reworked a bit, mainly to demonstrate that UDFs can call any other UDFs in the same file. Now, instead of using a `<CFQUERY>` tag within the body of the function, the new, convenient `GetFilmsQuery()` function is used instead. Note that the `FilmID` argument provided to `GetFilmTitle()` is in turn passed to `GetFilmsQuery()` internally, which means that the returned query contains data about the specified film only. It is then a simple matter to return the film's title using the `<CFRETURN>` tag.
- The `GetFilmURL()` function is the simplest of all the UDFs in this library. It simply returns a URL that points to a template called `ShowFilm.cfm`, passing along the specified `FilmID` as a URL parameter. The nice thing about this function is that it abstracts the idea of a film's Detail Page. If the URL that people should go to for more information about a film changes in the future, you can just edit the function in one place, rather than in multiple places throughout the application.
- The `MakeFilmPopupLink()` function is somewhat interesting because it calls three functions internally. It uses both `GetFilmURL()` and `GetFilmTitle()` to get the URL and title of the specified film, respectively. It then passes the returned values to the `JavaScriptPopupLink()` function, created in a separate UDF library file called `SimpleJavaScriptFunctions.cfm`. You will see the code for this function in a moment. For now, just take it on faith that the function returns the HTML and JavaScript code needed to create a link that opens a pop-up window.

Putting the UDF Library to Use

Listing 19.5 shows a new version of the Film List page (see Listings 19.1 and 19.3 for the previous versions). This version gets its work done with just a few lines of code, and it's more functional too! Now, when the user clicks a film's title, a small pop-up window displays more information about that film (Figure 19.3).

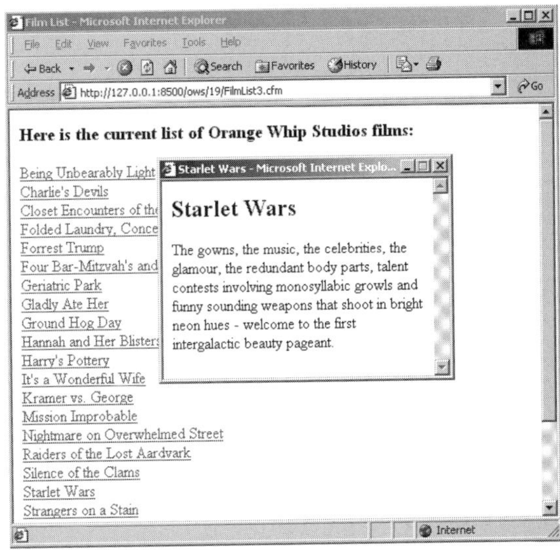

Figure 19.3

UDFs can encapsulate scripting, HTML, or other lower-level code.

Listing 19.5 FilmList3.cfm Using several UDFs together

```
<!--- Include the set of film-related user-defined functions --->
<CFINCLUDE TEMPLATE="FilmFunctions2.cfm">

<!--- Get a query object about films in database --->
<CFSET GetFilms = GetFilmsQuery()>

<HTML>
<HEAD><TITLE>Film List</TITLE></HEAD>
<BODY>
  <H3>Here is the current list of Orange Whip Studios films:</H3>

  <!--- Now it is extremely easy to display a list of film links --->
  <CFOUTPUT QUERY="GetFilms">
    #MakeFilmPopupLink(GetFilms.FilmID)#<BR>
  </CFOUTPUT>
</BODY>
</HTML>
```

First, a `<CFINCLUDE>` tag is used to include the new library of film-related UDFs. That makes it possible to call the `GetFilmsQuery()` function to get a query object full of information about the films in the company's database. The value returned by the function is assigned to the local `GetFilms` variable. From that point on, the `GetFilms` query object can be used just as if there was an actual `<CFQUERY NAME="GetFilms">` tag on the page.

Now it just takes a simple call to `MakeFilmPopupLink()` to create a pop-up–enabled link for each film in the `GetFilms` query. Through the magic of the UDF framework, that one line of code looks up the movie's title, obtains the correct URL to display details about the film, and generates the JavaScript code needed to pop up the detail page in a small window. And it's all eminently reusable.

Don't user-defined functions rock?

Creating General-Purpose UDFs

The functions in the FilmFunctions UDF library (refer to Table 19.4) are all related to the film concept, which is in turn somewhat related to the Films table in the ows database. As such, the library is really of interest only to the developers working on the Orange Whip Studios site. It's not going to be of much use to other ColdFusion developers.

It is, however, possible to create user-defined functions that have no ties to a particular application. You can think of such functions as *general-purpose functions*. They are useful for many different types of applications.

For instance, consider the `JavaScriptPopupLink()` function used internally by the FilmFunctions library in Listing 19.4. That function isn't expecting any input that is specific to Orange Whip Studios or any other type of application. And its purpose—to create pop-up windows easily—might come in handy in any Web-based application.

Things to Consider

You don't need to do anything special to create a general-purpose function. Just go ahead and use the same `<CFFUNCTION>`, `<CFARGUMENT>`, and `<CFRETURN>` syntax you have already learned about. Just keep these things in mind as you go along:

Keep the list of arguments as short as possible. ColdFusion will let you create UDFs with many, many arguments, but such functions quickly become unwieldy. If you feel like you need to have lots and lots of arguments, consider creating a CFML Custom Tag instead, as discussed in the next chapter.

Keep code reuse in mind. If the problem at hand has both an application-specific aspect and a general-purpose aspect, try to isolate the two parts of the problems in two different functions. For instance, the problem of displaying a pop-up window about a film has an application-specific aspect (the film) and a general-purpose aspect (the pop-up window). By creating two different functions, you can reuse the pop-up aspect in situations that don't have anything to do with films.

You haven't learned how to make them yet, but remember that it is also possible to create your own Custom Tags and Components (CFCs) as well as functions. Custom Tags are significantly more powerful and flexible than custom functions. Try to use UDFs for simple matters, especially quick retrieval and formatting. Use Custom Tags and Components for more involved processes, especially those you can think of as discrete actions rather than simple "massaging." See Chapter 20 for details.

Writing the SimpleJavaScriptFunctions Library

As an example of a general-purpose UDF library, let's consider the `SimpleJavaScriptFunctions.cfm` library we used earlier, in Listing 19.4. Presently, this library contains only one function, `JavaScriptPopupLink()`, which is responsible for creating a link that opens a pop-up window when clicked. This function supports four arguments, as listed in Table 19.5.

Table 19.5 `JavaScriptPopupLink()` Function Syntax

ARGUMENT	DESCRIPTION
`LinkURL`	Required. The URL for the page that should appear in the pop-up window when the user clicks the link.
`LinkText`	Required. The text of the link—that is, the text the user will click to open the pop-up window. This text will also appear in the browser's status bar when the pointer hovers over the link.
`PopupWidth`	Optional. The width of the pop-up window, in pixels. If this argument is not provided, a default width of `300` is used.
`PopupHeight`	Optional. The height of the pop-up window, in pixels. If this argument is not provided, a default width of `200` is used.
`PopupTop`	Optional. The vertical position of the pop-up window. If this argument is not provided, a default value of `200` is used.
`PopupLeft`	Optional. The horizontal position of the pop-up window. If this argument is not provided, a default value of `300` is used.

NOTE

The `PopupWidth`, `PopupHeight`, `PopupTop`, and `PopupLeft` arguments correspond to the `width`, `height`, `top`, and `left` values supported by the JavaScript `window.open()` method. I don't have the space to go into the ins and outs of these values here. Consult a JavaScript reference for details.

The function uses all these pieces of information to assemble the HTML code for an anchor element (that is, an `<A HREF>` tag) containing the appropriate JavaScript code to get the desired effect. The code is returned as the function's result (as a string).

Listing 19.6 is the ColdFusion code required to create `JavaScriptPopupLink()`.

NOTE

Please keep in mind that the goal here is not to teach you about JavaScript (that would take a whole book in itself), but rather to show you how you can distill something *like* JavaScript code and package it into a UDF for your ColdFusion pages. The nice thing about this kind of abstraction is that people can use the UDF without needing to understand the JavaScript code it generates.

Listing 19.6 `SimpleJavaScriptFunctions.cfm`—Creating a General-Purpose UDF

```
<!---
 Filename:    SimpleJavaScriptFunctions.cfm
 Created by: Nate Weiss (NMW)
 Purpose:     Creates a library of ColdFusion functions that
              encapsulate JavaScript ideas
--->

<!--- Function: JavaScriptPopupLink() --->
<!--- Returns an HTML link that opens a pop-up window via JavaScript --->
<CFFUNCTION NAME="JavaScriptPopupLink">
  <!--- One argument: FilmID --->
  <CFARGUMENT NAME="LinkURL" TYPE="string" REQUIRED="Yes">
  <CFARGUMENT NAME="LinkText" TYPE="string" REQUIRED="Yes">
```

Listing 19.6 (continued)

```
    <CFARGUMENT NAME="PopupWidth" TYPE="numeric" DEFAULT="300">
    <CFARGUMENT NAME="PopupHeight" TYPE="numeric" DEFAULT="200">
    <CFARGUMENT NAME="PopupTop" TYPE="numeric" DEFAULT="200">
    <CFARGUMENT NAME="PopupLeft" TYPE="numeric" DEFAULT="300">

    <!--- These variables are for this function's use only --->
    <CFSET var Features = "">
    <CFSET var LinkCode = "">

    <!--- Window features get passed to JavaScript's window.open() command --->
    <CFSET Features = "width=#ARGUMENTS.PopupWidth#,"
      & "height=#ARGUMENTS.PopupHeight#,top=#ARGUMENTS.PopupTop#,"
      & "left=#ARGUMENTS.PopupLeft#,scrollbars=yes">

    <!--- Create variable called LinkCode, which contains HTML / JavaScript --->
    <!--- needed to display a link that creates a pop-up window when clicked --->
    <CFSAVECONTENT VARIABLE="LinkCode">
      <CFOUTPUT>
        <a href="#ARGUMENTS.LinkURL#"
          onclick="
            popupWin = window.open('#ARGUMENTS.LinkURL#','myPopup','#Features#');
            popupWin.focus(); return false;"
          onmouseover="window.status = '#JSStringFormat(LinkText)#';return true;"
          onmouseout="window.status = ''; return true;"
        >#LinkText#</a>
      </CFOUTPUT>
    </CFSAVECONTENT>

    <!--- Return the completed link code --->
    <CFRETURN LinkCode>
  </CFFUNCTION>
```

NOTE

This listing includes some JavaScript code, such as `window.open()`, `focus()`, `window.status`, and `return true`. Unfortunately, I can't explain these items here. However, you will find these are among the very first things covered in even the most rudimentary JavaScript reference or online guide. So if you aren't familiar with these items, you won't have a hard time finding an explanation.

As with the earlier UDF examples in this chapter, the first thing this code does is define the function's arguments with the `<CFARGUMENT>` tag. This is actually the first UDF example that accepts more than one argument. As you can see, you can add as many arguments as you like. (Just don't get totally carried away, since functions with dozens of arguments will probably be somewhat harder to use.)

Next, a variable called `Features` is created; this is the list of "window features" that will be supplied to the JavaScript `window.open()` method. You can find out more about how to specify window features in a JavaScript reference guide, but the basic idea is that this describes the physical pop-up window, including its position and size. When the function executes, the value of `Features` will be something like this (depending on the actual arguments used):

```
width=300,height=200,top=200,left=300,scrollbars=yes
```

The next block of code uses the `<CFSAVECONTENT>` tag to create a variable named `LinkCode`. ColdFusion will process and evaluate all the code between the opening and closing `<CFSAVECONTENT>` tags, then assign the final result to the `LinkCode` variable. This makes it easier to create a variable that contains multiple lines, a variety of quotation marks, and so on. In this kind of situation, it's a lot easier than using the <CFSET> tag. You can even use tags like <CFLOOP> within this type of block. That said, a <CFSET> (or several <CFSET> tags) would work equally well. The code might just be a bit harder to follow.

Within the <CFSAVECONTENT> block, the basic idea is to generate a normal HTML <a> tag, with a normal `href` attribute. In addition to the `href` attribute, the <a> tag is also given `onclick`, `onmouseover`, and `onmouseout` attributes. These attributes contain JavaScript code that will execute when the user clicks the link, hovers over the link, and hovers away from the link, respectively.

NOTE

It is also necessary to use a pair of <CFOUTPUT> tags here to force ColdFusion to evaluate the variables and expressions within this block. The final result (after all number signs (#), tags, and functions have been evaluated) is "captured" by <CFSAVECONTENT> and placed into the `LinkText` variable. See Appendix B for details.

The result is the behavior shown earlier in Figure 19.3: when the user clicks the link, a pop-up window appears. If the user's browser doesn't support JavaScript, or if scripting has been disabled, the Film Details page simply appears in the main window (as a normal link would). You can use your browser's View Source option to examine the final HTML and JavaScript code that gets sent to the browser.

Another Example Library: ColorFunctions

At this point, you know just about everything you need to know for creating user-defined functions with ColdFusion MX. Our companion volume, *Advanced ColdFusion MX Application Development*, has a chapter called "Advanced User-Defined Functions," which covers a few scenarios not discussed here. It also discusses creating UDFs with <CFSCRIPT> instead of the <CFFUNCTION> tag.

Now it's up to you to create the UDFs you need for your own applications!

Just to get your brain spinning, I have included the code for another general-purpose UDF library called `ColorFunctions.cfm`. This UDF library contains three functions, as listed in Table 19.6.

Table 19.6 Functions in the ColorFunctions UDF Library

FUNCTION	DESCRIPTION
`ListGetRand(list)`	Picks one element at random from a comma-separated list. This really doesn't have anything to do with colors; this library includes it so the `RandomColor()` function can use it internally.
`GetRandColor()`	Returns a random hexadecimal color, in the form `RRGGBB`. The red, green, and blue portions of the color are each selected at random from the values `00` through `FF`, which ensures that the returned color is a member of the so-called browser safety palette and thus should display reasonably well on all monitors.
`MulticolorFormat(text)`	Accepts any text (say, a sentence or paragraph) and returns the same text with HTML <font> tags wrapped around each word. Each of the <font> tags specifies that the word should be displayed in a color picked at random by the `GetRandColor()` function.

Once you include this UDF library with a <CFINCLUDE> tag, you could use any of these functions in your own templates. For instance, on a Web page, the following would display the message "Hello, World" in a random color:

```
<CFOUTPUT>
  <DIV STYLE="color:#GetRandColor()#">Hello, World</DIV>
</CFOUTPUT>
```

And this would display the following sentence about two cute forest critters, with each word colored randomly:

```
<CFOUTPUT>
  #MulticolorFormat("The quick red fox jumped over the lazy bear.")#
</CFOUTPUT>
```

Listing 19.7 shows the <CFFUNCTION> code for the three functions listed above. The code for each of the individual functions is pretty simple. The purpose of this listing is mostly to get you thinking a bit about what kinds of operations UDFs can encapsulate. That said, you are invited to study this listing or adapt it to serve some other purpose. Refer to Appendix C, "ColdFusion Function Reference," for details about the `ListGetAt()`, `RandRange()`, and `ListLen()`, functions used here.

Listing 19.7 `ColorFunctions.cfm`—A Library of Functions Related to Colors

```
<!---
  Filename:   ColorFunctions.cfm
  Created by: Nate Weiss (NMW)
  Purpose:    Creates a library of user-defined functions
              related to colors in the browser safety palette
--->


<!--- Function: ListGetRandom() --->
<!--- Returns a random element from any comma-separated list --->
<CFFUNCTION NAME="ListGetRand">
  <!--- One argument: The comma-separated list --->
  <CFARGUMENT NAME="List" TYPE="string" REQUIRED="Yes">

  <CFRETURN ListGetAt(ARGUMENTS.List, RandRange(1, ListLen(ARGUMENTS.List)))>
</CFFUNCTION>


<!--- Function: GetRandColor() --->
<!--- Returns a random element from any comma-separated list --->
<CFFUNCTION NAME="GetRandColor">
  <!---
    This is a list of hexidecimal values that can be used to specify colors
    for use on Web pages. Any three of these can be combined to make a color,
    in the form RRGGBB. For instance, 9900CC is a nice shade of purple.
  --->
  <CFSET var HexList = "00,11,22,33,44,55,66,77,88,99,AA,BB,CC,DD,EE,FF">

  <!--- Choose 3 of the Hex values randomly and return them all together --->
  <CFRETURN ListGetRand(HexList) & ListGetRand(HexList) & ListGetRand(HexList)>
</CFFUNCTION>
```

Listing 19.7 (continued)

```
<!--- Function: MulticolorFormat() --->
<!--- Adds <font> tags to any text such that each word is colored randomly --->
<CFFUNCTION NAME="MulticolorFormat">
  <!--- One argument: the text to make multicolored --->
  <CFARGUMENT NAME="Text" TYPE="string" REQUIRED="Yes">

  <!--- This is what we will end up returning. Start with an empty string. --->
  <CFSET var String = "">

  <!--- Loop through the list of words, treating spaces as list delimiters --->
  <CFLOOP LIST="#Text#" INDEX="Word" DELIMITERS=" ">
    <!--- Create a <font> tag for this word, using a random color --->
    <CFSET String = String & ' <font color="#GetRandColor()#">#Word#</font>'>
  </CFLOOP>

  <!--- Return completed string --->
  <CFRETURN String>
</CFFUNCTION>
```

Sharing UDF Libraries with Others

Of course, you can download and use UDF function libraries that other people have written. Just save the .cfm file that contains the functions to an appropriate place on your server's drive, then include the file with `<CFINCLUDE>`, just like the other examples in this chapter. You can also share your own general-purpose UDF libraries with others for fun and/or profit.

One place to exchange UDF function libraries is the Macromedia Developer Exchange, at `http://devex.macromedia.com` (Figure 19.4).

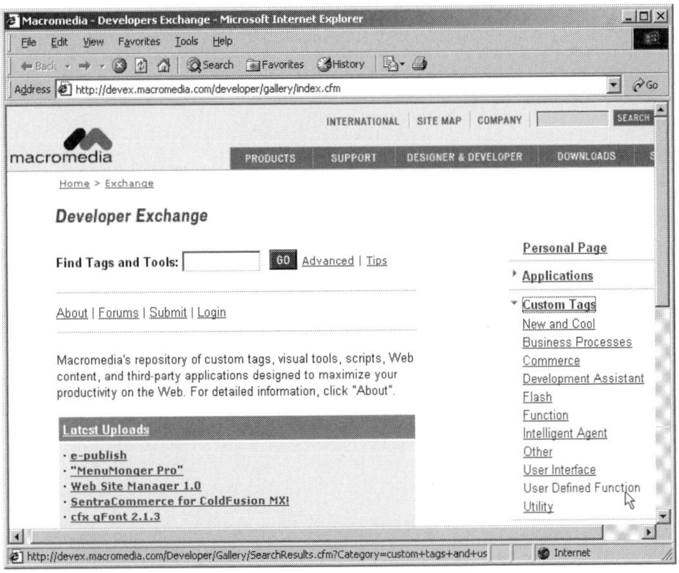

Figure 19.4
The Macromedia Developer Exchange is a good place to share UDFs.

Another great place to find or share user-defined functions is the Common Function Library Project, at www.cflib.com (Figure 19.5).

NOTE

The <CFFUNCTION> and related tags discussed in this chapter are new for ColdFusion MX. In previous versions of ColdFusion, the only way to create UDFs was with the less powerful <CFSCRIPT> tag, which is not discussed specifically in this book. If you come across a UDF that was created using <CFSCRIPT>, you can use it in your code just like the ones discussed in this chapter. For creating new UDFs, we strongly recommend using <CFFUNCTION> rather than the older, script-based method.

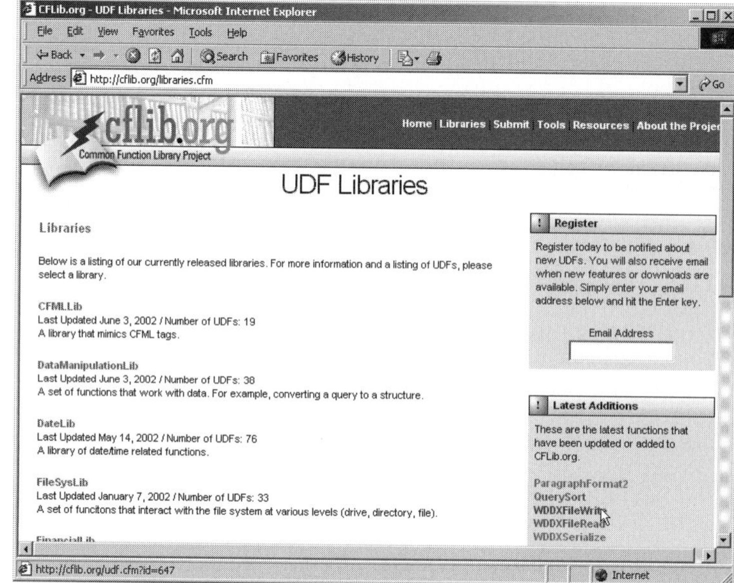

Figure 19.5

The Common Function Library Project's Web site is another great place to find user-defined functions.

CHAPTER 20

Building Reusable Components

IN THIS CHAPTER

Easy, Powerful Extensibility

In Chapter 19, "Building User-Defined Functions," you learned how to create your own user-defined functions (UDFs). UDFs are exciting because they allow you to add to the CFML language to better suit your needs. Once you have written a UDF, you can use it just like one of ColdFusion's own built-in functions. The notion of extending ColdFusion's own language is exciting, because it provides opportunities to reuse your code in many different places. That makes your job easier and more productive. Plus, it's just kind of fun!

Let's take a moment to recap the four basic ways of extending ColdFusion:

- **User-Defined Functions.** Again, if there is some function that you feel is missing from ColdFusion's list of built-in functions, or that would come in really handy for an application you're building, you can just make the function yourself. Chapter 19 discusses UDFs.
- **Custom Tags.** While UDFs allow you to make your own functions, custom tags allow you to create your own CFML tags. Of all the extensibility methods listed here, custom tags remain the most flexible and powerful. The first half of this chapter discusses custom tags.
- **ColdFusion Components (CFCs).** CFCs are similar conceptually to custom tags, but imply a more structured, object-oriented manner of programming. CFCs are also at the heart of ColdFusion MX's new Flash and Web Services integration. The second half of this chapter discusses CFCs.
- **CFX Tags.** It is also possible to write your own CFX tags in either Java or C++. For more information about writing CFX tags, see the ColdFusion MX documentation or consult this book's companion volume, *Advanced ColdFusion MX Application Development*.

Introducing CFML Custom Tags

The UDF framework introduced in Chapter 19 is brand new for ColdFusion MX and represents a major step forward, making ColdFusion application development faster than ever before. UDFs are probably the easiest and most straightforward way to extend the language.

That said, the most flexible way to extend ColdFusion is by creating your own tags. Like UDFs, custom tags enable you to add your own tags to the CFML language, for whatever purpose you want. Unlike UDFs, the custom tag framework has been around since ColdFusion 3.0, and has become a rich and mature part of the product. At the time of this writing, there are a great many more custom tags than UDFs, and custom tags are the bedrock of many existing ColdFusion applications. They excel at encapsulating concepts and processes.

You can solve many problems using either framework. The best news is that you can write extensions in ColdFusion's native language, CFML, regardless of which framework you choose for a particular task. This means you already know most of what you need, and can get started right away.

The Basic Idea

The idea behind custom tags is simple: to enable ColdFusion developers such as yourself to package chunks of ordinary CFML code into reusable modules. From that point on, you can refer to the modules by name, using the familiar tag-based syntax you already expect from ColdFusion. You get to define attributes for your tags, just as for regular CFML tags. Your tags can run queries, generate HTML, and perform calculations. They have almost no special requirements or limitations.

Generally, custom tags are self-contained and goal-oriented. They take care of whatever processing is necessary to get a particular task or a set of related tasks done. Truth is, custom tags can be many different things, depending on your needs.

Why Modularity Is a Good Thing

As you will soon see, custom tags are easy to write. However, as easy as they are, you generally need to put some thought into exactly how you want them to work. A process that might take half an hour to code as a normal ColdFusion template might require an extra 10 or 15 minutes to implement as a custom tag, because you will need to put some extra thought into how to modularize your code.

If it takes extra time, why bother with all this modularity business? The answer, of course, is that breaking your code into independent, manageable chunks has a number of significant advantages.

Modularity Means Having More Fun

Let's face it. The idea of creating your own tags—your very own extensions to the hip and stylish CFML language—is, well, it's just cool! And the fact that you get to write them using the ordinary ColdFusion syntax you already know and love makes it really easy to get excited about writing them. When you're excited as a programmer, you're naturally more creative, more ambitious, and more productive. There's nothing like a burst of enthusiasm to boost your productivity. It's as close to an adrenaline rush as many of us coders are going to get, at least at our day jobs.

Modularity Means Being Self-Contained

Because custom tags are modular, they usually end up being entirely self-contained. For instance, you might create a custom tag called `<CF_PlaceOrder>` that takes care of all aspects of placing an order, whatever that means in practice for your application. Because this custom tag is self contained, other developers can place the tag in their templates wherever they need to, without worrying about what your custom tag actually does internally.

Modules Are Easy to Maintain

In addition, when you're using a custom tag, you can make any changes in just one place. Again, consider a hypothetical custom tag called `<CF_PlaceOrder>`. If you need to add some new step to the actual processing of each order, you can update the custom tag without having to touch each template that uses the tag. Additionally, because custom tags generally represent self-contained, well-defined chunks of code that do just one thing and do it well, they are usually easier for various members of a team to maintain. Their single-mindedness and sense of purpose tend to make them more self-documenting and easier to understand than ordinary templates.

Modularity Encourages Code Reuse

Why reinvent the wheel? If someone else already has written code that gets a particular task done, it's almost always easier and more efficient to simply reuse that code, freeing you up to get on to the next item in your schedule. Conversely, if you write some code that solves a problem, why not package it in such a way that you can easily use it again later?

Modules Can Be Traded or Sold

You don't even have to know how to write a custom tag to take advantage of them. Hundreds of custom tags are available—most of them free—which you can download and use in your own applications. What's more, most publicly available custom tags are unencrypted, so you can adapt them to suit your needs if they do *almost* what you need them to do but not quite. Of course, you can share your custom tags with others if they help solve a common problem. And if one of your custom tags is particularly great, others will likely be glad to buy it from you.

How to Use Custom Tags

It is sometimes said that lazy people make the best programmers because they tend to solve problems by taking advantage of proven, working solutions that are already in place. Lazy or not, it's often a great idea to reuse work others have done. Before you get started on a project or before you tackle a piece of code, you should see whether someone has already written a custom tag that does what you need. If so, you can just use it in your code and move on to your next task. It's almost like getting the entire ColdFusion developer community to help you write the code for your application.

Finding Tags on the Developer Exchange

You can look for custom tags online in a number of places. By far the largest and most popular is the Developer Exchange portion of Macromedia's own Web site, which offers thousands of custom tags for the taking. In many situations, a simple search will reveal that someone else has already solved your problem for you.

The Developer Exchange is located at http://devex.macromedia.com . You can run keyword searches to find tags or browse through tags by category, popularity, or date of posting (Figure 20.1).

NOTE

Other items are available besides custom tags at the Developer Exchange, so when you run a search, be sure to specify that you want custom tags only.

NOTE

Another good place to look for custom tags is the CFXtras site, at `www.cfxtras.com`.

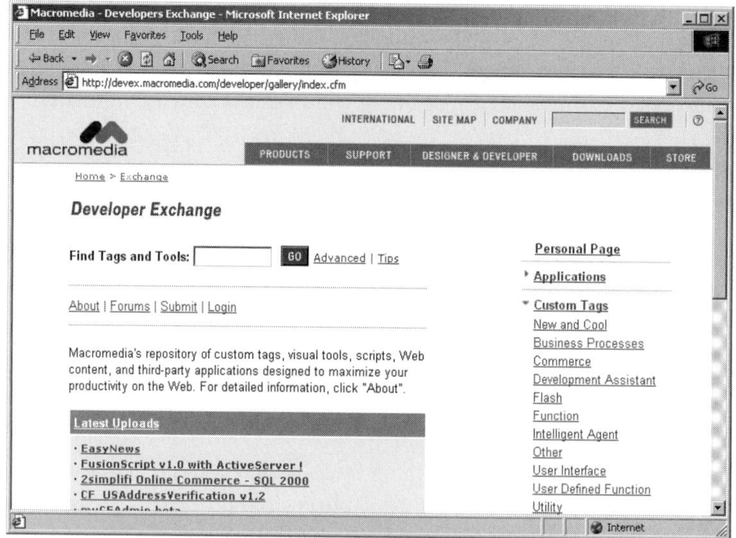

Figure 20.1

The Developer Exchange on the Macromedia Web site is a great place to look for publicly available custom tags.

How to "Install" a Custom Tag

A single ColdFusion template (.cfm) file represents each custom tag. Generally, the .cfm file and some type of documentation are placed together in a .zip file for easy downloading.

There isn't really any special installation step. All you have to do is place the custom tag template into the special `CustomTags` folder on your ColdFusion server's drive.

To install a custom tag, follow these steps:

1. Find the custom tag you want and download the .zip file that contains the tag. If you have been given the .cfm file directly rather than compressed in a .zip file, go to step 3.

2. Open the .zip file, using a utility such as WinZip from `www.winzip.com`, and find the custom tag template (.cfm) file itself. The template's filename will be the name of the custom tag, without the `CF_` prefix. So, if you have downloaded a custom tag called `<CF_PlaceOrder>`, you should look for a file called `PlaceOrder.cfm`.

3. Place the custom tag template file into the `CustomTags` folder, located within the `CFusionMX` folder on your ColdFusion server's drive. In a default Windows installation, this is the `c:\CFusionMX\CustomTags` folder.

That's it. The custom tag is now installed, and you can start using it in your code.

TIP

If you want to organize the custom tag templates you download (or write yourself) into subfolders within the `CustomTags` folder, go ahead. As long as they are somewhere within the `CustomTags` folder, ColdFusion will find them and let you use them in your applications.

NOTE

If you don't have access to the special `CustomTags` folder, or if you plan to use the custom tag in just one or two of your own templates, you can just place the custom tag template into the folder where you plan to use it. See "Placing Custom Tags in the Current Directory," later in this chapter.

NOTE

You can move the location of the special `CustomTags` folder, or create additional special custom tag folders. See Changing the "Custom Tag Search Path," later in this chapter.

NOTE

Some custom tags might require other tags or files to be present as well. The documentation that comes with the tag should point out what you need to know.

NOTE

If after you download a tag, you find that no ColdFusion template exists with the appropriate filename, you may have downloaded a *CFX tag*, which is different from a CFML custom tag. CFX tags are compiled with a language such as Java or C++ and must be registered in the ColdFusion Administrator before you can use them. Instead of a template (.cfm) file, they are represented by one or more Dynamic Link Library (.dll) or Java Class (.class) files. See Chapter 28, "ColdFusion Server Configuration," for details.

Using Custom Tags

After you install a custom tag by placing its template in the special `CustomTags` folder, it's ready for use in your code. So you can get your feet wet, this book's CD-ROM includes two custom tags in the folder for this chapter. The custom tags are .zip files, just as if you had downloaded them from the Developer Exchange (see Figure 20.1) or some other source. Table 20.1 provides information about the tags.

Before you try the following code listings, install these tags according to the directions in the last section. That is, extract the `CoolImage.cfm` and `TwoSelectsRelated.cfm` templates from the .zip files included on the CD-ROM, and place them in the special `CustomTags` folder on your ColdFusion server.

Table 20.1 Third-Party Custom Tags Included on the CD-ROM for This Chapter

CUSTOM TAG	WHAT IT DOES
`<CF_CoolImage>`	Creates a rollover image on the current page. When the user hovers the pointer over the image, it changes, usually to a glowing or highlighted version of the original image.
`<CF_TwoSelectsRelated>`	Places two correlated `<SELECT>` lists or drop-down lists on the current page. When the user selects an item in the first list, the choices in the second list change.

Using <CF_CoolImage>

Users and graphic designers seem to love rollover images, in which an image changes when you move your pointer over it, usually to suggest that the image is live and can (should! must!) be clicked. Normally, you must write or borrow some JavaScript to get this done.

Listing 20.1 shows how you can use the `<CF_CoolImage>` custom tag to place a rollover image easily on one of your pages. If you visit this listing in your Web browser, you will see that the image does indeed roll over when you move the pointer over it.

Listing 20.1 `UseCoolImage.cfm`—Using the `<CF_CoolImage>` Custom Tag to Create a Rollover Effect

```
<!---
  Filename: UsingCoolImage.cfm
  Author:   Nate Weiss (NMW)
  Purpose:  Demonstrates how to use a custom tag
--->

<HTML>
<HEAD><TITLE>Using a Custom Tag</TITLE></HEAD>
<BODY>

<H2>Using a Custom Tag</H2>
<P>Hover your mouse over the logo, baby, yeah!</P>

  <!--- Display a "Mouse Rollover" Image via groovy --->
  <!--- <CF_CoolImage> Custom Tag by Jeremy Allaire --->
  <!--- The tag will include all needed code for us --->
  <CF_CoolImage
    ImgName="MyImage"
    Src="Logo.gif"
    OverSrc="LogoOver.gif"
    Width="300"
    Height="139"
    Border="0"
    HREF="http://www.macromedia.com/"
    Alt="Click for Macromedia Home Page">

</BODY>
</HTML>
```

The attributes for `<CF_CoolImage>` are fairly self-explanatory and are not detailed here (you can look them up on the Developer Exchange if you want). The purpose of this listing is to show you how to use a custom tag in your code and give you a sense of what you can do with custom tags.

NOTE

If memory serves, this was one of the very first custom tags ever posted for public download, written by none other than Jeremy Allaire, one of the fathers of ColdFusion. I remember very fondly when I first saw it, only then realizing what custom tags were really all about. Others have since improved on this tag a bit, but it remains a classic and is quite interesting as a piece of history!

Thinking About Custom Tags as Abstractions

If you visit `UseCoolImage.cfm` and then view its HTML code using your browser's View Source option, you will see that all the appropriate JavaScript and HTML code has been generated for you, based on the attributes you provided to the tag in Listing 20.1. I don't have the space to go into a line-by-line explanation of the generated code here, but because the custom tag takes care of writing it correctly for you, you don't really need to understand it.

In fact, that's the great thing about the tag. It enables you to focus on the task at hand—inserting a rollover image—without worrying about the actual code you would normally need to write. It enables you to think about the rollover at a higher, or more abstract, level. Developers often refer to this type of phenomenon as *abstraction*.

The more concepts or coding steps a tag wraps up into one task-based or goal-oriented chunk, the more fully that tag becomes a helpful abstraction of the underlying concepts. You are free to make your custom tags do whatever you want them to and have them represent whatever level of abstraction you feel is appropriate.

NOTE

If you want to know more about the JavaScript code generated by `<CF_CoolImage>`, you can easily decipher it with the help of a JavaScript reference text or online JavaScript tutorial. You can also refer to the JavaScript reference built into Dreamweaver MX.

Using `<CF_TwoSelectsRelated>`

So you can begin to get a sense of the variety of effects and behaviors custom tags offer, here is another example, this time using the `<CF_TwoSelectsRelated>` custom tag, also included on this book's CD-ROM. This custom tag enables you to add two `<SELECT>` lists quickly to your page; these lists become actively correlated via JavaScript. Again, the goal of the tag is to present developers with an abstraction of the basic idea of related inputs, without making each developer concentrate on getting the tedious JavaScript code exactly right.

Listing 20.2 shows how to use the tag in your own applications. Here it displays a list of ratings. When the user clicks a rating in the first list, the corresponding list of films is displayed in the second list (Figure 20.2).

Listing 20.2 `UsingTwoSelectsRelated.cfm`—Using the `<CF_TwoSelectsRelated>` Tag to Display Correlated Information

```
<!--- Get ratings and associated films from database --->
<CFQUERY DATASOURCE="ows" NAME="GetRatedFilms">
  SELECT
    r.RatingID, r.Rating,
    f.FilmID, f.MovieTitle
  FROM FilmsRatings r INNER JOIN Films f
  ON r.RatingID = f.RatingID
  ORDER BY r.RatingID, f.MovieTitle
</CFQUERY>


<HTML>
<HEAD><TITLE>Using a Custom Tag</TITLE></HEAD>
<BODY>
<H2>Using a Custom Tag</H2>

  <!--- This custom tag will only work in a form --->
  <FORM>

    <!--- Show ratings and films in correlated SELECT lists --->
    <!--- via custom tag, which generates all needed script --->
    <CF_TwoSelectsRelated
      QUERY="GetRatedFilms"
      NAME1="RatingID"
      NAME2="FilmID"
      DISPLAY1="Rating"
      DISPLAY2="MovieTitle"
      SIZE1="5"
      SIZE2="5"
      FORCEWIDTH1="30"
      FORCEWIDTH2="50">

  </FORM>

</BODY>
</HTML>
```

This code queries the Orange Whip Studios database to get a list of ratings and related films. The query variable is then provided to the `QUERY` attribute of the `<CF_TwoSelectsRelated>` custom tag. When the tag executes, it outputs two ordinary `<SELECT>` tags—the first with a `NAME` attribute as provided to the `NAME1` attribute of the custom tag, and the second with a `NAME` attribute as provided to `NAME2`. The appropriate number of `<OPTION>` tags is also generated for each `<SELECT>` list, with each `<OPTION>`'s display text and `VALUE` attribute coming from the results of the `GetRatedFilms` query, as specified by the `VALUE1`, `VALUE2`, `DISPLAY1`, and `DISPLAY2` attributes provided to the custom tag. In addition, the appropriate JavaScript code is generated to give the lists an actively related effect. If you visit Listing 20.2 in your browser, you can test the behavior. And if you view the page's source code using your browser's View Source option, you will see that about 75 lines of HTML and JavaScript code were generated for you, depending on the actual records in the database.

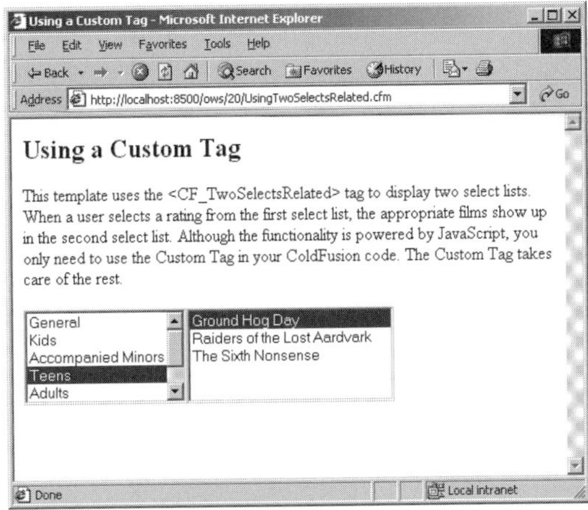

Figure 20.2

Some custom tags create user-interface widgets, such as these related select lists.

Again, the purpose of this listing is not to teach you the syntax for this custom tag in particular (you can learn more about that in the tag's documentation, included in the .zip file on the CD-ROM), as much as it is to give you an idea about how to use custom tags and the types of tasks they can do for you.

Changing the Custom Tag Search Path

As you have already learned, when you use a custom tag in one of your ColdFusion templates, the ColdFusion Application Server looks in the special `CustomTags` folder for the corresponding custom tag template. So, when you use the `<CF_TwoSelectsRelated>` custom tag in your own code, ColdFusion looks for the `TwoSelectsRelated.cfm` file in the `c:\CFUSION\CustomTags` folder (assuming you are running ColdFusion on a Windows machine and you've accepted the default installation options).

If you want, you can change the location of the special `CustomTags` folder or specify additional folders for ColdFusion to look in. For instance, say you want to place the custom tags for the Orange Whip Studios project in a folder called `C:\OrangeWhipCustomTags`, instead of `C:\CFUSION\CustomTags`. All you need to do is add the new folder to the custom tag search path. The custom tag search path is simply a list of folders ColdFusion looks through whenever you call a custom tag in one of your application templates. When you first install ColdFusion, only one folder is in the search path (the `CustomTags` folder within `CFusionMX`).

After you add a new folder to the search path, you are free to place some custom tags in the new folder and others in the original `CustomTags` folder. Now, when you first refer to a custom tag in your own templates, the ColdFusion server first looks in the special `CustomTags` folder (and its subfolders) and then in your newly specified folder (and any of its subfolders).

NOTE

If all this path searching sounds like a lot of overhead for ColdFusion to incur, don't worry. After ColdFusion successfully finds a custom tag template in the search paths you have configured, it remembers the template's location for all subsequent requests (until the server is restarted or until the server's template cache is exhausted). In other words, the custom tag search path is searched only once per custom tag per server restart, so there isn't much of a penalty for adding folders to the search path.

To add a folder to the custom tag search path, follow these steps:

1. Navigate to the Custom Tag Paths page of the ColdFusion Administrator.
2. Specify the path and name of the folder you want to add to the custom tag search path (Figure 20.3). You can use the Browse Server button to avoid having to type the folder's path manually.
3. Click the Add Path button. The new folder appears in the list of custom tag paths.
4. Now you can place your custom tag templates in the folder you just added or in the original.

You can also remove folders from the custom tag search path using the Delete button shown in Figure 20.3. After you remove a folder from the search path, ColdFusion will no longer find custom tag templates in that folder.

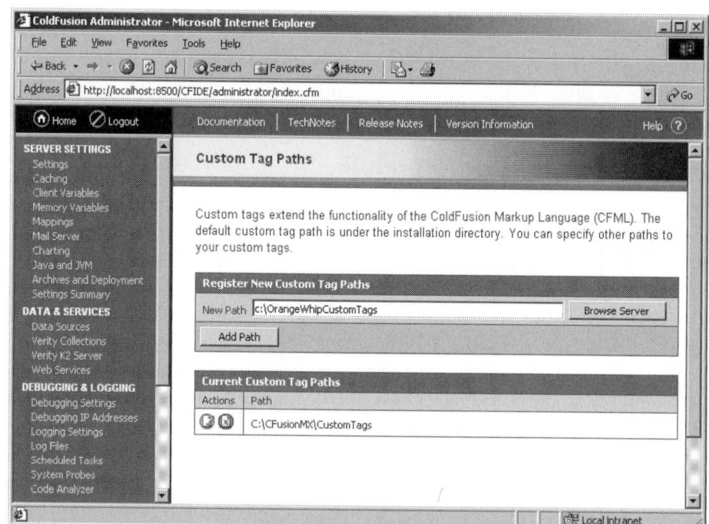

Figure 20.3

You can add folders to the custom tag search path with the ColdFusion Administrator.

NOTE

Throughout this chapter, you will find instructions to save files in the special `CustomTags` folder. Whenever the `CustomTags` folder is mentioned, you could also use any folders you have added to the custom tag search path.

Placing Custom Tags in the Current Directory

Sometimes placing custom tag templates in the special `CustomTags` folder is not possible or convenient (see the section "How to 'Install' a Custom Tag," earlier in this chapter). For instance, if an Internet Service Provider is hosting your ColdFusion application, you might not have access to the ColdFusion Administrator or the `CustomTags` folder.

In such a situation, you can place the custom tag template (`CoolImage.cfm`, for example) in the same folder as the template in which you want to use the custom tag. When ColdFusion encounters the custom tag in your code, it first looks for the appropriate file in the current folder. (It does not automatically look in the parent folder or subfolders of the current folder.) If ColdFusion can't find the `.cfm` file for the custom tag in the current folder, it then looks in the special `CustomTags` folder (and its subfolders).

Placing the custom tag template in the current folder is a good solution when:

- You don't have access to the special `CustomTags` folder.
- You are still developing and testing the custom tag.
- You know you won't use the custom tag extensively, so you don't mind its being available only to code templates in the current folder.
- You want to simplify the distribution of your application and would therefore rather not require that the custom tag template be dealt with separately.

These situations aside, it is generally recommended that you use the special `CustomTags` folder as described earlier in this chapter. You will find all your custom tags in one place, and you won't have to maintain multiple copies of the same custom tag template (one for each folder in which you want to use the tag).

Controlling Template Locations with <CFMODULE>

ColdFusion provides an alternative way to use custom tags in your templates, which is helpful in a number of situations. Instead of calling your custom tags using the usual `<CF_` prefix, you use the `<CFMODULE>` tag. You don't need to change anything in the custom tag template itself. You can use any custom tag with either method.

Introducing the <CFMODULE> Tag

The `<CFMODULE>` tag executes a ColdFusion template as a module, which is just another name for a CFML custom tag. Basically, you specify which custom tag you want to use with the `NAME` or `TEMPLATE` attribute. Then you add whatever additional attributes you need to pass to the tag, just as you would if you were calling the module using the normal `<CF_`-style custom tag syntax.

Table 20.2 explains the attributes you can supply to the `<CFMODULE>` tag.

TIP

You provide either the `NAME` attribute *or* the `TEMPLATE` attribute when using `<CFMODULE>`. You do not provide both.

Table 20.2 <CFMODULE> Tag Syntax

ATTRIBUTE	PURPOSE
NAME	The name of the custom tag you want to use, not including the <CF_ prefix. ColdFusion will look for the tag in the current folder and then the special CustomTags folder, just as it would if you were calling the custom tag normally. So, instead of using <CF_PlaceOrder> in your code, you would use <CFMODULE> with NAME="PlaceOrder".
TEMPLATE	The filename of the custom tag template, including the .cfm extension. You can provide a relative path to the template, just like the TEMPLATE attribute of the <CFINCLUDE> tag. ColdFusion will not automatically look for the tag in the special CustomTags folder because you are specifying the location explicitly. So, instead of using <CF_PlaceOrder> in your code, you might use <CFMODULE> with TEMPLATE="PlaceOrder.cfm".
ATTRIBUTECOLLECTION	Optional, and for special cases only. A structure that contains name-value pairs to consider as attributes. See the section "Passing Attributes with ATTRIBUTECOLLECTION," later in this chapter.

Calling Modules by Name

As mentioned previously, you can use <CFMODULE> to call modules either by name with the NAME attribute or by template location with the TEMPLATE attribute. In this section, you learn about calling modules by name.

Understanding the NAME Attribute

At its simplest, you can use <CFMODULE> to call custom tags by simply providing the name of the tag, without the customary <CF_ prefix. ColdFusion will use the same logic it does normally to find the corresponding template file (first looking in the current directory and then looking in the special CustomTags folder). Provide <CFMODULE> with whatever additional attributes you would normally supply to the custom tag.

For instance, you might have a custom tag called <CF_PlaceOrder> that's normally called with two attributes called OrderID and SendConfirmation, like this:

```
<!--- Place order --->
<CF_PlaceOrder
  OrderID="#MyOrderID#"
  SendConfirmation="Yes">
```

To call the tag with <CFMODULE>, you would use the following:

```
<!--- Delete movie --->
<CFMODULE
  NAME="PlaceOrder"
  OrderID="#MyOrderID#"
  SendConfirmation="Yes">
```

No huge advantage exists to using <CFMODULE> in this way versus the traditional <CF_ method. It is simply an alternative syntax you can use if you prefer.

NOTE

One advantage that can be helpful in certain situations is that this syntax can determine the NAME attribute dynamically. For example, you could create a string variable called CallThisModule, which would hold the name of the module you wanted to call, based on whatever logic you needed. You could then call <CFMODULE> with TEMPLATE="#CallThisModule#" to execute the module. There would be no way to accomplish this using the traditional <CF_ syntax.

Using Dot Notation to Avoid Conflicts

As you learned earlier, you can place custom tag templates anywhere within the special CustomTags folder. You can place them in the CustomTags folder itself, or you can create any number of folders and subfolders with the CustomTags folder (see the section "Using Custom Tags," earlier in this chapter).

In general, this is a great feature. The only problem is that more than one custom tag with the same filename could exist. For instance, what if two of your Web applications are running on the same ColdFusion server, and both use <CF_PlaceOrder> custom tags that do different things internally? You could place one in a subfolder of CustomTags called OrangeWhip and the other in a subfolder called PetStore, but you would have no way to tell ColdFusion which one of these to use at any given time. ColdFusion would simply use the first one it found for all requests, regardless of which folder the calling template was in.

To address this type of situation, ColdFusion allows you to use dot notation in <CFMODULE>'s NAME attribute, where the dots indicate subfolders within the special CustomTags folder.

For instance, to specify that you want to use the version of the PlaceOrder module located within the OrangeWhip subfolder of the CustomTags folder, you would use the following:

```
<!--- Place order via custom tag --->
<CFMODULE
  NAME="OrangeWhip.PlaceOrder">
```

To specify that you want to use the custom tag template PlaceOrder.cfm located in a folder called Commerce within a folder called OrangeWhip in the special CustomTags folder, you would use the following:

```
<!--- Delete movie --->
<CFMODULE
  NAME="OrangeWhip.Commerce.PlaceOrder"
  Action="Delete"
  FilmID="5">
```

As you can see, this special dot notation enables you to set up hierarchies of custom tag modules, simply by establishing subfolders nested within the CustomTags folder. This can be important if you'll be installing your application on a server along with other ColdFusion applications.

NOTE

If you prefer the <CF_ syntax to <CFMODULE> but are still worried about naming conflicts, you can generally address the issue by adding a consistent prefix to each of your custom tag filenames. Instead of naming a custom tag file PlaceOrder.cfm, for instance, you might call it owsPlaceOrder.cfm, making the chance of there being two tags with the same filename on the same server very unlikely. Then you could use the tag with <CF_owsPlaceOrder> syntax. It's a less formal solution, but it will generally work.

Calling Modules by Template Location

You can also use `<CFMODULE>` with its `TEMPLATE` attribute instead of the `NAME` attribute to explicitly specify the location of your custom tag template. Use this method in situations where you don't want ColdFusion to attempt to find your tag's template automatically (in the current folder, the `CustomTags` folder, or anywhere else).

NOTE

The `TEMPLATE` attribute effectively takes away the magic effect created by your custom tags as they appear to become part of ColdFusion. So using the word module instead of custom tag starts to make more sense.

The `TEMPLATE` attribute works just like the `TEMPLATE` attribute of the `<CFINCLUDE>` tag. You can provide a relative path to the template, using slashes to indicate subdirectories. You can also use the usual URL-style `../` notation to indicate the parent folder.

For instance, just as all images for the Orange Whip Studios project are stored in the `images` subfolder within the `ows` folder, you could keep all your modules in a subfolder called `modules`. Then, assuming you want to call a template from a different subfolder of `ows` (such as a subfolder called `20` for this chapter of this book), you could refer to the custom tag template using a relative path that starts with `../modules/`, as shown in the following code.

So, instead of this:

```
<!--- Place order --->
<CF_PlaceOrder
  OrderID="#MyOrderID#"
  SendConfirmation="Yes">
```

or this:

```
<!--- Delete movie --->
<CFMODULE
  NAME="PlaceOrder"
  OrderID="#MyOrderID#"
  SendConfirmation="Yes">
```

you might use something such as this:

```
<!--- Delete movie --->
<CFMODULE
  TEMPLATE="../modules/PlaceOrder.cfm"
  OrderID="#MyOrderID#"
  SendConfirmation="Yes">
```

NOTE

You can't provide an absolute file system–style path to the `TEMPLATE` attribute, so drive letters or UNC paths are not allowed.

Writing Custom Tags That Display Information

Now that you understand how to use existing custom tags, it's time to learn how to write your own. This section introduces you to the basic concepts involved in creating a custom tag. As you will soon see, it's an easy and productive way to write your code. And it's fun, too!

Writing Your First Custom Tag

It's traditional to illustrate a new language or technique with a "Hello, World" example. Listing 20.3 shows a custom tag that outputs a `"Hello, World"` message in the current Web page, formatted with ordinary HTML table syntax.

Make sure to save this listing as `HelloWorld.cfm`. Remember, you can save it in either the special `CustomTags` folder or the same folder you've been using as you follow along in this chapter.

Listing 20.3 `HelloWorld.cfm`—A Simple Custom Tag Template

```
<!---
  Filename: HelloWorld.cfm
  Author:   Nate Weiss (NMW)
  Purpose:  Creates the <CF_HelloWorld> custom tag example
--->

<TABLE BORDER="5" CELLPADDING="5">
  <TR><TH BGCOLOR="Yellow">
    <B>Hello, World, from Orange Whip Studios.</B><BR>
  </TH></TR>
  <TR><TD BGCOLOR="Orange">
    Orange whip... two orange whips... three orange whips!<BR>
  </TD></TR>
</TABLE>
```

Now you can use the custom tag just by adding a `CF_` prefix to the tag's filename (without the `.cfm` part). This means you have just created a custom tag called `<CF_HelloWorld>`, which you can use in code as shown in Listing 20.4.

Listing 20.4 `UsingHelloWorld.cfm`—Testing the `<CF_HelloWorld>` Custom Tag

```
<!---
  Filename: UsingHelloWorld.cfm
  Author:   Nate Weiss (NMW)
  Purpose:  Shows how <CF_HelloWorld> can be used in a ColdFusion page
--->

<HTML>
<HEAD><TITLE>Testing &lt;CF_HelloWorld&gt;</TITLE></HEAD>
<BODY>

  <!--- Display Hello World Message, via Custom Tag --->
  <CF_HelloWorld>

</BODY>
</HTML>
```

It's a start, but this custom tag is not terribly exciting. Of course, it will always output exactly the same thing. In fact, at this point, you could just replace the reference to the custom tag in Listing 20.4 with an ordinary `<CFINCLUDE>` tag and the results would be the same:

```
<!--- Display Hello World Message, via Custom Tag --->
<CFINCLUDE TEMPLATE="HelloWorld.cfm">
```

Things get a lot more interesting after you start making custom tags that accept attributes, just like ColdFusion's built-in tags.

Introducing the ATTRIBUTES Scope

To make your own custom tags really useful, you want them to accept tag attributes, just as normal CFML and HTML tags do. ColdFusion makes this very easy by defining a special `ATTRIBUTES` scope for use within your custom tag templates.

The `ATTRIBUTES` scope is a ColdFusion structure that is automatically populated with any attributes provided to the custom tag when it is actually used in code. For instance, if an attribute called `Message` is provided to a tag, as in `<CF_HelloWorld Message="Country and Western">`, then the special `ATTRIBUTES` scope will contain a `Message` value, set to `Country and Western`. You could output this value to the page by referring to `#ATTRIBUTES.Message#` between `<CFOUTPUT>` tags within the custom tag template.

Outputting Attribute Values

Listing 20.5 shows another custom tag called `<CF_HelloWorldMessage>`, which is almost the same as `<CF_HelloWorld>` from Listing 20.3. The difference is the fact that this tag accepts an attribute called `Message`, which gets displayed as part of the `"Hello, World"` message (Figure 20.4).

Listing 20.5 `HelloWorldMessage.cfm`—Defining Attributes for Your Custom Tags

```
<!---
  Filename: HelloWorldMessage.cfm
  Author:   Nate Weiss (NMW)
  Purpose:  Creates a custom tag that accepts attributes
--->

<!--- Tag Attributes --->
<CFPARAM NAME="ATTRIBUTES.Message" TYPE="string">

<!--- Output message in HTML table format --->
<CFOUTPUT>
  <TABLE BORDER="5" CELLPADDING="5">
    <TR><TH BGCOLOR="yellow">
      <B>Hello, World, from Orange Whip Studios.</B><BR>
    </TH></TR>
    <TR><TD BGCOLOR="orange">
      #ATTRIBUTES.Message#<BR>
    </TD></TR>
  </TABLE>
</CFOUTPUT>
```

The `<CFPARAM>` tag at the top of Listing 20.5 makes it clear that a `Message` parameter is expected to be provided to the tag and that it is expected to be a string value. The `<CFOUTPUT>` block near the end outputs the value of the `Message` parameter provided to the tag, as shown in Figure 20.4. Listing 20.6 shows how to supply the `Message` parameter that the tag now expects.

NOTE

To make this listing work, you must save the previous listing (Listing 20.5) as `HelloWorldMessage.cfm`, either in the same folder as Listing 20.6 or in the special `CustomTags` folder.

Listing 20.6 `UsingHelloWorldMessage.cfm`—Supplying Attributes to Your Custom Tags

```
<!---
  Filename: UsingHelloWorldMessage.cfm
  Author:   Nate Weiss (NMW)
  Purpose:  Shows how to use the <CF_HelloWorldMessage> custom tag
--->

<HTML>
<HEAD><TITLE>Testing &lt;CF_HelloWorldMessage&gt;</TITLE></HEAD>
<BODY>

  <!--- Display Hello World Message, via Custom Tag --->
  <CF_HelloWorldMessage
    Message="We're getting the band back together!">

</BODY>
</HTML>
```

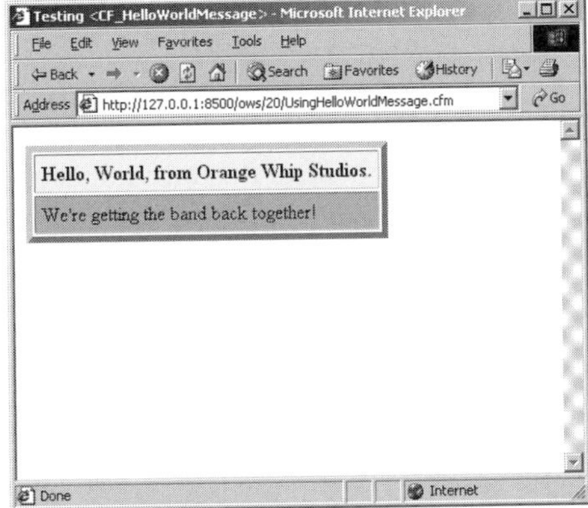

Figure 20.4
The `<CF_HelloWorldMessage>` custom tag displays any message in a consistent manner.

NOTE
Attribute names are not case sensitive. There is no way to determine whether a parameter was passed to a tag with code such as `Message="Hello"` or `MESSAGE="Hello"`. Of course, the case of each attribute's value is preserved, so there is a difference between `Message="Hello"` and `Message="HELLO"`.

Using `<CFPARAM>` to Declare Attributes

You don't have to include the `<CFPARAM>` tag in Listing 20.5. As long as the `Message` attribute is actually provided when the tag is used, and as long as the parameter is a string value, the `<CFPARAM>` tag doesn't do anything. It only has an effect if the attribute is omitted (or provided with a value that can't be converted to a string), in which case it displays an error message.

However, I strongly suggest that you declare each of a custom tag's attributes with a `<CFPARAM>` tag at the top of the tag's template, for the following reasons:

- Always having your custom tag's attributes formally listed as `<CFPARAM>` tags at the top of your templates makes your custom tag code clearer and more self-documenting.

- Specifying the expected data type with `<CFPARAM>`'s `TYPE` attribute acts as a convenient sanity check in case someone tries to use your tag in an unexpected way.
- If you declare all your tag's attributes using `<CFPARAM>` tags at the top of a tag's template, you know that the rest of the template will never run if the attributes are not provided properly when the tag is actually used. This prevents problems or data inconsistencies that could arise from partially executed code.
- As discussed in the next section, you can easily make any of your tag's attributes optional by simply adding a `DEFAULT` attribute for the corresponding `<CFPARAM>` tag.

See Chapter 9, "CFML Basics," for more information about the `<CFPARAM>` tag.

NOTE

You can use the `<CFTRY>` and `<CFCATCH>` tags to provide friendly error messages when the attributes passed to a custom tag do not comply with the rules imposed by the custom tag's `<CFPARAM>` tags. See the version of the `<CF_PlaceOrder>` custom tag presented in Chapter 31, "Error Handling," for an example.

Making Attributes Optional or Required

When you are first working on a new custom tag, one of the most important things to consider is which attributes your new tag will take. You want to ensure that the attribute names are as clear, intuitive, and self-describing as possible.

Often, you will want to make certain attributes optional, so they can be omitted when the tag is actually used. That way, you can provide lots of attributes (and thus flexibility and customizability) for your tags, without overburdening users of your tags with a lot of unnecessary typing if they just want a tag's normal behavior.

Using `<CFPARAM>` to Establish Default Values

The most straightforward way to declare an optional attribute for a custom tag is to provide a `DEFAULT` attribute to the corresponding `<CFPARAM>` tag at the top of the tag's template.

For instance, take a look at the version of the `<CF_HelloWorldMessage>` tag shown in Listing 20.7. This version is the same as the previous one (shown in Listing 20.5), except that it defines five new attributes: `TopMessage`, `TopColor`, `BottomColor`, `TableBorder`, and `TablePadding`. The values are given sensible default values using the `DEFAULT` attribute.

Listing 20.7 `HelloWorldMessage2.cfm`—Making Certain Attributes Optional

```
<!---
  Filename: HelloWorldMessage.cfm
  Author:   Nate Weiss (NMW)
  Purpose:  Creates a custom tag that accepts attributes
--->

<!--- Tag Attributes --->
<CFPARAM NAME="ATTRIBUTES.Message" TYPE="string">
<CFPARAM NAME="ATTRIBUTES.TopMessage" TYPE="string"
  DEFAULT="Hello, World, from Orange Whip Studios.">
```

Listing 20.7 (continued)

```
<CFPARAM NAME="ATTRIBUTES.TopColor" TYPE="string" DEFAULT="yellow">
<CFPARAM NAME="ATTRIBUTES.BottomColor" TYPE="string" DEFAULT="orange">
<CFPARAM NAME="ATTRIBUTES.TableBorder" TYPE="numeric" DEFAULT="5">
<CFPARAM NAME="ATTRIBUTES.TablePadding" TYPE="numeric" DEFAULT="5">

<!--- Output message in HTML table format --->
<CFOUTPUT>
  <TABLE BORDER="#ATTRIBUTES.TableBorder#" CELLPADDING="#ATTRIBUTES.TablePadding#">
    <TR><TH BGCOLOR="#ATTRIBUTES.TopColor#">
      <B>#ATTRIBUTES.TopMessage#</B><BR>
    </TH></TR>
    <TR><TD BGCOLOR="#ATTRIBUTES.BottomColor#">
      #ATTRIBUTES.Message#<BR>
    </TD></TR>
  </TABLE>
</CFOUTPUT>
```

So, if the tag is explicitly provided with a `TopColor` value when it is used, that value will be available as `ATTRIBUTES.TopColor`. If not, the `DEFAULT` attribute of the `<CFPARAM>` tag kicks in and provides the default value of `Yellow`. The same goes for the other new attributes: If values are supplied at run time, the supplied values are used; if not, the default values kick in.

NOTE

There's generally no harm in defining more attributes than you think people will usually need, as long as you supply default values for them. As a rule of thumb, you can try to provide attributes for just about every string or number your tag uses, rather than hard-coding them. This is what Listing 20.7 does.

Assuming you save Listing 20.7 as a custom tag template called `HelloWorldMessage.cfm`, you can now use any of the following in your application templates:

```
<CF_HelloWorldMessage
  Message="We're getting the band back together!">

<CF_HelloWorldMessage
  TopMessage="Message of the Day"
  Message="We're getting the band back together!">

<CF_HelloWorldMessage
  Message="We're getting the band back together!"
  TopColor="Beige"
  BottomColor="##FFFFFF"
  TableBorder="0">
```

Using Functions to Test for Attributes

Instead of using the `<CFPARAM>` tag, you can use the `IsDefined()` function to test for the existence of tag attributes. This is largely a matter of personal preference. For instance, instead of this:

```
<CFPARAM NAME="ATTRIBUTES.Message" TYPE="string">
```

you could use this:

```
<CFIF IsDefined("ATTRIBUTES.Message") EQ "No">
  <CFABORT SHOWERROR="You must provide a Message attribute">
</CFIF>
```

Or instead of this:

```
<CFPARAM NAME="ATTRIBUTES.TopColor" TYPE="string" DEFAULT="Yellow">
```

you could use this:

```
<CFIF NOT IsDefined("ATTRIBUTES.TopColor")>
  <CFSET ATTRIBUTES.TopColor="Yellow">
</CFIF>
```

NOTE

Since the `ATTRIBUTES` scope is implemented as a ColdFusion structure, you can also use CFML's various structure functions to test for the existence of tag attributes. For instance, instead of `IsDefined("Attributes.TopColor")`–shown in the previous code snippet–you could use `StructKeyExists(ATTRIBUTES, "TopColor")` to get the same effect.

NOTE

Because the special `ATTRIBUTES` scope exists only when a template is being called as a custom tag, you can use `IsDefined("ATTRIBUTES")` if you want to be able to detect whether the template is being visited on its own or included via a regular `<CFINCLUDE>` tag.

Who Are You Developing For?

Before you get started on a new custom tag, it's often helpful to think about who the your new tag's audience for your new tag will be. Keep the audience in mind as you think about the tag's functionality and what its attributes and default behavior should be.Custom tags generally fall into one of these two groups:

- **Application-Specific Tags.** These display something or perform an action that makes sense only within your application (or within your company). These tags generally either relate to your application's specific database schema or are in charge of maintaining or participating in business rules or processes specific to your company. This type of tag extends the CFML language to the exclusive benefit of your application, perhaps creating a kind of tool set for your code's internal use.
- **General-Purpose Tags.** These don't have anything specific to do with your application; instead, they provide some functionality you might need in a variety of scenarios. Rather than being of interest mainly to yourself or your programming team, these tags are of interest to the ColdFusion developer community at large. This type of tag extends the CFML language for all ColdFusion programmers who download or purchase the tag.

The type of code you use to write the two types of tags is not categorically different, but it is still helpful to keep the tag's audience in mind as you work, whether that audience is just yourself or ColdFusion developers all over the world. If you are creating an application-specific tag, think about the various people on your team or people who might need to look at the code in the future. If you are creating a general-purpose tag, imagine fellow developers using your tag in various contexts.

Then ask yourself these questions:

- **How can you name the tag so that its purpose is self-explanatory?** In general, the longer the tag name, the better. Also, the tag name should hint not only at what the tag does, but also at what it acts on. Something such as `<CF_DisplayMovie>` or `<CF_ShowMovieCallout>` is better than just `<CF_Movie>` or `<CF_Display>`, even if the shorter names are easier to type or seem obvious to you.
- **How can you name the attributes so that they are also self-explanatory?** Again, there is usually little harm in using long attribute names. Long names make the tags—and the code that uses them—more self-documenting.
- **Which attributes will the audience need, and which should be optional versus required?** A good rule of thumb is that the tag's optional attributes should have sensible enough default values so that the tag works in a useful way with only the required attributes. The optional attributes should be gravy.

NOTE

If you want to, try to make your tag's name and attribute names come together in such a way that the tag's use in code reads almost like a sentence. It's really great when you can understand a tag's purpose by simply looking at its usage in actual code templates.

Querying and Displaying Output

Now that you know how to create a custom tag that accepts a few attributes to control its behavior, it's time to try creating a custom tag that really gets something useful done. This section demonstrates how easy it is to create tags that look up and display information. You can then reuse these tags throughout your application.

Running Queries in Custom Tags

You can use any tag in the CFML language within a custom tag template, including `<CFQUERY>`, `<CFOUTPUT>`, and `<CFSET>`. Listing 20.8 turns the movie-display code from the `FeaturedMovie.cfm` template in Chapter 16, "Introducing the Web Application Framework," into a custom tag called `<CF_ShowMovieCallout>`.

The first half of the `FeaturedMovie.cfm` example randomly determines which of the available movies to show, and the second half queries the database for the selected movie and displays its title, description, and other information. This custom tag does the work of the second half of that example (that is, it just shows a movie's information, without the randomizing aspect). It takes just one required attribute, a numeric attribute called `FilmID`. Within the custom tag, you can use the `ATTRIBUTES.FilmID` value in the criteria for a `<CFQUERY>` to retrieve the appropriate film information.

At its simplest, this tag can be used like the following, which is a neat, tidy, and helpful abstraction of the CFML, HTML, and CSS code the tag generates:

```
<!--- Show movie number five, formatted nicely --->
<CF_ShowMovieCallout
  FilmID=5">
```

Listing 20.8 `ShowMovieCallout.cfm`—Querying and Displaying Information About a Particular Film Record

```
<!---
  <CF_ShowMovieCallout> Custom Tag
  Retrieves and displays the given film

  Example of Use:
  <CF_ShowMovieCallout
    FilmID="5">
--->

<!--- Tag Attributes --->
<!--- FilmID Attribute is Required --->
<CFPARAM NAME="ATTRIBUTES.FilmID" TYPE="numeric">
<!--- Whether to reveal cost/release dates (optional) --->
<CFPARAM NAME="ATTRIBUTES.ShowCost" TYPE="boolean" DEFAULT="Yes">
<CFPARAM NAME="ATTRIBUTES.ShowReleaseDate" TYPE="boolean" DEFAULT="Yes">
<!--- Optional formatting and placement options --->
<CFPARAM NAME="ATTRIBUTES.TableAlign" TYPE="string" DEFAULT="right">
<CFPARAM NAME="ATTRIBUTES.TableWidth" TYPE="string" DEFAULT="150">
<CFPARAM NAME="ATTRIBUTES.Caption" TYPE="string" DEFAULT="Featured Film">
<!--- Use "ows" datasource by default --->
<CFPARAM NAME="ATTRIBUTES.DataSource" TYPE="string" DEFAULT="ows">

<!--- Get important info about film from database --->
<CFQUERY NAME="GetFilm" DATASOURCE="#ATTRIBUTES.DataSource#">
  SELECT
    MovieTitle, Summary,
    AmountBudgeted, DateInTheaters
  FROM Films
  WHERE FilmID = #ATTRIBUTES.FilmID#
</CFQUERY>

<!--- Display error message if record not fetched --->
<CFIF GetFilm.RecordCount NEQ 1>
  <CFTHROW
    MESSAGE="Invalid FilmID Attribute"
    DETAIL="Film #ATTRIBUTES.FilmID# does not exist!">
</CFIF>


<!--- Format a few queried values in local variables --->
<CFSET ProductCost = Ceiling(Val(GetFilm.AmountBudgeted) / 1000000)>
<CFSET ReleaseDate = DateFormat(GetFilm.DateInTheaters, "mmmm d")>

<!--- Now Display The Specified Movie --->
<CFOUTPUT>
  <!--- Define formatting for film display --->
  <STYLE TYPE="text/css">
    TH.fm {background:RoyalBlue;color:white;text-align:left;
           font-family:sans-serif;font-size:10px}
    TD.fm {background:LightSteelBlue;
           font-family:sans-serif;font-size:12px}
```

Listing 20.8 (continued)

```
</STYLE>

<!--- Show info about featured movie in HTML Table --->
<TABLE
  WIDTH="#ATTRIBUTES.TableWidth#"
  ALIGN="#ATTRIBUTES.TableAlign#"
  BORDER="0"
  CELLSPACING="0">

  <TR><TH CLASS="fm">
    #ATTRIBUTES.Caption#
  </TH></TR>
  <!--- Movie Title, Summary, Rating --->
  <TR><TD CLASS="fm">
    <B>#GetFilm.MovieTitle#</B><BR>
    #GetFilm.Summary#<BR>
  </TD></TR>
  <!--- Cost (rounded to millions), release date --->
  <CFIF ATTRIBUTES.ShowCost OR ATTRIBUTES.ShowReleaseDate>
    <TR><TH CLASS="fm">
      <!--- Show Cost, if called for --->
      <CFIF ATTRIBUTES.ShowCost>
        Production Cost $#ProductCost# Million<BR>
      </CFIF>
      <!--- Show release date, if called for --->
      <CFIF ATTRIBUTES.ShowReleaseDate>
        In Theaters #ReleaseDate#<BR>
      </CFIF>
    </TH></TR>
  </CFIF>
 </TABLE>
 <BR CLEAR="all">
</CFOUTPUT>
```

TIP

It is often helpful to put an Example of Use comment at the top of your custom tag as shown here, even if you provide better documentation elsewhere. If nothing else, the hint will serve as a quick reminder to you if you need to revise the tag later.

At the top of this listing, a number of `<CFPARAM>` tags make clear what the tag's required and optional parameters will be. Only the `FilmID` attribute is required; because its `<CFPARAM>` tag doesn't have a `DEFAULT` attribute, ColdFusion will throw an error message if a `FilmID` is not provided at run time. The `ShowCost` and `ShowReleaseDate` attributes are Boolean values, meaning that either `Yes` or `No` (or an expression that evaluates to `True` or `False`) can be supplied when the tag is actually used; the `DEFAULT` for each is defined to be `Yes`. The `TableAlign`, `TableWidth`, `Caption`, and `DataSource` attributes are also given sensible default values so they can be omitted when the tag is used.

Next, the `<CFQUERY>` named `GetFilm` retrieves information about the appropriate film, using the value of `ATTRIBUTES.FilmID` in the `WHERE` clause. Then two local variables called `ProductionCost` and `ReleaseDate` are set to formatted versions of the `AmountBudgeted` and `DateInTheaters` columns returned by the query.

NOTE

These two variables are referred to as *local* because they exist only in the context of the custom tag template itself, not in the calling template where the tag is used. The `GetFilm` query is also a local variable. See the section "Local Variables in Custom Tags," later in this chapter, for more information.

Custom tags should be capable of dealing reasonably gracefully with unexpected situations. For that reason, a `<CFIF>` block is used right after the `<CFQUERY>` to ensure that the query retrieved one record as expected. If not, a `<CFTHROW>` tag halts all processing with a customized, diagnostic error message. For more information about `<CFTHROW>`, see Chapter 31.

NOTE

The error message generated by the `<CFTHROW>` tag will be displayed using the appropriate look-and-feel template if the `<CFERROR>` tag is used in `Application.cfm`, as discussed in Chapter 16.

The rest of the template is essentially unchanged from the `FeaturedMovie.cfm` template as it originally appeared in Chapter 16. The film's title, summary, and other information are shown in an attractive table format. The `<CFIF>` logic at the end of the template enables the display of the `Production Cost` and `Release Date` to be turned off by setting the `ShowCost` or `ShowReleaseDate` attributes of the tag to `No`.

After you've saved Listing 20.8 as a custom tag template called `ShowMovieCallout.cfm` (in the special `CustomTags` folder or in the same folder as the templates in which you want to use the tag), it is ready for use. Listing 20.9 shows how easily you can use the tag in your application's templates. The results are shown in Figure 20.5.

Listing 20.9 `UsingShowMovieCallout.cfm`—Using the `<CF_ShowMovieCallout>` Custom Tag

```
<!---
  Filename: UsingShowMovieCallout.cfm
  Author:   Nate Weiss (NMW)
  Purpose:  Demonstrates how to use the <CF_ShowMovieCallout> custom tag
--->

<HTML>
<HEAD><TITLE>Movie Display</TITLE></HEAD>
<BODY>
  <!--- Page Title and Text Message --->
  <h2>Movie Display Demonstration</h2>
  <P>Any movie can be displayed at any time by using
  the <B>&lt;CF_ShowMovieCallout&gt;</B> tag.  All you
  need to do is to pass the appropriate FilmID to the tag.
  If the formatting needs to be changed in the future, only
  the Custom Tag's template will need to be edited.<BR>

  <!--- Display Film info as "callout", via Custom Tag --->
  <CF_ShowMovieCallout
    FilmID="20">

</BODY>
</HTML>
```

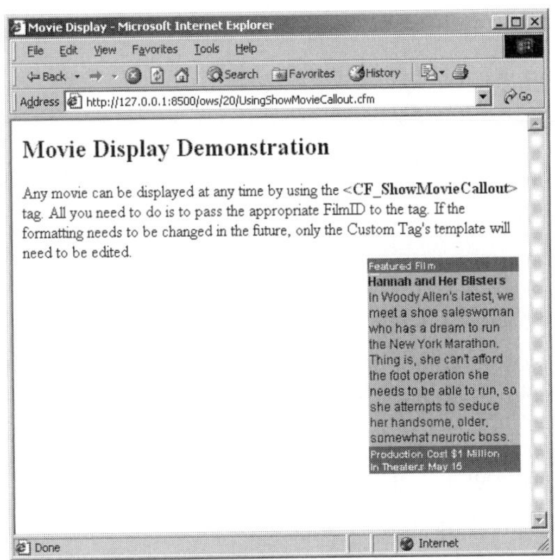

Figure 20.5

Using the `<CF_ShowMovieCallout>` tag, you can display any film with just one line of code.

Local Variables in Custom Tags

The previous section pointed out that the `GetFilm`, `ProductCost`, and `ReleaseDate` variables are local variables, meaning they exist only within the scope of the custom tag template itself.

This is an important aspect of ColdFusion's custom tag functionality. Whenever a custom tag is executed, it gets a private area in the server's memory to store its own variables. Unless you use a scope prefix (such as `ATTRIBUTES`, `APPLICATION`, or `SESSION`), all references to variables in the custom tag template refer only to this private area. The result is what some other programming languages call a name space—an interim memory space for the tag to do its work, without worrying about how it will affect the template in which it is used.

For instance, if you attempt to display the value of the `ProductCost` variable in Listing 20.9, after the `<CF_ShowMovieCallout>` tag, you would get an error message saying that the variable doesn't exist. The variable exists only within the custom tag's template itself. After the tag finishes its work, all its variables are discarded and are no longer available.

This is what enables custom tags to be so modular and independent. Because they don't affect the variables in the templates in which they run, they are free to create variables and run queries in any way they need to. All kinds of problems would arise if this were not the case.

For instance, what if Listing 20.9 needs to run its own query named `GetFilms` before it uses the `<CF_ShowMovieCallout>` tag? If it weren't for the fact that custom tags have their own local variables, the `<CFQUERY>` inside the custom tag template would overwrite any variable called `GetFilms` that was set before the tag was called. This could lead to all sorts of strange and unexpected behavior (especially if you were using a custom tag that you did not write, because you would need to know all the variable names the custom tag uses internally and to avoid using them in your templates).

In short, remember these important points:

- Variables in custom tags are always local, unless you specify a special scope name (discussed shortly).
- Variables set before the tag is used are not available within the custom tag itself.
- Similarly, variables set in the custom tag's template are not available as normal variables in code that uses the tag.
- The `ATTRIBUTES` scope enables you to pass specific values into the tag.
- The special `CALLER` scope, which you will learn about shortly, enables you to access or set specific variables in the calling template.

Custom Tags Versus `<CFINCLUDE>`

Earlier in this book, you learned about the `<CFINCLUDE>` tag, which enables you to put ordinary CFML code in a separate template and include it elsewhere, wherever you need to use it. You might be thinking that including a template with the `<CFINCLUDE>` tag is pretty similar to calling a custom tag. That's true, but custom tags are more sophisticated because they have their own variable name spaces, as explained above.

So although you can often get the same results using `<CFINCLUDE>` instead of creating a custom tag, your code will usually be harder to maintain and debug because variables set in the calling template might interfere with the way the included template behaves, and vice versa.

Custom Tags That Process Data

So far, this chapter has concentrated on creating custom tags that display information, such as the `<CF_ShowMovieCallout>` custom tag. Many of the custom tags you will write are likely to be similar to `<CF_ShowMovieCallout>` in that they will be in charge of wrapping up several display-related concepts (querying the database, including formatting, outputting the information, and so on).

However, you can also create custom tags that have different purposes in life: to process or gather information. This type of custom tag generally doesn't generate any HTML to be displayed on the current page. Instead, these tags just perform some type of processing, often returning a calculated result to the calling template.

NOTE

You might call these tags nonvisual, or perhaps number crunchers, just to set them apart from tags that generate something visual, such as the `<CF_ ShowMovieCallout>` and `<CF_HelloWorldMessage>` examples you have already seen.

Introducing the `CALLER` Scope

ColdFusion defines two special variable scopes that come into play only when you're creating custom tags:

- The `ATTRIBUTES` Scope—You have already learned about this scope, which passes specific information to a custom tag each time it is used.

- The CALLER Scope—Gives a custom tag a way to set and use variables in the template in which you're using the tag (the calling template).

The special CALLER scope is easy to understand and use. Within a custom tag template, you just prefix any variable name with CALLER (using dot notation) to access the corresponding variable in the calling template. Through the CALLER scope, you have full read-write access to all variables known to the calling template, meaning that you can set variables as well as access their current values. For instance, you can set variables in the calling template using an ordinary <CFSET> tag.

Returning Variables to the Calling Template

Let's say you are writing a custom tag called <CF_PickFeaturedMovie>, which will choose a movie from the list of available films. In the calling template, you plan on using the tag like so:

```
<CF_PickFeaturedMovie>
```

Inside the custom tag template (PickFeaturedMovie.cfm), you could set a variable using a special CALLER prefix, such as this:

```
<CFSET Caller.FeaturedFilmID = 5>
```

This prefix would make FeaturedFilmID available in the calling template as a normal variable. For instance, this code snippet would call the custom tag and then output the value of the variable it returns:

```
<CF_PickFeaturedMovie>
<CFOUTPUT>
  The featured Film ID is:
  #FeaturedFilmID#
</CFOUTPUT>
```

Of course, using these snippets, the value of FeaturedFilmID would always be 5, so the custom tag wouldn't be all that useful. Listing 20.10 shows how to expand the previous snippets into a useful version of the <CF_PickFeaturedMovie> custom tag. This tag borrows the featured movie selection code from the FeaturedMovie.cfm template that originally appeared in Chapter 16 and was adapted further in Chapter 17, "Working with Sessions." The purpose of the code is to select a single film's ID number in such a way that all films are rotated evenly on a per-session basis.

Listing 20.10 PickFeaturedMovie1.cfm—Setting a Variable in the Calling Template

```
<!---
  Filename: PickFeaturedMovie.cfm
  Author:   Nate Weiss (NMW)
  Purpose:  Creates the <CF_PickFeaturedMovie> custom tag
--->

<!--- Tag Attributes --->
<!--- Use "ows" datasource by default --->
<CFPARAM NAME="ATTRIBUTES.DataSource" TYPE="string" DEFAULT="ows">

<!--- Need to lock when accessing shared data --->
<CFLOCK SCOPE="SESSION" TIMEOUT="10">

  <!--- List of movies to show (list starts out empty) --->
  <CFPARAM NAME="SESSION.MovieList" TYPE="string" DEFAULT="">
```

Listing 20.10 (continued)

```
    <!--- If this is the first time we're running this,  --->
    <!--- Or we have run out of movies to rotate through --->
    <CFIF SESSION.MovieList EQ "">
      <!--- Get all current FilmIDs from the database --->
      <CFQUERY NAME="GetFilmIDs" DATASOURCE="#ATTRIBUTES.DataSource#">
        SELECT FilmID FROM Films
        ORDER BY MovieTitle
      </CFQUERY>

      <!--- Turn FilmIDs into a simple comma-separated list --->
      <CFSET SESSION.MovieList = ValueList(GetFilmIDs.FilmID)>
    </CFIF>

    <!--- Pick the first movie in the list to show right now --->
    <CFSET ThisMovieID = ListFirst(SESSION.MovieList)>
    <!--- Re-save the list, as all movies *except* the first --->
    <CFSET SESSION.MovieList = ListRest(SESSION.MovieList)>

    <!--- Return chosen movie to calling template --->
    <CFSET CALLER.FeaturedFilmID = ThisMovieID>
  </CFLOCK>
```

The `<CFPARAM>` tag at the top of this custom tag template establishes a single optional attribute for the tag called `DataSource`, which will default to `ows` if not provided explicitly. Except for the final `<CFSET>` line, the remainder of the code is copied literally from the version presented in Chapter 17. Because the final `<CFSET>` uses the special `CALLER` scope, the featured movie the tag has chosen is available for the calling template to use normally.

Listing 20.11 shows how you can put this version of the `<CF_PickFeaturedMovie>` custom tag to use in actual code. This code assumes you have saved Listing 20.10 as `PickFeaturedMovie.cfm` (not `PickFeaturedMovie1.cfm`) in the current directory or in the special `CustomTags` folder.

Listing 20.11 `UsingPickFeaturedMovie1.cfm`—Using a Variable Set by a Custom Tag

```
<!---
  Filename: UsingPickFeaturedMovie1.cfm
  Author:   Nate Weiss (NMW)
  Purpose:  Shows how <CF_PickFeaturedMovie> can be used in a ColdFusion page
--->

<HTML>
<HEAD><TITLE>Movie Display</TITLE></HEAD>
<BODY>
  <!--- Page Title and Text Message --->
  <h2>Movie Display Demonstration</h2>
  <P>The appropriate "Featured Movie" can be obtained by
  using the <B>&lt;CF_PickFeaturedMovie&gt;</B> tag.
  The featured movie can then be displayed using the
  <B>&lt;CF_ShowMovieCallout&gt;</B> tag.<BR>

  <!--- Pick rotating Featured Movie to show, via Custom Tag --->
  <CF_PickFeaturedMovie>

  <!--- Display Film info as "callout", via Custom Tag --->
```

Listing 20.11 (continued)

```
<CF_ShowMovieCallout
  FilmID="#FeaturedFilmID#">

</BODY>
</HTML>
```

NOTE

The `CALLER` scope is for use only within custom tag templates. Don't use it in your ordinary ColdFusion templates. Doing so won't generate an error message, but it could lead to unexpected results.

NOTE

If you are calling a custom tag from within another custom tag, the `CALLER` scope of the innermost tag will refer to the local variables in the first custom tag template, not the variables in the top-level page template. To access the variables of the top-level template from the innermost tag, you must use `CALLER.CALLER.VariableName` instead of `CALLER.VariableName`. In some cases, this can be a pain; the `REQUEST` scope provides an effective solution, as explained in the section "The `REQUEST` Scope," later in this chapter.

First, the `<CF_PickFeaturedMovie>` custom tag from Listing 20.10 is called. As the custom tag executes, it selects the film ID it feels is appropriate and saves the value in the `FeaturedFilmID` variable in the calling template (which, in this case, is Listing 20.11). Next, the featured movie is actually displayed to the user, using the `<CF_ShowMovieCallout>` custom tag presented earlier in this chapter.

NOTE

These two custom tags (`<CF_PickFeaturedMovie>` and `<CF_ShowMovieCallout>`) each do something useful on their own and can be used together, as shown here. As you design custom tags for your applications, this type of synergy between tags is a nice goal to shoot for.

Of course, to make Listing 20.11 work, you need to enable session management by including a `<CFAPPLICATION>` tag in the application's `Application.cfm` file (see Chapter 17 for details):

```
<!--- Name our application and enable application variables --->
<CFAPPLICATION
  NAME="OrangeWhipSite"
  SESSIONMANAGEMENT="Yes">
```

NOTE

The more a custom tag relies on variables in the calling template, the less modular it becomes. So, although the `CALLER` scope gives you read-write access to variables in the calling template, you should use it mainly for setting new variables, rather than accessing the values of existing ones. If you find that you are accessing the values of many existing variables in the calling template, it might be that you should just be writing a normal `<CFINCLUDE>` style template rather than a custom tag, or that the values should be passed into the tag explicitly as attributes.

Variable Names as Tag Attributes

In the version of the `<CF_PickFeaturedMovie>` custom tag shown in Listing 21.10, the selected film ID is always returned to the calling template as a variable named `FeaturedFilmID`. Often, allowing a custom tag to accept an additional attribute is helpful to determine the name of the return variable in which the custom tag will place information.

For instance, for the <CF_PickFeaturedMovie> custom tag, you might add an attribute called ReturnVariable, which determines the calling template to specify the variable in which to place the featured film's ID number.

So, to use the tag, you would change this line from Listing 20.10:

```
<!--- Pick rotating featured movie to show via custom tag --->
<CF_PickFeaturedMovie>
```

to this:

```
<!--- Pick rotating featured movie to show via custom tag --->
<CF_PickFeaturedMovie
  ReturnVariable="FeaturedFilmID">
```

This makes the custom tag less intrusive because it doesn't demand that any particular variable names be set aside for its use. If for whatever reason the developer coding the calling template wants the selected film to be known as MyFeaturedFilmID or ShowThisMovieID, he or she can simply specify that name for the ReturnVariable attribute. The calling template is always in control.

NOTE

Also, code that uses the <CF_PickFeaturedMovie> tag will be a bit more self-documenting and easier to understand because it is now evident from where exactly the FeaturedFilmID variable is coming.

NOTE

If you think about it, a number of ColdFusion's own CFML tags use the same technique. The most obvious example is the <CFQUERY> tag's NAME attribute, which tells the tag in which variable to store its results. The NAME attributes of the <CFDIRECTORY> and <CFSEARCH> tags are similar, as are the OUTPUT attribute for <CFWDDX> and the VARIABLE attributes for <CFFILE> and <CFSAVEOUTPUT>. See Appendix B, "ColdFusion Tag Reference," for details.

Using <CFPARAM> with TYPE="VariableName"

You have already seen the <CFPARAM> tag used throughout this chapter to make it clear which attributes a custom tag expects and to ensure that the data type of each attribute is correct. When you want the calling template to accept a variable name as one of its attributes, you can set the TYPE of the <CFPARAM> tag to variableName.

Therefore, the next version of the <CF_PickFeaturedMovie> custom tag will include the following lines:

```
<!--- Variable name to return selected FilmID as --->
<CFPARAM NAME="ATTRIBUTES.ReturnVariable" TYPE="variableName">
```

When the <CFPARAM> tag is encountered, ColdFusion ensures that the actual value of the attribute is a legal variable name. If it's not, ColdFusion displays an error message stating that the variable name is illegal. This makes for a very simple sanity check. It ensures that the tag isn't being provided with something such as ReturnValue="My Name", which likely would result in a much uglier error message later on because spaces are not allowed in ColdFusion variable names.

NOTE

In ColdFusion, variable names must start with a letter, and all the other characters can only be letters, numbers, and underscores. Any string that does not conform to these rules will not get past a <CFPARAM> of TYPE="variableName".

Setting a Variable Dynamically

After you've added the <CFPARAM> tag shown previously to the <CF_PickFeaturedMovie> custom tag template, the template can refer to Attributes.ReturnVariable to get the desired variable name. Now the final <CFSET> variable in Listing 20.10 just needs to be changed so that it uses the dynamic variable name instead of the hard-coded variable name of FeaturedFilmID. Developers sometimes get confused about how exactly to do this.

Here's the line as it stands now, from Listing 20.10:

```
<!--- Return chosen movie to calling template --->
<CFSET CALLER.FeaturedFilmID = ThisMovieID>
```

People often try to use syntax similar to the following to somehow indicate that the value of Attributes.ReturnVariable should be used to determine the name of the variable in the CALLER scope:

```
<!--- Return chosen movie to calling template --->
<CFSET CALLER.#Attributes.ReturnVariable# = ThisMovieID>
```

Or they might use this:

```
<!--- Return chosen movie to calling template --->
<CFSET #CALLER.##Attributes.ReturnVariable### = ThisMovieID>
```

These are not legal because ColdFusion does not understand that you want the value of Attributes.ReturnVariable evaluated before <CFSET> is actually performed. ColdFusion will just get exasperated with you and display an error message.

Using Quoted <CFSET> Syntax

ColdFusion provides a somewhat odd-looking solution to this problem. You simply surround the left side of the <CFSET> expression, the part before the equals (=) sign, with quotation marks. This forces ColdFusion to first evaluate the variable name as a string before attempting to actually perform the variable setting. The resulting code looks a bit strange, but it actually works very nicely and is relatively easy to read.

So, this line from Listing 20.10:

```
<!--- Return chosen movie to calling template --->
<CFSET CALLER.FeaturedFilmID = ThisMovieID>
```

can be replaced with this:

```
<!--- Return chosen movie to calling template --->
<CFSET "CALLER.#ATTRIBUTES.ReturnVariable#" = ThisMovieID>
```

Listing 20.12 shows the completed version of the <CF_PickFeaturedMovie> custom tag. This listing is identical to Listing 20.10, except for the first and last lines, which are the <CFPARAM> line and the updated <CFSET> line shown previously.

Listing 20.12 `PickFeaturedMovie2.cfm`—Revised Version of `<CF_PickFeaturedMovie>`—Custom Tag

```
<!---
  Filename: PickFeaturedMovie.cfm
  Author:   Nate Weiss (NMW)
  Purpose:  Creates the <CF_PickFeaturedMovie> custom tag
--->

<!--- Tag Attributes --->
<!--- Variable name to return selected FilmID as --->
<CFPARAM NAME="ATTRIBUTES.ReturnVariable" TYPE="variableName">
<!--- Use "ows" datasource by default --->
<CFPARAM NAME="ATTRIBUTES.DataSource" TYPE="string" DEFAULT="ows">

<!--- Need to lock when accessing shared data --->
<CFLOCK SCOPE="Session" TIMEOUT="10">

  <!--- List of movies to show (list starts out empty) --->
  <CFPARAM NAME="SESSION.MovieList" TYPE="string" DEFAULT="">

  <!--- If this is the first time we're running this,  --->
  <!--- Or we have run out of movies to rotate through --->
  <CFIF SESSION.MovieList EQ "">
    <!--- Get all current FilmIDs from the database --->
    <CFQUERY NAME="GetFilmIDs" DATASOURCE="#ATTRIBUTES.DataSource#">
      SELECT FilmID FROM Films
      ORDER BY MovieTitle
    </CFQUERY>

    <!--- Turn FilmIDs into a simple comma-separated list --->
    <CFSET SESSION.MovieList = ValueList(GetFilmIDs.FilmID)>
  </CFIF>

  <!--- Pick the first movie in the list to show right now --->
  <CFSET ThisMovieID = ListFirst(SESSION.MovieList)>
  <!--- Re-save the list, as all movies *except* the first --->
  <CFSET SESSION.MovieList = ListRest(SESSION.MovieList)>

  <!--- Return Chosen Movie to Calling Template --->
  <CFSET "CALLER.#ATTRIBUTES.ReturnVariable#" = ThisMovieID>
</CFLOCK>
```

Listing 20.13 shows how to use this new version of the custom tag. This listing is nearly identical to Listing 20.11, except for the addition of the `ReturnVariable` attribute. Note how much clearer the cause and effect now are. In Listing 20.11, the `FeaturedFilmID` variable seemed to appear out of nowhere. Here, it is very clear where the `ShowThisMovieID` variable is coming from.

NOTE

This listing assumes that you have saved the code shown in Listing 20.12 as a template called `PickFeaturedMovie.cfm` (not `PickFeaturedMovie2.cfm`). Of course, you would need to save it in the special `CustomTags` folder or in the same folder as this listing.

Listing 20.13 `UsingPickFeaturedMovie2.cfm`—Using the `ReturnVariable` Attribute

```
<!---
  Filename: UsingPickFeaturedMovie1.cfm
  Author:   Nate Weiss (NMW)
  Purpose:  Shows how <CF_PickFeaturedMovie> can be used in a ColdFusion page
--->

<HTML>
<HEAD><TITLE>Movie Display</TITLE></HEAD>
<BODY>
  <!--- Page Title and Text Message --->
  <h2>Movie Display Demonstration</h2>
  <P>The appropriate "Featured Movie" can be obtained by
  using the <B>&lt;CF_PickFeaturedMovie&gt;</B> tag.
  The featured movie can then be displayed using the
  <B>&lt;CF_ShowMovieCallout&gt;</B> tag.<BR>

  <!--- Pick rotating Featured Movie to show, via Custom Tag --->
  <CF_PickFeaturedMovie
    ReturnVariable="ShowThisMovieID">

  <!--- Display Film info as "callout", via Custom Tag --->
  <CF_ShowMovieCallout
    FilmID="#ShowThisMovieID#">

</BODY>
</HTML>
```

Using the `SetVariable()` Function

Another way to solve this type of problem is with the `SetVariable()` function. This function accepts two parameters. The first parameter is a string specifying the name of a variable, and the second parameter is the value you want to store in the specified variable. (The function also returns the new value as its result, which is not generally helpful in this situation.)

So, this line from Listing 20.12:

```
<!--- Return chosen movie to calling template --->
<CFSET "CALLER.#ATTRIBUTES.ReturnVariable#" = ThisMovieID>
```

could be replaced with this:

```
<!--- Return chosen movie to calling template --->
<CFSET Temp = SetVariable("CALLER.#Attributes.ReturnVariable#", ThisMovieID)>
```

And because the result of the function is unnecessary here, this line can be simplified to just this:

```
<!--- Return chosen movie to calling template --->
<CFSET SetVariable("CALLER.#Attributes.ReturnVariable#", ThisMovieID)>
```

Either method (the quoted `<CFSET>` syntax mentioned previously or the `SetVariable()` method shown here) produces the same results. Use whichever method you prefer.

Custom Tags That Encapsulate Business Rules

Often it's helpful to create custom tags to represent the business rules or logic your application needs to enforce or adhere to. After these custom tags are written correctly, you can rest assured that your application will not violate the corresponding business rules.

For instance, looking at the tables in the ows example database, it is easy to see that several tables will be involved when someone wants to place an order from Orange Whip Studios' online store. For each order, a record will be added to the MerchandiseOrders table, and several records can be added to the MerchandiseOrdersItems table (one record for each item the user has in the shopping cart). In addition, you will need to verify the user's credit-card number and perhaps send a confirmation email as an acknowledgment of the user's order. In a real-world application, you might also need to decrease the current number of items on hand after the order has been placed, and so on.

You could place all those steps in a single custom tag. It could be called something such as <CF_PlaceMerchandiseOrder> and take a few simple and easily understood parameters that represent everything necessary to complete an order successfully. The tag might look similar to this when used in code:

```
<!--- Place order for selected items and get new Order ID --->
<CF_PlaceMerchandiseOrder
  ContactID="4"
  MerchIDList="2,6,9"
  ShipToCurrentAddress="Yes"
  SendReceiptViaEmail="Yes"
  ReturnVariable="NewOrderID">
```

In fact, a version of the <CF_PlaceMerchandiseOrder> tag is developed in Chapter 27, "Online Commerce."

Custom Tags for General-Purpose Use

So far in this chapter, you have learned how to make custom tags that are mainly for internal use within your application or company. That is, although the <CF_ShowMovieCallout> custom tag can be enormously helpful in building projects for Orange Whip Studios, they probably are not all that helpful to the average ColdFusion programmer.

In contrast, sometimes you will find yourself writing a custom tag you know will be helpful not only to yourself but to other developers as well. If so, you can package it and make it available to others via the Developer Exchange on the Macromedia Web site, either free or for a charge.

For instance, perhaps you have a need to convert sentences to title case, meaning that the first letter of each word should be capitalized. You could write a custom tag, perhaps called <CF_TextToTitleCase>, to get the job done. After the tag is complete, you could share it with other developers you know or even post it for free download for the entire ColdFusion developer community to use.

Listing 20.14 shows code that creates the <CF_TextToTitleCase> custom tag. The tag has two required attributes—Input and Output. The tag looks at the text passed to it via the Input attribute, capitalizes the first letter of each word, and returns the capitalized version of the string back to the calling template by storing it in the variable specified by the Output attribute.

A third, optional attribute, `DontCapitalizeList`, can be supplied with a comma-separated list of words that should not be capitalized. If this attribute is not provided, it uses a default list of words: `a`, `an`, `the`, `to`, `for`, and `of`. If a word from the `INPUT` is in this list, it is appended to the `OUTPUT` string verbatim, its case preserved.

NOTE

The `Output` attribute here works just like the `ReturnVariable` attribute in some of the other examples in this chapter. Depending on the situation, simplified attribute names, such as `Input` and `Output`, can be easier for other developers to use. In other cases, more verbose attribute names, such as `TextToConvert` and `ReturnVariable`, might make more sense. Geeky as this might sound, coming up with the names is part of the fun.

Listing 20.14 `TextToTitleCase.cfm`—Source Code for `<CF_TextToTitleCase>`

```
<!---
  Filename: TextToTitleCase.cfm
  Author:   Nate Weiss (NMW)
  Purpose:  Creates the <CF_TextToTitleCase> custom tag
--->

<!--- Tag Parameters --->
<CFPARAM NAME="ATTRIBUTES.Input" TYPE="string">
<CFPARAM NAME="ATTRIBUTES.Output" TYPE="variableName">
<CFPARAM NAME="ATTRIBUTES.DontCapitalizeList" TYPE="string"
  DEFAULT="a,an,the,to,for,of">

<!--- Local Variables --->
<CFSET Result = "">

<!--- For each word in the input --->
<CFLOOP LIST="#ATTRIBUTES.Input#" INDEX="ThisWord" DELIMITERS=" ">
  <!--- Assuming this is a word that should be capitalized --->
  <CFIF ListFindNoCase(ATTRIBUTES.DontCapitalizeList, ThisWord) EQ 0>
    <!--- Grab the first letter, and convert it to uppercase --->
    <CFSET FirstLetter = UCase( Mid(ThisWord, 1, 1) )>
    <!--- Grab remaining letters, convert them to lowercase --->
    <CFSET RestOfWord = LCase( Mid(ThisWord, 2, Len(ThisWord)-1) )>

    <!--- Append the completed, capitalized word to result --->
    <CFSET Result = ListAppend(Result, FirstLetter & RestOfWord, " ")>

  <!--- If this is a word that should *not* be capitalized --->
  <CFELSE>
    <CFSET Result = ListAppend(Result, ThisWord, " ")>
  </CFIF>
</CFLOOP>

<!--- Return result to calling template --->
<CFSET "Caller.#ATTRIBUTES.Output#" = Result>
```

Listing 20.14 relies on the idea that you can think of a set of words (similar to a sentence) as a list, just like an ordinary, comma-separated list of values. The only difference is that the list is delimited by spaces instead of commas. Therefore, by supplying a space as the delimiter to ColdFusion's list functions, such as `ListAppend()`, you can easily treat each word individually or loop through the list of words in a sentence.

NOTE

For more information about lists, see the various list functions (such as `ListFind()`, `ListGetAt()`, and `ListDeleteAt()`) in Appendix C, "ColdFusion Function Reference." See also the discussion about CFML data types in Chapter 8, "Using ColdFusion."

First, two `<CFPARAM>` tags declare the tag's `Input` and `Output` attributes, and a variable called `Result` is set to an empty string. Then, a `<CFLOOP>` tag loops over the words supplied by the `Input` attribute. For each word, the first letter is capitalized and stored in the `FirstLetter` variable. The remaining letters, if any, are stored in the `RestOfWord` variable. So, when the `FirstLetter` and `RestOfWord` variables are concatenated using the `&` operator, they form the capitalized form of the current word. The `ListAppend()` function then appends the word to the list of capitalized words in `Result`, again using the space character as the delimiter. When the `<CFLOOP>` is finished, all the words in `Input` have been capitalized and the tag's work is done. It then passes the completed `Result` back to the calling template using the usual quoted `<CFSET>` syntax.

NOTE

Because of the way ColdFusion's list functionality behaves, consecutive space characters from the original string are not preserved in the tag's output. ColdFusion treats multiple delimiters as a single delimiter. So, if the `Input` contained three words with five spaces between each word, the resulting `Output` would still contain three words (in title case), but with only one space between each word. This is the defined, documented behavior and is not a bug. Depending on the situation, the multiple-delimiter behavior can work for you or against you. Just keep it in mind.

Listing 20.15 shows how you and other developers can use this custom tag in actual code. Figure 20.6 shows what the results look like in a browser.

Listing 20.15 `UsingTextToTitleCase.cfm`—Using `<CF_TextToTitleCase>`

```
<!---
  Filename: UsingTextToTitleCase.cfm
  Author:   Nate Weiss (NMW)
  Purpose:  Demonstrates how to use the <CF_TextToTitleCase> custom tag
--->

<HTML>
<HEAD><TITLE>Using &lt;CF_TextToTitleCase&gt;</TITLE></HEAD>
<BODY>
  <H2>Using &lt;CF_TextToTitleCase&gt;</H2>

  <!--- Text to convert to "Title Case" --->
  <CFSET OriginalText = "The rest of the band's around back.">

  <!--- Convert Text to Title Case, via Custom Tag --->
  <CF_TextToTitleCase
    Input="#OriginalText#"
    Output="FixedCase">

  <!--- Output the text, now in Title Case --->
  <CFOUTPUT>
    <P><B>Original Text:</B><BR>
    #OriginalText#<BR>
```

Listing 20.15 (continued)

```
      <P><B>Processed Text:</B><BR>
      #FixedCase#<BR>
    </CFOUTPUT>

  </BODY>
  </HTML>
```

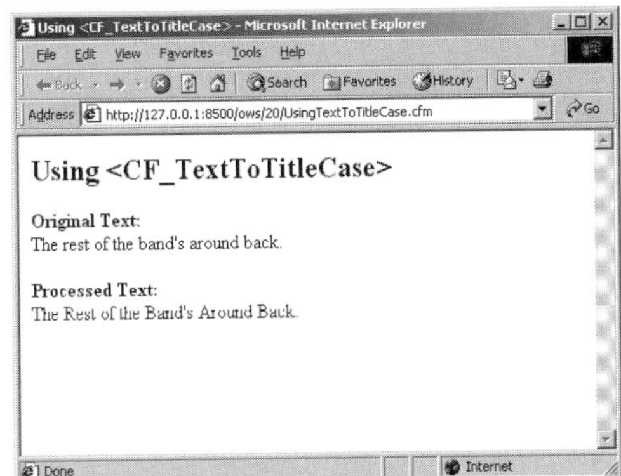

Figure 20.6
The `<CF_TextToTitleCase>` custom tag capitalizes the first letter of each word in a string.

Sharing Your Custom Tags

As explained in the section "Finding Tags on the Developer Exchange," earlier in this chapter, the Developer Exchange on the Macromedia Web site is the first place most ColdFusion developers go when they are looking for custom tags to purchase or download. If you want to share one of your custom tags with others, consider posting it to the Developer Exchange.

TIP

Many developers also make personal custom tag pages of their own. For instance, you can find many custom tags and other ColdFusion goodies by the authors of this book at `www.forta.com` and `www.nateweiss.com`.

Providing Documentation

If you are going to make one of your custom tags available to other developers, you should write some type of short documentation for the tag. No formal guidelines exist for doing this, but it is customary to write the documentation in a simple HTML (.htm) file and include it in a .zip file along with the custom tag template itself. So, for the `<CF_TextToTitleCase>` custom tag, you might create a documentation file called `CF_TextToTitleCase.htm`.

At the very least, your documentation should describe what the tag is meant to do and provide a list of its attributes. In general, the more detailed, the better. If your documentation is not clear, you might start getting questions via email from developers who are using the tag. Rest assured, they will find you!

NOTE

You will find that many developers don't know how to install a custom tag and often start fooling around in the ColdFusion Administrator or the Registry instead of just placing your template in the special `CustomTags` folder. It is therefore recommended that you quickly mention in your documentation how to install the tag.

In addition, it is recommended that you include a sample ColdFusion template (.cfm file) showing how to actually use the custom tag in code. For instance, for the `<CF_TextToTitleCase>` custom tag, you could simply include the `UsingTextToTitleCase.cfm` template from Listing 20.15.

Posting to the Developer Exchange

Posting your custom tag to the Developer Exchange on the Macromedia Web site is simple. If you are going to allow people to download your tag for free, all you need to do is create a .zip file that contains your custom tag template, plus any documentation or examples, as discussed previously. Then go to the Developers Exchange and follow the submit links to post your tag to the exchange.

Visit the Developers Exchange at `http://devex.macromedia.com`.

Selling Your Custom Tags

As of this writing, the Developer Exchange on Macromedia's Web site does not accept payment for commercial tags. Therefore, if you want to sell your custom tags, you must either set up a secured payment processing and download area of your own (see Chapter 27) or use a specialized third-party site to handle this for you.

NOTE

The CFXtras Web site at www.cfextras.com is a good example of such a site. Signing up as a tag author and selling your custom tags is easy. The site retains a portion of each payment made to you as a service fee.

Additional Custom Tag Topics

In this chapter, you have learned quite a bit about how to use and write custom tags and the various roles they can play in your applications. A number of advanced custom tag concepts remain that this book just can't cover completely.

The following topics are covered, however, in its companion volume, *Advanced ColdFusion MX Application Development.*

Paired Custom Tags

You can create paired custom tags that expect opening and closing tags to be placed in the calling template, just as CFML's own `<CFOUTPUT>` tag expects a matching `</CFOUTPUT>` tag to be present. ColdFusion provides a special structure called `ThisTag`, which you can use to create such tags.

For more information, see *Advanced ColdFusion MX Application Development.* You can also search for `ThisTag` in ColdFusion Studio's online documentation.

Associating Nested Custom Tags

You can also create families of custom tags for use together that can access each other's attributes and other information. The tags usually are nested—often to gather multiple sets of attributes. Many of ColdFusion's native tags have special subtags that gather additional information from you, the coder. For instance, consider the <CFMAILPARAM> tag, which is used only between opening and closing <CFMAIL> tags (see Chapter 26, "Interacting with Email"), or the <CFCATCH> and <CFRETHROW> tags, which are used only between <CFTRY> tags (see Chapter 31).

You generally create such tag families using the <CFASSOCIATE> tag, which this book's companion volume explains.

NOTE

A great example of this type of custom tag is the extremely popular <CF_DHTMLMenu> custom tag by Ben Forta. It is included on the CD-ROM for this chapter.

Passing Attributes with ATTRIBUTECOLLECTION

In addition to the special NAME and TEMPLATE attribute names (discussed in the section "Controlling Template Locations with <CFMODULE>," earlier in this chapter), a third attribute name exists, which you should avoid defining for your custom tags: ATTRIBUTECOLLECTION. ColdFusion reserves the ATTRIBUTECOLLECTION attribute name for a special use: If a structure variable is passed to a custom tag as an attribute called ATTRIBUTECOLLECTION, the values in the structure become part of the ATTRIBUTES scope inside the custom tag template.

That is, instead of doing this:

```
<!--- Display Hello World Message, via Custom Tag --->
<CF_HelloWorldMessage
  Message="We're getting the band back together!"
  TopColor="yellow"
  BottomColor="orange">
or this:
<!--- Display Hello World Message, via Custom Tag --->
<CFMODULE
  NAME="HelloWorldMessage"
  Message="We're getting the band back together!"
  TopColor="yellow"
  BottomColor="orange">
```

you could do this:

```
<!--- Delete movie --->
<CFSET Attribs = StructNew()>
<CFSET Attribs.Message = "We're getting the band back together!"">
<CFSET Attribs.TopColor = "yellow">
<CFSET Attribs.BottomColor = "orange">
<!--- Display Hello World Message, via Custom Tag --->
<CFMODULE
  NAME="HelloWorldMessage"
  ATTRIBUTECOLLECTION="#Attribs#">
```

This is most useful in certain specialized situations, perhaps if you are calling a custom tag recursively (using the custom tag within the custom tag's own template, so that the tag calls itself repeatedly when used). You would be able to call a tag a second time within itself, passing the second tag the same attributes that were passed to the first, by specifying `ATTRIBUTESCOLLECTION="#Attributes#"`.

The REQUEST Scope

In addition to the `CALLER` and `ATTRIBUTES` scopes, ColdFusion defines a third special variable scope called `REQUEST`, which is relevant to a discussion of custom tags. Although it is not specifically part of ColdFusion's custom tag framework, it comes into play only in situations in which you have custom tags that might in turn use other custom tags.

Making Variables Available to All Custom Tags

Consider a situation where you might want to create a custom tag that uses the `<CF_ShowMovieCallout>` tag from Listing 20.8 internally. The new custom tag defines an optional `DataSource` attribute, which defaults to `ows`. That value is then passed to the `<CF_ShowMovieCallout>` tag from Listing 20.8. Wouldn't it be more convenient to use the `DataSource` variable defined in the `Application.cfm` file, in a process similar to that of earlier templates? That way, if your application needed to use a different data source name, you could just make the change in one place, in `Application.cfm`.

But how could you refer to that `DataSource` variable? Normally, you would refer to it directly in the `DATASOURCE` attribute for each `<CFQUERY>` tag, as in the `DATASOURCE= "#DataSource#"` attribute that has appeared in previous chapters. Of course, in a custom tag template, that variable wouldn't exist because the tag has its own local variable scope. You could access the value using the `CALLER` scope, as in `DATASOURCE="#CALLER.DataSource#"`, but there is a problem with that, too. When the new tag calls `<CF_ShowMovieCallout>`, the code template for `<CF_ShowMovieCallout>` won't be capable of referring to `CALLER.DataSource` because there is no local variable named `DataSource` in the calling template. In this situation, `<CF_ShowMovieCallout>` could refer to `CALLER.CALLER.DataSource`. That would work, but your code will get messier and messier if you start nesting tags several levels deep.

The answer is the `REQUEST` scope, a special scope shared among all ColdFusion templates participating in the page request—whether they are included via `<CFINCLUDE>`, called as a custom tag, or called via `<CFMODULE>`.

This means you can change these lines in the `Application.cfm` file:

```
<!--- Any variables set here can be used by all our pages --->
<CFSET DataSource  = "ows">
<CFSET CompanyName = "Orange Whip Studios">
```

to this:

```
<!--- Any variables set here can be used by all our pages --->
<CFSET REQUEST.DataSource  = "ows">
<CFSET REQUEST.CompanyName = "Orange Whip Studios">
```

Then you will be able to provide the `REQUEST.DataSource` variable to the `DATASOURCE` attribute of every `<CFQUERY>` tag in your application, regardless of whether the query is in a custom tag.

Maintaining Per-Request Flags and Counters

You can also use the REQUEST scope to create custom tags that are aware of how many times they have been included on a page. For instance, if you look at the code for the <CF_ShowMovieCallout> tag in Listing 20.8, you will see that it includes a <STYLE> block defining how the callout box will appear. If you include this custom tag several times on the same page, that <STYLE> block will be included several times in the page's source, which will cause the final page to have a longer download time than it should.

You could use the REQUEST scope to ensure that the <STYLE> block gets included in the page's source code only once, by surrounding the block with a <CFIF> test that checks to see whether a variable called REQUEST.CalloutStyleIncluded has been set. If not, the <STYLE> block should be included in the page. If it has been set, the tag knows that the block has already been included on the page, presumably because the tag has already been used earlier on the same page.

So, the <STYLE> block in ShowMovieCallout.cfm would be adjusted to look similar to the following:

```
<!--- If the <STYLE> is not included in this page yet --->
<CFIF IsDefined("REQUEST.CalloutStyleIncluded") EQ "No">
  <!--- Define formatting for film display --->
  <STYLE TYPE="text/css">
    TH.fm {background:RoyalBlue;color:white;text-align:left;
           font-family:sans-serif;font-size:10px}
    TD.fm {background:LightSteelBlue;
           font-family:sans-serif;font-size:12px}
  </STYLE>

  <!--- Remember that the <STYLE> has been included --->
  <CFSET REQUEST.CalloutStyleIncluded = "Yes">
</CFIF>
```

Listing 20.16 provides the complete code for the revised ShowMovieCallout.cfm template.

Listing 20.16 ShowMovieCallout2.cfm—Tracking Variables Between Tag Invocations

```
<!---
  <CF_ShowMovieCallout> Custom Tag
  Retrieves and displays the given film

  Example of Use:
  <CF_ShowMovieCallout
    FilmID="5">
--->

<!--- Tag Attributes --->
<!--- FilmID Attribute is Required --->
<CFPARAM NAME="ATTRIBUTES.FilmID" TYPE="numeric">
<!--- Whether to reveal cost/release dates (optional) --->
<CFPARAM NAME="ATTRIBUTES.ShowCost" TYPE="boolean" DEFAULT="Yes">
<CFPARAM NAME="ATTRIBUTES.ShowReleaseDate" TYPE="boolean" DEFAULT="Yes">
<!--- Optional formatting and placement options --->
<CFPARAM NAME="ATTRIBUTES.TableAlign" TYPE="string" DEFAULT="right">
<CFPARAM NAME="ATTRIBUTES.TableWidth" TYPE="string" DEFAULT="150">
<CFPARAM NAME="ATTRIBUTES.Caption" TYPE="string" DEFAULT="Featured Film">
<!--- Use "ows" datasource by default --->
```

Listing 20.16 (continued)

```
<CFPARAM NAME="ATTRIBUTES.DataSource" TYPE="string" DEFAULT="ows">

<!--- Get important info about film from database --->
<CFQUERY NAME="GetFilm" DATASOURCE="#ATTRIBUTES.DataSource#">
  SELECT
    MovieTitle, Summary,
    AmountBudgeted, DateInTheaters
  FROM Films
  WHERE FilmID = #ATTRIBUTES.FilmID#
</CFQUERY>

<!--- Display error message if record not fetched --->
<CFIF GetFilm.RecordCount NEQ 1>
  <CFTHROW
    MESSAGE="Invalid FilmID Attribute"
    DETAIL="Film #ATTRIBUTES.FilmID# does not exist!">
</CFIF>


<!--- Format a few queried values in local variables --->
<CFSET ProductCost = Ceiling(Val(GetFilm.AmountBudgeted) / 1000000)>
<CFSET ReleaseDate = DateFormat(GetFilm.DateInTheaters, "mmmm d")>

<!--- Now Display The Specified Movie --->
<CFOUTPUT>
  <!--- If the <STYLE> not included in this page yet --->
  <CFIF IsDefined("REQUEST.CalloutStyleIncluded") EQ "No">
    <!--- Define formatting for film display --->
    <STYLE TYPE="text/css">
      TH.fm {background:RoyalBlue;color:white;text-align:left;
             font-family:sans-serif;font-size:10px}
      TD.fm {background:LightSteelBlue;
             font-family:sans-serif;font-size:12px}
    </STYLE>

    <!--- Remember that the <STYLE> has been included --->
    <CFSET REQUEST.CalloutStyleIncluded = "Yes">
  </CFIF>

  <!--- Show info about featured movie in HTML Table --->
  <TABLE
    WIDTH="#ATTRIBUTES.TableWidth#"
    ALIGN="#ATTRIBUTES.TableAlign#"
    BORDER="0"
    CELLSPACING="0">

    <TR><TH CLASS="fm">
      #ATTRIBUTES.Caption#
    </TH></TR>
    <!--- Movie Title, Summary, Rating --->
    <TR><TD CLASS="fm">
      <B>#GetFilm.MovieTitle#</B><BR>
      #GetFilm.Summary#<BR>
    </TD></TR>
    <!--- Cost (rounded to millions), release date --->
    <CFIF ATTRIBUTES.ShowCost OR ATTRIBUTES.ShowReleaseDate>
```

Listing 20.16 (continued)

```
        <TR><TH CLASS="fm">
          <!--- Show Cost, if called for --->
          <CFIF ATTRIBUTES.ShowCost>
            Production Cost $#ProductCost# Million<BR>
          </CFIF>
          <!--- Show release date, if called for --->
          <CFIF ATTRIBUTES.ShowReleaseDate>
            In Theaters #ReleaseDate#<BR>
          </CFIF>
        </TH></TR>
      </CFIF>
    </TABLE>
    <BR CLEAR="all">
  </CFOUTPUT>
```

NOTE

Because the REQUEST scope is not shared between page requests, you do not need to use the <CFLOCK> tag when setting or accessing REQUEST variables.

Introducing ColdFusion Components

As you have learned in this chapter, you can use custom tags to package whatever type of processing you wish. In the last chapter, you learned how to package custom processing with the simpler user-defined functions framework.

An important part of ColdFusion MX is its new ColdFusion Components framework. Think of the CFC framework as a special way to combine key concepts from custom tags and user-defined functions into *objects*. These objects might represent concepts (such as individual films or actors), or they might represent processes (such as searching, creating special files, or validating credit card numbers).

Unlike custom tags, which have been serving the developer community for years now, CFCs are new in ColdFusion MX.

About ColdFusion Components

In a way, you can think of CFCs as a structured, formalized variation on custom tags. Whereas custom tags are very free in form and don't necessarily imply any kind of "correct" way to go about your work as a developer, the CFC framework gently forces developers to work in a more systematic way. If you choose to use the CFC framework for parts of your application, you will find yourself thinking about those aspects in a slightly more theoretical, abstract manner.

Of course, there are lots of benefits. Because CFCs are more structured, the code is generally very easy to follow, figure out, and troubleshoot. In this respect, you can think of the CFC framework as a way to write smart code, guiding you to adopt some very sensible suggested practices as a developer.

But the most dramatic benefit to the structured nature of CFCs is the fact that the structure makes it possible for ColdFusion to look into your CFC code and find the important elements, such as what functions you have included in the CFC and what each function's arguments are. This knowledge allows ColdFusion to act as a kind of interpreter between your CFC and other types of applications, such as Dreamweaver MX, Flash MX and Web Services. So, if you want them to, these components become part of a larger world of interconnected clients and servers, rather than only being a part of your ColdFusion code.

CFCs Can Be Called in Many Different Ways

This chapter and the last chapter have been all about making it easier to reuse the code that you and other developers write. CFCs take the notion of code reuse to a whole new level by making it ridiculously easy to reuse your code not only within ColdFusion, but in other types of applications as well.

All of the following can share and use CFCs:

- ColdFusion Pages. Once you have written the code for a CFC, you can call its methods from your normal ColdFusion pages, much in the same way that you can call the user-defined functions and custom tags that you write. In this sense, you can think of CFCs as a third way of extending the CFML language.
- Flash MX. Client-side applications written with Flash MX can easily access ColdFusion Components. The Flash 6 player contains scriptable support for communicating with a ColdFusion server and interacting with your CFCs. In other words, CFCs become the logical gateway between your ColdFusion MX code and the Flash player. The integration between CFCs and Flash is tight. It is almost as easy to use CFCs within Flash code as it is within another ColdFusion page. In Chapter 23, "Integrating with Macromedia Flash," you will see how easy it is to use the CFCs developed in this chapter within the Flash client.
- Web Browsers. If you wish, you can allow Web browsers to visit and interact with your CFCs directly, without your even needing to create a separate ColdFusion page that uses the CFC. Of course, you can control whether this is allowed, whether the user would first need to log in, and so on.
- Other Applications That Support Web Services. You can turn any ColdFusion Component into a Web Service by adding just one or two additional attributes to your CFC code. It will then be available as a resource that can be used over the Internet by any other application that supports Web Services, like other Web application servers, the various pieces of the .NET and J2EE platforms, and other languages such as Perl.

In other words, if you love the idea of reusing code, you'll love the CFC framework even more than the UDF and custom tag frameworks.

CFCs Are Object-Oriented Tools

Depending on your background, you may be familiar with object-oriented programming (OOP). If not, you may have at least heard the term before. Whether you know OOP or not, the important news is that CFCs give you the most important real-world benefits of object-oriented programming without getting too complicated—exactly what you would expect from ColdFusion.

NOTE

Don't let the OOP term scare you–this isn't your father's object orientation. The introduction of CFCs hasn't turned ColdFusion or CFML into a complex, full-blown object-oriented language. CFCs are not obsessive-compulsive. Whether your father may be is a different story.

Without getting too deeply into the specifics, you can think of object-oriented programming as a general programming philosophy. The philosophy basically says that most of the concepts in an application represent objects in the real world, and should be treated as such. Some objects, like films or merchandise for sale, might be physical. Others, like expense records or individual orders for merchandise, might be more conceptual but still easy to imagine as objects. (Or they might just end up being objectified, like many of Orange Whip Studios' actors.)

ColdFusion's CFC framework is based on these object-oriented ideas:

- **Classes.** In traditional object-oriented programming, the notion of a class is extremely important. For your purposes here, just think of an object class as a type of object. For instance, Orange Whip Studios has made many films during its proud history. If you think of each individual film as an object, then it follows that you can consider the general notion of a film (as opposed to a particular film) as a class. Hence, each individual film object belongs to the same class, perhaps called Film. In ColdFusion you don't actually ever create a class, CFCs are your classes.
- **Methods.** In the object-oriented world, each type of object (that is, each class) will have a few *methods*. Methods are just functions that have been conceptually attached to a class. The idea is that a method represents something you can do to an object. For instance, think about a car as an object. You can start it, put it into gear, stop it, and so on. So, for a corresponding object class called car, it might have methods named `Car.StartEngine()`, `Car.ChangeGear()`, `Car.AvoidPedestrian()`, and so on.
- **Instances.** OK, if there is a class of object called Film, then you also need a word to refer to each individual film the studio makes. In the OOP world, this is described as an *instance*. Each individual film is an instance of the class called Film. Each instance of an object usually has some information associated with it, called its *instance data*. For instance, Film A has its own title and stars. Film B and Film C have different titles and different stars.
- **Properties.** Most real-world objects have properties that make them unique (or if not unique, at least distinguish them from other objects of the same type). For instance, a real-world car has properties such as its color, make, model, engine size, number of doors, license plate and vehicle identification number, and so on. At any given moment, it might have other properties such as whether it is currently running, who is currently driving it, and how much gas is in the fuel tank. Or, if you're talking about films, the properties might be the film's title, the director, how many screens it is currently shown on, or whether it is going to be released straight to video. Properties are generally stored as instance data.

CFCs and Method Inheritance

In addition to the OOP concepts just listed, ColdFusion's CFC framework also supports the notion of *inheritance*, which basically means that different object classes can be derived from a parent object class. So, there might be other types of objects that are related to the Film class, but have additional, more specific characteristics (perhaps ComedyFilm, which would track additional information about how funny it is, and ActionFilm, which would track how many explosions occur per minute).

NOTE

> Once you start talking about this concept, you usually need to start talking about other object-oriented vocabulary words, such as *subclassing, overriding, overloading, descendants, polymorphism,* and so on. If none of those words means anything to you, don't worry. The CFC framework implements the concept in a straightforward and simple way that sidesteps many of the thornier points of traditional OOP implementations. This isn't your father's inheritance.

You can learn all about CFC inheritance in this book's companion volume, *Advanced ColdFusion MX Application Development*. See also the `EXTENDS` attribute of the `<CFCOMPONENT>` tag in Appendix B.

The Two Types of Components

In general, you will find that most CFCs fall into two broad categories: *static* components and *instance-based* components.

Static Components

I'll use the term *static* to refer to any component where it doesn't make sense to create individual instances of the component. Often you can think of such components as *services* which are constantly listening for and answering requests. For instance, if you were creating a film-searching component that made it easy to search the current list of films, you probably wouldn't need to create multiple copies of the film-searching component.

Static components are kind of like Santa Claus, the Wizard of Oz, or your father—only one of each exists. You just go to that one and make your request.

Instance-Based Components

Other components represent ideas where it is very important to create individual instances of a component. For instance, consider a CFC called ShoppingCart that represents a user's shopping cart on your site. Many different shopping carts will exist in the world at any given time (one for each user). Therefore, you need to create a fresh instance of the ShoppingCart CFC for each new Web visitor, or perhaps each new Web session. You would expect most of the CFC's methods to return different results for each instance, depending on the contents of each user's cart.

Your First CFC

The best news about CFCs is that there is really very little to learn about them. For the most part, you just write functions in much the same way that you learned in Chapter 19. You just save them in a special file and surround them with a `<CFCOMPONENT>` tag. That's really about it.

Let's take a closer look.

The Structure of a CFC File

Each ColdFusion component is saved in its own file, with a `.cfc` extension. Except for one new tag, `<CFCOMPONENT>`, everything in the file is just ordinary CFML code. With the `.cfc` extension instead of .cfm, the ColdFusion server can easily detect which files represent CFC components.

Table 20.3 describes the various parts of a component definition file.

Table 20.3 The Parts of a Component

PART	DESCRIPTION
`<CFCOMPONENT>` block	Surrounds everything else in the CFC file. Just place an opening `<CFCOMPONENT>` tag at the top of your `.cfc` file, and a closing tag at the bottom.
`<CFFUNCTION>` blocks	Within the `<CFCOMPONENT>` tag, use `<CFFUNCTION>` blocks to create each of the component's methods. There are a few additional attributes in the `<CFFUNCTION>` tag for CFCs, but for the most part, you write these functions the same way you learned in Chapter 19. Within each `<CFFUNCTION>` tag, you will use `<CFARGUMENT>` to define the method's arguments, `<CFRETURN>` to return whatever result you want the method to return, and so on.
Initialization code	Any CFML code that is inside the `<CFCOMPONENT>` block but not within any of the `<CFFUNCTION>` tags will execute the first time an instance of the component is used. I call this *initialization code* because the main reason you would want code to run when the CFC is first created would be to set values in the `THIS` scope to their initial values.

Introducing the `<CFCOMPONENT>` Tag

The `<CFCOMPONENT>` tag doesn't have any required attributes, so in its simplest use, you can just wrap opening and closing `<CFCOMPONENT>` tags around everything else your CFC file contains (mainly `<CFFUNCTION>` blocks). That said, you can use two optional attributes, `HINT` and `DISPLAYNAME`, to make your CFC file more self-describing (see Table 20.4).

If you provide these optional attributes, ColdFusion MX and Dreamweaver MX can automatically show `HINT` and `DISPLAYNAME` in various places, to make life easier for you and the other developers that might be using the component. See the "Exploring CFCs in Dreamweaver MX" section, later in this chapter, for more on where you will see this information displayed.

Table 20.4 `<CFCOMPONENT>` Tag Syntax

ATTRIBUTE	DESCRIPTION
`HINT`	What your component does, in plain English (or whatever language you want, of course). I recommend that you provide this attribute.
`DISPLAYNAME`	An alternative, friendlier phrasing of the component's name. In general, I recommend that you make the component's actual name (that is, the filename) as self-describing as possible, rather than relying on the `DISPLAYNAME` to make its purpose clear.

NOTE

You can also use the EXTENDS attribute to make CFCs that inherit methods from other CFCs. This book does not discuss the notion of CFC inheritance, but see the companion volume, *Advanced ColdFusion MX Application Development.*

NOTE

As you will soon see, the <CFFUNCTION> and <CFARGUMENT> tags have HINT and DISPLAYNAME attributes too. That is, each aspect of a CFC that someone would need to know about to actually use it can be described more completely within the component code itself.

Using <CFFUNCTION> to Create Methods

The vast majority of a CFC is the ColdFusion code you write for each of the CFC's methods (remember, I use the word *method* to refer to a function attached to a CFC). To create a component's methods, you use the <CFFUNCTION> tag in much the same way you learned in Chapter 19. If the method has any required or optional arguments, you use the <CFARGUMENT> tag, again just as you learned in Chapter 19.

The <CFFUNCTION> and <CFARGUMENT> tags each take a few additional attributes that Chapter 19 didn't discuss because they are only relevant for CFCs. The most important new attributes are HINT and DISPLAYNAME, which all the CFC-related tags have in common. A summary of all <CFFUNCTION> and <CFARGUMENT> attributes is provided in Table 20.5 and Table 20.6.

Table 20.5 <CFFUNCTION> Syntax for CFC Methods

ATTRIBUTE	DESCRIPTION
NAME	Required. The name of the function (method), as discussed in Chapter 19.
HINT	Optional. A description of the method. Like the HINT attribute for <CFCOMPONENT>, this description will be visible in Dreamweaver MX to make life easier for you and the other developers on your team. It is also included in the automatic documentation that ColdFusion produces for your components.
DISPLAYNAME	Optional. Like the DISPLAYNAME attribute for <CFCOMPONENT> (see Table 20.4).
RETURNTYPE	Optional. The type of data that the function returns (for instance, a date or a string). While you are not required to specify the RETURNTYPE, I recommend that you do so. If you do, the return type will be conveniently displayed in Dreamweaver MX and by ColdFusion itself, making it a lot easier to keep track of which methods do what. Also, the RETURNTYPE is required if you want the method you're creating to be available as a Web Service.
ACCESS	Optional. This attribute defines how your method can be used. If ACCESS="Remote", then the method can be accessed over the Internet as a Web Service, by Web browsers, or by the Flash Player. If ACCESS="Public", then the method can be used internally by any of your ColdFusion pages (similar to a UDF or custom tag), but not by Flash, browsers, or Web Services. If ACCESS="Private", then the method can only be used internally by other methods in the same component. If ACCESS="Package", then the method can only be used internally by other methods in the same component, or other components in the same directory.

Table 20.5 (continued)

ATTRIBUTE	DESCRIPTION
ROLES	Optional. A list of security roles or user groups that should be able to use the method. This attribute only has meaning if you are using the <CFLOGIN> security framework discussed in Chapter 18, "Securing Your Applications." If a ROLES attribute is provided, and the current user has not logged in as a member of one of the allowed roles, then the user will not be able to access the method. The effect is similar to using the IsUserInRole() function to deny access within normal ColdFusion pages, as discussed in Chapter 18. For details about this attribute, see our companion book, *Advanced ColdFusion MX Application Development*.
OUTPUT	Optional. Whether the method is designed to generate output to the current page directly (like a <CFOUTPUT> block), rather than only generating a return value. See Appendix B for details.

NOTE

The valid data types you can provide for RETURNTYPE are: any, array, binary, boolean, date, guid, numeric, query, string, struct, uuid, and variableName. If the method is not going to return a value at all, use RETURNTYPE="void". If the method is going to return an instance of another component, you can provide that component's name (the filename without the .cfc) as the RETURNTYPE.

Table 20.6 <CFARGUMENT> Syntax for CFC Method Arguments

ATTRIBUTE	SYNTAX
NAME	Required. The name of the argument, as discussed in Chapter 19.
HINT	An explanation of the argument's purpose. Like the HINT attribute for <CFCOMPONENT> and <CFARGUMENT>, this description will be visible in Dreamweaver MX to make life easier for you and the other developers on your team. It is also included in the automatic documentation that ColdFusion produces for your components.
DISPLAYNAME	Optional. Like the DISPLAYNAME attribute for <CFCOMPONENT> (see Table 20.4).
TYPE	Optional. The data type of the argument, as discussed in Chapter 19. You can use any of the values mentioned in the note under Table 20.5 except for void.
REQUIRED	Optional. Whether the argument is required. See Chapter 19 for details.
DEFAULT	Optional. A default value for the argument, if REQUIRED="No". See Chapter 19.

NOTE

There is actually another CFC related tag, called <CFPROPERTY>. In this version of ColdFusion the <CFPROPERTY> tag doesn't affect how a CFC works; it only helps the CFC be more self-documenting, mainly for the benefit of Web Services, a topic which is beyond the scope of this book. Therefore, I'm not discussing it right away in an effort to keep the discussion as clear as possible while you are learning. See the "Documenting Properties With <CFPROPERTY>" section, near the end of this chapter, for details.

A Simple Example

Let's take a look at a simple example of CFC. Say you want to create a CFC called `FilmSearchCFC`, which provides a simplified way to search for films. You like the idea of being able to reuse this component within your ColdFusion pages, instead of having to write queries over and over again. You'd also like to be able to flick a switch and have the component available to the Flash Player or Web Services.

Listing 20.17 is a simple version of the `FilmSearchCFC`.

Listing 20.17 `FilmSearchCFC.cfc`—A Simple CFC

```
<!---
  Filename: FilmSearchCFC.cfc
  Author:   Nate Weiss (NMW)
  Purpose:  Creates FilmSearchCFC, a simple ColdFusion Component
--->

<!--- The <CFCOMPONENT> block defines the CFC --->
<!--- The filename of this file determines the CFC's name --->
<CFCOMPONENT>

   <!--- ListFilms() method --->
   <CFFUNCTION NAME="ListFilms" RETURNTYPE="query">

<!--- Optional SearchString argument --->
      <CFARGUMENT NAME="SearchString" REQUIRED="No" DEFAULT="">

      <!--- Run the query --->
      <CFQUERY NAME="GetFilms" DATASOURCE="#Request.Datasource#">
        SELECT FilmID, MovieTitle FROM Films
        <!--- If a search string has been specified --->
        <CFIF ARGUMENTS.SearchString NEQ "">
          WHERE (MovieTitle LIKE '%#ARGUMENTS.SearchString#%'
                 OR Summary LIKE '%#ARGUMENTS.SearchString#%')
        </CFIF>
        ORDER BY MovieTitle
      </CFQUERY>

      <!--- Return the query results --->
      <CFRETURN GetFilms>
   </CFFUNCTION>

</CFCOMPONENT>
```

NOTE

Earlier, I explained that there are two types of components: *static* components, which just provide functionality, and *instance-based* components, which provide functionality but also hold information. This CFC is an example of a static component. You will see how to create instance-based components shortly.

This version of the CFC only has one method, called `ListFilms()`, which queries the database for a listing of current films. The query object is returned as the method's return value (this is why `RETURNTYPE="query"` is used in the method's `<CFFUNCTION>` tag).

The `ListFilms()` method takes one optional argument called `SearchString`. If the `SearchString` argument is provided, then a WHERE clause is added to the database query so that only films with matching titles or summaries are selected. If the `SearchString` is not provided, then all films are retrieved from the database and returned by the new method.

As you can see, building a simple component is not much different from creating a user-defined function. Now that you've created the component, let's take a look at how to use it in your ColdFusion code.

TIP

You can use the Create Component dialog in Dreamweaver MX to create the basic skeleton of `<CFCOMPONENT>`, `<CFFUNCTION>`, `<CFARGUMENT>`, and `<CFRETURN>` tags. Then all you need to do is add the appropriate logic to the `<CFFUNCTION>` blocks. See the "Using the Create Component Dialog" section, later in this chapter.

Using the CFC in ColdFusion Pages

Once you have completed your CFC file, there are two basic ways to use the new component's methods in your ColdFusion code:

- With the `<CFINVOKE>` tag, as discussed next.
- With scriptlike syntax, in the form `Component.MethodName()`. To use this syntax, you must first create an instance of the CFC with the `<CFOBJECT>` tag.

In general, you will probably use the `<CFINVOKE>` syntax for static components (like the `FilmSearchCFC`), and the scriptlike syntax when interacting with a specific instance of a component. See "The Two Types of Components," earlier in this chapter.

Calling Methods with `<CFINVOKE>`

The most straightforward way to call a CFC method is with the `<CFINVOKE>` tag. `<CFINVOKE>` makes your CFC look a lot like a custom tag. To provide values to the method's arguments, as in the optional `SearchString` argument in Listing 20.17, you can either add additional attributes to `<CFINVOKE>` or you can nest a `<CFINVOKEARGUMENT>` tag within the `<CFINVOKE>` tag. Table 20.7 and Table 20.8 show the attributes supported by `<CFINVOKE>` and `<CFINVOKEARGUMENT>`.

Table 20.7 `<CFINVOKE>` Tag Syntax

ATTRIBUTE	DESCRIPTION
`COMPONENT`	The name of the component, as a string (the name of the file in which you saved the component, without the `.cfc` extension); or a component instance.
`METHOD`	The name of the method you want to use.
`RETURNVARIABLE`	A variable name in which to store whatever value the method decides to return.

Table 20.7 (continued)

ATTRIBUTE	DESCRIPTION
(method arguments)	In addition to the COMPONENT, METHOD, and RETURNVARIABLE attributes, you can also provide values to the method's arguments by providing them as attributes. For instance, the ListFilms() method from Listing 20.17 has an optional argument called SearchString. To provide a value to this argument, you could use SearchString="Raiders" or SearchString="#FORM.Keywords#". You can also provide arguments using the separate <CFINVOKEARGUMENT> tag (see Table 20.8).
ARGUMENTCOLLECTION	Optional, and for special cases only. This attribute lets you provide values for the method's arguments together in a single structure. It works the same way as the ATTRIBUTECOLLECTION attribute of the <CFMODULE> tag (see "Introducing the <CFMODULE> Tag," earlier in this chapter).

NOTE

For the COMPONENT attribute, you can use the component name alone (that is, the file without the .cfc extension) if the .cfc file is in the same folder as the file that is using the <CFINVOKE> tag. You can also specify a .cfc in another folder, using dot notation to specify the location of the folder relative to the Web server root, where the dots represent folder names. For instance, you could use the FilmSearchCFC component by specifying COMPONENT="ows.20.FilmSearchCFC". For more information, see the ColdFusion MX documentation.

NOTE

You can also save .cfc files in the special CustomTags folder or its subfolders. For the COMPONENT attribute of <CFINVOKE>, specify the location relative to the CustomTags folder, again using dots to separate the folder names. This is the same way that you can specify folder locations for the NAME attribute of the <CFMODULE> tag. See the "Using Dot Notation to Avoid Conflicts" section, earlier in this chapter. You can also start the COMPONENT attribute with a mapping from the Mappings page of the ColdFusion Administrator.

Table 20.8 <CFINVOKEARGUMENT> Tag Syntax

ATTRIBUTE	DESCRIPTION
NAME	The name of the argument. So, to provide a value to an argument called SearchString, you could use a <CFINVOKEARGUMENT> tag with NAME="SearchString".
VALUE	The value of the argument. To provide the value of a form field to the SearchString argument, you could use VALUE="#FORM.SearchString#".

Listing 20.18 shows how to use <CFINVOKE> to call the ListFilms() method of the FilmSearchCFC component created in Listing 20.17.

Listing 20.18 UsingFilmSearchCFC1.cfm—Invoking a Component Method

```
<!---
  Filename: UsingFilmSearchCFC1.cfm
  Author:   Nate Weiss (NMW)
  Purpose:  Uses the FilmSearchCFC component to display a list of films
```

Listing 20.18 (CONTINUED)

```
--->

<HTML>
<HEAD><TITLE>Film Search Example</TITLE></HEAD>
<BODY>

<!--- Invoke the ListFilms() method of the FilmSearchComponent --->
<CFINVOKE
  COMPONENT="FilmSearchCFC"
  METHOD="ListFilms"
  RETURNVARIABLE="FilmsQuery">

<!--- Now output the list of films --->
<CFOUTPUT QUERY="FilmsQuery">
  #FilmsQuery.MovieTitle#<BR>
</CFOUTPUT>

</BODY>
</HTML>
```

First, the `<CFINVOKE>` tag invokes the `ListFilms()` method provided by the `FilmSearchCFC1` component. Note that the correct value to provide to `COMPONENT` is the name of the component filename, but without the `.cfc` extension. So, when this page is visited with a browser, ColdFusion will see the `<CFINVOKE>` tag and look for the corresponding CFC file (`FilmSearchCFC.cfc`). It will then execute the code in the `<CFFUNCTION>` block with `NAME="ListFilms"`.

The `RETURNVARIABLE` attribute has been set to `FilmQuery`, which means that `FilmsQuery` will hold whatever value the method returns. The method in question, `ListFilms()`, returns a query object as its return value. Therefore, after the `<CFINVOKE>` tag executes, the rest of the example can refer to `FilmsQuery` just as if it were the results of a normal `<CFQUERY>` tag. Here, a simple `<CFOUTPUT>` block outputs the title of each film.

The result is a simple list of film titles, as shown in Figure 20.7.

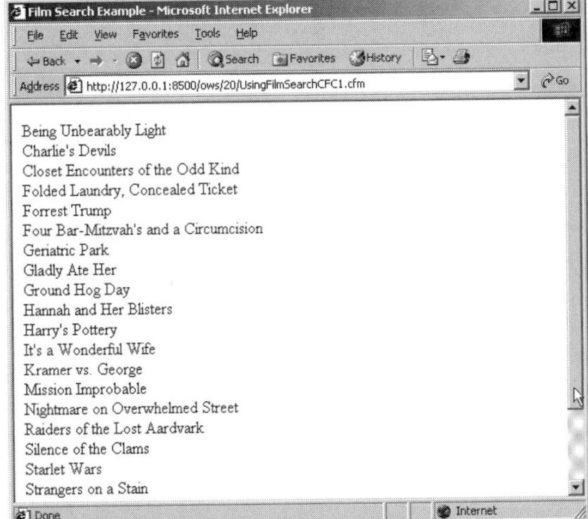

Figure 20.7

It's easy to execute a component's methods and use the results.

Supplying Arguments

The `ListFilms()` method from Listing 20.17 takes an optional argument called `SearchString`. This argument was not provided to the method in Listing 20.18, so the method will always return all films. Listing 20.19 shows how to supply values to method arguments by adding an attribute to the `<CFINVOKE>` tag.

Listing 20.19 `UsingFilmSearchCFC2.cfm`—Supplying Arguments with `<CFINVOKE>`

```
<!---
  Filename: UsingFilmSearchCFC2.cfm
  Author:   Nate Weiss (NMW)
  Purpose:  Uses the FilmSearchCFC component to display a list of films
--->

<HTML>
<HEAD><TITLE>Film Search Example</TITLE></HEAD>
<BODY>

<!--- FORM parameter called Keywords, empty by default --->
<CFPARAM NAME="FORM.Keywords" DEFAULT="">

<!--- Simple form to allow user to filter films --->
<CFFORM>
  <CFINPUT NAME="Keywords" VALUE="#FORM.Keywords#">
  <INPUT TYPE="Submit" VALUE="Filter">
</CFFORM>

<!--- Invoke the ListFilms() method of the FilmSearchComponent --->
<!--- Pass the user's search keywords to the SearchString argument --->
<CFINVOKE
  COMPONENT="FilmSearchCFC"
  METHOD="ListFilms"
  SearchString="#FORM.Keywords#"
  RETURNVARIABLE="FilmsQuery">

<!--- Now output the list of films --->
<CFOUTPUT QUERY="FilmsQuery">
  #FilmsQuery.MovieTitle#<BR>
</CFOUTPUT>

</BODY>
</HTML>
```

In this example, a very simple search form has been added at the top of the page, where the user can filter the list of films by typing in a keyword. The value that the user types is passed to the `SearchString` argument of the `ListFilms()` method. The method responds by returning only those films that contain the user's filter string in their title or summary (Figure 20.8).

NOTE

You can use the `<CFINVOKEARGUMENT>` tag to supply the `SearchString` argument (or any other argument), instead of providing the argument as an attribute of `<CFINVOKE>`. You can see this in action in the next example (Listing 20.20).

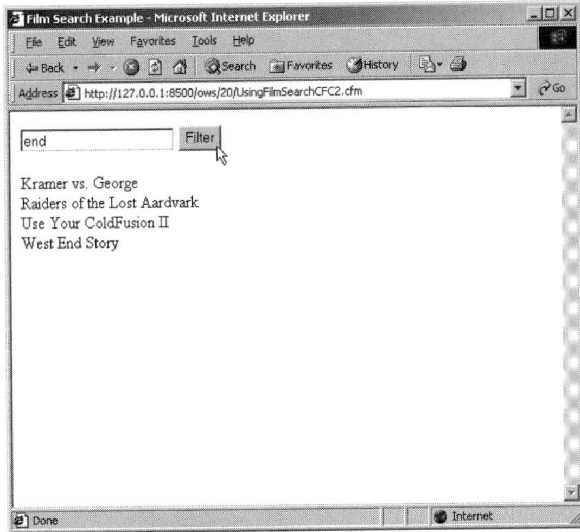

Figure 20.8

The <CFINVOKE> tag makes it easy to pass values to methods.

Calling an Instance's Methods

In the last listing, you saw how to use the <CFINVOKE> tag to call a CFC method. Calling methods this way is not much different from calling a custom tag with <CFMODULE>, or calling a UDF. There's nothing terribly object oriented about this yet.

It's also possible to create an instance of a CFC, and then call the instance's methods. If the CFC doesn't track instance data (like a shopping cart, say, or information about a particular film), then there isn't much of a functional difference. But it's worth taking a look at now, because it underscores the notion of a CFC as an object that provides functionality (in the form of methods).

To work with methods in this way, two steps are involved:

1 Create an instance of the CFC with the <CFOBJECT> tag.

2 Invoke whatever methods you want, using the <CFINVOKE> tag as you learned in the last section. But instead of specifying the component by name, you pass the component instance directly to the `COMPONENT` attribute. You can repeat this part as many times as you like, using the same component instance.

Table 20.9 shows the attributes you supply to the <CFOBJECT> tag to create an instance of a CFC.

Table 20.9 <CFOBJECT> Tag Syntax for CFC Instantiation

ATTRIBUTE	DESCRIPTION
`COMPONENT`	Required. The name of the component (that is, the CFC filename without the `.cfc` extension).
`NAME`	Required. A variable name in which to store the CFC instance. After the <CFOBJECT> tag executes, your code can refer to the variable named here to interact with the instance.

NOTE

You can use the <CFOBJECT> tag to create instances of other types of objects, not just CFCs. For instance, it can create instances of JavaBeans and Windows COM controls. Only the attributes relevant for CFCs are included in Table 20.9. For information on the other uses of <CFOBJECT>, see Appendix B or the companion book, *Advanced ColdFusion MX Application Development.*

Listing 20.20 is a simple example of CFC instantiation and method calling. This listing does the same thing as the previous one, except that it calls the `ListFilms()` method using an *instance* of the `FilmSearchCFC1` component, rather than the component itself.

Listing 20.20 `UsingFilmSearchCFC3.cfm`—Creating a Component Instance

```
<!---
  Filename: UsingFilmSearchCFC3.cfm
  Author:   Nate Weiss (NMW)
  Purpose:  Uses the FilmSearchCFC component to display a list of films
--->


<HTML>
<HEAD><TITLE>Film Search Example</TITLE></HEAD>
<BODY>

<!--- FORM parameter called Keywords, empty by default --->
<CFPARAM NAME="FORM.Keywords" DEFAULT="">

<!--- Simple form to allow user to filter films --->
<CFFORM>
  <CFINPUT NAME="Keywords" VALUE="#FORM.Keywords#">
  <INPUT TYPE="Submit" VALUE="Filter">
</CFFORM>

<!--- Create an instance of the CFC --->
<CFOBJECT
  COMPONENT="FilmSearchCFC"
  NAME="MyFilmSearcher">

<!--- Invoke the ListFilms() method of the CFC instance --->
<CFINVOKE
  COMPONENT="#MyFilmSearcher#"
  METHOD="ListFilms"
  RETURNVARIABLE="FilmsQuery">
  <!--- Pass the user's search keywords to the SearchString argument --->
  <CFINVOKEARGUMENT
    NAME="SearchString"
    VALUE="#FORM.Keywords#">
</CFINVOKE>

<!--- Now output the list of films --->
<CFOUTPUT QUERY="FilmsQuery">
  #FilmsQuery.MovieTitle#<BR>
</CFOUTPUT>

</BODY>
</HTML>
```

Calling Methods with Scriptlike Syntax

You've seen how you can call a component's methods using `<CFINVOKE>`. You can also call methods using a scriptlike syntax, where you call a CFC's methods in a way that makes them look more obviously like functions.

To call methods using the scriptlike syntax, you just use the method like a function (either a built-in CFML function or a UDF), as in a `<CFSET>` tag. The only difference is that you precede the function name with a component instance, separated with a dot. So, if you have a object instance called `MyFilmSearcher`, you could use this line to call its `ListFilms()` method:

```
<CFSET FilmsQuery = MyFilmSearcher.ListFilms()>
```

Functionally, this way of calling a method isn't any different than using `<CFINVOKE>`, but it is more concise, so you may prefer it. Listing 20.21 is the same as the previous listing, but with the `<CFINVOKE>` tag replaced with the script-style syntax.

Listing 20.21 `UsingFilmSearchCFC4.cfm`—Calling Methods Using Scriptlike Syntax

```
<!---
  Filename: UsingFilmSearchCFC4.cfm
  Author:   Nate Weiss (NMW)
  Purpose:  Uses the FilmSearchCFC component to display a list of films
--->


<HTML>
<HEAD><TITLE>Film Search Example</TITLE></HEAD>
<BODY>

<!--- FORM parameter called Keywords, empty by default --->
<CFPARAM NAME="FORM.Keywords" DEFAULT="">

<!--- Simple form to allow user to filter films --->
<CFFORM>
  <CFINPUT NAME="Keywords" VALUE="#FORM.Keywords#">
  <INPUT TYPE="Submit" VALUE="Filter">
</CFFORM>

<!--- Create an instance of the CFC --->
<CFOBJECT
  COMPONENT="FilmSearchCFC"
  NAME="MyFilmSearcher">

<!--- Invoke the CFC's ListFilms() method --->
<CFSET FilmsQuery = MyFilmSearcher.ListFilms(FORM.Keywords)>

<!--- Now output the list of films --->
<CFOUTPUT QUERY="FilmsQuery">
  #FilmsQuery.MovieTitle#<BR>
</CFOUTPUT>

</BODY>
</HTML>
```

Instantiating Components with `CreateObject()`

The past two examples have used the <CFOBJECT> tag to create an instance of a CFC. As an alternative, you can use the `CreateObject()` function to do the same thing. Provide the word `component` as the function's first argument, and the name of the desired CFC as the second argument. The function will return the component instance, which you can then use to call methods.

In other words, you could replace the <CFOBJECT> tag in Listing 20.21 with this line:

```
<CFSET MyFilmSearcher = CreateObject("component","FilmSearchCFC1")>
```

Neither <CFOBJECT> nor `CreateObject()` is better. Just use whichever one you prefer.

A More Complete CFC

Listing 20.22 shows a slightly more complex variation on the `FilmSearchCFC` component created in Listing 20.17. The idea behind this CFC is to provide not only a search facility, but also a way to get and display detailed information about films. To reflect this expanded role, I'll call this version `FilmDataCFC` instead of `FilmSearchCFC`.

CFCs as Collections of Functions

In addition to the `ListFilms()` method, Listing 20.22 also includes a new method, `GetFilmData()`, which takes a film's ID number as input and returns a structure containing the film's title, summary, and actors. You can think of this CFC as a collection of conceptually related functions, since both methods are about data retrieval pertaining to records in the `Films` database table. In a big-picture way, this is what many CFCs are all about: collecting related functionality into a single bundle.

Also, this listing uses the `HINT` attribute in the <CFCOMPONENT> tag and each of the <CFFUNCTION> and <CFARGUMENT> tags to allow the component to be self-documenting.

NOTE

In fact, once you create a CFC, you can view automatically-generated for it by visiting the `.cfc` file with your browser. For details, see Figure 20.11 in the "Exploring CFCs in Dreamweaver MX" section, later in this chapter.

Listing 20.22 `FilmDataCFC1.cfc`—Providing Descriptive Information About Methods

```
<!---
  Filename: FilmDataCFC1.cfc
  Author:   Nate Weiss (NMW)
  Purpose:  Creates the FilmDataCFC1 ColdFusion Component, which provides
            search and data retrieval services for films in the ows database.
--->

<!--- The <CFCOMPONENT> block defines the CFC --->
<!--- The filename of this file determines the CFC's name --->
<CFCOMPONENT
  HINT="Provides a simple interface for searching for and getting detailed
        information about films in the Orange Whip Studios database.">

   <!--- ListFilms() method --->
   <CFFUNCTION
```

Listing 20.22 (continued)

```
  NAME="ListFilms"
  RETURNTYPE="query"
  HINT="Returns a query object containing film information.">

  <!--- Optional SearchString argument --->
  <CFARGUMENT
    NAME="SearchString"
    TYPE="string"
    REQUIRED="No"
    HINT="Optional search criteria; if not given, all films are returned.">

  <!--- Optional SearchString argument --->
  <CFARGUMENT
    NAME="ActorID"
    TYPE="numeric"
    REQUIRED="No"
    HINT="Allows searching for films by actor.">

  <!--- Run the query --->
  <CFQUERY NAME="GetFilms" DATASOURCE="ows">
    SELECT FilmID, MovieTitle FROM Films
    WHERE 0=0
    <!--- If a search string has been specified --->
    <CFIF IsDefined("ARGUMENTS.SearchString")>
      AND (MovieTitle LIKE '%#ARGUMENTS.SearchString#%'
           OR Summary LIKE '%#ARGUMENTS.SearchString#%')
    </CFIF>
    <!--- If an actor's name has been specified --->
    <CFIF IsDefined("ARGUMENTS.ActorID")>
      AND FilmID IN
        (SELECT FilmID FROM FilmsActors
         WHERE ActorID = #ARGUMENTS.ActorID#)
    </CFIF>
    ORDER BY MovieTitle
  </CFQUERY>

  <!--- Return the query results --->
  <CFRETURN GetFilms>
</CFFUNCTION>


<!--- GetFilmData() method --->
<CFFUNCTION
  NAME="GetFilmData"
  RETURNTYPE="struct"
  HINT="Returns structured information about the specified film.">

  <!--- FilmID argument --->
  <CFARGUMENT
    NAME="FilmID"
    TYPE="numeric"
    REQUIRED="Yes"
    HINT="The film that you want information about.">

  <!--- This is what this method originally returns --->
  <!--- The var keyword makes it local to the method --->
```

Listing 20.22 (continued)

```
    <CFSET var FilmData = StructNew()>
    <CFSET FilmData.FilmID = ARGUMENTS.FilmID>

    <!--- Select data about the film from the database --->
    <CFQUERY NAME="GetFilm" DATASOURCE="ows">
      SELECT MovieTitle, Summary FROM Films
      WHERE FilmID = #ARGUMENTS.FilmID#
    </CFQUERY>

    <!--- Populate the FilmData structure with film info --->
    <CFSET FilmData.MovieTitle = GetFilm.MovieTitle>
    <CFSET FilmData.Summary = GetFilm.Summary>

    <!--- Run second query to get actor information --->
    <CFQUERY NAME="GetActors" DATASOURCE="ows">
      SELECT ActorID, NameFirst, NameLast
      FROM Actors
      WHERE ActorID IN
        (SELECT ActorID FROM FilmsActors
         WHERE FilmID = #ARGUMENTS.FilmID#)
    </CFQUERY>

    <!--- Make the GetActors query results part of the returned structure --->
    <CFSET FilmData.ActorsQuery = GetActors>

     <!--- Return the final structure --->
    <CFRETURN FilmData>
  </CFFUNCTION>

</CFCOMPONENT>
```

TIP

As the number of methods provided by each CFC increases, you will want to have some way of keeping track of them all. Dreamweaver MX addresses this need by allowing you to explore the methods and arguments for each CFC in the Components tree. See the "Exploring CFCs in Dreamweaver MX" section, later in this chapter.

TIP

You can use the Create Component dialog in Dreamweaver MX to create the basic skeleton of `<CFCOMPONENT>` and related tags. See the "Using the Create Component Dialog" section, later in this chapter.

The `ListFilms()` method was in the last version, but I've adapted it slightly here. It now accepts two optional arguments, `SearchCriteria` and `ActorName`, which can filter the returned query object based on keywords or the name of an actor.

Using the `FilmData` CFC

The code in Listing 20.22 creates two methods: the `ListFilms()` method can be used to display a list of films, and the `GetFilmData()` method can be used to display detailed information about a particular film. The next two listings show how you can use these methods together to create a simple film-browsing interface.

Listing 20.23 uses the `ListFilms()` method to display a list of films. This is not much different from the first listing that used the `FilmSearchCFC` component (Listing 20.18), as shown in Figure 20.7. The only real difference is each film is now presented as a link to a detail page, where the details about the selected film will be shown.

Listing 20.23 `UsingFilmDataCFC1.cfm`—Using a CFC in a Master-Detail Data Interface

```
<HTML>
<HEAD><TITLE>Using FilmDataCFC</TITLE></HEAD>
<BODY>
<H3>Orange Whip Studios Films</H3>

<!--- Invoke the ListFilms() method of the FilmSearchComponent --->
<CFINVOKE
  COMPONENT="ows.20.FilmDataCFC1"
  METHOD="ListFilms"
  RETURNVARIABLE="FilmsQuery">

<!--- Now output the list of films --->
<CFOUTPUT QUERY="FilmsQuery">
  <A HREF="UsingFilmDataCFC1_Detail.cfm?FilmID=#FilmID#">#MovieTitle#</A><BR>
</CFOUTPUT>

</BODY>
</HTML>
```

Listing 20.24 is the detail page a user gets if he or she clicks one of the links created by Listing 20.23. It simply calls the `GetFilmData()` method exposed by the `FilmDataCFC1` component, then displays the information using an ordinary `<CFOUTPUT>` block (Figure 20.9).

Figure 20.9

The GetFilmData() method can be used to produce a page such as this.

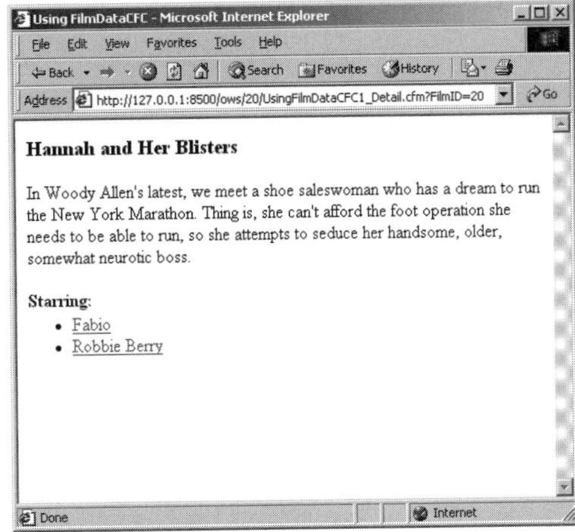

Listing 20.24 `UsingFilmDataCFC1_Detail.cfm`—Creating the Film Details Page

```
<HTML>
<HEAD><TITLE>Using FilmDataCFC</TITLE></HEAD>
<BODY>

<!--- We need to have a FilmID parameter in the URL --->
<CFPARAM NAME="URL.FilmID" TYPE="numeric">

<!--- Call the GetFilmData() method of the FilmDataCFC1 component --->
<CFINVOKE
  COMPONENT="ows.20.FilmDataCFC1"
  METHOD="GetFilmData"
  FilmID="#URL.FilmID#"
  RETURNVARIABLE="FilmData">

<!--- Produce the simple film display --->
<CFOUTPUT>
  <h3>#FilmData.MovieTitle#</h3>
  <p>#FilmData.Summary#</p>

  <!--- Include a list of actors --->
  <p><B>Starring:</B>
  <ul STYLE="margin-top:2px">
  <CFLOOP QUERY="FilmData.ActorsQuery">
    <li>
      <A
        HREF="UsingFilmDataCFC1.cfm?ActorID=#ActorID#"
        TITLE="Click for films this actor stars in.">#NameFirst# #NameLast#</A>
    </li>
  </CFLOOP>
  </ul>
</CFOUTPUT>

</BODY>
</HTML>
```

Note that the `<CFLOOP>` tag in this listing uses `FilmData.ActorsQuery` as its `QUERY` attribute. The `FilmData` variable is a structure returned by the `GetFilmData()` method created in Listing 20.22. If you look back at that listing, you will find that `GetFilmData()` returns a structure. The structure contains simple string properties such as `MovieTitle` and `Summary`, but it also contains a property called `ActorsQuery`, which is a query result set object returned by a `<CFQUERY>` tag. Because the `ActorsQuery` properties contains a query object, it can be used as the `QUERY` attribute of a `<CFLOOP>` (or, for that matter, of `<CFMAIL>`, `<CFGRAPHSERIES>`, or any other tag that accepts a query object).

NOTE

The `GetFilmData()` method demonstrates that although component methods can only return a single return value, you can easily have that return value be a structure that contains as much information as you need it to.

The result is a set of pages that allows the user to browse through films, using the actors in them as a way to get from film to film. When a user first visits Listing 20.23, a simple list of films appears. When the user clicks a film's title, he or she is brought to Listing 20.24, which displays details about the selected film, including a list of actors. The user can click each of the actor's names, which sends the user back to Listing 20.23. This time, though, the selected actor's ID number is passed to the `ListFilms()` method, which means that only that actor's films are shown. The user can click any of those films to see the other actors in the selected film, and so on.

Separating Logic from Presentation

The past three listings have shown that it is relatively easy to create a CFC and then use its methods to display data, perhaps to create some sort of master-detail interface. The process was basically to first create the CFC, and then create a normal ColdFusion page to interact with each of the methods.

When used in this fashion, the CFC is a container for *logic* (such as extraction of information from a database), leaving the normal ColdFusion pages to deal only with *presentation* of information. Many developers find that keeping a clean separation of logic and presentation in mind as a goal while coding often leads to good results.

This is especially true in a team environment where different people are working on the logic and the presentation. By keeping your interactions within databases and other logic packaged in CFCs, you can shield the people working on the presentation from the guts of your application. They can focus on making the presentation as attractive and functional as possible, probably without needing to know any CFML other than `<CFINVOKE>` and `<CFOUTPUT>`. And they can easily bring up the automatically generated documentation pages for each component to stay up to date on the methods each component provides.

Accessing a CFC via a URL

You have seen how to use CFC methods in your `.cfm` pages using the `<CFINVOKE>` and `<CFOBJECT>` tags. It is also possible to access methods directly with a Web browser. That is, if you place a `.cfc` file in a location that is accessible via a URL, people can use the component's methods by visiting that URL directly.

NOTE

In general, I recommend that you use CFCs by invoking their methods within a `.cfm` page (using `<CFINVOKE>` or the script-like method syntax), as you have seen already, rather than having browsers visit the CFC's methods directly. This keeps the separation of functionality and presentation clean. If you do decide to have your CFCs accessed directly via a URL, keep the parts of the code that output HTML in separate methods, as the example in this section does.

Visiting the Correct URL

Assuming you installed ColdFusion on your local machine and are saving this chapter's listings in the `ows/20` folder within your Web server's document root, the URL to access a component called `FilmDataCFC2` would be:

```
http://localhost:8500/ows/20/FilmDataCFC2.cfc
```

If you visit this URL with your browser, you will get the automatically generated documentation page for the component. (You will be asked for a password before the documentation page will appear; use your ColdFusion Administrator or RDS password).

To use one of the component's methods, just add a URL parameter named `method`, where the value of the parameter is the name of the method you want to call. For instance, to use the method called `ProduceFilmListHTML`, you would visit this URL with your browser:

```
http://localhost:8500/ows/20/FilmDataCFC2.cfc?method=ProduceFilmListHTML
```

NOTE

It is only possible to access a method via a URL if the `<CFFUNCTION>` block that creates the method contains an `ACCESS="Remote"` attribute. If you try to use the URL to access a method that has a different `ACCESS` level, ColdFusion will display an error message.

When calling a method via the URL, you can supply values for the method's arguments by including the arguments as name-value pairs in the URL. So, to call the `ProduceFilmHTML` method, supplying a value of 3 to the method's `FilmID` argument, you would use this URL:

```
http://localhost:8500/ows/20/FilmDataCFC2.cfc?method=ProduceFilmHTML&FilmID=3
```

To provide values for multiple arguments, just provide the appropriate number of name-value pairs, always using the name of the argument on the left side of the = sign and the value of the argument on the right side of the = sign.

NOTE

Remember that if the value of the argument might contain special characters such as spaces or slashes, then you need to escape the value with ColdFusion's `URLEncodedFormat()` function. This is the case for any URL parameter, not just for CFCs. In fact, it's the case for any Web application environment, not just ColdFusion.

NOTE

This is a bit of an advanced topic, but If you need to provide non-simple arguments such as arrays or structures, you can do so by creating a structure that contains all of your arguments (similar to creating a structure to pass to the `ATTRIBUTECOLLECTION` attribute of the `<CFMODULE>` tag, discussed earlier in this chapter), using the `<CFWDDX>` tag to convert the structure to a WDDX packet, then passing the packet as a single URL parameter called `ARGUMENTCOLLECTION`. Or, if you are accessing the CFC via a form, you can provide such a packet as a form field named `ARGUMENTCOLLECTION`. See Appendix B, "ColdFusion Function Reference," for details about `<CFWDDX>`.

Creating Methods That Generate HTML

Of course, just because it's possible to access a method with your browser doesn't mean the browser will understand what to do with the result. For instance, if you look at the `FilmDataCFC1` component from Listing 20.22, one of the methods returns a query and the other returns a structure. These are ColdFusion concepts; no browser is going to understand what to do with those results.

So, in order for a CFC to be able to do anything meaningful if accessed via a URL, you must make sure that any methods accessed in this way return HTML that the browser can understand. The most straightforward way to do this is to add additional methods to your CFC that produce the appropriate HTML. Internally, these methods can call the CFC's other methods to retrieve data or perform other processing. To make sure that only the HTML-generating methods are accessible via a URL, only those methods should have an `ACCESS="Remote"` attribute.

Listing 20.25 is a revised version of the `FilmDataCFC1` component from Listing 20.22. This version adds two new methods called `ProduceFilmListHTML()` and `ProduceFilmHTML()`. These methods basically contain the same code and produce the same result as Listing 20.23 and Listing 20.24, respectively. In other words, the component now takes care of both logic and presentation.

NOTE

I am explaining how CFCs can be accessed via a URL because it is a feature of ColdFusion MX. That said, in general I recommend that you use CFCs by invoking their methods within a `.cfm` page (using `<CFINVOKE>` or the script-like method syntax), as you have seen already, rather than having browsers visit the CFC's methods directly. This keeps the separation of functionality and presentation clean. If you do decide to have your CFCs accessed directly via a URL, keep the parts of the code that output HTML in separate methods, as the example in this section does.

Listing 20.25 `FilmDataCFC2.cfc`—Adding Methods That Generate HTML

```
<!---
  Filename: FilmDataCFC2.cfc
  Author:   Nate Weiss (NMW)
  Purpose:  Creates the FilmDataCFC2 ColdFusion Component, which provides
            search and data retrieval services for films in the ows database.
--->


<!--- The <CFCOMPONENT> block defines the CFC --->
<!--- The filename of this file determines the CFC's name --->
<CFCOMPONENT
  HINT="Provides a simple interface for searching for and getting detailed
        information about films in the Orange Whip Studios database.">

   <!--- ListFilms() method --->
   <CFFUNCTION
     NAME="ListFilms"
     RETURNTYPE="query"
     HINT="Returns a query object containing film information.">

     <!--- Optional SearchString argument --->
     <CFARGUMENT
       NAME="SearchString"
       TYPE="string"
       REQUIRED="No"
       HINT="Optional search criteria; if not given, all films are returned.">

     <!--- Optional SearchString argument --->
     <CFARGUMENT
       NAME="ActorID"
       TYPE="numeric"
       REQUIRED="No"
       HINT="Allows searching for films by actor.">

     <!--- Run the query --->
     <CFQUERY NAME="GetFilms" DATASOURCE="ows">
       SELECT FilmID, MovieTitle FROM Films
       WHERE 0=0
       <!--- If a search string has been specified --->
       <CFIF IsDefined("ARGUMENTS.SearchString")>
         AND (MovieTitle LIKE '%#ARGUMENTS.SearchString#%'
              OR Summary LIKE '%#ARGUMENTS.SearchString#%')
       </CFIF>
       <!--- If an actor's name has been specified --->
       <CFIF IsDefined("ARGUMENTS.ActorID")>
         AND FilmID IN
```

Listing 20.25 (continued)

```
          (SELECT FilmID FROM FilmsActors
           WHERE ActorID = #ARGUMENTS.ActorID#)
      </CFIF>
      ORDER BY MovieTitle
    </CFQUERY>

    <!--- Return the query results --->
    <CFRETURN GetFilms>
  </CFFUNCTION>


  <!--- GetFilmData() method --->
  <CFFUNCTION
    NAME="GetFilmData"
    RETURNTYPE="struct"
    HINT="Returns structured information about the specified film.">

    <!--- FilmID argument --->
    <CFARGUMENT
      NAME="FilmID"
      TYPE="numeric"
      REQUIRED="Yes"
      HINT="The film that you want information about.">

    <!--- This is what this method originally returns --->
    <!--- The var keyword makes it local to the method --->
    <CFSET var FilmData = StructNew()>
    <CFSET FilmData.FilmID = ARGUMENTS.FilmID>

    <!--- Select data about the film from the database --->
    <CFQUERY NAME="GetFilm" DATASOURCE="ows">
      SELECT MovieTitle, Summary FROM Films
      WHERE FilmID = #ARGUMENTS.FilmID#
    </CFQUERY>

    <!--- Populate the FilmData structure with film info --->
    <CFSET FilmData.MovieTitle = GetFilm.MovieTitle>
    <CFSET FilmData.Summary = GetFilm.Summary>

    <!--- Run second query to get actor information --->
    <CFQUERY NAME="GetActors" DATASOURCE="ows">
      SELECT ActorID, NameFirst, NameLast
      FROM Actors
      WHERE ActorID IN
        (SELECT ActorID FROM FilmsActors
         WHERE FilmID = #ARGUMENTS.FilmID#)
    </CFQUERY>

    <!--- Make the GetActors query results part of the returned structure --->
    <CFSET FilmData.ActorsQuery = GetActors>

    <!--- Return the final structure --->
    <CFRETURN FilmData>
  </CFFUNCTION>
```

Listing 20.25 (continued)

```
<!--- ProduceFilmListHTML() method --->
<CFFUNCTION
  NAME="ProduceFilmListHTML"
  ACCESS="Remote"
  HINT="Produces a simple HTML display">

  <!--- This variable is local to only to this function --->
  <CFSET var FilmsQuery = "">

  <!--- Call the ListFilms() method to get data about all films--->
  <!--- Pass along any arguments that were passed to this method --->
  <CFINVOKE
    METHOD="ListFilms"
    RETURNVARIABLE="FilmsQuery"
    ARGUMENTCOLLECTION="#ARGUMENTS#">

  <!--- Begin displaying output --->
  <CFOUTPUT>
    <!--- If an ActorID was provided as an argument, then we are --->
    <!--- only displaying films that star the specified actor --->
    <CFIF IsDefined("ARGUMENTS.ActorID")>
      <CFSET ActorData = GetFilmData(FilmsQuery.FilmID).ActorsQuery>
      <h3>Films Starring #ActorData.NameFirst# #ActorData.NameLast#</h3>
      <p><A href="FilmDataCFC2.cfc?method=ProduceFilmListHTML">
              ➥[List Of All Films]</A></p>
    <!--- Otherwise, all Orange Whip films are being displayed --->
    <CFELSE>
      <h3>Orange Whip Studios Films</h3>
    </CFIF>

    <!--- For each film, display the title as a link --->
    <!--- to this component's ProduceFilmHTML() method --->
    <CFLOOP QUERY="FilmsQuery">
      <A href="FilmDataCFC2.cfc?method=ProduceFilmHTML
           ➥&FilmID=#FilmID#">#MovieTitle#</A><BR>
    </CFLOOP>
  </CFOUTPUT>
</CFFUNCTION>


<!--- ProduceFilmHTML() method --->
<CFFUNCTION
  NAME="ProduceFilmHTML"
  ACCESS="Remote"
  HINT="Produces a simple HTML display">

  <!--- FilmID argument --->
  <CFARGUMENT
    NAME="FilmID"
    TYPE="numeric"
    REQUIRED="Yes"
    HINT="The ID number of the film to display information about">

  <!--- Call the GetFilmData() method to get basic film information --->
  <CFSET var FilmData = GetFilmData(ARGUMENTS.FilmID)>
```

Listing 20.25 (continued)

```
        <!--- Produce the simple film display --->
        <CFOUTPUT>
          <h3>#FilmData.MovieTitle#</h3>
          <p>#FilmData.Summary#</p>

          <!--- Include a list of actors --->
          <p><B>Starring:</B>
          <ul STYLE="margin-top:2px">
          <CFLOOP QUERY="FilmData.ActorsQuery">
            <li>
              <A href="FilmDataCFC2.cfc?method=ProduceFilmListHTML
                   ➥&ActorID=#ActorID#">#NameFirst# #NameLast#</A>
            </li>
          </CFLOOP>
          </ul>
        </CFOUTPUT>
      </CFFUNCTION>

    </CFCOMPONENT>
```

Within the `ProduceFilmListHTML()` method, the component's own `ListFilms()` method retrieves a list of films. Then an `<CFOUTPUT>` block generates the HTML that should be returned to the browser. This `<CFOUTPUT>` code is fairly similar to the code after the `<CFINVOKE>` in Listing 20.23. The main difference is that the `HREF` attributes of the links this code generates point to the `ProduceFilmHTML()` method of this same component instead of a normal ColdFusion page. That is, the HTML generated by this method contains links that will execute other methods of the same component.

NOTE

Take a look at the `ARGUMENTCOLLECTION="#ARGUMENTS#"` attribute used in the `<CFINVOKE>` tag in this listing. This means any arguments passed to the `ProduceFilmListHTML()` method will be passed along to the `ListFilms()` method as it is invoked. You can use this syntax whenever you want to call a method within another method and want the nested method to receive the same arguments as the outer method.

NOTE

Another interesting thing about this `<CFINVOKE>` tag is that it doesn't include a `COMPONENT` attribute. Normally, `COMPONENT` is a required attribute, but you can leave it out if you are using `<CFINVOKE>` within another method. ColdFusion assumes that you are referring to another method within the same component.

The code for the second new method, `ProduceFilmHTML()`, works similarly. Again, this new method calls one of the nonremote methods, `GetFilmData()`, to obtain the information it needs to display. For variety's sake, `GetFilmData()` is called via the scriptlike syntax, rather than the `<CFINVOKE>` tag.

NOTE

In general, methods that generate HTML or other output with `<CFOUTPUT>` should not also produce a return value. In other words, you generally shouldn't use `<CFOUTPUT>` and `<CFRETURN>` within the same method.

Now that you've completed this component, you can visit it using the following URL:

```
http://localhost:8500/ows/20/FilmDataCFC2.cfc?method=ProduceFilmListHTML
```

The result for the user is the same master-detail film-browsing interface created with Listings 20.23 and 20.24. The only difference is that the CFC is doing all the work on its own, rather than needing separate `.cfm` files to invoke it. As far as the user is concerned, the only difference is the `.cfc` extension in the URL.

NOTE

All of the methods, including the non-`Remote` ones (`ListFilms()` and `GetFilmData()`), are still available for use within normal ColdFusion pages via `<CFINVOKE>` or `<CFOBJECT>`.

Other Ways of Separating CFC Logic from Presentation

Listing 20.25 contains two logic methods and two presentation methods. Although only the presentation methods can be accessed directly with a Web browser (because of the `ACCESS="Remote"` attribute), they are all included in the same CFC file.

If you wanted, you could create a separate CFC for the presentation methods. You would just use the `<CFINVOKE>` tag within the presentation CFC to call the logic methods.

Another option would be to store the presentation methods in their own .cfc file, adding an `EXTENDS` attribute that specifies the name of the logic CFC. This would cause the presentation CFC to *inherit* the methods from the logic CFC so it could use them internally as shown in Listing 20.25. Component inheritance and a complete discussion of the `EXTENDS` attribute are beyond the scope of this chapter. For details, consult the ColdFusion MX documentation or this book's companion volume, *Advanced ColdFusion MX Application Development.*

Accessing a CFC via a Form

It is also possible to access a method directly from a browser using a form. Conceptually, this is very similar to accessing a method via a URL, as discussed in the previous section, "Accessing a CFC via a URL." Just use the URL for the `.cfc` file as the form's action, along with the desired method name. Then add form fields for each argument that you want to pass to the method when the form is submitted. For example, the following snippet would create a simple search form, which, when submitted, would cause a list of matching films to appear.

```
<CFFORM ACTION="FilmDataCFC2.cfc?method=ProduceFilmListHTML">
  <INPUT NAME="SearchString">
  <INPUT TYPE="Submit" VALUE="Search">
</CFFORM>
```

NOTE

Again, it is required that the method use `ACCESS="Remote"` in its `<CFFUNCTION>` tag. Otherwise, it cannot be accessed directly over the Internet via a Form or a URL.

Exploring CFCs in Dreamweaver MX

Once you've written your CFCs, they become a part of Macromedia Dreamweaver MX. You can explore each CFC's hints and methods, display automatic documentation for each CFC, and drag and drop methods into your ColdFusion pages. These features make it even easier for you and your team to reuse code with CFCs.

The heart of the Dreamweaver-CFC integration is the Components tab in the Application panel, which is displayed by default if you chose the HomeSite/Coder interface while you were installing Dreamweaver MX. If you don't see the Application panel, select Window > Components from the main menu.

TIP

As a shortcut, you can use Ctrl-F7 (or equivalent) to show the Application panel.

NOTE

If the tabs in the Application panel are grayed out (disabled), open a file that is associated with a site that uses ColdFusion as the Application Server type. You've probably already done this for the `ows` folder in your Web server's document root, so just open up any of the `.cfm` files within `ows`. That should enable the Application panel.

Viewing All of Your CFCs

Make sure the Application panel is expanded, then click the Components tab. You will notice a drop-down list at the top of the tab, with choices for CF Components or Web Services. Make sure CF Components is selected.

You should now see a tree with items for each folder on your Web server that contains a `.cfc` file. For instance, you should see an item for `ows.20` (the `20` folder within the `ows` folder); this will contain the CFCs created in this chapter.

NOTE

I am assuming that you have copied all the example files for this chapter from the CD-ROM to the `/ows/20` folder within your Web server's document root. If not, do so now, or just keep in mind that only the `.cfc` files that are actually present on your server will be shown in the tree in Dreamweaver MX.

Go ahead and expand the `ows.20` item in the tree. The CFCs for this chapter, including the `FilmSearchCFC`, `FilmDataCFC`, and `FilmRotationCFC` components, will display as nested items in the tree. You can expand each CFC to reveal its methods, and you can expand each method to reveal its input arguments (Figure 20.10).

NOTE

If you add or make a change to a CFC, click the Refresh button at the top right corner of the Components tab to make the tree reflect your changes.

NOTE

ColdFusion MX and Dreamweaver MX refer to the ability to display this kind of information about components as *component introspection.* The fact that the server can look into the component file to learn about its methods, return values, and arguments is a key feature of the new CFC framework. Component introspection makes many things possible, including the tight Dreamweaver MX integration you are seeing here, the Flash MX integration you will learn about in Chapter 23, and ColdFusion's exciting ability to automatically expose your CFCs as Web Services.

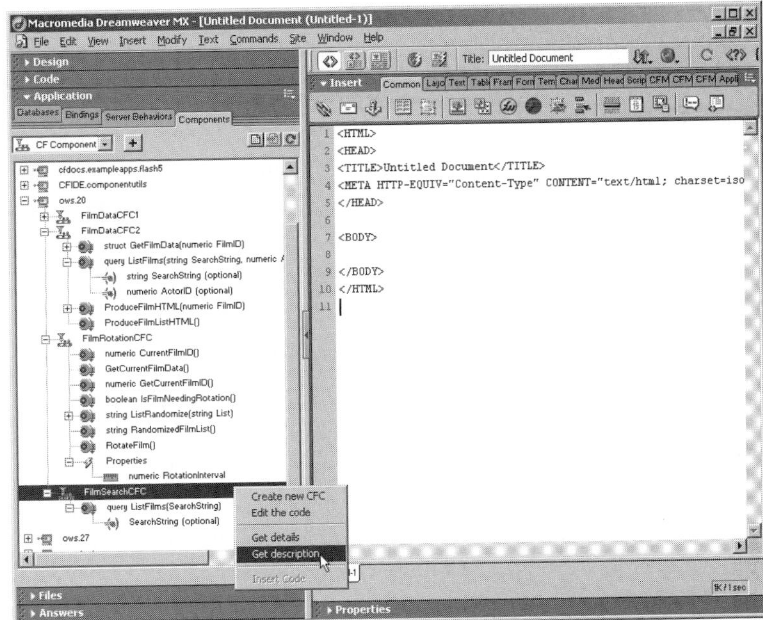

Figure 20.10

Dreamweaver MX makes it easy to keep track of your CFCs and their methods.

Jumping to CFC Code from the Tree

Once you have the Components tree showing in the Application tab (see the previous section, "Viewing All of Your CFCs"), you can double-click the items in the tree to open the corresponding `.cfc` file.

If you double-click:

- A component (like the `FilmDataCFC` item), Dreamweaver MX will open up the `.cfc` file, ready for your edits.
- A method within a component (like `GetFilmData` or `ListFilms`), Dreamweaver will open the file, then scroll down and highlight the corresponding `<CFFUNCTION>` block.
- An argument within a method (like `SearchString` or `FilmID`), Dreamweaver will open the file and scroll down to the corresponding `<CFARGUMENT>` tag.

Inserting `<CFINVOKE>` Tags via Drag and Drop

If you are working on a ColdFusion page and want to call one of your CFC's methods, Dreamweaver MX can automatically write the appropriate `<CFINVOKE>` code for you. Just click the method in the Components tree (see Figure 20.10), then drag it to the appropriate spot in your code. When you release the mouse, a `<CFINVOKE>` tag will be added to your code with the `COMPONENT`, `METHOD`, and other attributes already filled in for you. In addition, a `<CFINVOKEARGUMENT>` tag will be added for each of the method's required arguments. This can be a real time saver.

TIP

You can insert the same code by right-clicking the method and choosing Insert Code from the context menu.

Viewing CFC Details

To get more information about an item in the Components tree, right-click the item and then select Get Details from the context menu. A message box will appear, displaying detailed information about the component, method, or argument.

Viewing CFC Documentation

One of the coolest CFC features in ColdFusion MX is the ability to generate a documentation page automatically for each of your components. You can use the page as a live reference guide to the CFC. (If you are familiar with Java, this is analogous to a javadoc page).

To view the automatic reference page for a component, right-click the component (or any of its methods or arguments) in the Components tree and select Get Description from the context menu. Dreamweaver will launch your browser with the documentation page showing. For instance, the generated documentation page for the `FilmDataCFC` component is shown in Figure 20.11.

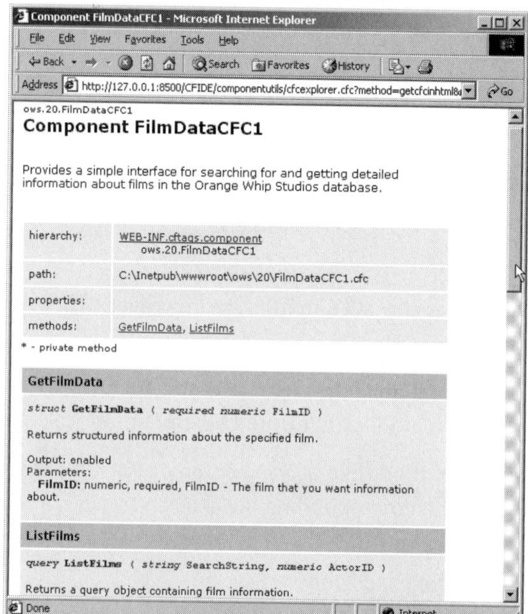

Figure 20.11

ColdFusion MX will generate an automatic reference page for any CFC.

Viewing CFC Documentation Without Dreamweaver

You don't have to use Dreamweaver to generate the documentation page for a CFC. You can view the documentation page at any time by just navigating your browser to the URL for the `.cfc` file. For instance, assuming you have installed ColdFusion on your local machine, you can get to the documentation page at `http://localhost:8500/ows/20/FilmDataCFC2.cfc`

TIP

Of course, once you have the generated documentation page open in your browser, you can always use your browser's File, Save As command to save the HTML file to some permanent location on your local hard drive. This way you can view or print the documentation even when you can't connect to the ColdFusion server.

Using the Create Component Dialog

Wizards aren't for everyone, but if you like them, Dreamweaver MX provides a very nice Create Component dialog box that you can use to create new `.cfc` files. This wizard-style interface makes it really easy to design a new CFC. You just fill in the blanks about your new component's name, hints, methods (functions), arguments, and so on.

To launch the Create Component dialog, click the button marked with a plus sign at the top of the Components tab in the Application panel. Or you can right-click anywhere in the Components tab and select Create New CFC from the context menu. The Create Component dialog will appear (Figure 20.12). Just fill in the desired blanks on each of the various pages. Except for the component's name and directory, you can leave whatever other items you wish blank.

When you click OK, Dreamweaver will generate the appropriate skeleton of `<CFCOMPONENT>`, `<CFFUNCTION>`, `<CFARGUMENT>`, and `<CFRETURN>` tags for you. All that remains is to add the appropriate method code to each of the `<CFFUNCTION>` blocks.

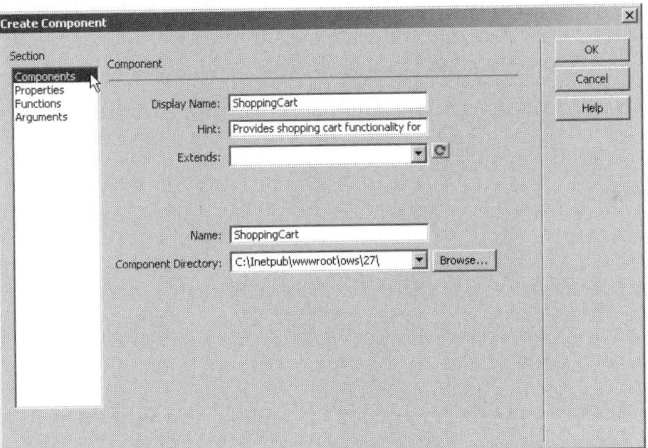

Figure 20.12

The Create Component dialog can make it easier to design a new CFC.

Components That Hold Instance Data

The ColdFusion components discussed so far in this chapter (the `FilmSearchCFC` and `FilmDataCFC` examples) have both been *static* components, meaning they don't hold any instance data. That is, although you can create an instance of a component with `<CFOBJECT>` before using it, there really isn't any need to do so. One instance of a component isn't going to behave any differently from any other instance, so it is fine to simply call the CFC's methods directly.

If you create components that hold instance data, though, each instance of the component lives on its own and has its own memory in which to store information. If your component is about films, then each instance might be an individual film and the instance data might be the film's title, budget, gross receipts, or even movie reviews. If your component is about shopping carts, then each instance of the component would represent a separate user's shopping cart, and the instance data would be the contents of the cart.

This section will explain how to create this type of component.

Introducing the `THIS` Scope

The CFC framework sets aside a special variable scope called `THIS`, which stands for *this instance* of a component. In this context, think of the word `THIS` as meaning *this film* or *this shopping cart* or *this object*, depending on what you intend your component to represent.

The `THIS` Scope Represents an Instance

The `THIS` scope is similar in its function to the `SESSION` scope you learned about in Chapter 17, except that instead of being a place to store information that will be remembered for the duration of a user's session, `THIS` is a place to store information that will be remembered for as long as a particular instance of a component continues to exist.

As an example, consider a fictional CFC called `ParrotCFC`. The idea behind the component is that each instance of the component represents one parrot. Each instance of the component needs to have a name, an age, a gender, a wingspan, a favorite word or cracker, and so on. This kind of information is exactly what the `THIS` scope was designed for. Your CFC code just needs to set variables in the `THIS` scope (perhaps `THIS.FavoriteWord` or `THIS.WingSpan`) to remember these values. ColdFusion will take care of making sure that each component's variables are kept separate.

Steps in the Process

Here are the steps involved:

1. Create the CFC file. Within the file, use the `THIS` scope as the component's personal memory space, keeping in mind that each instance of the component (that is, each parrot) will get its own copy of the `THIS` scope for its own use.
2. In your ColdFusion pages, create an instance of the CFC with `<CFOBJECT>` before you use any of the component's methods. If you want the instance to live longer than the current page request, you can place the instance in the `SESSION` or `APPLICATION` scope.
3. Now go ahead and use the instance's methods with the `<CFINVOKE>` tag as you learned in previous examples. Make sure that you specify the instance (that is, the individual parrot) as the `COMPONENT` attribute of the `<CFINVOKE>` tag, rather than as the name of the CFC.

In this scenario, each individual instance of the `ParrotCFC` has a life of its own. The `<CFOBJECT>` tag is what makes a particular parrot come to life. The `THIS` scope automatically maintains the parrot's characteristics.

Extending the metaphor, if the parrot is the pet of one of your Web users, then you can make the parrot follow the user around by having it live in the user's `SESSION` scope. Or if the parrot doesn't belong to a particular person but instead belongs to your application as a whole (perhaps the parrot is your site's mascot), then you could have it live in the `APPLICATION` scope. Or you might have a bunch of parrots that are looking for owners. You could keep these parrots (each one an instance of the `ParrotCFC` component) in an array in the `APPLICATION` scope. When a user wants to take one of the parrots home as a pet, you could move the parrot out of the array and into the `SESSION` scope.

OK, enough about the parrot. The idea here is to think of a CFC as an independent thing or object with its own properties. Then store individual instances of the object in the `APPLICATION` or `SESSION` scope if you want it to remain in memory for a period of time, or just leave it in the normal scope if you only need the instance to live for the current page request.

NOTE

Almost by definition, then, a component that doesn't refer to the `THIS` scope at all in its methods does not need to be instantiated with `<CFOBJECT>` before calling its methods, and can therefore be considered a *static* component. Any component that does use the `THIS` scope internally probably needs to be instantiated to function properly.

An Instance Data CFC Example

Let's take a look at a simple example of a CFC that holds instance data. The component is called `FilmRotationCFC`, and its purpose is to keep track of a featured film, much like the `FeaturedMovie.cfm` examples in Chapter 16.

Designing FilmRotationCFC

To demonstrate the use of multiple methods within an instantiated component, the `FilmRotationCFC` component will contain five methods, as listed in Table 20.10.

Table 20.10 Methods Provided by FilmRotationCFC

METHOD	DESCRIPTION
`CurrentFilmID()`	Returns the ID number of the currently featured film. Because this method uses `ACCESS="Private"`, it can only be used internally within the `FilmRotationCFC`.
`IsFilmNeedingRotation()`	Returns `TRUE` if the current film has been featured for more than the amount of time specified as the rotation interval (5 seconds by default). Returns `FALSE` if the current film should be left as is for now. This is a private method that can only be used internally.
`RotateFilm()`	Rotates the currently featured film if it has been featured for more than the amount of time specified as the rotation interval (5 seconds by default). Internally, this method calls `IsFilmNeedingRotation()` to find out if the current film has expired. If so, it sets the current film to be the next film in the rotation.
`GetCurrentFilmID()`	Rotates the current movie (if appropriate), then returns the currently featured film. Internally, this function calls `RotateFilm()` and then returns the value of `CurrentFilmID()`. This is a public method.

Table 20.10 (continued)

METHOD	DESCRIPTION
`GetCurrentFilmData()`	Returns the title, summary, and other information about the currently featured film. Internally, this function calls `GetCurrentFilmID()` and then returns the information provided by the `GetFilmData()` method of the `FilmDataCFC2` component. This method is included mainly to show how to call one component's methods from another component.
`RandomizedFilmList()`	Returns a list of all `FilmID` numbers in the `ows` database, in random order. Internally, this uses the `ListRandomize()` method to perform the randomization.
`ListRandomize(list)`	Accepts any comma-separated list and returns a new list with the same items in it, but in a random order. Because this method uses `ACCESS="Private"`, it can only be used internally within the `FilmRotationCFC`. This method really doesn't have anything to do with this CFC in particular; you could reuse it in any situation where you wanted to randomize a list of items.

TIP

In this CFC, I am adopting a convention of starting all public method names with the word `Get`. You might want to consider using naming conventions such as this when creating your own component methods.

TIP

It is conventional in many programming languages to start the name of any function that returns a Boolean value with the word `Is`. You might want to consider doing the same in your own CFCs.

Building FilmRotationCFC

Listing 20.26 shows the code for the `FilmRotationCFC` component. Because this component includes a number of methods, this code listing is a bit long. Don't worry. The code for each of the individual methods is quite short.

Listing 20.26 `FilmRotationCFC.cfc`—Building a CFC That Maintains Instance Data

```
<!---
  Filename: FilmRotationCFC.cfc
  Author:   Nate Weiss (NMW)
  Purpose:  Creates FilmRotationCFC, a ColdFusion Component
--->


<CFCOMPONENT>

  <!--- *** begin initialization code *** --->
  <CFSET THIS.FilmList = RandomizedFilmList()>
  <CFSET THIS.CurrentListPos = 1>
  <CFSET THIS.RotationInterval = 5>
  <CFSET THIS.CurrentUntil = DateAdd("s", THIS.RotationInterval, Now())>
  <!--- *** end initialization code *** --->
```

Listing 20.26 (continued)

```
<!--- Private function: RandomizedFilmList() --->
<CFFUNCTION
  NAME="RandomizedFilmList"
  RETURNTYPE="string"
  ACCESS="Private"
  HINT="For internal use. Returns a list of all Film IDs, in random order.">

  <!--- This variable is for this function's use only --->
  <CFSET var GetFilmIDs = "">

  <!--- Retrieve list of current films from database --->
  <CFQUERY NAME="GetFilmIDs" DATASOURCE="ows"
    CACHEDWITHIN="#CreateTimeSpan(0,1,0,0)#">
    SELECT FilmID FROM Films
    ORDER BY MovieTitle
  </CFQUERY>

  <!--- Return the list of films, in random order --->
  <CFRETURN ListRandomize(ValueList(GetFilmIDs.FilmID))>
</CFFUNCTION>



<!--- Private utility function: ListRandomize() --->
<CFFUNCTION
  NAME="ListRandomize"
  RETURNTYPE="string"
  HINT="Randomizes the order of the items in any comma-separated list.">

  <!--- List argument --->
  <CFARGUMENT
    NAME="List"
    TYPE="string"
    REQUIRED="Yes"
    HINT="The string that you want to randomize.">

  <!--- These variables are for this function's use only --->
  <CFSET var Result = "">
  <CFSET var RandPos = "">

  <!--- While there are items left in the original list... --->
  <CFLOOP CONDITION="ListLen(ARGUMENTS.List) GT 0">
    <!--- Select a list position at random --->
    <CFSET RandPos = RandRange(1, ListLen(ARGUMENTS.List))>
    <!--- Add the item at the selected position to the Result list --->
    <CFSET Result = ListAppend(Result, ListGetAt(ARGUMENTS.List, RandPos))>
    <!--- Remove the item from selected position of the original list --->
    <CFSET ARGUMENTS.List = ListDeleteAt(ARGUMENTS.List, RandPos)>
  </CFLOOP>

  <!--- Return the reordered list --->
  <CFRETURN Result>
</CFFUNCTION>



<!--- Private method: IsFilmNeedingRotation() --->
```

Listing 20.26 (continued)

```
<CFFUNCTION
  NAME="IsFilmNeedingRotation"
  ACCESS="Private"
  RETURNTYPE="boolean"
  HINT="For internal use. Returns TRUE if the film should be rotated now.">

  <!--- Compare the current time to the THIS.CurrentUntil time --->
  <!--- If the film is still current, DateCompare() will return 1 --->
  <CFSET var DateComparison = DateCompare(THIS.CurrentUntil, Now())>

  <!--- Return TRUE if the film is still current, FALSE otherwise --->
  <CFRETURN DateComparison NEQ 1>
</CFFUNCTION>


<!--- RotateFilm() method --->
<CFFUNCTION
  NAME="RotateFilm"
  ACCESS="Private"
  HINT="For internal use. Advances the current movie.">

  <!--- If the film needs to be rotated at this time... --->
  <CFIF IsFilmNeedingRotation()>
    <!--- Advance the instance-level THIS.CurrentListPos value by one --->
    <CFSET THIS.CurrentListPos = THIS.CurrentListPos + 1>

    <!--- If THIS.CurrentListPos is now more than the number of films, --->
    <!--- Start over again at the beginning (the first film) --->
    <CFIF THIS.CurrentListPos GT ListLen(THIS.FilmList)>
      <CFSET THIS.CurrentListPos = 1>
    </CFIF>

    <!--- Set the time that the next rotation will be due --->
    <CFSET THIS.CurrentUntil = DateAdd("s", THIS.RotationInterval, Now())>
  </CFIF>
</CFFUNCTION>


<!--- Private method: CurrentFilmID() --->
<CFFUNCTION
  NAME="CurrentFilmID"
  ACCESS="Private"
  RETURNTYPE="numeric"
  HINT="For internal use. Returns the ID of the current film in rotation.">

  <!--- Return the FilmID from the current row of the GetFilmIDs query --->
  <CFRETURN ListGetAt(THIS.FilmList, THIS.CurrentListPos)>
</CFFUNCTION>


<!--- Public method: GetCurrentFilmID() --->
<CFFUNCTION
  NAME="GetCurrentFilmID"
  ACCESS="Public"
  RETURNTYPE="numeric"
  HINT="Returns the ID number of the currently 'featured' film.">
```

Listing 20.26 (continued)

```
    <!--- First, rotate the current film --->
    <CFSET RotateFilm()>

    <!--- Return the ID of the current film --->
    <CFRETURN CurrentFilmID()>
  </CFFUNCTION>


  <!--- Public method: GetCurrentFilmData() --->
  <CFFUNCTION
    NAME="GetCurrentFilmData"
    ACCESS="Remote"
    HINT="Returns structured data about the currently 'featured' film.">

    <!--- This variable is local just to this function --->
    <CFSET var CurrentFilmData = "">

    <!--- Invoke the GetCurrentFilmID() method (in separate component) --->
    <!--- Returns a structure with film's title, summary, actors, etc. --->
    <CFINVOKE
      COMPONENT="FilmDataCFC2"
      METHOD="GetFilmData"
      FilmID="#GetCurrentFilmID()#"
      RETURNVARIABLE="CurrentFilmData">

    <!--- Return the structure --->
    <CFRETURN CurrentFilmData>
  </CFFUNCTION>
</CFCOMPONENT>
```

The most important thing to note and understand about this CFC is the purpose of the first few `<CFSET>` tags at the top of Listing 20.26. Because these lines sit directly within the body of the `<CFCOMPONENT>` tag, outside any `<CFFUNCTION>` blocks, they are considered *initialization code* that will be executed whenever a new instance of the component is created. Notice that each of these `<CFSET>` tags creates variables in the special `THIS` scope, which means they are assigned to each instance of the component separately. Typically, all that happens in a CFC's initialization code is that it sets instance data in the `THIS` scope.

NOTE

It is important to understand that these lines do not execute each time one of the instance's methods is called. They execute only when a new instance of the component is brought to life with the `<CFOBJECT>` tag.

The `<CFSET>` tags at the top of the listing create these instance variables:

- `THIS.FilmList` is a list of all current films in the order in which the component should show them. The component's `RandomizedFilmList()` method creates the sequence. Keep in mind that this order will be different for each instance of the CFC.
- `THIS.CurrentListPos` is the current position in the randomized list of films. The initial value is `1`, which means that the first film in the randomized list will be considered the featured film.

- THIS.RotationInterval is the number of seconds that a film should be considered featured before the component features the next film. Right now, the interval is 5 seconds.
- THIS.CurrentUntil is the time at which the current film should be considered expired. At that point, the CFC will select the next film in the randomized list of films. When the component is first instantiated, this variable is set to 5 seconds in the future.

Let's take a quick look at the <CFFUNCTION> blocks in Listing 20.26.

The RandomizedFilmList() method will always be the first one to be called, since it is used in the initialization code block. This method simply retrieves a record set of FilmIDs from the database. Then it turns the FilmIDs into a comma-separated list with ColdFusion's ValueList() function and passes the list to the CFC's ListRandomize() method. The resulting list (which is a list of films in random order) is returned as the method's return value.

The ListRandomize() method just uses a combination of ColdFusion's list functions to randomize the list supplied to the List argument. The basic idea is to pluck items at random from the original list, adding them to the end of a new list called Result. When there are no more items in the original list, the Result variable is returned as the method's return value. See Appendix C for details on the list functions used here.

The CurrentFilmID() method simply returns the FilmID in the current position of the CFC's randomized list of films. As long as THIS.CurrentListPos is set to 1, this method returns the first film's ID.

The IsFilmNeedingRotation() method uses DateCompare() to compare THIS.CurrentUntil to the current time. If the time has passed, this method returns TRUE to indicate that the current film is ready for rotation.

The RotateFilm() method is interesting because it actually makes changes to the variables in the THIS scope first created in the initialization code block. First, it uses IsFilmNeedingRotation() to see whether the current film has been featured for more than 5 seconds already. If so, it advances the This.CurrentListPos value by 1. If the new CurrentListPos value is greater than the length of the list of films, that means all films in the sequence have been featured, so the position is set back to 1. Lastly, the method uses ColdFusion's DateAdd() function to set the THIS.CurrentUntil variable to 5 seconds in the future.

The GetCurrentFilmID() method ties all the concepts together. Whenever this method is used, the RotateFilm() method is called (which will advance the current film to the next item in the sequence if the current one has expired). It then calls CurrentFilmID() to return the current film's ID.

Storing CFCs in the APPLICATION Scope

Now that the FilmRotationCFC component is in place, it is quite simple to put it to use. Listing 20.27 shows one way of using the component.

Listing 20.27 `UsingFilmRotationCFCa.cfm`—Instantiating a CFC at the Application Level

```
<!---
  Filename: UsingFilmRotationCFCa.cfm
  Author:   Nate Weiss (NMW)
  Purpose:  Demonstrates storage of CFC instances in shared memory scopes
--->

<HTML>
<HEAD>
  <TITLE>Using FilmRotationCFC</TITLE>
</HEAD>

<BODY>

<!--- If an instance of the FilmRotatorCFC component hasn't been created --->
<!--- yet, create a fresh instance and store it in the APPLICATION scope --->
<CFIF IsDefined("APPLICATION.FilmRotator") EQ False>
  <CFOBJECT
    COMPONENT="FilmRotationCFC"
    NAME="APPLICATION.FilmRotator">
</CFIF>
<!--- Invoke the GetCurrentFilmID() method of the FilmRotator CFC object --->
<CFINVOKE
  COMPONENT="#APPLICATION.FilmRotator#"
  METHOD="GetCurrentFilmID"
  RETURNVARIABLE="FeaturedFilmID">

<p>The callout at the right side of this page shows the currently featured film.
The featured film changes every five seconds.
Just reload the page to see the next film in the sequence.
The sequence will not change until the ColdFusion server is restarted.</p>

<!--- Show the current film in a callout, via custom tag --->
<CF_ShowMovieCallout
  FilmID="#FeaturedFilmID#">

</BODY>
</HTML>
```

The idea here is to keep an instance of `FilmRotationCFC` in the `APPLICATION.FilmRotator` variable. Keeping it in the `APPLICATION` scope means that the same instance will be kept in the server's memory until the ColdFusion server is restarted. All sessions that visit the page will share the instance.

First, a simple `IsDefined()` test sees if the CFC instance called `APPLICATION.FilmRotator` already exists. If not, the instance is created with the `<CFOBJECT>` tag. So, after this `<CFIF>` block, the instance is guaranteed to exist. Keep in mind that the CFC's initialization code block is executed when the instance is first created (refer to Listing 20.25).

NOTE

If you wanted the CFC instance to be available to all pages in the application, you could move the `<CFIF>` block in Listing 20.27 to your `Application.cfm` file.

Displaying the currently featured film is a simple matter of calling the `GetCurrentFilmID()` method with the `<CFINVOKE>` tag and passing it to the `<CF_ShowMovieCallout>` custom tag created near the beginning of this chapter. When a browser visits this listing, the currently featured movie is displayed (Figure 20.13). If you reload the page repeatedly, you will see that the featured movie changes every 5 seconds. If you wait long enough, you will see the sequence of films repeat itself. The sequence will continue to repeat until the ColdFusion server is restarted, at which point a new sequence of films will be selected at random.

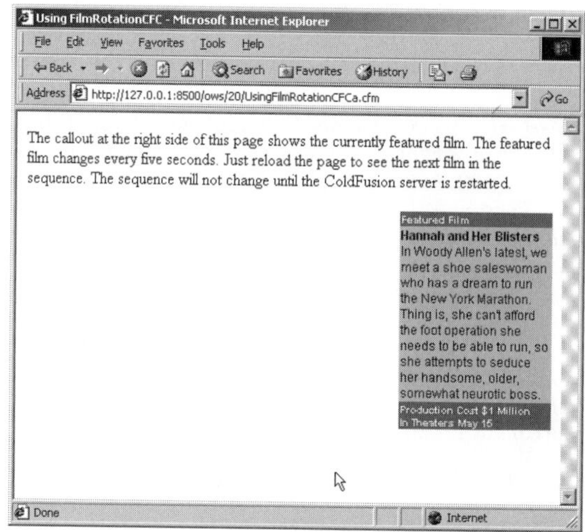

Figure 20.13
CFCs can be stored in shared variable scopes to provide interesting, controlled user experiences.

It's worth noting that you can use the scriptlike syntax to call methods of CFC instances in the `APPLICATION` scope. Depending on the situation, the scriptlike syntax may be more clear. Listing 20.28 does the same thing as Listing 20.27, except that it replaces the `<CFINVOKE>` tag with the scriptlike syntax. This shortens the whole listing considerably.

Listing 20.28 `UsingFilmRotationCFCb.cfm`—Using Scriptlike Syntax with Persisted CFCs

```
<!---
  Filename: UsingFilmRotationCFCb.cfm
  Author:   Nate Weiss (NMW)
  Purpose:  Demonstrates storage of CFC instances in shared memory scopes
--->

<HTML>
<HEAD>
  <TITLE>Using FilmRotationCFC</TITLE>
</HEAD>

<BODY>

<!--- If an instance of the FilmRotatorCFC component hasn't been created --->
<!--- yet, create a fresh instance and store it in the APPLICATION scope --->
<CFIF IsDefined("APPLICATION.FilmRotator") EQ False>
  <CFOBJECT
```

Listing 20.28 (continued)

```
    COMPONENT="FilmRotationCFC"
    NAME="APPLICATION.FilmRotator">
</CFIF>

<p>The callout at the right side of this page shows the currently featured film.
The featured film changes every five seconds.
Just reload the page to see the next film in the sequence.
The sequence will not change until the ColdFusion server is restarted.</p>

<!--- Show the current film in a callout, via custom tag --->
<CF_ShowMovieCallout
  FilmID="#APPLICATION.FilmRotator.GetCurrentFilmID()#">

</BODY>
</HTML>
```

Storing CFCs in the `SESSION` Scope

One of the neat things about CFCs is their independence. It is important to note that the code for the `RotateFilmCFC` component doesn't contain a single reference to the `APPLICATION` scope. In fact, it doesn't refer to any of ColdFusion's built-in scopes at all, except for the `THIS` scope.

This means it's possible to create some instances of the CFC that are kept in the `APPLICATION` scope, and others that are kept in the `SESSION` scope. All of the instances will work properly, and will maintain their own versions of the variables in the `THIS` scope.

To see this in action, go back to either Listing 20.27 or Listing 20.28 and change the code so that the CFC instance is kept in the `SESSION` scope instead of the `APPLICATION` scope. Now each Web session will be given its own `FilmRotator` object, stored as a session variable. You can see how this looks in Listing 20.29 (in the next section, "Modifying Properties from a ColdFusion Page").

To see the difference in behavior, open up the revised listing in two different browsers (say, Netscape 6 and Internet Explorer 6), and experiment with reloading the page. You will find that the films are featured on independent cycles, and that each session sees the films in a different order. If you view the page on different computers, you will see that each machine also has its own private, randomized sequence of featured films.

Instance Data as Properties

As I've been explaining, the code for the `FilmRotationCFC` component uses the `THIS` scope to store certain variables for its own use. You can think of these variables as *properties* of each component instance, because they are the items that make a particular instance special, that give it its individuality, its life.

Sometimes you will want to display or change the value of one of these properties from a normal ColdFusion page. ColdFusion makes it very easy to access an instance's properties. Basically, you can access any variable in a CFC's `THIS` scope as a property of the instance itself.

Modifying Properties from a ColdFusion Page

If you have a CFC instance called `SESSION.MyFilmRotator` and you want to display the current value of the `CurrentUntil` property (that is, the value of the variable that is called `THIS.CurrentUntil` within the CFC code), you could do so with the following in a normal `.cfm` page:

```
<CFOUTPUT>
  #TimeFormat(SESSION.MyFilmRotator.CurrentUntil)#
</CFOUTPUT>
```

Or to change the value of the `RotationInterval` property (referred to as `THIS.RotationInterval` in the `FilmRotationCFC.cfc` file) to 10 seconds instead of the usual 5 seconds, you could use this line:

```
<CFSET SESSION.MyFilmRotator.RotationInterval = 10>
```

After you changed the `RotationInterval` for the `SESSION.FilmRotator` instance, then that session's films would rotate every 10 seconds instead of every 5 seconds. Listing 20.29 shows how all this would look in a ColdFusion page.

Listing 20.29 `UsingFilmRotationCFCc.cfm`—Interacting with a CFC's Properties

```
<!---
  Filename: UsingFilmRotationCFCc.cfm
  Author:   Nate Weiss (NMW)
  Purpose:  Demonstrates storage of CFC instances in shared memory scopes
--->

<HTML>
<HEAD>
  <TITLE>Using FilmRotationCFC</TITLE>
</HEAD>

<BODY>

<!--- If an instance of the FilmRotatorCFC component hasn't been created --->
<!--- yet, create a fresh instance and store it in the SESSION scope --->
<CFIF IsDefined("SESSION.MyFilmRotator") EQ False>
  <CFOBJECT
    COMPONENT="FilmRotationCFC"
    NAME="SESSION.MyFilmRotator">

  <!--- Rotate films every two seconds --->
  <CFSET SESSION.MyFilmRotator.RotationInterval = 10>
</CFIF>

<!--- Display message --->
<CFOUTPUT>
  <p>
  The callout at the right side of this page shows the currently featured film.
  Featured films rotate every #SESSION.MyFilmRotator.RotationInterval# seconds.
  Just reload the page to see the next film in the sequence.
  The sequence will not change until the web session ends.</p>
```

Listing 20.28 (continued)

```
    The next film rotation will occur at:
    #TimeFormat(SESSION.MyFilmRotator.CurrentUntil, "h:mm:ss tt")#
  </CFOUTPUT>

  <!--- Show the current film in a callout, via custom tag --->
  <CF_ShowMovieCallout
    FilmID="#SESSION.MyFilmRotator.GetCurrentFilmID()#">

  </BODY>
  </HTML>
```

NOTE

You can experiment with changing the `RotationInterval` property to different values. Keep in mind that the code in the `<CFIF>` block will only execute once per session, so you may need to restart ColdFusion to see a change. Or if you are using J2EE Session Variables, you can just close and reopen your browser. Or you could move the `<CFSET>` line outside the `<CFIF>` block.

What all this means is that the CFC's methods can access an instantiated CFC's properties internally via the `THIS` scope, and your ColdFusion pages can access them via the instance object variable itself. As you learned in the introduction to this topic, CFCs can be thought of as containers for data and functionality, like many objects in the real world. You know how to access the data (properties) as well as the functionality (methods).

Documenting Properties With `<CFPROPERTY>`

As you learned earlier, you can easily view a CFC's methods in the Component tree in Dreamweaver MX's Application panel. You can also view them in the automatically generated reference page that ColdFusion produces if you visit a CFC's URL with your browser. Since a CFC's properties are also important, it would be nice if there was an easy way to view them too.

ColdFusion MX provides a tag called `<CFPROPERTY>` that allows you to provide information about each variable in the `THIS` scope that you want to document as an official property of a component. The `<CFPROPERTY>` tags must be placed at the top of the CFC file, just within the `<CFCOMPONENT>` tag, before any initialization code.

The syntax for the `<CFPROPERTY>` tag is shown in Table 20.11.

NOTE

The `<CFPROPERTY>` tag doesn't actively create a property in this version of ColdFusion. Adding the tag to a `.cfc` file doesn't cause your component to behave differently. It simply causes the information you provide in the `<CFPROPERTY>` tag to be included in the automatic documentation and in the Dreamweaver MX interface.

NOTE

If you are using the CFC framework to create Web Services, the `<CFPROPERTY>` tag becomes important, because the property will become part of the published description of the service. The topic of creating Web Services, while not much harder than creating ordinary CFCs, is beyond the scope of this book. For details, see our companion volume, "Advanced ColdFusion MX Application Development."

Table 20.11 <CFPROPERTY> Tag Syntax

ATTRIBUTE	DESCRIPTION
NAME	The name of the property. This should match the name of the variable in the THIS scope that is used within the component's methods.
TYPE	The data type of the property, such as numeric, string, or query.
REQUIRED	Whether the property is required.
DEFAULT	The initial value of the property.
HINT	An explanation of what the property does or represents.
DISPLAYNAME	An alternate name for the property.

So, to document the RotationInterval property officially, you could add the following <CFPROPERTY> tag to Listing 20.26, between the opening <CFCOMPONENT> tag and the series of <CFSET> tags:

```
<!--- Property: Rotation Interval --->
<CFPROPERTY
  NAME="RotationInterval"
  TYPE="numeric"
  REQUIRED="No"
  DEFAULT="5"
  HINT="The number of seconds between film rotations.">
```

NOTE

Remember that the <CFPROPERTY> doesn't actively create a property in this version of ColdFusion, so just because you add the <CFPROPERTY> tag to document the THIS.RotationInterval property, it doesn't mean that you can remove the <CFSET> tag that actually creates the variable and gives it its initial value.

CFCs, Shared Scopes, and Locking

In Chapter 16, you learned that it is important to keep the notion of *race conditions* in the back of your mind. In ColdFusion, a race condition is any type of situation where strange, inconsistent behavior might arise if multiple page requests try to change the values of the same variables at the same time. Race conditions aren't specific to ColdFusion development; they are something almost all Web developers should spend at least a bit of time thinking about. See Chapter 16 for more information about this important topic.

Since these last few examples have encouraged you to consider storing instances of your CFCs in the APPLICATION or SESSION scopes, you may be wondering whether there is the possibility of logical race conditions occurring in your code, and whether you should use the <CFLOCK> tag or some other means to protect against them if necessary.

The basic answer is that packaging your code in a CFC doesn't make it any more or less susceptible to race conditions. If the nature of the information you are accessing within a CFC's methods is such that it should not be altered or accessed by two different page requests at the same time, then you most likely should use the <CFLOCK> tag to make sure one page request waits for the other before continuing.

Direct Access to Shared Scopes from CFC Methods

If your CFC code is creating or accessing variables in the APPLICATION or SESSION scope directly (that is, if the words APPLICATION or SESSION appear in the body of your CFC's <CFFUNCTION> blocks), then I recommend that you place <CFLOCK> tags around those portions of the code. The <CFLOCK> tags should appear inside the <CFFUNCTION> blocks, not around them. Additionally, you probably want to place <CFLOCK> tags around any initialization code (that is, within <CFCOMPONENT> but outside any <CFFUNCTION> blocks) that refers to APPLICATION or SESSION. In either case, you would probably use SCOPE="SESSION" or SCOPE="APPLICATION" as appropriate; alternatively, you could use <CFLOCK>'s NAME attribute as explained in Chapter 16 if you wanted finer-grained control over your locks.

Locking Access to the THIS Scope

The FilmRotationCFC example in this chapter (Listing 20.26) doesn't manipulate variables in the APPLICATION or SESSION scopes; instead, the CFC is designed so that entire instances of the CFC can be stored in the APPLICATION or SESSION scope (or the SERVER scope, for that matter) as the application's needs change over time. This is accomplished by only using variables in the THIS scope, rather than referring directly to SESSION or APPLICATION, within the CFC's methods.

You may be wondering how to approach locking in such a situation. My recommendation is to create a unique lock name for each component when each instance is first instantiated. You can easily accomplish this with ColdFusion's CreateUUID() function. For instance, you could use a line like this in the component's initialization code, within the body of the <CFCOMPONENT> tag:

```
<CFSET THIS.LockName = CreateUUID()>
```

The THIS.LockName variable (or property, if you prefer) is now guaranteed to be unique for each instance of the CFC, regardless of whether the component is stored in the APPLICATION or the SERVER scope. You can use this value as the NAME of a <CFLOCK> tag within any of the CFC's methods. For instance, if you were working with a CFC called ShoppingCartCFC and creating a new method called AddItemToCart(), you could structure it according to this basic outline:

```
<CFFUNCTION NAME="AddItemToCart">
  <CFLOCK NAME="#THIS.LockName#" TYPE="Exclusive" TIMEOUT="10">
    <!--- Changes to sensitive data in THIS scope goes here --->
  </CFLOCK>
</CFFUNCTION>
```

In Chapter 27, a shopping-cart component is created that locks accesses to the THIS scope using this technique, so you can refer to the ShoppingCart.cfc example in that chapter for a complete example. For more information on the <CFLOCK> tag, especially when to use TYPE="Exclusive" or TYPE="ReadOnly", see the "Using Locks to Protect Against Race Conditions" section in Chapter 16.

Learning More About CFCs

Other CFC Examples In This Book

In Chapter 27, there is a CFC called `ShoppingCart`, which is another example of a component that is designed to be stored in the `SESSION` scope. You are encouraged to take a look at this example to see another way in which a helpful and independent CFC can be created that encapsulates a real-world concept or metaphorical object (in this case, a shopping cart).

In Chapter 23, you will learn how client-side applications created with Flash MX can easily connect to ColdFusion Components, call methods, and display or otherwise present the data or functionality that the CFCs expose. Take a look at this chapter to get your brain thinking about how CFCs aren't necessarily for the use of your ColdFusion code alone. They can be thought of as universal suppliers of information of functionality that don't particularly care whether the user of the information is a Flash movie, a ColdFusion page, or a Web Service.

Learning About Advanced CFC Concepts

This chapter has introduced you to the most important concepts about the new ColdFusion Components functionality in ColdFusion MX. That said, there is more to the CFC framework than I have been able to introduce you to here.

In our companion book, Advanced ColdFusion MX Application Development, you will find chapters on advanced CFC concepts such as:

- Component inheritance and method overriding using the `EXTENDS` attribute of the `<CFCOMPONENT>` tag.
- Securing access to individual CFC methods with the `ROLES` attribute of the `<CFFUNCTION>` tag.
- Use of the `GetMetaData()` function to determine a CFC's characteristics programmatically at runtime.
- Accessing component methods with JSP tag library style syntax, using the `<CFIMPORT>` tag.
- Exposure of CFC methods as Web Services so that other systems, including participants in Microsoft's .NET framework or systems that work under Sun's J2EE umbrella, can use the methods over the Internet.

The additional attributes and functions methods mentioned in this list are also explained briefly in Appendices B and C.

CHAPTER 21

Improving the User Experience

IN THIS CHAPTER

Usability Considerations

This chapter concentrates on issues regarding the overall user experience and various ways it can be improved. The term *user experience* is purposefully a bit vague and is hard to measure quantitatively. Different people will define it differently. For the purposes of this discussion, think of the quality of the user experience as being affected mainly by the combination of an application's performance, usability, and friendliness.

In other words, do people have a pleasant experience when they use your application?

Putting Yourself in the User's Shoes

One of the best ways to ensure that your application is pleasant for your users is to simply keep them in mind as you do your development work. When you are deep into a development project, perhaps rushing to meet a deadline, it's easy to just produce code that works well enough for you to move on to the next task, without asking yourself whether it's really good enough for the user.

So, even if you are not responsible for the design or navigation, you still should keep the user in mind as you put together each data-entry screen or code each query. If users are happy, your application will probably be successful. If they spend too much time waiting or get confused, your application will probably not be successful. In most situations, especially applications aimed at the general public, it's as simple as that.

Thinking About Navigation

Entire books have been written on great ways to set up navigation elements for Web sites. Navigation elements should not only look good, but also be clear and easy to use. There shouldn't be too many choices, especially on your application's first page. At the same time, you will notice that most Web sites try to ensure that the most important content is no more than three levels (clicks) deep into the navigation structure. Most usability scholars agree that the most important or most commonly used items should appear before the less important items, even at the cost of the sequence being somewhat less predictable.

Studying the navigation elements used by your favorite Web sites—the ones you use often—can be helpful. What do these sites have in common? What is the theory behind the navigation on each page? For instance, does it adapt itself to context, or does it remain consistent from page to page? Why are some elements on the home page but others on a second-level page? Try to come up with rules that explain which items appear on which pages, and where. For instance, some sites tend to put "verbs" (actions) in a toolbar at the top of each page and "nouns" (articles, accounts) in the left margin. Other sites might do the reverse. Try to come up with similar rules for what goes where within your own application.

TIP

Good discussions on navigation and other design elements can be found on a number of developer-related Web sites. One good place to start is the Dimitry's Design Lab section at the WebReference Web site (`www.webreference.com/dlab`).

Why It's Good to Be Predictable

When describing a book or a movie, the word predictable might not sound like much of a compliment. But when describing a Web application, predictability is almost always something that should be actively pursued and cherished. As users move from page to page, they will feel most comfortable if they can predict, even intuit, what is going to appear next.

Anticipating the User's Next Move

As you are putting together a page, don't just think about what the user is going to do on that page. Try to figure out what the user is likely to do next. If the user is filling out a registration form, he might want to know what your company's privacy policy is. Or, if he is reading a press release, he might appreciate links to the company's corporate information and facts about its management team.

In general, on any page, try to put yourself in the user's shoes and ask yourself whether it's clear how to get to the next step or the next piece of information.

Scripting, Rollovers, and Widgets

JavaScript and Dynamic HTML can go a long way toward making your applications more exciting to your users. They also can cause problems of their own. For instance, image rollovers are great when used judiciously but can really slow a page down if too many are used.

In particular, Dynamic HTML functionality is notorious for behaving differently from browser to browser, version to version, and platform to platform. If you are going to use Dynamic HTML, try to find cross-browser scripts you can adapt until you come to understand what the specific limitations are. As a start, `www.webreference.com`, `www.builder.com`, and `www.dhtmlzone.com` are good places to look for scripts that work reasonably well in various browsers.

You may want to consider using Flash instead of Dynamic HTML, since a Flash movie almost always behaves the same way no matter what browser or platform it is viewed with. For more information about using Flash in your ColdFusion applications, see Chapter 23, "Integrating with Macromedia Flash."

Dealing with Problems Gracefully

Hopefully, your application will never encounter any serious problems or error conditions. That said, even though ColdFusion MX is really great, your application is bound to run into a problem at some point. Try to ensure that any error messages seem friendly and encouraging to the user and won't make her to lose trust in your Web site.

For instance, consider customizing all error messages so that they match the look and feel of your site. For instructions, see the section "Customizing the Look of Error Messages" in Chapter 16, "Introducing the Web Application Framework." See also Chapter 31, "Error Handling."

Easing the Browser's Burden

If an application isn't running as fast as you want it to, you usually should look for a source of trouble on the server side, such a `<CFQUERY>` tag that is taking longer to execute than it should. However, you might also think about how much work the browser is doing to display your pages.

If you're having performance troubles, try turning on the debugging options in the ColdFusion Administrator so you can see the execution time for the page. This shows you how long the server is taking to complete your CFML template(s). If the server execution time is nice and short (under a couple of hundred milliseconds, say) but pages still seem to come up slowly for some users, then the problem is probably something like image size, the overuse of tables, or some other topic discussed in this section. If, on the other hand, the server execution time is long, then you need to work on the code in your CFML templates themselves.

Dealing with Image Size

No matter how ardently you strive to make your application generate sensible HTML, and no matter how hard you work to ensure that all your queries and other server-side code runs quickly, it is all too easy to slow down your pages with a lot of large images. Not only can such images take a long time to download, but they also take up room in the browser machine's memory, which can have an effect on the user's computer (depending on how much RAM and virtual memory are available).

Here are some suggestions to keep image size in check:

- **Create or resave your images using a program that knows how to compress or optimize images for use on the Web.** In general, you give up a bit of image quality for a smaller file size; the trade-off is generally worth it. Macromedia's Fireworks product also does a great job of compressing image files and generally optimizing them for display on the Web. Also, recent versions of Adobe Photoshop include a terrific Save for Web option on the File menu, which enables you to preview how your images will look after they are optimized. Other tools, some of them free or shareware, can provide similar results. One place to look for such programs is `www.shareware.com`.
- **Create or resave JPEG images using a progressive JPEG option, so the images can be displayed in increasingly finer detail as they are downloaded.** This is more pleasant for the user because she doesn't have to wait for the whole file to download

before she can get a sense of the image. Most graphic-manipulation packages let you save progressive JPEGs.

- **The `WIDTH` and `HEIGHT` attributes you supply to an C tag don't have to reflect the actual width and height of the image file.** You could, for instance, create an image file that is 50 by 50 pixels, yet provide `WIDTH` and `HEIGHT` attributes of `100` each. The image's file size would be much smaller, but it would take up the same amount of space on the page. Of course, it would appear pixelated, but depending on the nature of the artwork, that might be fine.
- **If you don't know an image's `WIDTH` and `HEIGHT`, you can determine them by reading the dimensions dynamically using a custom tag or CFX tag.** This occurs in situations such as dealing with images that have been uploaded from users (see Chapter 33, "Interacting with the Operating System"). A number of such tags are available from the ColdFusion Developers Exchange Web site. See Chapter 20, "Building Reusable Components," for details about the Developers Exchange.
- **Always try to provide a sensible `ALT` attribute for each `<IMG>` tag to describe the image. Most browsers display any text you provide in an** `ALT` tag while the image is loading or as a tool tip when the user hovers her mouse pointer over the image. This enables the user to anticipate what each image is before it is actually displayed.
- **Consider using the `LOWSRC` attribute for your larger `<IMG>` tags.** The `LOWSRC` attribute enables a smaller version of the image to be displayed while the full-size image is being downloaded. Consult the HTML Reference section of the Dreamweaver MX or HomeSite+ online help for details.

And, of course, you must think about whether larger images are really necessary. Can they be eliminated, or at least be made a bit smaller? Look at some of your favorite Web sites—the ones you actually use on a daily basis. How many images do you see? Most likely, not that many. Most popular Web sites use other techniques (especially type size and background colors) to give a page visual impact, and use images sparingly.

NOTE

In any case, always provide `WIDTH` and `HEIGHT` attributes for each `<IMG>` tag. This enables the browser to display the rest of the page correctly before it has loaded the images. Without `WIDTH` and `HEIGHT`, the browser might have to wait until all the images have loaded to display anything, or it might have to reflow the document several times as each image loads. (The exact behavior in the absence of `WIDTH` and `HEIGHT` varies a bit from browser to browser.)

Using Tables Wisely

HTML tables are a great way to display information in any type of rows-and-columns format, such as the next-n examples shown later in this chapter. Here are a few tips to help you make the most of them without placing an undue burden on the browser:

- **Whenever possible, provide `WIDTH` attributes for each `<TH>` or `<TD>` cell in the table.** This usually speeds up the display of the table. The exact behavior, however, varies from browser to browser.

- **You can specify the `WIDTH` attribute for an entire table as a percentage. For instance,** `WIDTH="100%"` tells the browser to make the table take up the entire available width of the page. You can also use percentages for the widths of each `<TH>` and `<TD>` cell. For instance, if three `<TD>` cells were in a table row, you could use `WIDTH="50%"` for the first one and `WIDTH="25%"` for the second two. This is helpful when you want content to spread itself evenly across the page regardless of screen resolution. If the user resizes the page, the table automatically resizes itself as well.
- **You can use tables as a way to add color, style, and callout sections to a page without needing to use solid images.** If you want to fill in a section of the screen with a light blue color, why send a light blue image to the browser when you can just include a light blue table cell instead, by seeing the cell's `BGCOLOR` to blue? It will almost surely be smaller in terms of file size and overall speed.
- **You should try not to use tables to control an entire page's layout.** Because tables usually cannot be displayed incrementally, a table often will not be displayed until the closing `</TABLE>` tag is encountered. So, if your whole page is laid out using a single, large table, the page might not be displayed at all until the whole page has been received (regardless of what you do with the `<CFFLUSH>` tag discussed later in this chapter). Sometimes, however, a table can be displayed incrementally. The exact behavior varies from browser to browser. See the `COLS` attribute for the `<TABLE>` tag in an HTML reference for details.

Using Frames Wisely

Frames are a nice way to separate sections of a page. A frame-based page usually takes a tiny bit longer to appear at first because the browser must fetch each frame by submitting a separate page request to the server. However, after the frameset is loaded, subsequent page requests can be pretty quick (assuming that only one frame needs to be replaced, rather than the whole page).

NOTE

However, some users find frames confusing–especially if a lot of them are used on a page, each with its own scroll bar. If you choose to use frames in your application, you should try to create a layout in which the content of each frame does not need to scroll.

Using External Script and Style Files

The use of JavaScript and Cascading Style Sheets (CSS) is not discussed specifically in this book, but they often become important parts of ColdFusion applications. CSS and JavaScript code usually are included as part of the HTML document itself, generally in the `<HEAD>` section. If you will use the same JavaScript functions or CSS classes over and over again on a number of pages, you should consider moving the script or CSS code into separate files.

This way, the browser must download the file only once, at the beginning of each session (depending on how the user has set up the browser's caching preferences), rather than as a part of each page. This can make your pages display more quickly, especially for modem users—and especially if your script or CSS code is rather long.

To move frequently used JavaScript functions into a separate file, just save the JavaScript code to a file with a .js extension. The file should not include opening and closing <SCRIPT> tags; it should contain only the JavaScript code itself. Next, in place of the original <SCRIPT> block, include a reference to the .js file using the SRC attribute of the <SCRIPT> tag, like this (the closing </SCRIPT> tag is required):

```
<SCRIPT LANGUAGE="JavaScript" SRC="MyScripts.js"></SCRIPT>
```

Similarly, to move frequently used CSS code into a separate file, save the CSS code to a file with a .css extension. The file should not include any <STYLE> tags—just the CSS code itself. Now, in place of the original <STYLE> block, include a reference to the .css file using the <LINK> tag:

```
<LINK REL="stylesheet" TYPE="text/css" HREF="MyStyles.css">
```

Browser Compatibility Issues

Not all browsers support all HTML tags. For instance, neither Internet Explorer nor Netscape 6 (or later) supports the <LAYER> tag that were introduced in Netscape Communicator 4.0, and Netscape browsers don't support the <MARQUEE> tag introduced by IE. Support for various tags also differs across browser versions—for instance, the <IFRAME> tag was not supported in Netscape browsers until version 6.0. Support for more advanced technologies, such as JavaScript and Dynamic HTML, differ even more widely from browser to browser.

You can use the automatic CGI.HTTP_USER_AGENT variable to determine which browser is being used to access the currently executing template. The HTTP_USER_AGENT value is a string provided by the browser for identification purposes. You can look at the string with ColdFusion's string functions to determine the browser and version number. For instance, the following line of code can be placed in Application.cfm to determine whether the a Microsoft Internet Explorer browser is being used:

```
<CFSET REQUEST.IsIE = HTTP_USER_AGENT contains "MSIE">
```

You then could use the REQUEST.IsIE variable in any of your application's pages (including custom tags or modules) to display Internet Explorer–specific content when appropriate:

```
<CFIF REQUEST.IsIE>
  <!--- Internet Explorer content goes here --->
<CFELSE>
  <!--- Non-IE content goes here --->
</CFIF>
```

Remembering Settings

One way to make your application more usable and helpful is to make it remember certain settings or actions as users interact with it. For instance, in Chapter 17, ColdFusion's Client Management feature was used to remember the words the user last searched for. When a user returns to the search page later, he finds that his most recent search phrase is already filled in for him. This can improve the user experience by both saving the user time and making him feel at home.

Remembering User Names and Passwords

If your application requires users to log in by providing a user name and password, you might consider adding some type of "remember me" option on the login form. This would cause the user name to be prefilled for the user when he next needs to log in. You can use the same basic technique used in the `SearchForm1.cfm` and `SearchForm2.cfm` templates from Chapter 17. Instead of using the `CLIENT` scope to remember the last search phrase, use it to remember and prefill the user name.

NOTE

Of course, this makes your application less secure, because anyone with physical access to the machine could see the person's user name. Do whatever makes sense for your application.

Other Helpful Settings to Remember

Many other things can be remembered between visits to save the user time and make him feel more at home:

- If the user has indicated which country he lives in, you could show him content relevant to his country each time he returns to your site, perhaps even translated into the appropriate language.
- If the user has a favorite color, you could store the color in the `CLIENT` scope and use it to set the `BGCOLOR` for the `<BODY>` tags at the top of each page.

Avoiding the Big Brother Effect

After you start thinking about remembering settings for users, it becomes clear that you probably could retain information on just about everything they do, on which pages, and when. However, if your application begins to flaunt its knowledge of users' actions in a way that is perceived as excessive, you might start to lose their trust. People like it when sites are personalized for them, but no one likes to feel as if their every move is being watched and recorded.

Also, be sure you aren't violating any type of privacy statement your company or client has made publicly available.

Creating Next-N Records Interfaces

Sooner or later, you probably will run into a situation in which you need to build what we call a next-n interface. A next-n interface is used in any Web page that enables the user to view a portion of a large number of records—say, 10 or 20 at a time. You probably have seen such interfaces yourself. They are common on search engine Web sites, which might have 1,000 records to look through. Instead of showing you all 1,000 records at once, the page provides buttons or links labeled Next and Back that let you move through them in more reasonable chunks.

Advantages of Next-N Interfaces

This type of interface has a number of advantages:

- **Familiarity.** Because next-n interfaces are so common, many users expect them whenever they are presented with a large number of records. If they see a ton of records without such an interface, your application might appear unfinished.
- **Performance.** As discussed earlier, good performance is part of providing a good user experience. Because next-n interfaces put an upper boundary on the size of the generated HTML, pages that use them usually are easier on both the browser machine and the ColdFusion server.
- **Readability.** Most importantly, next-n interfaces usually enable the user to more easily find the information she is looking for, simply because reading a small page is faster than reading a large one.

When to Create a Next-N Interface

It will usually be obvious when you need to add a next-n interface to a particular display page. Other times, though, it becomes evident only over time, as the number of records in the database grows. A year after an application is deployed, what seemed to be a nice, compact data-display page when you wrote it could get to the point where it is slow and unmanageable. So, you should consider creating some variation on the next-n interface presented in this chapter whenever you think the user might sometime need to look at a large number of records.

TIP

You might come up with an internal user interface policy stipulating that whenever a user will be presented with more than 50 records, a next-n interface should be implemented. You might pick a larger cutoff point if your users have fast connection speeds, or a smaller cutoff if many users will connect via slow modems.

Creating the Basic Interface

Say you have been asked to create a simple expense report area for Orange Whip Studio's intranet. The only instruction you have been given is to create a page in which employees can review all expenses. After talking with a few of the employees in the accounting department, you learn that they are usually most interested in viewing the most recent expenses. You decide to display the expense records in reverse order (the most recent expense first), with a next-10 interface. This way, users can see the new expenses right away and page through the older records 10 at a time.

This section presents four versions of a typical next-n interface, each version a bit more sophisticated than the one before it.

Limiting the Number of Records Shown

A number of approaches can be taken to create a next-n interface. Listing 21.1 demonstrates a simple, effective technique that easily can be adapted to suit your needs.

The code relies on a URL parameter named `StartRow`, which tells the template which records to display. The first time the page is displayed, `StartRow` defaults to `1`, which causes rows 1–10 to be displayed. When the user clicks the Next button, `StartRow` is passed as `11`, so rows 11–20 are displayed. The user can continue to click Next (or Back) to move through all the records.

NOTE

Before this listing will work, the `REQUEST.DataSource` variable needs to be set in your `Application.cfm` file, as shown in Listing 21.2. Listing 21.3, later in this chapter, also must be in place.

Listing 21.1 `NextN1.cfm`—A Simple Next-N Interface

```
<!---
  Filename:     NextN1.cfm
  Created by:   Nate Weiss (NMW)
  Purpose:      Displays Next N record-navigation interface
  Please Note  Includes NextNIncludeBackNext.cfm template
--->

<!--- Retrieve expense records from database --->
<CFQUERY NAME="GetExp" DATASOURCE="#REQUEST.DataSource#">
  SELECT
    f.FilmID, f.MovieTitle,
    e.Description, e.ExpenseAmount, e.ExpenseDate
  FROM
    Expenses e INNER JOIN Films f
    ON e.FilmID = f.FilmID
  ORDER BY
    e.ExpenseDate DESC
</CFQUERY>


<!--- Number of rows to display per Next/Back page  --->
<CFSET RowsPerPage = 10>
<!--- What row to start at? Assume first by default --->
<CFPARAM NAME="URL.StartRow" DEFAULT="1" TYPE="numeric">

<!--- We know the total number of rows from query   --->
<CFSET TotalRows = GetExp.RecordCount>
<!--- Last row is 10 rows past the starting row, or --->
<!--- total number of query rows, whichever is less --->
<CFSET EndRow = Min(URL.StartRow + RowsPerPage - 1, TotalRows)>
<!--- Next button goes to 1 past current end row  --->
<CFSET StartRowNext = EndRow + 1>
<!--- Back button goes back N rows from start row --->
<CFSET StartRowBack = URL.StartRow - RowsPerPage>


<!--- Page Title --->
<HTML>
<HEAD><TITLE>Expense Browser</TITLE></HEAD>
<BODY>
<CFOUTPUT><H2>#REQUEST.CompanyName# Expense Report</H2></CFOUTPUT>


<TABLE WIDTH="600" BORDER="0" CELLSPACING="0" CELLPADDING="1" COLS="3">
```

Listing 21.1 (continued)

```
    <!--- Row at top of table, above column headers --->
    <TR>
      <TD COLSPAN="2">
        <!--- Message about which rows are being displayed --->
        <CFOUTPUT>
          Displaying <B>#URL.StartRow#</B> to <B>#EndRow#</B>
          of <B>#TotalRows#</B> Records<BR>
        </CFOUTPUT>
      </TD>
      <TD></TD>
      <TD ALIGN="right">
        <!--- Provide Next/Back links --->
        <CFINCLUDE TEMPLATE="NextNIncludeBackNext.cfm">
      </TD>
    </TR>

    <!--- Row for column headers --->
    <TR>
      <TH WIDTH="100">Date</TH>
      <TH WIDTH="250">Film</TH>
      <TH WIDTH="150">Expense</TH>
      <TH WIDTH="100">Amount</TH>
    </TR>

    <!--- For each query row that should be shown now --->
    <CFLOOP QUERY="GetExp" StartRow="#URL.StartRow#" ENDROW="#EndRow#">
      <CFOUTPUT>
        <TR VALIGN="baseline">
          <TD WIDTH="100">#LSDateFormat(ExpenseDate)#</TD>
          <TD WIDTH="250">#MovieTitle#</TD>
          <TD WIDTH="150"><EM>#Description#</EM></TD>
          <TD WIDTH="100">#LSCurrencyFormat(ExpenseAmount)#</TD>
        </TR>
      </CFOUTPUT>
    </CFLOOP>

    <!--- Row at bottom of table, after rows of data --->
    <TR>
      <TD WIDTH="100"></TD>
      <TD WIDTH="250"></TD>
      <TD WIDTH="150"></TD>
      <TD WIDTH="100" ALIGN="right">
        <!--- Provide Next/Back links --->
        <CFINCLUDE TEMPLATE="NextNIncludeBackNext.cfm">
      </TD>
    </TR>
  </TABLE>


  </BODY>
  </HTML>
```

NOTE

This listing relies on the `STARTROW` and `ENDROW` attributes for the `<CFLOOP>` tag. See Chapter 9, "CFML Basics," and Appendix B, "ColdFusion Tag Reference," for detailed information about `<CFLOOP>`.

First, a query named GetExp is run, which retrieves all expense records from the Expenses table, along with the associated MovieTitle for each expense. The records are returned in reverse date order (most recent expenses first). Next, a variable called RowsPerPage is set to the number of rows that should be displayed to the user at one time. Of course, you can adjust this value to 20, 50, or whatever you feel is appropriate.

TIP

You could set the RowsPerPage variable in Application.cfm if you wanted to use the same value in a number of different next-n interfaces throughout your application.

The URL.StartRow parameter is established via the <CFPARAM> tag and given a default value of 1 if it is not actually supplied in the URL. Then, a TotalRows variable is set to the number of rows returned by the GetExp query.

TIP

Sometimes it's worth setting a variable just to keep your code clear. In this template, you could skip the <CFSET> for the TotalRows variable and just use GetExp.RecordCount in its place throughout the rest of the code. But the name of the TotalRows variable helps make the role of the value easier to understand, and virtually no performance penalty will exist for the extra line of code.

Next, a variable called EndRow is calculated, which determines the row that should be the last to appear on a given page. In general, the EndRow is simply RowsPerPage past the StartRow. However, the EndRow should never go past the total number of rows in the query, so the Min function is used to ensure that the value is never greater than TotalRows. This becomes important when the user reaches the last page of search results. The URL.StartRow and EndRow values are passed to the STARTROW and ENDROW attributes of the <CFLOOP> that displays the expense records, effectively throttling the display so it shows only the appropriate records for the current page.

StartRowNext and StartRowBack represent what the new StartRow value should be if the user clicks the Next or Back link. If the user clicks Next, the page is reloaded at one row past the current EndRow. If the user clicks Back, the display moves back by the value stored in RowsPerPage (which is 10 in this example).

After this small set of variables has been calculated, the rest of the template is really quite simple. An HTML table is used to display the expense results. The first row of the table displays a message about which rows are currently being shown. It also displays Next and Back links, as appropriate, by including the NextNIncludeBackNext.cfm template (see Listing 21.3). The next row of the table displays some simple column headings. Then, the <CFLOOP> tag is used to output a table row for each record returned by the GetExp query, but only for the rows from URL.StartRow through EndRow. Finally, the last row of the HTML table repeats the same Next and Back links under the expense records, using an identical <CFINCLUDE> tag.For now, don't worry about the fact that the query must be rerun each time the user clicks the Next or Back link. ColdFusion's query-caching feature can be used to ensure that your database is not queried unnecessarily. See Chapter 22, "Improving Performance," for details.

The Application.cfm file shown in Listing 21.2 establishes the REQUEST.DataSource and REQUEST.CompanyName variables used in Listing 21.1. Because they are set in the special REQUEST scope, these variables are available for use within any of this folder's templates, including any custom tags (see Chapter 20, "Building Reusable Components"). This is an excellent way to establish global settings for an application, such as data source names, and is used in most of the Application.cfm templates in the second half of this book. In addition, <CFAPPLICATION> is used to turn on session management, which is needed by some of the later examples in this chapter. See Chapter 17, "Working with Sessions," for more information about session management and session variables.

Listing 21.2 Application.cfm—Providing Application Settings for This Chapter's Examples

```
<!---
  Filename:     Application.cfm
  Created by:   Nate Weiss (NMW)
  Please Note  Executes for each page request
--->

<!--- Any variables set here can be used by all our pages --->
<CFSET REQUEST.DataSource = "ows">
<CFSET REQUEST.CompanyName = "Orange Whip Studios">

<!--- Name our app, and enable Client and Application vars --->
<CFAPPLICATION
  NAME="OrangeWhipSite"
  SESSIONMANAGEMENT="Yes">
```

Adding Next and Back Buttons

Listing 21.3 provides the code that includes the Back and Next links above and below the expense records. The idea here is simple: to show Back and Next links when appropriate. The Back link should be shown whenever the StartRowBack value is greater than 0, which should always be the case unless the user is looking at the first page of records. The Next link should be shown as long as the StartRowNext value is not after the last row of the query, which would be the case only when the user is at the last page of records.

Listing 21.3 NextNIncludeBackNext.cfm—Including Back and Next Buttons

```
<!---
  Filename:     NextNIncludeBackNext.cfm
  Created by:   Nate Weiss (NMW)
  Purpose:      Displays Back and Next links for record navigation
  Please Note  Included by the NextN.cfm templates in this folder
--->

<!--- Provide Next/Back links --->
<CFOUTPUT>
  <!--- Show link for Back, if appropriate --->
  <CFIF StartRowBack GT 0>
    <A HREF="#CGI.SCRIPT_NAME#?StartRow=#StartRowBack#">
      <IMG SRC="../images/BrowseBack.gif" WIDTH="40" HEIGHT="16"
        ALT="Back #RowsPerPage# Records" BORDER="0"></A>
  </CFIF>
  <!--- Show link for Next, if appropriate --->
  <CFIF StartRowNext LTE TotalRows>
    <A HREF="#CGI.SCRIPT_NAME#?StartRow=#StartRowNext#">
      <IMG SRC="../images/BrowseNext.gif" WIDTH="40" HEIGHT="16"
        ALT="Next #RowsPerPage# Records" BORDER="0"></A>
  </CFIF>
</CFOUTPUT>
```

As you can see, the Next and Back links always reload the current page, passing the appropriate `StartRow` parameter in the URL. Now the user can navigate through the all the query's records in digestible groups of 10. Figure 21.1 shows what the results look like in a browser.

NOTE

Because the `CGI.SCRIPT_NAME` variable is used for the Back and Next links, this code continues to provide the correct links even if you change the filename for Listing 21.1. If you find this confusing, you could replace the `CGI.SCRIPT_NAME` with the name of the template the user will be accessing (in this case, `NextN1.cfm`). See Appendix D, "Special ColdFusion Variables and Result Codes," for more information about this handy CGI variable.

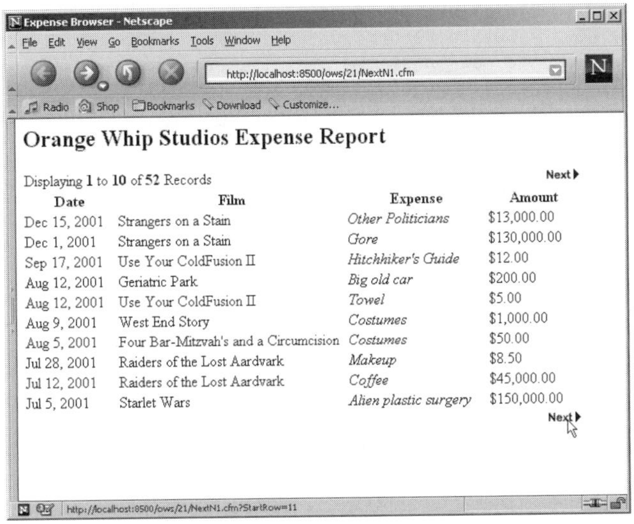

Figure 21.1

Creating a simple Next 10 interface for your users is easy.

Alternating Row Colors for Readability

Listing 21.4 is a revised version of Listing 21.1. This version just adds some basic formatting via CSS syntax and presents the rows of data with alternating colors, as shown in Figure 21.2.

Listing 21.4 `NextN2.cfm`—Adding CSS-Based Formatting to the Next-N Interface

```
<!---
  Filename:     NextN2.cfm
  Created by:   Nate Weiss (NMW)
  Purpose:      Displays Next N record-navigation interface
  Please Note  Includes NextNIncludeBackNext.cfm template
--->

<!--- Retrieve expense records from database --->
<CFQUERY NAME="GetExp" DATASOURCE="#REQUEST.DataSource#">
  SELECT
    f.FilmID, f.MovieTitle,
    e.Description, e.ExpenseAmount, e.ExpenseDate
  FROM
    Expenses e INNER JOIN Films f
```

Listing 21.4 (continued)

```
      ON e.FilmID = f.FilmID
    ORDER BY
      e.ExpenseDate DESC
  </CFQUERY>


  <!--- Number of rows to display per Next/Back page  --->
  <CFSET RowsPerPage = 10>
  <!--- What row to start at? Assume first by default --->
  <CFPARAM NAME="URL.StartRow" DEFAULT="1" TYPE="numeric">

  <!--- We know the total number of rows from query   --->
  <CFSET TotalRows = GetExp.RecordCount>
  <!--- Last row is 10 rows past the starting row, or --->
  <!--- total number of query rows, whichever is less --->
  <CFSET EndRow = Min(URL.StartRow + RowsPerPage - 1, TotalRows)>
  <!--- Next button goes to 1 past current end row  --->
  <CFSET StartRowNext = EndRow + 1>
  <!--- Back button goes back N rows from start row --->
  <CFSET StartRowBack = URL.StartRow - RowsPerPage>


  <!--- Page Title --->
  <HTML>
  <HEAD><TITLE>Expense Browser</TITLE></HEAD>
  <BODY>
  <CFOUTPUT><H2>#REQUEST.CompanyName# Expense Report</H2></CFOUTPUT>

  <!--- Simple Style Sheet for formatting --->
  <STYLE>
    TH       {font-family:sans-serif;font-size:smaller;
              background:navy;color:white}
    TD       {font-family:sans-serif;font-size:smaller}
    TD.DataA {background:silver;color:black}
    TD.DataB {background:lightgrey;color:black}
  </STYLE>

  <TABLE WIDTH="600" BORDER="0" CELLSPACING="0" CELLPADDING="1">
    <!--- Row at top of table, above column headers --->
    <TR>
      <TD WIDTH="500" COLSPAN="3">
        <!--- Message about which rows are being displayed --->
        <CFOUTPUT>
          Displaying <B>#URL.StartRow#</B> to <B>#EndRow#</B>
          of <B>#TotalRows#</B> Records<BR>
        </CFOUTPUT>
      </TD>
      <TD ALIGN="right">
        <!--- Provide Next/Back links --->
        <CFINCLUDE TEMPLATE="NextNIncludeBackNext.cfm">
      </TD>
    </TR>

    <!--- Row for column headers --->
    <TR>
      <TH WIDTH="100">Date</TH>
```

Listing 21.4 (CONTINUED)

```
      <TH WIDTH="250">Film</TH>
      <TH WIDTH="150">Expense</TH>
      <TH WIDTH="100">Amount</TH>
    </TR>

    <!--- For each query row that should be shown now --->
    <CFLOOP QUERY="GetExp" StartRow="#URL.StartRow#" ENDROW="#EndRow#">
      <!--- Use class "DataA" or "DataB" for alternate rows --->
      <CFSET Class = IIF(GetExp.CurrentRow MOD 2 EQ 0, "'DataA'", "'DataB'")>

      <CFOUTPUT>
        <TR VALIGN="baseline">
          <TD CLASS="#Class#" WIDTH="100">#LSDateFormat(ExpenseDate)#</TD>
          <TD CLASS="#Class#" WIDTH="250">#MovieTitle#</TD>
          <TD CLASS="#Class#" WIDTH="150"><I>#Description#</I></TD>
          <TD CLASS="#Class#" WIDTH="100">#LSCurrencyFormat(ExpenseAmount)#</TD>
        </TR>
      </CFOUTPUT>
    </CFLOOP>

    <!--- Row at bottom of table, after rows of data --->
    <TR>
      <TD WIDTH="100"></TD>
      <TD WIDTH="250"></TD>
      <TD WIDTH="150"></TD>
      <TD WIDTH="100" ALIGN="right">
        <!--- Provide Next/Back links --->
        <CFINCLUDE TEMPLATE="NextNIncludeBackNext.cfm">
      </TD>
    </TR>
  </TABLE>


  </BODY>
  </HTML>
```

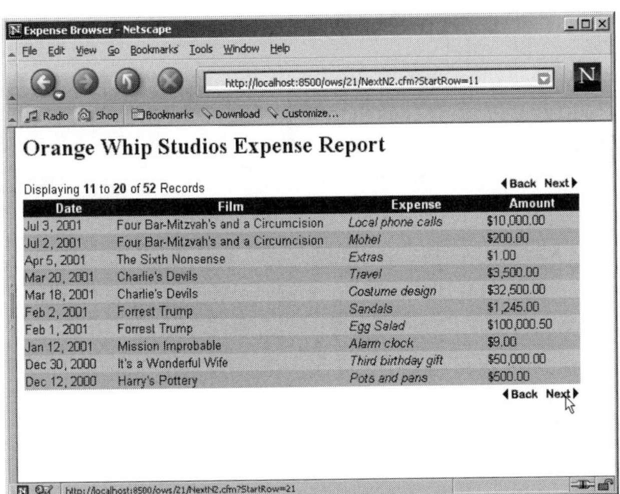

Figure 21.2

The background colors of table cells can be alternated to make the display easier to read.

Defining Styles

The <STYLE> block in Listing 21.4 specifies that all <TH> cells be displayed with white lettering on a navy background. Also, two style classes for <TD> cells are defined, called DataA and DataB. By displaying alternate rows with these two classes, the expenses are displayed with alternating background colors, as shown in Figure 21.2.

Inside the <CFLOOP> tag, the code alternates between the DataA and DataB style classes by using ColdFusion's MOD operator. MOD simply returns the modulus of two numbers, which is the remainder left over when the first number is divided by the second. When the CurrentRow is an even number, dividing it by 2 results in a remainder of 0, so the Class variable is set to DataA. Otherwise, Class is set to DataB. The Class variable is then used as the CLASS attribute for the <TD> cells that display each row of expenses. The result is the pleasant-looking rendition of the next-n interface shown in Figure 21.2.

TIP

The DataA and DataB style classes could vary in more than just background color. They could use different typefaces, font colors, boldface, and so on. See a CSS reference for details.

If you don't want to use CSS-based formatting, you could use the IIF() test in Listing 21.4 to switch between two color names instead of class names. Then, you would feed the result to the BGCOLOR attribute of the <TD> tags, instead of the CLASS attribute. This would ensure that the rows displayed with alternating colors, even for browsers that don't support CSS (CSS support appeared in version 4.0 of Internet Explorer and Netscape Communicator). Of course, you could also choose to alternate both the CLASS and BGCOLOR values.

A Note on the Use of IIF()

The line that sets the Class attribute uses the IIF() function, which enables you to choose between two expressions depending on a condition. The IIF() function is comparable to the ? and : operators used in JavaScript and some other languages. The first parameter is the condition; the second parameter determines what the result should be when the condition is True; and the third is what the result should be when condition is False.

When IIF() is used to switch between two strings, as shown previously in Listing 21.4, the second and third parameters must have two sets of quotes because they each will be evaluated as expressions. If the second parameter were written as "DataA" instead of "'DataA'", an error would result because ColdFusion would try to return the value of a variable called DataA, which does not exist. The inner set of single quotation marks tells ColdFusion that the literal string DataA should be returned. For details, see IIF() in Appendix C, "ColdFusion Function Reference."

The IIF() function is used here because it often improves code readability in cases such as this, due to its brevity. If, however, you find it confusing, you could achieve the same result by replacing the single <CFSET> line with this:

```
<CFIF GetExp.CurrentRow MOD 2 EQ 0>
  <CFSET Class = "DataA">
<CFELSE>
  <CFSET Class = "DataB">
</CFIF>
```

Letting the User Browse Page-by-Page

Many next-n interfaces you see on the Web provide numbered page-by-page links in addition to the customary Back and Next links. If there are 50 records to display, and 10 records are shown per page, the user can use links labeled 1–5 to jump to a particular set of 10 records. Not only does this give the user a way to move through the records quickly, but the collection of clickable page numbers also serves as a visual cue that provides a sense of how many records there are to look through.

For clarity, the page-by-page links are implemented in a separate file called `NextNInclude-PageLinks.cfm`. Listing 21.5 shows the code for this new file.

Listing 21.5 `NextNIncludePageLinks.cfm`—Creating Page-by-Page Links for Browsing Records

```
<!---
  Filename:      NextNIncludePageLinks.cfm
  Created by:    Nate Weiss (NMW)
  Purpose:       Displays Page 1, Page 2... links for record navigation
  Please Note  Included by the NextN.cfm templates in this folder
--->

<!--- Simple "Page" counter, starting at first "Page" --->
<CFSET ThisPage = 1>

<!--- Loop thru row numbers, in increments of RowsPerPage --->
<CFLOOP FROM="1" TO="#TotalRows#" STEP="#RowsPerPage#" INDEX="PageRow">
  <!--- Detect whether this "Page" currently being viewed --->
  <CFSET IsCurrentPage = (PageRow GTE URL.StartRow) AND (PageRow LTE EndRow)>

  <!--- If this "Page" is current page, show without link --->
  <CFIF IsCurrentPage>
    <CFOUTPUT><B>#ThisPage#</B></CFOUTPUT>
  <!--- Otherwise, show with link so user can go to page  --->
  <CFELSE>
    <CFOUTPUT>
      <A HREF="#CGI.SCRIPT_NAME#?StartRow=#PageRow#">#ThisPage#</A>
    </CFOUTPUT>
  </CFIF>

  <!--- Increment ThisPage variable --->
  <CFSET ThisPage = ThisPage + 1>
</CFLOOP>
```

Like the Back and Next code shown in Listing 21.3, this template is responsible for generating a number of links that reload the current template, passing the appropriate `StartRow` parameter in the URL.

First, a variable named `ThisPage` is set to `1`. This variable changes incrementally as each page-by-page link is displayed. Next, a `<CFLOOP>` tag is used to create each page-by-page link. Because the `STEP` attribute is set to the value of `RowsPerPage`, the `PageRow` variable rises in increments of `10` for each iteration of the loop, until it exceeds `TotalRows`. So, the first time through the loop, `ThisPage` and `PageRow` are both `1`. The second time through the loop, `ThisPage` is `2` and `PageRow` is `11`, and so on.

The next `<CFSET>` determines whether the user is already looking at the page of results currently being considered by the loop. If the current value of `PageRow` is between the `StartRow` and `EndRow` values (refer to Listing 21.4), `IsCurrentPage` is `True`. Now the page number can be displayed by outputting the value of `ThisPage`. If `ThisPage` is the page currently being viewed, it is shown in boldface. If not, the page number is presented as a link to the appropriate page by passing the value of `PageRow` in the URL as the `StartRow` parameter. Now the user can see where she is in the records by looking for the boldface number, and she can jump to other pages by clicking the other numbers, as shown in Figure 21.3.

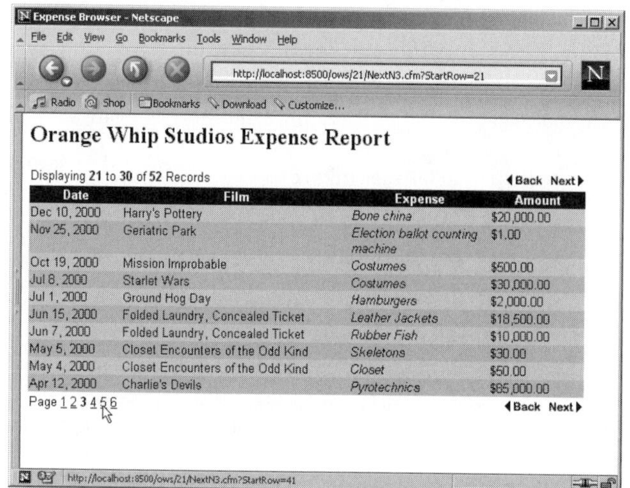

Figure 21.3

The completed interface includes Back, Next, page-by-page, and Show All links for easy navigation.

Now that the code has been written, it can be included in the next-n interface with a simple `<CFINCLUDE>` tag, like so:

```
<!--- Shortcut links for Pages of search results --->
Page <CFINCLUDE TEMPLATE="NextNIncludePageLinks.cfm">
```

The `NextN3.cfm` template (Listing 21.6, on this book's CD-ROM) builds on the previous version (refer to Listing 21.4) by adding this `<CFINCLUDE>` tag in the appropriate place. The code is otherwise unchanged. You can also see this `<CFINCLUDE>` tag in the next version of this template (see Listing 21.7).

Adding Show All and Filter Options

Although next-n interfaces are great for keeping your pages from getting too large to navigate comfortably, your users sometimes might need a way to see all the records at once (for instance, when they need to print a hard copy). Therefore, it's worth considering the addition of a Show All link, which essentially serves to override the next-n interface if the user so desires.

Listing 21.7 is the feature-complete version of the next-n interface, which now includes a Show All option, as well as the page-by-page navigation included in the previous version. As you can see, only a few lines of new code were necessary to put the Show All option into place.

This version of the template also gives the user a way to filter the records being displayed in the next-n interface. The user is able to filter the records by movie name, the text of the expense description, or by expense date. In general, this is a simple matter of inclucing a Filter form on the page, and then querying the database dynamically based on the user's entries. You learned all about this in Chapter 11, "ColdFusion Forms."

The only trick is the fact that this next-n page will be reloaded over and over as the user navigates through the records. The user shouldn't have to keep reentering his filter criteria over and over again, so session variables will be used to remember his filter throughout his interaction with the interface. Luckily, ColdFusion's session variables make it easy to provide this basic usability feature. Three session variables are used to remember the filter: `SESSION.ExpenseReport.UserFilter`, `SESSION.ExpenseReport.DateFrom`, and `SESSION.ExpenseReport.DateThru`. At the top of the template, `<CFPARAM>` tags are used to initialize these variables to empty strings. Next, a simple `<CFIF>` tests whether the user is currently submitting the Filter form. If so, his submission is saved in the three session variables. These session variables are then used in the page's `<CFQUERY>` to filter the records according to the user's wishes. The session variables are also used to prepopulate the three `<CFINPUT>` tags within the Filter form each time the page is reloaded, giving the user an easy way to experiment with various filters.

Listing 21.7 `NextN4.cfm`—Adding a Way to View All Records at Once

```
<!---
  Filename:      NextN4.cfm
  Created by:    Nate Weiss (NMW)
  Purpose:       Displays Next N record-navigation interface
  Please Note   Includes NextNIncludeBackNext.cfm and NextNIncludePageLinks.cfm
--->

<!--- Maintain ExpenseReport filtering variables at session level --->
<CFPARAM NAME="SESSION.ExpenseReport.UserFilter" TYPE="string" DEFAULT="">
<CFPARAM NAME="SESSION.ExpenseReport.DateFrom" TYPE="string" DEFAULT="">
<CFPARAM NAME="SESSION.ExpenseReport.DateThru" TYPE="string" DEFAULT="">

<!--- If the user is submitting the "filter" form, --->
<!--- we'll make their submission be the filter for rest of session --->
<CFIF IsDefined("FORM.UserFilter")>
  <CFSET SESSION.ExpenseReport.UserFilter = FORM.UserFilter>
  <CFSET SESSION.ExpenseReport.DateFrom   = FORM.DateFrom>
  <CFSET SESSION.ExpenseReport.DateThru   = FORM.DateThru>
</CFIF>

<!--- Retrieve expense records from database --->
<CFQUERY NAME="GetExp" DATASOURCE="#REQUEST.DataSource#">
  SELECT
    f.FilmID, f.MovieTitle,
    e.Description, e.ExpenseAmount, e.ExpenseDate
  FROM
    Expenses e INNER JOIN Films f
    ON e.FilmID = f.FilmID
  WHERE
    0=0
  <!--- If the user provided a filter string, --->
```

Listing 21.7 (continued)

```
    <!--- show only matching films and/or expenses --->
    <CFIF SESSION.ExpenseReport.UserFilter IS NOT "">
      AND (f.MovieTitle LIKE '%#SESSION.ExpenseReport.UserFilter#%' OR
           e.Description LIKE '%#SESSION.ExpenseReport.UserFilter#%')
    </CFIF>
    <!--- Also filter on From date, if provided --->
    <CFIF IsDate(SESSION.ExpenseReport.DateFrom)>
      AND e.ExpenseDate >= #CreateODBCDate(SESSION.ExpenseReport.DateFrom)#
    </CFIF>
    <!--- Also filter on Through date, if provided --->
    <CFIF IsDate(SESSION.ExpenseReport.DateThru)>
      AND e.ExpenseDate <= #CreateODBCDate(SESSION.ExpenseReport.DateThru)#
    </CFIF>
    ORDER BY
      e.ExpenseDate DESC
  </CFQUERY>


  <!--- Number of rows to display per Next/Back page  --->
  <CFSET RowsPerPage = 10>
  <!--- What row to start at? Assume first by default --->
  <CFPARAM NAME="URL.StartRow" DEFAULT="1" TYPE="numeric">
  <!--- Allow for Show All parameter in the URL --->
  <CFPARAM NAME="URL.ShowAll" TYPE="boolean" DEFAULT="No">

  <!--- We know the total number of rows from query   --->
  <CFSET TotalRows = GetExp.RecordCount>
  <!--- Show all on page if ShowAll passed in URL   --->
  <CFIF URL.ShowAll>
    <CFSET RowsPerPage = TotalRows>
  </CFIF>
  <!--- Last row is 10 rows past the starting row, or --->
  <!--- total number of query rows, whichever is less --->
  <CFSET EndRow = Min(URL.StartRow + RowsPerPage - 1, TotalRows)>
  <!--- Next button goes to 1 past current end row  --->
  <CFSET StartRowNext = EndRow + 1>
  <!--- Back button goes back N rows from start row --->
  <CFSET StartRowBack = URL.StartRow - RowsPerPage>


  <!--- Page Title --->
  <HTML>
  <HEAD><TITLE>Expense Browser</TITLE></HEAD>
  <BODY>
  <CFOUTPUT><H2>#REQUEST.CompanyName# Expense Report</H2></CFOUTPUT>

  <!--- Simple style sheet for formatting --->
  <STYLE>
    FORM     {font-family:sans-serif;font-size:smaller;}
    TH       {font-family:sans-serif;font-size:smaller;
              background:navy;color:white}
    TD       {font-family:sans-serif;font-size:smaller}
    TD.DataA {background:silver;color:black}
    TD.DataB {background:lightgrey;color:black}
  </STYLE>
```

Listing 21.7 (continued)

```
<!--- Simple form to allow user to filter results --->
<CFFORM ACTION="#CGI.SCRIPT_NAME#" METHOD="POST">
  <!--- Filter string --->
  <B>Filter:</B>
  <CFINPUT
    TYPE="Text"
    NAME="UserFilter"
    VALUE="#SESSION.ExpenseReport.UserFilter#"
    SIZE="15">

  <!--- From date --->
   
  <B>Dates:</B> from
  <CFINPUT
    TYPE="Text"
    NAME="DateFrom"
    VALUE="#SESSION.ExpenseReport.DateFrom#"
    SIZE="9"
    VALIDATE="date"
    MESSAGE="Please enter a valid date, or leave it blank.">

  <!--- Through date --->
  through
  <CFINPUT
    TYPE="Text"
    NAME="DateThru"
    VALUE="#SESSION.ExpenseReport.DateThru#"
    SIZE="9"
    VALIDATE="date"
    MESSAGE="Please enter a valid date, or leave it blank.">

  <!--- Submit button to activate/change/clear filter --->
  <INPUT
    TYPE="Submit"
    VALUE="Apply">
</CFFORM>


<TABLE WIDTH="600" BORDER="0" CELLSPACING="0" CELLPADDING="1">
  <!--- Row at top of table, above column headers --->
  <TR>
    <TD WIDTH="500" COLSPAN="3">
      <!--- Message about which rows are being displayed --->
      <CFOUTPUT>
        Displaying <B>#URL.StartRow#</B> to <B>#EndRow#</B>
        of <B>#TotalRows#</B> Records<BR>
      </CFOUTPUT>
    </TD>
    <TD WIDTH="100" ALIGN="right">
      <CFIF NOT URL.ShowAll>
        <!--- Provide Next/Back links --->
        <CFINCLUDE TEMPLATE="NextNIncludeBackNext.cfm">
      </CFIF>
    </TD>
  </TR>
```

Listing 21.7 (continued)

```
    <!--- Row for column headers --->
    <TR>
      <TH WIDTH="100">Date</TH>
      <TH WIDTH="250">Film</TH>
      <TH WIDTH="150">Expense</TH>
      <TH WIDTH="100">Amount</TH>
    </TR>

    <!--- For each query row that should be shown now --->
    <CFLOOP QUERY="GetExp" StartRow="#URL.StartRow#" ENDROW="#EndRow#">
      <!--- Use class "DataA" or "DataB" for alternate rows --->
      <CFSET Class = IIF(GetExp.CurrentRow MOD 2 EQ 0, "'DataA'", "'DataB'")>

      <CFOUTPUT>
        <TR VALIGN="baseline">
          <TD CLASS="#Class#" WIDTH="100">#LSDateFormat(ExpenseDate)#</TD>
          <TD CLASS="#Class#" WIDTH="250">#MovieTitle#</TD>
          <TD CLASS="#Class#" WIDTH="150"><I>#Description#</I></TD>
          <TD CLASS="#Class#" WIDTH="100">#LSCurrencyFormat(ExpenseAmount)#</TD>
        </TR>
      </CFOUTPUT>
    </CFLOOP>

    <!--- Row at bottom of table, after rows of data --->
    <TR>
      <TD WIDTH="500" COLSPAN="3">
        <CFIF NOT URL.ShowAll AND TotalRows GT RowsPerPage>
          <!--- Shortcut links for "Pages" of search results --->
          Page <CFINCLUDE TEMPLATE="NextNIncludePageLinks.cfm">
          <!--- Show All link --->
          <CFOUTPUT>
            <A HREF="#CGI.SCRIPT_NAME#?&ShowAll=Yes">Show All</A>
          </CFOUTPUT>
        </CFIF>
      </TD>
      <TD WIDTH="100" ALIGN="right">
        <CFIF NOT URL.ShowAll>
          <!--- Provide Next/Back links --->
          <CFINCLUDE TEMPLATE="NextNIncludeBackNext.cfm">
        </CFIF>
      </TD>
    </TR>
  </TABLE>

  </BODY>
  </HTML>
```

Aside from the addition of the filter form and accompanying session variables, not too much has changed in this version of the template. Near the top, a new URL parameter called `ShowAll` is introduced and given a default value of `No`. Two lines later, a simple `<CFIF>` test is used to set the `RowsPerPage` variable to the value of `TotalRows` if `URL.ShowAll` is `True`. Therefore, if the page is accessed with `ShowAll=Yes` in the URL, the page displays all the records in one large group.

The only other difference is the addition of a few `<CFIF>` tests throughout, so the Back, Next, and page-by-page links are not shown when in Show All mode. The final results are shown in Figure 21.4.

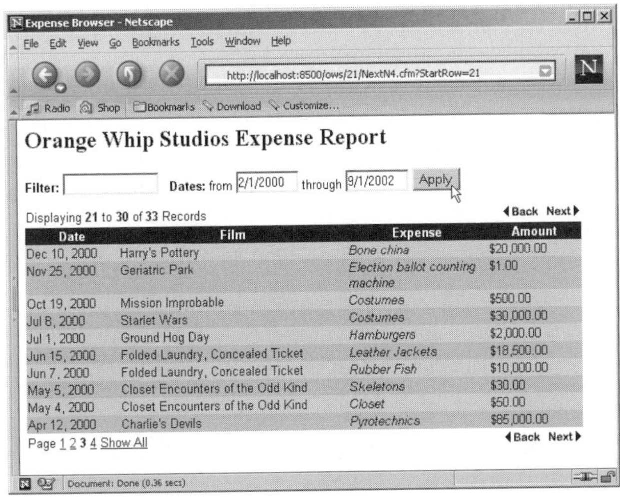

Figure 21.4

Users can apply filters and move back and next within the filtered results.

NOTE

Again, for now, don't worry about the fact that the query must be rerun each time the user clicks Next, Back, Show All, or one of the numbered page links. ColdFusion's query-caching feature can be used to ensure that your database is not hit too hard. See Chapter 22, "Improving Performance," for details.

Returning Page Output Right Away with <CFFLUSH>

By default, the output of all ColdFusion templates is automatically buffered by the server, which means the HTML for the entire page is sent to the browser at once, after all processing has been completed. In general, this isn't a problem. In fact, it enables ColdFusion to pull off a number of cool tricks internally (see the section "When You Can't Flush the Buffer," later in this chapter).

That said, in some instances you will want ColdFusion to return the HTML it generates right away, while the template is executing. The browser will be capable of receiving and displaying the HTML as it is generated. Meanwhile, ColdFusion can be finishing the remainder of the template. The act of telling ColdFusion to send back the generated output right away is called clearing the page buffer.

When to Clear the Buffer

The two basic situations in which you might want to clear the page buffer are as follows:

- **Large Pages.** If the template you are working on will output a lot of information, such as a long article all on one page, or some type of report that will have many records, you might want to flush the page buffer after every 1,000 characters of HTML have been generated. This causes the page to appear to display more quickly because the user can start reading the page before it has been completely received. It can also be easier on the ColdFusion server because the entire page will never have to be in its RAM at the same time.

- **Long-Running Pages**. Sometimes one of your templates might need to perform some type of operation that is inherently slow but doesn't necessarily output a large amount of HTML. For instance, if the user is placing an order (see Chapter 27, "Online Commerce"), verifying his credit card number could take 10 or 15 seconds. By clearing the page buffer several times during the order process, you can display a series of "please wait" messages so the user can see that something is actually happening.

In both of these situations, clearing the page buffer judiciously can make your applications appear to be more responsive because they give more feedback to the user sooner. That can mean a better user experience.

NOTE

In our opinion, you should not start clearing the page buffer regularly in all your ColdFusion templates. Just use it when you really think there would be a problem for ColdFusion to send back a particular page all at once. In particular, you should not place a `<CFFLUSH>` tag in your `Application.cfm` file. See the section "When You Can't Flush the Buffer," later in this chapter.

The Exception, Not the Rule

Most ColdFusion pages don't fall into either of the categories we've discussed. That is, most of your application's templates will not generate tons and tons of HTML code, and most of them will complete their executions normally in well under a second.

So, clearing the page buffer usually doesn't have much impact on the average ColdFusion template. And after the page buffer has been cleared, a number of features can no longer be used and will generate error messages (see the section "When You Can't Flush the Buffer," later in this chapter).

In short, the capability to flush the page buffer is helpful for dealing with certain special situations, as outlined previously. Unless the template you are working on will produce a large amount of output or will take a long time to process, just let ColdFusion buffer the page normally.

Introducing the `<CFFLUSH>` Tag

ColdFusion MX provides a tag called `<CFFLUSH>` that lets you clear the server's page buffer programmatically. As soon as ColdFusion encounters a `<CFFLUSH>` tag, it sends anything the template has generated so far to the browser. If the browser can, it displays that content to the user while ColdFusion continues working on the template.

The `<CFFLUSH>` tag takes just one attribute—`INTERVAL`—which is optional. You can use `<CFFLUSH>` without `INTERVAL`; that simply causes the page buffer to be flushed at the moment the tag is encountered. If you provide a number to `INTERVAL`, ColdFusion continues to flush the page cache whenever that many bytes have been generated by your template. So, `_INTERVAL="1000"` causes the page buffer to be cleared after every 1,000 bytes, which would usually mean after every 1,000th character or so.

NOTE

If you're not familiar with what a *byte* is, don't worry about it. Just think of the `INTERVAL` attribute as specifying a number of characters, rather than a number of bytes. Basically, each character in the normal English character set takes up a byte in a computer's memory.

Flushing the Output Buffer for Large Pages

Consider the Show All option shown in Listing 21.7, earlier in this chapter. Over time, hundreds or thousands of records could exist in the Expenses table, causing the Show All display to become extremely large. Therefore, it becomes a good candidate for the <CFFLUSH> tag.

For instance, near the top of Listing 21.7, you could change this code:

```
<!--- Show all on page if ShowAll is passed in URL   --->
<CFIF URL.ShowAll>
  <CFSET RowsPerPage = TotalRows>
</CFIF>
```

to this:

```
<!--- Show all on page if ShowAll is passed in URL   --->
<CFIF URL.ShowAll>
  <CFSET RowsPerPage = TotalRows>

  <!--- Flush the page buffer after every 5,000 characters --->
  <CFFLUSH INTERVAL="5000">
</CFIF>
```

Now, the page should begin to be sent to the user's browser in 5,000-character chunks, instead of all at once. The result is that the page should display more quickly when the Show All option is used. Note, however, that the difference might not be particularly noticeable until the Expenses table starts to get quite large. Even then, the difference will likely be more noticeable for modem users.

Flushing the Output Buffer for Long-Running Processes

You already have seen how <CFFLUSH> can help with templates that return large pages to the browser. You also can use <CFFLUSH> to help deal with situations in which a lengthy process needs to take place (such as verifying and charging a user's credit card or executing a particularly complex record-updating process).

Simulating a Long-Running Process

To keep the examples in this chapter simple, the following code snippet is used to simulate some type of time-consuming process. Because this code should never be used in an actual, real-world application, it is not explained in detail here. The basic idea is to create a <CFLOOP> that keeps looping over and over again until a specified number of seconds have passed.

For instance, this will force ColdFusion to spin its wheels for five seconds:

```
<CFSET InitialTime = Now()>
<CFLOOP CONDITION="DateDiff('s', InitialTime, Now()) LT 5"></CFLOOP>
```

See Appendix C for more information about the Now() and DateDiff() functions.

NOTE

The previous code snippet is a very inefficient way to cause ColdFusion to pause for a specified amount of time and should not be used in your own production code. It will cause ColdFusion to hog the CPU during the time period specified. It is used in this chapter only as a placeholder for whatever time-consuming process you might need to execute in your own templates.

Displaying a Please-Wait Type of Message

The FlushTest.cfm template shown in Listing 21.8 demonstrates how you can use the <CFFLUSH> tag to output page content before and after a lengthy process. Here, the user is asked to wait while an order is processed.

Listing 21.8 FlushTest.cfm—Displaying Messages Before and After a Lengthy Process

```
<!---
  Filename:      FlushTest.cfm
  Created by:    Nate Weiss (NMW)
  Purpose:       Demonstrates use of <CFFLUSH> for incremental page output
--->

<HTML>
<HEAD><TITLE>&lt;CFFLUSH&gt; Example</TITLE></HEAD>
<BODY>

  <!--- Initial Message --->
  <P><STRONG>Please Wait</STRONG><BR>
  We are processing your order.<BR>
  This process may take up to several minutes.<BR>
  Please do not Reload or leave this page until the process is complete.<BR>

  <!--- Flush the page output buffer --->
  <!--- The above code is sent to the browser right now --->
  <CFFLUSH>

  <!--- Time-consuming process goes here --->
  <!--- Here, ColdFusion is forced to wait for 5 seconds --->
  <!--- Do not use this CFLOOP technique in actual code! --->
  <CFSET InitialTime = Now()>
  <CFLOOP CONDITION="DateDiff('s', InitialTime, Now()) LT 5"></CFLOOP>

  <!--- Display "Success" message --->
  <P><STRONG>Thank You.</STRONG><BR>
  Your order has been processed.<BR>

</BODY>
</HTML>
```

As you can see, the code is very simple. First, a "please wait" message is displayed, using ordinary HTML tags. Then, the <CFFLUSH> tag is used to flush the page buffer, enabling the user to see the message immediately. Next, the time-consuming process is performed (you would replace the <CFLOOP> snippet with whatever is appropriate for your situation). The rest of the page can then be completed normally.

If you visit this template with your browser, you should see the "please wait" message alone on the page at first. After about five seconds, the thank-you message will appear. This gives your application a more responsive feel.

Displaying a Graphical Progress Meter

With the help of some simple JavaScript code, you can create a graphical progress meter while a particularly long process executes. The code shown in Listing 21.9 is similar to the previous listing, except that it assumes there are several steps in the time-consuming process the template needs to accomplish. When the page first appears, it shows an image of a progress indicator that reads `0%`. As each step of the lengthy process is completed, the image is updated so the indicator reads `25%`, `50%`, `75%`, and finally `100%`.

Listing 21.9 `FlushMeter.cfm`—Displaying a Progress Meter by Swapping Images via JavaScript

```
<!---
  Filename:     FlushMeter.cfm
  Created by:   Nate Weiss (NMW)
  Purpose:      Diplays a progress meter as a lengthy task is completed
--->


<HTML>
<HEAD><TITLE>&lt;CFFLUSH&gt; Example</TITLE></HEAD>
<BODY>

  <!--- Initial Message --->
  <P><STRONG>Please Wait</STRONG><BR>
  We are processing your order.<BR>

  <!--- Create the "Meter" image object --->
  <!--- Initially, it displays a blank GIF --->
  <IMG NAME="Meter" SRC="../images/PercentBlank.gif"
    WIDTH="200" HEIGHT="16" ALT="" BORDER="0">

  <!--- Flush the page buffer --->
  <CFFLUSH>

  <!--- Loop from 0 to 25 to 50 to 75 to 100 --->
  <CFLOOP FROM="0" TO="100" STEP="25" INDEX="i">
    <!--- Time-consuming process goes here --->
    <!--- Here, ColdFusion waits for 5 seconds as an example --->
    <!--- Do not use this technique in actual code! --->
    <CFSET InitialTime = Now()>
    <CFLOOP CONDITION="DateDiff('s', InitialTime, Now()) LT 2"></CFLOOP>

    <!--- Change the SRC attribute of the Meter image --->
    <CFOUTPUT>
      <SCRIPT LANGUAGE="JavaScript">
        document.images["Meter"].src = '../images/Percent#i#.gif';
      </SCRIPT>
    </CFOUTPUT>
    <CFFLUSH>
  </CFLOOP>

  <!--- Display "Success" message --->
  <P><STRONG>Thank You.</STRONG><BR>
  Your order has been processed.<BR>
</BODY>
</HTML>
```

First, an ordinary `<IMG>` tag is used to put the progress indicator on the page. The image's `SRC` attribute is set to the `PercentBlank.gif` image, which is just an empty, transparent (spacer) image that won't show up (except as empty space) on the page. The `<CFFLUSH>` tag is used to ensure that the browser receives the `<IMG>` tag code and displays the placeholder image right away.

Next, the `<CFLOOP>` tag is used to simulate some type of time-consuming, five-step process. Because of the `STEP` attribute, the value of `i` is `0` the first time through the loop, then `25`, then `50`, then `75`, and then `100`. Each time through the loop, a `<SCRIPT>` tag is output that contains JavaScript code to change the `src` property of the meter `<IMG>`, which causes the meter effect. The buffer is flushed with `<CFFLUSH>` after each `<SCRIPT>` tag, so the browser can receive and execute the script right away. The first time through the loop, the `<IMG>` is set to display the `Percent0.gif` file, then `Percent25.gif`, and so on. The end result is a simple progress meter that can help your users feel like they are still connected during whatever time-consuming processes they initiate. Figure 21.5 shows what the meter looks like in a browser.

NOTE

There isn't room here to fully cover the use of an image's `src` property to swap the images it displays. For more information, consult a JavaScript reference book, or the scripting reference section under HTML Reference in ColdFusion Studio's online help.

If the user's browser doesn't support JavaScript, the `<IMG>` tag will simply continue to display the `PercentBlank.gif` image, which the user won't even notice because it is invisible.

Figure 21.5

The `<CFFLUSH>` tag enables you to display progress indicators during lengthy processes.

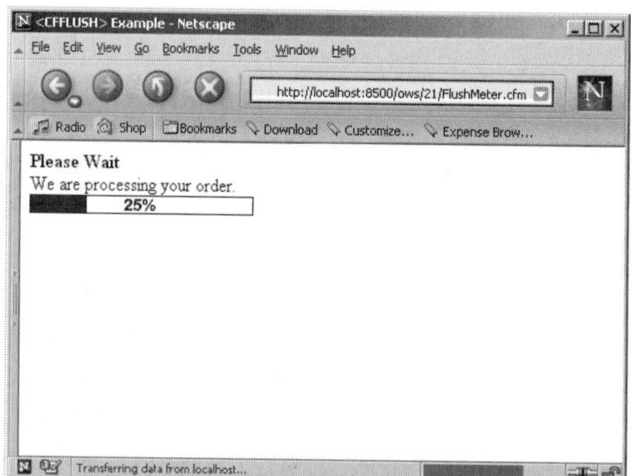

Flushing the Output Buffer Between Table Rows

In Listing 21.7, a Show All link was added to the next-n interface for browsing Orange Whip Studios' expenses. Depending on the number of rows in the `Expenses` table, that page could produce quite a bit of output. You might want to consider flushing the page output buffer after every few rows of data, so the user will start to see the rows while the page is being generated.

Listing 21.10 shows how you can add a `<CFFLUSH>` tag in the middle of an output loop, so that groups of rows are sent back to the browser right away. In this example, the rows are sent back in groups of five; in practice, you might want to choose a higher number of rows, such as 20 or 30.

Listing 21.10 NextN5.cfm—Sending Content to the Browser After Every Fifth Row of Data

```
<!---
  Filename:     NextN5.cfm
  Created by:   Nate Weiss (NMW)
  Purpose:      Displays Next N record-navigation interface
  Please Note  Includes NextNIncludeBackNext.cfm and NextNIncludePageLinks
--->

<!--- Retrieve expense records from database --->
<CFQUERY NAME="GetExp" DATASOURCE="#REQUEST.DataSource#">
  SELECT
    f.FilmID, f.MovieTitle,
    e.Description, e.ExpenseAmount, e.ExpenseDate
  FROM
    Expenses e INNER JOIN Films f
    ON e.FilmID = f.FilmID
  ORDER BY
    e.ExpenseDate DESC
</CFQUERY>


<!--- Number of rows to display per Next/Back page  --->
<CFSET RowsPerPage = 10>
<!--- What row to start at? Assume first by default --->
<CFPARAM NAME="URL.StartRow" DEFAULT="1" TYPE="numeric">
<!--- Allow for Show All parameter in the URL --->
<CFPARAM NAME="URL.ShowAll" TYPE="boolean" DEFAULT="No">

<!--- We know the total number of rows from query   --->
<CFSET TotalRows = GetExp.RecordCount>
<!--- Show all on page if ShowAll passed in URL   --->
<CFIF URL.ShowAll>
  <CFSET RowsPerPage = TotalRows>
</CFIF>
<!--- Last row is 10 rows past the starting row, or --->
<!--- total number of query rows, whichever is less --->
<CFSET EndRow = Min(URL.StartRow + RowsPerPage - 1, TotalRows)>
<!--- Next button goes to 1 past current end row  --->
<CFSET StartRowNext = EndRow + 1>
<!--- Back button goes back N rows from start row --->
<CFSET StartRowBack = URL.StartRow - RowsPerPage>


<!--- Page Title --->
<HTML>
<HEAD><TITLE>Expense Browser</TITLE></HEAD>
<BODY>
<CFOUTPUT><H2>#REQUEST.CompanyName# Expense Report</H2></CFOUTPUT>

<!--- simple style sheet for formatting --->
<STYLE>
  TH       {font-family:sans-serif;font-size:smaller;
            background:navy;color:white}
  TD       {font-family:sans-serif;font-size:smaller}
  TD.DataA {background:silver;color:black}
  TD.DataB {background:lightgrey;color:black}
```

Listing 21.10 (continued)

```
</STYLE>

<TABLE WIDTH="600" BORDER="0" CELLSPACING="0" CELLPADDING="1">
  <!--- Row at top of table, above column headers --->
  <TR>
    <TD WIDTH="500" COLSPAN="3">
      <!--- Message about which rows are being displayed --->
      <CFOUTPUT>
        Displaying <B>#URL.StartRow#</B> to <B>#EndRow#</B>
        of <B>#TotalRows#</B> Records<BR>
      </CFOUTPUT>
    </TD>
    <TD WIDTH="100" ALIGN="right">
      <CFIF NOT URL.ShowAll>
        <!--- Provide Next/Back links --->
        <CFINCLUDE TEMPLATE="NextNIncludeBackNext.cfm">
      </CFIF>
    </TD>
  </TR>

  <!--- Row for column headers --->
  <TR>
    <TH WIDTH="100">Date</TH>
    <TH WIDTH="250">Film</TH>
    <TH WIDTH="150">Expense</TH>
    <TH WIDTH="100">Amount</TH>
  </TR>

  <!--- For each query row that should be shown now --->
  <CFLOOP QUERY="GetExp" StartRow="#URL.StartRow#" ENDROW="#EndRow#">
    <!--- Use class "DataA" or "DataB" for alternate rows --->
    <CFSET Class = IIF(GetExp.CurrentRow MOD 2 EQ 0, "'DataA'", "'DataB'")>

    <!--- Actual data display --->
    <CFOUTPUT>
      <TR VALIGN="baseline">
        <TD CLASS="#Class#" WIDTH="100">#LSDateFormat(ExpenseDate)#</TD>
        <TD CLASS="#Class#" WIDTH="250">#MovieTitle#</TD>
        <TD CLASS="#Class#" WIDTH="150"><I>#Description#</I></TD>
        <TD CLASS="#Class#" WIDTH="100">#LSCurrencyFormat(ExpenseAmount)#</TD>
      </TR>
    </CFOUTPUT>

    <!--- If showing all records, flush the page buffer after every 5th row --->
    <CFIF URL.ShowAll>
      <CFIF GetExp.CurrentRow MOD 5 EQ 0>
        <!--- End the current table --->
        </TABLE>
        <!--- Flush the page buffer --->
        <CFFLUSH>
        <!--- Start a new table --->
        <TABLE WIDTH="600" BORDER="0" CELLSPACING="0" CELLPADDING="1">
        <!--- Simulate a time-intensive process --->
        <CFSET InitialTime = Now()>
        <CFLOOP CONDITION="DateDiff('s', InitialTime, Now()) LT 1"></CFLOOP>
```

Listing 21.10 (continued)

```
        </CFIF>
      </CFIF>

    </CFLOOP>

    <!--- Row at bottom of table, after rows of data --->
    <TR>
      <TD WIDTH="500" COLSPAN="3">
        <CFIF NOT URL.ShowAll AND TotalRows GT RowsPerPage>
          <!--- Shortcut links for "Pages" of search results --->
          Page <CFINCLUDE TEMPLATE="NextNIncludePageLinks.cfm">
          <!--- Show All Link --->
          <CFOUTPUT>
            <A HREF="#CGI.SCRIPT_NAME#?ShowAll=Yes">Show All</A>
          </CFOUTPUT>
        </CFIF>
      </TD>
      <TD WIDTH="100" ALIGN="right">
        <CFIF NOT URL.ShowAll>
          <!--- Provide Next/Back links --->
          <CFINCLUDE TEMPLATE="NextNIncludeBackNext.cfm">
        </CFIF>
      </TD>
    </TR>
  </TABLE>


  </BODY>
  </HTML>
```

This code listing is mostly unchanged from an earlier version (refer to Listing 21.4). The only significant change is the addition of the <CFIF> block at the end of the <CFLOOP> block. The code in this block executes only if the user has clicked the Show All link, and only if the current row number is evenly divisible by 5 (that is, every fifth row).

If both of these conditions apply, the current <TABLE> tag (the one opened near the top of the listing) is ended with a closing </TABLE> tag. The page buffer is then flushed using <CFFLUSH>, and a new table is started with an opening <TABLE> tag that matches the one from the top of the listing. In other words, the expense records are shown as a series of five-row tables that are each sent to the browser individually, rather than as one long table that gets sent to the browser at once. Because each of these mini tables is complete, with beginning and ending <TABLE> tags, the browser can display them as it receives them (most browsers can't properly render a table until the closing </TABLE> tag has been encountered).

After the page buffer is cleared, this template waits for one second, using the same time-delay technique that was used in the progress meter example (refer to Listing 21.9). Again, you should never use this technique in your actual code templates. It is used here only as a simple way of causing ColdFusion to pause for a moment, so you can see the effect of the page flushes.

If you visit Listing 21.10 with your Web browser and click the Show All link, you will see that the rows of data are presented to you in small groups, with a one-second pause between each group.

This shows that the buffer is being cleared, and that a user accessing a very long page over a slow connection would at least be able to begin viewing records before the entire page had been received.

NOTE

Of course, in practice, you wouldn't have the time-delay loop at all. It is included here only to make the effect easier to see while developing.

When You Can't Flush the Buffer

This section has introduced the <CFFLUSH> tag and pointed out several situations in which it can be helpful. However, because it causes the content your templates generate to be sent to the browser in pieces—rather than the whole page at once—certain ColdFusion tags and features that depend on being capable of manipulating the page as a whole cannot be used after a <CFFLUSH> tag.

Restrictions on Cookie Use

After the <CFFLUSH> tag has been used on a page, telling ColdFusion to set a cookie in the browser is no longer possible. This is because cookies are set by sending special HTTP headers to the browser, and all HTTP headers must be sent to the browser before any actual HTML content is. So, after a <CFFLUSH> tag has been used, sending additional headers to the browser is no longer possible, which in turn means that it's too late for ColdFusion to set any cookies.

If you really need to set a cookie after a <CFFLUSH>, you can use JavaScript to do it. For your convenience, a custom tag called <CF_SetCookieViaJS> has been included on the CD-ROM for this book. The custom tag supports three attributes—COOKIENAME, COOKIEVALUE, and EXPIRES—which correspond to the NAME, VALUE, and EXPIRES attributes for the regular <CFCOOKIE> tag. The EXPIRES attribute is optional.

So, instead of

```
<CFCOOKIE
  NAME="MyCookie"
  VALUE="My Value">
```

You would use

```
<CF_SetCookieViaJS
  CookieName="MyCookie"
  CookieValue="My Value">
```

Please note that the cookie will be set only if the user's browser supports JavaScript and if JavaScript has not been disabled.

NOTE

This example custom tag is not supported and is merely presented as a work-around for situations in which you must set a cookie after a <CFFLUSH> tag. Whenever possible, it is recommended that you set cookies using the usual <CFCOOKIE> and <CFSET> methods explained in Chapter 17.

NOTE

If you are somewhat familiar with JavaScript, you could study the `SetCookieViaJS.cfm` custom tag template (on the CD-ROM) as an example of how custom tags can be used to generate JavaScript code.

NOTE

The `PATH`, `SECURE`, and `DOMAIN` attributes from `<CFCOOKIE>` are not supported by this custom tag, but they could easily be added by editing the custom tag template. See Chapter 20 for information about building custom tags.

Restrictions on <CFLOCATION>

After a `<CFFLUSH>` tag has been encountered, you can no longer use the `<CFLOCATION>` tag to redirect the user to another page. This is because `<CFLOCATION>` works by sending a redirect header back to the browser. After the first `<CFFLUSH>` tag has been encountered on a page, the page's headers have already been sent to the browser; thus, it is too late to redirect the browser to another page using the usual methods provided by HTTP alone.

There are a few work-arounds to this problem. Both rely on the browser to interpret your document in a certain way, and they are not part of the standard HTTP protocol. That said, these methods should work fine with most browsers.

The first work-around is to include a `<META>` tag in the document, with an `HTTP-EQUIV` attribute set to `Refresh`. Then, provide the URL for the next page in the `CONTENT` attribute, as shown in the following. Most browsers interpret this as an instruction to go to the specified page as soon as the tag is encountered.

So, instead of this:

```
<CFLOCATION URL="MyNextPage.cfm">
```

you would use this:

```
<META HTTP-EQUIV="Refresh" CONTENT="0; URL=MyNextPage.cfm">
```

TIP

If you want the redirect to occur after five seconds rather than right away, you could change the `0` in the previous snippet to `5`. Consult an HTML reference for more information about this use of the `<META>` tag.

Another work-around is to use JavaScript. The following snippet could also be used in place of the `<CFLOCATION>` shown previously. However, if JavaScript is disabled or not supported by the client, nothing will happen. See the scripting reference in Dreamweaver MX or HomeSite+ for more information about this use of the `document.location` object:

```
<SCRIPT LANGUAGE="JavaScript">
<!--
  document.location.href ="MyNextPage.cfm";
//-->
</SCRIPT>
```

Other Restrictions

Several other tags cannot be used after a `<CFFLUSH>` tag has been encountered, for the same basic reasons the `<CFCOOKIE>` and `<CFLOCATION>` tags cannot be used (they all need to send special HTTP headers to the browser before your HTML code begins).

These tags cannot be used after a `<CFFLUSH>`:

- `<CFCONTENT>`
- `<<CFCOOKIE>`
- `<<CFFORM>`
- `<<CFHEADER>`
- `<<CFHTMLHEAD>`
- `<<CFLOCATION>`

CHAPTER 22

Improving Performance

IN THIS CHAPTER

Options in the ColdFusion Administrator

This chapter discusses a number of ways to improve the performance of your ColdFusion templates, some of which are a bit involved. Before getting into the specific solutions, you should be aware of a number of serverwide options provided by the ColdFusion Administrator that can affect the overall performance of your applications.

The Administrator options most likely to have a direct effect on performance are:

- **Limit Simultaneous Requests To.** This option on the Settings page of the Administrator should be set to a fairly low number (but not as low as 1) for best performance. The best value for your application will vary depending on how heavily it is used and how much processing is done per page request.
- **Enable Whitespace Management.** This option on the Settings page should be enabled for best performance.
- **Template Cache Size.** Ideally, this option on the Caching page should be set to a number greater than (or at least close to) the number of ColdFusion templates that get used on a regular basis.
- **Trusted Cache.** This option on the Caching page should be enabled for best performance, but only when your application has moved into a production mode (after you have completely finished writing your code).
- **Maintain Connections.** This option for each of your data sources should be enabled for best performance.

- **Limit Connections.** In general, if you choose Maintain Connections (above), this option should also be enabled for each of your data sources, and you should provide a sensible number for the Restrict Connections To field next to the Limit Connections check box. As a rough guide, consider starting with a value that is approximately the same as the number you provided for Limit Simultaneous Requests To, above.

You are encouraged to consult Chapter 28, "ColdFusion Server Configuration," for details on each of these options.

Improving Query Performance with Caching

Nearly all ColdFusion applications have a database at their heart, and most ColdFusion templates contain at least one `<CFQUERY>` or other database interaction. In fact, depending on the type of application you are building, your ColdFusion templates might be solely about getting information in and out of a database. In such a situation, ColdFusion is basically behaving as database middleware, sitting between your database and your Web server.

Because database access is such an integral part of ColdFusion development, the server provides a number of features to help you improve the performance of your database queries. This section helps you understand which options are available to you and how to make the most of them.

In particular, this section discusses the following:

- Query caching, which cuts down on the amount of interaction between your database and ColdFusion. This can improve performance dramatically.
- Helping ColdFusion deal with larger query results via the `BLOCKFACTOR` attribute.

NOTE

It used to be easier to think of ColdFusion as simply a database middleware application. In fact, very early versions of ColdFusion were so database centric that what we now call CFML was known as DBML, and tags such as `<CFOUTPUT>` and `<CFIF>` were known as `<DBOUTPUT>` and `<DBIF>`. With the addition of more services such as email, HTTP, LDAP, graphing, file manipulation, Flash and Web Services integration, ColdFusion has since expanded and matured into something much more interesting: a Web application server.

Understanding Query Caching

To improve performance, ColdFusion provides a wonderful feature called query caching. Basically, query caching allows ColdFusion to keep frequently used query results in its internal memory, rather than retrieving the results from the database over and over again.

You tell ColdFusion to cache a query by adding a `CACHEDWITHIN` or `CACHEDAFTER` attribute to the `<CFQUERY>` tag. If one of your templates is visited often and contains a query that will not return different results each time it runs, you can usually give the page an instant performance boost by simply using one of these two special attributes. Table 22.1 explains what each of the attributes does.

Table 22.1 <CFQUERY> Attributes Relevant for Query Caching

ATTRIBUTE	PURPOSE
CACHEDWITHIN	Optional. Tells ColdFusion to cache the query results for a period of time, which you can specify in days, hours, minutes, or seconds. You specify the time period using the CreateTimeSpan() function.
CACHEDAFTER	Optional. Tells ColdFusion to cache the query results based on a particular date and time. This attribute is generally less useful in real-world applications than CACHEDWITHIN. If you know that your database will be updated at a certain moment in time, perhaps after some type of external batch process, you can specify that date and time (as a ColdFusion date value) here.

Query caching is really easy to use. Say you use the following query in one of your ColdFusion templates:

```
<CFQUERY NAME="GetFilms" DATASOURCE="ows">
  SELECT * FROM Films
</CFQUERY>
```

Assuming that the data in the Films table doesn't change very often, it would probably be sufficient to only query the database occasionally, rather than with every page request. For instance, you might decide that the database really only needs to be checked for new or changed data every 15 minutes. Within each 15-minute period, the data from a previous query can just be reused. To get this effect, simply add a CACHEDWITHIN attribute that uses CreateTimeSpan() to specify a 15-minute interval, like this:

```
<CFQUERY NAME="GetFilms" DATASOURCE="ows"
  CACHEDWITHIN="#CreateTimeSpan(0,0,15,0)#">
  SELECT * FROM Films
</CFQUERY>
```

➜ See Appendix C, "ColdFusion Function Reference," for information about the CreateTimeSpan() function.

That's all you have to do. The first time the query runs, ColdFusion interacts with the database normally and retrieves the film records. But instead of discarding the records when the page request is finished—as it would do normally—ColdFusion stores the query results in the server's RAM. The next time the template is visited, ColdFusion uses the records in its memory instead of contacting the database again. It continues to do so for 15 minutes after the first query ran (or until the ColdFusion server is restarted). The next time the template is visited, the original records are flushed from the server's RAM and replaced with new records, retrieved afresh from the database.

There's more. Queries aren't cached on a per-page basis. They are cached on a serverwide basis. If two <CFQUERY> tags on two different pages specify exactly the same SQL code, DATASOURCE, and NAME, they will share the same cache. That is, the first time either page is accessed, the database is contacted and the records are retrieved. Then, for the next 15 minutes (or whatever interval you specify), a visit to either page will use the cached copy of the query results.

NOTE

If the two <CFQUERY> tags specify USERNAME, PASSWORD, DBTYPE, DBSERVER, or DBNAME attributes, all these attributes must be the same as well. If not, the two <CFQUERY> tags will be cached independently of one another (each will operate on its own 15-minute cycle).

NOTE

The SQL statements in the two `<CFQUERY>` tags must be exactly the same, even considering whitespace such as tabs, indenting, and spaces. If they're not the same, the two queries will be cached independently.

Clearly, if a query is at all time-consuming, the performance benefits can be tremendous. Every template that uses the cached query will be sped up. Plus, if the database and ColdFusion are on different machines, using query caching will likely cut down dramatically on network traffic. This tends to improve performance as well, depending on how your local network is configured.

NOTE

Of course, one possible disadvantage to caching a query is that changes to the actual data in the database will not show up in the cached version of the query, because the database is not actually being contacted. Any new records (or updates or deletes) will show up only after the cache interval has expired. For details and solutions, see the section "Refreshing a Cached Query Programmatically," later in this chapter.

Using Cached Queries

One obvious situation in which ColdFusion's query caching feature can be of great benefit is when you're building a Next N type of record-browsing interface, such as the one presented in Chapter 21, "Improving the User Experience."

Listing 22.1 takes the `NextN4.cfm` template from Listing 23.7 of Chapter 21 and adds a `CACHEDWITHIN` attribute to the `<CFQUERY>` at the top of the template. Now ColdFusion does not need to keep rerunning the query as the user browses through the pages of records.

Listing 22.1 `NextNCached.cfm`—Adding the `CACHEDWITHIN` Attribute to Speed Up Record Browsing

```
<!---
  Filename:      NextNCached.cfm
  Created by:    Nate Weiss (NMW)
  Purpose:       Displays Next N record-navigation interface
  Please Note   Includes NextNIncludeBackNext.cfm and NextNIncludePageLinks.cfm
--->

<!--- Maintain ExpenseReport filtering variables at session level --->
<CFPARAM NAME="SESSION.ExpenseReport.UserFilter" TYPE="string" DEFAULT="">
<CFPARAM NAME="SESSION.ExpenseReport.DateFrom" TYPE="string" DEFAULT="">
<CFPARAM NAME="SESSION.ExpenseReport.DateThru" TYPE="string" DEFAULT="">

<!--- If the user is submitting the "filter" form, --->
<!--- we'll make their submission be the filter for rest of session --->
<CFIF IsDefined("FORM.UserFilter")>
  <CFSET SESSION.ExpenseReport.UserFilter = FORM.UserFilter>
  <CFSET SESSION.ExpenseReport.DateFrom   = FORM.DateFrom>
  <CFSET SESSION.ExpenseReport.DateThru   = FORM.DateThru>
</CFIF>

<!--- Retrieve expense records from database --->
<CFQUERY NAME="GetExp" DATASOURCE="#REQUEST.DataSource#"
  CACHEDWITHIN="#CreateTimeSpan(0,0,15,0)#">
  SELECT
    f.FilmID, f.MovieTitle,
```

Listing 22.1 (continued)

```
    e.Description, e.ExpenseAmount, e.ExpenseDate
  FROM
    Expenses e INNER JOIN Films f
    ON e.FilmID = f.FilmID
  WHERE
    0=0
  <!--- If the user provided a filter string, --->
  <!--- show only matching films and/or expenses --->
  <CFIF SESSION.ExpenseReport.UserFilter IS NOT "">
    AND (f.MovieTitle LIKE '%#SESSION.ExpenseReport.UserFilter#%' OR
         e.Description LIKE '%#SESSION.ExpenseReport.UserFilter#%')
  </CFIF>
  <!--- Also filter on From date, if provided --->
  <CFIF IsDate(SESSION.ExpenseReport.DateFrom)>
    AND e.ExpenseDate >= #CreateODBCDate(SESSION.ExpenseReport.DateFrom)#
  </CFIF>
  <!--- Also filter on Through date, if provided --->
  <CFIF IsDate(SESSION.ExpenseReport.DateThru)>
    AND e.ExpenseDate <= #CreateODBCDate(SESSION.ExpenseReport.DateThru)#
  </CFIF>
  ORDER BY
    e.ExpenseDate DESC
</CFQUERY>


<!--- Number of rows to display per Next/Back page  --->
<CFSET RowsPerPage = 10>
<!--- What row to start at? Assume first by default --->
<CFPARAM NAME="URL.StartRow" DEFAULT="1" TYPE="numeric">
<!--- Allow for Show All parameter in the URL --->
<CFPARAM NAME="URL.ShowAll" TYPE="boolean" DEFAULT="No">

<!--- We know the total number of rows from query   --->
<CFSET TotalRows = GetExp.RecordCount>
<!--- Show all on page if ShowAll passed in URL   --->
<CFIF URL.ShowAll>
  <CFSET RowsPerPage = TotalRows>
</CFIF>
<!--- Last row is 10 rows past the starting row, or --->
<!--- total number of query rows, whichever is less --->
<CFSET EndRow = Min(URL.StartRow + RowsPerPage - 1, TotalRows)>
<!--- Next button goes to 1 past current end row  --->
<CFSET StartRowNext = EndRow + 1>
<!--- Back button goes back N rows from start row --->
<CFSET StartRowBack = URL.StartRow - RowsPerPage>


<!--- Page Title --->
<HTML>
<HEAD><TITLE>Expense Browser</TITLE></HEAD>
<BODY>
<CFOUTPUT><H2>#REQUEST.CompanyName# Expense Report</H2></CFOUTPUT>

<!--- Simple style sheet for formatting --->
<STYLE>
```

Listing 22.1 (continued)

```
    FORM      {font-family:sans-serif;font-size:smaller;}
    TH        {font-family:sans-serif;font-size:smaller;
               background:navy;color:white}
    TD        {font-family:sans-serif;font-size:smaller}
    TD.DataA {background:silver;color:black}
    TD.DataB {background:lightgrey;color:black}
  </STYLE>


  <!--- Simple form to allow user to filter results --->
  <CFFORM ACTION="#CGI.SCRIPT_NAME#" METHOD="POST">
    <!--- Filter string --->
    <B>Filter:</B>
    <CFINPUT
      TYPE="Text"
      NAME="UserFilter"
      VALUE="#SESSION.ExpenseReport.UserFilter#"
      SIZE="15">

    <!--- From date --->
     
    <B>Dates:</B> from
    <CFINPUT
      TYPE="Text"
      NAME="DateFrom"
      VALUE="#SESSION.ExpenseReport.DateFrom#"
      SIZE="9"
      VALIDATE="date"
      MESSAGE="Please enter a valid date, or leave it blank.">

    <!--- Through date --->
    through
    <CFINPUT
      TYPE="Text"
      NAME="DateThru"
      VALUE="#SESSION.ExpenseReport.DateThru#"
      SIZE="9"
      VALIDATE="date"
      MESSAGE="Please enter a valid date, or leave it blank.">

    <!--- Submit button to activate/change/clear filter --->
    <INPUT
      TYPE="Submit"
      VALUE="Apply">
  </CFFORM>


  <TABLE WIDTH="600" BORDER="0" CELLSPACING="0" CELLPADDING="1">
    <!--- Row at top of table, above column headers --->
    <TR>
      <TD WIDTH="500" COLSPAN="3">
        <!--- Message about which rows are being displayed --->
        <CFOUTPUT>
          Displaying <B>#URL.StartRow#</B> to <B>#EndRow#</B>
          of <B>#TotalRows#</B> Records<BR>
```

Listing 22.1 (continued)

```
      </CFOUTPUT>
    </TD>
    <TD WIDTH="100" ALIGN="right">
      <CFIF NOT URL.ShowAll>
        <!--- Provide Next/Back links --->
        <CFINCLUDE TEMPLATE="NextNIncludeBackNext.cfm">
      </CFIF>
    </TD>
  </TR>

  <!--- Row for column headers --->
  <TR>
    <TH WIDTH="100">Date</TH>
    <TH WIDTH="250">Film</TH>
    <TH WIDTH="150">Expense</TH>
    <TH WIDTH="100">Amount</TH>
  </TR>

  <!--- For each query row that should be shown now --->
  <CFLOOP QUERY="GetExp" StartRow="#URL.StartRow#" ENDROW="#EndRow#">
    <!--- Use class "DataA" or "DataB" for alternate rows --->
    <CFSET Class = IIF(GetExp.CurrentRow MOD 2 EQ 0, "'DataA'", "'DataB'")>

    <CFOUTPUT>
      <TR VALIGN="baseline">
        <TD CLASS="#Class#" WIDTH="100">#LSDateFormat(ExpenseDate)#</TD>
        <TD CLASS="#Class#" WIDTH="250">#MovieTitle#</TD>
        <TD CLASS="#Class#" WIDTH="150"><I>#Description#</I></TD>
        <TD CLASS="#Class#" WIDTH="100">#LSCurrencyFormat(ExpenseAmount)#</TD>
      </TR>
    </CFOUTPUT>
  </CFLOOP>

  <!--- Row at bottom of table, after rows of data --->
  <TR>
    <TD WIDTH="500" COLSPAN="3">
      <CFIF NOT URL.ShowAll AND TotalRows GT RowsPerPage>
        <!--- Shortcut links for "Pages" of search results --->
        Page <CFINCLUDE TEMPLATE="NextNIncludePageLinks.cfm">
        <!--- Show All link --->
        <CFOUTPUT>
          <A HREF="#CGI.SCRIPT_NAME#?&ShowAll=Yes">Show All</A>
        </CFOUTPUT>
      </CFIF>
    </TD>
    <TD WIDTH="100" ALIGN="right">
      <CFIF NOT URL.ShowAll>
        <!--- Provide Next/Back links --->
        <CFINCLUDE TEMPLATE="NextNIncludeBackNext.cfm">
      </CFIF>
    </TD>
  </TR>
</TABLE>

</BODY>
</HTML>
```

If you want, you can watch which queries ColdFusion is actually caching by turning on the Database Activity option in the Debugging Settings page of the ColdFusion Administrator. Whenever a query is returned from the cache, the execution time will be reported as `0ms`, accompanied by the words `Cached Query`, as shown in Figure 22.1. When the cache timeout expires, you will see the execution time reappear in milliseconds, as it does normally.

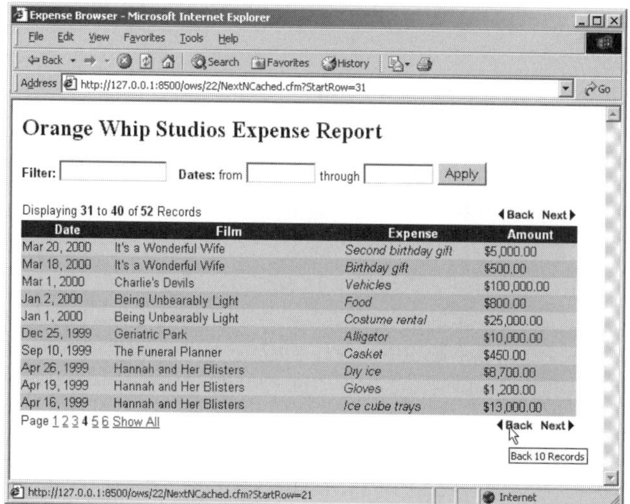

Figure 22.1

Cached queries are fetched directly from ColdFusion's internal memory, which can greatly improve performance.

Refreshing Cached Queries Programmatically

Query caching is used most frequently for queries that do not change often over time, or in situations where it is acceptable for your application to show information that might be slightly out of date. However, you might run into situations in which you want a query cached for several hours at a time (because the underlying data hardly ever changes), but where it is very important for any changes that *do* get made to the database to be reflected right away.

Flushing A Specific Cached Query After an Update

ColdFusion doesn't provide a specific attribute for flushing a particular cached query, but you can achieve the same effect by including a `<CFQUERY>` tag with a negative `CACHEDWITHIN` value right after a relevant change is made to the database. This will force ColdFusion to contact the database and fetch the updated records. From that point on, the updated version of the query results will be what is shared with other pages that use the same query.

NOTE

Of course, this technique is not effective if the database is being updated via some application other than ColdFusion. Your ColdFusion application needs to be aware of when to discard a cached version of a query.

For instance, say you are using the following cached query in your code:

```
<CFQUERY NAME="GetFilms" DATASOURCE="ows"
  CACHEDWITHIN="#CreateTimeSpan(0,3,0,0)#">
  SELECT * FROM Films
</CFQUERY>
```

Left to its own devices, this query's cache will only be refreshed every three hours. Now say that some other page updates one of the film records, perhaps using a `<CFUPDATE>` tag, like so:

```
<CFUPDATE DATASOURCE="ows" TABLENAME="Films">
```

Again, left to its own devices, the `SELECT` query will continue to show the cached records until the three-hour timeout expires. Only then will the changes that the `<CFUPDATE>` made be fetched from the database. However, you could force the updated records into the cache by placing the following query right after the `<CFUPDATE>`:

```
<CFQUERY NAME="GetFilms" DATASOURCE="ows"
  CACHEDWITHIN="#CreateTimeSpan(0,0,0,-1)#">
  SELECT * FROM Films
</CFQUERY>
```

Now, when the first `SELECT` query is next executed, it will read the updated records from the cache. Your application will always show the most current version of the records, even though it is usually reading the records from the query cache.

NOTE

The SQL statements in the two `<CFQUERY>` tags (the one that uses the `CACHEDWITHIN` of three hours and the one that uses the negative `CACHEDWITHIN` value) must be exactly the same, even considering indenting and other whitespace. The `NAME` and `DATASOURCE` attributes must also be identical, as well as any `USERNAME`, `PASSWORD`, `DBTYPE`, `DBSERVER`, or `DBNAME` attributes you might be providing. If not, ColdFusion will consider the queries separate for caching purposes, which means that the second query will not have the desired effect of refreshing the first.

Flushing All Cached Queries

As you just learned, you can use a negative value for a specific query's `CACHEDWITHIN` attribute to make sure a particular query gets removed from the query cache. This method is simple and straightforward, but you may also find that there are situations in which you would like to discard all cached query records. One way to do this is to simply restart the ColdFusion MX application server.

You can also refresh all cached queries programmatically, using the `<CFOBJECTCACHE>` tag. At this time, `<CFOBJECTCACHE>` takes one attribute, `ACTION`, which must always be set to `Clear`. When ColdFusion encounters this tag in your code, all cached queries are discarded. The next time each `<CFQUERY>` tag is encountered for the first time, it will re-contact the database and retrieve the current data from your tables.

Here is how the tag would look in your code:

```
<!--- Discard all cached queries --->
<CFOBJECTCACHE
  ACTION="Clear">
```

NOTE

This tag was present but undocumented in previous versions of ColdFusion. As of ColdFusion MX, it is a documented and supported part of the product.

Limiting the Number of Cached Queries

To ensure that your cached queries don't take up crippling amounts of the server's RAM, ColdFusion imposes a serverwide limit on the number of queries that can be cached at any given time. By default, the limit is set to 100 cached queries. If a new `<CFQUERY>` tag that uses `CACHEDWITHIN` or `CACHEDAFTER` is encountered after 100 queries are already in the cache, the oldest query is dropped from the cache and replaced with the new query.

You can increase this limit by editing the Limit the Maximum Number of Cached Queries on the Server field in the Caching page of the ColdFusion Administrator. Keep in mind that the final SQL code determines how a query is cached. If you use a ColdFusion variable in the SQL portion of a `<CFQUERY>` tag, and the query is run with 10 different variable values during a given period, that will count as 10 queries toward the limit of 100. See Chapter 28 for details about using the ColdFusion Administrator.

Controlling How Many Records Are Fetched at Once

NOTE

For ColdFusion MX, the `BLOCKFACTOR` attribute discussed in this section applies only to the Oracle native database drivers that ship with ColdFusion. If you are not using Oracle, you can skip this section. Future versions of ColdFusion may support `BLOCKFACTOR` with other types of databases.

Normally, ColdFusion retrieves each record from your database individually. That said, if you are using Oracle and know a query will return more than a few records, you can speed up ColdFusion a bit by giving it a hint about how many records are likely to be returned. To do so, provide a `BLOCKFACTOR` attribute in your `<CFQUERY>` tags. `BLOCKFACTOR` should be a reasonable guess as to how many records the query might return.

However, you should not provide a `BLOCKFACTOR` value that is less than the number of records the query returns. If you do, your database driver will tell ColdFusion that the specified `BLOCKFACTOR` is invalid, and ColdFusion will try again—this time repeatedly subtracting 1 from the value you supplied until `BLOCKFACTOR` does not exceed the total number of records. This could slow down your query. Unfortunately, ColdFusion can't determine the appropriate `BLOCKFACTOR` automatically.

For instance, if you know that the `Films` table will contain 25 or more records for the foreseeable future, you should provide a `BLOCKFACTOR` value of `25`, like this:

```
<CFQUERY NAME="GetFilms" DATASOURCE="ows" BLOCKFACTOR="25">
  SELECT * FROM Films
</CFQUERY>
```

The larger the number of records involved, the more effect `BLOCKFACTOR` is likely to have on overall query performance. Don't obsess about getting `BLOCKFACTOR` exactly right. Just think of it as a way to let ColdFusion know whether to expect a large number of records or just one or two. At the very least, consider providing a `BLOCKFACTOR="100"` attribute for all queries that will return hundreds or thousands of records.

NOTE

If you are using stored procedures with Oracle, it's worth noting that the <CFSTOREDPROC> tag also supports the BLOCKFACTOR attribute. See Chapter 30, "Working with Stored Procedures," for details.

NOTE

Currently, the maximum value BLOCKFACTOR allows is 100. If a query might return hundreds or thousands of records, you should still go ahead and set BLOCKFACTOR="100". Because ColdFusion will be retrieving the records in 100-record chunks, this can often improve performance rather dramatically.

Caching Page Output

You already have learned that ColdFusion allows you to cache query results. It also provides a page caching feature, which enables you to cache the complete page HTML each of your templates generates. Similar to query caching, ColdFusion's page caching feature is designed to improve the overall performance of your Web pages.

The idea is simple. If you have certain ColdFusion templates that can be somewhat time-consuming or that may get hit fairly often, you can tell ColdFusion to cache them for a specified period of time. This can have a huge effect on overall application performance. The caching can take place on the browser machine, on the server machine, or on both.

Introducing the <CFCACHE> Tag

If you want ColdFusion to cache a page, just place the <CFCACHE> tag at the top of the template, before any other CFML or HTML tags. The most important attribute for the <CFCACHE> tag is the ACTION attribute, which tells ColdFusion whether you want the page cached on the client machine, on the ColdFusion server machine, or on both.

Client-Side Page Caching

The <CFCACHE> tag can provide two types of caching: client-side page caching and server-side page caching. Both are of great benefit. First you will learn about client-side page caching, which is of particular relevance when you're putting together personalized pages that might take a bit of time to display. Then you will learn about server-side page caching, which is most useful for putting together nonpersonalized pages that get hit very often.

Finally, you will learn about how to use client-side and server-side page caching together, usually the best option.

Background

All modern Web browsers provide some type of internal page-caching mechanism. As you use your Web browser to visit sites, it makes local copies of the HTML for each page, along with local copies of any images or other media files the pages contain. If you go back to that same page later, the browser can show you the local copies of the files, rather than refetching them from the Web server.

Your browser also provides a few settings you can use to control where the cached files are kept and how large the collection of all cached files can get. If it weren't for your browser's cache, most casual Web browsing would be much slower than it is.

Normally, the browser just relies on these settings to determine whether to display a page from its local cache or to recontact the Web server. If you haven't adjusted any of these settings yourself, your own browser is probably set to use the cached copy of a page until you close the browser. When you reopen the browser and visit that same page, the browser recontacts the Web server and fetches the page afresh.

NOTE

To view the current cache settings for a Netscape browser, choose Edit > Preferences > Advanced > Cache. For Internet Explorer, choose Internet Options from the Tools menu, and then click the Settings button under Temporary Internet Files.

Gaining More Control

The `<CFCACHE>` tag gives you programmatic control over when the browser should use its local, cached copy to display a page to the user. You use the `TIMEOUT` attribute to tell ColdFusion how old the browser's cached version of the page can be before ColdFusion should refetch it from the server. If the browser fetched its local copy of the page after the date you specify, it uses the local copy to show the page to the user. If not, it visits the template normally. Table 22.2 summarizes the attributes relevant for this use of the `<CFCACHE>`.

Table 22.2 `<CFCACHE>` Tag Attributes Relevant for Client-Side Caching

ATTRIBUTE	PURPOSE
ACTION	Must be set to `ClientCache` to use client-side caching only. You can also set this attribute to several other values to enable server-side caching, which the next section describes. You can also set it to `CACHE`, which uses both client-side and server-side mechanisms (see the section "ColdFusion-Optimized Caching," later in this chapter).
TIMESPAN	The period of time that you would like the page to remain cached by the user's browser. You can specify this period using any combination of days, hours, minutes, or seconds, by providing a value returned by the `CreateTimeSpan()` function. In other words, this attribute works just like the `CACHEDWITHIN` attribute for `<CFQUERY>` that you learned about earlier in this chapter.

For instance, if you wanted the browser to feel free to use its local copy of a page for 6 hours at a time, you would include the following at the top of your ColdFusion template:

```
<!--- Let browser use a cached version of --->
<!--- this page, from up to six hours ago --->
<CFCACHE
  ACTION="ClientCache"
  TIMESPAN="#CreateTimeSpan(0, 6, 0, 0)#">
```

TIP

If you wanted to cache all pages in an application, you could simply place the `<CFCACHE>` tag at the top of your `Application.cfm` file. That would cause all page requests to be cached (except for form submissions, which never are).

The first time a user visits the page, ColdFusion processes the template normally and sends the generated page back to the browser. The browser then stores the page in its local cache. The next time the user visits the same page, the browser quickly contacts the server, providing the server with the exact date and time that the page was visited the first time (that is, the date and time the local copy was saved). If the browser tells the server that its local copy is not older than the date specified in `TIMEOUT`, the server then tells the browser to show the local copy to the user and immediately stop processing the rest of your template. Otherwise, ColdFusion tells the browser that the local copy is now out of date; processes the rest of your code normally; and returns the newly generated version to the browser, where it can be cached locally for the next 6 hours (or whatever interval you specify).

What It Means

In other words, using `<CFCACHE>`, you can keep the amount of interaction between the browser and server to a minimum. Yes, the browser will contact the Web server, and ColdFusion will begin executing your template code. But as soon as ColdFusion encounters the `<CFCACHE>` tag, which should be at the top of your CFML code, ColdFusion will often be able to tell the browser to just use its local copy of the page. This is a fast operation because only the initial handshake between browser and server is necessary to determine whether the local copy can be used.

This improves performance in three important ways:

- First, the browser can display the template more quickly. This is because it can just use the local copy instead of waiting for your template code to generate the template and refetch it over the Net. The longer the page and the more time-consuming your CFML code is, the greater the benefit.
- Second, the amount of work ColdFusion needs to do is lessened. As long as the browser's local copy is still valid, ColdFusion can stop processing your template as soon as it encounters the `<CFCACHE>` tag. This frees up ColdFusion to complete its next task more quickly, which benefits all your users. The more often the same users revisit your pages, the greater the benefit.
- Third, by reducing the number of times complete pages must be sent back to browsers, traffic on your local network is kept to a minimum. This makes better use of your network bandwidth. Again, the more often the same users revisit your pages, the greater the benefit.

TIP

With Netscape browsers, you can override the client-side cache for a particular page request by doing what Netscape calls a super reload (which means holding down the Shift key while clicking the browser's Reload button). This can be useful for testing your pages. You can do the same with most versions of Internet Explorer by holding down the Ctrl key (or equivalent) while clicking the browser's Refresh button.

Server-Side Page Caching

You can also use the <CFCACHE> tag to enable ColdFusion's server-side page caching mechanism. Similar to client-side caching, this method takes advantage of a previously generated version of your template code. However, server-side caching doesn't use the cached copy of the page that might be on the browser machine. Instead, it looks for a cached copy of the page that ColdFusion stores on the server's drive.

Enabling Server-Side Caching

To enable server-side caching for one of your templates, place a <CFCACHE> tag at the top of the template before your other CFML and HTML tags. As you can see in Table 22.3, a number of attributes are relevant for using <CFCACHE> to do server-side caching. However, they are all optional, and most of them are relevant only if your template is secured via SSL encryption or a user name and password. Most of the time, you can just specify `ACTION="Cache"` and whatever `TIMEOUT` you desire.

Table 22.3 <CFCACHE> Tag Attributes Relevant for Server-Side Caching

ATTRIBUTE	PURPOSE
`ACTION`	Set this attribute to `ServerCache` to enable server-side caching for your template. You can also set it to `ClientCache` to enable client-side caching only, as discussed in the previous section. Finally, you can set it to `Cache` (the default), which uses both client-side and server-side mechanisms (see the section "ColdFusion-Optimized Caching," later in this chapter).
`TIMESPAN`	As with client-side caching, this is the period of time that you would like the user's browser to cache the page. You can specify this period using any combination of days, hours, minutes, or seconds by providing a value returned by the `CreateTimeSpan()` function. In other words, this attribute works just like the `CACHEDWITHIN` attribute for <CFQUERY> that you learned about earlier in this chapter.
`DIRECTORY`	Optional. The directory in which you want ColdFusion to store cached versions of the page. If this is omitted, ColdFusion stores the cached versions in a `cache` directory within the `ColdFusionMX` directory (or wherever you installed ColdFusion).
`USERNAME`	Optional. If the template you want to cache normally requires the user to enter a user name and password, you must provide the appropriate user name here. Depending on the Web server software you are using, remember that the user name might be case sensitive.
`PASSWORD`	Optional. If the template you want to cache normally requires the user to enter a user name and password, you must provide the appropriate password here. Again, depending on your Web server, the password might be case sensitive.
`PROTOCOL`	Optional. Specify either `http://` (the default) or `https://`, depending on whether the template you want to cache is being served using SSL encryption. Normally, you can just omit this attribute.
`PORT`	Optional. If the Web server is serving documents at a nonstandard HTTP port, specify that port number here. Otherwise, you can omit this attribute, in which case it defaults to `80`, the port number usually used for the Web.

For instance, you could place the following snippet at the top of any of your ColdFusion templates. This tells ColdFusion that your template code only needs to execute once every 30 minutes (at most):

```
<!--- Let browser use a cached version of --->
<!--- this page, from up to six hours ago --->
<CFCACHE
  ACTION="ServerCache"
  TIMESPAN="#CreateTimeSpan(0, 0, 30, 0)#">
```

The first time the template is accessed, ColdFusion processes your code as it would normally do. Before it sends the generated page back to the browser, though, it also saves the page as a separate, static file on the server's drive. The next time the page is accessed, ColdFusion simply sends back the static version of the file without executing any code that appears after the `<CFCACHE>` tag. ColdFusion will continue to send this static version back to all visitors until 30 minutes have passed. After the 30 minutes have elapsed, the next page request reexecutes your template normally.

For most situations, that's all you have to do. Your visitors will immediately begin to see improved performance. The more often your pages are hit and the longer your template code takes to execute, the larger the benefit.

Listing 22.2 is a simple example that demonstrates the effect. The template uses the `TimeFormat()` function to output the current time. At the top of the template, the `<CFCACHE>` tag allows the page to be cached for 30 seconds at a time. Try visiting this page repeatedly in your browser.

Listing 22.2 `ServerSideCache.cfm`—Testing the Server-Side Cache Mechanism

```
<!---
  Filename: ServerSideCache.cfm
  Author:   Nate Weiss (NMW)
  Purpose:  Demonstrates use of server-side caching
--->

<!--- Cache this template for 30 seconds at a time --->
<CFCACHE
  ACTION="SERVERCACHE"
  TIMESPAN="#CreateTimeSpan(0, 0, 0, 30)#">

<HTML>
<HEAD><TITLE>Caching Demonstration</TITLE></HEAD>
<BODY>

  <!--- Display the current time --->
  <P>This page was generated at:
  <CFOUTPUT>#TimeFormat(Now(), "h:mm:ss tt")#</CFOUTPUT>

</BODY>
</HTML>
```

The first time you visit this template, it displays the current time. For the next 30 seconds, subsequent page accesses will continue to show that same time, which proves that your template code is not reexecuting. Regardless of whether you access the page using another browser or from another machine, click the browser's Reload or Refresh button, or close and reopen the browser, you will continue to see the original time message until the 30 seconds have elapsed. Then the next page request will once again reflect the current time, which will be used for the next 30 seconds.

NOTE

Remember, if you are using <CFCACHE> for server-side caching (that is, with an ACTION of Cache or ServerCache), the page will not be regenerated for each user. In particular, you should make sure that the page does not depend on any variables kept in the CLIENT, COOKIE, or SESSION scopes because the generated page will be shared with other users, without checking that their CLIENT, COOKIE, or SESSION variables are the same. So in general, you should not cache personalized pages using server-side caching. For personalized pages, enable client-side caching with ACTION="ClientCache" instead.

ColdFusion-Optimized Caching

So far, you have learned about client-side page caching (that is, using <CFCACHE> with ACTION="ClientCache") and server-side page caching (ACTION="ServerCache").

As noted earlier in Tables 24.2 and 24.3, you can use both types of caching together by specifying ACTION="Cache", or by omitting the ACTION attribute altogether. For each page request, ColdFusion will first determine whether the browser has an appropriate version of the page in its local cache. If not, ColdFusion determines whether it has an appropriate version of the page in its own server-side cache. Only if there isn't an appropriate version in either cache will your template code reexecute.

The result is greatly enhanced performance in most situations.

NOTE

In previous versions of ColdFusion, the default value for ACTION resulted in server-side caching only. In ColdFusion MX, the default is for both types of caching to be enabled. So, if you move an application to ColdFusion MX and the code does not provide an ACTION attribute, the server-side cache and client-side caches will both be enabled. This should not be a problem, since nearly any situation that would benefit from server-side caching will also benefit from client-side caching as well.

Caching Pages That Use URL Parameters

ColdFusion maintains a separate cached version of your page for each combination of URL parameters with which it gets accessed. Each version expires on its own schedule, based on the TIMEOUT parameter you provide. In other words, you don't need to do anything special to employ server-side caching with pages that use URL parameters to pass ID numbers or any other information.

ColdFusion does not cache the result of a form submission, regardless of whether the target page contains a <CFCACHE> tag, so <CFCACHE> is disabled whenever the CGI.REQUEST_METHOD variable is set to POST.

NOTE

Remember, if you are using <CFCACHE> for server-side caching, the page will not be regenerated for each user, so server-side caching should not be used for pages that are personalized in any way. The only type of caching that is safe for personalized pages is client-side caching (ACTION="ClientCache"). See the important caution in the previous section.

Specifying the Cache Directory

By default, ColdFusion stores the cached versions of your templates in a folder called cache, located within the ColdFusionMX directory (or wherever you installed ColdFusion). If after visiting Listing 22.2, you take a look in the directory in which you saved the listing, you will notice that

ColdFusion has placed a file there, with an extension of .tmp. If you open up this .tmp file in a text editor, you will see that it contains the final, evaluated code that the ColdFusion template generated. A new .tmp file will appear in the folder whenever you visit a different template that uses server-side caching. In addition, a different .tmp file will appear for each set of URL parameters supplied to the templates when they are visited.

If you want to store the .tmp files in some other location, you can use the `DIRECTORY` attribute to tell ColdFusion where to store them. You must provide a fully qualified file path to a folder on your server's drive (or on a local network, although this is not recommended).

For instance, the following would tell ColdFusion to store its cache files in a folder called `cachefiles`:

```
<!--- Cache this template for 30 seconds at a time --->
<CFCACHE
  ACTION="Cache"
  TIMESPAN="c:\cachefiles">
```

You would, of course, need to create the `cachefiles` directory on the server machine before this would work.

The `DIRECTORY` should not be within the Web server's document root. You don't want people to be able to request the .tmp files directly via their browsers.

Flushing the Page Cache

Earlier in this chapter, you learned about query caching and how to make a cached query refresh when the data in the underlying database tables changes. You have the same type of option for server-side page caching, via the `FLUSH` action provided by the `<CFCACHE>` tag. You can also delete ColdFusion's cache files manually.

Using `ACTION="FLUSH"`

To flush a page from the cache before it would time out on its own, simply use the `<CFCACHE>` tag with `ACTION="FLUSH"`. Table 22.4 shows the attributes relevant for flushing the server-side page cache.

Table 22.4 `<CFCACHE>` Tag Attributes Relevant for Server-Side Cache Flushing

ATTRIBUTE	PURPOSE
`ACTION`	Must be set to `Flush` to flush pages from the server-side cache.
`DIRECTORY`	Optional. The directory that contains the cached versions of your pages. In other words, provide the same value here that you provide to the `DIRECTORY` attribute in your other `<CFCACHE>` tags (the ones that enable caching).
`EXPIREURL`	Optional. A URL reference that represents which cache files to delete. If you don't provide this attribute, ColdFusion will flush the cache for all files in the specified directory. You can use an asterisk (*) in this attribute as a simple wildcard.

So if one of your templates makes some type of change that your application should reflect immediately, even in pages that would otherwise still be cached, you could use the following line to delete all cached pages in the current directory. You would place this code in the change template, right after the <CFQUERY> or whatever else is making the actual changes:

```
<!--- Flush the server-side page cache --->
<CFCACHE
  ACTION="Flush">
```

If you don't need to expire all cached pages from the directory, you can provide an `EXPIREURL` attribute. For instance, suppose you are using server-side caching to cache a template called `ShowMovie.cfm`, and that movie accepts a URL parameter called `FilmID`. After some kind of update to the `Films` table, you might want to flush the `ShowMovie.cfm` template from the cache, but only for the appropriate `FilmID`. To do so, you might use code like the following:

```
<!--- Flush the server-side page cache --->
<CFCACHE
  ACTION="Flush"
  EXPIREURL="ShowMovie.cfm?FilmID=#FORM.FilmID#">
```

Or to flush the cache for all versions of the `ShowMovie.cfm` template (regardless of URL parameters), leaving all other cached pages in the directory alone, you would use something like this:

```
<!--- Flush the server-side page cache --->
<CFCACHE
  ACTION="Flush"
  EXPIREURL="ShowMovie.cfm?*">
```

NOTE

The above snippets assume that the "change" template is in the same folder as the "display" pages that need to be flushed from the cache. If not, you can specify the appropriate directory using the `DIRECTORY` attribute.

Controlling Whitespace

One of the side effects of CFML's tag-based nature is the fact that whitespace characters (such as tabs, spaces, and return characters) that you use to indent your CFML code are usually passed on to the browser as part of the final generated page. In certain cases, this whitespace can considerably inflate the size of the generated HTML content, and this in turn can have a negative effect on performance. ColdFusion provides several options for dealing with these extraneous whitespace characters.

NOTE

ColdFusion's ability to automatically control whitespace is better than ever in ColdFusion MX. You will find that in most cases, you can just enable the automatic Whitespace Management feature (discussed in a moment) and never think about whitespace issues again. Nonetheless, it is worthwhile to discuss the other options available to you, just in case.

Understanding the Issue

In a ColdFusion template, you use CFML and HTML tags together. The processing instructions for the server are intermingled with what you actually want to generate. That is, there is no formal separation between the code and the content parts of your template. Most other Web scripting environments separate code from content, generally forcing you to put the HTML code you want to generate into some type of `Write()` function or special block delimited by characters such as `<%` and `%>` (depending on the language).

The fact that you get to use CFML tags right in the body of your document is a big part of what makes ColdFusion development so powerful, but it has a disadvantage. Often ColdFusion can't easily determine which whitespace characters in a template just indent the code for clarity and which should actually be sent to the browser as part of the final, generated page. When ColdFusion can't make the distinction, it errs on the side of caution and includes the whitespace in the final content.

Automatic Whitespace Control

The good news is that ColdFusion already does a lot to eliminate excess whitespace from your generated pages. ColdFusion includes an automatic whitespace elimination feature, enabled by default. As long as you haven't disabled this feature, it's already pulling much whitespace out of your documents for you, before the generated page is sent to the browser.

Enabling Whitespace Suppression

On the Settings page of ColdFusion Administrator, you'll see an option called Enable Whitespace Management. When this is enabled, portions of your template that contain only CFML tags will have the whitespace removed from them before the page is returned to the browser. Basically, ColdFusion looks at the template, finds the areas that contain only CFML tags, removes any whitespace (extra spaces, tabs, indents, new lines, or hard returns) from those areas, and then processes the template.

It's easy to see this in action. To do so, follow these steps:

1. Visit the `NextNCached.cfm` template (refer to Listing 22.1) via your Web browser.
2. Use the browser's View Source option to see the final HTML code that the template generated. Leave the source code's window open.
3. On the Settings page of ColdFusion Administrator, uncheck the Enable Whitespace Management option and submit the changes.
4. Visit the `NextNCached.cfm` template and view the source code again.

If you compare the two versions of the page source, you will see that the second version has a lot more blank lines and other whitespace in it. In particular, it has a lot more space at the very top, consisting of all the whitespace that surrounds the comments and various `<CFQUERY>`, `<CFPARAM>`, and `<CFSET>` tags at the top of Listing 22.1. The first version of the page source has eliminated that whitespace from the top of the document.

There are very few situations in which this automatic suppression of whitespace would be undesirable. In general, you should leave the Enable Whitespace Management option enabled in ColdFusion Administrator.

Controlling Whitespace Suppression Programmatically

You can turn off ColdFusion's automatic whitespace suppression feature for specific parts of your document. Such situations are few and far between because HTML usually ignores whitespace, so there is generally no need to preserve it.

However, in a few situations you wouldn't want ColdFusion to remove whitespace for you. For instance, a few rarely used HTML tags do consider whitespace significant. The <PRE> tag is one, and the <XMP> tag is another. If you are using either of these tags in a Web document, ColdFusion's whitespace suppression might eliminate the very space you are trying to display between the <PRE> or <XMP> tags. You might run into the same problem when composing an email message programmatically using the <CFMAIL> tag (see Chapter 26, "Interacting with Email").

In such a situation, you can use the SUPPRESSWHITESPACE="No" attribute of the <CFPROCESSINGDIRECTIVE> tag to disable the automatic suppression of whitespace. Place the tag around the block of code that is sensitive to whitespace characters, like so:

```
<CFPROCESSINGDIRECTIVE SUPPRESSWHITESPACE="No">
  <PRE>
    ...code that is sensitive to whitespace here...
  </PRE>
</CFPROCESSINGDIRECTIVE>
```

For details, see the <CFPROCESSINGDIRECTIVE> tag in Appendix B, "ColdFusion Tag Reference."

Suppressing Whitespace Output with <CFSILENT>

Unfortunately, ColdFusion cannot always correctly identify which parts of your code consist only of CFML tags and should therefore have whitespace automatically removed. This is most often the case with code loops created by <CFLOOP> and <CFOUTPUT>.

If you find that a particular portion of code generates a lot of unexpected whitespace, you can add the <CFSILENT> tag, which suppresses all output (even actual text and HTML tags). The <CFSILENT> tag takes no attributes. Simply wrap it around any code blocks that might generate extraneous whitespace when executed, such as <CFLOOP> or <CFOUTPUT> loops that perform calculations but don't generate any output the browser needs to receive.

NOTE

The <CFSILENT> tag doesn't just suppress whitespace output. It suppresses all output, even output you would generally want to send to the browser (such as HTML code and text).

Suppressing Specific White Space with <CFSETTING>

For situations in which ColdFusion's automatic suppression isn't suppressing all the whitespace in your generated pages (for instance, the first <CFLOOP> snippet in the previous section), but where <CFSILENT> is too drastic, you can use the <CFSETTING> tag to suppress output in a more selective manner.

The `<CFSETTING>` tag takes a few optional attributes, but the only one relevant to this discussion is the `ENABLECFOUTPUTONLY` attribute. When this attribute is set to `Yes`, it suppresses all output (similar to how the `<CFSILENT>` tag works), except for `<CFOUTPUT>` blocks. Any HTML code or text that should be sent to the browser must be between `<CFOUTPUT>` tags, even if the code doesn't include any ColdFusion variables or expressions. This is different from ColdFusion's normal behavior, where it assumes that it can send any non-CFML text or code to the browser.

So if you find that a section of code is generating a lot of whitespace, but you can't easily use `<CFSILENT>` because your code must be able to generate *some* output, then you should place a `<CFSETTING>` tag with `ENABLECFOUTPUTONLY="Yes"` just above the section of code, and a `<CFSETTING>` tag with `ENABLECFOUTPUTONLY="No"` just below the section. Within the section of code, make sure `<CFOUTPUT>` tags surround any item (even plain text) that you want to include in the final, generated version of the page. This gives you complete control over all generated whitespace and other characters.

➜ See Appendix B, "ColdFusion Tag Reference," for more information about the `<CFSETTING>` tag.

CHAPTER 23

Integrating with Macromedia Flash

IN THIS CHAPTER

One of the most exciting aspects of Macromedia's MX generation of products is the new focus on integration across the whole MX product line. In this chapter, you will learn about a particularly exciting type of integration: between ColdFusion MX and Macromedia Flash MX. By employing Flash and ColdFusion together, you can easily create fresh, engaging interfaces that make using your site more fun and more efficient.

Flash Integration Concepts

Macromedia Flash MX

Macromedia Flash MX is the application you use to create or design new Flash movies. It's an Integrated Development Environment (IDE), which contains the drawing tools, animation tools, and code editor you need to create an animation, advertisement, or interactive data presentation for your users.

For your convenience, a 30-day trial version of Flash MX is provided on the CD-ROM for this book.

The Flash 6 Player

The Flash 6 Player is a browser plug-in that displays Flash movies to Web visitors. Think of it as a minibrowser within your regular Web browser, except that instead of understanding HTML pages, it only understands Flash movies (`.swf` files). Nearly all browsers come with some version of the Flash Player already installed.

NOTE

For most of the examples in this chapter to work, each user needs to have version 6 of the player on their computer. With some browsers (particularly Internet Explorer on Windows), the upgrade happens automatically. Other users need to download and install the player from `www.macromedia.com`.

ColdFusion Components

In Flash MX, the preferred way to have the Flash Player interact with ColdFusion is to use ColdFusion Components (CFC). You learned how to create CFCs in Chapter 20, "Building Reusable Components." That chapter focused on creating CFCs for use within ColdFusion pages. The basic idea was to create a CFC with methods that performed whatever processing you needed, and then use those methods in your ColdFusion pages with the `<CFINVOKE>` tag.

In this chapter, you will learn how not only other ColdFusion pages, but the Flash Player itself can use those same CFCs.

Flash Remoting

Flash Remoting is the bridge between your CFCs on the ColdFusion server and the Flash player. Flash Remoting consists of two parts: the *Gateway*, automatically installed when you install ColdFusion MX; and the *Components*, a special set of scripting commands that you use within a Flash movie to interact with your CFCs (through the gateway).

ActionScript

ActionScript is the programming language that you use to control the various elements within a Flash movie. It lets you do things like start and stop animations, make things appear and disappear, and validate form entries. ActionScript is very similar to JavaScript, which is nice because if you know one you are well on your way to understanding the other. When you install the Flash Remoting Components, you are adding a set of functions to ActionScript. You then write simple ActionScript code to trigger interactions between your movie and the CFCs on your server.

Your First Flash Movie

In case you haven't used Flash before, I will now walk you through the process of creating a Flash movie and displaying it on a ColdFusion page. Unfortunately, I just don't have the space in this book to really teach you how to create nice-looking Flash movies. My intent here is mostly to help you understand what types of files are involved so you won't be completely mystified when a graphic artist hands them to you. :)

What You Need to Install

If you want to follow along with the creation of Flash movies in this chapter, you will need to install the following items:

- Macromedia Flash MX
- Flash Remoting Components
- Flash UI Components Set 2

For your convenience, the CD-ROM for this book includes the installation files for Macromedia Flash MX and the Flash Remoting Components. Simply click or double-click the appropriate Windows or Macintosh file to start the installation process.

To install the Flash UI Components Set 2, use the Macromedia Extension Manager to install `FUIComponentsSet2.mxp`, a Macromedia Extension Package file. The CD-ROM for this book also includes this file, in the directory for this chapter. To open Extension Manager, choose Help > Manage Extensions from Flash MX's main menu. When Extension Manager appears, choose File > Install Extension, then locate the `FUIComponentsSet2.mxp` file and click the Install button. An entry for Flash Components Set 2 should appear in the list of Installed Extensions. Make sure it is checked, then close the Extension Manager. Finally, close and reopen Flash MX itself.

NOTE

The version of Flash MX included on the CD-ROM is a free trial. After a certain number of days, you must purchase Flash MX to continue using it. There is no additional charge for the Flash Remoting Components.

NOTE

It's possible that updated versions of Flash or the Remoting Components will be available by the time you read this book. If so, they will be available for download from `www.macromedia.com`.

Creating a Movie

To create a basic Flash movie, perform the following steps:

1. Launch Flash MX. A new, untitled movie will appear, ready for you to draw on or add code to.
2. Use the drawing controls in the Tools panel to draw something on the *Stage*. The Stage is the large white area that represents the movie you want to show your users. It doesn't really matter what you draw; just draw a few circles or rectangles. If you need help, choose Help > Lessons, then look through the "Illustrating in Flash" lesson.
3. Save your work by choosing File > Save from the menu. It doesn't matter where you save your document; you can just save it to your desktop to keep things simple. Note that you are saving a Flash MX *Document*. Flash MX Documents always have a `.fla` extension. This is not the movie you will show your Web users. This file is only for the person creating the movie.
4. Publish the Flash movie by choosing File > Publish from the menu. After a moment, Flash launches your browser to a simple test page that displays your movie.

When you published the Flash movie, two files were created, in the same place where you saved the `.fla` file. The most important file is the Flash movie itself, which has a `.swf` extension. This is the file you would move into the Web server root to make it available to your Web users, much like a GIF or JPEG image. The other file is just a simple HTML file, created to help you see how the movie will look on a Web page.

NOTE

After a while, you may not want the HTML file created anymore, or you may want to store the files in a different location or with different filenames. To control what files are created when you publish the movie, choose File > Publish Settings from the main menu. For details, see the Flash MX documentation.

Placing the Movie on a ColdFusion Page

Now that you have seen your movie on a static HTML page, you may be wondering how to place the movie on a ColdFusion page. Since the tags needed to display a Flash movie are just standard HTML, you don't need to learn much.

Take a look at the HTML source code for the `.html` file created when you published your movie. To view the source code, just open the file in a text editor such as Macromedia Dreamweaver MX or Windows Notepad. Of course, you can also use the View Source command in your browser to view the source code.

The source code will include a set of nested `<OBJECT>`, `<PARAM>`, and `<EMBED>` tags, similar to this (I have added white space here for clarity):

```
<OBJECT
  classid="clsid:D27CDB6E-AE6D-11cf-96B8-444553540000"
  codebase="http://download.macromedia.com/pub/shockwave/cabs/flash/swflash.
  ➥cab#version=6,0,0,0"
  width="537"
  height="190"
  id="MyFirstMovie"
  align="">
  <PARAM name="movie" value="MyFirstMovie.swf">
  <PARAM name="quality" value="high">
  <PARAM name="bgcolor" value="#FFFFFF">
  <EMBED
    src="MyFirstMovie.swf"
    quality="high"
    bgcolor="#FFFFFF"
    width="537"
    height="190"
    name="MyFirstMovie"
    align=""
    type="application/x-shockwave-flash"
    pluginspage="http://www.macromedia.com/go/getflashplayer">
  </EMBED>
</OBJECT>
```

At this point, it's not terribly important for you to know what every one of these tags and attributes does. The basic idea is that the set of tags tells the browser the filename of the movie to display (here, `MyFirstMovie.swf`), as well as its width, height, and a few other display-related options.

NOTE

Because different browsers have historically supported different tags for displaying multimedia content such as movies, the code shown above provides most of these pieces of information twice, once in the form of `<OBJECT>` and `<PARAM>` tags, and again in the form of an `<EMBED>` tag. For more information, see the "Publishing" section of the "Using Flash" portion in the Flash MX documentation.

Copying and Pasting the HTML Code

One way to display your movie in a ColdFusion page is to simply copy and paste the `<OBJECT>` and `<EMBED>` source code from the `.html` file that Flash MX creates when you publish a movie. Just copy the source code and paste it into a `.cfm` file.

You will also need to copy the Flash movie (the `.swf` file) to the same location as your `.cfm` file so the browser can request it using just the filename. Alternatively, you can place the `.swf` in some other folder and then include the absolute or relative path to the file along with the filename. This all works the same way as it does for the `SRC` attribute of an ordinary `<IMG>` tag.

For instance, you might choose to keep the `.swf` file in the `images` subfolder of the `ows` folder. You would then need to use `../images/MyFirstMovie.swf` or `/ows/images/MyFirstMovie.swf` instead of just `MyFirstMovie.swf` in the two places where the filename appears in the `<OBJECT>` and `<EMBED>` code block. For details, see the Flash MX documentation or an HTML reference guide.

NOTE

The HTML source code usually includes a few number (`#`)signs in the `bgcolor` and `codebase` attributes. If the code appears between `<CFOUTPUT>` tags, you will need to escape the `#` signs by doubling them so ColdFusion doesn't think you are talking about a variable. For example, you would need to change `bgcolor="#FFFFFF"` to `bgcolor="##FFFFFF"`.

Inserting Movies with Dreamweaver MX

As you might expect, Dreamweaver MX makes it easy to display your Flash movies in your ColdFusion pages (or any other type of Web page, for that matter). There are a few different ways to do it, but they lead to the same result: the addition of the appropriate `<OBJECT>` and `<EMBED>` tags to your ColdFusion page.

To insert a Flash movie into the current page, do the following:

1. Choose Insert > Media > Flash from Dreamweaver MX's menu; the Select File dialog appears. Alternatively, you can click the Flash button on the Insert toolbar (it's on the Common tab).
2. Select the `.swf` file you want to use. You can choose a file in a different folder if you want, as long as it's accessible to your Web server. Dreamweaver will take care of inserting the correct path information.
3. Click OK. The appropriate `<OBJECT>`, `<PARAM>`, and `<EMBED>` tags are added to your document (Figure 23.1).

That's it. If you preview the page in your browser, you should see the Flash movie displayed as expected.

NOTE

If you want, you can adjust the Relative To option in the Select File dialog before clicking OK. The default is Document, which means a relative path will be used, probably starting with `../` if the `.swf` file is not contained within the current folder. If you select Site Root, an absolute path will be used (starting with `/ows/23` if the `.swf` file is in this chapter's folder). Choose Site Root if you'll be moving the `.cfm` file around later, but plan to keep the `.swf` file in the same place.

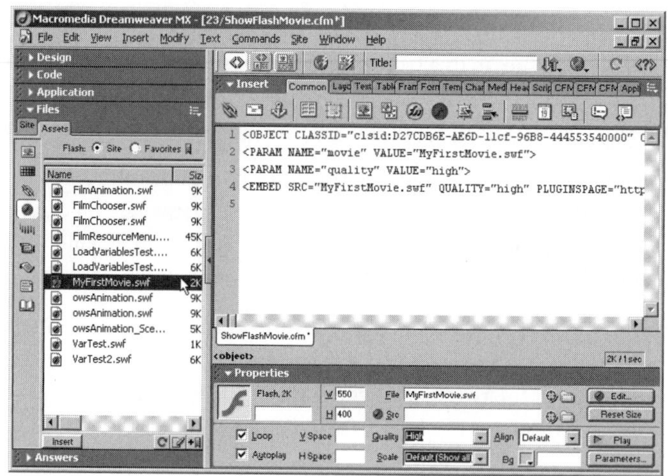

Figure 23.1

Dreamweaver MX makes it easy to add Flash movies to your pages.

Inserting Movies via Drag and Drop

Dreamweaver also lets you drag and drop Flash movies into your ColdFusion pages. Just do the following:

1. Create a new ColdFusion (`.cfm`) file, or open an existing one. Just make sure it is associated with a site. (This is probably already the case for any file within the `ows` folder or its subfolders.)

2. Make sure the Assets tab of the Files panel is showing. If not, choose Window > Assets from the menu.

3. Locate the `.swf` file you want to insert. If it is not displayed, click the Refresh button at the bottom of the Assets tab. Note that you can use the Flash button at the left side of the Assets tab to show only `.swf` files.

4. Drag the `.swf` file from the Assets tab into your document. The appropriate `<OBJECT>`, `<PARAM>`, and `<EMBED>` tags are added to your document.

TIP

Once you've added the `<OBJECT>` and `<EMBED>` block to your document, try placing your cursor on the `<OBJECT>` tag. The Properties panel will present a number of controls relevant for Flash files, as shown in Figure 23.1.

TIP

If you use Design View, a gray square will represent the Flash movie. You can right-click this area for some helpful options, such as opening the movie in Flash MX.

Using Flash Remoting

Now that you have an idea how to create basic Flash movies and understand how to place them in your CFML pages, I can move on to the fun part. If you haven't guessed, the fun part is getting your Flash movies to interact with ColdFusion. This allows the movies to do things like display information from a database, collect information from users, or other processes that would normally only be possible via HTML forms or links.

The advantage, of course, is that you can use all the animation and interactivity tools in Flash's arsenal to make data presentations, navigation widgets, and data-collection tools that are far richer and more interactive than is generally possible with HTML alone. You can combine these tools to create user interfaces which are more intuitive and usable than with HTML pages alone, and which look and behave exactly the same with any browser.

What makes all this possible is the new Flash MX concept of Remoting, which allows the Flash Player (which is running on the user's machine) to contact and interact easily with ColdFusion pages (which are running on your server) in real time, without needing to reload the page.

Going from the Flash world of old to the new world of Flash Remoting is kind of like going from static HTML pages to ColdFusion. All of a sudden, you can create a new kind of Flash movie that provides a rich, interactive, data-aware experience for your users. This has been possible with previous versions of Flash, but it has always meant jumping through a series of hoops, whereas Flash Remoting makes it easy and sustainable.

ColdFusion Pages as Services

Normally, you use ColdFusion to communicate with Web browsers. In turn, the ColdFusion pages you normally write are about generating HTML code, which the browser interprets and displays. The idea is similar with Flash Remoting, except that you use ColdFusion to communicate with the Flash Player instead of with a Web browser. And, instead of generating HTML code, your ColdFusion pages just output data that should be sent back to the Flash Player. The data is made available to ActionScript, which means you can write code (usually very simple code) that causes your Flash movie to display or respond in whatever way you see fit.

One of the key concepts in the Flash Remoting framework is the notion of a *service*. For purposes of this discussion, a service means any directory on your ColdFusion server. Within each directory, each individual ColdFusion page that knows how to talk to Flash is referred to as a *service function*. There's a bit of an assumption that these service functions for each service (that is, the `.cfm` files in each directory) have some kind of conceptual relationship to one another, but if not, that's okay.

In other words, a service is a collection of functions, and the code to power each one of those functions is written in CFML, as an ordinary ColdFusion page. You just change a few things about the code so that it knows to send information back to Flash instead of generating HTML.

Hey, come to think of it, you learned about another concept recently that can be thought of as a collection of functions: the concept of a ColdFusion component. So, if it's easy for Flash to consider a directory of .cfm pages as a set of service functions, maybe it's just as easy for it to consider the methods in a CFC as a set of service functions. Hmmm. More on that a bit later! :)

NOTE

Actually, Flash Remoting is about more than just connecting Flash to ColdFusion. You can also use it to connect Flash to Macromedia's JRun server, and support for other J2EE servers and .NET servers were in the works when this book went to press. So, the term *service* really refers to any directory on any server that supports Flash Remoting, regardless of what application server is powering it. For this chapter, though, the assumption is that you are using Flash Remoting to connect to ColdFusion MX.

Your First Flash Remoting Project

This section will walk you through the process of creating a user interface with Flash MX that connects to a ColdFusion page through Flash Remoting. This first example will be pretty simple, but it will get you well on your way to understanding how everything works together.

Getting Started

As you may already know, the Flash IDE includes a number of templates that you can use to get started with certain types of projects. There's one for pop-up ads, one for navigation menus, one for a photo slide show, and so on. Flash MX also includes a template for creating a movie that communicates with a server via Flash Remoting. Unfortunately, the template is somewhat poorly named and therefore easy to miss, but it's a sensible place to start for the first example.

To use the template for Flash Remoting, follow these steps:

1. From Flash MX's main menu, choose File > New from Template. The New Document dialog appears (Figure 23.2).
2. In the Category list, select Web.
3. In the Category Items list, select Basic (it may be the only item available).
4. Click Create. Your new Flash Document is created.

In most respects, the Flash Document created with this template isn't much different from what you get if you just create a totally blank document. The only difference is that a layer called Actions is present in the timeline. The first frame of this layer contains some skeletal ActionScript code that you can adapt to interact with a ColdFusion page.

Your timeline is probably docked near the top of the Flash MX workspace. Within the timeline, you will see a series of small gray and white rectangles, which represent the frames of your movie. The first frame should be marked with a lowercase *A*, indicating that the frame contains ActionScript code.

When you click this frame, the skeletal ActionScript code added by the template appears in the Actions panel. (If the Actions panel is not visible, choose Window > Actions from the main menu). The first line of the code reads `#include "NetServices.as"` (Figure 23.3).

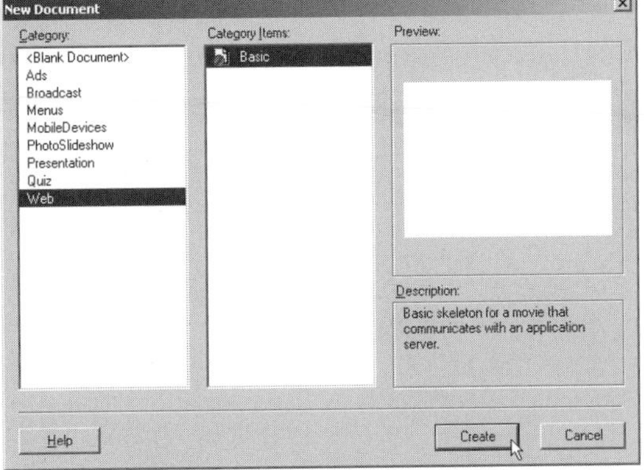

Figure 23.2

This template is a good way to get started with Flash Remoting.

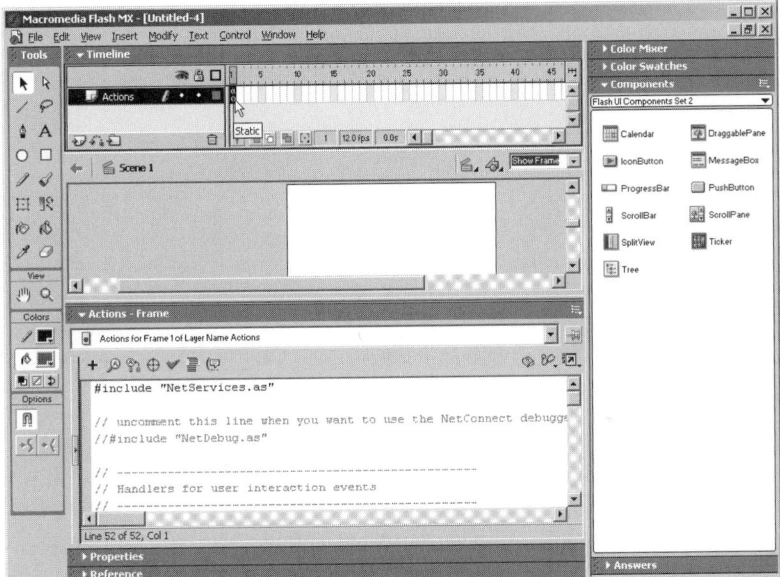

Figure 23.3

You use ActionScript code to interact with ColdFusion via Flash Remoting.

Listing 23.1 shows the skeletal ActionScript code produced by the Basic Web template. As you will soon see, it is easy to adapt this code so it interacts with ColdFusion pages of your choosing.

Listing 23.1 Template ActionScript Code for Flash Remoting

```
#include "NetServices.as"

// uncomment this line when you want to use the NetConnect debugger
//#include "NetDebug.as"

// -----------------------------------------------
// Handlers for user interaction events
// -----------------------------------------------

// This gets called when the "aaaa" button is clicked
```

Listing 23.1 (continued)

```
function aaaa_Clicked ()
{
  // ... put code here

  // For example, you could call the "bbbb" function of "my.service" by doing:
  // myService.bbbb(123, "abc");
}

// ---------------------------------------------
// Handlers for data coming in from server
// ---------------------------------------------

// This gets called with the results of calls to the server function "bbbb".
function bbbb_Result ( result )
{
  // ... put code here

  // For example, if result is a RecordSet, display it in a ListBox like this:
  // myListBox.setDataProvider(result);
}

// ---------------------------------------------
// Application initialization
// ---------------------------------------------

if (inited == null)
{
  // do this code only once
  inited = true;

  // set the default gateway URL (this is used only in authoring)
NetServices.setDefaultGatewayUrl("http://localhost:8100/flashservices/gateway");

  // connect to the gateway
  gateway_conn = NetServices.createGatewayConnection();

  // get a reference to a service
  myService = gateway_conn.getService("my.service", this);
}

stop();
```

NOTE

When you create the new document in Flash MX, the automatically-added code erroneously uses a URL that refers to port `8100` instead of `8500`, as shown in this listing. You will need to change it to `8500` before the code can work (you'll see this change in the next listing). Or, if you're not using ColdFusion in stand-alone mode, you should omit the port reference altogether. In other words, the first part of the URL should be the same as what you use to display the other examples in this book.

Drawing a Simple Search Interface

Your first Flash Remoting project will be a simple search interface for searching the list of Orange Whip Studios films (Figure 23.4). (With all this great Macromedia technology at its disposal, why does the studio keep churning out the same kinds of applications over and over again? That's Hollywood for you.)

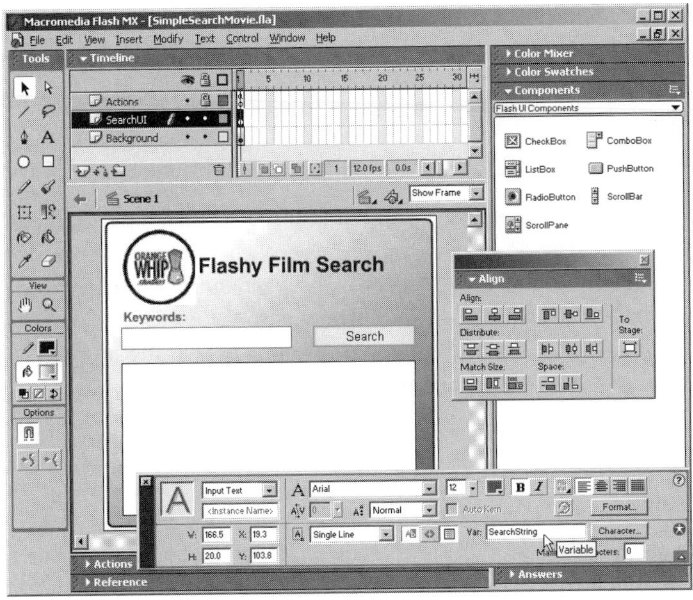

Figure 23.4

Flash Remoting makes it easy to power this simple search interface.

NOTE

If you don't want to follow the steps listed below, just open the completed `SimpleSearchMovie.fla` file. It's included with the listings for this chapter on the CD-ROM.

To create the visual part of the search interface, just follow these steps:

1. Lock the Actions layer by clicking the dot just under the padlock icon at the top of the timeline. This will keep you from accidentally drawing in the Actions layer.
2. Insert a new layer by choosing Insert > Layer from the main menu. Two layers should now show in the timeline: the Actions layer mentioned previously, and a new layer (probably named Layer 2).
3. Double-click the new layer's name in the timeline and rename it `SearchUI`.
4. Make sure the `SearchUI` layer is selected, then select the text tool from the Tools panel. Use the mouse to draw a text box. Make sure the text box remains selected. If you accidentally deselect it, just draw it again.
5. With the text box selected, use the Properties panel to change the Input Type from Static Text to Input Text. Enter `MySearchString` in the Var (Variable) field. Enable the Show Border Around Text option (to the left of the Var field).
6. In the Components panel, make sure the components from the Flash UI Components Set 2 drop-down list are showing. Add a PushButton component by dragging it from the Components Panel onto the stage, near the Text Box.
7. With PushButton selected, use the Properties panel to change the button's Label to `Search`. Change the Click Handler parameter to `SearchButton_Clicked`. Change the name in the Instance Name field from `<Instance Name>` to `SearchButton`.

8. Add another Text Box. This one should be Static Text instead of Input Text, and the Show Border Around Text option should be off. Double-click the Text Box and type `Keywords:`.

9. Add another Text Box. This one should be Dynamic Text. Using the Properties panel, change the Line Type from Single Line to Multiline. Set the Var field to `SearchResults`.

10. If you want, add a new layer called `Background`, making sure it appears at the bottom of the list of layers. Add the Orange Whip logo by importing the `logo_b.gif` file from the `ows/images` folder, add a border or background color with the paint bucket tool, and generally rearrange the various elements so it looks something like Figure 23.4. You may find it helpful to use the Align panel to line everything up right (open it by choosing Window > Align from the menu).

11. Save your work, using the filename `SimpleSearchMovie.fla`.

Adding ActionScript Code

Now that you've created a new Flash Document from the Flash Remoting template and have drawn the simple search interface on its Stage, the next thing to do is to edit the ActionScript code generated by the template. With this simple example, the necessary edits are quite minor.

Take a look at Listing 23.2, which is the original template code (shown in Listing 23.1) with the appropriate additions and changes to power this simple example. Since this code is in the first frame of the movie, it will execute when the movie first appears.

Listing 23.2 ActionScript Code for the First Frame of `SimpleSearchMovie.fla`

```
#include "NetServices.as"

// uncomment this line when you want to use the NetConnect debugger
// #include "NetDebug.as"

// -----------------------------------------------
// Application initialization
// -----------------------------------------------

if (inited == null)
{
  // do this code only once
  inited = true;

   // set the default gateway URL (this is used only in authoring)
NetServices.setDefaultGatewayUrl("http://localhost:8500/flashservices/gateway")

  // connect to the gateway
  gateway_conn = NetServices.createGatewayConnection();

  // get a reference to a service
  // In this case, the "service" is the /ows/23 directory in web server root
  myService = gateway_conn.getService("ows.23", this);
}
```

Listing 23.2 (continued)

```
// -------------------------------------------------
// Handlers for user interaction events
// -------------------------------------------------

// This gets called when the "SearchButton" button is clicked
function SearchButton_Clicked ()
{
  // ... put code here
  // For example, you could call the "bbbb" function of "my.service" by doing:
  // myService.bbbb(123, "abc");

  // In this case, we want to use the SimpleSearchProvider service function
  // (in other words, we want to execute SimpleSearchProvider.cfm)
  myService.SimpleSearchProvider({SearchString:MySearchString});
}

// -------------------------------------------------
// Handlers for data coming in from server
// -------------------------------------------------

// This gets called with the results of calls to the server function "bbbb".
function SimpleSearchProvider_Result ( result )
{
  // ... put code here
  // For example, if result is a RecordSet, display it in a ListBox by doing:
  // myListBox.setDataProvider(result);

  // In this case, we will simply set the SearchResults variable to whatever
  // was returned by ColdFusion.  Because the SearchResults variable is bound
  // to the multiline text box in the search UI, the result will display there
  SearchResults = result;
}


stop();
```

Unfortunately, it's not possible for me to provide a complete introduction to the syntax and semantics of ActionScript here. If you know JavaScript already, you'll find that this is essentially the same language. If not, you may need to consult a book on JavaScript to make sense of how the curly braces and parentheses are used, and how the `function` statement works.

TIP

There are some excellent resources in Flash MX's online help that will help you get up to speed with ActionScript concepts and syntax. For an introduction, choose Help > Learning Flash from Flash MX's main menu, then read the "Writing Scripts with ActionScript" and "Understanding the ActionScript Language" sections. For a reference guide, choose Help > ActionScript Dictionary.

What I *can* do, assuming that you understand the basic form of JavaScript or ActionScript, is explain what each line of code does. Let's get started.

The first line of Listing 23.2 reads:

```
#include "NetServices.as"
```

The purpose of this line is to include the functions created in the `NetServices.as` file, so they're available to the current document. The `NetServices.as` file is an ActionScript file—the .as extension stands for ActionScript—that was placed on your computer when you installed the Flash Remoting Components. `NetServices.as` is where nearly all the other objects and functions used in Listing 23.2 are defined. If you think of the `NetServices.as` file as similar to a file of user-defined functions, as discussed in Chapter 19, "Building User-Defined Functions," then this `#include` statement is like a `<CFINCLUDE>` tag that lets you use the functions in the current document.

Connecting to the Flash Remoting Gateway

The next line of Listing 23.2 reads:

```
if (inited == null)
```

This simply tests to see if a `ActionScript` variable called `inited` currently exists. If it does not exist (that is, if it is `null`), the code inside the block that follows (enclosed by the `{}` braces) executes. The first line of code inside the block sets the `inited` variable to `true`. In other words, the code in this block only needs to execute once to initialize the rest of the movie. You can use this technique whenever you want certain code to run just once, when the movie first appears.

The next line, which executes only once, reads:

```
// set the default gateway URL
NetServices.setDefaultGatewayUrl("http://localhost:8500/flashservices/gateway")
```

The `NetServices` object referred to here is defined in the `NetServices.as` file included at the top of the listing. The `NetServices` object provides a number of functions (or, if you prefer, *methods*) related to Flash Remoting. The first one used here is the `setDefaultGatewayUrl()` method, which expects a URL to the Flash Remoting Gateway on whatever server you are connecting to. This simply tells the Flash Player which server it should try to talk to. Change the `localhost` or the `:8500` parts as appropriate for how you installed ColdFusion.

NOTE

Assuming that you want to connect to the Remoting Gateway on your ColdFusion MX server, the default gateway URL should always point to `flashservices/gateway` as shown above. I am assuming that you are mostly interested in using Flash to access a ColdFusion server. If connecting to a different type of Remoting Gateway, such as a .NET server or a JavaBean, the default gateway URL might be slightly different.

The next line reads:

```
// connect to the gateway
gateway_conn = NetServices.createGatewayConnection();
```

This uses the `createGatewayConnection()` method, also provided by the `NetServices` object, to establish a conceptual connection to the Flash Gateway part of ColdFusion. The method returns a gateway *connection object* named `gateway_conn`. You can read all about connection objects in the ActionScript reference in Flash MX's online help; for now, just think of `gateway_conn` as representing your ColdFusion server.

The next line reads:

```
// get a reference to a service
myService = gateway_conn.getService("ows.23", this);
```

Any gateway connection object exposes a number of properties and methods. The most important method is `getService()`, which establishes a conceptual connection to a particular service on the gateway. Keep in mind that the *gateway* is just the ColdFusion server, and the *service* is the directory in which the relevant ColdFusion pages are located. Because the code listings for this chapter are located in the `ows/23` location in your Web server's document root, the service's name is specified as `ows.23` (simply use dots instead of slashes to specify the path to the correct folder). The method returns a *service object*, which can now be used to execute the ColdFusion pages in the `ows/23` directory.

NOTE

There is no need to provide a complete URL that includes `http://` or the server's name, because that was established earlier by `setDefaultGatewayUrl()`.

At this point, a connection to the ColdFusion server has been established. It only required three lines of code, which can be used as the first part of nearly any ActionScript code that needs to use Flash Remoting.

Executing a ColdFusion Page and Passing Parameters

Continuing this line-by-line tour of Listing 23.2, the next line reads:

```
function SearchButton_Clicked()
```

This creates a function called `SearchButton_Clicked`. If you recall, `SearchButton_Clicked` was specified as the Click Handler for the Search button in this simple search movie (see "Drawing a Simple Search Interface", earlier in this chapter). This simply means that the code in the `SearchButton_Clicked` function block will execute when a user clicks the Search button.

There is just one line of code in `SearchButton_Clicked`, which reads:

```
myService.SimpleSearchProvider({SearchString:MySearchString});
```

This line of code executes a ColdFusion template called `SimpleSearchProvider.cfm`. You will see this ColdFusion file shortly, in Listing 23.3. If you want, go ahead and take a look at it now, but for the moment all you really need to know is that it is a fairly ordinary page that takes a parameter called `SearchString`, runs a query to find a matching movie, and returns the title and summary of that movie. For now, it just returns a simple string, not anything fancy like a query object or an array or structure.

Remember that `myService` is a service object that essentially represents the `ows/23` folder on the ColdFusion server. Any ColdFusion page in this folder can be executed as a *service function*, simply by using its filename like a method, which is why `SimpleSearchProvider.cfm` becomes `SimpleSearchProvider()` here.

To pass parameters to the ColdFusion page, you can provide them as name-value pairs within curly braces. This is similar conceptually to passing URL parameters in a normal HTML link, except that instead of separating the name and the value with an equals (=) sign, you use a colon. And if you need to provide multiple parameters, separate them with a comma instead of an ampersand (&).

So if you don't need to send any parameters to `SimpleSearchProvider.cfm`, you would use:

```
mySerVice.SimpleSearchProvider()
```

To provide ColdFusion with a parameter called `SearchString`, where the value of the parameter is the current value of the Flash variable named `MySearchString`, you'd use:

```
myService.SimpleSearchProvider({SearchString:MySearchString})
```

If the name of the ColdFusion page was `BuyItem.cfm` instead of `SimpleSearchProvider.cfm`, and it needed parameters called `ItemID` and `Quantity`, you could use this, assuming that Flash variables called `MyItemID` and `MyQuantity` exist and contain sensible values:

```
myService.BuyItem({ItemID:MyItemID,Quantity:MyQuantity});
```

You can also provide numbers or strings instead of variables in the name-value pairs. If `SimpleSearchProvider.cfm` accepted an optional parameter called `MaxRows`, you could provide the parameters like so:

```
myService.SimpleSearchProvider({SearchString:"Britney Spears",MaxRows:100});
```

It is also possible to create an ActionScript object to represent the set of parameters you want to set. You then add properties to the object to represent each parameter, and then supply the object to the service function call. The following fictional function call:

```
myService.SimpleSearchProvider({SearchString:MySearchString,MaxRows:100});
```

would become:

```
var myParams = new Object;
myParams.SearchString = MySearchString;
myParams.MaxRows = 100;
myService.SimpleSearchProvider(myParams);
```

Accessing the Returned Value

Now that you know what code to use for executing a ColdFusion page, you maybe wondering how to access whatever data the ColdFusion page sends back to the Flash Player. To access the data, you need to create a special function called an *event handler* that executes when ColdFusion's response is received.

Basically, the idea is this: Depending on what it does, it is possible that the ColdFusion code to which your movie is connecting might take a few seconds to complete its work. Rather than halting the movie (which could be animated) while the ColdFusion template is working, the Flash Player lets the movie continue playing normally while the ColdFusion page is working. Then, when the ColdFusion page is completed and sends back whatever result it generates, your event handler is called, and takes care of displaying the information or doing whatever else is appropriate.

To create an event handler to receive data sent back from a ColdFusion page, create a function that follows this basic form:

```
function serviceFunctionName_Result(result) {
  // do something with result, which is what ColdFusion returned
}
```

Replace the `serviceFunctionName` part of the function name with the name of the service function that you are calling. In other words, the name of the event handler is simply the word `_Result` tacked onto the name of your ColdFusion page (without the .cfm extension). That's why the last function in Listing 23.2 looks like this, comments notwithstanding:

```
function SimpleSearchProvider_Result(result)
{
  // do something with result, which is what ColdFusion returned
  SearchResults = result;
}
```

Inside the event handler, the `result` variable will hold whatever value the ColdFusion page called `SimpleSearchProvider.cfm` returns. If the page returns a string, the `result` will hold that string. If it returns an array, that `result` will hold an ActionScript array, and so on. Structures and query objects can be returned as well.

For now, assume that `result` is a string created dynamically by the ColdFusion page, based somehow on the `SearchString` parameter provided when the page is called. The `SearchResults = result` statement within the event handler just sets the value of the Flash variable named `SearchResults` to the string sent back by the Remoting gateway. Because the larger, multiline text box in the Search user interface from Figure 23.4 is bound to the `SearchResults` variable (this was one of the steps you performed while drawing the interface), it will display the value of the string as soon as a response has been received from ColdFusion and this event handler is called.

NOTE

> If a specific event handler is not found (that is, if there is no corresponding function whose name ends in `_Result`), the Flash Player will look for a function named `onResult()` to pass the results to. This means you can create a function with `function serviceFunctionName(result)` if for some reason it doesn't make sense to write separate handlers for each ColdFusion page you will be executing. You might do this if you were going to execute different pages based on some kind of option the user selects, but the results should be treated the same way no matter which page is executed. See the Flash Remoting reference in Flash MX's online help for details.

Whew! That was a lot of explanation for just the short amount of code shown in Listing 23.2. But as you can see, each individual line is quite simple, and hardly anything at all needed to be changed from the code that the Flash template automatically included in the first frame of the movie. Now the only thing left to do is to create the `SimpleSearchProvider.cfm` page to which the Flash movie refers.

Creating the ColdFusion Code

Now that the Flash side of the search interface example is done, it is time to create the server side part of the application with ColdFusion. Creating a ColdFusion page that interacts with Flash is much like creating the normal ColdFusion pages you already know and love. You can run queries with <CFQUERY> and then loop over the records with <CFLOOP>. You can send dynamic email with <CFMAIL>, interact with custom tags, user-defined functions, CFCs, or whatever you like.

The only real difference is that instead of outputting content to the browser with <CFOUTPUT>, you return the content by setting a special variable called `FLASH.Result`.

Introducing the FLASH Scope

ColdFusion MX includes a new scope called `FLASH`, which contains several special variables that you can use to respond to the Flash Player when it executes one of your ColdFusion pages via Flash Remoting. Table 23.1 provides an explanation of the `FLASH` scope.

Table 23.1 Variables in the `FLASH` Scope

VARIABLE	DESCRIPTION
`FLASH.`variable name	The `FLASH` scope is similar conceptually to the `URL` or `FORM` scopes you are already familiar with. Any parameter passed by Flash is available as a variable with a corresponding name in the `FLASH` scope. So, if the Flash player passes a parameter called `SearchString` to one of your ColdFusion pages, that page can access the value as `FLASH.Params.SearchString`.
`FLASH.Result`	The value of this variable will be sent back to the Flash Player when your page has finished executing. So, if you have a query object called `SearchQuery` that you would like to send to Flash, just use a <CFSET> tag to set the value of `FLASH.Result` to `SearchQuery`.
`FLASH.PageSize`	This sets the number of records to send back at one time to the Flash Player. Currently relevant only if you are returning a query object (a record set) to the Flash Player. This is a somewhat advanced topic; I will touch on it later in the section about record sets.

NOTE

There is also an array in the `FLASH` scope called `FLASH.Params`, which provides an alternative way to access the values of parameters. In general, it is easier to ignore the `FLASH.Params` array and just refer to the parameters by name in the `FLASH` scope directly. See the Flash Remoting documentation for details.

Listing 23.3 is the `SimpleSearchProvider.cfm` template to which the `SimpleSearchMovie.fla` movie refers. Notice how ridiculously easy it is to accept the user's search string, run a query, and return a result to the Flash Player.

Listing 23.3 `SimpleSearchProvider.cfm`—Sending Data Back to the Flash Player

```
<!---
  Filename: SimpleSearchProvider.cfm
  Author:   Nate Weiss (NMW)
  Purpose:  Provides a simple film search service for a Flash MX movie
--->

<!--- We are expecting a SearchString parameter from Flash --->
<CFPARAM NAME="FLASH.SearchString" TYPE="string">
```

Listing 23.3 (CONTINUED)

```
<!--- Query the database for any matching film records --->
<CFQUERY NAME="SearchQuery" DATASOURCE="#REQUEST.DataSource#" MAXROWS="1">
  SELECT *
  FROM Films
  WHERE MovieTitle LIKE '%#FLASH.SearchString#%'
</CFQUERY>

<!--- Set the FLASH.Result variable to the summary of the returned film --->
<!--- This will be available as the "result" variable in the --->
<!--- SimpleSearchProvider_Result handler within the Flash movie --->
<CFSET FLASH.Result = SearchQuery.Summary>
```

That's really all you need. Because my example Flash movie is providing the user's typed keywords as a parameter called `SearchString`, there will be a corresponding variable called `FLASH.SearchString` that holds the user's search criteria. The `<CFPARAM>` tag at the top of the page makes sure this parameter is passed.

Next, an ordinary `<CFQUERY>` tag queries the `Films` database table for matching records. The user's actual search criteria is used in the `WHERE` part of the query by referring to the `Films.SearchString` variable. Note that a `MAXROWS="1"` attribute makes sure the query returns only one record (at most). Of course, you would normally want to return multiple records; I am just trying to keep the example as simple as possible for the moment.

TIP

If you wanted a more full-featured search mechanism, allowing the user to run **AND** versus **OR** searches and the like, you could use the Verity search engine by replacing the `<CFQUERY>` tag with a `<CFSEARCH>` tag. See Chapter 34, "Full-Text Searching," for details.

Note that this is almost the same as how one would respond to a similar request from a traditional HTML search form. One could even argue that it's *easier* to interact with Flash than with a regular Web browser, because you don't even have to learn about HTML or the slightly different ways various browsers may interpret HTML.

Testing the Example

At this point, the simple search example should be ready to use.

To test it out, you can do either of the following:

- *Publish* the movie by choosing File > Publish in Flash MX. After a moment, your browser should show the search interface on a blank Web page.
- *Test* the movie by choosing Control, Test Movie. This will display your movie directly in the Flash MX environment, rather than in a separate Web page.

In either case, you should now be able to type a film's title or part of its title in the search blank in the Flash movie. When you click Search, the ColdFusion code in Listing 23.3 will execute. When Listing 23.3 sends the result string back to the Flash Player, the `SimpleSearchProvider_Result()` event handler in Listing 23.2 will execute, which in turn causes the summary of the matching film (if any) to be displayed (Figure 23.5).

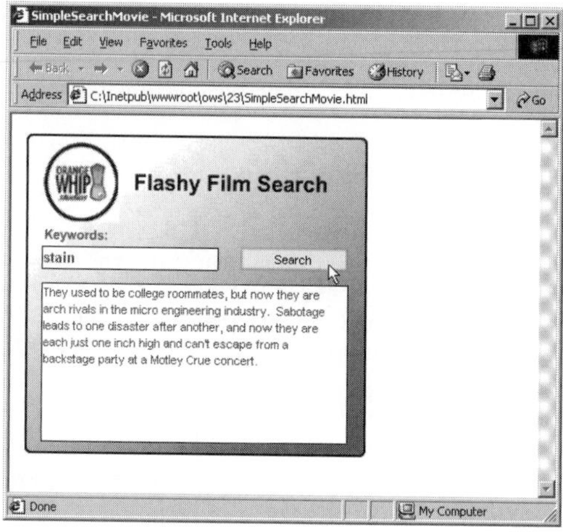

Figure 23.5

The Flash Remoting Gateway is contacted when the user clicks the Search button.

More About Returning Data to Flash

You've now learned the basic concepts involved in sending data back to ColdFusion. This section explains with a bit more detail exactly what kinds of data you can return to Flash, and how. The good news is that you can send almost any type of data native to ColdFusion (including structures, arrays, and record sets) back to the Flash Player just as effortlessly as you can send strings.

Returning Multiple Values to Flash

In Listing 23.3, only one piece of information was returned to the Flash Player: the summary of a matching film, which is a simple string. You aren't stuck with sending back one measly piece of information at a time. In fact, you can send back as much information as you want. Just treat the `FLASH.Result` variable as a structure, using dot notation to create subvariables within `FLASH.Result`. Each of the subvariables will be available to your Flash movie as corresponding subvariables of the ActionScript `result` variable.

For instance, instead of this line from the end of Listing 23.3:

```
<CFSET FLASH.Result = SearchQuery.Summary>
```

you could use the following:

```
<CFSET FLASH.Result.Title = SearchQuery.MovieTitle>
<CFSET FLASH.Result.Summary = SearchQuery.Summary>
<CFSET FLASH.Result.CurrentDate = DateFormat(Now())>
```

Then, in the ActionScript code in the Flash movie, you would change this line:

```
SearchResults = result;
```

to this:

```
SearchResults = result.Summary;
```

You could also use the `result.Title` and `result.CurrentDate` variables however you wanted. In fact, `result` is now an ActionScript object, as I'll discuss next.

Returning Structures to Flash

If you send a CFML structure back to Flash in the `FLASH.Result` variable, the information will be made available to your movie as a native ActionScript `Object` variable. It's not possible to explain everything about how to work with objects, but here is a quick example.

Say you created a structure with two values called `FirstName` and `LastName` your ColdFusion page, like so:

```
<CFSET s = StructNew()>
<CFSET s.FirstName = "Nate">
<CFSET s.LastName = "Weiss">
<CFSET FLASH.Result = s>
```

Then in your Flash movie you could refer to the first and last names as `result.FirstName` and `result.LastName`. You can find out how many values (or properties) the `result` object included by accessing `result.length`. You can loop through the values in `result` using a `for..in` loop, like so:

```
for (Prop in result) {
  // Within this loop, refer to Prop for the current property name
  // refer to result[Prop] for the value of the current property
}
```

Returning Arrays to Flash

If you return a CFML array to Flash in the `FLASH.Result` variable, a corresponding ActionScript array will be created. You can use the array just like any other ActionScript array. Keep in mind that ActionScript arrays (like JavaScript arrays) are zero-based, which means that the array positions start at `0` rather than at `1`.

Say you have this in your ColdFusion code:

```
<CFSET ar = ArrayNew(1)>
<CFSET ar[1] = 3>
<CFSET ar[2] = 1>
<CFSET ar[3] = 4>
<CFSET FLASH.Result = ar>
```

Then the Flash movie could access the first element in the array as `result[0]`, and the value of `result[0]` would be `3`. The number of elements in the array is available as `result.length`, and you can add, remove, or sort elements in the array using `result.push()`, `result.pop()`, and `result.sort()`, respectively. See the ActionScript dictionary in your Flash MX documentation for details on arrays.

Returning Queries to Flash

You can also return query objects to Flash using the `FLASH.Result` variable; the query becomes available in ActionScript as a Flash Remoting RecordSet object. This is discussed shortly, in the "Working with Record Sets in Flash" section.

Rich Text in Flash Text Boxes

It's worth taking a moment to point out that the Flash Player allows you to use very simple HTML tags to format text displayed in a text box. Flash only supports basic character-formatting tags: `<A>`, `<B>`, `<FONT>`, `<I>`, `<P>`, and `<U>`. While this doesn't give you the ability to lay out pages (you're meant to use the Flash MX environment for design and layout work), you do have the ability to manipulate text that you send back from ColdFusion by making certain parts of it bold, italic, or the like.

To experiment with this, go back to the simple search movie in Flash MX and use the Property panel to enable the Render Text as HTML option for the multiline text box that shows the search results. Then go back to Listing 23.3 to and remove the `MAXROWS` attribute so the query can return multiple records. Finally, change this line:

```
<CFSET FLASH.Result = SearchQuery.Summary>
```

to this:

```
<CFSAVECONTENT VARIABLE="Flash.Result">
  <CFOUTPUT QUERY="SearchQuery">
    <P><B>#MovieTitle#</B><BR>#Summary#<BR></P>
  </CFOUTPUT>
</CFSAVECONTENT>
```

Now test the movie again, typing in something like `the` as the search criterion so that you see multiple records (Figure 23.6). As you can see, the `<BR>` and `<P>` tags are interpreted as ends of lines, and the `<B>` tags are interpreted as bold, similar to how a browser would interpret these tags.

NOTE

In Figure 23.6, I also added a scroll bar to the text area to make it possible for a user to look through the records. You do this by dragging the ScrollBar from the Flash UI Components part of the Components panel. Refer to your Flash documentation for details about scroll bars.

NOTE

The SimpleSearchProvider2.cfm template on the CD-ROM is a revised version of Listing 23.3 that includes the changes mentioned here.

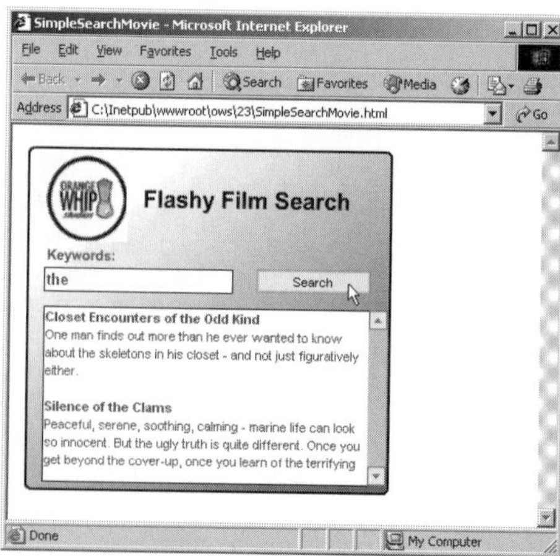

Figure 23.6
The Flash Player allows you to mark up text with simple HTML tags.

Working with Record Sets in Flash

One of ColdFusion's greatest strengths has always been its thoughtful treatment of the concept of a query record set. Whenever you use a `<CFQUERY>` tag to select information from a database, you get back a query record set object that contains rows and columns of information. Because it's such a natural way to think about data, and because it corresponds so closely to how relational database systems store data internally, it's hard to imagine any ColdFusion application that doesn't deal with query record sets in one way or another.

One of the Flash Remoting Components is a special ActionScript object called RecordSet, which is very similar conceptually to a query object in CFML. Whenever you use the `FLASH.Result` variable to send a query object back to the Flash Player, the data becomes available to ActionScript as an equivalent RecordSet object.

About RecordSet Objects

Take a look at the ColdFusion listing in Listing 23.4. It is very similar to Listing 23.3, which supplied information about a single film as a simple string. In contrast, this listing simply runs a `<CFQUERY>` named `MerchQuery` and then returns the entire query object to Flash.

Listing 23.4 `MerchRecordsetProvider.cfm`—Returning a Query Object to the Flash Player

```
<!---
  Filename: MerchRecordsetProvider.cfm
  Author:   Nate Weiss (NMW)
  Purpose:  Provides data to a Flash MX movie
--->

<!--- Query the database for merchandise records --->
<CFQUERY NAME="MerchQuery" DATASOURCE="#REQUEST.DataSource#">
  SELECT MerchID, MerchName
  FROM Merchandise
  ORDER BY MerchName
</CFQUERY>

<!--- This will be available as the "result" variable in the --->
<!--- MerchRecordsetProvider_Result handler within the Flash movie --->
<CFSET FLASH.Result = MerchQuery>
```

As you have learned, whatever value ColdFusion returns with the `FLASH.Result` variable becomes available to Flash as a native ActionScript variable called `result`. If the value of `FLASH.Result` is a string on the server, then `result` is a string in Flash. If `FLASH.Result` is an array, then `result` is an array, and so on. It follows that if the value of `FLASH.Result` is a query object, then `result` will be a `RecordSet` object.

Unlike strings, dates, numbers, structures, and arrays, which have obvious equivalents in JavaScript, there is no native JavaScript data type that corresponds in a helpful way to the ColdFusion concept of a query result set. The RecordSet object type, which is included automatically with `NetServices.as`, was designed to fill this need.

NOTE

If you are really into JavaScript or ActionScript, you can check out how the RecordSet object is implemented by opening the `RecordSet.as` file in the `Configuration/Include` folder within Flash MX's program folder. It's pure ActionScript.

RecordSet Functions

Table 23.2 lists the methods supported by the RecordSet object. This is by no means an exhaustive list; I am just trying to show you some of the most interesting methods. For a complete listing, you need to consult the ActionScript Dictionary part of the Flash Remoting online documentation (choose Window > Welcome to Flash Remoting to view this documentation).

NOTE

The only methods actually used in this chapter's listings are `getLength()` and `getItemAt()`. I am listing the other functions in this table mainly to give you an idea about what kinds of things the RecordSet object is capable of.

Table 23.2 Important RecordSet Methods

METHOD	DESCRIPTION
`myRS.getLength()`	Returns the number of records (rows) in the record set. Equivalent to the `RecordCount` property of queries in CFML.
`myRS.getItemAt(row)`	Returns the data in the row specified by the `row` argument. The record numbers are zero-based, so `getItemAt(0)` returns the first row of data, `getItemAt(1)` returns the second row, and so on. The data is returned as an ActionScript object (similar to a CFML structure), with properties that correspond to the record set's column names.
`myRS.filter()`	Provides an easy way to filter the records in a RecordSet object. This is similar conceptually to ColdFusion's Query of Queries feature (see Chapter 29, "More On SQL and Queries").
`myRS.setField()`	Provides a way to change the values in Flash's local copy of the record set. Similar conceptually to CFML's `QuerySetCell()` function.
`myRS.sortItemsBy()`	Sorts Flash's local copy of the record set by whatever column you specify.

NOTE

For details about the methods listed in Table 23.2, see the ActionScript dictionary in the Flash Remoting documentation.

For instance, the following snippet is an example of a event handler that loops through the record set returned by the `MerchRecordsetProvider.cfm` page (Listing 23.4). You can usually use code like this to loop through any given RecordSet object. Think of this as the ActionScript equivalent of a `<CFLOOP>` block that loops over a ColdFusion query object with the `QUERY` attribute.

```
function MerchRecordsetProvider_Result(result) {
  // For each record in the recordset...
  for (var i = 0; i < result.getLength(); i++) {
    // Use the record variable to refer to the current row of recordset
    var record = result.getItemAt(i);
```

```
        /*
          Now the rest of this block can refer to the current row's data
          as properties of the record variable, such as record.MerchName,
          record.MerchDescription, or record.MerchPrice.
        */
    };
}
```

The for statement at the top uses `result.getLength()` to find out the number of records in the `result` record set. The code within the `for` block will execute once for each row in the record set, incrementing the value of `i` for each pass through the loop. In other words, `i` is the current row number, starting with 0. Next, the `getItemAt()` method grabs the data from the current row of the record set and places it into the `record` variable. Now the rest of the code in the loop can refer to the current row's data as properties of the `record` variable, such as `record.MerchName`, `record.MerchDescription`, or `record.MerchPrice`.

NOTE

Unlike JavaScript, ActionScript is not case sensitive (except for statement keywords like `for`, `var`, and `function`), so you don't have to get the capitalization of column names or of the `record` variable itself exactly right. That said, it is generally easier to follow and maintain code that uses capitalization consistently.

A Complete Example

The next Flash example is a movie that displays a simple but effective Merchandise Browser for Orange Whip Studios. The idea is to provide an interesting way for users to look through the items for sale, without taking up too much space on the page and without reloading the page to show the details about each item. The example will also use a bit of animation to make the display seem livelier and to give the user a sense that the information about each product is looked up in real time. Actually, it's more than a sense; the information really will be looked up in real time.

The User Experience

The Flash Document used to create the Merchandise Browser example is included on the CD-ROM for this chapter. The filename is `MerchBrowser.fla`. Go ahead and open the file in Flash MX now, then view the movie by choosing Control > Test Movie or File > Publish Preview > Default. That should produce a working version of the example.

NOTE

You may need to adjust the URL used in the `NetServices.setDefaultGatewayUrl()` method before the example will operate properly (see Listing 23.5). The version of the file on the CD-ROM assumes you are using a ColdFusion on your local machine in stand-alone mode (that is, at port `8500`). If not, just adjust the URL accordingly.

The movie shows a list of merchandise available for sale in a scrolling list box (Figure 23.7). When the user selects an item in the list, details about the item slide out from underneath the list (Figure 23.8) in an animated fashion. The details include the product's name, description, and price (Figure 23.9).

Figure 23.7

The movie shows a list of products; the user can drill down by selecting items.

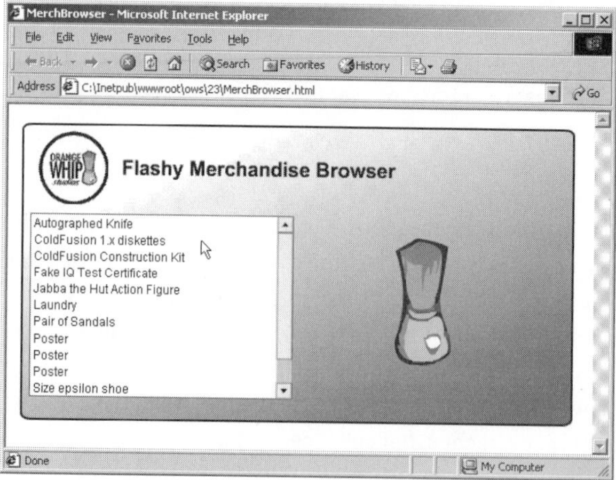

Figure 23.8

When the user selects an item, details slide out from under the list.

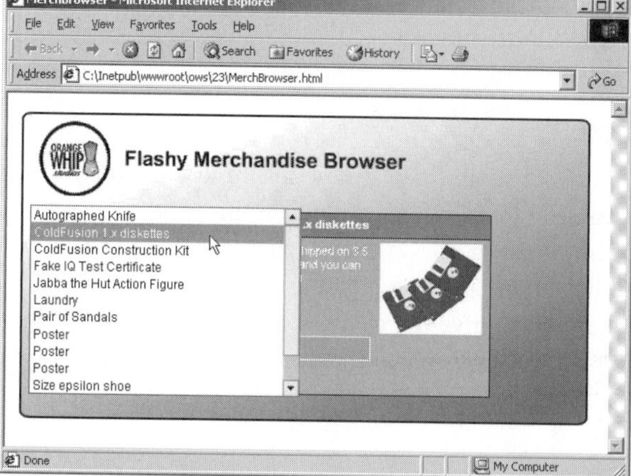

Figure 23.9

Flash Remoting allows you to create data-aware applications with rich, interactive user interfaces.

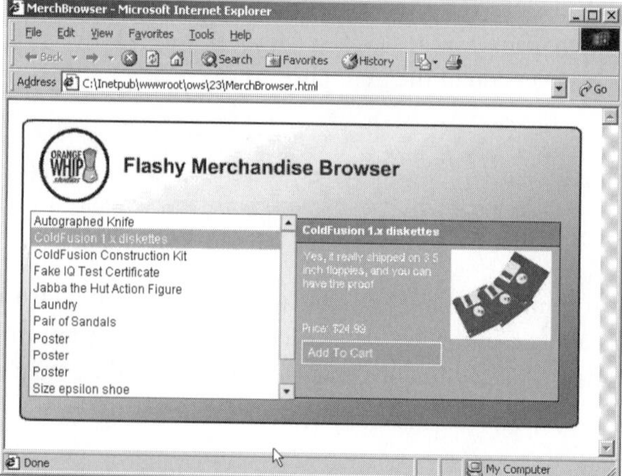

NOTE

The Add To Cart button shown in Figure 23.9 is not operational in this movie. I'll create a second version of this movie later, one that includes working cart functionality. See the "Instantiated CFCs" section, later in this chapter.

Of course, this is only an example, and Orange Whip Studios isn't any more likely to win design awards for this interface than to win Academy Awards for its films. My main goal here is to get you thinking about how you can use Flash to reinvent certain kinds of Web experiences, like master-detail record navigation or shopping carts. Information can slide in or fade out, giving users visual feedback about what exactly is happening as they make choices or push buttons. Of course, the point isn't just to be showy, but to make the user experience more engaging, more fun, and more efficient.

Building the Interface

Compared to the last example, this one is a bit involved, and requires more individual steps than I can reasonably list here. I recommend that you open and explore the `MerchBrowser.fla` file, rather than taking the time to reproduce it from scratch. That said, I would like to call your attention to the important elements in the movie so you can understand how the code works.

Figure 23.10 shows how the movie looks in the Flash MX workspace. Note that there are four layers in the timeline (at the top of the window). Also, unlike the last example, this one has more than one frame in the timeline. The various frames represent different moments in the animation that takes place while the user interacts with the movie. Figure 23.10 shows Frame 10, which is when the detail view is fully showing (refer to Figure 23.9). The frames before Frame 10 are when the detail view is sliding out from under the list of products; the frames after Frame 10 are when the details are sliding back under the list.

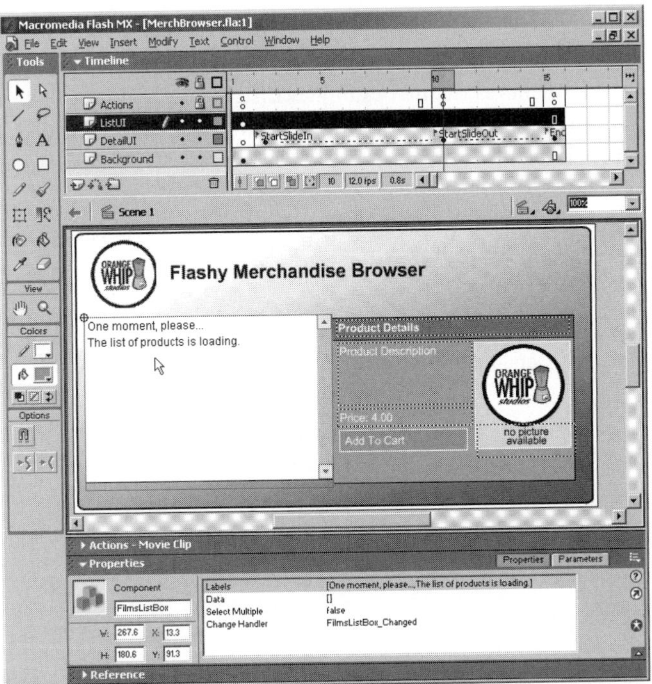

Figure 23.10

You can use Flash's concept of animation through time to make your pages more interactive.

Table 23.3 explains what is in each layer of the movie.

Table 23.3 Layers in `MerchBrowser.fla`

LAYER	DESCRIPTION
`Actions` layer	As is the custom, a separate layer called `Actions` holds actions (that is, blocks of ActionScript code) that should execute at different moments in the movie's animation sequence. The code in the first frame is similar conceptually to the code in the first frame of the first example (Listing 23.2). Note that since this layer isn't meant to hold any visual elements, it is locked so nothing gets placed on it accidentally.
`ListUI` layer	This layer contains a ListBox component called `MerchListBox`, which is what the user uses to browse the list of products. Note that this layer appears above the others in the timeline, which is why the ListBox always stays on top of other items (like the detail view that slides from under it).
`DetailUI` layer	This layer contains the animated detail view. The animation is pretty modest by Flash standards; just a simple slide from left to right. The layer contains several text box elements to show the selected product's name, description, and price. The actual animation was created with just a few mouse clicks and Flash's motion-tweening feature. Note that this is the only layer that changes from frame to frame. Note also that each of the layer's *keyframes* (turning points in the animation) are named with descriptive labels (`StartSlideIn`, `StartSlideOut`, and `EndSlideOut`).
`Background` layer	This layer contains a decorative background and some artwork, as shown in Figure 23.7.

Writing the ActionScript Code

Listing 23.5 shows the ActionScript code in the first frame of `MerchBrowser.fla`. The code here has many of the same elements as the first example (Listing 23.2). Considering that this movie appears to do more, it's pretty remarkable that not much additional code is needed. I will explain each of the important points in the code shortly.

Listing 23.5 ActionScript Code in the First Frame of `MerchBrowser.fla`

```
// Include support for Flash Remoting Components
#include "NetServices.as"

// uncomment this line when you want to use the NetConnect debugger
// #include "NetDebug.as"

// ---------------------------------------------
// Handlers for user interaction events
// ---------------------------------------------

// ---------------------------------------------
// Application initialization
// ---------------------------------------------

if (inited == null)
```

Listing 23.5 (continued)

```
{
  // do this code only once
  inited = true;

  // set the default gateway URL (this is used only in authoring)
NetServices.setDefaultGatewayUrl("http://localhost:8500/flashservices/gateway")

  // connect to the gateway
  gateway_conn = NetServices.createGatewayConnection();

  // get a reference to a service
  // In this case, the "service" is the /ows/23 directory in web server root
  myService = gateway_conn.getService("ows.23", this);

  // Call the service function that fills the ListBox with a list
  // of products (from ColdFusion) for the user to browse through
  myService.MerchRecordsetProvider();
}


// This function executes when the user selects an item in the ListBox
function MerchListBox_Changed() {
  // If this is the first time an item has been selected,
  // go straight to the frame that loads the detail information
  if (_currentFrame == 1) {
    gotoAndPlay("EndSlideOut");
  // Otherwise, go to the frame that slides the display back in (hides it)
  // When it finishes sliding, it will load the detail information
  } else {
    gotoAndPlay("StartSlideOut");
  }
}


// This function retrieves the detail information about the selected product.
// It is executed when the last frame of the movie is reached
// (when the detail view has finished hiding itself under the product list)
function getSelectedItemDetails() {
  myService.MerchDetailProvider({MerchID:MerchListBox.getValue()});
}


// -----------------------------------------------
// Handlers for data coming in from server
// -----------------------------------------------
function MerchRecordsetProvider_Result(result) {
  // First, remove any existing items from the list box
  MerchListBox.removeAll();

  //DataGlue.bindFormatStrings (MerchListBox, result, "#MerchName#", "#MerchID#");
  // For each record in the recordset...
  for (var i = 0; i < result.getLength(); i++) {
    // Use the record variable to refer to the current row of recordset
    var record = result.getItemAt(i);
    // Add item to the MerchListBox widget, which is like a <SELECT> in HTML
    MerchListBox.addItem(record.MerchName, record.MerchID);
```

Listing 23.5 (CONTINUED)

```
    };
  }


  // This executes when a merchandise detail record has been received
  function MerchDetailProvider_Result(result) {
    // The result variable is a recordset that contains just one row
    // The detailRecord variable will represent the row of data
    var detailRecord = result.getItemAt(0);

    // Display detail information in text boxes
    _root.TitleTextBox.text = detailRecord.MerchName;
    _root.DescriptionTextBox.text = detailRecord.MerchDescription;
    _root.PriceTextBox.text = "Price: " + detailRecord.MerchPrice;

    // If the ImageNameSmall column contains an image filename, display it
    if (detailRecord.ImageNameSmall.length > 0) {
      // Load and display the product image
      loadMovie("../images/" + detailRecord.ImageNameSmall, _root.ImageMovie);
      // Hide the OWS logo
      OWSLogo._visible = false;
    // If there is no image file for this record, display the OWS logo instead
    } else {
      // Unload any product image that might already be showing
      unloadMovie(_root.ImageMovie);
      // Make the OWS logo visible
      OWSLogo._visible = true;
    }

    // Now that the information about the merchandise has been placed,
    // make the display slide back into view, revealing the information
    gotoAndPlay("StartSlideIn");
  }


  // Stop here, so animation doesn't occur until user selects a product
  stop();
```

In addition to the code in the first frame, frames 10 and 15 contain a few additional lines of ActionScript code, as shown in Listing 23.6 and Listing 23.7.

Listing 23.6 ActionScript Code in Frame 10 of `MerchBrowser.fla`

```
// Stop the animation for now, so the detail view remains visible.
// The animation will remain stopped until the user selects a different
// item from the list of products.
stop();
```

Listing 23.7 ActionScript Code in Frame 15 of `MerchBrowser.fla`

```
// Retrieve detail information about the selected item in the product list
getSelectedItemDetails();

// Stop the animation for now, so detail view remains hidden behind list
// until the details have been retrieved.  The event handler for the
// MerchDetailProvider.cfm page will bring it back into view when ready.
stop();
```

Understanding the Code

You have now seen all the ActionScript code needed to create the Merchandise Browser example. Some of it is familiar to you from the first Flash movie we created (Listing 23.2). Let's go through the sequence of events that occurs within the movie, from when it first appears to what happens when users click the various elements in the movie.

The normal sequence of events is as follows:

1. When the movie first appears, the first thing the Flash Player does is execute the ActionScript code in the first frame (Listing 23.5).
2. The initialization block at the top of Listing 23.5 executes. Except for the last line, this block is the same as the one in Listing 23.2. The last line executes calls the `MerchRecordsetProvider.cfm` page from Listing 23.4 as a Flash Remoting service function.
3. On the ColdFusion server, the `<CFQUERY>` in Listing 23.4 is run, and the query records are passed back to Flash with `FLASH.Result`.
4. When the Flash Player receives the data from ColdFusion, it executes the `MerchRecordsetProvider_Result()` event handler.
5. Within `MerchRecordsetProvider_Result()`, the `MerchListBox` is populated with the data in the record set returned by ColdFusion. First, any existing items are removed from the list with the `removeAll()` method. Then a simple `for` loop loops through the record set, as discussed in the "RecordSet Functions" section earlier in this chapter. Within the loop, the list box's `addItem()` method adds an item to the list for each record in the record set. These items are conceptually similar to the individual `<OPTION>` elements in a normal HTML `<SELECT>` list. Each item will display a product's name, and the value of each item is the corresponding `MerchID` number.
6. The initial work of the movie is now complete. Because of the `stop()` action at the bottom of Listing 23.5, the timeline does not advance past the first frame. Nothing further will happen until the user selects a product from the list.
7. When the user selects a product, Flash Player executes the `MerchListBox_Changed()` function. This is because `MerchListBox_Changed` is specified as the Change Handler for the `MerchListBox` list box (you specify the Change Handler in the Properties panel).
8. Within `MerchListBox_Changed()`, the idea is to make sure the detail view returns to its hidden position, where it will remain hidden while the detail information for the selected movie is retrieved from the server. If this is the first time a product has been selected, then the `gotoAndPlay()` command sends the timeline directly to the `EndSlideOut` frame of the movie. Normally, though, `gotoAndPlay()`sends the timeline to the `StartSlideOut` frame, which starts the animation of the details sliding back under the product list. Either way, the `EndSlideOut` frame (the last frame of the movie) is reached eventually, which is what starts the process of contacting the server for the details of the newly selected product.

9. The code in the EndSlideOut frame of the movie (Listing 23.7) runs, simply executing the getSelectedItemDetails() function and halting the animation (now that the detail view is hidden under the product list).

10. Within getSelectedItemDetails(), the Flash Player requests detail information about the selected movie by calling the MerchDetailProvider.cfm ColdFusion page as a service function, passing the value of the currently selected item as a parameter called MerchID. You haven't seen this listing yet, but it takes the MerchID, runs a query to get the details about the item, and returns the query.

11. When the detail data is received from ColdFusion, the MerchRecordsetProvider_Result() event handler is called.

12. Within MerchRecordsetProvider_Result(), a variable named detailRecord gets the first row of data from the record set. This record set will only return one row, so there is no need for looping. The name, description, and price of the item is displayed in the TitleTextBox, DescriptionTextBox, and PriceTextBox text boxes, respectively.

13. Still within MerchRecordsetProvider_Result(), an if statement determines if the ImageNameSmall column of the record set contains a filename. If so, it displays the picture by calling the loadMovie() command. The picture will be displayed where the movie clip called ImageMovie is positioned (it's in the DetailUI layer). If an image is not available, a different movie clip called OWSLogo is shown in its place, visually indicating that there is no picture available.

14. Now that the details of the selected product are visible, the final step within MerchRecordsetProvider_Result() is to send the timeline to the StartSlideIn frame (that's Frame 2), which begins the animation of the details sliding out from under the product list.

15. The animation stops at Frame 10 because of the stop() command at Frame 10 (Listing 23.6), and remains at Frame 10 until the user selects a different product from the list, at which point the execution goes back to step 7, above.

That's it. Unfortunately it's not possible for me to explain all of the Flash concepts mentioned in this section, such as how to create animations with Flash's motion-tweening feature, what keyframes and movie clips are, and how to load images dynamically at run time. That said, this example should give you a solid understanding of how to incorporate Flash Remoting into your Flash MX movies. If you are new to Flash, it has also hopefully given you some idea about what is involved in creating new movies of your own.

Listing 23.8 shows the ColdFusion page that provides the detail information about each product to Flash. This is the page called by the getSelectedItemDetails() function when the movie reaches its last frame (that is, when the detail view is fully hidden).

Listing 23.8 `MerchDetailProvider.cfm`—Providing Details About the Selected Product

```
<!---
  Filename: MerchDetailProvider.cfm
  Author:   Nate Weiss (NMW)
  Purpose:  Provides film detail to a Flash movie
--->

<!--- We are expecting a MerchID parameter to be passed from Flash --->
<CFPARAM NAME="FLASH.MerchID" TYPE="numeric">

<!--- Query the database for merchandise records --->
<CFQUERY NAME="MerchQuery" DATASOURCE="#REQUEST.DataSource#" MAXROWS="1">
  SELECT MerchID, MerchName, MerchDescription, ImageNameSmall, MerchPrice
  FROM Merchandise
  WHERE MerchID = #FLASH.MerchID#
</CFQUERY>

<!--- Format the MerchPrice column in the appropriate currency format --->
<!--- (It's easier to do this with ColdFusion than with ActionScript) --->
<CFSET MerchQuery.MerchPrice = LSCurrencyFormat(MerchQuery.MerchPrice)>

<!--- This will be available as the "result" variable in the --->
<!--- MerchDetailProvider_Result handler within the Flash movie --->
<CFSET FLASH.Result = MerchQuery>
```

As you can see, this is a very simple template. The `<CFPARAM>` tag makes sure that Flash provides a parameter called `MerchID`. Then a simple query retrieves information from the corresponding record of the Merchandise table, and the query is passed back to Flash with `FLASH.Result`.

The only thing of note here is the fact that the `MerchPrice` column of the query is changed to hold the currency-formatted version of the price. This is done because the `LSCurrencyFormat()` function is easy to use in ColdFusion, whereas there is no direct equivalent in Flash. This underscores the fact that you can use any of the tools available to you as a ColdFusion developer within a page that serves Flash via Flash Remoting.

Calling CFC Methods from Flash

As you have seen, Flash Remoting makes it really easy to create ColdFusion pages that supply information to Flash, or perform whatever other type of processing you want to trigger from movies playing in the Flash Player. You just think of each directory that contains such ColdFusion pages as a service, and of each individual page as a service function.

Flash Remoting also makes it possible to use ColdFusion Components to supply information or other server-side processing to Flash MX. Nearly everything you do on the Flash side of things is exactly the same. The only difference is that each CFC constitutes a service, and each of the CFC's methods constitute service functions.

In other words, you can think of a service as a collection of functions. Whether you want to write those functions as pages in a directory or as methods of a CFC is up to you.

Of course, if you go the CFC route, you get all the other benefits of CFCs for free, including automatic documentation and integration with Dreamweaver MX. But the greatest benefit of going the CFC route is the fact that your CFCs can be used internally by your ColdFusion pages (via the `<CFINVOKE>` tag) or as Web Services, as well as by your Flash MX applications. See Chapter 20 for details about ColdFusion Components.

NOTE

I am talking about ColdFusion Components, special CFML code files executed on the server. ColdFusion Components are completely different from what Flash called components; the latter show up in the Components panel in Flash MX and usually present themselves visually within the player.

NOTE

I am assuming that you have already read about ColdFusion Components in Chapter 20. If not, you might want to take a glance at that chapter before continuing here. Or you can just keep reading to get a crash course in CFCs. :)

ColdFusion Components as Services

To demonstrate how easy it is to use ColdFusion Components in your Flash MX applications, you will now create a CFC that takes the place of the ColdFusion pages used by the Merchandise Browser example in the previous section. The Merchandise Browser calls two ColdFusion pages as service functions: `MerchRecordsetProvider.cfm` (Listing 23.4) and `MerchDetailProvider.cfm` (Listing 23.8).

Listing 23.9 creates a new ColdFusion Component called `MerchProviderCFC` which can be used instead. The component exposes two methods called `MerchRecordsetProvider()` and `MerchDetailProvider()` that correspond to the two ColdFusion pages already in place.

Listing 23.9 `MerchProviderCFC.cfc`—A CFC That Supplies Data to Flash, ColdFusion, or Other Applications

```
<!---
  Filename: MerchProviderCFC.cfc
  Author:   Nate Weiss (NMW)
  Purpose:  Creates a ColdFusion Component that supplies data about products
--->

<CFCOMPONENT
  HINT="Provides data about merchandise records.">

  <!--- GetMerchList() function --->
  <CFFUNCTION
    NAME="MerchRecordsetProvider"
    HINT="Returns a recordset of all products in the Merchandise table."
    RETURNTYPE="query"
    ACCESS="Remote">

    <!--- Query the database for merchandise records --->
    <CFQUERY NAME="MerchQuery" DATASOURCE="ows">
      SELECT MerchID, MerchName
      FROM Merchandise
      ORDER BY MerchName
```

Listing 23.9 (continued)

```
    </CFQUERY>

    <!--- Return the query --->
    <CFRETURN MerchQuery>
  </CFFUNCTION>


  <!--- GetMerchList() function --->
  <CFFUNCTION
    NAME="MerchDetailProvider"
    HINT="Returns details about a particular item in the Merchandise table."
    RETURNTYPE="query"
    ACCESS="Remote">

    <!--- MerchID argument (required) --->
    <CFARGUMENT
      NAME="MerchID"
      TYPE="numeric"
      REQUIRED="Yes"
      HINT="The ID number of the desired Merchandise record.">

    <!--- Query the database for merchandise records --->
    <CFQUERY NAME="MerchQuery" DATASOURCE="ows" MAXROWS="1">
      SELECT MerchID, MerchName, MerchDescription, ImageNameSmall, MerchPrice
      FROM Merchandise
      WHERE MerchID = #ARGUMENTS.MerchID#
    </CFQUERY>

    <!--- Format the MerchPrice column in the appropriate currency format --->
    <!--- (It's easier to do this with ColdFusion than with ActionScript) --->
    <CFSET MerchQuery.MerchPrice = LSCurrencyFormat(MerchQuery.MerchPrice)>

    <!--- Return the query --->
    <CFRETURN MerchQuery>
  </CFFUNCTION>

</CFCOMPONENT>
```

NOTE

Only methods that use `ACCESS="Remote"` in their `<CFFUNCTION>` blocks are accessible to Flash Remoting. See Chapter 20 for details.

If you compare the first `<CFFUNCTION>` block in this listing to the code in Listing 23.4, you will see that it is almost identical. The same query is run to get information about products from the database. The only difference is how the query is returned: instead of returning it specifically to the Flash Player with `FLASH.Return`, this code returns it to whatever program is calling the method with the `<CFRETURN>` tag.

In other words, the two versions of the code are the same, except for the fact that the CFC version isn't coded specifically for Flash, which means you get the bonus of being able to use this method internally within your ColdFusion pages. The `ACCESS="Remote"` attribute means the method can also be accessed as a Web Service.

The same goes for the second `<CFFUNCTION>` block; it is nearly identical to Listing 23.8, the ColdFusion page on which it is based. Instead of expecting a parameter called `MerchID` to be passed from the Flash Player specifically, it simply expects that an argument named `MerchID` be passed to the method, whether it is called by Flash, from a ColdFusion page via the `<CFINVOKE>` tag, or by some other means.

See Chapter 20 for further discussion of CFC concepts, and for details about `<CFFUNCTION>`, `<CFARGUMENT>`, and `<CFRETURN>`.

Calling CFC Methods

Once the CFC in Listing 23.9 is in place, it is really easy to make use of the component in your Flash MX applications. Just how easy is it? Well, to make the Merchandise Browser example use the new component to get its data instead of the ad-hoc ColdFusion pages it used previously, you change just one line of code.

Go back to the code for the first frame of the `MerchBrowser.fla` example (Listing 23.5) and change this line:

```
myService = gateway_conn.getService("ows.23", this);
```

to this:

```
myService = gateway_conn.getService("ows.23.MerchProviderCFC", this);
```

That's it! You can now publish or test the movie again, and it will behave in exactly the same way it did before.

As you can see, to create a service reference to a CFC, you simply refer to the CFC by name (that is, the filename without the `.cfc` extension). You specify the path to the CFC file's location in exactly the same way as you would with the `<CFINVOKE>` tag, by using dots to separate the folder names in the path (rather than slashes).

Once you've created the service reference variable, you can call its service functions (that is, the CFC's methods) by calling each function as a method of the variable, just as you did before. So, to call the `MerchRecordsetProvider()` method of the CFC in Listing 23.9, you can continue using the following line of code:

```
myService.MerchRecordsetProvider();
```

To call the `MerchDetailProvider()` method of the CFC and provide the `MerchID` parameter, you can use this line, which is also unchanged from the original version in Listing 23.5:

```
myService.MerchDetailProvider({MerchID:MerchListBox.getValue()});
```

Of course, if you were to change the name of this CFC method to `getMerchDetails()`, say, you would simply change the function call accordingly, like so:

```
myService.getMerchDetails({MerchID:MerchListBox.getValue()});
```

NOTE

You would also need to change the name of the event handler that executes when the data is received. Instead of `MerchDetailProvider_Result`, you would name it `getMerchDetails_Result`.

Instantiated CFCs

Flash Remoting doesn't provide a mechanism for directly accessing components stored in the `APPLICATION` or `SESSION` scopes as discussed in Chapter 20. When you call a method as a Flash service function, you are always calling the method statically, not via an instance of the component.

This doesn't mean you have to rule out the idea of instance-based components in your Flash-based applications entirely, however. Listing 23.10 creates a ColdFusion Component called `CallShoppingCartCFC`. It exposes two methods to Flash: `AddItem()` and `GetItemCount()`. Within the CFC code, each of these methods interact with an instance of the ShoppingCart CFC from Chapter 27, "Online Commerce."

NOTE

I am assuming that you have already copied all the listings for Chapter 27 from the CD-ROM to the `ows/27` folder on your ColdFusion server. If not, please do so now. See Chapter 27 for details on how the ShoppingCart component works internally.

In other words, the CFC in Listing 23.10 is a wrapper around the session-based instance of the Shopping Cart component. This means ColdFusion pages can use the cart instance, and you can still expose it to Flash via the wrapper component.

Listing 23.10 `CallShoppingCartCFC.cfc`—Using a Session-Based CFC Instance

```
<CFCOMPONENT>

  <!--- AddItem() function --->
  <CFFUNCTION
    NAME="AddItem"
    HINT="Adds an item to the session's shopping cart."
    ACCESS="Remote">

    <!--- Required argument: MerchID --->
    <CFARGUMENT
      NAME="MerchID"
      TYPE="numeric"
      REQUIRED="Yes">

    <!--- Call the Add() method of the ShoppingCart CFC --->
    <CFINVOKE
      COMPONENT="#SESSION.MyShoppingCart#"
      METHOD="Add"
      MerchID="#ARGUMENTS.MerchID#">

  </CFFUNCTION>


  <!--- GetItemCount() function --->
  <CFFUNCTION
    NAME="GetItemCount"
    RETURNTYPE="numeric"
    ACCESS="Remote">

    <!--- Call the List() method of the ShoppingCart CFC --->
    <CFINVOKE
      COMPONENT="#SESSION.MyShoppingCart#"
      METHOD="List"
```

Listing 23.10 (continued)

```
        RETURNVARIABLE="CartContents">

      <!--- Use Query-of-Queries to get the number of items in cart --->
      <CFQUERY DBTYPE="query" NAME="GetCount">
        SELECT SUM(Quantity) AS ItemCount
        FROM CartContents
      </CFQUERY>

      <!--- Return the total number of items to Flash --->
      <CFRETURN Val(GetCount.ItemCount)>
    </CFFUNCTION>
  </CFCOMPONENT>
```

NOTE

To make this CFC work, you need to enable session variables and place the `MyShoppingCart` instance of the `ShoppingCart.cfc` component in the `SESSION` scope with the `<CFINVOKE>` tag. The `Application.cfm` file included with this chapter's listings provides the needed code. See Chapter 27 for a discussion of the `<CFINVOKE>` and `<CFIF>` tags used in `Application.cfm`.

The CD-ROM for this book offers another version of the Merchandise Browser movie. The filename is `MerchBrowserCart.fla`. Visually, this version is exactly the same as the first one (`MerchBrowser.fla`), except that there is now a black Shopping Cart button in the upper-right corner (Figure 23.11). Additionally, the Add To Cart button in the detail view for each product now works as expected (it was not operational in the original version).

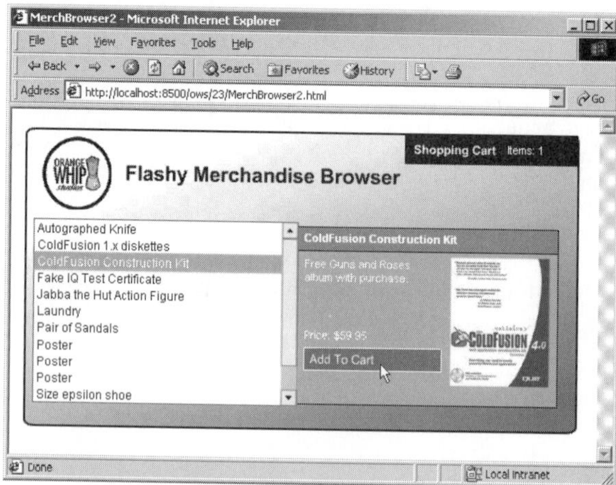

Figure 23.11

Users can add items to their shopping carts with the Add To Cart button.

The ActionScript code in the movie is the same as the previous version (Listing 23.5), except for a small number of additions. The code in the first frame of the new movie is shown in Listing 23.11.

Listing 23.11 ActionScript Code in the First Frame of `MerchBrowserCart.fla`

```
// Include support for Flash Remoting Components
#include "NetServices.as"

// uncomment this line when you want to use the NetConnect debugger
```

Listing 23.11 (continued)

```
// #include "NetDebug.as"

// -----------------------------------------------
// Handlers for user interaction events
// -----------------------------------------------

// -----------------------------------------------
// Application initialization
// -----------------------------------------------

if (inited == null)
{
  // do this code only once
  inited = true;

   // set the default gateway URL (this is used only in authoring)
NetServices.setDefaultGatewayUrl("http://localhost:8500/flashservices/gateway")

  // connect to the gateway
  gateway_conn = NetServices.createGatewayConnection();

  // get a reference to a service
  // In this case, the "service" is the MerchProviderCFC component
  myService = gateway_conn.getService("ows.23.MerchProviderCFC", this);
  cartService = gateway_conn.getService("ows.23.CallShoppingCartCFC", this);

  // Call the service function that fills the ListBox with a list
  // of products (from ColdFusion) for the user to browse through
  myService.MerchRecordsetProvider();
}


// This function executes when the user selects an item in the ListBox
function MerchListBox_Changed() {
  // If this is the first time an item has been selected,
  // go straight to the frame that loads the detail information
  if (_currentFrame == 1) {
    gotoAndPlay("EndSlideOut");
  // Otherwise, go to the frame that slides the display back in (hides it)
  // When it finishes sliding, it will load the detail information
  } else {
    gotoAndPlay("StartSlideOut");
  }
}


// This function retrieves the detail information about the selected product.
// It is executed when the last frame of the movie is reached
// (when the detail view has finished hiding itself under the product list)
function getSelectedItemDetails() {
  myService.MerchDetailProvider({MerchID:MerchListBox.getValue()});
}


// -----------------------------------------------
// Handlers for data coming in from server
// -----------------------------------------------
```

Listing 23.11 (continued)

```
function MerchRecordsetProvider_Result(result) {
  // First, remove any existing items from the list box
  MerchListBox.removeAll();

  //DataGlue.bindFormatStrings (MerchListBox, result, "#MerchName#", "#MerchID#");
  // For each record in the recordset...
  for (var i = 0; i < result.getLength(); i++) {
    // Use the record variable to refer to the current row of recordset
    var record = result.getItemAt(i);
    // Add item to the MerchListBox widget, which is like a <SELECT> in HTML
    MerchListBox.addItem(record.MerchName, record.MerchID);
  };
}


// This executes when a merchandise detail record has been received
function MerchDetailProvider_Result(result) {
  // The result variable is a recordset that contains just one row
  // The detailRecord variable will represent the row of data
  var detailRecord = result.getItemAt(0);

  // Display detail information in text boxes
  _root.TitleTextBox.text = detailRecord.MerchName;
  _root.DescriptionTextBox.text = detailRecord.MerchDescription;
  _root.PriceTextBox.text = "Price: " + detailRecord.MerchPrice;

  // If the ImageNameSmall column contains an image filename, display it
  if (detailRecord.ImageNameSmall.length > 0) {
    // Load and display the product image
    loadMovie("../images/" + detailRecord.ImageNameSmall, _root.ImageMovie);
    // Hide the OWS logo
    OWSLogo._visible = false;
  // If there is no image file for this record, display the OWS logo instead
  } else {
    // Unload any product image that might already be showing
    unloadMovie(_root.ImageMovie);
    // Make the OWS logo visible
    OWSLogo._visible = true;
  }

  // Now that the information about the merchandise has been placed,
  // make the display slide back into view, revealing the information
  gotoAndPlay("StartSlideIn");
}


// This function updates the Number Of Items display for the cart
function refreshCart() {
  // Use Flash Remoting to get the number of items in cart
  // When the number has been retrieved, execution will continue
  // in the GetItemCount_Result() function, below
  cartService.GetItemCount();
};

// This executes when the number of items in the cart is received
function GetItemCount_Result(result) {
```

Listing 23.11 (continued)

```
    CartItemCount = "Items: " + result;
  };

  // This executes when a user uses the Add To Cart button
  function addSelectedItemToCart() {
    cartService.AddItem({MerchID:MerchListBox.getValue()});
  }

  // This executes after an item has been added to the cart
  function AddItem_Result(result) {
    // Show the new number of items in the cart
    refreshCart();
  }


  // Show the number of items in the user's cart now
  refreshCart();

  // Stop here, so animation doesn't occur until user selects a product
  stop();
```

Near the top of the template, a new Flash Remoting service object is created, called `cartService`. This object represents the `CallShoppingCartCFC` component created in Listing 23.10. This is in addition to the `myService` object already being used to connect to the `MerchProviderCFC` component from Listing 23.9. I can call `CallShoppingCartCFC` methods using `cartService`; I will continue to call the other methods using `myService`.

In addition, several new functions have been added near the bottom of the listing, called`refreshCart()`, `GetItemCount_Result()`, `addSelectedItemToCart()`, and `AddItem_Result()`. Note that `refreshCart()` is called right away, just before the `stop()` command.

Aside from the code in Listing 23.11, the following code has been added to the Add To Cart button in the `DetailUI` layer:

```
on (release) {
  addSelectedItemToCart();
}
```

Finally, the following code has been added to the Shopping Cart button at the upper-right corner, in a new layer called `CartUI`:

```
on (release) {
  getURL("../27/StoreCart.cfm");
}
```

When this version of the movie first appears, the `refreshCart()` function in Listing 23.11 executes (in addition to all the other code that executes in the original version of the movie). Inside `refreshCart()`, the `cartService.GetItemCount()` service function is called, triggering the `GetItemCount()` method on the ColdFusion server (see Listing 23.10). When the server returns its response, which is the number of items in the current session's shopping cart, the `GetItemCount_Result()` event handler executes. Within `GetItemCount_Result()`, the Flash variable called `CartItemCount` is updated with the current number of items.

If the user clicks the Add To Cart button (refer to Figure 23.11), the `addSelectedItemToCart()` function is called. Within `addSelectedItemToCart()`, the `cartService.AddItem()` service method is called, executing the `AddItem()` CFC method from Listing 23.10. When the server responds, the `AddItem_Result()` event handler executes, calling the `refreshCart()` method to make sure the new number of items in the user's cart is correctly reflected.

The user can go to the HTML version of the shopping cart (created in Chapter 27) by clicking the Shopping Cart button in the upper-right corner. This causes the browser to navigate to the `StoreCart.cfm` page (from Chapter 27), where the user can check out, remove items, update quantities, or continue shopping.

A neat thing about this application is that it proves that both the Flash player and normal ColdFusion pages can use the same `SESSION` scope. If you make changes in the HTML version of the cart, the Flash movie will reflect them, and vice versa. This is because the Shopping Cart CFC, and thus the `THIS` scope used internally by the component, is maintained in the `SESSION` scope.

Other Cool Flash Remoting Features

The remainder of this chapter will introduce a number of miscellaneous topics related to Flash Remoting that I think you'll find interesting. Please refer to the Flash MX and ColdFusion MX documentation to learn all the details.

Debugging Flash Remoting Projects

The Flash Remoting Components include a special debugging tool called the NetConnection Debugger. This clever programming aid lets you monitor the interactions between your Flash MX applications in real time. Conceptually, the NetConnection Debugger is similar to the Server Debug window in Dreamweaver MX; its purpose is to make your life easier while building applications, especially complex ones.

To use the NetConnection Debugger, follow these steps:

1. Go to the Debugging Settings page of the ColdFusion Administrator and make sure the Enable Debugging check box is enabled. Also make sure the IP address of the machine on which you are using the Flash MX workspace is listed as the Debugging IP Addresses page.
2. Include the `NetDebug.as` file with `#include "NetDebug.as"` in the first frame of your movie. The template I used to build the examples in this chapter already include this line; you just need to uncomment it to enable the debugger.
3. Open the NetConnection Debugger panel by choosing Window > NetConnection Debugger from Flash MX's menu.
4. Choose Control > Test Movie to display your movie within the Flash MX workspace, or File > Publish Preview to view your movie in a browser.

The NetConnection Debugger window will show information about each interaction between Flash and your ColdFusion MX server (Figure 23.12). You see the same type of information here that you would normally see at the bottom of a ColdFusion page when you have the debugging options turned on. You can view SQL statements and query results as they take place on the server, the total execution time of each service function call, and more. This information can be incredibly helpful if you are trying to track down problems or performance bottlenecks in your application.

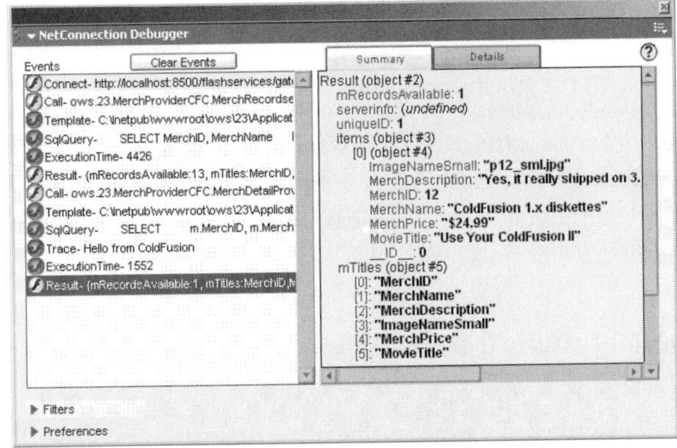

Figure 23.12

The NetConnection Debugger makes it easier to monitor and troubleshoot your Flash Remoting projects.

NOTE

Make sure to exclude the `NetDebug.as` file before you make your Flash application public. This reduces the size of your Flash movie file.

You can send helpful trace messages from the ColdFusion server to the NetConnection Debugger window by simply using the `<CFTRACE>` tag. For instance, if you add the following line to the `MerchDetailProvider` function in Listing 23.9, then the debugger will display the “Hello from ColdFusion” message. You can see this message in Figure 23.12, near the lower-left corner:

```
<CFTRACE TEXT="Hello from ColdFusion">
```

The Data Glue Object

You can use the Data Glue object to bind RecordSet objects to ListBox and other controls in your movies. Conceptually, this allows you to simply tell the Flash Player to display whatever data is in a record set in a ListBox, without having to write the looping code that would otherwise be required.

For instance, you can replace the following lines of code in Listing 23.5:

```
function MerchRecordsetProvider_Result(result) {
  // First, remove any existing items from the list box
  MerchListBox.removeAll();

  // For each record in the recordset...
  for (var i = 0; i < result.getLength(); i++) {
    // Use the record variable to refer to the current row of recordset
    var record = result.getItemAt(i);
```

```
      // Add item to the MerchListBox widget, which is like a <SELECT> in HTML
      MerchListBox.addItem(record.MerchName, record.MerchID);
    };
  }
```

with this:

```
function MerchRecordsetProvider_Result(result) {
  DataGlue.bindFormatStrings(MerchListBox, result, "#MerchName#", "#MerchID#");
}
```

To use this line, you just need to add `#include "DataGlue.as"` at the top of the code. The `DataGlue.as` file was installed along with the Flash Remoting Components.

DataGlue offers many other benefits as well. For more information about DataGlue, choose Help > Welcome to Flash Remoting from Flash MX's menu, and look in the Flash Remoting ActionScript Dictionary part of the documentation that appears. You can also find the same information in the Reference panel under the Remoting topic.

Incrementally Loading Record Sets

If you want to send very large record sets from ColdFusion to Flash, you may want to deliver and display a certain number of rows at a time, rather than requiring the Flash Player to wait until it has received the entire record set. The Flash Remoting framework makes it surprisingly easy to work with record set data right away, even if the entire record set has not yet been received.

To return records incrementally from ColdFusion, use the special `FLASH.PageSize` variable. For instance, to send a record set back to Flash ten rows at a time, include this line in your ColdFusion code before you return the record set with `FLASH.Result` or `<CFRETURN>`:

```
<CFSET FLASH.PageSize = 10>
```

Once you are sending records back to Flash incrementally, you may have to adapt the ActionScript code that works with the records. For instance, in loops, you will often need to use the `getNumberAvailable()` method, which returns the number of records that have actually been received, instead of `getLength()`, which includes records that have not yet been received. You'll have to make a number of other changes, which lie beyond the scope of this book.

NOTE

When possible, use the DataGlue object (discussed in the previous section, "The DataGlue Object") to bind record sets to ListBoxes or other visual components once you are using incremental record sets. The DataGlue framework will take care of displaying the records as they are received. That way, you don't have to worry about checking for the current number of records in your code.

For more information about incrementally receiving record sets on the Flash side, choose Help > Welcome to Flash Remoting from Flash MX's menu and look in the Flash Remoting ActionScript Dictionary part of the documentation that appears. Pay particular attention to the `setDeliveryMode()` and `getNumberAvailable()` methods of the RecordSet object. You can also find the same information in the Reference panel under the Remoting topic.

TIP

Once you set `FLASH.PageSize`, you can watch the records coming back to Flash in the smaller groups with the NetConnection Debugger.

Security and Logging In from Flash

If you want to secure the information you are providing from ColdFusion to Flash, you can do so using portions of the `<CFLOGIN>` framework introduced in Chapter 18, "Securing Your Applications." For instance, if you log in your users with `<CFLOGIN>` and `<CFLOGINUSER>` and supply role names to the `ROLES` attribute of your CFC's `<CFFUNCTION>` blocks, then only the users assigned to the appropriate roles can access the methods, even through Flash.

To try this out, edit this chapter's Application.cfm file so that it forces the user to log in via the `ForceUserLogin.cfm` template from Chapter 18 by adding this `<CFINCLUDE>` tag:

```
<!--- Force the user to log in --->
<CFINCLUDE TEMPLATE="../18/ForceUserLogin.cfm">
```

Now add a `ROLES="Admin"` attribute (careful, `Admin` is case sensitive) to the `<CFFUNCTION>` tags in Listing 23.9. Publish the Merchandise Browser movie, but rename the generated HTML file to `MerchBrowser.cfm` so that ColdFusion will process the page. Now visit `MerchBrowser.cfm` with your browser. You should be forced to log in. If you log in as an Admin user (for example, with user name `Ben` and password `Forta`), you will be permitted to see the list of products. If you log in as a non-Admin user, the list of products will never appear.

NOTE

The `ROLES` attribute is for CFCs only (see Appendix B, "ColdFusion Tag Reference," for details). You can also use the `IsUserInRole()` function to secure normal ColdFusion pages that supply data to Flash (see Chapter 18 for details about `IsUserInRole()`).

TIP

You can watch the process succeed or fail, and check out messages about users' failure to log in properly, in the NetConnection Debugger.

Other Integration Methods

This chapter has introduced you to the brave new world of Flash Remoting, which enables you to integrate ColdFusion MX and Flash MX in a feature-rich, sophisticated way. It is also possible for Flash to grab information from a ColdFusion server using the somewhat more humble `LoadVariables()`, available to Flash developers for years. Before Flash MX and Flash Remoting, this was the primary way for the Flash Player to interact with servers via the Internet.

NOTE

Actually, there are two forms of this function: `LoadVariables()` and `LoadVariablesNum()`. For purposes of this discussion, consider them synonymous. See the Flash MX documentation for details.

I don't have the space to cover the use of `LoadVariables()` completely here. However, I have included some examples of its use on the CD-ROM for this book, in the subfolder named `LoadVariablesExamples`. The examples use a CFML Custom Tag called `<CF_ExposeDataToFlash>` (also included in the folder) which makes it quite easy to output information in the format that the Flash Player expects when it calls a page with `LoadVariables()`.

The `<CF_ExposeDataToFlash>` custom tag has one attribute, `DATA`. To use the tag, pass a structure or a query object to the tag, like so:

```
<!--- To send a structure back to Flash --->
<CF_ExposeDataToFlash
  Data="#MyStructure#">
```

or like this:

```
<!--- To send a query back to Flash --->
<CF_ExposeDataToFlash
  Data="#Query#">
```

The examples on the CD-ROM include the following:

- `LoadVariablesTest.fla` is a simple example that connects to a ColdFusion page called `ExposeDataTest.cfm`. Inside `ExposeDataTest.cfm`, a structure is created that holds two values (`NAME` and `AGE`); the structure is then passed to the `<CF_ExposeDataToFlash>` custom tag. When `LoadVariables()` is called in the Flash movie, the result is the creation of local Flash variables called `NAME` and `AGE` . To view this example, visit the `LoadVariablesTest.html` file with your Web browser, using a http:// address.
- `FilmChooser.fla` is a slightly more advanced example that connects to a ColdFusion page called `ExposeFilmInfo.cfm`. Inside `ExposeFilmInfo.cfm`, a query runs to get a current list of films; the query object is then passed to the `<CF_ExposeDataToFlash>` custom tag. When `LoadVariables()` is called in the Flash movie, the result is that a number of variables are created to represent each row and column in the query. Visually, orange squares showing the title of each movie appear on the page and bounce around. To view this example, visit `FilmChooser.html` with your Web browser (using a http:// address).

You are invited to take a look inside these `.fla` and `.cfm` files to explore how the movies were built. The ActionScript code in each is quite simple; most of it occurs in the first frame of each movie.

NOTE

In general, I recommend that you use Flash Remoting instead of the `LoadVariables()` approach. It's more robust, faster, more flexible, and more formally supported. The only big reason I can think of to use `LoadVariables()` is if your application needs to work with older versions of ColdFusion or the Flash Player. Regarding the Flash Player, remember that for many users, the upgrade to version 6 (which corresponds to Flash MX) happens automatically.

CHAPTER 24

Enhancing Forms with Client-Side Java

IN THIS CHAPTER

ColdFusion MX includes a number of Java-based controls that you can add to your ColdFusion pages. The idea behind the controls is to pick up where HTML form controls leave off. Instead of being limited to simple checkboxes, radio buttons, and text input fields, the Java-based controls give you the ability to add trees, editable data grids, sliders, and other widgets to your pages.

Tags covered in this chapter include:

- `<CFFORM>`
- `<CFGRID>`, `<CFGRIDCOLUMN>`, `<CFGRIDROW>`, and `<CFGRIDUPDATE>`
- `<CFTREE>` and `<CFTREEITEM>`
- `<CFSLIDER>`
- `<CFTEXTINPUT>`

NOTE

The entire text of this chapter can be found on the included CD.

CHAPTER 25
Graphing

IN THIS CHAPTER

Many ColdFusion applications involve some type of data reporting. If you are building an online store, for instance, you might create a series of report-style pages that show the number of products sold per month. If you are building a community site, you might create a page that shows how many people tend to log on during which parts of the day. Or, if you are building a Web site for a movie studio (ahem), you might create a page that shows the expenses to date for each film, and which films are in danger of going over budget.

It'd be easy to imagine how each of these pages would turn out, if you could only use the skills you have already learned in this book. The pages would be easy to create with various uses of the `<CFQUERY>` and `<CFOUTPUT>` tags, and they could be absolutely packed with useful information. You might even come up with some really attractive, creative uses of HTML tables to make the information easier to digest.

But, as the saying goes, a picture is often as good as a thousand words (or a thousand totals, or subtotals). ColdFusion MX provides an exciting set of features that let you dynamically create charts and graphs that report on whatever data you want. Wouldn't all the reporting scenarios mentioned above be easier for users to digest if they contained nice-looking, colorful pie charts or bar graphs? Sure they would. And does ColdFusion make it really easy for you to add them? Of course it does.

Charting and Graphing Features

This section will give you an overview of the charting features included in ColdFusion MX. The charting functionality in ColdFusion MX is a significant step up from what was included in the last version of the product. Based on feedback from developers, Macromedia added three all-new chart-related tags to CFML for the ColdFusion MX release.

With ColdFusion MX, you can:

- Create many different types of graphs, including pie charts, bar graphs, line graphs, and scatter charts.
- Format your graphs with an extensive number of formatting options for controlling fonts, colors, labels, and more.
- Display the graphs on any ColdFusion page as JPEG images, PNG images, or interactive Flash charts.
- Allow users to *drill down* on data shown in your charts. For instance, you could allow people to click the wedges in a pie chart, revealing the data represented in that wedge.
- Combine several different charts, displaying them together on the page. For instance, you might create a scatter chart that shows individual purchases over time, and then add a line chart on top of it that shows average spending by other users.
- Save the charts to the server's drive for later use.

Building Simple Charts

Now that you have an idea of what you can do with ColdFusion's charting features, it's time to get started with some basic examples. Most of the time, you will create charts with just two CFML tags, `<CFCHART>` and `<CFCHARTSERIES>`.

NOTE

In ColdFusion 5, you created graphs with `<CFGRAPH>`, whereas you now create them with `<CFCHART>`. If you already use `<CFGRAPH>` in your applications, your `<CFGRAPH>` code should continue to work in ColdFusion MX, although the graphs may look slightly different. In any case, you should start using `<CFCHART>` as soon as possible, since `<CFGRAPH>` has been retired and may not work in future versions of the product.

Introducing `<CFCHART>` and `<CFCHARTSERIES>`

To display a chart on a ColdFusion page, you use the `<CFCHART>` tag. The `<CFCHART>` tag is what controls the height, width, and formatting of your chart, but it doesn't actually display anything. Within the `<CFCHART>` tag, you use the `<CFCHARTSERIES>` tag, which determines the type of chart (like `bar` or `pie`) and the actual data to show on the chart.

NOTE

Actually, you will occasionally want to place multiple `<CFCHARTSERIES>` tags within a `<CFCHART>` tag. See the "Combining Multiple Chart Series" section, later in this chapter.

Table 25.1 shows the most important attributes for the `<CFCHART>` tag, and Table 25.2 shows the most important attributes for `<CFCHARTSERIES>`.

NOTE

Because these tags have a large number of attributes (more than 40 in all), we are introducing only the most important attributes in this table. The rest are discussed in the "Formatting Your Charts" section, later in this chapter.

Table 25.1 Basic <CFCHART> Tag Syntax

ATTRIBUTE	DESCRIPTION
CHARTWIDTH	Optional. The width of the chart, in pixels. The default is 320.
CHARTHEIGHT	Optional. The height of the chart, in pixels. The default is 240.
XAXISTITLE	Optional. The text to display along the chart's x-axis.
YAXISTITLE	Optional. The text to display along the chart's y-axis.
ROTATED	Yes or No. If yes, the chart is rotated clockwise by 90 degrees. You can use this to create bar charts that point sideways rather than up and down, and so on. The default is No.
URL	Optional. The URL of a page to send the user to when various sections of the chart are clicked. You can pass variables in the URL so you know what part of the chart the user clicked. See "Drilling Down from Charts," later in this chapter.
FORMAT	Optional. The type of image format in which the chart should be created. The valid choices are flash (the default), jpg, or png.
SERIESPLACEMENT	Optional. For charts that have more than one data series, you can use this attribute—cluster, stacked, percent, or default—to control how the series are combined visually. Use cluster if the data series represent related pieces of information that should be presented next to one another, rather than added together visually. Use stacked or percent if the data series represent values that should be added up to a single whole value for each item you are plotting. See "Combining Multiple Chart Series," later in this chapter.

Table 25.2 Basic <CFCHARTSERIES> Syntax

ATTRIBUTE	DESCRIPTION
TYPE	Required. The type of chart to create. Usually, you will set this to either bar, line, area, or pie. Other chart types are cone, curve, cylinder, scatter, step, and pyramid. The ColdFusion documentation includes some nice pictures of these more unusual types of graphs.
QUERY	Optional. The name of a query that contains data to chart. If you don't provide a QUERY attribute, you will need to provide <CFCHARTDATA> tags to tell ColdFusion the data to display in the chart.
VALUECOLUMN	Required if a QUERY is provided. The name of the column that contains the actual value (the number to represent graphically) for each data point on the chart.
ITEMCOLUMN	Required if a QUERY is provided. The name of the column that contains labels for each data point on the chart.

NOTE

In this chapter, you will see the term *data point* often. Data points are the actual pieces of data that are displayed on a chart. If you are creating a pie chart, the data points are the slices of the pie. In a bar chart, the data points are the bars. In a line or scatter chart, the data points are the individual points that have been plotted on the graph.

NOTE

You don't have to have a query object to create a chart. You can also create data points manually using the `<CFCHARTDATA>` tag. See "Plotting Individual Points with `<CFCHARTDATA>`," near the end of this chapter.

Creating Your First Chart

Listing 25.1 shows how to use `<CFCHART>` and `<CFCHARTSERIES>` to create a simple bar chart. The resulting chart is shown in Figure 25.1. As you can see, it doesn't take much code at all to produce a reasonably helpful bar chart. Anyone can glance at this chart and instantly understand which films cost more than the average, and by how much.

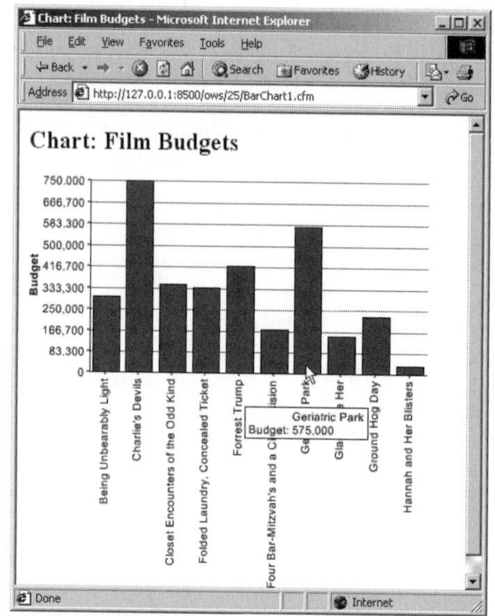

Figure 25.1

It's easy to create simple charts with `<CFCHART>` and `<CFCHARTDATA>`.

Listing 25.1 `BarChart1.cfm`—Creating a Simple Bar Chart from Query Data

```
<!---
  Filename: BarChart1.cfm
  Author:   Nate Weiss (NMW)
  Purpose:  Displays a simple bar chart
--->

<!--- Get information from the database --->
<CFQUERY NAME="ChartQuery" DATASOURCE="ows" MAXROWS="10">
```

Listing 25.1 (continued)

```
    SELECT FilmID, MovieTitle, AmountBudgeted
    FROM Films
    ORDER BY MovieTitle
  </CFQUERY>


  <HTML>
  <HEAD><TITLE>Chart: Film Budgets</TITLE></HEAD>
  <BODY>
  <H2>Chart: Film Budgets</H2>

  <!--- This defines the size and appearance of the chart --->
  <CFCHART
    CHARTWIDTH="400"
    CHARTHEIGHT="400"
    YAXISTITLE="Budget">

    <!--- Within the chart --->
    <CFCHARTSERIES
      TYPE="bar"
      QUERY="ChartQuery"
      VALUECOLUMN="AmountBudgeted"
      ITEMCOLUMN="MovieTitle">

  </CFCHART>


  </BODY>
  </HTML>
```

First, an ordinary `<CFQUERY>` tag is used to select film and budget information from the database. Then, a `<CFCHART>` tag is used to establish the size of the chart, and to specify that the word Budget appear along the y-axis (that is, at the bottom of the chart). Finally, within the `<CFCHART>` block, a `<CFCHARTSERIES>` tag is used to create a bar chart. ColdFusion is instructed to chart the information in the `ChartQuery` record set, plotting the data in the `AmountBudgeted` column and using the `MovieTitle` column to provide a label for each piece of information.

NOTE

For this example and the next few listings, we are using `MAXROWS="10"` in the `<CFQUERY>` tag to limit the number of films displayed in the chart to ten. This is simply to keep the pictures of the graphs simple while you are learning how to use the charting tags. Just eliminate the `MAXROWS` attribute to see all films displayed in the chart.

Rotating the Chart

You can use the `ROTATE` attribute of the `<CFCHART>` tag to rotate any chart clockwise by 90 degrees. So, if `ROTATE="Yes"` is added to Listing 25.1, the bars will be displayed horizontally instead of vertically, and the data labels will be on the left side of the chart rather than at the bottom. Listing 25.2 takes the chart from Listing 25.1, rotates it, and adjusts the width and height a bit so it looks nice when viewed with a browser (Figure 25.2).

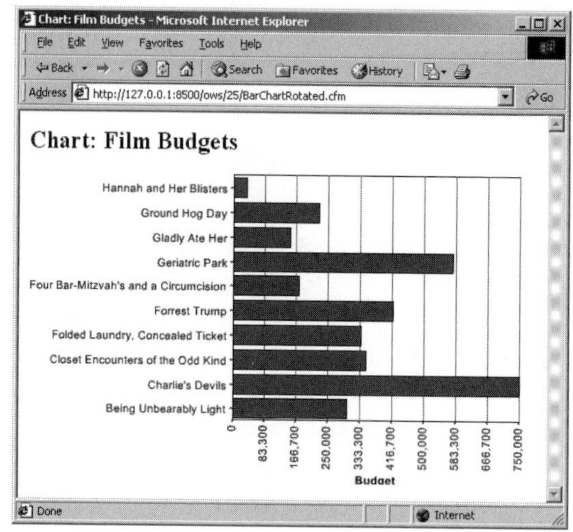

Figure 25.2

Some charts will have a more natural feel if presented horizontally.

Listing 25.2 `BarChartRotated.cfm`—Using the `ROTATE` Attribute for `<CFCHART>`

```
<!---
  Filename: BarChartRotated.cfm
  Author:   Nate Weiss (NMW)
  Purpose:  Displays a simple bar chart
--->

<!--- Get information from the database --->
<CFQUERY NAME="ChartQuery" DATASOURCE="ows" MAXROWS="10">
  SELECT FilmID, MovieTitle, AmountBudgeted
  FROM Films
  ORDER BY MovieTitle
</CFQUERY>


<HTML>
<HEAD><TITLE>Chart: Film Budgets</TITLE></HEAD>
<BODY>
<H2>Chart: Film Budgets</H2>

<!--- This defines the size and appearance of the chart --->
<CFCHART
  CHARTWIDTH="500"
  CHARTHEIGHT="300"
  YAXISTITLE="Budget"
  ROTATED="Yes">

  <!--- Within the chart --->
  <CFCHARTSERIES
    TYPE="bar"
    QUERY="ChartQuery"
    VALUECOLUMN="AmountBudgeted"
```

Listing 25.2 (continued)

```
        ITEMCOLUMN="MovieTitle">

    </CFCHART>


    </BODY>
    </HTML>
```

Sorting the Data First

You may want to consider thinking about how your data is sorted before displaying it in a chart. For instance, the charts shown in Figure 25.1 and Figure 25.2 list the movies in alphabetical order, which may not be particularly useful (depending on the purpose of the chart). Sorting the films by budget instead of by title will emphasize the spectrum of budgets assigned to various films.

Listing 25.3 shows how ColdFusion's query of queries feature can be used to change the sequence of the films in the chart (Figure 25.3).

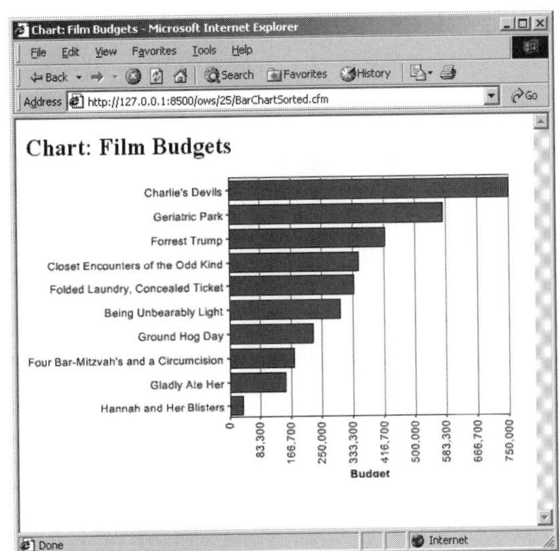

Figure 25.3
Changing the order of the data points can change the focus of a chart.

Listing 25.3 `BarChartSorted.cfm`—Using Query of Queries to Re-sort Data for Charting

```
<!---
  Filename: BarChartSorted.cfm
  Author:   Nate Weiss (NMW)
  Purpose:  Displays a simple bar chart
--->

<!--- Get information from the database --->
<CFQUERY NAME="ChartQuery" DATASOURCE="ows" MAXROWS="10">
```

Listing 25.3 (CONTINUED)

```
    SELECT FilmID, MovieTitle, AmountBudgeted
    FROM Films
    ORDER BY MovieTitle
  </CFQUERY>

  <!--- Get information from the database --->
  <CFQUERY NAME="SortedQuery" DBTYPE="query">
    SELECT *
    FROM ChartQuery
    ORDER BY AmountBudgeted
  </CFQUERY>


  <HTML>
  <HEAD><TITLE>Chart: Film Budgets</TITLE></HEAD>
  <BODY>
  <H2>Chart: Film Budgets</H2>

  <!--- This defines the size and appearance of the chart --->
  <CFCHART
    CHARTWIDTH="500"
    CHARTHEIGHT="300"
    YAXISTITLE="Budget"
    ROTATED="Yes">

    <!--- Within the chart --->
    <CFCHARTSERIES
      TYPE="bar"
      QUERY="SortedQuery"
      VALUECOLUMN="AmountBudgeted"
      ITEMCOLUMN="MovieTitle">

  </CFCHART>


  </BODY>
  </HTML>
```

Nothing has changed among the `<CFCHART>` and `<CFCHARTSERIES>` tags from the previous version (Listing 25.3). The only difference is the second `<CFQUERY>` tag, which reorders the records in the `ChartQuery` record set.

NOTE

Of course, you could just use an **ORDER BY AmountBudgeted** in the original query, rather than using query of queries. The QofQ technique was used in this listing mainly just to point out that QofQ and **<CFCHART>** can often be used together to manipulate and display your data.

Changing the Chart Type

So far, all the charts you've seen in this chapter have been bar charts. It's easy to change your code so that it displays a different kind of graph. Just change the `TYPE` attribute of the `<CFCHARTSERIES>` tag. Figure 25.4 shows the pie chart created by the `PieChart1.cfm` template (with this chapter's listings on the CD-ROM). The code for this page is almost the same as that used in the first example (Listing 25.1). The differences are that `TYPE="Pie"` is used in the `<CFCHARTSERIES>` tag, and a `PIESLICESTYLE="solid"` attribute has been added to `<CFCHART>`.

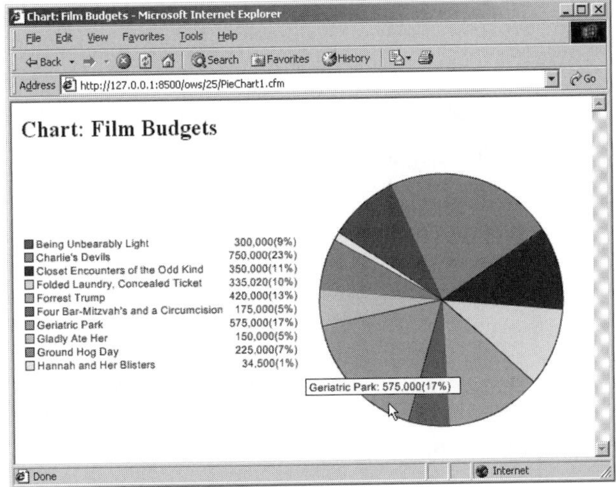

Figure 25.4
Pie charts emphasize the proportional differences between numbers, rather than the numbers themselves.

Formatting Your Charts

Now that you understand the basics of how to produce simple charts, it's time to learn about the formatting options available to make your charts look better and more closely meet your users' needs. In general, your goal should be to make the charts as easy on the eyes as possible, so that it is easy and pleasant for people to concentrate on the data.

Adding Depth with 3D Charts

One of the easiest ways to make a basic chart look more sophisticated is to give its appearance a 3D effect. Table 25.3 shows the `<CFCHART>` options available for adding a 3D look to your charts. Get out the red and blue glasses!

NOTE

Whether the 3D effect makes a chart any easier to read depends on the situation. It tends to look nice in simple creations, especially bar charts that contain a relatively small number of data points. Once a chart is trying to display a large number of data points, however, the 3D effect tends to get in the way visually.

NOTE

The `XOFFSET` and `YOFFSET` attributes have no discernible effect on pie charts in ColdFusion MX. You can make a pie chart display with a 3D appearance using `SHOW3D="Yes"`, but you can't control the offsets.

Listing 25.4 shows how to produce a 3D graph by adding these attributes to the code from Listing 25.2. The `XOFFSET` and `YOFFSET` have been tweaked to make the bars look like they are being looked at from the top a bit more than from the side. The results are shown in Figure 25.5.

Table 25.3 <CFCHART> Options for a 3D Effect

ATTRIBUTE	DESCRIPTION
SHOW3D	Whether to show the chart with a 3D effect. The default is No.
XOFFSET	The amount that the chart should be rotated on the x-axis. In other words, this controls to what extent the chart appears to be viewed from the side. You can use a value anywhere from -1 to 1, but in general you will want to experiment with low, positive numbers (between .01 and .3) for best results. A value of 0 means no 3D effect horizontally. The default is .1.
YOFFSET	Similarly, the amount that the chart should be turned around its y-axis. This controls the extent the chart seems to be viewed from the top. Again, you will probably want to experiment with low, positive numbers (between .01 and .3) for best results. A value of 0 means no 3D effect vertically. The default is .1.

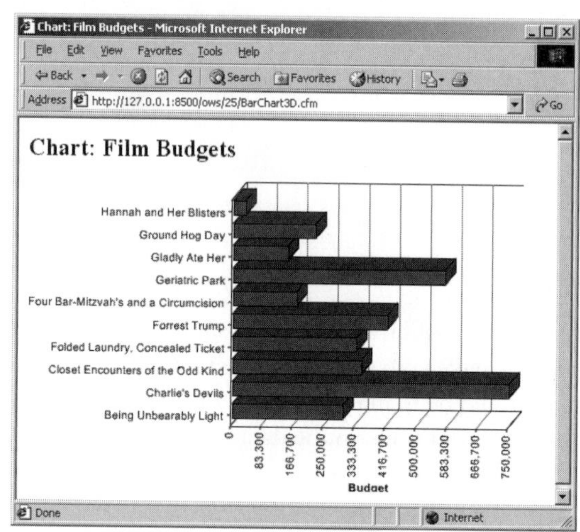

Figure 25.5 3D charts have a slick, professional feel.

Listing 25.4 BarChart3D.cfm—Adding a 3D Appearance

```
<!---
  Filename: BarChart3D.cfm
  Author:   Nate Weiss (NMW)
  Purpose:  Displays a simple bar chart
--->

<!--- Get information from the database --->
<CFQUERY NAME="ChartQuery" DATASOURCE="ows" MAXROWS="10">
  SELECT FilmID, MovieTitle, AmountBudgeted
  FROM Films
  ORDER BY MovieTitle
</CFQUERY>


<HTML>
<HEAD><TITLE>Chart: Film Budgets</TITLE></HEAD>
<BODY>
```

Listing 25.4 (continued)

```
<H2>Chart: Film Budgets</H2>

<!--- This defines the size and appearance of the chart --->
<CFCHART
  CHARTWIDTH="500"
  CHARTHEIGHT="300"
  YAXISTITLE="Budget"
  ROTATED="Yes"
  SHOW3D="Yes"
  XOFFSET=".03"
  YOFFSET=".06">

  <!--- Within the chart --->
  <CFCHARTSERIES
    TYPE="bar"
    QUERY="ChartQuery"
    VALUECOLUMN="AmountBudgeted"
    ITEMCOLUMN="MovieTitle">

</CFCHART>

</BODY>
</HTML>
```

Controlling Fonts and Colors

ColdFusion provides a number of formatting attributes that you can use to control fonts, colors, and borders. Some of the attributes are applied at the `<CFCHART>` level and others at the `<CFCHARTSERIES>` level, as listed in Table 25.4 and Table 25.5, respectively.

NOTE

All of the attributes that control color can accept Web-style hexadecimal color values, such as `FFFFFF` for white or `0000FF` for blue. In addition, any of the following named colors can be used: `Aqua`, `Black`, `Blue`, `Fuchsia`, `Gray`, `Green`, `Lime`, `Maroon`, `Navy`, `Olive`, `Purple`, `Red`, `Silver`, `Teal`, `White`, and `Yellow`.

Table 25.4 `<CFCHART>` Formatting Options

ATTRIBUTE	DESCRIPTION
`SHOWBORDER`	Whether a border should be drawn around the entire chart. The default is `No`.
`SHOWLEGEND`	Whether to display a legend that shows the meaning of each color used in the graph. This is applicable only to pie charts, or charts that use more than one `<CFCHARTSERIES>` tag. The default is `Yes`.
`BACKGROUNDCOLOR`	The background color of the portion of the chart that contains the actual graph (that is, excluding the space set aside for axis labels and legends).
`DATABACKGROUNDCOLOR`	The background color of the space set aside for axis labels and legends (everywhere except the part where the actual graph is shown).
`TIPBGCOLOR`	The background color for the pop-up tip window that appears when you hover the pointer over a data point.

Table 25.4 (CONTINUED)

ATTRIBUTE	DESCRIPTION
FOREGROUNDCOLOR	The foreground color to use throughout the chart. This controls the color of all text in the chart, as well as the lines used to draw the x- and y-axes, the lines around each bar or pie slice, and so on.
FONT	The font to use for text in the chart, such as legends and axis labels. In ColdFusion MX, you can choose between `arial`, `times`, and `courier`. In addition, you can choose `arialunicodeMS`, which you should use when using double-byte character sets. The default is `arial`.
FONTSIZE	The size of the font, expressed as a number. The default is `11`.
FONTBOLD	Whether text is displayed in bold. The default is `No`.
FONTITALIC	Whether text is displayed in italics. The default is `No`.
TIPSTYLE	Optional. Can be set to `mouseOver` (the default), `mouseDown`, or `off`. By default, a hint or tip message will display when the user hovers her pointer over a data point in a graph (an example of this is shown in Figure 25.1). The tip message includes the label and value of the data point, as well as the series label, if given (see Table 25.5). If you want the tip to be shown only when the user clicks a data point, you can use `TIPSTYLE="mouseDown"`, but this works only if `FORMAT="flash"`. If you don't want any tip to be shown at all, use `TIPSTYLE="off"`.
PIESLICESTYLE	Relevant only for pie charts. If `sliced` (the default) is used, the pie is shown with its slices separated by white space (this effect is sometimes called *exploded*). If `solid` is used, the pie is shown with its slices together in a circle, the way you would normally think of a pie chart. Unfortunately, there is no way to explode just one slice at a time, which is a common way to present pie charts. In general, you will probably want to use `PIESLICESTYLE="solid"`.

Table 25.5 `<CFCHARTSERIES>` Formatting Options

ATTRIBUTE	DESCRIPTION
SERIESCOLOR	A color to use for the main element of the data series.
SERIESLABEL	A label or title for the data series.
PAINTSTYLE	A style to use when filling in solid areas on the chart for this series. The default is `plain`, which uses solid colors. You can also provide `raise`, which gives each area a raised, buttonlike appearance; `shade`, which shades each area with a gradient fill, or `light`, which is a lighter version of `shade`.
COLORLIST	Relevant for pie charts only. A comma-separated list of colors to use for the slices of the pie. The first slice will have the first color in the list, the second slice will have the second color, and so on.
MARKERSTYLE	Relevant only for `line`, `curve`, and `scatter` charts. The look of the marker that appears at each data point. Can be set to `rectangle` (the default), `triangle`, `diamond`, `circle`, `letter`, `mcross`, `snow`, or `rcross`.

Listing 25.5 and Figure 25.6 (in the next section) show how some of these formatting attributes can be combined to improve the appearance of the bar charts you have seen so far.

Controlling Grid Lines and Axis Labels

One of the most important aspects of nearly any chart are the numbers and labels that surround the actual graphic on the x- and y-axes. Yes, the graphic itself is what lends the chart its ability to convey a message visually, but it is the numbers surrounding the graphic that give it a context. ColdFusion provides you with a number of options for controlling the *scale* of each axis (that is, the distance between the highest and lowest values that could be plotted on the chart), and for controlling how many different numbers are actually displayed along the axes.

Table 25.6 shows the `<CFCHART>` attributes related to grid lines and axis labels.

Table 25.6 `<CFCHART>` Options for Grid Lines and Labels

ATTRIBUTE	DESCRIPTION
`SCALEFROM`	The lowest number to show on the y-axis. For instance, if you want one of the budget chart examples shown previously to start at $20,000 instead of $0, you can do so with `SCALEFROM="20000"`.
`SCALETO`	The highest number to show on the y-axis. So, if the highest budget shown in the budget chart examples is $750,000, providing `SCALETO="1000000"` will cause the scale to go all the way up to 1 million, even though there aren't any data points that go up that high. The result is extra "empty space" above the highest value, giving the viewer the sense that the values plotted in the chart could have been higher than they actually are.
`GRIDLINES`	The number of grid lines to show for the data axis (generally the y-axis). This also affects the number of labeled tick marks along the axis. If you don't provide a value, ColdFusion attempts to use a sensible default value based on the size of the graph. For instance, in Figure 25.2 there are ten grid lines and tick marks (one for `0`, one for `83,300`, and so on), which seems about right.
`SHOWYGRIDLINES`	Whether to display grid lines for the y-axis. On most types of charts, these grid lines generally make it easier to understand what the value is for each piece of data. These grid lines are shown in Figure 25.1 (the horizontal lines) and Figure 25.2 (the vertical lines). The default is `Yes`.
`SHOWXGRIDLINES`	Whether to display grid lines for the x-axis. The default is `No`.
`SORTXAXIS`	Sorts the data in the x-axis (that is, the labels) alphabetically. In general, I recommend that you use `ORDER BY` to reorder the records within a normal `<CFQUERY>` tag, before your code gets to the `<CFCHART>` tag; that approach will be much more flexible (see the "Sorting the Data First" section earlier in this chapter).
`LABELFORMAT`	The format for the labels along the y-axis (in our examples so far, the labels that show the increasing amounts of money). You can set this to `number` (the default), `currency` (which on English systems adds a dollar sign [$]), `percent` (which multiplies by 100 and adds a percent sign [%]), or `date` (appropriate only if the data you are plotting are dates).

NOTE

You can't adjust the scale in such a way that it would obscure or chop off any of the actual data being shown in the chart. If your SCALEFROM value is higher than the lowest data point on the graph, ColdFusion will use the data point's value instead. For instance, if the lowest budget being plotted in one of the budget chart examples is $34,000 and you provide SCALEFROM="50000", ColdFusion will start the scale at $34,000. The inverse is also true; if you provide a SCALETO value that is lower than the highest data point, that point's value will be used instead.

Listing 25.5 shows how formatting, axis, and grid line options can be added to a chart to make it more appealing (Figure 25.6). You can't see the colors in this book, but different shades of light blue have been used for the data background and the overall chart background. The text is in a dark navy type, and the bars of the chart themselves have a green gradient. In addition, the axis labels have been formatted as currency.

Note that the scale of the chart now goes all the way up to $1.5 million, which has the effect of making the budget for *Charlie's Devils* look like less of a bloated anomaly. This graph gives the sense that perhaps there is room for film budgets to grow much bigger, whereas the previous versions of the chart (see Figure 25.5) made it look like *Charlie's Devils* was way overbudgeted.

Also note that the number of grid lines (that is, the number of numbered tick marks along the horizontal axis) has been set to 6 with the GRIDLINES attribute. This means that there will be five tick marks (in addition to the first one), evenly distributed from $0 to $1.5 million, which in turn means that the tick marks will be counting off round, intuitive intervals of $300,000 each. Compare these tick marks to those in Figure 25.5, which counted off odder-looking intervals of $83,300 each.

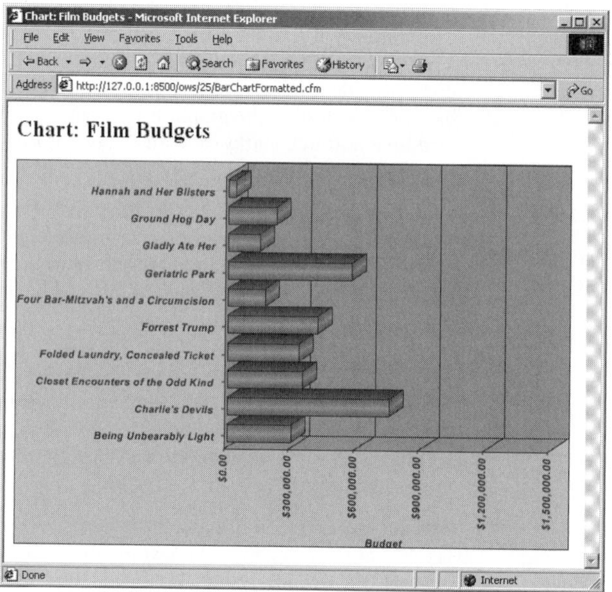

Figure 25.6

Formatting options, applied sensibly, can make your charts easier to read and understand.

Listing 25.5 `BarChartFormatted.cfm`—Adding Formatting, Grid Line, and Axis Options

```
<!---
  Filename: BarChartFormatted.cfm
  Author:   Nate Weiss (NMW)
  Purpose:  Displays a simple bar chart
--->

<!--- Get information from the database --->
<CFQUERY NAME="ChartQuery" DATASOURCE="ows" MAXROWS="10">
  SELECT FilmID, MovieTitle, AmountBudgeted
  FROM Films
  ORDER BY MovieTitle
</CFQUERY>


<HTML>
<HEAD><TITLE>Chart: Film Budgets</TITLE></HEAD>
<BODY>
<H2>Chart: Film Budgets</H2>

<!--- This defines the size and appearance of the chart --->
<CFCHART
  CHARTWIDTH="600"
  CHARTHEIGHT="400"
  YAXISTITLE="Budget"
  ROTATED="Yes"
  <!--- 3D appearance --->
  SHOW3D="Yes"
  XOFFSET=".04"
  YOFFSET=".04"
  <!--- Fonts and colors --->
  SHOWBORDER="Yes"
  FOREGROUNDCOLOR="003366"
  BACKGROUNDCOLOR="99DDDD"
  DATABACKGROUNDCOLOR="66BBBB"
  TIPBGCOLOR="FFFF99"
  FONTSIZE="11"
  FONTBOLD="Yes"
  FONTITALIC="Yes"
  <!--- Gridlines and axis labels --->
  SCALEFROM="0"
  SCALETO="1500000"
  GRIDLINES="6"
  SHOWYGRIDLINES="Yes"
  LABELFORMAT="currency">

  <!--- Within the chart --->
  <CFCHARTSERIES
    TYPE="bar"
    SERIESCOLOR="green"
    SERIESLABEL="Budget Details:"
    QUERY="ChartQuery"
    VALUECOLUMN="AmountBudgeted"
    ITEMCOLUMN="MovieTitle"
```

Listing 25.5 (CONTINUED)

```
        PAINTSTYLE="light">

    </CFCHART>


    </BODY>
    </HTML>
```

NOTE

When providing hexadecimal color values, the traditional number sign (`#`) is optional. If you provide it, though, you must escape the # by doubling it, so ColdFusion doesn't think you are trying to reference a variable. In other words, you could provide `BACKGROUNDCOLOR="99DDDD"` or `BACKGROUNDCOLOR="##99DDDD"` as you prefer, but not `BACKGROUNDCOLOR="#99DDDD"`.

Creating Sophisticated Charts

Now that you've been introduced to the basic principles involved in creating and formatting charts, we'd like to explain some of the more advanced aspects of ColdFusion MX's charting support. In the next section, you will learn how to combine several chart types into a single graph. Then you will learn how to create charts that users can click, enabling them to drill down on information presented in the graph.

Combining Multiple Chart Series

So far, all of the charts you have seen have contained only one `<CFCHARTSERIES>` tag. This makes sense, considering that the charts have been attempting to represent only one set of information at a time. It is also possible to create charts that represent more than one set of information, simply by adding additional `<CFCHARTSERIES>` tags within the `<CFCHART>` block. The additional `<CFCHARTSERIES>` tags can each display different columns from the same query, or they can display information from different queries or data sources altogether.

Multiple Series of the Same Type

The bar chart examples so far all show the budget for each film. It might be helpful to show not only the budget but also the actual expenses to date for each film, so that a glance at the chart will reveal which films are over budget and by how much.

Figure 25.7 shows just such a chart. There are now two bars for each film, clustered in pairs. One bar shows the budget for each film, and the other shows the actual expenses for the film to date, as recorded in the Expenses table. Listing 25.6 shows the code used to produce this chart.

Listing 25.6 `BarChartCombined.cfm`—Plotting Two Related Sets of Data on One Bar Chart

```
<!---
  Filename: BarChartCombined.cfm
  Author:   Nate Weiss (NMW)
  Purpose:  Displays a bar chart with two data series
--->
```

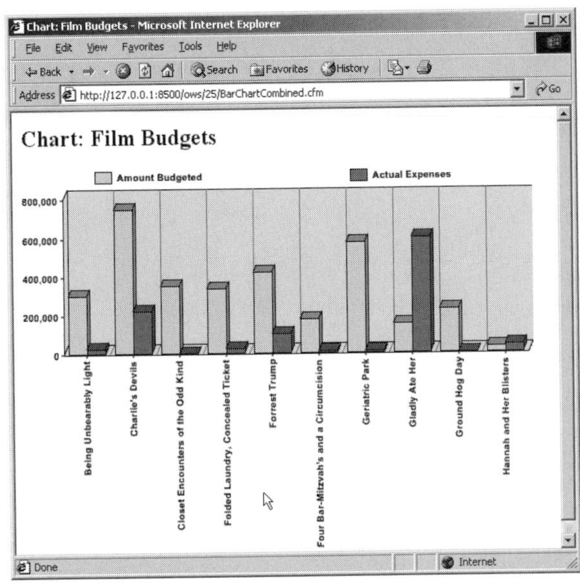

Figure 25.7

The ability to combine multiple data series makes <CFCHART> especially powerful and flexible.

Listing 25.6 (continued)

```
<!--- Get information from the database --->
<CFQUERY NAME="ChartQuery" DATASOURCE="ows" MAXROWS="10">
  SELECT FilmID, MovieTitle, AmountBudgeted,
    (SELECT SUM(ExpenseAmount) FROM Expenses
     WHERE FilmID = Films.FilmID) AS ExpenseTotal
  FROM Films
  ORDER BY MovieTitle
</CFQUERY>


<HTML>
<HEAD><TITLE>Chart: Film Budgets</TITLE></HEAD>
<BODY>
<H2>Chart: Film Budgets</H2>

<!--- This defines the size and appearance of the chart --->
<CFCHART
  CHARTWIDTH="550"
  CHARTHEIGHT="400"
  ROTATED="no"
  SERIESPLACEMENT="cluster"
  <!--- 3D appearance --->
  SHOW3D="Yes"
  XOFFSET=".01"
  YOFFSET=".03"
  <!--- Fonts and colors --->
  FONTSIZE="10"
  FONTBOLD="Yes"
  DATABACKGROUNDCOLOR="DDDDDD"
  <!--- Axes and gridlines --->
```

Listing 25.6 (CONTINUED)

```
    SCALETO="800000"
    GRIDLINES="5"
    SHOWXGRIDLINES="Yes"
    SHOWYGRIDLINES="No">

    <!--- This series of bars shows the budgets --->
    <CFCHARTSERIES
      TYPE="bar"
      QUERY="ChartQuery"
      ITEMCOLUMN="MovieTitle"
      VALUECOLUMN="AmountBudgeted"
      SERIESLABEL="Amount Budgeted"
      SERIESCOLOR="99FF99">

    <!--- This series of bars shows the expenses --->
    <CFCHARTSERIES
      TYPE="bar"
      QUERY="ChartQuery"
      ITEMCOLUMN="MovieTitle"
      VALUECOLUMN="ExpenseTotal"
      SERIESLABEL="Actual Expenses"
      SERIESCOLOR="FF4444">

  </CFCHART>

  </BODY>
  </HTML>
```

Nearly any time you have multiple columns of information in the same query, you can display them using code similar to that used in this listing. The unspoken assumption is that the data in the first row of the `AmountBudgeted` and `ExpenseTotal` columns are related to the same real-world item. In this case, that real-world item is the first film.

Combining Series of Different Types

You are free to use different `TYPE` values (`line`, `bar`, `area`, `scatter`, and so on) for each `<CFCHARTSERIES>` tag in the same chart. For instance, Figure 25.8 shows what happens if you change one of the series types to `area` and the other to `line`. Line graphs are generally used to represent a single concept that changes over time, rather than blocks of individual data like film budgets, but in this particular case the result is rather effective. You are invited to experiment with different combinations of bar charts to see the various possibilities for yourself.

NOTE

You can't combine pie charts with other types of charts. Any `<CFCHARTSERIES>` tags that try to mix pie charts with other types will be ignored.

You can also experiment with the `SERIESPLACEMENT` attribute to tell ColdFusion to change the way in which your chart series are combined. For instance, you can use `SERIESPLACEMENT="stacked"` to have the bars shown in Figure 25.7 displayed stacked on top of one another (as if their values represent concepts that should be combined, like different types of expenses), instead of side by side in pairs. Figure 25.9 shows the result if you use `SERIESPLACEMENT="stacked"`, if the expenses in the `ExpenseTotal` column of the `ChartQuery` record set are negative instead of positive by changing `SUM(ExpenseAmount)` to `0-SUM(ExpenseAmount)`.

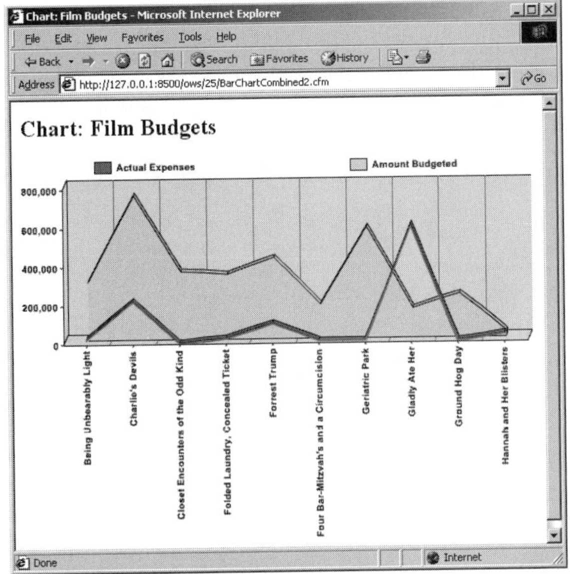

Figure 25.8

You can combine different types of graph types to create your own hybrid charts.

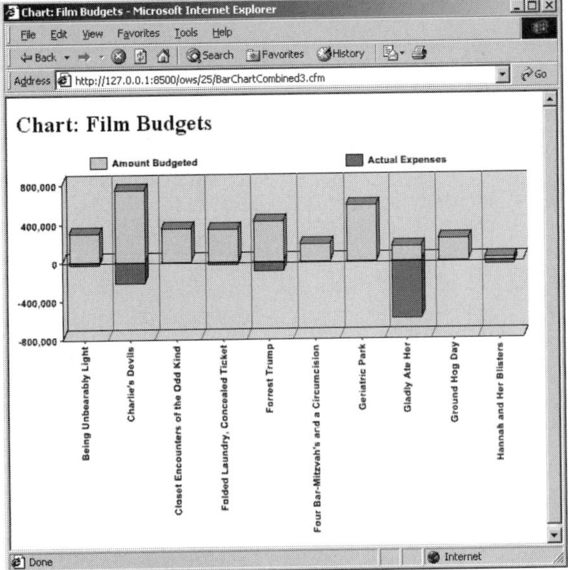

Figure 25.9

The ability to stack multiple data series gives you even greater flexibility.

Drilling Down from Charts

The <CFCHART> tag provides a URL attribute that you can use to create *clickable* charts, where the user is able to click the various data points in the chart to link to a different page. Of course, the page you bring users to when they click the chart is up to you. Generally, the idea is to allow users to *zoom in* or *drill down* conceptually on the data point they clicked.

For instance, if a chart is displaying information about film expenses, as in Figure 25.7, then clicking one of the expense bars might display an HTML table that lists the actual expense records. Or it might bring up a second chart, this one a pie chart that shows the distribution of the individual expenses for that particular film. In either case, your clickable chart can be thought of as a navigation element, not unlike a toolbar or a set of HTML links. It's a way for users to explore your data visually.

Creating a Clickable Chart

To create a clickable chart, simply add a URL attribute to the <CFCHART> tag. When the user clicks one of the data points in the chart (the slices of a pie chart, the bars in a bar chart, the points in a line graph, and so on), he will be sent to the URL you specify. So, if you want the browser to navigate to a ColdFusion page called FilmExpenseDetail.cfm when a chart is clicked, you would use URL="FilmExpenseDetail.cfm". You can use any type of relative or absolute URL that would be acceptable to use in a normal HTML link.

In order to make the detail page dynamic, though, it will need to know which data point the user clicked. To make this possible, ColdFusion allows you to pass the actual data that the user is clicking as URL variables. To do so, include any of the special values shown in Table 25.7 in the URL attribute. ColdFusion will create a dynamic URL for each data point by replacing these special values with the actual data for that data point.

Table 25.7 Special Values for Passing in <CFCHART> URLs

VARIABLE	DESCRIPTION
$VALUE$	The value of the selected row (that is, the value in the VALUECOLUMN attribute of the <CFCHARTSERIES> tag for the data point that was clicked). This is typically the value that you are most interested in passing in the URL.
$ITEMLABEL$	The label of the selected row (that is, the value in the ITEMCOLUMN for the data point that was clicked).
$SERIESLABEL$	The series label (that is, the value of the SERIESLABEL attribute of the <CFCHARTSERIES> tag). It is usually necessary to include this value in the URL only if you have multiple <CFCHARTSERIES> tags in your chart; this value becomes the way that the target page knows which series the user clicked.

For instance, consider the following <CFCHARTSERIES> tag:

```
<CFCHARTSERIES
  TYPE="pie"
  QUERY="ChartQuery"
  VALUECOLUMN="AmountBudgeted"
  ITEMCOLUMN="MovieTitle"
  URL="FilmExpenseDetail.cfm?MovieTitle=$ITEMLABEL$">
```

When the user clicks the slices in this pie chart, the title of the film he is clicking will be passed to the `FilmExpenseDetail.cfm` page as a URL parameter named `MovieTitle`. Within `FilmExpenseDetail.cfm`, the value will be available as `URL.MovieTitle`, which can be used just like any other variable in the `URL` scope.

Listing 25.7 shows how the `URL` attribute can be used to create a clickable chart. This listing creates a pie chart that breaks down the overall budget for Orange Whip Studios by film, just like the chart shown in Figure 25.4 does. When the user clicks a slice of the pie, he is presented with the detail page shown in Figure 25.10. You'll see the code for the detail page in a moment.

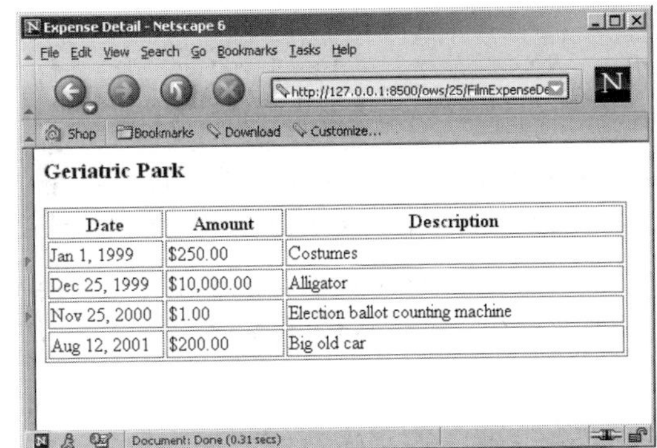

Figure 25.10
Users can click slices of a pie chart to view detail pages like this one.

Listing 25.7 `PieChartDrillDown.cfm`—Creating a Chart with Drill-Down Facilities

```
<!---
  Filename: PieChartDrillDown.cfm
  Author:   Nate Weiss (NMW)
  Purpose:  Displays a pie chart that can be drilled down on for detail records
--->

<!--- Get information from the database --->
<CFQUERY NAME="ChartQuery" DATASOURCE="ows" MAXROWS="10">
  SELECT FilmID, MovieTitle, AmountBudgeted
  FROM Films
  ORDER BY MovieTitle
</CFQUERY>

<HTML>
<HEAD><TITLE>Chart: Film Budgets</TITLE></HEAD>
<BODY>
<H2>Chart: Film Budgets</H2>

<!--- This defines the size and appearance of the chart --->
<CFCHART
  CHARTWIDTH="550"
  CHARTHEIGHT="300"
  PIESLICESTYLE="solid"
  SHOW3D="Yes"
  YOFFSET=".9"
  URL="FilmExpenseDetail.cfm?MovieTitle=$ITEMLABEL$&Budget=$VALUE$">
```

Listing 25.7 (CONTINUED)

```
    <!--- Within the chart --->
    <CFCHARTSERIES
      TYPE="pie"
      QUERY="ChartQuery"
      VALUECOLUMN="AmountBudgeted"
      ITEMCOLUMN="MovieTitle">

  </CFCHART>

  </BODY>
  </HTML>
```

Creating the Detail Page

Creating the detail page shown in Figure 25.10 is relatively straightforward. You simply use the URL parameters passed by the `URL` attribute of the `<CFCHART>` in Listing 25.7 to query the database for the appropriate Expense records. The records can then be displayed using normal `<CFOUTPUT>` and HTML table tags.

There is one bit of unpleasantness to deal with, though: Unfortunately, `<CFCHART>` doesn't provide a straightforward way to pass a unique identifier in URLs generated by `<CFCHART>`. The only things you can pass are the actual label and value of the data point displayed on the graph (with the special `$ITEMLABEL$` and `$VALUE$` values, respectively).

So, for the example at hand (see Listing 25.8), the only pieces of information that can be passed to the `FilmExpenseDetail.cfm` page are the film's title and budget, since those are the only values that the chart is aware of. Ordinarily, it would be far preferable to pass the `FilmID` in the URL, thereby eliminating any problems that would come up if there were two films with the same title. Since this isn't currently possible in ColdFusion MX, the film will have to be identified by its title (and budget) alone.

NOTE

Keep this limitation in mind when creating drill-down applications with `<CFCHART>`. If a data point cannot be safely and uniquely identified by the combination of the label and value displayed in the graph, you will probably not be able to implement drill-down.

Listing 25.8 `FilmExpenseDetail.cfm`—A Detail Page Displayed upon Drill-Down from Charts

```
<!---
  Filename: FilmExpenseDetail.cfm
  Author:   Nate Weiss (NMW)
  Purpose:  Displays detail records for a particular film
--->

<!--- These URL parameters will be passed by the chart --->
<CFPARAM NAME="URL.MovieTitle" TYPE="string">
<CFPARAM NAME="URL.Budget" TYPE="numeric">

<!--- Get information from the database --->
<CFQUERY NAME="FilmQuery" DATASOURCE="ows" MAXROWS="1">
  SELECT FilmID
  FROM Films
  WHERE MovieTitle = '#URL.MovieTitle#'
    AND AmountBudgeted = #URL.Budget#
```

Listing 25.8 (CONTINUED)

```
</CFQUERY>

<!--- Show an error message if we could not determine the FilmID --->
<CFIF FilmQuery.RecordCount NEQ 1>
  <CFTHROW
    MESSAGE="Could not retrieve film infomration."
    DETAIL="No film was identified based on the title and budget provided.">
</CFIF>

<!--- Now that we know the FilmID, we can select the --->
<!--- corresponding expense records from the database --->
<CFQUERY NAME="ExpenseQuery" DATASOURCE="ows">
  SELECT * FROM Expenses
  WHERE FilmID = #FilmQuery.FilmID#
  ORDER BY ExpenseDate
</CFQUERY>


<HTML>
<HEAD><TITLE>Expense Detail</TITLE></HEAD>
<BODY>

<CFOUTPUT>
  <!--- Page heading --->
  <H3>#URL.MovieTitle#</H3>

  <!--- HTML table for expense display --->
  <TABLE BORDER="1" WIDTH="500">
    <TR>
      <TH WIDTH="100">Date</TH>
      <TH WIDTH="100">Amount</TH>
      <TH WIDTH="300">Description</TH>
    </TR>

    <!--- For each expense in the query... --->
    <CFLOOP QUERY="ExpenseQuery">
    <TR>
      <TD>#LSDateFormat(ExpenseDate)#</TD>
      <TD>#LSCurrencyFormat(ExpenseAmount)#</TD>
      <TD>#Description#</TD>
    </TR>
    </CFLOOP>
  </TABLE>
</CFOUTPUT>

</BODY>
</HTML>
```

The purpose of the first query, at the top of the page, is to determine the `FilmID` to the `MovieTitle` parameter passed to the page (from the chart in Listing 25.7) measure, the `Budget` parameter is also included in the query criteria. This me happen to have the same title, they can still be correctly identified as long as ferent. For the rest of the page, `FilmQuery.FilmID` holds the ID number fo to retrieve any related information from the database.

NOTE

If no films are retrieved from the database (or if more than one is retrieved), an error message is displayed with the `<CFTHROW>` tag. For more information about `<CFTHROW>`, see Chapter 31, "Error Handling."

Other Drill-Down Possibilities

In Figure 25.10, the details for a particular data point on the chart is shown on a separate page. There are many other ways to approach the drill-down experience. For instance, you might want to show the detail information on the same page as the chart. One way to do this would be to change the `URL` attribute of the `<CFCHART>` so that it reloads the current page. There is a `PieChartDrillDown2.cfm` page on the CD-ROM, which is just like Listing 25.7 except that it uses its own filename in the `URL` attribute, like so:

```
URL="PieChartDrillDown2.cfm?MovieTitle=$ITEMLABEL$&Budget=$VALUE$"
```

Then, after the `<CFCHART>` block, the following code is used to include the detail page directly under the chart, as shown in Figure 25.11:

```
<!--- If user just clicked on the chart, display drill down page --->
<CFIF IsDefined("URL.MovieTitle") AND IsDefined("URL.Budget")>
  <CFINCLUDE TEMPLATE="FilmExpenseDetail.cfm">
</CFIF>
```

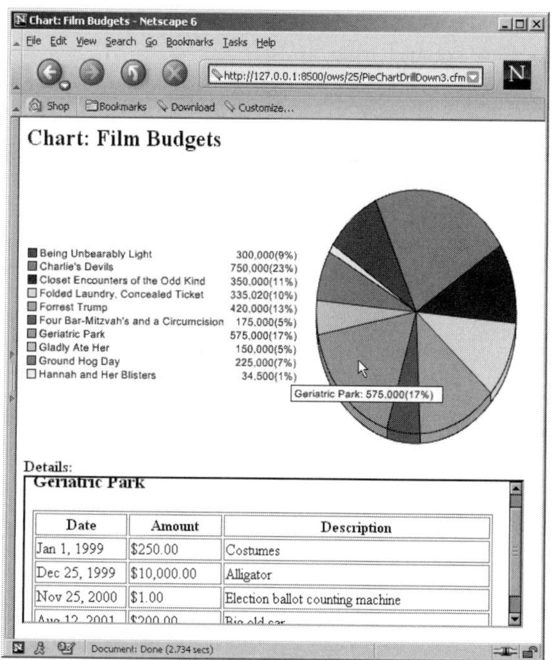

Figure 25.11

You can easily provide a chart and drill-down information on the same page.

TE

Even though this approach causes the chart page to be reloaded for each click, it shouldn't affect the server's performance very much, because ColdFusion automatically caches the chart images it generates. See the "Controlling the Chart Cache" section, later in his chapter.

NOTE

The <HTML>, <HEAD>, and <BODY> tags really should be removed from the detail page for the result to be considered proper, but most browsers will be able to display the results correctly even though two sets of these tags will be in the HTML source for the page. This is just an example.

Using JavaScript and <IFRAME>

Another way to get a similar effect is to place a scrolling window under the chart with a set of <IFRAME> tags. <IFRAME> was originally introduced by Microsoft Internet Explorer, and is now an official part of HTML. Netscape browsers started supporting <IFRAME> with version 6.

Listing 25.9 shows how to implement a chart and drill-down interface using <IFRAME>. The results are shown in Figure 25.12.

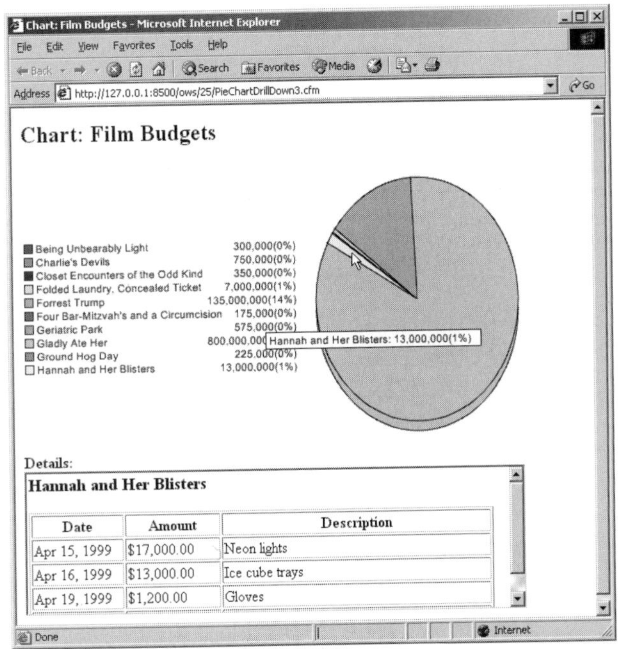

Figure 25.12 With a little help from JavaScript, you can create drill-down pages that use other window areas.

Listing 25.9 PieChartDrillDown3.cfm—Using <IFRAME> to Display Details in a Scrolling Window

```
<!---
  Filename: PieChartDrillDown.cfm
  Author:   Nate Weiss (NMW)
  Purpose:  Displays a pie chart that can be drilled down on for detail records
--->

<!--- Get information from the database --->
<CFQUERY NAME="ChartQuery" DATASOURCE="ows" MAXROWS="10">
  SELECT FilmID, MovieTitle, AmountBudgeted
  FROM Films
  ORDER BY MovieTitle
```

Listing 25.9 (CONTINUED)

```
</CFQUERY>

<HTML>
<HEAD><TITLE>Chart: Film Budgets</TITLE></HEAD>
<BODY>
<H2>Chart: Film Budgets</H2>

<!--- Script to power the drill-down --->
<SCRIPT LANGUAGE="JavaScript">
  function drillDown(movieTitle, budget) {
    // Build the url for the detail page
    var baseUrl = "FilmExpenseDetail.cfm";
    var url = baseUrl + "?MovieTitle=" + escape(movieTitle) + "&Budget=" + budget;

    // Navigate the sub-window to the url
    window.DetailFrame.document.location = url;
  }
</SCRIPT>

<!--- This defines the size and appearance of the chart --->
<CFCHART
  CHARTWIDTH="550"
  CHARTHEIGHT="300"
  PIESLICESTYLE="solid"
  SHOW3D="Yes"
  YOFFSET=".9"
  URL="javascript:drillDown('$ITEMLABEL$', $VALUE$)">

  <!--- Within the chart --->
  <CFCHARTSERIES
    TYPE="pie"
    QUERY="ChartQuery"
    VALUECOLUMN="AmountBudgeted"
    ITEMCOLUMN="MovieTitle">

</CFCHART>

<!--- This creates a sub-window for showing the detail page --->
<!--- Note <IFRAME> tags don't work in Netscape 4 or lower --->
<BR><B>Details:</B><BR>
<IFRAME
  SRC="about:blank"
  NAME="DetailFrame"
  WIDTH="540"
  MARGINHEIGHT="2"
  MARGINWIDTH="2"
  HEIGHT="150"></IFRAME>

</BODY>
</HTML>
```

This method requires a bit of JavaScript, which you can read more about in an HTML or JavaScript reference guide. The basic idea is that a function called `drillDown` has been created that is responsible for navigating the scrolling window to the correct detail page URL. This JavaScript function is provided as the URL attribute of the <CFCHART> tag, using the special javascript: pseudo-protocol (which is supported by all JavaScript-enabled browsers). Again, you will need to consult a JavaScript text for details, but the point is that you can use JavaScript to respond to the drill-down clicks any of your charts.

Using JavaScript with Pop-up Windows

You can also use the same basic JavaScript technique to open the detail page in a separate pop-up window. For instance, the PieChartDrillDown4.cfm page included with this chapter's listings on the CD-ROM is the same as the last version (Listing 25.9), except that this line:

```
window.DetailFrame.document.location = url;
```

has been replaced with this:

```
detailPopup = window.open(url, "dp", "width=530,height=150,scrollbars=yes");
detailPopup.focus();
```

The result is that the detail page is shown in a small pop-up window. See a JavaScript guide for more information about window.open() and focus() methods.

Drilling Down to Another Chart

Of course, you are free to drill down to a different chart that shows a different view or subset of the data, rather just drilling down to a simple HTML page. The second chart page, in turn, could drill down to another page, and so on. You could use any of the drill-down techniques discussed in this section to put together such a multilayered data-navigation interface.

Additional Charting Topics

The remainder of this chapter introduces various topics related to ColdFusion MX's charting features.

Plotting Individual Points with <CFCHARTDATA>

The most common way to provide the actual data to a <CFCHARTSERIES> tag is to specify a QUERY attribute, then tell ColdFusion which columns of the query to look in by specifying ITEMCOLUMN and VALUECOLUMN attributes. All of the examples you've seen so far in this chapter have supplied their data in this way.

It is also possible to omit the QUERY, ITEMCOLUMN, and VALUECOLUMN attributes and instead plot the data points individually using the <CFCHARTDATA> tag, nested within your <CFCHARTSERIES>. The <CFCHARTDATA> approach can come in handy if you want to permanently hard-code certain data points onto your charts, if you need to format your data in a special way, or if you come across any other situation in which you can't extract the desired data from a query in a completely straight-forward manner.

Table 25.8 shows the syntax for the <CFCHARTDATA> tag.

Table 25.8 <CFCHARTDATA> Syntax

ATTRIBUTE	DESCRIPTION
ITEM	The item associated with the data point you are plotting, such as a film title, a category of purchases, or a period of time—in other words, the information you would normally supply to the ITEMCOLUMN attribute of the <CFCHARTSERIES> tag.
VALUE	The value of the data point (a number). This is what you would normally supply to the VALUECOLUMN attribute of <CFCHARTSERIES>.

For instance, if you have a query called ChartQuery with two columns, ExpenseDate and ExpenseAmount, and you wanted to make sure the date was formatted to your liking when it was displayed on the chart, you could use:

```
<CFCHARTSERIES
  TYPE="line">
  <CFLOOP QUERY="ChartQuery">
    <CFCHARTDATA
      ITEM="#DateFormat(ExpenseDate, 'm/d/yy')#"
      VALUE="#ExpenseAmount#">
  </CFLOOP>
</CFCHARTSERIES>
```

instead of:

```
<CFCHARTSERIES
  TYPE="line"
  QUERY="ChartQuery"
  VALUECOLUMN="ExpenseAmount"
  ITEMCOLUMN="ExpenseDate">
```

Accessing Chart Images on the Server

Normally, when you use the <CFCHART> tag, ColdFusion creates the actual chart image, then creates the HTML needed to display that image on your Web page. If the chart is being created with FORMAT="Flash", your Web page includes the necessary <OBJECT> and <EMBED> tags to display the movie. If the chart is being created as a JPEG or PNG file, your Web page includes an <IMG> tag to display the movie (plus the appropriate <MAP> and <AREA> tags to implement the drill-down feature if you are using the URL attribute).

If you want, you can use the NAME attribute of the <CFCHART> tag to get direct access to the generated Flash or image file itself. If you provide a NAME attribute, the <CFCHART> tag does not display the chart on your Web page. Instead, it generates the resulting image and places it in a *binary object* variable with the name you specify. You haven't learned much about binary object variables in this book, but they can easily be written to disk with <CFFILE>. Once saved to your server's drive, they can be easily sent as an email attachment via <CFMAIL>, uploaded to another server via <CFFTP>, or whatever else you want.

For instance, assume for the moment that you are using FORMAT="jpg" in a <CFCHART> tag. To save the chart to a location of your choosing on the server's drive, just add a NAME="ChartContent" attribute. Then, after the <CFCHART> block, use <CFFILE> to save the file to disk, like so:

```
<CFFILE
  ACTION="Write"
  FILE="c:\MyDirectory\MyChartImage.jpg"
  OUTPUT="#ChartContent#">
```

You could then send the MyChartImage.jpg file as an email attachment via the <CFMAIL> and <CFMAILPARAM> tags.

NOTE

See Chapter 33, "Interacting with the Operating System," for details about <CFFILE>. See Chapter 26, "Interacting With Email," for details about <CFMAIL> and <CFMAILPARAM>.

Or, to send the binary contents of the image to the Web browser (rather than generating an <IMG> tag that embeds the image on a Web page, which is what <CFCHART> normally does), you could use NAME="ChartContent" as mentioned above, then use the <CFCONTENT> tag to stream the binary content back to the client, like this:

```
<CFCONTENT
  TYPE="image/jpeg"
  RESET="Yes"><CFOUTPUT>#ChartContent#</CFOUTPUT>
```

You could then display the chart using an <IMG> tag that points to the ColdFusion page that includes this <CFCONTENT> tag, like so:

```
<IMG SRC="MyChartContentPage.cfm" WIDTH="300" HEIGHT="200">
```

NOTE

For more information about <CFCONTENT>, see Chapter 32, "Generating Non-HTML Content."

Listing 25.10 is an interesting example; it creates a page that displays a small chart with the budget and expenses for a single film. The film represented by the chart is rotated on a per-session basis, meaning that the page will generate a different chart each time a user reloads the page (until the user has seen charts for all of the films, at which point the rotation starts over). Instead of outputting the chart normally, this example uses the NAME attribute and <CFCONTENT> tag as shown above to send the binary image itself back to the browser. In a moment, you will see how this example should be used.

The rotation logic is similar to the Featured Movie examples in Chapter 16, "Introducing the Web Application Framework," and the <CFCHART> syntax is similar to many of the other examples in this chapter.

Listing 25.10 RotatingChartStream.cfm—Sending the Chart Image Itself to the Browser

```
<!---
  Filename: RotatingChartStream.cfm
  Author:   Nate Weiss (NMW)
  Purpose:  Creates a simple chart and streams the image to the browser
--->
```

Listing 25.10 (continued)

```
<!--- Get a list of film ID numbers --->
<!--- Cache the query for good performance --->
<CFQUERY NAME="FilmQuery" DATASOURCE="ows"
  CACHEDWITHIN="#CreateTimeSpan(0,1,0,0)#">
  SELECT FilmID FROM Films
  ORDER BY MovieTitle
</CFQUERY>

<!--- Make sure we have a SESSION.ChartRotator.CurrentPos variable --->
<CFPARAM NAME="SESSION.ChartRotator.CurrentPos" TYPE="numeric" DEFAULT="0">
<!--- Increase the value of the variable by one --->
<CFSET SESSION.ChartRotator.CurrentPos = SESSION.ChartRotator.CurrentPos + 1>
<!--- If we have gotten to the end of the list of films, start over --->
<CFIF SESSION.ChartRotator.CurrentPos GT FilmQuery.RecordCount>
  <CFSET SESSION.ChartRotator.CurrentPos = 1>
</CFIF>

<!--- This is the FilmID that we should use for this request --->
<CFSET ShowFilmID = FilmQuery.FilmID[SESSION.ChartRotator.CurrentPos]>

<!--- Get information about the film --->
<CFQUERY NAME="FilmQuery" DATASOURCE="ows"
  CACHEDWITHIN="#CreateTimeSpan(0,1,0,0)#">
  SELECT AmountBudgeted, MovieTitle FROM Films
  WHERE FilmID = #ShowFilmID#
</CFQUERY>

<!--- Get information about the film's expenses --->
<CFQUERY NAME="ExpenseQuery" DATASOURCE="ows"
  CACHEDWITHIN="#CreateTimeSpan(0,1,0,0)#">
  SELECT SUM(ExpenseAmount) AS ExpenseTotal FROM Expenses
  WHERE FilmID = #ShowFilmID#
</CFQUERY>

<!--- This defines the size and appearance of the chart --->
<CFCHART
  CHARTWIDTH="200"
  CHARTHEIGHT="150"
  ROTATED="no"
  FORMAT="png"
  SERIESPLACEMENT="cluster"
  SHOWLEGEND="No"
  <!--- 3D appearance --->
  SHOW3D="Yes"
  XAXISTITLE="#FilmQuery.MovieTitle#"
  <!--- Fonts and colors --->
  FONTSIZE="9"
  DATABACKGROUNDCOLOR="DDDDDD"
  <!--- Axes and gridlines --->
  SCALETO="800000"
  GRIDLINES="5"
  SHOWXGRIDLINES="Yes"
  SHOWYGRIDLINES="No"
  NAME="ChartContent">
```

Listing 25.10 (continued)

```
    <!--- This series of bars shows the budget --->
    <CFCHARTSERIES
      TYPE="bar"
      QUERY="FilmQuery"
      VALUECOLUMN="AmountBudgeted"
      SERIESLABEL="Amount Budgeted"
      SERIESCOLOR="99FF99">

    <!--- This series of bars shows the expenses --->
    <CFCHARTSERIES
      TYPE="bar"
      QUERY="ExpenseQuery"
      ITEMCOLUMN="MovieTitle"
      VALUECOLUMN="ExpenseTotal"
      SERIESLABEL="Actual Expenses"
      SERIESCOLOR="FF4444">

  </CFCHART>

  <!--- Ask the browser not to cache the image on its drive --->
  <CFHEADER NAME="Expires" VALUE="0">

  <!--- Output the chart image directly to the browser --->
  <CFCONTENT
    TYPE="image/jpeg"
    RESET="Yes"><CFOUTPUT>#ChartContent#</CFOUTPUT>
```

NOTE

The purpose of the `<CFHEADER>` tag is to tell the browser not to cache each chart image, since they will be replaced so often. See Appendix B for details about `<CFHEADER>`.

Once Listing 25.10 is in place, you can use it by creating an ordinary Web page that uses Listing 25.10 as the `SRC` of an `<IMG>` tag. You can then use JavaScript to tell the browser to update the actual image shown every few seconds. Each time the browser reestablishes contact with the server, the server will respond with the chart for the next film. The result is a page that presents the user with a slide show of charts about individual films (Figure 25.13).

You could easily adapt this example so that the slide show displays some kind of data changing over time (month-by-month sales, for instance, or the price of a stock over the past 24 hours) (see Listing 25.11).

Listing 25.11 `ShowRotatingChart.htm`—Refetching the Chart from Listing 25.10 Every Few Seconds

```
<!---
  Filename: ShowRotatingChart.htm
  Author:   Nate Weiss (NMW)
  Purpose:  Displays the chart generated by RotatingChartStream.cfm
--->


<HTML>
<HEAD>
  <TITLE>Updating Chart</TITLE>
```

Listing 25.11 (CONTINUED)

```
  <!--- This function forces the image to be re-fetched from the server --->
  <SCRIPT LANGUAGE="JavaScript">
    function updateChart() {
      document.RotatingChart.src = document.RotatingChart.src;
    };
  </SCRIPT>
</HEAD>

<!--- Once the page has loaded, tell the browser to execute --->
<!--- the updateChart() function every two seconds --->
<BODY onload="setInterval('updateChart()', 2000)">

<H3>Self-Updating Mini Chart</H3>
<P>This chart will update every two seconds, without reloading the page:</P>

<!--- Include the initial chart image --->
<IMG
  SRC="RotatingChartStream.cfm"
  NAME="RotatingChart"
  WIDTH="200"
  HEIGHT="150"
  BORDER="0">

</BODY>
</HTML>
```

NOTE

It's worth pointing out that Listing 25.11 doesn't have to be a dynamic page, because there is no server-side processing needed to display the image on the page (only to generate the image).

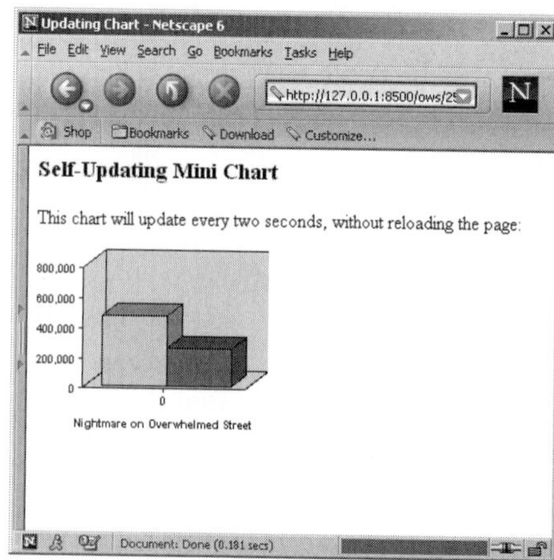

Figure 25.13

The chart on this page updates itself every 2 seconds, resulting in a slide-show effect.

Using Charts with Flash Remoting

It is possible to use the NAME attribute to capture the binary content of a chart and then make it available to the Macromedia Flash Player via Flash Remoting. This capability allows you to create a Flash movie that displays dynamically generated charts on the fly, perhaps as a part of a sophisticated data-entry or reporting interface, all without reloading the page to display an updated or changed chart. This topic is beyond the scope of this book, but you can consult Chapter 23, "Integrating with Macromedia Flash," for general information about connecting ColdFusion to Flash via Flash Remoting.

Controlling the Chart Cache

ColdFusion MX automatically caches charts for later use. Conceptually, the chart cache is the charting equivalent of the query caching feature you learned about in Chapter 22, "Improving Performance." Its purpose is to improve performance by automatically reusing the results of a <CFCHART> tag if all of its data and attributes are the same, rather than having to rerender each chart for every page request.

The Charting page of the ColdFusion MX Administrator contains a number of options that you can use to tweak the chart cache's behavior:

- Cache type: You can set this to Disk Cache (the default value) or Memory Cache. The Memory Cache setting will perform better under a high load, but it will require more of the server's memory to do so. The Disk Cache setting may not perform quite as quickly, but it will not have much of an impact on the server's RAM. We recommend leaving this value alone unless you are specifically experiencing performance problems with <CFCHART> under a heavy load.
- Maximum number of images in cache: You can increase this number to allow ColdFusion to store more charts in its cache, thereby improving performance if your application is serving up a number of different charts. If you are using the Memory Cache option, keep in mind that this will cause even more of the server's memory to be used for chart caching.
- Maximum number of chart requests: This is the maximum number of <CFCHART> tags that you want ColdFusion to be willing to process at the same time. Under a high load, a higher number here may improve responsiveness for individual page requests, but it will put more strain on your server.
- Disk cache location: If you are using the Disk Cache option, you may want to adjust this value: the location in which ColdFusion stores charts for later reuse.

For more information about the ColdFusion MX Administrator, see Chapter 28, "ColdFusion Server Configuration."

CHAPTER 26

Interacting with Email

IN THIS CHAPTER

Sending Email from ColdFusion

Clearly, ColdFusion's main purpose is to create dynamic, data-driven Web pages. However, ColdFusion also provides a set of email-related tags that enable you to send email messages that are just as dynamic and data-driven as your Web pages. You can also write ColdFusion templates that check and retrieve email messages, and even respond to them automatically.

NOTE

> `<CFMAIL>` sends standard, Internet-style email messages using the Simple Mail Transport Protocol (SMTP). SMTP is not explained in detail in this book; for now, all you need to know about SMTP is that it is the standard for sending email on the Internet. Virtually all email programs, such as Netscape, Outlook Express, Eudora, and so on send standard SMTP mail. The exceptions are proprietary messaging systems, such as Lotus Notes or older Microsoft Mail (MAPI-style) clients. If you want to learn more about the underpinnings of the SMTP protocol, visit the World Wide Web Consortium's Web site at www.wc3.org.

Introducing the `<CFMAIL>` Tag

You can use the `<CFMAIL>` tag to send email messages from your ColdFusion templates. After the server is set up correctly, you can use `<CFMAIL>` to send email messages to anyone with a standard Internet-style email address. As far as the receiver is concerned, the email messages you send with `<CFMAIL>` are just like messages sent via a normal email sending program, such as Netscape, Outlook Express, Eudora, or the like.

Table 26.1 shows the key attributes for the `<CFMAIL>` tag. These are the attributes you will use most often, and they are presented in a separate table here for clarity. Assuming that you have sent email messages before, you will understand what almost all of these attributes do right away.

NOTE

> Some additional `<CFMAIL>` attributes are introduced later in this chapter (see Table 26.2 in the "Sending Data-Driven Mail" section and Table 26.4 in the "Overriding the Default Mail Server Settings" section).

Table 26.1 Key <CFMAIL> Attributes for Sending Email Messages

ATTRIBUTE	PURPOSE
SUBJECT	Required. The subject of the email message.
FROM	Required. The email address that should be used to send the message. This is the address the message will be from when it is received. The address must be a standard Internet-style email address (see the section "Using Friendly Email Addresses," later in this chapter).
TO	Required. The address or addresses to send the message to. To specify multiple addresses, simply separate them with commas. Each must be a standard Internet-style email address (see the section "Using Friendly Email Addresses").
CC	Optional. Address or addresses to send a carbon copy of the message to. This is the equivalent to using the CC feature when sending mail with a normal email program. To specify multiple addresses, simply separate them with commas. Each must be a standard Internet-style email address (see the section "Using Friendly Email Addresses").
BCC	Optional. Address or addresses to send a blind carbon copy of the message to. Equivalent to using the BCC feature when sending mail with a normal email program. To specify multiple addresses, simply separate them with commas. Each must be a standard Internet-style email address (see the section "Using Friendly Email Addresses").
TYPE	Optional. `Text` or `HTML`. `Text` is the default, which means that the message will be sent as a normal, plain text message. `HTML` means that HTML tags within the message will be interpreted as HTML, so you can specify fonts and include images in the email message. See "Sending HTML-Formatted Mail," later in this chapter.
MAILERID	Optional. Can be used to specify the X-Mailer header that is sent with the email message. The X-Mailer header is meant to identify which software program was used to send the message. This header is generally never seen by the recipient of the message but can be important to systems in between, such as firewalls. Using the `MAILERID`, you can make it appear as if your message is being sent by a different piece of software. If you find that your outgoing messages are being filtered out when sent to certain users, try using a `MAILERID` that matches some other mail client (such as Outlook Express or some other popular, end-user mail client).
MIMEATTACH	Optional. A document on the server's drive that should be included in the mail message as an attachment. This is an older way to specify attachments, maintained for backward compatibility. It is now recommended that you use the `<CFMAILPARAM>` tag to specify attachments. See "Adding Attachments," later in this chapter, for details.
SPOOLENABLE	Optional. Controls whether the email message should be sent right away, before ColdFusion begins processing the rest of the template. The default value is `Yes`, which means that the message is created and then placed in a queue; the actual sending will take place as soon as possible, but not necessarily before the page request has been completed. If you use `SPOOLENABLE="No"`, the message will be sent right away; ColdFusion will not proceed beyond the `<CFMAIL>` tag until the sending has been completed. That is, `No` forces the mail sending to be a synchronous process; `Yes` (the default) lets it be an asynchronous process.

NOTE

The SPOOLENABLE attribute is new for ColdFusion MX. Previous versions of ColdFusion always behaved as if SPOOLENABLE were Yes.

Specifying a Mail Server in the Administrator

Before you can actually use the <CFMAIL> tag to send email messages, you need to specify a mail server in the ColdFusion Administrator. This is the mail server with which ColdFusion will interact to actually send the messages that get generated by your templates.

To set up ColdFusion to send email, follow these steps:

1. If you don't know it already, find out the host name or IP address for the SMTP mail server ColdFusion should use to send messages. Usually, this is the same server your normal email client program (Outlook Express, Eudora, and so on) uses to send your own mail, so you typically can find the host name or IP address somewhere in your mail client's Settings or Preferences. Often, the host name starts with something such as `mail` or `smtp`, as in `mail.orangewhipstudios.com`.
2. Open the ColdFusion Administrator, and navigate to the Mail Server page, as shown in Figure 26.1.
3. Provide the mail server's host name or IP address in the Mail Server field.
4. Check the Verify Mail Server Connection option.

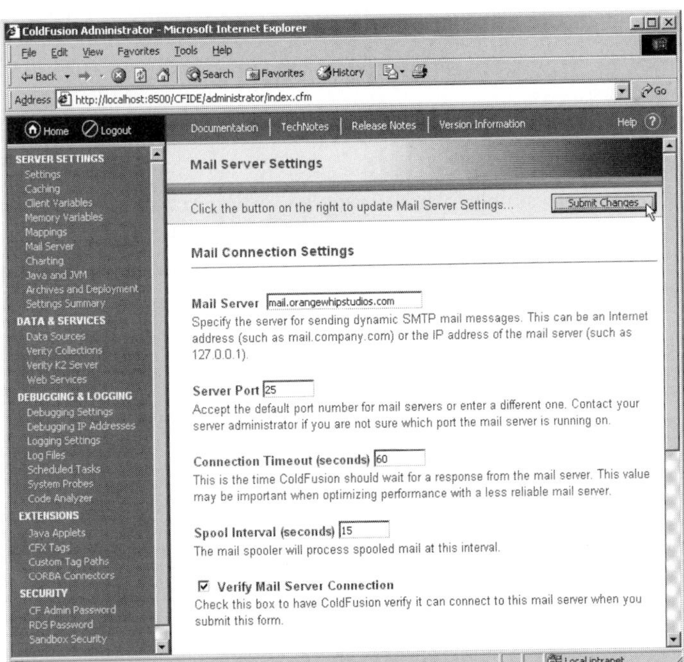

Figure 26.1

Before messages can be sent, ColdFusion needs to know which mail server to use.

5. If your mail server operates on a port other than the usual port number 25, provide the port number in the Server Port field. This is usually unnecessary.
6. Save your changes by clicking the Submit Changes button.

TIP

These settings can be overridden in individual ColdFusion templates by the `<CFMAIL>` tag. See the "Overriding the Default Mail Server Settings" section, later in this chapter.

NOTE

For more information about the other Mail Server options shown in Figure 26.1, see Chapter 28, "ColdFusion Server Configuration."

Sending Email Messages

Sending an email message via a ColdFusion template is easy. Simply code a pair of opening and closing `<CFMAIL>` tags, and provide the `TO`, `FROM`, and `SUBJECT` attributes as appropriate. Between the tags, type the actual message that should be sent to the recipient.

Of course, you can use ColdFusion variables and functions between the `<CFMAIL>` tags to build the message dynamically, using the `#` sign syntax you're used to. You don't need to place `<CFOUTPUT>` tags within (or outside) the `<CFMAIL>` tags; your `#` variables and expressions will be evaluated as if there were a `<CFOUTPUT>` tag in effect.

TIP

In fact, as you look through the examples in this chapter, you will find that the `<CFMAIL>` tag is basically a specially modified `<CFOUTPUT>` tag. It has similar behavior (variables and expressions are evaluated) and attributes (`GROUP`, `MAXROWS`, and so on, as listed in Table 26.4).

Sending a Simple Message

Listing 26.1 shows how easy it is to use the `<CFMAIL>` tag to send a message. The idea behind this template is to provide a simple form for people working in Orange Whip Studios' personnel department. Rather than having to open their normal email client programs, they can just use this Web page. It displays a simple form for the user to type a message and specify a recipient, as shown previously in Figure 26.1. When the form is submitted, the message is sent.

Listing 26.1 `PersonnelMail1.cfm`—Sending Email with ColdFusion

```
<!---
  Filename: PersonnelMail1.cfm
  Author:   Nate Weiss (NMW)
  Purpose:  A simple form for sending email
--->


<HTML>
<HEAD>
  <TITLE>Personnel Office Mailer</TITLE>
  <!--- Apply simple CSS formatting to <TH> cells --->
  <STYLE>
    TH {background:blue;color:white;text-align:right}
```

Listing 26.1 (continued)

```
  </STYLE>
</HEAD>
<BODY>

<H2>Personnel Office Mailer</H2>

<!--- If the user is submitting the Form... --->
<CFIF IsDefined("FORM.Subject")>

<!--- We do not want ColdFusion to suppress whitespace here --->
<CFPROCESSINGDIRECTIVE SUPPRESSWHITESPACE="No">

<!--- Send the mail message, based on form input --->
<CFMAIL
  SUBJECT="#FORM.Subject#"
  FROM="personnel@orangewhipstudios.com"
  TO="#FORM.ToAddress#"
  BCC="personneldirector@orangewhipstudios.com"
>This is a message from the Personnel Office:
#FORM.MessageBody#

If you have any questions about this message, please
write back or call us at extension 352.  Thanks!</CFMAIL>

</CFPROCESSINGDIRECTIVE>

  <!--- Display "success" message to user --->
  <P>The email message was sent.<BR>
  By the way, you look fabulous today.
  You should be in pictures!<BR>

<!--- Otherwise, display the form to user... --->
<CFELSE>
  <!--- Provide simple form for recipient and message --->
  <CFFORM ACTION="#CGI.SCRIPT_NAME#" METHOD="POST">

    <TABLE CELLPADDING="2" CELLSPACING="2">
      <!--- Table row: Input for Email Address --->
      <TR>
        <TH>EMail Address:</TH>
        <TD>
          <CFINPUT
            TYPE="Text"
            NAME="ToAddress"
            REQUIRED="Yes"
            SIZE="40"
            MESSAGE="You must provide an email address.">
        </TD>
      </TR>

      <!--- Table row: Input for E-mail Subject --->
      <TR>
        <TH>Subject:</TH>
        <TD>
          <CFINPUT
            TYPE="Text"
            NAME="Subject"
```

Listing 26.1 (continued)

```
                REQUIRED="Yes"
                SIZE="40"
                MESSAGE="You must provide a subject for the email.">
            </TD>
          </TR>

          <!--- Table row: Input for actual Message Text --->
          <TR>
            <TH>Your Message:</TH>
            <TD>
              <TEXTAREA
                NAME="MessageBody"
                COLS="30"
                ROWS="5"
                WRAP="Hard"></TEXTAREA>

            </TD>
          </TR>

          <!--- Table row: Submit button to send message --->
          <TR>
            <TD></TD>
            <TD>
              <INPUT
                TYPE="Submit"
                VALUE="Send Message Now">
            </TD>
          </TR>
        </TABLE>
      </CFFORM>
    </CFIF>

    </BODY>
    </HTML>
```

There are two parts to this listing, divided by the large `<CFIF>/<CFELSE>` block. When the page is first visited, the second part of the template executes, which displays the form shown in Figure 26.2.

When the form is submitted, the first part of the template kicks in, which actually sends the email message with the `<CFMAIL>` tag. The message's subject line and "to" address are specified by the appropriate form values, and the content of the message itself is constructed by combining the `#FORM.MessageBody#` variable with some static text. Additionally, each message sent by this template is also sent to the personnel director as a blind carbon copy, via the `BCC` attribute.

Around the `<CFMAIL>` tag, the `<CFPROCESSINGDIRECTIVE>` tag is used to turn off ColdFusion's default whitespace-suppression behavior. This is needed in this template because the `<CFMAIL>` tag that follows is written to output the exact text of the email message, which includes "newlines" and other whitespace characters that should be included literally in the actual email message. Without the `<CFPROCESSINGDIRECTIVE>` tag, ColdFusion would see the newlines within the `<CFOUTPUT>` tags as evil whitespace, deserving to be ruthlessly suppressed.

NOTE

For more information about whitespace suppression and the `<CFPROCESSINGDIRECTIVE>` tag, see the "Controlling Whitespace" section in Chapter 22, "Improving Performance."

NOTE

There is a reason why the opening and closing `<CFMAIL>` tags are not indented in this listing. If they were, the spaces or tabs used to do the indenting would show up in the actual email message. You will generally need to make exceptions to your usual indenting practices when using `<CFMAIL>`. The exception would be when using `TYPE="HTML"`, as discussed in the "Sending HTML-Formatted Mail" section, because whitespace is not significant in HTML.

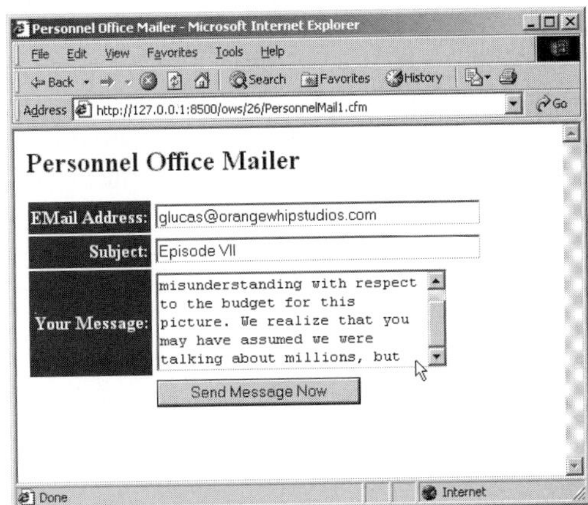

Figure 26.2
Creating a Web-based mail-sending mechanism for your users is easy.

Using Friendly Email Addresses

The email addresses provided to the `TO`, `FROM`, `CC`, and `BCC` attributes can all be specified as just the email address itself (such as `bforta@orangewhipstudios.com`), or as a combination of the address and the address's friendly name. The friendly name is usually the person's real-life first and last names.

To specify a friendly name along with an email address, place the friendly name between double quotation marks, followed by the actual email address between angle brackets. So, instead of

```
bforta@orangewhipstudios.com
```

you would provide

```
"Ben Forta" <bforta@orangewhipstudios.com>
```

To provide such an address to the `FROM`, `TO`, `CC`, or `BCC` attribute of the `<CFMAIL>` tag, you must double up each double quotation mark shown above, assuming that you are already using double quotation marks around the whole attribute value. So, you might end up with something such as the following:

```
<CFMAIL
  SUBJECT="Dinner Plans"
  FROM="""Nate Weiss"" <nweiss@orangewhipstudios.com>"
  TO="""Belinda Foxile"" <bfoxile@orangewhipstudios.com>">
```

Or, if you find the use of the doubled-up double quotation marks confusing, you could surround the `FROM` and `TO` attributes with single quotation marks instead of double quotation marks, which would allow you to provide the double-quotation characters around the friendly name normally, like so:

```
<CFMAIL
  SUBJECT="Dinner Plans"
  FROM='"Nate Weiss" <nweiss@orangewhipstudios.com>'
  TO='"Belinda Foxile" <bfoxile@orangewhipstudios.com>'>
```

Now, when the message is sent, the "to" and "from" addresses shown in the recipient's email program can be shown with each person's real-life name along with his email address. How the friendly name and email address are actually presented to the user is up to the email client software.

The version of the `PersonnelMail.cfm` template shown in Listing 26.2 is nearly the same as the one from Listing 26.1, except that this version collects the recipient's friendly name in addition to his email address. Additionally, this version uses a bit of JavaScript to attempt to pre-fill the email address field based on the friendly name. When the user changes the value in the `FirstName` or `LastName` field, the `ToAddress` field is filled in with the first letter of the first name, plus the whole last name.

NOTE

There isn't space to go through the JavaScript code used in this template in detail. It is provided to give you an idea of one place where JavaScript can be useful. Consult a JavaScript reference or online tutorial for details. One good place to look is the JavaScript section of the Reference tab of the Code panel in Dreamweaver MX.

Limiting Input

This version of the form makes it impossible to send messages to anyone outside of Orange Whip Studios, by simply hard-coding the `@orangewhipstudios.com` part of the email address into the `<CFMAIL>` tag itself. Also, it forces the user to select from a short list of Subject lines, rather than being able to type his own Subject, as shown in Figure 26.3.

In a real-world application, you probably would make different choices about what exactly to allow the user to do. The point is that by limiting the amount of input required, you can make it simpler for users to send consistent email messages, thus increasing the value of your application. This can be a lot of what differentiates Web pages that send mail from ordinary email programs, which can be more complex for users to learn.

Listing 26.2 `PersonnelMail2.cfm`—Providing Friendly Names Along with Email Addresses

```
<!---
  Filename: PersonnelMail2.cfm
  Author:   Nate Weiss (NMW)
  Purpose:  A simple form for sending email
--->

<HTML>
<HEAD>
  <TITLE>Personnel Office Mailer</TITLE>
```

Listing 26.2 (continued)

```
  <!--- Apply simple CSS formatting to <TH> cells --->
  <STYLE>
    TH {background:blue;color:white;
        font-family:sans-serif;font-size:12px;
        text-align:right;padding:5px;}
  </STYLE>

  <!--- Function to guess email based on first/last name --->
  <SCRIPT LANGUAGE="JavaScript">
    function guessEmail() {
      var guess;

      with (document.mailForm) {
        guess = FirstName.value.substr(0,1) + LastName.value;
        ToAddress.value = guess.toLowerCase();
      };
    };
  </SCRIPT>
</HEAD>

<!--- Put cursor in FirstName field when page loads --->
<BODY <CFIF NOT IsDefined("FORM.Subject")>
        onLoad="document.mailForm.FirstName.focus()"
      </CFIF>>

<!--- If the user is submitting the form... --->
<CFIF IsDefined("FORM.Subject")>
  <CFSET RecipEmail = ListFirst(FORM.ToAddress, "@") & "@orangewhipstudios.com">

  <!--- We do not want ColdFusion to suppress whitespace here --->
  <CFPROCESSINGDIRECTIVE SUPPRESSWHITESPACE="No">

  <!--- Send the mail message, based on form input --->
  <CFMAIL
    SUBJECT="#Form.Subject#"
    FROM="""Personnel Office"" <personnel@orangewhipstudios.com>"
    TO="""#FORM.FirstName# #FORM.LastName#"" <#RecipEmail#>"
    BCC="personneldirector@orangewhipstudios.com"
>This is a message from the Personnel Office:

#UCase(FORM.Subject)#

#FORM.MessageBody#

If you have any questions about this message, please
write back or call us at extension 352.  Thanks!</CFMAIL>

  </CFPROCESSINGDIRECTIVE>

  <!--- Display "success" message to user --->
  <P>The email message was sent.<BR>
  By the way, you look fabulous today.
  You should be in pictures!<BR>
```

Listing 26.2 (continued)

```
<!--- Otherwise, display the form to user... --->
<CFELSE>
  <!--- Provide simple form for recipient and message --->
  <CFFORM ACTION="#CGI.SCRIPT_NAME#" NAME="mailForm" METHOD="POST">

    <TABLE CELLPADDING="2" CELLSPACING="2">
      <!--- Table row: Input for Recipient's Name --->
      <TR>
        <TH>Recipient's Name:</TH>
        <TD>
          <CFINPUT
            TYPE="Text"
            NAME="FirstName"
            REQUIRED="Yes"
            SIZE="15"
            MESSAGE="You must provide a first name."
            onChange="guessEmail()">

          <CFINPUT
            TYPE="Text"
            NAME="LastName"
            REQUIRED="Yes"
            SIZE="20"
            MESSAGE="You must provide a first name."
            onChange="guessEmail()">
        </TD>
      </TR>

      <!--- Table row: Input for EMail Address --->
      <TR>
        <TH>EMail Address:</TH>
        <TD>
          <CFINPUT
            TYPE="Text"
            NAME="ToAddress"
            REQUIRED="Yes"
            SIZE="20"
            MESSAGE="You must provide the recipient's email.">@orangewhipstudios.com
        </TD>
      </TR>

      <!--- Table row: Input for EMail Subject --->
      <TR>
        <TH>Subject:</TH>
        <TD>
          <CFSELECT
            NAME="Subject">
            <OPTION>Sorry, but you have been fired.
            <OPTION>Congratulations! You got a raise!
            <OPTION>Just FYI, you have hit the glass ceiling.
            <OPTION>The company dress code, Capri Pants, and you
            <OPTION>All your Ben Forta are belong to us.
          </CFSELECT>
        </TD>
```

Listing 26.2 (CONTINUED)

```
        </TR>

        <!--- Table row: Input for actual Message Text --->
        <TR>
          <TH>Your Message:</TH>
          <TD>
            <TEXTAREA
              NAME="MessageBody"
              COLS="50"
              ROWS="5"
              WRAP="Hard"></TEXTAREA>

          </TD>
        </TR>

        <!--- Table row: Submit button to send message --->
        <TR>
          <TD></TD>
          <TD>
            <INPUT
              TYPE="Submit"
              VALUE="Send Message Now">
          </TD>
        </TR>
      </TABLE>
    </CFFORM>
  </CFIF>

  </BODY>
  </HTML>
```

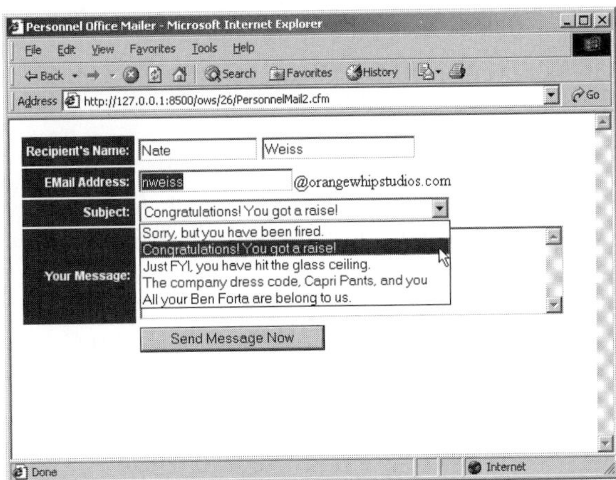

Figure 26.3

Web-based forms can make sending email almost foolproof.

Figure 26.4 shows what an email message generated by Listing 26.2 might look like when received and viewed in a typical email client (here, Microsoft Outlook Express 5).

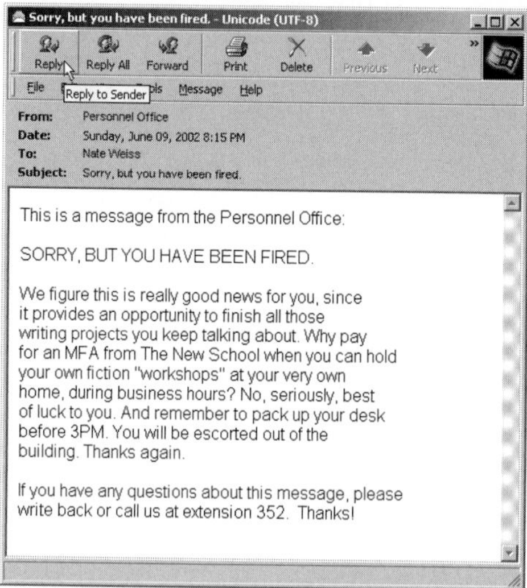

Figure 26.4

Providing a friendly name along with an email address makes for a more personal-feeling email message.

Sending Data-Driven Mail

In the last section, you learned that `<CFMAIL>` can be thought of as an extended version of the `<CFOUTPUT>` tag because ColdFusion variables and expressions are evaluated without the need for an explicit `<CFOUTPUT>` within the `<CFMAIL>`. The similarity between the two tags doesn't end there. They also share attributes specific to the notion of looping over query records. This capability enables you to send data-driven email messages using nearly the same syntax and techniques that you use to output data-driven HTML code.

Table 26.2 shows the `<CFMAIL>` attributes relevant to sending data-driven mail. Each of these attributes behaves the same way as the corresponding attributes for `<CFOUTPUT>`. Instead of causing HTML output to be repeated for each row in a query, these attributes have to do with repeating email message content for each row in a query.

Table 26.2 Additional `<CFMAIL>` Attributes for Sending Data-Driven Email Messages

ATTRIBUTE	PURPOSE
`QUERY`	Optional. A query to use for sending data-driven email. Very similar to the `QUERY` attribute of the `<CFOUTPUT>` tag.
`STARTROW`	Optional. A number that indicates which row of the query to consider when sending data-driven email. The default is to start at the first row. Equivalent to the `STARTROW` attribute of the `<CFOUTPUT>` tag.
`MAXROWS`	Optional. A maximum number of query rows to consider when sending data-driven email. Equivalent to the `MAXROWS` attribute of the `<CFOUTPUT>` tag.

Table 26.2 (continued)

ATTRIBUTE	PURPOSE
GROUP	Optional. A column name from the query that indicates groups of records. Additional output or processing can occur when each new group is encountered. You can indicate nested groups by providing a comma-separated list of column names. Equivalent to the GROUP attribute of the <CFOUTPUT> tag.
GROUPCASESENSITIVE	Optional. Whether to consider text case when determining when a new group of records has been encountered in the column(s) indicated by GROUP. Equivalent to the GROUPCASESENSITIVE attribute of the <CFOUTPUT> tag.

NOTE

You may be thinking that a few of these additional attributes aren't really necessary. In today's ColdFusion, you usually can achieve the same results using a <CFLOOP> tag around a <CFMAIL> tag to send out multiple messages or using <CFLOOP> within <CFMAIL> to include queried information in the message itself. However, the <CFMAIL> tag appeared in CFML before the <CFLOOP> tag existed, which is one reason why these attributes exist today.

Including Query Data in Messages

By adding a QUERY attribute to the <CFMAIL> tag, you easily can include query data in the email messages your application sends. Adding the QUERY attribute to <CFMAIL> is similar to adding QUERY to a <CFOUTPUT> tag—the content inside the tags will repeat for each row of the query.

Additionally, if you add a GROUP attribute, you can nest a pair of <CFOUTPUT> tags within the <CFMAIL> tag. If you do, the inner <CFOUTPUT> block is repeated for every record from the query, and everything outside the <CFOUTPUT> block is output only when the value in the GROUP column changes. This is just like the GROUP behavior of the <CFOUTPUT> tag itself; see Chapter 10, "Creating Data-Driven Pages," for more information about grouping query results.

Listing 26.3 shows how the <CFMAIL> tag can be used with the QUERY and GROUP attributes to send data-driven email messages. This example creates a CFML custom tag called <CF_SendOrderConfirmation>, which takes one attribute called OrderID, like this:

```
<!--- Send Confirmation E-Mail, via Custom Tag --->
<CF_SendOrderConfirmation
  OrderID="3">
```

The idea is for the tag to compose an order confirmation type of email message for the person who placed the order, detailing the items she purchased and when. If you have ever purchased something online, you likely received such a confirmation email immediately after placing your order. This custom tag is used in Chapter 27, "Online Commerce," after a user makes an actual purchase.

NOTE

You should save this listing as a file called SendOrderConfirmation.cfm, either in the special CustomTags folder or just in the same folder as the other examples from this chapter. See Chapter 20, "Building Reusable Components," for information about the CustomTags folder and CFML custom tags in general.

Listing 26.3 `SendOrderConfirmation1.cfm`—Sending a Data-Driven Email Message

```
<!---
  Filename: SendOrderConfirmation1.cfm
  Author:   Nate Weiss (NMW)
  Purpose:  Sends an email message to the person who placed an order
--->

<!--- Tag attributes --->
<CFPARAM NAME="ATTRIBUTES.OrderID" TYPE="numeric">

<!--- Retrieve order information from database --->
<CFQUERY DATASOURCE="#REQUEST.Datasource#" NAME="GetOrder">
  SELECT
    c.ContactID, c.FirstName, c.LastName, c.Email,
    o.OrderDate, o.ShipAddress, o.ShipCity,
    o.ShipState, o.ShipZip, o.ShipCountry,
    oi.OrderQty, oi.ItemPrice,
    m.MerchName,
    f.MovieTitle
  FROM
    Contacts c,
    MerchandiseOrders o,
    MerchandiseOrdersItems oi,
    Merchandise m,
    Films f
  WHERE
    o.OrderID = #ATTRIBUTES.OrderID#
    AND c.ContactID = o.ContactID
    AND m.MerchID   = oi.ItemID
    AND o.OrderID   = oi.OrderID
    AND f.FilmID    = m.FilmID
  ORDER BY
    m.MerchName
</CFQUERY>

<!--- Re-Query the GetOrders query to find total $ spent --->
<!--- The DBTYPE="Query" invokes CF's "Query Of Queries" --->
<CFQUERY DBTYPE="Query" NAME="GetTotal">
  SELECT SUM(ItemPrice * OrderQty) AS OrderTotal
  FROM GetOrder
</CFQUERY>

<!--- We do not want ColdFusion to suppress whitespace here --->
<CFPROCESSINGDIRECTIVE SUPPRESSWHITESPACE="No">

<!--- Send email to the user --->
<!--- Because of the GROUP attribute, the inner <CFOUTPUT> --->
<!--- block will be repeated for each item in the order --->
<CFMAIL
  QUERY="GetOrder"
  GROUP="ContactID"
  GROUPCASESENSITIVE="No"
  STARTROW="1"
  SUBJECT="Thanks for your order (Order number #ATTRIBUTES.OrderID#)"
  TO="""#FirstName# #LastName#"" <#Email#>"
  FROM="""Orange Whip Online Store"" <orders@orangewhipstudios.com>"
```

Listing 26.3 (continued)

```
>Thank you for ordering from Orange Whip Studios.
Here are the details of your order, which will ship shortly.
Please save or print this email for your records.

Order Number:  #ATTRIBUTES.OrderID#
Items Ordered: #RecordCount#
Date of Order: #DateFormat(OrderDate, "dddd, mmmm d, yyyy")#
               #TimeFormat(OrderDate)#

--------------------------------------------------------
<CFOUTPUT>
#CurrentRow#. #MerchName#
   (in commemoration of the film "#MovieTitle#")
   Price: #LSCurrencyFormat(ItemPrice)#
   Qty:   #OrderQty#
</CFOUTPUT>
--------------------------------------------------------
Order Total: #LSCurrencyFormat(GetTotal.OrderTotal)#

This order will be shipped to:;;
#FirstName# #LastName#
#ShipAddress#
#ShipCity#
#ShipState# #ShipZip# #ShipCountry#

If you have any questions, please write back to us at
orders@orangewhipstudios.com, or just reply to this email.
</CFMAIL>

</CFPROCESSINGDIRECTIVE>
```

The first thing this listing needs to do is to retrieve all the relevant information about the order from the database, including the orderer's name and shipping address; the name, price, and quantity of each item ordered; and the title of the movie that goes along with each item. This is all obtained using a single query called `GetOrder`, which is somewhat long but is fairly straightforward.

The `GetOrders` query returns one row for each item that was ordered in the specified `OrderID`. Because there is, by definition, only one row for each `OrderID` and only one `ContactID` for each order, the columns from the `MerchandiseOrders` and `Contacts` tables (marked with the `o` and `c` aliases in the query) will have the same values for each row. Therefore, the query can be thought of as being grouped by the `ContactID` column (or any of the other columns from the `MerchandiseOrders` or `Contacts` tables).

Next, ColdFusion's query of queries feature is used to get the grand total of the order, which is simply the sum of each price times the quantity ordered. This query returns just one row (because there is no `GROUP BY` clause) and just one column (called `OrderTotal`), which means that the total can be output at any time by referring to `GetTotal.OrderTotal`. For more information about `DBTYPE="Query"`, the query of queries feature, and the `SUM` function used in this query, see Chapter 29, "More on SQL and Queries."

TIP

You could forgo the `GetTotal` query and just add the prices by looping over the `GetOrders` query, as in the `OrderHistory2.cfm` template from Chapter 18. However, getting the total via the query of queries feature is a quick and convenient way to obtain the total, using familiar SQL-style syntax.

NOTE

In general, you should use the `<CFPROCESSINGDIRECTIVE>` tag with `SUPPRESSWHITESPACE="No"` whenever you send data-driven email. The exception would be if you were using `TYPE="HTML"` in the `<CFMAIL>` tag, in which case you should leave the whitespace-suppression options alone. See the section "Sending HTML-Formatted Mail," later in the chapter, for details.

Now the `<CFMAIL>` tag is used to actually send the confirmation message. Because the `QUERY` attribute is set to the `GetOrder` query, the columns in that query can be freely referred to in the `TO` attribute and the body of the email message itself. Columns specific to each item ordered are referred to within the `<CFOUTPUT>` block. Columns specific to just the order in general are referred to outside the `<CFOUTPUT>` block, which will be repeated only once because there is only one group of records as defined by the `GROUP` attribute (that is, all the query records have the same `ContactID` value).

The custom tag you just created is used in Chapter 27, "Online Commerce," after a user makes an actual purchase.

Sending Bulk Messages

You easily can use ColdFusion to send messages to an entire mailing list. Simply execute a query that returns the email addresses of all the people the message should be sent to, and then refer to the email column of the query in the `<CFMAIL>` tag's `TO` attribute.

Listing 26.4 shows how easy sending a message to a mailing list is. This listing is similar to the Personnel Office Mailer templates from earlier (refer to Listings 26.1 and 26.2). It enables the user (presumably someone within Orange Whip Studios' public relations department) to type a message, which will be sent to everyone on the studio's mailing list.

Listing 26.4 `SendBulkMail.cfm`—Sending a Message to Everyone on a Mailing List

```
<!---
  Filename: SendBulkMail.cfm
  Author:   Nate Weiss (NMW)
  Purpose:  Creates form for sending email to everyone on the mailing list
--->

<HTML>
<HEAD>
  <TITLE>Mailing List</TITLE>
  <!--- Apply simple CSS formatting to <TH> cells --->
  <STYLE>
    TH {background:blue;color:white;
        font-family:sans-serif;font-size:12px;
        text-align:right;padding:5px;}
  </STYLE>
</HEAD>

<!--- Put cursor in FirstName field when page loads --->
<BODY>
```

Listing 26.4 (continued)

```
<!--- Page Title --->
<H2>Send Message To Mailing List</H2>

<!--- If the user is submitting the form... --->
<CFIF IsDefined("FORM.Subject")>
  <!--- Retrieve "mailing list" records from database --->
  <CFQUERY DATASOURCE="#REQUEST.DataSource#" NAME="GetList">
    SELECT FirstName, LastName, EMail
    FROM Contacts
    WHERE MailingList = 1
  </CFQUERY>

  <!--- Send the mail message, based on form input --->
  <CFMAIL
    QUERY="GetList"
    SUBJECT="#Form.Subject#"
    FROM="""Orange Whip Studios"" <mailings@orangewhipstudios.com>"
    TO="""#FirstName# #LastName#"" <#EMail#>"
    BCC="personneldirector@orangewhipstudios.com"
>#FORM.MessageBody#

----------------------------------------------------
We respect your privacy here at Orange Whip Studios.
To be removed from this mailing list, reply to this
message with the word "Remove" in the subject line.
----------------------------------------------------
</CFMAIL>

  <!--- Display "success" message to user --->
  <P>The email message was sent.<BR>
  By the way, you look fabulous today.
  You should be in pictures!<BR>

<!--- Otherwise, display the form to user... --->
<CFELSE>
  <!--- Provide simple form for recipient and message --->
  <CFFORM ACTION="#CGI.SCRIPT_NAME#" NAME="mailForm" METHOD="POST"
    onSubmit="return confirm('Are you sure? This message will be sent to everyone on
the mailing list.  This is your last chance to cancel the bulk mailing.')">

    <TABLE CELLPADDING="2" CELLSPACING="2">
      <!--- Table row: Input for email Subject --->
      <TR>
        <TH>Subject:</TH>
        <TD>
          <CFINPUT
            TYPE="Text"
            NAME="Subject"
            REQUIRED="Yes"
            SIZE="40"
            MESSAGE="You must provide a subject for the email.">
        </TD>
       </TR>

      <!--- Table row: Input for actual Message Text --->
      <TR>
        <TH>Your Message:</TH>
```

Listing 26.4 (continued)

```
            <TD>
              <TEXTAREA
                NAME="MessageBody"
                COLS="30"
                ROWS="5"></TEXTAREA>

            </TD>
          </TR>

          <!--- Table row: Submit button to send message --->
          <TR>
            <TD></TD>
            <TD>
              <INPUT
                TYPE="Submit"
                VALUE="Send Message Now">
            </TD>
          </TR>
        </TABLE>
      </CFFORM>
    </CFIF>

    </BODY>
    </HTML>
```

Like Listings 26.1 and 26.2, this listing presents a simple form to the user, in which a subject and message can be typed. When the form is submitted, the `<CFIF>` block at the top of the template is executed.

The `GetList` query retrieves the name and email address for each person in the `Contacts` table who has consented to be on the mailing list (that is, where the Boolean `MailingList` column is set to `1`, which represents true or yes). Then, the `<CFMAIL>` tag is used to send the message to each user. Because of the `QUERY="GetList"` attribute, `<CFMAIL>` executes once for each row in the query.

A few lines of text at the bottom of the message let each recipient know that he can remove himself from the mailing list by replying to the email message with the word "Remove" in the subject line. Listing 26.11—in the "Creating Automated POP Agents" section of this chapter—demonstrates how ColdFusion can respond to these remove requests.

Sending HTML-Formatted Mail

As noted in Table 26.1, you can set the optional `TYPE` attribute of the `<CFMAIL>` tag to `HTML`, which enables you to use ordinary HTML tags to add formatting, images, and other media elements to your mail messages.

The following rules apply:

- The recipient's email client program must be HTML enabled. Most modern email clients (for instance, version 4 or later of Outlook Express or Netscape Communicator) know how to display the contents of email messages as HTML. However, if the message is read in a program that is not HTML enabled, the user will see the message literally, including the actual HTML tags.

- The mail message should be a well-formed HTML document. This includes opening and closing `<HTML>`, `<HEAD>`, and `<BODY>` tags.
- All references to external URLs must be fully qualified, absolute URLs, including the `http://` or `https://`. In particular, this includes the `HREF` attribute for links and the `SRC` attribute for images.

The version of the `<CF_SendOrderConfirmation>` tag in Listing 26.5 expands on the previous version (refer to Listing 26.3) by adding a `UseHTML` attribute. If the tag is called with `UseHTML="Yes"`, an HTML-formatted version of the confirmation email is sent, including small pictures of each item that was ordered (see Figure 26.5). If `UseHTML` is `No` or is omitted, the email is sent as plain text (as in the previous version).

NOTE

Although it is not something that is supported by ColdFusion directly, you can use `<CFMAIL>` to send *multipart mail messages*, which include both a plain-text and HTML-formatted version of the same message. This would enable you to send the same message to all users, without needing to know whether their mail clients can render HTML-formatted mail messages. The downside is that the doubling-up makes each mail message that much larger. Search the ColdFusion Developers Exchange for CFML custom tags that provide multipart mail functionality.

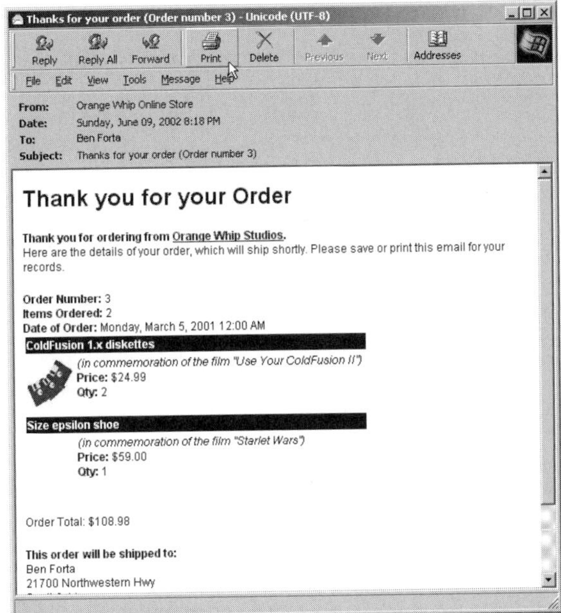

Figure 26.5

As long as the recipient's email program supports HTML, your messages can include formatting, images, and so on.

Listing 26.5 `SendOrderConfirmation2.cfm`—Using HTML Tags to Format a Mail Message

```
<!---
  Filename: SendOrderConfirmation2.cfm
  Author:   Nate Weiss (NMW)
  Purpose:  Sends an email message to the person who placed an order
--->
```

Listing 26.5 (continued)

```
<!--- Tag attributes --->
<CFPARAM NAME="ATTRIBUTES.OrderID" TYPE="numeric">
<CFPARAM NAME="ATTRIBUTES.UseHTML" TYPE="boolean" DEFAULT="Yes">

<!--- Local variables --->
<CFSET ImgSrcPath  = "http://#CGI.HTTP_HOST#/ows/images">

<!--- Retrieve order information from database --->
<CFQUERY DATASOURCE="#REQUEST.Datasource#" NAME="GetOrder">
  SELECT
    c.ContactID, c.FirstName, c.LastName, c.Email,
    o.OrderDate, o.ShipAddress, o.ShipCity,
    o.ShipState, o.ShipZip, o.ShipCountry,
    oi.OrderQty, oi.ItemPrice,
    m.MerchName, m.ImageNameSmall,
    f.MovieTitle
  FROM
    Contacts c,
    MerchandiseOrders o,
    MerchandiseOrdersItems oi,
    Merchandise m,
    Films f
  WHERE
    o.OrderID = #ATTRIBUTES.OrderID#
    AND c.ContactID = o.ContactID
    AND m.MerchID   = oi.ItemID
    AND o.OrderID   = oi.OrderID
    AND f.FilmID    = m.FilmID
  ORDER BY
    m.MerchName
</CFQUERY>

<!--- Display an error message if query returned no records --->
<CFIF GetOrder.RecordCount EQ 0>
  <CFTHROW
    MESSAGE="Failed to obtain order information."
    DETAIL="Either the Order ID was incorrect, or order has no detail records.">
<!--- Display an error message if email blank or not valid --->
<CFELSEIF (GetOrder.Email does not contain "@")
  OR (GetOrder.Email does not contain ".")>
  <CFTHROW
    MESSAGE="Failed to obtain order information."
    DETAIL="Email addresses need to have an @ sign and at least one 'dot'.">
</CFIF>

<!--- Query the GetOrders query to find total $$ --->
<CFQUERY DBTYPE="Query" NAME="GetTotal">
  SELECT SUM(ItemPrice * OrderQty) AS OrderTotal
  FROM GetOrder
</CFQUERY>


<!--- *** If we are sending HTML-Formatted Email *** --->
<CFIF ATTRIBUTES.UseHTML>

  <!--- Send Email to the user --->
```

Listing 26.5 (continued)

```
<!--- Because of the GROUP attribute, the inner <CFOUTPUT> --->
<!--- block will be repeated for each item in the order --->
<CFMAIL
  QUERY="GetOrder"
  GROUP="ContactID"
  GROUPCASESENSITIVE="No"
  STARTROW="1"
  SUBJECT="Thanks for your order (Order number #ATTRIBUTES.OrderID#)"
  TO="""#FirstName# #LastName#"" <#Email#>"
  FROM="""Orange Whip Online Store"" <orders@orangewhipstudios.com>"
  TYPE="HTML">

  <HTML>
  <HEAD>
    <STYLE TYPE="text/css">
      BODY {font-family:sans-serif;font-size:12px;color:navy}
      TD   {font-size:12px}
      TH   {font-size:12px;color:white;
            background:navy;text-align:left}
    </STYLE>
  </HEAD>
  <BODY>

  <H2>Thank you for your Order</H2>

  <P><B>Thank you for ordering from
  <A HREF="http://www.orangewhipstudios.com">Orange Whip Studios</A>.</B><BR>
  Here are the details of your order, which will ship shortly.
  Please save or print this email for your records.<BR>

  <P>
  <STRONG>Order Number:</STRONG> #ATTRIBUTES.OrderID#<BR>
  <STRONG>Items Ordered:</STRONG> #RecordCount#<BR>
  <STRONG>Date of Order:</STRONG>
  #DateFormat(OrderDate, "dddd, mmmm d, yyyy")#
  #TimeFormat(OrderDate)#<BR>

  <TABLE>
    <CFOUTPUT>
      <TR VALIGN="top">
        <TH COLSPAN="2">
          #MerchName#
        </TH>
      </TR>
      <TR>
        <TD>
          <!--- If there is an image available... --->
          <CFIF ImageNameSmall NEQ "">
            <IMG SRC="#ImgSrcPath#/#ImageNameSmall#"
              ALT="#MerchName#"
              WIDTH="50" HEIGHT="50" BORDER="0">
          </CFIF>
        </TD>
        <TD>
          <EM>(in commemoration of the film "#MovieTitle#")</EM><BR>
          <STRONG>Price:</STRONG> #LSCurrencyFormat(ItemPrice)#<BR>
```

Listing 26.5 (continued)

```
            <STRONG>Qty:</STRONG>    #OrderQty#<BR> <BR>
          </TD>
        </TR>
      </CFOUTPUT>
    </TABLE>

    <P>Order Total: #LSCurrencyFormat(GetTotal.OrderTotal)#<BR>

    <P><STRONG>This order will be shipped to:</STRONG><BR>
    #FirstName# #LastName#<BR>
    #ShipAddress#<BR>
    #ShipCity#<BR>
    #ShipState# #ShipZip# #ShipCountry#<BR>

    <P>If you have any questions, please write back to us at
    <a href="orders@orangewhipstudios.com">orders@orangewhipstudios.com</a>,
    or just reply to this email.<BR>
    </BODY>
    </HTML>
  </CFMAIL>


<!--- *** If we are NOT sending HTML-Formatted Email *** --->
<CFELSE>

<!--- We do not want ColdFusion to suppress whitespace here --->
<CFPROCESSINGDIRECTIVE SUPPRESSWHITESPACE="No">

<!--- Send email to the user --->
<!--- Because of the GROUP attribute, the inner <CFOUTPUT> --->
<!--- block will be repeated for each item in the order --->
<CFMAIL
  QUERY="GetOrder"
  GROUP="ContactID"
  GROUPCASESENSITIVE="No"
  STARTROW="1"
  SUBJECT="Thanks for your order (Order number #ATTRIBUTES.OrderID#)"
  TO="""#FirstName# #LastName#"" <#Email#>"
  FROM="""Orange Whip Online Store"" <orders@orangewhipstudios.com>"
>Thank you for ordering from Orange Whip Studios.
Here are the details of your order, which will ship shortly.
Please save or print this email for your records.

Order Number:  #ATTRIBUTES.OrderID#
Items Ordered: #RecordCount#
Date of Order: #DateFormat(OrderDate, "dddd, mmmm d, yyyy")#
               #TimeFormat(OrderDate)#

-----------------------------------------------------
<CFOUTPUT>
#CurrentRow#. #MerchName#
   (in commemoration of the film "#MovieTitle#")
   Price: #LSCurrencyFormat(ItemPrice)#
   Qty:   #OrderQty#
</CFOUTPUT>
```

Listing 26.5 (CONTINUED)

```
-----------------------------------------------------
Order Total: #LSCurrencyFormat(GetTotal.OrderTotal)#

This order will be shipped to:
#FirstName# #LastName#
#ShipAddress#
#ShipCity#
#ShipState# #ShipZip# #ShipCountry#

If you have any questions, please write back to us at
orders@orangewhipstudios.com, or just reply to this email.
</CFMAIL>

</CFPROCESSINGDIRECTIVE>

</CFIF>
```

In most respects, Listing 26.5 is nearly identical to the prior version (refer to Listing 26.3). A simple `<CFIF>` determines whether the tag is being called with `UseHTML="Yes"`. If so, `<CFMAIL>` is used with `TYPE="HTML"` to send an HTML-formatted message. If not, a separate `<CFMAIL>` tag is used to send a plain-text message. Note that the `<CFPROCESSINGDIRECTIVE>` tag is needed only around the plain-text version of the message because HTML is not sensitive to whitespace.

As already noted, a fully qualified URL must be provided for images to be correctly displayed in email messages. To make this easier, a variable called `ImgSrcPath` is defined at the top of the template, which will always hold the fully qualified URL path to the `ows/images` folder. This variable can then be used in the `SRC` attribute of any `<IMG>` tags within the message. For instance, assuming that you are visiting a copy of ColdFusion server on your local machine, this variable will evaluate to something such as `http://localhost/ows/images/`.

NOTE

The `CGI.HTTP_HOST` variable can be used to refer to the host name of the ColdFusion server. The `CGI.SERVER_NAME` also could be used to get the same value. For details, see Appendix D, "Special ColdFusion Variables and Result Codes."

In addition, Listing 26.5 does two quick checks after the `GetOrder` query to ensure that it makes sense for the rest of the template to continue. If the query fails to return any records, the `OrderID` passed to the tag is assumed to be invalid, and an appropriate error message is displayed. An error message is also displayed if the `Email` column returned by the query is blank or appears not to be a valid email address (specifically, if it doesn't contain both an `@` sign and at least one dot (`.`) character).

TIP

The error messages created by the `<CFTHROW>` tags in this example can be caught with the `<CFCATCH>` tag, as discussed in Chapter 31, "Error Handling."

NOTE

If the recipient doesn't use an HTML-enabled mail client to read the message, the message will be shown literally, including the actual HTML tags. Therefore, you should send messages of `TYPE="HTML"` only if you know the recipient is using an HTML-enabled email client program.

Adding Custom Mail Headers

All SMTP email messages contain a number of mail headers, which give Internet mail servers the information necessary to route the message to its destination. Mail headers also provide information used by the email client program to show the message to the user, such as the message date and the sender's email address.

ColdFusion allows you to add your own mail headers to mail messages, using the `<CFMAILPARAM>` tag.

TIP

You can see what these mail headers look like by using an ordinary email client program. For instance, in Outlook Express, highlight a message in your Inbox, select Properties from the File menu, and then click the Details tab.

Introducing the `<CFMAILPARAM>` Tag

ColdFusion provides a tag called `<CFMAILPARAM>` that can be used to add custom headers to your mail messages. It also can be used to add attachments to your messages, which is discussed in the next section. The `<CFMAILPARAM>` tag is allowed only between opening and closing `<CFMAIL>` tags. Table 26.3 shows which attributes can b provided to `<CFMAILPARAM>`.

Table 26.3 `<CFMAILPARAM>` Tag Attributes

ATTRIBUTE	PURPOSE
`NAME`	The name of the custom mail header you want to add to the message. You can provide any mail header name you want; a common one is `Reply-To`, as discussed in this section. (You must provide a `NAME` or `FILE` attribute, but not both in the same `<CFMAILPARAM>` tag.)
`VALUE`	The actual value for the mail header specified by `NAME`. The type of string you provide for `VALUE` will depend on which mail header you are adding to the message. For instance, if `NAME="Reply-To"`, the `VALUE` should be the email address that should be used when people reply to the message. Required if the `NAME` attribute is provided.
`FILE`	The filename of document or other file that should be sent as an attachment to the mail message. The filename must include a fully qualified, filesystem-style path—for instance a drive letter if ColdFusion is running on a Windows machine. (You must provide a `NAME` or `FILE` attribute, but not both in the same `<CFMAILPARAM>` tag.)

Specifying the Reply-To Address

Before you use `<CFMAILPARAM>` to add a custom header to a mail message, you first need to know the name of the mail header you want to add and what its value should be. This book doesn't discuss all possible mail headers. You will need to refer to the SMTP specification or reference for a list of mail header names.

That said, probably the most common use of the `<CFMAILPARAM>` tag is to provide a Reply-To address for a mail message. As the name implies, the Reply-To address is the address that is used when a user uses the Reply feature in her email client program. If a Reply-To address is present in the mail message, the reply will be sent to that address. If not, the reply is sent to the From address. In other words, the Reply-To address is a way to override the From address for the purpose of sending reply messages.

To include a Reply-To address for a message, simply add a `<CFMAILPARAM>` tag between the opening and closing `<CFMAIL>` tags, supplying a `NAME` of Reply-To and the desired email address as the `VALUE`. This would look something like the following:

```
<!--- Include "Reply-To" address --->
<CFMAILPARAM
  NAME="Reply-To"
  VALUE="help@orangewhipstudios.com">
```

Or, to include a friendly name (as discussed in the "Using Friendly Email Addresses" section, earlier in this chapter), you would use something such as this:

```
<!--- Include "Reply-To" address --->
<CFMAILPARAM
  NAME="Reply-To"
  VALUE="""Customer Service"" <help@orangewhipstudios.com>">
```

Adding Attachments

As noted in Table 26.3, you can also use the `<CFMAILPARAM>` tag to add a file attachment to a mail message. Simply place a `<CFMAILPARAM>` tag between the opening and closing `<CFMAIL>` tags, specifying the attachment's filename with the `FILE` attribute. The filename must be provided as a fully qualified filesystem path, including the drive letter and/or volume name. It can't be expressed as a relative path or URL.

NOTE

The filename you provide for `FILE` must point to a location on the ColdFusion server's drives (or a location on the local network). It can't refer to a location on the browser machine. ColdFusion has no way to grab a document from the browser's drive. If you want a user to be able to attach a file to a `<CFMAIL>` email, you first must have the user upload the file to the server. See Chapter 33, "Interacting with the Operating System," for details about file uploads.

TIP

The attachment does not have to be within your Web server's document root. In fact, you might want to ensure that it is not, if you want people to be able to access it only via email, rather than via the Web.

So, to add a Word document called `BusinessPlan.doc` as an attachment, you might include the following `<CFMAILPARAM>` tag between your opening and closing `<CFMAIL>` tags:

```
<!-- Attach business plan document to message --->
<CFMAILPARAM
  FILE="c:\OwsMailAttachments\BusinessPlan.doc">
```

TIP

To add multiple attachments to a message, simply provide multiple `<CFMAILPARAM>` tags, each specifying one `FILE`.

NOTE

As noted in Table 26.1, you also can use the older MIMEATTACH attribute of the <CFMAIL> tag to add an attachment, instead of coding a separate <CFMAILPARAM> tag. However, it is recommended that you use <CFMAILPARAM> instead because it is more flexible (it allows you to add more than one attachment to a single message).

Overriding the Default Mail Server Settings

Earlier in this chapter, you learned about the settings on the Mail/Mail Logging page of the ColdFusion Administrator (refer to Figure 26.1). These settings tell ColdFusion with which mail server to communicate to send the messages your templates generate. In most situations, you can simply provide these settings once, in the ColdFusion Administrator, and forget about them. ColdFusion will use the settings to send all messages.

However, you might encounter situations in which you want to specify the mail server settings within individual <CFMAIL> tags. For instance, your company might have two mail servers set up, one set aside for bulk messages and another for ordinary messages. Or, you might not have access to the ColdFusion Administrator for some reason, perhaps because your application is sitting on a shared ColdFusion server at an Internet service provider (ISP).

To specify the mail server for a particular <CFMAIL> tag, add the SERVER attribute, as explained in Table 26.4. You also can provide the PORT and TIMEOUT attributes to completely override all mail server settings from the ColdFusion Administrator.

NOTE

If you need to provide these attributes for your <CFMAIL> tags, consider setting a variable called REQUEST.MailServer in your Application.cfm file and then specifying SERVER="#REQUEST.MailServer#" for each <CFMAIL> tag.

Table 26.4 Additional <CFMAIL> Attributes for Overriding the Mail Server Settings in the ColdFusion Administrator

ATTRIBUTE	PURPOSE
SERVER	Optional. The host name or IP address of the mail server ColdFusion should use to actually send the message. If omitted, this defaults to the Mail Server setting on the Mail/Mail Logging page of the ColdFusion Administrator.
PORT	Optional. The port number on which the mail server is listening. If omitted, this defaults to the Server Port setting on the Mail/Mail Logging page of the ColdFusion Administrator. The standard port number is 25. Unless your mail server has been set up in a nonstandard way, you should never need to specify the PORT.
TIMEOUT	Optional. The number of seconds ColdFusion should spend trying to connect to the mail server. If omitted, this defaults to the Connection Timeout setting on the Mail/Mail Logging page of the ColdFusion Administrator.

Retrieving Email with ColdFusion

You already have learned how the <CFMAIL> tag can be used to send mail messages via your ColdFusion templates. You also can create ColdFusion templates that receive and process incoming mail messages. What your templates do with the messages is up to you. You might display each message to the user, or you might have ColdFusion periodically monitor the contents of a particular mailbox, responding to each incoming message in some way.

Introducing the <CFPOP> Tag

To check or receive email messages with ColdFusion, you use the <CFPOP> tag, providing the username and password for the email mailbox you want ColdFusion to look in. ColdFusion will connect to the appropriate mail server in the same way that your own email client program connects to retrieve your mail for you.

Table 26.5 lists the attributes supported by the <CFPOP> tag.

NOTE

The <CFPOP> tag can only be used to check email that is sitting on a mail server that uses the Post Office Protocol (POP, or POP3). POP servers are by far the most popular type of mailbox server, largely because the POP protocol is very simple. Some mail servers use the newer Internet Mail Access Protocol (IMAP, or IMAP4). The <CFPOP> tag can't be used to retrieve messages from IMAP mailboxes. Perhaps a future version of ColdFusion will include a <CFIMAP> tag; until then, some third-party solutions are available at the Developers Exchange Web site (`http://devex.macromedia.com`).

Table 26.5 <CFPOP> Tag Attributes

ATTRIBUTE	PURPOSE
ACTION	GetHeaderOnly, GetAll, or Delete. Use GetHeaderOnly to quickly retrieve just the basic information (the subject, who it is from, and so on) about messages, without retrieving the messages themselves. Use GetAll to retrieve actual messages, including any attachments (which might take some time). Use Delete to delete a message from the mailbox.
SERVER	Required. The POP server to which ColdFusion should connect. You can provide either a host name, such as pop.orangewhipstudios.com, or an IP address.
USERNAME	Required. The username for the POP mailbox ColdFusion should access. This is likely to be case sensitive, depending on the POP server.
PASSWORD	Required. The password for the POP mailbox ColdFusion should access. This is likely to be case sensitive, depending on the POP server.
NAME	ColdFusion places information about incoming messages into a query object. You will loop through the records in the query to perform whatever processing you need for each message. Provide a name (such as GetMessages) for the query object here. This attribute is required if the ACTION is GetHeaderOnly or GetAll.

Table 26.5 (CONTINUED)

ATTRIBUTE	PURPOSE
MAXROWS	Optional. The maximum number of messages that should be retrieved. Because you don't know how many messages might be in the mailbox you are accessing, it is usually a good idea to provide MAXROWS unless you are providing MESSAGENUMBER (later in this table).
STARTROW	Optional. The first message that should be retrieved. If, for instance, you already have processed the first 10 messages currently in the mailbox, you could specify STARTROW="11" to start at the 11th message.
MESSAGENUMBER	Optional. If the ACTION is GetHeaderOnly or GetAll, you can use this attribute to specify messages to retrieve from the POP server. If the ACTION is DELETE, this is the message or messages you want to delete from the mailbox. In either case, you can provide either a single message number or a comma-separated list of message numbers.
ATTACHMENTPATH	Optional. If the ACTION is GetAll, you can specify a directory on the server's drive in which ColdFusion should save any attachments. If you don't provide this attribute, the attachments will not be saved.
GENERATEUNIQUEFILENAMES	Optional. This attribute should be provided only if you are using the ATTACHMENTPATH attribute. If Yes, ColdFusion will ensure that two attachments that happen to have the same filename will get unique filenames when they are saved on the server's drive. If No (the default), each attachment is saved with its original filename, regardless of whether a file with the same name already exists in the ATTACHMENTPATH directory.
PORT	Optional. If the POP server specified in SERVER is listening for requests on a nonstandard port, specify the port number here. The default value is 110, which is the standard port used by most POP servers.
TIMEOUT	Optional. This attribute indicates how many seconds ColdFusion should wait for each response from the POP server. The default value is 60.

When the <CFPOP> tag is used with ACTION="GetHeaderOnly", it will return a query object that contains one row for each message in the specified mailbox. The columns of the query object are shown in Table 26.6.

Table 26.6 Columns Returned by <CFPOP> When ACTION="GetHeaderOnly"

COLUMN	EXPLANATION
MESSAGENUMBER	A number that represents the slot the current message is occupying in the mailbox on the POP server. The first message that arrives in a user's mailbox is message number one. The next one to arrive is message number two. When a message is deleted, any message behind the deleted message moves into the deleted message's slot. That is, if the first message is deleted, the second message becomes message number one. In other words, the MESSAGENUMBER is not a unique identifier for the message. It is simply a way to refer to the messages currently in the mailbox.
DATE	The date the message was originally sent. Unfortunately, this date value is not returned as a native CFML Date object. You must use the ParseDateTime() function to turn the value into something with which you can use ColdFusion's date functions (see Listing 26.6, later in this chapter, for an example).
SUBJECT	The subject line of the message.
FROM	The email address that the message is reported to be from. This address might or might not contain a friendly name for the sender, delimited by quotation marks and angle brackets (see the section "Using Friendly Email Addresses," earlier in this chapter). It is worth noting that the FROM address is not guaranteed to be a real email address that can actually receive replies.
TO	The email address to which the message was sent. This address might or might not contain a friendly name for the sender, delimited by quotation marks and angle brackets (see the section "Using Friendly Email Addresses").
CC	The email address or addresses to which the message was CC'd, if any. You can use ColdFusion's list functions to get the individual email addresses. Each address might or might not contain a friendly name for the sender, delimited by quotation marks and angle brackets (see the section "Using Friendly Email Addresses").
REPLYTO	The address to use when replying to the message, if provided. If the message's sender did not provide a Reply-To address, the column will contain an empty string, in which case it would be most appropriate for replies to go to the FROM address. This address might or might not contain a friendly name for the sender, delimited by quotation marks and angle brackets (see the section "Using Friendly Email Addresses").

If the <CFPOP> tag is used with ACTION="GetAll", the returned query object will contain all the columns from Table 26.6, plus the columns listed in Table 26.7.

Table 26.7 Additional Columns Returned by `<CFPOP>` When `ACTION="GetAll"`

COLUMN	EXPLANATION
`BODY`	The actual body of the message, as a simple string. This string usually contains just plain text, but if the message was sent as an HTML-formatted message, it contains HTML tags. You can check for the presence of a `Content-Type` header value of `text/html` to determine whether the message is HTML formatted (see Listing 26.8, later in this chapter, for an example).
`HEADER`	The raw, unparsed header section of the message. This usually contains information about how the message was routed to the mail server, along with information about which program was used to send the message, the MIME content type of the message, and so on. You need to know about the header names defined by the SMTP protocol (see the section "Adding Custom Mail Headers," earlier in this chapter) to make use of the `HEADER`.
`ATTACHMENTS`	If you provided an `ATTACHMENTPATH` attribute to the `<CFPOP>` tag, this column contains a list of the attachment filenames as they were named when originally attached to the message. The list of attachments is separated by tab characters. You can use ColdFusion's list functions to process the list, but you must specify `Chr(9)` (which is the tab character) as the delimiter for each list function, as in `ListLen(ATTACHMENTS, Chr(9))`.
`ATTACHMENTFILES`	If you provided an `ATTACHMENTPATH` attribute to the `<CFPOP>` tag, this column contains a list of the attachment filenames as they were saved on the ColdFusion server (in the directory specified by `ATTACHMENTPATH`). You can use the values in this list to delete, show, or move the files after the message has been retrieved. Like the `ATTACHMENTS` column, this list is separated by tab characters.

Retrieving the List of Messages

Most uses for `<CFPOP>` tag call for using all three of the `ACTION` values it supports. Whether you are using the tag to display messages to your users (such as a Web-based system for checking mail) or an automated agent that responds to incoming email messages on its own, the sequence of events probably involves these steps:

1. Log in to the mail server with `ACTION="GetHeaderOnly"` to get the list of messages currently in the specified mailbox. At this point, you can display or make decisions based on who the message is from, the date, or the subject line.
2. Use `ACTION="GetAll"` to retrieve the full text of individual messages.
3. Use `ACTION="Delete"` to delete messages.

Listing 26.6 is the first of three templates that demonstrate how to use `<CFPOP>` by creating a Web-based system for users to check their mail. This template asks the user to log in by providing the information ColdFusion needs to access her email mailbox (her username, password, and mail server). It then checks the user's mailbox for messages and displays the From address, date, and subject line for each. The user can click each message's subject to read the full message.

Listing 26.6 `CheckMail.cfm`—The Beginnings of a Simple POP Client

```
<!---
  Filename: CheckMail.cfm
  Author:   Nate Weiss (NMW)
  Purpose:  Creates a very simple POP client
--->

<HTML>
<HEAD><TITLE>Check Your Mail</TITLE></HEAD>
<BODY>

<!--- Simple CSS-based formatting styles --->
<STYLE>
  BODY {font-family:sans-serif;font-size:12px}
  TH   {font-size:12px;background:navy;color:white}
  TD   {font-size:12px;background:lightgrey;color:navy}
</STYLE>
<H2>Check Your Mail</H2>

<!--- If user is logging out, --->
<!--- or if user is submitting a different username/password --->
<CFIF IsDefined("URL.Logout") OR IsDefined("FORM.POPServer")>
  <CFSET StructDelete(SESSION, "Mail")>
</CFIF>

<!--- If we don't have a username/password --->
<CFIF NOT IsDefined("SESSION.Mail")>
  <!--- Show "mail server login" form --->
  <CFINCLUDE TEMPLATE="CheckMailLogin.cfm">
</CFIF>


<!--- If we need to contact server for list of messages --->
<!--- (if just logged in, or if clicked "Refresh" link) --->
<CFIF NOT IsDefined("SESSION.Mail.GetMessages") OR IsDefined("URL.Refresh")>
  <!--- Flush page output buffer --->
  <CFFLUSH>

  <!--- Contact POP Server and retieve messages --->
  <CFPOP
    ACTION="GetHeaderOnly"
    NAME="SESSION.Mail.GetMessages"
    SERVER="#SESSION.Mail.POPServer#"
    USERNAME="#SESSION.Mail.Username#"
    PASSWORD="#SESSION.Mail.Password#"
    MAXROWS="50">
</CFIF>


<!--- If no messages were retrieved... --->
<CFIF SESSION.Mail.GetMessages.RecordCount EQ 0>
  <P>You have no mail messages at this time.<BR>

<!--- If messages were retrieved... --->
<CFELSE>
  <!--- Display Messages in HTML Table Format --->
```

Listing 26.6 (continued)

```
    <TABLE BORDER="0" CELLSPACING="2" CELLSPACING="2" COLS="3" WIDTH="550">
      <!--- Column Headings for Table --->
      <TR>
        <TH WIDTH="100">Date Sent</TH>
        <TH WIDTH="200">From</TH>
        <TH WIDTH="200">Subject</TH>
      </TR>
      <!--- Display info about each message in a table row --->
      <CFOUTPUT QUERY="SESSION.Mail.GetMessages">
        <!--- Parse Date from the "date" mail header --->
        <CFSET MsgDate = ParseDateTime(Date)>
        <!--- Let user click on Subject to read full message --->
        <CFSET LinkURL = "CheckMailMsg.cfm?MsgNum=#MessageNumber#">

        <TR VALIGN="baseline">
          <!--- Show parsed Date and Time for message--->
          <TD>
            <STRONG>#DateFormat(MsgDate)#</STRONG><BR>
            #TimeFormat(MsgDate)# #ReplyTo#
          </TD>
          <!--- Show "From" address, escaping brackets --->
          <TD>#HTMLEditFormat(From)#</TD>
          <TD><STRONG><A HREF="#LinkURL#">#Subject#</A></STRONG></TD>
        </TR>
      </CFOUTPUT>
    </TABLE>

    <!--- "Refresh" link to get new list of messages  --->
    <STRONG><A HREF="CheckMail.cfm?Refresh=Yes">Refresh Message List</A></STRONG><BR>
    <!--- "Log Out" link to discard SESSION.Mail info --->
    <A HREF="CheckMail.cfm?Logout=Yes">Log Out</A><BR>
  </CFIF>


  </BODY>
  </HTML>
```

This template maintains a structure in the `SESSION` scope called `SESSION.Mail`. The `SESSION.Mail` structure holds information about the current user's POP server, username, and password. It also holds a query object called `GetMessages`, which is returned by the `<CFPOP>` tag when the user's mailbox is first checked.

At the top of the template, a `<CFIF>` test checks to see whether a `URL` parameter named `Logout` has been provided. If so, the `SESSION.Mail` structure is deleted from the server's memory, which effectively logs the user out. You will see how this works later. The same thing happens if a `FORM` parameter named `POPServer` exists, which indicates that the user is trying to submit a different username and password from the login form (explained in a moment).

Next, a similar `<CFIF>` tests checks to see whether the `SESSION.Mail` structure exists. If not, the template concludes that the user has not logged in yet, so it displays a simple login form by including the `CheckMailLogin.cfm` template (see Listing 26.7). This is the same basic login-check technique explained in Chapter 18. In any case, all code after this `<CFIF>` test is guaranteed to execute only if the user has logged in. The `SESSION.Mail` structure will contain `Username`, `Password`, and `POPServer` values, which can later be passed to all `<CFPOP>` tags for the remainder of the session.

The next `<CFIF>` test checks to see whether ColdFusion needs to access the user's mailbox to get a list of current messages. ColdFusion should do this whenever `SESSION.Mail.GetMessages` does not exist yet (which means that the user has just logged in) or if the page has been passed a `Refresh` parameter in the URL (which means that the user has just clicked the Refresh Message List link, as shown in Figure 26.6). If so, the `<CFPOP>` tag is called with `ACTION="GetHeaderOnly"`, which means that ColdFusion should just get a list of messages from the mail server (which is usually pretty fast), rather than getting the actual test of each message (which can be quite slow, especially if some of the messages have attachments). Note that the `<CFPOP>` tag is provided with the username, password, and POP server name that the user provided when she first logged in (now available in the `SESSION.Mail` structure).

NOTE

The `SESSION.Mail.GetMessages` object returned by the tag contains columns called `Date`, `Subject`, `From`, `To`, `CC`, `ReplyTo`, and `MessageNumber`, as listed previously in Table 26.6. Because it is a query object, it also contains the automatic `CurrentRow` and `RecordCount` attributes returned by ordinary `<CFQUERY>` tags.

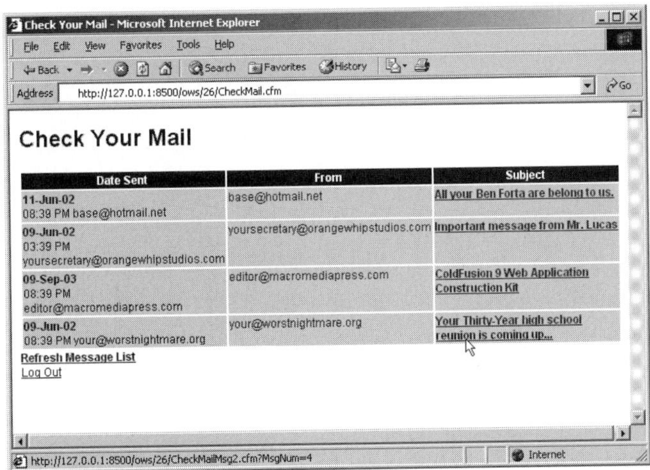

Figure 26.6

The `<CFPOP>` tag enables email messages to be retrieved via ColdFusion templates.

At this point, the template has retrieved the list of current messages from the user's mailbox, so all that's left to do is to display them to the user. The remainder of Listing 26.6 simply outputs the list of messages in a simple HTML table format, using an ordinary `<CFOUTPUT>` block that loops over the `SESSION.Mail.GetMessages` query object. Within this loop, the code can refer to the `Date` column of the query object to access a message's date or to the `Subject` column to access the message's subject line. The first time through the loop, these variables refer to the first message retrieved from the user's mailbox. The second time, the variables refer to the second message, and so on.

Just inside the `<CFOUTPUT>` block, a ColdFusion date variable called `MsgDate` is created using the `ParseDateTime()` function with the optional `POP` attribute. This is necessary because the `Date` column returned by <CFPOP> does not contain native CFML date value as you might expect. Instead, it contains the date in the special date format required by the mail-sending protocol (SMTP). The ParseDateTime() function is needed to parse this special date string into a proper CFML Date value you can provide to ColdFusion's date functions (such as the DateFormat() and DateAdd() functions).

NOTE

Unfortunately, the format used for the date portion of mail messages varies somewhat. The ParseDateTime() function does not properly parse the date string that some incoming messages have. If the function encounters a date that it cannot parse correctly, an error message results. Some custom tag solutions to this problem are available at the ColdFusion Developers Exchange Web site (http://devex.macromedia.com). Search for POP and Date.

Inside the <CFOUTPUT> block, the basic information about the message is output as a table row. The date of the message is shown using the DateFormat() and TimeFormat() functions. The Subject line of the message is presented as a link to the CheckMailMsg.cfm template (see Listing 26.8), passing the MessageNumber for the current message in the URL. Because the MessageNumber identifies the message in a particular slot in the mailbox, the user can click the subject to view the whole message.

At the bottom of the template, the user is provided with Refresh Message List and Log Out links, which simply reload the listing with either Refresh=Yes or Logout=Yes in the URL.

NOTE

Because email addresses can contain angle brackets (see the section "Using Friendly Email Addresses," earlier in this chapter), you should always use the HTMLEditFormat() function when displaying an email address returned by <CFPOP> in a Web page. Otherwise, the browser will think the angle brackets are meant to indicate an HTML tag, which means that the email address will not show up visibly on the page (although it will be part of the page's HTML if you view source). Here, HTMLEditFormat() is used on the From column, but you should use it whenever you output the To, CC, or ReplyTo columns as well.

Listing 26.7 is a template that presents a login form to the user when he first visits CheckMail.cfm. It is included via the <CFINCLUDE> tag in Listing 26.6 whenever the SESSION.Mail structure does not exist (which means that the user has either logged out or has not logged in yet).

Listing 26.7 CheckMailLogin.cfm—A Simple Login Form, Which Gets Included by CheckMail.cfm

```
<!---
  Filename: CheckMailLogin.cfm
  Author:   Nate Weiss (NMW)
  Purpose:  Provides a login form for the simple POP client
--->

<!--- If user is submitting username/password form --->
<CFIF IsDefined("FORM.POPServer")>
  <!--- Retain username, password, server in SESSION --->
  <CFSET SESSION.Mail = StructNew()>
  <CFSET SESSION.Mail.POPServer = FORM.POPServer>
  <CFSET SESSION.Mail.Username  = FORM.Username>
  <CFSET SESSION.Mail.Password  = FORM.Password>
  <!--- Remember server and username for next time --->
  <CFSET CLIENT.MailServer      = FORM.POPServer>
  <CFSET CLIENT.MailUsername    = FORM.Username>

<CFELSE>
  <!--- Use server/username from last time, if available --->
```

Listing 26.7 (continued)

```
  <CFPARAM NAME="CLIENT.MailServer" TYPE="string" DEFAULT="">
  <CFPARAM NAME="CLIENT.MailUsername" TYPE="string" DEFAULT="">

  <!--- Simple form for user to provide mailbox info --->
  <CFFORM ACTION="#CGI.SCRIPT_NAME#" METHOD="POST">
    <P>To access your mail, please provide the
    server, username and password.<BR>

    <!--- FORM field: POPServer --->
    <P>Mail Server:<BR>
    <CFINPUT TYPE="Text" NAME="POPServer"
      VALUE="#CLIENT.MailServer#" REQUIRED="Yes"
      MESSAGE="Please provide your mail server.">
    (example: pop.yourcompany.com)<BR>

    <!--- FORM field: Username --->
    Mailbox Username:<BR>
    <CFINPUT TYPE="Text" NAME="Username"
      VALUE="#CLIENT.MailUsername#" REQUIRED="Yes"
      MESSAGE="Please provide your username.">
    (yourname@yourcompany.com)<BR>

    <!--- FORM field: Password --->
    Mailbox Password:<BR>
    <CFINPUT TYPE="Password" NAME="Password"
      REQUIRED="Yes"
      MESSAGE="Please provide your username."><BR>

    <INPUT TYPE="Submit" VALUE="Check Mail"><BR>
  </CFFORM>

  </BODY></HTML>
  <CFABORT>
</CFIF>
```

When the user first visits `CheckMail.cfm`, Listing 26.7 gets included. At first, the `FORM.POPServer` variable will not exist, so the `<CFELSE>` part of the code executes, which presents the login form to the user. When the form is submitted, it posts the user's entries to the `CheckMail.cfm` template, which in turn calls this template again. This time, `FORM.POPServer` exists, so the first part of the `<CFIF>` block executes. The `SESSION.Mail` structure is created, and the `POPServer`, `Username`, and `Password` values are copied from the user's form input into the structure so that they can be referred to during the rest of the session (or until the user logs out.

NOTE

If you accidentally enter an incorrect username or password while testing this listing, you will get a rather ugly error message. You can intercept the error so that the user is kindly asked to try again, without it seeming like anything has really gone so wrong. A revised version of this listing that does just that is included in Chapter 31, "Error Handling."

NOTE

As a convenience to the user, Listing 26.7 stores the POPServer and Username values (which the user provides in the login form) as variables in the CLIENT scope. These values are passed to the VALUE attributes of the corresponding form fields the next time the user needs to log in. This way, the user must enter only his password on repeat visits.

Receiving and Deleting Messages

Listing 26.8 is the `CheckMailMsg.cfm` template the user will be directed to whenever she clicks the subject line in the list of messages (refer to Figure 26.6). This template requires that a URL parameter called `MsgNum` be passed to it, which indicates the `MESSAGENUMBER` of the message the user clicked. In addition, the template can be passed a `Delete` parameter, which indicates that the user wants to delete the specified message.

Listing 26.8 `CheckMailMsg.cfm`—Retrieving the Full Text of an Individual Message

```
<!---
  Filename: CheckMailMsg.cfm
  Author:   Nate Weiss (NMW)
  Purpose:  Allows the user to view a message on their POP server
--->

<HTML>
<HEAD><TITLE>Mail Message</TITLE></HEAD>
<BODY>

<!--- Simple CSS-based formatting styles --->
<STYLE>
  BODY {font-family:sans-serif;font-size:12px}
  TH   {font-size:12px;background:navy;color:white}
  TD   {font-size:12px;background:lightgrey;color:navy}
</STYLE>

<H2>Mail Message</H2>

<!--- A message number must be passed in the URL --->
<CFPARAM NAME="URL.MsgNum" TYPE="numeric">
<CFPARAM NAME="URL.Delete" TYPE="boolean" DEFAULT="No">

<!--- If we don't have a username/password --->
<!--- send user to main CheckMail.cfm page --->
<CFIF IsDefined("SESSION.Mail.GetMessages") EQ "No">
  <CFLOCATION URL="CheckMail.cfm">
</CFIF>

<!--- If the user is trying to delete the message --->
<CFIF URL.Delete>
  <!--- Contact POP Server and delete the message --->
  <CFPOP
    ACTION="Delete"
    MESSAGENUMBER="#URL.MsgNum#"
    SERVER="#SESSION.Mail.POPServer#"
    USERNAME="#SESSION.Mail.Username#"
    PASSWORD="#SESSION.Mail.Password#">

  <!--- Send user back to main "Check Mail" page --->
  <CFLOCATION URL="CheckMail.cfm?Refresh=Yes">


<!--- If not deleting, retrieve and show the message --->
<CFELSE>
```

Listing 26.8 (continued)

```
<!--- Contact POP Server and retrieve the message --->
<CFPOP
  ACTION="GetAll"
  NAME="GetMsg"
  MESSAGENUMBER="#URL.MsgNum#"
  SERVER="#SESSION.Mail.POPServer#"
  USERNAME="#SESSION.Mail.Username#"
  PASSWORD="#SESSION.Mail.Password#">

<CFSET MsgDate = ParseDateTime(GetMsg.Date, "POP")>

<!--- If message was not retrieved from POP server --->
<CFIF GetMsg.RecordCount NEQ 1>
  <CFTHROW
    MESSAGE="Message could not be retrieved."
    DETAIL="Perhaps the message has already been deleted.">
</CFIF>

<!--- We will provide a link to Delete message --->
<CFSET DeleteURL = "#CGI.SCRIPT_NAME#?MsgNum=#MsgNum#&Delete=Yes">

<!--- Display message in a simple table format --->
<TABLE BORDER="0" CELLSPACING="0" CELLPADDING="3">
  <CFOUTPUT>
    <TR>
      <TH BGCOLOR="Wheat" ALIGN="left" NOWRAP>
        Message #URL.MsgNum# of #SESSION.Mail.GetMessages.RecordCount#
      </TH>
      <TD ALIGN="right" BGCOLOR="beige">
        <!--- Provide "Back" button, if appropriate --->
        <CFIF URL.MsgNum GT 1>
          <A HREF="CheckMailMsg.cfm?MsgNum=#Val(URL.MsgNum - 1)#">
            <IMG SRC="../images/BrowseBack.gif"
              WIDTH="40" HEIGHT="16" ALT="Back" BORDER="0"></A>
        </CFIF>
        <!--- Provide "Next" button, if appropriate --->
        <CFIF URL.MsgNum LT SESSION.Mail.GetMessages.RecordCount>
          <A HREF="CheckMailMsg.cfm?MsgNum=#Val(URL.MsgNum + 1)#">
            <IMG SRC="../images/BrowseNext.gif"
              WIDTH="40" HEIGHT="16" ALT="Next" BORDER="0"></A>
        </CFIF>
      </TD>
    </TR>
    <TR>
      <TH ALIGN="right">From:</TH>
      <TD>#HTMLEditFormat(GetMsg.From)#</TD>
    </TR>
    <CFIF GetMsg.CC NEQ "">
    <TR>
      <TH ALIGN="right">CC:</TH>
      <TD>#HTMLEditFormat(GetMsg.CC)#</TD>
    </TR>
    </CFIF>
    <TR>
      <TH ALIGN="right">Date:</TH>
      <TD>#DateFormat(MsgDate)# #TimeFormat(MsgDate)#</TD>
```

Listing 26.8 (CONTINUED)

```
        </TR>
        <TR>
          <TH ALIGN="right">Subject:</TH>
          <TD>#GetMsg.Subject#</TD>
        </TR>
        <TR>
          <TD BGCOLOR="Beige" COLSPAN="2">
            <STRONG>Message:</STRONG><BR>

            <CFIF GetMsg.Header contains "Content-Type: text/html">
              #GetMsg.Body#
            <CFELSE>
              #HTMLCodeFormat(GetMsg.Body)#
            </CFIF>
          </TD>
        </TR>
      </CFOUTPUT>
    </TABLE>

    <CFOUTPUT>
      <!--- Provide link back to list of messages --->
      <STRONG><A HREF="CheckMail.cfm">Back To Message List</A></STRONG><BR>
      <!--- Provide link to Delete message --->
      <A HREF="#DeleteURL#">Delete Message</A><BR>
      <!--- "Log Out" link to discard SESSION.Mail info --->
      <A HREF="CheckMail.cfm?Logout=Yes">Log Out</A><BR>
    </CFOUTPUT>
  </CFIF>

  </BODY>
  </HTML>
```

First, as a sanity check, the user is sent back to the `CheckMail.cfm` template (refer to Listing 26.6) if the `SESSION.Mail.GetMessages` query does not exist. This would happen if the user's session had timed out or if the user had somehow navigated to the page without logging in first. In any case, sending her back to `CheckMail.cfm` causes the login form to be displayed.

Next, a `<CFIF>` test is used to see whether `Delete=Yes` was passed in the URL. If so, the message is deleted using the `ACTION="Delete"` attribute of the `<CFPOP>` tag, specifying the passed `URL.MsgNum` as the `MESSAGENUMBER` to delete. The user is then sent back to `CheckMail.cfm` with `Refresh=Yes` in the URL, which causes `CheckMail.cfm` to re-contact the mail server and repopulate the `SESSION.Mail.GetMessages` query with the revised list of messages (which should no longer include the deleted message).

If the user is not deleting the message, the template simply retrieves and displays it in a simple HTML table format. To do so, `<CFPOP>` is called again, this time with `ACTION="GetAll"` and the `MESSAGENUMBER` of the desired message. Then the columns returned by `<CFPOP>` can be displayed, much as they were in Listing 26.6. Because the `ACTION` was `GetAll`, this template could use the `BODY` and `HEADER` columns listed previously in Table 26.7. The end result is that the user has a convenient way to view, scroll through, and delete messages, as shown in Figure 26.7.

At the bottom of the template, the user is provided with the links to log out or return to the list of messages. She is also provided with a link to delete the current message, which simply reloads the current page with `Delete=Yes` in the URL, causing the Delete logic mentioned previously to execute.

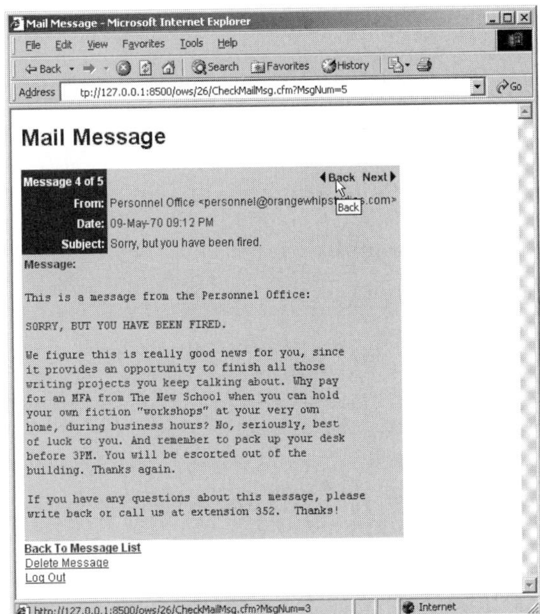

Figure 26.7

With `<CFPOP>`, retrieving and displaying the messages in a user's POP mailbox is easy.

Receiving Attachments

As noted previously in Table 26.5, the `<CFPOP>` tag includes an `ATTACHMENTPATH` attribute that, when provided, tells ColdFusion to save any attachments to a message to a folder on the server's drive. Your template can then process the attachments in whatever way is appropriate (move the files to a certain location, parse through them, display them to the user, or whatever your application needs).

Retrieving the Attachments

Listing 26.9 is a revised version of the `CheckMailMsg.cfm` template from Listing 26.8. This version enables the user to download and view any attachments that might be attached to each mail message. The most important change in this version is the addition of the `ATTACHMENTPATH` attribute, which specifies that any attachments should be placed in a subfolder named `Attach` (within the folder that the template itself is in).

Listing 26.9 `CheckMailMsg2.cfm`—Allowing the User to Access Attachments

```
<!---
  Filename: CheckMailMsg.cfm
  Author:   Nate Weiss (NMW)
  Purpose:  Allows the user to view a message on their POP server
--->
```

Listing 26.9 (continued)

```
<HTML>
<HEAD><TITLE>Mail Message</TITLE></HEAD>
<BODY>

<!--- Simple CSS-based formatting styles --->
<STYLE>
  BODY {font-family:sans-serif;font-size:12px}
  TH   {font-size:12px;background:navy;color:white}
  TD   {font-size:12px;background:lightgrey;color:navy}
</STYLE>

<H2>Mail Message</H2>

<!--- A message number must be passed in the URL --->
<CFPARAM NAME="URL.MsgNum" TYPE="numeric">
<CFPARAM NAME="URL.Delete" TYPE="boolean" DEFAULT="No">


<!--- Store attachments in "Attach" subfolder --->
<CFSET AttachDir = ExpandPath("Attach")>
<!--- Set a variable to hold the Tab character --->
<CFSET TAB = Chr(9)>

<!--- Create the folder if it doesn't already exist --->
<CFIF NOT DirectoryExists(AttachDir)>
  <CFDIRECTORY
    ACTION="Create"
    DIRECTORY="#AttachDir#">
</CFIF>

<!--- If we don't have a username/password --->
<!--- send user to main CheckMail.cfm page --->
<CFIF IsDefined("SESSION.Mail.GetMessages") EQ "No">
  <CFLOCATION URL="CheckMail.cfm">
</CFIF>

<!--- If the user is trying to delete the message --->
<CFIF URL.Delete>
  <!--- Contact POP Server and delete the message --->
  <CFPOP
    ACTION="Delete"
    MESSAGENUMBER="#URL.MsgNum#"
    SERVER="#SESSION.Mail.POPServer#"
    USERNAME="#SESSION.Mail.Username#"
    PASSWORD="#SESSION.Mail.Password#">

  <!--- Send user back to main "Check Mail" page --->
  <CFLOCATION URL="CheckMail.cfm?Refresh=Yes">


<!--- If not deleting, retrieve and show the message --->
<CFELSE>

  <!--- Contact POP Server and retrieve the message --->
  <CFPOP
    ACTION="GetAll"
    NAME="GetMsg"
```

Listing 26.9 (continued)

```
    MESSAGENUMBER="#URL.MsgNum#"
    SERVER="#SESSION.Mail.POPServer#"
    USERNAME="#SESSION.Mail.Username#"
    PASSWORD="#SESSION.Mail.Password#"
    ATTACHMENTPATH="#AttachDir#"
    GENERATEUNIQUEFILENAMES="Yes">

  <!--- Parse message's date string to CF Date value --->
  <CFSET MsgDate = ParseDateTime(GetMsg.Date, "POP")>

  <!--- If message was not retrieved from POP server --->
  <CFIF GetMsg.RecordCount NEQ 1>
    <CFTHROW
      MESSAGE="Message could not be retrieved."
      DETAIL="Perhaps the message has already been deleted.">
  </CFIF>

  <!--- We will provide a link to Delete message --->
  <CFSET DeleteURL = "#CGI.SCRIPT_NAME#?MsgNum=#MsgNum#&Delete=Yes">

  <!--- Display message in a simple table format --->
  <TABLE BORDER="0" CELLSPACING="0" CELLPADDING="3">
    <CFOUTPUT>
      <TR>
        <TH BGCOLOR="Wheat" ALIGN="left" NOWRAP>
          Message #URL.MsgNum# of #SESSION.Mail.GetMessages.RecordCount#
        </TH>
        <TD ALIGN="right" BGCOLOR="beige">
          <!--- Provide "Back" button, if appropriate --->
          <CFIF URL.MsgNum GT 1>
            <A HREF="CheckMailMsg.cfm?MsgNum=#Val(URL.MsgNum - 1)#">
              <IMG SRC="../images/BrowseBack.gif"
                WIDTH="40" HEIGHT="16" ALT="Back" BORDER="0"></A>
          </CFIF>
          <!--- Provide "Next" button, if appropriate --->
          <CFIF URL.MsgNum LT SESSION.Mail.GetMessages.RecordCount>
            <A HREF="CheckMailMsg.cfm?MsgNum=#Val(URL.MsgNum + 1)#">
              <IMG SRC="../images/BrowseNext.gif"
                WIDTH="40" HEIGHT="16" ALT="Next" BORDER="0"></A>
          </CFIF>
        </TD>
      </TR>
      <TR>
        <TH ALIGN="right">From:</TH>
        <TD>#HTMLEditFormat(GetMsg.From)#</TD>
      </TR>
      <CFIF GetMsg.CC NEQ "">
      <TR>
        <TH ALIGN="right">CC:</TH>
        <TD>#HTMLEditFormat(GetMsg.CC)#</TD>
      </TR>
      </CFIF>
      <TR>
        <TH ALIGN="right">Date:</TH>
        <TD>#DateFormat(MsgDate)# #TimeFormat(MsgDate)#</TD>
      </TR>
      <TR>
```

Listing 26.9 (continued)

```
            <TH ALIGN="right">Subject:</TH>
            <TD>#GetMsg.Subject#</TD>
          </TR>
          <TR>
            <TD BGCOLOR="Beige" COLSPAN="2">
              <STRONG>Message:</STRONG><BR>

              <CFIF GetMsg.Header contains "Content-Type: text/html">
                #GetMsg.Body#
              <CFELSE>
                #HTMLCodeFormat(GetMsg.Body)#
              </CFIF>
            </TD>
          </TR>
          <!--- If this message has any attachments --->
          <CFSET NumAttachments = ListLen(GetMsg.Attachments, TAB)>
          <CFIF NumAttachments GT 0>
            <TR>
              <TH ALIGN="right">Attachments:</TH>
              <TD>
                <!--- For each attachment, provide a link  --->
                <CFLOOP FROM="1" TO="#NumAttachments#" INDEX="i">
                  <!--- Original filename, as it was attached to message  --->
                  <CFSET ThisFileOrig = ListGetAt(GetMsg.Attachments, i, TAB)>
                  <!--- Full path to file, as it was saved on this server --->
                  <CFSET ThisFilePath = ListGetAt(GetMsg.AttachmentFiles, i, TAB)>
                  <!--- Relative URL to file, so user can click to get it --->
                  <CFSET ThisFileURL  = "Attach/#GetFileFromPath(ThisFilePath)#">
                  <!--- Actual link --->
                  <A HREF="#ThisFileURL#">#ThisFileOrig#</A><BR>
                </CFLOOP>
              </TD>
            </TR>
          </CFIF>
        </CFOUTPUT>
      </TABLE>

      <CFOUTPUT>
        <!--- Provide link back to list of messages --->
        <STRONG><A HREF="CheckMail.cfm">Back To Message List</A></STRONG><BR>
        <!--- Provide link to Delete message --->
        <A HREF="#DeleteURL#">Delete Message</A><BR>
        <!--- "Log Out" link to discard SESSION.Mail info --->
        <A HREF="CheckMail.cfm?Logout=Yes">Log Out</A><BR>
      </CFOUTPUT>
    </CFIF>

    </BODY>
    </HTML>
```

The first change is the addition of a variable called `AttachDir`, which is the complete path to the directory on the server that will hold attachment files. Additionally, a variable called `TAB` is created to hold a single Tab character (which is character number `9` in the standard character set). This way, the rest of the code can refer to `TAB` instead of `Chr(9)`, which improves code readability.

NOTE

This code uses the variable name `TAB` in all caps instead of `Tab` to indicate the notion that the variable holds a *constant value*. A constant value is simply a value that will never change (that is, the Tab character will always be represented by ASCII code `9`). Developers often spell constants with capital letters to make them stand out. There is no need to do this, but you might find it helpful as you write your ColdFusion templates.

NOTE

This code uses the `ExpandPath()` function to set `AttachDir` to the subfolder named `Attach` within the folder that the template itself is in. See Appendix C, "ColdFusion Function Reference," for details about `ExpandPath()`.

Next, a `DirectoryExists()` test checks to see whether the `AttachDir` directory exists yet. If not, the directory is created via the `<CFDIRECTORY>` tag. See Chapter 33 for details about creating directories on the server. After the directory is known to exist, it is safe to provide the value of `AttachDir` to the `ATTACHMENTPATH` attribute of the `<CFPOP>` tag.

NOTE

This code also sets `GENERATEUNIQUEFILENAMES` to `Yes` so there is no danger of two attachment files with the same name (from different messages, say) being overwritten with one another. It is generally recommended that you do this to prevent the risk of two `<CFPOP>` requests interfering with one another.

Now, near the bottom of the template, the `ATTACHMENTS` and `ATTACHMENTFILES` columns of the `GetMsg` query object are examined to present any attachments to the user. As noted previously in Table 26.7, these two columns contain tab-separated lists of the message's file attachments (if any). Unlike most ColdFusion lists, these lists are separated with Tab characters, so any of ColdFusion's list functions must specify the Tab character as the delimiter.

For instance, the `NumAttachments` variable is set to the number of file attachments using a simple call to the `ListLen()` function. If at least one attachment exists, a simple `<CFLOOP>` block iterates through the list of attachments. Each time through the loop, the `ThisFileOrig` variable holds the original filename of the attachment (as the sender attached it), the `ThisFilePath` variable holds the unique filename used to save the file in `AttachDir`, and the `ThisFileURL` variable holds the appropriate relative URL for the file on the server. It is then quite easy to provide a simple link the user can click to view or save the file (as shown in Figure 26.8).

Deleting Attachments After Use

One problem with Listing 26.9 is the fact that the attachment files that get placed into `AttachDir` are never deleted. Over time, the directory would fill up with every attachment for every message that was ever displayed by the template. It would be nice to delete the files when the user was finished looking at the message, but because of the stateless nature of the Web, you don' t really know when that is. You could delete each user's attachment files when he logs out, but the user could close his browser at any time, without logging out.

NOTE

Developers familiar with Active Server Pages (ASP) might point out that ASP provides a way to fire a template just before a session variable (similar to ColdFusion's `SESSION` scope) is discarded from the server's RAM. This template could take care of deleting the files in `AttachDir` that were created by each session. Unfortunately, there is no ColdFusion equivalent to ASP's `OnSessionEnd` event.

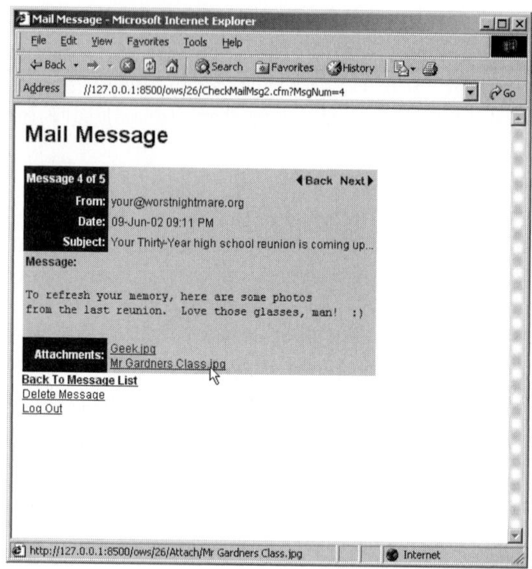

Figure 26.8

The <CFPOP> tag can retrieve files attached to messages in a mailbox.

The most straightforward solution to this problem, strange at it might seem, is to simply create a ColdFusion template that deletes all files from the `AttachDir` folder that are older than, say, one hour. Then, use ColdFusion's template scheduler to execute the template once an hour, or whatever interval you feel is appropriate. This will keep the folder from filling up with old attachment files.

Listing 26.10 provides a template that deletes all files from `AttachDir` after they are more than one hour old. You could schedule this template to run periodically, using the ColdFusion Administrator. See Chapter 35, "Event Scheduling," for details.

Listing 26.10 `DeleteAttachments.cfm`—Deleting Attachment Files Previously Saved by <CFPOP>

```
<!---
  Filename: DeleteAttachments.cfm
  Author:   Nate Weiss (NMW)
  Purpose:  Deletes attachment files previously saved on server with <CFPOP>
--->
<!--- Attachments are stored in "Attach" subfolder --->
<CFSET AttachDir = ExpandPath("Attach")>

<!--- Get a list of all files in the directory --->
<CFDIRECTORY
  DIRECTORY="#AttachDir#"
  NAME="GetFiles">

<!--- For each file in the directory --->
<CFLOOP QUERY="GetFiles">
  <!--- If it's a file (rather than a directory) --->
  <CFIF GetFiles.Type NEQ "Dir">
    <!--- If it's older than one hour --->
    <CFIF DateDiff("h", DateLastModified, Now()) GT 1>
      <!--- Get full filename of this file --->
```

Listing 26.10 (continued)

```
        <CFSET ThisFile = ExpandPath("Attach\#GetFiles.Name#")>

        <!--- Go ahead and delete the file --->
        <CFFILE
          ACTION="DELETE"
          FILE="#ThisFile#">
      </CFIF>
    </CFIF>
  </CFLOOP>
```

Another Approach

`CheckMailMsg3.cfm` (on this book's CD-ROM) is yet another version of `CheckMailMsg.cfm` that uses a different approach to provide the user with access to the attachments. When the user first views the message, the attachment filenames are displayed on the page, but the actual attachments are immediately deleted from disk. If the user clicks an attachment, the page is accessed again, this time passing the name of the desired attachment in the URL. The template code reexecutes, this time returning the requested file via the `<CFCONTENT>` tag. See Chapter 32, "Generating Non-HTML Content," for details about the `<CFCONTENT>` and `<CFHEADER>` tags used in this template.

The end result is that the user can access the files without the files ever needing to be stored on the server's drive. There is a significant downside, however, which is that the message is being re-retrieved from the server whenever the user clicks an attachment. If the attachments are many or large, this could mean quite a bit of extra processing time for ColdFusion. In general, the previous approach (Listing 26.9 coupled with Listing 26.10) is likely to serve you better in the long run.

NOTE

An interesting side effect of this approach is that the attachment files do not need to reside within the Web server's document root because they will be accessed only via `<CFCONTENT>`. Therefore, the `AttachDir` folder is set to the value returned by the `GetTempDirectory()` function, which is a reasonable place to store files that need to exist for only a short time. See Appendix C for information about `GetTempDirectory()`.

Creating Automated POP Agents

You can create automated agents that watch for new messages in a particular mailbox and respond to the messages in some kind of intelligent way. First, you create an agent template, which is just an ordinary ColdFusion template that checks a mailbox and performs whatever type of automatic processing is necessary. This template should not contain any forms or links because it will not be viewed by any of your users. Then, using the ColdFusion scheduler, you schedule the template to be visited automatically every 10 minutes, or whatever interval you feel is appropriate.

Creating the Agent Template

Listing 26.11 creates a simple version of a typical agent template: an unsubscribe agent, which responds to user requests to be removed from mailing lists. If you look at the `SendBulkMail.cfm` template (refer to Listing 26.4), you will notice that all messages sent by the template include instructions for users who want to be removed from Orange Whip Studios' mailing list.

The instructions tell the user to send a reply to the email with the word `Remove` in the subject line. Therefore, the main job of this template is to check the mailbox to which the replies will be sent (which is `mailings@orangewhipstudios.com` in this example). The template then checks each message's subject line. If it includes the word `Remove`, and the sender's email address is found in the `Contacts` table, the user is removed from the mailing list by setting the user's `MailingList` field to `0` in the database. The next time the `SendBulkMail.cfm` is used to send a bulk message, the user will be excluded from the mailing.

Listing 26.11 `ListUnsubscriber.cfm`—Automatically Unsubscribing Users from a Mailing List

```
<!---
  Filename: ListUnsubscriber.cfm
  Author:   Nate Weiss (NMW)
  Purpose:  A simple automated POP agent for unsubscribing from mailing lists
--->

<!--- Mailbox info for "mailings@orangewhipstudios.com" --->
<CFSET POPServer = "pop.orangewhipstudios.com">
<CFSET Username  = "mailings">
<CFSET Password  = "ThreeOrangeWhips">

<!--- We will delete all messages in this list --->
<CFSET MsgDeleteList = "">

<HTML>
<HEAD><TITLE>List Unsubscriber Agent</TITLE></HEAD>
<BODY>
<H2>List Unsubscriber Agent</H2>

<P>Checking the mailings@orangewhipstudios.com mailbox for new messages...<BR>
This may take a minute, depending on traffic and the number of messages.<BR>

<!--- Flush output buffer so the above messages --->
<!--- are shown while <CFPOP> is doing its work --->
<CFFLUSH>

<!--- Contact POP Server and retrieve messages --->
<CFPOP
  ACTION="GetHeaderOnly"
  NAME="GetMessages"
  SERVER="#POPServer#"
  USERNAME="#Username#"
  PASSWORD="#Password#"
  MAXROWS="20">

<!--- Short status message --->
<CFOUTPUT>
  <P><STRONG>#GetMessages.RecordCount# messages to process.</STRONG><BR>
</CFOUTPUT>

<!--- For each message currently in the mailbox... --->
<CFLOOP QUERY="GetMessages">
  <!--- Short status message --->
  <CFOUTPUT>
    <P><STRONG>Message from:</STRONG> #HTMLEditFormat(GetMessages.From)#<BR>
  </CFOUTPUT>
```

Listing 26.11 (continued)

```
<!--- If the subject line contains the word "Remove" --->
<CFIF GetMessages.Subject does not contain "Remove">
  <!--- Short status message --->
  Message does not contain "Remove".<BR>
<CFELSE>
  <!--- Short status message --->
  Message contains "Remove".<BR>

  <!--- Which "word" in From address contains @ sign? --->
  <CFSET AddrPos = ListContains(GetMessages.From, "@", "<> ")>
  <!--- Assuming one of the "words" contains @ sign, --->
  <CFIF AddrPos EQ 0>
    <!--- Short status message --->
    Address not found in From line.<BR>
  <CFELSE>

    <!--- Email address is that word in From address --->
    <CFSET FromAddress = ListGetAt(GetMessages.From, AddrPos, "<> ")>

    <!--- Who in mailing list has this email address? --->
    <CFQUERY NAME="GetContact" DATASOURCE="#REQUEST.DataSource#" MAXROWS="1">
      SELECT ContactID, FirstName, LastName
      FROM Contacts
      WHERE Email = '#FromAddress#'
      AND MailingList = 1
    </CFQUERY>

    <!--- Assuming someone has this address... --->
    <CFIF GetContact.RecordCount EQ 0>
      <!--- Short status message --->
      <CFOUTPUT>Recipient #FromAddress# not on list.<BR></CFOUTPUT>
    <CFELSE>
      <!--- Short status message --->
      <CFOUTPUT>Removing #FromAddress# from list.<BR></CFOUTPUT>

      <!--- Update the database to take them off list --->
      <CFQUERY DATASOURCE="#REQUEST.DataSource#">
        UPDATE Contacts SET
          MailingList = 0
        WHERE ContactID = #GetContact.ContactID#
      </CFQUERY>

      <!--- Short status message --->
      Sending confirmation message via email.<BR>

      <!--- Mail user a confirmation note --->
      <CFMAIL
        TO="""#GetContact.FirstName# #GetContact.LastName#"" <#FromAddress#>"
        FROM="""Orange Whip Studios"" <mailings@orangewhipstudios.com>"
        SUBJECT="Mailing List Request"
      >You have been removed from our mailing list.</CFMAIL>

    </CFIF>
  </CFIF>
</CFIF>

<!--- Add this message to the list of ones to delete. --->
```

Listing 26.11 (continued)

```
    <!--- If you wanted to only delete some messages, you --->
    <!--- would put some kind of <CFIF> test around this. --->
    <CFSET MsgDeleteList = ListAppend(MsgDeleteList, GetMessages.MessageNumber)>
  </CFLOOP>


  <!--- If there are messages to delete --->
  <CFIF MsgDeleteList NEQ "">
    <!--- Short status message --->
    <P>Deleting messages...

    <!--- Flush output buffer so the above messages --->
    <!--- are shown while <CFPOP> is doing its work --->
    <CFFLUSH>

    <!--- Contact POP Server and delete messages --->
    <CFPOP
      ACTION="Delete"
      SERVER="#POPServer#"
      USERNAME="#Username#"
      PASSWORD="#Password#"
      MESSAGENUMBER="#MsgDeleteList#">

    Done.<BR>
  </CFIF>

  </BODY>
  </HTML>
```

The code in Listing 26.11 is fairly simple. First, the `<CFPOP>` tag is used to retrieve the list of messages currently in the appropriate mailbox. Because the template needs to look only at the Subject line of each message, this template only ever needs to perform this `GetHeaderOnly` action (it never needs to retrieve the entirety of each message via `ACTION="GetAll"`).

Then, for each message, a series of tests are performed to determine whether the message is indeed a removal request from someone who is actually on the mailing list. First, it checks to see whether the Subject line contains the word `Remove`. If so, it now must extract the sender's email address from the string in the message's `From` line (which might contain a friendly name or just an email address). To do so, the template uses `ListContains()` to determine which word in the `From` line—if any—contains an `@` sign, where each word is separated by angle brackets or spaces. If such a word is found, that word is assumed to be the user's email address and is stored in the `FromAddress` variable via the `ListGetAt()` function.

Next, the query named `GetContact` is run to determine whether a user with the email address in question and who hasn't already been removed from the mailing list does indeed exist. If the query returns a row, the email is coming from a legitimate email address, and so represents a valid removal request.

NOTE

The `GetContact` query uses `MAXROWS="1"` just in case two users exist in the database with the email address in question. If so, only one is removed from the mailing list.

The next <CFQUERY> updates the sender's record in the Contacts table, setting the MailingList column to 0, effectively removing her from the mailing list. Finally, the sender is sent a confirmation note via a <CFMAIL> tag, so she knows her remove request has been received and processed.

The <CFLOOP> then moves on to the next message in the mailbox, until all messages have been processed. With each iteration, the current MessageNumber is appended to a simple ColdFusion list called MsgDeleteList. After all messages have been processed, they are deleted from the mailbox using the second <CFPOP> tag at the bottom of the template. As the template executes, messages are output for debugging purposes, so you can see what the template is doing if you visit using a browser (see Figure 26.9).

NOTE

If you use the <CFFLUSH> tag before each <CFPOP> tag, as this template does, the messages output by the page is displayed in real time as the template executes. See Chapter 21, "Improving the User Experience," for details about <CFFLUSH>.

Figure 26.9

Automated POP agents can scan a mailbox for messages and act appropriately.

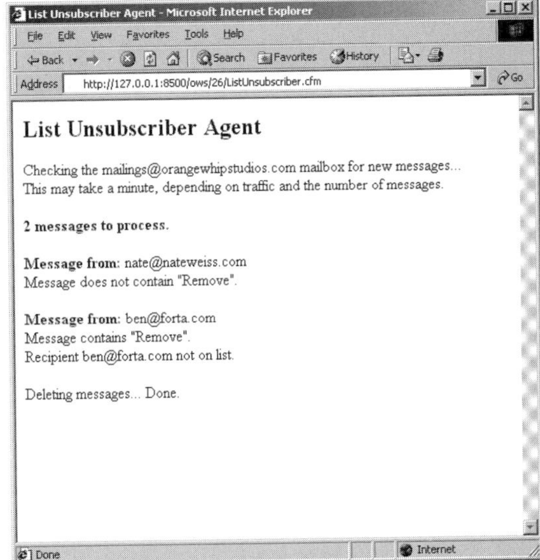

Scheduling the Agent Template

After you have your agent template working properly, you should schedule for automatic, periodic execution using the ColdFusion Administrator or the <CFSCHEDULE> tag. See Chapter 35 for details.

Other Uses for POP Agents

This example simply created a POP-based agent template that responds to unsubscribe requests. It could be expanded to serve as a full-fledged list server, responding to both subscribe and unsubscribe requests. It could even be in charge of forwarding incoming messages back out to members of the mailing list.

NOTE

That said, ColdFusion was not designed to be a round-the-clock, high-throughput, mail-generating engine. If you will be sending out tens of thousands of email messages every hour, you should probably think about a different solution. You wouldn't want your ColdFusion server to be so busy tending to its mail delivery duties that it wasn't capable of responding to Web page requests in a timely fashion.

Other POP-based agents could be used to create auto-responder mailboxes that respond to incoming messages by sending back standard messages, perhaps with files attached. You could also create a different type of agent that examines incoming help messages for certain words and sends back messages that should solve the user's problem.

CHAPTER 27
Online Commerce

IN THIS CHAPTER

Building Ecommerce Sites

For better or worse, more and more of today's World Wide Web is about selling goods and services, rather than providing freely available information for educational or other purposes. Once the realm of researchers, educators, and techies, the Net is now largely seen as a way to sell to a larger market with less overhead.

Whether this counts as progress is a debate I'll leave for the history books. What it means for you as a Web developer is that sooner or later, you will probably need to build some type of ecommerce Web application, hopefully with ColdFusion.

Common Commerce-Site Elements

No two commerce projects are exactly alike. Nearly every company will have its own idea about what its commerce application should look and feel like, complete with a wish list and feature requirements.

That said, a number of common elements appear in one shape or another on most online commerce sites. If your project is about selling goods or services to the general public, it probably makes sense to implement a format that's reasonably familiar to users. This section discusses some of the features nearly all shopping sites have in common.

Storefront Area

Most online shopping experiences start at some type of storefront page, which presents the user with a top-level view of all the items or services for sale. Depending on the number of items, these are usually broken down into various categories. From the main storefront page, users generally navigate to the item they want to purchase and then add the item to a virtual shopping cart.

Depending on the company, the storefront area might be its home page and might occupy nearly all of its Web site. This is often the case with an online bookstore or software reseller, for instance. In other situations, the storefront is just a section of a larger site. For instance, Orange Whip Studios' online store is just a place to buy merchandise, such as posters and movie memorabilia. It's an important part of the site, but information about upcoming releases, star news, and investor relations will probably be the primary focus.

NOTE

The `Store.cfm` template presented in this chapter is Orange Whip Studios' storefront page.

Promotions and Featured Items

Most shopping sites also ensure that certain items really jump out at the user by displaying them prominently, labeled as sale items, featured products, or by some other promotional term. These items are often sprinkled in callouts throughout the company's site to make them easy to find.

NOTE

The `<CF_MerchDisplay>` Custom Tag provided in this chapter offers a simple way to display featured merchandise throughout Orange Whip Studios' Web site.

Shopping Cart

Of course, one of the most important aspects of most commerce sites is the shopping cart. Shopping carts are so ubiquitous on today's Web that users have come to expect them and navigate through them almost intuitively.

If you implement a shopping cart for your application, you should ensure that it looks and feels like carts on other sites, especially those in similar industries. Typically, the user can see the contents of his or her cart on a designated page. From there, the user should be able to remove items from the cart, change quantities, review the total price of items in the cart, and enter a checkout process.

NOTE

The `StoreCart.cfm` template discussed in this chapter provides a simple shopping cart for the Orange Whip Studios' online store.

Checkout Process

Again, most users coming to your site will have a preconceived idea of what the checkout process should be like, so you should make it as straightforward and predictable as possible. This means asking the user to fill out one or two pages of forms, on which he or she provides information such as shipping addresses and credit-card data. Then the user clicks some type of Purchase Now button, which generates an order number and usually charges the user's credit card in real time.

NOTE

The `StoreCheckout.cfm` and `StoreCheckoutForm.cfm` templates in this chapter provide the checkout experience for Orange Whip Studios' virtual visitors.

Order Status and Package Tracking

If you are selling physical goods that need to be shipped after a purchase, users will expect to be able to check the status of their orders online. At a minimum, you should provide an email address to which users can write, but you should also consider building a page that allows them to check the status of current and past orders in real time.

Many users will also expect to be able to track shipped packages online. You can usually accomplish this via a simple link to the shipping carrier's Web site—such as `www.ups.com` or `www.fedex.com`—perhaps passing a tracking number in the URL. Visit the Web site of your shipping carrier for details (look for some type of developer's section).

NOTE

There isn't space in this chapter to discuss how to build such an order-tracking page, but the `OrderHistory.cfm` template discussed in Chapter 18, "Securing Your Applications," is a solid start that gets you most of the way there.

Using a Secure Server

Before you deploy your commerce site on a production server, you should certainly consider investing in a Secure Sockets Layer (SSL) server certificate from a company such as VeriSign (`www.verisign.com`). You can then use the certificate to set up a secure Web server that employs encryption when communicating with Web browsers. This secured server might or might not reside on the same machines as the company's regular Web servers.

NOTE

Many people are unwilling to place an order at a site that does not use SSL security, and rightly so. Of course, the decision is yours, but you are strongly urged to use a secured server for collecting any kind of personal information such as credit card numbers.

The secured Web-server instance may have its own document root (perhaps `c:\inetpub\secroot` instead of `c:\inetpub\wwwroot`), or it may share the same document root that your normal web pages are served from. This will depend on your preferences and the Web-server software you are using. According to your needs, you'll place some or all of your commerce application on the secure server. A typical scenario would put your checkout and order-history pages on the secure server and leave the storefront and cart pages on the regular Web server. If so, the URL for the checkout page would likely be something like `https://secure.orangewhipstudios.com/ows/Checkout.cfm` (instead of `http://www.orangewhipstudios.com/ows/Checkout.cfm`).

NOTE

You configure SSL encryption at the Web-server level; it doesn't relate directly to ColdFusion. Consult your Web server's documentation for details on how to enable SSL and HTTPS with the software you are using.

Creating Storefronts

Before creating code for the shopping cart and checkout process, you should create a simple framework for displaying the products and services your company will be offering for purchase. Then you can organize the items into an online storefront.

Displaying Individual Items

Listing 27.1 creates a CFML Custom Tag called <CF_MerchDisplay>. The tag displays a single piece of merchandise for sale, including a picture of the item and the appropriate Add To Cart link. You can use this to display a series of items in Orange Whip Studios' storefront page, as well as to feature individual items as callouts on the home page and throughout the site.

After you have this tag is in place, you can use it like this (where `SomeMerchID` is the name of a variable that identifies the desired item from the `Merchandise` table):

```
<!--- Show item for sale, via custom tag --->
<CF_MerchDisplay
  MerchID="#SomeMerchID#"
  ShowAddLink="Yes">
```

This Custom Tag is similar conceptually to the <CF_ShowMovieCallout> Custom Tag covered in Chapter 20, "Building Reusable Components." The two <CFPARAM> tags at the top force the tag to accept two attributes: the desired `MerchID` (which is required) and `ShowAddLink` (which is optional). If `ShowAddLink` is `Yes` or is not provided, the Custom Tag displays the merchandise item with a link for the user to add the item to the shopping cart. If `ShowAddLink` is `No`, the same content is displayed, but without the Add To Cart link.

NOTE

To make this Custom Tag available to ColdFusion, you should save Listing 27.1 as a file called `MerchDisplay.cfm`, either within the special `CustomTags` folder or in the same folder as the templates that will call it. See Chapter 20 for more information about where to save Custom Tag templates and about CFML Custom Tags in general.

Listing 27.1 `MerchDisplay.cfm`—Ceating a Custom Tag to Display Individual Items for Sale

```
<!---
  Filename:     MerchDisplay.cfm
  Created by:   Nate Weiss (NMW)
  Purpose:      Provides simple online shopping interface
  Please Note  Used by Store.cfm page
--->

<!--- Tag Attributes --->
<!--- MerchID to display (from Merchandise table) --->
<CFPARAM NAME="ATTRIBUTES.MerchID" TYPE="numeric">
<!--- Controls whether to show "Add To Cart" link --->
<CFPARAM NAME="ATTRIBUTES.ShowAddLink" TYPE="boolean" DEFAULT="Yes">

<!--- Get information about this part from database --->
<!--- Query-Caching cuts down on database accesses. --->
<CFQUERY NAME="GetMerch" DATASOURCE="#REQUEST.DataSource#"
  CACHEDWITHIN="#CreateTimeSpan(0,1,0,0)#">
  SELECT
    m.MerchName, m.MerchDescription, m.MerchPrice,
    m.ImageNameSmall, m.ImageNameLarge,
    f.FilmID, f.MovieTitle
  FROM
    Merchandise m INNER JOIN Films f
    ON m.FilmID = f.FilmID
  WHERE
    m.MerchID = #ATTRIBUTES.MerchID#
```

Listing 27.1 (continued)

```
</CFQUERY>

<!--- Exit tag silently (no error) if item not found --->
<CFIF GetMerch.RecordCount NEQ 1>
  <CFEXIT>
</CFIF>

<!--- URL for "Add To Cart" link/button --->
<CFSET AddLinkURL = "StoreCart.cfm?AddMerchID=#ATTRIBUTES.MerchID#">


<!--- Now display information about the merchandise --->
<CFOUTPUT>
  <TABLE WIDTH="300" CELLSPACING="0" BORDER="0">
    <TR>
      <!--- Pictures go on left --->
      <TD ALIGN="center">
        <!--- If there is an image available for item  --->
        <!--- (allow user to click for bigger picture) --->
        <CFIF GetMerch.ImageNameLarge NEQ "">
          <A HREF="../images/#GetMerch.ImageNameLarge#">
            <IMG SRC="../images/#GetMerch.ImageNameSmall#" BORDER="0"
            ALT="#GetMerch.MerchName# (click for larger picture)"></A>
        </CFIF>
      </TD>
      <!--- Item description, price, etc., go on right --->
      <TD STYLE="font-family:arial;font-size:12px">
        <!--- Name of item, associated movie title, etc --->
        <STRONG>#GetMerch.MerchName#</STRONG><BR>
        <FONT SIZE="1">From the film: #GetMerch.MovieTitle#</FONT><BR>
        #GetMerch.MerchDescription#<BR>
        <!--- Display Price --->
        <B>Price: #LSCurrencyFormat(GetMerch.MerchPrice)#</B><BR>

        <!--- If we are supposed to show an "AddToCart" link --->
        <CFIF ATTRIBUTES.ShowAddLink>
          <IMG SRC="../images/Arrow.gif" WIDTH="10" HEIGHT="9" ALT="" BORDER="0">
          <A HREF="#AddLinkURL#">Add To Cart</A><BR>
        </CFIF>
      </TD>
    </TR>
  </TABLE>
</CFOUTPUT>
```

After the two <CFPARAM> tags, a simple query named `GetMerch` gets the relevant information about the piece of merchandise, based on the `MerchID` passed to the tag. If for some reason the `MerchID` no longer exists, the tag simply stops its processing via the <CFEXIT> tag (no error message is displayed and processing in the calling template continues normally). Next, a variable called `AddLinkURL` is constructed, which is the URL to which the user will be sent if he or she decides to add the item to the shopping cart.

TIP

Using the `CACHEDWITHIN` attribute to cache the `GetMerch` query in the server's RAM keeps database interaction to a minimum, which improves performance. See the section "Improving Query Performance with Caching" in Chapter 22, "Improving Performance," for details.

The rest of the template is straightforward. An HTML table displays a picture of the part (if available), based on the value of the `ImageNameSmall` column in the `Merchandise` table. The user can see a larger version of the image by clicking it.

This makes it easy to display various items for sale throughout a site, based on whatever logic your application calls for. For instance, assuming you've already run a query called `GetMerch` that includes a `MerchID` column, you could select a random `MerchID` from one of the query's rows, like so:

```
<!--- Pick an item at random to display as a "Feature" --->
<CFSET RandNum     = RandRange(1, GetMerch.RecordCount)>
<CFSET RandMerchID = GetMerch.MerchID[RandNum]>
```

The following could then display the randomly selected merchandise:

```
<!--- Display featured item --->
<CF_MerchDisplay
  MerchID="#RandMerchID#">
```

Collecting Items into a Store

Depending on the nature of the company, the actual store part of a Web site can be a sprawling, category-driven affair or something quite simple. Because Orange Whip Studios has a relatively low number of products for sale (less than 20 rows exist in the `Merchandise` table), the best thing might be to create a one-page store that just displays all items for sale.

Listing 27.2 outputs all the items currently available for sale in a two-column display, using ordinary HTML table tags. Because the job of actually displaying the product's name, image, and associated links is encapsulated within the `<CF_MerchDisplay>` Custom Tag, this simple storefront template turns out to be quite short.

Figure 27.1 shows what this storefront looks like in a user's browser.

Listing 27.2 `Store.cfm`—Displaying All Items for Sale

```
<!---
  Filename:     Store.cfm
  Created by:   Nate Weiss (NMW)
  Purpose:      Provides simple online shopping interface
  Please Note  Relies upon CF_MerchDisplay custom tag
--->

<!--- Get list of merchandise from database --->
<CFQUERY NAME="GetMerch" DATASOURCE="#REQUEST.DataSource#"
  CACHEDWITHIN="#CreateTimeSpan(0,1,0,0)#">
  SELECT MerchID, MerchPrice
  FROM Merchandise
  ORDER BY MerchName
</CFQUERY>

<!--- Show header images, etc., for Online Store --->
<CFINCLUDE TEMPLATE="StoreHeader.cfm">

<!--- Show merchandise in a HTML table --->
<P>
```

Listing 27.2 (continued)

```
<TABLE>
  <TR>
    <!--- For each piece of merchandise --->
    <CFLOOP QUERY="GetMerch">
      <TD>
        <!--- Show this piece of merchandise --->
        <CF_MerchDisplay
          MerchID="#MerchID#">
      </TD>

      <!--- Alternate left and right columns --->
      <CFIF CurrentRow MOD 2 EQ 0></TR><TR></CFIF>
    </CFLOOP>
  </TR>
</TABLE>

</BODY>
</HTML>
```

Figure 27.1

Orange Whip Studios' online store enables users to peruse the merchandise available for sale.

TIP

By altering the `ORDER BY` part of the query, you could display the items in terms of popularity, price, or some other measure.

The `Store.cfm` template in Listing 27.2 displays a common storefront page header at the top of the page by including a file called `StoreHeader.cfm` via a `<CFINCLUDE>` tag. Listing 27.3 creates that header template, which displays Orange Whip Studios' logo, plus links marked Store Home, Shopping Cart, and Checkout. It also establishes a few default font settings via a `<STYLE>` block.

Listing 27.3 `StoreHeader.cfm`—Common Header for All of Orange Whip's Shopping Pages

```
<!---
  Filename:   StoreHeader.cfm
  Created by: Nate Weiss (NMW)
  Purpose:    Provides consistent navigation within store
--->


<!--- "Online Store" page title and header --->
<CFOUTPUT>
  <HTML>
  <HEAD><TITLE>#REQUEST.CompanyName# Online Store</TITLE></HEAD>
  <BODY>
  <STYLE TYPE="text/css">
    BODY {font-family:arial,helvetica,sans-serif;font-size:12px}
    TD   {font-size:12px}
    TH   {font-size:12px}
  </STYLE>

  <TABLE BORDER="0" WIDTH="100%">
    <TR>
      <TD WIDTH="101">
        <!--- Company logo, with link to company home page --->
        <A HREF="http://www.orangewhipstudios.com">
          <IMG SRC="../images/logo_c.gif"
            WIDTH="101" HEIGHT="101" ALT="" BORDER="0" ALIGN="left"></A>
      </TD>
      <TD>
        <HR>
        <STRONG>#REQUEST.CompanyName#</STRONG><BR>
        Online Store<BR CLEAR="all">
        <HR>
      </TD>
      <TD WIDTH="100" ALIGN="left">
        <!--- Link to "Shopping Cart" page --->
        <IMG SRC="../images/Arrow.gif" WIDTH="10" HEIGHT="9" ALT="" BORDER="0">
        <A HREF="Store.cfm">Store Home</A><BR>
        <!--- Link to "Shopping Cart" page --->
        <IMG SRC="../images/Arrow.gif" WIDTH="10" HEIGHT="9" ALT="" BORDER="0">
        <A HREF="StoreCart.cfm">Shopping Cart</A><BR>
        <!--- Link to "Checkout" page --->
        <IMG SRC="../images/Arrow.gif" WIDTH="10" HEIGHT="9" ALT="" BORDER="0">
        <A HREF="StoreCheckout.cfm">Checkout</A><BR>
      </TD>
    </TR>
  </TABLE>
   <BR>
</CFOUTPUT>
```

NOTE

This listing displays all the items for sale on the same page. If you will be selling many items, you might want to create a Next N interface for browsing through the merchandise in groups of 10 or 20 items per page. See Chapter 21, "Improving the User Experience," for information about how to build Next N interfaces.

Creating Shopping Carts

Not all shopping-cart experiences are alike, but most are reasonably similar. After you have built one cart application, others will come naturally and quickly. This section presents one way of implementing a shopping cart, which you can adapt for your own applications. First I'll discuss several approaches for remembering shopping-cart contents. Then you'll assemble a simple cart, using just a few ColdFusion templates.

NOTE

This section discusses a number of concepts introduced in Chapter 17, "Working with Sessions," including the definition of a Web-based session, as well as ColdFusion's special `CLIENT` and `SESSION` scopes. It is recommended that you read (or at least look through) Chapter 17 before you continue here.

Storing Cart Information

One of the first things to consider when building a shopping cart is how to store the shopping-cart information. Most users expect to be able to add items to a cart, go somewhere else (perhaps back to your storefront page or to another site for comparison shopping), and then return later to check out. This means you need to maintain the contents of each user's cart somewhere on your site.

No matter how you decide to store the information, you usually have at least two pieces of information to maintain:

- Items Added to the Cart—In most situations, each item will have its own unique identifier (in the sample database, this is the `MerchID` column in the Merchandise table), so remembering which items the user has added to the cart is usually just a matter of remembering one or more ID numbers.
- Desired Quantity—Generally, when the user first adds an item to the cart, you should assume he or she wants to purchase just one of that item. The user can usually increase the quantity for each item by adding the same item to the cart multiple times or by going to a View Cart page and entering the desired quantity in a text field.

As far as these examples are concerned, these two pieces of information, considered together, comprise the user's shopping cart. In many situations, this is all you need to track. Sometimes, though, you also need to track some kind of option for each item, such as a color or discounted price. Typically you can deal with these extra modifiers in the same way that you'll deal with the quantity in this chapter.

In any case, you can store this information in a number of ways. The most common approaches are summarized here.

`CLIENT`-Scoped Lists

Perhaps the simplest approach is to simply store the item IDs and quantities as variables in the `CLIENT` scope. As you learned in Chapter 17, the `CLIENT` scope can only store simple values, rather than arrays, structures, and so on. So the simplest option is probably to maintain two variables in the `CLIENT` scope, a ColdFusion-style list of `MerchIDs` and a list of associated quantities.

Aside from its simplicity, one nice thing about this approach is that the user's cart will persist between visits, without your having to write any additional code (see Chapter 17 for details about how long `CLIENT` variables are maintained and how they can be stored in the server's registry, in a database, or as a cookie on the user's machine). Also, client variables can be set up so that they work within all servers in a cluster.

This chapter includes example code for a Custom Tag called `<CF_ShoppingCart>`, which uses `CLIENT`-scoped lists to provide shopping-cart experiences for Orange Whip's visitors.

NOTE

While it's true that the `CLIENT` scope can only hold simple values, you can use the `<CFWDDX>` tag as a way to store a complex value like an array or structure as a client variable. I'm not going to show how to do that in this chapter, but you can read more about `<CFWDDX>` in Appendix B, "ColdFusion Tag Reference." There are also two chapters devoted to WDDX in our companion book, "Advanced ColdFusion MX Application Development."

SESSION-Scoped Structures and Arrays

Another approach would be to maintain each user's shopping-cart data in the `SESSION` scope. Unlike the `CLIENT` scope, the `SESSION` scope can contain structured data, such as structures and arrays. This means your code can be a lot more elegant and flexible, especially if you have to track more information about each item than just the desired quantity. However, `SESSION` variables are RAM resident and not cluster aware as ColdFusion MX ships, so you might want to stay away from this approach if you plan to run a number of ColdFusion servers together in a cluster. See Chapter 17 for more pros, cons, and techniques regarding session variables.

This chapter provides sample code for a ColdFusion Component (CFC) called `ShoppingCart`, which uses a `SESSION`-scoped array of structures to provide a shopping-cart experience.

Cart Data in a Database

Another approach is to create additional tables in your database to hold cart information. If you require your users to register before they add items to their carts, you could use their `ContactID` (or whatever unique identifiers you were using for users) to associate cart contents with users. Therefore, you might have a table called `CartContents`, with columns such as `ContactID`, `MerchID`, `Quant`, `DateAdded`, and whatever additional columns you might need, such as `Color` or `Size`. If you don't require users to register before using the cart, you could use the automatic `CLIENT.CFID` variable as a reasonably unique identifier for tracking cart contents.

This approach gives you more control than the others, in particular the capability to maintain easily queried historical information about which items users have added to carts most often and so on (as opposed to items that have actually been purchased). It would also work in a clustered environment. You would, however, probably need to come up with some type of mechanism for flushing very old cart records from the database because they would not automatically expire in the way that `SESSION` and `CLIENT` variables do.

TIP

You could handle this periodic table flushing via a scheduled template, as explained in Chapter 35, "Event Scheduling."

Building a Shopping Cart

Now that a storefront has been constructed with Add To Cart links for each product, it is now time to build the actual shopping cart. This section creates two versions of a ColdFusion template called `StoreCart.cfm`.

If the `StoreCart.cfm` template is visited without any URL parameters, it displays the items in the cart and gives the user the opportunity to either change the quantity of each item or check out, as shown in Figure 27.2. If a `MerchID` parameter is passed in the URL, that item is added to the user's cart before the cart is actually displayed. You will notice that the Add To Cart links generated by the `<CF_MerchDisplay>` Custom Tag (refer to Listing 27.1) do exactly that.

The Simplest Approach

The version of the `StoreCart.cfm` template in Listing 27.4 is probably one of the simplest shopping-cart templates possible. As suggested in the "Storing Cart Information" section earlier in this chapter, each user's cart data is stored using two comma-separated lists in the `CLIENT` scope. The `CLIENT.CartMerchList` variable holds a comma-separated list of merchandise IDs, and `CLIENT.CartQuantList` holds a comma-separated list of corresponding quantities.

TIP

The next version of the template improves upon this one by moving the task of remembering the user's cart into a CFML Custom Tag. It is recommended that you model your code after the next version of this template, rather than this one. Just use this listing as a study guide to make yourself familiar with the basic concepts at hand.

NOTE

To make the links to the shopping-cart page work correctly, you should save Listing 27.4 as `StoreCart.cfm`, not `StoreCart1.cfm`.

NOTE

This listing uses client variables, which means you need to enable the `CLIENT` scope in `Application.cfm`. The `Application.cfm` file for this chapter (Listing 27.8) does this, using the usual `<CFAPPLICATION>` syntax. It also creates some additional code used by the CFC version of this shopping cart, discussed in the "A ColdFusion Component Version of the Shopping Cart" section, later in this chapter.

Listing 27.4 `StoreCart1.cfm`—A Simple Shopping Cart

```
<!---
  Filename:    StoreCart.cfm
  Created by: Nate Weiss (NMW)
  Purpose:     Provides a simple shopping cart interface
--->

<!--- Show header images, etc., for Online Store --->
<CFINCLUDE TEMPLATE="StoreHeader.cfm">

<!--- URL parameter for MerchID --->
<CFPARAM NAME="URL.AddMerchID" TYPE="string" DEFAULT="">
```

Listing 27.4 (CONTINUED)

```
<!--- These two variables track MerchIDs / Quantities  --->
<!--- for items in user's cart (start with empty cart) --->
<CFPARAM NAME="CLIENT.CartMerchList" TYPE="string" DEFAULT="">
<CFPARAM NAME="CLIENT.CartQuantList" TYPE="string" DEFAULT="">

<!--- If MerchID was passed in URL --->
<CFIF IsNumeric(URL.AddMerchID)>
  <!--- Get position, if any, of MerchID in cart list --->
  <CFSET CurrentListPos=ListFind(CartMerchList, URL.AddMerchID)>
  <!--- If this item *is not* already in cart, add it --->
  <CFIF CurrentListPos EQ 0>
    <CFSET CLIENT.CartMerchList=ListAppend(CLIENT.CartMerchList, URL.AddMerchID)>
    <CFSET CLIENT.CartQuantList=ListAppend(CLIENT.CartQuantList, 1)>
  <!--- If item *is* already in cart, change its qty --->
  <CFELSE>
    <CFSET CurrentQuant=ListGetAt(CLIENT.CartQuantList, CurrentListPos)>
    <CFSET UpdatedQuant=CurrentQuant + 1>
    <CFSET CLIENT.CartQuantList=ListSetAt(CLIENT.CartQuantList, CurrentListPos,
UpdatedQuant)>
  </CFIF>

<!--- If no MerchID passed in URL --->
<CFELSE>
  <!--- For each item currently in user's cart --->
  <CFLOOP FROM="1" TO="#ListLen(CLIENT.CartMerchList)#" INDEX="i">
    <CFSET ThisMerchID=ListGetAt(CLIENT.CartMerchList, i)>

    <!--- If FORM field exists for this item's Quant --->
    <CFIF IsDefined("FORM.Quant_#ThisMerchID#")>
      <!--- The FORM field value is the new quantity --->
      <CFSET NewQuant=FORM["Quant_#ThisMerchID#"]>
      <!--- If new quant is 0, remove item from cart --->
      <CFIF NewQuant EQ 0>
        <CFSET CLIENT.CartMerchList=ListDeleteAt(CLIENT.CartMerchList, i)>
        <CFSET CLIENT.CartQuantList=ListDeleteAt(CLIENT.CartQuantList, i)>
      <!--- Otherwise, Update cart with new quantity --->
      <CFELSE>
        <CFSET CLIENT.CartQuantList=ListSetAt(CLIENT.CartQuantList, i, NewQuant)>
      </CFIF>
    </CFIF>
  </CFLOOP>

  <!--- If user submitted form via "Checkout" button --->
  <CFIF IsDefined("FORM.IsCheckingOut")>
    <CFLOCATION URL="StoreCheckout.cfm">
  </CFIF>
</CFIF>

<!--- Stop here if user's cart is empty --->
<CFIF CLIENT.CartMerchList EQ "">
  There is nothing in your cart.
  <CFABORT>
</CFIF>
```

Listing 27.4 (continued)

```
<!--- Create form that submits to this template --->
<CFFORM ACTION="#CGI.SCRIPT_NAME#">
  <TABLE>
    <TR>
      <TH COLSPAN="2" BGCOLOR="Silver">Your Shopping Cart</TH>
    </TR>
    <!--- For each piece of merchandise --->
    <CFLOOP FROM="1" TO="#ListLen(CLIENT.CartMerchList)#" INDEX="i">
      <CFSET ThisMerchID=ListGetAt(CLIENT.CartMerchList, i)>
      <CFSET ThisQuant=ListGetAt(CLIENT.CartQuantList, i)>
      <TR>
        <TD>
          <!--- Show this piece of merchandise --->
          <CF_MerchDisplay
            MerchID="#ThisMerchID#"
            ShowAddLink="No">
        </TD>
        <TD>
          <!--- Display Quantity in Text entry field --->
          <CFOUTPUT>
            Quantity:
            <INPUT TYPE="Text"
              NAME="Quant_#ThisMerchID#"
              SIZE="3"
              VALUE="#ThisQuant#">
          </CFOUTPUT>
        </TD>
      </TR>
    </CFLOOP>
  </TABLE>

  <!--- Submit button to update quantities --->
  <INPUT TYPE="Submit" VALUE="Update Quantities">

  <!--- Submit button to Check out --->
  <INPUT TYPE="Submit" VALUE="Checkout" NAME="IsCheckingOut">
</CFFORM>
```

The `<CFFORM>` section at the bottom of this template is what displays the contents of the user's cart, based on the contents of the `CLIENT.CartMerchList` and `CLIENT.CartQuantList` variables. Suppose for the moment that the current value of `CartMerchList` is `5,8` (meaning the user has added items number 5 and 8 to the cart) and that `CartQuantList` is `1,2` (meaning the user wants to buy one of item number 5 and two of item number 8). If so, the `<CFLOOP>` near the bottom of this template will execute twice. The first time through the loop, `ThisMerchID` will be `5` and `ThisQuant` will be `1`. Item number 5 is displayed with the `<CF_MerchDisplay>` tag, and then a text field called `Quant_5` is displayed, prefilled with a value of `1`. This text field enables the user to adjust the quantities for each item.

At the very bottom of the template, two submit buttons are provided, labeled Update Quantities and Checkout. Both submit the form, but the Checkout button sends the user on to the Checkout phase after the cart quantities have been updated.

Updating Cart Quantities

Three <CFPARAM> tags are at the top of Listing 27.4. The first makes it clear that the template can take an optional `AddMerchID` parameter. The next two ensure that the `CLIENT.CartMerchList` and `CLIENT.CartQuantList` variables are guaranteed to exist (if not, they are initialized to empty strings, which represent an empty shopping cart).

If a numeric `AddMerchID` is passed to the page, the first <CFIF> block executes. The job of this block of code is to add the item indicated by `URL.AddMerchID` to the user's cart. First, the `ListFind()` function sets the `CurrentListPos` variable. This variable is `0` if the `AddMerchID` value is not in `CLIENT.CartMerchList` (in other words, if the item is not in the user's cart). Therefore, this function places the `AddMerchID` value in the user's cart by appending it to the current `CartMerchList` value, and by appending a quantity of `1` to the current `MerchQuantList` value.

If, on the other hand, the item is already in the user's cart, `CurrentListPos` is the position of the item in the comma-separated lists that represent the cart. Therefore, the current quantity for the passed `AddMerchID` value can be obtained with the `ListGetAt()` function and stored in `CurrentQuant`. The current quantity is incremented by `1`, and the updated quantity is placed in the appropriate spot in `CLIENT.CartQuantList`, via the `ListSetAt()` function.

The large <CFELSE> block executes when the user submits the form, using the Update Quantities or Checkout button (see Figure 27.2). The <CFLOOP> loops through the list of items in the user's cart. Again, supposing that `CLIENT.CartMerchList` is currently `5,8`, `ThisMerchID` is set to `5` the first time through the loop. If a form variable named `FORM.Quant_5` exists, that form value represents the user's updated quantity for the item. If the user has specified an updated quantity of `0`, it is assumed that the user wants to remove the item from the cart, so the appropriate values in `CartMerchList` and `CartQuantList` are removed using the `ListDeleteAt()` function. If the user has specified some other quantity, the quantity in `CartQuantList` is simply updated, using the `ListSetAt()` function.

Finally, if the user submitted the form using the Checkout button, the browser is directed to the `CartCheckout.cfm` template via the <CFLOCATION> tag.

At this point, the shopping cart is quite usable. The user can go to the `Store.cfm` template (refer to Figure 27.1) and add items to the shopping cart. Once at the shopping cart (see Figure 27.2), the user can update quantities or remove items by setting the quantity to `0`.

Encapsulating the Shopping Cart in a Custom Tag

Although the version of `StoreCart.cfm` in Listing 27.4 works just fine, the code itself is a bit messy. It contains quite a few list functions, which don't necessarily have to do with the conceptual problem at hand (the user's cart). Worse, other templates that need to refer to the user's cart (such as the Checkout template) must use nearly all the same list functions over again, resulting in quite a bit of code for you to maintain.

Using the Custom Tag skills you learned in Chapter 20, you can create a Custom Tag that represents the abstract notion of the user's shopping cart.

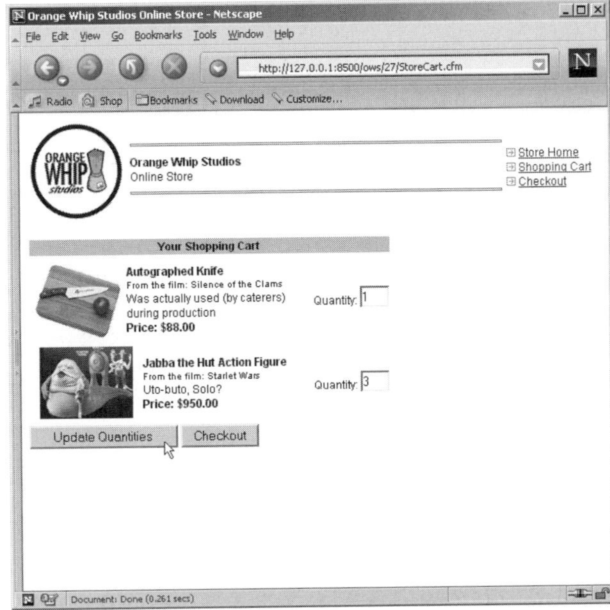

Figure 27.2

From the Shopping Cart page, users can update quantities or proceed to the Checkout phase.

Building `<CF_ShoppingCart>`

The code in Listing 27.5 creates a Custom Tag called `<CF_ShoppingCart>`, which encapsulates all the list-manipulation details necessary to maintain the user's shopping cart. After you save Listing 27.5 as `ShoppingCart.cfm` in the special `CustomTags` folder (or just in the same folder where you'll be using it), it will be capable of accomplishing any of the tasks shown in Table 27.1.

Table 27.1 Syntax Supported by the `<CF_ShoppingCart>` Custom Tag Example

DESIRED ACTION	SAMPLE CODE
Add an item to the user's cart	`<CF_ShoppingCart Action="Add" MerchID="5">`
Update the quantity of an item	`<CF_ShoppingCart Action="Update" MerchID="5" Quantity="10">`
Remove an item from the cart	`<CF_ShoppingCart Action="Remove" MerchID="5">`
Remove all items from cart	`<CF_ShoppingCart Action="Empty">`
Retrieve all items in cart	`<CF_ShoppingCart Action="List" ReturnVariable="GetCart">`

`ACTION="List"` returns the cart's contents as a ColdFusion query object; the query object will contain two columns, `MerchID` and `Quantity`.)

NOTE

Because the various `ACTION` tasks provided by this Custom Tag all relate to a single concept (a shopping cart), you can think of the Custom Tag as an object-based representation of the cart. That makes it an ideal candidate for turning into a ColdFusion Component (CFC). See Chapter 20 for further discussion of Custom Tags and CFCs as objects.

Listing 27.5 `ShoppingCart.cfm`—Constructing the `<CF_ShoppingCart>` Custom Tag

```
<!---
  Filename:    ShoppingCart.cfm
  Created by: Nate Weiss (NMW)
  Purpose:     Creates the <CF_ShoppingCart> Custom Tag
--->

<!--- Tag Parameters --->
<CFPARAM NAME="ATTRIBUTES.Action" TYPE="string">


<!--- These two variables track MerchIDs / Quantities  --->
<!--- for items in user's cart (start with empty cart) --->
<CFPARAM NAME="CLIENT.CartMerchList" TYPE="string" DEFAULT="">
<CFPARAM NAME="CLIENT.CartQuantList" TYPE="string" DEFAULT="">


<!--- This tag is being called with what ACTION? --->
<CFSWITCH EXPRESSION="#ATTRIBUTES.Action#">

  <!--- *** ACTION="Add" or ACTION="Update" *** --->
  <CFCASE VALUE="Add,Update">
    <!--- Tag attributes specific to this ACTION --->
    <CFPARAM NAME="ATTRIBUTES.MerchID" TYPE="numeric">
    <CFPARAM NAME="ATTRIBUTES.Quantity" TYPE="numeric" DEFAULT="1">

    <!--- Get position, if any, of MerchID in cart list --->
    <CFSET CurrentListPos = ListFind(CLIENT.CartMerchList, ATTRIBUTES.MerchID)>
    <!--- If this item *is not* already in cart, add it --->
    <CFIF CurrentListPos EQ 0>
      <CFSET CLIENT.CartMerchList =
        ListAppend(CLIENT.CartMerchList, ATTRIBUTES.MerchID)>
      <CFSET CLIENT.CartQuantList =
        ListAppend(CLIENT.CartQuantList, ATTRIBUTES.Quantity)>
    <!--- If item *is* already in cart, change its qty --->
    <CFELSE>
      <!--- If Action="Add", add new Qty to existing --->
      <CFIF ATTRIBUTES.Action EQ "Add">
        <CFSET ATTRIBUTES.Quantity =
          ATTRIBUTES.Quantity + ListGetAt(CLIENT.CartQuantList, CurrentListPos)>
      </CFIF>
      <!--- If new quantity is zero, remove item from cart --->
      <CFIF ATTRIBUTES.Quantity EQ 0>
        <CFSET CLIENT.CartMerchList =
          ListDeleteAt(CLIENT.CartMerchList, CurrentListPos)>
        <CFSET CLIENT.CartQuantList =
          ListDeleteAt(CLIENT.CartQuantList, CurrentListPos)>
      <!--- If new quantity not zero, update cart quantity --->
```

Listing 27.5 (CONTINUED)

```
      <CFELSE>
        <CFSET CLIENT.CartQuantList =
          ListSetAt(CLIENT.CartQuantList, CurrentListPos, ATTRIBUTES.Quantity)>
      </CFIF>
    </CFIF>
  </CFCASE>


  <!--- *** ACTION="Remove" *** --->
  <CFCASE VALUE="Remove">
    <!--- Tag attributes specific to this ACTION --->
    <CFPARAM NAME="ATTRIBUTES.MerchID" TYPE="numeric">
    <!--- Treat "Remove" action same as "Update" with Quant=0 --->
    <CF_ShoppingCart
      ACTION="Update"
      MerchID="#ATTRIBUTES.MerchID#"
      Quantity="0">
  </CFCASE>


  <!--- *** ACTION="Empty" *** --->
  <CFCASE VALUE="Empty">
    <CFSET CLIENT.CartMerchList = "">
    <CFSET CLIENT.CartQuantList = "">
  </CFCASE>


  <!--- *** ACTION="List" *** --->
  <CFCASE VALUE="List">
    <!--- Tag attributes specific to this ACTION --->
    <CFPARAM NAME="ATTRIBUTES.ReturnVariable" TYPE="variableName">

    <!--- Create a query, to return to calling template --->
    <CFSET q = QueryNew("MerchID,Quantity")>

    <!--- For each item in CLIENT lists, add row to query --->
    <CFLOOP FROM="1" TO="#ListLen(CLIENT.CartMerchList)#" INDEX="i">
      <CFSET QueryAddRow(q)>
      <CFSET QuerySetCell(q, "MerchID",  ListGetAt(CLIENT.CartMerchList, i))>
      <CFSET QuerySetCell(q, "Quantity", ListGetAt(CLIENT.CartQuantList, i))>
    </CFLOOP>

    <!--- Return query to calling template --->
    <CFSET "Caller.#ATTRIBUTES.ReturnVariable#" = q>
  </CFCASE>


  <!--- If an unknown ACTION was provided, display error --->
  <CFDEFAULTCASE>
     <CFTHROW
       MESSAGE="Unknown ACTION passed to &lt;CF_ShoppingCart&gt;"
       DETAIL="Recognized ACTION values are <B>List</B>, <B>Add</B>,
               <B>Update</B>, <B>Remove</B>, and <B>Empty</B>.">
  </CFDEFAULTCASE>
</CFSWITCH>
```

NOTE

Some of the <CFSET> tags in this template are broken somewhat unusually across two lines (the left side of the expression on one line and the right side on the next line) to make them easier to read in this book. In your actual code templates, you would probably have the whole <CFSET> statement on one line, but this listing does show that ColdFusion can deal uncomplainingly with expressions spanning multiple lines.

Similar to the <CF_Film> Custom Tag in Chapter 20, this Custom Tag supports its various tasks by requiring an `ACTION` attribute (required by the <CFPARAM> tag at the top of Listing 27.5), and then handling each of the supported actions in separate <CFCASE> tags within a large <CFSWITCH> block. If the `ACTION` is `Add` or `Update`, the first <CFCASE> tag executes. If the `ACTION` is `Remove`, the second one executes, and so on.

If `ACTION="Add"` or `ACTION="Update"`, the tag accepts two additional parameters—`MerchID` (required) and `Quantity` (optional, defaulting to `1`). The <CFCASE> block for these actions is similar to the top portion of Listing 27.4, using `ListFind()` to determine whether the item is already in the user's cart and then adding it to the cart with `ListAppend()` or updating the quantity using `ListSetAt()`. Also, if `ACTION="Update"` and `Quantity="0"`, the item is removed from the user's cart.

If the tag is called `ACTION="Remove"`, the tag just calls itself again, using `ACTION="Update"` and `Quantity="0"` to remove the item from the user's cart. So `Remove` is just a synonym for an `Update` that sets the quantity to `0`.

If `ACTION="Empty"`, the `CLIENT.CartMerchList` and `CLIENT.CartQuantList` are emptied by setting them both to empty strings. This has the effect of removing all items from the user's cart.

Finally, if `ACTION="List"`, the tag creates a new ColdFusion query object using the `QueryNew()` function, which the calling template will be capable of using as if it were generated by an ordinary <CFQUERY> tag. The new query has two columns, `MerchID` and `Quantity`. For each item in the `CartMerchList` and `CartQuantList` lists, a row is added to the query using `QueryAddRow()`; then the `MerchID` and `Quantity` columns of the just-inserted row are set using the `QuerySetCell()` function. The end result is a simple two-column query that contains a row for each item in the user's cart. The query object is returned to the calling template with the name specified in the tag's `ReturnVariable` attribute.

TIP

It's worth learning more about returning nondatabase queries from Custom Tags. Check out `QueryNew()`, `QueryAddRow()`, and `QuerySetCell()` in Appendix C, "ColdFusion Function Reference."

NOTE

One of the goals for this Custom Tag is to ensure that no other template will need to refer to the `CLIENT.CartMerchList` and `CLIENT.CartQuantList` variables. The Custom Tag will therefore be a clean abstraction of the concept of a user's cart, including the storage method (currently the two lists in the `CLIENT` scope). If you later decide to use `SESSION` variables or a database table to hold each user's cart data, you only have to change the code in the Custom Tag template. See Chapter 20 for more discussion about attaining the holy grail of abstraction via Custom Tags.

Putting <CF_ShoppingCart> to Work

The version of `StoreCart.cfm` in Listing 27.6 is a revision of the one in Listing 27.4. As far as the user is concerned, it behaves the same way. However, it removes all references to the internal storage mechanisms (the `CLIENT` variables, list functions, and so on). As a result, the code reads well, and it will be clearer to future coders and easier for you to reuse and maintain.

NOTE

To make the links to the shopping-cart page work correctly, you should save Listing 27.6 as `StoreCart.cfm`, not `StoreCart2.cfm`.

Listing 27.6 `StoreCart2.cfm`—Using `<CF_ShoppingCart>` to Rebuild the `StoreCart.cfm` Template

```
<!---
  Filename:   StoreCart.cfm
  Created by: Nate Weiss (NMW)
  Purpose:    Provides a simple shopping cart interface
--->

<!--- Show header images, etc., for Online Store --->
<CFINCLUDE TEMPLATE="StoreHeader.cfm">

<!--- If MerchID was passed in URL --->
<CFIF IsDefined("URL.AddMerchID")>
  <!--- Add item to user's cart data, via custom tag --->
  <CF_ShoppingCart
    Action="Add"
    MerchID="#URL.AddMerchID#">

<!--- If user is submitting cart form --->
<CFELSEIF IsDefined("FORM.MerchID")>
  <!--- For each MerchID on Form, Update Quantity --->
  <CFLOOP LIST="#Form.MerchID#" INDEX="ThisMerchID">
    <!--- Update Quantity, via Custom Tag --->
    <CF_ShoppingCart
      Action="Update"
      MerchID="#ThisMerchID#"
      Quantity="#FORM['Quant_#ThisMerchID#']#">
  </CFLOOP>

  <!--- If user submitted form via "Checkout" button, --->
  <!--- send on to Checkout page after updating cart. --->
  <CFIF IsDefined("FORM.IsCheckingOut")>
    <CFLOCATION URL="StoreCheckout.cfm">
  </CFIF>
</CFIF>

<!--- Get current cart contents, as a query object --->
<CF_ShoppingCart
  Action="List"
  ReturnVariable="GetCart">

<!--- Stop here if user's cart is empty --->
<CFIF GetCart.RecordCount EQ 0>
  There is nothing in your cart.
```

Listing 27.6 (continued)

```
    <CFABORT>
  </CFIF>


  <!--- Create form that submits to this template --->
  <CFFORM ACTION="#CGI.SCRIPT_NAME#">
    <TABLE>
      <TR>
        <TH COLSPAN="2" BGCOLOR="Silver">Your Shopping Cart</TH>
      </TR>
      <!--- For each piece of merchandise --->
      <CFLOOP QUERY="GetCart">
        <TR>
          <TD>
            <!--- Show this piece of merchandise --->
            <CF_MerchDisplay
              MerchID="#GetCart.MerchID#"
              ShowAddLink="No">
          </TD>
          <TD>
            <!--- Display Quantity in Text entry field --->
            <CFOUTPUT>
              Quantity:
              <INPUT TYPE="Hidden"
                NAME="MerchID"
                VALUE="#GetCart.MerchID#">
              <INPUT TYPE="Text" SIZE="3"
                NAME="Quant_#GetCart.MerchID#"
                VALUE="#GetCart.Quantity#">
            </CFOUTPUT>
          </TD>
        </TR>
      </CFLOOP>
    </TABLE>

    <!--- Submit button to update quantities --->
    <INPUT TYPE="Submit" VALUE="Update Quantities">

    <!--- Submit button to Check out --->
    <INPUT TYPE="Submit" VALUE="Checkout" NAME="IsCheckingOut">
  </CFFORM>
```

If the template receives an `AddMerchID` parameter in the URL, the `<CF_ShoppingCart>` tag is called with `ACTION="Add"` to add the item to the user's cart. If the user submits the shopping cart form with the Update Quantities or Checkout button, the template loops through the merchandise elements on the form, calling `<CF_ShoppingCart>` with `ACTION="Update"` for each one.

Then, to display the items in the user's cart, the `<CF_ShoppingCart>` tag is called again, this time with `Action="List"`. Because `GetCart` is specified for the `ReturnVariable` attribute, the display portion of the code just needs to use a `<CFLOOP>` over the `GetCart` query, calling `<CF_MerchDisplay>` for each row to get the merchandise displayed to the user.

A ColdFusion Component Version of the Shopping Cart

If you think about it, the `<CF_ShoppingCart>` tag seems to embody some of the object-based ideas that are in keeping with the ColdFusion Components framework introduced in Chapter 20. In that chapter, you learned that CFCs often represent some kind of high-level idea that you can think of as a widget or object. Each type of object can provide its own set of functions or methods. You also learned that each instance of a CFC is often populated with its own data.

A shopping cart shares all of these properties, which we have already seen brought to life by `<CF_ShoppingCart>`. Think of the cart as a type of object. The object can execute different actions, like `Add`, `Update`, and `List`. We can think of these actions as the object's methods. Most important, each instance of the shopping-cart object holds its own data. That is, each individual user's shopping cart is structurally the same (all spawned from the same object type, with the same methods and so on), but holds a different set of items.

It seems, then, that a shopping cart would be an ideal candidate for turning into a ColdFusion component. As you will see in this section, it is quite easy to turn the code for the `<CF_ShoppingCart>` Custom Tag into a ColdFusion Component called `ShoppingCart`. That will give Orange Whip Studios the option to expose the shopping cart as a Web Service in the future. It will also open up the possibility of creating a slick Flash version of the shopping experience for visitors, because of Flash MX's ability to interact easily with ColdFusion Components via the Flash Remoting service.

NOTE

See Chapter 23, "Integrating with Macromedia Flash MX," for details about calling CFCs from Flash movies. See Chapter 20 for more information about ColdFusion Components in general.

Building the `ShoppingCart` Component

The first step in converting the shopping-cart code from the Custom Tag implementation to a CFC implementation is largely a matter of changing the large `<CFSWITCH>` block from the Custom Tag into a `<CFCOMPONENT>` tag, and changing each of the `<CFCASE>` tags to `<CFFUNCTION>` tags. Obviously, that's not all you must do, but you'll see that the CFC code within each `<CFFUNCTION>` is strongly related to the corresponding `<CFCASE>` from the Custom Tag (see Listing 27.5).

Listing 27.7 provides code for a simple component-based shopping cart. The most obvious change is the introduction of CFC framework tags like `<CFCOMPONENT>` and `<CFFUNCTION>` to establish the CFC's methods. Table 27.2 shows the methods exposed by the CFC.

Remember that once you create this CFC, you can view automatically generated documentation for it by visiting the URL for the `.cfc` file with your browser, or by choosing Get Description from the right-click menu for the component in the Components tab of the Application panel in Dreamweaver MX. The automatic documentation page for the ShoppingCart component is shown in Figure 27.3.

Table 27.2 Methods Exposed by the `ShoppingCart` CFC

METHOD	WHAT IT DOES
`Add(MerchID, Quantity)`	Adds an item to the shopping cart. The `Quantity` argument is optional (defaults to 1).
`Update(MerchID, Quantity)`	Updates the quantity of a particular item in the shopping cart.
`Remove(MerchID)`	Removes an item from the shopping cart.
`Empty()`	Removes all items from the shopping cart.
`List()`	Returns a query that contains all items currently in the shopping cart.

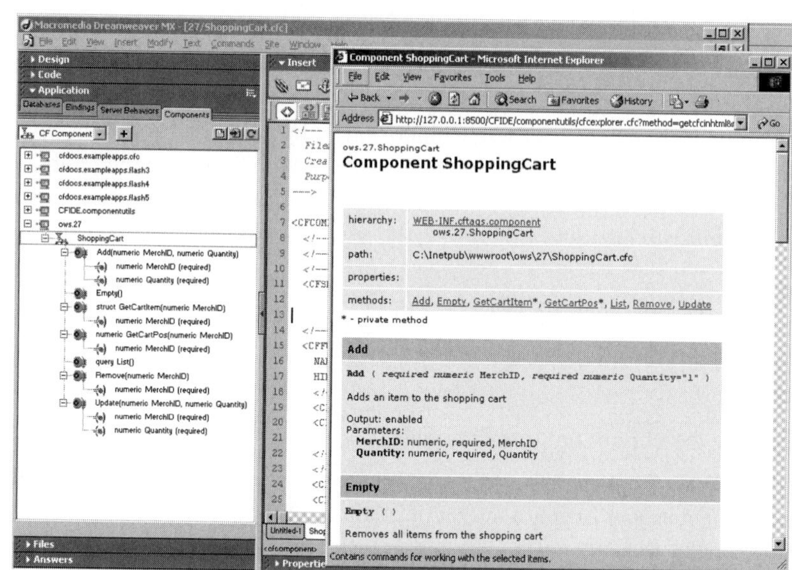

Figure 27.3 Dreamweaver MX helps you explore a CFC's methods through automatic component introspection.

Listing 27.7 `ShoppingCart.cfc`—Creating the `ShoppingCart` Component

```
<!---
  Filename:     ShoppingCart.cfc
  Created by:   Nate Weiss (NMW)
  Purpose:      Creates a CFC called ShoppingCart
--->

<CFCOMPONENT>
  <!--- Initialize the cart's contents --->
  <!--- Because this is outside of any <CFFUNCTION> tag, --->
  <!--- it only occurs when the CFC is first created --->
  <CFSET This.CartArray = ArrayNew(1)>


  <!--- *** ADD Method *** --->
  <CFFUNCTION
    NAME="Add"
```

Listing 27.7 (continued)

```
    HINT="Adds an item to the shopping cart">
    <!--- Two Arguments: MerchID and Quantity --->
    <CFARGUMENT NAME="MerchID" TYPE="numeric" REQUIRED="Yes">
    <CFARGUMENT NAME="Quantity" TYPE="numeric" REQUIRED="No" DEFAULT="1">

    <!--- Get structure that represents this item in cart, --->
    <!--- then set its quantity to the specified quantity --->
    <CFSET CartItem = GetCartItem(MerchID)>
    <CFSET CartItem.Quantity = CartItem.Quantity + Arguments.Quantity>
  </CFFUNCTION>


  <!--- *** UPDATE Method *** --->
  <CFFUNCTION
    NAME="Update"
    HINT="Updates an item's quantity in the shopping cart">
    <!--- Two Arguments: MerchID and Quantity --->
    <CFARGUMENT NAME="MerchID" TYPE="numeric" REQUIRED="Yes">
    <CFARGUMENT NAME="Quantity" TYPE="numeric" REQUIRED="Yes">

    <!--- If the new quantity is greater than zero --->
    <CFIF Quantity GT 0>
      <!--- Get structure that represents this item in cart, --->
      <!--- then set its quantity to the specified quantity --->
      <CFSET CartItem = GetCartItem(MerchID)>
      <CFSET CartItem.Quantity = Arguments.Quantity>
    <!--- If new quantity is zero, remove the item from cart --->
    <CFELSE>
      <CFSET This.Remove(MerchID)>
    </CFIF>
  </CFFUNCTION>


  <!--- *** REMOVE Method *** --->
  <CFFUNCTION
    NAME="Remove"
    HINT="Removes an item from the shopping cart">
    <!--- One Argument: MerchID --->
    <CFARGUMENT NAME="MerchID" TYPE="numeric" REQUIRED="Yes">

    <!--- What position is this item occupying in the cart? --->
    <CFSET CartPos = GetCartPos(MerchID)>

    <!--- Assuming the item was found, remove it from cart --->
    <CFIF CartPos GT 0>
      <CFSET ArrayDeleteAt(This.CartArray, CartPos)>
    </CFIF>
  </CFFUNCTION>


  <!--- *** EMPTY Method *** --->
  <CFFUNCTION
    NAME="Empty"
    HINT="Removes all items from the shopping cart">

    <!--- Empty the cart by clearing the This.CartArray array --->
```

Listing 27.7 (continued)

```
    <CFSET ArrayClear(This.CartArray)>
  </CFFUNCTION>


  <!--- *** LIST Method *** --->
  <CFFUNCTION
    NAME="List"
    HINT="Returns a query object containing all items in shopping cart.  The query
object has two columns: MerchID and Quantity."
    RETURNTYPE="query">

    <!--- Create a query, to return to calling process --->
    <CFSET q = QueryNew("MerchID,Quantity")>

    <!--- For each item in cart, add row to query --->
    <CFLOOP FROM="1" TO="#ArrayLen(This.CartArray)#" INDEX="i">
      <CFSET QueryAddRow(q)>
      <CFSET QuerySetCell(q, "MerchID",  This.CartArray[i].MerchID)>
      <CFSET QuerySetCell(q, "Quantity", This.CartArray[i].Quantity)>
    </CFLOOP>

    <!--- Return completed query --->
    <CFRETURN q>
  </CFFUNCTION>


  <!--- Internal GetCartPos() Method --->
  <CFFUNCTION
    NAME="GetCartPos"
    RETURNTYPE="numeric"
    ACCESS="private">
    <!--- Argument: MerchID --->
    <CFARGUMENT NAME="MerchID" TYPE="numeric" REQUIRED="Yes">

    <!--- Get position, if any, of MerchID in cart query --->
    <CFSET CurrentArrayPos = 0>
    <CFLOOP FROM="1" TO="#ArrayLen(This.CartArray)#" INDEX="i">
      <CFIF This.CartArray[i].MerchID EQ Arguments.MerchID>
        <CFSET CurrentArrayPos = i>
        <CFBREAK>
      </CFIF>
    </CFLOOP>

    <!--- Return the position --->
    <CFRETURN CurrentArrayPos>
  </CFFUNCTION>


  <!--- Internal GetCartItem() Method --->
  <CFFUNCTION
    NAME="GetCartItem"
    RETURNTYPE="struct"
    ACCESS="private">
    <!--- One Argument: MerchID --->
    <CFARGUMENT NAME="MerchID" TYPE="numeric" REQUIRED="Yes">
```

Listing 27.7 (continued)

```
    <!--- Get the position of the item in This.CartArray --->
    <CFSET CartPos = GetCartPos(MerchID)>

    <!--- If item for this MerchID was found, we will return it --->
    <CFIF CartPos GT 0>
      <CFSET CartItem = This.CartArray[CartPos]>
    <!--- If item was not found, create new one and add to cart --->
    <CFELSE>
      <CFSET CartItem = StructNew()>
      <CFSET CartItem.MerchID = Arguments.MerchID>
      <CFSET CartItem.Quantity = 0>
      <CFSET ArrayAppend(This.CartArray, CartItem)>
    </CFIF>

    <!--- In either case, return the item --->
    <CFRETURN CartItem>
  </CFFUNCTION>

</CFCOMPONENT>
```

Aside from the structural makeup of the code, you've made another important change here. While the Custom Tag version used comma-separated lists stored in the `CLIENT` scope to remember the items in each user's cart, this new component version uses an array called `CartArray` to hold the cart's contents. Each time the user selects merchandise to purchase, a CFML structure will be created to hold information about that particular item. So if the user has selected three items for purchase, the array will have a length of three. Each item in the array will be a structure that has two properties: the `MerchID` for the item, and the `Quantity`.

Most important, the `CartArray` array is stored in the special `THIS` scope provided by the CFC framework. As you learned in Chapter 20, the THIS scope is a place where you can store information specific to each instance of a CFC. Storing `CartArray` in the `THIS` scope means that the array will automatically live for as long as the CFC does. In other words, this shopping cart still tracks the same information as the Custom Tag version; it just does so differently.

Take a look at the component's `GetCartPos()` method (the second-to-last `<CFFUNCTION>` block in Listing 27.7). Because of the `ACCESS="private"` attribute, this is a private method that you can only use within the component itself. The purpose of this method is to return the index position of a particular item within the cart's `THIS.CartArray` array, based on the item's `MerchID`. If the item is not in the cart at all, then the method returns `0`. A simple `<CFLOOP>` block makes the function do its work. The rest of the code in the CFC will use this method often.

This CFC includes another private method, called `GetCartItem()`. The purpose of this method is similar to that of `GetCartPos()`; it returns information about an item in the cart, based on the item's `MerchID`. But instead of returning the item's index position, this method returns the actual structure kept in the `THIS.CartArray` array. If the item isn't in the cart yet, this method automatically adds it to the cart by creating a new structure for the item and then appending it to `THIS.CartArray`. In other words, this method always returns a structure, even if the desired item wasn't in the cart when the method was called.

NOTE

In this example code, the structure returned by `GetCartItem()` will contain two keys, `MerchID` and `Quantity`. If the item wasn't in the cart yet when the method was called, the `Quantity` will be set to `0`. You can easily adjust the code to have the CFC remember other information as needed.

Together, these two private methods do most of the grunt work that makes this component work. The rest of the methods are very simple.

For instance, the `Add()` method at the top of Listing 27.7 gets its work done with just two lines of code. First, it gets the structure for the given item by calling the private `GetCartItem()` method. Then it adds the desired quantity to the item's existing quantity using simple addition in a `<CFSET>`. The `Update()` method does its work using virtually the same two lines unless the the quanity provided is `0`, in which case the CFC's `Remove()` method is called to remove the item from the cart. That `Remove()` function is also really simple. It just gets the position of the given item in the user's cart via the `GetCartPos()` method, then deletes the item (if found) with ColdFusion's `ArrayDeleteAt()` function.

In fact, once you've built the private methods, none of the code for the other (public) methods is at all difficult to write. The `Empty()` method is the simplest of all; it simply discards all items from the `THIS.CartArray` variable with the `ArrayClear()` function. And the code for the `List()` function is very similar to the corresponding code in Listing 27.5.

Using the `ShoppingCart` Component

Now that the `ShoppingCart` component has been built, it is easy to put it to work. The first thing to do to is to make sure each user gets his or her own `ShoppingCart` instance. Take a look at Listing 27.8, a simple `Application.cfm` file. The `<CFSET>` and `<CFAPPLICATION>` lines are nothing new; they have been used in most `Application.cfm` files since Chapter 16, "Introducing the Web Application Framework."

The new thing here is the addition of the `<CFOBJECT>` tag and surrounding `IsDefined()` test at the bottom of the template.

Listing 27.8 `Application.cfm`—Creating a New CFC Instance for Each User

```
<!---
  Filename:     Application.cfm
  Created by:   Nate Weiss (NMW)
  Please Note  Executes for each page request
--->

<!--- Any variables set here can be used by all our pages --->
<CFSET REQUEST.DataSource  = "ows">
<CFSET REQUEST.CompanyName = "Orange Whip Studios">

<!--- Name our app, and enable Application vars --->
<CFAPPLICATION
  NAME="OrangeWhipSite"
  CLIENTMANAGEMENT="Yes"
  SESSIONMANAGEMENT="Yes">

<!--- If user's session has just begun, create a --->
```

Listing 27.8 (continued)

```
<!--- new, empty ShoppingCart instance for user. --->
<CFIF NOT IsDefined("SESSION.MyShoppingCart")>

  <!--- This creates the new CFC instance --->
  <CFOBJECT
    NAME="SESSION.MyShoppingCart"
    COMPONENT="ShoppingCart">

</CFIF>
```

So, when a user first visits the application, the code inside the `<CFIF>` block executes, which means that a new instance of the `ShoppingCart` CFC is created and stored in the `SESSION` scope. The CFC instance remains in ColdFusion's memory for the remainder of the user's visit (or until the server is restarted or the user's session expires). That's all you need to do to give each user a shopping cart.

NOTE

Note that the component code itself (in Listing 27.7) did not refer to the `SESSION` scope at all. Instead, it referred only to the `THIS` scope provided by the CFC framework. It is only now, when the CFC is instantiated, that it becomes attached to the notion of a session.

Now all that remains is to go back to the `StoreCart2.cfm` template from Listing 27.6 and replace the calls to the `<CF_ShoppingCart>` tag with calls to the CFC's methods. Listing 27.9 is the resulting template.

NOTE

To keep the various links between pages intact, remember to save this template as `StoreCart.cfm`, not `StoreCart3.cfm`.

Listing 27.9 `StoreCart3.cfm`—Putting the `ShoppingCart` CFC to Work

```
<!---
  Filename:    StoreCart.cfm
  Created by:  Nate Weiss (NMW)
  Purpose:     Provides a simple shopping cart interface
--->

<!--- Show header images, etc., for Online Store --->
<CFINCLUDE TEMPLATE="StoreHeader.cfm">

<!--- If MerchID was passed in URL --->
<CFIF IsDefined("URL.AddMerchID")>
  <!--- Add item to user's cart data --->
  <CFINVOKE
    COMPONENT="#SESSION.MyShoppingCart#"
    METHOD="Add"
    MERCHID="#URL.AddMerchID#">

<!--- If user is submitting cart form --->
<CFELSEIF IsDefined("FORM.MerchID")>
  <!--- For each MerchID on Form, Update Quantity --->
  <CFLOOP LIST="#Form.MerchID#" INDEX="ThisMerchID">
    <!--- Add item to user's cart data --->
    <CFINVOKE
      COMPONENT="#SESSION.MyShoppingCart#"
      METHOD="Update"
```

Listing 27.9 (continued)

```
        MERCHID="#ThisMerchID#"
        QUANTITY="#FORM['Quant_#ThisMerchID#']#">
    </CFLOOP>

    <!--- If user submitted form via "Checkout" button, --->
    <!--- send on to Checkout page after updating cart. --->
    <CFIF IsDefined("FORM.IsCheckingOut")>
      <CFLOCATION URL="StoreCheckout.cfm">
    </CFIF>
  </CFIF>

  <!--- Get current cart contents, as a query object --->
  <CFSET GetCart = SESSION.MyShoppingCart.List()>

  <!--- Stop here if user's cart is empty --->
  <CFIF GetCart.RecordCount EQ 0>
    There is nothing in your cart.
    <CFABORT>
  </CFIF>


  <!--- Create form that submits to this template --->
  <CFFORM ACTION="#CGI.SCRIPT_NAME#">
    <TABLE>
      <TR>
        <TH COLSPAN="2" BGCOLOR="Silver">Your Shopping Cart</TH>
      </TR>
      <!--- For each piece of merchandise --->
      <CFLOOP QUERY="GetCart">
        <TR>
          <TD>
            <!--- Show this piece of merchandise --->
            <CF_MerchDisplay
              MerchID="#GetCart.MerchID#"
              ShowAddLink="No">
          </TD>
          <TD>
            <!--- Display Quantity in Text entry field --->
            <CFOUTPUT>
              Quantity:
              <INPUT TYPE="Hidden"
                NAME="MerchID"
                VALUE="#GetCart.MerchID#">
              <INPUT TYPE="Text" SIZE="3"
                NAME="Quant_#GetCart.MerchID#"
                VALUE="#GetCart.Quantity#">
            </CFOUTPUT>
          </TD>
        </TR>
      </CFLOOP>
    </TABLE>

    <!--- Submit button to update quantities --->
    <INPUT TYPE="Submit" VALUE="Update Quantities">

    <!--- Submit button to Check out --->
    <INPUT TYPE="Submit" VALUE="Checkout" NAME="IsCheckingOut">
  </CFFORM>
```

As you learned in Chapter 20, there are two basic ways to invoke a CFC's methods from a ColdFusion template: with the `<CFINVOKE>` tag, or using script-style method syntax in a `<CFSET>` or other expression. This listing shows both.

For instance, in Listing 27.6, the following code retrieved the contents of the user's cart:

```
<!--- Get current cart contents, via Custom Tag --->
<CF_ShoppingCart
  Action="List"
  ReturnVariable="GetCart">
```

In Listing 26.9, the equivalent line is:

```
<!--- Get current cart contents, as a query object --->
<CFSET GetCart = SESSION.MyShoppingCart.List()>
```

The following `<CFINVOKE>` syntax would do the same thing:

```
<!--- Add item to user's cart data --->
<CFINVOKE
  COMPONENT="#SESSION.MyShoppingCart#"
  METHOD="List"
  RETURNVARIABLE="GetCart">
```

Similarly, this line calls the CFC's `Add` method:

```
<!--- Add item to user's cart data --->
<CFINVOKE
  COMPONENT="#SESSION.MyShoppingCart#"
  METHOD="Add"
  MERCHID="#URL.AddMerchID#">
```

You could change it to the following, which would do the same thing:

```
<CFSET SESSION.MyShoppingCart.Add(URL.AddMerchID)>
```

As you can see, the `<CFINVOKE>` syntax is a bit more self-explanatory because the arguments are explicitly named. However, the script-style syntax is usually much more concise and perhaps easier to follow logically. Use whatever style you prefer.

Payment Processing

Now that Orange Whip Studios' storefront and shopping-cart mechanisms are in place, it is time to tackle the checkout process. While by no means difficult, this part generally takes the most time to get into place because you must make some decisions about how to accept and process the actual payments from your users.

Depending on the nature of your application, you might have no need for real-time payment processing. For instance, if your company operates by billing your customers at the end of each month, you probably just need to perform some type of query to determine the status of the user's account, rather than worrying about collecting a credit-card number and charging the card right when the user checks out.

However, most online shopping applications call for getting a credit-card number from a user at checkout time and charging the user's credit-card account in real time. That is the focus of this section.

Payment-Processing Solutions

Assuming that you will be collecting credit-card information from your users, the first thing you should decide is how you will process the credit-card charges that come through your application. ColdFusion does not ship with any specific functionality for processing credit-card transactions. However, a number of third-party packages enable you to accept payments via credit cards and checks.

NOTE

Because it is quite popular, the examples in this chapter use the Payflow Pro payment-processing service from VeriSign (www.verisign.com). But VeriSign's service is just one of several solutions available to you. You are encouraged to investigate other payment-processing software to find the service or package that makes the most sense for your project.

Processing a Payment

The exact ColdFusion code you use to process payments will vary according to the payment-processing package you decide to use. This section uses VeriSign's Payflow Pro as an example. Please understand, however, that other options are available and that Payflow Pro shouldn't necessarily be considered as superior or better suited than other solutions just because I discuss it here.

Getting Started with Payflow Pro

If you want to try the payment-processing code examples that follow in this section, you must download and install the Java version of the Payflow Pro software.

NOTE

At the time of this writing, the items discussed here were available for free download from VeriSign's Web site. It was necessary to sign up for a free test vendor account first to download and use the software.

To get started, do the following:

1. Go to VeriSign's Web site and register for a free test vendor account.
2. Download and install the Pure Java version of the Payflow Pro software. At the time of this writing, that meant unzipping the downloaded software to an appropriate location on your computer's hard drive. The guts of the software is the Java archive file named `Verisign.jar`. For purposes of this discussion, we will assume that you are using Windows and have unzipped the downloaded files so that the `Verisign.jar` file is at this location: `c:\versign\payflowpro\java`
3. On the Java and JVM page of the ColdFusion Administrator, add the full path of the `Verisign.jar` file to the Class Path field (for instance, `c:\versign\payflowpro\java\Verisign.jar`). If the Class Path field already contains a value, add the path at the end, separated with a comma. Make sure to restart the ColdFusion MX service to make the changes take effect.

NOTE

The Payflow Pro software on your server needs to communicate with VeriSign's network over the Internet, so your ColdFusion server must be capable of accessing the Internet before you can start testing. Depending on your situation, you might need to configure Payflow Pro so it can get past your firewall or proxy software, or take other special steps. See the Payflow Pro documentation for details. Please understand that successful installation of VeriSign's software is not the primary focus of this chapter.

The `<CF_VerisignPayflowPro>` Custom Tag

VeriSign provides a Java CFX tag called `<CFX_PAYFLOWPRO>` for ColdFusion developers. Unfortunately, at the time of this writing, the `<CFX_PAYFLOWPRO>` tag did not work correctly with ColdFusion MX. This situation may be remedied by the time you read this book, in which case you can just use the official `<CFX_PAYFLOWPRO>` tag provided by VeriSign. See VeriSign's site for details.

To take the place of VeriSign's own `<CFX_PAYFLOWPRO>`, I have provided a CFML Custom Tag called `<CF_VerisignPayflowPro>`. This Custom Tag is a wrapper around the Pure Java API that VeriSign provides. While this API was designed with Java coders in mind, you can use it quite easily with CFML. Table 27.3 shows the attributes supported by the Custom Tag. Even if you don't end up needing this custom tag, it makes for an interesting example of what you can do with ColdFusion and APIs designed for Java.

Table 27.3 shows the attributes supported by `<CF_VerisignPayflowPro>`.

Table 27.3 Attributes Supported by `<CF_VerisignPayflowPro>`

ATTRIBUTE	DESCRIPTION
`CertPath`	The full path to the location of your VeriSign vendor certificates. For testing, you can just use the test certificate included in the Java API download from VeriSign. If you are using Windows, then the correct value is `c:\versign\payflowpro\java\certs` or something similar.
`ServerName`	The Payflow server to connect to for payment processing the payment. For testing, you should use `test-payflow.verisign.com`. When you are ready to process real payments, you would change this to `payflow.verisign.com`. If needed, you can also provide `ServerPort` and `ServerTimeout` attributes.
`PayflowVendor`	Your Payflow vendor user name. This is the same user name you use to log in to the Payflow Manager on VeriSIlgn"s Wweb site. This value is case-sensitive, so make sure to get it exactly right.
`PayflowPassword`	Your Payflow vendor password, also case -sensitive.
`ReturnVariable`	A variable name thatwhere you would like to place the results of the transaction placed into. After the tag runs, a structure will exist with whatever name you specify here. The structure will always contain `RESULT`,, `RESPCODE`, and `PNREF` values, plus whatever other values are appropriate for the transaction you are attempting. See the Payflow documentation for details about the meaning of these values.
`ACCT`	The credit-card number (or other account number) that you want to charge.

Table 27.3 (CONTINUED)

ATTRIBUTE	DESCRIPTION
EXPDATE	The four-digit expiration date, in the form MMYY.
AMT	The amount of the sale.
TENDER	Optional. The type of account to charge. The default is C for credit card. See the Payflow documentation for other values.
TRXTYPE	Optional. The type of transation. The default is S for sale. You can also provide C (Credit), A (Authorization), D (Delayed Capture), V (Void), F (Voice Authorization), or I (Inquiry). See the Payflow documentation for details.
ORIGID	If the TRXTYPE is D (Delayed Capture), V (Void), F (Voice Authorization), or I (Inquiry), then you must also provide the original transaction number here. Most likely, you would supply the PNREF value returned by some previous transaction (see ReturnVariable, above).
COMMENT1 and COMMENT2	Optional. Use these attributes to record any comments along with the transaction.
AVSSTREET and AVSZIP	Optional. Use these attributes to use AVS address verification, most likely when usingwith TRXTYPE="A". See the Payflow documentation for details.
PARMLIST	Optional. If for some reason you need to provide additional information, you can create your own Payflow parameter list and provide it here, in which case the ACCT, EXPDATE, AMT, TENDER, TRXTYPE, COMMENT1, COMMENT2, AVSSTREET, and AVSZIP attributes will be ignored. See the Payflow documentation for details about parameter lists.

NOTE

I don't have the space to discuss the code used to build the <CF_VerisignPayflowPro> tag in detail here. In general, connecting to native Java objects is conceptually beyond the scope of this book. That is why I've provided this Custom Tag, so that you can have a complete working example without needing to understand how the Java API is used (aren't Custom Tags great?). That said, I invite you to examine the code for <CF_VerisignPayflowPro>, which is included on the CD-ROM. You may find it a useful guide for creating your own CFML wrappers around other Java APIs. For more information about using native Java objects in ColdFusion templates, see the ColdFusion MX documentation or this book's companion volume, *Advanced ColdFusion MX Application Development.*

Writing a Custom Tag Wrapper to Accept Payments

To make the <CF_VerisignPayflowPro> tag easier to use in your own ColdFusion templates, and to make it easier to switch to some other payment-processing solution in the future, you might consider hiding all payment-package–specific code within a more abstract, general-purpose Custom Tag that encapsulates the notion of processing a payment.

Listing 27.10 creates a CFML Custom Tag called <CF_ProcessPayment>. It accepts a Processor attribute to indicate which payment-processing software should process the payment. As you will see, this example supports Processor="PayflowPro" and Processor="JustTesting". You would need to expand the tag by adding the package-specific code necessary for any additional software.

NOTE

Actually, the tag also includes code for `Processor="CyberCash"`. CyberCash was a payment processing solution that was similar to Payflow Pro; it is no longer in operation. The last edition of this book used CyberCash as the main example. I am including the CyberCash-specific code in Listing 27.10 so that you can see how different payment processing solutions could be handled within a single custom tag. The CyberCash setting will not actually work though, because their servers will no longer respond to requests.

The idea here is similar to the idea behind the `<CF_ShoppingCart>` tag created earlier in this chapter: Keep all the mechanics in the Custom Tag template, so each individual page can use simpler, more goal-oriented syntax. In addition to the `Processor` attribute, this sample version of the `<CF_ProcessPayment>` tag accepts the following attributes:

- `OrderID`—This is passed along to the credit-card company as a reference number.
- `OrderAmount`, `CreditCard`, `CreditExpM`, `CreditExpY`, and `CreditName`—These describe the actual payment to be processed.
- `ReturnVariable`—This indicates a variable name the Custom Tag should use to report the status of the attempted payment transaction. The returned value is a ColdFusion structure that contains a number of status values.

Listing 27.10 `ProcessPayment.cfm`—Creating the `<CF_ProcessPayment>` Custom Tag

```
<!---
  Filename:      ProcessPayment.cfm
  Created by:    Nate Weiss (NMW)
  Please Note  Creates the <CF_ProcessPayment> Custom Tag
  Purpose:       Handles credit card and other transactions
--->


<!--- Tag Parameters --->
<CFPARAM NAME="ATTRIBUTES.Processor" TYPE="string">
<CFPARAM NAME="ATTRIBUTES.OrderID" TYPE="numeric">
<CFPARAM NAME="ATTRIBUTES.OrderAmount" TYPE="numeric">
<CFPARAM NAME="ATTRIBUTES.CreditCard" TYPE="string">
<CFPARAM NAME="ATTRIBUTES.CreditExpM" TYPE="string">
<CFPARAM NAME="ATTRIBUTES.CreditExpY" TYPE="string">
<CFPARAM NAME="ATTRIBUTES.ReturnVariable" TYPE="variableName">
<CFPARAM NAME="ATTRIBUTES.CreditName" TYPE="string">


<!--- Depending on the PROCESSOR attribute --->
<CFSWITCH EXPRESSION="#ATTRIBUTES.Processor#">

  <!--- If PROCESSOR="PayflowPro" --->
  <CFCASE VALUE="PayflowPro">
    <!--- Force expiration into MM and YY format --->
    <CFSET ExpM  = NumberFormat(ATTRIBUTES.CreditExpM, "00")>
    <CFSET ExpY  = NumberFormat(Right(ATTRIBUTES.CreditExpY, 2), "00")>

    <!--- Attempt transaction with Payflow Pro --->
    <CF_VerisignPayflowPro
      CertPath="c:\verisign\payflowpro\java\certs"
      ServerName="test-payflow.verisign.com"
```

Listing 27.10 (continued)

```
      PayflowPartner="VeriSign"
      PayflowVendor="YOUR_INFO_HERE"
      PayflowPassword="YOUR_INFO_HERE"
      ACCT="#ATTRIBUTES.CreditCard#"
      EXPDATE="#ExpM##ExpY#"
      AMT="#NumberFormat(ATTRIBUTES.OrderAmount, '9.00')#"
      COMMENT1="Orange Whip OrderID: #ATTRIBUTES.OrderID#"
      COMMENT2="Customer Name on Card: #ATTRIBUTES.CreditName#"
      ReturnVariable="PayflowResult">

    <!--- Values to return to calling template --->
    <CFSET s = StructNew()>
    <!--- Always return IsSuccessful (Boolean) --->
    <CFSET s.IsSuccessful = PayflowResult.RESULT EQ 0>
    <!--- Always return status of transaction --->
    <CFSET s.Status = PayflowResult.RESPMSG>
    <!--- If Successful, return the Auth Code --->
    <CFIF s.IsSuccessful>
      <CFSET s.AuthCode     = PayflowResult.AUTHCODE>
      <CFSET s.OrderID      = ATTRIBUTES.OrderID>
      <CFSET s.OrderAmount  = ATTRIBUTES.OrderAmount>
    <!--- If not successful, return the error --->
    <CFELSE>
      <CFSET s.ErrorCode    = PayflowResult.RESULT>
      <CFSET s.ErrorMessage = PayflowResult.RESPMSG>
    </CFIF>
    <!--- Return values to calling template --->
    <CFSET "Caller.#ATTRIBUTES.ReturnVariable#" = s>

  </CFCASE>


  <!--- If PROCESSOR="JustTesting" --->
  <!--- This puts the tag into a "testing" mode --->
  <!--- Where any transaction will always succeed --->
  <CFCASE VALUE="JustTesting">
    <!--- Values to return to calling template --->
    <CFSET s = StructNew()>
    <!--- Always return IsSuccessful (Boolean) --->
    <CFSET s.IsSuccessful = True>
    <!--- Always return status of transaction --->
    <CFSET s.Status = "success">
    <!--- Return other data, as if transaction succeeded --->
    <CFSET s.AuthCode     = "DummyAuthCode">
    <CFSET s.OrderID      = ATTRIBUTES.ORDERID>
    <CFSET s.OrderAmount  = ATTRIBUTES.OrderAmount>

    <!--- Return values to calling template --->
    <CFSET "Caller.#ATTRIBUTES.ReturnVariable#" = s>
  </CFCASE>


  <!--- If PROCESSOR="CyberCash" --->
  <!--- *** This is now defunct but remains as an example --->
  <CFCASE VALUE="CyberCash">
```

Listing 27.10 (continued)

```
<!--- Force expiration into MM and YY format --->
<CFSET ExpM  = NumberFormat(ATTRIBUTES.CreditExpM, "00")>
<CFSET ExpY  = NumberFormat(Right(ATTRIBUTES.CreditExpY, 2), "00")>

<!--- Attempt to process the transaction --->
<CFX_CYBERCASH
  VERSION="3.2"
  CONFIGFILE="C:\mck-3.3.1-NT\test-mck\conf\merchant_conf"
  MO_ORDER_ID="8767767#ATTRIBUTES.OrderID#"
  MO_VERSION="3.3.1"
  MO_PRICE="USD #NumberFormat(ATTRIBUTES.OrderAmount, '9.00')#"
  CPI_CARD_NUMBER="#ATTRIBUTES.CreditCard#"
  CPI_CARD_EXP="#ExpM#/#ExpY#"
  CPI_CARD_NAME="#ATTRIBUTES.CreditName#"
  OUTPUTPOPQUERY="Charge">

<!--- Values to return to calling template --->
<CFSET s = StructNew()>
<!--- Always return IsSuccessful (Boolean) --->
<CFSET s.IsSuccessful = Charge.STATUS EQ "success">
<!--- Always return status of transaction --->
<CFSET s.Status = Charge.STATUS>
<!--- If Successful, return the Auth Code --->
<CFIF s.IsSuccessful>
  <CFSET s.AuthCode     = Charge.AUTH_CODE>
  <CFSET s.OrderID      = ATTRIBUTES.ORDERID>
  <CFSET s.OrderAmount  = ATTRIBUTES.OrderAmount>
<!--- If not successful, return the error --->
<CFELSE>
  <CFSET s.ErrorCode    = Charge.ERROR_CODE>
  <CFSET s.ErrorMessage = Charge.ERROR_MESSAGE>
</CFIF>
<!--- Return values to calling template --->
<CFSET "Caller.#ATTRIBUTES.ReturnVariable#" = s>
</CFCASE>

<!--- If the PROCESSOR attribute is unknown --->
<CFDEFAULTCASE>
  <CFTHROW MESSAGE="Unknown PROCESSOR attribute.">
</CFDEFAULTCASE>
</CFSWITCH>
```

NOTE

The `CERTPATH` attribute for the `<CF_VerisignPayflowPro>` tag needs to point to your own `certs` folder, wherever it is located (see the previous section, "Getting Started with Payflow Pro").

NOTE

You need to provide your own account information for the PayflowVendor and PayflowPassword attributes before you can expect this code to work. You may also need to alter the PayflowPartner attribute if someone other than VeriSign is providing your payment services.

At the top of Listing 27.10, eight `<CFPARAM>` tags establish the tag's various attributes (all of the attributes are required). Then a `<CFSWITCH>` tag executes various payment-processing code, based on the `Processor` attribute passed to the Custom Tag. The syntax specific to `<CF_VerisignPayflowPro>` is the only code fleshed out in this template; you would add syntax for other packages in separate `<CFCASE>` blocks.

The actual code in the `<CFCASE>` block is quite simple. Most of the Custom Tag's attributes are fed directly to the `<CF_VerisignPayflowPro>` tag. You need to tweak some of the values just a bit to conform to what the CFX tag expects. For instance, the Custom Tag expects the expiration month and year to be provided as simple numeric values, but the Payflow tag wants them provided as a single string in `MM/YY` format.

After the `<CF_VerisignPayflowPro>` tag executes, a new structure named `s` is created using `StructNew()`. Next, a Boolean value called `IsSuccessful` is added to the structure. Its value will be `True` if the `RESULT` code returned by the Payflow servers is 0 (which indicates success); otherwise, it will be `False`. The calling template can look at `IsSuccessful` to tell whether the payment was completed successfully. Additionally, if the order was successful, `AuthCode`, `OrderID`, and `OrderAmount` values are added to the structure. If it was not successful, values called `ErrorCode` and `ErrorMessage` are added to the structure, so the calling template can understand exactly what went wrong. Then the whole structure is passed back to the calling template using the quoted `<CFSET>` return variable syntax (explained in Chapter 20).

Thus, the generic `<CF_ProcessPayment>` tag is able to support Payflow Pro.

NOTE

A similar `<CFCASE>` block is also provided, which will execute if `Processor="JustTesting"` is passed to the tag. This provides an easy way to test the checkout functionality even if you don't want to bother registering for Payflow Pro. Just change the `Processor` attribute to `JustTesting` in Listing 27.11.

NOTE

If you adapt this Custom Tag to handle other payment processors, try to return the same value names (`IsSuccessful`, `AuthCode`, and so on) to a structure. In this way, you will build a common API to deal with payment processing in an application-agnostic way.

Processing a Complete Order

In addition to explaining how to build commerce applications, this chapter emphasizes the benefits of hiding the mechanics of complex operations within goal-oriented Custom Tag wrappers that can accomplish whole tasks on their own. Actual page templates that use these Custom Tags end up very clean, dealing only with the larger concepts at hand, rather than including a lot of low-level code. That's the difference, for instance, between the two versions of the `StoreCart.cfm` template (Listings 29.4 and 29.6).

In keeping with that notion, Listing 27.11 creates another Custom Tag, called `<CF_PlaceOrder>`. This tag is in charge of handling all aspects of accepting a new order from a customer, including:

- Inserting a new record into the `MerchandiseOrders` table
- Inserting one or more detail records into the `MerchandiseOrdersItems` table (one detail record for each item ordered)

- Attempting to charge the user's credit card, using the `<CF_ProcessPayment>` Custom Tag created in the previous section (refer to Listing 27.10)
- For a successful charge, sending an order-confirmation message to the user via email, using the `<CF_SendOrderConfirmation>` Custom Tag created in Chapter 26, "Interacting with Email"
- For an unsuccessful charge (because of an incorrect credit-card number, expiration date, or the like), ensuring that the just-inserted records from `MerchandiseOrders` and `MerchandiseOrdersItems` are not actually permanently committed to the database

Listing 27.11 `PlaceOrder.cfm`—Creating the `<CF_PlaceOrder>` Custom Tag

```
<!---
  Filename:     PlaceOrder.cfm (creates <CF_PlaceOrder> Custom Tag)
  Created by:   Nate Weiss (NMW)
  Please Note  Depends on <CF_ProcessPayment> and <CF_SendOrderConfirmation>
  Purpose:      Handles all operations related to placing a customer's order
--->

<!--- Tag Parameters --->
<CFPARAM NAME="ATTRIBUTES.Processor" TYPE="string" DEFAULT="PayflowPro">
<CFPARAM NAME="ATTRIBUTES.MerchList" TYPE="string">
<CFPARAM NAME="ATTRIBUTES.QuantList" TYPE="string">
<CFPARAM NAME="ATTRIBUTES.ContactID" TYPE="numeric">
<CFPARAM NAME="ATTRIBUTES.CreditCard" TYPE="string">
<CFPARAM NAME="ATTRIBUTES.CreditExpM" TYPE="string">
<CFPARAM NAME="ATTRIBUTES.CreditExpY" TYPE="string">
<CFPARAM NAME="ATTRIBUTES.CreditName" TYPE="string">
<CFPARAM NAME="ATTRIBUTES.ShipAddress" TYPE="string">
<CFPARAM NAME="ATTRIBUTES.ShipCity" TYPE="string">
<CFPARAM NAME="ATTRIBUTES.ShipCity" TYPE="string">
<CFPARAM NAME="ATTRIBUTES.ShipState" TYPE="string">
<CFPARAM NAME="ATTRIBUTES.ShipZIP" TYPE="string">
<CFPARAM NAME="ATTRIBUTES.ShipCountry" TYPE="string">
<CFPARAM NAME="ATTRIBUTES.HTMLMail" TYPE="boolean">
<CFPARAM NAME="ATTRIBUTES.ReturnVariable" TYPE="variableName">


<!--- Begin "order" database transaction here --->
<!--- Can be rolled back or committed later --->
<CFTRANSACTION ACTION="BEGIN">
  <!--- Insert new record into Orders table --->
  <CFQUERY DATASOURCE="#REQUEST.DataSource#">
    INSERT INTO MerchandiseOrders (
      ContactID,
      OrderDate,
      ShipAddress, ShipCity,
      ShipState, ShipZip,
      ShipCountry)
    VALUES (
      #ATTRIBUTES.ContactID#,
      <CFQUERYPARAM CFSQLTYPE="CF_SQL_TIMESTAMP"
        VALUE="#DateFormat(Now())# #TimeFormat(Now())#">,
      '#ATTRIBUTES.ShipAddress#', '#ATTRIBUTES.ShipCity#',
      '#ATTRIBUTES.ShipState#', '#ATTRIBUTES.ShipZip#',
```

Listing 27.11 (continued)

```
        '#ATTRIBUTES.ShipCountry#'
      )
    </CFQUERY>

    <!--- Get just-inserted OrderID from database --->
    <CFQUERY DATASOURCE="#REQUEST.DataSource#" NAME="GetNew">
      SELECT MAX(OrderID) AS NewID
      FROM MerchandiseOrders
    </CFQUERY>

    <!--- For each item in user's shopping cart --->
    <CFLOOP FROM="1" TO="#ListLen(ATTRIBUTES.MerchList)#" INDEX="i">
      <CFSET ThisMerchID = ListGetAt(ATTRIBUTES.MerchList, i)>
      <CFSET ThisQuant   = ListGetAt(ATTRIBUTES.QuantList, i)>

      <!--- Add the item to "OrdersItems" table --->
      <CFQUERY DATASOURCE="#REQUEST.DataSource#">
        INSERT INTO MerchandiseOrdersItems
          (OrderID, ItemID, OrderQty, ItemPrice)
        SELECT
          #GetNew.NewID#, MerchID, #ThisQuant#, MerchPrice
        FROM Merchandise
        WHERE MerchID = #ThisMerchID#
      </CFQUERY>
    </CFLOOP>

    <!--- Get the total of all items in user's cart --->
    <CFQUERY DATASOURCE="#REQUEST.DataSource#" NAME="GetTotal">
      SELECT SUM(ItemPrice * OrderQty) AS OrderTotal
      FROM MerchandiseOrdersItems
      WHERE OrderID = #GetNew.NewID#
    </CFQUERY>

    <!--- Attempt to process the transaction  --->
    <CF_ProcessPayment
      Processor="#ATTRIBUTES.Processor#"
      OrderID="#GetNew.NewID#"
      OrderAmount="#GetTotal.OrderTotal#"
      CreditCard="#ATTRIBUTES.CreditCard#"
      CreditExpM="#ATTRIBUTES.CreditExpM#"
      CreditExpY="#ATTRIBUTES.CreditExpY#"
      CreditName="#ATTRIBUTES.CreditName#"
      ReturnVariable="ChargeInfo">

    <!--- If the order was processed successfully --->
    <CFIF ChargeInfo.IsSuccessful>
      <!--- Commit the transaction to database --->
      <CFTRANSACTION ACTION="Commit"/>
    <CFELSE>
      <!--- Rollback the Order from the Database --->
      <CFTRANSACTION ACTION="RollBack"/>
    </CFIF>
  </CFTRANSACTION>


  <!--- If the order was processed successfully --->
  <CFIF ChargeInfo.IsSuccessful>
```

Listing 27.11 (continued)

```
    <!--- Send Confirmation E-Mail, via Custom Tag --->
    <CF_SendOrderConfirmation
      OrderID="#GetNew.NewID#"
      UseHTML="#ATTRIBUTES.HTMLMail#">
  </CFIF>

  <!--- Return status values to callling template --->
  <CFSET "Caller.#ATTRIBUTES.ReturnVariable#" = ChargeInfo>
```

At the top of the template is a rather large number of `<CFPARAM>` tags that define the various attributes for the `<CF_PlaceOrder>` Custom Tag. The `Processor`, `ReturnVariable`, and four `Credit` attributes are passed directly to `<CF_ProcessPayment>`. The `MerchList` and `QuantList` attributes specify which item is actually being ordered, in the same comma-separated format that the `CLIENT` variables use in Listing 27.4. The `ContactID` and the six `Ship` attributes are needed for the `MerchandiseOrders` table. The `HTMLMail` attribute sends an email confirmation to the user if the payment is successful.

After the tag attributes have been defined, a large `<CFTRANSACTION>` block starts. The `<CFTRANSACTION>` tag is ColdFusion's representation of a database transaction. You saw it in action in Chapter 13, "Using Forms to Add or Change Data," and you will learn about it more formally in Chapter 29, "More On SQL and Queries," and Chapter 31, "Error Handling." The `<CFTRANSACTION>` tag tells the database to consider all queries and other database operations within the block as a single transaction, which other operations cannot interrupt.

The use of `<CFTRANSACTION>` in this template accomplishes two things. First, it makes sure that no other records are inserted between the first `INSERT` query and the `GetNew` query that comes right after it. This in turn ensures that the ID number retrieved by the `GetNew` query is indeed the correct one, rather than a record some other process inserted. Second, the `<CFTRANSACTION>` tag allows any database changes (inserts, deletes, or updates) to be rolled back if some kind of problem occurs. A rollback is basically the database equivalent of the Undo function in a word processor—it undoes all changes, leaving the database in the same state as at the start of the transaction. Here, the transaction is rolled back if the credit-card transaction fails (perhaps because of an incorrect credit-card number), which means that all traces of the new order will be removed from the database.

After the opening `<CFTRANSACTION>` tag, the following actions are taken:

1. A new order record is inserted into the `MerchandiseOrders` table.
2. The `GetNew` query obtains the `OrderID` number for the just-inserted order record.
3. A simple `<CFLOOP>` tag inserts one record into the MerchandiseOrdersItems table for each item supplied to the `MerchList` attribute. Each record includes the new `OrderID`, the appropriate quantity from the `QuantList` attribute, and the current price for the item (as listed in the Merchandise table). (The `INSERT/SELECT` syntax used here is explained in Chapter 29.)
4. The `GetTotal` query obtains the total price of the items purchased by adding up the price of each item times its quantity.
5. The `<CF_ProcessPayment>` tag (refer to Listing 27.10) attempts to process the credit-card transaction. The structure of payment-status information is returned as a structure named `ChargeInfo`.

6. If the charge was successful, the database transaction is committed by using the `<CFTRANSACTION>` tag with `ACTION="Commit"`. This permanently saves the inserted records in the database and ends the transaction.
7. If the charge was not successful, the database transaction is rolled back with a `<CFTRANSACTION>` tag of `ACTION="RollBack"`. This permanently removes the inserted records from the database and ends the transaction.
8. If the charge was successful, a confirmation email message is sent to the user, using the `<CF_SendOrderConfirmation>` Custom Tag from Chapter 26. Because this tag performs database interactions of its own, it should sit outside the `<CFTRANSACTION>` block.
9. Finally, the `ChargeInfo` structure returned by `<CF_PlaceOrder>` is passed back to the calling template so it can understand whether the order was placed successfully.

Creating the Checkout Page

Now that you've created the `<CF_PlaceOrder>` Custom Tag, actually creating the Checkout page for Orange Whip Studios' visitors is a simple task. Listing 27.12 provides the code for the `StoreCheckout.cfm` page, which users can access via the Checkout link at the top of each page in the online store or by clicking the Checkout button on the `StoreCart.cfm` page (refer to Figure 27.2).

Listing 27.12 `StoreCheckout.cfm`—Allowing the User to Complete the Online Transaction

```
<!---
  Filename:     StoreCheckout.cfm (save with Chapter 27's listings)
  Created by:   Nate Weiss (NMW)
  Purpose:      Provides final Checkout/Payment page
  Please Note  Depends on <CF_PlaceOrder> and StoreCheckoutForm.cfm
--->

<!--- Show header images, etc., for Online Store --->
<CFINCLUDE TEMPLATE="StoreHeader.cfm">

<!--- Get current cart contents, as a query object --->
<CFSET GetCart = SESSION.MyShoppingCart.List()>

<!--- Stop here if user's cart is empty --->
<CFIF GetCart.RecordCount EQ 0>
  There is nothing in your cart.
  <CFABORT>
</CFIF>

<!--- If user is not logged in, force them to now --->
<CFIF NOT IsDefined("SESSION.Auth.IsLoggedIn")>
  <CFINCLUDE TEMPLATE="LoginForm.cfm">
  <CFABORT>
</CFIF>

<!--- If user is attempting to place order --->
<CFIF IsDefined("FORM.IsPlacingOrder")>

  <CFTRY>
```

Listing 27.12 (continued)

```
    <!--- Attempt to process the transaction  --->
    <CF_PlaceOrder
      Processor="JustTesting" <!--- Change to PayflowPro to use VeriSign --->
      ContactID="#SESSION.Auth.ContactID#"
      MerchList="#ValueList(GetCart.MerchID)#"
      QuantList="#ValueList(GetCart.Quantity)#"
      CreditCard="#FORM.CreditCard#"
      CreditExpM="#FORM.CreditExpM#"
      CreditExpY="#FORM.CreditExpY#"
      CreditName="#FORM.CreditName#"
      ShipAddress="#FORM.ShipAddress#"
      ShipState="#FORM.ShipState#"
      ShipCity="#FORM.ShipCity#"
      ShipZIP="#FORM.ShipZIP#"
      ShipCountry="#FORM.ShipCountry#"
      HTMLMail="#FORM.HTMLMail#"
      ReturnVariable="OrderInfo">

    <!--- If any exceptions in the "ows.MerchOrder" family are thrown... --->
    <CFCATCH TYPE="ows.MerchOrder">
      <P>Unfortunately, we are not able to process your order at the moment.<BR>
      Please try again later.  We apologize for the inconvenience.<BR>
      <CFABORT>
    </CFCATCH>
  </CFTRY>


  <!--- If the order was processed successfully --->
  <CFIF OrderInfo.IsSuccessful>

    <!--- Empty user's shopping cart, via custom tag --->
    <CF_ShoppingCart
      ACTION="Empty">

    <!--- Display Success Message --->
    <CFOUTPUT>
      <H2>Thanks For Your Order</H2>
      <P><B>Your Order Has Been Placed.</B><BR>
      Your order number is: #OrderInfo.OrderID#<BR>
      Your credit card has been charged:
      #LSCurrencyFormat(OrderInfo.OrderAmount)#<BR>
      <P>A confirmation is being Emailed to you.<BR>
    </CFOUTPUT>

    <!--- Stop here. --->
    <CFABORT>
  <CFELSE>
    <!--- Display "Error" message --->
    <FONT COLOR="Red">
      <STRONG>Your credit card could not be processed.</STRONG><BR>
      Please verify the credit card number, expiration date, and
      name on the card.<BR>
    </FONT>

    <!--- Show debug info if viewing page on server --->
```

Listing 27.12 (continued)

```
      <CFTRACE
        Inline="True"
        Var="OrderInfo">
    </CFIF>
  </CFIF>


  <!--- Show Checkout Form (Ship Address/Credit Card) --->
  <CFINCLUDE TEMPLATE="StoreCheckoutForm.cfm">
```

First, the standard page header for the online store is displayed with the `<CFINCLUDE>` tag at the top of Listing 27.12. Next, the `List` method of the `ShoppingCart` CFC gets the current contents of the user's cart. If `GetCart.RecordCount` is `0`, the user's cart must be empty, so the template displays a short your-cart-is-empty message and stops further processing. Next, the template ensures that the user has logged in, using the same `<CFINCLUDE>` file developed in Chapter 18.

Of course, if you want to use the client variable–based `<CF_ShoppingCart>` Custom Tag instead of the session variable–based `ShoppingCart` CFC, you can easily do so by changing the first `<CFSET>` line (near the top of Listing 27.12) to this:

```
<!--- Get current cart contents, as a query object --->
<CF_ShoppingCart
  Action="List"
  ReturnVariable="GetCart">
```

At the bottom of the template, a `<CFINCLUDE>` tag includes the form shown in Figure 27.4, which asks the user for shipping and credit-card information. The form is self-submitting, so when the user clicks the Place Order Now button, the code in Listing 27.12 is executed again. This is when the large `<CFIF>` block kicks in.

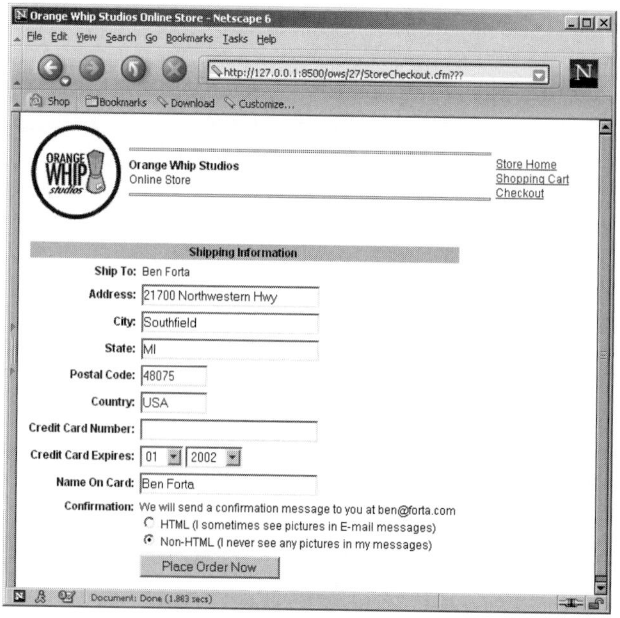

Figure 27.4

Users provide credit-card information on the Checkout page.

Within the <CFIF> block, the <CF_PlaceOrder> tag attempts to complete the user's order. If all goes well, the order will be committed to the database, the confirmation email message will be sent, the `OrderInfo.IsSuccessful` value will be `True`, and the new order's ID number will be returned as `OrderInfo.OrderID`.

If the order is actually successful, the user's cart is emptied using a final call to <CF_ShoppingCart>, and a thanks-for-your-order message appears, as shown in Figure 27.5. If not, an error message appears and the checkout form (see Listing 27.13) is displayed again. Also, the <CFTRACE> tag displays additional diagnostic information if the debugging options are on in the ColdFusion Administrator.

Listing 27.13 is the `StoreCheckoutForm.cfm` template included via the <CFINCLUDE> tag at the bottom of Listing 27.12. This template uses <CFFORM> and <CFINPUT> to display a Web-based form with some simple data validation (such as the `VALIDATE="creditcard"` attribute for the `CreditCard` field). As a convenience to the user, it prefills the shipping-address fields based on the address information currently in the `Contacts` table. The resulting form was shown in Figure 27.4.

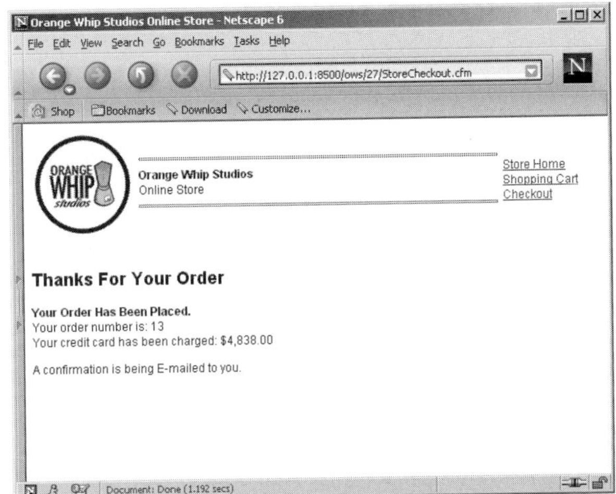

Figure 27.5 Credit-card numbers can be verified and charged in real time to facilitate immediate confirmation of orders.

Listing 27.13 `StoreCheckoutForm.cfm`—Collecting Shipping and Credit-Card Information from the User

```
<!---
  Filename:     StoreCheckoutForm.cfm
  Created by:   Nate Weiss (NMW)
  Please Note  Included by StoreCheckout.cfm
  Purpose:      Displays a simple checkout form
--->

<!--- Get the user's contact info from database --->
<CFQUERY NAME="GetContact" DATASOURCE="#REQUEST.DataSource#">
  SELECT
    FirstName, LastName, Address,
    City, State, Zip, Country, Email
  FROM Contacts
  WHERE ContactID = #SESSION.Auth.ContactID#
```

Listing 27.13 (CONTINUED)

```
</CFQUERY>

<!--- Used to pre-fill user's choice of HTML or Plain email --->
<CFPARAM NAME="FORM.HTMLMail" TYPE="string" DEFAULT="Yes">


<CFOUTPUT>
  <CFFORM ACTION="#CGI.SCRIPT_NAME#" METHOD="POST" PRESERVEDATA="Yes">
    <INPUT TYPE="Hidden" NAME="IsPlacingOrder" VALUE="Yes">

    <TABLE BORDER="0" CELLSPACING="4">
      <TR>
        <TH COLSPAN="2" BGCOLOR="Silver">Shipping Information</TH>
      </TR>

      <TR>
        <TH ALIGN="right">Ship To:</TH>
        <TD>
          #GetContact.FirstName# #GetContact.LastName#
        </TD>
      </TR>
      <TR>
        <TH ALIGN="right">Address:</TH>
        <TD>
          <CFINPUT
            NAME="ShipAddress" SIZE="30"
            REQUIRED="Yes" VALUE="#GetContact.Address#"
            MESSAGE="Please don't leave the Address blank!">
        </TD>
      </TR>
      <TR>
        <TH ALIGN="right">City:</TH>
        <TD>
          <CFINPUT
            NAME="ShipCity" SIZE="30"
            REQUIRED="Yes" VALUE="#GetContact.City#"
            MESSAGE="Please don't leave the City blank!">
        </TD>
      </TR>
      <TR>
        <TH ALIGN="right">State:</TH>
        <TD>
          <CFINPUT
            NAME="ShipState" SIZE="30"
            REQUIRED="Yes" VALUE="#GetContact.State#"
            MESSAGE="Please don't leave the State blank!">
        </TD>
      </TR>
      <TR>
        <TH ALIGN="right">Postal Code:</TH>
        <TD>
          <CFINPUT
            NAME="ShipZIP" SIZE="10"
            REQUIRED="Yes" VALUE="#GetContact.ZIP#"
            MESSAGE="Please don't leave the ZIP blank!">
        </TD>
```

Listing 27.13 (continued)

```
</TR>
<TR>
  <TH ALIGN="right">Country:</TH>
  <TD>
    <CFINPUT
      NAME="ShipCountry" SIZE="10"
      REQUIRED="Yes" VALUE="#GetContact.Country#"
      MESSAGE="Please don't leave the Country blank!">
  </TD>
</TR>
<TR>
  <TH ALIGN="right">Credit Card Number:</TH>
  <TD>
    <CFINPUT
      NAME="CreditCard" SIZE="30"
      REQUIRED="Yes" VALIDATE="creditcard"
      MESSAGE="You must provide a credit card number.">
  </TD>
</TR>
<TR>
  <TH ALIGN="right">Credit Card Expires:</TH>
  <TD>
    <SELECT NAME="CreditExpM">
      <CFLOOP FROM="1" TO="12" INDEX="i">
        <OPTION VALUE="#i#">#NumberFormat(i, "00")#
      </CFLOOP>
    </SELECT>
    <SELECT NAME="CreditExpY">
      <CFLOOP FROM="#Year(Now())#" TO="#Val(Year(Now())+10)#" INDEX="i">
        <OPTION VALUE="#i#">#i#
      </CFLOOP>
    </SELECT>
  </TD>
</TR>
<TR>
  <TH ALIGN="right">Name On Card:</TH>
  <TD>
    <CFINPUT
      NAME="CreditName" SIZE="30" REQUIRED="Yes"
      VALUE="#GetContact.FirstName# #GetContact.LastName#"
      MESSAGE="You must provide the Name on the Credit Card.">
  </TD>
</TR>
<TR VALIGN="baseline">
  <TH ALIGN="right">Confirmation:</TH>
  <TD>
    We will send a confirmation message to you at
    #GetContact.EMail#<BR>
    <INPUT TYPE="RADIO" NAME="HTMLMail" VALUE="Yes"
      <CFIF FORM.HTMLMail EQ "Yes">CHECKED</CFIF>>
    HTML (I sometimes see pictures in Email messages)<BR>
    <INPUT TYPE="Radio" NAME="HTMLMail" VALUE="No"
      <CFIF FORM.HTMLMail EQ "No">CHECKED</CFIF>>
    Non-HTML (I never see any pictures in my messages)<BR>
  </TD>
```

Listing 27.13 (continued)

```
        </TR>
        <TR>
          <TD></TD>
          <TD>
            <INPUT TYPE="Submit" VALUE="Place Order Now">
          </TD>
        </TR>
      </TABLE>

    </CFFORM>
  </CFOUTPUT>
```

The online store for Orange Whip Studios is now complete. Users can add items to their shopping carts, adjust quantities, remove items, and check out. And all the code has been abstracted in a reasonable and maintainable fashion, thanks to ColdFusion's wonderful Custom Tag feature.

Other Commerce-Related Tasks

For a real-world online commerce site, your application pages will need to take care of some other tasks. This book doesn't cover these tasks explicitly, but they should be well within your reach now that you have been introduced to the basic concepts and have walked through the construction of the main shopping experience for your users.

Order Tracking

Most users who place orders online will expect some mechanism to allow them to check the status of their orders, and they generally expect that mechanism to be online. Depending on what your site sells, simply making an email address available for status inquiries might be enough. However, some type of secure order-tracking page will usually satisfy more people and cut down on support costs.

The `OrderHistory.cfm` templates from Chapter 18 are a great start. You would just need to ensure that the user has a way to see the `ShipDate` as well as the `OrderDate`, and you might even add a button the user could use to cancel an order.

Order Fulfillment

This chapter hasn't even touched upon the notion of actually fulfilling an order after it has been placed. How this works will depend entirely on the company for which you are building your commerce application. For instance, you might provide an Order Queue page for employees in Orange Whip Studios' shipping department. This Order Queue page could be similar to the `OrderHistory.cfm` templates (see the previous section, "Order Tracking"), except that it would show all pending orders, not just the ones for a particular user.

Or you might decide that an email message should be sent to the shipping department using the `<CFMAIL>` tag. If your company's needs are simple, it might be sufficient to simply `BCC` the shipping department on the email message sent by the `<CF_SendOrderConfirmation>` Custom Tag from Chapter 26.

Cancellations, Returns, and Refunds

If you are taking money from your visitors, there is always the possibility that you will need to give some of it back at some point. You must ensure that your company has some means for dealing with returns and refunds, including the ability to credit back any charges made to the user's credit card.

You might build your own Web-based interface for refunds and cancellations, using the `<CF_VerisignPayflowPro>` tag (which does support items such as refunds), if that is the payment-processing mechanism you are using. Many payment-processing services provide their own Web-based systems, which your company's accounting or customer service departments can use to handle such special cases.

Inventory Tracking

The examples in this chapter assume that all items in the `Merchandise` table are always available for sale. Orange Whip Studios might not need to be concerned about its merchandise ever selling out, but your company probably does. At a minimum, you should probably add an `InStock` Boolean field to the `Merchandise` table and ensure that users can't add items to their carts unless the `InStock` field is `1`. More sophisticated applications might call for maintaining a `NumberOnHand` field for each item, which gets decremented each time an item is ordered and incremented each time new shipments come in from the supplier.

Reporting

Of course, once a company is doing business online, it will need to know how much business its online store is generating. You should supply your company's executives with some type of reporting functionality that shows purchase trends over time, which products are profitable, and so on. To build such reports, you could use Crystal Reports with the `<CFREPORT>` tag (see Appendix B, "ColdFusion Tag Reference") or build your own reporting templates, perhaps illustrating the data visually using ColdFusion's dynamic graphing and charting capabilities (see Chapter 25, "Graphing").

PART 4

Enhancing Forms with Client-Side Java

IN THIS PART

CHAPTER 28

ColdFusion Server Configuration

IN THIS CHAPTER

The ColdFusion Administrator

The ColdFusion Administrator is a Web-based console that gives you an easy way to adjust the way ColdFusion MX behaves. Macromedia graciously provides this simple, straightforward Administrator so that we developers don't have to fiddle around with configuration files or registry settings to get ColdFusion to behave the way we need it to.

Because the Administrator is Web-based, you can use it to monitor and configure your ColdFusion MX server from nearly anywhere, armed with nothing more than a browser and a password.

Most parts of the Administrator are about the following:

- Tweaking and monitoring the server's performance
- Telling ColdFusion where to find various external resources, such as databases, Verity full-text search collections, and mail servers
- Installing extensions to the CFML language, in the form of CFX tags, Web Services, CORBA connectors, and Java applets
- Administrative tasks, such as backing up applications, reviewing log files, and securing portions of the server

This chapter will walk you through each part of the ColdFusion Administrator, explaining the purpose of each setting, and making some recommendations along the way. Let's begin.

Launching the ColdFusion Administrator

To enter the ColdFusion Administrator, just visit its URL with your Web browser. Of course, the URL needs to contain the host name or IP address for the ColdFusion server that you wish to configure. If ColdFusion is installed on your local machine, you would use this URL:

```
http://localhost/CFIDE/administrator
```

Or, if you installed ColdFusion in standalone mode, then you need to include the `:8500` port number part, like so:

```
http://localhost:8500/CFIDE/administrator
```

Or, if you wanted to configure the ColdFusion server at Orange Whip Studios, you might use the following URL:

```
http://www.orangewhipstudios.com/CFIDE/administrator
```

TIP

If you installed ColdFusion on a Windows machine, an Administrator shortcut was placed in the Macromedia ColdFusion MX program group (within the Windows Start menu) during installation. You can just use that shortcut to start the Administrator.

TIP

Of course, you can create a browser bookmark to the ColdFusion Administrator, just like any other Web page. If you are using Internet Explorer, you might want to the ColdFusion Administrator to your Links Toolbar so its always just a click away.

When you visit the ColdFusion Administrator for the first time during your browser session, you will be asked to log in (Figure 28.1). Just supply the ColdFusion Administrator password that you selected while ColdFusion was being installed.

NOTE

The password is case sensitive, so make sure you enter it exactly as it was originally provided.

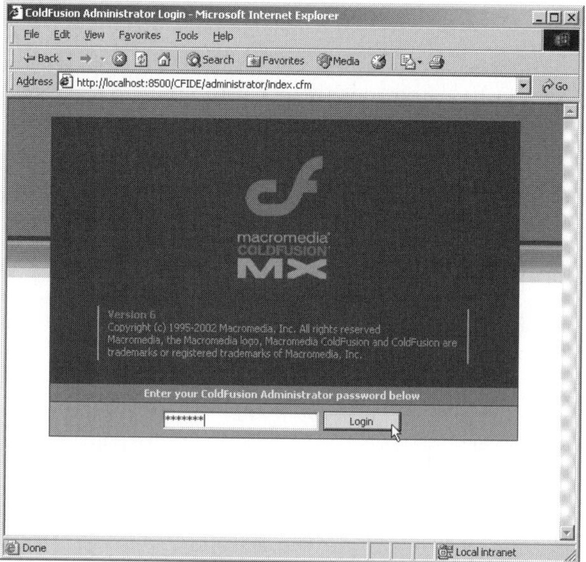

Figure 28.1

To enter the ColdFusion Administrator, provide the password you chose during installation.

The Administrator Home Page

Once you log in, the Administrator's home page appears (Figure 28.2). As you can see, the Administrator is designed much like many other Web interfaces, with a toolbar along the top and a navigation column along the left hand side. The main area of the page is a collection of helpful links to various online resources related to ColdFusion and the CFML developer community.

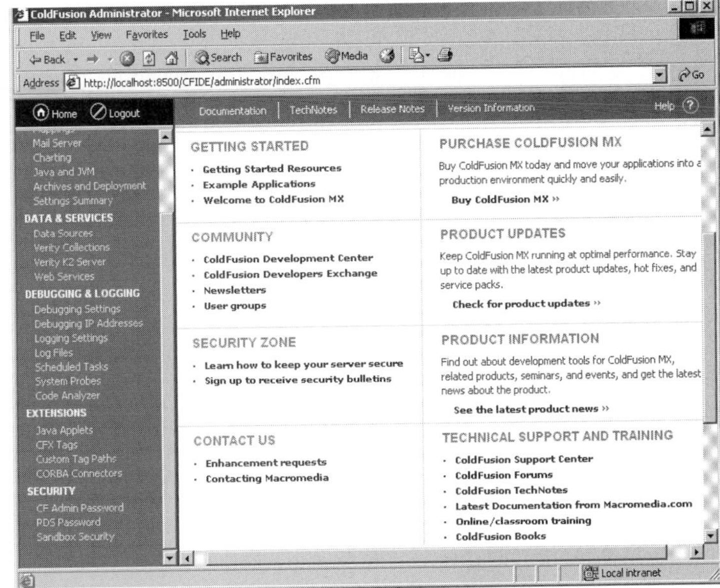

Figure 28.2

The home page of the ColdFusion Administrator is packed with useful links.

Some of the links you'll find here are:

- The ColdFusion Support Forums, where you can exchange questions, answers, problems and solutions with other ColdFusion developers everywhere. You'll find that the ColdFusion developer community is quite a helpful and responsive bunch.
- The ColdFusion Development Center, which contains all sorts of articles, tutorials, downloadable code snippets, and other information sure to be of interest to ColdFusion developers.
- Macromedia's Security Zone, where is where security bulletins, patches, or other security-related materials and links will be made available.
- Support and training, in the form of phone technical support from Macromedia, online and classroom training, and books about ColdFusion. Of course, you're already pretty well covered in terms of the book part.

Let's take a moment for a quick look at the various navigation elements always available within the ColdFusion Administrator:

- **Home and Logout**. At the top left corner, you will find Home and Logout links. Home will always return you to the Administrator home page shown in Figure 28.2, and Logout will log you out and return you to the login page shown in Figure 28.1.
- **Left Navigation Column**. Along the left hand side, you will find quite a few links to the various pages within the Administrator, grouped under the headings Server Settings, Data & Services, Debugging & Logging, Extensions, and Security. This chapter will walk you through each of these pages, one at a time.

- **Documentation.** The blue Documentation link at the top of the page brings you to a handy, online version of the ColdFusion MX documentation set, including an online CFML reference. The documentation is fully searchable.
- **TechNotes and Release Notes**. Links for TechNotes and Release Notes also appear at the top of the page. Both of these links will bring you to the Macromedia website. The TechNotes link is particularly handy, since Macromedia frequently publishes new TechNotes (short articles) on various topics such as frequently asked programming questions, security, and so on.
- **Version Information.** The blue Version Information link at the top of the page will display a summary page that shows the exact version number and build number of ColdFusion MX that you are using, as well as information about the Java Virtual Machine that ColdFusion is running under. If you originally installed the trial version of ColdFusion and have just purchased a license, this page is where you enter your new license number (Figure 28.3).

TIP

If you get confused at any time during your visit to the ColdFusion Administrator, the Help link at the top right corner of the screen will provide you with context-sensitive help about whatever Administrator page you happen to be on.

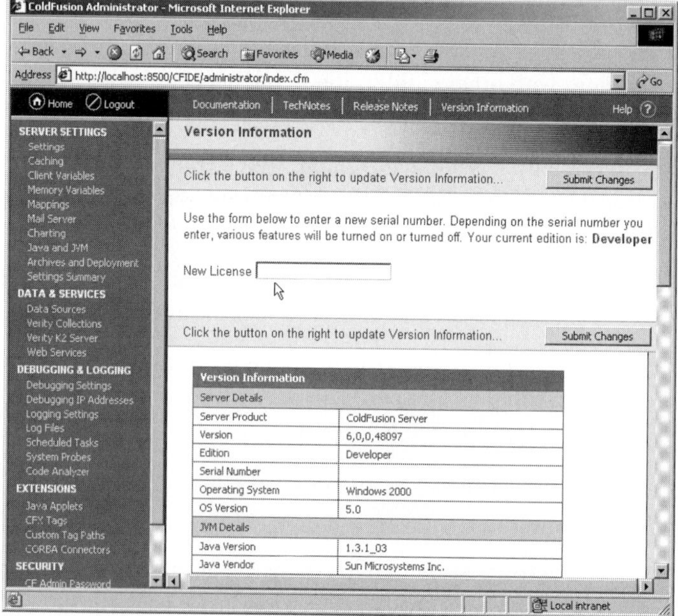

Figure 28.3

After purchasing a license for ColdFusion, enter your new serial number here.

Server Settings

Let's begin our page by page tour of the ColdFusion Administrator with the Server Settings section, which makes up the first part of the left-hand navigation column. The pages in this section pertain mostly to tweaking the server's performance. Aside from the Data Sources page in the next section, this is the most important portion of the ColdFusion Administrator, and the part that you will probably become most familiar with.

The Settings Page

The Settings page (Figure 28.4) contains various options related to tweaking the server's performance and responsiveness to page requests from your users. It also contains options for controlling what happens when errors occur.

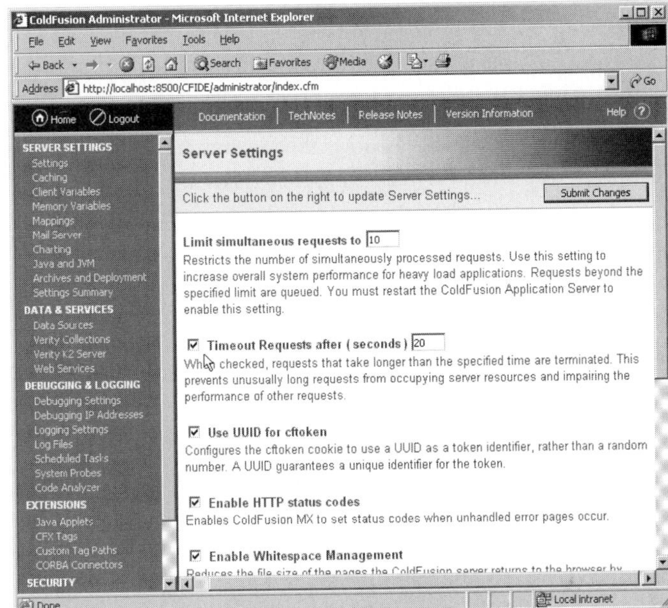

Figure 28.4

The Settings page is for tweaking performance and error handling options.

Limit simultaneous requests to

NOTE

This first option is important and a bit challenging conceptually, so I will spend the next page or so to explain it. Don't worry, not all of the Administrator options require this much explanation! :)

ColdFusion is fast and efficient, but it obviously can't handle an absolutely unlimited amount of page requests at once. At some point, any server will become overwhelmed if it tries to serve too many users at once. This setting allows you to tweak your server's performance by adjusting the maximum number of page requests that it is willing to process at the same moment in time.

NOTE

If you change this setting, you need to restart the ColdFusion MX Application Server for the changes to take effect.

To understand this setting, let's use a metaphor. Let's say your ColdFusion Server is a short-order cook in a busy downtown diner. This cook, who goes by the name of Gus, is new to the job and can handle five orders (page requests) at a time efficiently. However, at lunch hour, when office workers crowd the diner, Gus is suddenly flooded with twenty orders at a time. Bewildered by the avalanche of orders, Gus tries to fill all the orders at once. Unfortunately, because of his lack of experience, Gus's efficiency plunges, all the orders take longer, and the diner patrons become impatient.

Gus knows that if he had more experience, or if the kitchen were better organized, he could handle more orders at one time. Oh well. Gus can think on his feet though, and has a clever idea. He instructs the waitresses to herd the hungry patrons into one line and take five orders at a time. That way, Gus stays at peak efficiency and can cook the maximum number of orders.

I suppose you can see where this metaphor is going. Of course, Gus is analogous to the ColdFusion server, the lunch orders are like requests for ColdFusion pages, and Gus's customers are like your application's users. Gus is able to improve the efficiency of his kitchen because he understands the maximum number of lunch orders he can handle at once.

That's really important. Gus somehow knows the maximum number of orders he can work on at once without slowing way down. When it comes to this setting in the ColdFusion Administrator, the trick is to figure out the number of page requests that your server can process at once before it slows way down.

Because this setting can have a big impact on an application's performance, it would be nice if there was a hard and fast rule that you could use to determine the best value to provide. Unfortunately, there is no hard and fast rule. To understand why, let's think some more about Gus's situation.

Gus can limit the number of simultaneous orders to five, but unfortunately he can't tell ahead of time what the customers are actually going to order. If three or four out of five particular orders are really complicated, his efficiency will still go down; he really ought to take fewer orders at once for a while. On the other hand, if the next five orders are really simple, his efficiency will go back up. Also, if Gus gets a new stove (which might be like getting a new processor for your server), or more counter space installed (which might be like getting more RAM), or moves the refrigerator closer to the stove (which might be like getting a faster connection to your databases), his efficiency will go up and he could start taking more orders at once. If the kitchen deteriorates or becomes cluttered (like an aging hard drive or poor network connection), his efficiency will go down.

So, Gus's efficiency, and thus the maximum number of orders he should process, relies upon two main factors:

- The nature of the lunch orders
- The nature of his working environment

When talking about the ColdFusion server's efficiency, the maximum number of pages it should process simultaneously relies upon two main analogous factors:

- The complexity of the pages being requested
- The physical capacity of your server

Gus's level of experience directly translates into your server's hardware specifications. The more powerful your hardware, such as a greater amount of RAM, faster processors, quicker hard drives, and faster network connections to your databases, the more requests it can handle at one time.

Therefore, depending on your hardware specifications, reducing the number of requests forces ColdFusion to devote its resources to a small number of tasks, thus executing all tasks more quickly. If you think your server can handle more requests, try your ColdFusion applications with the increased setting under load in a staging environment.

Here are some helpful rules of thumb:

1. Start with a value of 5, which is a pretty reasonable starting point.
2. If your server has more than one processor, it is reasonable to assume that it will be able to handle more requests at once. Add more requests (perhaps around 5) for each processor.
3. If your server really kicks some serious butt in some other way, like amount or type of RAM, type or number of disk controllers, network connections, or other physical characteristics, increase the number of simultaneous requests per processor. If the server is starting to show its age, lower the number.
4. If all of your pages execute very quickly during development, then you can probably increase the number a bit further per processor. On the other hand, if they take more than a second or two to complete their work, even when the server is not under load, then you should decrease the number.
5. If most of your pages are very fast, but there are a small number of pages that you know will take a long time to execute because of their very nature, then you should probably increase the number of simultaneous requests (so that the fast pages aren't blocked by the slow pages at runtime). In addition, you could use the `<CFLOCK>` tag to make sure that a large number of the slow pages aren't allowed to execute all at once. For instance, you could place a `<CFLOCK>` tag with `NAME="VerySlowProcess"` and `TYPE="Exclusive"` attributes around code that you know will be time consuming or just generally hard on the server. See Chapter 16, Introducing the Web Application Framework, for more information about locking.
6. If your application uses shared variables, especially `APPLICATION` variables, in such a way that you often need to request an exclusive lock to protect against race conditions, then you will probably want to decrease the number of simultaneous requests (so that fewer locks actually block one another at runtime). See Chapter 16, Introducing the Web Application Framework, for more information about race conditions.

NOTE

This setting is not available in the ColdFusion MX for J2EE Application Servers version of ColdFusion, which means that it won't be available if you are running ColdFusion under IBM WebSphere, BEA WebLogic, or Sun ONE Application Server. It is available only for ColdFusion MX installations that use Macromedia JRun as the underlying engine (that includes the traditional Professional or Enterprise editions). It modifies an underlying setting in the jrun.xml configuration file which tells JRun how many concurrent threads to use.

Timeout requests after (seconds)

This setting brings us back to Gus for a moment (bear with me). Let's say that Gus is doing his usual thing, working on five orders at once. But, for whatever reason, one of the orders is taking way longer than usual (maybe he burned a burger, or dropped an order of fries on the ground, or ran out of egg salad and so has started making more). That order is taking up all of Gus's resources, keeping him from being able to start on the next person's order.

Always wanting to be more efficient, Gus puts a new policy into place. If any order takes him longer than 3 minutes to complete, he'll simply throw it away and forget about it! This will irritate the person who was waiting for that order, but it will allow him to complete more orders overall.

Again, the analogy is pretty clear here. If you want to make sure that ColdFusion spends no more than twenty or thirty seconds working on a particular page request, go ahead and check the Timeout requests after checkbox, and provide the appropriate value for the number of seconds. If a page takes longer than the number of seconds you specify, the page will simply halt and display an error message.

I strongly suggest that you enable this option, and set it to a relatively low number to start off with, perhaps `20` or `30`. The idea is that any page that takes longer than twenty or thirty seconds has probably encountered some kind of serious problem (perhaps an unresponsive database) and thus won't be able to produce the desired output anyway, so it might as well be cut off so the server can move on to other page requests which will hopefully be easier for it to generate quickly.

You can override the request timeout you provide for this setting on a page-by-page basis. Just use the `<CFSETTING>` tag, specifying the maximum number of seconds that you would like the page to be allowed to execute as the `REQUESTTIMEOUT` attribute. This use of `<CFSETTING>` allows you to provide a reasonably short timeout value in the Administrator, while still allowing certain pages (which you know really should take a while) to run for as long as they need to. For instance, if you wanted a particular page to run for up to five minutes (perhaps it performs a large file transfer operation with `<CFFTP>`), you would use the following code, near at the top of the page:

```
<!--- Allow this page to execute for up to five minutes --->
<CFSETTING
  REQUESTTIMEOUT="300">
```

Keep in mind, however, that a long-running page could block other pages from executing. If you have set the maximum number of simultaneous requests to 10 (as discussed in the previous section), and ten different page requests for the page with the `<CFSETTING>` shown above were received around the same time, then the server would essentially unable to respond to any other page requests for up to five whole minutes. You might, therefore, want to use the `<CFLOCK>` tag to make sure that only one instance of the long-running page is able to execute at the same time. You would use `<CFLOCK>` attribute with a `NAME` attribute that was unique to that particular ColdFusion file, like this:

```
<CFTRY>
  <CFLOCK
    NAME="MyLongRunningFTPTransferPage"
    TYPE="EXCLUSIVE"
    TIMEOUT="30">

    <!--- Allow this page to execute for up to five minutes --->
    <CFSETTING
      REQUESTTIMEOUT="300">

    <!---
      ...long running code would go here...
    --->
  </CFLOCK>
```

```
  <!--- If the lock can't be obtained, display a message and stop --->
  <CFCATCH TYPE="Lock">
    Sorry, but another user is currently using this page.
    Because this page is hard on the server, only one person is
    allowed to execute it at once. Please try again in a few minutes.
    <CFABORT>
  </CFCATCH>
</CFTRY>
```

Alternatively, you could use a NAME value that was the same for all long-running pages; this would ensure that only one of the long-running pages was allowed to execute at one time. For more information about <CFSETTING>, see Appendix B, ColdFusion Tag Reference. For more information about <CFLOCK>, see Chapter 16, "Introducing the Web Application Framework."

NOTE

Of course, you can customize the look of the error message that appears if a page takes longer than the number of seconds you specify. See the Site-Wide Error Handler setting, later in this section, and the discussion of the <CFERROR> tag in Chapter 16, "Introducing the Web Application Framework."

Use UUID for cftoken

As you learned in Chapter 17, Working with Sessions, ColdFusion uses values called CFID and CFTOKEN to identify each browser machine. The CFTOKEN value is used as a kind of password that allows each user to be connected to their client variables on the server. In addition, this value is also used (in concert with the notion of a session timeout) to connect each user with their session variables on the server.

Historically, ColdFusion used a random number for the CFTOKEN value. You can use this option to have ColdFusion use a universally unique identifier (UUID) instead, which will guarantee that the CFTOKEN is unique, even across multiple servers in a cluster.

While it is rather unlikely that this value will have a real world impact on your application, it is safer to enable this setting if possible. I recommend that you go ahead and enable this option unless you have an existing application that uses the CFTOKEN internally in some manner and depends on it being a number.

NOTE

If you need to be able to generate unique identifiers for your own use within your application, you can use the CreateUUID() function. See Appendix C, ColdFusion Function Reference, for details.

Enable HTTP status codes

This setting allows ColdFusion to return true HTTP status codes in the header of its response if an unexpected error occurs. For instance, if a user requests a ColdFusion page that doesn't exist on the server, ColdFusion will be able to return a true error message (HTTP status code number 404) that other machines can understand to mean not found. If this option is unchecked, ColdFusion would simply display a page that contained a message saying the page could not be found in English (which is fine for humans but not so helpful for proxy servers, search engines, or machines trying to access Web Services on your server).

Similarly, if ColdFusion needs to report an error message, the HTTP status code of the server's response will be set to 500 if this option is checked. If left unchecked, the error message is displayed, but the status code remains set to the normal HTTP status code, 200, which means that other automated systems on the network can't really tell that anything has gone wrong.

Enable Whitespace Management

When enabled, this option makes sure that extraneous whitespace (such as the various hard returns, spaces, and tabs that you use to indent your ColdFusion code) is removed from any generated HTML code before it is sent back to browsers. The idea is that since whitespace is not significant to HTML, then whitespace in your ColdFusion templates should, in general, be ignored as well.

I recommend that this option be enabled in nearly all cases. There are a few special situations in which you would not want whitespace to be removed (for instance, if you are using `<PRE>` blocks in your pages), but you can always turn off the whitespace management on a case-by-case basis with the `<CFPROCESSINGDIRECTIVE>` tag. For more information about whitespace management, see Chapter 22, Improving Performance.

Missing Template Handler

You can create a ColdFusion page that will be executed and displayed whenever a user requests a ColdFusion page that doesn't actually exist on the server. This page will take the place of the standard Not Found message that would ordinarily appear. The missing template handler can contain whatever ColdFusion code that you wish. Just specify its location here, in the ColdFusion Administrator. Make sure to include the complete filesystem path to the file (including the `c:\` or whatever is appropriate), not just its name.

NOTE

Some web servers provide options that will make sure that the requested file actually exists before passing the page request to ColdFusion. For instance, Microsoft IIS provides a Check That File Exists option for each file extension mapping (choose Configuration from the Home Directory tab of your site's Properties dialog in the Internet Information Services Manager). If you enable this option for .cfm files, ColdFusion will never requests for nonexistent files, and thus the Missing Template Handler you specify in the ColdFusion Administrator will never be used. For details, consult the documentation for your Web server software.

Site-wide Error Handler

You can also create a ColdFusion page that will be executed and displayed whenever an uncaught error (exception) is displayed. This page will take the place of the standard error message that would ordinarily appear. Again, just specify its location here, in the ColdFusion Administrator. Make sure to include the complete filesystem path to the file (including the `c:\` or whatever is appropriate), not just its name.

NOTE

You can still specify customized error handling pages on a page-by-page or application-by-application basis with the `<CFERROR>` tag, as explained in Chapter 16, Introducing the Web Application Framework.

The Caching Page

The term *cache* is a general term that refers to the use of a temporary area of a computer's memory or disk drive to store information that can be time-consuming to retrieve or calculate normally. The idea is to perform the action or calculation once, store it in the cache, and then use the information in the cache (the *cached version*) for subsequent requests, rather than performing the action or calculation over and over again. In general, there always needs to be some limit placed on the amount of information in the cache; otherwise the size of the cache would become unwieldy and thus become inefficient.

The Caching page of the ColdFusion Administrator (Figure 28.5) is for controlling two types of caches within the server: the internal cache that ColdFusion uses to cache your ColdFusion code files, and the database cache that ColdFusion uses whenever you use the `CACHEDWITHIN` or `CACHEDAFTER` attributes in a `<CFQUERY>` tag.

Figure 28.5

Enable the Trusted Cache option on your production servers for best performance.

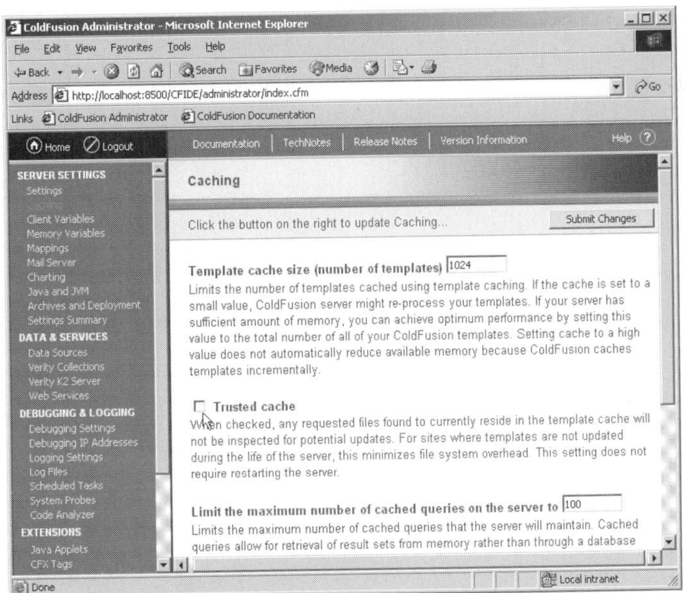

NOTE

There is also a cache setting specific to `<CFCHART>`. For details, refer to The Charting Page section, later in this chapter.

NOTE

Don't confuse the Caching options on this page of the Administrator with the `<CFCACHE>` tag, which is for caching individual pages. For details about `<CFCACHE>`, see Chapter 22, Improving Performance.

Template cache size (number of templates)

As you know, ColdFusion MX converts your ColdFusion templates to compiled Java classes in the background. Whenever someone visits one of your ColdFusion pages, ColdFusion checks to see if the page has been converted to a Java class, and whether the Java class is up to date (that is, whether the .cfm file has been changed since the Java class was compiled). The same goes for any included pages, custom tags and components. Certain aspects of this decision-making process, as well as the compiled Java classes themselves, are cached in memory to improve performance.

This setting allows you to tweak the size of this template cache to tweak performance. Ideally, you would want the cache to be big enough to hold all of your templates; however, doing so might cause ColdFusion to use a large amount of your server's available memory. I recommend that you use the following steps as a rough guideline:

1 Count the number of ColdFusion (.cfm and .cfc) files in your application(s). Don't count files that you think will be used pretty infrequently.

2 Find the approximate average of the size (in KB) of the .class files in the web-inf/cfclasses folder. The average is likely to be in the neighborhood of 8-10KB.

3 Multiply these two numbers (the number of files and the average .class size).

You can use the result as a rough estimate of what the template cache size would be in a close-to-perfect world. Your server may not have enough memory for you to be able to set the cache size to this number; if not, just give the cache as much room as you reasonably can. If, on the other hand, your computation is much less than the current template cache size setting, then you can probably reduce the setting to the number you found without sacrificing performance.

NOTE

Remember, a *template* is just another name for a ColdFusion page. Any .cfm or .cfc file is a *template*.

NOTE

This setting has changed for ColdFusion MX. Previous versions of ColdFusion had a similar setting called Template Cache Size, but it referred to the amount of ColdFusion code that it would keep stored in a parsed, optimized state (known as p-code). ColdFusion MX doesn't have a p-code state, since your CFML code becomes pure, compiled Java code behind the scenes. Another difference is that the old setting was expressed in terms of amount of memory (KB); the new setting for ColdFusion MX is expressed as a simple number of templates.

Trusted cache

Normally, when a user requests one of your ColdFusion pages, the server needs to check to see if the .cfm file has been changed since the last time the page was executed. If so, it recompiles the .cfm file into an updated version of the corresponding Java class; if not, the existing version of the Java class can be used. The same goes for any included files, custom tags, or ColdFusion components. It doesn't take much time for the server to check whether each file has changed, but even that little bit of time is for naught if you know that your ColdFusion files will not be changing over time.

Checking this option tells ColdFusion not to bother checking whether each ColdFusion file has changed. This can improve performance quite a bit, especially if the server is receiving a lot of page requests.

In general, you should enable this option on your production servers, since the files would not normally be changing often. Leave it unchecked on your development servers. When you move files from development to production, uncheck the option, or delete all the files in the `CFusionMX/wwwroot/WEB-INF/cfclasses` folder and then restart the ColdFusion MX Application Server.

Limit the number of cached queries on the server to

As you learned in Chapter 22, Improving Performance, you can use the `CACHEDWITHIN` or `CACHEDAFTER` attributes of the `<CFQUERY>` tag to reuse query results so they don't have to be retrieved from the database with each and every page request. Of course, it's not possible for the server to cache an unlimited number of query result sets in memory; there's only so much memory to go around.

By default, ColdFusion will allow up to 100 cached result sets to reside in its memory; when the 101st query needs to be cached, the query that was cached first will be removed from the cache. Increasing the number will allow more cached result sets to remain in memory at once; decreasing the number will reduce the amount of RAM that the cached queries will use up.

Like some of the options discussed earlier (particularly the number of simultaneous requests), this setting is a matter of balance, and there is no hard and fast rule about what the best value is. Setting the value too high could cause ColdFusion to use too much memory, which might negatively impact the overall performance of your applications. Setting the value too low will reduce the likelihood of a page request being able to take advantage of a previously cached query, which would also negatively impact performance.

In general, if you use cached queries relatively extensively in your code, and you find that your server still has plenty of available RAM after your applications have been running for a while, then you can increase the value. On the other hand, if you find that your server is tending to run out of available RAM, then you should try decreasing this value.

The Client Variables Page

In Chapter 17, Working with Sessions, you learned about the `CLIENT` variable scope, which allows you to create variables that become associated with a particular web browser. You can use `CLIENT` variables to create pages that show personalized information or that otherwise maintain state between each user's visits and page requests.

Choosing a Client Variable Storage Mechanism

In general, the idea behind `CLIENT` variables is to store the actual variables on the server, so that the burden (and responsibility) for remembering the values isn't placed on each browser machine. There are two methods for storing values on the server: in a database, or in the registry. (For Windows servers, *registry* refers to the Windows Registry, which is a special information store that is built into the operating system; for other servers, *registry* refers to a special text file that Macromedia ships with ColdFusion.) Because the values are stored on the server side, the total size of all the accumulated client variables can become quite large over time. Either the database or the registry will have to become large enough to store the total size of all client variables for all users.

You can also choose to have your client variables stored as a cookie on the browser machine. This takes care of the problem of your servers having to store every client variable for every user, but there are some pretty significant tradeoffs. Conceptually, you are trusting the browser to store the values for you. Savvy users know how to delete cookies to save disk space; they may do so at any time, which means that you have no way to prevent your application's client variables from being deleted. Some users will disable cookies altogether, which means that your client variables won't work at all. Perhaps most importantly, browsers are not required to store an unlimited amount of information in cookies, which means that the combined length of all client variables for each user cannot be very large.

Macromedia recommends that you only use the default registry option for development, and that you should create a database storage mechanism for your staging or production machines—even if it's just a lowly Access database). You can set the database to be the default storage mechanism (as discussed in the next section) so that your code doesn't have to change as you move your applications out of development.

That said, the registry option is generally fine as long as your ColdFusion applications (at least, the that use client variables) will not be visited by a very large number of unique visitors. So, for intranet applications that are only used by a limited number of people, it is probably fine to just use the default registry option. If, on the other hand, your client-variable-aware applications are going to be used by lots and lots of people, then you should consider using a database. You can also use the cookie option, if the information in the client variables is not critical and is not particularly verbose.

NOTE

Multiple ColdFusion servers can use the same database to store client variables. This allows you to share client variables among all the servers in a cluster, if your database system can handle the load.

Choosing the Default Storage Mechanism

To choose the default storage mechanism used for client variables, make the appropriate selection under the heading Select Default Storage Mechanism for Client Sessions (Figure 28.6), then click Apply.

NOTE

You can override this setting on an application-by-application basis by specifying a `CLIENTSTORAGE` attribute in your `<CFAPPLICATION>` tag. For details, see Chapter 17.

Editing a Storage Mechanism's Options

If you are using the registry or a database to store your client variables, ColdFusion MX provides several options which you can use to manage how your client variables are stored on the server. To edit the options for one of these storage mechanisms, click on its Edit icon (Figure 28.6). The Add/Edit Client Store page appears (Figure 28.7).

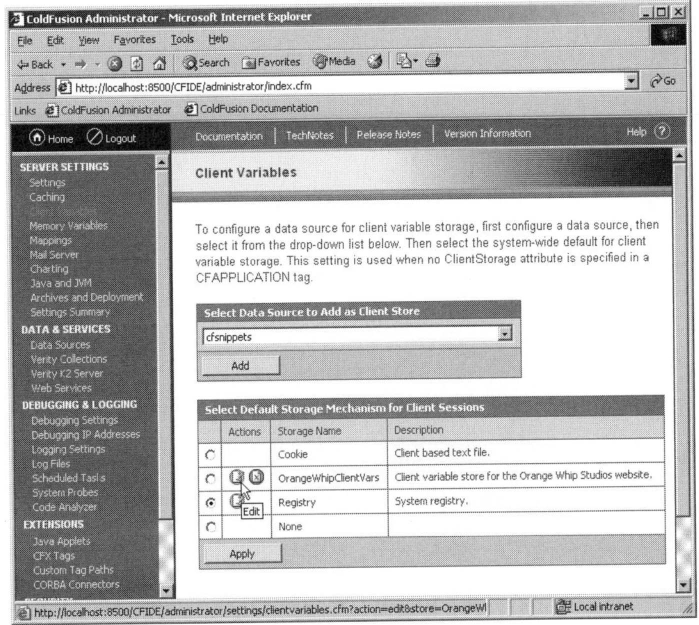

Figure 28.6

You can store client variables in a database, as cookies, or in the registry.

The available options are:

- **Description**—This is simply a place for you to type an optional description of the storage mechanism. This option is available only for databases; it is not available for the Registry storage mechanism.
- **Purge data for clients that remain unvisited for**—This option allows you to tweak the length of time that each client's variables are kept on the server. 90 days is the default. Increasing this value allows each user's variables to be kept longer, but may cause the overall size of the database or registry to grow considerably. Decreasing the value conserves space on the server side, but means that the personalized effect that your client bring to the table are more likely to expire between a user's visits. It is important to note that is not individual client variables that expire after 90 days (or whatever period you specify); it is the client record itself that expires. That is, if a particular client (that is, a particular browser) fails to return to one of your pages after 90 days, all of that client's `CLIENT` variables are purged at once. See Chapter 17 for details.
- **Disable global client variable updates**—By default, this option is unchecked, which means that ColdFusion updates the automatic `CLIENT.HitCount` and `CLIENT.LastVisit` variables with every page request in every application that uses client variables. If you check this option, ColdFusion will only update these variables on each page that actually changes the value of a client variable. In general, I recommend that you check this option unless your application is depending on up-to-the-minute accuracy from these automatic variables.

NOTE

If you are using the same database for multiple servers in a cluster, make sure that the checkbox for Purge Data For Clients option is only checked for one of the servers in the cluster.

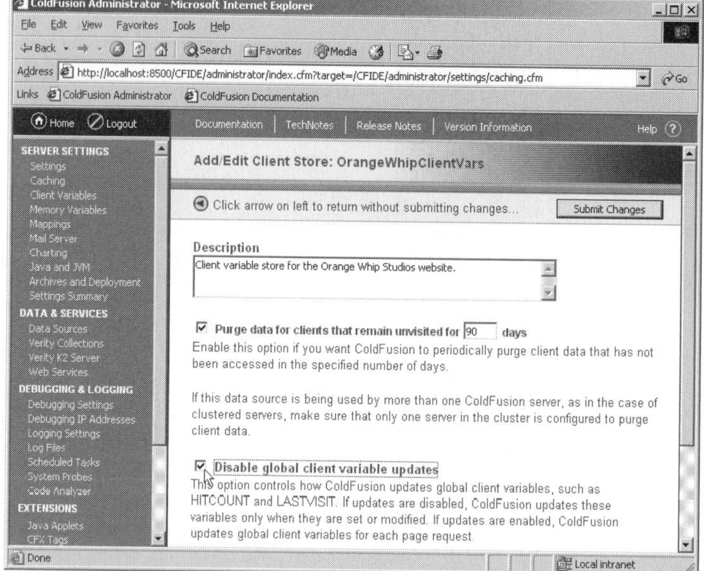

Figure 28.7

These options allow you to tweak the size and performance of your server-side client variable stores.

Creating a New Database Storage Mechanism

To create a new database storage mechanism for client variables, perform the following steps:

1. Create a new database, using whatever tools your database software provides. I recommend that you always use a separate database to store client variables, rather than a database that contains tables you've designed yourself. That said, you can just use your application's existing database if you wish.
2. Create a ColdFusion data source for the new database, using the Data Sources page of the ColdFusion Administrator (see the Data Sources Page section, later in this chapter).
3. On the Client Variables page of the Administrator, choose the new data source under Select Data Source to Add as Client Store (refer to Figure 28.6), then click Add.
4. Fill in the options for the new storage mechanisms (refer to Figure 28.7), then click Submit Changes. The new storage mechanism can then be used as the value of the `CLIENTSTORAGE` attribute for `<CFAPPLICATION>`, or selected as the default storage mechanism (refer to Figure 28.6).

The options for new database storage mechanisms are the same as what was discussed in the previous section, except for one option which is available only for new databases: Create Client Database Tables. This option should be checked if this is truly a new database, which has never been used for client variables before. If the database has already been set up for client variables in the past (perhaps when you set it up for another server in a cluster), then uncheck this option.

The Memory Variables Page

In Chapter 16, you learned about `APPLICATION` variables, which allow you to maintain counters, flags, and other variables on an application-wide basis. In Chapter 17, you learned about `SESSION` variables, which provide a way to track variables for your users on a per-session basis.

This page of the Administrator (Figure 28.8) allows you to change how these variables are tracked, and for how long. Either type of variable can be disabled by un-checking the Enable Application Variables or Enable Session Variables checkboxes.

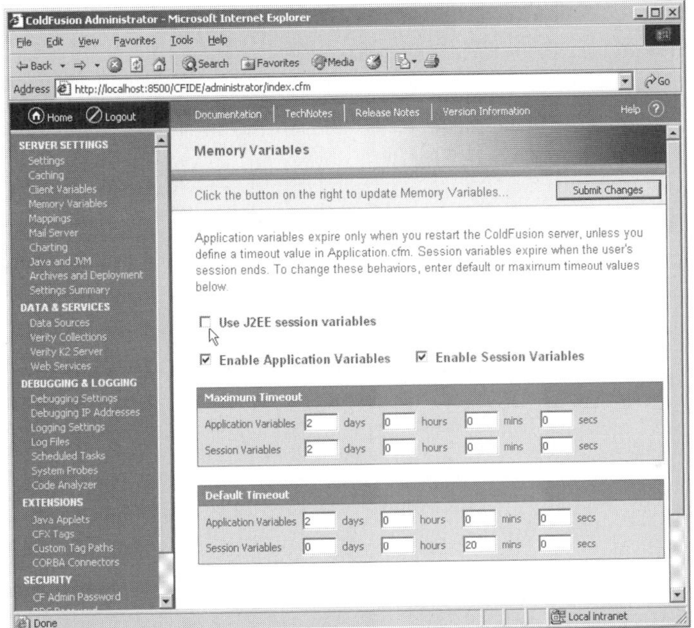

Figure 28.8

The Memory Variables page allows you to adjust the way application and session variables are stored.

You can edit the Default Timeout for each type of variable, by typing in the desired number of days, minutes, hours, and seconds. This default value will be used whenever you do not specify a `SESSIONTIMEOUT` or `APPLICATIONTIMEOUT` attribute in your `<CFAPPLICATION>` tags. For instance, you can a longer timeout session timeout if users are complaining that their session variables disappear while they are filling out long forms or making complex decisions. You can use a shorter timeout if you suspect that too much memory is being used to store your session variables.

You can also adjust the Maximum Timeout for each type of variable, which gives you a way to make sure that no individual `<CFAPPLICATION>` tag is specifying a `SESSIONTIMEOUT` or `APPLICATIONTIMEOUT` that is unreasonably long. If `<CFAPPLICATION>` tag specifies a timeout that exceeds the maximum value you supply here, the maximum value is used instead.

You can also enable the Use J2EE Session Variables option if you want your session variables to be sharable with other J2EE applications. This will also cause your session variables to be lost when the user closes the browser. (Normally, session variables only expire after the session timeout has been reached). For details, see Chapter 17.

The Mail Server Page

In Chapter 26, Interacting with Email, you learned to create ColdFusion pages that send dynamic, personalized email messages with the `<CFMAIL>` tag. ColdFusion can also send automatically generated reports to server administrators in case of problems, as you will learn in the System Probes Page section, later in this chapter. Use the Mail Server page (Figure 28.9) to establish an SMTP email server connection for ColdFusion to use for these purposes.

NOTE

See Chapter 26, "Interacting with Email," to learn more about how to generate email with the `<CFMAIL>` tag.

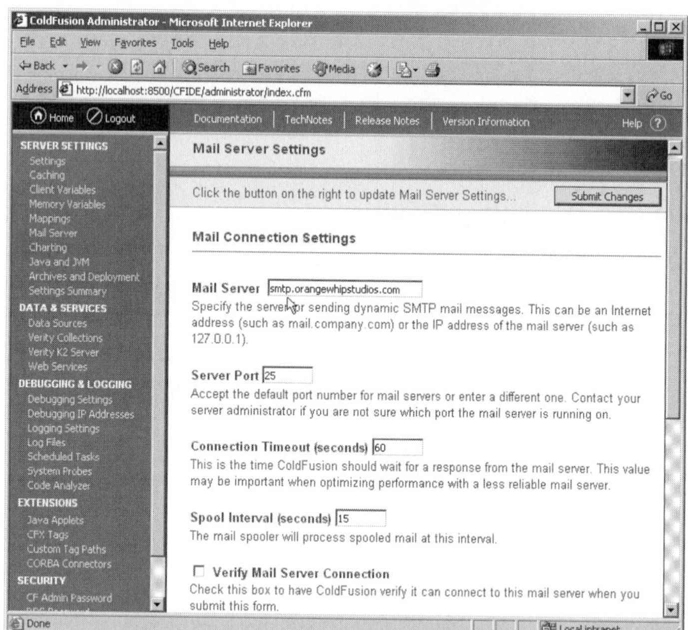

Figure 28.9

Use the Mail/Mail Logging page to specify server settings, set logging options, and verify e-mail servers.

To set up a mail server, do the following:

1. Enter either the Internet domain name or the IP address for your company's outgoing mail server (also known as an SMTP server) in the Mail Server text box.
2. Enter your e-mail server's port number. This is almost always 25, so you can usually leave the port number alone.

3. The Connection Timeout setting enables you to set the number of seconds ColdFusion should wait for a response from the e-mail server. In general, the default value of 60 seconds is sensible. If your mail server is far away or available only via a slow network connection, it is possible that you would need to increase this value.

4. The Spool Interval setting enables you to specify the number of seconds ColdFusion waits before checking to see if new email messages are waiting to be sent out. You can decrease this value if it is critical that your messages be sent out very soon after they are created; you can increase the value to conserve server resources. Note that this value is ignored whenever you use the `SPOOLENABLE="No"` attribute in your `<CFMAIL>` tags (this attribute is new in ColdFusion MX; see Chapter 26 for details).

5. Click the Verify Mail Server check box for ColdFusion to make sure it can contact the email server when the Submit Changes button is clicked. This isn't required, but it is recommended.

The Mail Logging settings give you the ability to either log the e-mail messages generated by ColdFusion by severity (including Information, Warning, and Error) or just log all ColdFusion-generated e-mails. The logs are saved in the `/CFusionMX/Log` folder, and are viewable using the log viewer pages within the ColdFusion Administrator (see the Log Files Page section, later in this chapter).

Charting

In Chapter 25, Graphing, you learned how to use ColdFusion MX's new `<CFCHART>` tag to create dynamic charts and graphs that create visual representations of your application's data. ColdFusion MX automatically caches charts for later use. Conceptually, the chart cache is the charting equivalent of the query caching feature you learned about in Chapter 22, "Improving Performance". Its purpose is to improve performance by automatically reusing the results of a `<CFCHART>` tag if all of its data and attributes are the same, rather than having to re-render each chart for every page request.

The Charting page of the ColdFusion MX Administrator contains a number of options that you can use to tweak the way the chart cache behaves:

- Cache Type: You can set this to Disk Cache (the default value) or Memory Cache. The memory cache setting will perform better under high load, but will require more of the server's memory to do so. The disk cache setting may not perform quite as quickly, but it will not have much of an impact on the server's RAM. We recommend leaving this value alone unless you are specifically experiencing performance problems with `<CFCHART>` under heavy load.

- Maximum number of images in cache: You can increase this number to allow ColdFusion to store more charts in its cache, thereby improving performance if your application is serving up lots of different charts. If you are using the Memory Cache option, keep in mind that this will cause even more of the server's memory to be used for chart caching.

- Maximum number of chart requests: The maximum number of `<CFCHART>` tags that you want ColdFusion to be willing to process at the same moment in time. Under high load, a higher number here may improve responsiveness for individual chart requests, but it will put more overall strain on your server.
- Disk cache location: If you are using the Disk Cache option, you may adjust this value, which is the location in which ColdFusion stores charts for later reuse.

Java and JVM

As you know, ColdFusion MX runs on top of the Java platform. Your ColdFusion pages are translated into Java classes, and those classes are executed within the context of a Java Virtual Machine (JVM). The Java and JVM page of the Administrator (Figure 28.10) allows you to adjust which JVM is used to execute your pages. You can also make other JVM-related adjustments, such as the amount of memory that the JVM is allowed to use while executing your pages.

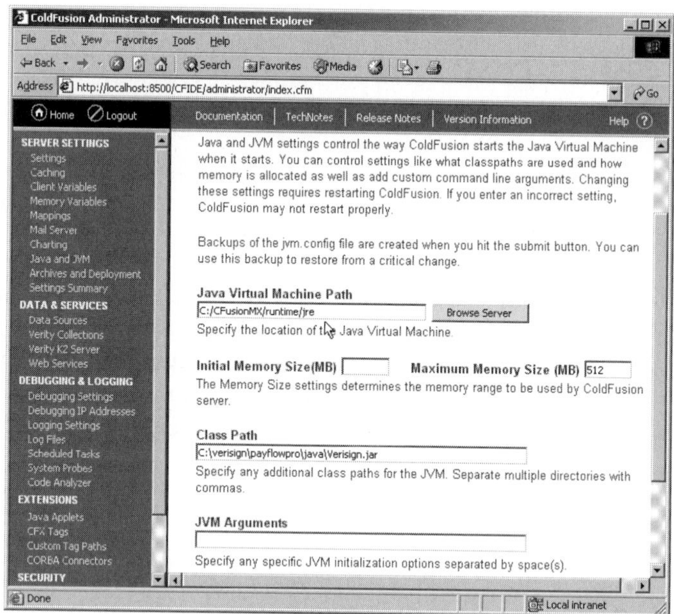

Figure 28.10

The Java and JVM page allows you to adjust how ColdFusion interacts with the Java Virtual Machine.

Java Virtual Machine Path

In theory, ColdFusion MX should be able to use any up to date JVM. At the time of this writing, the only officially supported virtual machine is the one that ships with ColdFusion MX (Sun's JVM version 1.3.1_03) . By default, this version of Sun's virtual machine is installed and configured for you when you install ColdFusion MX.

At some point in the future, you may wish to download and install a different JVM, presumably because it offers a new feature, a smaller footprint, faster performance, or some other desirable trait. Once the new JVM has been successfully installed, change the Java Virtual Machine Path setting in the ColdFusion Administrator (shown in Figure 28.10), then restart the ColdFusion MX Application Server.

NOTE

Before using a different JVM on your production servers, you should definitely test your applications with that same JVM on some kind of development, staging, or beta-testing server. You should also see whether the JVM is officially supported by Macromedia.

NOTE

You can always find out what JVM ColdFusion is running under by clicking on the Version Information link at the top of the ColdFusion Administrator (refer to Figure 28.3).

Initial Memory Size

This setting allows you to provide an initial amount of your server's memory that the JVM should claim when the ColdFusion MX Application Server is started. By default, this setting is left blank, which means that the JVM will make its own decisions about how much memory it should claim at startup. If your server encounters a lot of traffic, the JVM will generally need to claim more memory. You may be able to save the JVM some time by telling it to claim a larger amount of memory at startup. In general, this could make the whole startup process (which includes the initial processing of your pages) more efficient.

If you provide a value for this setting, it is strongly recommended that you specify a size of at least 32 MB.

Maximum Memory Size

In a default ColdFusion MX installation, the JVM is instructed to use no more than 512 MB of memory for the ColdFusion runtime and your ColdFusion pages. If your server has considerably more than 512 MB of RAM installed, you may want to allow the JVM to use more of it, which would generally improve performance. Simply specify the maximum amount of memory that you wish the JVM (and thus the ColdFusion server, and thus your ColdFusion pages) to be able to use, in megabytes.

NOTE

Don't set this value to anything lower than 32 MB, because ColdFusion will probably not be able to start with any less than that amount of memory.

Class Path

If your applications use any external Java objects that in turn refer to other Java classes (that is, any Java classes that are not provided by the JVM itself), you can tell ColdFusion where to find the class files by adjusting the Class Path setting in the ColdFusion Administrator. By *Java objects*, I mean any Java classes that you are accessing via `<CFOBJECT>` or `CreateObject()`, any servlets or JSP tag libraries that you are using via `<CFIMPORT>`, CFX tags that have been written in Java, and so on.

In general, you will either be specifying the path to a directory, or the path to a Java Archive (.jar) file. If you need to specify multiple directories or archives, separate them with commas. Whatever Java objects you are using should include documentation that tells exactly which files need to be accessible via the class path.

NOTE

If you're familiar with invoking Java on the command line, this Administrator setting is equivalent to the `-classpath` or `-cp` options.

NOTE

ColdFusion always adds some additional directories and archives of its own, in addition to the class path you provide here. If you are curious, you can view the complete class path being used internally by clicking on the Version Information link at the top of the Administrator (see Figure 28.3).

JVM Arguments

If you want any additional arguments to be passed to the JVM when the ColdFusion server is started, you can specify them here. Separate multiple arguments with spaces. Presumably, you would provide such arguments if they were required by an external Java object that you wanted to use, or if the argument was suggested by the JVM vendor to improve performance or stability. The exact purpose and effect of the arguments will depend on the JVM and classes you are using.

Archives and Deployment

At any point during your application's development, you can use the ColdFusion Administrator to create a *ColdFusion archive* of your application. ColdFusion archives are files that can contain all the files needed to run your application, such as your ColdFusion (.cfm) pages, image files, XML files, desktop database files, Macromedia Flash movies, and any other files that your application depends on.

But ColdFusion archives can include more than just your application files; they can also include any Administrator settings that your application depends on. In other words, the idea behind the ColdFusion archive feature is to give you a way to create a single file that contains everything needed to make your application work. It's a great way to back up your work.

ColdFusion archives are also about deployment. Once you have created an archive for your application, you can copy the single archive file to another ColdFusion server. Your application can then be installed in one step. All of your application's files will be unpacked from the archive and placed in the appropriate places on the server, and all of the required configuration changes (such as setting up data sources and mappings) will be made automatically. In most cases, this means that you can move your applications from your development servers to your staging or production servers without having to manually copy individual files or make changes manually in each server's ColdFusion Administrator.

Creating a New ColdFusion Archive Definition

There are two steps to creating a ColdFusion archive for your application. First, you use the ColdFusion Administrator to create a new *archive definition*. The archive definition is just a list of the files and settings that should be included in the archive. Once the archive definition has been created, you can use the definition *build* an actual archive (.car) file at any time. The archive will include a snapshot of the current files and settings. When the files change and you want to create a new snapshot, you can build the archive again, using the same definition.

To create an archive definition, simply type a name in the Archive Name field in the Create New Archive section of the Archives and Deployment page (Figure 28.11), then click Create. The Archive Wizard appears, which walks you through the processes of selecting which files and which settings should be included in the archive each time it is built. The first step of the Archive Wizard simply asks you to provide an optional description to explain the purpose of the archive (Figure 28.12).

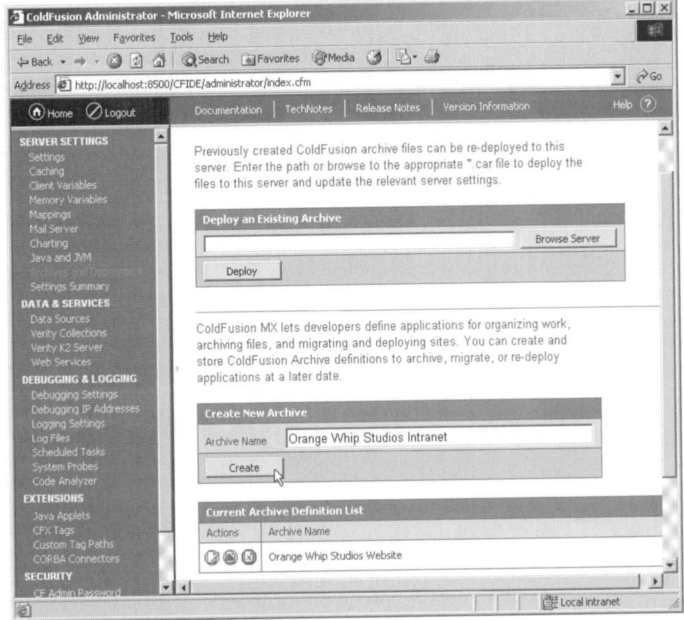

Figure 28.11

You can create an archive definition for your application, which will let you take a snapshot of it at any time.

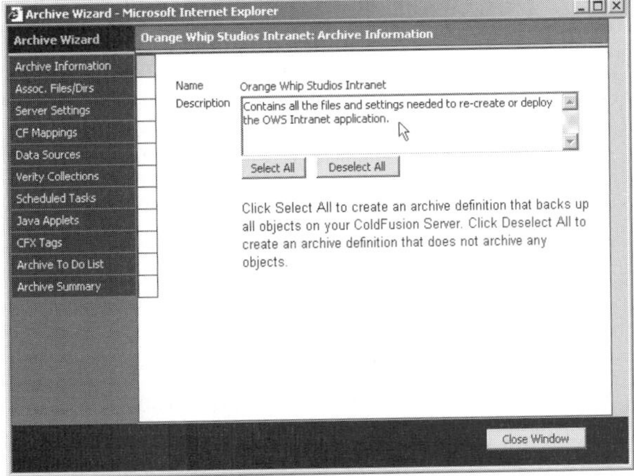

Figure 28.12

The Archive Wizard walks you through the process of creating a new archive definition.

NOTE

In addition, there are Select All and Deselect All buttons on this screen. Clicking the Select All button is a shortcut for checking all the options on subsequent steps of the wizard; Deselect All unchecks them all.

When you are done entering the description, click the Assoc. Files/Dirs link in the left hand column. The second step of the wizard appears, which allows you to specify which files should be included in the archive (Figure 28.13). For instance, your application might rely on all files in the ows folder within your web server's document root, plus all custom tags within the ows folder within the CFusionMX/CustomTags folder. If so, you would add those two paths with the Add Path button, which would result in a display similar to Figure 28.13.

Figure 28.13

You can specify which files to include each time the archive is built.

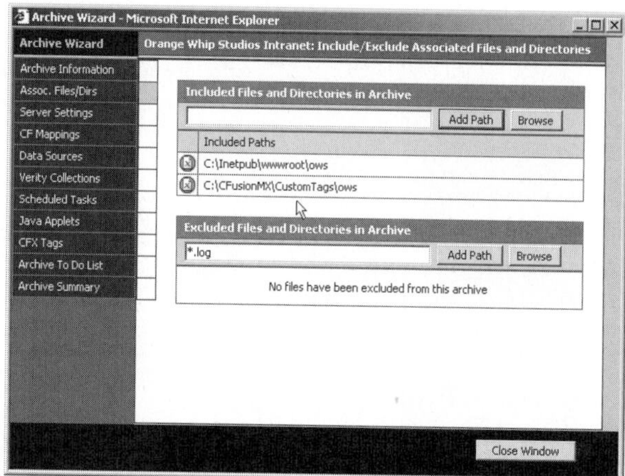

You can now navigate through the remaining parts of the Archive Wizard by clicking on the various links in the left margin. Most of these links correspond to portions of the ColdFusion Administrator; within each of these wizard steps, you simply select which specific settings should be included in the archive.

For instance, when you select the Data Sources portion of the Archive Wizard, you are presented with a list of all currently defined data sources (Figure 28.14). Simply select the data source settings that you want included in the archive. Later, when the archive is deployed, these data sources will be automatically re-created, rather than you having to do it manually in the ColdFusion Administrator.

NOTE

Selecting a data source in the Archive Wizard just means that the data source definition (that is, the Administrator settings) will be included in the archive. It doesn't mean that the database itself will be included in the archive. If you are using a file-based database such as Access, you could include the .mdb file in the archive using the previous step (shown in Figure 28.13); assuming that you are using a server-based database system such as Oracle or SQLServer, you probably want your application to continue connecting to the same external database server.

The same basic process applies to the other portions of the Archive Wizard. When you are finished making your selections, click Close Window to return to the ColdFusion Administrator.

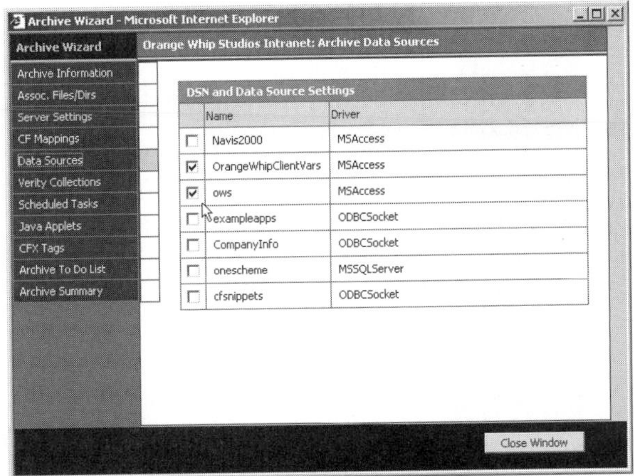

Figure 28.14

Data sources, directory mappings, and other Administrator settings can all be restored whenever the archive is deployed.

Building an Archive

Now that you have created an archive definition, you can take a snapshot of your application at any time by building an archive (.car) file. Just click on the Build Archive icon for your archive definition at the bottom of the Archives and Deployment page (see Figure 28.11). The Build CAR File Archive wizard appears with some summary information about what will be included in the archive.

When you click Next, the Archive File Location step appears, which allows you to choose a file location for the new archive file (Figure 28.15). The new archive file will be saved to this location on the server's drive. You can use the Browse Server button to browse for the directory location. You must specify a filename with a .car extension. If you choose a .car file that already exists, it will be overwritten without warning.

TIP

You may want to incorporate the current date in the name of the archive file, as shown in Figure 28.15.

When you click Next again, the archive will be built. You will see status messages while ColdFusion adds items to the archive. When the build process is complete, a Build Successful message will be displayed.

You now look in the folder you specified for the archive location. You will see your new archive there. You can now burn the archive to a CD or tape to back up your work, or copy the archive to another ColdFusion server to deploy your application in one step (see Deploying an Archive in the next section).

CAUTION

ColdFusion may show the Build Successful message before the archive is actually complete. Make sure the archive has finished building (by watching the size of the archive until it stops increasing) before you copy the file to another location.

NOTE

ColdFusion Archive (.car) files are similar conceptually and structurally to ZIP (.zip) archives or Java Archive (.jar) files. A program like WinZip will be able to make some sense of the file, but it will probably not be able to unpack the files correctly. The archive files are designed to only be unpacked by a ColdFusion server.

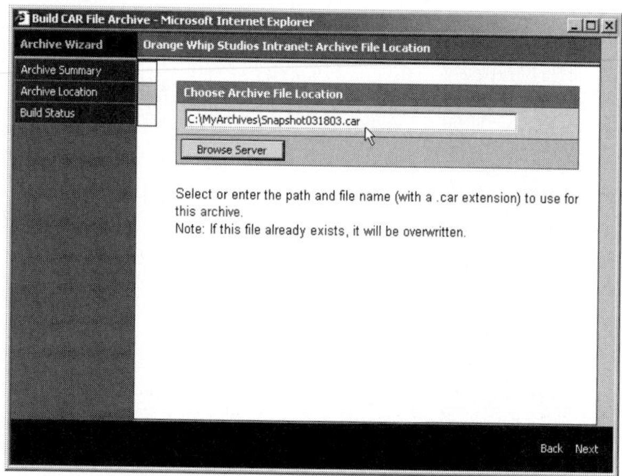

Figure 28.15

The archive file will be created on the server at the location you specify.

Deploying an Archive

It is easy to restore all the files and settings stored in an archive, or to deploy an archive to a new ColdFusion server. Just follow these steps:

1. If necessary, copy the .car file to a folder on the server's drive (or place it at a location that is accessible to the ColdFusion MX service on your local network).
2. In the Deploy an Existing Archive field (shown in Figure 28.11), provide the location and filename of the .car file. You can use the Browse Server button to browse for and select the archive file without typing.
3. Click the Deploy button. The Archive Wizard appears, displaying information about what files and settings are contained in the archive.
4. When you click Next, the Deploy Location step appears (Figure 28.16). You can use this page to provide a different location for each of the folders that were originally added to the archive. You might want to change the locations if you are deploying the archive to a ColdFusion server whose document root is on a different drive or folder location than the server you created the archive on. You might also want to change the locations if you don't want the files in the archive to overwrite the files that are currently on your server, or if you just want to test the archive functionality.
5. When you click Next again, the archive will be deployed. All the files in the archive will be unpacked and placed in the appropriate locations on your server, and the settings for any datasources, directory mappings, CFX tags, or other items that you selected while creating the archive definition will be added or changed in the ColdFusion Administrator for you.

CAUTION

When you deploy an archive, any existing files on the server will be overwritten with the version of the files in the archive. If you are using an archive file that contains an older version of your application, make sure to specify different folder locations before you deploy (see Figure 28.16).

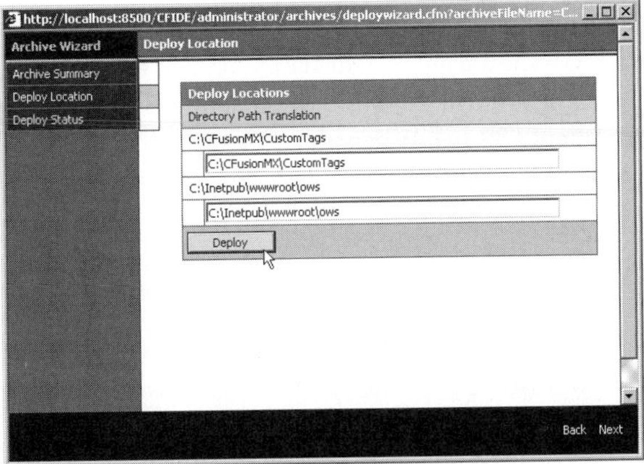

Figure 28.16

You can restore the files in the archive to their original locations on the server or to new locations.

Editing and Deleting Archive Definition

You can edit or delete an existing archive definition at any time by clicking the Edit Archive Definition or Delete Archive icons at the bottom of the Archives and Deployment page (see Figure 28.11).

NOTE

Deleting an archive definition just removes the definition from the Administrator, not any actual archive (.car) files that you may have built with the definition in the past. You need to delete the archive files yourself.

Settings Summary

The Settings Summary page provides a quick overview of all ColdFusion Administrator settings. Detailed information about all data sources, CFX tags, mappings, Verity full-text archives, and nearly all other settings discussed in this chapter are displayed. Most of the information from the Version Information page (see Figure 28.3) is included in the report as well. You can print this page to get a hardcopy record of all ColdFusion settings on the server.

Data & Services

The Data & Services section of the ColdFusion Administrator contains pages that let you create, edit, and delete data sources and Verity full-text search collections. You can also create aliases for Web Services.

The Data Sources Page

The Data Sources page provides tools to manage the list of data sources available to ColdFusion. Any data source listed here can be used as the `DATASOURCE` attribute of a `<CFQUERY>` (or `<CFINSERT>`, `<CFUPDATE>`, `<CFGRIDUPDATE>`, or `<CFSTOREDPROC>`) tag. If you have been following along with the examples in this book, you have probably already used this page of the ColdFusion Administrator to set up the ows data source.

Adding a new data source

To create a new data source, type a name for the data source in the Data Source Name field and choose the correct driver type (Oracle, MySQL, Microsoft SQLServer, or whatever is appropriate) from the drop down list (Figure 28.17). When you click the Add button, the configuration page for your new data source appears. This page will contain slightly different fields, depending on what type of data source you are adding.

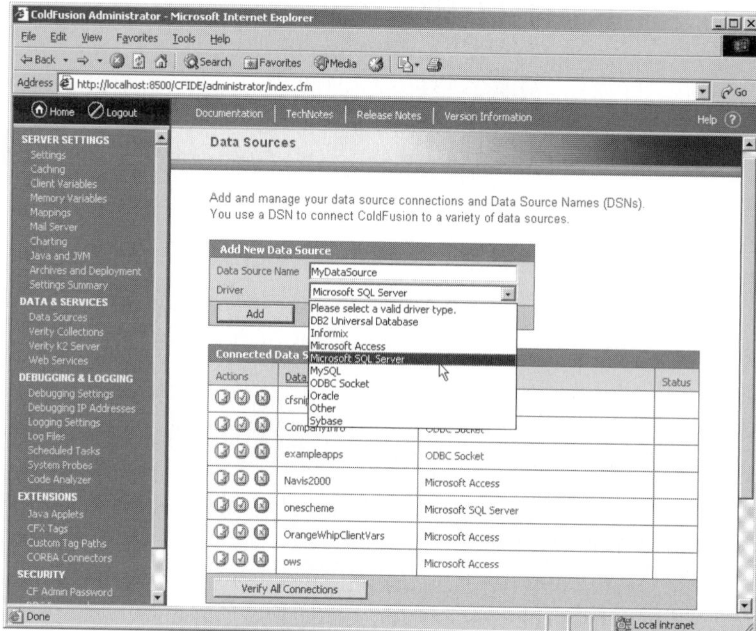

Figure 28.17

To create a new data source, select the appropriate driver from the drop-down list.

For instance, for a Microsoft SQLServer data source, you are prompted for the Database (the name of the database as it appears in the SQLServer Enterprise Manager), the Server (the name or IP address of the SQLServer machine), Port (the TCP/IP port, typically 1433), your SQLServer Username and Password, and an optional description for the new datasource (Figure 28.18). If SQLServer is installed on the same machine as your ColdFusion server, you can enter `localhost` for the Server name.

For an Oracle data source, the fields are almost identical, except that the Server field has been replaced with a field for the Oracle SID Name. Similar adjustments are made for other database types, but the basic type of information collected for each is the same. When you click Submit, ColdFusion attempts to connect to your database. If the connection is successful, the data source is created and can be used right away in a `<CFQUERY>` or other database manipulation tag. If the connection is not successful, an error message is displayed; verify that the username, password, and other information you are providing is correct and try again. Keep in mind that some of the values are likely to be case sensitive.

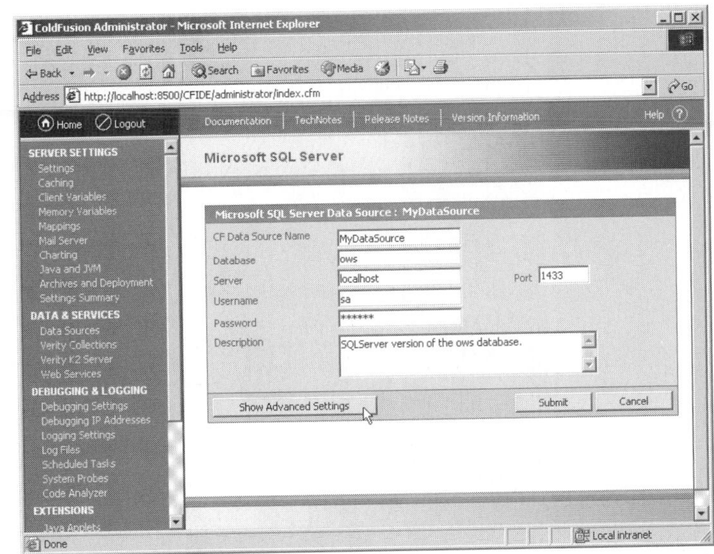

Figure 28.18

Fill in the database location or server, username, password, or whatever other information is required by the database driver.

Editing or deleting a data source

To edit or delete a data source, just use the Edit or Delete icons in the Connected Data Sources list in the Data Sources page (see Figure 28.17). Please note that deleting a data source just removes it from the list in the ColdFusion Administrator and makes it unavailable to `<CFQUERY>` and other CFML tags; it doesn't delete the database itself.

Verifying your data sources

You can verify your data source connections at any time by clicking on the Verify icon in the Connected Data Sources list in the Data Sources page (shown in Figure 28.17). You will see a message letting you know whether ColdFusion is currently able to connect to the database. You can verify all data source connections at once by clicking the Verify All Connections button at the bottom of the page.

Adjusting advanced data source settings

While creating or editing a data source, you can click the Show Advanced Settings button (shown in Figure 28.18) to configure additional options for the data source. Again, some of the advanced fields are different depending on the type of database. Figure 28.19 shows the advanced settings available for SQLServer databases; other types of databases will have nearly all of these settings in common.

NOTE

Most ColdFusion applications have absolutely no reason to be able to alter the structure of your database. Therefore, I recommend that you make it a habit to disable the `CREATE`, `DROP`, `ALTER`, `GRANT`, and `REVOKE` commands. It can't do any harm!

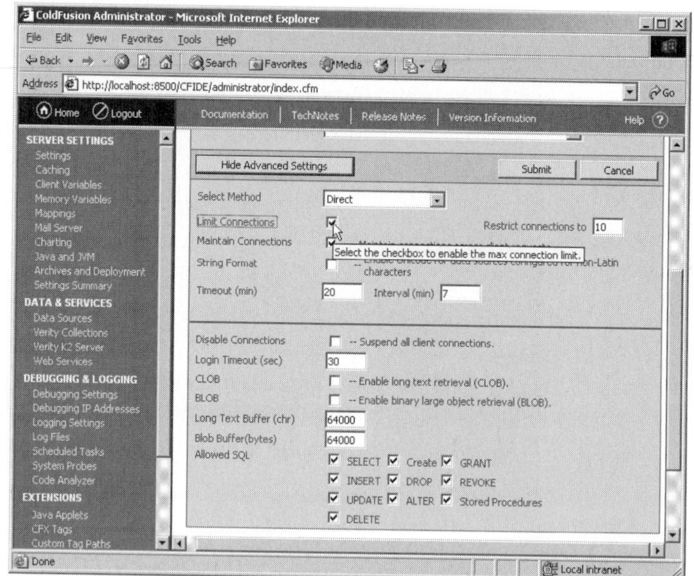

Figure 28.19

You can provide advanced settings to tweak performance and security options.

The advanced settings that will be available for all database types are listed in Table 28.1.

Table 28.1 ADVANCED DATA SOURCE SETTINGS

OPTION	DESCRIPTION
Limit Connections	By default, ColdFusion will use multiple connections to a single data source if different page requests are executing queries at the same time. If you wish to give ColdFusion a limit on the number of connections for the data source, check this checkbox and specify the maximum number of connections in the Restriction connections to field, discussed next.
Restrict connections to	If the Limit Connections option is checked, ColdFusion will open no more connections to the data source at the same time. Limiting the number of connections to a reasonable number may improve the performance of your database server and cause ColdFusion to use less memory. Another reason to limit the number of connections would be to comply with whatever licensing requirements your database system imposes.
Maintain Connections	Check this option to allow ColdFusion to keep database connections open between page requests. Enabling this option improves performance because ColdFusion doesn't have to keep re-establishing a fresh database connection whenever a new `<CFQUERY>` or similar tag is encountered. The degree of performance improvement will vary depending on the type of database you are using, and the speed of the network connection to the database. If a data source is not going to be used often, you may want to disable this option to minimize network utilization. In particular, people often disable this option when using Access databases that aren't used very often, so that the database's design doesn't remain locked.

Table 28.1 (CONTINUED)

OPTION	DESCRIPTION
Timeout	Assuming the Maintain Connections option is checked, these two settings determine how long the connection to the data source will remain open. By default, ColdFusion checks each connection every 7 minutes (the Interval) to see if the connection has been used during the last 20 minutes (the Timeout). If not, the connection is closed. These settings have no effect if you have unchecked the Maintain Connections option. If it takes a particularly long time for ColdFusion to connect to your database (you can check this by Verifying the connection as discussed in the previous section), you might want to increase the Timeout accordingly.
Disable Connections	Check this box to disable the data source. This option is helpful if you want to do temporary maintenance on a database, but don't want to have to delete and then re-create the data source.
Login Timeout	The amount of time, in seconds, that ColdFusion will wait while it attempts to connect to the data source. In general, the default value of 30 seconds should be more than sufficient.
Enable long text retrieval	If this option is checked, ColdFusion will allow an unlimited amount of text to be retrieved from so-called CLOB (character large object) columns in your database tables. Different database systems use different terms to describe such columns (in Access, CLOB columns are called *Memo* fields; in SQLServer, they are called *text* or *ntext* fields). If this option is left unchecked, then only the number of characters specified in the Long Text Buffer option (discussed next) will be retrieved.
Long Text Buffer	The maximum number of characters that will be retrieved from a character or text type of database column. This limit is ignored if the Enable long text retrieval option is checked.
Enable binary long object retrieval	If checked, ColdFusion will retrieve an unlimited amount of data from any BLOB (binary large object) columns. Again, different database systems use different terms, such as *image* or something similar, for these columns. If unchecked, then the byte limit specified in the Blob Buffer (discussed next) will be imposed.
Blob Buffer	The maximum number of bytes to retrieve from a BLOB column. Ignored if the Enable binary long object retrieval option is checked.
Allowed SQL	These options allow you make sure that only the desired kinds of SQL commands can be used via ColdFusion. To make sure that only ordinary data operations can be executed, check only the SELECT, INSERT, UPDATE, and DELETE options. To make a database be read-only as far as ColdFusion is concerned, uncheck everything except for SELECT.

NOTE

> Many database systems include *system stored procedures* that can alter the structure of a database. Therefore, I recommend that you disable the Stored Procedures option unless you are specifically using stored procedures in your ColdFusion code. For more information about stored procedures and the `<CFSTOREDPROC>` tag, see Chapter 30, Working with Stored Procedures.

Again, there may be one or two additional options in the Advanced Settings area, depending on the type of database you are using. You can consult your database documentation for information about what such options do. In addition, you can click on the Help icon at the top right corner of the ColdFusion Administrator for context sensitive help.

The Verity Collections Page

In Chapter 34, Full-Text Searching, you will learn about using the Verity functionality built into ColdFusion MX to add sophisticated search features to your applications. CFML includes three tags related to Verity: `<CFSEARH>`, `<CFINDEX>`, and `<CFCOLLECTION>`. All three tags have a `COLLECTION` attribute, which refers to what Verity calls a *collection*. A collection is to Verity as data sources are to databases: it's a name that you can use to refer to or search a particular set of data.

Creating and Deleting Collections

To create a collection, simply provide a name for the new collection and click Create Collection (Figure 28.20). By default, the new collection will be created in the CFusionMX/verity/collections folder; if you want the collection files to be kept somewhere else, you can specify the location in the Path field.

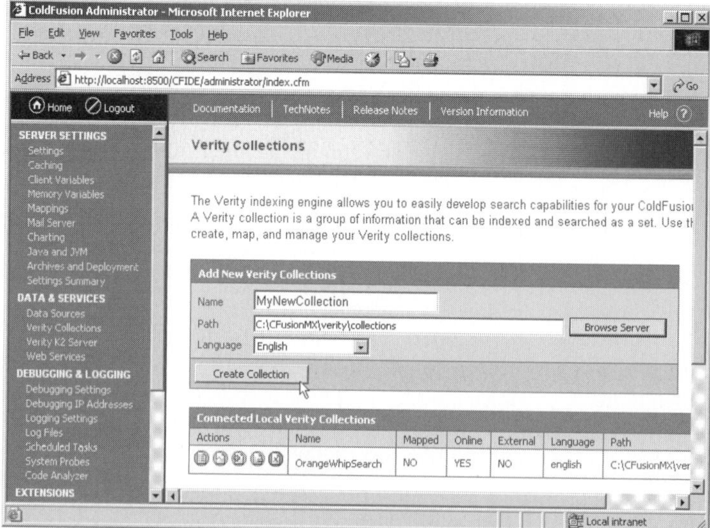

Figure 28.20

The Verity Collections page allows you to manage and index your full-text collections.

NOTE

If the documents you will be searching are in a language other than English, choose the appropriate language from the drop-down list. If you are working with non-roman character sets (especially double-byte character sets), you may want to consult the Internationalization and Localization chapter in our companion volume, *Advanced ColdFusion MX Application Development* (Macromedia Press).

To delete a collection, just click the Delete Collection icon for the collection in the Connected Local Verity Connections list.

NOTE

You can also create and delete collections programmatically with the `<CFCOLLECTION>` tag, rather than using the ColdFusion Administrator. For details, see Chapter 34.

Indexing a Collection

Once a collection has been created, it must be *indexed* before it will be able to return any useful search results. Basically, indexing is the process of telling Verity what information to make searchable.

There are two ways to index a collection:

- You can use the ColdFusion Administrator to tell Verity to make document files (such as static HTML pages, PDF documents, XML document files, and Microsoft Word documents) searchable. This is the simplest (but most limited) method.
- You can also use the `<CFINDEX>` tag to do the same thing programmatically in your ColdFusion code. The `<CFINDEX>` method also allows you to index text in a database, thus making it possible to create search interfaces for dynamic pages. For more information about the `<CFINDEX>` tag and indexing collections in general, please refer to Chapter 34.

To index a collection with the ColdFusion Administrator, click on the collection name or the Index Collection icon in the Connected Local Verity Collections list (see Figure 28.20). The Index Verity Collections page appears (Figure 28.21).

In the File Extensions field, specify what document types you want Verity to make searchable (separate the extensions with commas as shown in Figure 28.21). In the Directory Path field, provide the location of the files. Check the Recursively Index Sub Directories option if you want Verity to index files in folders that are nested within the location you specify.

In the Return URL field, enter the URL that corresponds to the location you specified for the Directory Path. The correct URL will depend on how you have configured and organized your web server. Just provide whatever URL can be used by a web browser to access the files via the Web. For details, see Chapter 34.

When you click Submit, the indexing process will begin.

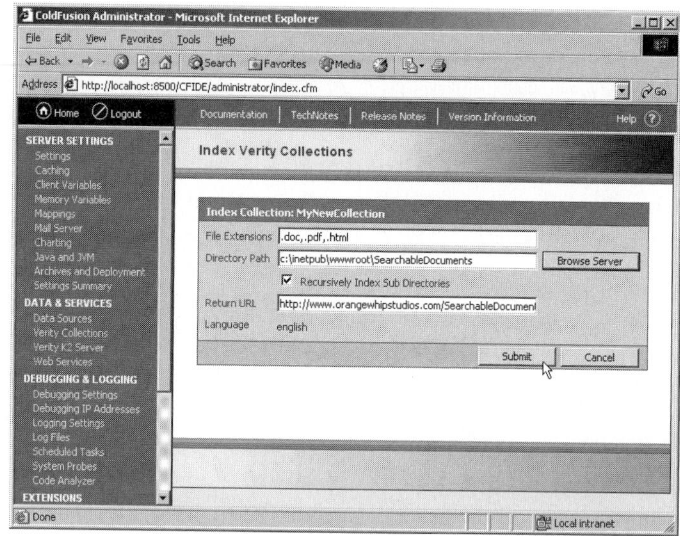

Figure 28.21

You can make static documents searchable by indexing them with Verity.

NOTE

If there are a large number of documents to index, the process may take a while. If you want the indexing to take place automatically during the night or some other time when your application is under lighter load, please consult Chapter 35, Event Scheduling.

The Verity K2 Server Page

In ColdFusion MX, you can use K2 functionality to get improved performance and functionality from Verity. For details, please refer to Chapter 34.

The Web Services Page

ColdFusion MX allows you to use (*consume*) web services via the `<CFINVOKE>` or `<CFOBJECT>` tags, or via the `CreateObject()` function. Consumption of Web Services is not something that is covered specifically in this book; it is covered in full in our companion volume, Advanced ColdFusion MX Application Development (Peachpit).

You can use the Web Services page of the ColdFusion Administrator to create aliases for the Web Services that you plan to use. You can then use the alias name instead of providing the full URL for the web service in every `<CFINVOKE>` tag. If the Web Service requires a username and password, they can be associated with the alias as well, which means that the username and password don't have to appear in your ColdFusion code at all.

To create an alias for a Web Service, enter the alias in the Web Service Name field (Figure 28.22). Provide the URL for the service's WSDL description in the WDSL URL field (if the service requires a username and password, enter them as well), then press the Add Web Service button. The new alias will appear in the Active ColdFusion Services list at the bottom of the page. You can now use the alias name as the `WEBSERVICE` attribute for `<CFINVOKE>`, `<CFOBJECT>`, or `CreateObject()` where you would normally need to provide the complete WSDL URL.

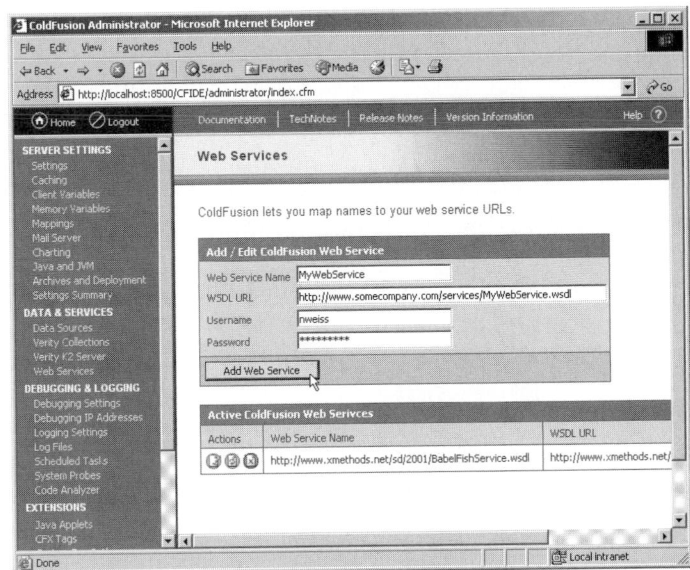

Figure 28.22

You can create aliases to make it easier to manage the Web Services your applications consume.

Debugging & Logging

The Debugging & Logging section of the ColdFusion Administrator provides a set of tools that can help you understand what your applications are doing, where and when any performance bottlenecks are occurring, and whether any error messages are occurring without your knowledge. There is also a rich set of debugging options that make it easier to troubleshoot errors while coding. In short, this section is all about making it easier for you to identify and avoid problems, both during and after the development process.

The Debugging Settings Page

In Chapter 14, Debugging and Troubleshooting, you learned how to take advantage of ColdFusion's debugging output to help you troubleshoot your applications. Enabling the debugging output causes all kinds of helpful information to appear at the bottom of your ColdFusion pages.

The Debugging Settings page (Figure 28.23) allows you to customize what exactly appears in the debugging output. This page also lets you monitor the ColdFusion server externally, via the command line or the System Monitor in Windows.

Enable Debugging

Check this option to enable debugging output. Information about variables, queries, execution times, and more will begin appearing at the bottom of each page processed by ColdFusion. You can customize which information is included in the debugging output (discussed next).

TIP

Even when this option is enabled, you can make sure that only the appropriate people (presumably yourself and the other developers on your team) see the debugging output by restricting the output by IP address. This is discussed shortly, in the Debugging IP Addresses section.

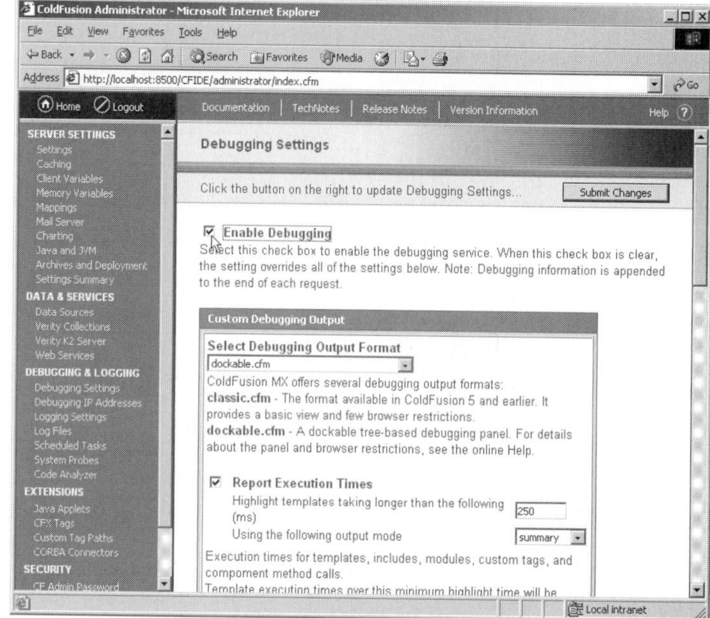

Figure 28.23

You can enable and customize ColdFusion's debugging output.

Custom Debugging Output

You can customize what exactly is included in the debugging output and how it is displayed with the options in this section. Most of these options are self-explanatory; others are covered in detail in Chapter 14. Table 28.2 provides a summary of the options available in this section.

Table 28.2 Custom Debugging Output Options

OPTION	DESCRIPTION
Select Debugging Output Format	ColdFusion MX lets you switch between debugging output formats. As of this writing, the output formats that ship with the product are *classic output*, which displays the debugging output in the no-nonsense format familiar to veteran ColdFusion developers, and the *dockable format*, which displays the output in a less obtrusive, more interactive style. You can even create your own output formats by creating new ColdFusion templates in the CFusionMX/wwwroot/WEB-INF/debug folder. Check out the code in the existing templates to see how it's done.

Table 28.2 (continued)

OPTION	DESCRIPTION
Report Execution Times	It is usually helpful to see execution times in your debugging output, so you can understand how long each of your ColdFusion files takes to execute. Enable this option to include execution times in the debugging output.
Highlight execution time	By default, ColdFusion will highlight the execution time of any template that takes more than 250 milliseconds to execute. Increase the value to highlight fewer execution times, or decrease the value to highlight more of them.
Execution time output mode	You can choose between *summary* and *tree*. *Summary* shows the amount of time that ColdFusion spends processing each ColdFusion file involved in the page request (such as `<CFINCLUDE>` files, custom tags, and ColdFusion Components); if a file is used more than once, the execution times are totaled so that the actual display shows one execution time per ColdFusion file. *Tree* provides more detail, showing execution times for every single use of a file, and displaying the various included files in a tree-like format so you can easily see which pages are being included by which. In other words, the *tree* mode is better for applications which use lots of separate files to process each page request. That said, the tree mode can take a bit longer to display, so you might want to enable it only when you need the extra level of precision.
Database Activity	Check this option to include database-related information, such as query execution times, in the debugging output.
Exception Information	Check this option to include information about each exception raised while the template was executing.
Tracing Information	Check this option to allow messages included by the `<CFTRACE>` tag to be shown in the page output. Uncheck the option to turn off the messages included by `<CFTRACE>`. Note that even when this option is enabled, `<CFTRACE>` messages will only be visible to the IP addresses listed in the Debugging IP Addresses page, discussed shortly.
Variables	These options allow you to include variables from the various built-in variable scopes, such as `CLIENT`, `SESSION`, `APPLICATION`, `URL`, `FORM`, and so on. You can uncheck the scopes you're not interested in at the moment to reduce the amount of debugging information displayed so you can concentrate on the task at hand.

Enable Robust Exception Information

This option controls whether certain nitty-gritty details are included in the debugging output. If this option is enabled, the debugging output will include such detailed items as the physical path of your ColdFusion files, the exact SQL code executed by each <CFQUERY> tag, the names of your data-sources, and the Java stack trace for each error that occurs.

NOTE

In general, these are the details that reveal information about your server and how your ColdFusion, and SQL code is constructed, as well as the makeup of any external Java objects that you may be using. For this reason, do not enable this option on production machines; if you must, be extra careful about the list of IP addresses that see the debugging information.

Enable Performance Monitoring

If you are using ColdFusion with Windows, you can monitor the ColdFusion MX server with the standard Performance Monitor application that comes with Windows. This is the same application that you use to monitor internal Windows processes such as memory management and CPU utilization, or other Microsoft applications such as IIS or SQLServer.

Check this option to tell ColdFusion to make information available to the Performance Monitor. When enabled, the Performance Object called ColdFusion MX Server will be available for display and monitoring within the Performance Monitor.

To monitor performance with the Performance Monitor, follow these steps:

1. Make sure the Enable Debugging option is checked, since it affects all options on this page of the Administrator.
2. Make sure the Enable Performance Monitoring option is checked.
3. Launch the Performance Monitor using the shortcut in the Macromedia ColdFusion MX program group.

The Performance Monitor will show a live graph of the various counters available, such as the number of database interactions per second, the average page execution time, and the number of currently executing page requests (Figure 28.24). If you wish, you can also add counters from other Performance Objects, such as the IIS object (to monitor the IIS web server) or the Processor object (to monitor the CPU itself). Use the Help icon on the Performance Monitor toolbar for more information.

NOTE

The performance monitor is part of Microsoft's Windows NT lineage, so it's included with Windows XP, 2000, and NT. It's not included in Windows 95, 98, or ME.

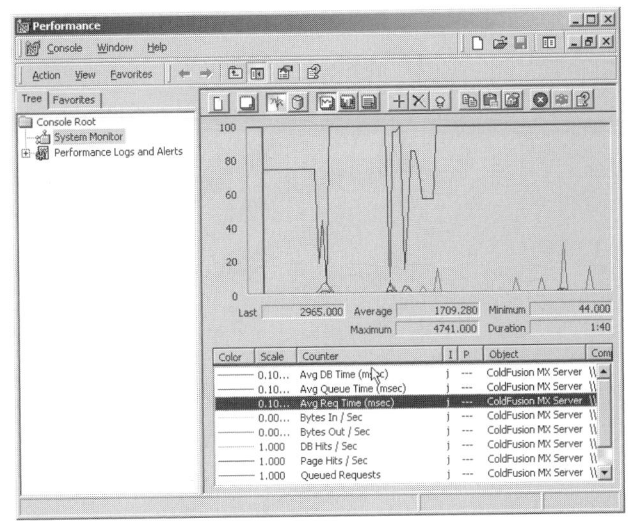

Figure 28.24

On Windows machines, you can use the Performance application to Monitor your ColdFusion server.

Enable CFSTAT

For non-Windows servers, you can use the CFSTAT command line utility to take the place of the Performance Monitor. It doesn't show up as a nice graph, but it displays the same information.

To use CFSTAT, follow these steps:

1. Make sure the Enable Debugging option is checked, since it affects all options on this page of the Administrator.
2. Make sure the Enable CFSTAT option is checked.
3. Do whatever is appropriate for the operating system you're using to execute the `cfstat` executable in the CFusionMX/bin folder. It's helpful to add a command line switch of `1`, so that the statistics will be updated once per second (Figure 28.25). UNIX and Linux users already know what to do here; if you're using Windows, launch a Command Prompt window (in the Accessories program group), then type: `\CFusionMX\bin\cfstat`

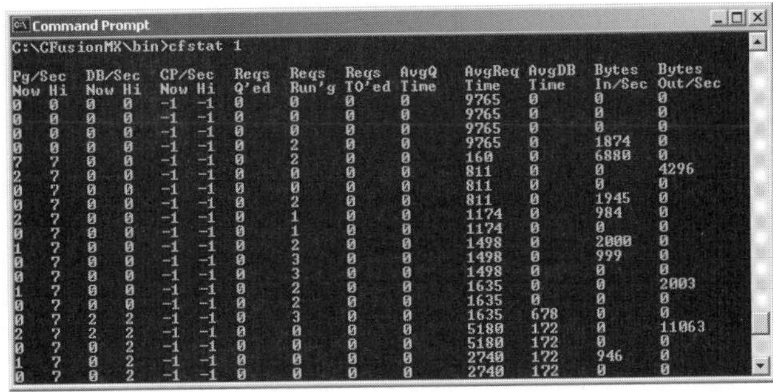

Command Prompt

C:\CFusionMX\bin>cfstat 1

Pg/Sec Now	Pg/Sec Hi	DB/Sec Now	DB/Sec Hi	CP/Sec Now	CP/Sec Hi	Reqs Q'ed	Reqs Run'g	Reqs TO'ed	AvgQ Time	AvgReq Time	AvgDB Time	Bytes In/Sec	Bytes Out/Sec
0	0	0	0	-1	-1	0	0	0	0	9765	0	0	0
0	0	0	0	-1	-1	0	0	0	0	9765	0	0	0
0	0	0	0	-1	-1	0	0	0	0	9765	0	0	0
0	0	0	0	-1	-1	0	2	0	0	9765	0	1874	0
7	7	0	0	-1	-1	0	2	0	0	160	0	6880	0
2	7	0	0	-1	-1	0	0	0	0	811	0	0	4296
0	7	0	0	-1	-1	0	0	0	0	811	0	0	0
0	7	0	0	-1	-1	0	2	0	0	811	0	1945	0
2	7	0	0	-1	-1	0	1	0	0	1174	0	984	0
0	7	0	0	-1	-1	0	1	0	0	1174	0	0	0
1	7	0	0	-1	-1	0	2	0	0	1498	0	2000	0
0	7	0	0	-1	-1	0	3	0	0	1498	0	999	0
0	7	0	0	-1	-1	0	3	0	0	1498	0	0	0
1	7	0	0	-1	-1	0	2	0	0	1635	0	0	2003
0	7	0	0	-1	-1	0	2	0	0	1635	0	0	0
0	7	2	2	-1	-1	0	3	0	0	1635	678	0	0
2	7	2	2	-1	-1	0	0	0	0	5180	172	0	11063
0	7	0	2	-1	-1	0	0	0	0	5180	172	0	0
1	7	0	2	-1	-1	0	0	0	0	2740	172	946	0
0	7	0	2	-1	-1	0	0	0	0	2740	172	0	0

Figure 28.25

You can use the CFSTAT utility to monitor your ColdFusion server's performance.

Table 28.3 shows the command line arguments (also called switches) supported by CFSTAT.

Table 28.3 `CFSTAT` Command Line Arguments

ARGUMENT	DESCRIPTION
1, 2, etc.	Refresh interval. You can provide any number as an argument to `cfstat`, which will cause it to display updated statistics on a separate line every few seconds, as shown in Figure 28.25. So, `cfstat 2` updates the statistics every 2 seconds, and so on.
`-s`	Use the `-s` option with a refresh interval to cause CFSTAT to accumulate statistics for the desired number of seconds, and then display the aggregated statistics on a single line at the end of the period. So, `cfstat -s 30` will collect statistics for 30 seconds; at the end of the 30 seconds, a single line of statistics will report on what happened during those 30 seconds.
`-n`	Use the `-n` option to omit the column headers that normally appear above the statistics (shown in Figure 28.25).
`/?`	Use `cfstat /?` to get further help on using CFSTAT, including the meaning of each statistic it displays.

The Debugging IP Addresses Page

While ColdFusion's debugging output is certainly helpful to you as a developer, you probably don't want your users or beta testers to see it. You may also want to get rid of it from time to time while you work, to keep in mind what your pages will look like without it.

Rather than having to turn off the debugging output on or off for the entire server at once, ColdFusion allows you to turn it on only for specific IP addresses. This way, you can turn on debugging but still make it show up for only the appropriate people. Also, you can remove your own IP address from the list to get rid of the display on your own computer, without affecting everyone else on your team.

To add an IP address, type it in the IP Address field and click Add. To remove an IP address, select it from the list and click Remove Selected.

TIP

To add your own IP address with one click, you can just click the Add Current button.

The Logging Settings Pages

As you learned in Chapter 14, ColdFusion keeps detailed log files that can be extremely helpful for monitoring or debugging an application. This page controls how ColdFusion maintains the log files, and allows you to turn on some additional log files that aren't kept by default.

NOTE

You can log your own messages in ColdFusion's logs with the `<CFLOG>` tag. You can even create your own log files for each of your applications. For details, see Appendix B, "ColdFusion Tag Reference."

Log directory

By default, ColdFusion stores all log files in the `CFusionMX/logs` folder (for a default Windows installation, that would be `c:\CFusionMX\logs`). You can use this option to change the location of the log files.

Maximum file size

When log files get very large, they can become unwieldy and hard to read. Use this option to set the maximum amount of information to keep in each log file. The default value is 5000 KB (around 5 megabytes). When a log file exceeds this size, its contents are copied into an *log archive* file. Log archives are the same as the original log files, except that they are given an extension of .1, .2, and so on instead of .log.

Maximum number of archives

So, a new archive file will be created each time the log file reaches 5000 KB (or whatever you specify). If you don't want an indefinite number of these archive files hanging around forever, you can tell ColdFusion to only maintain a certain number of archives for each log file. By default, a limit of 10 archives is used. If, when the actual log file reaches 5000 KB, there are already 10 archives present (perhaps application.1 through application.10), the oldest archive file is deleted.

Log slow pages

If you enable this option, a special entry in the server.log file will be made for any ColdFusion pages that take longer than the specified number of seconds to execute. You can use this information to identify bottlenecks in your application.

Log all CORBA calls

In you happen to be using CORBA objects in your application, enable this option to have ColdFusion log all CORBA interactions to the server.log file. The use of CORBA objects is not covered in this book; for more information, see `<CFOBJECT TYPE="Corba">` in Appendix B, ColdFusion Tag Reference. This topic is also covered in detail in the Extending ColdFusion with CORBA chapter in our companion volume, Advanced ColdFusion MX Application Development.

Enable logging for scheduled tasks

If you are using ColdFusion's built in task scheduler (see The Scheduled Tasks Page section, later in this chapter), you can enable this option to have all scheduler-related actions logged to a special log file called scheduler.log.

The Log Files Page

The Log Files page (Figure 28.26) allows you to view and manage all of the log files on your server. Each .log file in the CFusionMX/log folder (or whatever log file location you have specified) is listed. For each log, icons are provided to view, archive, download, or delete the log. When viewing a log, you can click on the Launch Filter button to launch the Log Viewer filter window (Figure 28.27). For more information about viewing and searching log files, please refer to Chapter 14.

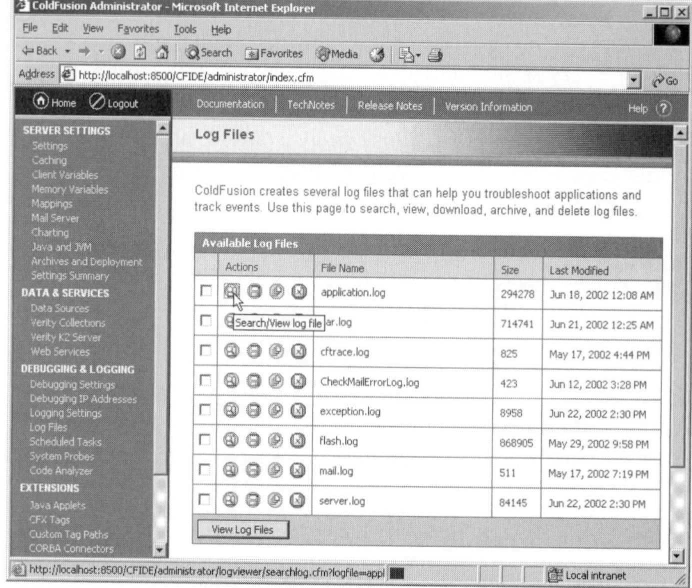

Figure 28.26

Use the log files age to view, manage, and download ColdFusion's logs.

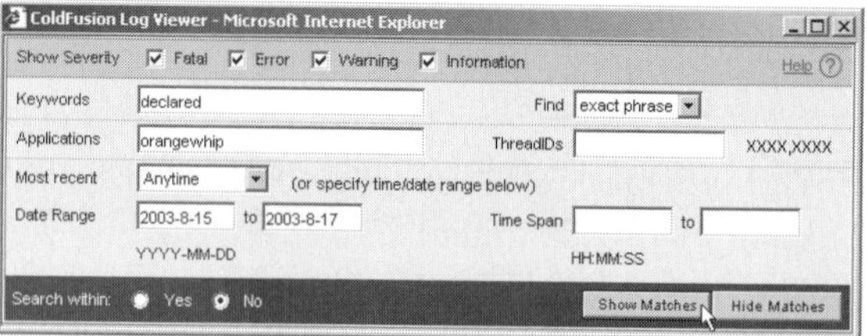

Figure 28.27

Use the Log Viewer to search your log files for specific entries.

The Scheduled Tasks Page

In Chapter 35, Event Scheduling, you will learn all about ColdFusion's built-in task scheduler, which allows you to create ColdFusion pages that run every few minutes or hours, or that execute at a certain time of day (Figure 28.28). Such pages are usually used to do things like sending mail, indexing Verity collections, deleting temporary files that are no longer needed, and other administrative tasks.

For more information about scheduling tasks, see Chapter 35, Event Scheduling.

NOTE

You can also schedule tasks programmatically with the `<CFSCHEDULE>` tag, instead of using the ColdFusion Administrator. For details, see Appendix B or Chapter 35.

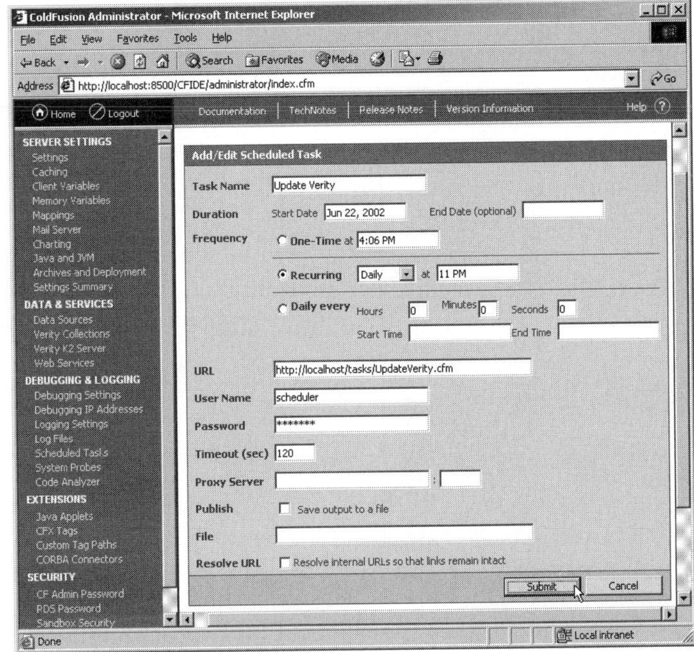

Figure 28.28

Use the scheduler to create pages that execute automatically based on time.

The System Probes Page

The System Probes page allows you to set up *probes* that check to see whether a particular page is executing normally. If not, ColdFusion can send you an email message so that you are among the very first to know when problems occur.

Managing System Probes

The System Probes page list all currently defined probes (Figure 28.29). Icons are provided to edit or delete each probe. There is also a Disable/Enable icon for each probe which you can use to temporarily turn a probe on or off. Finally, you can use the Run Probe icon to run a probe immediately, rather than waiting for it to run at its normally scheduled time or interval.

System Probe Options

At the bottom of the System Probes page, you will find a number of options to control the way ColdFusion handles notification when a probe finds a problem:

- **Notification Email Recipients**—Provide a list of email addresses that ColdFusion should use when sending out a notification that a probe has found a problem. Everyone you specify here will receive a notification about every failed probe.
- **Notification Sent From**—Specify a valid email address that ColdFusion's notification messages should use as their *from* field.

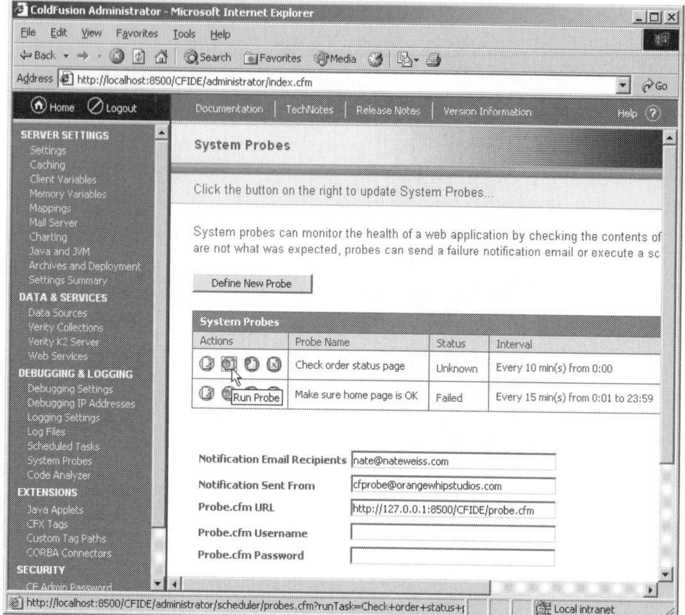

Figure 28.29

Use system probes to make sure your pages continue to run properly.

- **Probe.cfm URL**—Internally, the probe mechanism needs to be able to execute the Probe.cfm template in the CFIDE folder within your web server root. If for some reason you need to move the template or place it on a different virtual server, edit the URL accordingly. The Probe.cfm template is encrypted; you are not meant to be able to edit or customize it.
- **Probe.cfm Username and Password**—If you have used your web server software to secure access to the Probe.cfm file with a username and password, enter that username and password here.

Creating a New Probe

To create a new probe, click the Define New Probe button. The Add/Edit System Probe page appears (Figure 28.30). Table 28.4 briefly explains each of the fields on this page. When you are finished, click the Submit button to create the probe.

Table 28.4 Options Available for Each System Probe

OPTION	DESCRIPTION
Probe Name	A name for the new probe.
Frequency	The frequency at which you want the probe to check your ColdFusion page. You can specify the frequency in terms of hours, minutes, and seconds. You must supply an Start Time; if you wish you may also provide an End Time.
URL	The URL of the ColdFusion page (or other document) that you want the probe to check. Any URL that can be accessed via a browser is acceptable. The page does not have to be on the same server, or even on the same local network.
User Name	If the page requires authentication, supply a valid user name here.

Table 28.4 (CONTINUED)

OPTION	DESCRIPTION
Password	If the page requires authentication, supply the corresponding password.
Timeout	The number of seconds to wait for the page to respond. If the page does not respond within the specified timeout, ColdFusion will consider the probe to have failed and will notify people accordingly.
Proxy Server	If there is a proxy server between the ColdFusion server and the page being tested, enter the address and port number for the proxy server here.
Probe Failure	Check this option to have ColdFusion examine the actual text returned by the page being tested. You can use the *contains* option to make sure that the page is generating the content that it is supposed to, by entering a string that should appear near the bottom of the page. Or you could use the *does not contain* option to make sure that the page doesn't contain an error message or some other canary in the coal mine.
Failure Actions	You can have ColdFusion send out an email message whenever the probe finds a problem. The message will be sent to and from the addresses discussed in the previous section.
Publish	Enable this option if you want ColdFusion to save the content returned by the page you are checking. If you enable this option, fill in the File field as well.
File	Relevant only when the Publish option is checked. The path and filename to save the tested page's content to. The content will be saved to the server's drive at the location you specify here.
Resolve URL	Relevant only when the Publish option is checked. Enable this option if you want ColdFusion to resolve any internal URLs (such as URLs for images and links) so that the saved version of the page can be viewed correctly in a browser.

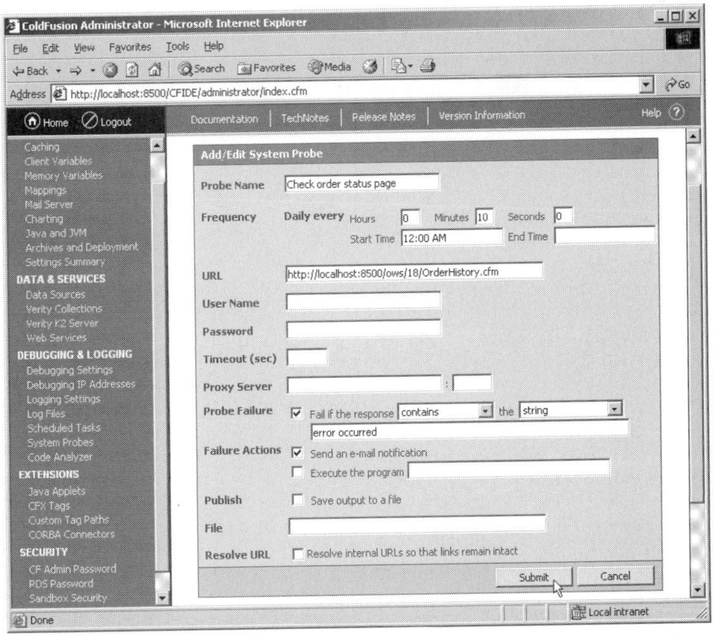

Figure 28.30

System probes help monitor your application's health.

The Code Analyzer Page

While ColdFusion MX is very close to being completely compatible with earlier versions of ColdFusion, a few details have changed which could cause problems with existing applications. The Code Analyzer page (Figure 28.31) can help you identify most of the potential compatibility issues ahead of time, before you even try to run your application under ColdFusion MX.

To run the analyzer, specify the location of the application files you would like to test in the Directory to Analyze field, then press Run Analyzer. If you click the Advanced Options button, you will be able to tell ColdFusion which files to inspect (the default is all .cfm files), which incompatibilities to check for (the default is to check for all incompatibilities), and whether to display only serious problems (the Warn vs. Info options).

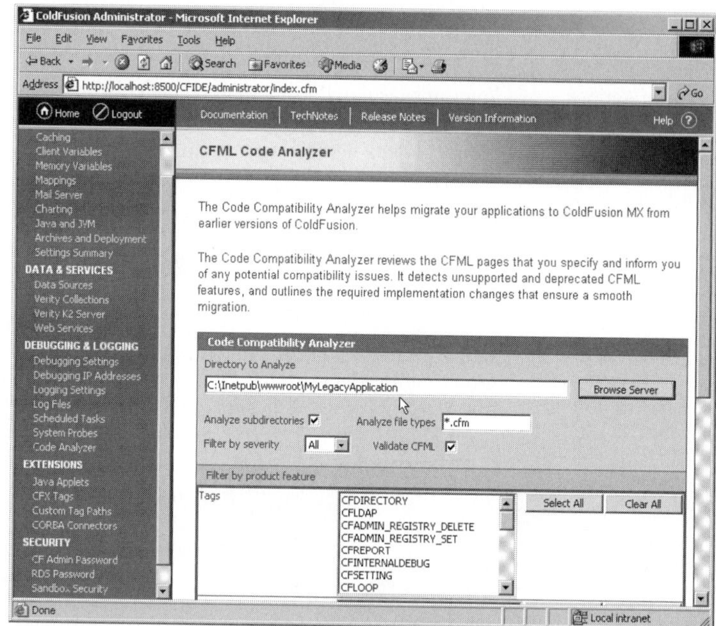

Figure 28.31
The Code Analyzer will check for incompatibilities within existing ColdFusion applications.

Extensions

In Chapter 20, Building Reusable Components, you learned how to create CFML Custom Tags to package your code into manageable, reusable components. There are other ways to extend ColdFusion as well, by writing CFX tags with Java or C++, by using CORBA objects, and more. The Extensions section of the Administrator allows to manage certain options related to extensibility.

The Java Applets Page

You can use the Java Applets page to create aliases for client-side Java applets that you use often throughout your applications. These aliases allow you to add the applets to individual pages with slightly simpler, more manageable code. Once the alias has been created, you include the actual applet in your pages with the `<CFAPPLET>` tag. For details, please refer to Chapter 34, Enhancing Forms with Client-Side Java.

The CFX Tags Page

It is possible to create new tags for ColdFusion that are written with Java or C++, rather than CFML. These are called CFX tags. CFX tags are usually created to add some kind of capability that is intrinsically easier or more sensible to implement with Java or C++ than with ColdFusion code. For instance, if you already have C++ code available that completes a particular task, why translate it into the corresponding ColdFusion code when you can just create a CFX tag that leverages the existing C++ code?

Development of CFX tags is discussed in detail in our companion volume, Advanced ColdFusion MX Application Framework. For now, let's assume that the tag has already been created, or that you simply want to use a CFX tag that you downloaded or purchased from another company.

Before a CFX tag can be used in your ColdFusion pages, it must be registered using the ColdFusion Administrator. The first thing you will need to know is whether the CFX tag in question was written with Java or C++. If you have been given a .class file (or files), then the CFX was written with Java. If it has a .dll extension, then it was created with C++.

NOTE

> Actually, although it's not officially supported, it's possible to create CFX tags with other tools, such as Delphi. If the CFX tag in question was created in any language other than Java, treat it as if it was created with C++ for the purposes of registering it with the Administrator.

Registering a Java CFX

To register a Java CFX, follow these steps:

1. On the CFX Tags page, click Register Java CFX. The Add/Edit Java CFX Tag page appears (Figure 28.32).
2. Enter the name of the CFX tag in the Tag Name field. The name must start with `CFX_` (but it's not case-sensitive).
3. Enter the name of the class file that implements the CFX tag in the Class Name field. You should type the name of the .class file (but without the .class extension). The class name is case-sensitive, so make sure to get the canalization exactly right. The actual .class file (as well as any other classes or files that the .class file depends on) must be located somewhere within the Java class path (see the Java and JVM Page section, earlier in this chapter).
4. If you wish, provide a description for the CFX tag.
5. Click the Submit button to register the CFX tag. Assuming that there are no problems with the CFX tag internally, and assuming that the .class file can be found in the Java class path, you can now use the CFX tag in your ColdFusion pages.

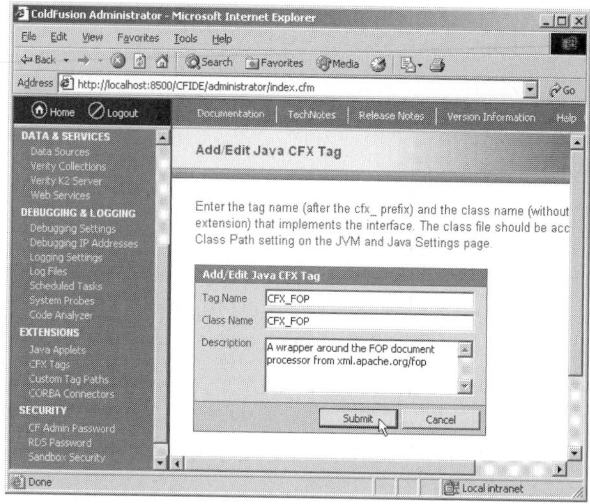

Figure 28.32
CFX tags must be registered in the Administrator before they can be used.

Registering a C++ CFX

To register a CFX tag that was written in C++, follow these steps:

1. On the CFX Tags page, click Register C++ CFX. The Add/Edit C++ CFX Tag page appears (Figure 28.33).
2. Enter the name of the CFX tag in the Tag Name field. The name must start with `CFX_` (but it's not case-sensitive).
3. Enter the name and location of the file that implements the CFX tag in the Class Name field. Most likely, this is a dynamic link library (.dll) file. You can use the Browse Server button to locate the file without typing.
4. Leave the Procedure field set to `ProcessTagRequest` unless you have been told otherwise by whoever created the CFX.
5. If you wish, provide a description for the CFX tag.
6. Click the Submit button to register the CFX tag. Assuming that there are no problems with the CFX tag internally, you can now use the CFX tag in your ColdFusion pages.

The Custom Tag Paths Page

In Chapter 20, Creating Reusable Components, you learned how to create CFML Custom Tags. You also learned that placing the custom tag file in the special CFusionMX/CustomTags folder directory automatically makes it available to all your ColdFusion pages. You can use the Custom Tag Paths page to change the location of the special CustomTags folder, or to create additional folders that behave just like the CustomTags folder (Figure 28.34).

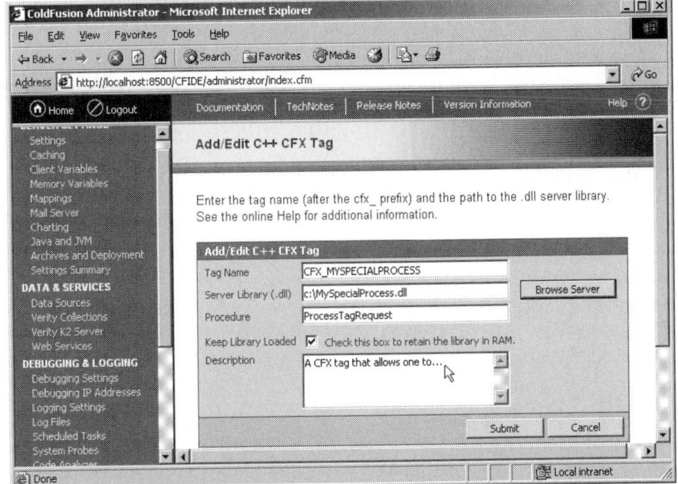

Figure 28.33

Once registered, Java and C++ tags can be used the same way in your ColdFusion pages.

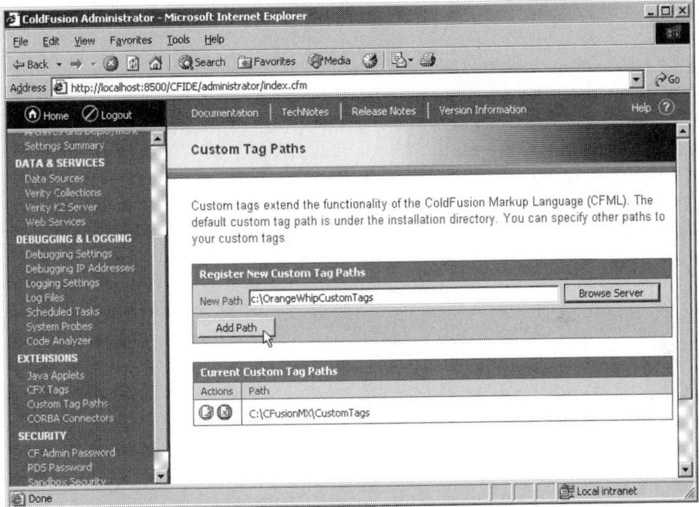

Figure 28.34

You can place custom tag files in any of the folders listed on this page.

To add a new custom tag path, enter the location in the New Path field and click Add Path. Once the path has been created, you can now place custom tag files within the folder you specified, and they will be found automatically, just as if they were placed in the built-in CFusionMX/CustomTags folder.

To edit or delete an existing tag path, use the icons provided for each entry in the Current Custom Tag Paths list.

The CORBA Connectors Page

If you plan to invoke CORBA objects or services within your ColdFusion pages, you need to set up a CORBA connector for the ORB you plan to use to broker your requests. ColdFusion ships with support for the Borland's VisiBroker product. If you need support for a different ORB vendor's product, you will need to contact Macromedia.

Assuming that you intend to use the VisiBroker support rather than some other ORB, you need to add a connector for VisiBroker by following these steps:

1. Click the Register CORBA Connector button on the CORBA Connectors page of the Administrator. The Edit CORBA Connector page appears (Figure 28.35).
2. In the ORB Name field, enter a descriptive name for the connector, such as `visibroker`.
3. In the ORB Class Name field, enter: `coldfusion.runtime.corba.VisibrokerConnector`
4. Leave the Classpath field blank.
5. In the ORB Property File field, enter the path to the vbjorb.properties file in ColdFusion's lib folder. For a default Windows installation, the correct path would be: `C:\CFusionMX\lib\vbjorb.properties`
6. Click Submit to create the connector.
7. Edit the SVCnameroot property in the vbjorb.properties file appropriately so that ColdFusion is able to find the root.

In addition, you will need to provide the appropriate value to the SVCnameroot property in the vbjorb.properties file. You will also need to make sure that the vbjorb.jar file is present (this file is distributed with VisiBroker) and that the path to vbjorb.jar is part of ColdFusion's Java class path setting (see the Java and JVM Page section, earlier in this chapter).

For a complete discussion of using CORBA with ColdFusion, see the Extending ColdFusion with CORBA chapter in our companion volume, Advanced ColdFusion MX Application Development.

Security

ColdFusion provides a number of security-related features. Some of these features are about adding login and role-based security mechanisms to your own applications. These mechanisms are discussed in Chapter 18, Securing Your Applications. The options in the Security portion of the ColdFusion Administrator, in contrast, are about securing the server itself so that only the proper people have the ability to administer ColdFusion. You can also lock down various parts of the server (tags, files, data sources, and so on) so that each application only has the right to use its own files and data.

NOTE

Your web server software also provides its own security measures. You should become familiar with them as well.

The CF Admin Password Page

Use the CF Admin Password page to change the password that you use to log in to the ColdFusion Administrator. Alternatively, you can disable the password altogether by clearing the Use a

ColdFusion Administration Password checkbox (Figure 28.35). It is important to understand that if the checkbox is cleared, then anyone will be able to access the Administrator unless you configure your web server software to secure the CFIDE/Administrator portion of the server's document root.

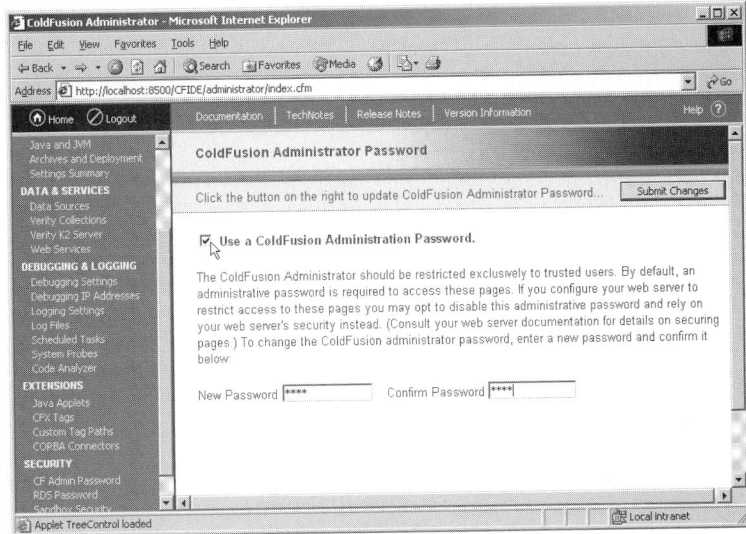

Figure 28.35

Use this page to change the ColdFusion Administrator password.

The RDS Password Page

The RDS password is what controls access to ColdFusion's file structure via Macromedia Dream-Weaver MX (or HomeSite+, or the older ColdFusion Studio product). Without this password, Dreamweaver MX can't directly browse through the database tables on the server, view CFCs, upload files via RDS, and so on. Use the RDS Password page to change the RDS password, or to disable the password altogether. If you disable the password, then anyone will be able to access your server's directories and other resources, so it is strongly recommended that you always use an RDS password and keep it safe.

The Sandbox Security Page

ColdFusion MX includes a new feature called *sandbox security*. This feature is mostly aimed at Internet Service Providers or people running large enterprise-wide servers, where a server may have many different ColdFusion applications that are written by many different developers. In such a situation, there needs to be some way to keep one set of developers from accessing the data sources that are being used by another set of developers. Similarly, there needs to be some way to keep one application from being able to use `<CFFILE>` or `<CFDIRECTORY>` to read or destroy files that are important to another application.

The idea behind sandbox security is to let you tell the server that the ColdFusion pages in certain directories either have more or fewer privileges than all other ColdFusion pages. For each of these special directories (sandboxes), you can tell ColdFusion to:

- Allow or forbid ColdFusion pages from accessing certain data sources via `<CFQUERY>`, `<CFINSERT>`, `<CFUPDATE>`, or similar tags.
- Allow or forbid ColdFusion pages from using accessing certain files or directories via `<CFDIRECTORY>`, `<CFFILE>`, `<CFEXECUTE>`, and related tags and functions
- Allow or forbid ColdFusion pages from using certain CFML tags and functions altogether
- Allow or forbid ColdFusion pages from accessing other servers over the Internet with the `<CFHTTP>`, `<CFFTP>`, `<CFMAIL>` or similar tags.

NOTE

Earlier versions of ColdFusion also contained a feature that covered similar conceptual ground and was sometimes called sandbox security or advanced security (the terms were used somewhat interchangeably), but the ColdFusion MX implementation is so different that it might as well be considered an entirely new feature.

Thinking about Sandboxes

There are basically two ways to go about managing sandboxes for your ColdFusion server:

- If there is a particular application (or developer) that you don't trust to behave nicely, you can create a sandbox for its root directory that denies it access to everything but what it actually needs. All other applications, including those created in the future, will be unaffected.
- If you would rather consider all applications to be untrusted (or if the applications shouldn't be considered to trust one another), you can create a larger sandbox for your entire document root that denies access to everything. You then create smaller sandboxes for each individual application, specifically granting access to only what that application needs.

In general, the second approach is the most flexible, and doesn't require very much extra effort at all.

Creating and Editing Security Sandboxes

To create a new security sandbox, enter the path to the directory you want to make more or less omniscient in the Add Security Sandbox field (you can use the Browse Server button to specify the directory without typing). When you click the Add button, the new sandbox is added to the Defined Directory Permissions list (Figure 28.36).

TIP

If you want, you can select an existing sandbox from the drop down list, which will cause all the access rights from the selected sandbox to be copied to the sandbox you're creating. This can be a real timesaver if you are creating multiple sandboxes with similar access rights.

To edit a sandbox (including one that you just added), just click on the Edit icon for the sandbox. To remove a sandbox, click the Delete icon.

NOTE

You can't delete the two built-in system directory sandboxes, which are used internally by ColdFusion. These sandboxes are what allow the ColdFusion Administrator to continue functioning even if you place the rest of the ColdFusion pages in a very restrictive sandbox.

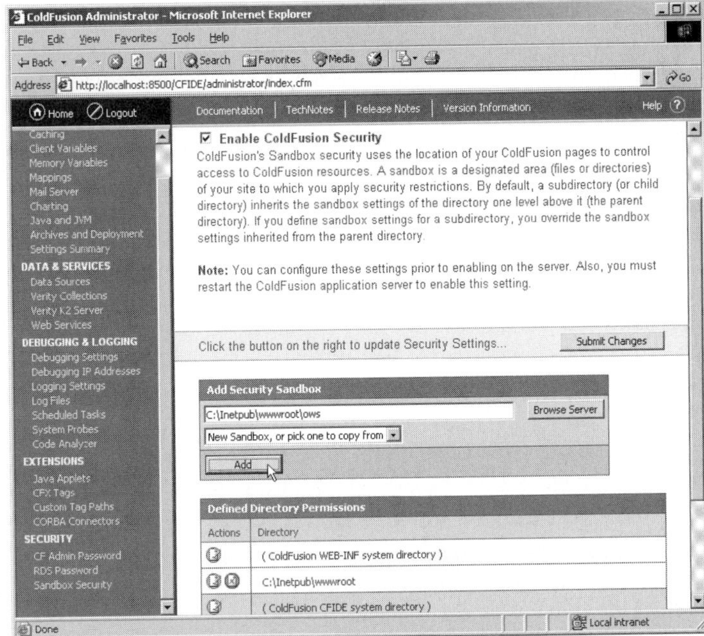

Figure 28.36

You can add new security sandboxes to control access to the server.

Restricting Access to Data Sources

When you click the Edit icon for a sandbox, the Security Permissions page appears. This page has are five tabs across the top, the first of which being Data Sources (Figure 28.37).

ColdFusion pages in the sandbox directory you're editing will be able to access all the data sources in the Enabled Data Sources list (on the left). To disable access to a data source, select it and click the >> button to move it into the Disabled Data Sources list. Continue to move the data sources back and forth until only the appropriate data sources are enabled.

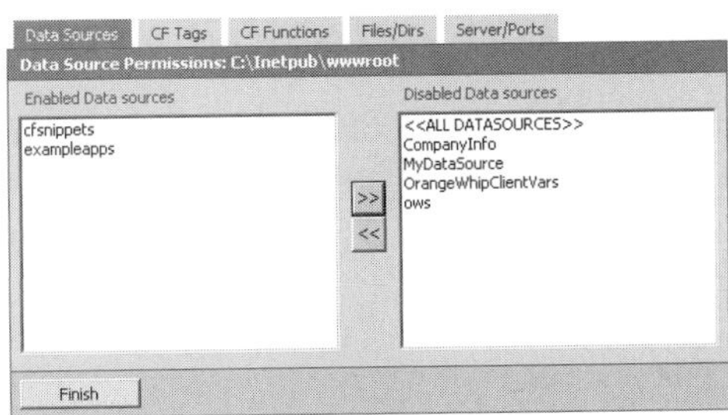

Figure 28.37

You can easily keep applications from being able to access each other's databases.

For instance, say you were editing a sandbox for your web server's document root directory (perhaps c:\inetpub\wwwroot). The list in Figure 28.37 enables only the cfsnippets and exampleapps datasources for that sandbox. The assumption is that since these are just example databases, they can be safely accessed by anyone. All other data sources should be considered private, accessible only to the applications that actually need them. Once the sandbox for the document root was set up as shown in Figure 28.37, you could set up a smaller sandbox for the ows folder (perhaps c:\inetpub\wwwroot\ows) that enabled the ows data source. The combination of these two sandboxes would mean that only the ColdFusion files in the ows folder (and its subfolders) would be able to use `DATASOURCE="ows"` in a `<CFQUERY>` or other database-related tag. If some other ColdFusion page attempted to use the data source, an error message would be displayed whenever the page was accessed with a browser.

NOTE

The special `<<ALL DATASOURCES>>` item behaves like a wildcard. It represents all datasources that exist now as well as ones that are created in the future. If you move this item to the disabled side of the page, that means that the sandbox will not have access to any data sources at all (unless access is specifically granted by some other, nested sandbox).

Restricting Access to Tags and Functions

You can restrict access to CFML tags and functions for each sandbox. For instance, the configuration shown in Figure 28.38 would keep all ColdFusion pages on the server from being able to access the `<CFDIRECTORY>`, `<CFEXECUTE>`, `<CFFILE>`, and `<CFFTP>` tags. You could then grant specific applications the right to use these tags by creating nested sandboxes, making sure the appropriate tags are in the Enabled Tags list for each application's sandbox.

The CF Functions tab works the same way.

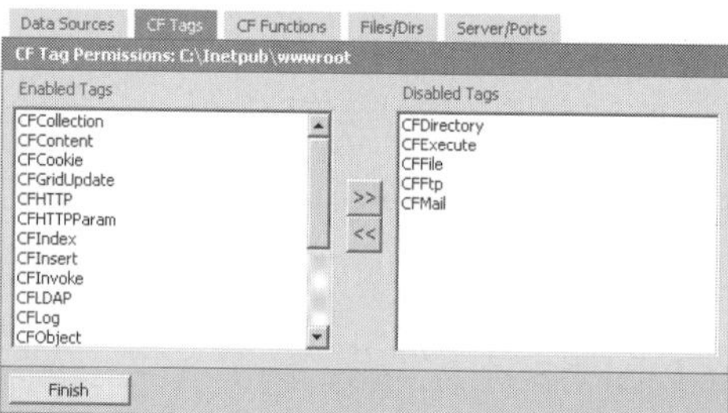

Figure 28.38

You can grant or deny access to any tags you feel are dangerous.

Restricting Access to Files and Directories

Use the Files/Dirs tab to keep the `<CFFILE>`, `<CFDIRECTORY>`, `<CFEXECUTE>`, and similar tags and functions from being able to freely access or change the files on the server's drive. When you create a sandbox, two paths are automatically added to the Secured Files and Directories list (Figure 28.39).

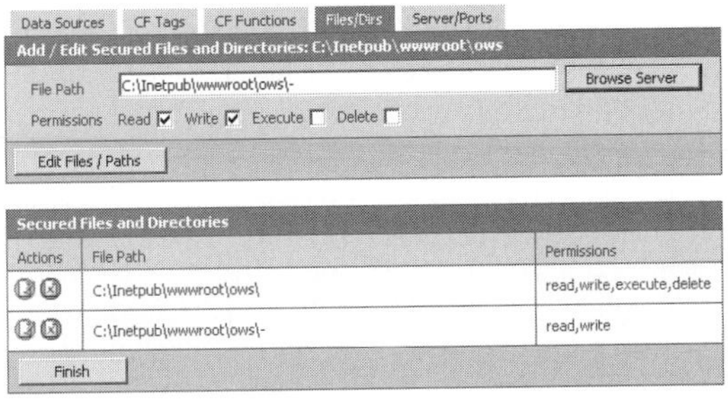

Figure 28.39

You can edit the file permissions for the ColdFusion pages in each security sandbox.

The sandbox being edited in this figure is for the ows folder within my web server's document root. Note that two Secured Paths appear in the list; these were created automatically by ColdFusion when I created the sandbox. The first Secured Path (the one without the trailing - character) refers to the files in the ows folder itself, but not any of its subfolders. The second entry, because of the trailing - sign, refers to all subfolders (even nested subfolders) within ows. In the figure, I am altering the Permissions options (for ows and its subfolders) such that the ColdFusion pages in the ows application will be able to use `<CFFILE>` and `<CFDIRECTORY>` to read, create, and change files in this part of the server, but will not be able to delete files with `<CFILE>` or execute files with `<CFEXECUTE>`.

If I wanted my application to be able to accept file uploads from users, I might decide to create a new `uploads` folder within the ows directory. I would probably want the `<CFFILE>` and `<CFDIRECTORY>` to be able to work freely in this new `uploads` folder, but not elsewhere on the server. I would add a new Secured Path by typing the path to the uploads folder in the File Path field, make sure the Read, Write, and Delete permissions are checked, and then clicking the Edit Files/Paths button. I would then delete the two Secured Paths that ColdFusion created for me, leaving `<CFFILE>` and `<CFDIRECTORY>` able to access the uploads folder but not any other files in the ows directory. (This is assuming that a larger sandbox for the web server's entire document root has been created which has denied access to all files via removal of its two automatic Secured Path entries.)

NOTE

Restricting the files and directories that can be accessed via the `<CFFILE>` and `<CFDIRECTORY>` tags is separate from enabling or disabling the tags themselves. To disable the actual tags for a sandbox, use the CF Tags tab (discussed in the previous section).

Restricting Access to Other Servers and Ports

For each sandbox, you can restrict the ability of ColdFusion pages to access other servers on the Internet via the `<CFHTTP>`, `<CFMAIL>`, `<CFPOP>`, `<CFLDAP>`, or `<CFFTP>`. By default, any of these tags can access any machine on the Internet. For each sandbox, you can add entries for specific machines and IP ports. From that point forward, the tags can only access the machines and IP ports you added. Any attempt to access some other machine or port number will fail.

For instance, you might want to let most of your applications be able to use the `<CFHTTP>` tag, but you want to make sure that the `<CFHTTP>` tag can only be used to retrieve pages from certain sites, for instance Google and Yahoo!. You don't want ColdFusion code to be able to retrieve pages from arbitrary URLs on the Internet. This is easily accomplished by specifically enabling IP port 80 for each of the desired sites (Figure 38.40).

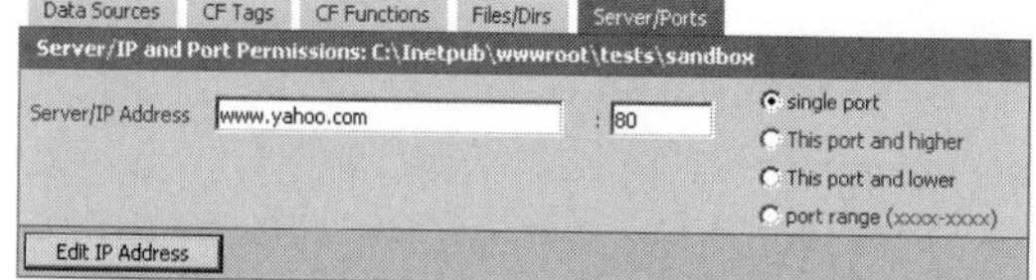

Figure 28.40
Sandboxes allow ColdFusion pages to access just the servers that you feel are appropriate.

Table 28.5 shows the IP ports that you would typically want to allow access to in order to enable the various tasks supported by ColdFusion's internet protocol tags.

Table 28.5 IP Ports Typically Used by Internet Protocol Tags

TASK	PORT NUMBER
Sending mail with `<CFMAIL>`	25
Checking mail with `<CFPOP>`	110
Retrieving pages with `<CFHTTP>`	80 for normal Web URLs (starting with http://), or 443 for secured URLs (starting with https://)
Transferring files with `<CFFTP>`	21
Accessing user data with `<CFLDAP>`	389

CHAPTER 29

More About SQL and Queries

IN THIS CHAPTER

Advanced SQL Topics

You have already learned quite a bit about SQL in this book. In Chapter 5, "Introducing SQL," you learned how to retrieve records using SELECT, WHERE, and ORDER BY. In Chapter 6, "SQL Data Manipulation," you learned how to change the data in your database with INSERT, UPDATE, and DELETE and how to use the AS keyword to create aliases. You have also seen how the <CFQUERY> tag lets you create SQL statements dynamically, based on form parameters and other variables.

This chapter introduces you to some additional topics related to querying your databases with Macromedia ColdFusion MX. This section explains certain aspects of SQL that haven't been discussed yet, and which will be particularly relevant when putting together report style pages.

Later in this chapter, the "Additional <CFQUERY> Topics" section explains how to use several advanced features of the <CFQUERY> tag, including ColdFusion's "query of queries" (also known as In Memory Queries) feature.

NOTE

The discussion in this section assumes that you have already read Chapters 5 and 6 or that you have used SQL on your own in the past. If not, it's recommended that you take a few minutes to look through Chapters 5 and 6 (especially Chapter 5) before reading on here.

Getting Unique Records with DISTINCT

In Chapter 5, you learned how to use the SELECT statement to retrieve records from your database tables, with or without WHERE or ORDER BY clauses. You can add DISTINCT to these SELECT statements in situations in which you don't want to retrieve duplicate rows from your tables.

In general, all you have to do is add the DISTINCT keyword directly after the SELECT keyword. As an example, Listing 29.1 shows the results of two queries side by side. The first query retrieves the descriptions for all expenses logged in the Expenses table. The second query is exactly the same as the first, except it uses the `DISTINCT` keyword to ensure that any repeats in the result set are eliminated before the query results are returned to ColdFusion. As you can see from Figure 29.1, the first query returns multiple entries for Costumes and Extras, whereas the second query does not.

TIP

It's often appropriate to remove duplicated values when creating report-style pages. Even if duplicated entries don't yet exist in your database, keep `DISTINCT` in the back of your mind when putting together such pages.

Listing 29.1 `Distinct.cfm`—Using `DISTINCT` to Eliminate Duplicates

```
<!---
  Filename:   Distinct.cfm
  Created by: Nate Weiss (NMW)
  Purpose:    Demonstrates use of SQL DISTINCT keyword
--->

<!--- Retrieve Expense Descriptions from Expense table; --->
<!--- This query may include any repeated descriptions  --->
<CFQUERY NAME="GetExp" DATASOURCE="#REQUEST.DataSource#">
  SELECT Description
  FROM Expenses
  ORDER BY Description
</CFQUERY>

<!--- Retrieve Expense Descriptions from Expense table; --->
<!--- The DISTINCT means we won't get any repeated rows --->
<CFQUERY NAME="GetUniqueExp" DATASOURCE="#REQUEST.DataSource#">
  SELECT DISTINCT Description
  FROM Expenses
  ORDER BY Description
</CFQUERY>

<HTML>
<HEAD><TITLE>Film Expenses</TITLE></HEAD>
<BODY>
<H2>What Are We Spending Money On?</H2>

<TABLE BORDER="1">
  <TR VALIGN="Top">
    <!--- First, ordinary SELECT records --->
    <TD>Ordinary SELECT statement:
      <OL>
      <CFOUTPUT QUERY="GetExp">
        <LI>#GetExp.Description#</LI>
      </CFOUTPUT>
      </OL>
    </TD>
    <!--- Now the SELECT DISTINCT records --->
    <TD>SELECT DISTINCT statement:
      <OL>
      <CFOUTPUT QUERY="GetUniqueExp">
        <LI>#GetUniqueExp.Description#</LI>
      </CFOUTPUT>
      </OL>
    </TD>
```

Listing 29.1 (continued)

```
    </TR>
  </TABLE>

  </BODY>
  </HTML>
```

NOTE

You could get the same unique effect in other ways. For instance, you could just run the first query and then add a `GROUP="Description"` attribute to the `<CFOUTPUT>` tag, causing ColdFusion to display a record only if its `Description` value were different from the previous row's (see Chapter 10, "Creating Data-Driven Pages," for more information about `GROUP`). However, the `DISTINCT` approach would be more efficient because the duplicate records never leave the database in the first place.

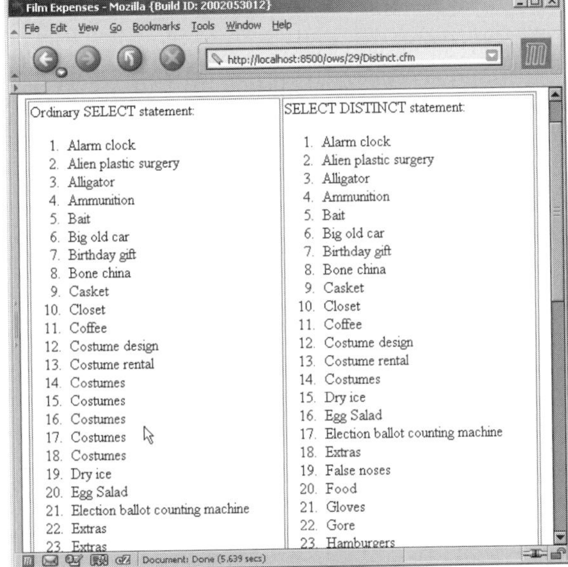

Figure 29.1

The value Costumes, which appears several times in the `Expenses` table, appears only once when `DISTINCT` is used.

NOTE

It is important to understand that the `DISTINCT` keyword applies to all columns in each row being returned by the query, not just the first column. So, if the `SELECT` statements in Listing 29.1 were selecting the `ExpenseAmount` column as well as the `Description` column, rows would be eliminated only in the unlikely event that the descriptions *and* expense amounts were exactly the same.

Summarizing Data with Aggregate Functions

SQL provides a number of aggregate functions for your use. Aggregate functions are used to crunch information from any number of rows into a summarized overview of your data. Again, you will find yourself using these functions most often when trying to present some type of big picture to your users, such as with report-style summaries or overviews in your ColdFusion applications.

NOTE

Aggregate functions are sometimes called *set functions*, or *set-based functions*.

Standard Aggregate Functions

There are five standard aggregate functions, which any SQL-compliant database system should support: `COUNT`, `SUM`, `AVG`, `MIN`, and `MAX`. Table 29.1 explains what each of these functions does and the types of columns they can generally be used with (although certain database systems might make exceptions).

Table 29.1 Standard SQL Aggregate Functions

FUNCTION	ON NUMERIC COLUMNS	ON DATE COLUMNS	ON CHARACTER COLUMNS
`COUNT(*)`	Counts the number of rows in a table	(same)	(same)
`COUNT(column)`	Counts the number of values found in a column	(same)	(same)
`SUM(column)`	Adds the total of the values found in a column	(not allowed)	(not allowed)
`AVG(column)`	Computes the average of values found in a column	(not allowed)	(not allowed)
`MIN(column)`	Finds the smallest value	Finds the earliest date	Finds the first value in a column (alphabetically)
`MAX(column)`	Finds the largest value	Finds the latest date	Finds the last value in a column (alphabetically)

NOTE

Some database systems might support additional aggregate or aggregate-like functions, such as `FIRST` and `LAST`, and related keywords, such as `PIVOT`, `CUBE`, and `ROLLUP`. Consult your database documentation for details.

Listing 29.2 shows how aggregate functions can be used in a ColdFusion template. This example uses `COUNT`, `SUM`, `AVG`, `MIN`, and `MAX` on numeric and date values in Orange Whip Studios' `Expenses` table. The query result set that is returned contains just one row of data (the computed, summarized information from the database) and seven columns (ExpenseCount, DateMin, DateMax, and so on). The results are shown in Figure 29.2.

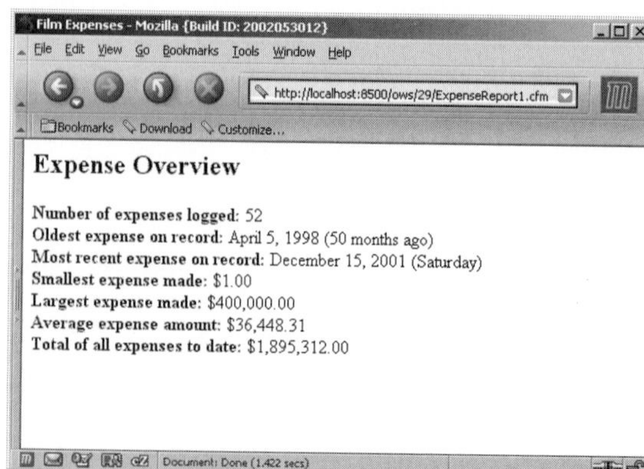

Figure 29.2

Aggregate functions can be used to report on trends in your data.

Listing 29.2 `ExpenseReport1.cfm`—Using Aggregate Functions on All Records of a Table

```
<!---
  Filename:   ExpenseReport1.cfm
  Created by: Nate Weiss (NMW)
  Purpose:    Demonstrates use of SQL aggregate functions
--->

<!--- Retrieve summarized expense data from database --->
<CFQUERY NAME="GetExp" DATASOURCE="#REQUEST.DataSource#">
  SELECT
    COUNT(*) AS ExpenseCount,
    MIN(ExpenseDate)   AS DateMin,
    MAX(ExpenseDate)   AS DateMax,
    MIN(ExpenseAmount) AS ExpenseMin,
    MAX(ExpenseAmount) AS ExpenseMax,
    SUM(ExpenseAmount) AS ExpenseSum,
    AVG(ExpenseAmount) AS ExpenseAvg
  FROM Expenses
</CFQUERY>


<HTML>
<HEAD><TITLE>Film Expenses</TITLE></HEAD>
<BODY>
<H2>Expense Overview</H2>

<!--- Output high-level expense summary --->
<CFOUTPUT>
  <B>Number of expenses logged:</B>
    #GetExp.ExpenseCount#<BR>

  <B>Oldest expense on record:</B>
    #LSDateFormat(GetExp.DateMin, "mmmm d, yyyy")#
    (#DateDiff("m", GetExp.DateMin, Now())# months ago)<BR>

  <B>Most recent expense on record:</B>
    #LSDateFormat(GetExp.DateMax, "mmmm d, yyyy (dddd)")#<BR>

  <B>Smallest expense made:</B>
    #LSCurrencyFormat(GetExp.ExpenseMin)#<BR>

  <B>Largest expense made:</B>
    #LSCurrencyFormat(GetExp.ExpenseMax)#<BR>

  <B>Average expense amount:</B>
    #LSCurrencyFormat(GetExp.ExpenseAvg)#<BR>

  <B>Total of all expenses to date:</B>
    #LSCurrencyFormat(GetExp.ExpenseSum)#<BR>
</CFOUTPUT>

</BODY>
</HTML>
```

NOTE

Queries that use only aggregate functions in their `SELECT` lists, such as the query in Listing 29.2, will never return more than one row.

NOTE

It's important to note that no "source" columns are being selected on their own by the query in this listing (the only columns the query returns are the temporary ones named with the AS keyword). To mix ordinary column references and aggregate columns in the same `SELECT` list, you also must add a `GROUP BY` clause (discussed in the next section). Otherwise, you will get an error message from the database driver.

Getting More Selective with `WHERE`

You can use `WHERE` and aggregates in the same query to get summarized records about only certain rows in your database tables. For instance, if a parameter named `FilmID` might be passed to the page in the URL, you could show the summarized expense information for just that film by adding the following to the `<CFQUERY>` tag in Listing 29.2 (right after the `FROM` line of the query):

```
<!--- Limit expense summary to single film, if provided --->
<CFIF IsDefined("URL.FilmID")>
  WHERE FilmID = #URL.FilmID#
</CFIF>
```

The results would look the same when viewed in a browser, except that the various totals and dates would apply only to the `FilmID` (if any) specified in the URL. When no `FilmID` parameter is provided, the data for all expenses would continue to be shown (as shown previously in Figure 29.2).

NOTE

Be careful not to confuse `WHERE` with `HAVING` (discussed later in this section). As a rule, you almost always should use `WHERE` when specifying criteria. `HAVING` is generally used for special cases only.

Breaking It Down with `GROUP BY`

So far, you have seen how aggregate functions can be used to run simple computations that return only one row of data, which reports the computed sums (or averages, or counts) of all matching records at once. You'll often want to break down the computations further, returning a separate set of summary data results for each value in a particular column. You can get this effect by adding a `GROUP BY` clause to your query.

To use `GROUP BY`, the columns for which you want summarized data are added in two places: the query's `SELECT` list and the new `GROUP BY` clause, which should come right after the `FROM` part of your query (but before any `ORDER BY` clause).

Behind the scenes, your database breaks down your data into groups, one for each value found in your `GROUP BY` columns. Each of your aggregate functions is computed separately for each group. When the results are returned to ColdFusion, one row will exist for each unique value in your `GROUP BY` column(s). That is, there will be one row for each group.

Listing 29.3 shows how `GROUP BY` can be used to apply aggregate functions, such as `SUM`, to each group in the `Expenses` table. Here, the results are broken down (or grouped) by `FilmID`. The results are shown in Figure 29.3.

Listing 29.3 ExpenseReport2.cfm—Using GROUP BY with Aggregate Functions to Break Down Your Data

```
<!---
  Filename:   ExpenseReport2.cfm
  Created by: Nate Weiss (NMW)
  Purpose:    Demonstrates use of SQL aggregate functions
--->

<!--- Retrieve summarized expense data from database --->
<CFQUERY NAME="GetExp" DATASOURCE="#REQUEST.DataSource#">
  SELECT
    f.FilmID, f.MovieTitle,
    SUM(ExpenseAmount) AS ExpenseSum
  FROM Expenses e, Films f
  WHERE e.FilmID = f.FilmID
  GROUP BY f.FilmID, f.MovieTitle
  ORDER BY f.MovieTitle
</CFQUERY>


<HTML>
<HEAD><TITLE>Film Expenses</TITLE></HEAD>
<BODY>
<H2>Expense Overview</H2>

<!--- Output film-level expense summary --->
<CFTABLE
  QUERY="GetExp"
  HTMLTABLE="Yes"
  BORDER="Yes"
  COLHEADERS="Yes">

  <CFCOL
    HEADER="Film Title"
    TEXT="#MovieTitle#">
  <CFCOL
    HEADER="Amount"
    TEXT="#LSCurrencyFormat(ExpenseSum)#"
    ALIGN="RIGHT">

</CFTABLE>

</BODY>
</HTML>
```

NOTE

If you specify more than one column in the GROUP BY part of your query, the results will include one record for each unique permutation of values among the specified columns. That is, each unique permutation of values in the GROUP BY columns is what defines a new group.

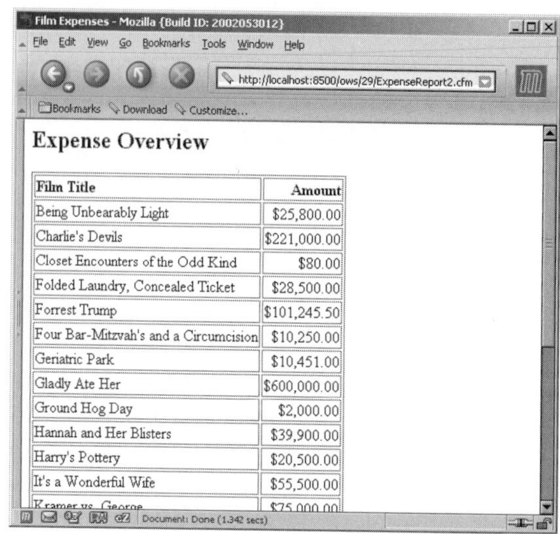

Film Expenses - Mozilla {Build ID: 2002053012}
File Edit View Go Bookmarks Tools Window Help
http://localhost:8500/ows/29/ExpenseReport2.cfm
Bookmarks Download Customize...
Expense Overview
Film Title Amount
Being Unbearably Light $25,800.00
Charlie's Devils $221,000.00
Closet Encounters of the Odd Kind $80.00
Folded Laundry, Concealed Ticket $28,500.00
Forrest Trump $101,245.50
Four Bar-Mitzvah's and a Circumcision $10,250.00
Geriatric Park $10,451.00
Gladly Ate Her $600,000.00
Ground Hog Day $2,000.00
Hannah and Her Blisters $39,900.00
Harry's Pottery $20,500.00
It's a Wonderful Wife $55,500.00
Document: Done (1.342 secs)

Figure 29.3

Aggregate functions become more powerful when combined with `GROUP BY` to break down the results.

Filtering Summarized Records with `HAVING`

You've seen how you can use `WHERE` to cause only certain rows to be considered by aggregate functions such as `SUM` and `MAX`. That's fine for filtering totals based on something fixed, such as an ID number. But what if you wanted to apply a different type of filtering criteria, based on what the values are after the aggregate functions do their work, not before?

The `HAVING` keyword lets you do just that. You get to provide criteria using the same syntax you use in a `WHERE` clause, using the =, <, and > operators. The difference is that the `HAVING` criteria is applied to the final grouped rows just before they are returned to ColdFusion, whereas the `WHERE` criteria is applied before any of the values are considered for grouping in the first place.

To use `HAVING`, place it directly after the `GROUP BY` part of your query (but before the `ORDER BY` part, if any). For instance, if you wanted to keep films with a small amount of expenses from being shown in the report from Listing 29.3, you could change the query code from this

```
WHERE e.FilmID = f.FilmID
GROUP BY f.FilmID, f.MovieTitle
```

to this

```
WHERE e.FilmID = f.FilmID
GROUP BY f.FilmID, f.MovieTitle
HAVING SUM(ExpenseAmount) > 1000
```

Now only those groups that have a total expense of more than `1000` will be returned to ColdFusion. Note that this is very different from the following:

```
WHERE e.FilmID = f.FilmID
AND ExpenseAmount > 1000
GROUP BY f.FilmID, f.MovieTitle
```

This snippet simply means that no individual expenses that are less than `1,000` will be considered; the total amount for any group (film) could exceed `1,000`. The `HAVING` snippet, by contrast, considers only the total for each film, with no regard to how big the individual payments are.

Of course, you can combine both concepts, like so:

```
WHERE e.FilmID = f.FilmID
AND ExpenseAmount < 50000
GROUP BY f.FilmID, f.MovieTitle
HAVING SUM(ExpenseAmount) > 1000
```

The previous snippet shows total spending only for films that have `1,000` or more in expenses. However, in coming up with these totals, it ignores any individual expenses that are very large (more than `50,000`). This might be useful to an executive at Orange Whip Studios who probably doesn't care about movies that are spending very small amounts of money (less than `1,000` total) and who also probably already knows about the really big expenditures (more than `50,000` each). This report lets the executive focus on the middle ground, where movie executives seem to feel most at home.

Listing 29.4 is a simple revision of the template from Listing 29.3, which presents the data returned from this last version of the query. Figure 29.4 shows the results.

NOTE

Compared with everything else you're learning in this chapter, `HAVING` is relatively obscure, and you may not find yourself using it much. That said, it's still good to know everything that's available to you.

Listing 29.4 `ExpenseReport3.cfm`—Using `GROUP BY`, `HAVING`, `WHERE`, and Aggregate Functions Together

```
<!---
  Filename:    ExpenseReport3.cfm
  Created by: Nate Weiss (NMW)
  Purpose:     Demonstrates use of SQL aggregate functions
--->

<!--- These values will control the filtering --->
<CFSET FilterMinTotal = 1000>
<CFSET FilterMaxIndiv = 50000>

<!--- Retrieve summarized expense data from database --->
<CFQUERY NAME="GetExp" DATASOURCE="#REQUEST.DataSource#">
  SELECT
    f.FilmID, f.MovieTitle,
    SUM(ExpenseAmount) AS ExpenseSum
  FROM Expenses e, Films f
  WHERE e.FilmID = f.FilmID
  AND ExpenseAmount < #FilterMaxIndiv#
  GROUP BY f.FilmID, f.MovieTitle
  HAVING SUM(ExpenseAmount) > #FilterMinTotal#
  ORDER BY f.MovieTitle
</CFQUERY>


<HTML>
<HEAD><TITLE>Film Expenses</TITLE></HEAD>
<BODY>
```

Listing 29.4 (continued)

```
<H2>Expense Overview</H2>
<CFOUTPUT>
  <!--- Note that we are filtering out small numbers --->
  For clarity, films that haven't reported more than <BR>
  #LSCurrencyFormat(FilterMinTotal, "international")#
  have been ommitted from this list.<BR>
  In addition, large payments
  (over #LSCurrencyFormat(FilterMaxIndiv, "international")#) <BR>
  have not been considered in the totals.<BR>
</CFOUTPUT>

<!--- Output film-level expense summary --->
<CFTABLE
  QUERY="GetExp"
  HTMLTABLE="Yes"
  BORDER="Yes"
  COLHEADERS="Yes">

  <CFCOL
    HEADER="Film Title"
    TEXT="#MovieTitle#">
  <CFCOL
    HEADER="Amount"
    TEXT="#LSCurrencyFormat(ExpenseSum)#"
    ALIGN="RIGHT">

</CFTABLE>

</BODY>
</HTML>
```

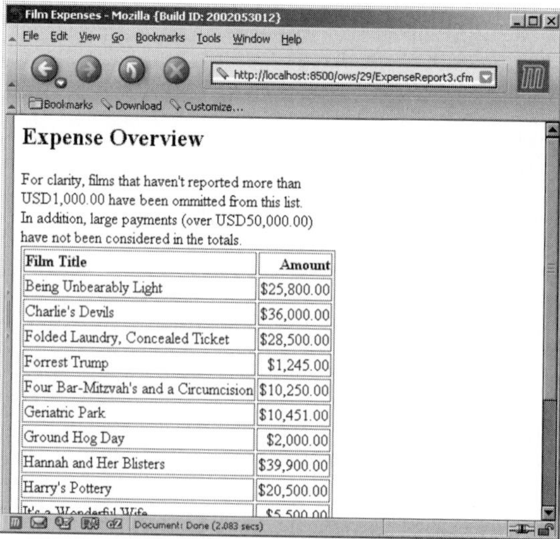

Figure 29.4

The HAVING keyword lets you filter records based on the results of your aggregate functions.

Selecting Related Data with Joins

The design of the tables in Orange Whip Studios' database calls for a number of relationships between the various tables. This section focuses on the relationships between the `Films`, `Actors`, and `FilmsActors` tables.

You will recall that the `Films` and `Actors` tables contain relatively straightforward information about the studio's films and actors (the title of each movie, the name of each actor, and so on). That is, the principal purpose of these two tables is to remember the attributes of each film and actor. In contrast, the principal purpose of the `FilmsActors` table is to connect each film with its actors (and vice versa). Yes, there are a couple of extra columns in `FilmsActors` (the `Salary` and `IsStarringRole` columns), but the really important columns are the `FilmID` and `ActorID` columns. Because of these two columns, the database is able to track the relationship between the other two tables (`Films` and `Actors`).

Because tables such as `FilmsActors` define the relationship, or connection, between other tables, they can be thought of as connector tables. Much of the SQL language's power comes from its capability to return records from several tables at once, using something called a join. A join is simply a way to describe the relationship between tables, right in a SQL query statement. This means you can use join syntax in a `SELECT` query, for example, to easily retrieve information about the actors who have appeared in each film.

NOTE

For clarity, this section refers to tables such as `Films` and `Actors` as data tables and tables such as `FilmsActors` as connector tables. These aren't official SQL terms; they are used here just to keep the discussion as clear as possible.

Joining Two Tables

When you need to join two tables in a query, you actually have your choice of several syntax forms. The simplest and most common method is to add a piece of criteria in the query's `WHERE` clause, using this basic form:

```
SELECT Columns
FROM TableA, TableB
WHERE TableA.SomeID = TableB.SomeID
```

Applying this to the `Films` and `FilmsActors` tables, say, might translate to

```
SELECT Films.FilmID, Films.MovieTitle, FilmsActors.ActorID
FROM Films, FilmsActors
WHERE Films.FilmID = FilmsActors.FilmID
```

The `WHERE` keyword is clearly being used in a new way here. Rather than merely specifying selection criteria, it is used here to bind the `Films` and `FilmsActors` tables together. Translated into plain English, this statement might read, "Using the `FilmID` as a guide, show me the `FilmID` and `MovieTitle` for each row in the `Films` table, along with the corresponding `ActorID` numbers from the `FilmsActors` table."

Listing 29.5 shows how the previous join query can be used in a ColdFusion template. For each film, the query results include one record for each actor in that film, as shown in Figure 29.5.

Listing 29.5 `FilmCast1.cfm`—Retrieving Data from Two Tables at Once, Using a Join

```
<!---
  Filename:    FilmCast1.cfm
  Created by: Nate Weiss (NMW)
  Purpose:     Demonstrates the use of SQL joins
--->


<!--- Retrieve Films and Related Actors from database --->
<CFQUERY NAME="GetFilmInfo" DATASOURCE="#REQUEST.DataSource#">
  SELECT
    Films.FilmID, Films.MovieTitle,
    FilmsActors.ActorID
  FROM Films, FilmsActors
  WHERE Films.FilmID = FilmsActors.FilmID
  ORDER BY Films.MovieTitle
</CFQUERY>

<HTML>
<HEAD><TITLE>Films and Actors</TITLE></HEAD>
<BODY>
<H2>Films And Actors</H2>

<!--- Display retrieved information in HTML table --->
<CFTABLE QUERY="GetFilmInfo" HTMLTABLE BORDER COLHEADERS>
  <CFCOL HEADER="Film ID" TEXT="#FilmID#">
  <CFCOL HEADER="Film Title" TEXT="#MovieTitle#">
  <CFCOL HEADER="Actor ID" TEXT="#ActorID#">
</CFTABLE>

</BODY>
</HTML>
```

NOTE

If a film has no associated actors (that is, if there are no rows in the `FilmsActors` table with the same `FilmID`), no records are returned for that film. Therefore, the query results return records only for those combinations of film and actor that can actually be found in both tables. If you wanted to get information about all films, including those with no corresponding actors, you would need to use an outer join (see the section "Using Outer Joins," later in this chapter).

The `WHERE` clause in this listing is absolutely critical to understand. The conceptual relationship between the two tables hinges on the fact that the rows of the `Films` table in which the `FilmID` is `1` correspond to the rows in the `FilmsActors` table in which the `FilmID` is `1`, and so on. The `WHERE` clause explains this fact to your database system.

NOTE

Notice the simple dot notation used to specify which columns are in which tables. Now that two tables are participating in the `SELECT`, this dot notation is necessary. Otherwise, your database system wouldn't know which table to retrieve the `FilmID` from (because a column called `FilmID` exists in each one).

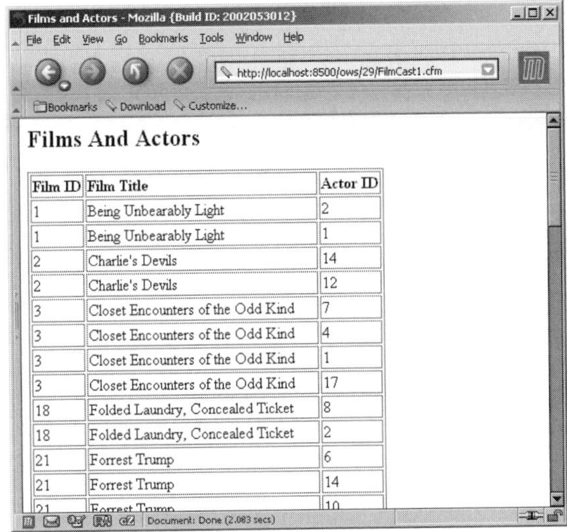

Films And Actors

Film ID	Film Title	Actor ID
1	Being Unbearably Light	2
1	Being Unbearably Light	1
2	Charlie's Devils	14
2	Charlie's Devils	12
3	Closet Encounters of the Odd Kind	7
3	Closet Encounters of the Odd Kind	4
3	Closet Encounters of the Odd Kind	1
3	Closet Encounters of the Odd Kind	17
18	Folded Laundry, Concealed Ticket	8
18	Folded Laundry, Concealed Ticket	2
21	Forrest Trump	6
21	Forrest Trump	14
21	Forrest Trump	10

Figure 29.5

Two tables can be queried together using simple join syntax.

TIP

You actually have to use the dot notation only for columns that exist in both tables (that is, where the column name alone would be ambiguous). However, it is recommended that you use the dot notation for all columns in any query that involves more than one table, simply to make your code clearer and remove any possibility of (gasp!) human error.

Joining Three Tables

Joining three tables is not much different from joining two tables; you simply specify two join conditions in your `WHERE` clause, using `AND` between them. When querying against a relationship established by a connector table, you often need to join three tables together in order to provide user-friendly pages.

So, to retrieve each actor's last name instead of just the actors' ID numbers, you would join the `Films` table to the `FilmsActors` table (as you have already seen) and then join the `FilmsActors` table to the `Actors` table (to pick up the last name associated with each actor's ID number). The resulting query would look like this:

```
SELECT Films.FilmID, Films.MovieTitle, Actors.NameLast
FROM Films, FilmsActors, Actors
WHERE Films.FilmID = FilmsActors.FilmID
  AND FilmsActors.ActorID = Actors.ActorID
```

Listing 29.6 shows how this three-table join can be used to revise the previous example (refer to Listing 29.5) to create a much friendlier display for your users. Now, instead of just seeing each actor's ID number, your users can see each actor's first and last names, as shown in Figure 29.6. If you wanted to display other information from the `Actors` table, you could just add them to the query's `SELECT` list.

Listing 29.6 `FilmCast2.cfm`—Joining Three Tables at Once

```
<!---
  Filename:   FilmCast2.cfm
  Created by: Nate Weiss (NMW)
  Purpose:    Demonstrates the use of SQL joins
--->


<!--- Retrieve Films and Related Actors from database --->
<CFQUERY NAME="GetFilmInfo" DATASOURCE="#REQUEST.DataSource#">
  SELECT
    Films.FilmID, Films.MovieTitle,
    Actors.NameFirst, Actors.NameLast
  FROM Films, FilmsActors, Actors
  WHERE Films.FilmID        = FilmsActors.FilmID
    AND FilmsActors.ActorID = Actors.ActorID
  ORDER BY Films.MovieTitle, Actors.NameLast
</CFQUERY>

<HTML>
<HEAD><TITLE>Films and Actors</TITLE></HEAD>
<BODY>
<H2>Films And Actors</H2>

<!--- Display retrieved information in HTML table --->
<CFTABLE QUERY="GetFilmInfo" HTMLTABLE BORDER COLHEADERS>
  <CFCOL HEADER="Film ID" TEXT="#FilmID#">
  <CFCOL HEADER="Film Title" TEXT="#MovieTitle#">
  <CFCOL HEADER="Actor (First Name)" TEXT="#NameFirst#">
  <CFCOL HEADER="Actor (Last Name)" TEXT="#NameLast#">
</CFTABLE>

</BODY>
</HTML>
```

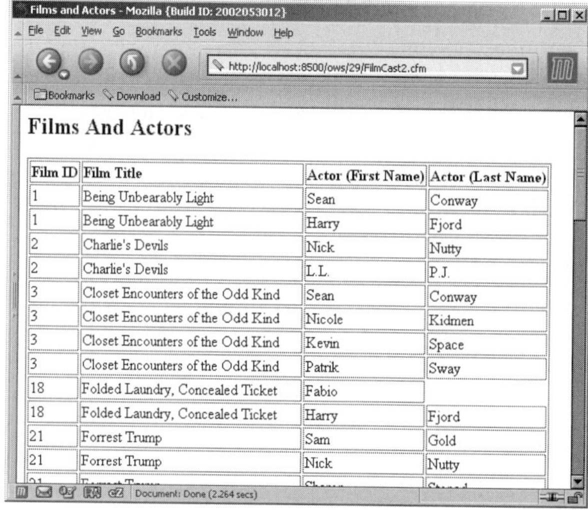

Figure 29.6

Three-table joins are common when you need to display names, labels, or titles from related data tables.

TIP

To create queries that join four or more tables together, just continue to add additional lines of criteria in your `WHERE` clause, using the `AND` keyword between each one.

Improving Readability with Table Aliases

When you start using table joins more frequently, you will probably find it helpful to use table aliases to make the queries easier to read (and easier to type!). A table alias is just a temporary nickname for a table, good only within the context of the current query. You can define a very short table alias that is only one or two letters long, allowing you to remove clutter from the remainder of the query statement.

To define a table alias, just provide a short nickname right after the table's real name in the `FROM` part of your query. Now you can use the short alias in the other parts of the query, in place of the actual table name. Many developers choose to use just the first letter or two of the table name (in lowercase) for an alias. For instance, this query

```
SELECT Films.FilmID, Films.MovieTitle, Actors.NameLast
FROM Films, FilmsActors, Actors
WHERE Films.FilmID = FilmsActors.FilmID
  AND FilmsActors.ActorID = Actors.ActorID
```

could become this, which is relatively easy on the eyes (like the actors themselves):

```
SELECT f.FilmID, f.MovieTitle, a.NameLast
FROM Films f, FilmsActors fa, Actors a
WHERE f.FilmID   = fa.FilmID
  AND fa.ActorID = a.ActorID
```

If you prefer, you can use the `AS` keyword between the table's real name and the alias, like so:

```
SELECT f.FilmID, f.MovieTitle, a.NameLast
FROM Films AS f, FilmsActors AS fa, Actors AS a
WHERE f.FilmID   = fa.FilmID
  AND fa.ActorID = a.ActorID
```

The Two Types of Join Syntax

So far, you have seen how tables can be joined using the `WHERE` part of a query. This is the simplest and most common method, but there is another. The two types of join syntax generate the same results (except in very rare circumstances that are well beyond the scope of this book, and which you are unlikely to encounter). You can use whichever syntax you like better.

The two forms of join syntax are

- `WHERE JOIN` syntax—You have already learned about this simple syntax.
- `INNER JOIN` syntax—This is somewhat more complex-looking but is formally preferred by some SQL scholars, mainly because it keeps your table relationships separate from any filter criteria (that is, it gets the join description out of the `WHERE` clause).

The first join syntax describes the join as part of the query's `WHERE` criteria, as you have already seen:

```
SELECT f.FilmID, f.MovieTitle, fa.ActorID
FROM Films f,
     FilmsActors fa
WHERE f.FilmID   = fa.FilmID
```

The `INNER JOIN` syntax describes the join in the `FROM` part of the query, instead of the `WHERE` part. Instead of separating the table names with commas, you separate them with the words `INNER JOIN`. Each pair of table names is followed by the word `ON`, followed by the equality condition that describes the join. For instance, the `WHERE`-style join shown above would translate into the following:

```
SELECT Films.FilmID, Films.MovieTitle, FilmsActors.ActorID
FROM Films INNER JOIN
     FilmsActors ON Films.FilmID = FilmsActors.FilmID
```

Or, adding table aliases to improve readability somewhat, it would look like this:

```
SELECT f.FilmID, f.MovieTitle, fa.ActorID
FROM Films f INNER JOIN
     FilmsActors fa ON f.FilmID = fa.FilmID
```

To join three or more tables using `INNER JOIN` syntax, use parentheses to isolate the individual `INNER JOIN` pieces from one another, like so:

```
SELECT f.FilmID, f.MovieTitle, a.NameFirst, a.NameLast
FROM (Films f INNER JOIN
     FilmsActors fa ON f.FilmID = fa.FilmID) INNER JOIN
     Actors a ON fa.ActorID =  a.ActorID
```

Listings 29.7 and 29.8 are revisions of Listings 29.5 and 29.6, respectively, using `INNER JOIN` syntax instead of the `WHERE`-style of join syntax. Use whichever syntax you find more straightforward.

Listing 29.7 `FilmCast1a.cfm`—Using `INNER JOIN` Syntax to Join Two Tables

```
<!---
  Filename:    FilmCast1a.cfm
  Created by: Nate Weiss (NMW)
  Purpose:    Demonstrates the use of SQL joins
--->


<!--- Retrieve Films and Related Actors from database --->
<CFQUERY NAME="GetFilmInfo" DATASOURCE="#REQUEST.DataSource#">
  SELECT f.FilmID, f.MovieTitle, fa.ActorID
  FROM Films f INNER JOIN
       FilmsActors fa ON f.FilmID = fa.FilmID
  ORDER BY f.MovieTitle
</CFQUERY>

<HTML>
<HEAD><TITLE>Films and Actors</TITLE></HEAD>
<BODY>
<H2>Films And Actors</H2>
```

Listing 29.7 (continued)

```
<!--- Display retrieved information in HTML table --->
<CFTABLE QUERY="GetFilmInfo" HTMLTABLE BORDER COLHEADERS>
  <CFCOL HEADER="Film ID" TEXT="#FilmID#">
  <CFCOL HEADER="Film Title" TEXT="#MovieTitle#">
  <CFCOL HEADER="Actor ID" TEXT="#ActorID#">
</CFTABLE>

</BODY>
</HTML>
```

Listing 29.8 `FilmCast2a.cfm`—Using `INNER JOIN` Syntax to Join Three Tables

```
<!---
  Filename:   FilmCast2a.cfm
  Created by: Nate Weiss (NMW)
  Purpose:    Demonstrates the use of SQL joins
--->


<!--- Retrieve Films and Related Actors from database --->
<CFQUERY NAME="GetFilmInfo" DATASOURCE="#REQUEST.DataSource#">
  SELECT
    f.FilmID, f.MovieTitle,
    a.NameFirst, a.NameLast
  FROM (Films f INNER JOIN
        FilmsActors fa ON f.FilmID = fa.FilmID) INNER JOIN
        Actors a ON fa.ActorID =  a.ActorID
  ORDER BY f.MovieTitle, a.NameLast
</CFQUERY>

<HTML>
<HEAD><TITLE>Films and Actors</TITLE></HEAD>
<BODY>
<H2>Films And Actors</H2>

<!--- Display retrieved information in HTML table --->
<CFTABLE QUERY="GetFilmInfo" HTMLTABLE BORDER COLHEADERS>
  <CFCOL HEADER="Film ID" TEXT="#FilmID#">
  <CFCOL HEADER="Film Title" TEXT="#MovieTitle#">
  <CFCOL HEADER="Actor (First Name)" TEXT="#NameFirst#">
  <CFCOL HEADER="Actor (Last Name)" TEXT="#NameLast#">
</CFTABLE>

</BODY>
</HTML>
```

Using Outer Joins

So far, all of the joins in this chapter have been inner joins, which means that only those records that match up in both tables are included in the results. From time to time, you will run into situations in which you need to use an outer join, which means that all records in one of the tables are returned, regardless of whether any matching records exist in the other.

For instance, say you need to create a simple report page—similar to Listing 29.5 or 29.6—but that shows each film and the rating it has been given. You decide to join the `Films` table to the `Ratings` table, using the `RatingID` column as the join criteria. Putting your new join skills to work, you come up with something like this:

```
SELECT f.FilmID, f.MovieTitle, r.Rating
FROM Films f INNER JOIN
     FilmsRatings r ON f.RatingID = r.RatingID
ORDER BY f.MovieTitle
```

The query seems to work fine, and no one notices any problems for the first few weeks your application is up and running. But after a while, people start complaining that some movies never show up on the list. After a bit of trial and error, you realize that whenever a movie doesn't have a rating (when the `RatingID` column is null, or blank), it gets excluded from the query results. This is because inner joins return records only when matching rows exist in both tables.

To solve the problem, you need to change the query to use an outer join instead of an inner join. To do so, you simply change the words `INNER JOIN` to `OUTER JOIN`, preceded by either `LEFT` or `RIGHT`, depending on whether the outer table (the table that should always get included in the query results) is on the left or the right side of the `OUTER JOIN` statement.

So, the query statement shown previously could become this:

```
SELECT f.FilmID, f.MovieTitle, r.Rating
FROM Films f LEFT OUTER JOIN
     FilmsRatings r ON f.RatingID = r.RatingID
```

or this:

```
SELECT f.FilmID, f.MovieTitle, r.Rating
FROM FilmsRatings r RIGHT OUTER JOIN
     Films f ON f.RatingID = r.RatingID
```

These two queries will behave in exactly the same way. They will always return all records from the `Films` table, regardless of whether any corresponding rows exist in the `Ratings` table. When matching records exist in `Ratings`, a row gets added to the query results for each combination of film and rating, just like with a normal inner join.

But, because these are outer joins, the film is included in the results even when no matching rating exists for a film (when the film's `RatingID` is null or is set to some number that doesn't exist in the `Ratings` table). Any columns from the `Ratings` table—in this case, just the `Rating` column—are simply returned as blank columns. For instance, in the above examples, the `Rating` column will be set to an empty string for any films that don't have ratings.

NOTE

Technically, the `Rating` column isn't returned to ColdFusion as an empty string; it's returned as a null value. However, ColdFusion converts null values to empty strings as it receives them, so as far as your CFML code is concerned, the column is an empty string. You would need to test for it as such in any `<CFIF>` statements. See "Working with `NULL` Values," later in this chapter, for details.

Listing 29.9 shows how this outer join query can be used in an actual template. To test this template, add a few new films to the `Films` table, being sure to leave the `RatingID` as null, `0`, or some other unknown rating ID number. Then, visit Listing 29.9 with your browser. The new films will appear, but their ratings will be blank, as shown in Figure 29.7. If you then change Listing 29.9 so that it uses ordinary inner join syntax, you will see that the new films disappear altogether when you revisit the page.

Listing 29.9 `FilmRatings.cfm`—Using an Outer Join to Show All Films, Even Those with No Corresponding Rating

```
<!---
  Filename:    FilmRatings.cfm
  Created by: Nate Weiss (NMW)
  Purpose:     Demonstrates use of SQL outer joins
--->

<!--- Retrieve Films and Related Actors from database --->
<CFQUERY NAME="GetFilmInfo" DATASOURCE="#REQUEST.DataSource#">
  SELECT
    f.FilmID, f.MovieTitle,
    r.Rating
  FROM Films f LEFT OUTER JOIN
       FilmsRatings r ON f.RatingID = r.RatingID
  ORDER BY f.MovieTitle
</CFQUERY>

<HTML>
<HEAD><TITLE>Film Ratings</TITLE></HEAD>
<BODY>
<H2>Film Ratings</H2>

<!--- Display retrieved information in HTML table --->
<CFTABLE QUERY="GetFilmInfo" HTMLTABLE BORDER COLHEADERS>
  <CFCOL HEADER="Film ID" TEXT="#FilmID#">
  <CFCOL HEADER="Film Title" TEXT="#MovieTitle#">
  <CFCOL HEADER="Rating" TEXT="#Rating#">
</CFTABLE>

</BODY>
</HTML>
```

NOTE

If you want, you can leave the word `OUTER` out of your outer join queries. That is, `LEFT JOIN` and `LEFT OUTER JOIN` are synonyms; so are `RIGHT JOIN` and `RIGHT OUTER JOIN`. However, we recommend that you leave the word `OUTER` in there to emphasize what is going on.

NOTE

Some database systems place restrictions on whether you can use inner and outer joins together in the same `SELECT` statement. See your database documentation for details.

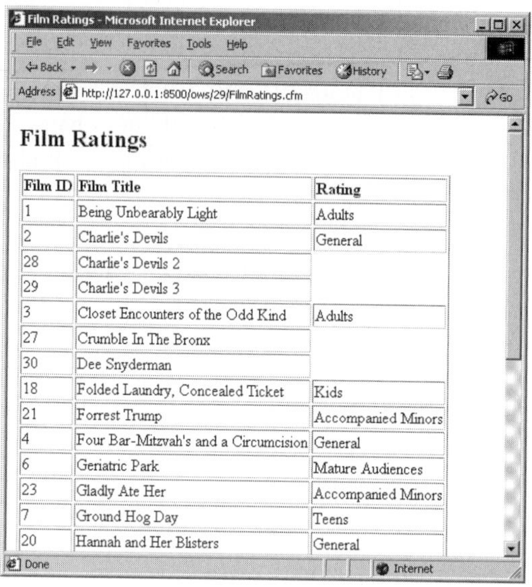

Film ID	Film Title	Rating
1	Being Unbearably Light	Adults
2	Charlie's Devils	General
28	Charlie's Devils 2	
29	Charlie's Devils 3	
3	Closet Encounters of the Odd Kind	Adults
27	Crumble In The Bronx	
30	Dee Snyderman	
18	Folded Laundry, Concealed Ticket	Kids
21	Forrest Trump	Accompanied Minors
4	Four Bar-Mitzvah's and a Circumcision	General
6	Geriatric Park	Mature Audiences
23	Gladly Ate Her	Accompanied Minors
7	Ground Hog Day	Teens
20	Hannah and Her Blisters	General

Figure 29.7

Because an outer join is used, unrated movies simply show up with a blank rating, instead of being eliminated from the list altogether.

Subqueries

SQL allows you to nest complete `SELECT` statements within other statements for various purposes. These nested queries are known as subqueries. Although subqueries cover similar conceptual ground as joins, you need to be aware of both, because subqueries provide great flexibility and really allow your queries to get into those hard-to-reach places.

Subqueries can be included in your queries in a number of ways. The most common are

- In the `WHERE` part of a SQL statement to correlate data in various tables.
- In the `SELECT` part of a SQL statement to return an additional column.

Either way, the subquery itself is put inside parentheses and can contain just about any valid `SELECT` statement. The subquery can use dot notation to refer to tables outside the parentheses, but not vice versa (the main statement can't reach in and refer to tables inside the parentheses, but the subquery can reach out and refer to tables in the main statement).

NOTE

Most database systems support subqueries, but some of them place certain restrictions on their use. If you run into problems, consult your database system's documentation for details.

Subqueries in `WHERE` Criteria

The simplest way to include a subquery in your SQL statements is as part of your `WHERE` criteria, using the `=` operator. In general, this type of subquery statement is best for quickly and easily looking up information based on some type of ID number.

Say you were constructing a set of pages that will enable the folks in Orange Whip Studios' accounting department to view a list of merchandise orders. On the first page, the user sees a list of all orders, retrieved straightforwardly from the `MerchandiseOrders` table. Each order can be clicked to view the name and other information about the person who placed the order. This link (for each order's contact information) passes the `OrderID` in the URL. Therefore, the code in the contact details page must retrieve information from the `Contacts` table, based on the given `OrderID`.

The following statement, which uses a subquery, does this job nicely:

```
<CFQUERY NAME="GetContact" DATASOURCE="ows">
  SELECT * FROM Contacts
  WHERE ContactID =
    (SELECT ContactID FROM MerchandiseOrders
     WHERE OrderID = #URL.OrderID#)
</CFQUERY>
```

NOTE

This example uses the = operator to include the subquery in the larger query statement, but you also could use <>, >, <, >=, or <= in place of =.

When this query is executed, your database system works on it from the inside out, starting with the subquery. Say the `URL.OrderID` value is passed as `2`. The subquery looks in the `MerchandiseOrders` table and finds that the corresponding `ContactID` number is `4`. Now the outer query statement is run, using the value of `4` in place of the subquery, almost as if the outer query had used `WHERE ContactID = 4`.

The result is that all contact information from the `Contacts` table is returned to ColdFusion, based only on the `OrderID`. This type of subquery technique is great for situations such as this, in which there is a conceptual step-by-step process to go through (first, get the `ContactID` from the `MerchandiseOrders` table; then use that to retrieve the correct record from the `Contacts` table).

NOTE

When you include a subquery in a SQL statement with the = operator, be sure that only one record will ever be found by the subquery. If the subquery part of the statement shown previously were to return more than one record, a database error message would be displayed. If the subquery might return more than one record, you should use the `IN` operator (discussed shortly) instead of =.

Subqueries Are Often Just Alternatives

Take another look at the previous subquery code snippet. There are other ways that the same information could be retrieved from the database. For instance, you could simply use two separate `<CFQUERY>` tags, which represent the two steps mentioned previously. First, you could get the correct `ContactID`, like so:

```
<CFQUERY NAME="GetID" DATASOURCE="ows">
  SELECT ContactID FROM MerchandiseOrders
  WHERE OrderID = #URL.OrderID#
</CFQUERY>
```

Then, you would pass the retrieved `ContactID` to a second query, like so:

```
<CFQUERY NAME="GetContact" DATASOURCE="ows">
  SELECT * FROM Contacts
  WHERE ContactID = #GetID.ContactID#
</CFQUERY>
```

This method returns the same information to ColdFusion; you are free to use either method. However, you can expect slightly better performance from the subquery approach, because only one database operation is necessary. Also, if you conceptually ask your questions all at once, your database system often can make optimizations based on indexes and other tuning algorithms, which usually are bypassed if you run two separate queries. As a general rule of thumb, the fewer times ColdFusion must interact with the database, the better.

You also could get the same information by using a join, which you learned about in the last section. The following query (which uses a join) returns the same results as the subquery statement shown earlier or the two `<CFQUERY>` tags shown most recently:

```
<CFQUERY NAME="GetContact" DATASOURCE="ows">
  SELECT c.*
  FROM Contacts c INNER JOIN MerchandiseOrders o
    ON c.ContactID = o.ContactID
  WHERE o.OrderID = #URL.OrderID#
</CFQUERY>
```

Again, you are free to use the join syntax instead of the subquery syntax. They will both return the same data to ColdFusion. In this case, you could theoretically expect slightly better performance from the subquery because it implies that there is only one relevant `ContactID` and only one matching `OrderID` (whereas the database system would potentially need to scan all rows of the tables to see how many matching records might exist). Whether any real-world performance difference exists between the two, however, depends on the database system being used, how the columns are indexed, and other factors too numerous to discuss here. In fact, many database systems will decide to treat a subquery and a join in exactly the same manner internally. In general, deciding whether to use a subquery or a join in any given situation is often a matter of personal choice. Joins are frequently more powerful, mainly because they can return multiple columns from all tables at once. Subqueries are often easier to write and understand, and can sometimes be more efficient. The best rule of thumb is to simply use the method that springs to mind first as you are thinking about the query you need to write. You can always make changes later.

NOTE

As a rule, joins are a bit more likely to run faster than subqueries, so use a join when in doubt. That said, you should feel free to experiment and use whichever seems more straightforward for a given situation.

Using Subqueries with `IN`

You just saw how a subquery can be introduced into a larger query statement by including it on the right side of the = operator in the `WHERE` clause. That type of subquery is useful when you know the subquery will never return more than one record. If the subquery can return any number of records, you must introduce the subquery using the `IN` keyword. Conceptually, the values found by the subquery will be turned into a comma-separated list. Then, the comma-separated list is used to complete the outer query statement.

For instance, to get information from the `Merchandise` table about the items included in a particular order, you could do the following:

```
SELECT * FROM Merchandise
WHERE MerchID IN
 (SELECT ItemID FROM MerchandiseOrdersItems
  WHERE OrderID = #URL.OrderID# )
```

You also can nest subqueries within other subqueries. For instance, this statement first retrieves all the `OrderID` numbers from the `MerchandiseOrders` table that a particular contact has made. The list of order numbers is passed to the middle subquery, which retrieves a list of corresponding `ItemID` numbers from the `MerchandiseOrdersItems` table. Finally, the list of item numbers is passed to the outermost query, which retrieves the list of merchandise. The result is a set of records that provide information about all of the merchandise items a particular customer has ordered:

```
SELECT * FROM Merchandise WHERE MerchID IN
  (SELECT ItemID FROM MerchandiseOrdersItems
   WHERE OrderID IN
     (SELECT OrderID FROM MerchandiseOrders
      WHERE ContactID = #URL.ContactID#))
```

Again, you could get this same information using join syntax. The following join returns the same information that the previous snippet's nested subquery syntax does:

```
SELECT m.*
FROM Merchandise m, MerchandiseOrders o, MerchandiseOrdersItems oi
WHERE m.MerchID = oi.ItemID AND o.OrderID = oi.OrderID
AND o.ContactID = #URL.ContactID#
```

The different syntaxes will feel more natural to different developers. The thought process to get to the first query is more step-by-step, whereas the second requires a more relational mind-set. In general, you can just use the approach that seems more intuitive to you.

NOTE

The `IN` keyword isn't just for subqueries. It's for any situation in which you need to provide a comma-separated list of values as criteria. For instance, you could use `WHERE OrderID IN (4,7,9)` to get information about order numbers 4, 7, and 9. Or, if you have several check boxes named `OrderID` on a form, you could use `WHERE OrderID IN (#FORM.OrderID#)` to retrieve information about the orders the user checked.

Using Subqueries with `NOT IN`

One interesting way to use subqueries is with the `NOT IN` operator. You can use `NOT IN` just like `IN`, as discussed previously. The difference is that the outer query will retrieve records that do not correspond to the values found by the subquery. In other words, the query as a whole will return the opposite set of records.

So, to select the merchandise items a user has not ordered in the past, you could do the following. This is the same as the first example in the previous section, "Using Subqueries with `IN`," except that it adds the word `NOT` to invert the results:

```
SELECT * FROM Merchandise
WHERE MerchID NOT IN
 (SELECT ItemID FROM MerchandiseOrdersItems
  WHERE OrderID = #URL.OrderID# )
```

Listing 29.10 shows how to use several nested `IN` and `NOT IN` subqueries together to create a lightweight collaborative filtering effect. The term collaborative filtering is sometimes used to describe the online merchandising technique of presenting a user with a list of suggested items based on what similar people have ordered in the past. The technique can be seen most visibly at Amazon.com ("People who bought Raiders of the Lost Aardvark also bought The Mommy Returns"). The listing that follows is relatively simple and might not count as true collaborative filtering. However, it does show how subqueries can be used to create something fairly similar.

The idea behind this listing is simple: It updates the `StoreCart.cfm` template from Chapter 27, "Online Commerce." When the user prepares to check out by visiting the version of `StoreCart.cfm` shown in Listing 29.10, the `GetSimilar` query is run. `GetSimilar` looks at the items in the user's cart and finds the completed orders in which the items have appeared. In addition, if the user has logged in, the query uses a `NOT IN` subquery to ensure that the user's own orders are not included in the list of completed orders being considered.

Then, for each of the other completed orders, the query retrieves all items that were included in those orders (not counting the items in the current user's cart). These items are then shown to the user with the message "People who have purchased items in your cart have also bought the following," as shown in Figure 29.8.

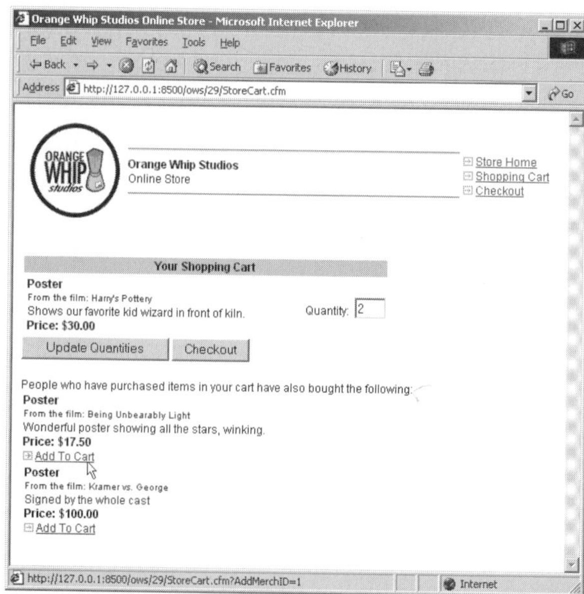

Figure 29.8

You can use `IN` and `NOT IN` subqueries to build interesting takes on your data, such as this lightweight collaborative filtering example.

Listing 29.10 `StoreCart3.cfm`—Using Subqueries to Mimic a Collaborative Filtering Feature

```
<!---
  Filename:    StoreCart.cfm (save as StoreCart.cfm)
  Created by:  Nate Weiss (NMW)
  Purpose:     Displays the current user's shopping cart
  Please Note Depends on the <CF_ShoppingCart> custom tag
--->

<!--- Show header images, etc., for Online Store --->
<CFINCLUDE TEMPLATE="StoreHeader.cfm">

<!--- If MerchID was passed in URL --->
<CFIF IsDefined("URL.AddMerchID")>
  <!--- Add item to user's cart data, via custom tag --->
  <CF_ShoppingCart
    Action="Add"
    MerchID="#URL.AddMerchID#">

<!--- If user is submitting cart form --->
<CFELSEIF IsDefined("FORM.MerchID")>
  <!--- For each MerchID on Form, Update Quantity --->
  <CFLOOP LIST="#Form.MerchID#" INDEX="ThisMerchID">
    <!--- Update Quantity, via Custom Tag --->
    <CF_ShoppingCart
      Action="Update"
      MerchID="#ThisMerchID#"
      Quantity="#FORM['Quant_#ThisMerchID#']#">  </CFLOOP>

  <!--- If user submitted form via "Checkout" button, --->
  <!--- send on to Checkout page after updating cart. --->
  <CFIF IsDefined("FORM.IsCheckingOut")>
    <CFLOCATION URL="../27/StoreCheckout.cfm">
  </CFIF>
</CFIF>

<!--- Get current cart contents, via Custom Tag --->
<CF_ShoppingCart
  Action="List"
  ReturnVariable="GetCart">


<!--- Stop here if user's cart is empty --->
<CFIF GetCart.RecordCount EQ 0>
  There is nothing in your cart.
  <CFABORT>
</CFIF>



<!--- Create form that submits to this template --->
<CFFORM ACTION="#CGI.SCRIPT_NAME#">
  <TABLE>
    <TR>
      <TH COLSPAN="2" BGCOLOR="Silver">Your Shopping Cart</TH>
    </TR>
    <!--- For each piece of merchandise --->
```

Listing 29.10 (continued)

```
      <CFLOOP QUERY="GetCart">
        <TR>
          <TD>
            <!--- Show this piece of merchandise --->
            <CF_MerchDisplay
              MerchID="#GetCart.MerchID#"
              ShowAddLink="No">
          </TD>
          <TD>
            <!--- Display Quantity in Text entry field --->
            <CFOUTPUT>
              Quantity:
              <INPUT TYPE="Hidden"
                NAME="MerchID"
                VALUE="#GetCart.MerchID#">
              <INPUT TYPE="Text" SIZE="3"
                NAME="Quant_#GetCart.MerchID#"
                VALUE="#GetCart.Quantity#"><BR>
            </CFOUTPUT>
          </TD>
        </TR>
      </CFLOOP>

    </TABLE>

    <!--- Submit button to update quantities --->
    <INPUT TYPE="Submit" VALUE="Update Quantities">

    <!--- Submit button to Check out --->
    <INPUT TYPE="Submit" VALUE="Checkout" NAME="IsCheckingOut">
  </CFFORM>



  <!--- Convert current cart contents to comma-sep list --->
  <CFSET CurrentMerchList = ValueList(GetCart.MerchID)>

  <!--- Run query to suggest other items for user to buy --->
  <CFQUERY NAME="GetSimilar" DATASOURCE="#REQUEST.DataSource#"
    CACHEDWITHIN="#CreateTimeSpan(0,0,5,0)#" MAXROWS="3">
    <!--- We want all items NOT in user's cart... --->
    SELECT ItemID
    FROM MerchandiseOrdersItems
    WHERE ItemID NOT IN (#CurrentMerchList#)
    <!--- ...but that *were* included in other orders --->
    <!--- along with items now in the user's cart... --->
    AND OrderID IN
      (SELECT OrderID FROM MerchandiseOrdersItems
       WHERE ItemID IN (#CurrentMerchList#)
       <!--- ...not including this user's past orders! --->
       <CFIF IsDefined("SESSION.Auth.ContactID")>
       AND OrderID NOT IN
         (SELECT OrderID FROM MerchandiseOrders
```

Listing 29.10 (continued)

```
        WHERE ContactID = #SESSION.Auth.ContactID#)
     </CFIF> )
</CFQUERY>

<!--- If at least one "similar" item was found --->
<CFIF GetSimilar.RecordCount GT 0>
  <P>People who have purchased items in your cart have also bought the
following:<BR>

    <!--- For each similar item, display it, via Custom Tag --->
    <!--- (show five suggestions at most) --->
    <CFLOOP QUERY="GetSimilar">
      <CF_MerchDisplay
        MerchID="#GetSimilar.ItemID#">
    </CFLOOP>
</CFIF>
```

NOTE

This `StoreCart.cfm` listing is meant to work with the other listings from Chapter 27. For all the links to work properly, you should save Listing 29.10 as `StoreCart.cfm` in the same folder with Chapter 27's listings. We have also included most of the relevant files with this chapter's listings on the CD-ROM, so everything except checking out should work if you copy all the files from the CD-ROM to your ColdFusion server.

Calculating New Columns with Subqueries

Another convenient place to use subqueries is in the `SELECT` part of an ordinary query statement. Simply include the subquery in the `SELECT` list, as if it were a column. Within the subquery, add criteria to its `WHERE` clause using dot notation, similar to a join. The idea is to somehow connect the subquery to the outer query, usually based on a common ID number of some type.

For instance, to get a list of all contacts in the `Contacts` table, along with a simple count of the number of orders that each contact has made, you could use the following query:

```
SELECT ContactID, FirstName, LastName,
  (SELECT COUNT(*) FROM MerchandiseOrders o
   WHERE c.ContactID = o.ContactID) AS OrderCount
FROM Contacts c
```

You could get this same information using an outer join, as discussed earlier in this chapter, as shown below:

```
SELECT c.ContactID, c.FirstName, c.LastName,
  COUNT(o.OrderID) AS OrderCount
FROM Contacts c LEFT OUTER JOIN MerchandiseOrders o
ON c.ContactID = o.ContactID
GROUP BY c.ContactID, c.FirstName, c.LastName
```

NOTE

Because an aggregate function is in this join query's `SELECT` list, all other columns must be repeated in the `GROUP BY` list. Depending on the situation and the database system being used, queries that have a long `GROUP BY` list can start to perform somewhat poorly when the number of rows in the tables gets to be large.

Combining Record Sets with UNION

You can use SQL's UNION operator to combine the results from two different queries. Compared with joins, subqueries, aggregates, and the like, UNION is pretty simple. UNION is simply about combining the results of two different SELECT statements. Each SELECT can be based on the same table or different tables.

Say someone at Orange Whip Studios has asked you to come up with a simple report page that shows which actors and directors are involved with each of the studio's films. For each film, the people's last names should be sorted alphabetically.

Listing 29.11 shows how the UNION operator makes this task easy. The <CFQUERY> in this template contains two SELECT statements. The first retrieves information about the actors in each film. If it were run on its own, it would return four columns: MovieTitle, NameFirst, NameLast, and Credit. The second SELECT retrieves information about the directors of each film. Run on its own, it would also return four columns, with slightly different names (MovieTitle, FirstName, LastName, and Credit). The UNION statement causes the records from both statements to be returned together, in the order specified by the ORDER BY at the end of the query (first by MovieTitle and then by the last names of each actor or director involved with that movie). The results are shown in Figure 29.9.

NOTE

ColdFusion MX's query of queries feature enables you to perform UNIONs between queries that come from different data sources or database systems. See the section "Queries of Queries," later in this chapter.

Figure 29.9

UNION statements allow you to combine the results of several SELECT statements.

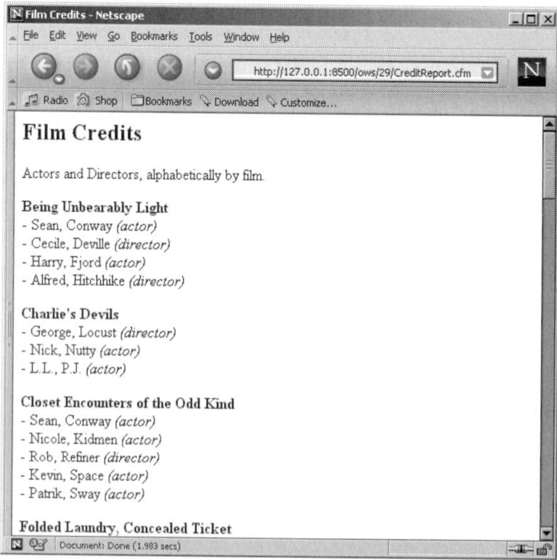

NOTE

Even though the column names are not exactly the same, this query is still valid (see the following list of rules and considerations). Use the column names in the first `SELECT` statement in your ColdFusion code.

Listing 29.11 `CreditReport.cfm`—Using `UNION` to Combine Two Result Sets

```
<!---
  Filename:   CreditReport.cfm
  Created by: Nate Weiss (NMW)
  Purpose:    Demonstrates use of SQL UNION statements
--->

<HTML>
<HEAD><TITLE>Film Credits</TITLE></HEAD>
<BODY>
<H2>Film Credits</H2>
Actors and Directors, alphabetically by film.

<!--- Retrieve Films and Actors, then --->
<!--- Retrieve Films and Directors, then order everyone --->
<!--- by related Film Title and the person's last name. --->
<CFQUERY NAME="GetExp" DATASOURCE="#REQUEST.DataSource#">
    SELECT
      f.FilmID, f.MovieTitle,
      a.NameFirst, a.NameLast, 'actor' AS Credit
    FROM
      Films f, Actors a, FilmsActors fa
    WHERE
      f.FilmID  = fa.FilmID AND
      a.ActorID = fa.ActorID
  UNION
    SELECT
      f.FilmID, f.MovieTitle,
      d.FirstName, d.LastName, 'director' AS Credit
    FROM
      Films f, Directors d, FilmsDirectors fd
    WHERE
      f.FilmID     = fd.FilmID AND
      d.DirectorID = fd.DirectorID
  ORDER BY
    f.MovieTitle, NameLast
</CFQUERY>

<!--- For each film, show the title --->
<CFOUTPUT QUERY="GetExp" GROUP="FilmID">
  <P><B>#MovieTitle#</B><BR>

  <!--- Within each film, show each person involved --->
  <CFOUTPUT>
    - #NameFirst#, #NameLast# <I>(#Credit#)</I><BR>
  </CFOUTPUT>
</CFOUTPUT>

</BODY>
</HTML>
```

NOTE

The `Credit` column for the first `SELECT` statement has a constant value of `actor`. Every row returned by that statement will hold the actual word `actor` in the `Credit` column. The same column for the second `SELECT` has a constant value of `director`. This allows the user to see whether each person is an actor or a director (otherwise, there would be no way to tell, because they are all mixed together in alphabetical order). This is not something that is done very often, but you can actually return constant values from any query. Just provide the constant value (a string in single quotes or a number without any quotes) where you would normally provide the column name; then give the new psdeuocolumn an alias using the `AS` keyword.

TIP

You can use more than one `UNION` in a SQL statement–which means that you can combine records from more than two `SELECT` statements.

When you are using `UNION` in your queries, the following rules and considerations apply:

- All of the `SELECT` statements must specify the same number of columns.
- The columns' data types—`Text`, `Numeric`, `Date`, and so on—must match. However, the text width or numeric precision of the columns might not need to, depending on the type of database you are using. See your database documentation for details.
- The column names in the `SELECT` statements *don't* have to match. In fact, the column names from the first `SELECT` are the only ones that matter and are the only ones that will be returned to ColdFusion.
- Duplicate rows (rows that are the same from more than one of the `SELECT` statements) are automatically eliminated. This is true unless you use `UNION ALL` instead of `UNION`.
- There might be only one `ORDER BY` statement, at the very end, and it refers only to column names from the first `SELECT` statement. It arranges all the rows from all the queries involved in the `UNION`, intermingling the rows with one another.
- With most database systems, you may not use `DISTINCT` and `UNION` in the same query.
- So-called BLOb (Binary Large Object) columns, which allow unlimited amounts of data to be stored (such as `Memo` columns in Access or `Image` columns in SQLServer), generally cannot be used in `UNION` statements. Some database systems might make an exception to this rule if you are using `UNION ALL` instead of `UNION`.

Working with `NULL` Values

One of the most confusing concepts to encounter when starting out with databases is the idea of a null value. A null value indicates that there is literally nothing recorded in the table for that row and column (in layman's terms, the value was left blank). For instance, consider the `MerchandiseOrders` table's `ShipDate` column. When the order is indeed shipped, the date is recorded here. Until that point, there is nothing in the column; its value is `NULL`.

Setting Values to NULL

To indicate that you want to set a column to a null value, use the keyword NULL where you would normally provide a value. It is important to understand that you should not surround the NULL keyword with quotation marks; that would set the column to the four-character string NULL rather than the single, special value of NULL.

If you need to record a null value when a form field has been left blank, ColdFusion's <CFIF> and <CFELSE> tags come in handy. For instance, imagine a form with OrderID and ShipDate fields on it. The following code snippet would set the ShipDate column to whatever the user provides, as long as it is a valid date. If the form field has been left blank, or if ColdFusion doesn't recognize it as a date value, it will be set to NULL to indicate that no date is known:

```
UPDATE MerchandiseOrders
SET ShipDate = <CFIF IsDate(FORM.ShipDate)>
                '#DateFormat(FORM.ShipDate, "m/d/yyyy")#'
               <CFELSE> NULL </CFIF>
WHERE OrderID = #FORM.OrderID#
```

Testing for NULL Values in SQL Code

SQL statements that deal with null values can produce unexpected results if you don't know what to watch out for. There isn't room to get into the formal theory behind null values here, but the basic idea is that a null value by its very definition is not equal or unequal to anything—not even another null value. Therefore, the following statement should not return any records, even if null values exist for ShipDate in the table:

```
SELECT * FROM MerchandiseOrders
WHERE ShipDate = NULL
```

Instead, to retrieve the orders that have not yet shipped, you must use the special IS NULL operator, which is used only for testing for NULL values. In addition, a special IS NOT NULL operator is available, which can be used to return values that do not have NULL values.

So, the following could be used to find orders that have not yet shipped:

```
SELECT * FROM MerchandiseOrders
WHERE ShipDate IS NULL
```

Conversely, to find records that have already been shipped, you would use this:

```
SELECT * FROM MerchandiseOrders
WHERE ShipDate IS NOT NULL
```

NOTE

Some database systems, especially older ones, don't make a distinction between = NULL and IS NULL. You should still avoid using = to test for null values in your tables, though, to ensure that your applications will continue to work while the database system is brought up to date.

It is also important to note that any comparison against a null value (not just equality comparisons done with the = operator) must, by definition, not result in a match. Therefore, inequality tests (with the <> operator) and other comparisons (such as < or >=) often produce what end users might consider to be counterintuitive results. You need to take a bit of extra time to think about how any null values might affect your application's queries. For instance, at first glance, you would probably expect the following snippet to return all films except for one (The Lice Storm):

```
SELECT * FROM MerchandiseOrders
WHERE MovieTitle <> 'The Lice Storm'
```

Strange as it might seem, if any of the films have a null value in the `MovieTitle` column (perhaps the studio's focus groups haven't yet determined a title), those films will not be returned by the previous snippet, because null values are not allowed to pass an inequality test. To get all rows except The Lice Storm, including ones that have `NULL` titles, you would need to use the following:

```
SELECT * FROM MerchandiseOrders
WHERE (MovieTitle <> 'The Lice Storm' OR MovieTitle IS NULL)
```

Testing for `NULL` Values in CFML Code

The situation is further complicated by the fact that CFML doesn't include the concept of a null value (which is somewhat surprising, given the database-centric nature of the product). When ColdFusion receives a `NULL` value from a database query, it converts the value into an empty string.

NOTE

SQL purists generally wince when they hear this, because it means that there is no way to tell the difference between a `NULL` value and a value that has actually been set to an empty string. In practice, though, this isn't usually much of a problem, because such a distinction rarely is significant in a real-world application. Would there ever be a need, for instance, to distinguish between a film title that hasn't yet been named (a null value) and a film that has actually been named `""` (an empty string)? Probably not. So yes, it would be nice if ColdFusion maintained null values in query objects, but the fact that it does not isn't a deal breaker.

So, if you want to display a date only when it is has not been set to a null value in the database, you can test for an empty string in your CFML code, like so:

```
<CFIF GetOrders.ShipDate EQ "">
  (this order has not shipped yet)
<CFELSE>
  Shipped on: #LSDateFormat(GetOrders.ShipDate)#
</CFIF>
```

Working with Date Values

Working with date values in databases and ColdFusion can be confusing. The confusion often stems from the fact that a date value in a database is recorded conceptually as a moment in history, rather than as a simple string (such as `4/15/01`). How exactly the date is stored internally is up to the database system (often it's stored as a very long number that represents the number of milliseconds before or after some fixed reference point). Only when the figure is returned to ColdFusion and then output using a CFML function such as `DateFormat()` or `LSDateFormat()` does it look like a date to us humans.

NOTE

This discussion assumes that you are storing your dates in actual date-type columns in your database tables. Depending on the database system you're using, these columns can be called *date* columns, *date/time* columns, or something similar.

Specifying Dates in <CFQUERY> Tags

First, the bad news: Not all database systems agree on the syntax that should be used to specify a date in a query. Some are willing to parse the date based on a number of formats; others have a strict format that must be used at all times. The good news is that the ODBC specification defines a common format that can be used for any ODBC data source. The JDBC specification uses the same format, and ColdFusion conveniently provides a `CreateODBCDate()` function that can be used to automatically put dates into this format in your `<CFQUERY>` tags. Since all database connections in ColdFusion MX use JDBC under the hood, you can nearly always use `CreateODBCDate()` to specify dates in queries.

NOTE

It's admittedly a bit strange that you use a function with ODBC in the name to specify dates, even when you're not using an ODBC data source. Chalk it up to history; it's just the way things have evolved over time.

So, for almost all data sources, you can use `CreateODBCDate()` to correctly format the date in your `INSERT` and `UPDATE` queries. Here's a sample snippet that updates a column based on a form field called `DateInTheaters`:

```
<CFQUERY DATASOURCE="ows">
  UPDATE Films
  SET DateInTheaters = #CreateODBCDate(FORM.DateInTheaters)#
  WHERE FilmID = #FORM.FilmID#
</CFQUERY>
```

NOTE

If your situation is such that you can use `<CFUPDATE>` or `<CFINSERT>` to update your database, you don't even have to worry about this part. ColdFusion takes care of writing the correct query syntax for you.

Alternatively, you can substitute the `CreateODBCDate()` function with a `<CFQUERYPARAM>` tag that uses a `CFSQLTYPE` attribute of `CF_SQL_DATE`. ColdFusion will take care of adapting your SQL statement so the date is sent to the database in a format it will understand.

You will learn more about `<CFQUERYPARAM>` later in this chapter. For now, just think of it as a way to tell ColdFusion to convert the `VALUE` you supply into whatever format is appropriate for the type of database you are using (ODBC or otherwise). The query shown previously, then, would become this:

```
<CFQUERY DATASOURCE="ows">
  UPDATE Films
  SET DateInTheaters =
    <CFQUERYPARAM CFSQLTYPE="CF_SQL_DATE" VALUE="#FORM.DateInTheaters#">
  WHERE FilmID = #FORM.FilmID#
</CFQUERY>
```

As of ColdFusion MX, the decision to use `CreateODBCDate()` or `<CFQUERYPARAM>` as shown above is up to you; both will do the same thing. The distinction was more important in previous versions of ColdFusion, which didn't use JDBC as a common ground for all data sources. For more about `<CFQUERYPARAM>`, see the section "Parameterized Queries," later in this chapter.

Dates in Query Criteria

Developers often get confused about how to work with columns that contain both date and time information. For instance, consider the `ShipDate` column of the `MerchandiseOrders` table in the Orange Whip Studios database. This column contains the date and time the order was shipped. The date and time are not stored separately. They are stored as one value, which you can think of as a moment in history.

If, when a date is being recorded in a database, a time is not supplied, the database will store the time as midnight at the beginning of that day. If, later, you retrieve that date value with a `SELECT` statement and output the time portion of it with CFML's `TimeFormat()` function, the time will display as `12:00 AM`.

All of this makes perfect sense. But you will often need to query the database based on a date value, where the time portions of the date values can feel like they are working against you. For instance, say you are allowing the user to see all orders made on a particular day. You decide to allow the user to specify the date in a form field called `SearchDate`, using a `<CFINPUT>` tag, like this:

```
<CFINPUT
  NAME="SearchDate"
  VALIDATE="date"
  REQUIRED="Yes" MESSAGE="You must provide a date first!">
```

The user expects to be able to type a simple date into this field (perhaps `3/18/2001`) to see all orders placed on that date. You decide, quite sensibly, to write a query such as the following, which executes when the form is submitted:

```
<CFQUERY NAME="GetOrders" DATABASE="ows">
  SELECT * FROM MerchandiseOrders
  WHERE OrderDate = #CreateODBCDate(FORM.SearchDate)#
</CFQUERY>
```

When you test the template, though, you find that it doesn't work as planned. Users expect to see all orders placed on the date they specify, no matter what time the order was placed during that day. However, your code never seems to find any records. This is because no time is specified in the query criteria, so the database assumes a time of midnight. If the user types `3/18/2001` in the search field, your query is sent as something such as the following to your database system (conceptually):

```
SELECT * FROM MerchandiseOrders
WHERE OrderDate = '3/18/2001 12:00 AM'
```

After you see it this way, it becomes clear what's going on. Your query will return only records that were shipped at exactly midnight on whatever day the user specifies. You need to translate the user-specified date into a range between two moments in time (the beginning of that day and the end).

The following will work as expected, returning all orders placed on or after midnight at the beginning of the specified day, all the way up to (but not including) midnight at the end of that same day:

```
<CFQUERY NAME="GetOrders" DATABASE="ows">
  SELECT * FROM MerchandiseOrders
  WHERE OrderDate >= #CreateODBCDate(FORM.SearchDate)#
    AND OrderDate <  #CreateOBDCDate(DateAdd("d", Form.SearchDate, 1))#
</CFQUERY>
```

The following query will also work as expected and can be used interchangeably with the one shown previously. It uses a special keyword provided by SQL, called `BETWEEN`:

```
<CFQUERY NAME="GetOrders" DATABASE="ows">
  SELECT * FROM MerchandiseOrders
  WHERE OrderDate BETWEEN
    #CreateODBCDate(FORM.SearchDate)# AND
    #CreateOBDCDate(DateAdd("d", Form.SearchDate, 1))#
</CFQUERY>
```

NOTE

You could substitute all the `CreateODBCDate()` functions shown in this section with a `<CFQUERYPARAM>` tag, as explained earlier in the section "Specifying Dates in `<CFQUERY>` Tags."

Understanding Views

Many database systems support something called a view. The idea behind a view is to be able to save the SQL code for a particular `SELECT` query as a permanent part of the database. From that point on, the name of the view can be used like a table name in other queries.

Creating a View

Again, the exact syntax needed to create a view might vary depending on your database system, but you usually can create one by typing the words `CREATE VIEW`, then a name for the view, then the word `AS`, and then the actual `SELECT` statement you want to use to create the view, like so:

```
CREATE VIEW OrdersPending AS
SELECT * FROM MerchandiseOrders
WHERE ShipDate IS NULL
```

After you execute this SQL statement once (either via a `<CFQUERY>` tag; by executing it with ColdFusion Studio's Query Builder; or via whatever command-line, graphical, or other query tools your database system provides), it becomes a part of your database. You can now refer to the `OrdersPending` view in your queries as if it were a table. It's as if you have created a virtual or shadow table that always contains the same data as the `MerchandiseOrders` table, except that all the orders that have already shipped (where the `ShipDate` is not a null value) are excluded.

For instance, the following would return all pending orders:

```
SELECT * FROM OrdersPending
ORDER BY OrderDate
```

NOTE

The exact definition of what a view is called, how you create it, and what it can do varies a bit depending on the database system you use. For instance, if you use `CREATE VIEW` with an Access database, Access will create what it normally calls a query.

Advantages of Using Views

You almost never would need to create a view when building a ColdFusion application, but they can be helpful. Here, the `OrdersPending` view makes it easier to separate the abstract idea of a pending order from its implementation in the database (the `NULL` value). If you are working on a part of the application that deals only with pending orders (a section of the company intranet for the shipping department, say), you can use the `OrdersPending` view in each of your queries, instead of having to remember to use `ShipDate IS NULL` each time.

Also, if in the future you decide to keep pending orders in a different table, you would need to change only the definition of the view, rather than having to alter each individual query. In this respect, views become a method of abstraction, somewhat comparable to CFML's custom tags. They become a tool for separating your application's logic from the physical details of how the data is stored behind the scenes.

In fact, if your database is being designed by a different person in your team, or if you are connecting ColdFusion to some type of legacy database already in place, your database administrator may decide to give you access to only the `OrdersPending` view rather than the underlying `MerchandiseOrders` table. You might not even know the difference. This way, the administrator knows that your ColdFusion application will not be capable of displaying inappropriate records (in this case, orders that have already shipped).

You can also create views that involve more than one table by using ordinary join syntax in the `SELECT` statement that follows `CREATE VIEW`. For instance, you could create a view called `ActorsInFilms`, which uses a join to select the `FilmID` and `MovieTitle` of each film, plus the `ActorID` and name of each actor in that film. The `CREATE VIEW` statement would look like this:

```
CREATE VIEW ActorsInFilms AS
SELECT f.FilmID, f.MovieTitle, a.ActorID, a.NameFirst, a.NameLast
FROM Actors a, Films f, FilmsActors fa
WHERE a.ActorID = fa.ActorID AND f.FilmID = fa.FilmID
```

After the previous snippet is executed once, you can retrieve the title and actors for any film without having to use any joins at all. For instance:

```
SELECT * FROM ActorsInFilms
WHERE FilmID = #URL.FilmID#
```

NOTE

Views that involve more than one table are considered read-only by most database systems. You can `SELECT` from them but not make changes via `INSERT`, `UPDATE`, or `DELETE`.

Additional <CFQUERY> Topics

The remainder of this chapter discusses several advanced features provided by the `<CFQUERY>` tag. Each of these features provides you with finer-grained control over how ColdFusion interacts with your database or database server.

Query of Queries (In Memory Queries)

One of the most interesting and unique features in ColdFusion MX is its improved query of queries (QofQ) capability. As the name implies, this feature lets you retrieve information from queries that have already been run, using standard SQL syntax. The feature is simple but has many uses. This section introduces you to the query of queries feature and suggests several ways to put it to use in your ColdFusion applications.

NOTE

The ColdFusion MX documentation refers to this feature as *Query of Queries* and also as *In-Memory Queries* (IMQ). I will use the term Query of Queries in this discussion because that is what the feature has been called in the past.

The Basics

Considering all the problems it can solve, the actual process of using the query of queries feature is surprisingly straightforward. Perhaps the nicest thing about it is that it enables you to get new benefits from the SQL skills you already have.

To use the QofQ feature, follow these steps:

1. Run one or more ordinary queries using the `<CFQUERY>` tag in the way that you are already familiar with. These are the queries you will be able to query further in a moment. You can think of these as source queries.
2. Create a new `<CFQUERY>` tag, this time with `DBTYPE="query"`. This tells ColdFusion you don't intend to contact a traditional database (via a database driver). Instead, you will query the results returned by the queries from step 1.
3. Within this new `<CFQUERY>` tag, write SQL code that retrieves the records you want, using the names of the source queries as if they were table names. You can't do everything you would be able to within a traditional database query, but the most important SQL concepts and keywords are supported.
4. Now you can use the results of the query normally, just as you would any other query. You can output its records in a `<CFOUTPUT>` block, loop through them using `<CFLOOP>`, and so on. You can even query the records again, using yet another query of queries.

Using QofQ for Heterogeneous Data Analysis

Say Orange Whip Studios has some type of legacy database in place that predates your ColdFusion application. Perhaps the studio is experimenting with direct phone sales, trying to get people to buy collector's editions of coins (complete with certificates of authenticity) that commemorate the studio's classic films.

This database has just one table, called `Calls`, which contains the `ContactID` of each person called and columns named `CallID`, `CallDate`, `Status`, and `Comments`. Using the ColdFusion Administrator, you set up a new ODBC data source called DirectSales and then write a query that retrieves all the records from the Calls table, like so:

```
<CFQUERY DATASOURCE="DirectSales" NAME="GetCalls">
  SELECT ContactID, CallID, CallDate, Status, Comments
  FROM Calls
</CFQUERY>
```

Next, you run a second query against the Contacts table, using the usual ows data source:

```
<CFQUERY DATASOURCE="ows" NAME="GetContacts">
  SELECT ContactID, FirstName, LastName
  FROM Contacts
</CFQUERY>
```

Now you can use the QofQ feature to join the results of the GetCalls and GetContacts queries, like so:

```
<CFQUERY DBTYPE="query" NAME="GetJoined">
  SELECT *
  FROM GetCalls, GetContacts
  WHERE GetCalls.ContactID = GetContacts.ContactID
</CFQUERY>
```

That's it. Now you can use the GetJoined query just like the results of any other <CFQUERY> tag. Its results will contain one row for each row of the GetCalls and GetContacts queries that contain the same ContactID. All columns from the original query will be included.

NOTE

What makes this particularly interesting is the fact that the records from the two source queries need not have come from the same database or even the same type of database system. In fact, as you will see shortly, the source queries don't even have to come from databases at all. Any ColdFusion tag or function that returns a query object, such as the <CFDIRECTORY>, <CFPOP>, or <CFSEARCH> tags, can be requeried using the query of queries feature.

SQL Statements Supported by Query of Queries

In general, you can use just about any type of SQL statement in a QofQ query. There are a few exceptions, though. The absolute nitty-gritty can be found in the ColdFusion MX documentation, but the important things to keep in mind are all listed in Table 29.2.

Table 29.2 SQL Functionality Supported by Query of Queries

SQL CONCEPT	QUERY OF QUERIES NOTES
Table Joins	Fully supported, as long as you use basic WHERE syntax for joining the tables (as opposed to the alternate INNER JOIN syntax). For details, see "The Two Types of Join Syntax," earlier in this chapter.
Outer Joins	Unfortunately, Outer Joins are not supported by ColdFusion MX's query of queries feature. Only normal table joins (inner joins) are supported. Of course, this doesn'tdoesn't restrict you from using outer joins in ordinary <CFQUERY> tags; the restriction only applies only when using query-of-queries. Also, you are free to query a database directly using an outer join and then re-query it with QofQ. The only thing you can't do is to actually use the OUTER JOIN keywords inside a <CFQUERY> of DBTYPE="query".

Table 29.2 (continued)

SQL Concept	Query of Queries Notes
Unions	Fully supported. For information about unions, see "Combining Recordsets Sets with `UNION`," earlier in this chapter.
Aggregate functions, `GROUP BY` and `HAVING`	Supported. For more information, see the "Summarizing Data with Aggregate Functions" section, earlier in this chapter.
Case Sensitivity	Most database systems consider `WHERE` conditions without regard to upper- or lower case. However, `WHERE` conditions are case-sensitive when using QofQ. To get non-case-sensitive behavior, you need to use the `UPPER()` or `LOWER()` functions. For details, see the "Case-Sensitivity and Query of Queries" section, later in this chapter.
Reserved Words	ColdFusion MX's QofQ feature defines a list of reserved words—-including `CHECK`, `SIZE`, and `ZONE`—that can't be used as column or table names without escaping them with square brackets. See "Reserved Words and Query of Queries," later in this chapter.
Null values	Works normally, except that null values will pass inequality tests. For example, if you include `WHERE RatingID <> 3` in a QofQ, all records except for the ones with a `RatingID` of 3 will be returned, even rows where the `RatingID` was `NULL`. The proper, SQL-compliant behavior would be for the null rows to be omitted from the results. For more information about null values, see "Working with `NULL` Values" earlier in this chapter.
Reserved Words	ColdFusion MX's QofQ feature defines a list of reserved words that can't be used as column or table names without escaping them with square brackets. See "Reserved Words and Query of Queries," later in this chapter.

Using QofQ to Reduce Database Interaction

In Chapter 22, "Improving Performance," you learned about ColdFusion's query-caching mechanism, which allows you to transparently share query results between page requests, thereby cutting down on the interaction with the database system. You can use the QofQ feature in combination with query caching to reduce the actual communication with the database system even further.

You can use QofQ and query caching together in many ways; most are variations on the following basic idea. First, you write a source query using a normal `<CFQUERY>` tag that queries your database in the usual way and uses the `CACHEDWITHIN` attribute to cache the query's results. For instance, you might retrieve all records from the `Films` table and cache them for 30 minutes at a time, like so:

```
<CFQUERY DATASOURCE="ows" NAME="GetFilms"
  CACHEDWITHIN="#CreateTimeSpan(0,0,30,0)#">
  SELECT * FROM Films
  ORDER BY MovieTitle
</CFQUERY>
```

Now you can get information about individual film records by querying the `GetFilms` query, instead of running a separate query. For instance, if you wanted to retrieve a film record based on a URL parameter called `FilmID`, you could use code such as the following, which uses the query of queries feature to fetch a single row from the `GetFilms` query:

```
<CFQUERY DBTYPE="query" NAME="GetThisFilm">
  SELECT * FROM GetFilms
  WHERE FilmID = #URL.FilmID#
</CFQUERY>
```

The `GetThisFilm` query can now be used to output the film record. The net effect is that you have access to all the data you need, even though the database is hit only once every 30 minutes (at most). If you accept the notion that cutting down on database communication typically has a positive impact on overall system performance, then using QofQ in this way makes a lot of sense.

But why is this necessarily better than simply letting ColdFusion run separate cached queries for each individual record? That is, why not just use another version of `GetThisFilm` (rather than the combination of the `GetFilms` and `GetThisFilm` shown previously)? Consider:

```
<CFQUERY DATASOURCE="ows" NAME="GetThisFilm "
  CACHEDWITHIN="#CreateTimeSpan(0,0,30,0)#">
  SELECT * FROM Films
  WHERE FilmID = #URL.FilmID#
</CFQUERY>
```

The answer is that neither approach is inherently better than the other; it depends on the situation. For the moment, let's suppose that 100 films exist in the `Films` table and that the individual film records are all being accessed about five times in any 30-minute period. The first approach retrieves all 100 records at the beginning of the 30 minutes and serves the individual queries from the cached source query; however, all 100 records must be remembered in ColdFusion's RAM. The second approach contacts the database more often (up to 100 times during a 30-minute period, once for each film), but each query is very small and takes up only a tiny amount of memory in ColdFusion's RAM.

So, all other things being equal, the first approach probably makes the most sense when a significant number of the individual records will actually be accessed during the 30-minute period. If it turns out that only 3 out of the 100 records are accessed during the 30 minutes, the memory being used by the other 97 is essentially wasted; therefore, the second approach is probably a bit more efficient. On the other hand, if almost all of the individual records are actually accessed during the 30 minutes, the first approach is likely to be more efficient.

NOTE

Also, depending on the situation, the cached `GetFilms` query might be capable of being used by a large number of other QofQ queries in the application. Some pages might retrieve individual records using `WHERE`, as shown previously. Other pages might need to obtain counts or summaries from the data using aggregate functions and `GROUP BY` statements in QofQ queries. Still other pages might simply need to display the records as is, using the cached query results directly. Using the query of queries feature, you could tell all these pages to use the same cached version of the `GetFilms` query, so there is still only one access to the database every 30 minutes, even though the query is being massaged and reinterpreted by the various pages in various ways.

But ColdFusion Is Not a Database Server

It is critical to understand that ColdFusion's query of queries feature, while certainly very useful, is unlikely to be better at searching through large sets of records than a dedicated database system. Whereas database systems can rely on indexes, active query optimizers, and other tools to find the correct record in a large database table, ColdFusion's query of queries feature just iterates through the rows, looking for the correct values. This is what database server products call an iterative table scan, which is unlikely to scale well in extreme conditions.

So, if the number of records in the cached `GetFilms` query becomes very large over time (say, 100,000 records instead of 100), the performance of the first approach will start to degrade because ColdFusion will have to look through all of them each time it needs to find an individual record. In contrast, a decent database system should be capable of returning the correct record very quickly, regardless of the size of the table (especially if a well-tuned index exists on the `FilmID` column), making the second approach more efficient.

To put it another way, the existence of the query of queries feature in ColdFusion MX does not mean that ColdFusion should be considered a database server, competing directly with high-performance database products such as MySQL, Oracle, and Microsoft SQLServer. The fact that query records are maintained in ColdFusion's RAM does not automatically mean ColdFusion will be capable of requerying the records more efficiently than your database server would. Today's database servers are very sophisticated animals indeed and are difficult for ColdFusion to outperform.

As a general rule of thumb, a practice of caching queries of 1,000 records or less (and then requerying those records using QofQ) is likely to serve you very well. When the record count starts to climb toward five digits, the benefit of having the records already in RAM will eventually be overcome by the sheer weight of the large record set and will probably be further hampered by ColdFusion's iterative approach to requerying the data.

A Real-World Example

In Chapter 21, "Improving the User Experience," several versions of a next-n interface were created, allowing the user to click through records on pages 10 rows at a time. Then, in Chapter 22, the next-n interface was revised to use ColdFusion's query-caching feature via the `CACHEDWITHIN` attribute to improve perfomance.

The code in Listing 29.12 revises the next-n interface again, this time using ColdFusion's query of queries feature to allow the user to re-sort the records by clicking the column names. Upon the user's first visit to the page, the records are sorted by date (with the most recent expense first), just as in the previous versions of the template. Then, if the user clicks the `Film` column, the page reloads with the records sorted alphabetically by film title. If the user clicks the `Film` column again, the sort order is reversed. A small triangle image indicates which column the records are sorted by, and in what order.

NOTE

This listing uses `<CFINCLUDE>` tags to include the `NextNIncludePageLinks.cfm` and `NextNIncludeBackNext.cfm` templates from Chapter 21. Either save this template in the same directory as Chapter 21's listings or copy the included templates into the folder you are using for this chapter. For your convenience, the included files have been duplicated in the folder for this chapter on the CD-ROM.

Listing 29.12 `NextN6.cfm`—Allowing Users to Re-sort Cached Query Results

```
<!---
  Filename:     NextN6.cfm
  Created by:   Nate Weiss (NMW)
  Purpose:      Displays Next N record-navigation interface
  Please Note  Includes NextNIncludeBackNext.cfm and NextNIncludePageLinks.cfm
--->

<!--- Maintain ExpenseReport filtering variables at session level --->
<CFPARAM NAME="SESSION.ExpenseReport.UserFilter" TYPE="string" DEFAULT="">
<CFPARAM NAME="SESSION.ExpenseReport.DateFrom" TYPE="string" DEFAULT="">
<CFPARAM NAME="SESSION.ExpenseReport.DateThru" TYPE="string" DEFAULT="">
<!--- Also which column is being sorted on, and in which direction --->
<CFPARAM NAME="SESSION.ExpenseReport.SortCol" TYPE="string" DEFAULT="d">
<CFPARAM NAME="SESSION.ExpenseReport.SortAsc" TYPE="boolean" DEFAULT="No">

<!--- If user is asking to change sort order --->
<CFIF IsDefined("URL.SortCol") AND IsDefined("URL.SortDir")>
  <!--- Save new order column/order in SESSION scope --->
  <CFSET SESSION.ExpenseReport.SortCol = URL.SortCol>
  <CFSET SESSION.ExpenseReport.SortAsc = URL.SortDir>
  <!--- Send user back to first row of query results --->
  <CFSET URL.StartRow = 1>
</CFIF>

<!--- If the user is submitting the "filter" form, --->
<!--- we'll make their submission be the filter for rest of session --->
<CFIF IsDefined("FORM.UserFilter")>
  <CFSET SESSION.ExpenseReport.UserFilter = FORM.UserFilter>
  <CFSET SESSION.ExpenseReport.DateFrom   = FORM.DateFrom>
  <CFSET SESSION.ExpenseReport.DateThru   = FORM.DateThru>
</CFIF>

<!--- Retrieve expense records from database --->
<CFQUERY NAME="GetExp" DATASOURCE="#REQUEST.DataSource#"
  CACHEDWITHIN="#CreateTimeSpan(0,0,15,0)#">
  SELECT
    f.FilmID, f.MovieTitle,
    e.Description, e.ExpenseAmount, e.ExpenseDate
  FROM
    Expenses e INNER JOIN Films f
    ON e.FilmID = f.FilmID
  WHERE
    0=0
  <!--- If the user provided a filter string, --->
  <!--- show only matching films and/or expenses --->
  <CFIF SESSION.ExpenseReport.UserFilter IS NOT "">
    AND (f.MovieTitle LIKE '%#SESSION.ExpenseReport.UserFilter#%' OR
```

Listing 29.12 (continued)

```
        e.Description LIKE '%#SESSION.ExpenseReport.UserFilter#%')
  </CFIF>
  <!--- Also filter on From date, if provided --->
  <CFIF IsDate(SESSION.ExpenseReport.DateFrom)>
    AND e.ExpenseDate >= #CreateODBCDate(SESSION.ExpenseReport.DateFrom)#
  </CFIF>
  <!--- Also filter on Through date, if provided --->
  <CFIF IsDate(SESSION.ExpenseReport.DateThru)>
    AND e.ExpenseDate <= #CreateODBCDate(SESSION.ExpenseReport.DateThru)#
  </CFIF>
  ORDER BY
    e.ExpenseDate DESC
</CFQUERY>


<!--- If user's current sort order differs from the --->
<!--- default, use Q-of-Q to re-sort original query --->
<CFIF NOT (SESSION.ExpenseReport.SortCol EQ "d" AND SESSION.ExpenseReport.SortAsc EQ
"No")>
  <!--- Re-query "GetExp" with appropriate ORDER BY --->
  <CFQUERY NAME="GetExp" DBTYPE="query">
    SELECT * FROM GetExp
    ORDER BY
    <!--- Use appropriate sort column --->
    <CFSWITCH EXPRESSION="#SESSION.ExpenseReport.SortCol#">
      <CFCASE VALUE="f">MovieTitle</CFCASE>
      <CFCASE VALUE="e">Description</CFCASE>
      <CFCASE VALUE="a">ExpenseAmount</CFCASE>
      <CFDEFAULTCASE>   ExpenseDate</CFDEFAULTCASE>
    </CFSWITCH>
    <!--- Appropriate sort direction --->
    <CFIF SESSION.ExpenseReport.SortAsc>ASC<CFELSE>DESC</CFIF>
  </CFQUERY>
</CFIF>

<!--- Number of rows to display per Next/Back page  --->
<CFSET RowsPerPage = 10>
<!--- What row to start at? Assume first by default --->
<CFPARAM NAME="URL.StartRow" DEFAULT="1" TYPE="numeric">
<!--- Allow for Show All parameter in the URL --->
<CFPARAM NAME="URL.ShowAll" TYPE="boolean" DEFAULT="No">

<!--- We know the total number of rows from query   --->
<CFSET TotalRows = GetExp.RecordCount>
<!--- Show all on page if ShowAll passed in URL   --->
<CFIF URL.ShowAll>
  <CFSET RowsPerPage = TotalRows>
</CFIF>
<!--- Last row is 10 rows past the starting row, or --->
<!--- total number of query rows, whichever is less --->
<CFSET EndRow = Min(URL.StartRow + RowsPerPage - 1, TotalRows)>
<!--- Next button goes to 1 past current end row  --->
<CFSET StartRowNext = EndRow + 1>
<!--- Back button goes back N rows from start row --->
<CFSET StartRowBack = URL.StartRow - RowsPerPage>
```

Listing 29.12 (continued)

```
<!--- Page Title --->
<HTML>
<HEAD><TITLE>Expense Browser</TITLE></HEAD>
<BODY>
<CFOUTPUT><H2>#REQUEST.CompanyName# Expense Report</H2></CFOUTPUT>

<!--- Simple style sheet for formatting --->
<STYLE>
  FORM     {font-family:sans-serif;font-size:smaller;}
  TH       {font-family:sans-serif;font-size:smaller;
            background:navy;color:white}
  TD       {font-family:sans-serif;font-size:smaller}
  TD.DataA {background:silver;color:black}
  TD.DataB {background:lightgrey;color:black}
  A.Head    {color:white}
  A.Head:visited {color:white}
</STYLE>


<!--- Simple form to allow user to filter results --->
<CFFORM ACTION="#CGI.SCRIPT_NAME#" METHOD="POST">
  <!--- Filter string --->
  <B>Filter:</B>
  <CFINPUT
    TYPE="Text"
    NAME="UserFilter"
    VALUE="#SESSION.ExpenseReport.UserFilter#"
    SIZE="15">

  <!--- From date --->
   
  <B>Dates:</B> from
  <CFINPUT
    TYPE="Text"
    NAME="DateFrom"
    VALUE="#SESSION.ExpenseReport.DateFrom#"
    SIZE="9"
    VALIDATE="date"
    MESSAGE="Please enter a valid date, or leave it blank.">

  <!--- Through date --->
  through
  <CFINPUT
    TYPE="Text"
    NAME="DateThru"
    VALUE="#SESSION.ExpenseReport.DateThru#"
    SIZE="9"
    VALIDATE="date"
    MESSAGE="Please enter a valid date, or leave it blank.">

  <!--- Submit button to activate/change/clear filter --->
  <INPUT
    TYPE="Submit"
    VALUE="Apply">
</CFFORM>
```

Listing 29.12 (CONTINUED)

```
<TABLE WIDTH="600" BORDER="0" CELLSPACING="0" CELLPADDING="1">
  <!--- Row at top of table, above column headers --->
  <TR>
    <TD WIDTH="500" COLSPAN="3">
      <!--- Message about which rows are being displayed --->
      <CFOUTPUT>
        Displaying <B>#URL.StartRow#</B> to <B>#EndRow#</B>
        of <B>#TotalRows#</B> Records<BR>
      </CFOUTPUT>
    </TD>
    <TD WIDTH="100" ALIGN="right">
      <CFIF NOT URL.ShowAll>
        <!--- Provide Next/Back links --->
        <CFINCLUDE TEMPLATE="NextNIncludeBackNext.cfm">
      </CFIF>
    </TD>
  </TR>

  <!--- Row for Column Headers --->
  <TR>
    <CFOUTPUT>
      <!--- For each of the four columns... --->
      <CFLOOP LIST="Date,Film,Expense,Amount" INDEX="Col">
        <!--- Use 1st letter of column as "Alias" to pass in URL --->
        <CFSET Alias = LCase(Left(Col, 1))>
        <!--- If user already viewing by this col, link should   --->
        <!--- reverse order; otherwise, order should be ASC for  --->
        <!--- all columns except Date, when order should be DESC --->
        <CFIF SESSION.ExpenseReport.SortCol EQ Alias>
          <CFSET SortDir = NOT SESSION.ExpenseReport.SortAsc>
        <CFELSE>
          <CFSET SortDir = Col NEQ "Date">
        </CFIF>
        <!--- URL for when user clicks on column name --->
        <CFSET SortLink = "#CGI.SCRIPT_NAME#?SortCol=#Alias#&SortDir=#SortDir#">
        <TH>
          <!--- Show column heading as link that changes order --->
          <A HREF="#SortLink#" CLASS="Head">#Col#</A>
          <!--- If this is current column, show icon to indicate current sort --->
          <CFIF SESSION.ExpenseReport.SortCol EQ Alias>
            <CFSET SortImgSrc = IIF(SESSION.ExpenseReport.SortAsc, "'SortA.gif'",
            ➥"'SortD.gif'")>
            <IMG SRC="../images/#SortImgSrc#" WIDTH="12" HEIGHT="12" ALT="">
          </CFIF>
        </TH>
      </CFLOOP>
    </CFOUTPUT>
  </TR>

  <!--- For each query row that should be shown now --->
  <CFLOOP QUERY="GetExp" StartRow="#URL.StartRow#" ENDROW="#EndRow#">
    <!--- Use class "DataA" or "DataB" for alternate rows --->
    <CFSET Class = IIF(GetExp.CurrentRow MOD 2 EQ 0, "'DataA'", "'DataB'")>

    <CFOUTPUT>
```

Listing 29.12 (continued)

```
      <TR VALIGN="baseline">
        <TD CLASS="#Class#" WIDTH="100">#LSDateFormat(ExpenseDate)#</TD>
        <TD CLASS="#Class#" WIDTH="250">#MovieTitle#</TD>
        <TD CLASS="#Class#" WIDTH="150"><I>#Description#</I></TD>
        <TD CLASS="#Class#" WIDTH="100">#LSCurrencyFormat(ExpenseAmount)#</TD>
      </TR>
    </CFOUTPUT>
  </CFLOOP>

  <!--- Row at bottom of table, after rows of data --->
  <TR>
    <TD WIDTH="500" COLSPAN="3">
      <CFIF NOT URL.ShowAll AND TotalRows GT RowsPerPage>
        <!--- Shortcut links for "Pages" of search results --->
        Page <CFINCLUDE TEMPLATE="NextNIncludePageLinks.cfm">
        <!--- Show All link --->
        <CFOUTPUT>
          <A HREF="#CGI.SCRIPT_NAME#?&ShowAll=Yes">Show All</A>
        </CFOUTPUT>
      </CFIF>
    </TD>
    <TD WIDTH="100" ALIGN="right">
      <CFIF NOT URL.ShowAll>
        <!--- Provide Next/Back links --->
        <CFINCLUDE TEMPLATE="NextNIncludeBackNext.cfm">
      </CFIF>
    </TD>
  </TR>
</TABLE>

</BODY>
</HTML>
```

Most of the code in this template is identical to the versions presented in Chapters 21 and 22. The most important additions are discussed here.

First, two `<CFPARAM>` tags have been added, which define `SESSION.ExpenseReport.SortCol` and `SESSION.ExpenseReport.SortAsc` variables to track the user's current sort column and sort direction. The `NextNSortCol` value will be `d`, `f`, `e`, or `a` to signify the `ExpenseDate`, `MovieTitle`, expense `Description`, and `ExpenseAmount` columns, respectively. The Boolean `NextNSortAsc` value will be `True` if the column is being sorted in ascending order, and will be `False` if it is being sorted in descending order.

A `<CFIF>` block at the top of the template changes the sort order and sort direction for the user's session if URL parameters called `SortCol` and `SortDir` are provided. If provided, the values provided in the URL are copied to the two new `SESSION` variables, which causes the template to remember to show the records in the new sort order for the rest of the session. In addition, the `StartRow` variable is set to `1`, so the user is always shown the first page of records whenever the sort is changed.

After the cached `GetExp` query, a second `<CFQUERY>` tag that uses the query of queries feature is used to re-sort the cached query results, depending on the current values of the two `SESSION` variables.

For instance, if `SESSION.ExpenseReport.SortCol` is `f` and `SESSION.ExpenseReport.SortAsc` is `True`, the resulting `ORDER BY` statement would be `MovieTitle ASC`, thereby providing the user with the desired sorting effect. Simple `<CFIF>` logic skips this requerying step if the user is viewing the template with the default sort options.

The rest of the code is largely unchanged from prior versions. The only other major change is in the middle of the template, where the column headings are displayed.

A `<CFLOOP>` is used to output the four columns. For each column, the `Alias` variable is set to the first letter of the column name; this is passed in the URL when the user clicks a column heading. Then, a `SortDir` variable is set to `True` or `False`, depending on whether the results are already being sorted by that column. The `SortDir` determines the direction in which the records should be sorted if the user clicks the column heading. For instance, for the `Date` column, if the user is already viewing the records by date, the `SortDir` is the opposite of the current `SESSION.ExpenseReport.SortAsc` value. If the user is currently viewing records by some other column, the `SortDir` is `NO`, meaning the sort direction is changed to a descending sort if the user clicks the `Date` column.

The column name is then displayed as a link, passing the appropriate values as URL parameters called `SortCol` and `SortDir`. Plus, if the column heading being output corresponds with the current sort order, a small triangle icon is displayed (`SortA.gif` or `SortD.gif`), depending on whether the column is currently sorted in ascending or descending order, respectively. The results are shown in Figure 29.10.

NOTE

In this example, the query of queries feature is used to reorder the original, cached result set. The same basic technique could be used for other types of requerying needs. For instance, the second QofQ query might retrieve a subset of the original records, using some type of `WHERE` filter criteria.

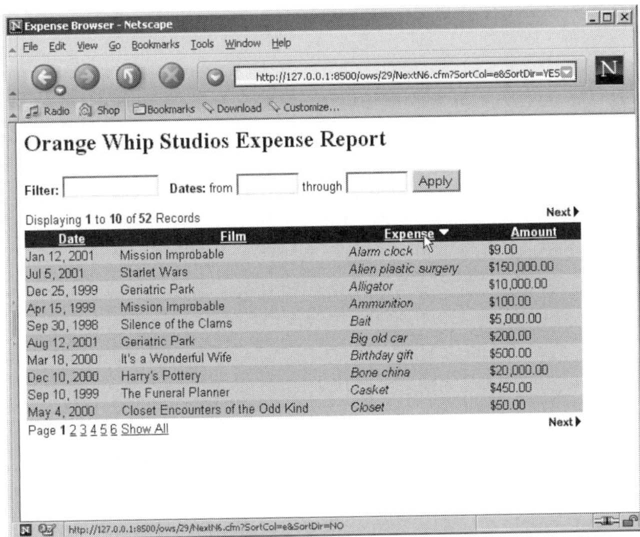

Figure 29.10

When users click a column header, the results are re-sorted using a QofQ query.

Using QofQ with Nondatabase Queries

The query of queries feature can be used on any ColdFusion query object. Most commonly, this is the result of a <CFQUERY> tag that retrieves records from a database. However, a number of other CFML tags return information as ColdFusion query objects, which means they can be requeried using QofQ.

Table 29.3 provides a short list of tags that return query objects. More information about each of these tags is available in Appendix B, "ColdFusion Tag Reference."

Table 29.3 CFML Tags That Return Query Objects, Which Can Be Requeried Using QofQ

CFML TAG	RETURNS QUERY OBJECT THAT CONTAINS
<CFDIRECTORY>	A listing of files in a particular directory (when used with ACTION="List"). See Chapter 33, "Interacting with the Operating System."
<CFFTP>	A listing of files on a remote FTP server (when used with ACTION="ListDir").
<CFLDAP>	Directory listings retrieved from a remote LDAP server (when used with ACTION="Query").
<CFPOP>	Incoming mail messages, as retrieved from a remote email mailbox (when used with ACTION="GetHeaderOnly" or ACTION="GetAll"). See Chapter 26, "Interacting with Email."
<CFQUERY>	Any database query.
<CFSEARCH>	Search results found by a Verity full-text search operation. See Chapter 34, "Full-Text Searching."
<CFPROCRESULT>	A result set returned by a stored procedure in a database. See Chapter 30, "Working with Stored Procedures."
Custom Tags	CFML custom tags can use the QueryNew() function to create and return query objects, filled with rows and columns of whatever data is appropriate. The <CF_ShoppingCart> custom tag from Chapter 27 is an example of such a tag. For more about CFML custom tags, see Chapter 20, "Building Reusable Components."
User-Defined Functions	UDFs can query objects by specifying RETURNTYPE="query" in a <CFFUNCTION> tag. For details, see Chapter 19, "Building User-Defined Functions."
ColdFusion Components	CFC methods can also return query objects, also by specifying RETURNTYPE="query" in the corresponding <CFFUNCTION> tag. For details, see Chapter 20.
CFX Tags	Many CFX tags return query objects, filled with whatever specialized data is appropriate. For information about writing your own CFX tags (using Java or C++), see our companion volume, Advanced ColdFusion MX Application Development.

For instance, Listing 29.13 shows how ColdFusion's query of queries feature can be used to combine result sets from two different query objects. Here, QofQ is used to get around a limitation of the `<CFDIRECTORY>` tag. It is a good example of how QofQ can add flexibility and power to CFML tags that return query objects (refer to Table 29.3).

The purpose of this listing is to display all the GIF and JPEG images in a particular directory. As explained in Chapter 36, the `<CFDIRECTORY>` tag can be used to easily obtain a list of files, and it even provides a `FILTER` attribute that enables you to filter the files based on DOS-style wildcards. For instance, a `FILTER` of `*.jpg` returns all JPEG files in a directory, and a `FILTER` of `*.gif` lists all the GIF files. Unfortunately, `<CFDIRECTORY>` doesn't allow you to provide a single filter that returns all GIF and JPEG files together as a single, sorted query object.

Listing 29.13 overcomes this limitation by using separate `<CFDIRECTORY>` tags to retrieve the GIF and JPEG directory listings. Then, the query of queries feature is used to combine the two result sets as a single query object, sorted by filename.

Listing 29.13 `MultiDirectory1.cfm`—Combining the Results of Two `<CFDIRECTORY>` Tags with `UNION`

```
<!---
  Filename:      MultiDirectory1.cfm
  Created by:    Nate Weiss (NMW)
  Purpose:       Displays a list of all GIF and JPEG files in images folder
--->

<!--- Directory to scan for images --->
<CFSET Dir = ExpandPath("../images")>

<!--- First, get query object of JPEG files --->
<CFDIRECTORY
  ACTION="LIST"
  DIRECTORY="#Dir#"
  FILTER="*.jpg"
  NAME="GetJPG">

<!--- Next, get query object of GIF files --->
<CFDIRECTORY
  ACTION="LIST"
  DIRECTORY="#Dir#"
  FILTER="*.gif"
  NAME="GetGIF">

<!--- Use CF's Query-of-Queries feature to --->
<!--- combine the queries with a SQL UNION --->
<!--- Sort the resulting query by filename --->
<CFQUERY DBTYPE="query" NAME="GetAll">
  SELECT * FROM GetJPG
  UNION
  SELECT * FROM GetGIF
  ORDER BY Name
</CFQUERY>


<HTML>
<HEAD><TITLE>Images Folder</TITLE></HEAD>
<BODY>
<H2>Images Folder</H2>
```

Listing 29.13 (continued)

```
<!--- Display all files together as a list --->
<CFOUTPUT>
  <P>There are #GetAll.RecordCount# images in #Dir#:<BR>

  <CFLOOP QUERY="GetAll">
    <P>
      #CurrentRow#. #GetAll.Name#<BR>
      <IMG SRC="../images/#Name#"><BR>
    </P>
  </CFLOOP>
</CFOUTPUT>

</BODY>
</HTML>
```

First, the `ExpandPath()` function is used to get the absolute filesystem path of Orange Whip Studios' `images` folder. It is assumed that the `images` folder and the current folder are both contained within the same parent folder.

Next, two `<CFDIRECTORY>` tags are used to retrieve listings of all JPEG and GIF files in the `images` folder. The query objects returned by the two tags are named `GetJPG` and `GetGIF`, respectively.

Now the two query objects can be combined in the QofQ query named `GetAll`. The SQL syntax used here is extremely simple. All that's needed is a standard `UNION` statement that retrieves all records from both source queries and sorts the combined result set by filename (see the section "Combining Record Sets with `UNION`," earlier in this chapter). The result is a single ColdFusion query object that can be used just like any other. It contains a row for each GIF and JPEG file. The images and filenames are then displayed using a standard `<CFLOOP>` block that loops over the `GetAll` query, as shown in Figure 29.11.

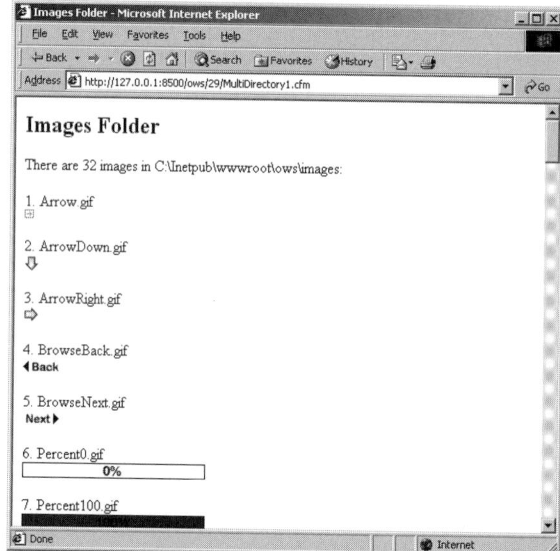

Figure 29.11

The query of queries feature makes obtaining flexible directory listings easier.

You can wrap such QofQ operations in CFML custom tags. Listing 29.14 takes the code from Listing 29.13 and turns it into a custom tag called `<CF_GetDirectoryContents>`. The custom tag takes `Directory`, `Filter`, `Sort`, and `Name` attributes, which correspond to the same attributes of ColdFusion's native `<CFDIRECTORY>` tag. The advantage of this custom tag is that its `Filter` attribute accepts multiple wildcard filters. The individual filters are separated with semicolons, like so:

```
<CF_GetDirectoryContents
  Directory="c:\inetpub\wwwroot\ows\images\"
  Filter="*.gif;*.jpg"
  Name="GetAll">
```

NOTE

Because this is a custom tag template, it should be saved in the special `CustomTags` folder. As an alternative, you can just save a copy of it in the folder where you intend to use it (the same folder you are using for the other code listings in this chapter).

Listing 29.14 `GetDirectoryContents.cfm`—Creating the `<CF_GetDirectoryContents>` Custom Tag

```
<!---
  Filename:     GetDirectoryContents.cfm
  Created by:   Nate Weiss (NMW)
  Purpose:      Creates the <CF_GetDirectoryContents> custom tag
  Please Note  This example uses Query-of-Queries to combine query objects
--->

<!--- Tag Parameters --->
<CFPARAM NAME="ATTRIBUTES.Directory">
<CFPARAM NAME="ATTRIBUTES.Filter" TYPE="string" DEFAULT="*.*">
<CFPARAM NAME="ATTRIBUTES.Sort" TYPE="string" DEFAULT="Name">
<CFPARAM NAME="ATTRIBUTES.Name" TYPE="variableName">

<!--- For each filter (filters separated by semicolons) --->
<CFLOOP LIST="#ATTRIBUTES.Filter#" INDEX="ThisFilter" DELIMITERS=";">

  <!--- Get query object of matching files --->
  <CFDIRECTORY
    ACTION="LIST"
    DIRECTORY="#ATTRIBUTES.Directory#"
    FILTER="#ThisFilter#"
    NAME="GetFiles">

  <!--- If this is first time through loop, --->
  <!--- Save GetFiles as our "ResultQuery". --->
  <CFIF NOT IsDefined("ResultQuery")>
    <CFSET ResultQuery = GetFiles>
  <!--- If ResultQuery already exists, add --->
  <!--- GetFiles's records to it via UNION --->
  <CFELSE>
    <CFQUERY DBTYPE="query" NAME="ResultQuery">
      SELECT * FROM ResultQuery
      UNION
      SELECT * FROM GetFiles
      ORDER BY #ATTRIBUTES.Sort#
    </CFQUERY>
  </CFIF>
```

Listing 29.14 (continued)

```
</CFLOOP>

<!--- Return completed resultset to calling template --->
<CFSET "Caller.#ATTRIBUTES.Name#" = ResultQuery>
```

First, four `<CFPARAM>` tags are used to establish the tag's parameters. Then, a `<CFLOOP>` tag is used to loop through the semicolon-delimited list provided to the tag's `Filter` attribute. If the `Filter` is provided as `*.gif;*.jpg`, the loop runs twice. The first time through the loop, `ThisFilter` is `*.gif`, and so on.

Within the loop, the `<CFDIRECTORY>` tag called `GetFiles` is used to retrieve the files in the directory that correspond to the current `ThisFilter` value. Then, if this is the first time through the loop, the `GetFiles` object is set to a new variable named `ResultQuery`, which is what gets passed back to the calling template when the tag is finished with its work. The next time through the loop, the results of the `GetFiles` query are added to the `ResultsQuery`, using the `UNION` technique from Listing 29.13.

When the loop is finished, the `ResultsQuery` variable contains the complete file listing. It is returned to the calling template using quoted `<CFSET>` syntax. See Chapter 20 for details.Listing 29.15 shows how this custom tag can be used in a normal ColdFusion template. It is the same as Listing 29.13, except that the `<CFDIRECTORY>` and `<CFQUERY>` tags have been replaced with the `<CF_GetDirectoryContents>` custom tag. Refer to Figure 29.11 to see what the results will look like.

Listing 29.15 `MultiDirectory2.cfm`—Executing a QofQ Operation Via the `<CF_GetDirectoryContents>` Custom Tag

```
<!---
  Filename:     MultiDirectory2.cfm
  Created by:   Nate Weiss (NMW)
  Purpose:      Displays a list of all GIF and JPEG files in images folder
--->

<!--- Directory to scan for images --->
<CFSET Dir = ExpandPath("../images")>

<!--- Get GIF and JPG file listing, via custom tag --->
<CF_GetDirectoryContents
  Directory="#Dir#"
  Filter="*.gif;*.jpg"
  Name="GetAll">

<HTML>
<HEAD><TITLE>Images Folder</TITLE></HEAD>
<BODY>
<H2>Images Folder</H2>

<!--- Display all files together as a list --->
<CFOUTPUT>
  <P>There are #GetAll.RecordCount# images in #Dir#:<BR>

  <CFLOOP QUERY="GetAll">
    <P>
      #CurrentRow#. #GetAll.Name#<BR>
```

Listing 29.15 (continued)

```
      <IMG SRC="../images/#Name#"><BR>
    </P>
  </CFLOOP>
</CFOUTPUT>

</BODY>
</HTML>
```

Joining Database and Nondatabase Queries

You have seen how ColdFusion's QofQ feature can be used to join or combine query objects returned by database queries or nondatabase tags, such as `<CFDIRECTORY>`. You also can use QofQ to merge the results of database queries with nondatabase query objects, using `UNION` or join syntax.

Listing 29.16 is another revision of the `StoreCart.cfm` templates created in Chapter 27. Similar to the version in Listing 29.10, this template displays suggestions to the user using a pseudocollaborative filtering technique. In addition, this version displays a subtotal for each item in the user's cart, along with a grand total of all the items. Versions provided up to this point did not display totals.

NOTE

Because this listing relies on other templates from Chapter 27, you should save this template in the same folder you use for Chapter 27's listings.

Listing 29.16 `StoreCart4.cfm`—Using Several QofQ Queries Together, with Database and Nondatabase Source Queries

```
<!---
  Filename:    StoreCart.cfm (save as StoreCart.cfm)
  Created by:  Nate Weiss (NMW)
  Purpose:     Displays the current user's shopping cart
  Please Note Depends on the <CF_ShoppingCart> custom tag
--->

<!--- Show header images, etc., for Online Store --->
<CFINCLUDE TEMPLATE="StoreHeader.cfm">

<!--- If MerchID was passed in URL --->
<CFIF IsDefined("URL.AddMerchID")>
  <!--- Add item to user's cart data, via custom tag --->
  <CF_ShoppingCart
    Action="Add"
    MerchID="#URL.AddMerchID#">

<!--- If user is submitting cart form --->
<CFELSEIF IsDefined("FORM.MerchID")>
  <!--- For each MerchID on Form, Update Quantity --->
  <CFLOOP LIST="#Form.MerchID#" INDEX="ThisMerchID">
    <!--- Update Quantity, via Custom Tag --->
    <CF_ShoppingCart
      Action="Update"
      MerchID="#ThisMerchID#"
      Quantity="#FORM['Quant_#ThisMerchID#']#">
```

Listing 29.16 (continued)

```
    </CFLOOP>

    <!--- If user submitted form via "Checkout" button, --->
    <!--- send on to Checkout page after updating cart. --->
    <CFIF IsDefined("FORM.IsCheckingOut")>
      <CFLOCATION URL="../27/StoreCheckout.cfm">
    </CFIF>
  </CFIF>

  <!--- Get current cart contents, via Custom Tag --->
  <CF_ShoppingCart
    Action="List"
    ReturnVariable="GetCart">


  <!--- Stop here if user's cart is empty --->
  <CFIF GetCart.RecordCount EQ 0>
    There is nothing in your cart.
    <CFABORT>
  </CFIF>


  <!--- Retrieve items in user's cart from database --->
  <CFQUERY NAME="GetMerch" DATASOURCE="ows">
    SELECT MerchID, MerchPrice
    FROM Merchandise
    WHERE MerchID IN (#ValueList(GetCart.MerchID)#)
  </CFQUERY>

  <!--- Use QofQ to join queried records against cart data --->
  <!--- The SubTotal column is Quantity times MerchPrice --->
  <CFQUERY NAME="GetPrices" DBTYPE="query">
    SELECT
      GetMerch.MerchID AS MerchID,
      GetCart.Quantity AS Quantity,
      (GetCart.Quantity * GetMerch.MerchPrice) AS SubTotal
    FROM GetMerch, GetCart
    WHERE GetMerch.MerchID = GetCart.MerchID
  </CFQUERY>

  <!--- Use QofQ again to get a grand total of all items --->
  <CFQUERY NAME="GetTotal" DBTYPE="query">
    SELECT SUM(SubTotal) AS GrandTotal
    FROM GetPrices
  </CFQUERY>

  <!--- Create form that submits to this template --->
  <CFFORM ACTION="#CGI.SCRIPT_NAME#">
    <TABLE>
      <TR>
        <TH COLSPAN="2" BGCOLOR="Silver">Your Shopping Cart</TH>
      </TR>
      <!--- For each piece of merchandise --->
      <CFLOOP QUERY="GetPrices">
        <TR>
```

Listing 29.16 (CONTINUED)

```
        <TD>
          <!--- Show this piece of merchandise --->
          <CF_MerchDisplay
            MerchID="#GetPrices.MerchID#"
            ShowAddLink="No">
        </TD>
        <TD>
          <!--- Display Quantity in Text entry field --->
          <CFOUTPUT>
            Quantity:
            <INPUT TYPE="Hidden"
              NAME="MerchID"
              VALUE="#GetPrices.MerchID#">
            <INPUT TYPE="Text" SIZE="3"
              NAME="Quant_#GetPrices.MerchID#"
              VALUE="#GetPrices.Quantity#"><BR>
            Subtotal: #LSCurrencyFormat(SubTotal)#
          </CFOUTPUT>
        </TD>
      </TR>
    </CFLOOP>

    <TR>
      <TD></TD>
      <TD>
        <!--- Display Grand Total for all items in cart --->
        <CFOUTPUT>
          <B>Total: #LSCurrencyFormat(GetTotal.GrandTotal)#</B>
        </CFOUTPUT>
      </TD>
    </TR>
  </TABLE>

  <!--- Submit button to update quantities --->
  <INPUT TYPE="Submit" VALUE="Update Quantities">

  <!--- Submit button to Check out --->
  <INPUT TYPE="Submit" VALUE="Checkout" NAME="IsCheckingOut">
</CFFORM>



<!--- Convert current cart contents to comma-sep list --->
<CFSET CurrentMerchList = ValueList(GetCart.MerchID)>

<!--- Run query to suggest other items for user to buy --->
<CFQUERY NAME="GetSimilar" DATASOURCE="#REQUEST.DataSource#"
  CACHEDWITHIN="#CreateTimeSpan(0,0,5,0)#" MAXROWS="3">
  <!--- We want all items NOT in user's cart... --->
  SELECT ItemID
  FROM MerchandiseOrdersItems
  WHERE ItemID NOT IN (#CurrentMerchList#)
  <!--- ...but that *were* included in other orders --->
  <!--- along with items now in the user's cart... --->
```

Listing 29.16 (continued)

```
      AND OrderID IN
        (SELECT OrderID FROM MerchandiseOrdersItems
         WHERE ItemID IN (#CurrentMerchList#)
         <!--- ...not including this user's past orders! --->
         <CFIF IsDefined("SESSION.Auth.ContactID")>
         AND OrderID NOT IN
           (SELECT OrderID FROM MerchandiseOrders
            WHERE ContactID = #SESSION.Auth.ContactID#)
         </CFIF> )
   </CFQUERY>

   <!--- If at least one "similar" item was found --->
   <CFIF GetSimilar.RecordCount GT 0>
     <P>People who have purchased items in your cart have also bought the
   following:<BR>

      <!--- For each similar item, display it, via Custom Tag --->
      <!--- (show five suggestions at most) --->
      <CFLOOP QUERY="GetSimilar">
        <CF_MerchDisplay
          MerchID="#GetSimilar.ItemID#">
      </CFLOOP>
   </CFIF>
```

Listing 29.16 is identical to Listing 29.10 in most respects. The important additions are the `GetMerch`, `GetPrices`, and `GetTotal` prices near the middle of the template.

First, for each item in the user's cart the `GetMerch` query retrieves the `MerchID` and `MerchPrice` from the database. This works because the `ValueList` function returns a comma-separated list of values in the `MerchID` column of the `GetCart` query object that was returned by the `<CF_ShoppingCart>` custom tag. Therefore, the `IN` criteria causes the database to return just the records that are actually in the user's cart at the moment.

Next, a QofQ query named `GetPrices` is used to calculate the subtotals for each item in the user's cart by joining the `MerchID` columns from the `GetMerch` query, which came from a database, and the `GetCart` query, which did not. The resulting query contains three columns for each item in the cart: `MerchID`, `Quantity`, and `SubTotal`.

Finally, a second QofQ query called `GetTotal` calculates the grand total of all items in the user's cart by applying the aggregate `SUM()` function against the `SubTotal` column from the `GetPrices` query. The result is a query with one value, `GrandTotal`, which represents the total value of all cart items. This proves that you can use QofQ to retrieve information from query objects that were themselves created with QofQ.

Now outputting the rest of the page, including the subtotals and totals, is a simple matter. Note that the `<CFLOOP>` that displays each item now iterates over the `GetPrices` query created by the first QofQ. The results are shown in Figure 29.12.

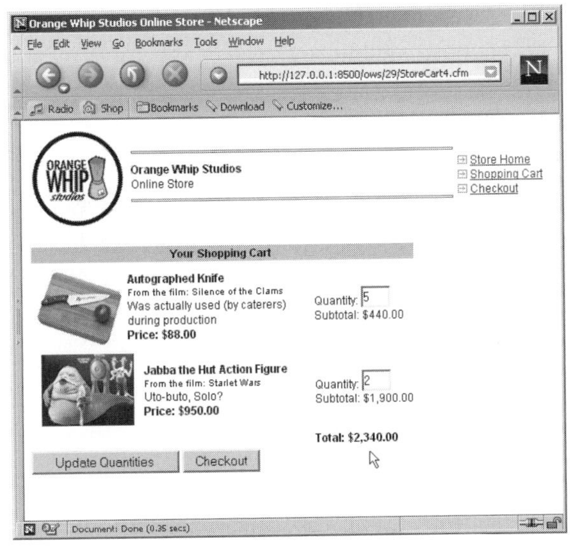

Figure 29.12

Using ColdFusion's query of queries feature to SUM data that lives both inside and outside a database.

Case Sensitivity and Query of Queries

Most database systems consider `WHERE` conditions without regard to upper- or lowercase. However, `WHERE` conditions are case sensitive when using QofQ. For instance, consider the following QofQ query:

```
<CFQUERY DBTYPE="query" NAME="GetThisFilm">
  SELECT * FROM GetFilms
  WHERE MovieTitle LIKE '%#FORM.SearchString#%'
</CFQUERY>
```

This snippet will return all films with titles that include the words provided by the user in the form field called `#SearchString#`. However, the search will be case sensitive; if the user types `encounters` as the search criteria, movies with *Encounters* in the title will not be found (because of the capital *E*). In most situations, you probably don't want case-sensitive behavior from QofQ.

QofQ provides functions called `UPPER()` and `LOWER()`, which can be used to subvert the default case-sensitive behavior. Just use `UPPER()` or `LOWER()` around the column name that you want to query, and then use CFML's `UCase()` or `LCase()`, respectively, around the actual query criteria. (Whether you use the combination of `UPPER()` and `UCase()` or the combination of `LOWER()` and `LCase()` doesn't matter.) So, to make the previous snippet behave as expected, you would do the following:

```
<CFQUERY DBTYPE="query" NAME="GetThisFilm">
  SELECT * FROM GetFilms
  WHERE LOWER(MovieTitle) LIKE '%#LCase(FORM.SearchString)#%'
</CFQUERY>
```

Now, when ColdFusion examines each row of the source query, it compares the lowercase version of each title with the lowercase version of the user's search criteria. This results in the expected, non–case-sensitive behavior.

Reserved Words and Query of Queries

ColdFusion MX's QofQ feature defines a list of reserved words that can't be used as column or table names without taking special steps. For instance, QofQ considers `SIZE` a reserved word. If you have a query object that you want to requery with QofQ, and one of its columns is named `SIZE`, you will receive an error message unless you escape the column name with square brackets.

For instance, instead of:

```
<CFQUERY DBTYPE="query" NAME="GetThisFilm">
  SELECT Name, Size
  FROM GetFiles
  WHERE Size > 25
</CFQUERY>
```

you would need to use this:

```
<CFQUERY DBTYPE="query" NAME="GetThisFilm">
  SELECT Name, [Size]
  FROM GetFiles
  WHERE [Size] > 25
</CFQUERY>
```

The following are the reserved words around which you need to use square brackets within a QofQ query: `ABSOLUTE`, `ACTION`, `ADD`, `ALL`, `ALLOCATE`, `ALTER`, `AND`, `ANY`, `ARE`, `AS`, `ASC`, `ASSERTION`, `AT`, `AUTHORIZATION`, `AVG`, `BEGIN`, `BETWEEN`, `BIT`, `BIT_LENGTH`, `BOTH`, `BY`, `CASCADE`, `CASCADED`, `CASE`, `CAST`, `CATALOG`, `CHAR`, `CHAR_LENGTH`, `CHARACTER`, `CHARACTER_LENGTH`, `CHECK`, `CLOSE`, `COALESCE`, `COLLATE`, `COLLATION`, `COLUMN`, `COMMIT`, `CONNECT`, `CONNECTION`, `CONSTRAINT`, `CONSTRAINTS`, `CONTINUE`, `CONVERT`, `CORRESPONDING`, `COUNT`, `CREATE`, `CROSS`, `CURRENT`, `CURRENT_DATE`, `CURRENT_TIME`, `CURRENT_TIMESTAMP`, `CURRENT_USER`, `CURSOR`, `DATE`, `DAY`, `DEALLOCATE`, `DEC`, `DECIMAL`, `DECLARE`, `DEFAULT`, `DEFERRABLE`, `DEFERRED`, `DELETE`, `DESC`, `DESCRIBE`, `DESCRIPTOR`, `DIAGNOSTICS`, `DISCONNECT`, `DISTINCT`, `DOMAIN`, `DOUBLE`, `DROP`, `ELSE`, `END`, `END-EXEC`, `ESCAPE`, `EXCEPT`, `EXCEPTION`, `EXEC`, `EXECUTE`, `EXISTS`, `EXTERNAL`, `EXTRACT`, `FALSE`, `FETCH`, `FIRST`, `FLOAT`, `FOR`, `FOREIGN`, `FOUND`, `FROM`, `FULL`, `GET`, `GLOBAL`, `GO`, `GOTO`, `GRANT`, `GROUP`, `HAVING`, `HOUR`, `IDENTITY`, `IMMEDIATE`, `IN`, `INDICATOR`, `INITIALLY`, `INNER`, `INPUT`, `INSENSITIVE`, `INSERT`, `INT`, `INTEGER`, `INTERSECT`, `INTERVAL`, `INTO`, `IS`, `ISOLATION`, `JOIN`, `KEY`, `LANGUAGE`, `LAST`, `LEADING`, `LEFT`, `LEVEL`, `LIKE`, `LOCAL`, `LOWER`, `MATCH`, `MAX`, `MIN`, `MINUTE`, `MODULE`, `MONTH`, `NAMES`, `NATIONAL`, `NATURAL`, `NCHAR`, `NEXT`, `NO`, `NOT`, `NULL`, `NULLIF`, `NUMERIC`, `OCTET_LENGTH`, `OF`, `ON`, `ONLY`, `OPEN`, `OPTION`, `OR`, `ORDER`, `OUTER`, `OUTPUT`, `OVERLAPS`, `PAD`, `PARTIAL`, `POSITION`, `PRECISION`, `PREPARE`, `PRESERVE`, `PRIMARY`, `PRIOR`, `PRIVILEGES`, `PROCEDURE`, `PUBLIC`, `READ`, `REAL`, `REFERENCES`, `RELATIVE`, `RESTRICT`, `REVOKE`, `RIGHT`, `ROLLBACK`, `ROWS`, `SCHEMA`, `SCROLL`, `SECOND`, `SECTION`, `SELECT`, `SESSION`, `SESSION_USER`, `SET`, `SIZE`, `SMALLINT`, `SOME`, `SPACE`, `SQL`, `SQLCODE`, `SQLERROR`, `SQLSTATE`, `SUBSTRING`, `SUM`, `SYSTEM_USER`, `TABLE`, `TEMPORARY`, `THEN`, `TIME`, `TIMESTAMP`, `TIMEZONE_HOUR`, `TIMEZONE_MINUTE`, `TO`, `TRAILING`, `TRANSACTION`, `TRANSLATE`, `TRANSLATION`, `TRIM`, `TRUE`, `UNION`, `UNIQUE`, `UNKNOWN`, `UPDATE`, `UPPER`, `USAGE`, `USER`, `USING`, `VALUE`, `VALUES`, `VARCHAR`, `VARYING`, `VIEW`, `WHEN`, `WHENEVER`, `WHERE`, `WITH`, `WORK`, `WRITE`, `YEAR`, `ZONE`.

Parameterized Queries

ColdFusion enables you to create parameterized queries by placing `<CFQUERYPARAM>` tags within the SQL code you supply to `<CFQUERY>`. The value of each `<CFQUERYPARAM>` tag is sent to the database.

Behind the scenes, as ColdFusion sends your query to the database, it substitutes a SQL bind parameter for each `<CFQUERYPARAM>` tag you supply. Unfortunately, a proper definition of a SQL bind parameter would be beyond the scope of this book. In a nutshell, bind parameters enable a database client (here, ColdFusion) to send a SQL statement to the database with placeholders in it, followed by the actual values for each placeholder. This method is a bit more formalized than the usual method of sending completed, ad hoc query statements to the database.

NOTE

Most database systems support bind parameters. If the database you are using does not, ColdFusion simply inserts the correct value into your query for you.

Theoretically, depending on the database system, this could result in slightly faster performance, because the database system might be capable of compiling a parameterized query for later reuse. If your knowledge of your database system is such that you believe the use of SQL bind parameters would result in a performance boost, `<CFQUERYPARAM>` is the way to implement them in your ColdFusion applications. In practice, however, real-world testing suggests that you will not see an actual performance boost of any noticeable margin.

There are other reasons to use parameterized queries in your templates, though. In some cases, the tag can prevent a certain type of hack and can make your query code more database independent. This section introduces the `<CFQUERYPARAM>` tag and explains how to use it in your code and why.

Introducing <CFQUERYPARAM>

At its simplest, you can parameterize a query by adding a `<CFQUERYPARAM>` tag to a query wherever you would normally provide a variable name. For instance, suppose you want to run a query called `GetFilm`, which retrieves a record from the `Films` table, based on a `FilmID` value passed in the URL.

Normally, you would do this:

```
<CFQUERY NAME="GetFilm" DATASOURCE="ows">
  SELECT * FROM Films
  WHERE FilmID = #URL.FilmID#
</CFQUERY>
```

Instead, you could do the following, which supplies the dynamic part of the query (the value of `URL.FilmID`) as a SQL bind parameter:

```
<CFQUERY NAME="GetFilm" DATASOURCE="ows">
  SELECT * FROM Films
  WHERE FilmID = <CFQUERYPARAM VALUE="#URL.FilmID#">
</CFQUERY>
```

In general, you should provide ColdFusion with the data type of the corresponding column in your database via the CFSQLTYPE attribute. This lets ColdFusion send the data to the database system correctly (rather than relying on the database to convert the parameteron the fly), which reduces overhead. Because the FilmID column contains integers, you would specify a CFSQLTYPE of CF_SQL_INTEGER:

```
<CFQUERY NAME="GetFilm" DATASOURCE="ows">
  SELECT * FROM Films
  WHERE FilmID = <CFQUERYPARAM VALUE="#URL.FilmID#" CFSQLTYPE="CF_SQL_INTEGER">
</CFQUERY>
```

In most situations, you can use <CFQUERYPARAM> with just the VALUE and SQLTYPE attributes, as shown previously. A number of other attributes can be used to deal with special situations, as listed in Table 29.4. Table 29.5 shows the values you can supply to the CFSQLTYPE attribute and helps you understand which CFSQLTYPE to use for corresponding column data types in Access, SQLServer, and Oracle databases.

Table 29.4 Attributes for the <CFQUERYPARAM> Tag

ATTRIBUTE	PURPOSE
VALUE	Required. The value you want ColdFusion to send to your database system in place of the <CFQUERYPARAM> tag.
CFSQLTYPE	Optional. One of the CFSQLTYPE values listed in Table 29.6. If you do not provide this attribute, the parameter is treated as a CFSQLCHAR.
MAXLENGTH	Optional. The maximum number of characters to allow for the VALUE. If you provide this attribute, it should reflect the maximum number of characters (width) allowed by the corresponding column in your database.
SCALE	Optional. The number of decimal places to allow. If you provide this attribute, it should reflect the numeric scale defined for the corresponding column in your database (see your database documentation about the concepts of scale and precision for numeric columns). Applicable only if the CFSQLTYPE is CF_SQL_NUMERIC or CF_SQL_DECIMAL.
LIST	Optional. If set to Yes, indicates that the value you are supplying to VALUE should be treated as a comma-separated list of values. Typically, you use this if the <CFQUERYPARAM> tag is being placed between the parentheses of SQL's IN keyword. ColdFusion takes care of quoting each element in the list for you, if appropriate for the data type of the column. If you want to use a different delimiter for the list (instead of a comma), provide the delimiter as the SEPARATOR attribute (see the following).
SEPARATOR	The delimiter character to use to separate the VALUE into separate values. Relevant only if LIST="Yes". The default is a comma.
NULL	Optional. Set this attribute to Yes to send a null value to the database, instead of the VALUE. The default, of course, is No.

Table 29.5 Which CFSQLTYPE to Use with Which Native Data Type

CFSQLTYPE	USE WITH ACCESS	USE WITH SQLSERVER	USE WITH ORACLE
CF_SQL_BIGINT		bigint	
CF_SQL_BIT	Yes/No	bit	
CF_SQL_CHAR		char, nchar	CHAR, NCHAR
CF_SQL_DATE			
CF_SQL_DECIMAL		numeric, decimal	
CF_SQL_DOUBLE		double, float	
CF_SQL_FLOAT		double, float	
CF_SQL_IDSTAMP		timestamp	
CF_SQL_INTEGER	AutoNumber	int	
CF_SQL_LONGVARCHAR	Memo	text	LONG, CLOB, NCLOB
CF_SQL_MONEY	Currency	money	
CF_SQL_MONEY4		smallmoney	
CF_SQL_NUMERIC	Number	numeric, decimal	NUMBER
CF_SQL_REAL		real	
CF_SQL_REFCURSOR		cursor	
CF_SQL_SMALLINT		smallint	
CF_SQL_TIME			
CF_SQL_TIMESTAMP	Date/Time	datetime,	DATE_smalldatetime
CF_SQL_TINYINT		tinyint	
CF_SQL_VARCHAR	Text	varchar, nvarchar, uniqueidentifier	VARCHAR2, NVAR CHAR2, VARCHAR

NOTE

ColdFusion MX also supports two additional SQL types: CF_SQL_BLOB and CF_SQL_CLOB. See the ColdFusion documentation for details.

Using Parameterized Queries for Database Independence

In the section "Specifying Dates in <CFQUERY> Tags," earlier in this chapter, you learned how the <CFQUERYPARAM> tag can be used to avoid having to provide dates in the format required for the particular database system you are using. This approach can be especially helpful if you are creating custom tags or complete ColdFusion applications that need to interact with different types of databases. As long as your queries use standard SQL statements, and as long as tricky data types such as dates are handled with <CFQUERYPARAM>, you can feel reasonably confident that the queries will work on just about any database ColdFusion encounters.

Using Parameterized Queries for Security

Parameterized queries can also help you prevent a certain type of database hack. The hack depends on the fact that many database systems enable you to execute multiple SQL statements in the same `<CFQUERY>` tag. If your queries are being built dynamically, using information being passed via URL or form parameters, your database could be subject to this form of attack.

For instance, take another look at this unparameterized query:

```
<CFQUERY NAME="GetFilm" DATASOURCE="ows">
  SELECT * FROM Films
  WHERE FilmID = #URL.FilmID#
</CFQUERY>
```

Normally, you would expect that the value of `URL.FilmID` to be a number. But what if it's not? What if the user changes the URL parameter from `2`, say, to a value that includes actual SQL code? For instance, consider what would happen if some pesky user changed a template's URL from this:

```
ShowFilm.cfm?FilmID=2
```

to this:

```
ShowFilm.cfm?FilmID=2%3BDELETE%20FROM%20Films
```

You guessed it. The actual SQL sent to the database would be:

```
SELECT * FROM Films
WHERE FilmID = 2;DELETE FROM Expenses
```

Most database systems would consider the semicolon to indicate the start of a new SQL statement, and would thus dutifully carry out the `DELETE` statement, removing all records from your `Expenses` table. Try explaining this one to your colleagues in the accounting department!

NOTE

Of course, this isn't a bug or security hole in ColdFusion itself, or in your database or database driver. Both ColdFusion and your database are only doing what they are being told to do.

If you use the `<CFQUERYPARAM>` tag in your query, specifying the appropriate data type with `CFSQLTYPE`, it becomes impossible for users to violate your database in this way because the `<CFQUERYPARAM>` tag displays an error message if the URL parameter doesn't contain the expected type of information.

So, the unsafe, unparameterized query shown previously would become the following, which should defeat the type of attack described in this section:

```
<CFQUERY NAME="GetFilm" DATASOURCE="ows">
  SELECT * FROM Films
  WHERE FilmID = <CFQUERYPARAM VALUE="#URL.FilmID#" CFSQLTYPE="CF_SQL_INTEGER">
</CFQUERY>
```

NOTE

There are other ways to deal with this problem. For instance, you could put a `<CFPARAM>` tag at the top of the template, with `NAME="URL.FilmID"` and `TYPE="numeric"`. This would prevent users from being able to cause damage, because an error message would be generated by the `<CFPARAM>` tag if the value is not a simple number, stopping all further template execution. Another option is to use `#Val(URL.FilmID)#` instead of just `#URL.FilmID#` in the original `<CFQUERY>` tag.

NOTE

Or you could just use a simple <CFIF> test at the top of the template that uses the IsNumeric() function to ensure that URL.FilmID is valid; if not, you could skip the query or abort all processing with <CFABORT>.

Parameterized Queries and Query Caching

Unfortunately, parameterized queries cannot be used with ColdFusion's query-caching feature. If you attempt to use <CFQUERYPARAM> in a query that also uses the CACHEDWITHIN or CACHEDAFTER attribute, ColdFusion displays an error message. See Chapter 22 for more information about CACHEDWITHIN and CACHEDAFTER.

Building Query Results Programmatically

ColdFusion provides functions that enable you to create new query objects programmatically. These functions are called QueryNew(), QueryAddRow(), and QuerySetCell(). For instance, the <CF_ShoppingCart> custom tag created in Chapter 27 uses these functions to return a query object that represents the items currently in a user's shopping cart.

Furthermore, Listing 29.5 showed you how query results that are built using these functions can be requeried further, using ColdFusion's query of queries feature. You can find out more about QueryNew(), QueryAddRow(), and QuerySetCell()in Appendix C, "ColdFusion Function Reference".

Using Database Transactions

ColdFusion provides a tag called <CFTRANSACTION>, which can be used to explicitly specify the beginning and end of a database transaction. A database transaction is a way of telling your database system that several SQL statements should be thought of as representing a single unit of work.

For instance, in the Orange Whip Studios project, the series of related inserts that need to occur to record a merchandise order should be thought of as a single transaction. An order really hasn't been properly recorded unless the appropriate records have been added to both the MerchandiseOrders and MerchandiseOrdersItems tables. During the moments between those inserts, the database is in what's called an inconsistent state, meaning that the data doesn't properly represent the real-world facts yet. Database transactions ensure that your database doesn't expose this inconsistent state to other connections.

Using <CFTRANSACTION> is simple:

- Whenever you need to make several related changes to your database, you should use a <CFTRANSACTION> tag around the <CFQUERY> tags that perform all the various steps. This tells your database system that the changes made by the queries should not be considered a permanent part of the database until the transaction has completed all its work.
- Until the transaction has finished its work, any changes made to the database during the transaction will not be visible to any other connections that might be querying the database at the same time. This means that queries made by other ColdFusion page requests will be incapable of interrupting your database transaction or catching the

database in an inconsistent state (for instance, between the moments during which two related changes are made).

- Because changes made to the database during the transaction are not considered a permanent part of the database until the transaction is finished, you are actually free to undo all the changes at any time during the transaction. This is called rolling back the transaction and is supported by ColdFusion via `ACTION="Rollback"` (see Table 29.7). Or, you can permanently commit the transaction using `ACTION="Commit"`. After a transaction is committed, it can't be rolled back.

Table 29.6 shows the attributes supported by `<CFTRANSACTION>` in ColdFusion MX.

Table 29.6 `<CFTRANSACTION>` Tag Attributes

ATTRIBUTE	DESCRIPTION
`ACTION`	Can be set to `BEGIN`, `COMMIT`, or `ROLLBACK`. If you do not provide an `ACTION`, it defaults to `BEGIN`.
`ISOLATION`	Can be set to `Read_Uncommitted`, `Read_Committed`, `Repeatable_Read`, or `Serializable`. These values allow you to control the appropriate balance between concurrency and consistency. Consult your database documentation to find out which isolation levels are actually supported by your database system and how your database vendor has chosen to implement the various isolation levels.

Database scholars generally define the concept of a database transaction as having a number of properties, often referred to as the so-called *ACID Properties* (atomicity, consistency, isolation, and durability). If you are interested in the theory behind database transactions, you are encouraged to consult your database's documentation (or a dedicated SQL text) to learn about them formally.

A complete discussion about database transactions is, unfortunately, beyond the scope of this book. Again, you are encouraged to consult your database system's documentation to find out more about how transactions are implemented in the database software you are using.

Using the `<CFTRANSACTION>` Tag

You have already seen `<CFTRANSACTION>` used in several of this book's listings. In general, this book's examples use `<CFTRANSACTION>` to explicitly mark the beginning and end of database transactions to accomplish one of two things:

- To correctly retrieve an automatically generated ID number after a new record is inserted into the database
- To be able to commit or roll back changes within the transaction, based on the success or failure of some type of external processing

Using Transactions for ID Number Safety

In Chapter 13, "Using Forms to Add or Change Data," you learned how the `<CFTRANSACTION>` tag should be used around the two-step process that's often necessary when inserting a new record into a database. First, the actual insert is performed (via `<CFINSERT>` or a SQL `INSERT` statement), then the SQL `MAX()` function is used to retrieve the ID number of the just-inserted record.

The examples in this book always use `<CFTRANSACTION>` around such a multistep process. Without `<CFTRANSACTION>`, the wrong ID number could occasionally be retrieved if the ColdFusion template was being visited by several users at the same time. With `<CFTRANSACTION>`, you are assured that you will get back the correct number because no other database operations are allowed to affect the state of each transaction until it is finished. Conceptually, you are asking your database to freeze just before the changes are made and unfreeze only after the changes are complete.

You generally end up with code that follows this basic pattern:

```
<CFTRANSACTION>
  <!--- 1) insert record, via <CFINSERT> or SQL INSERT --->
  <!--- 2) get new id number, via a SELECT MAX() query --->
</CFTRANSACTION>
```

See Chapter 13 for a complete example that uses `<CFTRANSACTION>` in this manner.

NOTE

The mechanics of how the database actually preserves the integrity of the transaction varies somewhat from database to database. Some of them implement transactions by simply blocking all other access to the relevant database (or table or portions of the table) until your transaction is finished. Others use a more sophisticated approach, in which simultaneous transactions each affect their own version of the data. Consult your database documentation for details.

Using Transactions for the Ability to Undo

In Chapter 27, a CFML custom tag called `<CF_PlaceOrder>` was created, which takes care of all the various steps that must be completed each time a user decides to buy merchandise from Orange Whip Studios. The custom tag inserts a new record into the `MerchandiseOrders` table and inserts several new records into the `MerchandiseOrdersItems` table. It also attempts to charge the user's credit card and is smart enough to undo all the changes to the database if for whatever reason the user's credit card can't be successfully charged at the time. The `<CFTRANSACTION>` tag makes this possible.

When using `<CFTRANSACTION>` to enable rollback processing, you usually end up with code that follows this basic pattern:

```
<CFTRANSACTION ACTION="Begin">
  ... database changes here ...
  <CFIF Everything Goes Well>
    <CFTRANSACTION ACTION="Commit"/>
  <CFELSE>
    <CFTRANSACTION ACTION="Rollback"/>
  </CFIF>
</CFIF>
```

NOTE

The trailing forward slashes at the end of the previous `ACTION="Commit"` and the `ACTION="Rollback"` are important. Be sure to include the slashes when performing a `Commit` or `Rollback` in your own code.

If you take a look at the code for the `<CF_PlaceOrder>` tag in Chapter 27, you will see that it follows this pattern. First, the transaction is begun, using the opening `<CFTRANSACTION>` tag. Within the transaction, the various `INSERT` queries needed to record the order are executed. Because the queries are being executed within the safe space of the transaction, you do not need to worry about what might happen if only part of the database changes were able to take place.

Then, after the records have been inserted and there has been an attempt to charge the user's credit card, a `<CFIF>` statement is used to determine whether the credit card charge was successful. If so, the transaction is committed via an `ACTION="Commit"`. If not, the transaction is rolled back via an `ACTION="Rollback"`.

NOTE

With two important exceptions, you can't use more than one data source within a single `<CFTRANSACTION>` block. The first exception is when you're using ColdFusion's query of queries feature; queries of `DBTYPE="query"` are always allowed, even in transactions that involve other data sources. The second exception is after an explicit `COMMIT`; you can run queries that refer to other data sources after a transaction has been committed. Otherwise, any queries that need to use other data sources must be placed outside the `<CFTRANSACTION>` block.

Transactions and CFML Error Handling

Database transactions commonly are committed or rolled back based on the results of ColdFusion's structured exception-handling mechanisms. In general, this means using `<CFTRANSACTION>` inside a `<CFTRY>` block. Within the `<CFTRY>` block, any database errors are caught using the `<CFCATCH>` tag, which causes the transaction to be rolled back with an `ACTION="Rollback"`. For details, see Chapter 31, "Error Handling."

Transactions and Stored Procedures

In general, it often makes the most sense to create stored procedures that encapsulate an entire database transaction. Rather than creating several `<CFQUERY>` tags and wrapping `<CFTRANSACTION>` around them, you would just make a single stored procedure that takes care of performing all the steps. Within the stored procedure, you would use whatever syntax your database requires to ensure the database server considers the whole process to be a single database transaction.

This way, everything about the transaction is owned conceptually by the database server and occurs entirely under its watch. Also, the stored procedure can then be used by other systems within your company (not just ColdFusion).

You will learn all about stored procedures in Chapter 30, "Working with Stored Procedures."

NOTE

With Oracle systems, you use the `SET TRANSACTION`, `COMMIT`, and `ROLLBACK` statements to declare the beginning and end of a transaction within a stored procedure. With SQLServer, you use `BEGIN TRANSACTION`, `COMMIT TRANSACTION`, and `COMMIT TRANSACTION`.

CHAPTER 30

Working with Stored Procedures

IN THIS CHAPTER

This chapter will introduce you to *stored procedures*, which is a relatively advanced featured supported by most server-based database systems. A stored procedure is a chunk of SQL code that's given a name and stored as a part of your database, along with your actual data tables. You can think stored procedures as the database equivalent of Custom Tags, as discussed in Chapter 20. After a stored procedure has been created, you can invoke it in your ColdFusion templates using the `<CFSTOREDPROC>` tag.

Tags covered in this chapter:

- `<CFSTOREDPROC>`
- `<CFPROCPARAM>`
- `<CFPROCRESULT>`

NOTE

The entire text of this chapter can be found on the included CD.

CHAPTER 31

Error Handling

IN THIS CHAPTER

Catching Errors as They Occur

Unless you are a really, really amazing developer—and an incredibly fast learner—you have seen quite a few error messages from ColdFusion, both during development and after deployment of your applications. ColdFusion is generally very good about providing diagnostic messages that help you understand what the problem is. Error messages are a developer's friends. These clever little helpers selflessly provide hints and observations about the state of your code so you can fix it as soon as possible. It's an almost romantic relationship.

Unfortunately, your users aren't likely to see error messages through the rose-colored glasses coders tend to wear. They are likely to call or page you or flood your in-box with unfriendly email until you get the error message (which they perceive as some kind of ugly monster) under control.

Wouldn't it be great if you could have your code watch for certain types of errors and respond to them on the fly, before the user even sees the error? After all, as a developer, you often know the types of problems that might occur while a particular chunk of code does its work. If you could teach your code to recover from predictable problems on its own, you could lead a less stressful and healthier (albeit somewhat lonelier) coding lifestyle.

This, and more, is what this chapter is all about. ColdFusion provides a small but powerful set of structured exception-handling tags, which enable you to respond to problems as they occur.

NOTE

Many ColdFusion developers do not use the structured exception tags discussed in this chapter, perhaps because they sound too complicated (or out of an optimistic feeling that nothing will ever go wrong). The truth is, the structured exception framework is really easy to use and will likely save you time in the long run. Give the techniques shown in this chapter a shot. This is ColdFusion, after all. How hard can it be?

What Is an Exception?

When ColdFusion displays an error message, it is responding to an exception. Whenever a CFML tag or function is incapable of doing whatever your code has asked it to do—such as connect to a database or process a variable—it lets ColdFusion know what exactly went wrong and provides information about why. This process of reporting a problem is called raising an exception. After the tag or function raises an exception, ColdFusion's job is to respond to the exception. Out of the box, ColdFusion responds to nearly all exceptions in the same way: by displaying an error message that describes the exception. ColdFusion's logs also note the fact that the exception occurred. If you want, you can use ColdFusion's exception-handling tags to respond to an exception in some different, customized way. When you do this, you are telling ColdFusion to run special code of your own devising, instead of displaying an error message as it would normally. This process of responding to an exception with your own code is called catching an exception.

NOTE

After your code has caught an exception, ColdFusion no longer considers itself responsible for displaying any type of error message, and suppresses the error message.

NOTE

Although subtle distinctions exist between the exact meanings of each term, for now you can just consider exception, exception condition, error, and error condition to all mean the same thing: the state that occurs whenever an operation can't be completed. For purposes of this discussion, also consider raising and throwing to be synonyms as well. Raising an exception, throwing an error, and throwing an exception all mean pretty much the same thing.

NOTE

As you learned in Chapter 16, "Introducing the Web Application Framework," you can customize the look and feel of ColdFusion's error messages. If all you want to do is change the way error messages look, you can skip this chapter and just use what you learned in Chapter 16. If, however, you want to take active recovery steps when an error occurs, read on.

Introducing `<CFTRY>` and `<CFCATCH>`

ColdFusion provides two basic CFML tags for handling exception conditions:

- The `<CFTRY>` tag—A paired tag you place around the portions of your templates that you think might fail under certain conditions. The `<CFTRY>` tag does not take any attributes. You simply place opening and closing `<CFTRY>` tags around the block of code you want ColdFusion to attempt to execute.
- The `<CFCATCH>` tag—Used to catch exceptions that occur within a `<CFTRY>` block. `<CFCATCH>` takes only one attribute, `TYPE`, as shown in Table 31.1. `TYPE` tells ColdFusion what type of problem you are interested in responding to. If that type of problem occurs, ColdFusion executes the code between the `<CFCATCH>` tags. Otherwise, it ignores the code between the `<CFCATCH>` tags.

Table 31.1 <CFCATCH> Tag Attributes

ATTRIBUTE	DESCRIPTION
TYPE	The type of exceptions to catch or respond to. It can be any of the types shown in Table 31.2. For instance, if you are interested in trying to recover from errors that occur while executing <CFQUERY> or another database-related operation, you would use a <CFCATCH> of TYPE="Database".

Table 31.2 Predefined Exception Types

EXCEPTION TYPE	DESCRIPTION
Any	Catches any exception, even those you might not have any way of dealing with (such as an "out of memory" message). Use this exception value if you need to catch errors that do not fall into one of the other exception types in this table. If possible, use one of the more specific exception types listed in this table.
Application	Catches application-level exception conditions. Your own CFML code reports these exceptions, using the <CFTHROW> tag. In other words, catch errors of TYPE="APPLICATION" if you want to catch your own custom errors.
Database	Catches database errors, which could include errors such as inability to connect to a database, an incorrect column or table name, a locked database record, and so on.
Expression	Catches errors that occur while attempting to evaluate a CFML expression. For instance, if you refer to an unknown variable name or provide a function parameter that doesn't turn out to make sense when your template actually executes, an exception of type Expression is thrown.
Lock	Catches errors that occur while attempting to process a <CFLOCK> tag. Most frequently, this type of error is thrown when a lock cannot be obtained within the TIMEOUT period specified by the <CFLOCK> tag, which usually means that some other page request that uses a lock with the same name or scope is taking a long time to complete its work.
MissingInclude	Catches errors that arise when you use a <CFINCLUDE> tag but the CFML template you specify for the TEMPLATE attribute cannot be found.
Object	Catches errors that occur while attempting to process a <CFOBJECT> tag or CreateObject() function, or while attempting to access a property or method of an object returned by <CFOBJECT> or CreateObject().
Security	Catches errors that occur while using one of ColdFusion's built-in security-related tags, such as <CFAUTHENTICATE> (see Appendix B, "ColdFusion Tag Reference").
Template	Catches general application page errors that occur while processing a <CFINCLUDE>, <CFMODULE>, or <CFERROR> tag.
SearchEngine	Catches errors that occur while performing full-text searches or other Verity-related tasks, such as indexing. For details about Verity, see Chapter 34, "Full-Text Searching."

TIP

You can also provide your own exception types for the `TYPE` attribute of the `<CFCATCH>` tag. For details, see the "Throwing and Catching Your Own Errors" section, later in this chapter.

NOTE

The dedicated `SearchEngine` exception type is new for ColdFusion MX. In previous versions of ColdFusion, Verity-related errors result in exceptions of type `Application`.

Basic Exception Handling

The easiest way to understand exception handling is to actually go through the process of adding `<CFTRY>` and `<CFCATCH>` to an existing template. Listings 31.1 and 31.2 show the effects of ColdFusion's exception-handling tags, using a before-and-after scenario.

A Typical Scenario

Say you have been asked to create a page that enables users to select from two separate drop-down lists. The first drop-down provides a list of films; the second drop-down shows a list of film ratings. Each drop-down list has a Go button next to it, which presumably takes the user to some type of detail page when clicked.

Here's the catch: For whatever reason, you know ahead of time that the database tables populating these drop-down lists (the Films and FilmsRatings tables) will not always be available. There might be any number of reasons for this. Perhaps you are connecting to a database server that is known to crash often, that goes down during certain times of the day for maintenance, or that is accessed via an unreliable network connection.

Your job is to make your new drop-down list page operate as gracefully as possible, even when the database connections fail. At the very least, users should not see an ugly database error message. If you can pull off something more elegant, such as querying some kind of backup database in the event that the normal database tables are not available, that's even better. It seems that your yearly review is coming up, and you've received a hint that you might get a hefty raise if you can pull off this project with aplomb. Let's see whether ColdFusion can help you get that raise.

A Basic Template, Without Exception Handling

Listing 31.1 is the basic template, before the addition of any error handling. This template works just fine as long as no problems occur while the user is connecting to the database. It runs two queries and displays two drop-down lists, as shown in Figure 31.1. If an error occurs, though, the user sees an ugly error message and can't get any further information.

NOTE

The examples in this chapter assume the creation of an `Application.cfm` file that sets the `REQUEST.DataSource` variable and also turns on Session and Client management via the `<CFAPPLICATION>` tag (as discussed in Chapter 16). For your convenience, the CD-ROM includes the appropriate `Application.cfm` file for this chapter.

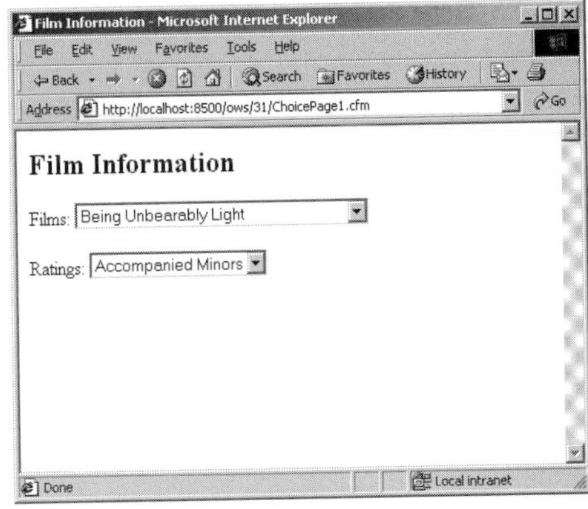

Figure 31.1

This is what the drop-down page looks like, as long as no errors occur.

Listing 31.1 `ChoicePage1.cfm`—A Basic Display Template, Without Any Error Handling

```
<!---
  Filename:   ChoicePage1.cfm
  Created by: Nate Weiss (NMW)
  Purpose:    Provides navigation elements for films and ratings
--->

<HTML>
<HEAD><TITLE>Film Information</TITLE></HEAD>
<BODY>
<H2>Film Information</H2>

<!--- Retrieve Ratings from database --->
<CFQUERY NAME="GetRatings" DATASOURCE="#REQUEST.DataSource#">
  SELECT RatingID, Rating
  FROM FilmsRatings
  ORDER BY Rating
</CFQUERY>

<!--- Retrieve Films from database --->
<CFQUERY NAME="GetFilms" DATASOURCE="#REQUEST.DataSource#">
  SELECT FilmID, MovieTitle
  FROM Films
  ORDER BY Films.MovieTitle
</CFQUERY>


<!--- Create self-submitting form --->
<CFFORM ACTION="#CGI.SCRIPT_NAME#" METHOD="Post">
  <!--- Display Film names in a drop-down list --->
  <P>Films:
  <CFSELECT
    QUERY="GetFilms" NAME="FilmID"
    VALUE="FilmID" DISPLAY="MovieTitle"/>
```

Listing 31.1 (CONTINUED)

```
    <!--- Display Rating names in a drop-down list --->
    <P>Ratings:
    <CFSELECT
      QUERY="GetRatings" NAME="RatingID"
      VALUE="RatingID" DISPLAY="Rating"/>

  </CFFORM>

  </BODY>
  </HTML>
```

This template doesn't contain anything new yet. Two `<CFQUERY>` tags named `GetRatings` and `GetFilms` run, and the results from each query appear in a drop-down list that enables the user to select a film or rating. If any of this looks unfamiliar, take a look back at Chapter 13, "Using Forms to Add or Change Data."

If for whatever reason `GetRatings` and `GetFilms` can't execute normally, an error message appears, leaving the user with nothing useful (other than a general impression that you don't maintain your site very carefully). For instance, if you go into the ColdFusion Administrator and sabotage the connection by providing an invalid filename in the Database File field for the `ows` data source, you'll see the error shown in Figure 31.2.

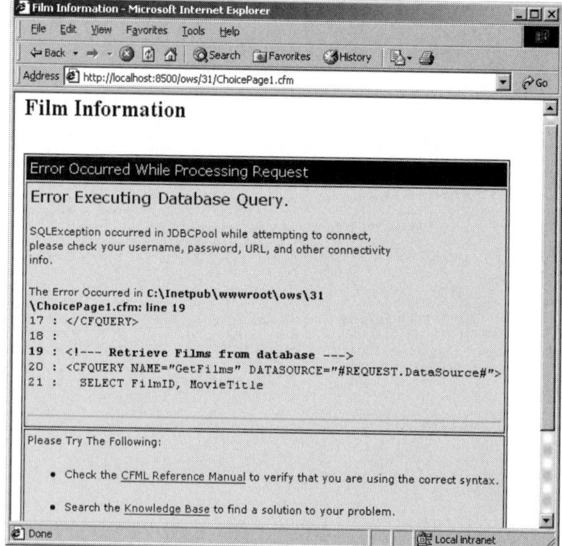

Figure 31.2

If an error occurs while connecting to the database, the default error message is displayed.

Adding `<CFTRY>` and `<CFCATCH>`

To add ColdFusion's structured exception handling to Listing 31.1, simply wrap a pair of opening and closing `<CFTRY>` tags around the two `<CFQUERY>` tags. Then add a `<CFCATCH>` block that specifies an exception `TYPE` of `Database`, just before the closing `</CFTRY>` tag. The code inside the `<CFCATCH>` tag will execute whenever either of the `<CFQUERY>` tags raises an exception.

Listing 31.2 is a revised version of Listing 31.1. The code is almost exactly the same, except for the addition of the <CFTRY> and <CFCATCH> blocks, which display a basic "Sorry, we are not able to connect" error message. Now, if any problems occur when connecting to the database, the error message appears as shown in Figure 31.3. This really isn't much better than what the user saw in Figure 31.2, but it's a start.

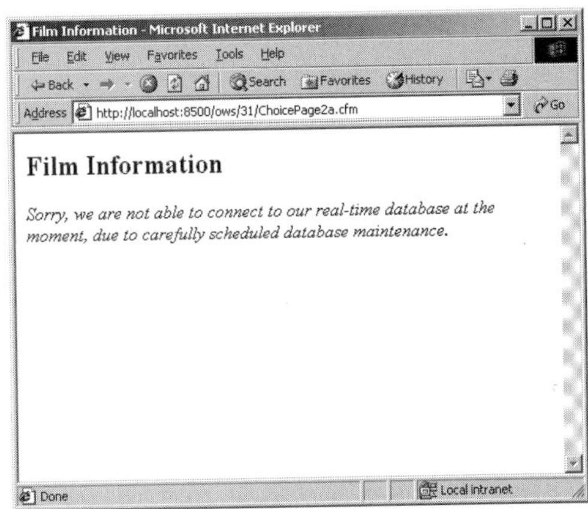

Figure 31.3

You can use a <CFCATCH> block in its simplest form to display context-specific error messages.

Listing 31.2 ChoicePage2a.cfm—Adding a Simple <CFTRY> Block to Catch Database Errors

```
<!---
  Filename:   ChoicePage2a.cfm
  Created by: Nate Weiss (NMW)
  Purpose:    Provides navigation elements for films and ratings
--->

<HTML>
<HEAD><TITLE>Film Information</TITLE></HEAD>
<BODY>
<H2>Film Information</H2>

<CFTRY>
  <!--- Retrieve Ratings from database --->
  <CFQUERY NAME="GetRatings" DATASOURCE="#REQUEST.DataSource#">
    SELECT RatingID, Rating
    FROM FilmsRatings
    ORDER BY Rating
  </CFQUERY>

  <!--- Retrieve Films from database --->
  <CFQUERY NAME="GetFilms" DATASOURCE="#REQUEST.DataSource#">
    SELECT FilmID, MovieTitle
    FROM Films
    ORDER BY Films.MovieTitle
  </CFQUERY>

  <!--- If any database errors occur during above query, --->
  <CFCATCH TYPE="Database">
```

Listing 31.2 (continued)

```
      <!--- Let user know that the Films data can't be shown right now --->
      <CFOUTPUT>
        <!--- Let user know that the Films data can't be shown right now --->
        <I>Sorry, we are not able to connect to our real-time database at the moment,
        due to carefully scheduled database maintenance.<BR></I>
      </CFOUTPUT>

      <!--- Stop processing at this point --->
      <CFABORT>
    </CFCATCH>
  </CFTRY>

  <!--- Create self-submitting form --->
  <CFFORM ACTION="#CGI.SCRIPT_NAME#" METHOD="Post">
    <!--- If, after all is said and done, we were able to get Film data --->
    <CFIF IsDefined("GetFilms")>
      <!--- Display Film names in a drop-down list --->
      <P>Films:
      <CFSELECT QUERY="GetFilms" NAME="FilmID"
        VALUE="FilmID" DISPLAY="MovieTitle"/>
    </CFIF>

    <!--- If, after all is said and done, we were able to get Ratings data --->
    <CFIF IsDefined("GetRatings")>
      <!--- Display Rating names in a drop-down list --->
      <P>Ratings:
      <CFSELECT QUERY="GetRatings" NAME="RatingID"
        VALUE="RatingID" DISPLAY="Rating"/>
    </CFIF>

  </CFFORM>

  </BODY>
  </HTML>
```

Even though it's rather simplistic, take a close look at Listing 31.2. First, the `<CFTRY>` block tells ColdFusion that you are interested in trapping exceptions. Within the `<CFTRY>` block, all of the queries needed by the page execute. If any type of problem occurs—anything from a crashed database server to a mere typo in your SQL code—the code inside the `<CFCATCH>` block executes, displaying the static message shown in Figure 31.3. Otherwise, the `<CFCATCH>` block is skipped entirely.

NOTE

It's important to note that the `<CFCATCH>` block in Listing 31.2 includes a `<CFABORT>` tag to halt all further processing. If it were not for the `<CFABORT>` tag, ColdFusion would continue processing the template, including the code that follows the `<CFTRY>` block. This would just result in a different error message because the `<CFSELECT>` tags would be referring to queries that never ended up running.

NOTE

Because all this code does so far is display a custom error message without taking any specific action to help the user, Listing 31.2 really isn't any better than the templates in Chapter 16, which used the `<CFERROR>` tag to customize the display of error messages. The advantages of using `<CFTRY>` and `<CFCATCH>` will become apparent shortly. In practice, you will often use `<CFTRY>` and `<CFCATCH>` along with `<CFERROR>`.

Understanding What Caused the Error

When it catches an exception, ColdFusion populates a number of special variables that contain information about the problem that actually occurred. These variables are available to you via the special CFCATCH scope. Your code can examine these CFCATCH variables to get a better understanding of what exactly went wrong, or you can just display the CFCATCH values to the user in a customized error message.

Table 31.3 lists the variables available to you within a <CFCATCH> block.

Table 31.3 CFCATCH Variables Available After an Exception Is Caught

VARIABLE	DESCRIPTION
CFCATCH.Type	The type of exception that was caught. This will be one of the exception types listed in Table 31.2.
CFCATCH.Message	The text error message that goes along with the exception that was caught. Nearly all ColdFusion errors include a reasonably helpful Message value; this is the message that shows up at the top of normal error messages. For instance, the value of CFCATCH.Message for the exception shown in Figure 31.2 is ODBC Error Code = S1000 (General error).
CFCATCH.Detail	Detail information that goes along with the caught exception. Most ColdFusion errors include a helpful Detail value. For the error shown in Figure 31.2, it's the value of CFCATCH. Detail begins with [Microsoft] and ends with Data Source = "OWS".
CFCATCH.SqlState	Available only if CFCATCH.TYPE is Database. A standardized error code that should be reasonably consistent for the same type of error, even between different database systems.
CFCATCH.NativeErrorCode	Available only if CFCATCH.TYPE is Database. The native error code reported by the database system when the problem occurred. These error codes are not usually consistent between database systems.
CFCATCH.ErrNumber	Available only if CFCATCH.TYPE is Expression. This code identifies the type of error that threw the exception. We recommend that you do not use this value to check for specific errors, because the values are not documented and have been known to change from version to version of ColdFusion. It is generally better to examine the text of the CFCATCH.Detail or CFCATCH.Message values.
CFCATCH.MissingFileName	Available only if CFCATCH.TYPE is MissingInclude. The name of the ColdFusion template that could not be found.
CFCATCH.LockName	Available only if CFCATCH.TYPE is Lock. The name of the lock, if any, that was provided to the <CFLOCK> tag that failed.
CFCATCH.LockOperation	Available only if CFCATCH.TYPE is Lock. At this time, this value will always be Timeout, Create Mutex, or Unknown.
CFCATCH.ErrorCode	Available only when you throw your own exceptions with <CFTHROW>. The value, if any, that was supplied to the ERRORCODE attribute of the <CFTHROW> tag that threw the exception.

Table 31.3 (continued)

VARIABLE	DESCRIPTION
`CFCATCH.ExtendedInfo`	Available only when you throw your own exceptions with `<CFTHROW>`. The value, if any, that was supplied to the `EXTENDEDINFO` attribute of the `<CFTHROW>` tag.
`CFCATCH.TagContext`	An array of structures that contains information about the ColdFusion templates involved in the page request when the exception occurred. This value is used primarily for creating your own debugging templates, not for exception handling as discussed in this chapter. For details, see the ColdFusion documentation.

Listing 31.3 is a slightly revised version of Listing 31.2. This time, the message shown to the user includes information about the exception, by outputting the value of `CFCATCH.SqlState`. One possible result is shown in Figure 31.4; this figure was taken after changing a column name in one of the queries to an unknown name.

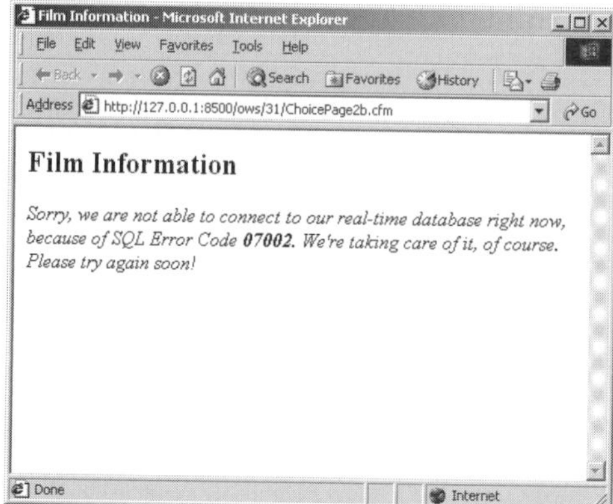

Figure 31.4

You can use the `CFCATCH` variables to examine or display diagnostic information.

Listing 31.3 `ChoicePage2a.cfm`—Displaying the SQL Error Code for a Database Error

```
<!---
  Filename:   ChoicePage2b.cfm
  Created by: Nate Weiss (NMW)
  Purpose:    Provides navigation elements for films and ratings
--->

<HTML>
<HEAD><TITLE>Film Information</TITLE></HEAD>
<BODY>
<H2>Film Information</H2>

<CFTRY>
  <!--- Retrieve Ratings from database --->
  <CFQUERY NAME="GetRatings" DATASOURCE="#REQUEST.DataSource#">
    SELECT RatingID, Rating
    FROM FilmsRatings
    ORDER BY Rating
  </CFQUERY>
```

Listing 31.3 (continued)

```
<!--- Retrieve Films from database --->
<CFQUERY NAME="GetFilms" DATASOURCE="#REQUEST.DataSource#">
  SELECT FilmID, MovieTitle
  FROM Films
  ORDER BY Films.MovieTitle
</CFQUERY>

<!--- If any database errors occur during above query, --->
<CFCATCH TYPE="Database">
  <!--- Let user know that the Films data can't be shown right now --->
  <CFOUTPUT>
    <I>Sorry, we are not able to connect to our real-time database right now,
    because of SQL Error Code <B>#CFCATCH.ErrorCode#</B>.
    We're taking care of it, of course. Please try again soon!</I><BR>
  </CFOUTPUT>

  <!--- Stop processing at this point --->
  <CFABORT>
 </CFCATCH>
</CFTRY>

<!--- Create self-submitting form --->
<CFFORM ACTION="#CGI.SCRIPT_NAME#" METHOD="Post">
  <!--- If, after all is said and done, we were able to get Film data --->
  <CFIF IsDefined("GetFilms")>
    <!--- Display Film names in a drop-down list --->
    <P>Films:
    <CFSELECT QUERY="GetFilms" NAME="FilmID"
      VALUE="FilmID" DISPLAY="MovieTitle"/>
  </CFIF>

  <!--- If, after all is said and done, we were able to get Ratings data --->
  <CFIF IsDefined("GetRatings")>
    <!--- Display Rating names in a drop-down list --->
    <P>Ratings:
    <CFSELECT QUERY="GetRatings" NAME="RatingID"
      VALUE="RatingID" DISPLAY="Rating"/>
  </CFIF>

</CFFORM>

</BODY>
</HTML>
```

NOTE

This template only outputs the value of `CFCATCH.SqlState`. Of course, if you want to give the user more information, you are free to use the other `CFCATCH` variables from Table 31.3 that are relevant to the type of exception.

Writing Templates That Work Around Errors

As shown in Figure 31.4, you can use `<CFTRY>` and `<CFCATCH>` to respond to errors by displaying a customized error message. But that's really not so different from the way you learned to use `<CFERROR>` in Chapter 16. The real value of `<CFTRY>` and `<CFCATCH>` is the fact that they enable you to create templates that actively respond to or work around exception conditions. In other words, they let you write Web pages that continue to be at least somewhat helpful to your users, even after an error has occurred.

Working Around a Failed Query

Take a look at Listing 31.4, which is similar to the other listings you have looked at so far in this chapter. This version isolates each `<CFQUERY>` within its own `<CFTRY>` block. Within each `<CFTRY>` block, if any database errors occur, the user sees a static message, but the template execution doesn't stop.

NOTE

No errors are thrown when you first visit this page with your browser. To see the results shown in Figure 31.5, sabotage one of the queries in some way and then visit the template again. For instance, change one of the columns in the SQL statement to an invalid column name–or go into the `Application.cfm` file and change the `Request.DataSource` variable to a data source name that doesn't exist.

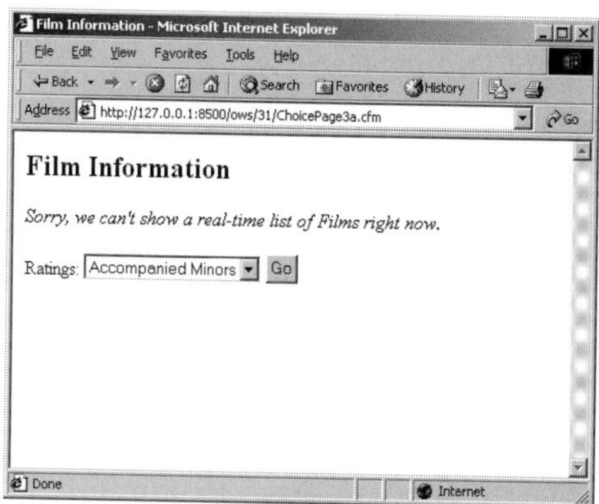

Figure 31.5 ColdFusion's exception-handling capabilities enable your templates to recover gracefully from error conditions.

Listing 31.4 `ChoicePage3a.cfm`—Using `<CFTRY>` and `<CFCATCH>` to Display Information Only When It Is Actually Available

```
<!---
  Filename:   ChoicePage3a.cfm
  Created by: Nate Weiss (NMW)
  Purpose:    Provides navigation elements for films and ratings
--->

<HTML>
<HEAD><TITLE>Film Information</TITLE></HEAD>
<BODY>
<H2>Film Information</H2>

<!--- Create self-submitting form --->
<CFFORM ACTION="#CGI.SCRIPT_NAME#" METHOD="Post">

  <!--- Attempt database operation --->
  <CFTRY>
    <!--- Retrieve Films from database --->
```

Listing 31.4 (continued)

```
    <CFQUERY NAME="GetFilms" DATASOURCE="#REQUEST.DataSource#">
      SELECT FilmID, MovieTitle
      FROM Films
      ORDER BY Films.MovieTitle
    </CFQUERY>

    <!--- If any database errors occur during above query, --->
    <CFCATCH TYPE="Database">
      <!--- Let user know that the Films data can't be shown right now --->
      <P><I>Sorry, we can't show a real-time list of Films right now.<BR></I>
    </CFCATCH>
  </CFTRY>


  <!--- Attempt database operation --->
  <CFTRY>
    <!--- Retrieve Ratings from database --->
    <CFQUERY NAME="GetRatings" DATASOURCE="#REQUEST.DataSource#">
      SELECT RatingID, Rating
      FROM FilmsRatings
      ORDER BY Rating
    </CFQUERY>

    <!--- If any database errors occur during above query, --->
    <CFCATCH TYPE="Database">
      <!--- Let user know that the Ratings data can't be shown right now --->
      <P><I>Sorry, we can't show a real-time list of Ratings right now.<BR></I>
    </CFCATCH>
  </CFTRY>


  <!--- If, after all is said and done, we were able to get Film data --->
  <CFIF IsDefined("GetFilms")>
    <!--- Display Film names in a drop-down list --->
    <P>Films:
    <CFSELECT
      QUERY="GetFilms" NAME="FilmID"
      VALUE="FilmID" DISPLAY="MovieTitle"/>
    <INPUT TYPE="Submit" VALUE="Go">
  </CFIF>

  <!--- If, after all is said and done, we were able to get Ratings data --->
  <CFIF IsDefined("GetRatings")>
    <!--- Display Ratings in a drop-down list --->
    <P>Ratings:
    <CFSELECT
      QUERY="GetRatings" NAME="RatingID"
      VALUE="RatingID" DISPLAY="Rating"/>
    <INPUT TYPE="Submit" VALUE="Go">
  </CFIF>

</CFFORM>

</BODY>
</HTML>
```

For instance, if for some reason the GetFilms query fails to run properly, a "not able to get a real-time list of Films" message is displayed. Template execution then continues normally, right after the first <CFTRY> block. Because the <CFQUERY> couldn't complete its work, the GetFilms variable does not exist; otherwise, everything is fine.

At the bottom of the template, an IsDefined() check, which ascertains whether the corresponding query actually exists, protects the display of each drop-down list. If the GetFilms query is completed without error, the first <CFIF> test passes and the Films drop-down list is displayed. If not, the code inside the <CFIF> block is skipped.

So, if the first query causes an error, the user simply sees a friendly little status message, as shown in Figure 31.5, instead of the Films drop-down list. Assuming that the second query can execute successfully, however, the Ratings drop-down list still displays normally.

The result is a page that remains useful when a problem with the database partially disables it. It is, in a small but very helpful way, self-healing.

NOTE

To see the results shown in Listing 31.5, sabotage the GetFilms query in some way, such as changing the value supplied to the DATASOURCE attribute to a data source name that doesn't exist.

Listing 31.5 shows a slightly different way to structure the code. Almost all the code lines are the same as Listing 31.4, just ordered differently. Instead of placing both <CFSELECT> tags together at the end of the template, Listing 31.5 outputs each <CFSELECT> in the corresponding <CFTRY> block, right after the query that populates it. If one of the queries fails, the <CFSWITCH> block immediately takes over, thus skipping over <CFSELECT> for the failed query.

The result is a template that behaves in exactly the same way as Listing 31.4. Depending on your preference and on the situation, placing code in self-contained <CFTRY> blocks as shown in Listing 31.5 can make your templates easier to understand and maintain. On the other hand, in many situations, the approach taken in Listing 31.4 is more sensible because it keeps the database access code separate from the HTML generation code. Use whichever approach results in the simplest-looking, most straightforward code.

Listing 31.5 ChoicePage3b.cfm—An Alternative Way of Structuring the Code in Listing 31.4

```
<!---
  Filename:   ChoicePage3b.cfm
  Created by: Nate Weiss (NMW)
  Purpose:    Provides navigation elements for films and ratings
--->

<HTML>
<HEAD><TITLE>Film Information</TITLE></HEAD>
<BODY>
<H2>Film Information</H2>
```

Listing 31.5 (continued)

```
<!--- Create self-submitting form --->
<CFFORM ACTION="#CGI.SCRIPT_NAME#" METHOD="Post">

  <!--- Attempt database operation --->
  <CFTRY>
    <!--- Retrieve Films from database --->
    <CFQUERY NAME="GetFilms" DATASOURCE="#REQUEST.DataSource#">
      SELECT FilmID, MovieTitle
      FROM Films
      ORDER BY Films.MovieTitle
    </CFQUERY>

    <!--- Display Film names in a drop-down list --->
    <P>Films:
    <CFSELECT
      QUERY="GetFilms" NAME="FilmID"
      VALUE="FilmID" DISPLAY="MovieTitle"/>
    <INPUT TYPE="Submit" VALUE="Go">

    <!--- If any database errors occur during above query, --->
    <CFCATCH TYPE="Database">
      <!--- Let user know that the Films data can't be shown right now --->
      <P><I>Sorry, we can't show a real-time list of Films right now.<BR></I>
    </CFCATCH>
  </CFTRY>


  <!--- Attempt database operation --->
  <CFTRY>
    <!--- Retrieve Ratings from database --->
    <CFQUERY NAME="GetRatings" DATASOURCE="#REQUEST.DataSource#">
      SELECT RatingID, Rating
      FROM FilmsRatings
      ORDER BY Rating
    </CFQUERY>

    <!--- Display Rating names in a drop-down list --->
    <P>Ratings:
    <CFSELECT
      QUERY="GetRatings" NAME="RatingID"
      VALUE="RatingID" DISPLAY="Rating"/>
    <INPUT TYPE="Submit" VALUE="Go">

    <!--- If any database errors occur during above query, --->
    <CFCATCH TYPE="Database">
      <!--- Let user know that the Ratings data can't be shown right now --->
      <P><I>Sorry, we can't show a real-time list of Ratings right now.<BR></I>
    </CFCATCH>
  </CFTRY>

</CFFORM>

</BODY>
</HTML>
```

Working Around Errors Silently

Listing 31.6 is another version of Listing 31.4. This time, no action of any type is taken in the `<CFCATCH>` block (not even the display of an error message). Because nothing needs to be placed between the `<CFCATCH>` and `</CFCATCH>` tags, they can be coded using the shorthand notation of `<CFCATCH/>` alone. The trailing slash is just an abbreviated way of providing an empty tag pair.

TIP

> You can use this trailing-slash notation whenever you're using a CFML tag that requires a closing tag, but you don't actually need to place anything between the tags. Most of the templates in this chapter use this shorthand in their `<CFSELECT>` tags.

The result is a template that recovers silently from database errors, without even acknowledging that anything has gone wrong. If the `GetFilms` query can't execute, the Films drop-down list just doesn't appear. As far as the user is concerned, no error has occurred. The template simply displays what it can and gracefully omits what it cannot.

Listing 31.6 `ChoicePage3c.cfm`—Handling Errors Silently, Without Letting the User Know Anything Went Wrong

```
<!---
  Filename:    ChoicePage3c.cfm
  Created by:  Nate Weiss (NMW)
  Purpose:     Provides navigation elements for films and ratings
--->

<HTML>
<HEAD><TITLE>Film Information</TITLE></HEAD>
<BODY>
<H2>Film Information</H2>

<!--- Create self-submitting form --->
<CFFORM ACTION="#CGI.SCRIPT_NAME#" METHOD="Post">

  <!--- Attempt database operation --->
  <CFTRY>
    <!--- Retrieve Films from database --->
    <CFQUERY NAME="GetFilms" DATASOURCE="#REQUEST.DataSource#">
      SELECT FilmID, MovieTitle
      FROM Films
      ORDER BY Films.MovieTitle
    </CFQUERY>

    <!--- Display Film names in a drop-down list --->
    <P>Films:
    <CFSELECT
      QUERY="GetFilms" NAME="FilmID"
      VALUE="FilmID" DISPLAY="MovieTitle"/>
    <INPUT TYPE="Submit" VALUE="Go">

    <!--- Silently catch any database errors from above query --->
    <CFCATCH TYPE="Database"/>
  </CFTRY>
```

Listing 31.6 (continued)

```
<!--- Attempt database operation --->
<CFTRY>
  <!--- Retrieve Ratings from database --->
  <CFQUERY NAME="GetRatings" DATASOURCE="#REQUEST.DataSource#">
    SELECT RatingID, Rating
    FROM FilmsRatings
    ORDER BY Rating
  </CFQUERY>

  <!--- Display Ratings in a drop-down list --->
  <P>Ratings:
  <CFSELECT
    QUERY="GetRatings" NAME="RatingID"
    VALUE="RatingID" DISPLAY="Rating"/>
  <INPUT TYPE="Submit" VALUE="Go">

  <!--- Silently catch any database errors from above query --->
  <CFCATCH TYPE="Database"/>
</CFTRY>

</CFFORM>

</BODY>
</HTML>
```

Writing Templates That Recover from Errors

Listings 31.4 to 31.6 created templates that serve your users by skipping blocks of code that rely on failed queries. Depending on the situation, you can often go a step further, creating templates that continue to provide the basic functionality they are supposed to (albeit in some type of scaled-back manner), even when a problem occurs.

For instance, Listing 31.7 creates yet another version of the drop-down page example. It looks similar to Listing 31.4, except for the first `<CFCATCH>` block, which has been expanded. The idea here is to use a backup copy of the Films database table, which exists for the sole purpose of providing a fallback when the primary database system can't be reached.

Listing 31.7 `ChoicePage4.cfm`—Querying a Backup Text File When the Primary Database Is Unavailable

```
<!---
  Filename:    ChoicePage4.cfm
  Created by: Nate Weiss (NMW)
  Purpose:     Provides navigation elements for films and ratings
--->

<HTML>
<HEAD><TITLE>Films</TITLE></HEAD>
<BODY>
<H2>Film Information</H2>

<CFTRY>
  <!--- Retrieve Films from live database --->
  <CFQUERY NAME="GetFilms" DATASOURCE="#REQUEST.DataSource#">
```

Listing 31.7 (CONTINUED)

```
    SELECT FilmID, MovieTitles
    FROM Films
    ORDER BY Films.MovieTitle
   </CFQUERY>

   <!--- If any database errors occur during above query, --->
   <CFCATCH TYPE="Database">

     <!--- Location of our emergency backup file --->
     <CFSET BackupFilePath = ExpandPath("FilmsBackup.xml")>

     <!--- Read contents of the WDDX/XML in from backup file --->
     <CFFILE
       ACTION="READ"
       FILE="#BackupFilePath#"
       VARIABLE="WddxPacket">

     <!--- Convert the XML back into original query object --->
     <CFWDDX
       ACTION="WDDX2CFML"
       INPUT="#WddxPacket#"
       OUTPUT="GetFilms">

     <!--- Let user know that emergency version is being used --->
     <I><P>NOTE:
     We are not able to connect to our real-time Films database at the moment.
     Instead, we are using data from our archives to display the Films list.
     Please try again later today for an up to date listing.<BR></I>
   </CFCATCH>
  </CFTRY>

  <!--- Attempt database operation --->
  <CFTRY>
   <!--- Retrieve Ratings from database --->
   <CFQUERY NAME="GetRatings" DATASOURCE="#REQUEST.DataSource#">
    SELECT RatingID, Rating
    FROM FilmsRatings
    ORDER BY Rating
   </CFQUERY>

   <!--- Silently catch any database errors from above query --->
   <CFCATCH TYPE="Database"/>
  </CFTRY>


  <!--- Create self-submitting form --->
  <CFFORM ACTION="#CGI.SCRIPT_NAME#" METHOD="Post">

   <!--- If, after all is said and done, we were able to get Film data --->
   <CFIF IsDefined("GetFilms")>
    <!--- Display Film names in a drop-down list --->
    <P>Films:
    <CFSELECT
      QUERY="GetFilms" NAME="FilmID"
```

Listing 31.7 (continued)

```
        VALUE="FilmID" DISPLAY="MovieTitle"/>
      <INPUT TYPE="Submit" VALUE="Go">
    </CFIF>

    <!--- If, after all is said and done, we were able to get Ratings data --->
    <CFIF IsDefined("GetRatings")>
      <!--- Display Ratings in a drop-down list --->
      <P>Ratings:
      <CFSELECT
        QUERY="GetRatings" NAME="RatingID"
        VALUE="RatingID" DISPLAY="Rating"/>
      <INPUT TYPE="Submit" VALUE="Go">
    </CFIF>

  </CFFORM>

  </BODY>
  </HTML>
```

If the `<CFQUERY>` named GetFilms fails for whatever reason, the code in the `<CFCATCH>` block will execute in an attempt to save the day. The idea behind this code is to read information about films from a previously saved XML file called FilmsBackup.xml. The backup file is in the WDDX format, which is a special type of XML used to convert any type of data (such as a query record set) quickly and easily into a simple string format that can be saved to disk.

NOTE

Unfortunately, we don't have enough space to explain WDDX in detail in this book. If you want, open the FilmsBackup.xml file in a text editor and take a look at the format. You'll find it fairly self-explanatory.

NOTE

This process (converting a variable in the server's RAM memory into a string) is called *serialization*. The reverse process (parsing the XML-formatted string back into the original variable in the server's memory) is called *deserialization*. For more information and examples regarding XML, WDDX, serialization, and deserialization, please consult our companion volume, Advanced ColdFusion MX Application Development. The ColdFusion documentation also contains a few simple examples.

First, the `<CFFILE>` tag is used to read the contents of the `FilmsBackup.xml` file into a string variable called `WddxPacket`. At this point, the variable holds the XML code that represents the backup film data. Now the `<CFWDDX>` tag is used to convert the XML code into a normal query object called `GetFilms`. You can use this query object just like the results of a normal `<CFQUERY>` tag. In other words, the rest of this template can continue working as if the `<CFQUERY>` at the top of the page hadn't caused an error.

The result is a version of the template that still provides the basic functionality it is supposed to, even when the first `GetFilms` query fails. Assuming that the backup file can be processed correctly, the user is presented with the expected drop-down list of films. The user also sees a message that alerts him or her to the fact that the list is populated not from the live database, but rather from an archived backup copy, as shown in Figure 31.6.

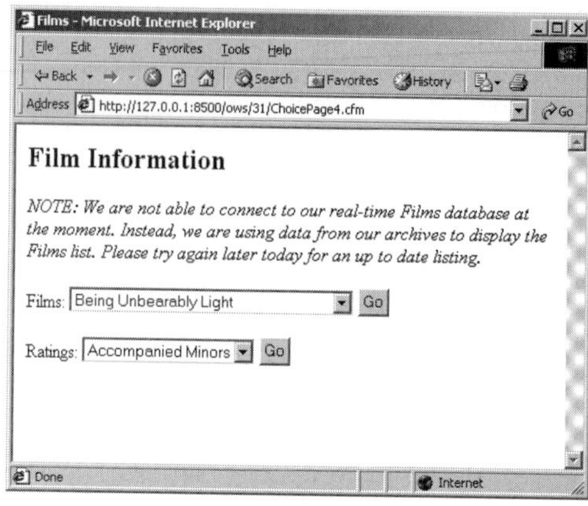

Figure 31.6

This version of the template uses a backup text file if the usual database is not accessible.

Nesting <CFTRY> Blocks

You can nest <CFTRY> blocks within one another. There are generally two ways you can nest the blocks, depending on the behavior you want.

If you nest a <CFTRY> within another <CFTRY> block (but not within a <CFCATCH>), this doubly protects the code inside the inner <CFTRY>. This type of nesting typically follows this basic form:

```
<CFTRY>
  <CFTRY>
    <!--- Important code goes here --->

    <CFCATCH></CFCATCH>
  </CFTRY>
  <CFCATCH></CFCATCH>
</CFTRY>
```

If something goes wrong, ColdFusion will see whether any of the <CFCATCH> tags within the inner <CFTRY> are appropriate (that is, whether a <CFCATCH> of the same TYPE as the exception itself exists). If so, the code in that block executes. If not, ColdFusion looks to see whether the <CFCATCH> tags within the outer <CFTRY> block are appropriate. If it doesn't find any appropriate <CFCATCH> blocks there either, it considers the exception uncaught, so the default error message displays.

Alternatively, you can essentially create a two-step process by nesting a <CFTRY> within a <CFCATCH> that belongs to another <CFTRY>. This second type of nesting is typically structured like this:

```
<CFTRY>
  <!--- important code here --->
  <CFCATCH>
    <CFTRY>
      <!--- fallback code here --->
      <CFCATCH>
        <!--- last chance code here --->
      </CFCATCH>
    </CFTRY>
  </CFCATCH>
</CFTRY>
```

If the code in the outer <CFTRY> fails, the inner <CFTRY> attempts to deal with the situation in some other way. If the code in the inner <CFTRY> also fails, its <CFCATCH> tags can catch the error and perform some type of last-ditch processing (such as displaying an error message).

Listing 31.8 is an example that includes both of these forms of <CFTRY> nesting. It builds upon Listing 31.7 by adding two <CFTRY> blocks within the larger <CFTRY> block that begins near the top of the template.

Listing 31.8 `ChoicePage5.cfm`—Nesting <CFTRY> Blocks Within Each Other Unavailable

```
<!---
  Filename:   ChoicePage5.cfm
  Created by: Nate Weiss (NMW)
  Purpose:    Provides navigation elements for films and ratings
--->

<HTML>
<HEAD><TITLE>Films</TITLE></HEAD>
<BODY>
<H2>Film Information</H2>

<CFTRY>
  <!--- Location of our emergency backup file --->
  <CFSET BackupFilePath = ExpandPath("FilmsBackup.xml")>

  <!--- Retrieve Films from live database --->
  <CFQUERY NAME="GetFilms" DATASOURCE="#REQUEST.DataSource#">
    SELECT FilmID, MovieTitle
    FROM Films
    ORDER BY Films.MovieTitle
  </CFQUERY>

  <!--- If the backup file has never been created --->
  <CFIF FileExists(BackupFilePath) EQ False>
    <!--- Now we'll make sure that our backup file exists --->
    <!--- If it doesn't exist yet, we'll try to create it --->
    <CFTRY>

      <!--- Convert the query to WDDX (an XML vocabulary) --->
      <CFWDDX
        ACTION="CFML2WDDX"
        INPUT="#GetFilms#"
        OUTPUT="WddxPacket">

      <!--- Save the XML on server's drive, as our backup file --->
      <CFFILE
        ACTION="WRITE"
        FILE="#BackupFilePath#"
        OUTPUT="#WddxPacket#">

      <!--- Silently ignore any errors while creating backup file --->
      <!--- (the worst that happens is the backup file doesn't get made) --->
      <CFCATCH TYPE="Any"/>
    </CFTRY>
  </CFIF>
```

Listing 31.8 (continued)

```
    <!--- If any database errors occur during above query, --->
    <CFCATCH TYPE="Database">
      <CFTRY>
        <!--- Read contents of the WDDX/XML in from backup file --->
        <CFFILE
          ACTION="READ"
          FILE="#BackupFilePath#"
          VARIABLE="WddxPacket">

        <!--- Convert the XML back into original query object --->
        <CFWDDX
          ACTION="WDDX2CFML"
          INPUT="#WddxPacket#"
          OUTPUT="GetFilms">

        <!--- Let user know that emergency version is being used --->
        <I><P>NOTE:
        We are not able to connect to our real-time Films database at the moment.<BR>
        Instead, we are using data from our archives to display the Films list.<BR>
        Please try again later today for an up to date listing.<BR></I>

        <!--- If any problems occur while trying to use the backup file --->
        <CFCATCH TYPE="Any">
          <!--- Let user know that the Films data can't be shown right now --->
          <I>Sorry, we are not able to provide you with a list of films.<BR></I>
        </CFCATCH>
      </CFTRY>

    </CFCATCH>
  </CFTRY>


  <!--- Attempt database operation --->
  <CFTRY>
    <!--- Retrieve Ratings from database --->
    <CFQUERY NAME="GetRatings" DATASOURCE="#REQUEST.DataSource#">
      SELECT RatingID, Rating
      FROM FilmsRatings
      ORDER BY Rating
    </CFQUERY>

    <!--- Silently catch any database errors from above query --->
    <CFCATCH TYPE="Database"/>
  </CFTRY>


  <!--- Create self-submitting form --->
  <CFFORM ACTION="#CGI.SCRIPT_NAME#" METHOD="Post">

    <!--- If, after all is said and done, we were able to get Film data --->
    <CFIF IsDefined("GetFilms")>
      <!--- Display Film names in a drop-down list --->
      <P>Films:
      <CFSELECT
```

Listing 31.8 (continued)

```
        QUERY="GetFilms" NAME="FilmID"
        VALUE="FilmID" DISPLAY="MovieTitle"/>
      <INPUT TYPE="Submit" VALUE="Go">
    </CFIF>

    <!--- If, after all is said and done, we were able to get Ratings data --->
    <CFIF IsDefined("GetRatings")>
      <!--- Display Ratings in a drop-down list --->
      <P>Ratings:
      <CFSELECT
        QUERY="GetRatings" NAME="RatingID"
        VALUE="RatingID" DISPLAY="Rating"/>
      <INPUT TYPE="Submit" VALUE="Go">
    </CFIF>

  </CFFORM>

  </BODY>
  </HTML>
```

The first of the nested `<CFTRY>` blocks attempts to create the FilmsBackup.xml file if it has not been created already (or if it has been deleted for some reason). A new version of the backup data is serialized using `<CFWDDX>`, then written to the server's drive using `<CFFILE>`. If any errors occur during this file-creation process, they will silently be ignored (no error message is shown). In other words, if the backup file doesn't exist, this nested `<CFTRY>` will attempt to create it. But if `<CFTRY>` can't do so, it just moves on.

NOTE

Since the first nested `<CFTRY>` sits within an outer `<CFTRY>` that catches all exceptions of `TYPE="Database"`, the nested `<CFTRY>` will be skipped altogether if `<CFQUERY>` causes a database error.

NOTE

If you want to test this code, delete the FilmsBackup.xml file from the directory you're using for this chapter's examples, then visit this template in your browser. Provided that the query itself doesn't have a problem, the backup file should be re-created.

The second nested `<CFTRY>` is within the outer `<CFTRY>` tag's `<CFCATCH>` block. This is the portion of the code that attempts to read the backup file if the `<CFQUERY>` fails (as introduced in Listing 31.7). Remember, because of where it is now nested, this inner `<CFTRY>` block will only be encountered if there is a problem retrieving the live film data from the database. This inner `<CFTRY>` tells ColdFusion that if the database query fails and there is a problem with the emergency `<CFFILE>` and `<CFWDDX>` code, then the template should just give up and display a "Sorry, we are not able to provide you with a list of films" message.

In other words, this version of the template has double protection: It has a fallback plan if the database query fails, and it knows how to degrade gracefully even if the fallback plan fails. This is quite an improvement over the original version of the template (refer to Listing 31.1), which could do no better than display a user-unfriendly error message when something went wrong (refer to Figure 31.2).

Deciding Not to Handle an Exception

When your code catches an exception with `<CFCATCH>`, it assumes all responsibility for dealing with the exception in an appropriate way. After your code catches the exception, ColdFusion is no longer responsible for logging an error message or halting further page processing.

For instance, take a look back at Listing 31.8 (`ChoicePage5.cfm`). The `<CFCATCH>` tags in this template declare themselves fit to handle any and all database-related errors by specifying a `TYPE="Database"` attribute in the `<CFCATCH>` tag. No matter what type of database-related exception gets raised, those `<CFCATCH>` tags will catch the error.

The purpose of the first `<CFCATCH>` block in Listing 31.8 is to attempt to use the backup version of the database when the first `<CFQUERY>` fails. This backup plan is activated no matter what the actual problem is. Even a simple syntax error or misspelled column name in the SQL statement will cause the `FilmsBackup.xml` file to be used.

It would be a better policy for the backup version of the database to be used only when the original query failed due to a connection problem. Other types of errors, such as syntax errors and so on, should probably not be caught and dealt with in the same way.

ColdFusion provides the `<CFRETHROW>` tag for exactly this type of situation. This section explains how to use `<CFRETHROW>` and when to use it.

Exceptions and the Notion of Bubbling Up

Like the error or exception constructs in many other programming languages, ColdFusion's exceptions can do something called bubbling up.

Say that you have some code that includes several layers of nested `<CFTRY>` blocks and that an exception has taken place in the innermost block. If the exception is not caught in the innermost `<CFTRY>` block, ColdFusion looks in the containing `<CFTRY>` block, if any, to see whether it contains any appropriate `<CFCATCH>` tags. If not, the exception continues to bubble up through the layers of `<CFTRY>` blocks until it is caught. If the error bubbles up through all the layers of the `<CFTRY>` blocks (that is, if none of the `<CFCATCH>` tags in the `<CFTRY>` blocks choose to catch the exception), that is when ColdFusion displays its default error message.

Using `<CFRETHROW>`

The `<CFRETHROW>` tag is basically the opposite of `<CFCATCH>`. After `<CFCATCH>` catches an error, `<CFRETHROW>` can uncatch the error. It is then free to bubble up to the next containing `<CFTRY>` block, if any.

The `<CFRETHROW>` tag takes no attributes and can be used only inside a `<CFCATCH>` tag. Typically, you will decide to use it by testing the value of one of the special `CFCATCH` variables shown previously in Table 31.3.

For instance, with Microsoft Access databases, if someone is currently making structural changes to a table (that is, if the table is open in Design View), then no other programs (including ColdFusion) are allowed to query it. If a ColdFusion template happens to execute a query while the table is being designed, an exception will be raised with a message like this: "The table 'Films' is already opened exclusively by another user." If you catch this error with a `<CFCATCH TYPE="Database">` (as in most of the examples in this chapter), the `CFCATCH.SQLState` variable will be set to `HY000`. If you want your code to handle only errors of this specific type, letting all other errors bubble up normally, you would use code similar to the following within a `<CFCATCH>` block:

```
<CFIF CFCATCH.SQLState NEQ "HY000">
  <CFRETHROW>
</CFIF>
```

Listing 31.9, a revision of Listing 31.8, uses the basic `<CFIF>` test shown in the previous snippet to ensure that the backup data file (`FilmsBackup.xml`) is used only if the database exception has a `SQLState` value of `HY000`.

Listing 31.9 `ChoicePage6.cfm`—Using `<CFRETHROW>` to Process Only Database Errors of Code `HY000`

```
<!---
  Filename:   ChoicePage6.cfm
  Created by: Nate Weiss (NMW)
  Purpose:    Provides navigation elements for films and ratings
--->

<HTML>
<HEAD><TITLE>Films</TITLE></HEAD>
<BODY>
<H2>Film Information</H2>

<CFTRY>
  <!--- Location of our emergency backup file --->
  <CFSET BackupFilePath = ExpandPath("FilmsBackup.xml")>

  <!--- Retrieve Films from live database --->
  <CFQUERY NAME="GetFilms" DATASOURCE="#REQUEST.DataSource#">
    SELECT FilmID, MovieTitle
    FROM Films
    ORDER BY Films.MovieTitle
  </CFQUERY>

  <!--- Now we'll make sure that our backup file exists --->
  <!--- If it doesn't exist yet, we'll try to create it --->
  <!--- Also, re-create it whenever server is restarted --->
  <CFTRY>
    <!--- If the server has just been restarted, or --->
    <!--- if the backup file has never been created --->
    <CFIF (IsDefined("APPLICATION.GetFilmsBackupCreated") EQ False)
       OR (FileExists(BackupFilePath) EQ False)>

      <!--- Convert the query to WDDX (an XML vocabulary) --->
      <CFWDDX
        ACTION="CFML2WDDX"
        INPUT="#GetFilms#"
        OUTPUT="WddxPacket">

      <!--- Save the XML on server's drive, as our backup file --->
      <CFFILE
        ACTION="WRITE"
        FILE="#BackupFilePath#"
        OUTPUT="#WddxPacket#">
```

Listing 31.9 (continued)

```
        <!--- Remember that we just created the emergency file --->
        <!--- This will be forgotten when server is restarted; thus, backup --->
        <!--- file will be refreshed on first successful query after restart --->
        <CFSET APPLICATION.GetFilmsBackupCreated = True>
      </CFIF>

      <!--- Silently ignore any errors while creating backup file --->
      <!--- (the worst that happens is the backup file doesn't get made) --->
      <CFCATCH TYPE="Any"/>
    </CFTRY>

    <!--- If any database errors occur during above query, --->
    <CFCATCH TYPE="Database">

      <!--- Unless this is SQL Error S0001, un-catch the exception --->
      <CFIF CFCATCH.SQLState NEQ "HY000">
        <CFRETHROW>

      <!--- If it is SQL Error, S0001, attempt to get data from txt file --->
      <CFELSE>

        <CFTRY>
          <!--- Read contents of the WDDX/XML in from backup file --->
          <CFFILE
            ACTION="READ"
            FILE="#BackupFilePath#"
            VARIABLE="WddxPacket">

          <!--- Convert the XML back into original query object --->
          <CFWDDX
            ACTION="WDDX2CFML"
            INPUT="#WddxPacket#"
            OUTPUT="GetFilms">

          <!--- Let user know that emergency version is being used --->
          <I><P>NOTE:
          We are not able to connect to our real-time Films database at the
          ➥moment.<BR>
          Instead, we are using data from our archives to display the Films list.<BR>
          Please try again later today for an up to date listing.<BR></I>

          <!--- If any problems occur while trying to use the backup file --->
          <CFCATCH TYPE="Any">
            <!--- Let user know that the Films data can't be shown right now --->
            <I>Sorry, we are not able to provide you with a list of films.<BR></I>
          </CFCATCH>
        </CFTRY>

      </CFIF>
    </CFCATCH>
  </CFTRY>

  <!--- Attempt database operation --->
  <CFTRY>
    <!--- Retrieve Ratings from database --->
    <CFQUERY NAME="GetRatings" DATASOURCE="#REQUEST.DataSource#">
      SELECT RatingID, Rating
```

Listing 31.9 (continued)

```
      FROM FilmsRatings
      ORDER BY Rating
    </CFQUERY>

    <!--- Silently catch any database errors from above query --->
    <CFCATCH TYPE="Database"/>
  </CFTRY>


  <!--- Create self-submitting form --->
  <CFFORM ACTION="#CGI.SCRIPT_NAME#" METHOD="Post">

    <!--- If, after all is said and done, we were able to get Film data --->
    <CFIF IsDefined("GetFilms")>
      <!--- Display Film names in a drop-down list --->
      <P>Films:
      <CFSELECT
        QUERY="GetFilms" NAME="FilmID"
        VALUE="FilmID" DISPLAY="MovieTitle"/>
      <INPUT TYPE="Submit" VALUE="Go">
    </CFIF>

    <!--- If, after all is said and done, we were able to get Ratings data --->
    <CFIF IsDefined("GetRatings")>
      <!--- Display Ratings in a drop-down list --->
      <P>Ratings:
      <CFSELECT
        QUERY="GetRatings" NAME="RatingID"
        VALUE="RatingID" DISPLAY="Rating"/>
      <INPUT TYPE="Submit" VALUE="Go">
    </CFIF>

  </CFFORM>

  </BODY>
  </HTML>
```

To test the exception-handling behavior of this template, try opening the ows.mdb file (in the ows/data folder within your Web server's root directory) and choosing Design for the Films table. Now visit Listing 31.9 with your Web browser. That should cause error HY000, so the backup version of the Films table will be used (refer to Figure 31.6). Now close the ows.mdb file and sabotage the first <CFQUERY> in some other way—for instance, by changing one of the column names to something invalid. That should cause the <CFRETHROW> tag to fire, which in turn causes the error to be raised again. Because there are no other <CFCATCH> tags to handle the reraised exception, ColdFusion displays its usual error message (which you could customize with <CFERROR>, as discussed in Chapter 16).

Of course, you are free to have as many <CFIF> tests as you need to make the decision whether to rethrow the error. For instance, if you wanted your <CFCATCH> code to handle only errors of types HY000, S1005, and S1010 instead of only HY000, you could replace the <CFIF> test in Listing 31.19 with something like the following:

```
<CFIF ListFindNoCase("HY000,S1005,S1010", CFCATCH.SQLState) EQ 0>
  <CFRETHROW>
</CFIF>
```

NOTE

Listing 31.9 also contains a simple check for the presence of an application variable called `APPLICATION.GetFilmsBackupCreated`. If this variable does not exist, it creates a new version of the backup file, just as if the backup file didn't exist. It then sets the `APPLICATION.GetFilmsBackupCreated` variable to True. In other words, this version of the template attempts to create a fresh version of the backup template whenever the server is restarted. The idea is to keep the backup file somewhat current (not months or years old), without negatively affecting performance. If you wanted, you could replace this simple test with code that refreshed the age of the backup file once per day, or according to other similar logic.

Examining Exception Messages to Improve Usability

In Chapter 26, "Interacting With Email," you learned how to create a simple web page that people can use to check their email. In that chapter, the ColdFusion template that does most of the work is called `CheckMail.cfm`. When a user visits this page for the first time, they are prompted for the host name of their POP mail server, plus their username and password.

One of the usability problems with that example is that it will display a rather ugly and potentially confusing error message if the user provides an incorrect mail server address, or accidentally types their username or password incorrectly. It would be a lot more helpful if the application would just let the user know what the problem is, encouraging her to check her input and try again.

Listing 31.10 uses a `<CFTRY>` block to do just that. The `<CFPOP>` tag, which is what will throw an exception if the email can't be retrieved (for whatever reason), is surrounded by `<CFTRY>` tags. If the `<CFPOP>` operation throws an exception, it is caught by the large `<CFCATCH>` block underneath. Within the `<CFCATCH>` block, the text of the `CFCATCH.Detail` variable is examined to attempt to determine what exactly went wrong.

The result is a template that simply asks the user to verify her log-in credentials if her messages can't be retrieved, as shown in Figure 31.7.

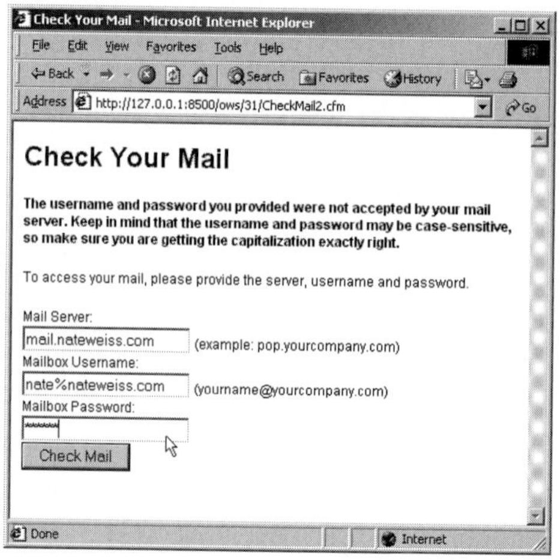

Figure 31.7

If a POP server can't be reached, the exception can be caught so that the user will see a sensible message.

Listing 31.10 CheckMail.cfm—Catching Advanced Exceptions Raised During a <!---

```
 Filename:   CheckMail.cfm
 Created by: Nate Weiss (NMW)
 Purpose:    Uses exception handling while retrieving email with <CFPOP>
--->

<!--- Include UDF function library, which includes the --->
<!--- TryToParsePOPDateTime() function used near the end of this page --->
<CFINCLUDE TEMPLATE="POPDateFunctions.cfm">


<HTML>
<HEAD><TITLE>Check Your Mail</TITLE></HEAD>
<BODY>

<!--- Simple CSS-based formatting styles --->
<STYLE>
  BODY {font-family:sans-serif;font-size:12px}
  TH   {font-size:12px;background:navy;color:white}
  TD   {font-size:12px;background:lightgrey;color:navy}
</STYLE>
<H2>Check Your Mail</H2>

<!--- If user is logging out, --->
<!--- or if user is submitting a different username/password --->
<CFIF IsDefined("URL.Logout") OR IsDefined("FORM.POPServer")>
  <CFSET StructDelete(SESSION, "Mail")>
</CFIF>

<!--- If we don't have a username/password --->
<CFIF NOT IsDefined("SESSION.Mail")>
  <!--- Show "mail server login" form --->
  <CFINCLUDE TEMPLATE="CheckMailLogin.cfm">
</CFIF>


<!--- If we need to contact server for list of messages --->
<!--- (if just logged in, or if clicked "Refresh" link) --->
<CFIF NOT IsDefined("SESSION.Mail.GetMessages") OR IsDefined("URL.Refresh")>

  <!--- Attempt to contact mail server --->
  <!--- If attempt is unsuccessful, try to catch the most common errors --->
  <CFTRY>

    <!--- Contact POP Server and retrieve messages --->
    <CFPOP
      ACTION="GetHeaderOnly"
      NAME="SESSION.Mail.GetMessages"
      SERVER="#SESSION.Mail.POPServer#"
      USERNAME="#SESSION.Mail.Username#"
      PASSWORD="#SESSION.Mail.Password#"
      MAXROWS="50">

    <!--- If an error occurs... --->
    <CFCATCH TYPE="APPLICATION">
      <CFDUMP VAR="#CFCATCH#">
```

Listing 31.10 (continued)

```
<!--- If the problem seems to be related to javax.mail, then --->
<!--- examine the message further and try to deal with the problem --->
<CFIF CFCATCH.Detail contains "javax.mail">

  <!--- If the username/password were rejected by mail server --->
  <CFIF CFCATCH.Detail contains "javax.mail.AuthenticationFailedException">
    <!--- Explain what happened --->
    <CFOUTPUT>
      <P><B>The username and password you provided were not accepted by
      your mail server. Keep in mind that the username and password may be
      case-sensitive, so make sure you are getting the capitalization
      exactly right.</B><BR>
    </CFOUTPUT>

  <!--- If the mail server cannot be found or can't be connected to --->
  <CFELSEIF CFCATCH.Detail contains "java.net.UnknownHostException">
    <!--- Explain what happened --->
    <CFOUTPUT>
      <P><B>The mail server you specified (#SESSION.Mail.POPServer#) does
      not appear to be working. Please check the name and try again.</B><BR>
    </CFOUTPUT>

  <!--- If some error occurs... --->
  <CFELSE>
    <!--- Display a generic error message --->
    <CFOUTPUT>
      <P><B>We're sorry, we weren't able to retrieve your messages at
      this time. The problem may be with your mail server,
      or some other network issue.</B><BR>
    </CFOUTPUT>

    <!--- Create a message to store in the log --->
    <CFSET LogMsg = "Couldn't get mail from #SESSION.Mail.POPServer#."
      & "Message: #CFCATCH.Message# Detail: #CFCATCH.Detail#">

    <!--- Log the problem. --->
    <!--- Appends to CheckMailErrorLog.log in CFusionMX/Logs folder --->
    <CFLOG
      FILE="CheckMailErrorLog"
      TEXT="#LogMsg#">

  </CFIF>

  <!--- Discard login information from SESSION scope --->
  <!--- This will force user to re-provide credentials --->
  <CFSET StructDelete(SESSION, "Mail")>

  <!--- Show "mail server login" form again --->
  <CFSET StructDelete(FORM, "POPServer")>
  <CFINCLUDE TEMPLATE="CheckMailLogin.cfm">

  <!--- Stop processing at this point --->
  <CFABORT>

<!--- If the problem does not seem to be related to javax.mail, --->
<!--- then just rethrow the error and let it expose itself normally. --->
```

Listing 31.10 (CONTINUED)

```
        <CFELSE>
          <CFRETHROW>
        </CFIF>
      </CFCATCH>

    </CFTRY>
  </CFIF>



  <!--- If no messages were retrieved... --->
  <CFIF SESSION.Mail.GetMessages.RecordCount EQ 0>
    <P>You have no mail messages at this time.<BR>

  <!--- If messages were retrieved... --->
  <CFELSE>
    <!--- Display Messages in HTML Table Format --->
    <TABLE BORDER="0" CELLSPACING="2" CELLSPACING="2" COLS="3" WIDTH="550">
      <!--- Column Headings for Table --->
      <TR>
        <TH WIDTH="100">Date Sent</TH>
        <TH WIDTH="200">From</TH>
        <TH WIDTH="200">Subject</TH>
      </TR>
      <!--- Display info about each message in a table row --->
      <CFOUTPUT QUERY="SESSION.Mail.GetMessages">
        <!--- Let user click on Subject to read full message --->
        <CFSET LinkURL = "CheckMailMsg2.cfm?MsgNum=#MessageNumber#">

        <TR VALIGN="baseline">
          <!--- Show parsed and formatted Date and Time for message--->
          <!--- If it can't be parsed, it will just be displayed as is --->
          <TD>
            #TryToFormatPOPDateTime(SESSION.Mail.GetMessages.Date)#
          </TD>
          <!--- Show "From" address, escaping brackets --->
          <TD>#HTMLEditFormat(From)#</TD>
          <TD><STRONG><A HREF="#LinkURL#">#Subject#</A></STRONG></TD>
        </TR>
      </CFOUTPUT>
    </TABLE>

    <!--- "Refresh" link to get new list of messages  --->
    <B><A HREF="CheckMail.cfm?Refresh=Yes">Refresh Message List</A></B><BR>
    <!--- "Log Out" link to discard SESSION.Mail info --->
    <A HREF="CheckMail.cfm?Logout=Yes">Log Out</A><BR>
  </CFIF>

  </BODY>
  </HTML>
```

NOTE

Most of the code in Listing 31.10 is unchanged from the version in Chapter 26, "Interacting With Email," so only the `<CFTRY>` block near the top of the listing will be discussed here. For a discussion of the rest of the code, especially the use of the `<CFPOP>` tag, please refer to Chapter 26.

The <CFTRY> and <CFCATCH> blocks in this listing rely on the fact that ColdFusion MX will throw predictable error messages when a <CFPOP> operation fails. Internally, <CFPOP> uses the javax.mail package provided by Java; when a problem occurs, the Java runtime engine throws an exception, which is caught by ColdFusion internally. In a <CFCATCH> block, the text of the Java exception will be available in the `CFCATCH.Message` and `CFCATCH.Detail` variables (refer to Table 31.3).

NOTE

Don't worry about the fact that the javax.mail package is used internally by ColdFusion. You don't need to know how to use javax.mail, or any other Java package, to use ColdFusion. I only mention it here to help you understand where the origin of the error messages.

To create this listing, the first thing I did was to find out what error messages would be displayed if I entered an incorrect username or password, or entered an incorrect mail server address. I simply used the original version of the `CheckMail.cfm` page from Chapter 26 and purposefully entered incorrect values in the login form. I found that if I supplied an incorrect mail server address (for instance, `fake.mailserver.net`), I would receive an error message that read:

```
This exception was caused by: javax.mail.MessagingException:
Connect failed; nested exception is: java.net.UnknownHostException:
fake.mailserver.net.
```

And, if I entered a correct mail server but an incorrect username or password, I would receive an error message that read:

```
This exception was caused by: javax.mail.AuthenticationFailedException: password
rejected
```

Both of the error messages contain the string `javax.mail`, so the first thing the <CFCATCH> block in Listing 31.10 does is to check to see if the `CFCATCH.Detail` variable includes `javax.mail`. If it does, it checks to see if it contains `javax.mail.AuthenticationFailedException`; if so, it displays an error message to check the username and password. If not, it checks to see if the message detail contains `java.net.UnknownHostException`; if so, it displays an error message to check the mail server name.

If neither of these two messages were found, the <CFELSE> blocks executes, the assumption being that some other minor mail-related exception has occurred. A generic error message is displayed, and the problem is logged with the <CFLOG> tag. So, any exceptions that contain the string `javax.mail` will be logged in a separate log file called `CheckMailErrorLog.log` in the `CFusionMX/logs` folder. This will help you debug other types of mail server-related problems.

No matter which of these three `javax.mail` related messages is displayed, the code then proceeds to deletes the `Mail` structure from the `SESSION` scope, which effectively logs the user out of the web-based mail application. The <CFINCLUDE> tag is then used to show the login form again so that the user can try logging in again. Finally, the <CFABORT> is used to halt any further processing.

It's worth noting that if the `CFCATCH.Detail` variable does not include the string `javax.mail`, it is assumed that some other more serious or unforeseen error has occurred, possibly not related to mail at all. In such a case, the <CFRETHROW> tag is used to allowed to resurface on its own.

Using Exception Handling In UDFs

In Chapter 19, "Building User Defined Functions," you learned how to create your own user defined functions (UDFs) using ColdFusion MX's new `<CFFUNCTION>` tag. Because you write UDFs using ordinary CFML code, you are free to use `<CFTRY>` and `<CFCATCH>` to catch exceptions that might occur while a UDF does its work.

Creating the UDFs

Listing 31.11 shows how you can use exception handling within a UDF. This listing creates a user defined function called `TryToParsePOPDateTime()`. The idea behind this function is to provide a sensible remedy to the fact that ColdFusion's own `ParseDateTime()` function, which is meant to be able to convert the date strings included in mail messages to CFML date objects, will sometimes fail to parse the date correctly. Basically, the problem is that different systems format the date differently. Some of the date formats can be parsed by `ParseDateTime()` if the `"POP"` option is used; some can't be parsed by that function but can be parsed by `LSParseDateTime()`, and others can be parsed by `ParseDateTime()` without the `"POP"` option. The function created in this listing accepts a date (which is presumably from the `Date` column of a mail message retrieved with `<CFPOP>`) as a string and tries to convert the date using each of the three strategies.

Listing 31.11 `POPDateFunctions.cfm`—Using Exception Handling Within a UDF

```
<!---
  Filename: POPDateFunctions.cfm
  Author:   Nate Weiss (NMW)
  Purpose:  A small library of functions related to POP dates
--->

<!---
  TryToParsePOPDateTime(date_string)
  Function that tries to parse a date string from an incoming email message.
  It attempts to parse the string using ParseDateTime() with "POP" option,
  then LSParseDateTime(), then ParseDateTime() without "POP" option. If all
  attempts fail, this function returns the original date string, unmodified.
--->
<CFFUNCTION NAME="TryToParsePOPDateTime">
  <!--- Required argument: DateString --->
  <CFARGUMENT NAME="DateString" TYPE="string" REQUIRED="Yes">

  <!--- Local variable to hold this function's result --->
  <!--- Start off by just setting it to original date string --->
  <CFSET var Result = ARGUMENTS.DateString>

  <!--- Attempt 1 --->
  <CFTRY>
    <CFSET Result = ParseDateTime(DateString, "POP")>

    <!--- If attempt 1 fails... --->
    <CFCATCH TYPE="Expression">
      <!--- Attempt 2 --->
      <CFTRY>
        <CFSET Result = LSParseDateTime(DateString)>
```

Listing 31.11 (continued)

```
          <!--- If attempts 2 fails... --->
          <CFCATCH TYPE="Expression">
            <!--- Attempt 3 --->
            <CFTRY>
              <CFSET Result = ParseDateTime(DateString)>

              <!--- If attempt 3 fails, give up. --->
              <!--- Result will just be the original date string, --->
              <!--- from the initial <CFSET> at top of this function. --->
              <CFCATCH TYPE="Expression"></CFCATCH>
            </CFTRY>

          </CFCATCH>
        </CFTRY>

      </CFCATCH>
    </CFTRY>

    <!--- Return the result --->
    <CFRETURN Result>
  </CFFUNCTION>


  <!---
    TryToFormatPOPDateTime(date_string)
    Attempts to parse a date, then formats it if possible
  --->
  <CFFUNCTION NAME="TryToFormatPOPDateTime">
    <!--- Required argument: DateString --->
    <CFARGUMENT NAME="DateString" TYPE="string" REQUIRED="Yes">

    <!--- Attempt to parse the date --->
    <CFSET var Result = TryToParsePOPDateTime(ARGUMENTS.DateString)>

    <!--- If it was parsed successfully, format it with DateFormat() --->
    <CFIF IsDate(Result)>
      <CFSET Result = "<B>#DateFormat(Result)#</B><BR>#TimeFormat(Result)#">
    </CFIF>

    <!--- Return the result --->
    <CFRETURN Result>
  </CFFUNCTION>
```

As you can see, this listing is not much more than three separate attempts to set the `Result` variable with the value returned by the `ParseDateTime()` and `LSParseDateTime()` functions. Each attempt is protected by its own `<CFTRY>` block, such that if the first attempt fails, the second attempt executes, and so on. Even if all three attempts fail, the function still does something reasonably useful: it returns the original date string. For details on the `ParseDateTime()` and `LSParseTime()` functions, see Appendix C, "ColdFusion Function Reference."

NOTE

As a learning exercise, you could adapt the innermost `<CFCATCH>` block so that it parsed the date on its own, using string functions like `GetToken()`, `Len()`, and the like. See Appendix C, "ColdFusion Function Reference," for a listing of all the string-manipulation functions available to you.

This listing also includes a function called `TryToFormatPOPDateTime()`, which calls the new `TryToParsePOPDateTime()` function internally, then formats it using `DateFormat()` and `TimeFormat()` if possible. If `TryToParsePOPDateTime()` was not able to return a parsed date object, then `TryToFormatPOPDateTime()` just returns whatever string was passed to it. In other words, you can pass any string to this second function. If it can be parsed as a string, a formatted version will be returned; if not, the original string is returned.

Using the UDFs

If you look back at Listing 31.11, you will see that it is already using these functions. The code from Listing 31.12 is included as a UDF library with the `<CFINCLUDE>` tag at the top of the listing. Then, near the end of the listing, the `TryToFormatPOPDateTime()` function is used to display each message's date in the most sensible way possible. Any dates that cannot be parsed by the UDFs are simply displayed to the user exactly as they were included in the original mail message.

Throwing and Catching Your Own Errors

You can throw custom exceptions whenever your code encounters a situation that should be considered an error within the context of your application, perhaps because it violates some type of business rule. Therefore, custom exceptions give you a way to teach your ColdFusion code to treat certain conditions—which ColdFusion wouldn't be capable of identifying as problematic on its own—as exceptions, just like the built-in exceptions thrown by ColdFusion itself.

Introducing `<CFTHROW>`

To throw your own custom exceptions, you use the `<CFTHROW>` tag. The exceptions you raise with `<CFTHROW>` can be caught with a `<CFTRY>`/`<CFCATCH>` block, just like the exceptions ColdFusion throws internally. If your custom exception is not caught (or is caught and then rethrown via the `<CFRETHROW>` tag), ColdFusion simply displays the text you provide for the `MESSAGE` and `DETAIL` attributes in a standard error message.

Table 31.4 lists the attributes you can provide for the `<CFTHROW>` tag. All of them are optional, but it is strongly recommended that you at least provide the `MESSAGE` attribute whenever you use `<CFTHROW>`.

Table 31.4 `<CFTHROW>` Tag Attributes

ATTRIBUTE	DESCRIPTION
`TYPE`	A string that classifies your exception into a category. You can provide either `TYPE="APPLICATION"`, which is the default, or a `TYPE` of your own choosing. You cannot provide any of the predefined exception types listed in Table 31.1. You can specify custom exception types that include dots, which enables you to create hierarchical families of custom exceptions. See the next section, "Creating Custom Exception Families."
`MESSAGE`	A text message that briefly describes the error you are raising. If the exception is caught in a `<CFCATCH>` block, the value you provide here is available as `CFCATCH.Message`. If the exception is not caught, ColdFusion displays this value in an error message to the user. This value is optional, but it is strongly recommended that you provide it.

Table 31.4 (CONTINUED)

ATTRIBUTE	DESCRIPTION
DETAIL	A second text message that describes the error in more detail, or any background information or hints that will help other people understand the cause of the error. If the exception is caught in a <CFCATCH> block, the value you provide here is available as CFCATCH.Detail. If the exception is not caught, ColdFusion displays this value in an error message to the user.
ERRORCODE	An optional error code of your own devising. If the exception is caught in a <CFCATCH> block, the value you provide here is available as CFCATCH.ErrorCode.
EXTENDEDINFO	A second optional error code of your own devising. If the exception is caught in a <CFCATCH> block, the value you provide here will be available as CFCATCH.ExtendedInfo.

Throwing Custom Exceptions

Say you are working on a piece of code that performs some type of operation (such as placing an order) based on a ContactID value. As a kind of sanity check, you should verify that ContactID is actually valid before going further.

If you find that ContactID is not valid, you can throw a custom error using the <CFTHROW> tag, like so:

```
<CFTHROW
  MESSAGE="Invalid Contact ID"
  DETAIL="No record exists for that Contact ID.">
```

This exception can be caught using a <CFCATCH> tag, as shown in the following. Within this <CFIF> block, you can take whatever action is appropriate in the face of an invalid contact ID (perhaps inserting a new record into the Contacts table or using <CFMAIL> to send a message to your customer service manager):

```
<CFCATCH TYPE="APPLICATION">
  <CFIF Message EQ "Invalid Contact ID">
    <!--- recovery code here --->
  </CFIF>
</CFIF>
```

This <CFCATCH> code catches the Invalid Contact ID exception because the exception's type is APPLICATION, which is the default exception type used when no TYPE attribute is provided to <CFTHROW>. If you want, you can specify your own exception type, like so:

```
<CFTHROW
  TYPE="InvalidContactID"
  MESSAGE="Invalid Contact ID"
  DETAIL="No record exists for that Contact ID.">
```

This exception will be caught by any <CFCATCH> tag that has a matching TYPE, like this one:

```
<CFCATCH TYPE="InvalidContactID">
  <!--- recovery code here --->
</CFCATCH>
```

NOTE

You can also use the `<CFABORT>` tag with the `SHOWERROR` attribute to throw a custom exception. If the exception is caught, the text you provide for `SHOWERROR` becomes the `CFCATCH.Message` value. However, the use of `<CFTHROW>` is preferred because you can provide more complete information about the error you are raising, via `TYPE`, `DETAIL`, and other attributes shown in Listing 31.5.

Creating Custom Exception Families

You can create hierarchical families of exceptions by including dots (periods) in the `TYPE` attribute you provide to the `<CFTHROW>` tag. If you do so, you can catch whole groups of exceptions using a single `<CFCATCH>` tag.

For instance, you could throw an error such as the following:

```
<CFTHROW
  TYPE="OrangeWhipStudios.InternalData.InvalidContactID"
  MESSAGE="Invalid Contact ID"
  DETAIL="No record exists for that Contact ID.">
```

You could catch the previous exception with a matching `<CFCATCH>` tag, like this one:

```
<CFCATCH TYPE="OrangeWhipStudios.InternalData.InvalidContactID">
```

If no `<CFCATCH>` matches the `TYPE` exactly, ColdFusion looks for a `<CFCATCH>` tag that matches the next most specific type of exception, using the dots to denote levels of specificity. So this `<CFCATCH>` tag would catch the error thrown by the previous `<CFTHROW>`:

```
<CFCATCH TYPE="OrangeWhipStudios.InternalData">
```

If no `<CFCATCH>` such as the previous one was present, this `<CFCATCH>` would catch the error, which would also catch other errors in the `OrangeWhipStudios` hierarchy, such as `OrangeWhipStudios.InternalData.InvalidMerchID` and `OrangeWhipStudios.DatabaseNotAvailable`:

```
<CFCATCH TYPE="OrangeWhipStudios">
```

Custom Exceptions and Custom Tags

Listing 31.12 is an example of a ColdFusion template that includes several `<CFTHROW>` tags that know how to report helpful diagnostic information when problems arise. It is a revision of the `<CF_PlaceOrder>` custom tag from Chapter 27, "Online Commerce." This version performs all the same operations as the original version; the main difference is the addition of several sanity checks at the top of the template, which ensure that the various ID numbers passed to the tag make sense. If not, custom exceptions are thrown, which the calling template can catch with `<CFCATCH>` if it wants. If the calling template does not catch the exceptions thrown by the tag, ColdFusion displays the exception to the user in the form of an error message.

NOTE

This template relies on many of the templates from Chapter 27. To test this template, save it as `PlaceOrder.cfm` in the same folder as the examples from Chapter 27.

Listing 31.12 `PlaceOrder.cfm`—Throwing Your Own Exceptions with `<CFTHROW>`

```
<!---
  Filename:    PlaceOrder.cfm
  Created by:  Nate Weiss (NMW)
  Purpose:     Processes a user's user, charging credit card, etc
  Please Note Relies upon <CF_ProcessPayment> custom tag
--->

<!--- Tag Parameters --->
<CFPARAM NAME="ATTRIBUTES.Processor" TYPE="string" DEFAULT="PayflowPro">
<CFPARAM NAME="ATTRIBUTES.MerchList" TYPE="string">
<CFPARAM NAME="ATTRIBUTES.QuantList" TYPE="string">
<CFPARAM NAME="ATTRIBUTES.ContactID" TYPE="numeric">
<CFPARAM NAME="ATTRIBUTES.CreditCard" TYPE="string">
<CFPARAM NAME="ATTRIBUTES.CreditExpM" TYPE="string">
<CFPARAM NAME="ATTRIBUTES.CreditExpY" TYPE="string">
<CFPARAM NAME="ATTRIBUTES.CreditName" TYPE="string">
<CFPARAM NAME="ATTRIBUTES.ShipAddress" TYPE="string">
<CFPARAM NAME="ATTRIBUTES.ShipCity" TYPE="string">
<CFPARAM NAME="ATTRIBUTES.ShipCity" TYPE="string">
<CFPARAM NAME="ATTRIBUTES.ShipState" TYPE="string">
<CFPARAM NAME="ATTRIBUTES.ShipZIP" TYPE="string">
<CFPARAM NAME="ATTRIBUTES.ShipCountry" TYPE="string">
<CFPARAM NAME="ATTRIBUTES.HTMLMail" TYPE="boolean">
<CFPARAM NAME="ATTRIBUTES.ReturnVariable" TYPE="variableName">

<CFTRY>
  <!--- Make sure the MerchList and QuantList Attributes make sense --->
  <CFIF (ListLen(ATTRIBUTES.MerchList) EQ 0)
    OR ListLen(ATTRIBUTES.MerchList) NEQ ListLen(ATTRIBUTES.QuantList)>
    <!--- If not, throw an error --->
    <CFTHROW
      MESSAGE="Invalid MerchList or QuantList attribute"
      DETAIL="Both must have same number of list elements, and cannot be empty.">
  </CFIF>

  <!--- Quick query to verify the ContactID is valid --->
  <CFQUERY NAME="GetCount" DATASOURCE="#REQUEST.DataSource#">
    SELECT Count(*) AS ContactCount
    FROM Contacts
    WHERE ContactID = #ATTRIBUTES.ContactID#
  </CFQUERY>

  <!--- If any of the MerchIDs are not valid, throw custom error --->
  <CFIF GetCount.ContactCount NEQ 1>
    <CFTHROW
      TYPE="ows.MerchOrder.InvalidContactID"
      MESSAGE="Invalid Contact ID"
      DETAIL="The ContactID you provided (#ATTRIBUTES.ContactID#) is not valid."
      ERRORCODE="1">
  </CFIF>

  <!--- Quick query to verify that all MerchIDs are valid --->
  <CFQUERY NAME="GetCount" DATASOURCE="#REQUEST.DataSource#">
    SELECT Count(*) AS ItemCount
    FROM Merchandise
    WHERE MerchID IN (#ATTRIBUTES.MerchList#)
  </CFQUERY>
```

Listing 31.12 (continued)

```
    <!--- If any of the MerchIDs are not valid, throw custom error --->
    <CFIF GetCount.ItemCount NEQ ListLen(ATTRIBUTES.MerchList)>
      <CFTHROW
        TYPE="ows.MerchOrder.InvalidMerchID"
        MESSAGE="Invalid Merchandise ID"
        DETAIL="At least one of the MerchID values you supplied is not valid."
        ERRORCODE="2">
    </CFIF>

    <!--- If any database problems came up during above validation steps --->
    <CFCATCH TYPE="Database">
      <CFTHROW
        TYPE="ows.MerchOrder.ValidationFailed"
        MESSAGE="Order Validation Failed"
        DETAIL="A database problem occured while attempting to validate the order.">
    </CFCATCH>
  </CFTRY>

  <!--- Begin "order" database transaction here --->
  <!--- Can be rolled back or committed later --->
  <CFTRANSACTION ACTION="BEGIN">
    <CFTRY>
      <!--- Insert new record into Orders table --->
      <CFQUERY DATASOURCE="#REQUEST.DataSource#">
        INSERT INTO MerchandiseOrders (
          ContactID,
          OrderDate,
          ShipAddress, ShipCity,
          ShipState, ShipZip,
          ShipCountry)
        VALUES (
          #ATTRIBUTES.ContactID#,
          <CFQUERYPARAM CFSQLTYPE="CF_SQL_TIMESTAMP"
            VALUE="#DateFormat(Now())# #TimeFormat(Now())#">,
          '#ATTRIBUTES.ShipAddress#', '#ATTRIBUTES.ShipCity#',
          '#ATTRIBUTES.ShipState#', '#ATTRIBUTES.ShipZip#',
          '#ATTRIBUTES.ShipCountry#'
        )
      </CFQUERY>

      <!--- Get just-inserted OrderID from database --->
      <CFQUERY DATASOURCE="#REQUEST.DataSource#" NAME="GetNew">
        SELECT MAX(OrderID) AS NewID
        FROM MerchandiseOrders
      </CFQUERY>

      <!--- For each item in user's shopping cart --->
      <CFLOOP FROM="1" TO="#ListLen(ATTRIBUTES.MerchList)#" INDEX="i">
        <CFSET ThisMerchID = ListGetAt(ATTRIBUTES.MerchList, i)>
        <CFSET ThisQuant   = ListGetAt(ATTRIBUTES.QuantList, i)>

        <!--- Add the item to "OrdersItems" table --->
        <CFQUERY DATASOURCE="#REQUEST.DataSource#">
          INSERT INTO MerchandiseOrdersItemsf
            (OrderID, ItemID, OrderQty, ItemPrice)
          SELECT
            #GetNew.NewID#, MerchID, #ThisQuant#, MerchPrice
```

Listing 31.12 (continued)

```
        FROM Merchandise
        WHERE MerchID = #ThisMerchID#
      </CFQUERY>
    </CFLOOP>

    <!--- Get the total of all items in user's cart --->
    <CFQUERY DATASOURCE="#REQUEST.DataSource#" NAME="GetTotal">
      SELECT SUM(ItemPrice * OrderQty) AS OrderTotal
      FROM MerchandiseOrdersItems
      WHERE OrderID = #GetNew.NewID#
    </CFQUERY>

    <!--- Attempt to process the transaction  --->
    <CF_ProcessPayment
      Processor="#ATTRIBUTES.Processor#"
      OrderID="#GetNew.NewID#"
            OrderAmount="#GetTotal.OrderTotal#"
            CreditCard="#ATTRIBUTES.CreditCard#"
            CreditExpM="#ATTRIBUTES.CreditExpM#"
      CreditExpY="#ATTRIBUTES.CreditExpY#"
            CreditName="#ATTRIBUTES.CreditName#"
      ReturnVariable="ChargeInfo">

    <!--- If the order was processed successfully --->
    <CFIF ChargeInfo.IsSuccessful>
      <!--- Commit the transaction to database --->
      <CFTRANSACTION ACTION="Commit"/>
    <CFELSE>
      <!--- Rollback the Order from the Database --->
      <CFTRANSACTION ACTION="RollBack"/>
    </CFIF>

    <!--- If any errors occur while processing the order --->
    <CFCATCH TYPE="Any">
      <!--- Rollback the Order from the Database --->
      <CFTRANSACTION ACTION="RollBack"/>
      <!--- Throw a custom exception --->
      <CFTHROW
        TYPE="ows.MerchOrder.OrderFailed"
        MESSAGE="Order Could Not Be Completed"
        DETAIL="The order (ID #GetNew.NewID#) was rolled back from the database."
        ERRORCODE="3">
    </CFCATCH>
  </CFTRY>
</CFTRANSACTION>

<!--- If the order was processed successfully --->
<CFIF ChargeInfo.IsSuccessful>
  <!--- Send Confirmation E-Mail, via Custom Tag --->
  <CF_SendOrderConfirmation
    OrderID="#GetNew.NewID#"
    UseHTML="#ATTRIBUTES.HTMLMail#">
</CFIF>

<!--- Return status values to callling template --->
<CFSET "Caller.#ATTRIBUTES.ReturnVariable#" = ChargeInfo>
```

The first use of <CFTHROW> just performs a bit of simple data validation on the MerchList and QuantList attributes. The custom tag needs these two lists to have the same number of elements; additionally, neither list should be allowed to be empty. If the ListLen() function reports that the lists contain different numbers of elements, or if the lists are empty, an exception is raised with a MESSAGE that reads Invalid MerchList or QuantList attribute.

Next, the <CFTHROW> tag is used again to raise an exception of type ows.MerchOrder.InvalidContactID if the ContactID attribute passed to the custom tag is not a valid contact ID number. First, the GetCount query counts the number of records in the Contacts table with the given ContactID. If the ID number is legitimate, the query returns a ContactCount of 1. If not, the custom exception is thrown.

Similar logic is used to ensure that all the merchandise IDs in the MerchList attribute are legitimate. If the ItemCount value returned by the second GetCount query is the same as the number of items in the list, all the merchandise IDs must be legitimate (and must not contain any duplicate values). If not, a custom exception of type ows.MerchOrder.InvalidMerchID is thrown.

The whole top portion of the template (the portion that performs the sanity checks) is also wrapped in its own <CFTRY> block, so a custom exception of type ows.MerchOrder.ValidationFailed is thrown if any database errors occur while performing either of the GetCount queries.

NOTE

Listing 31.12 has also added a <CFTRY> block around the main portion of the template, where the order is actually processed. This <CFTRY> tag uses <CFTRANSACTION> to roll back any changes to the database if a problem occurs. See the next section, "Exceptions and Database Transactions," for an explanation.

Listing 31.13 is a revised version of the StoreCheckout.cfm template, also from Chapter 27. It calls the <CF_PlaceOrder> custom tag from Listing 31.12, catching any of the custom exceptions the custom tag might throw. Because all of the exceptions that the tag throws start with ows.MerchOrder, a single <CFCATCH> of TYPE="owsMerchOrder" can catch them all.

NOTE

This template relies on many of the templates from Chapter 27, "Online Commerce." To test this template, save it as StoreCheckout.cfm in the same folder as the examples from Chapter 27. Make sure that you've also saved Listing 31.12 as PlaceOrder.cfm in the same folder.

Listing 31.13 StoreCheckout.cfm—Catching Custom Exceptions Thrown by a Custom Tag

```
<!---
  Filename:    StoreCheckout.cfm
  Created by:  Nate Weiss (NMW)
  Purpose:     Places an order for all items in user's shopping cart
  Please Note Relies upon <CF_PlaceOrder> custom tag
--->


<!--- Show header images, etc., for Online Store --->
<CFINCLUDE TEMPLATE="StoreHeader.cfm">

<!--- Get current cart contents, via Custom Tag --->
<CF_ShoppingCart
  Action="List"
  ReturnVariable="GetCart">
```

Listing 31.13 (continued)

```
<!--- Stop here if user's cart is empty --->
<CFIF GetCart.RecordCount EQ 0>
  There is nothing in your cart.
  <CFABORT>
</CFIF>

<!--- If user is not logged in, force them to now --->
<CFIF NOT IsDefined("SESSION.Auth.IsLoggedIn")>
  <CFINCLUDE TEMPLATE="LoginForm.cfm">
  <CFABORT>
</CFIF>

<!--- If user is attempting to place order --->
<CFIF IsDefined("FORM.IsPlacingOrder")>

  <CFTRY>
    <!--- Attempt to process the transaction  --->
    <CF_PlaceOrder
      Processor="JustTesting"
      ContactID="#SESSION.Auth.ContactID#"
      MerchList="#ValueList(GetCart.MerchID)#"
      QuantList="#ValueList(GetCart.Quantity)#"
            CreditCard="#FORM.CreditCard#"
            CreditExpM="#FORM.CreditExpM#"
      CreditExpY="#FORM.CreditExpY#"
            CreditName="#FORM.CreditName#"
      ShipAddress="#FORM.ShipAddress#"
      ShipState="#FORM.ShipState#"
      ShipCity="#FORM.ShipCity#"
      ShipZIP="#FORM.ShipZIP#"
      ShipCountry="#FORM.ShipCountry#"
      HTMLMail="#FORM.HTMLMail#"
      ReturnVariable="OrderInfo">

    <!--- If any exceptions in the "ows.MerchOrder" family are thrown... --->
    <CFCATCH TYPE="ows.MerchOrder">
      <P>Unfortunately, we are not able to process your order at the moment.<BR>
      Please try again later.  We apologize for the inconvenience.<BR>
      <CFABORT>
    </CFCATCH>
  </CFTRY>


  <!--- If the order was processed successfully --->
  <CFIF OrderInfo.IsSuccessful>

    <!--- Empty user's shopping cart, via custom tag --->
    <CF_ShoppingCart
      ACTION="Empty">

    <!--- Display Success Message --->
    <CFOUTPUT>
      <H2>Thanks For Your Order</H2>
      <P><B>Your Order Has Been Placed.</B><BR>
      Your order number is: #OrderInfo.OrderID#<BR>
      Your credit card has been charged:
      #LSCurrencyFormat(OrderInfo.OrderAmount)#<BR>
```

Listing 31.13 (continued)

```
        <P>A confirmation is being E-mailed to you.<BR>
      </CFOUTPUT>

      <!--- Stop here. --->
      <CFABORT>
    <CFELSE>
      <!--- Display "Error" message --->
      <FONT COLOR="Red">
        <STRONG>Your credit card could not be processed.</STRONG><BR>
        Please verify the credit card number, expiration date, and
        name on the card.<BR>
      </FONT>

      <!--- Show debug info if viewing page on server --->
      <CFIF CGI.REMOTE_ADDR EQ "127.0.0.1">
        <CFOUTPUT>
          Status:  #OrderInfo.Status#<BR>
          Error:   #OrderInfo.ErrorCode#<BR>
          Message: #OrderInfo.ErrorMessage#<BR>
        </CFOUTPUT>
      </CFIF>
    </CFIF>
  </CFIF>


  <!--- Show Checkout Form (Ship Address/Credit Card) --->
  <CFINCLUDE TEMPLATE="StoreCheckoutForm.cfm">
```

This listing is the same as the original version from Chapter 27, except for the addition of the <CFTRY> and <CFCATCH> blocks. Please see Chapter 27 for a complete discussion.

Exceptions and Database Transactions

Listing 31.12 uses <CFTRY> and <CFCATCH> together with the <CFTRANSACTION> tag so that the database transaction can be rolled back if any errors occur. The <CFTRY> block is wrapped around all the database interactions, as well as the call to the <CF_ProcessPayment> custom tag.

If any database errors or syntax errors occur while the order is being processed (even inside <CF_ProcessPayment>), the <CFCATCH> tag near the end of Listing 31.12 catches them. The <CFCATCH> tag uses <CFTRANSACTION> with ACTION="Rollback", which has the effect of undoing all the database changes made since the beginning of the first <CFTRANSACTION> tag. This greatly minimizes the risk that any erroneous or inconsistent order information will get recorded in the MerchandiseOrders or MerchandiseOrdersItems tables.

In many respects, you can think of <CFTRANSACTION> as the database equivalent of <CFTRY> because they are both about recovering gracefully when problems arise. Used together, they become even more powerful.

NOTE

It is generally preferable to keep transactions contained within stored procedures whenever possible. However, when that isn't possible, you can use <CFTRY> and <CFTRANSACTION> together as shown here. For more information, see Chapter 29, "More on SQL and Queries" and Chapter 30, "Working with Stored Procedures."

CHAPTER 32

Generating Non-HTML Content

IN THIS CHAPTER

Normally, ColdFusion is used to generate Web pages and Web pages only. However, there is no law that says you can't use it to generate other types of text-based output, such as comma-separated text or various types of XML for delivery to cell phones or voice-activated systems. You can even use it to dynamically produce binary content, such as images, Word documents, or Excel spreadsheets.

Tags covered in this chapter:

- `<CFCONTENT>`
- `<CFHEADER>`

NOTE

The entire text of this chapter can be found on the included CD.

CHAPTER 33

Interacting with the Operating System

IN THIS CHAPTER

ColdFusion provides the developer with many tools with which to interact with the operating system. These tools include functions and tags to create and manipulate files and directories using on the server, execute other applications installed on the server, and more. This chapter shows how these tags can be used to interact with the file system and operating system.

Tags and functions covered in this chapter include:

- `<CFFILE>`
- `<CFDIRECTORY>`
- `<CFEXECUTE>`
- `FileExists()` and `DirectoryExists()`
- `ExpandPath()`
- `GetTempFile()` and `GetTempDirectory()`

NOTE

The entire text of this chapter can be found on the included CD.

CHAPTER 34

Full-Text Searching

IN THIS CHAPTER

Getting to Know Verity

By now you're convinced that Macromedia ColdFusion MX is the greatest package on the planet for publishing database data to the Web—but you have not yet learned how to create that most popular of Web-based applications: the search engine. The success of Yahoo!, Google, and other search engines has made the concept of a Web-based search tool nearly as ubiquitous on the Internet as the word *ubiquitous* itself. An intelligent search tool is a must-have for an increasing number of sites. This chapter shows how to integrate the Verity search technology into your ColdFusion applications.

ColdFusion includes a variety of Verity search technology that can be integrated with ColdFusion applications. This technology includes:

- Two tools for indexing and searching large amounts of textual data.
- A "spider" for creating text indexes of linked documents.
- A programming interface for searching the indexes.
- A number of index optimization utilities.

You can think of the combination of these tools as "the Verity search engine." The Verity search engine excels at finding words in large chunks of unstructured text, such as the documents human beings tend to write. As a developer, you tell it what to search—and what to search for—and it faithfully tries to find it.

NOTE

In this chapter the word Verity refers to ColdFusion's integration with search technology (specifically, the Verity K2 server and Verity VDK) from a company called Verity. Just as people tend to say Netscape when they are really referring to the program called Navigator (which is made by Netscape Communications), ColdFusion developers tend to just say Verity when they are talking about putting together full-text search applications.

Verity can search a variety of files in a variety of languages, and it does all the fancy stuff you'd expect from a sophisticated search engine, such as handling `AND`s, `OR`s, wildcards, and so on. If you've ever used the search interface provided by LEXIS/NEXIS, you can expect the same type of functionality from your own applications that use Verity.

Conceptually, the Verity layer you learn about in this chapter is similar to the ODBC/SQL layer you learned so much about earlier in this book. The main difference is that while ODBC and SQL excel at accessing neat rows and columns of information in structured database tables, Verity excels at accessing messy chunks of text, strewn about in various folders on your hard drives.

Much of the inner workings of the Verity are thoughtfully hidden from ColdFusion developers. In a nutshell, here's how you integrate text searching into your ColdFusion applications. First you choose the indexing technology—either Verity's VDK, K2, or Spider technology—and index your textual data with the ColdFusion administrator or the `<CFINDEX>` tag. Then you build a search form for users. Then you build an *action* template that employs the `<CFSEARCH>` tag and formats the search results.

Searching for Different Types of Files with Verity

ColdFusion's Verity functionality supports more than 200 file types, including native files such as documents produced with many of the Microsoft Office applications. This feature provides great flexibility when it comes to making files searchable via a Web browser.

For instance, in an intranet situation, employees can continue to use the word-processing and spreadsheet applications they use every day. All they have to do is save the documents in a folder tree that is indexed in a Verity collection. With literally a few lines of code, you can turn those documents into a fully searchable company library. And with K2 server support in ColdFusion 5, these libraries can include *enterprise-level* volumes of information. Table 34.1 shows the various types of files Verity can index and search.

Table 34.1 File Types Verity Can Index and Search

CATEGORY	FILE TYPE	LIMITED TO VERSIONS
Word processing	Applix Words	4.2, 4.3, 4.4
	Lotus AmiPro	2.3
	Folio Flat File	v3.1
	Lotus Ami Professional Write Plus	
	Lotus Word Pro	96, 97
	Microsoft RTF	
	Microsoft Word	2, 6, 95, 97, 2000
	Microsoft Word Mac	4, 5, 6
	Microsoft Word PC	4, 5, 6
	Microsoft Works	
	Microsoft Write	

Table 34.1 (continued)

CATEGORY	FILE TYPE	LIMITED TO VERSIONS
Word processing	PDF (Verity PDF Filter)	
	WordPerfect	5.x, 6, 7, 8
	WordPerfect Mac	2, 3
	XyWrite	4.12
Text-based files	Text files (Verity Text Filter)	
	HTML (Verity Zone Filter)	
	ASCII Text (All versions)	
	ANSI Text (All versions)	
	Unicode	
Spreadsheets	Applix Spreadsheets	4.3, 4.4
	Corel QuattroPro	7, 8
	Lotus 1-2-3	v2, 3, 4, 5, 96, 97
	Microsoft Excel	3, 4, 5, 96, 97, 2000
	Microsoft Works spreadsheet	
Presentations	Corel Presentations	7.0, 8.0
	Lotus Freelance	96, 97
	Microsoft PowerPoint	4.0, 95, 97, 2000

NOTE

The term document files is used in reference to files that are being indexed with Verity. As you can see, Verity can handle 1-2-3 spreadsheets, PowerPoint presentations, and so on. Document files means any word processor, spreadsheet, or other file type listed in Table 34.1.

Different file types can be freely mixed and matched in a Verity collection. Don't worry about keeping the HTML and Word files in separate folders or collections. Store them wherever you want.

Integrating ColdFusion with Other Search Engines

Including Verity functionality is a terrific way to add search capability to your application, making it behave somewhat like a mini-Google. However, it has nothing to do with actually integrating with Google, AltaVista, Yahoo!, or any other commercial search engines. If you want to integrate with one of these search engines, you certainly can include standard `HREF` links from your application to a commercial search engine—but doing so has nothing to do with the Verity functionality explained in this chapter.

You also could place on one of your pages a search form that has an appropriate URL (within the commercial search engine's domain) as its `ACTION` parameter. Many of the commercial search engines have instructions about how to set this up—such as what to name the form `<INPUT>` tags, for instance. See their sites for details.

Finally, you could use the `<CFHTTP>` tag to place a search request to a commercial search engine and display the results on your page with the `#CFHTTP.FileContent#` variable.

➜ See Appendix B, "ColdFusion Tag Reference," for information about this extremely flexible tag.

Creating a Search Tool for Your Documents

Say that Orange Whip Studio's Human Resources Department wants to make the company's personnel policies available online so that employees can see what they are allowed to do (and not do) at any time. These policies are published internally and are not accessible to a large number of employees. As we're just getting started, lets' work with the Verity VDK server as its significantly easier to work with.

The documents are saved as various Word, plain-text, and Excel files. Collect all the documents into one folder on your Web server's local drive; explore what is necessary to make these documents searchable and retrievable from a Web browser using ColdFusion's Verity functionality as the back end. It's really pretty simple.

TIP

If you want to follow the examples in this section exactly, make a copy of the folder named **HR** from this chapter's directory on the CD-ROM. You can place the folder directly off your Web server's document root or use any random folder of your own documents that you like. Just be sure that the folder is accessible to your Web server.

Creating a New Collection for the Documents

Verity's search functionality centers around a concept of a collection. A Verity *collection* is a mass of documents you want Verity to keep track of and make searchable. (Note that a collection also can consist of a query result set, which is explored later in this chapter.)

After Verity has been told which documents belong to a collection, it can index the documents and compile metadata about them for its own use. This index enables it to search through your documents quickly, without actually parsing through them line by line at run time. Conceptually, the key to Verity's strength is its capability to invest a certain amount of time up front in indexing and compiling information about your documents. You get the payoff on that investment when your users run their searches; Verity has already studied the documents and can therefore return information about them very quickly.

Again, you might find it useful to think of Verity collections as being the full-text search equivalent of ODBC data sources. Just as you need to set up an ODBC data source before you can use `<CFQUERY>` to retrieve data with SQL, you need to set up a collection before you can get started with Verity. Just as with setting up a new ODBC data source, you go to the ColdFusion Administrator to set up a new collection.

Creating a New Verity VDK Collection

To set up a new collection, go to the ColdFusion Administrator and click the Verity Collections link in the Data & Services section, as shown in Figure 34.1.

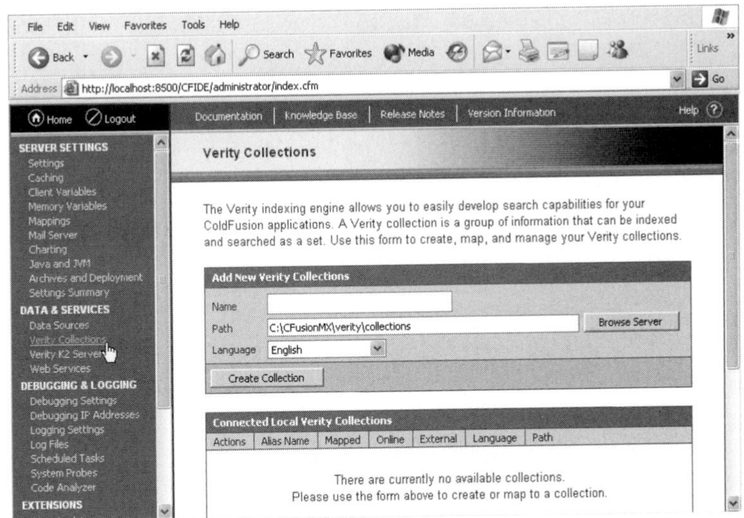

Verity Collections
The Verity indexing engine allows you to easily develop search capabilities for your ColdFusion applications. A Verity collection is a group of information that can be indexed and searched as a set. Use this form to create, map, and manage your Verity collections.
Add New Verity Collections
Name
Path
C:\CFusionMX\verity\collections
Browse Server
Language
English
Create Collection
Connected Local Verity Collections
Actions
Alias Name
Mapped
Online
External
Language
Path
There are currently no available collections.
Please use the form above to create or map to a collection.

Figure 34.1
All collections on your server are shown on the Verity Collections page of the ColdFusion Administrator.

Here's how to create the Verity collection to which your human resources documents will belong. Enter "HRDocs" as the name of the new collection in the top portion of the page.

You can change the path if you want the collection to be stored in a location other than the default (`C:\CFusionMX\verity\collections` in), but you might as well use the default unless you have a specific reason not to (such as drive space or file-permissions issues).

Click the Create Collection button. After a moment, your new collection will appear in the list of "Connected Local Verity Collections", along with any other existing collections.

NOTE

The path you fill in when creating a new collection is simply where Verity's internal data about your documents will be kept. This is *not* the path to where the actual documents are.

NOTE

Suppose you already have an existing collection on another server. If you type in the UNC path to that collection, ColdFusion will automatically recognize the existence of the collection and will map this entry to it. This is useful when you have several ColdFusion servers–perhaps operating in a cluster–that all need to be capable of searching the same information. By creating this mapped collection, the Verity engine uses the index files maintained by the other ColdFusion server. When the collection is reindexed on the other server, all collections that are mapped to it reflect the new data in search results. This approach keeps you from having to maintain separate collections on each ColdFusion server.

Specifying a Language

If you have the optional ColdFusion International Search Pack, you can specify a language other than English when creating a new collection. The language should match the language the documents were written in. Verity can pull off a few neat tricks when it knows which language the documents are written in, such as understanding the role of accented characters. It also uses knowledge of the language to pull off variations on the same word stem or root.

You must choose the language when you create the collection. Simply select the language from the drop-down list in the Administrator before you click the Create Collection button (see Figure 34.2). The International Search Pack supports the following languages: Arabic, two forms of Chinese, Czech, Danish, Dutch, English, Finnish, French, German, Greek, Hebrew, Hungarian, Italian, Japanese, Korean, three forms of Norwegian, Polish, Portuguese, Russian, Spanish, Swedish and Turkish. Support for the language pack was added to ColdFusion in version 3.1.

You must choose the language when you create the collection. Simply select the language from the drop-down list in the Administrator before you click the Create Collection button. Try not to mix documents written in different languages in the same collection. If you have documents in several languages, make separate collections for them.

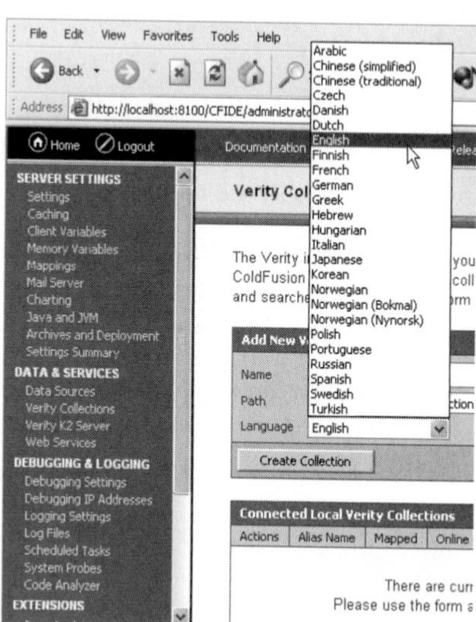

Figure 34.2

You can build the collection on documents written in one of 25 languages if you have the International Search Pack installed.

Indexing the Collection

Creating the collection simply results in the creation of the basic Verity infrastructure that will be used for the collection. You must *index* the collection in order to make the collection *searchable.*

Indexing is simple and can be done via the ColdFusion Administrator or through the `<CFINDEX>` tag. Let's start by indexing a collection through the ColdFusion Administrator.

Indexing Your Files with the ColdFusion Administrator

With the Verity Collections page selected, click on the Index icon (the leftmost icon) for the collection to be indexed, as shown in Figure 34.3. This step loads the Index Verity Collections page, as shown in Figure 34.4. The form is used to specify the text content that is to be made searchable.

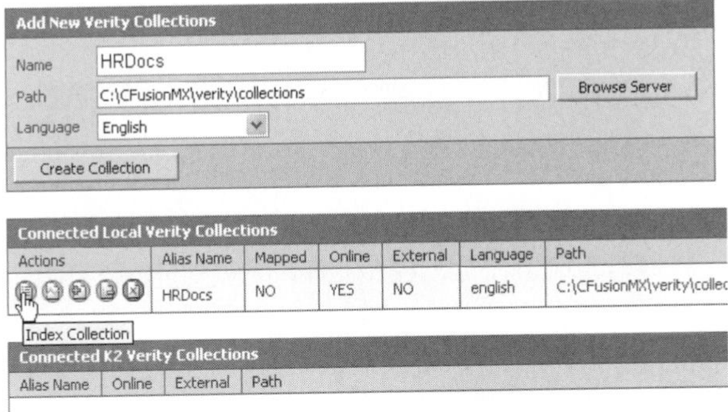

Figure 34.3
You begin the indexing process in the ColdFusion Administrator on the Verity Collections page.

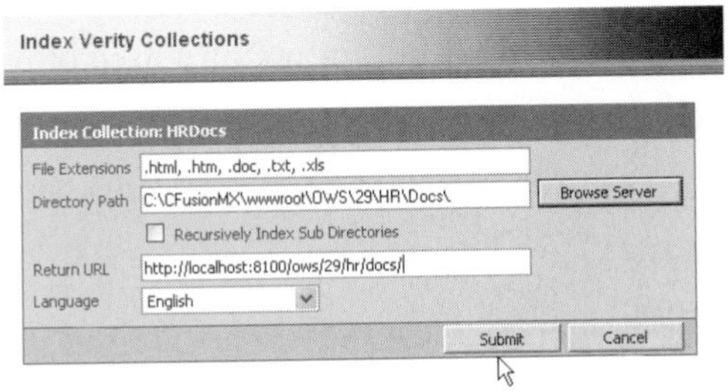

Figure 34.4
The Index Verity Collections page is used to specify the content to be made searchable.

Enter the file extensions: `.html, .htm, .doc, .txt, .xls`.

The `directory path` specifies the location on the server's disk where the data to be made searchable is located. Enter `C:\CFusionMX\wwwroot\OWS\29\HR\Docs`.

NOTE
This data is located on the CD. If you've installed the CD, it will be installed on your disk. Note that it is assumed that you've configured ColdFusion to use the standalone web server. If you haven't done so the directory path may be different.

The `return URL` specifies the URL that will be used to return any content if the user searches for it. It is the path the web server uses to find the content. Enter `http://localhost:8500/ows/34/hr/docs/`.

NOTE
Again, it's assumed that you're using the standalone web server. If you aren't the directory path may be different.

Select `English` as the `language` of the content to be indexed.

At this point, click the Submit button to index the content. When indexing is complete (it will take a second or two), you'll be returned to the Verity Collection list page and the message "Collection HRDocs Indexed" will be displayed at the top as shown in Figure 34.5.

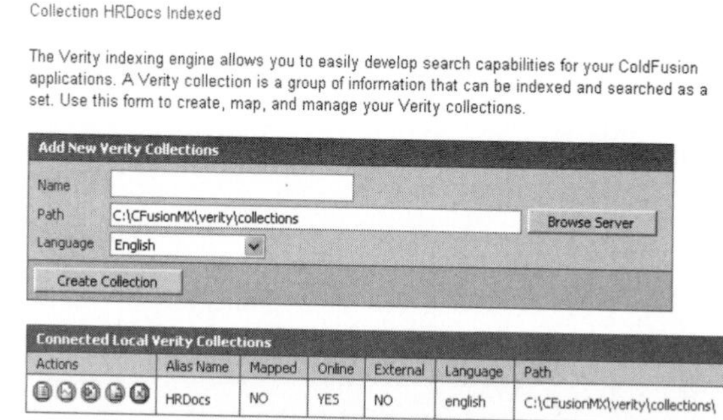
Collection HRDocs Indexed
The Verity indexing engine allows you to easily develop search capabilities for your ColdFusion applications. A Verity collection is a group of information that can be indexed and searched as a set. Use this form to create, map, and manage your Verity collections.
Add New Verity Collections
Name
Path
C:\CFusionMX\verity\collections
Browse Server
Language
English
Create Collection
Connected Local Verity Collections
Actions
Alias Name
Mapped
Online
External
Language
Path
HRDocs
NO
YES
NO
english
C:\CFusionMX\verity\collections\

Figure 34.5
The Verity Collections page indicates that the collection was indexed.

You now know how to index your documents. Or do you? Well, you know one way, but you'll find that this method is not suited for all occasions. This method is handy for the following situations:

- When the documents change infrequently, or not on a fixed or predictable schedule.
- When the documents live outside your ColdFusion application, such as in a folder full of Word files that employees might save and edit without your application knowing about it.
- Testing and development.
- Less complicated in-house applications.

But other situations are likely to require the programmatic approach:

- When the documents are always changing.
- When it's critical that new documents become searchable right away.
- When it's important that your application is as self-tuning as possible—like when you are working as an outside consultant.
- More complicated applications.

Let's see how the programmatic approach is used.

Indexing Your Files with the `<CFINDEX>` Tag

You've learned how to index a collection using the ColdFusion administrator, but that approach isn't always good enough. Sometimes, you'll need a ColdFusion application to do the indexing itself, programmatically.

The `<CFINDEX>` tag cues Verity to wake up and index (or reindex) the files in the folder you specify. This is the second step in the overall process of making a Verity application come alive. (The first step is creating the collection in the ColdFusion Administrator, and the third is actually searching the collection with the `<CFSEARCH>` tag, which is covered shortly.)

The template in Listing 34.1 uses the `<CFINDEX>` tag to index the content of the HR\Docs subdirectory. This content consists of some MS Word and Excel documents as well as some text and HTML files.

Listing 34.1 `INDEXING.CFM`—Indexing the HRDocs Collection

```
<!---
Lock the indexing function as we're working with
a shared resource.
--->
<CFLOCK TYPE="EXCLUSIVE" TIMEOUT="30">
<!--- Index the HRDocs collection --->
<CFINDEX
  COLLECTION="HRDocs"
  ACTION="REFRESH"
  TYPE="PATH"
  KEY="c:\CfusionMX\WWWROOT\OWS\34\HR\Docs\"
  EXTENSIONS=".htm, .html, .txt, .doc, .xls"
  RECURSE="Yes"
  LANGUAGE="english"
  URLPATH="http://localhost:8500/ows/34/HR/Docs"
>
</CFLOCK>
<HTML>
<HEAD>
    <TITLE>Personnel Policy Documents - Indexing Finished</TITLE>
</HEAD>
<BODY>
<FONT>Personnel Policy Documents</FONT> <BR>
<FONT><B>Indexing Finished</B></FONT>
</BODY>
</HTML>
```

NOTE

The `<CFLOCK>` tag is necessary because we are working on a shared resource on the server and we need to be assured that we'll have exclusive access to it. Whenever you use `<CFCOLLECTION>` or `<CFINDEX>`, be sure to lock these tags for exclusive execution.

Because the `<CFINDEX>` tag tells Verity to index your actual documents, the `<CFINDEX>` tag's various parameters simply give Verity the particulars about what you want it to do. Take a look at each of the parameters:

- **`COLLECTION`.** Tells Verity which collection to use.
- **`ACTION`.** Tells Verity you're interested in refreshing any data currently in the collection with new information. Other values are possible for `ACTION` other than `REFRESH`, and are discussed in the section "Maintaining Collections" later in this chapter.

- **TYPE.** Tells Verity you're interested in adding documents from a directory path on your Web server. You learn about another possible value for TYPE later, when using Verity to index database data rather than document files is covered. Refer to the section "Indexing Your Table Data: Verity to the Rescue," later in this chapter.
- **KEY.** Tells Verity from which directory path to add documents. This parameter must evaluate to the complete file system path to the actual documents you want to index.
- **EXTENSIONS.** Tells Verity which documents in the specified folder should be indexed. This parameter is useful if you want only certain types of documents to become searchable.
- **RECURSE.** Tells Verity whether you want it to index files in subfolders of the folder you specified with the KEY parameter. Possible values are YES and NO—usually, you specify YES for this parameter.
- **LANGUAGE.** Tells Verity in which language the documents are written. For the possible values, see the section "Specifying a Language," earlier in this chapter.
- **URLPATH.** Tells Verity to maintain URLs for each document, as it indexes, by appending the filename to the value you supply with this parameter. If RECURSE="YES" and the file is in a subfolder, the folder name is appended as well. As long as the value you supply here is the URL version of the value you supplied for KEY, Verity automatically records the correct URL for each file as it indexes. You see this in action later when you use the #URL# column returned by the <CFSEARCH> tag. This is discussed later in the section " The Search Results Page."

That's about all there is to indexing document files. Now all you have to do is ensure that the code in Listing 34.1 runs whenever new documents are saved to the C:\CfusionMX\wwwroot\ows\34\HR\Docs folder.

Creating a Search Interface

Now that you've created the HRDocs collection and you've learned both techniques for indexing it, you can start putting together the ColdFusion templates to make your documents searchable. You'll see that the code you use to do this is similar in concept to the examples in Chapter 11, "ColdFusion Forms."

Building the search interface involves constructing two pages. You need a simple search form page for users to enter their search criteria. This form's action template will actually conduct the search, using <CFSEARCH> and it can also display the search results.

The Search Form Page

Roll up your sleeves because we're writing more code: it's time to build a search form. Refer to Listing 34.2 and check out Figure 34.6.

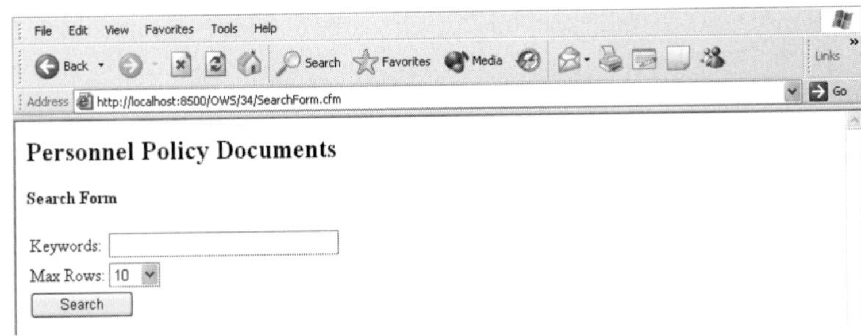

Figure 34.6
The search form enables you to specify text to search for in the collection.

This search form is similar to the search forms you worked through in Chapter 11. Refer to that chapter if you need to refresh your memory about the `<INPUT>` and `<SELECT>` tags that appear in Listing 34.2.

Listing 34.2 `SEARCHFORM.CFM`—The Search Form Page

```
<HTML>
<HEAD>
    <TITLE>Search Form</TITLE>
</HEAD>
<BODY>

<H2>Personnel Policy Documents</H2>
<P><B>Search Form</B>

<!--- Create search form --->
<FORM action="SearchResult.cfm" method="post">
<INPUT type="hidden" name="StartRow" value="1">

<TABLE>
<TR>
   <TD>Keywords:</TD>
   <TD><INPUT type="text" name="Criteria" size="30"></TD>
</TR>
<TR>
   <TD>Max Rows:</TD>
   <TD>
       <SELECT name="MaxRows">
       <OPTION> 10<OPTION> 25<OPTION> 100
       </SELECT>
   </TD>
</TR>
<TR>
   <TD colspan=2><INPUT type="submit" value="   Search   "></TD>
</TR>
</TABLE>
</FORM>
</BODY>
</HTML>
```

Figure 34.2 shows that the search form template contains a form that collects two pieces of information from the user. Most importantly, it collects the keywords the user wants to search for (the INPUT named Criteria). It also collects the maximum number of hits to display per page of search results (the <SELECT> named MaxRows).

The Search Results Page

This form submits these two pieces of information to the SEARCHRESULT.CFM template, which contains the code that actually runs the Verity search and displays the results of the search to the user.

Take a look at that template now. As Listing 34.3 shows, it contains only one ColdFusion tag that you're not familiar yet—the <CFSEARCH> tag.

Listing 34.3 SEARCHRESULT.CFM—The Search Results Page

```
<!--- Run the search against the HRDocs collection --->
<CFSEARCH
   name = "GetResults"
   collection = "HRDocs"
   criteria = "#Form.Criteria#"
   maxRows = "#Evaluate(Form.MaxRows + 1)#"
   startRow = "#Form.StartRow#"
>

<!--- Display results --->
<HTML>
<HEAD>
    <TITLE>Search Results</TITLE>
</HEAD>
<BODY bgcolor="ffffff">
<H2>Personnel Policy Documents</H2>
<B>Search Results</B>
<P>
<!--- no files found for specified criteria? --->
<CFIF GetResults.RecordCount is 0>
   <B>No files found for specified criteria</B>
<CFELSE>
   <!--- At least one file found --->
   <TABLE cellspacing=0 cellpadding=2>
   <TR bgcolor="cccccc">
      <TD><B>No</B></TD>
      <TD><B>Score</B></TD>
      <TD><B>File</B></TD>
      <TD><B>Title</B></TD>
   </TR>

   <CFOUTPUT query="GetResults" maxRows="#Form.MaxRows#">
   <TR bgcolor="#IIf(CurrentRow Mod 2, DE('ffffff'),
    DE('ffffcf'))#">

      <!--- current row information --->
      <TD>#Evaluate(Form.StartRow + CurrentRow - 1)#</TD>

      <!--- score --->
```

Listing 34.3 (continued)

```
<TD>#Score# </TD>
<!--- file name with the link returning the file --->
<TD>
   <!--- HREF to file is produced using either FILE protocol
      or HTTP, depending on whether this is a web document.
      so, we'll look at the file ext to determine if it's
      a web doc or not --->
   <CFSET FileName=GetFileFromPath(Key)>
   <CFSET Ext=Right(FileName,
    Evaluate(Find(".", Reverse(FileName))-1))>
   <CFIF ( Find(Ext,"htm,html,cfm,asp,dbm") GT 0)>
      <!--- If it's a web doc, use URL returned --->
      <A HREF="#GetResults.URL#">#GetFileFromPath(Key)#</A>
   <CFELSE>
      <!--- It's not a web doc, use file path in KEY from
       result --->
      <A HREF="#Key#">#GetFileFromPath(Key)#</A>
   </CFIF>
</TD>

<!--- title for HTML files --->
<TD>#Title# </TD>
</TR>
</CFOUTPUT>
</TABLE>

<!--- CFSEARCH tried to retrieve one more file than the
 number specified in the Form.MaxRows parameter. If
 number of retrieved files is greater than MaxRows we
 know that there is at least one file left. The following
 form contains only one button which reloads this template
 with the new StartRow parameter. --->
<CFIF GetResults.RecordCount gt Form.MaxRows>
   <FORM action="SearchResult.cfm" method="post">
   <CFOUTPUT>
      <INPUT type="hidden" name="Criteria"
       value="#Replace(Form.Criteria, """", "'", "ALL")#">
      <INPUT type="hidden" name="MaxRows" value="#Form.MaxRows#">
      <INPUT type="hidden" name="StartRow"
       value="#Evaluate(Form.StartRow + Form.MaxRows)#">
      <INPUT type="submit" value="    More ...    ">
   </CFOUTPUT>
   </FORM>
</CFIF> <!--- GetResults.RecordCount gt Form.MaxRows --->

</CFIF> <!--- GetResults.RecordCount is 0 --->

</BODY>
</HTML>
```

Clearly, the focus of this template is the `<CFSEARCH>` tag near the top. The `<CFSEARCH>` tag tells Verity to actually run a search—take the search criteria the user supplies and try to find documents that match.

Do you remember that Verity searches are similar to ODBC/SQL queries? With that similarity in mind, it's worth noting that the <CFSEARCH> tag acts a lot like the <CFQUERY> tag when you're dealing with database tables.

Take a look at the specific parameters you're supplying to the <CFSEARCH> tag in Listing 34.3. As you do so, keep in mind that most of these parameters look similar to the type of parameters you'd supply to a <CFQUERY> tag.

NOTE

The MAXROWS and STARTROW parameters listed here are used in the templates the wizard generated to create a Next 10 Records feature–the user can move through pages of search results–just like the ones you use on commercial search engines. The Next 10 Records functionality isn't explained in this chapter because it's not directly related to Verity. See Chapter 10, "Creating Data-Driven Pages," for an explanation of how to use MAXROWS and STARTROW to put together Next 10 Records types of solutions.

Here are the parameters for <CFSEARCH>, as used in Listing 34.3:

- **NAME.** Gives the search a name. Whatever results are found by Verity are available (for your use as a developer) as a query that has the name you supply here. You can use the search results in <CFOUTPUT> tags and in any of the other ways you normally use query results.
- **COLLECTION.** Tells Verity in which collection to search for documents. In this case, I'm directing it to the HRDocs collection I created and indexed in this chapter.
- **CRITERIA.** Is probably the most important parameter here. This is what you're actually asking Verity to look for. You're simply passing to this parameter whatever the user types in the search form.
- **MAXROWS.** Tells Verity to return only a certain number of rows. This is similar to using the MAXROWS parameter with the <CFQUERY> tag. Here, you're taking whatever the user indicated in the MaxRows SELECT on the search form and adding one to it.
- **STARTROW.** Tells Verity to return only the search results from a certain row in the search results on down. Here, you're taking the value specified by the hidden field named StartRow on the search form, so this value is always 1 for now. In other words, you're telling Verity to start returning the search results starting with the very first row.

TIP

<CFSEARCH> also takes a, TYPE parameter. You can use TYPE="SIMPLE" or TYPE="EXPLICIT" in your search templates. TYPE="SIMPLE" places the STEM and MANY operators into effect automatically (see Appendix E, "Verity Search Language Reference," for information on the STEM and MANY operators). Unless you specify EXPLICIT, SIMPLE is used by default. I recommend that you do not use EXPLICIT unless you have a specific reason to do so.

After the <CFSEARCH> is executed, the rest of Listing 34.3 displays the results to the user; it's fairly straightforward. See Figure 34.7. The main thing to keep in mind is that now that the <CFSEARCH> has found its results, you will treat it just as if it were a <CFQUERY> named GetResults.

First, a <CFIF> tag performs the now-familiar check to ensure that the built-in RecordCount variable is not 0 (which would mean Verity didn't find any results). See Chapter 10 for more information on the RecordCount variable.

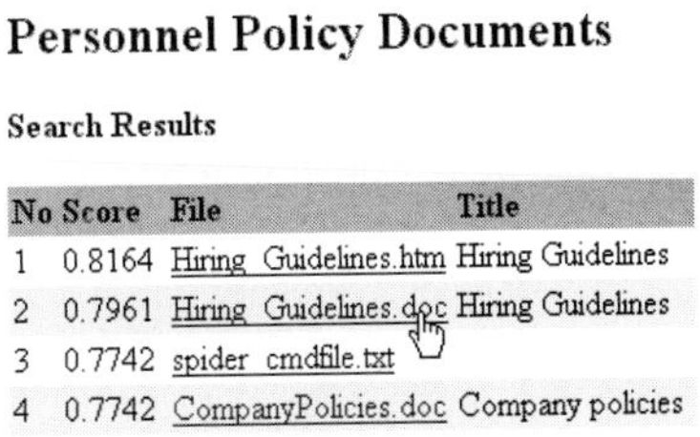

No	Score	File	Title
1	0.8164	Hiring_Guidelines.htm	Hiring Guidelines
2	0.7961	Hiring_Guidelines.doc	Hiring Guidelines
3	0.7742	spider_cmdfile.txt	
4	0.7742	CompanyPolicies.doc	Company policies

Personnel Policy Documents

Search Results

Figure 34.7

Your search results page shows a relevancy score, filename, and title (when available) for each document found.

Provided there are results to display, your code moves into the large `<CFELSE>` block that encompasses the remainder of the template. `<TABLE>`, `<TR>`, and `<TD>` tags are used to establish an HTML table in which to display the results, with headers. Refer to Chapter 10 for more examples of building tables row by row with query results.

Most of the important stuff happens in the large `<CFOUTPUT>` block that follows. The `QUERY="GetResults"` parameter in the `<CFOUTPUT>` tag causes this code to be executed once for each row in the search results, where each row represents a document found. Unlike a resultset returned by a `<CFQUERY>`—where you've specified which columns your resultset will contain by including them in the `SELECT` part of your SQL statement—resultsets returned by Verity searches always contain the same, predefined column names, which are shown in Table 34.2.

Table 34.2 Columns Returned by Verity Searches

COLUMN	CONTAINS
`Key`	The document's filename.
`TITLE`	The title of the document, if Verity is capable of determining what the title is. For example, if the file is an HTML document, Verity obtains the title from the `<TITLE>` tags in the document's `<HEAD>` section. Verity might not provide a title for other types of documents.
`SCORE`	The relevancy score for the document, which indicates how closely the document matched the search criteria. The score is always a value between `0` and `1`, where a score of `1` indicates a perfect match.
`URL`	The URL that can be used to obtain the file from your Web server. The information in this column is based on the information you supplied to the `<CFINDEX>` tag with its `URLPATH` parameter. If you did not specify a `URLPATH` parameter when indexing the collection, this column is blank.
`CUSTOM1`	The value of a custom field you specify when you populate the collection with `<CFINDEX>`. This information will be useful later when you build searches against collections consisting of database query results. See the section, "Indexing Additional Columns with Custom Fields."
`CUSTOM2`	This is the value of a second custom field you specify when you populate the collection with `<CFINDEX>`. Again, this is used in the same way as `CUSTOM1`.
`RECORDSSEARCHED`	The number of records Verity searched. In other words, the number of records in the collection(s).

The code in Listing 34.3 uses these columns to display the score, title, and filename for each document. It also uses the URL column in an HTML anchor tag's HREF attribute to provide a link to the document.

In addition, three predefined variables are available to you after a search runs. Table 34.3 explains these variables.

Table 34.3 Properties Available After a <CFSEARCH> Tag Executes

PROPERTY	INDICATES
ColumnList	Comma-separated list of the columns in this query result.
CurrentRow	This works just like the CurrentRow column returned by a <CFQUERY>. In a <CFOUTPUT> block that uses the search results in its QUERY parameter, CurrentRow is 1 for the first document returned by the <CFSEARCH>, 2 for the second document, and so on. See Chapter 10 for more discussion on CurrentRow.
RecordCount	Just as with <CFQUERY>, this is the number of matches Verity found. In this example, you access this variable using #GetResults.RecordCount# in your code.

You saw RecordCount in action in Listing 34.3. RecordsSearched can be used in much the same way, if you want to let the user know how many documents were searched to find his hits. For example, code like this:

```
<CFOUTPUT>
#GetResults.RecordCount# out of #GetResults.RecordsSearched#
documents found.
</CFOUTPUT>
```

would display something like:

```
10 out of 4363 documents found.
```

Running a Search

Your search tool should be operational. Pull up the search form in your browser and type "employee" in the blank. When you click Search, you should get a list of relevant documents from the OWS Human Resources Department, as shown in Figure 34.7.

NOTE

Listing 34.3 has a reference to a file called OPENFILE.CFM. That code is in the template to provide access to documents that do not reside in the Web server's document root, and it goes into effect only if the URL path is left blank when the collection is indexed. This OPENFILE template uses the <CFCONTENT> tag to get its job done. See Appendix B for more information on using the <CFCONTENT> tag.

Refining Your Search

Often, typing a few keywords isn't enough to find the documents you want. Verity provides a wealth of search operators to help you get the job done. By including special words such as AND, OR, and NOT in your search criteria, or by using various wildcards, your users can tweak their searches so they find exactly what they're looking for.

As you read through this section, note how Verity search criteria end up looking similar to SQL statements. It's nice that some common ground exists between the two, but it's also important to keep in mind that Verity's search language is not the same thing as SQL.

Using AND, OR, and NOT

If you want to refine your search a little, you can use special search operators in your search criteria to get more specific. Only the most common search operators are discussed at _this point. Many others are available for your use. See Appendix D, "Special ColdFusion Variables and Result Codes," for all the details on each of the search operators in Verity's search language.

Table 34.4 briefly describes the effect of using AND, OR, and NOT in your search criteria. These operators are very similar to the AND, OR, and NOT Boolean operators discussed in Chapter 5, "Introduction to SQL."

Table 34.4 Basic Search Operators

OPERATOR	EFFECT	EXAMPLE
AND	Searches for documents that have both words in it	`Verity AND Macromedia`
OR	Searches for documents that have either word in it	`Verity OR Macromedia`
NOT	Eliminates documents in which the word is found	`Verity NOT Macromedia`

TIP

A comma can be used instead of OR in search criteria. A search for `Verity, Macromedia` is therefore the same as a search for `Verity OR Macromedia`.

Using Parentheses and Quotation Marks

Search criteria can look ambiguous after more than two search words are present. For instance, if you typed in `Verity AND Macromedia OR ColdFusion`, what would that mean exactly? Documents that definitely contain Verity but that only need to contain Verity or ColdFusion? Documents that contain ColdFusion in addition to documents that contain both Verity and Macromedia?

Use parentheses and quotation marks to indicate this type of criteria, in which the order of evaluation needs to be specified. They make your intentions clear to Verity and are fairly easy to explain to users. Table 34.5 summarizes the use of parentheses and quotation marks.

Table 34.5 Examples: Quotation Marks and Parentheses

CHARACTER	PURPOSE	EXAMPLES
(Parentheses)	Determines how ANDs `Macromedia Fusion AND (Cold NOT Hot) OR (Cold AND Fusion)` and ORs are treated.	Words within parentheses are considered a unit and are considered first.
"Quotation Marks"	Quoted words or phrases ares earched for literally. Useful when you want to search for the actual words *and* or *or*.	`"Simple AND Explicit" Macromedia AND "not installed"`

Using Wildcards

Verity provides a few wildcards you can use in your searches, so you can find documents based on incomplete search words or phrases. The wildcards should look pretty familiar to you if you've used the `LIKE` operator with SQL queries, as discussed in Chapter 6, "SQL Data Manipulation. Table 34.6 summarizes the use of wildcard operators.

Table 34.6 The Two Most Common Wildcards

WILDCARD	PURPOSE
*	Similar to the `%` wildcard in SQL, `*` stands in for any number of characters (including 0). A search for `Fu*` would find `Fusion`, `Fugazi`, and `Fuchsia`.
?	Just as in SQL, `?` stands in for any single character. More precise—and thus generally less helpful—than the `*` wildcard. A search for `?ar?et` would find both `carpet` and `target`, but not `Learjet`.

➜ These aren't the only wildcards available for your use. See the `WILDCARD` operator in "Evidence Operators," in Appendix E, "Verity Search Language Reference."

Taking Case Sensitivity into Account

By default, a Verity search automatically becomes case sensitive whenever the characters provided as the `CRITERIA` parameter are of mixed case. A search for `employee`—or for `EMPLOYEE`—finds `employee`, `Employee`, or `EMPLOYEE`, but a search for `Employee` finds only `Employee`, not `employee` or `EMPLOYEE`. You might want to make this fact clear to your users by providing a message on your search forms, such as `"Type in all uppercase or all lowercase unless you want the search to be case sensitive."`

To have your application always ignore case regardless of what the user types, use ColdFusion's `LCase` function to convert the user's search words to lowercase when you supply them to `<CFSEARCH>`. For instance, by replacing the `<CFSEARCH>` in Listing 34.3 with the code in Listing 34.4, you guarantee that the search criteria passed to Verity is not of mixed case—you know the search will not be case sensitive.

Listing 34.4 Using `LCase` to Force Case-Insensitivity

```
<CFSEARCH
    name = "GetResults"
    collection = "HRDocs"
    criteria = "#LCase(Form.Criteria)#"
    maxRows = "#Evaluate(Form.MaxRows + 1)#"
    startRow = "#Form.StartRow#"
>
```

Indexing SQL Data

You've seen how easy it is to use ColdFusion's Verity VDK functionality to index all sorts of files on your system. What if you want to index and search information in your database files? ColdFusion enables you to build a Verity index from data in your database as if the data was a bunch of document files.

In this section you see how Verity enables you to neatly get around the limitations that make SQL less than ideal for true text-based searching. By the time you're finished, you'll have a good understanding of when you should unleash Verity's rich search capabilities on your database data and when you're better off leaving things to SQL instead.

➜ The examples in this section use the code listings directory located on the CD-ROM. The tables are populated with some example data with which to work.

Doing it without Verity

You don't need to use Verity to make your database searchable, but it can make implementing a search interface much easier and enable your users to more easily find what they want. Take a look at what you'd need to do to search your data using the tools you already know: `<CFQUERY>` and SQL.

Say you want to set up a little search tool to enable your users to search the OWS database's `Merchandise` table. You want the user to be able to type a word or two into a form field and click Search to get the matching item.

The code in Listing 34.5 is a simple search form. This will remind you a lot of the search forms explained in Chapter 11. The form is displayed in a browser, as shown in Figure 34.8.

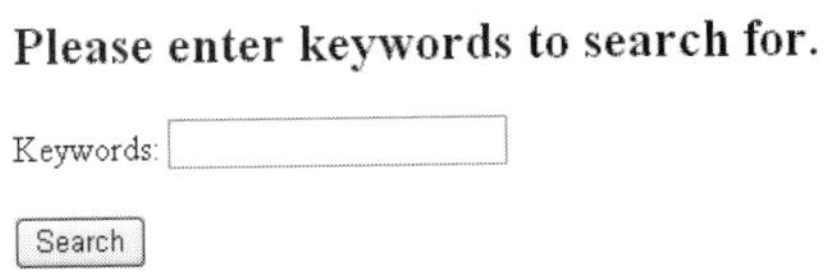

Figure 34.8

The Merchandise Search form lets you search against SQL data.

Please enter keywords to search for.

Keywords: [ ]

[Search]

Listing 34.5 `MERCHANDISESEARCH_FORM.CFM`—A Simple Merchandise Search Form

```
<!--- Create a search form --->
<HTML>
<HEAD>
   <TITLE>Merchandise Search</TITLE>
</HEAD>

<BODY>

<H2>Please enter keywords to search for.</H2>

<FORM ACTION="MerchandiseSearch_Action.cfm" METHOD="POST">
Keywords: <INPUT TYPE="text" NAME="Criteria"><BR>
<P><INPUT TYPE="submit" VALUE="Search">
</FORM>

</BODY>
</HTML>
```

Again borrowing heavily from Chapter 10, you could come up with the code in Listing 34.6 for searching and displaying the results from the `Merchandise` table. Note that the `LIKE` keyword is used along with the `%` wildcard to search any part of the description. See Chapter 10 if you need to jog your memory on the use of the `LIKE` keyword.

Listing 34.6 MERCHANDISESEARCH_ACTION.CFM—Code for Searching the Inventory

```
<!--- Execute SQL query to do the searching --->
<CFQUERY NAME="GetResults" DATASOURCE="ows">
  SELECT MerchID, MerchDescription
  FROM Merchandise
  WHERE (MerchDescription LIKE '%#Form.Criteria#%')
</CFQUERY>

<!--- Display the query results --->
<HTML>
<HEAD>
   <TITLE>Search Results</TITLE>
</HEAD>

<BODY>
<H2><CFOUTPUT>
#GetResults.RecordCount# Merchandise record(s) found for "#Form.Criteria#".
</CFOUTPUT>
</H2>

<!--- loop through each row outputting the description --->
<UL>
<CFOUTPUT QUERY="GetResults">
  <LI>#MerchDescription#
</CFOUTPUT>
</UL>

</BODY>
</HTML>
```

This would work fine as long as your application required only simple searching. If the user entered "*poster*" for the search criteria, SQL's `LIKE` operator would faithfully find all the merchandise that had the word `poster` somewhere in the description, as shown in Figure 34.9.

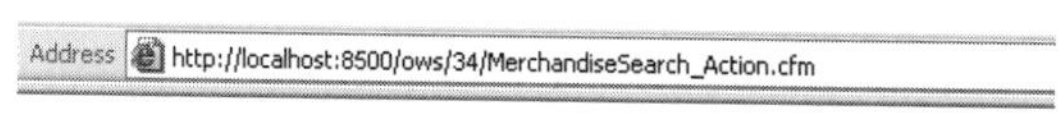

1 Merchandise record(s) found for "poster".

- Wonderful poster showing all the stars, winking.

Figure 34.9

Your Verity-free code works fine for simple, one-word searches.

What if the user entered something such as West End Tee? No records would be found because no records have those exact words in them (although one merchandise item does have the phrase "...West End Story Tee"). That's a limitation your users probably won't find acceptable.

Maybe you need to modify your `<CFQUERY>` a little, to account for multiple-word searches. Listing 34.7 contains a revised query that should take multiple words into account. Each word is treated separately because the `<CFLOOP>` adds an additional `AND` condition to the query for each word in the user's input. Only books that contain all the words entered in the blank will be found. See Chapter 9, "CFML Basics," for a detailed discussion of the `<CFLOOP>` tag.

Listing 34.7 MERCHANDISESEARCH_ACTION2.CFM—Getting SQL to Account for Multiple Words

```
<!--- Run the query, building 'where clause' dynamically --->
<CFQUERY NAME="GetResults" DATASOURCE="ows">
  SELECT MerchID, MerchDescription
  FROM Merchandise
  WHERE (0=0
  <CFLOOP LIST="#Form.Criteria#" INDEX="ThisWord" DELIMITERS=" ">
    AND (MerchDescription LIKE '%#ThisWord#%')
  </CFLOOP>)
</CFQUERY>

<!--- Display the results --->
<HTML>
<HEAD>
   <TITLE>Search Results</TITLE>
</HEAD>

<BODY>
<H2><CFOUTPUT>
#GetResults.RecordCount# Merchandise record(s) found for "#Form.Criteria#".
</CFOUTPUT>
</H2>

<UL>
<CFOUTPUT QUERY="GetResults">
  <LI>#MerchDescription#
</CFOUTPUT>
</UL>

</BODY>
</HTML>
```

Now the appropriate merchandise item will be found if the user enters *West End Tee*. What if your user wants to search for *Tee, West End*? There are other reasons SQL searches won't cut it when a real search engine is needed. For example, if the search phrase includes symbols such as apostrophes or hyphens, SQL won't find matches unless the user's criteria is an exact match.

This is the kind of intelligence users have come to expect from a real search engine. Theoretically, you could come up with various `CFLOOP`s and `CFIF`s that build SQL code to cover all those scenarios, but that many `WHERE`s, `LIKE`s, `AND`s, and `OR`s would be a real pain to code, debug, and maintain. In addition, performance degrades as the number of merchandise items grows. Indexing the text columns won't improve performance because the `LIKE` operator can't take advantage of indexes when a wildcard operator precedes the search string. There has to be a better way.

Indexing Your Table Data: Verity to the Rescue

ColdFusion's Verity functionality provides a well-performing, easy-to-implement solution that addresses all these concerns. You create a custom Verity collection filled with documents that aren't really documents at all. Each document is actually just a record from your database tables.

It works like this: You write a `<CFQUERY>` that retrieves the data you want to make searchable. You pass this data to a `<CFINDEX>` tag, which indexes the data as if it were documents. Additionally, you tell Verity which column from the query should be considered a document "filename," which column should be considered a document "title," and which column(s) should be considered a document's "body." Figure 34.10 illustrates the idea.

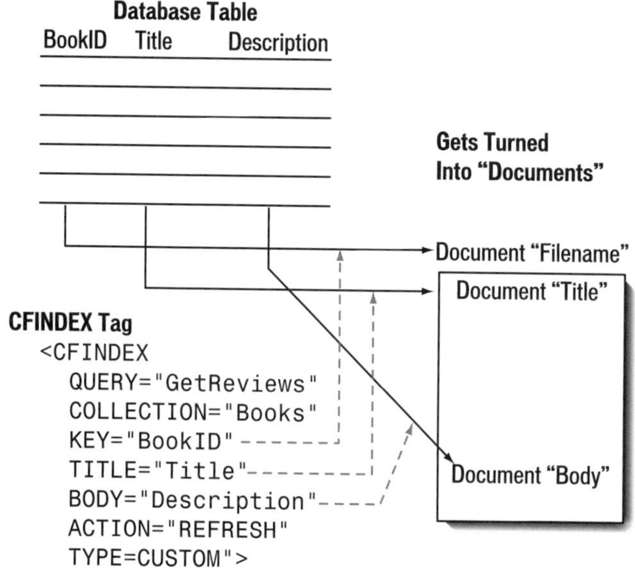

Figure 34.10
Database data becomes searchable, just like regular documents.

Assume you've just used the ColdFusion Administrator to create a new Verity collection called `Merchandise`, as discussed earlier in this chapter. You'll populate this new collection with data from the `Merchandise` database table.

Take a look at the code in Listing 34.8. Notice that the `<CFINDEX>` tag looks similar to Listing 34.1, in which you indexed your document files. The central differences here are the fact that you're setting `TYPE` to `CUSTOM` instead of `PATH` and that you're referring to column names from a `<CFQUERY>`.

Listing 34.8 `INDEXDATA.CFM`—Code to Index a Collection with Database Data

```
<!--- Run query to retrieve all merchandise to be searched --->
<CFQUERY NAME="GetResults" DATASOURCE="OWS">
  SELECT MerchID, MerchName, MerchDescription
  FROM Merchandise
</CFQUERY>

<!---
Lock the index operation as it uses a shared resource
--->
<CFLOCK TYPE="EXCLUSIVE" TIMEOUT="15">
<!--- Build 'custom' index on query result above --->
```

Listing 34.8 (continued)

```
<CFINDEX
   ACTION="REFRESH"
   COLLECTION="Merchandise"
   KEY="MerchID"
   TYPE="CUSTOM"
   TITLE="MerchName"
   QUERY="GetResults"
   BODY="MerchDescription"
>
</CFLOCK>
<HTML>
<HEAD>
   <TITLE>Indexing Complete</TITLE>
</HEAD>
<BODY>

<H2>Indexing Complete</H2>

</BODY>
</HTML>
```

The `<CFQUERY>` part is very simple—just get the basic information about the books. (Obviously, if you only want certain books to be indexed, a `WHERE` clause could be added to the `<CFQUERY>`'s SQL statement.) Next comes a `<CFINDEX>` tag, which looks a lot like the `<CFINDEX>` tag you used earlier to index your normal document files.

This time around, though, you specify a few new parameters that are necessary when indexing a database table instead of normal documents:

- **`ACTION="REFRESH"`.** As before, this tells Verity that you're supplying new data.
- **`TYPE="CUSTOM"`.** Says that you're dealing with table data, rather than document files.
- **`QUERY="GetResults"`.** Specifies from which `<CFQUERY>` to get the data.
- **`KEY, TITLE, BODY`.** Specifies which query columns should be treated like which parts of a document.

That's really about all there is to it. After the `INDEXDATA.CFM` template is executed, you should be able to search the `Merchandise` collection in much the same way as you searched the `HRDocs` collection in Listing 34.3.

The code in Listing 34.9 searches through the newly indexed Merchandise collection, based on whatever criteria the user types in the search form. Except for the introduction of the `<CFSEARCH>` tag, this code is virtually unchanged from Listing 34.6; the results are displayed to the user as shown in Figure 34.11.

TIP

Listing 34.5's Merchandise search form–be sure to change the `ACTION` parameter of the `FORM` tag to `"MerchandiseSearch_Action3.cfm"`.

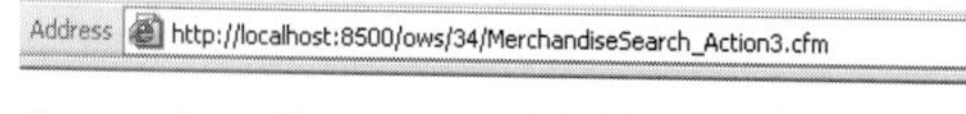

1 merchandise item(s) found for "poster".

- Poster

Figure 34.11 <CFSEARCH> and <CFQUERY> can work well together, through SQL's `IN` keyword and ColdFusion's `ValueList` function.

Listing 34.9 `MERCHANDISESEARCH_ACTION3.CFM`—Searching and Displaying Records from a Database

```
<!--- Search collection built on SQL query --->
<CFSEARCH COLLECTION="Merchandise"
   NAME="GetResults"
   CRITERIA="#Form.Criteria#"
>

<HTML>
<HEAD>
   <TITLE>Search Results</TITLE>
</HEAD>
<BODY>
<!--- Display results --->
<H2><CFOUTPUT>
#GetResults.RecordCount# merchandise item(s) found for "#Form.Criteria#".
</CFOUTPUT></H2>

<UL>
<CFOUTPUT QUERY="GetResults">
  <LI>#Title#
</CFOUTPUT>
</UL>
</BODY>
</HTML>
```

As you can see, exposing your database data to Verity was easy. You really didn't have to do much work at all. Of course, the user will notice a tremendous difference: All Verity's `AND`, `OR`, `NOT`, wildcarding, and other searching niceties are suddenly very much available.

Displaying a Summary for Each Record

In addition to the score and title, Verity also provides a summary for each record in the search results. The summary is the first three sentences—or the first 500 characters—of the information you specified for the body when you indexed the collection with the `<CFINDEX>` tag. The summary helps the user to eyeball which documents he is interested in.

To display the summary to the user, refer to it in your ColdFusion templates in the same way you refer to the key, score, or title. Figure 34.12 shows what the search results will look like to the user.

Figure 34.12

Displaying the document summary is a slick, professional-looking touch.

Address http://localhost:8500/ows/34/MerchandiseSearch_Action4.cfm

1 books found for "poster".

77% **Poster**
Wonderful poster showing all the stars, winking.

Listing 34.10 MERCHANDISESEARCH_ACTION4.CFM—Code to Include a Summary for Each Document

```
<!--- Search Verity collection --->
<CFSEARCH
   COLLECTION="Merchandise"
   NAME="GetResults"
   CRITERIA="#Form.Criteria#"
>

<HTML>
<HEAD>
   <TITLE>Search Results</TITLE>
</HEAD>

<BODY>
<H2><CFOUTPUT>
#GetResults.RecordCount# books found for "#Form.Criteria#".
</CFOUTPUT></H2>

<!--- Use definition list to disply Verity output
  score, title and summary from each item found. --->
<DL>
<CFOUTPUT QUERY="GetResults">
  <DT><I>#NumberFormat(Round(Score * 100))#%</I>
      <B>#Title#</B>
  <DD><FONT SIZE="-1">#Summary#</FONT>
</CFOUTPUT>
</DL>
</BODY>
</HTML>
```

Don't expect Verity summaries to always show the parts of the document that contain the search keywords; that's not how Verity summarization works. Verity selects each record's summary at the time the collection is indexed, and it is always the same for any given record, regardless of whatever the search criteria were that found it. The summary does not necessarily contain the keywords that were used as the search criteria.

Indexing Multiple Query Columns as the Body

In Listing 34.8 you indexed the `Merchandise` collection with the results from a query. In that listing, you declared that the `MerchDescription` column from the `Merchandise` table should be considered the body of each book record (by setting the `BODY` parameter of the `<CFINDEX>` tag to `"MerchDescription"`).

By default, when your application runs a Verity search, only the Body part of each record is actually searched for matching words. The information in the Title part of the record is not searched.

There are two ways to make the title searchable. One is to specify the title in the `CRITERIA` parameter, using relational operators and the `SUBSTRING` operator.

➜ See the section "Indexing Additional Columns with Custom Fields."

An easier way is to go back to your `<CFINDEX>` tag and supply the information you're giving to the `TITLE` parameter to the `BODY` parameter as well. The `BODY` parameter can take a comma-separated list of column names (`"MerchName,MerchDescription"`), rather than only one column name (`"MerchDescription"`). The searchable part of each record in your database is composed of the `MerchName` of the item, followed by the `MerchDescription` of the item.

There's no need to stop there. You can put a bunch of column names in the `BODY` parameter, as shown in Listing 34.11. For each row returned by the query, ColdFusion concatenates the `MerchDescription` and `MerchName` columns and presents them to Verity as the `BODY` of each document. The result is that all textual information about the merchandise description and name is now part of your collection and instantly searchable. You don't have to change a thing about the code in any of your search templates.

Listing 34.11 `INDEXDATA2.CFM`—Supplying More Than One Column to the `BODY` Parameter

```
<!--- Produce query results to be indexed --->
<CFQUERY NAME="GetResults" DATASOURCE="OWS">
  SELECT MerchID, MerchName, MerchDescription
  FROM Merchandise
</CFQUERY>

<!---
Lock the index operation as it uses a shared resource
--->
<CFLOCK TYPE="EXCLUSIVE" TIMEOUT="15">
<!--- Index both MerchName and MerchDescription fields --->
<CFINDEX
   ACTION="REFRESH"
   COLLECTION="Merchandise"
   TYPE="CUSTOM"
   KEY="MerchID"
   TITLE="MerchName"
   QUERY="GetResults"
   BODY="MerchName,MerchDescription"
>
</CFLOCK>
<HTML>
<HEAD>
   <TITLE>Indexing Complete</TITLE>
</HEAD>
<BODY>

<H2>Indexing Complete</H2>
</BODY>
</HTML>
```

It's important to note that when you supply several columns to the BODY parameter, Verity does not maintain the information in separate columns, fields, or anything else. The underlying table's structure is not preserved; all the information is pressed together into one big, searchable mass. Don't expect to be able to refer to a #MerchName# variable, for instance, in the same way you can refer to the #Title# and #Score# variables after a <CFSEARCH> is executed.

That might or might not feel like a limitation, depending on the nature of the applications you're building. In a way, it's just the flip side of Verity's concentrating on text in a natural-language kind of way, rather than being obsessed with columns the way SQL is.

However, ColdFusion and Verity do enable you to store a limited amount of information in a more database-like way, using something called *custom fields*.

Indexing Additional Columns with Custom Fields

ColdFusion enables you to index up to two additional Verity fields when you're indexing database data. The fields—CUSTOM1 and CUSTOM2—are treated similarly to the Title field you've already worked with. These custom fields come in handy when you have precise, code-style data you want to keep associated with each record.

In Listing 34.12, you adjust the code from Listing 34.8 to fill the CUSTOM1 field with your FilmID. Conceptually, it's as if Verity were making a little note on each document that it makes from the rows of your query. The CUSTOM1 note is the FilmID. This example doesn't use the CUSTOM2 attribute, but it is used exactly the same way as CUSTOM1.

Listing 34.12 INDEXDATA3.CFM—Adding Custom Fields to a Collection

```
<!--- Produce query results to be indexed --->
<CFQUERY NAME="GetResults" DATASOURCE="OWS">
  SELECT MerchID, MerchName, MerchDescription, FilmID
  FROM Merchandise
</CFQUERY>

<!---
Lock the index operation as it uses a shared resource
--->
<CFLOCK TYPE="EXCLUSIVE" TIMEOUT="15">
<!--- Index both MerchName and MerchDescription fields --->
<CFINDEX
   ACTION="REFRESH"
   COLLECTION="Merchandise"
   TYPE="CUSTOM"
   KEY="MerchID"
   TITLE="MerchName"
   QUERY="GetResults"
   BODY="MerchName,MerchDescription"
   CUSTOM1="FilmID"
>
</CFLOCK>
<HTML>
<HEAD>
   <TITLE>Indexing Complete</TITLE>
```

Listing 34.12 (continued)

```
</HEAD>
<BODY>

<H2>Indexing Complete</H2>

</BODY>

</HTML>
```

Now that Verity knows the `FilmID` for each record in the collection, you easily can create a more sophisticated search tool that enables the user to select films along with her search words, similar to Listing 34.13. Figure 34.13 shows what the search form looks like.

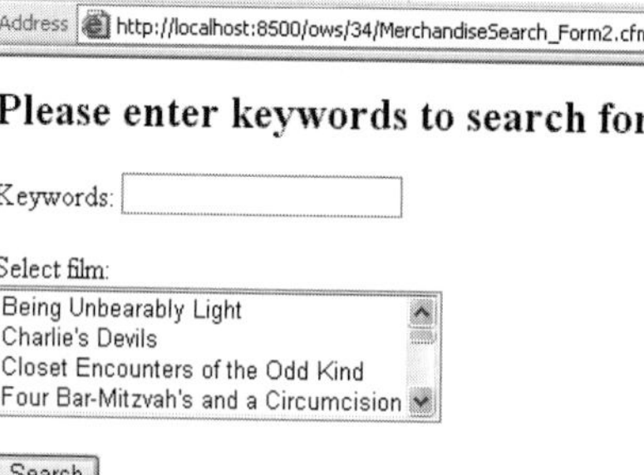

Figure 34.13

Custom fields provide a simple way to handle search forms such as this one.

Listing 34.13 `MERCHANDISESEARCH_FORM2.CFM`—Search Form with User Interface

```
<!--- Get the movie titles for drop down list --->
<CFQUERY NAME="GetFilms" DATASOURCE="ows">
   SELECT FilmID, MovieTitle
   FROM Films
</CFQUERY>

<HTML>
<HEAD>
   <TITLE>Merchandise Search</TITLE>
</HEAD>

<BODY>
<!--- Search criteria form includes ability to search for
   merchandise by movie title. --->
<H2>Please enter keywords to search for.</H2>
<FORM ACTION="MerchandiseSearch_Action5.cfm" METHOD="POST">
Keywords: <INPUT TYPE="text" NAME="Criteria"><BR>
<P>Select film:<BR>
<SELECT SIZE="4" NAME="FilmID">
<CFOUTPUT QUERY="GetFilms"><OPTION VALUE="#FilmID#">#MovieTitle#
</CFOUTPUT>
</SELECT>
<P><INPUT TYPE="submit" VALUE="Search">
</FORM>

</BODY>
</HTML>
```

Now you just need to teach the receiving template how to deal with the user's entries for the FilmID field. To specify the additional criteria, use Verity's MATCHES operator, which you use here for the first time.

The MATCHES operator searches specific document fields—rather than the body—and *finds only exact matches*. Document fields you can use MATCHES with include CF_CUSTOM1, CF_CUSTOM2, CF_TITLE, and CF_KEY, all of which correspond to the values you supply to the <CFINDEX> tag when you index the data.

TIP

Depending on the situation, you could use the Verity operators **CONTAINS**, **STARTS**, **ENDS**, and **SUBSTRING** in place of **MATCHES** in the this code. You also could use numeric operators, such as =, <, and >, with the **CF_CUSTOM2** field. See the section "Relational Operators" in Appendix E for more information.

Listing 34.14 demonstrates the use of the MATCHES search operator. At the top of the template, you use some <CFIF>, <CFELSE>, and <CFELSEIF> tags to decide what you're going to ask Verity to look for. If the user specifies a specific film (using the <SELECT> list, FilmID), you will ignore the keywords. If the FilmID is blank, search for the keywords the user enters—but, be sure he specified either keywords or a film.

Depending on which field the user might have left blank, the TheCriteria variable will have slightly different values. The TheCriteria variable is then supplied to the <CFSEARCH> tag in its CRITERIA parameter.

Listing 34.14 MERCHANDISESEARCH_ACTION5.CFM—Using the MATCHES Search Operator

```
<!--- Setup search criteria. Can be either merchandise for a
   specific film or search against merchandise name & desc or both--->
<CFIF IsDefined("Form.FilmID")>
   <!--- FilmID is specified --->
   <CFSET TheCriteria = "CF_CUSTOM1 <MATCHES> #Form.FilmID#">
<CFELSEIF (Form.Criteria NEQ "")>
   <!--- Film and keywords were specified --->
   <CFSET TheCriteria = "#Form.Criteria#">
<CFELSE>
   <!--- Neither keywords nor FilmID were specified --->
   <CFABORT SHOWERROR="Please enter your criteria">
</CFIF>
<!--- Execute the search --->
<CFSEARCH
   COLLECTION="Merchandise"
   NAME="GetResults"
   CRITERIA="#TheCriteria#"
>
<HTML>
<HEAD>
   <TITLE>Search Results</TITLE>
</HEAD>

<BODY>
<!--- Indicate number of 'records' returned --->
<H2><CFOUTPUT>#GetResults.RecordCount# merchandise item(s) found.</CFOUTPUT></H2>
```

Listing 34.14 (CONTINUED)

```
<P ALIGN="RIGHT">
<!--- Display the criteria used in the search --->
<CFOUTPUT>Actual Criteria Used:#HTMLEditFormat(TheCriteria)#
</CFOUTPUT>
</P>

<!--- Display results in a definition list --->
<DL>
<CFOUTPUT QUERY="GetResults">
  <DT><I>#NumberFormat(Round(Score * 100))#%</I>
      <B>#Title#</B>
  <DD><FONT SIZE="-1"><I>FilmID #Custom1#.</I> #Summary#</FONT>
</CFOUTPUT>
</DL>

</BODY>
</HTML>
```

As you can see in Listing 34.14, this code presents the `FilmID` to the user by using the `#Custom1#` variable in the `<CFOUTPUT>` block, along with the summary, score, and other information. Also note that this code displays the criteria that are actually being passed to Verity at the top of the page, so you can fool around with the template a bit if you want and see the effect your `<CFIF>` logic is having. The results are presented in Figure 34.14.

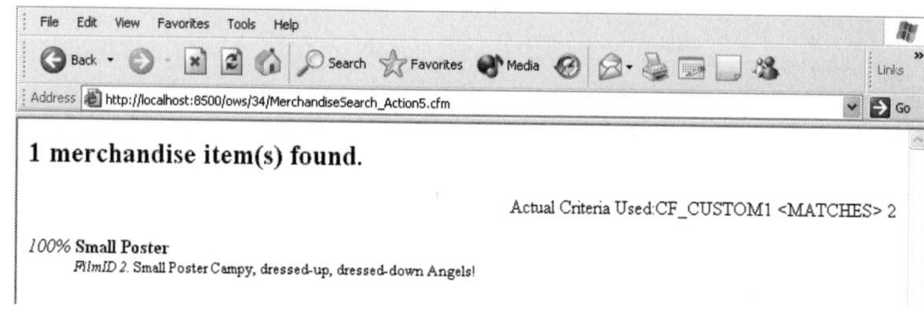

Figure 34.14
Custom fields let you display related information about each record found.

Combining Verity Searches with SQL Queries On-the-Fly

The custom fields you just learned about give you a lot of flexibility. In most cases, you'll be able to search and display records straight from your Verity collection(s), without bothering the underlying database tables.

You might encounter situations in which you want to get information from Verity and from your database tables, presenting the information together to the user. This is quite easy to pull off: Use ColdFusion's `ValueList` function along with SQL's `IN` operator.

Say you want to run a Verity search on the Merchandise collection, but you want to be able to show the current, up-to-the minute price on each item. You consider the idea of feeding the MerchPrice column to `CUSTOM1` or `CUSTOM2`, but you know that Orange Whip Studios changes the prices, well, hourly! So you decide you must get the live value directly from the database table.

You run a <CFSEARCH> just as you already have, but you won't display anything from it. Instead, you just use Verity's results as criteria for a normal SQL query. Verity supplies you with the key value for each document it finds, which you know happens to be the MerchID from your Merchandise table. You'll supply those MerchIDs to a normal <CFQUERY>.

Listing 34.15 shows how to use <CFSEARCH> results to drive a <CFQUERY> in this manner. Figure 34.15 shows the results.

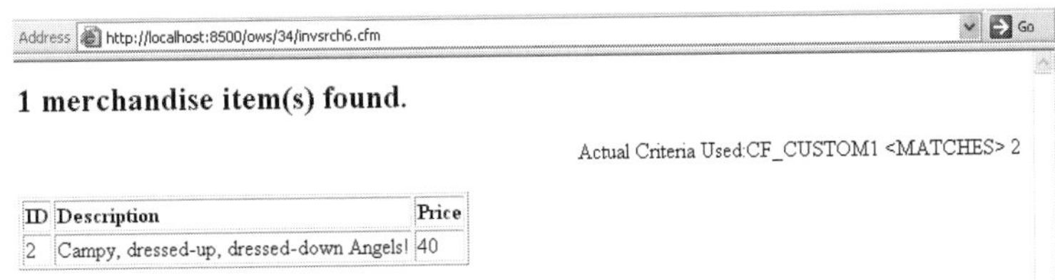

Figure 34.15
<CFSEARCH> and <CFQUERY> can work well together, through SQL's IN keyword and ColdFusion's ValueList function.

Listing 34.15 INVSRCH6.CFM—Using Verity Results as Criteria for a Normal SQL Query

```
<!--- Set up search criteria for Verity search --->
<CFIF IsDefined("Form.FilmID")>
   <!--- FilmID is specified --->
   <CFSET TheCriteria = "CF_CUSTOM1 <MATCHES> #Form.FilmID#">
<CFELSEIF (Form.Criteria NEQ "")>
   <!--- Film and keywords were specified --->
   <CFSET TheCriteria = "#Form.Criteria#">
<CFELSE>
   <!--- Neither keywords nor FilmID were specified --->
   <CFABORT SHOWERROR="Please enter your criteria">
</CFIF>

<!--- Execute Verity search; results 'Key' value is MerchID --->
<CFSEARCH
   COLLECTION="Merchandise"
   NAME="GetResults"
   CRITERIA="#TheCriteria#"
>
<!--- If no results found must stop. If we let GetPrices
   query run, an error would result from GetResults.Key
   begin a null string. --->
<CFIF GetResults.Key EQ "">
   <CFABORT SHOWERROR="No matching merchandise.">
</CFIF>

<!--- Assuming the search found something, feed results from
   Verity search (key = MerchID) into SQL query using ValueList
   function. --->
<CFQUERY NAME="GetPrices" DATASOURCE="ows">
   SELECT MerchID, MerchDescription, MerchPrice
   FROM Merchandise
   WHERE MerchID IN (#ValueList(GetResults.Key)#)
</CFQUERY>

<!--- Display the results --->
```

Listing 34.15 (continued)

```
<HTML>
<HEAD>
   <TITLE>Search Results</TITLE>
</HEAD>

<BODY>
<H2><CFOUTPUT>#GetPrices.RecordCount# merchandise item(s) found.</CFOUTPUT></H2>

<P ALIGN="RIGHT">
<CFOUTPUT>Actual Criteria Used:#HTMLEditFormat(Variables.TheCriteria)#
</CFOUTPUT>
</P>

<CFTABLE QUERY="GetPrices" COLHEADERS HTMLTABLE BORDER>
  <CFCOL HEADER="ID" TEXT="#MerchID#">
  <CFCOL HEADER="Description" TEXT="#MerchDescription#">
  <CFCOL HEADER="Price" TEXT="#MerchPrice#">
</CFTABLE>

</BODY>
</HTML>
```

NOTE

When you use this strategy, the search results no longer are sorted by relevance. Instead, they are sorted according to the ORDER BY part of your SQL statement. This can be a good or a bad thing, depending on your situation. Keep it in mind.

Understanding Verity and Your Table's Key Values

When you're indexing table data, it's important to understand that Verity doesn't think of the concept of a key in the same way that your database tables do. Specifically, Verity does not assume or enforce any rules about uniqueness of values you feed it with <CFINDEX>'s KEY parameter. This means Verity can and will index two separate documents that have the same key value. This can lead to problems, especially if the data you're indexing is derived from two tables that have a master-detail relationship to one another.

For instance, say you want to include the names of the people who placed orders for each of the merchandise items into the Verity collection. As you learned in Chapter 29, "More About SQL and Queries," creating a join query that retrieves this information from your database tables is fairly simple.

The problem is that any number of orders can be placed for each piece of merchandise. Therefore, if seven customers have ordered an item, seven rows will exist for that item in the result set. This poses a problem. Verity will dutifully index each of these rows as a separate document, without understanding that the seven rows all represent the same item. So, a search that matches with the description of the item finds all seven records and displays them to the user. This can make your application look buggy.

ColdFusion provides no built-in way out of this. <CFINDEX> doesn't have a GROUP parameter like CFOUTPUT does; you can't use GROUP when you're displaying the records because the seven rows aren't guaranteed to be in consecutive rows when Verity finds them. You need to either avoid this kind of situation altogether or figure out some way of processing the data between <CFQUERY> and <CFINDEX>.

Here's one approach. The code in Listing 34.16 takes the query results and manually creates a second query, line by line. The new query has the same structure as the original, except that it is guaranteed to have only one row for each MerchID. If the original query had more than one row for a particular MerchID (because of multiple orders), the customer names from all the rows would be turned into a comma-separated list when they were put into the new query. The result is a query that can be used to index a Verity collection without problems.

Listing 34.16 INDEXDATA4.CFM—Creating a Query Result to Store One Record for Each Type of Merchandise Item Purchased

```
<!--- Select merchandise and customer names by joining
   Contacts, Merchandise and MerchandiseOrders --->
<CFQUERY NAME="GetResults" DATASOURCE="OWS">
SELECT
   M.MerchID, M.MerchName, M.MerchDescription,
   C.LastName
FROM
   Contacts C, Merchandise M, MerchandiseOrders O,
   MerchandiseOrdersItems OI
WHERE
   M.MerchID = OI.ItemID AND
   OI.OrderID = O.OrderID AND
   O.ContactID = C.ContactID
ORDER BY
   M.MerchID
</CFQUERY>

<!--- Create new query object with same column names --->
<CFSET MerchCustomers = QueryNew(GetResults.ColumnList)>

<!--- This CFOUTPUT groups by Merchandise item --->
<CFOUTPUT QUERY="GetResults" GROUP="MerchID">
  <!--- Make a comma-separated list of all papers for each MerchID --->
  <CFSET LastNameList = "">
  <!--- This CFOUTPUT loops on individual rows (merchandise items
     from GetResults query and builds a list of the names of
     customers who have purchased that item. --->
  <CFOUTPUT><CFSET LastNameList = ListAppend(LastNameList,
  GetResults.LastName)>
  </CFOUTPUT>
  <!--- Make new row in MerchCustomers, with other data just copied from
     GetResults; add list of customers who have purchased each item
     to the field, LastName. --->
  <CFSET Temp = QueryAddRow(MerchCustomers)>
  <CFSET Temp = QuerySetCell(MerchCustomers,"MerchID",GetResults.MerchID)>
  <CFSET Temp = QuerySetCell(MerchCustomers,"MerchName",GetResults.MerchName)>
  <CFSET Temp = QuerySetCell(MerchCustomers,"MerchDescription",
 GetResults.MerchDescription)>
  <CFSET Temp = QuerySetCell(MerchCustomers,"LastName",LastNameList)>
 </CFOUTPUT>
```

Listing 34.16 (continued)

```
<!---
Lock the indexing function as we're working with
a shared resource.
--->
<CFLOCK TYPE="EXCLUSIVE" TIMEOUT="30">
<!--- Now build index on this new query result --->
<CFINDEX
   ACTION="UPDATE"
   COLLECTION="Merchandise"
   KEY="MerchID"
   TYPE="CUSTOM"
   TITLE="MerchDescription"
   QUERY="MerchCustomers"
   BODY="MerchDescription,LastName"
>
</CFLOCK>
<HTML>
<HEAD>
   <TITLE>Indexing Complete</TITLE>
</HEAD>

<BODY>

<H2>Indexing Complete</H2>

</BODY>
</HTML>
```

After this code is run, if the user types a company name in a search form, the `<CFSEARCH>` finds books the specified company has actually ordered.

Searching on More Than One Collection

To specify more than one Verity collection in a `<CFSEARCH>` tag, just specify all the collection names for the `COLLECTION` parameter and separate them with commas. All the collections are searched for matching documents.

If you want to allow your users to choose from several collections, you could add the code from Listing 34.17 to your search form.

Listing 34.17 `MERCHANDISESEARCH_FORM3.CFM`—Form Enables User to Search More Than One Collection

```
<HTML>
<HEAD>
   <TITLE>Collection Search</TITLE>
</HEAD>

<BODY>
<!--- This form enables user to search multiple collections --->
<H2>Please enter keywords to search for.</H2>

<FORM ACTION="search_action.cfm" METHOD="POST">
<INPUT TYPE="Hidden" NAME="Collections_required"
       VALUE="You must choose at least one collection.">
```

Listing 34.17 (continued)

```
Keywords: <INPUT TYPE="text" NAME="Criteria"><BR>
<!--- Identify each collection that can be searched --->
<INPUT TYPE="Checkbox" NAME="Collections" VALUE="Merchandise">Merchandise
<INPUT TYPE="Checkbox" NAME="Collections" VALUE="HRDocs">Personnel Policies

<P>
<INPUT TYPE="submit" VALUE="Search">

</FORM>
</BODY>
</HTML>
```

Because of the convenient way check boxes are handled by ColdFusion, the value of the `Form.Collections` variable is set to `"Merchandise,HRDocs"` if the user checks both boxes. You would pass the variable directly to the `COLLECTION` parameter of the receiving template's `<CFSEARCH>` tag.

NOTE

Note that you can freely mix normal document collections with database-table collections within a single `<CFSEARCH>` operation.

Displaying Records in a Different Order

The search results returned by a `<CFSEARCH>` tag are ranked in *order of relevance*. The closest matches—the ones with the highest score—are first, and the weakest matches are last.

Verity provides a few ways to tweak the way the score is computed (see the "Score Operators" section in Appendix E), which gives you a little bit of control over how the documents are ordered. What if you wanted to display the search results in, say, alphabetical order by title?

No built-in function is available to handle this in ColdFusion, though you could write a new query to sort the `<CFSEARCH>` query results. Another approach is to use a custom tag. Listing 34.18 provides a CFML custom tag developed by Nate Weiss that you can use to order your Verity results. Actually, you can use it to sort the output of any ColdFusion tag that presents its data as a query, such as `<CFPOP>`, `<CFLDAP>`, and so on.

Listing 34.18 `QUERYSORT.CFM`—A Custom Tag That Sorts Query (and Verity) Results

```
<!---  Example of use
<CF_QuerySort
  QUERY="MyQuery"
  SORTCOLUMN="MyColumn"
  SORTORDER="Desc"                <- optional, defaults to Asc
  SORTTYPE="Numeric"              <- optional, defaults to Textnocase
  SORTEDQUERY="MySortedQuery">   <- optional, defaults to "Sorted"
 --->

<!--- COLD FUSION 3.1 OR HIGHER NEEDED --->
<CFIF Val(ListGetAt(Server.ColdFusion.ProductVersion, 1)) &"."&
  Val(ListGetAt(Server.ColdFusion.ProductVersion, 2)) less than
  "3.1">This tag only works in Cold Fusion 3.1 and higher.
  <CFABORT>
</CFIF>
```

Listing 34.18 (continued)

```
<!--- SUSPEND OUTPUT --->
<CFSETTING ENABLECFOUTPUTONLY="YES">

<!--- REQUIRED PARAMETERS --->
<CFPARAM NAME="Attributes.QUERY">
<CFPARAM NAME="Attributes.SortColumn">
<!--- OPTIONAL PARAMETERS --->
<CFPARAM NAME="Attributes.SortType" DEFAULT="Textnocase">
<CFPARAM NAME="Attributes.SortOrder" DEFAULT="Asc">
<CFPARAM NAME="Attributes.SortedQuery" DEFAULT="Sorted">

<!--- ESTABLISH LOCAL VERSIONS OF QUERIES --->
<CFSET MyArray = ArrayNew(1)>
<CFSET MyQuery = Evaluate("Caller.#Attributes.Query#")>
<CFSET NewQuery = QueryNew(MyQuery.ColumnList)>
<CFIF MyQuery.RecordCount greater than 999999>
   <CFABORT SHOWERROR="Only Queries  with less than one million rows can
    be sorted.  Your Query has #MyQuery.RecordCount# rows.">
</CFIF>

<!--- ADD ROWNUMBER TO END OF EACH ROW'S VALUE --->
<CFOUTPUT QUERY="MyQuery">
  <CFSET MyArray[CurrentRow] =
    Evaluate("MyQuery.#Attributes.SortColumn#") &
    NumberFormat(CurrentRow, "000009")>
  <CFSET Temp = QueryAddRow(NewQuery)>
</CFOUTPUT>

<!--- SORT ARRAY --->
<CFSET Temp = ArraySort(MyArray, Attributes.SortType, Attributes.SortOrder)>

<!--- POPULATE NEW QUERY, ROW BY ROW, WITH APPROPRIATE ROW
   OF OLD QUERY --->
<CFLOOP FROM=1 TO=#MyQuery.RecordCount# INDEX="This">
  <CFSET Row = Val(Right(MyArray[This], 6))>
  <CFLOOP LIST="#MyQuery.ColumnList#" INDEX="Col">
    <CFSET Temp = QuerySetCell(NewQuery, Col,
       Evaluate("MyQuery.#Col#[Row]"), This)>
  </CFLOOP>
</CFLOOP>

<!--- PASS SORTED QUERY BACK TO CALLING TEMPLATE --->
<CFSET "Caller.#Attributes.SortedQuery#" = NewQuery>

<!--- RESTORE OUTPUT --->
<CFSETTING ENABLECFOUTPUTONLY="NO">
```

If you save the `QUERYSORT.CFM` file to your server's CustomTags directory, sorting your Verity results should be easy, as shown in Listing 34.19.

Listing 34.19 `SORTED.CFM`—Sorting Verity Results by Title

```
<!--- Run the search --->
<CFSEARCH
   COLLECTION="Merchandise"
   NAME="GetResults"
   CRITERIA="#Form.Criteria#"
```

Listing 34.19 (continued)

```
>

<!--- sort query result on Title --->
<CF_QUERYSORT
   QUERY="GetResults"
   SORTEDQUERY="GetResults"
   SORTCOLUMN="Title"
>

<HTML>
<HEAD>
   <TITLE>Search Results</TITLE>
</HEAD>

<BODY>
<!--- Display the reuslts --->
<H2><CFOUTPUT>#GetResults.RecordCount# merchandise item(s) found for
"#Form.Criteria#".
</CFOUTPUT>
</H2>

<UL>
<CFOUTPUT QUERY="GetResults">
  <LI>#Title#
</CFOUTPUT>
</UL>

</BODY>
</HTML>
```

Maintaining Collections

In some situations, you might be able to simply create a Verity collection, index it, and forget about it. If the documents or data that make up the collection never change, you're in luck—you get to skip this whole section of the chapter.

It's likely, though, that you'll have to refresh that data at some point. Even when you don't have to refresh it, you might want to get it to run more quickly.

Repopulating Your Verity Collection

Whenever the original documents change from what they were when you indexed them, your collection will be a little bit out of sync with reality. The search results will be based on Verity's knowledge of the documents back when you did your indexing. If a document or database record has since been edited so that it no longer has certain words in it, it might be found in error if someone types in a search for those words. If the document is deleted altogether, Verity will still find it in its own records, which means your application might show a bad link that leads nowhere.

In a perfect world, Verity would dynamically watch your document folders and data tables and immediately reflect any changes, additions, or deletions in your collections. Unfortunately, the world isn't perfect, and this stuff doesn't happen automatically for you. The good news is that it's no major chore.

If You Index Your Collections Interactively

If you recall, there are two ways of indexing a Verity collection: interactively with the ColdFusion Administrator or programmatically with the `<CFINDEX>` tag. If you did it interactively, there's not much I need to tell you; just go back to the Verity page in the Administrator and click the Purge button for your collection. Click the Index button, and do the same thing you did the first time. This should bring your collection up to date.

NOTE

You'd do the same basic thing if the location of the documents had changed.

If You Index Your Collections Programmatically

If you indexed the collection using `<CFINDEX>`—and you used `ACTION="REFRESH"` in the `<CFINDEX>` tag, as shown in Listing 34.1 and Listing 34.8—you should be able to bring your collection up to date simply by running it again.

TIP

You might consider scheduling this refresh template to be executed automatically at the end of each week, during off-peak hours. The indexing process can be resource intensive. It is therefore best to schedule this type of activity during off-peak hours.

➜ For more information on ColdFusion's built-in template scheduler, see Chapter 35, "Event Scheduling."

Instead of `ACTION="REFRESH"`, you can use `ACTION="UPDATE"` in your `<CFINDEX>` tag. This updates information on documents already indexed but without deleting information on documents that no longer exist. You also can use `ACTION="PURGE"` to completely remove all data from the collection. The `ACTION="REFRESH"` previously recommended is really the same thing as a `PURGE` followed by an `UPDATE`.

Deleting/Repopulating Specific Records

If your application is aware of the moment that a document or table record is deleted or edited, you might want to update the Verity collection right then, so your collection stays in sync with the actual information. Clearly, you don't have to repopulate the entire collection just because one record has changed. ColdFusion and Verity address this by enabling you to delete items from a collection via the key value.

For instance, after an edit has been made to the Merchandise database table, you could use the code shown in Listing 34.20 to remove the record from the Merchandise collection and put the new data in its place. This should run much more quickly than a complete repopulation. This listing assumes that a form that passes the `MerchID` as a hidden field has just been submitted and contains some other fields that are meant to allow them to update certain columns in the Merchandise table (the description, perhaps) for a particular item.

Listing 34.20 DELADD.CFM—Deleting and Re-Adding a Specific Record to a Collection

```
<!--- Perform the update to the database table --->
<CFUPDATE DATASOURCE="OWS" TABLENAME="Merchandise">

<!--- Retrieve updated data back from the database --->
<CFQUERY NAME="GetMerchandise" DATASOURCE="OWS">
  SELECT MerchID, MerchName, MerchDescription
  FROM Merchandise
  WHERE MerchID = #Form.MerchID#
</CFQUERY>

<!---
Lock the index operation as it uses a shared resource
--->
<CFLOCK TYPE="EXCLUSIVE" TIMEOUT="30">
<!--- Delete the old record from the Verity collection --->
<CFINDEX ACTION="DELETE"
  COLLECTION="Merchandise"
  KEY="#Form.MerchID#">

<!--- Get updated version back into the Verity collection --->
<CFINDEX
  ACTION="UPDATE"
  COLLECTION="Merchandise"
  TYPE="CUSTOM"
  QUERY="GetMerchandise"
  KEY="MerchID"
  TITLE="MerchName"
  BODY="MerchDescription"
>
</CFLOCK>
<HTML>
<HEAD>
   <TITLE>Update Complete</TITLE>
</HEAD>

<BODY>

<H2>Update Complete</H2>

</BODY>
</HTML>
```

Administrating Collections with <CFCOLLECTION>

The <CFCOLLECTION> tag enables you to administer collections programmatically in your own templates, as an alternative to using the ColdFusion Administrator. If you want your application to be capable of creating, deleting, and maintaining a collection on its own, the <CFCOLLECTION> tag is here to help.

This section might be especially interesting if you are developing prebuilt applications that other people will deploy on their servers without your help, or if you are presented with a project in which you want to completely remove any need for anyone to interact with the ColdFusion Administrator interface. For example, you could use <CFCOLLECTION> in a template that acted as a setup script, creating the various files, Registry entries, database tables, and Verity collections your application needs to operate.

Optimizing a Verity Collection

After a Verity collection gets hit many times, performance can start to degrade. Depending on your application, this might never become a problem. If you notice your Verity searches becoming slower over time, you might want to try optimizing your collection. Optimizing your collection is similar conceptually to running Disk Defragmenter on a Windows machine.

Two ways to optimize a collection are available: You can use the ColdFusion Administrator or create a ColdFusion template that uses the <CFCOLLECTION> tag to optimize the collection programmatically.

To optimize a collection with the ColdFusion Administrator, highlight the collection in the ColdFusion Administrator and click Optimize (refer to Figure 34.3). Verity whirs around for a minute or two as the collection is optimized. Because optimization can take some time—especially with large collections—you should optimize a collection during off-peak hours if possible.

To optimize a collection with the <CFCOLLECTION> tag, just include the tag in a simple ColdFusion template. The tag must include an ACTION="OPTIMIZE" parameter, and the collection name must be provided in the COLLECTION parameter. For instance, the code in Listing 34.21 can be used to optimize the HRDocs collection created earlier in this chapter.

NOTE

You might find that you want to optimize your collections on a regular basis. You could schedule the template shown in Listing 34.21 to be automatically run once a week, for example, by using the ColdFusion scheduler. See Chapter 32.

Listing 34.21 OPTIMIZE.CFM—Optimizing a Collection with the <CFCOLLECTION> Tag

```
<!---
Lock the index operation as it uses a shared resource
--->
<CFLOCK TYPE="EXCLUSIVE" TIMEOUT="30">
<!--- Optimize the Verity collection --->
<CFCOLLECTION
  ACTION="OPTIMIZE"
  COLLECTION="HRDocs">
</CFLOCK>
<HTML>
<HEAD>
   <TITLE>Optimizing Verity Collection</TITLE>
</HEAD>

<BODY>
<H2>Optimizing Complete</H2>
The HRDocs collection has been optimized successfully.
</BODY>
</HTML>
```

TIP

Use `ACTION="OPTIMIZE"` in a `<CFCOLLECTION>` tag when coding for ColdFusion 4.0 and later. In previous versions of ColdFusion, the way to optimize a collection programmatically was to use `ACTION="OPTIMIZE"` in a `<CFINDEX>` tag. This use of `<CFINDEX>` is now obsolete.

Repairing or Deleting a Collection

If Verity's internal index files for a collection become damaged, ColdFusion provides repairing functionality that enables you to get the collection back up and running quickly in most cases. Most likely, you will never need to repair a Verity collection. However, if you do need to, use the `<CFCOLLECTION>` tag with `ACTION="REPAIR"`. For instance, you could use the code shown in Listing 34.21—just change the `ACTION` parameter to `REPAIR`.

TIP

You also can use the Repair button on the Verity VDK Collections page in the ColdFusion Administrator (refer to Figure 34.3) to repair a collection. Simply highlight the collection to be repaired, and then click the Repair icon (second from left).

NOTE

Searches cannot be made against a collection while it is being repaired.

To delete a collection altogether, use the `<CFCOLLECTION>` tag with `ACTION="DELETE"`. Again, you could use the basic code shown in Listing 34.21 by simply changing the `ACTION` to `DELETE`. After the collection has been deleted, ColdFusion displays an error message if a `<CFSEARCH>` tag that uses that collection name is encountered. The collection name will no longer appear in the ColdFusion Administrator, and Verity's index files will be removed from your server's hard drive. Note that only Verity's internal index files will be deleted, not the actual documents that had been made searchable by the collection.

TIP

Alternatively, you could use the Delete button on the Verity page of the ColdFusion Administrator (refer to Figure 34.3) to delete the collection (rightmost icon).

Creating a Collection Programmatically

The `<CFCOLLECTION>` tag also can be used to create a collection from scratch. Basically, you supply the same information to the tag as you would normally supply to the ColdFusion Administrator when creating a new collection there. Provide a name for the new collection in the tag's `NAME` parameter, and provide the path for the new collection's internal index files with the `PATH` parameter.

Under most circumstances, you would supply the same path that appears by default in the ColdFusion Administrator, which typically would be `c:\CFUSION\Verity\Collections\` on Windows platforms, as shown at the top of Figure 34.1. Verity will create a new subfolder within the directory that you specify as the `PATH`.

Listing 34.22 demonstrates how to use `<CFCOLLECTION>` to create a new collection called `MoreHRDocs`.

NOTE

If you have the ColdFusion International Search Pack installed on your ColdFusion server, you also can provide a LANGUAGE attribute to specify a language other than English. The languages you can supply with the LANGUAGE attribute include Danish, Dutch, English, Finnish, French, German, Italian, Norwegian, Portuguese, Spanish, and Swedish.

Listing 34.22 CREATE.CFM—Creating a Collection with the <CFCOLLECTION> Tag

```
<!---
Lock the index operation as it uses a shared resource
--->
<CFLOCK TYPE="EXCLUSIVE" TIMEOUT="30">
<!--- Create the Verity collection --->
<CFCOLLECTION
  ACTION="CREATE"
  COLLECTION="MoreHRDocs"
  PATH="c:\CFUSIONMX\Verity\Collections\">
</CFLOCK>
<HTML>
<HEAD>
   <TITLE>Creating Verity Collection</TITLE>
</HEAD>
<BODY>

<H2>Collection Created</H2>
The MoreHRDocs collection has been created successfully.
</BODY>

</HTML>
```

NOTE

Remember that the newly created collection cannot be searched yet because no information has been indexed. You still need to use the <CFINDEX> tag-after the <CFCOLLECTION> tag-to index documents or data from your database tables, as discussed earlier in this chapter.

If the collection already exists on another server in your local network, you can create a mapping to it simply by using the UNC directory name when you create the collection. ColdFusion will recognize the earlier Verity collection and will create the mapping to it (rather than creating a new collection in that location).

NOTE

You also can use these techniques to map to an existing collection that was produced by Verity outside of ColdFusion.

After the mapping has been created, you can use the HRDocs collection name normally in <CFSEARCH> and <CFINDEX> tags. The Verity engine installed on the local ColdFusion server does the indexing and searching work, but it accesses the index files that are located on the other ColdFusion server.

NOTE

Depending on how your local network is configured, you might have permissions issues to deal with before ColdFusion can access the files on the other server. On Windows NT, you might need to go to the Services applet in the Control Panel; there you adjust the Windows NT username that the Macromedia ColdFusion service logs in as.

NOTE

If you delete a collection that is mapped to a Verity collection on another server, Verity's internal index files on the other ColdFusion server do not get deleted—only the mapping itself does. The same goes for collections created using the Map an Existing Collection option in the ColdFusion Administrator, as shown previously in Figure 34.3.

Expanding Verity's Power

ColdFusion version 5 introduced a more powerful way of using the Verity search engine. When you install ColdFusion MX (Professional and Enterprise editions), a somewhat limited version of Verity's K2 server technology is installed as well.

The K2 server is significantly faster than the VDK version. When using ColdFusion Professional Edition, you can index 150,000 documents, and when using ColdFusion Enterprise, you can index 250,000 documents!

Before you can use the K2 server, you must create *aliases* to the collections you want the K2 server to search and make sure the server is started (it does not automatically run, the way ColdFusion's Verity VDK search technology does). You then use `<CFSEARCH>` as you normally would, but you refer to the K2 server alias name for the collection (in the `COLLECTION` attribute) rather than the collection name itself. ColdFusion will then recognize that you are not searching one of the Verity VDK Collections and will direct your search to the Verity K2 server. The section "Starting the Verity K2 Server," later in this chapter describes how you configure the K2 server and create these aliases.

Here's a simple outline of what's involved:

1. Edit the `k2server.ini` file to set the proper port for the K2 server and to identify aliases to Verity collections you want to search with the K2 server.
2. Start the K2 server from the command line. It will read the settings specified in the `k2server.ini` file.
3. Creating an entry in the ColdFusion Administrator for your K2 Server host.
4. Verify that the K2 server is running.
5. You're now ready to run your `CFSEARCH`es against the aliases named in the `k2server.ini` file.

Editing the `k2server.ini` File

The K2 server uses an initialization file that contains a lot of its basic configuration settings. A sample, named `k2server.ini`, ships with ColdFusion server and is located in the `lib\` directory under the ColdFusion installation directory (typically, `c:\cfusionmx\lib`).

NOTE

Before editing the K2Server.ini file, save an un-edited backup copy of is as K2Server_original.ini or something to that effect.

Two basic sections must be edited in the `K2server.ini` file. First, you must enter a valid port number for the server to run on (the default is 9901) in the `[Server]` section. Second, you must create an entry for each VDK collection you want to search with the K2 server.

Listing 34.23 shows the setting you must make to the `[Server]` section of the `k2server.ini` file. Note that you only need to change this if port 9901 won't work for you.

Listing 34.23 The `[Server]` section of your `k2server.ini`

```
portNo=9901
```

Listing 34.24 shows the entries you must make in the section for each collection you want to be searched by the K2 server. You must specify the path to the existing Verity VDK collection. Note that if the collection was built by indexing a group of files, you should point to the file subdirectory. If it was built by indexing a query or some other custom data, you should point to the custom subdirectory instead. You also must specify the value of the `onLine` parameter.

With the online parameter set to `0`, the server starts with the collection offline. A value of `1` starts the server with the collection in a hidden state, and a value of `2` starts the server with the collection online. When hidden, a collection can't be searched, but it is primed and tested.

Listing 34.24 The `[COLL-n]` Section of Your `k2erver.ini`

```
[Coll-0",,"")>
collPath=c:\cfusionmx\verity\collections\HRDocs\file
collAlias=HRDocs_k2
topicSet=
knowledgeBase=
onLine=2
```

NOTE

Note again that the path to the collection you want to include will be somewhat different from the example in Listing 34.24. It will be in the verity\collections subdirectory below the directory in which you installed ColdFusion. As mentioned earlier in the chapter, the final subdirectory you point to will be either `\file` (as in Listing 34.24) or `\custom`. If the collection consists of a ColdFusion query result, use `\custom`; if it consists of a group of files, use `\file`.

Note that you must add new `COLL-`*n* sections for each VDK collection you want the K2 server to search, where *n* is a number starting from `0`. Be sure to increment `n` in each new `COLL-`*n* section you add.

Starting the Verity K2 Server

You must ensure that your the K2 server is up and running on your machine before you can use it in your searches.

If the K2 server isn't running, you must start it. Assuming you used the default directory when you installed ColdFusion, you can do this from the Windows command line with the following code, as demonstrated in Figure 34.16.

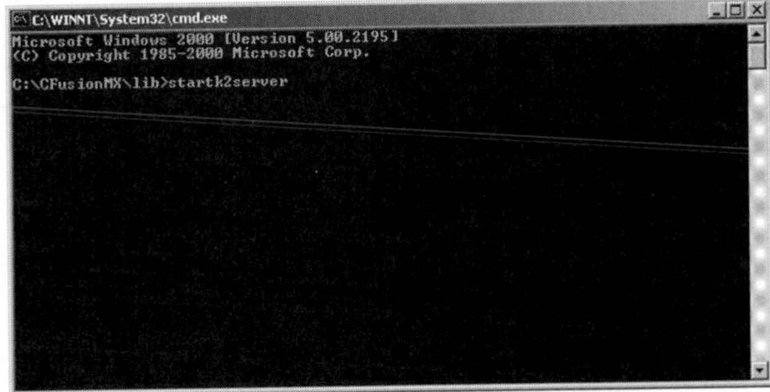

Figure 34.16

Use this command line (in the right directory) to start the K2 server.

Check the Windows Task Manager; under the Processes tab, look for `k2server.exe`, as shown in Figure 34.17.

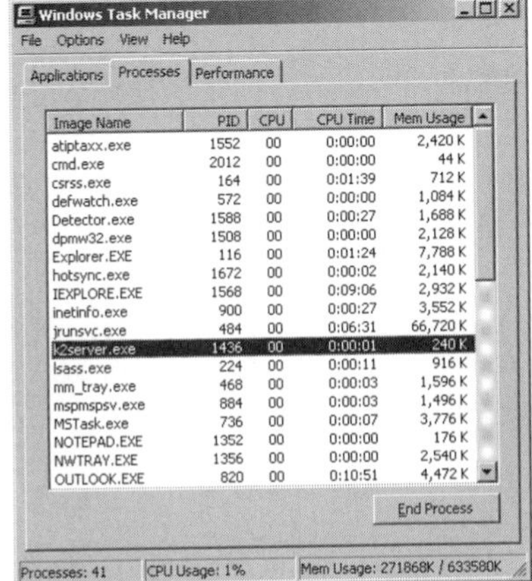

Figure 34.17

You can tell whether the K2 Server is running by checking the Windows Task Manager.

NOTE

Note that you can also run the K2 Server as a service under Windows. This is not recommended, however, as you must stop and restart it each time you modify or delete K2 collections.

You must now create an entry in the ColdFusion Administrator for your server. This is done on the Verity K2 Server page, as seen in Figure 34.18. Simply enter the host address or name in the `K2 Server Host Name` field and enter the port number you used in the `k2server.ini` file (defaults to 9901). Click connect. You should now see an entry in the `Connected Verity Collections` and `Connected Verity K2 Collections` lists for each collection that you specified in your `k2server.ini` file, as seen in the bottom of Figure 34.18.

By the way, you can also programmatically check to see if the K2 server is running using the new `IsK2ServerOnline()` function, as in Listing 34.25. Note that this won't work until you've registered the server in the ColdFusion Administrator.

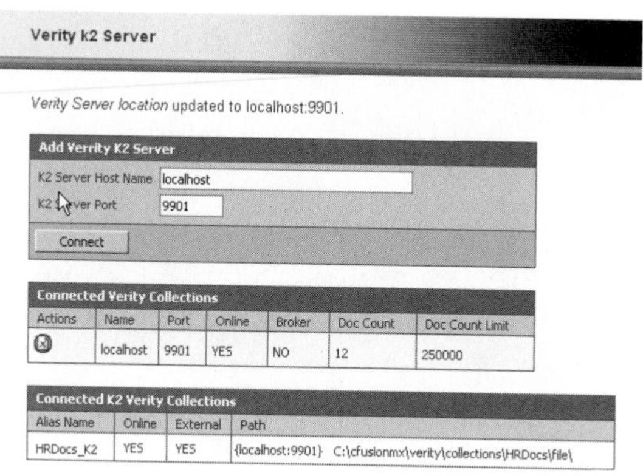

Figure 34.18 Creating an entry for your K2 Server in the CF Administrator.

Listing 34.25 Use `IsK2ServerOnline()` to Programmatically Check to See if the Server is Running

```
<CFIF NOT IsK2ServerOnline()>
   <CFABORT SHOWERROR="The K2 search engine is not on-line at
    this time">
<CFELSE>
   <P>Server is up
</CFIF>
```

NOTE

You should stop the K2 server when it's no longer needed. You do this under Windows by pressing the Ctrl-C key combination in the command window in which it's running. Doing so results in a prompt to terminate the batch job. Confirm this and close the command window. Under Linux/Unix platforms, use the script stopk2server.

Searching with the Verity K2 Server

As mentioned earlier, to use the Verity K2 Server in your searches, you use `<CFSEARCH>` as you have learned earlier in this chapter. The only change is that instead of referring to one of the VDK collections in the `COLLECTION` parameter, you refer to the alias name specified in the `collAlias` setting in one of the `[COLL-n]` sections in your `k2server.ini` file.

In Listing 34.24, the HRDocs collection was given the alias `HRDocs_k2`. To search this collection with the K2 Server, you'd use `<CFSEARCH>` as demonstrated in Listing 34.26.

Listing 34.26 Use `<CFSEARCH>` to Search K2 Server Collection Aliases

```
<!--- Check to see if the server is up and running. --->
<CFIF NOT IsK2ServerOnline()>
   <CFABORT SHOWERROR="The K2 search engine is not on-line at
    this time">
<CFELSE>
   <!--- Search the K2 collection alias --->
   <CFSEARCH COLLECTION="HRDocs_k2" CRITERIA="money"
     NAME="getresults">
   <!--- Display the query result --->
   <CFDUMP VAR="#getresults#"></CFIF>
</CFELSE>
```

Understanding Verity's Search Syntax

You've explored a number of ways to index information and make it searchable on the Web. You've also discovered using AND, OR, and wildcards, which make your search criteria work more easily for you.

It doesn't stop at AND and OR. Verity provides a fairly rich set of operators you can use in your search criteria. Your users probably won't use these operators along with their _keywords when they are running a search—most people won't go beyond ANDs and ORs. However, you might, in certain circumstances, want to use some of these operators behind the scenes. Table 34.7 lists all the operators available by category.

➜ See Appendix D for explanations of each of the operators listed in Table 34.7.

Table 34.7 Verity Operator Quick Reference

CATEGORY	OPERATOR	PURPOSE	DESCRIPTION
Concept Operators	AND	To find *documents* where:	All words/conditions are found.
	OR		Any one word/condition is found.
Evidence Operators	STEM	To find *words* that:	Are derived from the search words.
	WORD		Match the search words.
	WILDCARD		Match search words with *, ?, and so on.
Proximity Operators	NEAR	To find *words* that are:	Close together.
	NEAR/N		Within *n* words of each other.
	PARAGRAPH		In the same paragraph.
	PHRASE		In the same phrase.
	SENTENCE		In the same sentence.
Relational Operators	CONTAINS	To find *words* that are:	Within a specific field (see following).
	MATCHES		The text of an entire field.
	STARTS		At the start of a specific field.
	ENDS		At the end of a specific field.
	SUBSTRING		Within a specific field as (fragments).
	=,<, >, <=, >=		For numeric and date values.

Table 34.7 (CONTINUED)

CATEGORY	OPERATOR	PURPOSE	DESCRIPTION
Search Modifiers	`CASE`	To change Verity's behavior so that:	The search is case-sensitive.
	`MANY`		Documents are ranked by relevance.
	`NOT`		Matching documents should not be found.
	`ORDER`		Words must appear in documents in order.

The document fields you can specify with relational operators, such as `CONTAINS`, `STARTS`, `ENDS`, and so on, are:

- `CF_TITLE`
- `CF_KEY`
- `CF_URL`
- `CF_CUSTOM1`
- `CF_CUSTOM2`

These fields correspond to the values (`TITLE`, `KEY`, `URL`, and so on) you specify in the `<CFINDEX>` tag used to index a collection.

Finally, it's worth noting that ColdFusion employs a limited version of the Verity engine and K2 Server. For example, you can't index more than 250,000 documents with the ColdFusion Enterprise version of the Verity K2 Server. You can overcome these limitations by upgrading to the commercial versions of the Verity products from Verity.

Spidering Your Local Documents

The Verity Spider is a command-line driven utility for creating collections by *spidering* through a group of documents. By spidering, I'm referring to the act of walking through all the links in the documents and then *indexing the linked documents*. The version of the Verity Spider that ships with ColdFusion can be extremely handy but is limited to working with documents and links within your host.

NOTE

ike the other Verity tools you've learned about in this chapter, the Verity Spider is actually a separate Verity product that can be purchased on its own. The stand alone version is not limited to spidering only local documents.

There are typically several steps involved in using the spider; here's a rough outline of what is involved:

1. Identify the content to be spidered.
2. Use the `vspider.exe` command-line utility to create the collection based on this content.
3. Use the ColdFusion Administrator to register the collection.
4. Use `<CFSEARCH>` to search the collection as you would any collection.

Running the Verity Spider from the Command Line

As mentioned earlier in this chapter, the CD comes with some content that you can index. It is installed in directory `OWS\34` below your web server's root. The documents to be indexed are in the `hr\` and `hr\docs` sub-directories. Assuming you're using Windows and you've followed the installation defaults, we'll be referring to:

```
C:\cfusionmx\wwwroot\ows\34\hr\docs\
```

NOTE

The rest of the discussion in this section assumes you've set up ColdFusion under Windows with the default installation parameters and that you're using the stand alone web server provided with ColdFusion MX. This means your web site root URL is `http://localhost:8500/` and your default installation directory is `c:\cfusionmx\`.

`vspider.exe` is the command-line utility that builds the collections.

NOTE

You need to have a few directories on your environmental PATH in order to make the `vspider.exe` utility to work properly. This other directories contain libraries that `vspider.exe` uses. Specifically add these to directories to your path:

```
c:\cfusionmx\lib
c:\cfusionmx\lib\platform\bin
```

(This assumes that you've followed the ColdFusion installation defaults. If not, use the paths based on where you installed ColdFusion.)

NOTE

The value of *platform* is different in each platform. In Windows it is *`_nti40`*. In Solaris it's *`_solaris`* and *`_ssol26`*, In Linux it's *`_ilnx21`*, In HPUX it's *`_hpux11`*.

`vspider.exe` has many, many command-line options. Because you'll normally use several at a time, you'll want to create a command file containing your various options and then pass a reference to this file to `vspider.exe` on the command line. This is a much better alternative to typing all the various commands each time, not only because it's so easy to make a mistake when typing, but also because this way, you can re-use the commands as needed. You use Notepad or your favorite plain-text editor to create the command file.

We'll save the commands in Listing 34.27 in a text file named `hrdocs_spider.txt` and store it in the `c:\cfusionmx\wwwroot\ows\29\` directory.

Listing 34.27 These Verity Spider commands are saved in a file that is passed to `vspider.exe` on the command-line.

```
-collection c:\cfusionmx\verity\collections\spider_hr_docs
-start http://localhost:8500/ows/34/hr/docs/Hiring_Guidelines.htm
-indinclude *
```

The commands tell `vspider.exe` to create a new collection named spider_ur_docs by starting from the URL `http://localhost:8500/ows/34/hr/docs/Hiring_Guidelines.htm` and to include all key data.

NOTE

The name of the collection is the last sub-directory, spider_hr_docs. This is where the collection is created, thus this is its name.

To run the spider, open a command window and change directories to `c:\cfusionmx\wwwroot\ows\34\`.

Execute the command-line:

```
vspider -cmdfile hrdocs_spider.txt
```

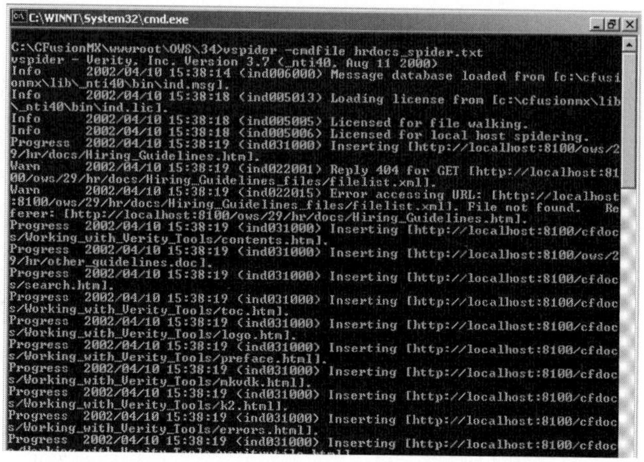

Figure 34.19

Executing the vspider.exe command line.

You should get the output shown in Figure 34.19. (Note again that you must have included the Verity libraries on your path.) Looking at this figure, you might notice that a lot of documents being indexed weren't in the folder that Verity was instructed to start in, `http://localhost:8500/ows/34/hr/docs/`. That's because, the document we're starting from, `Hiring_guidelines.htm` contains the line:

```
Also read: http://localhost:8500/cfdocs/Working_with_Verity_Tools/contents.htm
```

So, this is what spidering does, right? The `vspider.exe` utility read that link and indexed it. And of course, that document contained the links to *a lot* of other documents; and that's what all the commotion is about in Figure 34.19.

Searching a Verity Spider Collection

You search your Verity Spider collections the same way you search other Verity collections: using `<CFSEARCH>`. However, before you can search this collection, you must add a reference to it in the ColdFusion Administrator, using the Verity Collections link. Enter the name of the collection, spider_hr_docs, as shown in Figure 34.20.

TIP

If in the future, you create collections that are not in ColdFusion's default collections directory (i.e., `c:\cfusionmx\verity\collections\`), you can still add a reference to them; just change the value of the `Path` in the `Add New Verity Collection` form.

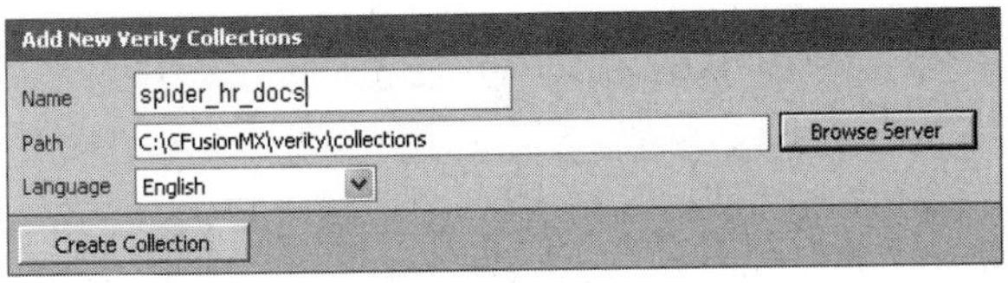

Figure 34.20

Creating a reference to the spider-built collection in the ColdFusion Administrator.

Add New Verity Collections

Name: spider_hr_docs

Path: C:\CFusionMX\verity\collections [Browse Server]

Language: English

[Create Collection]

Once you have this collection "registered" in the ColdFusion Administrator, you're ready to search it. Assuming we use the same search form as before (change the value of the form's `ACTION` attribute to point to the new action template), the code in Listing 34.28 will execute the search and display the results. Typical results for a search are displayed in Figure 34.21.

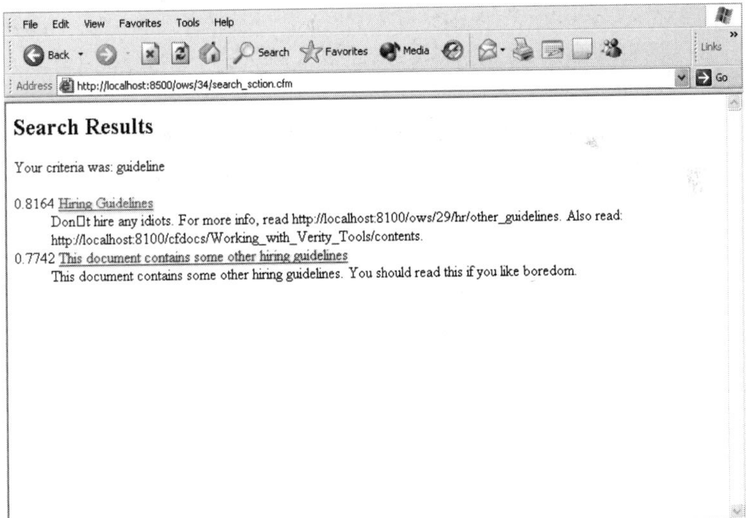

Figure 34.21

Search results from search the spider-built collection.

Listing 34.28 `SEARCH_ACTION.CFM`—Searching Against a Spider-Built Index

```
<!--- Execute search against spider-built collection --->
<CFSEARCH NAME="SpiderSearchResult" COLLECTION="spider_hr_docs"
 CRITERIA="#Form.Criteria#">
<HTML>
<HEAD>
   <TITLE>Spider Search Results</TITLE>
</HEAD>
<BODY>

<H2>Search Results</H2>
<P>Your criteria was: <CFOUTPUT>#FORM.Criteria#</CFOUTPUT>
<!--- Loop through the reuslts, displaying links to
   underlying documents --->
<DL>
<CFOUTPUT QUERY="SpiderSearchResult">
   <DT>#SpiderSearchResult.Score# <A
HREF="#SpiderSearchResult.URL#">#SpiderSearchResult.Title#</A></DT>
   <DD>#SpiderSearchResult.Summary#</DD>
</CFOUTPUT>
</DL>
</BODY>
</HTML>
```

CHAPTER 35
Event Scheduling

IN THIS CHAPTER

The automated scheduling of activities is a part of everyday life. We schedule automatic monthly mortgage payments from our bank accounts, the recording of various television shows with our VCRs, notifications from our handheld devices and many other activities. By scheduling these events to occur in an automated fashion, we free up other resources to focus on issues that require our explicit interaction. It simply makes our lives easier knowing that the scheduled activity is going to get done without requiring our attention or time.

In this chapter, you'll learn how to employ Macromedia ColdFusion MX's built in task scheduler. You'll learn about other types of task schedulers and how to determine how each different scheduling mechanism can be appropriately used. This chapter also presents examples of creating, modifying and deleting tasks through code and through the ColdFusion Administrator. Finally, you'll see how task execution is logged.

NOTE

The entire text of this chapter can be found on the included CD.

CHAPTER 36

Managing Your Code

IN THIS CHAPTER

Coding Standards

When developing an application with Macromedia ColdFusion MX, remember that *how* you code can sometimes have as much of an effect on your application's performance as *what* you code. Opinions differ within the community as to which coding methodology is the best choice and how one can—and should—perform certain CFML operations. In truth, the best methodology is simply to have a methodology. Chapter 37, "Development Methodologies," discusses some of the more prevalent ColdFusion development methodologies in greater detail.

What you need to understand prior to implementing a specific methodology is that your choices as a developer can cause degradation in your application's performance. Even though you can code exactly the same functionality a hundred different ways, you should consider some general guidelines when writing your code to keep your application performing at the best level possible.

NOTE

The coding standards covered here outline some issues you should be cautious about as you develop any application with ColdFusion. This chapter describes some of the most common things you can do as a developer to improve application performance. As you gain more experience and confidence, you can add your own suggestions to this list.

The guidelines are as follows:

- Avoid overuse of subqueries in a select statement
- Don't reassign variable values with each request
- Don't use if statements to test for the existence of variables
- Use `<CFSWITCH>` and `<CFCASE>` in place of `<CFIF>`
- Don't overuse the # sign
- Avoid overuse of the `<CFOUTPUT>` tag
- Comment, comment, comment

Avoid Overuse of Subqueries in a Select Statement

Using subqueries within a select statement can in some cases cause a database to create an inefficient execution plan for the overall query. The database has no way to know what the results of the subquery contained in your SQL statement will be, so it is forced to examine the table as many times as there are possible subquery results.

In other words, if you can break a large query containing a nested query into two or three smaller queries, you will generally see page execution time improve.

Don't Reassign Variable Values with Each Request

Developers commonly define certain variables—a data source, for example—inside the `application.cfm` file. There is nothing wrong with doing this, but keep in mind when working with your `application.cfm` file that it loads with each and every page request. Because of this, you should avoid forcing ColdFusion to reassign values to all of the variables inside the `application.cfm` if they are already present in `application.cfm`.

One way to avoid this unnecessary processing is to encapsulate variable assignments within a `<CFIF>` statement. In this way, you can check whether a variable value has already been assigned, instead of asking ColdFusion to perform this work again. The following example assumes that you are assigning a value to the variable `application.datasource` within your `application.cfm` page. This example demonstrates the concept of testing for the existence of this variable and writing a value for the variable only if one is not already present:

```
<CFLOCK SCOPE="Application" TYPE="exclusive" TIMEOUT="10">
<CFIF NOT IsDefined("Application.DataSource")>
    <CFSET application.datasource = "MyDSN">
</CFIF>
</CFLOCK>
```

It's not advisable to do this "if `IsDefined()` logic" for a whole bunch of variables that are normally assigned together in one place in your code. In this scenario, you could test for the existence of one and if it isn't defined, assign values to all of the variables within one `<CFLOCK>` block.

Don't Use If Statements to Test for the Existence of Variables

If you know that you need to evaluate a specific variable inside a ColdFusion template, you likely must check to see whether that variable is already present. If it's not, you should create it and assign a default value to it. You can do this with the `<CFIF>` statement, as shown in the following code:

```
<CFIF NOT IsDefined("myCat")>
    <CFSET MYCAT = "Carbon">
</CFIF>
```

This method of testing for the existence of a variable will work, but it is not the most efficient way to perform the task. As a matter of fact, the ColdFusion Markup Language provides an even easier method of testing for the existence of variables and assigning default values. The following example accomplishes the same thing that the previous `<CFIF>` evaluation accomplished, but much more efficiently:

```
<CFPARAM NAME="myCat" DEFAULT="Carbon">
```

Use <CFSWITCH> and <CFCASE> in Place of <CFIF>

If you want to have several pieces of code run depending on the value of a single parameter, you might assume that you should just create multiple `<CFIF>` statements to check for the value of the desired parameter and then run the code inside your `<CFIF>` if that value is met. To demonstrate how this would work, let's think about a task that many developers replicate when first working with ColdFusion. Suppose you are returning a list of users from a database. You want to list these users in alphabetical order by either first name or last name, depending on how the user of your application prefers to see these results. To accomplish this, you must allow the user to pass in a simple parameter, perhaps on the URL, telling your application to order the results by either last or first names. You could accomplish this as shown in the following example:

```
<CFQUERY NAME="ListTheUsers" DATASOURCE="MyDSN">
SELECT User.FirstName, User.LastName
FROM   tbl_Users
<CFIF URL.OrderBy EQ "LastName">
   ORDERBY LastName DESC
</CFIF>
<CFIF URL.OrderBy EQ "FirstName">
   ORDERBY FirstName DESC
</CFIF>
</CFQUERY>
```

Though the preceding code will accomplish your goal, ColdFusion provides a more efficient way to complete this type of evaluation—using the `<CFSWITCH>` and `<CFCASE>` tags, as shown in the following example:

```
<CFQUERY NAME="ListTheUsers" DATASOURCE="MyDSN">
SELECT User.FirstName, User.LastName
FROM   tbl_Users
<CFSWITCH EXPRESSION="URL.OrderBy">
   <CFCASE VALUE="LastName">
      ORDERBY LastName DESC
   </CFCASE>
   <CFCASE VALUE="FirstName">
      ORDERBY FirstName DESC
   </CFCASE>
   <CFDEFAULTCASE>
      ORDERBY LastName DESC
   </CFDEFAULTCASE>
</CFSWITCH>
</CFQUERY>
```

Both of these examples produce the same results, but using the `<CFSWITCH>/<CFCASE>` tags doesn't force evaluation of logic unless the specific watched-for conditions are met, making this method more efficient than a long list of `<CFIF>` statements.

Don't Overuse the # Sign

As you get started with ColdFusion, one of the characters you will type most often is the # sign. Surrounding a variable, function call, or variable-function combination with the # sign flags that bit of code so that ColdFusion knows it is a variable to evaluate. Otherwise, the ColdFusion engine would have no way of distinguishing what you wanted it to evaluate from other text within your CFML templates.

Anytime you use a variable as a parameter for a standard CFML tag, the pound signs are not necessary. Take the following example:

```
<CIF #MyName# = "John">
    <!--- Some conditional ColdFusion code --->
</CFIF>
```

This is the same thing as:

```
<CIF MyName = "John">
    <!--- Some conditional ColdFusion code --->
</CFIF>
```

Notice how having the # signs around the `MyName` variable makes no difference in how the code is processed.

Now, let's assume that you want to run a special bit of code if in fact `MyName` is John. The following example demonstrates this:

```
<CFIF MyName = "John">
    <CFSET FormAction = "updateData.cfm?MyName=#MyName#">
</CFIF>
```

Notice how when you want to use the `MyName` variable as part of a URL, you must use # signs to let ColdFusion know that you want this variable evaluated so that the string `John` will be passed to the page you're calling. Without the # signs here, ColdFusion passes the string `MyName` to the next page.

Avoid Overuse of the `<CFOUTPUT>` Tag

In general, you should try to use as few `<CFOUTPUT>` tags per page as possible. Overusing the `<CFOUTPUT>` tag can put undue strain on the ColdFusion parser, and under heavy load conditions this can potentially slow down your application. Because of this, you should try to combine code that requires `<CFOUTPUT>` statements into a single `<CFOUTPUT>` block as much as possible. The following example demonstrates overuse of `<CFOUTPUT>`:

```
<INPUT TYPE="text" VALUE="<CFOUTPUT>#Variable1#</CFOUTPUT>"
<INPUT TYPE="text" VALUE="<CFOUTPUT>#Variable2#</CFOUTPUT>"
<INPUT TYPE="text" VALUE="<CFOUTPUT>#Variable3#</CFOUTPUT>"
```

This code will work as you would expect it to, but the multiple output statements create a lot of extra work for ColdFusion's parser. The following example demonstrates a much better way to achieve the same result:

```
<CFOUTPUT>
    <INPUT TYPE="text" VALUE="#Variable1#">
    <INPUT TYPE="text" VALUE="#Variable2#">
    <INPUT TYPE="text" VALUE="#Variable3#">
</CFOUTPUT>
```

All of this said, you can go to the opposite extreme. It's also a bad idea to force ColdFusion to parse a lot of content that does not include any CFML. In other words, if you have large blocks of HTML or text that contain only a few CFML expressions, you should use individual `<CFOUTPUT>` tags. The problem is that ColdFusion must process every token within the body of the `<CFOUTPUT>` tag, so you don't want it to have to process a lot of content that contains no CFML.

Comment, Comment, Comment

Nothing is more frustrating than having to dig into another developer's code attempting to resolve a problem or add functionality, only to discover that he or she hasn't commented any of the code.

Trying to follow the flow of uncommented code is like finding your way around an unfamiliar city without a map. You have no idea what the person before you was doing or what his or her thought process was in developing the code. This can make your job extremely difficult when you are working with another developer's uncommented code base.

Be conscientious when developing your own application, and effectively comment your own CFML code. Place comments so that they will make it easier for someone else to come in behind you and pick up work right where you left off. Ensure that your comments are clear, concise, easy to understand, and relevant. Don't spend time restating the obvious, either. For example, this comment is of no practical value:

```
<!--- Set MyVar to part of YourVar --->
<CFSET MyVar = Right(YourVar, 3)>
```

Anyone can tell that `MyVar` is being set to part of the value `YourVar`. Whoever has to maintain this code will gain more insight from a comment like this:

```
<!--- Set MyVar to portion of YourVar containing file extension --->
<CFSET MyVar = Right(YourVar, 4)>
```

In a few weeks, you may not even remember how you accomplished a specific task within your code. Having comments for guidance will help you recall what you were thinking when you wrote the code.

Documentation

By nature, the first thing any ColdFusion developer wants to do when presented with a project is open Macromedia Dreamweaver MX and start coding away. That's understandable, because writing the code is the fun part and it's what most of us became ColdFusion developers to actually do.

Still, you must consider a few other things if you really want your project to succeed. One of the most important of these is ensuring that you document every step of it as clearly and completely as possible.

Finding out exactly what works for you in the way of project documentation is a deeply personal process. Keep in mind that there really is no right or wrong in this regard. So long as you are aware that you must document your project completely, from start to finish, how you choose to do it is not that important.

Table 36.1 outlines some key steps you should take along the path to complete documentation of a project of any size to ensure that you have a complete record.

Table 36.1 Steps to Complete Documentation of a Project

ITEM	DESCRIPTION
List of Key Players	Make sure you have a record of all the people involved in the project, along with a description of their specific roles and responsibilities.
Application Diagram	One of the first steps in building a successful ColdFusion application is to lay out that application on paper before you begin to code. This way, by the time you start development, you will already have solved many problems.
Problem and Solution Guide	As you begin to work through the development of your application, you will undoubtedly encounter some unexpected—and perhaps complex—problems. Keep a good record of what these problems were and how you resolved them. Not only do these documents add to your understanding of the current application, but they also provide a valuable reference should you run into similar problems in the future.
List of Resources	Keep a good record of all resources involved in the development of a specific application: in this instance, all CFML templates, their functions in the application, and their archived locations, as well as any data sources or third-party software used in conjunction with the application.

Part of building complete documentation for any project is making sure you completely and clearly commented all the CFML templates used in your application. Remember to comment your code along the way so you or anyone else can come back to any file and easily determine its function and logical flow.

Version Control

In the development of any ColdFusion application, the ability to control access to the templates you're developing, to track changes, and to roll back to earlier versions if necessary is an important part of ensuring that you complete the application on time—and successfully.

Developers today often work in teams, sometimes dispersed over large geographic distances. In such a case, it is also important to know that what you are working on doesn't affect what someone else has already done or will be doing in the near future.

Oftentimes, a developer will experiment with code, only to find that a change has just created a template that no longer functions. Worse still, someone else can change a template so that it no longer functions, in which case it is extremely helpful to have the ability to roll back to a stable version of the code.

Implementing some form of version control speaks to all these issues. Having version control in place enables you to know which developer, regardless of where he or she is located, made changes to any given template. You can revert to previous versions of code if you encounter an unexpected error, and you can allow large groups of people to work on the same project without having to worry about their stepping on each other's work.

Planning for Version Control

Before you jump into implementing a version-control solution, you need to ask yourself some questions about how you'll be designing, implementing, and managing your project. You should consider all the people involved in working on it.

You can save yourself some time by answering the following questions before you attempt to implement a specific version-control solution:

- Should I define this as a single project?— Chances are, if the application you are developing is of any size, you should consider dividing the development into multiple subprojects beneath the banner of a larger, all-encompassing project. For example, you may be developing an administrative section of the site, as most developers do at some point. This type of functionality is a good candidate for a subproject that could reside in a layer below the larger application project.
- Who are you working with on this project?—Chances are, if you're implementing source control, you aren't the sole developer. You must clearly define the role and responsibilities of each person involved with the development process so that you can determine which members of the team need access to which resources. Try to avoid giving team members unnecessary access to resources for which they are not directly responsible or on which they shouldn't be working.
- Where will the source files reside?—Determine where you want to store the project database and source files. Choose a location convenient for all those involved with the project.

After you've answered all these questions, you can begin to think about what kind of version-control system you want to implement.

Version-Control Systems

Several good third-party tools provide version control for ColdFusion code. Most of these tools share some key functionality:

- The capability to control access to source files
- The capability to log changes to files as they occur
- Maintenance of old source files to provide rollback capabilities
- An easy way to compare an older version of the source to the current version

Having a version-controlling system in place is particularly important when your development team is large or members of the team are widely scattered. It is also very important to have version controlling in place if your project is likely to have a long life span, in which case several builds of the application might exist at any given time.

After you understand why it's important to consider putting a version-control system in place, you can begin to examine which software is right for you. Though most of these systems have similar core functionality, the degree to which they allow you to manipulate the source code, track changes, and roll back coding errors depends on their quality and price. The various products available run the gamut from freeware tools to extremely pricey, all encompassing solutions.

For the purposes of this book, we'll look at one of the most popular and widely used version-control products on the market today: Microsoft Visual SourceSafe (VSS).

Microsoft Visual SourceSafe

VSS enables you to create and manage projects that consist of many types of files, from CFML code and images to sound and video files.

When working with a project managed in VSS, you set up a project database that enables you to store recent and past versions of source files (including code and supporting documentation), track access to those files, and re-create previous versions of any file.

When any user working with you on a project wants to make changes to a file, he or she must *check out* the file, which effectively prevents any other users from modifying the same file while it is in the checked-out state.

If not all your developers are in the same location as your source file's database, third-party plug-ins for VSS enable those offsite developers to access the VSS database using a standard TCP/IP connection and a Web browser. This enables developers working in separate physical locations to contribute safely to the same project without having to worry about gaining access to specific network resources.

If you are using Macromedia's Dreamweaver MX to develop your CFML code, you can use the Files panel within Dreamweaver to integrate directly with VSS. In this instance, the machine on which you are running your copy of Dreamweaver will act as a VSS client, connecting to a predefined VSS server to work on a project.

Integrating VSS with Dreamweaver MX

To integrate a Visual SourceSafe project with Dreamweaver MX, you must first create the VSS project by following the instructions included with the VSS software. When you're done, you should have a project like the one in Figure 36.1. I've created a few example files in directory 36 on the CD. If you set up your VSS project to control these files, you can follow along easily with the example.

After setting up the VSS project, you must create what Dreamweaver refers to as a *site*. With a file open in Dreamweaver, select New Site from the Site menu. In the Site Definition dialog box, enter the name of your site as seen in Figure 36.2. Next, rather than going through the wizard-style process, click the Advanced tab.

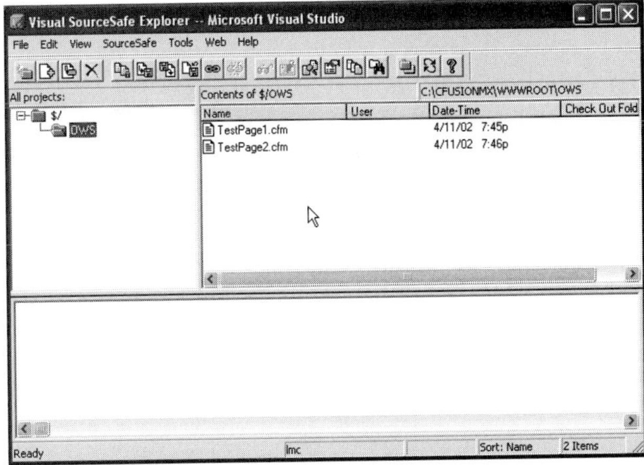

Figure 36.1

Create your VSS project before integrating it with Dreamweaver.

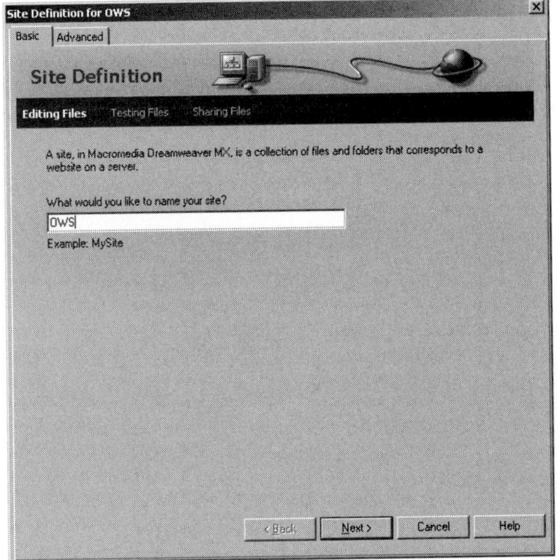

Figure 36.2

Select New Site from the Site menu and use the `Site Definition` dialog to name your site.

Select `Remote Access` from the `Category` list, as seen in Figure 36.3. Then select `SourceSafe Database` from the list of site access methods. Click the Settings button to provide Dreamweaver your VSS account information as in Figure 36.4.

Down below, you can indicate whether you want Dreamweaver to automatically check your files back in to the VSS server upon saving. You can also enable check-out and check-in. Note that if you do so (and it's recommended), two more fields appear in this dialog; enter your check-out name and e-mail address in these. Other VSS users will see this information when you have files checked out. See Figure 36.5.

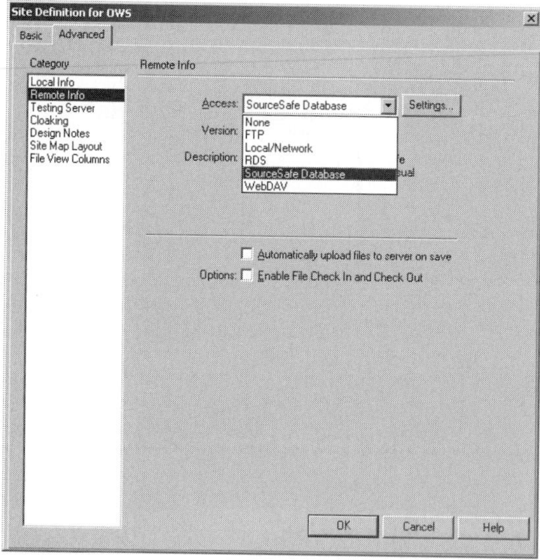

Figure 36.3

In the Remote Access category, select SourceSafe Database as your site access method.

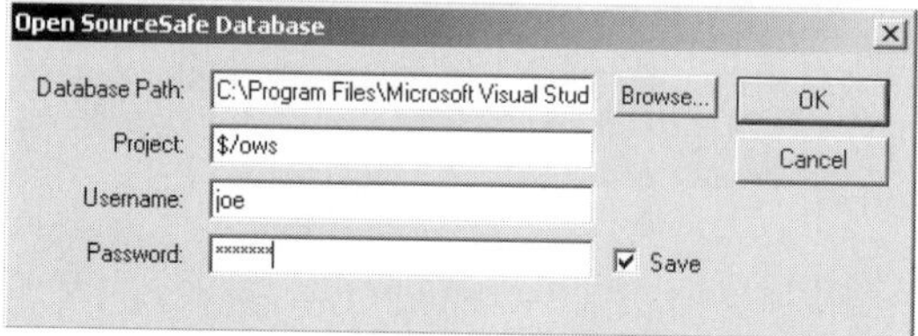

Figure 36.4

Enter your VSS account information.

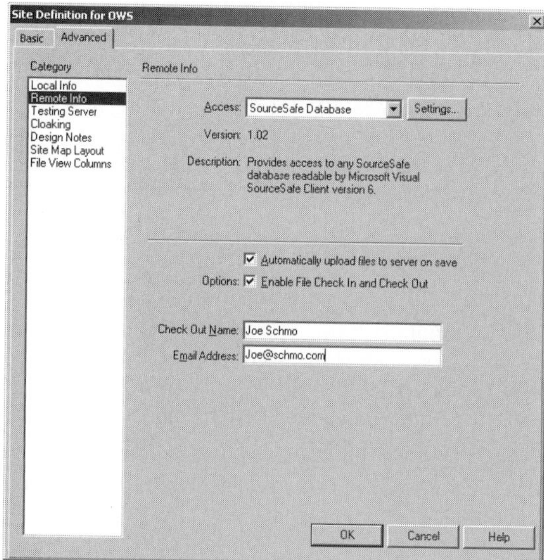

Figure 36.5

If you want Dreamweaver to check files out and back in, you'll also need to provide the name and e-mail address other VSS users will see.

At this point, you're essentially done setting up Dreamweaver to act as a client for VSS. You can set up other options related to your Dreamweaver site. If you want to begin working with your VSS files through Dreamweaver, click OK.

You should now have access to the files in the VSS project. Select the Files panel; you should see a list of the new site you created (OWS in our examples), as in Figure 36.6.

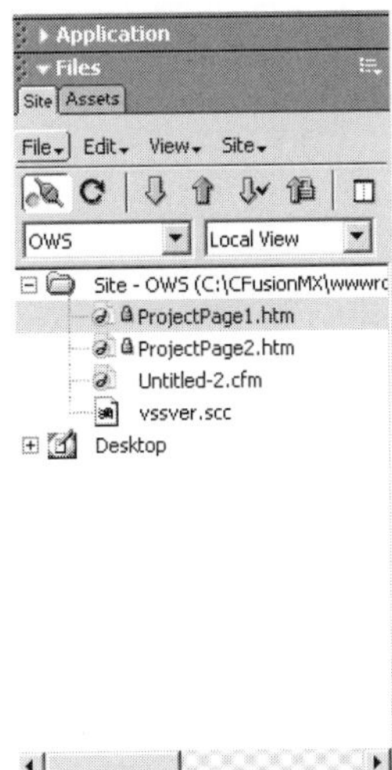

Figure 36.6

Once you've defined your access to the site through VSS, you can check files in or out via the `Files` panel.

Assuming you indicated that you want the ability to check files in and out, you will have the option of doing just that. Check out ProjectPage1.htm in our example. Modify it, and then select Save from Dreamweaver's `File` menu. VSS will prompt you to enter a comment upon saving the file, as in Figure 36.7.

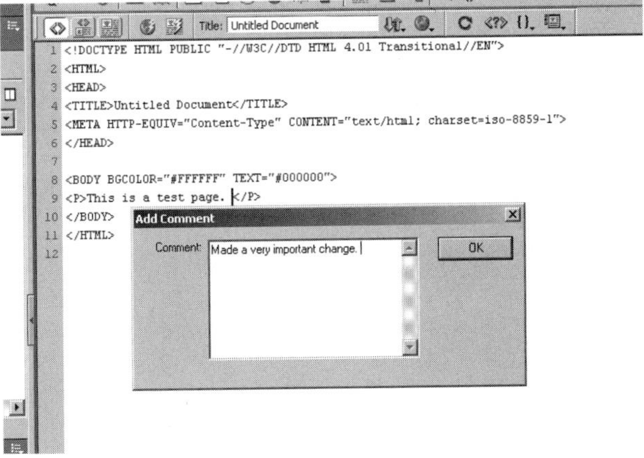

Figure 36.7

Saving a checked-out, modified file brings up the VSS prompt for a comment.

Multiple Users and Integration with Dreamweaver MX

When you are dealing with multiple developers, all of whom will be accessing your VSS source database through a Dreamweaver *site*, you must perform a few special steps to ensure that all your developers can share access to the version-control software through the Dreamweaver MX project.

In this case, each of the developer's computer accessing the source database through Dreamweaver MX will act as a client of the version-controlling software, as demonstrated in Figure 36.8. When you double-click one of the files that the VSS project controls, VSS prompts you to indicate whether you want to check out dependent files as well.

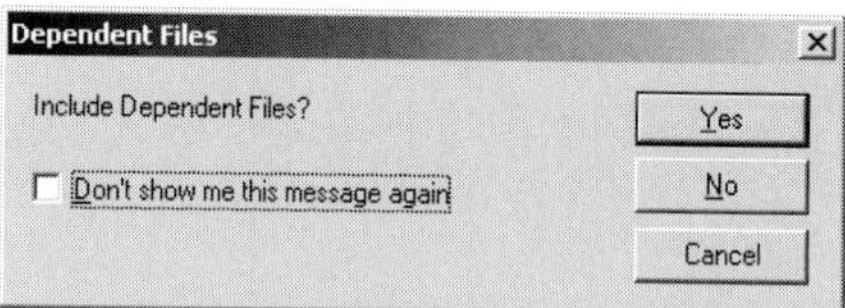

Figure 36.8

Attempting to open a checked-in file produces a prompt to check out dependent files.

If you try to check out a file that another user has checked out, for example, VSS will provide a message like the one in Figure 36.9. Note, however, that Dreamweaver will only list files that are available to check out. When another user checks out a file after you've opened the site in Dreamweaver, the file still appears in your list of files. However, you can refresh the list whenever you like by clicking the `Refresh` icon in the `Files` panel.

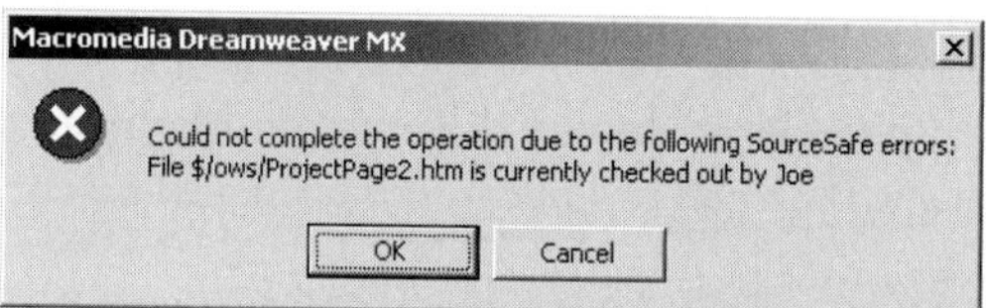

Figure 36.9

When another user has checked out a file and you try to check it out from your Dreamweaver site, VSS provides an error message.

Note that creating and saving new files in this site will result in a prompt to add a comment, as in Figure 36.10. As you probably know from your use of VSS, you can review these comments using the VSS reporting mechanisms to get a history of all the comments and changes made to a file.

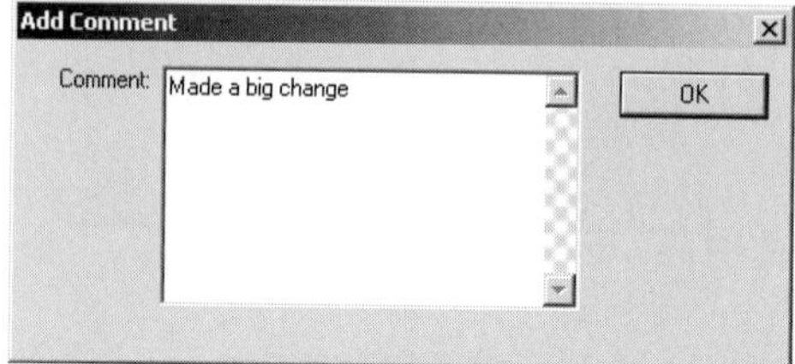

Figure 36.10

Checking a file back in or saving it results in a prompt from VSS for you to enter a comment.

CHAPTER 37

Development Methodologies

IN THIS CHAPTER

Why Use a Development Methodology?

If you've been building Web applications for a while, you've probably run into this situation: You're asked to work on something that you originally wrote many months ago. Perhaps you're asked to change the way a complex set of forms works. As you pour over your old code, you're bewildered and having a bit of difficulty figuring out which pages call which and why you did certain things the way you did. Sound familiar?

Of course, this can happen to the most experienced developer. You should recognize that when you spend *n* hours developing an application, you will probably spend 2*n* or 3*n* hours maintaining the application over time. The predicament just described can be largely avoided—or at least significantly mitigated—by employing a well-defined and well-thought-out development methodology.

A good development methodology defines naming conventions for files—and perhaps other elements. It provides an organizational structure for your application directories and source files (Web pages, Macromedia ColdFusion MX templates, graphical images, and other content). It also probably provides directives on how to structure your program code.

Employing these types of conventions allows you to more easily maintain your code. It also enables a team of developers—all employing the same methodology—to debug and support each other's code. Take it one step further, and it's easy to imagine how a methodology employed by unrelated individuals can produce code that can be understood and maintained by anyone who uses the methodology.

A robust methodology also lets you build large applications with many, many sections and pages. It provides a meaningful way of organizing all the content and program logic so as to make it easier to maintain.

So, development methodologies are useful to individuals because we can't remember how we programmed something a long time ago (or sometimes, just last week!). Development methodologies are useful to teams and remote programmers because they make the team members more interchangeable and better able to support each other's efforts. And development methodologies are useful when organizing large applications with many components and pages.

This chapter takes a detailed look at one methodology—Fusebox—and provides an overview of several others. Let's say you need to build a simple contact manager for Orange Whip Studios. In this chapter, you construct a simple contact manager in Fusebox so you can better understand how this framework addresses a common application.

Fusebox

First developed in 1998, Fusebox is the granddaddy of all ColdFusion development methodologies. Steve Nelson and Gabe Roffman are responsible for creating the original Fusebox specification, and Joshua Cyr was perhaps the first person to employ the methodology on a real application. Many ColdFusion developers have subsequently contributed to and popularized it.

Partly because of its longevity, but mostly because of its practicality, Fusebox is perhaps the most widely used ColdFusion development methodology. (It's worth noting that it isn't specific to ColdFusion per se. It can be applied—and has been developed—for other development environments.)

The Fusebox specification, now in its third release, lets you write applications that can be easily ported and reused. Fusebox 3 does a great job of providing a framework for separating business logic from presentation logic. This is a valuable feature because it enhances your ability to update code and improves your application's scalability and portability.

Fusebox provides a set of directory and file-naming conventions that help anyone familiar with the methodology to easily understand someone else's code. Fusebox employs a number of core files that are used for controlling program flow and managing global variables. The third release also provides *Fusedocs*—an XML-based approach for documenting and/or technically specifying your applications.

In the next section, you'll learn how Fusebox applications work.

How Fusebox Works

First it's important to understand a little bit of Fusebox jargon. A *circuit* refers to a self-contained, cohesive chunk of functionality. Perhaps you can think of a circuit as a module within an application. Each Fusebox app has at least a *home circuit*, which is the root directory for a Fusebox app. You create additional circuits as subdirectories when your application requires them.

Each circuit contains one or more *fuses*. A fuse is a small unit of application functionality. For example, a simple contact management application (like our example, discussed below) contains fuses that display a list of contacts, display individual contacts, edit contacts, delete contacts, and so on.

The logical flow in a Fusebox application is what some refer to as a "star" type of organization, as depicted in Figure 37.1. The flow of all application logic begins and ends in the index.cfm template. Each fuse in a circuit is represented by an "arm" in the star. The star or circuit translates into a simple `<CFSWITCH>` statement. Each fuse is identified by a *fuseaction* variable, and there is one `<CFCASE>` in the switch for each fuseaction.

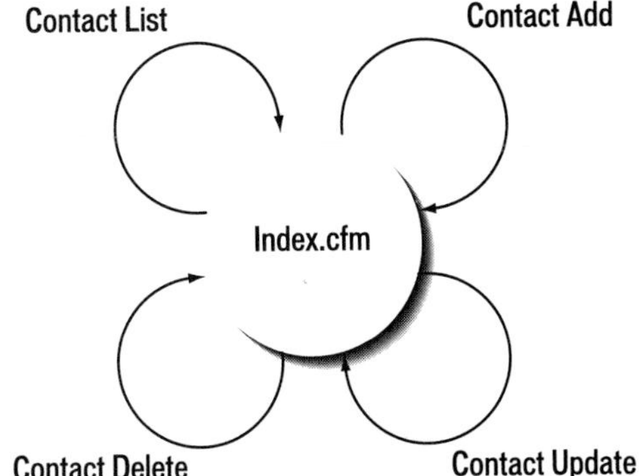

Figure 37.1

Fusebox uses a "star" application flow, in which all branching starts in and returns to the `index.cfm` template.

All Fusebox applications include a set of *core files*. They can be downloaded from `www.fusebox.org`. They are part of the Fusebox specification, controlling the logic and providing some of Fusebox's core functionality. You must edit and add your own code to some of these templates, while others are to be left untouched (unless you want to alter Fusebox's normal behavior in some way, such as changing Fusebox's default handling of internal errors). The core files are included in the home circuit of a Fusebox application, and some must be included in each circuit below the home circuit. The core Fusebox files are described in Table 37.1. To them, you add a variety of ColdFusion templates that contain the business logic of your app.

So, a Fusebox application consists of one or more circuits (directories) that contain a set of Fusebox core files and your own application logic templates.

How does all this stuff work together? Well I must admit, it doesn't appear simple, but it all works through a series of `<CFINCLUDE>` tags and isn't really all that complicated. Take a look at Figure 37.2. A Fusebox application starts by calling `index.cfm`—a Fusebox file that you normally don't touch.

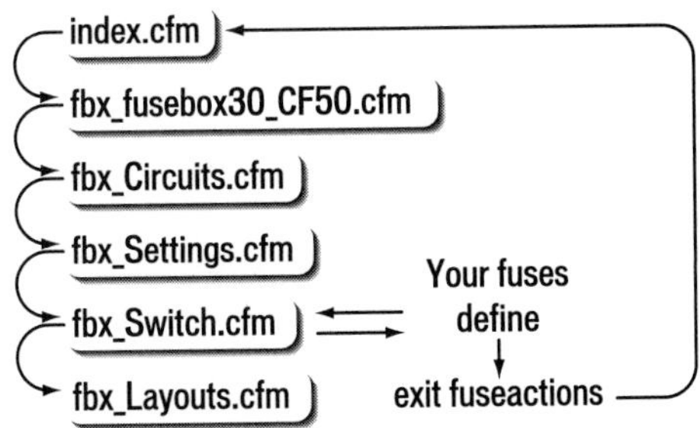

Figure 37.2

A Fusebox application is simply a series of `<CFINCLUDE>`s involving the core Fusebox files and your fuses (`dsp_xxx.cfm`, `qry_yyy.cfm`, and so on)

NOTE

At this point, I'd recommend reviewing the files on the CD for this chapter.

The `index.cfm` file looks at your ColdFusion server and determines which `fbx_Fusebox`*`nn`*`CF`*`ii`*`.cfm` file to include (this is a core file that you don't touch).

Table 37.1 Important Fusebox Files

FILENAME	EDITABLE?	FUNCTION
`fbx_Settings.cfm`	Yes	Contains "global" variable definitions for the current circuit and any child circuits. This file must be included in each of your app's circuits.
`fbx_Fusebox`*ii*`CF`*nn*`.cfm`	No	Fusebox library files, where *ii* indicates the Fusebox version and *nn* indicates the ColdFusion version. You'll also find some that end with *nix.cfm;* these are for use in various Unix/Linux dialects.
`fbx_Circuits.cfm`	Yes	Creates a structure that identifies all of your app's circuits and the directory associated with each one.
`fbx_Layouts.cfm`	Yes	Creates a structure that identifies your application's layout file(s). A layout file is a template of HTML code that creates the "shell" of a page. You do not need to use any layout files, but you do need to include the fbx_Layouts.cfm file in each of your app's circuits.
`fbx_Switch.cfm`	Yes	A `<CFSWITCH>` statement that invokes your various templates based on your application functionality. You edit this template to define your own fuseactions (cases). Each `<CFCASE>` in the switch processes one fuseaction.
`index.cfm`	No	Loads the appropriate Fusebox library file, based on your OS and your version of ColdFusion. This is not technically a core file, but it is required for your application to function.
`fbx_Savecontent.cfm`	No	Functions like ColdFusion's `<CFSAVECONTENT>` tag. It saves all generated output from the current page into a variable. This is not technically a core file; it'sneeded only if you're using a version of ColdFusion prior to 5.0.

This `fbx_Fusebox`*nn*`CF`*ii*`.cfm` file then includes `fbx_Circuits.cfm`, which you edit to create the `fusebox.circuits` structure. This structure includes an entry for each of your application's circuits. Each entry maps a circuit—a logical name—to a physical directory, relative to the home directory for the app.

The `fbx_Fusebox…cfm` file next includes the `fbx_Settings.cfm` template that you have modified to include your application's (and circuits') global variables, such as your database's data source name.

The `fbx_Fusebox`*nn*`CF`*ii*`.cfm` file then includes your `fbx_Switch.cfm` file. This is the core Fusebox file that you modify to identify your fuseactions in a big `<CFSWITCH>` statement. Within each fuse (`<CFCASE>`, for example), you identify the template to be included (`dsp_contactlist.cfm`, for instance) and also define the exit points from that template. These are called *exit fuseactions*—or *XFAs*, in Fusebox parlance.

XFAs are variables that define a fuse's exit points. They define the various ways that the user exits a fuse in your application. Their use will become clearer in our example below.

After the templates identified in the fuseaction are included, `fbx_FuseboxnnCFii.cfm` includes `fbx_Layouts.cfm`. You edit this template to define the layout template for your circuit. The template you identify is executed, and `fbx_FuseboxnnCFii.cfm` produces any content defined by your fuseaction and the layout template.

NOTE

Note that when `fbx_Switch.cfm` is included and executes, one of your fuses is executed. This might be a template that displays a list of contacts. That template may contain `HREF` anchors used to link to a detailed view of an individual contact. Each `HREF` is an *exit point* from the fuseaction that loaded the contact list template. Each `HREF` will point to `index.cfm` *and* an XFA and will provide something to identify the specific record to be retrieved.

There's one more concept worth discussing before you dig into some code: file-naming conventions. You don't have to follow these conventions per se, but their value will become clear quickly. You use a set of prefixes to name your templates, based on each template's technical function within your application. These prefixes are presented in Table 37.2.

Table 37.2 Fusebox Filename Prefixes

PREFIX	FUNCTION
`act`	Action templates execute some type of business logic on the server, often in response to a form submission. Most often, these are database updates, but they may include other sorts of processing.
`dsp`	Displays templates. These typically contain HTML code that formats some output.
`qry`	Queries or stored procedures. You typically put SQL code that retrieves data in a *qry* template. If the code updates a database, you'd typically put it in an *act* (action) template.
`fbx`	Fusebox files that are core files—in other words, part of the Fusebox specification and/or referenced in Fusebox core files.

Building a Simple Contact Manager with Fusebox

Now that you understand a bit of the mechanics behind Fusebox, let's review an example of how the Fusebox methodology could be used by Orange Whip Studios to build a simple contact manager. The main templates used in this application are described in Table 37.3 and are included on the CD. This section assumes you've installed these files.

The contact manager enables Orange Whip Studios to list, view, create, update, and delete contact records.

NOTE

Assuming you've installed the files for this chapter from the CD, take a look at the `fbx_Layouts.cfm` template. You'll see that it defines this circuit's layout template, `DefaultLayout.cfm`, as shown in Listing 37.1. This file is used by `fbx_FuseboxnnCFii.cfm` as a template for the basic presentation layout of this circuit. Therefore, the content produced by `DefaultLayout.cfm` is also used.

Table 37.3 Fusebox Contact Manager Templates

TEMPLATE	DESCRIPTION
`qry_GetAllContacts.cfm`	Runs a query to get a list of all contacts.
`qry_GetContactRecord.cfm`	Selects a specified contact or returns an empty record set.
`dsp_ContactList.cfm`	Displays a list of contacts, grouped by last name.
`dsp_ContactForm.cfm`	Displays a form for creating and modifying contact records.
`dsp_ContactDetail.cfm`	Displays a form for viewing contact records.
`act_ContactUpdate.cfm`	Uses SQL to either insert, update, or delete contact records.
`DefaultLayout.cfm`	Acts as a template for those fuseactions that generate content.

Listing 37.1 Here are the active ingredients from `fbx_Layouts.cfm`

```
<cfset fusebox.layoutFile = "DefaultLayout.cfm">
```

NOTE

Note that all the code presented in the following sections is on the CD. However, each Fusebox template also contains some *Fusedocs code* in the header, which I have left out of the listings for the sake of brevity.

Defining Circuits

As you know, the `fbx_Circuits.cfm` template (see Listing 37.2) is used to define your application's circuits. In our simple contact manager application, we need only one circuit, the home circuit.

Listing 37.2 `fbx_Circuits.cfm`—The `fbx_Circuits.cfm` template defines your application's circuits in the `fusebox.circuits` structure.

```
<!---
Module:         fbx_Circuits.cfm
Author:         M Jeo, L Chalnick
Function:       Defines our application's circuits. This app has only a
                home circuit, which is named 'home'.
Date created:   4/25/2002
--->
<cfset fusebox.circuits=StructNew()>
<cfset fusebox.circuits.home="home">
```

If our contact manager app was more complex, we might want to create other circuits. For example, let's say there was a requirement for tracking phone calls with contacts. We might want to create a circuit to handle this additional functionality. Assuming we created a subdirectory (off our application root directory) for this circuit, named `/calls`, we would add this line to our `fbx_Circuits.cfm` file:

```
<CFSET fusebox.circuits.phonecalls="home/calls">
```

Fusebox 3 supports the notion of nested circuits—child circuits that inherit from parent circuits. This is discussed further toward the end of this section.

NOTE

A hidden benefit in this implementation of circuits is not obvious but is worth noting: It removes the physical structure of your application from the logical structure. This not only makes your app more portable, but also makes it a bit harder to hack.

Defining Global Variables

Let's now look at the `fbx_Settings.cfm` file for this application, seen in Listing 37.3.

Listing 37.3 `fbx_Settings.cfm`—This template defines the global variables used in our application.

```
<!---
Module:          fbx_Settings.cfm
Author:          M Jeo, L Chalnick
Function:        Defines our application's global variables. These
                 include a data source, a logical name for index.cfm,
                 and a default fuseaction.
Date created:    4/25/2002
--->

<!--- define variables used in this application --->
<CFAPPLICATION NAME="FuseActionContact">
<CFPARAM NAME="DSN" DEFAULT="ows">
<CFPARAM NAME="self" DEFAULT="index.cfm">
<CFPARAM NAME="PageTitle" DEFAULT="Simple Contact Manager">

<!--- Default fuse action to use, in case no fuseaction
was given. --->
<CFPARAM NAME="attributes.fuseaction"
DEFAULT="home.contactlist">

<!---
Uncomment this if you wish to have code specific that only executes if the circuit
running is the home circuit.
<cfif fusebox.IsHomeCircuit>
   <!--- put settings here that you want to execute only when this is the
application's home circuit (for example "<cfapplication>" )--->
<CFELSE>
   <!--- put settings here that you want to execute only when this is not an
application's home circuit --->
</cfif>

--->
```

NOTE

Note the variable `self`. This is simply a way of abstracting the name for the default file that will be invoked for every call to Fusebox. This is used in all internal URLs so that your code doesn't point to `index.cfm` per se, but instead points to `self`.

Your Contact Manager's Fuse Box

As you may recall, `fbx_Switch.cfm` is the core Fusebox template in which you define all of the application's fuseactions. It's sometimes referred to as the *fuse box*. The various fuseactions refer to your application's specific templates. These are named with a prefix that identifies their technical function and a suffix that describes their business function.

It is also the responsibility of each fuseaction to define the XFAs or exit fuseactions. These are the logical exit points for this fuseaction.

Let's take look at the contact manager app's `fbx_Switch.cfm` template in Listing 37.4.

Listing 37.4 `fbx_Switch.cfm`—Your application's switch invokes all the fuseactions.

```
<!---
Module:         fbx_Switch.cfm
Author:         M Jeo, L Chalnick
Function:       The contact manager's fusebox determines which
                fuse to execute (based on the value of the
                fusebox.fuseaction parameter) and which circuit
                it's found in (based on the fusebox.circuit
                parameter.
Date created:   4/25/2002
--->

<!--- These exit fuse actions will be available for all switches --->
<CFSWITCH EXPRESSION = "#fusebox.fuseaction#">
   <CFCASE VALUE="contactlist">
      <CFSET XFA.contactform = "home.contactform">
      <CFSET XFA.contactdetail = "home.contactdetail">
      <CFSET XFA.contactlist = "home.contactlist">
      <CFSET PageTitle = "Contact Listing">
      <CFINCLUDE TEMPLATE="qry_getallcontacts.cfm">
      <CFINCLUDE TEMPLATE="dsp_contactlist.cfm">
   </CFCASE>
   <CFCASE VALUE="contactdetail">
      <CFSET XFA.contactdetail = "home.contactdetail">
      <CFSET XFA.contactform = "home.contactform">
      <CFSET XFA.contactlist = "home.contactlist">
      <CFSET XFA.deletecontact = "home.deletecontact">
      <CFSET PageTitle = "Display Contact">
      <CFINCLUDE TEMPLATE="qry_GetContactRecord.cfm">
      <CFINCLUDE TEMPLATE="dsp_contactdetail.cfm">
   </CFCASE>
   <CFCASE VALUE="contactform">
      <CFSET XFA.contactdetail = "home.contactdetail">
      <CFSET XFA.contactform = "home.contactform">
      <CFSET XFA.contactlist = "home.contactlist">
      <CFSET XFA.deletecontact = "home.deletecontact">
      <CFSET XFA.contactFormAction = "home.#Attributes.event#Contact">
      <CFSET PageTitle = "Contact Form">
      <CFINCLUDE TEMPLATE="qry_GetContactRecord.cfm">
      <CFINCLUDE TEMPLATE="dsp_contactform.cfm">
   </CFCASE>
   <CFCASE VALUE="updatecontact">
      <CFSET XFA.contactdetail = "home.contactdetail">
      <CFINCLUDE TEMPLATE="act_contactupdate.cfm">
   </CFCASE>
   <CFCASE VALUE="addcontact">
      <CFSET XFA.contactlist = "home.contactlist">
      <CFINCLUDE TEMPLATE="act_contactupdate.cfm">
   </CFCASE>
   <CFCASE VALUE="deletecontact">
      <CFSET XFA.contactform = "home.contactform">
      <CFSET XFA.contactlist = "home.contactlist">
```

Listing 37.4 (continued)

```
        <CFSET XFA.deletecontact = "home.deletecontact">
        <CFINCLUDE TEMPLATE="act_contactupdate.cfm">
    </CFCASE>

    <CFDEFAULTCASE>
        <!---This will just display an error message and is
         useful in catching typos of fuseaction names while
         developing--->
        <CFOUTPUT>This is the cfdefaultcase tag. I
        received a fuseaction called
        "#attributes.fuseaction#" and I don't know what to
        do with it.</CFOUTPUT>
    </CFDEFAULTCASE>
</CFSWITCH>
```

As you can see `fbx_Switch.cfm` defines the various fuseactions and associated exit fuseactions. This template is the central switch for all of your application's business logic. You can see that by looking at this file, you can get a darn good idea of what all the templates in this application do and how they're invoked.

If no `fuseaction` is passed, the contact list is displayed because `contactlist` is the default `fuseaction` defined in `fbx_Settings.cfm` (refer to Listing 37.3).

The Layout Template

This contains the HTML template used to format each page in the circuit. The layout file is identified in `fbx_Layouts.cfm` like this:

```
<CFSET fusebox.layoutFile = "DefaultLayout.cfm">
```

So, as you saw in Figure 37.2, `fbx_Fusebox`*nn*`_CF`*ii*`.cfm` includes this template, `DefaultLayout.cfm` (see Listing 37.5), after including the `fbx_Switch.cfm` template.

Listing 37.5 `DefaultLayout.cfm`—This acts as an HTML template for each page in the contact manager.

```
<!---
Module:          DefaultLayout.cfm
Author:          M Jeo, L Chalnick
Function:        Defines the basic HTML layout for this circuit.
                 This includes a standard head and body. Note that
                 the variable, PageTitle, is used to set the value
                 for the <TITLE> and in the <BODY>. The value of
                 PageTitle is defined in each fuseaction.
                 This page also includes a <SELECT> menu.
Date created:    4/25/2002
--->
<CFPARAM NAME="attributes.con_id" DEFAULT="0">
<!doctype html public "-//W3C//DTD HTML 4.0 Transitional//EN">
<HTML>
<HEAD>
    <TITLE><CFOUTPUT>#Variables.PageTitle#</CFOUTPUT></TITLE>
    <LINK REL="STYLESHEET" TYPE="text/css" HREF="default.css">
```

Listing 37.5 (continued)

```
    <SCRIPT language="JavaScript" TYPE="text/javascript">
       function gotoURL() {
          URLpass =
self.document.menu_form.event[self.document.menu_form.event.selectedIndex].value;
          if (URLpass != '') {
             self.document.location = URLpass;
          }
       }
    </SCRIPT>
</HEAD>
<BODY>
   <h2>Simple Contact Manager</h2>
   <FORM NAME="menu_form" ACTION="index.cfm" METHOD="post">
   <CFOUTPUT>
   <INPUT TYPE="hidden" NAME="con_id"
     VALUE="#attributes.con_id#">
   </CFOUTPUT>
   <TABLE CELLPADDING="5" WIDTH="100%" CELLSPACING="0">
   <TR BGCOLOR="#efefef">
      <TD> <!---/// Events ///--->
         <SELECT NAME="event" SIZE="1"
          onChange="gotoURL();">
            <OPTION VALUE="">---- Contacts ----</OPTION>
            <CFOUTPUT>
               <OPTION
                VALUE="#self#?fuseaction
                 =#XFA.contactform#&event=add">Add
                 a New Contact</OPTION>
               <CFIF val(attributes.con_id) gt 0>
                  <OPTION VALUE="#self#?fuseaction=
                  #XFA.contactform#&event=
                  update&con_id=#attributes.con_id#"
                  >Edit Contact</OPTION>
                  <OPTION VALUE="#self#?fuseaction=
                  #XFA.deletecontact#&event=
                  delete&con_id=#attributes.con_id#"
                  >Delete</OPTION>
               </CFIF>
               <OPTION VALUE="">----------------------------------------</OPTION>
               <OPTION VALUE="#self#?fuseaction=
               #XFA.contactlist#">Display All</OPTION>
            </CFOUTPUT>
         </SELECT>
         <INPUT TYPE="button" VALUE="Go"
          onClick="gotoURL();">
      </TD>

      <TD ALIGN="right">
         <FONT SIZE="+1"><B><CFOUTPUT>
          #Variables.PageTitle#</CFOUTPUT>
         </B></FONT>
      </TD>
   </TR>
   </TABLE>
   </FORM>
   <cfoutput>#fusebox.layout#</cfoutput>
```

Listing 37.5 (continued)

```
        <P> </P>
        <TABLE CELLPADDING="5" WIDTH="100%" CELLSPACING="0">
        <TR BGCOLOR="#efefef">
           <TD CLASS="smallText">&copy; 2002, Orange
            Whip Studios</TD>
        </TR>
        </TABLE>
    </BODY>
    </HTML>
```

It may not be readily apparent how this template works, but it is rather simple. The Fusebox framework (specifically, `fbx_Fuseboxnn_CFii.cfm`) collects all of the output from each fuse and stores it in the variable, `fusebox.layout`. This is handled in a little chunk of code around line 240, as seen in Listing 37.6. Note that in versions of ColdFusion older than 5, `<CFSAVECONTENT>` doesn't exist, so this has to be handled differently (it is done with a custom tag).

Listing 37.6 This snippet from `fbx_Fusebox30_CF50.cfm` uses `<CFSAVECONTENT>` to store output from your fuseactions in a variable named `fusebox.layout`.

```
<cfsavecontent variable="fusebox.layout">
   <cfoutput>
   <cfinclude template="#FB_.fuseboxpath#fbx_Switch.cfm">
   </cfoutput>
</cfsavecontent>
```

So the output from your fuseactions (invoked by `fbx_Switch.cfm`) is stored in a variable, and this variable, `fusebox.layout`, is used in your layout template to generate the body of a page (as you can see near the bottom of Listing 37.5). Figure 37.3 indicates which portions of the contact listing are produced by the `DefaultLayout.cfm` template as opposed to the `dsp_ContactList.cfm` template.

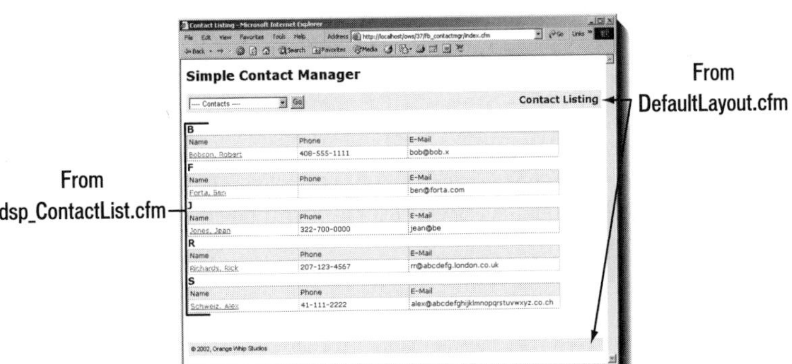

Figure 37.3 You can see which portions of the contact list the layout template produces.

Adding a New Contact

Let's explore the application's logic flow through the `contactlist` fuse. First, we'll assume that you've configured your Web server so that index.cfm is the default template for the folder in which this application resides.

To add a new contact, select Add a New Contact from the drop-down menu. You could choose any other mechanism to implement a navigational menu—there's nothing special about it. When you make a selection from the list, it executes JavaScript that redirects the user to the URL provided in the `<OPTION> VALUE` attribute, as shown in Listing 37.7.

Listing 37.7 A snippet from Listing 37.5 that is used to add a new contact.

```
<OPTION VALUE="#self#?fuseaction=#XFA.contactform#&event=add">Add a New
Contact</OPTION>
```

So, adding a new contact invokes `index.cfm` (as you may recall from the note above, the variable `self` points to `index.cfm`) with a `fuseaction` of `XFM.contactform` and sets an additional parameter, `event`, to `add`. Looking at Listing 37.4, you can see that this `fuseaction` runs the `qry_GetContactRecord.cfm` and then the `dsp_ContactForm.cfm` templates.

NOTE

If you've been working with ColdFusion for a while, you might recognize that it's often convenient to use the same HTML form for adding and modifying simple data. When you're editing, you use a query to retrieve a specific record to work on; then you populate all the form fields with the values from your query. But when you're adding, you must do something to populate the fields with null values. How can you do this with one form?

If you look at `qry_GetContactRecord.cfm` in Listing 37.8, you'll see it uses the same query to retrieve a record set. This way, you have all the same field values you need to populate the form.

Listing 37.8 `qry_GetContactRecord.cfm`—This query is run prior to adding or modifying a contact.

```
<!---
Module:         qry_GetContactRecord.cfm
Author:         M Jeo, L Chalnick
Function:       Query's a specific contact. A specific contact
                will not be identified when adding a new
                contact, so contact id will be set to 0
                and the query will return an empty recordset.
Date created:   4/25/2002
--->
<CFPARAM NAME="Attributes.Con_ID" DEFAULT="0">

<CFQUERY NAME="GetContactDetail" DATASOURCE="#DSN#">
   SELECT ContactID, FirstName, LastName, Phone, Address,
   City, State, Zip, Country, Email, UserLogin,
   UserPassword, MailingList
   FROM Contacts
   <CFIF attributes.Con_ID NEQ 0>
      WHERE ContactID = #Attributes.Con_ID#
   <CFELSE>
      <!--- When adding, will return empty result set --->
      WHERE 0 = 1
   </CFIF>
</CFQUERY>
```

After the fuse box includes `qry_GetContactRecord.cfm`, it includes `dsp_ContactForm.cfm`, which is displayed in Listing 37.9. This template displays the contact record in an editable form.

Listing 37.9 `dsp_ContactForm.cfm`—This template presents contact records in an editable form.

```
<!---
Module:         dsp_ContactForm.cfm
Author:         M Jeo, L Chalnick
Function:       This template presents the form that is be used to update
                and add contacts.
Date created:   4/25/2002
--->
<cfoutput>
<table border="0">
<cfform action="#self#?fuseaction=#XFA.contactFormAction#" method="post">
<input type="Hidden" name="con_id" value="#GetContactDetail.ContactID#">
<!--- Hidden field to store the event type ( update or add ) --->
<input type="Hidden" name="event" value="#attributes.event#">
<tr valign="top">
   <td colspan="2">* indicates required field</td>
</tr>
<tr valign="top">
   <td>Name:</td>
   <td><cfinput type="Text" name="FirstName" value="#GetContactDetail.FirstName#"
size="25" required="Yes" message="First Name is required">
      <cfinput type="Text" name="LastName" value="#GetContactDetail.LastName#"
size="25" required="Yes" message="Last Name is required">*</td>
</tr>
<tr valign="top">
   <td>Address:</td>
   <td>
      <input type="Text" name="Address" value="#GetContactDetail.Address#"
size="50">
   </td>
</tr>
<tr valign="top">
   <td>City/State/Zip</td>
   <td>
      <input type="Text" name="City" value="#GetContactDetail.City#" size="25">
      <input type="Text" name="State" value="#GetContactDetail.State#" size="3">
      <input type="Text" name="Zip" value="#GetContactDetail.Zip#" size="10">
   </td>
</tr>
<tr valign="top">
   <td>Country:</td>
   <td>
      <input type="Text" name="Country" value="#GetContactDetail.Country#">
   </td>
</tr>
<tr valign="top">
   <td>Phone:</td>
   <td><input type="Text" name="phone" value="#GetContactDetail.phone#"></td>
</tr>
<tr valign="top">
   <td>E-Mail:</td>
   <td><input type="Text" name="email" value="#GetContactDetail.email#"
size="50"></td>
</tr>
<tr valign="top">
   <td>Login Name:</td>
   <td><cfinput type="Text" name="UserLogin" value="#GetContactDetail.userlogin#"
```

Listing 37.9 (continued)

```
required="Yes" message="Login name is required">*</td>
</tr>
<tr valign="top">
   <td>Password:</td>
   <td><cfinput type="password" name="UserPassword"
value="#GetContactDetail.userpassword#" required="Yes" message="Password is
required">*</td>
</tr>
<tr valign="top">
   <td>Mailing List?:</td>
   <td><input type="Checkbox" name="MailingList" #iif(getcontactdetail.mailinglist
eq 0, de(""), de("CHECKED"))#></td>
</tr>
<tr valign="top">
   <td> </td>
   <td>
       <br>
      <cfif attributes.event eq "update">
         <input type="submit" value="Save Changes">
      <cfelse>
         <input type="submit" value="Add Contacts">
      </cfif>
      <input type="button" value="Cancel" onClick="history.back();">
   </td>
</tr>
</cfform>
</table>
</cfoutput>
```

Now you'll see how XFAs are used. In `fbx_Switch.cfm` (see Listing 37.4), you can see in the `contactform` fuse that `XFA.contactFormAction` is being set to `home.#Attributes.event#Contact` and that `XFA.contactFormAction` is being used in the `FORM ACTION` attribute in `dsp_ContactForm.cfm`; see Listing 37.9. (Note that URL parameters are converted to the `ATTRIBUTES` scope by `fbx_Fusebox....cfm.`) So, this `ATTRIBUTES.event` variable is used in the form's action to dynamically generate the name of the `fuseaction`. In this case, the `fuseaction` will be set to *add*`contact` because `event` was set to `add` back in the drop-down menu in Listing 37.7.

When `fbx_Switch.cfm` (refer to Listing 37.4) executes with a `fuseaction` of `addcontact`, it executes the template `act_ContactUpdate.cfm` with `XFA.contactlist` set to `home.contactlist`. The `act_ContactUpdate.cfm` (see Listing 37.10) template uses the value of the `event` parameter and then runs either an insert, an update, or a delete query and uses the value of `XFA.contactlist` to determine what to do next—in other words, how to exit this fuse.

Listing 37.10 `act_contactupdate.cfm`—The action template performs insert, update, or delete queries.

```
<!---
Module:         act_ContactUpdate.cfm
Author:         M Jeo, L Chalnick
Function:       This action template is used to add/edit/delete contacts.
Date created:   4/25/2002
--->

<cfif attributes.event eq "update">
   <cfif isdefined("Attributes.MailingList")>
```

Listing 37.10 (continued)

```
      <cfset variables.mailinglist = 1>
   <cfelse>
      <cfset variables.mailinglist = 0>
   </cfif>
   <cfquery name="UpdateContact" datasource="#DSN#">
      UPDATE Contacts SET
         FirstName = '#Attributes.FirstName#',
         LastName = '#Attributes.LastName#',
         Address = <cfif attributes.address neq
"">'#Attributes.Address#'<cfelse>Null</cfif>,
         City = <cfif attributes.city neq "">'#Attributes.city#'<cfelse>Null</cfif>,
         State = <cfif attributes.state neq
"">'#Attributes.state#'<cfelse>Null</cfif>,
         Zip = <cfif attributes.zip neq "">'#Attributes.zip#'<cfelse>Null</cfif>,
         Country = <cfif attributes.country neq
"">'#Attributes.country#'<cfelse>Null</cfif>,
         Email = <cfif attributes.email neq
"">'#Attributes.email#'<cfelse>Null</cfif>,
         Phone = <cfif attributes.phone neq
"">'#Attributes.phone#'<cfelse>Null</cfif>,
         UserLogin = '#Attributes.userlogin#',
         UserPassword = '#Attributes.UserPassword#',
         MailingList = #Variables.MailingList#
       WHERE ContactID = #Attributes.con_id#
   </cfquery>
   <cflocation
url="#self#?fuseaction=#XFA.contactdetail#&con_id=#Attributes.con_id#">
<cfelseif attributes.event eq "add">
   <cfif isdefined("Attributes.MailingList")>
      <cfset variables.mailinglist = 1>
   <cfelse>
      <cfset variables.mailinglist = 0>
   </cfif>
   <cfquery name="UpdateContact" datasource="#DSN#">
      INSERT INTO Contacts (FirstName, LastName, Address, City, State, Zip, Country,
         Email, Phone, UserLogin, UserPassword, MailingList)
      VALUES (
         '#Attributes.FirstName#',
         '#Attributes.LastName#',
         <cfif attributes.address neq "">'#Attributes.Address#'<cfelse>Null</cfif>,
         <cfif attributes.city neq "">'#Attributes.city#'<cfelse>Null</cfif>,
         <cfif attributes.state neq "">'#Attributes.state#'<cfelse>Null</cfif>,
         <cfif attributes.zip neq "">'#Attributes.zip#'<cfelse>Null</cfif>,
         <cfif attributes.country neq "">'#Attributes.country#'<cfelse>Null</cfif>,
         <cfif attributes.email neq "">'#Attributes.email#'<cfelse>Null</cfif>,
         <cfif attributes.phone neq "">'#Attributes.phone#'<cfelse>Null</cfif>,
         '#Attributes.userlogin#', '#Attributes.userpassword#',
         #Variables.MailingList# )
   </cfquery>
   <cflocation url="#self#?fuseaction=#XFA.contactlist#">
<cfelse>

   <cfif isdefined("Attributes.do_delete")>
      <cfquery name="DELETEContact" datasource="#DSN#">
         DELETE FROM Contacts
         WHERE ContactID = #Attributes.con_id#
      </cfquery>
```

Listing 37.10 (continued)

```
         <cflocation url="#self#?fuseaction=#XFA.contactlist#">

      <cfelse>

         <cfquery name="GetContactDetail" datasource="#DSN#">
            SELECT FirstName, LastName
            FROM Contacts
            WHERE ContactID = #Attributes.Con_ID#
         </cfquery>

         <cfoutput>
         <h1>Confirm Delete</h1>
         Are you sure you want to delete <b>#GetContactDetail.firstname#
   #GetContactDetail.lastname#</b>?
         <form action="#self#?fuseaction=#XFA.deletecontact#" method="post">
            <input type="hidden" name="event" value="delete">
            <input type="hidden" name="con_id" value="#Attributes.Con_ID#">
            <input type="submit" name="do_delete" value="Yes">
            <input type="button" value="No" onclick="history.back();">
         </form>
         </cfoutput>
      </cfif>
   </cfif>
```

The other templates in this example work in a similar fashion: Everything executes via `fbx_Switch.cfm`, which is included in `index.cfm`. Note that when following the Fusebox methodology, you do not normally use the ColdFusion `Application.cfm` file (although you now can—in earlier versions of Fusebox, it was verboten). One of the early goals of Fusebox was to provide a mechanism for running an entire application as a custom tag. Because `Application.cfm` is not automatically invoked inside custom tags, it wasn't considered useful. So, you instead use the `fbx_Settings.cfm` template, as it is included prior to each call to one of your fuses.

Note also that you are not supposed to invoke fuses directly. You always invoke fuses through the box (`fbx_switch.cfm`, normally invoked through `index.fm`) by passing it the appropriate `fuseaction` param. For example:

```
<A HREF="index.cfm?fuseaction=#XFA.search#">Search the site</A>
```

Benefits

The example demonstrates that you can tell a lot about how a Fusebox application works by looking at the `fbx_Switch.cfm` file. In a properly constructed Fusebox application, everything traces back to `fuseaction`. This makes understanding and maintaining a Fusebox application much easier: You just follow the `fuseactions`.

The example also demonstrates how Fusebox enables you separate much of the business logic layer from the presentation layer. The back-end SQL code that lists contacts is in its own template, as is the SQL code that creates (or inserts or deletes) contacts. The code for viewing a contact is in its own template, as is the code for editing a contact. The `DefaultLayout.cfm` template includes much of the basic UI and HTML that formats each page.

This separation results in a more portable application because it breaks links between business and presentation layers. You can change the presentation layer significantly with very little if any impact on the business layer. Likewise, you can change much of the internal operations of the business layer without affecting the presentation layer (as long as you accept the same input and generate the same output). This approach often results in more transportable, scalable code.

The example presented here is quite simple and includes only one circuit. Additional circuits are included in more complex applications. This involves employing additional directories. In older versions of Fusebox, you'd point directly to those directories in your URL. But now you use the `fbx_Circuits.cfm` template to map different circuits (directories) to logical *circuit names*, and you refer to these circuit names in your application. The benefit here is that your application's internal directory structure is obfuscated, making some kinds of hacks more difficult.

Many ColdFusion developers use Fusebox. If you learn to use this methodology, you'll certainly be in a great position to work and share code with other developers.

More to the point, Fusebox will make you more productive. You'll derive all the general benefits associated with employing a development methodology that were outlined earlier in the chapter. Maintaining Fusebox code that is old or written by someone else will be much easier. Understanding an application's structure is really just a question of following the `fuseactions`. You'll also be able to tell what a file does by where it's located and what it is named.

Also, note that because Fusebox applications are quite modular—they originally were intended to be written as custom tags—they can be swapped in and out of larger applications relatively easily.

As you can see from the example, you can also use this methodology to separate much of the application logic from the presentation. This makes for applications that will scale better and be easier to maintain.

Drawbacks

Understanding how Fusebox applications work is not trivial. Fusebox has become a lot more complicated with release 3 of the specification and associated files. Some will argue that unless you're building applications that will be deployed with a variety of clients (both HTTP and WAP browsers, for example) or that need to be very portable (as they'll be reused many times), that the overhead involved in "doing it with Fusebox" is just too much.

Ironically, some people believe that Fusebox applications can be harder to debug than non-Fusebox applications. All templates are included in the `fbx_Switch.cfm` template (or the template that includes it, like `index.cfm`) and refer back to it. So when something isn't working, it can be harder to tell which template the offending code came from.

This architecture also makes it quite difficult for your Web log reporting software to get an accurate hit count on individual pages because every page in the application appears to be `index.cfm`.

Fusebox's file-naming convention is based on files' technical roles in the application, rather than their functional roles. You should be careful to use filenames that also describe the business function being performed.

Other Methodologies and Frameworks

The next four methodologies to be investigated are not quite as well known as Fusebox. cfObjects was architected by Ralph Fiol of ActiveTier Technologies in late 1999 and introduced to the ColdFusion developer community in early 2000. Blackbox was developed by Dan Chick (with assistance from Joel Mueller and Mike Imhoff) in 1999. As you might expect from Blackbox's name, it has some similarities to Fusebox. Similarly, some analogies exist between SmartObjects and cfObjects. SmartObjects was developed by Benjamin Pate in the summer of 2000. Like cfObjects, SmartObjects allows you to write object-oriented ColdFusion applications. Switch_Box was developed by Joseph Flanigan and is an interesting blend of some Fusebox elements and some object-oriented concepts.

cfObjects and SmartObjects

cfObjects is a fascinating framework that brings the basic principles of object-oriented programming to the ColdFusion development environment—a markedly non–object-oriented platform. cfObjects brings the promise of being able to separate presentation from application logic, originally described in SmallTalk's Model-View-Controller architecture.

Employing this methodology enables you to write ColdFusion applications that use classes, encapsulation, polymorphism, and inheritance. Confused? Well, object-oriented programming can indeed be confusing for the uninitiated. If you need a brief review of these concepts, please read the sidebar titled "A Review of Object-Oriented Programming Concepts."

NOTE

> The basic idea is that you design your code based around logical *objects* or *classes*. A class represents a prototype of an object and defines the object's attributes and behaviors. For example, in a contact management application, you might have classes for contacts and phone calls. These objects have attributes (*properties*) and behaviors (*methods*). A contact will have properties such as first name, last name, company name, address, and phone number.
>
> When you actually create a contact, it is referred to as an *instance* of the contact class.
>
> The contact class will probably employ methods such as Fetch, Remove, and List. Methods are similar to procedures-they're the code that does most of the work.
>
> If you think about it, you could create the same methods for most of the other objects in the contact management system. For example, the phone call object probably needs Fetch and List capabilities, too. This demonstrates the concept of *polymorphism*-the notion that functions with the same name can be used to do different things in the same application. In this example, both the contact object and phone call object will have Fetch, Remove, and List methods.
>
> In a contact management system, you'll want to track phone calls you make. A follow-up is a certain type of phone call related to an earlier phone call. In the object-oriented contact management application, you might want to create a special class of phone call called a follow-up. You could create it as a subclass of your phone call class. This would save time because your subclass would *inherit* the property methods of its parent class, so you would only have to produce those that are new or modified.

The cfObjects methodology dictates the use of a directory structure, some file-naming conventions, and some tag-naming conventions, and requires the use of some specific tags. Moreover, you also must use a set of framework tags that are available from the `www.cfobjects.com` Web site.

The framework tags provide low-level services that you'll use throughout your applications, such as initializing your application, creating objects, and declaring methods. The Web site contains an excellent tutorial on the methodology. It's strongly recommended that you go through the tutorial before sitting down to code anything.

SmartObjects is intended to be easier to learn and use than cfObjects, while providing a similar set of benefits (that is, the benefits of object-oriented programming). It also supports multiple inheritance—the capability to encapsulate functions from more than one base class.

Similar to cfObjects, the methodology consists of a set of framework templates and a set of special directories and templates you create.

You create classes in their own directories. In each class directory, you create a file named `Public.cfm`. This defines the class and registers it using the framework's custom tag, `Class.cfm`. You specify the class name, its base classes (from which it inherits properties and methods), and its methods.

You use the custom tag `Object.cfm` to create instances of objects. As with cfObjects, instances of objects are implemented as structures. Each of an object's methods is a template in the object's directory.

Both of these object-oriented frameworks were developed prior to the introduction of ColdFusion Components (CFCs) in ColdFusion MX. As you may know by now, CFCs provide ColdFusion with some very powerful object-oriented features and benefits. CFCs, however, are not intended to act as the sole basis for writing your code; in other words, you shouldn't be replacing all of your application logic with CFCs. CFCs do not provide an entire framework for developing applications. But their introduction does mitigate some of the usefulness of cfObjects and SmartObjects.

Blackbox and Switch_Box

The Blackbox framework intends to provide many of the benefits of Fusebox, but in a somewhat less restrictive manner. The notion is that other developers might prefer their own file-naming conventions, for example. Blackbox also enables you to structure your applications so that all the URLs don't all point back to `index.cfm`.

How does it do this? It uses a special custom tag called `Blackbox.cfm` and a simple directory structure that you provide. It does not employ a true file-naming convention or tell you how to structure your application.

To a certain degree, the `Blackbox.cfm` template takes the place of some of the core Fusebox templates, including `fbx_Switch.cfm`. But instead of being a long `switch/case` statement that you code, it is a custom tag that navigates your application directory tree looking for a directory and template specified in two attributes that you pass it.

You create your application directory and put the `Blackbox.cfm` custom tag in it, along with templates you'll use to invoke the major sections of your application. You then create a directory named `Blackbox` in your application's root. Now, think of the logical sections of your application: You'll create a subdirectory of `/Blackbox` for each logical section.

Most of the functionality in your application is written through custom tags that are `<CFINCLUDE>`d in the `Blackbox.cfm` custom tag. The `Blackbox.cfm` tag itself is executed inside your application templates. This means your URLs will look like this:

```
http://localhost/MyApp/Contacts.cfm
http://localhost/MyApp/PhoneCalls.cfm
```

In Fusebox, on the other hand, your URLs might look like this:

```
http://localhost/MyApp/index.cfm?FuseAction=Contacts
http://localhost/MyApp/index.cfm?FuseAction=PhoneCalls
```

You might assume from its name that Switch_Box is another derivative of the Fusebox framework. But this would be far from accurate. It incorporates some object-oriented terminology and concepts, as well as bringing some its own unique concepts to the table.

This intriguing framework is built around the notion that application structure need not—and in fact should not—be tied to application logic. Your application's logical components are abstracted from the physical components.

In Switch_Box apps, URLs point to only one file, and this file includes a set of core files. Rather than pointing to directory structures and/or files in your URLs, you provide logical names. These names are interpreted into *message vectors* (sort of a combination of hierarchical object names and method names) by the core files and the core database table (which you include in your apps). These message vectors are mapped to specific files by core files that are part of the framework.

The framework also provides a security infrastructure that you can use to restrict access to logical parts of the application. It too employs some core files and a set of tables. All application files are executed by being included in either your initial `.cfm` file or one of the core files. The framework also employs the convention of naming files with a `.cfi` extension (which stands for *ColdFusion Include*). The advantage is that files named this way cannot be directly invoked by mischievous users spoofing URLs, thus providing a further layer of security.

Switch_Box also includes a Web-based user interface, referred to as *the Framework*, for generating many parts of your applications. It allows you to organize the various parts of your application as a logical tree (and employs `<CF_TREE>` to these ends). You complete a form, and the Framework generates the core table entries for you. Very cool!

The primary benefits of Switch_Box are that it does a very good job of isolating the presentation layer from the business logic layer. It goes further by abstracting the logical construction of the physical organization of your directories and files. There is *a lot* to Switch_Box. It provides much more functionality than the other frameworks we've discussed. As you might expect, there will definitely be a learning curve.

Issues to Consider with All Development Methodologies

Recognize that adopting a methodology is not a decision to take lightly. It can be a significant commitment. Varying learning curves are associated with the methodologies you've looked at in this chapter. Some require that you structure your applications a certain way, which might be contrary to what you or others you work with are accustomed to. For example, a commitment to an object-oriented methodology by a team of less-experienced programmers can prove to be challenging.

Another important point is that different methodologies exploit different features of the CFML language, and this language is not static. It has evolved quite significantly over the years. For example, ColdFusion MX represents a complete rewrite (in Java). The point is, you should be concerned with the effect that future changes might have on the approach taken by the methodology.

A final note: Most application-development tools provide some degree of a programming framework themselves. They often include features that support certain types of coding. There is some inherent danger in coding approaches that attempt to circumvent the way the developer (Macromedia in this case) intended for the product to be used.

Conclusions

ColdFusion provides a rich development environment in which the developer has a great deal of freedom. If you're in the business of developing ColdFusion (or any other) applications, however, it might make sense to adopt a methodology when developing applications. The most significant benefit from taking this approach is that you and others you work with will be able to more easily maintain the applications you create. Other benefits will vary a bit from one methodology to the next. However, all of the methodologies discussed in this chapter are intended to help you build more modular reusable code. Along with generally good coding practices, all these methodologies also help you write code more efficiently.

It's important to note that you do not need to use any of these methodologies to produce good ColdFusion applications. You should, however, adopt some sort of methodical approach to developing applications—perhaps something you and your associates develop on your own—so that you can still attain the benefits associated with using a methodology.

→ For more information on cfObjects, see `www.cfobjects.com`.

→ For more information on Fusebox, see `www.fusebox.org`.

→ For more information on SmartObjects, see `www.cfblackbox.com`.

→ For more information on Switch_Box, see `www.switch-box.org`.

→ For more information on Black Box, see `www.black-box.org`.

PART 5

Appendices

IN THIS PART

APPENDIX A

Installing ColdFusion MX, Dreamweaver MX, and the Sample Files

IN THIS APPENDIX

The goal of an install program is threefold: qualifying the computer, transferring files, and configuring the application to work with your operating system. If all goes well, you'll have a working application when the install is finished. In the unlikely event that things don't go smoothly, you'll need some help to get things right.

In this chapter, we're going to take a look at install processes for ColdFusion MX and Dreamweaver MX. We'll take a look at the minimum requirements for these applications, the install process, and a behind the scenes look at what the install does in the process of configuring the application for your operating system. We'll also walk you through installing the samples and examples used in the lessons in this book.

Introduction

This chapter is divided into three parts: the install process specific to ColdFusion MX, the install process specific for Dreamweaver MX, and instructions on how to install the sample files from the accompanying CD-ROM.

Let's get started.

ColdFusion MX

ColdFusion MX is supported on Windows, Linux, and UNIX systems. The supported platforms for Windows are Win9x (that is, Windows 98 and Windows ME), Windows NT 4.0, Windows 2000, and Windows XP. This includes the Professional, Server, Advanced Server, and Datacenter versions of the relevant operating systems as well. In addition to Windows, Linux, Solaris, and HP/UX are supported. There are some limitations to specific vendors and versions.

The Different Flavors of ColdFusion MX

Like the previous version, ColdFusion MX is sold in two versions: Professional and Enterprise. ColdFusion MX Enterprise contains powerful server management and scalability tools, security enhancements, additional database drivers, and other sophisticated features. The evaluation version of ColdFusion MX is called is functionally equivalent to the Enterprise edition. The Developer edition of ColdFusion MX is bundled with this book's accompanying CD-ROM.

Pre-Installation Checklist

To verify that ColdFusion MX will function at peak performance on your hardware platform, make sure you follow the steps listed here:

- Check your hardware's specs. If your RAM or disk space is inadequate or your processor cannot handle the load, an upgrade will be necessary.
- Check your operating system's configuration. Just having a copy of Windows 2000 does not guarantee ColdFusion MX will function perfectly.

Checking Your Hardware

At present, Macromedia supports three hardware platforms for ColdFusion MX: Intel-based systems running Windows NT 4.0; Windows 2000/XP; or Linux, Sun Sparc-processor systems running Solaris, and Hewlett Packard PA-RISC systems running HP-UX.

Intel-Based Systems

ColdFusion MX can be installed on Intel-based systems under Windows 98, Windows ME, Windows NT 4.0, Windows 2000, Windows XP, and several Linux distributions. The minimum recommended hardware is a Pentium-class machine.

Windows NT, Windows 2000 and Windows XP systems should have no less than 256MB of RAM to run ColdFusion MX and 400MB of free disk space.

All supported Linux distributions require the same system specifications as Windows.

NOTE

For all platforms, keep in mind that installing additional RAM usually improves system performance to some extent. Also, the applications you create with ColdFusion MX will take up additional hard disk space.

Solaris Systems

To use ColdFusion MX on Solaris systems, the system must be running Solaris with a SPARC processor. When installing ColdFusion MX on a Solaris system, your system must have 256MB of RAM and 350MB of free disk space. ColdFusion MX supports Solaris 7 and 8 with the latest operating system patches installed.

HP-UX Systems

To use ColdFusion MX on HP systems, the system must be running HP-UX with a PA-RISC 1.1 or 2.0 processor. In addition, 256MB of RAM and 350MB of free disk space are required.

Choosing Your Hardware

You probably already know which hardware platform you will use for ColdFusion MX because it's likely the hardware you already own. If you have yet to decide, the following points should be kept in mind during your deliberations:

- Virtually all ColdFusion MX code will execute perfectly across all supported platforms. That means if you jump ship to another platform during or after development, your applications will require little, if any, porting.
- Intel-based systems are the most popular hardware platforms in the world, with the largest number of options and vendors. Also, Intel-based systems experts can be found more easily than those for any other platform.
- Depending on a variety of configuration options, Sun SPARC, and HP-UX systems might provide more scalability and performance than Windows.

NOTE

The CD-ROM contains evaluation versions of ColdFusion MX and Dreamweaver MX for all supported platforms. ColdFusion MX reverts to the more restrictive developer edition when the evaluation period has expired.

Checking Your Operating System

The steps involved to ensure your operating system is properly configured to run ColdFusion depend on the operating system.

Windows

Both ColdFusion MX Professional and Enterprise run on Windows NT 4.0 Workstation and Server, Windows 2000 Professional and Server, and Windows XP Professional. If you use Windows 98 or ME, you should use ColdFusion MX Developer.

The TCP/IP protocol must be installed for your Windows system to take advantage of ColdFusion MX's network extensibility features such as web services, mail, HTTP, and LDAP. If you can browse Web sites on the Internet or your intranet using a Web browser, TCP/IP is installed on your system.

If you receive error messages that the proper protocols have not been installed, do the following:

- For Windows 98 and Windows ME, right-click the Network Neighborhood icon on the desktop and select the Properties option to display the Network properties dialog box shown in Figure A.1. The TCP/IP protocol should be shown in the Configuration tab. If it is not present, click the Add button to install it.

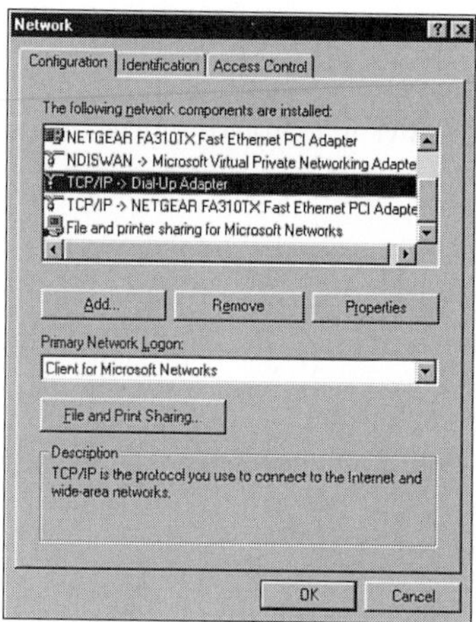

Figure A.1

Windows 98 and Windows ME Network Properties dialog with TCP/IP protocol installed.

The Network dialog box in Windows 98 shows installed clients, protocols, and adapters.

- If you use Windows NT 4.0, right-click the Network Neighborhood icon and select Properties. The Network dialog box will appear listing all available protocols (see Figure A.2). If TCP/IP does not appear, click the Add button to install it.

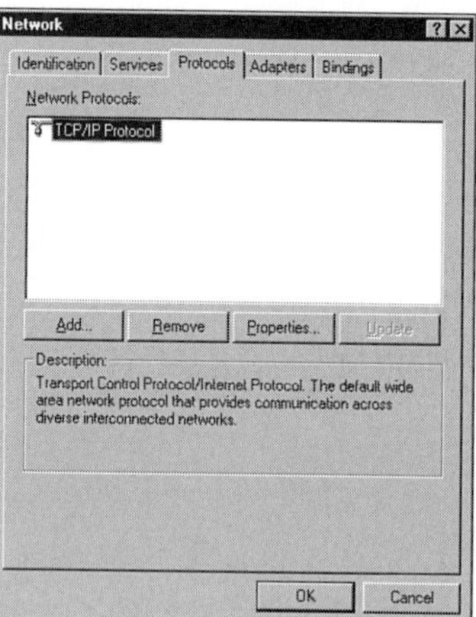

Figure A.2

Windows NT Network Properties dialog with TCP/IP protocol installed.

The Protocols tab in the Windows NT Network dialog box displays the installed protocols.

- If you use Windows 2000, right-click the My Network Places icon and select Properties. The Network and Dial-Up Connections dialog box will appear. In it, right-click the connection you want to configure (for example, Local Area Connection) to display the Properties dialog box shown in Figure A.3. If TCP/IP has been installed, it will be listed. If TCP/IP does not appear, click the Install… button to add it.

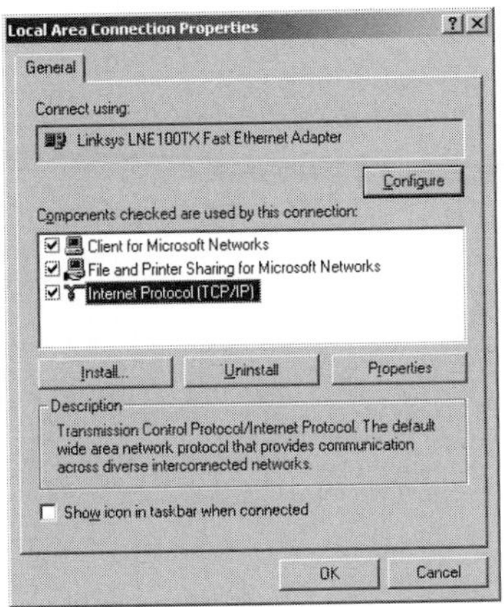

Figure A.3

Windows 2000 Network Properties dialog with TCP/IP protocol installed.

The Properties dialog box in Windows 2000's Network and Dial-Up Connections displays the installed protocols (Figure A.4).

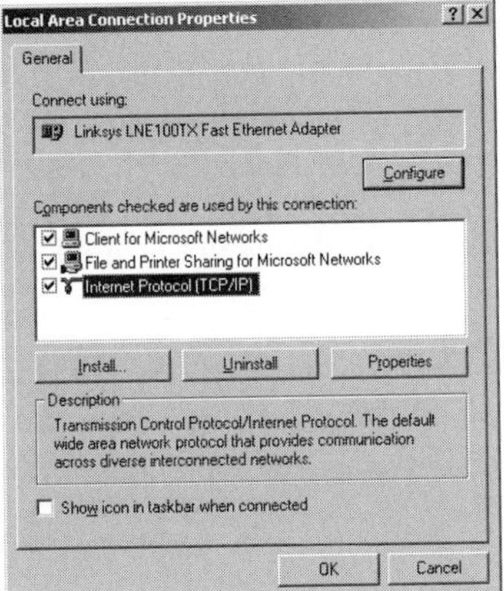

Figure A.4

Windows XP Network Properties dialog with TCP/IP protocol installed.

To test whether your system's TCP/IP is working, open a command prompt and type `ping 127.0.0.1`. If the ping succeeds, TCP/IP is working.

Linux

The rise in popularity of the Linux platform has taken the Web development community by storm. Today, ColdFusion MX supports RedHat Linux 7.x and SuSE Linux 7.x.

NOTE

Instalation procedures are similar for the different Linux distributions, however the procedures for manually configuring the various supported web servers, especially Apache, depend on the distribution. Consult the ColdFusion MX documentation for more information.

Solaris

ColdFusion MX requires Solaris 7 or 8. ColdFusion MX also needs the latest available patches and packages.

All patches and packages can be found at `http://sunsolve.sun.com`.

HP-UX

ColdFusion MX on HP-UX requires HP-UX 11 or 11i with the latest patches installed. The CD-ROM must be mounted prior to running the installation program. Detailed instructions are included in the section "Installing ColdFusion on HP-UX."

Choosing Your Operating System

You'll probably use the operating system with which you are the most familiar for your ColdFusion development.

You'll likely use the operating system you currently use for your ColdFusion development. If you're still undecided, here are some considerations:

- Essentially the same from a Web development perspective, Windows 98 and ME serves as a very capable environment for developing and debugging ColdFusion applications. In addition, a multitude of applications are available for the three platforms.

Windows 98 and ME are intended for home use and should not be used in a deployment and production environment.

- Windows NT 4.0 (Workstation and Server) and Windows 2000 (Professional, Server, Advanced Server, and DataCenter) and Windows XP (Home and Professional) feature stability and scalability enhancements that make them ideal for deployment and production environments.

The main difference between the Workstation/Professional/Home versions of Windows NT 4.0, Windows 2000, and Windows XP is the number of concurrent sessions the operating system can accommodate. Workstation/Professional can handle 10 concurrent connections. However, the Server editions do not have this limitation. Consult each version of Windows for detailed specifications.

While HP-UX 11 (and soon Windows XP) is a 64-bit operating system, ColdFusion MX supports only 32-bit operating systems at this time.

Solaris 9 is not officially supported at the time of publication, however Macromedia expects that it will be supported in the future.

- You should use the operating system with which you are the most familiar. If you have used Windows almost exclusively, a switch to a different operating system can cause more problems than it solves.

- You must consider what the purpose of your ColdFusion MX application will be. If you're developing a Web application that must provide the highest level of scalability and reliability, a UNIX-based operating system is probably your best choice.
- As the most popular operating system, Windows expertise and support are easier to come by than other operating systems. When tight deadlines loom, the last thing you want to be doing is searching discussion boards for a solution to an obscure bug.

Checking Your Web Server

As explained in Chapter 1, "Introducing ColdFusion," Web servers are separate software programs that enable two-way communication between your system and other Web servers. A great number of Web servers are available for a great number of operating systems. You must choose the Web server that is compatible with your operating system and ColdFusion.

ColdFusion MX supports most popular Web servers for the operating systems it supports. The Windows install program will detect and configure Microsoft's Internet Information Server (IIS), Apache, and Netscape's iPlanet. On non-Windows systems, the install program can configure Apache and iPlanet. On all platforms, an embedded web server is also available. This configuration is often referred to as "standalone."

Ask five Webmasters which Web server is best and you'll likely receive five different answers. Each Web server has advantages and disadvantages. Here are a few things to keep in mind when choosing which Web server is right for you:

- Windows 98 and ME use the Personal Web Server (PWS). PWS provides only basic Web server functionality and should not be used as a production Web server.
- Microsoft's Internet Information Server (IIS) is completely free and comes bundled with Windows NT 4 and Windows 2000. One of IIS's principal advantages is its capability to use Windows' user lists and security options. This eliminates the complexity of maintaining multiple lists of passwords and security privileges. On the other hand, IIS users must have a network login to have a Web server login. At the time of this writing, the latest version of IIS for Windows NT is 4.0. Windows 2000 users should use IIS 5. Go to Microsoft's Web site to download the latest version (`http://www.microsoft.com`).

Windows NT 4.0 comes bundled with IIS 2.0. If you plan to use IIS, you should upgrade to IIS 4.0 for critical enhancements that make Web development on Windows much easier. Windows 2000 includes IIS 5. Windows XP includes IIS 6.

- iPlanet Web Server is one of the most popular commercial web servers. It runs on Windows NT 4.0, Linux (with glibc-2.1.3-11 or later, gcc/egcs libstdc++ 2.9, and 2.2 kernel or later), HP-UX, and Sun Solaris. Enterprise Edition features Web-based administration and can be integrated with any LDAP-based directory server. At the time of this writing, the latest version of the server is 6.0. Visit iPlanet's Web site to download an evaluation copy (`http://www.iplanet.com`).

NOTE

iPlanet was a collaboration between Sun Microsystems and Netscape, a division of AOL/Time Warner. Recently, Sun has assumed all future development and marketing of iPlanet products and is rebranding them as "Sun ONE." iPlanet Web Server will likely be renamed iPlanet Web Server.

- Apache is one of the oldest and still the most popular Web server on the Web. Completely free of charge, the Apache Web server is an open-source software project available for most operating systems, including Windows NT 4.0, Windows 2000, Linux, Solaris, and HP-UX. Despite its popularity, Apache is more difficult to install than IIS and iPlanet Web Server. Also, support is provided through the Apache development community. The more recent 2.x version of Apache has provided many advances, enhancing performance, scalability, and extensibility. The older 1.3.x version is still supported. You may go to the Apache web site to download the Web server (www.apache.org).

Because the applications you develop with ColdFusion are portable among all supported Web servers, your production Web server can differ from the Web server used for development with minimal changes in your ColdFusion code.

After you have installed a Web server, you must verify that it is working properly. To do this, start a Web browser and go to the URL `http://localhost/`. If everything is working, your Web server's default home page should appear.

If the home page doesn't display, you must do a little troubleshooting. First, type `ping 127.0.0.1` at a command prompt. If the ping is successful, TCP/IP is working. More than likely, the problem lies with the Web server. For more information, consult the Web server's documentation.

Upgrading from ColdFusion 4.5.x and 5

On the Windows platform, the ColdFusion MX install automatically detects the presence of ColdFusion 4.5.x and 5. If an earlier version is detected, you will be prompted within the install to upgrade.

If you elect to upgrade, your existing settings and data will be preserved, however, the earlier version of ColdFusion will be removed.

If you decline the upgrade, ColdFusion will be configured to run in standalone mode—no external web servers will be configured.

On all other platforms, detection is not available. Instead, you must respond to the installer with the applicable answer when it asks you if a previous version of ColdFusion is installed on the machine.

If you respond that there is a previous version, you'll be prompted to upgrade and migrate the settings of the existing version. Selecting to not to upgrade when a previous version is available allows both the earlier version of ColdFusion and ColdFusion MX to co-exist on the same system. In this case, ColdFusion MX runs on the built-in web server.

On UNIX and Linux, if you respond that there is no previous version, you'll not be prompted to upgrade or migrate any existing version of ColdFusion. In addition, any existing version of ColdFusion will be broken.

Additionally, if you are upgrading from a previous version of ColdFusion, make sure to read the "Migrating to ColdFusion MX" guide in the documentation.

Final Installation Checklist

Ready to install ColdFusion? Almost. Before you begin the actual installation, quickly go through this final checklist to make sure your i's are dotted and your t's are crossed:

- Double-check your hardware's compliance with ColdFusion MX's system requirements.
- Make sure ColdFusion MX supports your operating system and that the required patches and packages have been properly installed. Don't forget the TCP/IP requirements of Windows.
- Verify that ColdFusion MX supports your Web server, as shown in Table A.1. Also, validate that your Web server is working by entering `http://localhost/` in a Web browser.

That's it. Let's install ColdFusion MX!

Installing ColdFusion MX On Windows

To begin with, the ColdFusion MX install uses Microsoft's Windows Installer technology. In essence, this means that the install is not a standalone executable—it requires the Windows Installer service to be present and up-to-date before the install can be performed.

The Windows Installer service is native to Windows 2000 and Windows XP. On all other Windows operating systems, it must be installed. Fortunately today myriads of install program use the Windows Installer service so odds are you've already got the required files on your system.

If the Windows Installer service is not on your system it will be installed by the install bootstrapping logic. This means that the executable that you launch to install ColdFusion MX contains the necessary logic and files to detect and install the service.

Also included in the install executable is the database that provides install information to the Windows Installer service. When extracted, this database has an .msi extension. More than likely you won't see this file. While it is extracted at runtime, the file is deleted after the install is finished.

With all of that said, let's look through the install sequence. The first dialog that you'll see is shown in Figure A.5.

While this dialog is displayed, the bootstrapping executable (the executable that was launched from the CD Browser or you double-clicked directly) extracts the install database and the Windows Installer service install logic. In addition, the bootstrap logic evaluates the existence and version of the current Windows Installer service. If non-existent or out-of-date, the updated service is installed.

These files are extracted to your temporary folder. After the install is finished, these files are deleted from your system.

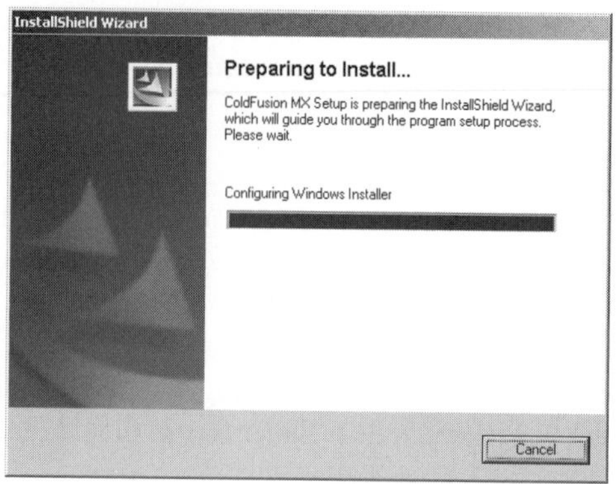

Figure A.5
When launched, the bootstrapping executable verifies the current version of the Windows Installer service.

If the Windows Installer service needs to be installed, you may see a noticeable delay (around a minute or two) on this dialog. If problems develop on this dialog, then the Windows Installer service itself is probably to blame. You can download the latest Windows Installer service directly from Microsoft's website (www.microsoft.com) and search for "Windows Installer." You'll be looking for the Windows Installer Redistributable for your specific operating system. There are two versions: one for Win9x systems (ANSI) and another for everyone else (Unicode).

The next dialog that you'll see is the Welcome dialog. While this dialog is displayed, the install is searching for several things. First, your system is queried for a pre-existing version of ColdFusion. The Property and Signature fields on this dialog represent internal install references and can be ignored. Second, your system is queried for any known web servers. This dialog is shown in Figure A.6.

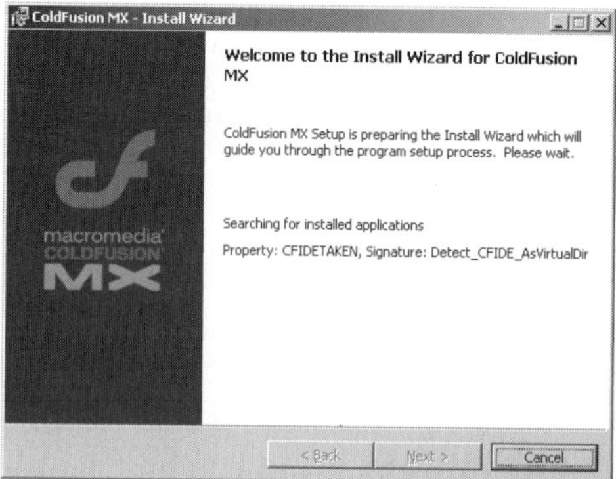

Figure A.6
The Welcome dialog is displayed while your system is queried for a pre-existing version of ColdFusion.

To locate pre-existing versions of ColdFusion, the detection logic searches for a specific registry key value. This key value is created by earlier ColdFusion installations. The key resides within HKEY_LOCAL_MACHINE. The registry key is SOFTWARE\Allaire\ColdFusion\CurrentVersion. The value name is RootDirectory. The value data is the installed location of ColdFusion. If this key is detected, you'll be prompted to upgrade to ColdFusion MX. This registry location is shown if Figure A.7.

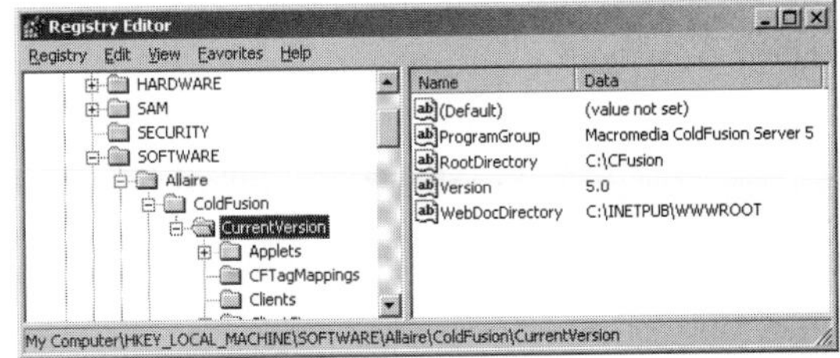

Figure A.7

Earlier versions of ColdFusion are detected through the system registry.

To locate web servers, the detection logic searches for a series of well-known registry keys. In the case of IIS, the install searches under the NT Services registry key. This is shown in Figure A.8.

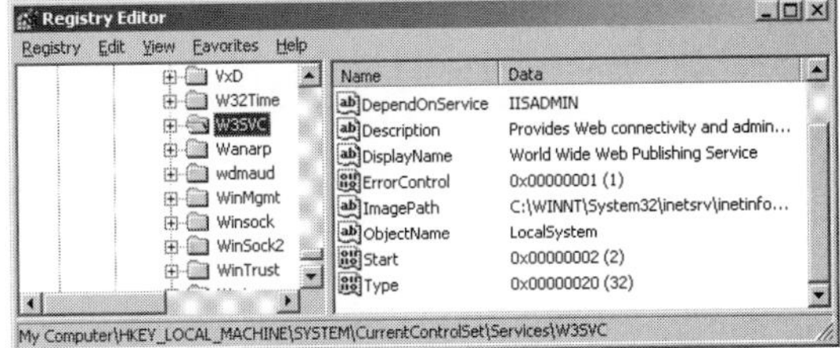

Figure A.8

To detect the existence of Microsoft's Internet Information Services (IIS), the system registry is queried.

For the Apache Group web server, the install searches under the application specific registry space. This is shown in Figure A.9.

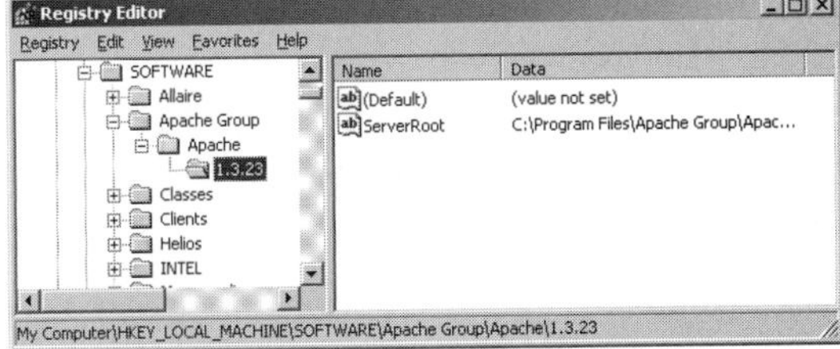

Figure A.9

To detect the existence of the Apache Group web server, the system registry is queried.

For iPlanet Web Server, the install searches under the application specific registry space. This is shown in Figure A.10.

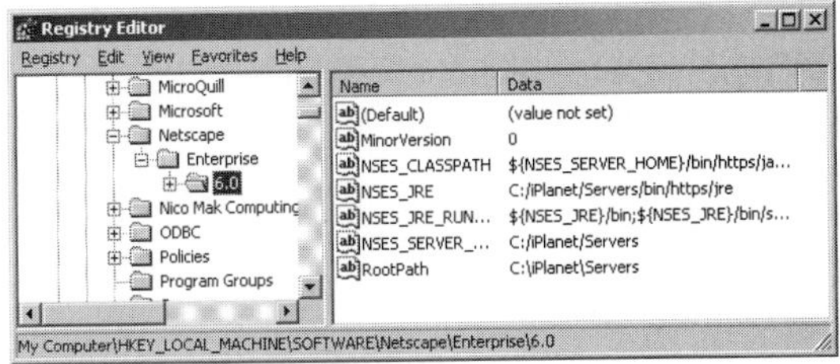

Figure A.10

To detect the existence of iPlanet web server, the system registry is queried.

The upgrade dialog, when triggered by the pre-existence of an earlier version of ColdFusion, is shown in Figure A.11.

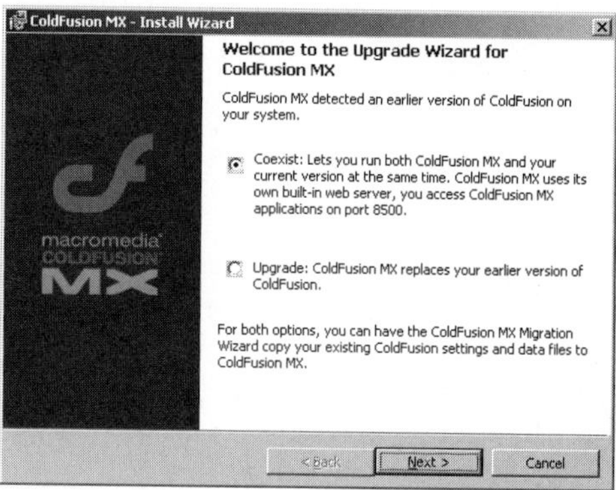

Figure A.11

Detecting a previous version of ColdFusion triggers the upgrade dialog.

You have two installation options, Coexist with the existing version of ColdFusion or Upgrade to ColdFusion MX.

Coexistence really means that ColdFusion MX will be installed in Standalone mode—no external web servers are configured during the installation. The idea being that an earlier version of ColdFusion is already using a web server.

On the other hand, selecting Upgrade will preserve any existing user data and settings and remove the previous version. The existing user data and settings will be migrated to the installation of ColdFusion MX.

TIP

Standalone mode is the simplest to use for development, as no Web server is needed. Most of the examples in this book assume that standalone mode is being used.

If you select Upgrade, the process will take upwards of five minutes or so depending on the amount of user data. A series of banner dialogs will be displayed to keep you informed of the process.

After the Upgrade is complete, two registry keys are set. The current and future installers use these keys to keep track of your computer's state.

The first identifies the old ColdFusion registry data as already upgraded. This will keep future versions of ColdFusion MX from detecting the old version. This registry key is stored under the old ColdFusion registry key. In the above example, this would be SOFTWARE\Allaire\ColdFusion\CurrentVersion. The value name is CFMX_Upgrade and the value data is "Yes."

The second registry key is made under the current ColdFusion MX registry key. This key is located under HKEY_LOCAL_MACHINE. The key is SOFTWARE\Macromedia\Install Data\CfusionMX. When an upgrade is selected, the key name Migrate is created and the value data is "1." ColdFusion MX uses this key as a prompt to continue the migration after the install is finished.

Independent of any of the selections you've made up to this point, the next dialog that you'll see is the standard Welcome dialog. This dialog is shown in Figure A.12.

Selecting Next from the Welcome dialog brings you to the License Agreement dialog. This dialog is shown in Figure A.13.

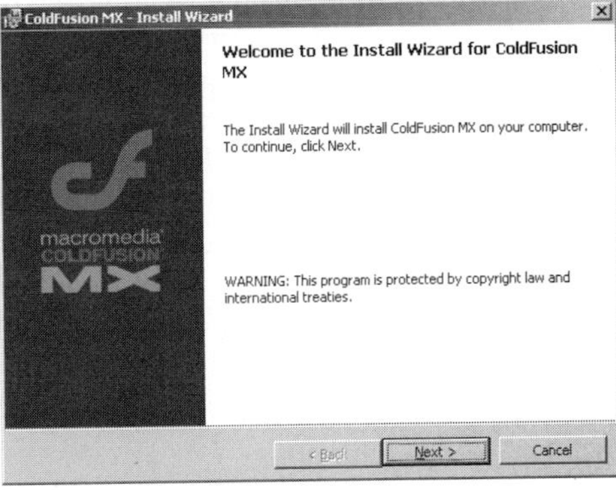

Figure A.12

The Welcome dialog is a standard artifact of the install process.

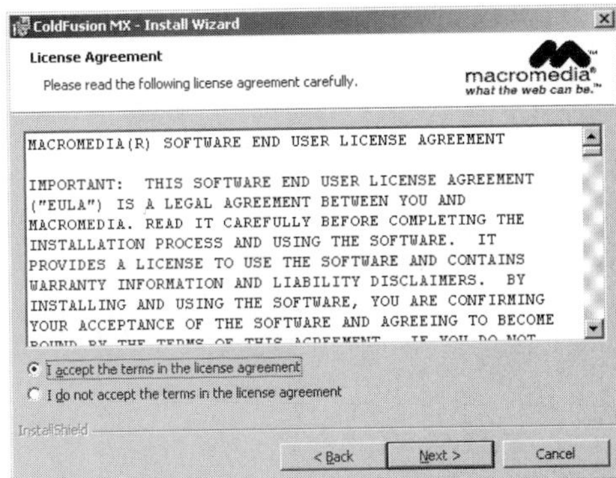

Figure A.13

The ever-ubiquitous License Agreement dialog follows the Welcome dialog.

Selecting Next from the License Agreement dialog brings you to the Customer Information dialog. In addition, to providing your name and organization, you'll also provide your ColdFusion MX serial number. If you're upgrading from a previous version of ColdFusion and you've purchased an Upgrade version of ColdFusion MX you must also provide the serial number from your earlier version of ColdFusion. This dialog is shown in Figure A.14.

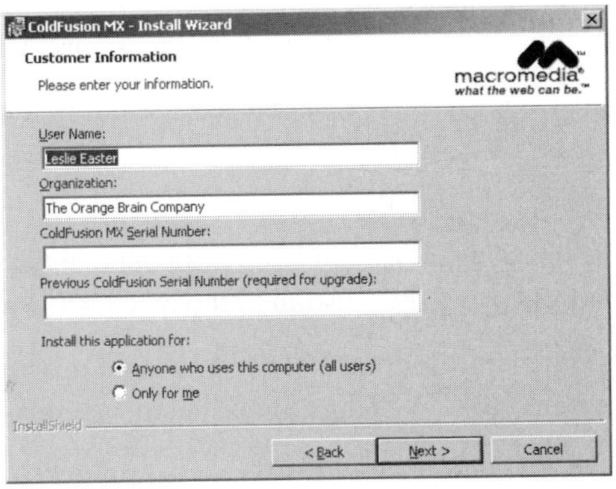

Figure A.14

The User Information dialog of the Cold-Fusion MX install.

Leaving the serial number field blank entitles you to an evaluation version of ColdFusion MX. The evaluation version of ColdFusion MX has full functionality for a limited time.

If you've provided a serial number and, if necessary, your previous version of ColdFusion serial number, selecting the Next button causes these numbers to be evaluated. Incorrect numbers are detected and a message will be displayed describing the error.

The serial numbers are stored for later evaluation by ColdFusion MX itself. You can change or upgrade from an evaluation version directly within the ColdFusion MX administrator.

Unless you've selected Co-exist in the upgrade dialog, the next dialog that you should see is the Web Server selection dialog. This dialog allows you to select from the available (and detected) web servers.

If Co-exist was your choice in the upgrade dialog, your selection will be Standalone automatically and this dialog will be skipped.

The Web Server selection dialog is shown in Figure A.15.

Figure A.15

The Web Server Selection dialog of the ColdFusion MX install.

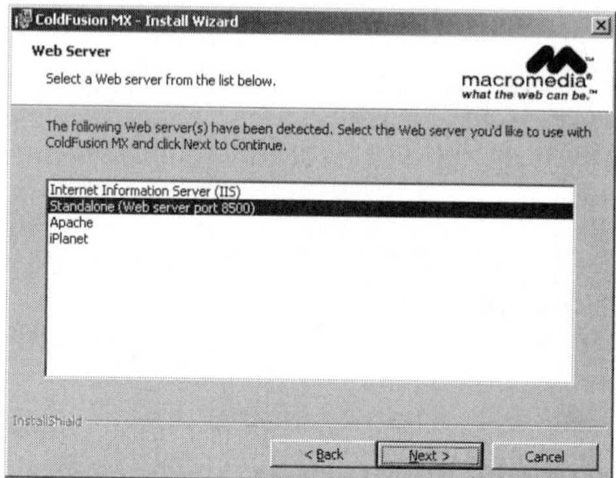

Web server detection is done through well-known registry keys. The detection logic was performed when the install program first started. If you're using a web server that is not readily detected or not one of the ones supported by ColdFusion MX, you may manually configure the web server.

After selecting the Next button, you will be prompted to enter the locations to install ColdFusion MX as well as specify the Webroot folder. This dialog is shown in Figure A.16.

The Webroot folder is specific to the Web server that you've selected. In most cases, the default values should suffice. However, the may be cases where you know more about your system than the install was able to deduce. Feel free to edit the path appropriately.

After selecting Next from the destination dialog, you'll have the opportunity to specify which features you'd like to install. This is done from the Custom Setup dialog shown in Figure A.17.

On a production server, the Documentation and Sample Apps should not be installed. This option is intended for a development system only. To change the installation status, click on the icon to the left of the Feature name.

After selecting the Features you would like installed, select the Next button to continue. The next dialog is the Select Passwords dialog. This dialog is shown in Figure A.18.

The first option is the administrator password into the ColdFusion MX Administrator. The second password is used when a client application requests access to ColdFusion. This is the case for a product like Dreamweaver MX.

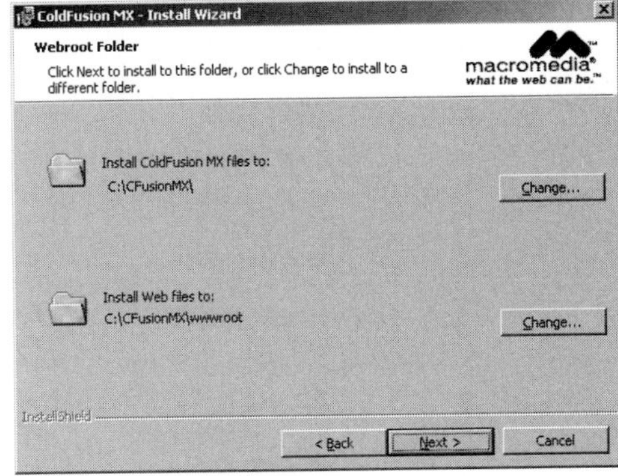

Figure A.16

The Path Selection dialog of the ColdFusion MX install.

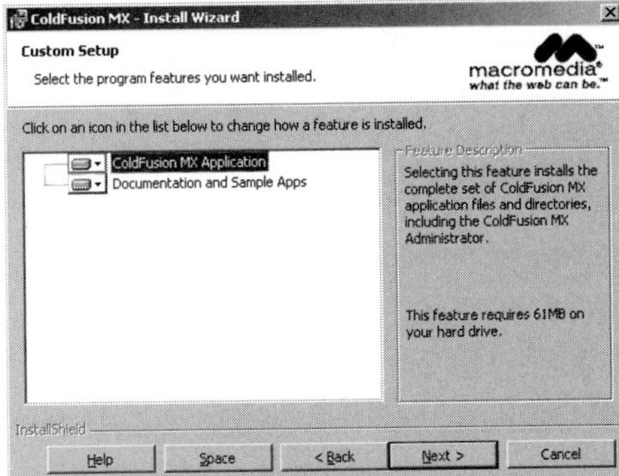

Figure A.17

The Feature Selection dialog of the ColdFusion MX install.

Figure A.18

The Select Passwords dialog of the ColdFusion MX install.

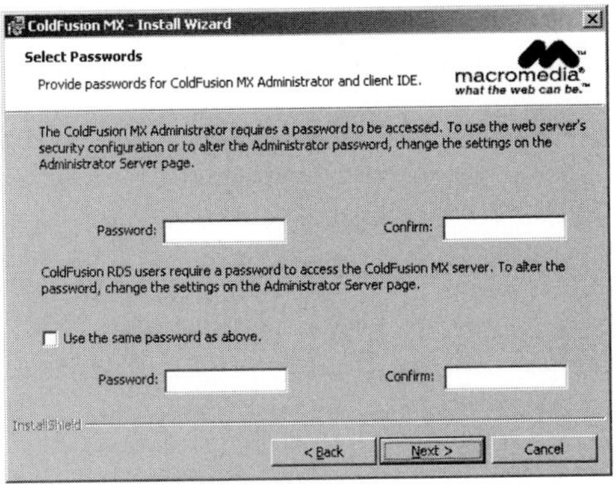

Selecting Next at this point, brings up the Ready to Install dialog. This dialog is shown in Figure A.19.

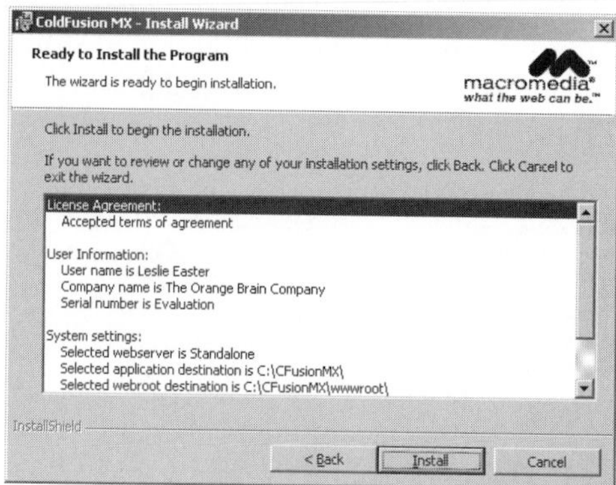

Figure A.19
The Summary dialog of the ColdFusion MX install.

This dialog displays all of the options that have been made up to this point. From here, the file transfer and system configuration takes place. Review the contents of this dialog and use the Back button to make any changes.

Selecting Next starts the file transfer. This dialog is shown in Figure A.20.

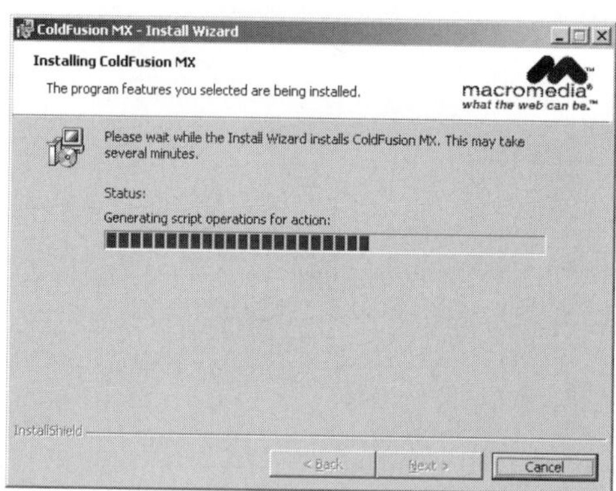

Figure A.20
The File Transfer dialog of the ColdFusion MX install.

This dialog is displayed during the file transfer and configuration process. At times the progress may appear to stall temporarily. This is typically due to some configuration process.

After the file transfer process is finished and ColdFusion MX is configured, you'll see the Install Wizard Completed dialog. This dialog is shown in Figure A.21. Selecting Next launches the ColdFusion MX Read Me file.

From this point on, ColdFusion MX can be accessed through the Start Menu.

Figure A.21
The Install Completed dialog of the ColdFusion MX install.

Installing ColdFusion MX On non-Windows

On UNIX and Linux, the ColdFusion MX install is provided through an InstallAnywhere bin file. InstallAnywhere is a commercially available install development environment.

The non-Windows install supports Linux, Solaris, and HP-UX. You'll need to make sure that the file you're using matches the operating system that you're running on.

In addition, make sure that all of the latest patches and updates are installed for your particular type and version of operating system. Most install issues are resolved when the operating system is completely up-to-date. For example, while Red Hat 7.1 ships with glibc-2.2.2-10, ColdFusion MX requires glibc-2.2.4-24.

Before you launch the install file, be sure that you are logged on as root. Identify the appropriate install file based on your platform. This is pretty straight-forward as the name of the operating system is embedded in the filename. See Table A.1 for name references.

Table A.1 Bin Files by Name

OPERATING SYSTEM	BIN FILENAME
Linux	coldfusion-60-linux-en.bin
Solaris	coldfusion-60-solaris-en.bin
HP-UX	coldfusion-60-hpux-en.bin

Next, make sure that the appropriate attributes have been assigned to the install file. The install file must be made executable. Use the chmod command to set the executable flag. This can be done from the command line as follows:

```
chmod 755 coldfusion-60-linux-en.bin
```

If you're running directly off of the CD-ROM this step is unnecessary as the executable bit has already been set.

Finally, the install program does consume a large amount of temporary disk space. By default the install will attempt to use /tmp or / to cache the temporary files. You'll need to have approximately 300MB of free disk space at either location. If you don't, there is a workaround.

The InstallAnywhere image will use the path location identified by the IATEMPDIR environment variable as an alternative temporary storage location. Setting this value for a Bourne shell (sh) as well as ksh, bash, and zsh shells is as follows:

```
$ IATEMPDIR=/your/free/space/directory
$ export IATEMPDIR
```

Setting this value for C (csh) and tcsh shells is as follows:

```
$ setenv IATEMPDIR /your/free/space/directory
```

After this preliminary work, the install and system are ready to go. After launching the bin file, the contents are extracted and the install initializes. You should see something very similar to the following after executing the bin file.

```
[root@MySystem]# ./coldfusion-60-linux-en.bin
Preparing to install...
Extracting the JRE from the installer archive...
Unpacking the JRE...
Extracting the installation resources from the installer archive...
Configuring the installer for this system's environment...

Launching installer...

Preparing CONSOLE Mode Installation...

===============================================================================
Macromedia ColdFusion MX     (created with InstallAnywhere by Zero G)

-------------------------------------------------------------------------------

===============================================================================
Welcome to ColdFusion MX
------------------------

Welcome to the Macromedia ColdFusion MX installation!

Respond to each prompt to proceed to the next step in the
installation. You may cancel this installation at any time by typing 'quit'.

PRESS <ENTER> TO CONTINUE:
```

Pressing Enter displays the License Agreement text. Multiple Enter strokes will get you through the text. I've abbreviated the output somewhat, but you should still recognize it as something like the following.

```
===============================================================================
License Agreement
-----------------
```

```
Installation and use of Macromedia ColdFusion MX requires acceptance of the
following License Agreement:

MACROMEDIA(R) SOFTWARE END USER LICENSE AGREEMENT

<Actual license text is not shown>

DO YOU ACCEPT THE TERMS OF THIS LICENSE AGREEMENT? (Y/N):y
```

Typing Y at this point continues the install. You'll next be confronted with a prompt as to whether a previous version of ColdFusion exists on the system. There is no auto-detection available. However, this is something that you should be immediately aware of. Make the appropriate selection.

```
=========================================================================
Existing Coldfusion Installation?
--------------------------------

Is there already a version of ColdFusion installed on this computer? (Y/N)
```

You should not attempt to subvert the install program. If ColdFusion pre-exists on the system and you select N at this point, the ColdFusion MX installation will break the previous version of ColdFusion. On the other hand, if ColdFusion exists and you select Y, you'll be asked if you want to upgrade. Selecting Y to upgrade migrates the existing ColdFusion settings to ColdFusion MX.

A previous version of ColdFusion and ColdFusion MX can co-exist. This puts ColdFusion MX into "standalone" mode. Co-existence is achieved automatically by declining the upgrade.

Next we move on to the serial number prompt.

```
=========================================================================
Serial Number
-------------

Please enter the ColdFusionMX product serial number. A serial number is not required
to install the ColdFusion MX Evaluation Version. Enter "eval" to default to
Evaluation Version. You can change this serial number in the ColdFusion
Administrator at a later date.

Enter Serial Number: eval
```

Next we move to the install folder prompt.

```
=========================================================================
Choose Install Folder
---------------------

Please select the install directory for ColdFusion MX. By default, ColdFusion MX
installs in the /opt/coldfusionmx directory. If you do not accept this default, you
must specify a full path to your desired install directory. (For example, entering
"/usr/foobar" installs ColdFusion MX in /usr/foobar, not /usr/foobar/coldfusionmx.)

Where Would You Like to Install ColdFusion MX?

  Default Install Folder: /opt/coldfusionmx

ENTER AN ABSOLUTE PATH, OR PRESS <ENTER> TO ACCEPT THE DEFAULT:
```

Provide the path where you'd like to see ColdFusion MX installed. Unlike previous versions of ColdFusion, you are not required to use the "Cfusion" path.

After you've entered the path, you must select a Web Server. This is done at the following prompt.

```
===============================================================================
Select Webserver
----------------

Please select the web server to serve your ColdFusion MX web pages. ColdFusion MX
can use its own built-in web server or a third-party web server. (You can switch to
a different web server later; for instructions, see the installation documentation.)

  ->1- Internal (Port Based) Web server
    2- Apache 1.3.x - 2.x
    3- Netscape/iPlanet

Please Select a Webserver: 2
```

The first option is also referred to as standalone. Make your selection here and the applicable configuration is performed for you.

Just in case, you tried to sneak your pre-existing ColdFusion through the install, a warning is displayed that alerts you to the potential problem.

```
===============================================================================
Warning
-------

You cannot use the same web server for ColdFusion MX and an earlier version of
ColdFusion. If you select the same web server for ColdFusion MX, the earlier version
of ColdFusion will be disabled.

PRESS <ENTER> TO CONTINUE:
```

There's really nothing to do at this prompt. Select Enter to move to the Web Server configuration prompt. In this case, we'll walk through the Apache configuration. Standalone and iPlanet have similar prompts.

```
===============================================================================
Apache Configuration (httpd.conf)
---------------------------------

You have selected Apache as your web server. This installation will now ask you some
questions about your Apache program.  Where is your Apache configuration file
(httpd.conf) located? (For example, on Red Hat Linux it is in the /etc/httpd/conf
directory.)

Enter File Location: /etc/httpd/conf
```

Based on the web server you've selected, in this case Apache, enter the path and name of the Apache configuration file.

You'll get a similar prompt for the Web Root.

```
===============================================================================
Document (web) Root
-------------------
```

```
Please enter the document root for your web server. (Your web server serves web
pages from this directory.) For example, the document root directory on Red Hat
Linux is /var/www/html/.

Enter Location: /var/www/html
```

Based on the web server you've selected, in this case Apache, enter the path of the document root directory. This path must already exist.

Next you'll be asked for the Web server program file.

```
========================================================================
Apache Binary Location
--------------------->

Please enter the location of the Apache program binary file (for example,
/usr/sbin/httpd) on Red Hat Linux). If you have more than one instance of Apache on
your computer, enter the binary file location for the Apache web server that will
use ColdFusion MX. (Note: this is not the Apache start and stop script.)

Enter Location (e.g. /usr/sbin/httpd): /usr/sbin/httpd
```

Provide the location and you'll next be asked to enter the location of the start and stop scripts.

```
========================================================================
Apache Start/Stop Script
-----------------------

Please enter the location of the file that you use to start and stop the Apache web
server. For example, this would be /etc/init.d/httpd on Red Hat Linux and it could
be /usr/local/apache/bin/apachectl on hand-compiled versions.

Apache Start/Stop Script: /etc/init.d/httpd
```

Provide the path to these files and you'll next need to define the runtime user account.

```
========================================================================
Select Runtime User
------------------

Like all UNIX applications, ColdFusion MX runs under a specific user account name.
Select a user account that already exists on the system, preferably the same user
account as for the web server. Do not use root.

Enter User: nobody
```

The user name that you enter must be a existing, valid user. After typing the user name, you'll next get an opportunity to set the ColdFusion MX Administrator password.

```
========================================================================
Administrator Password
---------------------

You change ColdFusion MX settings in the ColdFusion Administrator. To access the
ColdFusion Administrator, you must provide a password in the login page. The
password you enter below must be at least three (3) characters long.

Enter Password: admin
```

The password appears in plaintext. You should consider this a temporary password to use the first time you launch ColdFusion MX. After the initial launch it's prudent to change the password from within the ColdFusion MX Administrator.

Next, you'll need to provide a password for client applications that interact with ColdFusion MX.

```
===============================================================================
RDS (Remote Deployment System) Password
------------------------------------


By default, ColdFusion RDS users must provide a password to access a ColdFusion MX
server. (You can change this password later in the ColdFusion Administrator.) The
password you enter below must be at least three (3) characters long.

Enter Password: admin
```

Enter this password with much the same approach as the Administrator password. That is, once ColdFusion MX is up and running go through the Administrator panel to change the RDS password.

Next you'll be asked if you want ColdFusion MX to start automatically when the system starts up.

```
===============================================================================
Init System
-----------


Would you like ColdFusion MX to start at System Boot? Please note, this is only
supported on Solaris and Red Hat Linux. If you say no to this, you can add
ColdFusion MX to system boot post install by running /opt/coldfusionmx/bin/cfmx-
init.sh. (Y/N): n
```

This was the default behavior of previous versions of ColdFusion. With ColdFusion MX, you may select whether or not you want this to happen.

From here, you can confirm you install settings.

```
===============================================================================>
Pre-Installation Summary
-----------------------


Please review the following before continuing:

Product Name:
    Macromedia ColdFusion MX

Install Folder:
    /opt/coldfusionmx

Java VM Installation Folder:
    /opt/coldfusionmx/jre

Disk Space Information (for Installation Target):
    Required:  410,806,016 bytes
    Available: 13,279,735,808 bytes

PRESS <ENTER> TO CONTINUE:
```

And then the file transfer and configuration portion of the install begins. Note that because configuration occurs during various portions of the file transfer, you may notice significant delays in the progress bar. This is normal behavior. Be patient.

```
===============================================================================
Installing...
-------------

[==================|==================|==================|==================]

[------------------|------------------|------------------|------------------
```

Once this portion of the install is finished, we're just about done. The final step is to launch the ColdFusion MX start script.

```
===============================================================================
Installation Successful
-----------------------

Congratulations! Macromedia ColdFusion MX is now installed in:

/opt/coldfusionmx

To finish configuring ColdFusion MX and to start the server, please run the
following command:

/opt/coldfusionmx/bin/coldfusion start


PRESS <ENTER> TO EXIT THE INSTALLER:
```

Until the ColdFusion MX server is started, configuration is not finished. It's extremely important to finish the installation by starting the ColdFusion MX server.

Once that final step is achieved, you're ready to get started with ColdFusion MX.

Dreamweaver MX

The Dreamweaver MX install is fairly straight-forward. It requires a Windows platform and is standard in its flow. This is install does not leverage the Windows Installer technology, but instead relies on the industry standard InstallShield.

NOTE

Dreamweaver MX requires at least MDAC 2.6 although the install will continue if this condition isn't met. MDAC is a Microsoft redistributable and can be found at `www.microsoft.com/data/download.htm` or simply searching the Microsoft website for "MDAC."

Launching the setup.exe either through the CD Browser or by directly double-clicking the setup.exe cause the install program to extract temporary files to your system and process the InstallScript compiled file. During this time the dialog shown in Figure A.22 is displayed.

The actual install program starts with the Welcome dialog shown in Figure A.23.

This is a standard dialog and selecting Next is the most reasonable option. Doing so displays the License Agreement dialog shown in Figure A.24.

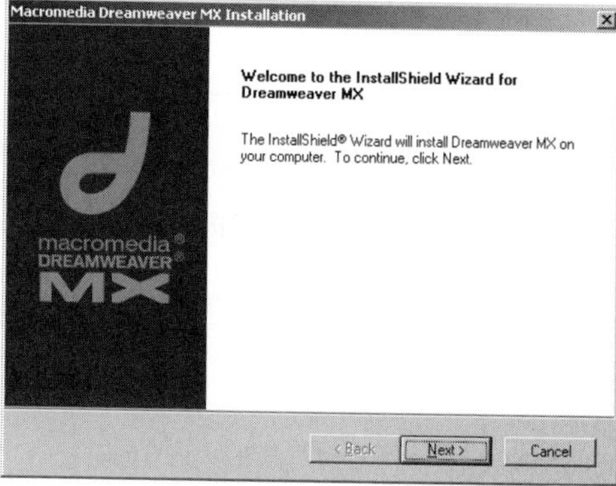

Figure A.22
As the Dreamweaver MX install readies itself; this dialog is displayed to show progress.

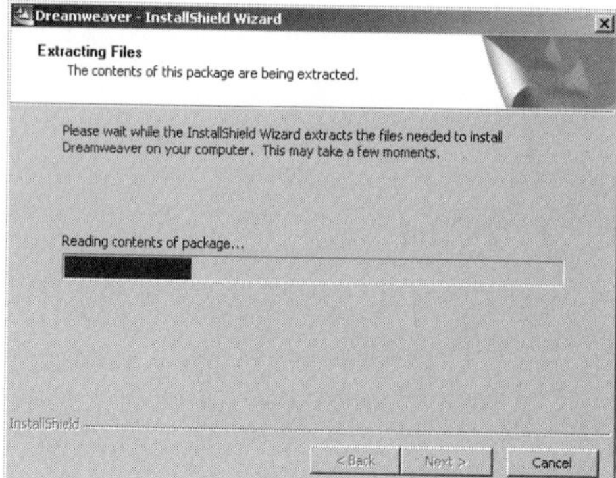

Figure A.23
Watch the status bar as Dreamweaver MX installs.

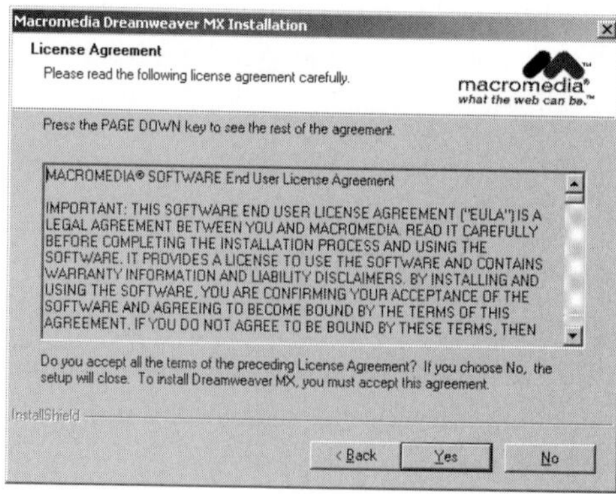

Figure A.24
The license agreement dialog is a mainstay in the install process.

You're encouraged to read the text and Select Yes if you feel the agreement is reasonable and is something that you can abide by. Selecting Next displays the User Information dialog shown in Figure A.25.

Fill in the applicable information. Notice that while ColdFusion MX does not require a serial number, Dreamweaver MX does. You must provide a complete user name and a valid serial number to continue.

Selecting Next takes you to the Destination Location dialog. This dialog is shown in Figure A.26.

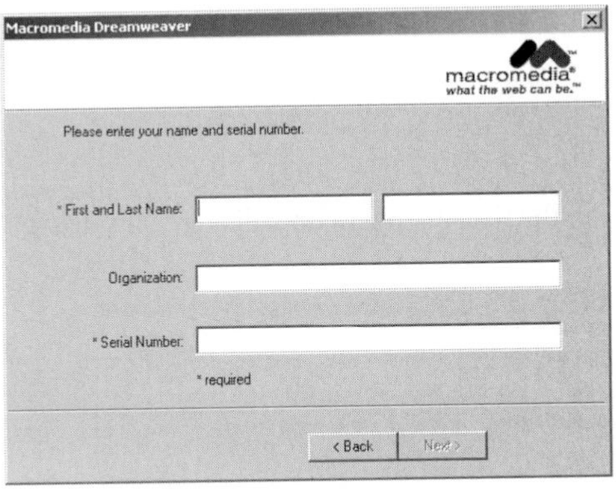

Figure A.25
Another mainstay of the install process is the user information dialog.

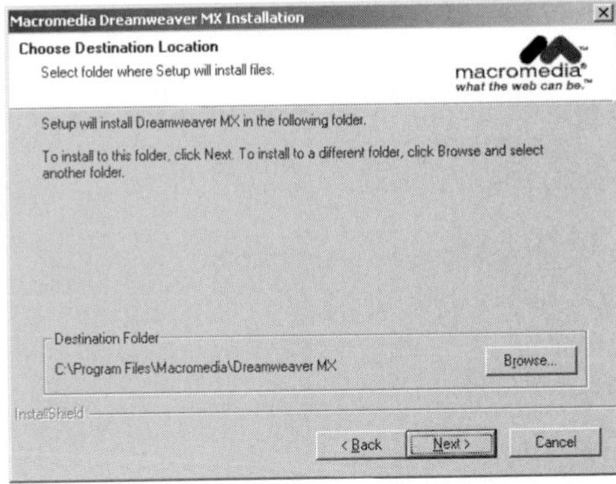

Figure A.26
The Destination Location dialog allows you to direct where the application is installed.

In most cases, the default location should be fine. You, however, are the best judge of the final destination. Make your selections and select Next to continue.

This dialog allows you to select which document type (by extension), you'd like associated with Dreamweaver MX (Figure A.27). This means nothing more than if you double-click on a file with the corresponding extension, Dreamweaver MX automatically loads the document. This could be handy at times, but also a bit of a nuisance if you're using multiple editors. Here again, you're the best judge on what's desirable for your system.

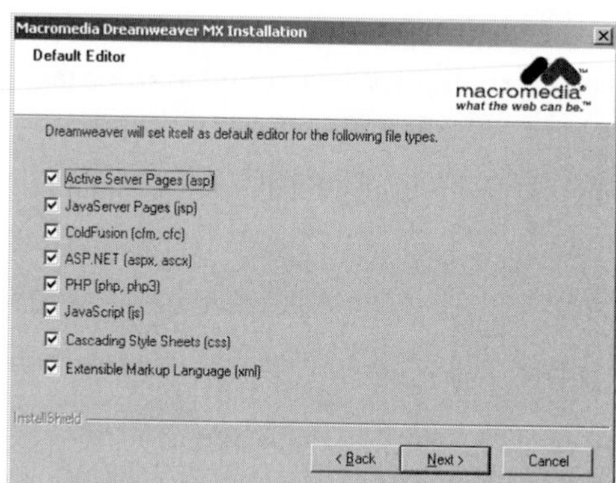

Figure A.27

Associated file extensions with Dreamweaver MX is the function of this dialog.

Selecting the Next button brings up the Start Copying Files dialog. This dialog is shown in Figure A.28.

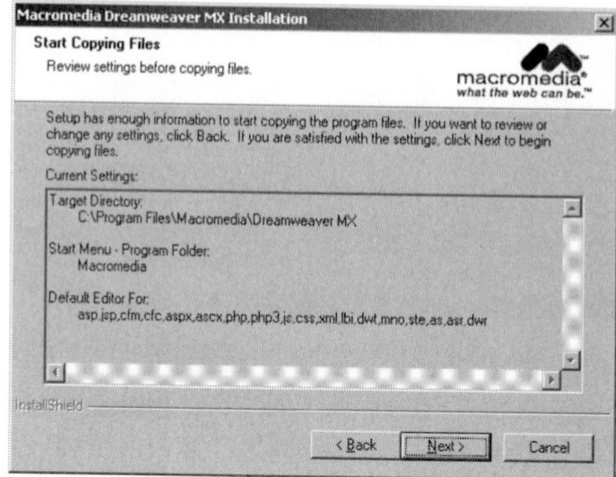

Figure A.28

A time to reflect on your selections thus far.

Once you're satisfied with the options you've selected up to this point, select Next to start the file transfer.

The File Transfer dialog is shown in Figure A.29.

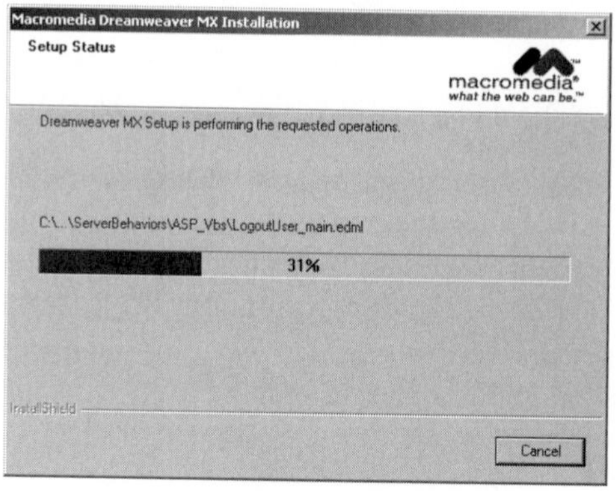

Figure A.29

The always fascinating file transfer dialog.

This dialog is displayed while files are being transferred to your computer. Additionally, application configuration is done during this period. You may see delays in the progress bar that reflects this activity. Once the file transfer is done, you'll be presented with the final dialog. This dialog is shown in Figure A.30.

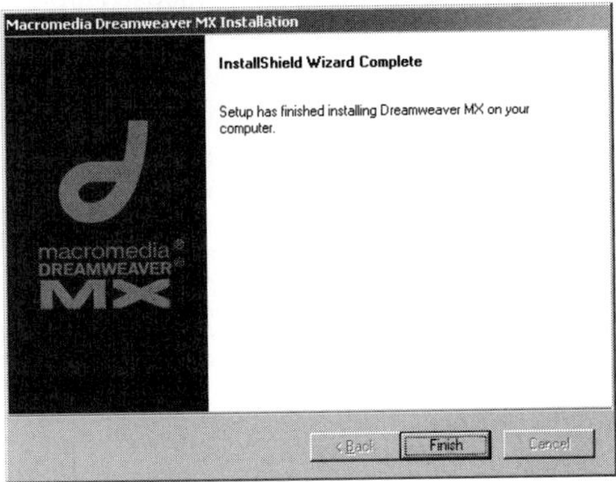

Figure A.30
You're done! Enjoy Dreamweaver MX.

You've finished with the Dreamweaver MX install and ready for business. Dreamweaver MX can be launched from the Start Menu.

Samples & Data Files

The best way to learn a product is by using it—and so in this book you learn ColdFusion by building applications, some really simple and some quite sophisticated. The applications you'll create are for a fictitious company named *Orange Whip Studios*, or *ows* for short.

Building the applications involves writing code, using databases, and accessing images and other files. So that you need not create all of these manually they have been included on the accompanying CD-ROM. You may install all of these files or just the ones you need, the choice is yours.

What To Install

The *ows* files are in a directory named `ows` on the CD-ROM. This directory contains subdirectories which each contain the files that make up the applications. Note the following sub-directories:

- The `data` directory contains the Microsoft Access database used by the example applications.
- The `images` directory contains GIF and JPEG images used in many of the applications.
- The `sql` directory contains a SQL query utility used in Chapters 5, "Introducing SQL," and 6, "SQL Data Manipulation."
- The numbered directories contain files created in specific chapters in this book with the directory number corresponding to the chapter number (so, directory `8` contains the files created in Chapter 8).

All readers should install the `data` and `images` directories as the instructions in this book will not walk you through creating the tables or designing the images. Without the databases most of the examples will not work, and without the images your screens will not look like the screenshots in the book.

The `sql` directory is optional and should only be installed if you have no other tool or utility with which to learn SQL.

CAUTION

To ensure database and server security, do not install the files in the `sql` directory on production servers.

The numbered directories should not be installed unless you plan to not try the examples yourself (this is not advised). These files are provided so that you may refer to them as needed (or even copy specific files to save time), but to truly learn ColdFusion you'll want to perform every lesson in the book and will thus create the files yourself.

Installing the OWS Files

To install the *ows* files, simply copy the ows directory from the CD-ROM to your Web server root. If you are using ColdFusion MX in standalone mode using installation defaults then the Web root will be:

```
c:\cfusionmx\wwwroot
```

If you are using Microsoft IIS the Web root will likely be:

```
c:\inetpub\wwwroot
```

➜ Web server roots are explained in Chapter 1, "Introducing ColdFusion".

To install the *ows* files do the following:

1. Create a directory named ows beneath the Web server root.
2. Copy the `data` and `images` directories from the ows directory on the CD-ROM into the just created ows directory. You may copy the entire directory, you need not copy the files individually.
3. Copy the `sql` directory if needed.
4. Copy the chapter directories if needed. If you plan to create the files yourself (as recommended) then you'll be creating your own files in the ows directory as you work through the book. As such, you may want to copy these files into another location (not the newly created ows directory) so that they will be readily available for browsing if needed, but not in the way of your own development.

And with that, you're ready to start learning ColdFusion.

IN THIS APPENDIX

ColdFusion Tag Reference

ColdFusion tags are the CFML extensions to HTML. These tags are the instructions to ColdFusion to perform database queries, process results, generate output, control program flow, handle errors, send and receive e-mail, and much more.

In this chapter, the tags are presented in alphabetical order and are cross-referenced to related tags wherever appropriate.

Tag Groups by Function

This section groups ColdFusion tags by functional category. For the tag description, refer to the page number.

Database Manipulation

Table B.1 Database Manipulation Tags

TAG	DESCRIPTION
<CFINSERT>	Add a single row to a database table.
<CFOBJECTCACHE>	Manipulate cached query objects.
<CFPROCPARAM>	Pass and retrieve parameters to and from <CFSTOREDPROC> invoked stored procedures.
<CFPROCRESULT>	Specify the result sets to be retrieved with <CFSTOREDPROC> invoked stored procedures.
<CFQUERY>	Submit SQL statements to a data source that is either previously configured or dynamically generated, or to another query.

Table B.1 (continued)

TAG	DESCRIPTION
`<CFQUERYPARAM>`	Define `<CFQUERY>` query parameters and their data types.
`<CFSTOREDPROC>`	Invoke a SQL stored procedure.
`<CFTRANSACTION>`	Group multiple `<CFQUERY>` uses into a single transaction.
`<CFUPDATE>`	Update a single row in a database table.

Data Output

Table B.2 Data Output Tags

TAG	DESCRIPTION
`<CFCHART>`	Generates and then displays a graph as an HTML object.
`<CFCHARTDATA>`	Defines data used with `<CFCHART>`.
`<CFCHARTSERIES>`	Defines a series of data used with `<CFCHART>`.
`<CFCOL>`	Specify columns in a `<CFTABLE>` HTML table.
`<CFCONTENT>`	Set the MIME-type so as to be able to send non-HTML documents to a client's browser.
`<CFFLUSH>`	Flushes ColdFusion's output buffer, sending the contents back to the Web browser.
`<CFGRAPH>`	Deprecated. Use `<CFCHART>`.
`<CFGRAPHDATA>`	Deprecated. Use `<CFCHARTDATA>`.
`<CFHEADER>`	Control the contents of specific HTTP headers.
`<CFOUTPUT>`	Resolves and outputs ColdFusion variables and expressions.
`<CFPROCESSINGDIRECTIVE>`	Suppress whitespace between the start and end tags and is also used to specify page encoding.
`<CFTABLE>`	Create a complete data-driven HTML `<TABLE>` automatically.

Extensibility

Table B.3 Extensibility Tags

TAG	DESCRIPTION
`<CFARGUMENT>`	Defines an argument in a function defined with `<CFFUNCTION>`.
`<CFCOMPONENT>`	Defines a ColdFusion component object.
`<CFFUNCTION>`	Defines a function.
`<CFIMPORT>`	Copies a Java Server Page (JSP) tag library into a CFML page.

Table B.3 (continued)

TAG	DESCRIPTION
<CFINVOKE>	Works with web services and components to invoke methods.
<CFINVOKEARGUMENT>	Used with <CFINVOKE> to provide an argument to the method.
<CFOBJECT>	Enables you to use COM, Java, and CORBA objects within your ColdFusion applications.
<CFPROPERTY>	Enables you to define a component's properties.
<CFREPORT>	Provides an interface to reports created with the Crystal Reports Professional report writer.
<CFRETURN>	Returns an expression from a function.
<CFXML>	Creates a ColdFusion XML document.

Variable Manipulation

Table B.4 Variable Manipulation Tags

TAG	DESCRIPTION
<CFCOOKIE>	Set cookies, persistent client-side variables, on the client browser.
<CFDUMP>	Output the contents of simple variables, queries, structures, arrays, serialized WDDX packets and XML documents for debugging.
<CFPARAM>	Specify default values for parameters and flag parameters that are required.
<CFSAVECONTENT>	Save the output of a page or portion of a page in a variable.
<CFSET>	Assign a value to a variable.

Flow Control

Table B.5 Flow Control Tags

TAG	DESCRIPTION
<CFABORT>	Immediately halt processing of a ColdFusion template.
<CFBREAK>	Break out of a looping process but does not stop ColdFusion processing, in contrast to <CFABORT>.
<CFCASE>	Specify a case statement within a <CFSWITCH> block.
<CFCATCH>	Create catch blocks to catch errors in a <CFTRY> block.
<CFDEFAULTCASE>	Specify a default case statement within a <CFSWITCH> block.
<CFELSE>	The else portion of a <CFIF> statement.
<CFELSEIF>	The else if portion of a <CFIF> statement.

Table B.5 (continued)

TAG	DESCRIPTION
<CFEXIT>	Abort the processing of a custom tag without aborting processing of the calling template.
<CFIF>	Perform conditional processing.
<CFLOCATION>	Redirect a browser to a different URL.
<CFLOOP>	Implement programmatic looping.
<CFRETHROW>	Force the current error to be invoked again within a `<CFCATCH>` block.
<CFSCRIPT>	Mark blocks of ColdFusion script.
<CFSILENT>	Suppress generated output.
<CFSWITCH>	Create a ColdFusion switch statement.
<CFTHROW>	Force an error condition in a `<CFTRY>` block.
<CFTRACE>	Log debugging information about the state of an application.
<CFTRY>	Catch exceptions thrown by ColdFusion or explicitly with `<CFTHROW>` or `<CFRETHROW>`.

Internet Protocols

Table B.6 Internet Protocol Tags

TAG	DESCRIPTION
<CFFTP>	Interface to FTP, the Internet standard file transfer protocol.
<CFHTTP>	Interface to HTTP, the Internet standard hypertext transfer protocol.
<CFHTTPPARAM>	Pass parameters to a `<CFHTTP>` request.
<CFLDAP>	Interact with LDAP servers.
<CFMAIL>	Generate SMTP mail from within ColdFusion templates.
<CFMAILPARAM>	Specify `<CFMAIL>` headers or provide file attachments.
<CFPOP>	Retrieve and manipulate mail in a POP3 mailbox.

File Management

Table B.7 File Management Tags

TAG	DESCRIPTION
<CFDIRECTORY>	Obtain directory lists; manipulate directories.
<CFFILE>	Perform file-management operations, including uploading files from a browser; moving, renaming, copying, and deleting files; and reading and writing files.

Web Application Framework

Table B.8 Web Application Framework Tags

TAG	DESCRIPTION
<CFAPPLICATION>	Define the scope of an application and specify several aspects of the application's configuration.
<CFERROR>	Override the standard ColdFusion error messages and replace them with error-handling templates you specify.

ColdFusion Forms

Table B.9 Form Tags

TAG	DESCRIPTION
<CFAPPLET>	Embed user-supplied Java applets in <CFFORM> forms.
<CFFORM>	Enable the use of other tags (<CFGRID>, <CFINPUT>, <CFSELECT>, <CFTEXTINPUT>, <CFSLIDER>, <CFTREE>, or any Java applets using <CFAPPLET>).
<CFGRID>	Create a Java applet data grid.
<CFGRIDCOLUMN>	Specify a <CFGRID> column explicitly.
<CFGRIDROW>	Specify a <CFGRID> data row.
<CFGRIDUPDATE>	Activate backend support for <CFGRID> in edit mode.
<CFINPUT>	Embed JavaScript client-side validation code in your HTML forms.
<CFSELECT>	Simplify the process of creating data-driven <SELECT> form controls.
<CFSLIDER>	Create a Java applet slider control.
<CFTEXTINPUT>	Create a Java applet text input control.
<CFTREE>	Create a Java applet tree control.
<CFTREEITEM>	Specify tree elements for a <CFTREE> tree control.

Security

Table B.10 Security Tags

TAG	DESCRIPTION
<CFLOGIN>	Provide a shell for authenticating users.
<CFLOGINUSER>	Provide user authentication information to security framework.
<CFLOGOUT>	Log user out of security framework.
<CFAUTHENTICATE>	Obsolete (no longer in use)
<CFIMPERSONATE>	Obsolete (no longer in use).

CFML Utilities

Table B.11 Utility Tags

TAG	DESCRIPTION
<CFASSOCIATE>	Associate subtags, or child tags, with base tags.
<CFCACHE>	Improve the performance of pages in which content doesn't need to be dynamically created each time the page is requested; ColdFusion instead returns static HTML output created during prior processing.
<CFEXECUTE>	Execute processes on the ColdFusion server machine.
<CFHTMLHEAD>	Write text into the header section of your Web page.
<CFINCLUDE>	Include the contents of another template in the one being processed.
<CFLOCK>	Place exclusive or read-only locks around a block of code.
<CFLOG>	Produce user-defined log files.
<CFMODULE>	Execute a custom tag explicitly stating its full or relative path.
<CFREGISTRY>	Directly manipulate the system Registry.
<CFSCHEDULE>	Programmatically create, update, delete, and execute tasks in the ColdFusion Administrator's scheduler.
<CFSERVLET>	Deprecated (no longer in use).
<CFSERVLETPARAM>	Deprecated (no longer in use).
<CFSETTING>	Control various aspects of page processing, such as controlling the output of HTML code in your pages or enabling and disabling debug output.
<CFWDDX>	Serialize and deserialize ColdFusion data structures to the XML-based WDDX format.

Verity Search

Table B.12 Verity Tags

TAG	DESCRIPTION
<CFCOLLECTION>	Programmatically create and administer Verity collections.
<CFINDEX>	Populate Verity collections with index data.
<CFSEARCH>	Performs searches against Verity collections (in much the same way).

Alphabetical List of ColdFusion Tags

<CFABORT>

Description: The <CFABORT> tag is used to halt processing of a ColdFusion template immediately. It optionally presents a user-defined error message. See Table B.13 for attributes.

Syntax:

```
<CFABORT SHOWERROR=?Error text?>
```

Table B.13 <CFABORT> Attributes

ATTRIBUTE	DESCRIPTION	NOTES
SHOWERROR	Error message text	Optional.

Example: The following example aborts the template processing if the user has not properly logged in, as evidenced by the existence of a session variable:

```
<!--- If a user is not logged in, an error is thrown --->
<CFIF NOT IsDefined("SESSION.LoggedIn")>
    <CFABORT SHOWERROR="You are not authorized to use this function!">
</CFIF>
```

TIP

<CFABORT> can be used to terminate the processing of a template safely if an error condition occurs. For example, if your template was expecting a URL parameter to be passed, you could use the `ParameterExists` or `IsDefined` function to verify its existence and terminate the template with an appropriate error message if it did not exist.

➜ *See also* <CFEXIT>, <CFBREAK>

<CFAPPLET>

Description: <CFAPPLET> is used to embed user-supplied Java applets in CFFORM forms. Table B.14 shows the complete list of attributes supported by <CFAPPLET>. In addition, you can pass your own attributes as long as they have been registered along with the applet itself.

Syntax:

```
<CFAPPLET ALIGN="Alignment"
        APPLETSOURCE="Registered Name"
        HEIGHT="Height"
        HSPACE="Horizontal Spacing" NAME="Field Name"
        NOTSUPPORTED="Text for non-Java browsers"
VSPACE="Vertical Spacing"
        WIDTH="Width">
```

Table B.14 <CFAPPLET> Attributes

ATTRIBUTE	DESCRIPTION	NOTES
ALIGN	Applet alignment	Optional; valid values are LEFT, RIGHT, BOTTOM, TOP, TEXTTOP, MIDDLE, ABSMIDDLE, BASELINE, and ABSBOTTOM.
APPLETSOURCE	Name of the	Required registered applet.
HEIGHT	Number of pixels	Optional; height of applet.
HSPACE	Number of pixels	Optional; horizontal space around applet.
NAME	Form field name	Required.
NOTSUPPORTED	Text to display on browsers that do not support Java.	Optional.
VSPACE	Number of pixels	Optional; vertical space around applet.
WIDTH	Number of pixels	Optional; width of applet.
PARAM*n*	Parameter names	Optional; parameter names registered with the applet.

Example: The following example embeds a Java calculator applet into <CFFORM>:

```
<!--- Creates form --->
<CFFORM ACTION="process.cfm">
    <!--- Creates calculator applet --->
    <CFAPPLET APPLETSOURCE="calculator"
        NAME="calc"
        NOTSUPPORTED="Your browser does not support Java."
        VSPACE=400
        WIDTH=200>
</CFFORM>
```

NOTE

Before you can use an applet with <CFAPPLET>, it must be registered with the ColdFusion Administrator.

NOTE

<CFAPPLET> must be used within <CFFORM> and </CFFORM> tags.

NOTE

Controls embedded with <CFAPPLET> are accessible only by users with Java-enabled browsers.

➜ *See also* <CFFORM>, <CFGRID>, <CFSLIDER>, <CFTEXTINPUT>, <CFTREE>

<CFAPPLICATION>

Description: <CFAPPLICATION> is used to define the scope of an application and to specify several aspects of the application's configuration. These include the use of session and client variables. This tag should be included in all templates that are part of the application and therefore intended for use in your application.cfm template. See Table B.15 for <CFAPPLICATION> attributes.

Syntax:

```
<CFAPPLICATION APPLICATIONTIMEOUT ="Timeout"
        CLIENTMANAGEMENT ="Yes or No"
        CLIENTSTORAGE="Storage Type"
        NAME="Application Name"
        SESSIONMANAGEMENT ="Yes or No"
        SESSIONTIMEOUT ="Timeout"
        SETCLIENTCOOKIES="Yes or No"
        SETDOMAINCOOKIES="Yes or No">
```

Table B.15 <CFAPPLICATION> Attributes

ATTRIBUTE	DESCRIPTION	NOTES
APPLICATIONTIMEOUT	Time interval	Optional; application variable timeout; defaults to value in ColdFusion Administrator.
CLIENTMANAGEMENT	YES or NO	Optional; defaults to NO. Enable or disable client variables.
CLIENTSTORAGE	Mechanism for storage of client ODBC data source name.	Optional; defaults to REGISTRY; other values are COOKIE and any information.
NAME	Name of application	Required if you are using application variables; can be up to 64 characters long.
SESSIONMANAGEMENT	YES or NO	Optional; defaults to NO. Enable or disable session variables.
SESSIONTIMEOUT	Time interval	Optional; session variable timeout; defaults to value in ColdFusion Administrator.
SETCLIENTCOOKIES	YES or NO	Optional; enable or disable client cookies; defaults to YES.
SETDOMAINCOOKIES	YES or NO	Enables use of CFID and CFTOKEN cookies across an entire domain, rather than just a single host.Intended for use in a CF Server cluster.

Example: The following example is designed for use in an `Application.cfm` file. It names part of an application `Administration` and enables session variables. It then looks for the presence of a particular session variable and redirects the user to the specified directory if the session variable doesn't exist:

```
<!--- creates ColdFusion application, enables session management, and sets session
timeout --->
<CFAPPLICATION NAME="Administration"
        SESSIONMANAGEMENT="Yes"
        ③SESSIONTIMEOUT="CreateTimeSpan(0,0,45,0)">
<!--- If user is not logged in, he or she is sent to the login page --->
<CFIF NOT IsDefined("SESSION.LoggedIn")>
        <CFLOCATION URL="/Login">
</CFIF>
```

TIP

Use the `CreateTimeSpan()` function to create the time interval parameters required in the `SESSIONTIMEOUT` and `APPLICATIONTIMEOUT` attributes. See Appendix C, "ColdFusion Function Reference," for further details.

➜ *See also* <CFCOOKIE>, <CFSET>

<CFARGUMENT>

Description: <CFARGUMENT> is used inside <CFFUNCTION> to define arguments to the function. <CFFUNCTION> is used to define methods within a ColdFusion component—so these three tags are frequently used together. Note that a component method does not require arguments, but <CFARGUMENT> can be used only within a <CFFUNCTION> body. Use the `ARGUMENT` scope to reference argment variables. <CFARGUMENT> attributes are shown in Table B.16.

Syntax:

```
<CFARGUMENT NAME ="Argument name"
        TYPE ="Data type of argument"
        REQUIRED="Yes or No"
        DEFAULT="Default value for argument">
```

Table B.16 <CFARGUMENT> Attributes

ATTRIBUTE	DESCRIPTION	NOTES
NAME	Time interval	Required; name of argument; string.
TYPE	Data type name	Optional; indicates type of data that this argument uses.
REQUIRED	YES or NO	Optional; defaults to No. Indicates whether or not this argument is required.
DEFAULT	Data value	The default value to be used by this argument. When this attributed is used, `REQUIRED` must be set to No.

Example: In the following example, a ColdFusion component is defined with one function that has one argument. This component is used to search for all merchandise for a specified film. If merchandise is found, it returns a query result containing the merchandise. The FilmID is passed to the component with <CFARGUMENT>:

```
<!--- Looks for merchandise for specified film and returns what
      it finds --->
<CFCOMPONENT>
   <CFFUNCTION NAME="CheckMerchandise">
      <CFARGUMENT NAME="FilmID" TYPE="Integer" REQUIRED="Yes">

      <!--- Find all merchandise for specified film --->
      <CFQUERY NAME="GetMerchandise" DATASOURCE="ows">
         SELECT MerchID, MerchName, MerchDescription, MerchPrice
         FROM Merchandise
         WHERE FilmID=#ARGUMENTS.FilmID#
      </CFQUERY>
```

```
      <!--- Return query result --->
      <CFRETURN #GetMerchandise#>
   </CFFUNCTION>
</CFCOMPONENT>
```

➜ *See also* <CFFUNCTION>, <CFCOMPONENT>, <CFRETURN>

<CFASSOCIATE>

Description: The <CFASSOCIATE> tag is used to associate subtags, or child tags, with base tags. This tag can be used only inside custom tag templates. It is used in the subtag to make the subtag data available in the base tag. The subtag data is stored in a structure in the base tag. See Table B.17 for <CFASSOCIATE> attributes.

Syntax:

```
<CFASSOCIATE BASETAG="CF_TAG"
        DATACOLLECTION="structure">
```

Table B.17 <CFASSOCIATE> Attributes

ATTRIBUTE	DESCRIPTION	NOTES
BASETAG	Base tag name	Required; name of base tag associated with this subtag.
DATACOLLECTION	Name of the structure in the base tag to store attributes	Optional; defaults to structureof AssocAttribs is used.

Example: The following example associates a subtag with a base tag:

```
<!--- In the subtag CF_USERINFO --->
<CFPARAM NAME="ATTRIBUTES.LoginName" DEFAULT="">
<CFPARAM NAME="ATTRIBUTES.Password" DEFAULT="">
<CFPARAM NAME="ATTRIBUTES.Privilege" DEFAULT="">
<CFASSOCIATE BASETAG="CF_CHECKUSER">
<!--- In the base tag, CF_CHECKUSER --->
<CFIF Len(AssocAttribs. ATTRIBUTES.LoginName) EQ 0>
   <CFEXIT>
</CFIF>
```

➜ *See also* <CFMODULE>

<CFBREAK>

Description: <CFBREAK>, which must be used inside the <CFLOOP> and </CFLOOP> tag, is used to break out of a looping process. Unlike <CFABORT>, it does not stop ColdFusion processing. <CFBREAK> has no attributes.

Syntax:

```
<CFBREAK>
```

Example: The following example queries all films from the `Films` table. It then loops through the list, comparing them to a `FORM` parameter, `FORM.LastFilmID`. If it finds a match, it saves the title of the selected film, breaks out of the loop, and continues processing:

```
<!--- Queries database --->
<CFQUERY NAME="GetMovies" DATASOURCE="#DSN#">
    SELECT FilmID, MovieTitle
    FROM Films
</CFQUERY>

<!--- Loops through query results --->
<CFLOOP QUERY="GetMovies">
    <!--- Tests for equality between query results and form variable --->
    <CFIF GetMovies.FilmID EQ FORM.LastFilmID>
        <!--- If equality found, variable is set --->
        <CFSET SelectedFilm=GetMovies.MovieTitle>
        <!--- Stops only loop processing --->
        <CFBREAK>
    </CFIF>
</CFLOOP>
```

➜ *See also* `<CFLOOP>`, `<CFABORT>`, `<CFEXIT>`

<CFCACHE>

Description: The `<CFCACHE>` tag is used to improve the performance on pages in which content doesn't need to be dynamically created each time the page is requested by storing copies on the client or server. ColdFusion instead returns static HTML output created during the last run of the page; so this tag should only be used when dynamic content is not required. Table B.18 shows the complete list of `<CFCACHE>` attributes. Available `ACTION` attribute values are shown in Table B.19.

This tag can now cache pages that have been secured through ColdFusion MX's authentication framework as well as pages that depend on session state. You use this tag in pages that are to be cached. The combination of a page's URL and its parameters are evaluated as unique.

Syntax:

```
<CFCACHE ACTION="action"
   DIRECTORY="server directory for cache"
   EXPIREURL="URL wildcard"
   PORT="port number"
   PROTOCOL="HTTP or HTTPS"
   USERNAME="user name"
   PASSWORD="password"
   TIMESPAN="time value">
```

Table B.18 `<CFCACHE>` Attributes

ATTRIBUTE	DESCRIPTION	NOTES
`ACTION`	Action	Optional. See Table B.19.
`DIRECTORY`	Absolute path	Optional. The absolute path to the server directory that holds the cached pages. Defaults to CACHE below the directory in which ColdFusion was installed.

Table B.18 (continued)

ATTRIBUTE	DESCRIPTION	NOTES
`EXPIREURL`	URL wildcard	Optional; used with `ACTION=FLUSH`. ColdFusion matches against URLs in the cache. You can include wildcard such as "*/dirname/file.*"
`PASSWORD`	Password	Optional; this password will be used if basic authentication is required.
`PORT`	Web server port	Optional; defaults to `80`. Port from which page is being requested.
`PROTOCOL`	`HTTP` or `HTTPS`	Optional; defaults to `HTTP`. Identifies protocol used to create pages from cache.
`TIMESPAN`	Time value	Interval before page is automatically flushed from cache. Can use either an integer (or fraction) for days or a value created by CreateTimeSpan().
`USERNAME`	User name	Optional; can be used if basic authentication is required.

Table B.19 `<CFCACHE>` Actions

ACTION	DESCRIPTION
`CACHE`	Indicates that server-side caching is to be used. This is the default action.
`FLUSH`	Cached page is to be refreshed.
`CLIENTCACHE`	Indicates that client-side caching is to be used.
`OPTIMAL`	Indicates that an optimal combination of client- and server-side caching is to be used.
`SERVERCACHE`	Indicates serve-rside caching only.

Example: This example caches the static content from a dynamic template for up to 36 hours (unless it's explicitly flushed sooner):

```
<!--- Cache page for 1 and one half days --->
<CFCACHE TIMESPAN="1.5" ACTION="cache">
<HTML>
<HEAD>
<TITLE>Page to be Cached</TITLE>
</HEAD>
<BODY>
<H1>This page is cached</H1>
<P>The last version of this page was on: <CFOUTPUT>#DateFormat(Now())#</CFOUTPUT>
</BODY>
</HTML>
```

NOTE

`<CFCACHE>` uses `<CFHTTP>` to retrieve the contents of your page, so if there is an HTTP error accessing the page the contents are not cached. If ColdFusion generates an error, the error result will be cached.

<CFCASE>

Description: <CFCASE>, which must be used with <CFSWITCH>, specifies individual case statements. A default case can be specified using the <CFDEFAULTCASE> tag. See Table B.20 for The complete list of <CFCASE> attributes.

Syntax:

```
<CFSWITCH EXPRESSION="expression">
    <CFCASE VALUE="value">
    HTML or CFML code here
    </CFCASE>
    <CFDEFAULTCASE>
    HTML or CFML code here
    </CFDEFAULTCASE>
</CFSWITCH>
```

Table B.20 <CFCASE> Attributes

ATTRIBUTE	DESCRIPTION	NOTES
VALUE	Case value	This attribute is required.
DELIMITERS	Character separator	Optional; Defaults to ",".

Example: The following example checks whether a state is a known state and displays an appropriate message:

```
<!--- Evaluates passed expression (UCase(state)) --->
<CFSWITCH EXPRESSION="#UCase(state)#">
    <!--- If case matches CA, California is used. --->
    <CFCASE VALUE="CA">California</CFCASE>
    <!--- If case matches AR, Arkansas is used. --->
    <CFCASE VALUE="AR">Arkansas</CFCASE>
    <!--- If case matches MI, Michigan is used. --->
    <CFCASE VALUE="MI">Michigan</CFCASE>
    <!--- If case doesn't match, the following message is displayed. --->
    <CFCASEDEFAULT>One of the other 47 states</CFCASEDEFAULT>
</CFSWITCH>
```

➜ *See also* <CFSWITCH>, <CFCASEDEFAULT>

<CFCATCH>

Description: <CFCATCH>, which must be used with <CFTRY>, catches exceptions thrown by ColdFusion or explicitly with <CFTHROW> or <CFRETHROW>. All code between <CFTRY> and </CFTRY> can throw exceptions, and exceptions are caught by <CFCATCH> blocks. Explicit <CFCATCH> blocks can be created for various error types, or one block can catch all errors. <CFCATCH> attributes are listed in Table B.21 A special structure variable, CFCATCH, is available in your <CFCATCH> blocks. Its elements are described in Table B.22, and its variable elements are described in Table B.23.

Syntax:

```
<CFTRY>
    <CFCATCH TYPE="type">
    </CFCATCH>
</CFTRY>
```

Table B.21 <CFCATCH> Attributes

ATTRIBUTE	DESCRIPTION	NOTES
TYPE	Exception type	Optional; values listed in Table B.22.

Table B.22 <CFCATCH> TYPE Values

TYPE
ANY
APPLICATION
Custom_Type
DATABASE
EXPRESSION
LOCK
MISSINGINCLUDE
OBJECT
SECURITY
SYNCHRONIZATION
TEMPLATE

Table B.23 CFCATCH Variable Elements

TYPE	ONLY FOR TYPE	DESCRIPTION
DETAIL		A detailed error message; helps determine which tag threw the exception.
ERRNUMBER	EXPRESSION	Internal expression error number.
ERRORCODE	*Custom type*	Developer-specified error code.
EXTENDEDINFO	APPLICATION	Developer's custom error *Custom type* message.
LOCKNAME	LOCK	Name of the affected lock; set to anonymous if the lock was unnamed.
LOCKOPERATION	LOCK	Operation that failed; TIMEOUT, CREATE MUTEX, or UNKNOWN.
MESSAGE		Diagnostic message; can be null.
MISSINGFILENAME	MISSINGINCLUDE	Name of file that could not be included.
NATIVEERRORCODE	DATABASE	The native error code from the database driver; -1 if no native code provided.

Table B.23 (continued)

TYPE	ONLY FOR TYPE	DESCRIPTION
SQLSTATE	DATABASE	Another error code from the database driver; -1 if no native code provided.
TAGCONTEXT		Tag stack; name and position of each tag in the stack.
TYPE		Exception type, as specified in <CFCATCH>.

Example: This example traps for an error when attempting to create a new directory programmatically:

```
<!--- Sets the trap for errors --->
<CFTRY>
    <!--- Creates directory --->
        <CFDIRECTORY ACTION="CREATE" DIRECTORY="#FORM.UserDir#">
        <!--- Catches any type of error --->
        <CFCATCH TYPE="ANY">
        <!--- Tests output for certain phrase --->
        <CFIF CFCATCH.Detail CONTAINS "when that file already exists">
            <P>Cannot create directory: this directory already exists.
            <!--- If the output doesn't contain phrase, it outputs the error
            details and aborts --->
        <CFELSE>
        <CFOUTPUT>#CFCATCH.Detail#</CFOUTPUT>
        </CFIF>
            <CFABORT>
        </CFCATCH>
</CFTRY>
<P>Directory created.
```

You will find other useful examples in the entries for <CFRETHROW>, <CFAUTHENTICATE>, and <CFTRANSACTION>.

➜ *See also* <CFTRY>, <CFTHROW>, <CFRETHROW>

<CFCHART>

Description: <CFCHART>, Enables you to create charts rendered as JPG, PNG or Flash objects in your web pages. It largely replaces <CFGRAPH> from previous versions of ColdFusion. You can produce dynamic bar (vertical or horizontal), line, and pie charts built from query results. Three sets of similar attributes are available to support the three types of charts. You also can employ the child tags <CFCHARTDATA> and <CFCHARTSERIES> to add individual data points and series of data points to the chart. Table B.24 shows <CFCHART> attributes.

Syntax:

```
<CFCHART
    BACKGROUNDCOLOR="Web color or hex value"
    BORDERBACKGROUNDCOLOR="Web color or hex value"
    BORDERCOLOR="Web color or hex value"
    BORDERWIDTH="Integer number of pixels"
```

```
CHARTHEIGHT="Integer number of pixels"
CHARTWIDTH="Integer number of pixels"
DATABACKGROUNDCOLOR="Web color or hex value"
FONT="Arial or Courier or Times"
FONTSIZE="Integer font size in points"
FONTBOLD="Yes o No"
FONTITALIC="Yes or cNo"
FORMAT="Flash or Jpg or Png"
FOREGROUNDCOLOR="Web color or hex value"
GRIDLINES="Integer number of lines"
ITEMCOLUMN="Query column"
ITEMLABELFONT="Arial or Courier or Times"
ITEMLABELSIZE="Number of points"
ITEMLABELORIENTATION="Horizontal or Vertical"
LABELFORMAT="Number, Currency, Percent, Date"
MARKERSIZE="Number of pixels, integer"
NAME="Text name of chart"
PIESLICESTYLE="Solid, Sliced"
ROTATED="Yes or No"
SCALEFROM="Integer minimum value"
SCALETO="Integer maximum value"
SERIESPLACEMENT="Defult, cluster, Stacked, Percent"
SHOW3D="Yes or No"
SHOWBORDER="Yes or No"
SHOWLEGEND="Yes or No"
SHOWMARKERS="Yes or No"
SHOWXGRIDLINES = "Yes or No"
SHOWYGRIDLINES = "Yes or No"
TIPSTYLE="MouseDown, MouseOver or Off"
TIPBGCOLOR="Web color or hex value"
URL="address of page to go to on Click"
XAXISTITLE="Title for X-Axis"
YAXISTITLE="Title for Y-Axis"
XOFFSET=number between -1 and 1"
YOFFSET=number between -1 and 1">
```

Table B.24 <CFCHART> Attributes

ATTRIBUTE	DESCRIPTION	NOTES
BACKGROUNDCOLOR	Web color or hex value	Optional. Color to use on background of chart.
BORDERBACKGROUNDCOLOR	Web color or hex value	Optional. Color for border background.
BORDERCOLOR	Web color or hex value	Optional. Hex color value. or Web color name.
BORDERWIDTH	Integer number of pixels	Optional. Width of border in pixels.
CHARTHEIGHT	Integer number of pixels	Optional. Width of border in pixels.
CHARTWIDTH	Integer number of pixels	Optional. Width of chart in pixels.
DATABACKGROUNDCOLOR	Web color or hex value	Optional. Hex color value or Web color name.
FONT	Font name	Optional. Name of font to be used on chart. Defaults to Arial.

Table B.24 (continued)

ATTRIBUTE	DESCRIPTION	NOTES
FONTSIZE	Font size in points	Optional. Integer, font size.
FONTBOLD	Yes or No	Optional. Indicates whether to bold the fonts. Defaults to No.
FONTITALIC	Yes or No	Optional. Indicates whether to italicize the fonts. Defaults to No.
FORMAT	Flash or Jpg or Png	Optional. Indicates file format for graphical image. Defaults to Flash.
FOREGROUNDCOLOR	Web color or hex value	Optional, Hex color value or Web color name for font and other foreground items (e.g., legend border color). Defaults to Black.
GRIDLINES	Integer	Optional, number of lines.
LABELFORMAT	Number, Currency, Percent, Date	Optional, label format, defaults to as is.
MARKERSIZE	Integer	Optional. Number of pixels.
NAME	String, var name	Optional. Name of string variable required for storing binary graph data java.io.ByteArrayInputStream. Used primarily by Flash gateways.
PIESLICESTYLE	Text	Optional. Sliced or Solid; defaults to Sliced.
ROTATED	Yes or No	Optional. Defaults to No.
SCALEFROM	Integer	Optional. Lowest value for Y axis in chart.
SCALETO	Integer	Optional. Highest value for Y axis in chart.
SERIESPLACEMENT	Text	Optional. Default, Cluster, Stacked, Percent. Default value is "Default".
SHOW3D	Yes or No	Optional. Defaults to No. Gives chart data a 3-D appearance.
SHOWBORDER	Yes or No	Optional. Defaults to No. Puts border around perimeter of chart.
SHOWLEGEND	Yes or No	Optional. Defaults to Yes. Results in the display of a data item legend.
SHOWMARKERS	Yes or No	Optional. Defaults to No. Results in data item markers being displayed.
SHOWXGRIDLINES	Yes or No	Optional. Defaults to No. Displays horizontal grid lines.

Table B.24 (continued)

ATTRIBUTE	DESCRIPTION	NOTES
SHOWYGRIDLINES	Yes or No	Optional. Defaults to Yes. Displays vertical grid lines.
TIPSTYLE	Text	Optional. Must be either MouseDown, MouseOver or Off. Defaults to MouseOver.
TIPBGCOLOR	Web color or hex value	Optional. Hex color value.or Web color name.
URL	URL	Optional. Address of page to go to on click of the chart.
XAXISTITLE	Text	Optional. Title for X-Axis.
YAXISTITLE	Text	Optional Title for Y-Axis.
XOFFSET		Number Optional. Number between -1 and 1.

Example: The following example creates a bar chart with a series. The series is built from a query result of amounts budgeted for various OWS films.

```
<!--- Get budget data --->
<CFQUERY NAME="GetBudget" DATASOURCE="OWS">
   SELECT FilmID, MovieTitle, AmountBudgeted AS Amt
   FROM Films
   order by filmID
</CFQUERY>

<!--- Define bar chart depicting budget per film --->
<CFCHART xAxisTitle="Film"
   yAxisTitle="Dollars"
   font="Arial"
   backgroundColor="##CCCC99"
   gridlines="20"
   scaleFrom=10000
   scaleTo=500000
   CHARTWIDTH=800
   CHARTHEIGHT=600
>
   <cfchartSeries
      type="BAR"
      query="GetBudget"
      itemColumn="MovieTitle"
      valueColumn="Amt"
      seriesLabel="Budget"
   >
</CFCHART>
```

➜ *See also* <CFCHARTDATA>, <CFCHARTSERIES>

<CFCHARTDATA>

Description: The <CFCHARTDATA> tag is used to produce graphs from hard-coded data items (as opposed to data points generated from query results). The <CFCHARTDATA> tag must be used in the body of a <CFCHARTSERIES> tag. And <CFCHARTSERIES> tags are used within the body of a <CFCHART> tag, which defines the "shell" of the chart. See Table B.25 for <CFCHARTDATA> attributes.

Syntax:

```
<CFCHARTDATA
   ITEM="Text"
   VALUE="Number">
```

Table B.25 <CFCHARTDATA> Attributes

ATTRIBUTE	DESCRIPTION	NOTES
ITEM	Text label	Optional; label for the data point.
VALUE	Number	Required; data point value; number.

Example: The following example presents a simple pie chart in which the data points are hard-coded.

```
<!--- Create pie chart itself --->
<CFCHART
   SHOWBORDER="Yes"
   SHOW3D="Yes"
   PIESLICESTYLE="solid"
   BACKGROUNDCOLOR="Gray"
   FOREGROUNDCOLOR="blue"
   CHARTWIDTH="640"
   CHARTHEIGHT="480"
   FORMAT="png"
>
   <!--- create pie slices --->
   <CFCHARTSERIES TYPE="pie" SERIESLABEL="Genre"
    COLORLIST="White,##00ff6e,Blue,Red,##eeff33">

      <!--- Specifies individual data points --->
      <CFCHARTDATA ITEM="Drama" VALUE="85000">
      <CFCHARTDATA ITEM="Comedy" VALUE="37500">
      <CFCHARTDATA ITEM="Action" VALUE="125000">
      <CFCHARTDATA ITEM="Horror" VALUE="95000">
      <CFCHARTDATA ITEM="Sci-Fi" VALUE="95000">

   </CFCHARTSERIES>
</CFCHART>
```

➜ *See also* <CFCHART>, <CFCHARTSERIES>

<CFCHARTSERIES>

Description: The <CFCHARTSERIES> tag, which must be used with the <CFCHART> tag, enables you to define series of data points to your charts. This series can be produced dynamically from query results or can be added as individual points using <CFCHARTDATA>. See Table B.26 for the <CFCHARTSERIES> attributes.

Syntax:

```
<CFCHARTSERIES
   TYPE="Chart type"
   QUERY="Query name"
   ITEMCOLUMN="Query column name"
   VALUECOLUMN="Query column name"
   SERIESLABEL="Label Text"
   SERIESCOLOR="Hex value or Web color"
   PAINTSTYLE="Plain, Raise, Shade, Light"
   MARKERSTYLE="Style"
   COLORLIST = "List">
</CFCHARTSERIES>
```

Table B.26 `<CFCHARTDATA>` Attributes

ATTRIBUTE	DESCRIPTION	NOTES
TYPE	Text label	Optional. Type of chart. Choices include Bar, Line, Pyramid, Area, Cone, Curve, Cylinder, Step, Scatter and Pie.
QUERY	Number	Optional. Query name to use to build series dynamically.
ITEMCOLUMN	Text	Optional. Name of column from query from which to get data item names.
VALUECOLUMN	Text	Optional. Name of column from query from which to get data item values.
SERIESCOLOR	Text	Optional. Can specify from the 256 standard Web colors in any valid HTML format.
PAINTSTYLE	Text	Optional. Specifies a chart style from one of the following: Plain, Raise, Shade or Light.
MARKERSTYLE	Text	Optional. Defaults to Rectangle. Indicates style of marker to be used from one of the following: Rectangle, Triangle, Diamond, Circle, LetterX, Mcross, Snow, Rcross.
COLORLIST	Comma-delimited list	Optional. Specifies colors for data points from the 256 for each data standard Web colors. If there are more colors than data points, the list starts over.

Example: The following example builds on the example in `<CFCHART>` by adding a second series. So in this chart, one series presents budget per film and another provides actual expenses per film and enables the viewer to visually compare the expenses to the budget.

```
<!--- Get expense and then budget data;
      expenses are summed by film --->
<CFQUERY NAME="GetExpenses" DATASOURCE="OWS">
   SELECT E.FilmID, MovieTitle, Sum(ExpenseAmount) As Amt
   FROM Films F INNER JOIN Expenses E ON F.FilmID = E.FilmID
```

```
   GROUP BY E.FilmID, MovieTitle
   order by E.filmID
</CFQUERY>

<CFQUERY NAME="GetBudget" DATASOURCE="OWS">
   SELECT FilmID, MovieTitle, AmountBudgeted AS Amt
   FROM Films
   order by filmID
</CFQUERY>

<!--- Define chart --->
<CFCHART xAxisTitle="Film"
   yAxisTitle="Dollars"
   font="Arial"
   backgroundColor="##CCCC99"
   gridlines="20"
   scaleFrom=10000
   scaleTo=500000
   CHARTWIDTH=800
   CHARTHEIGHT=600
>
   <cfchartSeries
      type="BAR"
      query="GetExpenses"
      itemColumn="MovieTitle"
      valueColumn="Amt"
      seriesLabel="Expenses"
   >
   <cfchartSeries
      type="BAR"
      query="GetBudget"
      itemColumn="MovieTitle"
      valueColumn="Amt"
      seriesLabel="Budget"
   >
</CFCHART>
```

➜ *See also* <CFCHART>, <CFCHARTDATA>

<CFCOL>

Description: <CFCOL>, which must be used with <CFTABLE>, defines table columns. The <CFCOL> attributes are listed in Table B.27.

Syntax:

```
<CFCOL HEADER="Header Text"
    WIDTH="Width"
    ALIGN="Alignment"
    TEXT="Body Text">
```

Table B.27 <CFCOL> Attributes

ATTRIBUTE	DESCRIPTION	NOTES
HEADER	Header text	Optional; text for header.
WIDTH	Number of characters	Data wider than this for column width value will be truncated.
ALIGN	Column alignment	Left, Right, or Center.
TEXT	Text that is to be displayed in the column	This can be a combination of text and ColdFusion variables.

Example: This example queries a database and displays the output using <CFTABLE> and <CFCOL>:

```
<!--- Query gets data --->
<CFQUERY NAME="GetFilms" DATASOURCE="OWS">
    SELECT FilmID, MovieTitle
    FROM Films
</CFQUERY>

<H1>Use of CFTABLE and CFCOL</H1>
<!--- Table is created from query results --->
<CFTABLE QUERY="GetFilms">
    <!--- Table columns are specified --->
    <CFCOL HEADER="Film ID" WIDTH="8" ALIGN="Right" TEXT="<EM>#FilmID#</EM>">
    <CFCOL HEADER="Name" WIDTH="30" ALIGN="Left" TEXT="#MovieTitle#">
</CFTABLE>
```

➜ *See also* <CFTABLE>, <CFOUTPUT>, <CFQUERY>

<CFCOLLECTION>

Description: The <CFCOLLECTION> tag can be used to create and administer Verity collections programmatically. The complete list of <CFCOLLECTION> attributes is shown in Table B.28. Table B.29 lists the values for the ACTION attribute.

Syntax:

```
<CFCOLLECTION
    ACTION="action"
    COLLECTION="collection"
    LANGUAGE="language"
    PATH="path">
```

Table B.28 <CFCOLLECTION> Attributes

ATTRIBUTE	DESCRIPTION	NOTES
ACTION	Action	Required; see Table B.29. Default is LIST.
COLLECTION	Collection name	Required; name of the collection to be indexed. If using external collections, this must be a fully qualified path to the collection.

Table B.28 (continued)

ATTRIBUTE	DESCRIPTION	NOTES
LANGUAGE	Collection language	Optional language; defaults to English.
NAME	Query result name	Required if ACTION is LIST. The name of the query result set.
PATH	Collection path	Required if ACTION is CREATE.

Table B.29 <CFCOLLECTION> Actions

ACTION	DESCRIPTION
CREATE	Creates a new collection.
DELETE	Deletes a collection.
LIST	Produces a query result listing the Verity and K2 collections registered with the ColdFusion server. Query result will be named with the value of the NAME attribute.
MAP	Assigns an alias to a collection.
OPTIMIZE	Purges and reorganizes a collection.
REPAIR	Fixes a corrupt collection.

The action CREATE creates a directory for the use of Verity, using the PATH attribute value. The COLLECTION attribute is used to create a subdirectory within the PATH directory. So, if PATH=MyDir and COLLECTION=MyCollection, the CREATE action would create a directory named c:\MyDir\MyCollection\.

The MAP action enables ColdFusion to reference a collection with an alias. This alias can be used in <CFINDEX> and to reuse a collection from an earlier installation of ColdFusion. The PATH attribute specifies the fully qualified path to the collection. Based on the example in the preceding paragraph, this would be c:\MyDir\MyCollection\.

Example: This example provides a form you can use to invoke any <CFCOLLECTION> action.

```
<!--- Here is the form page --->
<HTML>
<HEAD>
  <TITLE>CFCOLLECTION Example</TITLE>
</HEAD>
<BODY>
<!--- Form is created --->
<FORM ACTION="CollectionProcessor.cfm"
    METHOD="post">
<!--- Hidden form field that is passed to action page --->
<INPUT TYPE="Hidden" NAME="CollectionName_required">
<!--- Text input field is created --->
<P>Collection name: <INPUT TYPE="Text" NAME="CollectionName">
<BR>(note: When Action is Map, enter the collection Alias name to use.)
<!--- Menu is created that selects the <CFCOLLECTION> action --->
```

```
<P>Action:
<SELECT NAME="Actions">
    <OPTION SELECTED>Create
    <OPTION>Delete
    <OPTION>Map
    <OPTION>Optimize
    <OPTION>Repair
</SELECT>
<!--- Submit button is created --->
<P><INPUT TYPE="Submit">
</FORM>
</BODY>
</HTML>

<!--- This is the form's action template, CollectionProcessor.cfm. --->
<!--- Form passes ACTION and COLLECTION attributes to <CFCOLLECTION> tag --->
<CFCOLLECTION ACTION="#FORM.Actions#"
    COLLECTION="#FORM.CollectionName#">
```

NOTE

<CFCOLLECTION> works at the collection level only. To add content to a collection, use <CFINDEX>.

➜ *See also* <CFINDEX>, <CFSEARCH>

<CFCOMPONENT>

Description: The <CFCOMPONENT> tag is used to create ColdFusion components. These are much like objects that can have their own behaviors (methods) and properties. Again, like objects, ColdFusion components can inherit functionality from "parent" components identified by the EXTENDS attribute. The EXTENDS attribute identifies the current component's parent, from which it inherits methods and properties. Any text or CFML output within the tag body can be suppressed by setting the OUTPUT attribute to No. <CFCOMPONENT> attributes are shown in Table B.30.

Syntax:

```
<CFCOMPONENT EXTENDS="Component name" OUTPUT="Yes or No">
```

Table B.30 <CCFCOMPONENT> Attributes

ATTRIBUTE	DESCRIPTION	NOTES
EXTENDS	Text	Optional, implements object-oriented notion of inheritance. Name or pathname (dot notation, see following example) to another component that this component is based on.
OUTPUT	YES or NO	Defaults to No. "No" suppresses output from the body of the tag and "Yes" enables it.

Example:

```
<!--- This component inherits functionality from
      a component named Merchandise and adds a new
      function to it. --->
<CFCOMPONENT EXTENDS="Merchandise">
```

```
    <CFFUNCTION NAME="CheckFilmOrderCount">
       <CFARGUMENT NAME="FilmID" TYPE="Integer" REQUIRED="Yes">

       <!--- Find count of orders for merch for specified film --->
       <CFQUERY NAME="OrdersCount" DATASOURCE="ows">
          SELECT Distinct Count(MOI.OrderID) AS OrdersForFilm
          FROM MerchandiseOrdersItems MOI
             INNER JOIN Merchandise M ON MOI.ItemID = M.MerchID
          WHERE M.FilmID=#ARGUMENTS.FilmID#
       </CFQUERY>

       <!--- Return count --->
       <CFRETURN #OrdersCount.OrdersForFilm#>
    </CFFUNCTION>
</CFCOMPONENT>
```

NOTE

Components stored in the same directory are part of a *package*. They can be addressed with dot notation to indicate each subdirectory. For example, to invoke mycomponent.cfm in the directory c:\inetpub\webroot\components\myapp\, you could address it, `components.myapp.mycomponent`.

➜ *See also* <CFARGUMENT>, <CFFUNCTION>, <CFRETURN>, <CFMODULE>

<CFCONTENT>

Description: The <CFCONTENT> tag enables you to send non-HTML documents to a client's browser. <CFCONTENT> lets you specify the MIME type of the file and an optional filename to transmit. See Table B.31 for the complete list of supported attributes.

Syntax:

```
<CFCONTENT TYPE="MIME Type"
    FILE="File Name"
    DELETEFILE="Yes or No"
    RESET="Yes or No">
```

Table B.31 <CFCONTENT> Attributes

ATTRIBUTE	DESCRIPTION	NOTES
TYPE	Content MIME Type	Required.
FILE	Filename	Optional attribute that specifies the fully qualified path of a file to be transmitted to the user's browser.
RESET	YES or NO	Optional. It discards output preceding call to <CFCONTENT>. Defaults to YES.
DELETEFILE	YES or NO	Optional; deletes file once sent; useful if serving dynamically created graphics.

NOTE

Because <CFCONTENT> needs to write to the HTTP header, you cannot use it if you've already flushed the header from the ColdFusion output buffer with <CFFLUSH>.

NOTE

If you use the <CFCONTENT> tag in a distributed ColdFusion environment where the Web server and ColdFusion Server run on different systems, the file attribute must refer to a path on the Web server system, not the ColdFusion Server system.

Example: The following example sends tab-delimited output (which can be easily read by a spreadsheet) to the browser. Note the use of tab-delimited field titles immediately following the <CFCONTENT> tag:

```
<!--- Query gets the data --->
<CFQUERY NAME="GetFilmBudgets"
    DATASOURCE="OWS">
    SELECT DISTINCT FilmID, MovieTitle, AmountBudgeted
    FROM Films
    WHERE AmountBudgeted > 1000000.00
</CFQUERY>

<!--- If the query does not return any results, a message is displayed
      and processing stops. --->
<CFIF GetFilmBudgets.RecordCount EQ 0>
    <P>No films with budgets over one million dollars
    <CFABORT>
</CFIF>
<!--- Content is set to tab-delimited --->
<CFCONTENT TYPE="TEXT/TAB-DELIMITED"
    RESET>
FilmID#chr(9)#Title#chr(9)#Budget
<!--- Query results are outputted and formatted --->
<CFOUTPUT QUERY="GetFilmBudgets">
#FilmID##chr(9)##MovieTitle#[ic:ccc]#chr(9)##AmountBudgeted#
</CFOUTPUT>
```

This next example sends a Microsoft Word document:

```
<CFCONTENT TYPE="application/msword"
    FILE="C:\MyDocs\Proposal.DOC">
```

This final example sends a dynamically created map to the user and then deletes it upon completion of the transmission:

```
<CFCONTENT TYPE="image/gif"
    FILE="C:\Images\Maps\Temp123.gif"
    DELETEFILE>
```

<CFCOOKIE>

Description: <CFCOOKIE> enables you to set *cookies*, persistent client-side variables, on the client browser. Cookies enable you to set variables on a client's browser, which are then returned every time a page is requested by a browser. Cookies can be sent securely if required. The tag attributes are described in Table B.32.

To access a returned cookie, specify its name and precede it with the `COOKIE` designator, as in `#COOKIE.USER_ID#`.

Users can configure their browsers to refuse cookies. You must never make assumptions about the existence of the cookie. Always use the `IsDefined` function to check for the existence of the cookie before referencing it.

Syntax:

```
<CFCOOKIE NAME="Cookie Name"
    VALUE="Value"
    EXPIRES="Expiration"
    SECURE="Yes/No"
    PATH="URL Path"
    DOMAIN=".domain">
```

Table B.32 `<CFCOOKIE>` Attributes

ATTRIBUTE	DESCRIPTION	NOTES
DOMAIN	The domain for which the cookies are valid	Required only if PATH is used. Separate multiple domains with a ; character.
EXPIRES	Cookie expiration date	Optional; the cookie expiration date can be specified as a date (as in "10/1/97"), or as relative days (as in "100"), NOW, or NEVER.
NAME	Name of cookie	Required.
PATH	Subset of the specified domain to which the cookie applies	Optional; separate multiple paths with a ; character.
SECURE	YES or NO	Optional; specifies that cookie must be sent securely. If it is specified and the browser does not support SSL,the cookie is not sent.
VALUE	Cookie value	Required.

Example: The following example assumes a login form (not presented here) has been used to capture a user's name and password. These are then compared to what is in the database. If there's a match, a secure UserID cookie is created on the user's browser; the cookie will expire in 60 days:

```
<!--- Query gets the data --->
<CFQUERY NAME="CheckUser"
    DATASOURCE="OWS">
    SELECT UserID, UserName
    FROM Users
    WHERE UserName = '#FORM.UserName#'
    AND Password = '#FORM.UserPassword#'
</CFQUERY>

<!--- If the query returns no results, a cookie is placed
      on the user's system --->
<CFIF RecordCount EQ 1>
    <CFCOOKIE NAME="USER_ID"
        VALUE="CheckUser.UserID"
        EXPIRES="#DateFormat(DateAdd('d', 60, Now()), 'mm/dd/yy')#"
        SECURE="Yes">
    <!--- If a result is returns, an error is thrown and message displayed. --->
<CFELSE>
    <CFABORT SHOWERROR="Invalid login. Go back and try again.">
</CFIF>
```

This next example deletes the `UserID` cookie:

```
<CFCOOKIE NAME="OrderID" EXPIRES="Now">
```

NOTE

Starting in MX, it is okay to use <CFCOOKIE> and <CFLOCATION> on the same page. In earlier versions of ColdFusion, the cookie would not be created.

TIP

If you use the SECURE attribute to specify that the cookie must be sent securely, it is sent only if the browser supports SSL. If the cookie cannot be sent securely, it is not sent at all.

NOTE

Cookies are domain-specific, meaning they can be set so just the server that set them can retrieve them.

NOTE

Because <CFCOOKIE> needs to write to the HTTP header, you cannot use it if you've already flushed the header from the ColdFusion output buffer with <CFFLUSH>.

➜ *See also* <CFAPPLICATION>, <CFFLUSH>

<CFDEFAULTCASE>

Description: <CFDEFAULTFCASE>, which must be used with a <CFSWITCH> statement, specifies a default case. <CFCASE> can specify individual cases. <CFDEFAULTCASE> has no attributes.

Syntax:

```
<CFDEFAULTCASE>
HTML or CFML
</CFDEFAULTCASE>
```

Example: The following example checks to see whether a state is a known state and displays an appropriate message:

```
<!--- Evaluates passed expression (UCase(state)) --->
<CFSWITCH EXPRESSION="#UCase(state)#">
    <!--- If case matches CA, California is used. --->
    <CFCASE VALUE="CA">California</CFCASE>
    <!--- If case matches AR, Arkansas is used. --->
    <CFCASE VALUE="AR">Arkansas</CFCASE>
    <!--- If case matches MI, Michigan is used. --->
    <CFCASE VALUE="MI">Michigan</CFCASE>
    <!--- If case doesn't match, the following message is displayed. --->
    <CFCASEDEFAULT>One of the other 47 states</CFCASEDEFAULT>
</CFSWITCH>
```

➜ *See also* <CFSWITCH>, <CFCASE>

<CFDIRECTORY>

Description: <CFDIRECTORY> is used for all directory manipulation, including obtaining directory lists and creating or deleting directories. <CFDIRECTORY> is a flexible and powerful tag and has many attributes, some of which are mutually exclusive. The values passed to the ACTION attribute dictate what other attributes can be used.

The attributes for <CFDIRECTORY> are listed in Table B.33. The possible ACTION values for <CFDIRECTORY> are listed in Table B.34. LIST is assumed if no ACTION is specified. Table B.35 contains the list of columns returned if ACTION="LIST".

When ACTION="LIST" is specified, the tag creates a query containing the file list from the specified directory.

Syntax:

```
<CFDIRECTORY ACTION="Action Type"
    DIRECTORY="Directory Name"
    FILTER="Search Filter"
    MODE="Unix Permissions Mode"
    NAME="Query Name"
    NEWDIRECTORY="New Directory Name"
    SORT="Sort Order">
```

Table B.33 <CFDIRECTORY> Attributes

ATTRIBUTE	DESCRIPTION	NOTES
ACTION	Tag action	Optional; defaults to LIST if omitted.
DIRECTORY	Directory name	Required.
FILTER	Filter spec	Optional; only valid if ACTION="LIST". It can contain wildcard characters.
MODE	Permissions mode	Optional; only valid if ACTION="CREATE". It is used only by the Solaris version of ColdFusion and is ignored by the Windows versions.
NAME	Query name	Required if ACTION="LIST". Query to hold retrieved directory listing.
NEWDIRECTORY	New directory name	Required if ACTION="RENAME"; ignored by all other actions.
SORT	Sort order for use when ACTION="LIST"	Optional comma -delimited list of columns to sort by; each can use ASC for ascending or DESC for descending. Default is ascending.

Table B.34 <CFDIRECTORY> Actions

ACTION	DESCRIPTION
CREATE	Creates a new directory.
DELETE	Deletes a directory.
LIST	Obtains a list of directory contents.
RENAME	Renames a directory.

Table B.35 `<CFDIRECTORY> LIST` Columns

ACTION	DESCRIPTION
`ATTRIBUTES`	File attributes.
`DATELASTMODIFIED`	Last modified date.
`MODE`	Permissions mode (Solaris, HP-UX, and Linux only).
`NAME`	File or directory name
`SIZE`	Size in bytes.
`TYPE`	Type `F` for file or `D` for directory.

Example: This first example is a template that processes a form in which the user has specified a directory name. The example traps for errors:

```
<!--- Sets trap for errors --->
<CFTRY>
    <!--- Creates directory --->
    <CFDIRECTORY ACTION="CREATE" DIRECTORY="#FORM.UserDir#">
    <!--- Catches all errors --->
    <CFCATCH TYPE="ANY">
    <!--- If error contains certain phrase, an error message
    is displayed and processing stops --->
    <CFIF CFCATCH.Detail CONTAINS "when that file already exists">
        <P>Cannot create directory: this directory already exists.
    <!--- If error doesn't contain certain phrase, error details
    are displayed. --->
    <CFELSE>
        <CFOUTPUT>#CFCATCH.Detail#</CFOUTPUT>
    </CFIF>
    <!--- Processing stops --->
    <CFABORT>
    </CFCATCH>
</CFTRY>
<P>Directory created.
```

This next example retrieves a directory list, sorted by filename. The resulting query is displayed in a table:

```
<!--- Creates directory --->
<CFDIRECTORY ACTION="LIST"
    DIRECTORY="C:\INETPUB\WWWROOT\TEST\"
    NAME="Stuff"
    SORT="Name">
<!--- Creates table from query --->
<CFTABLE QUERY="Stuff" COLHEADERS="YES" HTMLTABLE="YES" BORDER="YES">
    <CFCOL HEADER="<B>Name</B>" ALIGN="LEFT" TEXT="Name">
    <CFCOL HEADER="<B>Size</B>" ALIGN="LEFT" TEXT="Size">
</CFTABLE>
```

CAUTION

Due to the inherent danger in using it, this tag can be disabled in the ColdFusion Administrator using Sandbox Security.

➜ *See also* `<CFFILE>`

<CFDUMP>

Description: <CFDUMP> enables you to debug variable values. It can output the contents of simple variables, queries, structures, arrays, and serialized WDDX packets. The attribute for this tag is presented in Table B.36.

Syntax:

```
<CFDUMP Var="Variable Name">
```

Table B.36 <CFDUMP> Attributes

ATTRIBUTE	DESCRIPTION	NOTES
VAR	Variable name	Required; name of variable to dump.

Example: The following example dumps the contents of a variable immediately after it executes. The values being dumped get progressively more complex. Note how you must enclose variable names in the pound sign. Note also that <CFDUMP> will work on nested types of variables.

```
<!--- Creates variable --->
<CFSET TheTime=Now()>
<!--- Dumps content of variable --->
<CFDUMP VAR="#TheTime#">

<!--- Query gets data --->
<CFQUERY NAME="GetContacts"
    DATASOURCE="OWS">
    SELECT LastName, FirstName
    FROM Contacts
</CFQUERY>
<!--- Dumps contents of query --->
<CFDUMP VAR="#GetContacts#">

<!--- Creates variable with structure--->
<CFSET Meals=StructNew()>
<!--- Populates variable --->
<CFSET Meals["Breakfast"]="Cereal">
<CFSET Meals["Lunch"]=StructNew()>
<CFSET Meals["Lunch"]["MainCourse"]="Sandwich">
<CFSET Meals["Lunch"]["Beverage"]="Bloody Mary">
<!--- Dumps contents of variable --->
<CFDUMP VAR="#Meals#">
```

<CFELSE>

Description: The <CFELSE> tag, which must be used with the <CFIF> set of tags, is used to provide conditional branching logic. Like the <CFELSEIF> tag, the <CFELSE> tag is entirely optional. Although you can use as many <CFELSEIF> tags as necessary in a <CFIF> statement, you can use only one <CFELSE>. If it is used, <CFELSE> must always be the last compare performed.

Syntax:

```
<CFIF Condition>
    <CFELSEIF Condition>
    <CFELSE>
</CFIF>
```

Example: This example checks whether a FORM variable named LastName exists:

```
<!--- If the condition is met, a variable is set --->
<CFIF IsDefined("FORM.LastName")>
<CFSET Lname=FORM.LastName)>
<!--- If the condition is not met, an alternative variable is set --->
<CFELSE>
<CFSET Lname="")>
```

The following example is a complete conditional statement that uses <CFELSEIF> to perform additional comparisons. It also uses <CFELSE> to specify a default for values that pass none of the compares:

```
<!--- Checks if a value meets a condition --->
<CFIF State IS "MI">
    Code for Michigan only goes here
<!--- If first condition is not met, checks if the value meets a second
      condition --->
<CFELSEIF State IS "IN">
    Code for Indiana only goes here
<!--- If first or second conditions are not met, checks if a value meets
      a third condition --->
<CFELSEIF (State IS "OH") OR (State IS "KY")>
    Code for Ohio or Kentucky goes here
<!--- If first, second, or third conditions are not met, the value is set --->
<CFELSE>
    Code for all other states goes here
</CFIF>
```

➜ *See also* <CFIF>, <CFELSEIF>

<CFELSEIF>

Description: The <CFELSEIF> tag, which must be used with the <CFIF> set of tags and the <CFELSE> tag, is used to provide conditional branching logic. Like the <CFELSE> tag, the <CFELSEIF> tag is entirely optional. Although you can use as many <CFELSEIF> tags as necessary in a <CFIF> statement, you can use only one <CFELSE>. If it is used, <CFELSE> must always be the last compare performed.

Syntax:

```
<CFIF Condition>
    <CFELSEIF Condition>
    <CFELSE>
</CFIF>
```

Example: This example checks to see whether a FORM variable named LastName exists:

```
<!--- If the condition is met, a variable is set --->
<CFIF IsDefined("FORM.LastName")>
    <CFSET Lname=FORM.LastName)>
<!--- If the condition is not met, an alternative variable is set --->
<CFELSE>
    <CFSET Lname="")>
```

The following example is a complete conditional statement that uses `<CFELSEIF>` to perform additional comparisons. It also uses `<CFELSE>` to specify a default for values that pass none of the compares:

```
<!--- Checks if a value meets a condition --->
<CFIF State IS "MI">
    Code for Michigan only goes here
<!--- If first condition is not met, checks if the value meets a second
      condition --->
<CFELSEIF State IS "IN">
    Code for Indiana only goes here
<!--- If first or second conditions are not met, checks if a value meets
      a third condition --->
<CFELSEIF (State IS "OH") OR (State IS "KY")>
    Code for Ohio or Kentucky goes here
<!--- If first, second, or third conditions are not met, the value is set --->
<CFELSE>
    Code for all other states goes here
</CFIF>
```

➜ *See also* `<CFIF>`, `<CFELSE>`

<CFERROR>

Description: `<CFERROR>` enables you to override the standard ColdFusion error messages and replace them with special error-handling templates that you specify. `<CFERROR>` requires that you specify the type of error message to be overridden and the template containing the error message to be displayed. Table B.37 provides attribute values.

Four types of error messages are available in ColdFusion. `REQUEST` errors occur while processing a template, and `VALIDATION` errors occur when `FORM` field validation errors occur. Trapping for `EXCEPTION` errors enables you to trap any unhandled errors. You also can specify an `EXCEPTION`-handling template in the ColdFusion Administrator. Table B.38 shows the available error message variables for `REQUEST`, `MONITOR`, `EXCEPTION` error types. Table B.39 shows the available error message variables for `VALIDATION` error types.

You cannot use CFML in error-handling templates for `REQUEST` errors; only HTML/JavaScript is allowed. Templates that handle `EXCEPTION` errors, however, are capable of using CFML. `MONITOR`, `REQUEST`, and `EXCEPTION` error-handling templates also have access to a special error structure named `ERROR`.

Syntax:

```
<CFERROR Type="Error Type"
    TEMPLATE="Error Message Template
    MAILTO="Administrator's e-mail address"
    EXCEPTION="Exception type">
```

Table B.37 <CFERROR> Attributes

ATTRIBUTE	DESCRIPTION	NOTES
EXCEPTION	Identifies the exception type	Required if the TYPE is EXCEPTION or MONITOR.
MAILTO	The administrator's e-mail address	The e-mail address of the administrator to be notified of error messages. This value is available with the error message template as#ERROR.MailTo#.
TEMPLATE	Error message template	Required; name of the template containing the error-handling code.
TYPE	Type of error message	Optional; values are REQUEST, VALIDATION, and EXCEPTION. If this attribute is omitted the default value of REQUEST is used. An ERROR variable is created for REQUEST,MONITOR, and EXCEPTION types. This is described in Table B.38. The values for VALIDATION errors are presented in Table B.39.

Table B.38 ColdFusion Error Message Variables for REQUEST, MONITOR, and EXCEPTION Error Types

VARIABLE	DESCRIPTION
#ERROR.BROWSER#	The browser the client was running, with version and platform information if provided by the browser.
#ERROR.DATETIME#	The date and time that the error occurred; can be passed to any of the date/time manipulation functions as necessary.
#ERROR.DIAGNOSTICS#	Detailed diagnostic error message returned by ColdFusion.
#ERROR.GENERATEDCONTENT#	Content generated by the failed template. This variable is not available to REQUEST error types.
#ERROR.HTTPREFERER#	URL of the page from which the template was accessed.
#ERROR.MAILTO#	Administrator's e-mail address; can be used to send notification of the error.
#ERROR.QUERYSTRING#	The URL query string of the request.
#ERROR.REMOTEADDRESS#	Client's IP address.
#ERROR.TEMPLATE#	Template being processed when the error occurred.

Table B.39 ColdFusion Error Message Variables for the `VALIDATION` Error Type

VARIABLE	DESCRIPTION
`#ERROR.InvalidFields#`	List of the invalid form fields.
`#ERROR.ValidationFooter#`	Text for footer of error message.
`#ERROR.ValidationHeader#`	Text for header of error message.

Example: The following example establishes an error-message template for `REQUEST` errors in the `application.cfm` file and shows what an error template might look like:

```
<!--- Application.cfm template --->
<!--- Application is created --->
<CFAPPLICATION NAME="MyApp">
<!--- Request errors --->
<CFERROR TYPE="REQUEST"
    NAME="ERROR_REQUEST.CFM"
    MAILTO="admin@orangeWhipStudios.com">
<!--- Exception errors --->
<CFERROR TYPE="EXCEPTION"
    NAME="ERROR_EXCEPTION.CFM">

<!--- Error_Exception.cfm template --->
<!--- Mail with error details is sent to the administrator --->
<CFMAIL
    FROM="system@orangeWhipStudios.com"
    TO="admin@orangeWhipStudios.com"
    SUBJECT="Error on OWS application">
    An error has occurred:
    #ERROR.Detail#
</CFMAIL>

<HTML>
<HEAD>
    <TITLE>Application Error</TITLE>
</HEAD>
<BODY>
<!--- If certain template is returned, an error message is displayed --->
<CFIF Error.Template EQ "GetCustomers.cfm">
    <H2>An error occurred getting customer records.</H2>
<!--- If certain template is not returned, an alternative message is displayed --->
<CFELSE>
    <H2>An Error Has Occurred</H2>
</CFIF>
<P>The administrator has been notified.
</BODY>
</HTML>
</HTML>
```

NOTE

The `<CFERROR>` tag is best used in the `Application.cfm` template.

<CFEXECUTE>

Description: <CFEXECUTE> enables you to execute processes on the ColdFusion server machine. <CFEXECUTE> is frequently used to execute a server program at a regular interval using <CFSCHEDULE>. Table B.40 describes the tag attributes.

NOTE

Don't put any CFML tags or functions between the start and end tags.

Syntax:

```
<CFEXECUTE NAME="ExecutableName"
    ARGUMENTS="CommandLine"
    OUTPUTFILE="Pathname For Output"
    TIMEOUT="Time interval in seconds">
</CFEXECUTE>
```

Table B.40 <CFEXECUTE> Attributes

ATTRIBUTE	DESCRIPTION	NOTES
NAME	Name of executable	Required.
ARGUMENTS	Any command-line parametersthat must be passed	Optional; only used if the program needs to be passed command-line arguments.
OUTPUTFILE	Pathname to file into which output from program should be written	Optional; if not specified, any output appears on the page in which this tag is used.
TIMEOUT	Number of seconds program should be given before it's timed out	Optional; defaults to 0. If 0 ColdFusion spawns another thread to execute the program.

Example: This example invokes PKZip to produce a user-specified Zip file by passing it an array of arguments:

```
<!--- args array is created --->
<CFSCRIPT>
    args = ArrayNew(1);
    args[1] = "-a";
    args[2] = "c:\temp\test.zip";
    args[3] = "c:\inetput\wwwwroot\MyApp\UTIL.*";
</CFSCRIPT>
<!--- Executes pkzip, passes arg array, and specifies output file --->
<CFTRY>
    <CFEXECUTE NAME="c:\utils\pkzip.exe "
    ARGUMENTS="#args#"
    OUTPUTFILE="C:\TEMP\TESTOUT.TXT">
    </CFEXECUTE>
<!--- Catches and outputs any arguments --->
<CFCATCH TYPE="Any">
    <CFOUTPUT>#CFCATCH.Message#</CFOUTPUT>
</CFCATCH>
</CFTRY>
```

NOTE

The arguments can be passed as an array or as a string.

➜ See also <CFSCHEDULE>

<CFEXIT>

Description: <CFEXIT> aborts the processing of a custom tag without aborting processing of the calling template. When used in a regular template, <CFEXIT> acts just like <CFABORT>. When called within a custom tag, however, <CFEXIT> does not terminate processing of the calling template (like <CFABORT>), but instead returns processing to it. Table B.41 presents the values for the METHOD attribute.

Syntax:

```
<CFEXIT METHOD="Method">
```

Table B.41 Methods Used in <CFEXIT>

METHODS	DESCRIPTION
ExitTag	Default; aborts current tag processing, similar to <CFABORT>. If used in a custom tag, this causes processing to continue after end tag.
ExitTemplate	Exits the currently processing tag. If used where a custom tag's execution mode is Start, this will continue processing from the first child tag in the current custom tag's body. If used where a custom tag's execution mode is End, it will continue processing after the end tag.
Loop	Re-executes body in current custom tag. This method can be used only when a custom tag's execution mode is End. In this case, it will continue processing from the first child tag in the current custom tag's body. In all other contexts, it will return an error.

Example: This example checks whether a particular attribute was passed. It stops the custom tag's processing if the attribute is missing but enables processing to continue in the calling template after the custom tag:

```
<!--- if attribute is not present, the custom tag stops processing --->
<CFIF NOT IsDefined("ATTRIBUTES.MyAttrib")>
    <CFEXIT>
</CFIF>
...
```

➜ See also <CFABORT>

<CFFILE>

Description: <CFFILE> is used to perform file-management operations, including uploading files from a browser; moving, renaming, copying, and deleting files; and reading and writing files. Table B.42 shows the tag attributes for <CFFILE>.

<CFFILE> is a flexible and powerful tag; it has several attributes, many of which are mutually exclusive. The values passed to the ACTION attribute dictate which other attributes can be used. These values are described in Table B.43. Table B.44 describes the options you have when dealing with filename conflicts arising from file upload operations.

<CFFILE> creates a FILE object after every <CFFILE> operation. You can use the variables in this object as you would any other ColdFusion variables, enabling you to check the results of an operation. However, only one FILE object exists, and as soon as you execute a new <CFFILE> tag, the prior FILE object is overwritten with the new one. FILE object variables are described in Table B.45.

Syntax:

```
<CFFILE ACCEPT="Filter"
    ACTION="Action Type"
    DESTINATION="Destination Directory or File Name"
    FILE="File Name"
    FILEFIELD="Field Containing File Name"
    NAMECONFLICT="Conflict Option"
    OUTPUT="Text To Output"
     SOURCE="Source File Name"
     VARIABLE="Variable Name">
```

Table B.42 <CFFILE> Attributes

ATTRIBUTE	DESCRIPTION	NOTES
ACCEPT	File type filter	This optional attribute restricts the types of files that can be uploaded, and can be used only if ACTION is UPLOAD. The filter is specified as a MIME type ("image/*", which allows all image types, but nothing else); multiple MIME types can be specified separated by commas.
ACTION	Desired action	This attribute is required.
DESTINATION	Destination file location	This attribute can be used only if ACTION is one of the following: COPY, MOVE, RENAME, or UPLOAD. Destination can be a filename or a fully qualified file path.
FILE	Name of local file to access	This attribute can be used only if ACTION is APPEND, DELETE, READ, READBINARY, or WRITE, in which case it is required.
FILEFIELD	Name of the FILE type	This attribute can be used only if <INPUT> containing ACTION is UPLOAD, in which case it is the file required.
MODE	Identifies file access permissions for uploaded file	This is used only in Unix-type installations. See Table B.43.
NAMECONFLICT	What to do in case of name conflicts	This optional attribute can be used if ACTION is UPLOAD. It specifies the course to take if a name conflict arises from the upload.If this attribute is omitted, the default value of "ERROR"is used.
OUTPUT	Text to output to file	This attribute can be used only if ACTION is WRITE or APPEND.
SOURCE	Source filename	Name of the source file to be written to, copied, or moved. Can be used only if ACTION is COPY, MOVE, or RENAME.
VARIABLE	Variable to store file	This attribute can be used only if contents of read ACTION is READ or READBINARY, in which case it is required.

Table B.43 <CFFILE> Actions

ACTION	DESCRIPTION
APPEND	Appends one text file to the end of another.
COPY	Copies a file.
DELETE	Deletes a specified file.
MOVE	Moves a specified file from one directory to another, or from one filename to another.
READ	Reads the contents of a text file.
READBINARY	Reads the contents of a binary file.
RENAME	Does the same thing as MOVE; see MOVE.
UPLOAD	Receives an uploaded file.
WRITE	Writes specified text to the end of a text file.

Table B.44 File Upload Name Conflict Options

OPTION	DESCRIPTION
ERROR	The file will not be saved, and ColdFusion will immediately terminate template processing.
SKIP	Neither saves the file nor generates an error message.
OVERWRITE	Overwrites the existing file.
MAKEUNIQUE	Generates a unique filename and saves the file with that new name. To find out what the new name is, inspect the #FILE.ServerFile# field.

Table B.45 <CFFILE> FILE Object Variables

FIELD	DESCRIPTION
#FILE.ATTEMPTEDSERVERFILE#	The original attempted filename; will be the same as #FILE.ServerFile# unless the name had to be changed to make it unique.
#FILE.CLIENTDIRECTORY#	The client directory from where the file was uploaded, as reported by the client browser.
#FILE.CLIENTFILE#	The original filename as reported by the client browser.
#FILE.CLIENTFILEEXT#	The original file extension, as reported by the client browser.
#FILE.CLIENTFILENAME#	The original filename as reported by the client browser, but without the file extension.
#FILE.CONTENTSUBTYPE#	The MIME subtype of an uploaded file.
#FILE.CONTENTTYPE#	The primary MIME type of an uploaded file.

Table B.45 (continued)

FIELD	DESCRIPTION
#FILE.DATELASTACCESSED#	The last date and time the file was accessed.
#FILE.FILEEXISTED#	Yes if file already existed; No if not.
#FILE.FILESIZE#	Size of file that was uploaded.
#FILE.FILEWASAPPENDED#	Yes if file was overwritten; No if not.
#FILE.FILEWASOVERWRITTEN#	Yes if file was overwritten; No if not.
#FILE.FILEWASRENAMED#	Yes if file was renamed; No if not.
#FILE.FILEWASSAVED#	Yes is file was saved; No if not.
#FILE.OLDFILESIZE#	Size of file that was overwritten.
#FILE.SERVERDIRECTORY#	The server directory in which the uploaded file was saved.
#FILE.SERVERFILEEXT#	The file extension of the uploaded file on the server (does not include period).
#FILE.SERVERFILE#	The name of the file as saved on the server (takes into account updated filename if it was modified to make it unique).
#FILE.SERVERFILENAME#	The name of the uploaded file on the server, without an extension.
#FILE.TIMECREATED#	Time when the file was uploaded.
#FILE.TIMELASTMODIFIED#	Date and time uploaded file was last modified.

Note that when you're uploading files under a Unix-type operating system, you also can use the optional MODE attribute. The possible values for MODE are described in Table B.46.

Table B.46 Mode Values Used When Uploading to Unix Systems

MODE	DESCRIPTION
644	Assigns owner read/write and assigns other/group read permissions.
666	Assigns read/write permissions to all.
777	Assigns read, write, and execute permissions to all.

Example: The two basic categories of use for <CFFILE> are uploading files and file management, including copying, moving, renaming, and so on.

The following example includes both types of use. It includes a form that is used to specify a file to be uploaded and the <CFFILE> code from the form's action template that does the uploading.

It checks to ensure the file is less than 50K (this arbitrary file size was chosen just to illustrate the use of the CFFILE variable). The example uses <CFTRY> and <CFCATCH> tags to trap this user-defined error. If the file is less than 50K, the progress is reported to the user.

It then checks the file extension to ensure that it is a GIF. This again is arbitrary and is included just to demonstrate this technique for limiting file types that can be uploaded.

The last part of the example moves the file to a different directory and reports to the user.

```
<!--- Code in the upload form. Must use ENCTYPE=MULTIPART/FORM-DATA --->
<FORM ENCTYPE="MULTIPART/FORM-DATA"
    ACTION="Upload_Action.cfm"
    METHOD="POST">
<!--- An INPUT of type FILE is required --->
<P>File to upload:
<INPUT TYPE="FILE"
    NAME="UploadFile"
    SIZE="40">
<P><INPUT TYPE="SUBMIT"
    NAME="Upload"
    VALUE="Upload">
</FORM>

<!--- Code in the upload form's action template --->
<CFTRY>
<CFFILE
    ACTION="Upload"
    FILEFIELD="UploadFile"
    DESTINATION="D:\TEMP\"
    NAMECONFLICT="MakeUnique">

<!--- Make sure file isn't more than 50k --->
<CFIF CFFILE.FileSize GT 51250>
    <CFTHROW TYPE="SizeError"
    MESSAGE="File too large. Cannot be more than 50k.">
</CFIF>
<CFIF CFFILE.ClientFileExt NEQ "gif">
    <CFTHROW TYPE="ExtError"
    MESSAGE="File is wrong type. You can only upload GIF files.">
</CFIF>

<CFCATCH TYPE="SizeError">
    <CFABORT SHOWERROR="#CFCATCH.Message#">
</CFCATCH>
<CFCATCH TYPE="ExtError">
    <CFABORT SHOWERROR="#CFCATCH.Message#">
</CFCATCH>
</CFTRY>

<!--- Report on status to user --->
<P>File uploaded successfully:
<CFOUTPUT>
    <P>Filename on client: #CFFILE.ClientFile#
    <P>Filename on server: #CFFILE.ServerFile#
    <P>File size: #CFFILE.FileSize#
</CFOUTPUT>

<!--- Now move file to a different folder --->
<CFFILE
```

```
    ACTION="Move"
    SOURCE="D:\TEMP\#CFFILE.ServerFile#"
    DESTINATION="D:\JUNK\#CFFILE.ServerFile#">
<P>File successfully moved to D:\JUNK\<CFOUTPUT>#CFFILE.ServerFile#</CFOUTPUT>
```

CAUTION

Be careful to use `<CFLOCK>` when using `<CFFILE>` because it uses a shared resource (the server's file system) that multiple ColdFusion threads can try to access simultaneously.

➜ *See also* `<CFDIRECTORY>`, `<CFFTP>`, `<CFLOCK>`

<CFFLUSH>

Description: `<CFFLUSH>` flushes ColdFusion's output buffer, sending the contents back to the Web browser. You can control the point at which the flush takes place with the `INTERVAL` attribute by entering the number of bytes. The attributes for this tag are presented in Table B.47.

Syntax:

```
<CFFLUSH INTERVAL="number of bytes">
```

Table B.47 `<CFFLUSH>` Attributes

ATTRIBUTE	DESCRIPTION	NOTES
`INTERVAL`	Number of bytes	Optional; specifies number of bytes that must be accumulated before buffer is flushed.

NOTE

Several ColdFusion tags are used to write data into the ColdFusion output buffer, including `<CFHEADER>`, `<CFHTMLHEAD>`, `<CFCOOKIE>`, `<CFFORM>`, `<CFCONTENT>`, and `<CFLOCATION>`. A run error will be generated if you try to use these tags after having flushed part of the HTML document (such as the HTTP header or HTML `<HEAD>`) to which these tags need to write.

Example: The following example employs `<CFFLUSH>` to get some output out of the buffer as a page with many queries is built. This gives the user some intermediate feedback as to what is taking place.

```
<!--- Query gets all films --->
<CFQUERY NAME="GetAllFilms" DATASOURCE="OWS">
    SELECT *
    FROM Films
</CFQUERY>

<!--- Query results are flushed to browser --->
<H1>Retrieved all Films</H1>
<CFFLUSH>

<!--- Query gets all actors --->
<CFQUERY NAME="GetAllActors" DATASOURCE="OWS">
    SELECT *
    FROM Actors
</CFQUERY>

<!--- Query results are flushed to the browser --->
```

```
<H1>Retrieved all Actors</H1>
<CFFLUSH>

<!--- Query gets all films and actors --->
<CFQUERY NAME="GetAllFilmsActors" DATASOURCE="OWS">
    SELECT *
    FROM FilmsActors
</CFQUERY>

<H1>Retrieved Everything</H1>
```

<CFFORM>

Description: `<CFFORM>` is an alternative to the standard HTML `<FORM>` tag. The `<CFFORM>` tag is not useful by itself. However, it enables you to use other tags (`<CFGRID>`, `<CFINPUT>`, `<CFSELECT>`, `<CFTEXTINPUT>`, `<CFSLIDER>`, `<CFTREE>`, or any Java applets of your own using `<CFAPPLET>`), which do add a great deal of functionality to HTML forms. The code generated by `<CFFORM>` is standard `FORM` HTML and JavaScript code. The attributes for this tag are presented in Table B.48.

Note that ColdFusion can create JavaScript functions and event handlers in the code that is returned to the browser. These functions are necessary to provide the functionality you specify in your input objects, such as required fields and other validations.

Syntax:

```
<CFFORM ACTION="Action Page"
    ENABLECAB="header"
    ENABLEJAR="header"
    ENCTYPE="mimetype"
    ONSUBMIT="javascript function"
    ONLOAD="javascript function"
    ONRESET="javascript function"
    PASSTHROUGH="HTML attribs"
    PRESERVEDATA="YES or NO"
    TARGET="window"></CFFORM>
```

Table B.48 `<CFFORM>` Attributes

ATTRIBUTE	DESCRIPTION	NOTES
`ACTION`	Form action page	Required.
`ENABLECAB`	Header value	Optional; allows the downloading Java classes in Microsoft cabinet files. If `Yes`, users are asked upon opening the page whether they want to download the CAB file.
`ENABLEJAR`	Header value	Optional; allows the downloading of Java JAR files. If `Yes`, users are asked upon opening the page whether they want to download the JAR file.
`ENCTYPE`	MIME type used to	Optional; default value is encode data sent via `application/x-www-form-urlencoded.`
`NAME`	Form name	Optional; if used, you must ensure that the form name is unique.

Table B.48 (continued)

ATTRIBUTE	DESCRIPTION	NOTES
ONLOAD	JavaScript OnLoad function	Optional name of JavaScript function to be executed when form is loaded.
ONRESET	JavaScript OnReset function	Optional name of JavaScript function to be executed when form is reset.
ONSUBMIT	JavaScript OnSubmit function	Optional name of JavaScript function to be executed prior to form submission.
PASSTHROUGH	HTML <FORM> attributes and values not supported directly by <CFFORM>	Optional; you can pass *attribute=value* pairs that aren't explicitly supported by<CFFORM> and they're passed on to the browser.
PRESERVEDATA	YES or NO	Optional; enables Java controls in form (for example, <CFSLIDER>) to maintain their most recent values when the form acts as its own action template.
TARGET	Target window	Optional target window.

Example: The following is a simple <CFFORM>:

```
<!--- ColdFusion form with class PASSTHROGH --->
<CFFORM ACTION="Test_Action.cfm" PASSTHROUGH="CLASS=""DataEntry""">
<P>First Name: <CFINPUT NAME="FirstName" REQUIRED="Yes"
    MESSAGE="You must enter a First Name.">
<P>Last Name: <CFINPUT NAME="LastName" REQUIRED="Yes"
    MESSAGE="You must enter a Last Name.">
<INPUT TYPE="Submit" VALUE="Save">
</CFFORM>
```

Note that the CLASS attribute and value will be passed through ColdFusion to the browser. Here is some of the code that is returned to the browser by ColdFusion:

```
<!--- ColdFusion form with JavaScript --->
<FORM NAME="DataEntryTest"
    ACTION="Test_Action.cfm"
    METHOD=POST
    onSubmit="return CF_checkCFForm_1(this)"
    CLASS="This">
<P>First Name: <INPUT TYPE="Text" NAME="FirstName">
<P>Last Name: <INPUT TYPE="Text" NAME="LastName">
<INPUT TYPE="Submit" VALUE="Save">
</FORM>
```

You can see that ColdFusion passed the CLASS attribute/value pair through to the browser. Also note how it added the onSubmit() JavaScript event to the <FORM> tag. This is due to the use of <CFINPUT> to produce required fields. ColdFusion also creates the JavaScript function CF_CheckCFForm_1() to process the required field validation.

NOTE

<CFFORM> automatically embeds METHOD="POST" in your form.

NOTE

If you specify a value in quotation marks, you must escape the quotation marks by doubling them, for example:

```
PASSTHROUGH="STYLE= ""DataEntry"" "
```

NOTE

Because <CFFORM> must write to the HTML <HEAD>, you cannot use it if you've already flushed the <HEAD> from the ColdFusion output buffer with <CFFLUSH>.

➜ *See also* <CFAPPLET>, <CFGRID>, <CFINPUT>, <CFSELECT>, <CFSLIDER>, <CFTEXTINPUT>, <CFTREE>

<CFFTP>

Description: <CFFTP> is the ColdFusion interface to the Internet standard file transfer protocol. It enables your ColdFusion program to function as an FTP client, interacting with remote file systems. It is a very powerful and complex tag; Table B.49 lists its attributes. Values for the ACTION attribute are presented in Table B.50. Table B.51 lists the status variables for <CFFTP>.

When calls to <CFFTP> are completed—assuming STOPONERROR is set to No (the default)—a series of variables is set so you can determine the success or failure of the operation. Table B.52 lists the complete set of error codes and their meanings.

<CFFTP> can be used to retrieve remote directory lists. Lists are returned in ColdFusion query format, and Table B.53 lists the query columns.

<CFFTP> is designed to be used two ways: either for single operations or to batch operations together. To use the batch mode (called *cached mode*), you must specify a unique name in the CONNECTION attribute that you can use in future <CFFTP> calls.

Syntax:

```
<CFFTP ACTION="Action"
    AGENTNAME=""
    ASCIIEXTENSIONLIST="List"
    ATTRIBUTES="Attributes"
    CONNECTION="Connection Name"
    DIRECTORY="Directory"
    EXISTING="Name"
    FAILIFEXISTS="Yes or No"
    ITEM="Name"
    LOCALFILE="Name"
    NAME="Query Name"
    NEW="Name"
    PASSWORD="Password"
    PORT="Port"
    PROXYBYPASS=""
    PROXYSERVER=""
    REMOTEFILE="Name"
    RETRYCOUNT="Count"
    SERVER="Server Address"
    STOPONERROR="Yes or No"
    TIMEOUT="Seconds"
    TRANSFERMODE="Mode"
    USERNAME="User Name">
```

Table B.49 <CFFTP> Attributes

ATTRIBUTE	DESCRIPTION	NOTES
ACTION	Action	Required.
ASCIIEXTENSIONLIST	ASCII extensions	Optional; semicolon-delimited list of extensions to be treated as ASCII extensions if using TRANSFERMODE of "AutoDetect," default is "txt;htm;html;cfm;cfml;shtm; shtml;css;asp;asa."
ATTRIBUTES	Attributes list	Comma-delimited list of attributes; specifies the file attributes for the local file. Possible values are READONLY, HIDDEN, SYSTEM, ARCHIVE, DIRECTORY, COMPRESSED, TEMPORARY, and NORMAL.
CONNECTION	Connection name	Optional; used to cache connections to perform operations without logging in again.
DIRECTORY	Directory on which operation is to be performed	Required if ACTION is CHANGEDIR, CREATEDIR, LISTDIR, or EXISTSDIR.
EXISTING	Current name of file or directory on remote system	Required if ACTION is RENAME.
FAILIFEXISTS	YES or NO	Optional; indicates whether a GETFILE action will fail if a local file with the same name already exists; defaults to YES.
ITEM	Item (file) name	Required if ACTION is EXISTS or REMOVE.
LOCALFILE	Local filename	Required if ACTION is GETFILE or PUTFILE.
NAME	Query name	Required if ACTION is LISTDIR; see Table B.52 for column list.
NEW	New item (file) name when file is being renamed	Required if ACTION is RENAME.
PASSIVE	Allows you to enable or disable passive mode	Optional; defaults to NO.
PASSWORD	Login password	Required when ACTION is OPEN.
PROXYSERVER	Name of proxy server	Used if you must go through a proxy server.
PROXYBYPASS		
PORT	Server port	Optional attribute; defaults to 21.
REMOTEFILE	Remote filename	Required if ACTION is EXISTSFILE, GETFILE, or PUTFILE.
RETRYCOUNT	Number of retries	Optional retry count; defaults to 1.

Table B.49 (continued)

ATTRIBUTE	DESCRIPTION	NOTES
SERVER	Server name; DNS or address of FTP server	Required when not using an IP cached connection.
STOPONERROR	YES or NO	Optional; defaults to NO. When it's NO, three status variables are produced, as found in Table B.53.
TIMEOUT	Timeout seconds	Optional; timeout value in seconds.
TRANSFERMODE	Transfer mode	Optional; values can be ASCII, BINARY, or AUTODETECT (default).
USERNAME	Login username	Required when ACTION is OPEN.

Table B.50 <CFFTP> Actions

ACTION	DESCRIPTION
CHANGEDIR	Changes directory.
CLOSE	Closes a cached connection.
CREATEDIR	Creates a directory.
EXISTS	Checks whether an object exists.
EXISTSDIR	Checks for a directory's existence.
EXISTSFILE	Checks for a file's existence.
GETCURRENTDIR	Gets current directory.
GETCURRENTURL	Gets current URL.
GETFILE	Retrieves a file.
LISTDIR	Retrieves directory list.
OPEN	Opens a cached connection.
PUTFILE	Sends a file.
REMOVE	Deletes a file.
REMOVEDIR	Removes a directory.
RENAME	Renames a file.

Table B.51 <CFFTP> Status Variables

VARIABLE	DESCRIPTION
#CFFTP.ErrorCode#	Error codes (see Table B.53).
#CFFTP.ErrorText#	Error text.
#CFFTP.Succeeded#	Success; YES or NO.

NOTE

The status variables in Table B.51 are produced only when the `STOPONERROR` attribute is set to `NO`. It's set to `YES` by default.

Table B.52 `<CFFTP>` Query Columns

COLUMN	DESCRIPTION
ATTRIBUTES	Comma-delimited list of attributes.
ISDIRECTORY	YES if directory; NO if file.
LASTMODIFIED	Date and time last modified.
LENGTH	File length.
MODE	An octal format string listing Unix permissions.
NAME	Object name.
PATH	Full path to object.
URL	Full URL to object.

Table B.53 `<CFFTP>` Error Codes

CODE	DESCRIPTION
0	Operation succeeded.
1	System error (OS or FTP protocol error).
2	An Internet session could not be established.
3	FTP session could not be opened.
4	File transfer mode not recognized.
5	Search connection could not be established.
6	Invoked operation valid only during a search.
7	Invalid timeout value.
8	Invalid port number.
9	Not enough memory to allocate system resources.
10	Cannot read contents of local file.
11	Cannot write to local file.
12	Cannot open remote file for reading.
13	Cannot read remote file.
14	Cannot open local file for writing.
15	Cannot write to remote file.
16	Unknown error.
18	File already exists.
21	Invalid retry count specified.

CAUTION

Because it can be rather dangerous, `<CFFTP>` can be disabled using the Basic Security settings in the ColdFusion Administrator.

Example: The following example opens a connection and caches it using the `CONNECTION` attribute. It reads the directory and outputs the resulting query (identified by the `NAME` attribute). This query is then displayed with a simple `<CFTABLE>`.

The next call to `<CFFTP>` uses the cached connection named in the first call. It is used to upload a file from the local ColdFusion server to the remote FTP server by using the `PUTFILE ACTION`. It then displays the value of the `CFFILE.Succeeded` to verify the success.

If the file was uploaded successfully, the file is deleted and the operation's success is displayed. A new directory listing is displayed.

```
<!--- FTP server is queried for directory listing --->
<CFFTP SERVER="ftp.someserver.com"
    USERNAME="joeuser"
    PASSWORD="myPassword"
    ACTION="LISTDIR"
    DIRECTORY="c:\temp\"
    NAME="MyDocs"
    CONNECTION="MyConn">

<HTML>
<HEAD>
    <TITLE>CFFTP Example</TITLE>
</HEAD>

<BODY>

<!--- Contents of FTP query is displayed in a table --->
<P>Directory of files
<CFTABLE BORDER="Yes" HTMLTABLE="yes" QUERY="MyDocs">
    <CFCOL HEADER="Name" TEXT="#Name#" ALIGN="LEFT">
    <CFCOL HEADER="Length" TEXT="#Length#" ALIGN="RIGHT">
</CFTABLE>

<!--- Uploads file and outputs results --->
<CFFTP
    ACTION="PUTFILE"
    LOCALFILE="c:\temp\tcmnote.txt"
    REMOTEFILE="c:\temp\tcmnote.txt">
<p>Uploaded? <CFOUTPUT>#CFFTP.Succeeded#</CFOUTPUT>

<!--- If upload succeeds, temp file is removed --->
<CFIF CFFTP.Succeeded>
    <CFFTP ACTION="REMOVE" ITEM="c:\temp\tcmnote.txt">

<!--- If delete succeeds, temp file is removed and results are outputted--->
<p>tcmote.txt Deleted? <CFOUTPUT> #CFFTP.Succeeded#</CFOUTPUT>

<!--- Contents of FTP query is displayed in a table --->
<CFFTP ACTION="LISTDIR"
    DIRECTORY="c:\temp\"
    NAME="MyDocs">
<P>Directory of files
<CFTABLE BORDER="Yes" HTMLTABLE="yes" QUERY="MyDocs">
```

```
    <CFCOL HEADER="Name" TEXT="#Name#" ALIGN="LEFT">
    <CFCOL HEADER="Length" TEXT="#Length#" ALIGN="RIGHT">
</CFTABLE>
</CFIF>

</BODY>
</HTML>
```

➜ *See also* <CFHTTP>, <CFFILE>

<CFFUNCTION>

Description: This tag is used to define a function or *method* in a ColdFusion component. It defines one of the components behaviors. It must be used in the body of a <CFCOMPONENT>.

Table B.54 describes the different ways that a component method defined with <CFFUNCTION> can be executed. In short you can executes methods using <CFINVOKE> or by calling the methods from URLs, form submission, CFScripts, Flash gateways or from web services. You can pass parameters to methods (by using <CFARGMENT> tags to specify the parameters) and you can return values from them (by using <CFRETURN> within the body of the <CFFUNCTION>). See Table B.55 for a list of <CFFUNCTION> attributes.

To return a value from a function you should specfy a data type to be returned (using the RETURNTYPE attribute) and <CFRETURN> to return the data.

Syntax:

```
<CFFUNCTION
   NAME="Function name"
   RETURNTYPE="Data type to be returned"
   ROLES="Comma-delimited list of roles"
   ACCESS="Access type"
   OUTPUT="YES or NO">…</CFFUNCTION>
```

Table B.54 Different ways of executing methods defined by <CFFUNCTION>

INVOCATION METHOD	DESCRIPTION
<CFINVOKE>	Used in ColdFusion templates or other ColdFusion components to execute a method. Parameters are directly passed as attributes. Return value defined in an attribute.
URL	You use the component name as part of the URL before the query string and specify the method name and params as part of the query string.
Form submission	The FORM's ACTION attribute points to the path of the .cfc that contains the method. INPUT fields are used to pass parameter values.
CFScript	You use the CreateObject() CFscript function to first create an object for the component. Then you invoke that component's methods as you would the functions of any object.
Flash gateway	You use the Netservices functions in your ActionScript. You need to use the Flash MX authoring environment and the Flash 6 player.
Web services	Web service can invoke remote ColdFusion component methods as other web services.

Table B.55 <CFFUNCTION> Attributes

ATTRIBUTE	DESCRIPTION	NOTES
NAME	Text	Required; name of function.
RETURNTYPE	Text	Optional; name of data type that will be returned.
ROLES	List	Optional; comma-delimited list of security roles who have access to this function.
ACCESS	List	Optional; comma-delimited list of access types from which this function can be invoked. The complete list is private, package, public, remote.
OUTPUT	Yes or No	Optional; indicates whether output from this function are to be processed as HTML or hidden as if the function ran in the body of <CFSILENT>.

NOTE

Because <CFFUNCTION> tags are only used in the body of <CFCOMPONENT> tags, they cannot be run in .cfm files, only in ColdFusion components or .cfc files.

Example: The following example demonstrates a method that produces the value of all outstanding orders. Use of this method is restricted to users who have authenticated with the application in the Manager role.

```
<!--- Returns the value of all outstanding orders, but only
      for users how have authenticated as managers.  --->
<CFCOMPONENT>
   <CFFUNCTION NAME="GetOpenOrderTotal"
    RETURNTYPE="Number" ROLES="Manager">
      <CFQUERY NAME="GetOpenOrderTtl" DATASOURCE="OWS">
         SELECT SUM(OI.ItemPrice) AS OpenOrderTotal
         FROM MerchandiseOrders O
           INNER JOIN MerchandiseOrdersItems OI
           ON O.OrderID = OI.OrderID
         WHERE
            O.ShipDate IS NULL
      </CFQUERY>
      <CFRETURN #GetOpenOrderTtl.OpenOrderTotal#>
   </CFFUNCTION>
</CFCOMPONENT>
```

➜ *See also* <CFCOMPONENT>, <CFARGUMENT>, <CFRETURN>, <CFINVOKE>, <CFOBJECT>

<CFGRAPH>

The <CFGRAPH> tag has been deprecated. See <CFCHART> and related tags.

<CFGRAPHDATA>

The <CFGRAPHDATA> tag has been deprecated. See <CFCHART> and related tags.

<CFGRID>

Description: <CFGRID> embeds a Java grid control in your <CFFORM> forms. Grids are similar to spreadsheet-style interfaces, and <CFGRID> grids can be used to browse, select, and even edit data. Grids can be populated either by a query or by specifying each row using the <CFGRIDROW> tag. <CFGRIDCOLUMN> can be used to configure the individual columns with a grid. <CFGRID> attributes are presented in Table B.56.

<CFGRID> must be used between <CFFORM> and </CFFORM> tags.

Syntax:

```
<CFGRID ALIGN="Alignment"
    APPENDKEY="Yes or No"
    AUTOWIDTH="Yes or No"
    BGCOLOR="Color"
    BOLD="Yes or No"
    COLHEADERALIGN="Alignment"
    COLHEADERBOLD="Yes or No"
    COLHEADERFONT="Font Face"
    COLHEADERFONTSIZE="Font Size"
    COLHEADERITALIC="Yes or No"
    COLHEADERS="Yes or No"
    COLHEADERSTEXTCOLOR="Color specification"
    DELETE="Yes or No"
    DELETEBUTTON="Button Text"
    FONT="Font Face"
    FONTSIZE="Font Size"
    GRIDDATAALIGN="Alignment"
    GRIDLINES="Yes or No"
    HEIGHT="Control Height"
    HIGHLIGHTHREF="Yes or No"
    HREF="URL"
    HREFKEY="Key"
    HSPACE="Horizontal Spacing"
    INSERT="Yes or No"
    INSERTBUTTON="Button Text"
    ITALIC="Yes or No"
    MAXROWS="Number"
    NAME="Field Name"
    NOTSUPPORTED="Non Java Browser Code"
    ONERROR="Error Function"
    ONVALIDATE="Validation Function"
    PICTUREBAR="Yes or No"
    QUERY="Query"
    ROWHEADER="Yes or No"
    ROWHEADERALIGN="Alignment"
    ROWHEADERBOLD="Yes or No"
    ROWHEADERFONT="Font Face"
    ROWHEADERFONTSIZE="Font Size"
    ROWHEADERWIDTH="Width"
    ROWHEADERITALIC="Yes or No"
    ROWHEADERTEXTCOLOR="Color specification"
    SELECTCOLOR="Color"
    SELECTMODE="Mode"
    SORT="Yes or No"
```

```
    SORTASCENDINGBUTTON="Button Text"
    SORTDESCENDINGBUTTON="Button Text"
    TARGET="Target Window"
    TEXTCOLOR="Color specification"
    VSPACE="Vertical Spacing"
WIDTH="Control Width">
```

Table B.56 <CFGRID> Attributes

ATTRIBUTE	DESCRIPTION	NOTES
ALIGN	Control alignment	Optional; possible values are TOP, LEFT, BOTTOM, BASELINE, TEXTTOP, ABSBOTTOM, MIDDLE, ABSMIDDLE, and RIGHT.
APPENDKEY	YES or NO	Optional; appends item key to URL. If the value is YES, a variable named GRIDKEY is appended to the URL containing the item selected. It defaults to YES.
AUTOWIDTH	YES or NO	Optional; sizes grid based on the width of the data, within the HEIGHT and WIDTH attributes.
BGCOLOR	Background color	Optional; possible values are BLACK, BLUE, RED, CYAN, DARKGRAY, GRAY, LIGHTGRAY,MAGENTA, ORANGE, PINK, WHITE, YELLOW, or any color specified in RGB form.
BOLD	YES or NO	Optional; boldfaces grid control text; defaults to NO.
COLHEADERALIGN	Column header alignment	Optional; can be LEFT, CENTER, or RIGHT; default is LEFT.
COLHEADERBOLD	YES or NO	Optional; boldfaces column header text; defaults to NO.
COLHEADERFONT	Column header font	Optional font to use for column header.
COLHEADERFONTSIZE	Column header font size in points	Optional font size to use for column header.
COLHEADERITALIC	YES or NO	Optional; italicizes column header text; defaults to NO.
COLHEADERS	YES or NO	Optional; displays column headers; default is YES.
COLHEADERSTEXTCOLOR	Color for text	Optional; can be specified as BLACK (default), BLUE, RED, MAGENTA, CYAN, ORANGE, DARKGRAY, PINK, GRAY, WHITE, LIGHTGRAY, or YELLOW. It can also be specified as a hex value, such as ##999999 (a hex value preceded by two pound signs).
DELETE	YES or NO	Optional; if YES, allows records to be deleted from the grid. Default is NO.

Table B.56 (continued)

ATTRIBUTE	DESCRIPTION	NOTES
DELETEBUTTON	Delete button text	Optional text to use for the Delete button; default is Delete.
FONT	Font face	Optional font face to use.
FONTSIZE	Font size	Optional font size.
GRIDDATAALIGN	Data alignment	Data alignment; can be LEFT, RIGHT, or CENTER; can be overridden at the column level.
GRIDLINES	YES or NO	Optional; displays grid lines; default is YES.
HEIGHT	Control height	Optional height in pixels.
HIGHLIGHTHREF	YES or NO	Optional attribute; if Yes, links are highlighted and underlined; defaults to YES.
HREF	URL	Optional URL to go to upon item selection; if populated by a query, this can be a query column.
HREFKEY	Primary key column	Optional name of column to be used as the primary key.
HSPACE	Control horizontal spacing	Optional horizontal spacing in pixels.
INSERT	YES or NO	Optional; if YES, allows records to be added to the grid; default is NO.
INSERTBUTTON	Insert button text	Optional text to use for the Insert button; default is INSERT.
ITALIC	Italic face text	Optional attribute; must be YES or NO if specified; defaults to NO.
MAXROWS	Number	Optional; number of rows you want to show in the grid.
NAME	Unique control	Required.
NOTSUPPORTED	Text to be used for non-Java browsers	Optional text (or HTML code) to be displayed on non–Java-capable browsers.
ONERROR	JavaScript error function	Optional override to your own JavaScript error message function.
ONVALIDATE	JavaScript validation function	Optional override to your own JavaScript validation function.
PICTUREBAR	Displays picture bar with icons	Optional; if YES, a button bar with icons is displayed for insert, delete, and sort; default is NO.
QUERY	Query to populate grid	Optional name of query to be used to populate the grid.
ROWHEADER	YES or NO	Optional; displays row header if YES; default is YES.

Table B.56 (continued)

ATTRIBUTE	DESCRIPTION	NOTES
ROWHEADERALIGN	Row header alignment	Optional attribute; can be LEFT, CENTER, or RIGHT; default is LEFT.
ROWHEADERBOLD	YES or NO	Optional; displays row header in bold font; defaults to NO.
ROWHEADERFONT	Row header font	Optional font to use for row header.
ROWHEADERFONTSIZE	Row header	Optional font size to use for row header. font size
ROWHEADERITALIC	YES or NO	Optional; displays row header in italics; default is NO.
ROWHEADERTEXTCOLOR	Color for text	Optional; can be specified as BLACK (default), BLUE, RED, MAGENTA, CYAN, ORANGE, DARKGRAY, PINK, GRAY, WHITE, LIGHTGRAY, or YELLOW. Can also be specified as a hex value, such as ##999999 (a hex value preceded by two pound signs).
ROWHEADERWIDTH	Row header width	Optional row header width in pixels.
ROWHEIGHT	Row height	Optional height of row in pixels.
SELECTCOLOR	Selection color	Optional attribute; possible values are BLACK (default), BLUE, RED, CYAN, DARKGRAY, GRAY, LIGHTGRAY, MAGENTA, ORANGE, PINK, WHITE, YELLOW, or any color specified in RGB form.
SELECTMODE	Selection mode	Optional attribute; can be EDIT, SINGLE, ROW, COLUMN or BROWSE; default is BROWSE.
SORT	YES or NO	Optional; if YES, allows grid data to be sorted; defaults to NO.
SORTASCENDINGBUTTON	Sort ascending button text	Optional text to use for the sort ascending button; default is A -> Z.
SORTDESCENDINGBUTTON	Sort descending button text	Optional text to use for the sort descending button; default is Z -> 1.
TARGET	URL to target window	Optional name of target window for HREF URL.
TEXTCOLOR	Color for text	Optional; can be specified as BLACK (default), RED, BLUE, MAGENTA, CYAN, ORANGE, DARKGRAY, PINK, GRAY, WHITE, LIGHTGRAY, or YELLOW. Can also be specified as a hex value, such as ##999999 (a hex value preceded by two pound signs).
VSPACE	Control vertical spacing	Optional vertical spacing in pixels.
WIDTH	Control width	Optional width in pixels.

Example: The following example creates two grids based on query results. The first query is then used to produce a read-only grid containing film budget information. The second query is used to produce a grid in which the user can edit and delete expense records. The last example demonstrates a grid produced with hard-coded data using <CFGRIDROW>.

```
<!--- Queries get raw data --->
<CFQUERY NAME="GetBigBudgetFlicks" DATASOURCE="ows">
    SELECT FilmID, MovieTitle, AmountBudgeted
    FROM Films
</CFQUERY>

<CFQUERY NAME="GetExpenses" DATASOURCE="ows">
    SELECT E.ExpenseID, E.FilmID, F.MovieTitle, E.ExpenseAmount, E.Description
    FROM Expenses E INNER JOIN Films F ON E.FilmID = F.FilmID
</CFQUERY>

<HTML>
<HEAD>
<TITLE>CFGRID Example</TITLE>
</HEAD>

<BODY>
<!--- Form created --->
<CFFORM ACTION="CFGRID_Action.cfm"
    METHOD="POST"
    NAME="GridForm">

<H3>Films Budgets</H3>

<!--- Grid created from first query --->
<CFGRID NAME="FilmBudgets"
    QUERY="GetBigBudgetFlicks"
    COLHEADERBOLD="Yes"
    COLHEADERFONT="Gill Sans MT"
    SELECTMODE="BROWSE"
    WIDTH="400"
    HEIGHT="300">
<!--- Grid column created --->
<CFGRIDCOLUMN NAME="FilmID"
    HEADER="Film ID">
<!--- Grid column created --->
<CFGRIDCOLUMN NAME="MovieTitle"
    HEADER="Title">
<!--- Grid column created --->
<CFGRIDCOLUMN NAME="AmountBudgeted"
    NUMBERFORMAT="___,___,___,___.__"
    DATAALIGN="RIGHT"
    HEADER="Budget"
    HEADERALIGN="RIGHT">
</CFGRID>

<h3>Film Expenses</H3>
<!--- Editable grid --->
<CFGRID NAME="FilmExpenses"
```

```
        QUERY="GetExpenses"
        COLHEADERBOLD="Yes"
        COLHEADERFONT="Gill Sans MT"
        SELECTMODE="EDIT"
        WIDTH="580"
        HEIGHT="300"
        DELETE="Yes"
        DELETEBUTTON="Del?">
    <!--- key column created but not displayed --->
    <CFGRIDCOLUMN NAME="ExpenseID"
       DISPLAY="No">
    <!--- selectable columns created --->
    <CFGRIDCOLUMN SELECT="Yes"
        NAME="FilmID"
        HEADER="Film ID">
    <CFGRIDCOLUMN SELECT="Yes"
        NAME="MovieTitle"
        HEADER="Title">
    <CFGRIDCOLUMN NAME="ExpenseAmount"
        SELECT="Yes"
        NUMBERFORMAT="___,___,___,___.__"
        DATAALIGN="RIGHT"
        HEADER="Amount"
        HEADERALIGN="RIGHT">
    <CFGRIDCOLUMN SELECT="yes"
        NAME="Description">
    </CFGRID>

    <P><INPUT TYPE="Submit" VALUE="Save">

    <!--- grid created from hard-coded data--->
    <CFGRID NAME="AnnualBudget">
    <!--- grid columns created --->
        <CFGRIDCOLUMN NAME="Q1">
        <CFGRIDCOLUMN NAME="Q2">
        <CFGRIDCOLUMN NAME="Q3">
        <CFGRIDCOLUMN NAME="Q4">
    <!--- grid row populated --->
    <CFGRIDROW DATA="400000, 500000, 600000, 700000">
    </CFGRID>

    </CFFORM>

    </BODY>
    </HTML>
```

The action template (CFGRID_ACTION.CFM) for the form developed in the previous example is presented in the following example for <CFGRIDUPDATE>.

NOTE

The <CFGRID> control is accessible only by users with Java-enabled browsers.

→ *See also* <CFGRIDCOLUMN>, <CFGRIDROW>, <CFFORM>, <CFGRIDUPDATE>, <CFINPUT>, <CFSELECT>, <CFSLIDER>, <CFTEXTINPUT>, <CFTREE>

<CFGRIDCOLUMN>

Description: <CFGRIDCOLUMN>, which must be used with <CFGRID>, can be used to configure the individual columns in a grid. <CFGRIDCOLUMN> attributes are presented in Table B. 57.

Syntax:

```
<CFGRIDCOLUMN BOLD="Yes or No"
    BGCOLOR="Color specification"
    COLHEADERTEXTCOLOR="Color specification"
    DATAALIGN="Alignment"
    DISPLAY="Yes or No"
    FONT="Font Face"
    FONTSIZE="Font Size"
    HEADER="Header Text"
    HEADERALIGN="Alignment"
    HEADERBOLD="Yes or No"
    HEADERFONT="Font Face"
    HEADERFONTSIZE="Font Size"
    HEADERITALIC="Yes or No"
    HREF="URL"
    HREFKEY="Key"
    ITALIC="Yes or No"
    NAME="Column Name"
    NUMBERFORMAT="Format Mask"
    SELECT="Yes or No"
    TARGET="Target Window"
    TYPE="Type"
    WIDTH="Column Width"
TEXTCOLOR="Color specification"
    VALUES="Values list"
    VALUESDISPLAY="List of values"
    VALUESDELIMITER="Delimiter character">
```

Table B.57 <CFGRIDCOLUMN> Attributes

ATTRIBUTE	DESCRIPTION	NOTES
BGCOLOR	Color for text	Optional; can be specified as BLACK (default), RED, BLUE, MAGENTA, CYAN, ORANGE, DARKGRAY, PINK, GRAY, WHITE, LIGHTGRAY, or YELLOW. Can also be specified as a hex value, such as ##999999 (a hex value preceded by two pound signs).
BOLD	Boldface text	Optional; must be YES or NO if specified; defaults to NO.
HEADERTEXTCOLOR	Color for text	Optional; can be specified as BLACK (default), RED, BLUE, MAGENTA, CYAN, ORANGE, DARKGRAY, PINK, GRAY, WHITE, LIGHTGRAY, or YELLOW. Can also be specified as a hex value, such as ##999999 (a hex value preceded by two pound signs).
DATAALIGN	Data alignment	Optional; can be LEFT, CENTER, or RIGHT; default is LEFT.
DISPLAY	Display column	Optional; if NO, column is hidden; default is YES.

Table B.57 (continued)

ATTRIBUTE	DESCRIPTION	NOTES
FONT	Font face	Optional font face to use.
FONTSIZE	Font size	Optional font size.
HEADER	Header text	Optional header text; defaults to column name. Value is significant only when the <CFGRID> COLHEADERS attribute is YES (default).
HEADERALIGN	Header alignment	Optional; can be LEFT, CENTER, or RIGHT; default is LEFT.
HEADERBOLD	Header in bold	Optional; if YES, header is displayed in a bold font; default is NO.
HEADERFONT	Header font	Optional font to use for header.
HEADERFONTSIZE	Header font size	Optional font size to use for header.
HEADERITALIC	Header in italics	Optional; if YES, header is displayed in an italic font; default is NO.
HREF	URL	URL for selection in this column; can be absolute or relative.
HREFKEY	Primary key	Optional primary key to use for this column.
ITALIC	Italic face text	Optional; must be YES or NO if specified; defaults to NO.
NAME	Column name	Required; if using a query to populate the grid, this must be a valid column name.
NUMBERFORMAT	Number formatting	Optional; uses NumberFormat() function masks; see that function for mask details.
SELECT	Allow selection	Optional; if NO, selection or editing is not allowed in this column.
TARGET	Target window	Optional target window for HREF.
TEXTCOLOR	Color for text	Optional; can be specified as BLACK (default), RED, BLUE, MAGENTA, CYAN, ORANGE, DARKGRAY, PINK, GRAY, WHITE, LIGHTGRAY, or YELLOW. Can also be specified as a hex value, such as ##999999 (a hex value preceded by two pound signs).
TYPE	Data type	Optional; can be image or numeric. If it's an image, an appropriate graphic is displayed for the cell value. Built-in images are in the following bulleted list.
VALUES	List or range	Optional; enables you to format a column as a drop-down box. You specify a hard-coded list of delimited values (for example, Joe,Bob,Jenny) or a range of values, such as 1-10.

Table B.57 (continued)

ATTRIBUTE	DESCRIPTION	NOTES
VALUESDISPLAY	List to dislay	Optional; this is used with the VALUES attribute to specify the list to be displayed.
VALUESDELIMITER	Delimiter character	Optional; character to act as delimiter in VALUES and VALUESDISPLAY lists. Defaults to ,.
WIDTH	Column width	Optional column width in pixels. Columns are sized as wide as the longest value by default.

The built-in image types for use in the TYPE attribute are:

- Image
- CD
- Computer
- Document
- Element
- Folder
- Floppy
- Fixed
- Remote

Example: The following example creates two grids based on query results. The first query is then used to produce a read-only grid containing film budget information. The second query is used to produce a grid in which the user can edit and delete expense records.

```
<!--- Queries get raw data --->
<CFQUERY NAME="GetBigBudgetFlicks" DATASOURCE="ows">
    SELECT FilmID, MovieTitle, AmountBudgeted
    FROM Films
</CFQUERY>

<CFQUERY NAME="GetExpenses" DATASOURCE="ows">
    SELECT E.ExpenseID, E.FilmID, F.MovieTitle, E.ExpenseAmount, E.Description
    FROM Expenses E INNER JOIN Films F ON E.FilmID = F.FilmID
</CFQUERY>

<HTML>
<HEAD>
    <TITLE>CFGRID Example</TITLE>
</HEAD>

<BODY>
<!--- Form created --->
```

```
<CFFORM ACTION="CFGRID_Action.cfm"
    METHOD="POST"
    NAME="GridForm">

<H3>Films Budgets</H3>

<!--- Grid created from first query --->
<CFGRID NAME="FilmBudgets"
    QUERY="GetBigBudgetFlicks"
    COLHEADERBOLD="Yes"
    COLHEADERFONT="Gill Sans MT"
    SELECTMODE="BROWSE"
    WIDTH="400"
    HEIGHT="300">
<!--- Grid column created --->
<CFGRIDCOLUMN NAME="FilmID"
    HEADER="Film ID">
<!--- Grid column created --->
<CFGRIDCOLUMN NAME="MovieTitle"
    HEADER="Title">
<!--- Grid column created --->
<CFGRIDCOLUMN NAME="AmountBudgeted"
    NUMBERFORMAT="___,___,___,___.__"
    DATAALIGN="RIGHT"
    HEADER="Budget"
    HEADERALIGN="RIGHT">
</CFGRID>

<h3>Film Expenses</H3>
<!--- Editable grid --->
<CFGRID NAME="FilmExpenses"
    QUERY="GetExpenses"
    COLHEADERBOLD="Yes"
    COLHEADERFONT="Gill Sans MT"
    SELECTMODE="EDIT"
    WIDTH="580"
    HEIGHT="300"
    DELETE="Yes"
    DELETEBUTTON="Del?">
<!--- key column created but not displayed --->
<CFGRIDCOLUMN NAME="ExpenseID"
    DISPLAY="No">
<!--- selectable columns created --->
<CFGRIDCOLUMN SELECT="Yes"
    NAME="FilmID"
    HEADER="Film ID">
<CFGRIDCOLUMN SELECT="Yes"
    NAME="MovieTitle"
    HEADER="Title">
<CFGRIDCOLUMN NAME="ExpenseAmount"
    SELECT="Yes"
    NUMBERFORMAT="___,___,___,___.__"
    DATAALIGN="RIGHT"
    HEADER="Amount"
    HEADERALIGN="RIGHT">
<CFGRIDCOLUMN SELECT="yes"
    NAME="Description">
```

```
</CFGRID>

<P><INPUT TYPE="Submit" VALUE="Save">

</CFFORM>

</BODY>
</HTML>
```

➜ *See also* <CFGRID>, <CFGRIDROW>

<CFGRIDROW>

Description: <CFGRIDROW>, which must be used with the <CFGRID> tag, can be used to populate rows in a grid with a comma-delimited list of data. Table B.58 shows <CFGRIDROW> attributes.

Syntax:

```
<CFGRIDROW DATA="Data">
```

Table B.58 <CFGRIDROW> Attributes

ATTRIBUTE	DESCRIPTION	NOTES
DATA	Row data	Comma-delimited list of data to be displayed; one item for each column in the grid.

Example: The following example demonstrates a grid produced with hard-coded data using <CFGRIDROW>.

```
<HTML>
<HEAD>
    <TITLE>CFGRID Example</TITLE>
</HEAD>

<BODY>
<!--- Form created --->
<CFFORM ACTION="CFGRID_Action.cfm"
    METHOD="POST"
    NAME="GridForm">

<!--- grid created from hard-coded data--->
<CFGRID NAME="AnnualBudget">
<!--- grid columns created --->
    <CFGRIDCOLUMN NAME="Q1">
    <CFGRIDCOLUMN NAME="Q2">
    <CFGRIDCOLUMN NAME="Q3">
    <CFGRIDCOLUMN NAME="Q4">
<!--- grid row populated --->
<CFGRIDROW DATA="400000, 500000, 600000, 700000">
</CFGRID>

</CFFORM>

</BODY>
</HTML>
```

➜ *See also* <CFGRID>, <CFGRIDCOLUMN>

<CFGRIDUPDATE>

Description: <CFGRIDUPDATE> provides the action backend to support <CFGRID> in edit mode. <CFGRIDUPDATE> performs all inserts, deletes, and updates in one simple operation. <CFGRIDUPDATE> can be used only in an action page to which a form containing a <CFGRID> control was submitted. <CFGRIDUPDATE> attributes are listed in Table B.59.

Syntax:

```
<CFGRIDUPDATE DATASOURCE="ODBC Data Source Name"
    DBNAME="database name"
    DBPOOL="pool"
    GRID="Grid Name"
    KEYONLY="Yes or No""
    PASSWORD="Password"
    PROVIDER="provider"
    PROVIDERDSN="data source"
    TABLENAME="Table Name"
    TABLEOWNER="Table Owner Name"
    TABLEQUALIFIER="Table Qualifier"
    USERNAME= "User Name">
```

Table B.59 <CFGRIDUPDATE> Attributes

ATTRIBUTE	DESCRIPTION	NOTES
CONNECTSTRING	Deprecated	This attribute has been deprecated.
DATASOURCE	ODBC data source	Required.
DBNAME	Sybase database name	Optional; used only if using native Sybase drivers.
DBPOOL	Database connection pool name	Optional database pool name.
DBSERVER	Deprecated	This attribute has been deprecated.
DBTYPE	Deprecated	This attribute has been deprecated.
GRID	Grid name	Required; the name of the grid in the submitted form with which to update the table.
KEYONLY	WHERE clause construction	If YES, the WHERE clause generated by <CFGRID> contains just the primary; default is YES.
PASSWORD	ODBC login password	Optional ODBC login password.
PROVIDER	OLE-DB COM provider	Optional; only used if using OLE-DB.
PROVIDERDSN	Data source OLE-DB COM provider	Optional; used only if using OLE-DB.
TABLENAME	Table name	Required.
TABLEOWNER	Table owner	Optional ODBC table owner.
TABLEQUALIFIER	Table qualifier	Optional ODBC table qualifier.
USERNAME	ODBC username	Optional ODBC username.

Example: The following example updates an Expenses table based on a grid in the calling form named FilmExpenses. See the example in <CFGRID>:

```
<!--- Updates database with values entered in grid --->
<CFGRIDUPDATE DATASOURCE="OWS"
    TABLENAME="Expenses"
    GRID="FilmExpenses">
```

➜ *See also* <CFFORM>, <CFGRID>

<CFHEADER>

Description: <CFHEADER> enables you to control the contents of specific HTTP headers. You can either provide values for HTTP header elements or specify an HTTP response code and text. The attributes for this tag are presented in Table B.60.

Syntax:

```
<CFHEADER NAME="Header Name"
    VALUE="Value">
```

or

```
<CFHEADER STATUSCODE="HTTP code number"
    STATUSTEXT="Explanation of code">
```

Table B.60 <CFHEADER> Attributes

ATTRIBUTE	DESCRIPTION	NOTES
NAME	Name for header to be set	Required if you're not supplying a STATUSCODE.
VALUE	Header value	Optional; Used in conjunction with NAME attribute to specify header value.
STATUSCODE	HTTP number code	Required if you're not specifying a NAME.
STATUSTEXT	Explains STATUSCODE	Optional; Used in conjunction with STATUSCODE attribute to supply explanation of STATUSCODE.

Example: The following example sets several header values to prevent the template from being cached:

```
<!--- header value is set to no cache --->
<CFHEADER NAME="Pragma"
    VALUE="no-cache">
<!--- header value sets cache to expire immediately --->
<CFHEADER NAME="Expires"
    VALUE="0">
<!--- header value is set to no cache in multiple ways --->
<CFHEADER NAME="cache-control" VALUE="no-cache, no-store,
    must-revalidate, max-age=0">
<!--- writes expiration date into http header --->
<CFHTMLHEAD TEXT='<META HTTP-EQUIV="Expires"
    CONTENT="Mon, 01 Jan 2001 00:00:01 GMT">'>
```

NOTE

There is usually little need to use <CFHEADER> because ColdFusion sets the HTTP headers automatically to optimum values.

NOTE

Because <CFHEADER> needs to write to the HTTP header, you cannot use it if you've already flushed the header from the ColdFusion output buffer with <CFFLUSH>.

➜ *See also* <CFFLUSH>

<CFHTMLHEAD>

Description: <CFHTMLHEAD> writes text into the header section of your Web page. It can be placed anywhere in your page, effectively enabling you to write your <HEAD> section from in or below the <BODY> section of a page. The <HEAD> section can contain <META> tags and well as <SCRIPT> tags (JavaScript) and <CFHTMLHEAD> is frequently used to do this write these sorts of tags. Attributes for this tag are presented in Table B.61.

Syntax:

```
<CFHTMLHEAD TEXT="Text">
```

Table B.61 <CFHTMLHEAD> Attributes

ATTRIBUTE	DESCRIPTION	NOTES
TEXT	Text to place in <HEAD>	Required.

NOTE

Because <CFHTMLHEAD> needs to write to the HTML <HEAD>, you cannot use it if you've already flushed the <HEAD> section from the ColdFusion output buffer with <CFFLUSH>.

Example: See <CFHEADER>.

➜ *See also* <CFFLUSH>

<CFHTTP>

Description: <CFHTTP> enables you to process HTTP GET and POST requests within your ColdFusion code, making ColdFusion perform like a browser. If you're using the POST method, parameters can be passed using the <CFHTTPPARAM> tag. <CFHTTPPARAM> can be used only between <CFHTTP> and </CFHTTP> tags. <CFHTTPPARAM> can be used only between <CFHTTP> and </CFHTTP> tags.

<CFHTTP> attributes are listed in Table B.62. <CFHTTP> sets special variables upon completion that you can inspect; they are listed in Table B.63.

Syntax:

```
<CFHTTP COLUMNS="Column Names"
    DELIMITER="Delimiter Character"
    FILE="File Name"
    FIRSTROWASHEADERS = "Yes or No"
    METHOD="Get|Post"
    NAME="Query Name"
    PASSWORD="Password"
```

```
    PATH="Directory"
    PORT="Port number"
    PROXYPORT="Port number"
    PROXYSERVER="Host Name"
    REDIRECT="Yes or No"
    RESOLVEURL="Yes or No"
    TEXTQUALIFIER="Text Qualifier"
    THROWONERROR="Yes or No"
    URL="Host Name"
    USERAGENT="Brower's user agent value"
    USERNAME="User Name">
</CFHTTP>
```

Table B.62 <CFHTTP> Attributes

ATTRIBUTE	DESCRIPTION	NOTES
COLUMNS	Query columns	Optional; queries columns for retrieved datl.
DELIMITER	Column delimiter	Required if NAME is used; default delimiter is a comml.
FILE	Filename	Required only if PATH is used; file to save.
FIRSTROWASHEADERS	YES or NO	Optional; YES value causes first row of results to be processed as headers if the COLUMNS attribute is NOT specified. If NO and COLUMNS is NOT specified, ColdFusion processes first row of query results and creates column names. If COLUMNS is specified then FIRSTROWASHEADERS attribute is ignored.
METHOD	Submission method	Required; must be either GET or POST; use POST to use <CFHTTPPARAM>.
NAME	Query name	Optional; name of query to be constructed with HTTP results.
PASSWORD	User password	Optional; user password if required by server.
PATH	File path	Optional; path to save file if method is POST.
PORT	TCP/IP port number	Optional; defaults to 80.
PROXYSERVER	Server name	Optional name of proxy server to use.
PROXYPORT	TCP/IP port number	Optional; defaults to 80.
REDIRECT	YES or NO	Optional; defaults to NO; indicates whether execution is to be redirected upon tag failure.
RESOLVEURL	Resolve URL	Optional; defaults to NO; if YES, fully resolves embedded URLs.
TEXTQUALIFIER	Text qualifier	Required if NAME is used; delimiter indicating start and end of column.
TIMEOUT	Timeout period in seconds	Optional; timeout period can be defined in the browser URL, the CF Administrator, and this tag.

Table B.62 (continued)

ATTRIBUTE	DESCRIPTION	NOTES
THROWONERROR	YES or NO	Optional; defaults to NO; indicates whether an exception should be thrown on an error; enables you to trap an error with a <CFTRY>...<CFCATCH> block. The error codes are found in the CFHTTP.StatusCode variable.
URL	Host URL	Required; must be DNS name or IP address of a valid host.
USERAGENT	User agent request	Optional; enables your <CFHTTP> call to spoof a specific browser.
USERNAME	Username	Optional; username if required by server.

Table B.63 <CFHTTP> Returned Variables

FIELD	DESCRIPTION
#CFHTTP.FILECONTENT#	Content returned by HTTP request.
#CFHTTP.MIMETYPE#	MIME type of returned data.
#CFHTTP.RESPONSEHEADER#	Response header name/value pair(s). If there are more than one, they're returned in an array.
#CFHTTP.HEADER#	Raw response header.
#CFHTTP.STATUSCODE#	HTTP error code associated with the error that occurs if THROWONERROR is set to YES.

Example: This example uses Altavist1.com's Babblefish to translate the expression "Say 'Hello' in French" into French. It does this by mimicking the Altavist1.com form found at http://world.altavist1.com/. It will work as long as Altavist1.com doesn't change the URLs or names of fields in this form.

The example uses a <CFHTTP> call with METHOD set to POST, passing the parameters on to the form's action page (identified in the URL attribute as http://world.altavist1.com/tr) using calls to <CFHTTPPARAM>.

The action page is itself a form and is returned in the CFHTTP.FileContent variable. This variable is parsed looking for two values that were determined to delimit the translated value in the action page.

```
<P>Say 'Hello' in French.
<!--- cftry sets trap for errors --->
<CFTRY>
<!--- mimics altavista form --->
    <CFHTTP METHOD="POST"
        URL="http://world.altavist1.com/tr"
        THROWONERROR="Yes">
    <CFHTTPPARAM TYPE="FORMFIELD" NAME="doit" VALUE="done">
    <CFHTTPPARAM TYPE="FORMFIELD" NAME="tt" VALUE="urltext">
```

```
    <CFHTTPPARAM TYPE="FORMFIELD" NAME="lp" VALUE="en_fr">
    <CFHTTPPARAM TYPE="FORMFIELD" NAME="urltext"
    ③VALUE="Say 'Hello' in French.">
    </CFHTTP>
<!--- if any errors are returned, details are displayed
and processing stops. --->
<CFCATCH TYPE="Any">
    <CFOUTPUT>#cfhttp.StatusCode#</CFOUTPUT>
    <P>Failure!<CFABORT>
    </CFCATCH>
</CFTRY>
<!--- if no errors are returned, success message is displayed --->
<P>Success!

<!--- Now parse the French out of the action page's form.
 The value we're looking for is inside a textarea named 'q'
 in the action page. --->
<CFSET nStart=Find('name="q"', CFHTTP.FileContent) +9>
<CFSET nEnd=Find('</textarea>', CFHTTP.FileContent, nStart+1) >
<CFSET French=Mid(CFHTTP.FileContent, nStart, nEnd-nStart)>
<!--- answer is displayed --->
<P><EM><CFOUTPUT>#French#</CFOUTPUT></EM>
```

➜ *See also* <CFHTTPPARAM>, <CFFTP>

<CFHTTPPARAM>

Description: <CFHTTPPARAM>, which must be used with the <CFHTTP> tag, enables you to pass parameters when using POST operations. <CFHTTPPARAM> can be used only between <CFHTTP> and </CFHTTP> tags.

<CFHTTPPARAM> attributes are listed in Table B.64.

Syntax:

```
<CFHTTPPARAM FILE="File Name"
    NAME="Field Name"
    TYPE="Type"
    VALUE="Value">
```

Table B.64 <CFHTTPPARAM> Attributes

ATTRIBUTE	DESCRIPTION	NOTES
FILE	Filename	Required if TYPE is File.
NAME	Field name	This attribute is required.
TYPE	Field type	This attribute is required; must be URL, FORMFIELD, COOKIE, CGI, or FILE.
VALUE	Field value	This attribute is optional unless TYPE is File.

Example: See <CFHTTP>.

➜ *See also* <CFHTTP>

<CFIF>

Description: The <CFIF> set of tags is used to provide conditional branching logic (along with <CFSWITCH>, <CFCASE>, and related tags).

Every <CFIF> tag must have a matching </CFIF> tag. The <CFELSEIF> and <CFELSE> tags are entirely optional. You can use as many <CFELSEIF> tags as necessary in a <CFIF> statement, but only one <CFELSE>. If it is used, <CFELSE> must always be the last compare performed.

<CFIF> uses operators to compare values. Table B.65 shows these operators. Conditions can also be combined to perform more complex comparisons using the Boolean operators shown in Table B.66.

You can compare any values, including static text and numbers, ColdFusion fields, database column values, and function results.

Syntax:

```
<CFIF Condition>
    <CFELSEIF Condition>
    <CFELSE>
</CFIF>
```

Table B.65 ColdFusion Conditional Operators

OPERATOR	ALTERNATIVE	DESCRIPTION
IS	EQUAL, EQ	Checks that the right value is equal to the left value.
IS NOT	NOT EQUAL, NEQ	Checks that the right value is not equal to the left value.
CONTAINS		Checks that the right value is contained within the left value.
DOES NOT CONTAIN		Checks that the right value is not contained within the left value.
GREATER THAN	GT	Checks that the left value is greater than the right value.
LESS THAN	LT	Checks that the left value is less than the right value
GREATER THAN OR EQUAL	GTE	Checks that the left value is greater than or equal to the right value.
LESS THAN OR EQUAL	LTE	Checks that the left value is less than or equal to the right value.

Table B.66 ColdFusion Boolean Operators

OPERATOR	DESCRIPTION
AND	Conjunction; returns TRUE only if both expressions are true.
OR	Disjunction; returns TRUE if either expression is true.
NOT	Negation.

Example: This example checks to see whether a `FORM` variable named `LastName` exists:

```
<!--- If the condition is met, a variable is set --->
<CFIF IsDefined("FORM.LastName")>
    <CFSET Lname=FORM.LastName)>
<!--- If the condition is not met, an alternative variable is set --->
<CFELSE>
    <CFSET Lname="")>
</CFIF>
```

The following example checks to see whether both the `FirstName` and `LastName` `FORM` variables exist:

```
<!--- Checks if two conditions are met --->
<CFIF (IsDefined("FORM.FirstName")) AND (IsDefined("FORM.LastName"))>
```

You could use the following to check for either a first name or a last name:

```
<!--- Checks if either of two conditions are met --->
<CFIF (IsDefined("FORM.FirstName")) OR (IsDefined("FORM.LastName"))>
```

Often, you will want to verify that a field is not empty and that it does not contain blank spaces. The following example demonstrates how this can be accomplished:

```
<!--- Checks that a condition is not met --->
<CFIF Trim(FORM.LastName) IS NOT "">
```

You can use the `CONTAINS` operator to check whether a value is within a range of values. Take a look at both of these examples:

```
<!--- Checks if a value contains certain sets of characters --->
<CFIF "KY,MI,MN,OH,WI" CONTAINS State>
<!--- Checks if a value contains certain sets of characters --->
<CFIF TaxableStates CONTAINS State>
```

By combining conditions within parentheses, more complex expressions can be created. For example, the following condition checks to see whether payment is by check or credit card; if payment is by credit card, it checks to ensure that there is an approval code:

```
<!--- Checks if multiple values fulfill multiple conditions --->
<CFIF (PaymentType IS "Check") OR ((PaymentType IS "Credit")
 AND (ApprovalCode IS NOT ""))>
```

The following example is a complete conditional statement that uses `<CFELSEIF>` to perform additional comparisons. It also uses `<CFELSE>` to specify a default for values that pass none of the compares:

```
<!--- Checks if a value meets a condition --->
<CFIF State IS "MI">
    Code for Michigan only goes here
<!--- If first condition is not met, checks if the value meets
      a second condition --->
<CFELSEIF State IS "IN">
    Code for Indiana only goes here
<!--- If first or second conditions are not met, checks if a value meets
      a third condition --->
<CFELSEIF (State IS "OH") OR (State IS "KY")>
    Code for Ohio or Kentucky goes here
<!--- If first, second, or third conditions are not met, the value is set --->
<CFELSE>
    Code for all other states goes here
</CFIF>
```

Note that <CFPARAM> can be used as a shortcut for this functionality. The code

```
<CFPARAM NAME="MyVariable"
    DEFAULT="123">
```

is the same as this code:

```
<CFIF NOT IsDefined("MyVariable")>
    <CFSET MyVariable=123>
</CFIF>
```

➜ *See also* <CFELSE>, <CFELSEIF>, <CFSWITCH>, <CFPARAM>, Iif()

<CFIMPERSONATE>

This tag has been deprecated and is no longer in use. Please refer to ColdFusion's new security framework tags: <CFLOGIN>, <CFLOGOUT> and <CFLOGINUSER>.

<CFIMPORT>

Description: <CFIMPORT> enables you to import and use JSP tag library (that conforms to the JSP 1.1. tag extension API) on a ColdFusion template. The JSP tags can only be accessed on the page that imported them. When importing multiple tag libraries, if tags with the same name are imported more than once, the first import takes precedence. You can define a prefix to use when accessing the imported tags. <CFIMPORT> attributes are shown in Table B.67.

Syntax:

```
<CFIMPORT TAGLIB="Location of tag library"
    PREFIX="Prefix name for imported tags" />
```

Table B.67 <CFIMPORT> Attributes

ATTRIBUTE	DESCRIPTION	NOTES
TAGLIB	URI or path	Required; you can use a URL to point to a JAR application or you can use a path to point to a tag library descriptor file.
PREFIX	Name	Optional; this value will be used as a prefix to access all imported JSP tags on current page.

NOTE

This tag must be included at the top of each page in which you intend to use the imported tags; it should not be <CFINCLUD>ed in the page. Also note that it should not be placed in application.cfm as it will not be propagated from there.

Example: The following code imports a library of JSP tags in a .JAR file. In the bottom half of the example, an imported JSP tag is employed using its imported prefix.

```
<!--- Import a library of statistics functions --->
<CFIMPORT TAGLIB="/myjavaserverpages/libraries/statstags.jar"
   PREFIX="Math">

<!--- Now we'll use one of the math tags. This one produces
```

```
  the standard deviation based on a list of values. --->
<CFOUTPUT>
<Math:stddev hi="2032,493,34,3673,232,45232,24,333,4335,32"/>
</CFOUTPUT>
```

➜ *See also* <CFINVOKE>

<CFINCLUDE>

Description: <CFINCLUDE> includes the contents of another template in the one being processed. This is one mechanism ColdFusion developers can employ to reuse code. Table B.68 shows the <CFINCLUDE> attributes.

Syntax:

```
<CFINCLUDE TEMPLATE="Template File Name">
```

Table B.68 <CFINCLUDE> Attributes

ATTRIBUTE	DESCRIPTION	NOTES
TEMPLATE	Name of template to include	This attribute is required. Only relative paths are supported.

Example: The following example includes the footer file in the current directory if it exists and a default footer if not:

```
<!--- if file exists, it is included in the page
being processed --->
<CFIF FileExists("FOOTER.CFM")>
    <CFINCLUDE TEMPLATE="FOOTER.CFM">
<!--- if file doesn't exist, a default template is used --->
<CFELSE>
    <CFINCLUDE TEMPLATE="/DEFAULT/FOOTER.CFM">
</CFIF>
```

NOTE

<CFINCLUDE> can help you reuse templates. You can use <CFINCLUDE> to break out common components (such as page headers and footers or commonly used queries), which enables you to share them among multiple templates.

CAUTION

Be careful about defining variables in templates that are being included in other templates because their variables share the same scope. Therefore, if the included template defines a variable that is previously defined in the including template, the original variable value will be overwritten. Note that ColdFusion custom tags enable you to avoid these problems and reuse code.

➜ *See also* <CFLOCATION>

<CFINDEX>

Description: <CFINDEX> is used to populate Verity collections with index data. A collection must be created with either the ColdFusion Administrator or <CFCOLLECTION> before it can be populated. <CFINDEX> can be used to index physical files (in which case, the filename is returned in searches) or query results (in which case the primary key is returned in searches). Table B.69 lists `<CFINDEX>` attributes. Table B.70 shows the values for the `ACTION` attribute.

Syntax:

```
<CFINDEX ACTION="Action"
    BODY="Text"
    COLLECTION="Collection Name"
    CUSTOM1="Data"
    CUSTOM2="Data"
    EXTENSIONS="File Extensions"
    KEY="Key"
    LANGUAGE="Language from optional International Search Pack"
    QUERY="Query Name"
    RECURSE="Yes or No"
    TITLE="Text"
    TYPE="Type"
    URLPATH="Path">
```

Table B.69 <CFINDEX> Attributes

ATTRIBUTE	DESCRIPTION	NOTES
ACTION	Action	Required attribute.
BODY	Body to index	Required if TYPE is CUSTOM; invalid if TYPE is DELETE. ASCII text to be indexed. If indexing a query, this must be the column (or comma-delimited list of columns) to be indexed.
COLLECTION	Collection name	Required; name of the collection to be indexed; if using external collections, this must be a fully qualified path to the collection.
CUSTOM1	Custom data	Optional attribute for storing data during indexing; specify a valid query column name.
CUSTOM2	Custom data	Optional attribute for storing data during indexing; usage is the same as CUSTOM1.
EXTENSIONS	File extensions	Optional; comma-delimited list of extensions of files to be indexed; only used if TYPE is PATH.
EXTERNAL	Deprecated	This attribute has been deprecated.
KEY	Unique key	Optional; used to indicate what makes each record unique. If TYPE is FILE, this should be the document filename; if TYPE is PATH, this should be a full path to the document; if TYPE is CUSTOM, this should be any unique identifier (for example, key field in a query result).
LANGUAGE	Specify a language	Optional; requires installation of the International Search Pack.
QUERY	Query name to be indexed	Optional; use when TYPE=CUSTOM.
RECURSE	YES or NO	Optional; used when TYPE=PATH; if it's YES, all subdirectories are indexed, too.

Table B.69 (continued)

ATTRIBUTE	DESCRIPTION	NOTES
`TITLE`	Document title	Required if `TYPE` is `Custom`; specified title for collection or query column name. Enables searching collections by title and the display of a title other than the actual key.
`TYPE`	Index type	Optional attribute, must be `FILE`, `PATH`, or `CUSTOM`. If `PATH` is used, specify the full filepath.
`URLPATH`	URL path	Optional attribute; specifies the URL path for files when `TYPE=File` or `TYPE=Path`.

Table B.70 `<CFINDEX>` Actions

ACTION	DESCRIPTION
`DELETE`	Deletes a key from a collection.
`PURGE`	Clears all data from a collection.
`REFRESH`	Clears all data from a collection and repopulates it.
`UPDATE`	Updates a collection and adds a key if it does not exist.

Example: The first example updates an existing collection built from a query. This index enables users to search for Orange Whip Studios merchandise based on merchandise name, description, or film name:

```
<!--- query gets raw data --->
<CFQUERY NAME="GetFilmsMerchandise" DATASOURCE="ows">
    SELECT M.MerchID, F.MovieTitle, M.MerchName, M.MerchDescription
    FROM Merchandise M, Films F
    WHERE M.FilmID = F.FilmID
</CFQUERY>
<!--- updates collection with query results --->
<CFINDEX
    ACTION="UPDATE"
    BODY="MerchName, MerchDescription, MovieTitle"
    COLLECTION="FilmsMerchandise"
    KEY="MerchID"
    QUERY="GetFilmsMerchandise"
    TYPE="CUSTOM">
```

The second example creates a collection and populates it with the contents of documents in a specific path:

```
<!--- collection is created --->
<CFCOLLECTION ACTION="CREATE" COLLECTION="CFInstallTest"
    PATH="C:\CFUSION\Verity\Collections">
<!--- collection is updated with files from a specific directory --->
<CFINDEX ACTION="UPDATE"
    TYPE="PATH"
    COLLECTION="CFInstallTest"
```

```
EXTENSIONS=".htm, .html, .cfm"
KEY="C:\Inetpub\wwwroot\CFDOCS\testinstallation"
RECURSE="Yes"
URLPATH="http://localhost/CFDOCS/testinstallation">
```

➜ *See also* <CFCOLLECTION>, <CFSEARCH>

<CFINPUT>

Description: <CFINPUT> is an enhancement to the standard HTML <INPUT> tag. <CFINPUT> enables you to embed JavaScript client-side validation code in your HTML forms automatically. <CFINPUT> must be used between <CFFORM> and </CFFORM> tags; it is not a Java control. Attributes are presented in Table B.71.

Syntax:

```
<CFINPUT CHECKED
    MAXLENGTH="Length"
    MESSAGE="Message Text"
    NAME="Field Name"
    ONERROR="JavaScipt Error Function"
    ONVALIDATE="JavaScript Validation Function"
    PASSTHROUGH="HTML attributes"
    RANGE="Range Values"
    REQUIRED="Yes or No"
    SIZE="Field Size"
    TYPE="Type"
    VALIDATE="Validation Type"
    VALUE="Initial Value">
```

Table B.71 <CFINPUT> Attributes

ATTRIBUTE	DESCRIPTION	NOTES
CHECKED	Checked state	Optional; only valid if type is RADIO or CHECKBOX and if present radio button or check box is prechecked.
MAXLENGTH	Maximum number of characters	Optional.
MESSAGE	Validation failure message	Optional message to display upon validation failure.
NAME	Unique control name	Required.
ONERROR	JavaScript error function	Optional override to your own JavaScript error message function.
ONVALIDATE	JavaScript validation function	Optional override to your own JavaScript validation function.
PASSTHROUGH	HTML attributes	Optional; for including HTML attributes not explicitly supported by <CFINPUT>.
RANGE	Range minimum and maximum	Optional range for numeric values only;must be specified as two numbers separated by a comma.
REQUIRED	YES or NO	Optional; indicates that value must be supplied; defaults to NO.

Table B.71 (continued)

ATTRIBUTE	DESCRIPTION	NOTES
SIZE	Field size	Optional number of characters to display before needing horizontal scrolling.
TYPE	Input type	Must be TEXT, RADIO, CHECKBOX, or PASSWORD.
VALIDATE	Field validation	Optional field validation type (see Table B.72).
VALUE	Initial value	Optional initial field value.

Table B.72 <CFINPUT> Validation Types

TYPE	DESCRIPTION
CREDITCARD	Correctly formatted credit card number verified using mod10 algorithm.
DATE	Date in mm/dd/yy format.
EURODATE	European date in dd/mm/yy format.
FLOAT	Number with decimal point.
INTEGER	Number with no decimal point.
SOCIAL_SECURITY_NUMBER	Social security number formatted as 999-99-9999 (using hyphens or spaces as separators).
TELEPHONE	Phone number in 999-999-9999 format (using hyphens or spaces as separators); area code and exchange must not begin with 0 or 1.
TIME	Time in hh:mm or hh:mm:ss format.
ZIPCODE	U.S. ZIP code, in either 99999 or 99999-9999 format.

Example: The following example creates a simple form with several fields. These fields employ several types of data validation using <CFINPUT>.

```
<!--- creates form --->
<CFFORM ACTION="process.cfm">
<!--- creates text field --->
<P>Enter your name: <CFINPUT TYPE="text" NAME="name" REQUIRED="Yes"
    MESSAGE="NAME is required!">
<P>Enter your phone number:
<!--- creates text field and validates telephone number format--->
<CFINPUT TYPE="text" NAME="phone" VALIDATE="telephone"
    MESSAGE="You entered an invalid phone number!">
<!--- creates menu --->
<P>Select credit card:
<SELECT NAME="ccnumber">
    <OPTION>MasterCard
    <OPTION>Visa
    <OPTION>Amex
</SELECT>
<!--- creates text field and validates credit card format --->
```

```
<P>CC#: <CFINPUT TYPE="text" NAME="ccnumber" VALIDATE="creditcard" MAXLENGTH="12"
    MESSAGE="Please enter a valid credit card number!">
<!--- creates submit button --->
<p><INPUT TYPE="Submit" VALUE="Save">
</CFFORM>
```

NOTE

<CFINPUT> does not support input fields of type HIDDEN.

➜ *See also* <CFFORM>, <CFGIRD>, <CFSELECT>, <CFSLIDER>, <CFTEXTINPUT>, <CFTREE>

<CFINSERT>

Description: <CFINSERT> adds a single row to a database table. <CFINSERT> requires that the data source and table names be provided. All other attributes are optional. Table B.73 shows the attributes for this tag. The data source can be a preconfigured data source or defined dynamically by using the value "query". In this case, you also must provide a CONNECTSTRING.

Syntax:

```
<CFINSERT DATASOURCE="ODBC data source"
    DBNAME="database name"
    FORMFIELDS="List of File to Insert"
    PASSWORD="Password"
    PROVIDER="provider"
    PROVIDERDSN="data source"
    TABLENAME="Table Name"
    TABLEOWNER="owner"
    TABLEQUALIFIER="qualifier"
    USERNAME="User Name">
```

Table B.73 <CFINSERT> Attributes

ATTRIBUTE	DESCRIPTION	NOTES
DATASOURCE	Name of ODBC data source or "Query"	Required; can be an existing data source or defined dynamically. In the later case, use "Query."
FORMFIELDS	List of fields to insert	Optional attribute; specifies the fields to be inserted, if they are present. Any fields present that are not in the list will not be inserted.
PASSWORD	ODBC data source password	Optional; used to override the ODBC login password specified in the ColdFusion Administrator.
TABLENAME	Name of table to insert data into	Required; some ODBC data sources require fully qualified table names.
TABLEOWNER	Table owner name	Optional; used by databases that support table ownership.
TABLEQUALIFIER	Table qualifier	Optional; used by databases that support full qualifiers.
USERNAME	ODBC data source login name	Optional; used to override the ODBC login name specified in the ColdFusion Administrator.

NOTE

Your form field names must match the column names in the destination table for <CFINSERT> to work correctly.

TIP

If your form contains fields that are not part of the table into which you are inserting data, use the FORMFIELDS attribute to instruct ColdFusion to ignore those fields.

TIP

For more control over the insertion of rows into a database table, use the <CFQUERY> tag, specifying INSERT as the SQL statement.

Example: In the first example, a simple data entry form is used to collect data to be inserted into the Merchandise table:

```
<!--- creates form --->
<FORM ACTION="testinsert_act.cfm" METHOD="post">
    <P>film id: <INPUT TYPE="Text" MAXLENGTH="5" NAME="filmid" value="18">
    <P>merchandise name: <INPUT TYPE="Text" NAME="MerchName" MAXLENGTH="100">
    <P>merchandise desc: <input type="Text" NAME="Merchdescription">
    <P>merchandise price: <input TYPE="Text" NAME="merchprice">
    <p><INPUT TYPE="Submit">
</FORM>
```

This <CFINSERT> tag inserts this form data:

```
<!--- inserts data into database ---><CFINSERT DATASOURCE="OWS"
TABLENAME="Merchandise">
```

However, if the form contains additional fields that don't correspond to the fields in the Merchandise table, you must use the FORMFIELDS attribute to identify the form fields to be inserted:

```
<!--- inserts certain form fields into database --->
<CFINSERT DATASOURCE="OWS" TABLENAME="Merchandise"
    FORMFIELDS="FilmID,MerchName,MerchDescription,MerchPrice">
```

➜ *See also* <CFQUERY>, <CFUPDATE>, <CFSTOREDPROC>

<CFINVOKE>

Description: <CFINVOKE> is used to instantiate a ColdFusion component and execute a method in the component. It can also be used to execute a method on a component that was previously instantiated. Note that you can pass values to the method three ways:

1. As additional, custom attributes in the <CFINVOKE> tag.
2. Through the ARGUMENTCOLLECTION attribute.
3. Through use of <CFINVOKEARGUMENT> tag in the body of the <CFINVOKE> tag.

A method return value can be specified using the RETURNVAIRABLE attribute. See Table B.74 for a list and description of <CFINVOKE> attributes.

NOTE

There are several methods to instantiate components. You can use <CFINOKE>, you can use CFScript's CreateObject() function or you can use <CFOBJECT>.

NOTE

Components invoked with <CFINOKE> are extant only long enough to execute whatever method is being called. If you need the component to remain extant, use <CFOBJECT> or `CreateObject()` (in a CFScript) to instantiate it.

Syntax:

```
<CFINVOKE COMPONENT="Name of component"
    METHOD="Name of method"
    RETURNVARIABLE="Name of return variable"
    ARGUMENTCOLLECTION="Name of a structure containing arguments">…</CFINVOKE>
```

Table B.74 <CFINVOKE> Attributes

ATTRIBUTE	DESCRIPTION	NOTES
COMPONENT	Name of component	Optional; required if METHOD is NOT specified.
METHOD	Name of method	Optional; required if COMPONENT is NOT specified.
RETURNVARIABLE	Name of variable	Optional; name of a variable that will contain a return value from the method being invoked. That method must contain a <CFRETURN>.
ARGUMENTCOLLECTION	Structure name	Optional; name of a structure containing argument name/value pairs. This is an alternative to explicitly including all of the arguments as individual <CFINVOKE> attributes.

NOTE

You must specify both the COMPONENT and METHOD attributes to invoke a method on an component that has not yet been instantiated.

Example: The first example demonstrates the use of <CFINVOKE> to create an instance of the component, `Orders.cfc` and to execute its `OrderTotal` method, passing it a pair of date ranges through the use of <CFINVOKEARGUMENT> tags:

```
<!--- Invokes Orders component and passes some values to
   the OrderTotal method. --->
<CFINVOKE COMPONENT="Orders" METHOD="OrderTotal"
   RETURNVARIABLE="OpenOrderTotal">
   <CFINVOKEARGUMENT NAME="StartDate" VALUE="1/1/2002">
   <CFINVOKEARGUMENT NAME="EndDate" VALUE="3/22/2002">
</CFINVOKE>

<!--- Display the returned value --->
<CFOUTPUT>#OpenOrderTotal#</CFOUTPUT>
```

This next example demonstrates use of arguments as attributes to <CFINVOKE>:

```
<!--- Invokes Orders component and passes some values to
   the OrderTotal method. --->
<CFINVOKE COMPONENT="Orders" METHOD="OrderTotal"
   RETURNVARIABLE="OpenOrderTotal" StartDate="1/1/2002"
    EndDate="3/22/2002">
</CFINVOKE>

<!--- Display the returned value --->
<CFOUTPUT>#OpenOrderTotal#</CFOUTPUT>
```

The last example demonstrates the use of `CreateObject()` to instantiate the component. It also demonstrates use of an argument structure with `<CFINVOKE>`:

```
<!--- Create structure for passing arguments and instantiate
   object. --->
<CFSCRIPT>
   DateRange = StructNew();
   DateRange.StartDate = "1/1/2002";
   DateRange.EndDate = "3/22/2002";
   CreateObject("Component", "Orders");
</CFSCRIPT>
<!--- Now execute the method and pass it the structure of
   arguments. --->
<CFINVOKE COMPONENT="Orders" METHOD="OrderTotal"
   RETURNVARIABLE="OpenOrderTotal"
   ARGUMENTCOLLECTION="#DateRange#">
</CFINVOKE>
<CFOUTPUT>#OpenOrderTotal#</CFOUTPUT>
```

➜ *See also* `<CFINVOKEARGUMENT>`, `<CFCOMPONENT>`, `<CFFUNCTION>`, `<CFARGUEMNT>`, `<CFRETURN>`

<CFINVOKEARGUMENT>

Description: `<CFINVOKEARGUMENT>` is used to pass parameters to a ColdFusion component. See Table B.75 for a list and description of `<CFINVOKEARGUMENT>` attributes. Arguments passed to component methods are referenced with the `ARGUMENTS` scope inside the component.

NOTE

There are other methods of passing values to ColdFusion components. These include including your own custom attributes in a `<CFINVOKE>` tag and using the `CFARGUMENTCOLLECTION` attribute in `<CFINVOKE>`.

Syntax:

```
<CFINVOKEARGUMENT NAME="Name of argument"
    VALUE="Value to be passed">
```

Table B.75 `<CFINVOKEARGUMENT>` Attributes

ATTRIBUTE	DESCRIPTION	NOTES
`NAME`	Name of argument	Required; name of argument to be passed.
`VALUE`	Name of method	Required; value to be passed to method.
`ARGUMENTCOLLECTION`	Structure name	Optional; name of a structure containing argument name/value pairs. This is an alternative to explicitly including all of the arguments as individual `<CFINVOKE>` attributes.

NOTE

Arguments are passed by value, not by reference, meaning that any changes the invoked method makes to the argument will *not* be reflected in the value of the argument once control returns from the component.

Example: This example demonstrates the use of <CFINVOKEARGUMENT> to pass to an actor's name, which is used as a selection criteria in the Films component:

```
<!--- Here it the code that invokes the comopnent,
   passing it the actor's name. --->
<CFINVOKE COMPONENT="Films" METHOD="GetFilms">
   <CFINVOKEARGUMENT NAME="NameFirst" VALUE="Sam">
   <CFINVOKEARGUMENT NAME="NameLast" VALUE="Gold">
</CFINVOKE>

<!--- Here is the component that processes this request --->
<CFCOMPONENT>
   <CFFUNCTION NAME="GetFilms">
      <CFARGUMENT NAME="NameLast" REQUIRED="Yes">
      <CFARGUMENT NAME="NameFirst" REQUIRED="Yes">
      <CFQUERY NAME="FindActorsFilms" DATASOURCE="OWS">
         SELECT FilmID
         FROM FilmsActors FA INNER JOIN Actors A
           ON FA.ActorID = A.ActorID
         WHERE
         A.NameFirst = '#ARGUMENTS.NameFirst#'
           AND A.NameLast = '#ARGUMENTS.NameLast#'
      </CFQUERY>
      <CFRETURN #FindActorsFilms.FilmID#>
   </CFFUNCTION>
</CFCOMPONENT>
```

➜ *See also* <CFINVOKE>, <CFCOMPONENT>, <CFFUNCTION>, <CFARGUEMNT>, <CFRETURN>

<CFLDAP>

Description: <CFLDAP> is used for all interaction with LDAP servers. It can be used to search an LDAP server, as well as to add, change, or delete data. Table B.76 lists the attributes for <CFLDAP>.

Syntax:

```
<CFLDAP ACTION="Action"
    ATTRIBUTES="Attributes List"
    DN="Name"
    FILTER="Filter"
    MAXROWS="Number"
    MODIFYTYPE="Modification type"
    NAME="Query Name"
    PASSWORD="Password"
    PORT="Port Number"
    REBIND="Yes or No"
    REFERRAL="Hops"
    SCOPE="Scope"
    SECURE="Security type"
    SEPARATOR="Separator character"
    SERVER="Server Address"
    SORT="Sort Order"
    SORTCONTROL="Ascending or Descending"
    START="Start Position"
    STARTROW="Number"
    TIMEOUT="Timeout"
         USERNAME="Name">
```

Table B.76 <CFLDAP> Attributes

ATTRIBUTE	DESCRIPTION	NOTES
ACTION	Action	Required; specifies one of the actions in Table B.77.
ATTRIBUTES	Desired attributes	Required if ACTION is QUERY, ADD, MODIFY, or MODIFYDN; comma-delimited list of desired attributes; query specified in NAME attribute will contain these columns.
DN	Distinguished name	Required if ACTION is ADD, MODIFY, MODIFYDN, or DELETE.
MAXROWS	Maximum rows to	Optional attribute. retrieve
MODIFYTYPE	Adds, deletes, or replaces attribute	Optional; ADD, DELETE, or REPLACE. Used to modify an attribute.
NAME	Query name	Name of query for returned data; required if ACTION is QUERY.
PASSWORD	User password	Optional user password; might be required for update operations.
PORT	Port number	Optional port number; defaults to 389 if not specified.
REBIND	Rebinds referral callback	Optional; YES or NO; reissues query using original credentials.
REFERRAL	Number of hops	Optional; specifies number of hops a referral is limited to.
SCOPE	Search scope	Optiona;l search scope if ACTION is QUERY; valid values are ONELEVEL, BASE, and SUBTREE; default is ONELEVEL.
SECURE	Type of security	Optional; CFSSL_BASIC or CFSSL_CLIENT_AUTH. Must include additional information specified in Table B.78.
SEPARATOR	Separator character	Optional; the character LDAP will use to separate values in multivalued attributes.
SERVER	Server name	Required DNS name or IP address of LDAP server.
SORT	Sort order	Optional attribute; used if ACTION is QUERY; specifies the sort order as a comma-delimited list; can use ASC for ascending and DESC for descending; default is ASC.
SORTCONTROL	How to sort query results	Optional; enter NOCASE; default is case sensitive ASC or DESC.
START	Start name	Required if ACTION is QUERY; distinguished name to start search at.
STARTROW	Start row	Optional start row; defaults to 1.
TIMEOUT	Timeout value	Optional timeout value; defaults to 1 minute.
USERNAME	User login name	Optional user login name; might be required for update operations.

Table B.77 <CFLDAP> Actions

ACTION	DESCRIPTION
ADD	Adds an entry to an LDAP server.
DELETE	Deletes an entry from an LDAP server.
MODIFY	Updates an entry on an LDAP server.
MODIFYDN	Updates the distinguished name of an entry on an LDAP server.
QUERY	Performs a query against an LDAP server (default action).

Table B.78 Variables for Use with the SECURE Attribute

SECURE VALUE	DESCRIPTION
CFSSL_BASIC	You must provide the name of the certificate database file (in Netscape cert7.db format).
Certificate_db	Actual name of certificate database file. Can be an absolute path or simple filename.

Example: The following example retrieves a list of names from a public directory:

```
<!--- creates variable --->
<CFSET Name="John Doe">
<!--- queries LDAP server, starts and filters on variable,
sorts results --->
<CFLDAP SERVER="ldap.bigfoot.com"
    ACTION="QUERY"
    NAME="results"
    START="cn=#Name#,c=US"
    FILTER="(cn=#Name#)"
    ATTRIBUTES="cn,o,mail,p"
    SORT="cn ASC">
<CFTABLE QUERY="results" BORDER="yes" HTMLTABLE="Yes">
    <CFCOL HEADER="Name" TEXT="#cn#">
    <CFCOL HEADER="Org" TEXT="#o#">
    <CFCOL HEADER="Email" TEXT="<A HREF='mailto:#mail#'>#mail#</A>">
</CFTABLE>
```

<CFLOCATION>

Description: <CFLOCATION> is used to redirect a browser to a different URL. See Table B.79 for a description of this tag's attributes.

Syntax:

```
<CFLOCATION ADDTOKEN="Yes|No"
    URL="URL">
```

Table B.79 <CFLOCATION> Attributes

ATTRIBUTE	DESCRIPTION	NOTES
ADDTOKEN	Adds session tokens	Optional attribute; default is YES.
URL	URL (or relative URL) to redirect to	This attribute is required.

Example: The following example redirects the user to a login page if she's not already logged in (as indicated by the presence of a session variable named LoggedIn):

```
<!--- checks for user's login status --->
<CFIF NOT IsDefined("SESSION.LoggedIn")>
    <!--- if not logged in, user is sent to login page --->
    <CFLOCATION URL="login.cfm">
</CFIF>
```

NOTE

Because <CFLOCATION> needs to write to the HTTP header, you cannot use it if you've already flushed the header from the ColdFusion output buffer with <CFFLUSH>.

NOTE

If your template creates cookies and then redirects the user to another template with <CFLOCATION>, the cookies will not be created. In this situation, use <META HTTP-EQUIV="refresh">, JavaScript, or some other directive to redirect the user.

NOTE

Unlike <CFINCLUDE>, any text or CFML after the <CFLOCATION> tag is ignored by ColdFusion.

➜ *See also* <CFINCLUDE>

<CFLOCK>

Description: <CFLOCK> is used to synchronize access to blocks of code. Once inside a locked block of code, all other threads are queued until the thread with the exclusive lock relinquishes control. Table B.80 lists the <CFLOCK> attributes.

Syntax:

```
<CFLOCK NAME="lock name"
    SCOPE="Application or Session or Server"
    TYPE="Readonly or Exclusive"
    TIMEOUT="timeout"
    THROWONTIMEOUT="Yes or No">
</CFLOCK>
```

Table B.80 <CFLOCK> Attributes

ATTRIBUTE	DESCRIPTION	NOTES
NAME	Name for a lock	Optional; only one request with a given name can execute at a time.
SCOPE	Scope of lock	Optional; should not be used with NAME. SCOPE is set to APPLICATION, SERVER, or SESSION. This identifies the scope of the shared item being locked.
TIMEOUT	Timeout interval	This attribute is required.
TYPE	Lock type	Optional; READONLY or EXCLUSIVE.
THROWONTIMEOUT	Timeout handling	This optional attribute specifies how timeouts should be handled; an exception is thrown if YES; processing continues if NO; defaults to YES.

This tag is intended for use over small sections of code in which you are accessing a shared resource, such as certain types of variables (SESSION, APPLICATION, and SERVER variables), server filesystems, or other shared resources (for example, <CFFILE>). Set TYPE to READONLY when you're just checking and not updating a session variable, and use TYPE=EXCLUSIVE when you're writing to a variable.

Example: The following example locks a session variable to check for its existence. Then, if the SESSION variable isn't defined, an exclusive lock is issued for the purpose of writing to it and the user is redirected to the login part of the application:

```
<!--- locks LoggedIn session variable --->
<CFLOCK TYPE="ReadOnly" SCOPE="SESSION">
<!--- sets LoggedIn variable according to whether
or not the user is logged in --->
<CFSET LoggedIn=IsDefined("SESSION.LoggedIn")>
</CFLOCK>
<!--- if the user is not logged in, variable is
locked and set to False --->
<CFIF NOT LoggedIn>
    <CFLOCK TYPE="Exclusive" SCOPE="SESSION">
    <CFSET Session.LoggedIn=False>
    </CFLOCK>
    <!--- user is directed to login page --->
    <CFLOCATION URL="/Login/Login_Form.cfm">
</CFIF>
```

CAUTION

Avoid unnecessary use of <CFLOCK>. Restricting access to chunks of code can affect performance.

➜ *See also* <CFCATCH>, <CFTRY>

<CFLOG>

Description: <CFLOG> enables you to produce user-defined log files. They can be targeted to run only for specified applications or tasks. This ability to produce logs on an application basis is intended primarily for ISPs. The attributes for this tag are presented in Table B.81.

Syntax:

```
<CFLOG APPLICATION="Yes or No"
    TEXT="text"
    LOG="log type"
    FILE="filename"
    TYPE="message type"
    THREAD="yes"
    DATE="yes"
    TIME="yes"
    APPLICATION="yes or no">
```

Table B.81 <CFLOG> Attributes

ATTRIBUTE	DESCRIPTION	NOTES
APPLICATION	YES or NO	Optional; indicates whether to log the application name (from <CFAPPLICATION>) if one was used. Defaults to YES.
DATE	YES	Optional; indicates that you want to log the system date. NO option has been deprecated.
FILE	Full filename	Optional; specifies the name of a custom log file.
LOG	Log type	Optional; USER, APPLICATION, or SCHEDULER. It defaults to USER if FILE is specified but LOG isn't; it defaults to APPLICATION if neither FILE nor LOG is specified. APPLICATION logs information only for the application named in the current <CFAPPLICATION> tag. SCHEDULER logs execution of tasks in the ColdFusion scheduler.
TEXT	Message for log	Required; text of entry to be written to log.
THREAD	YES	Optional; causes thread ID to be logged. NO option has been deprecated.
TIME	YES	Optional; causes system time to be logged. NO option has been deprecated.
TYPE	Message type	Optional; see Table B.82 for a list of message types.

Table B.82 Message Types in Order of Severity

TYPE	DESCRIPTION
INFORMATION	Simple informational message.
WARNING	A problem of some sort might have occurred.
ERROR	An error has occurred.
FATAL INFORMATION	Fatal error has occurred.

Example: This example involves writing to a custom log for the current application. It is invoked when a user makes more than three unsuccessful login attempts:

```
<!--- checks whether login attempts are greater than 3 --->
<CFIF FORM.LoginAttempts GT 3>
    <!--- creates log with user's IP address --->
    <CFLOG TEXT="Invalid login attempt: #CGI.REMOTE_ADDR#"
    FILE = "C:\INETPUB\WWWROOT\OWS\OWS_SECURITY.LOG"
    TYPE="Information">
</CFIF>
```

<CFLOGIN>

Description: `<CFLOGIN>` is part of ColdFusion's security framework. This tag acts as a shell for authenticating users. When you authenticate users within the body of this tag, ColdFusion can track their authentication properties, such as the roles or groups that they are in. This tag has no attributes. You write the code that does the authenticating in the body of `<CFLOGIN>`. Use `<CFLOGINUSER>` after authenticating the user to pass the a user's user name and roles to ColdFusion's security framework. The attributes for `<CFLOGIN>` are presented below in Table B.83.

NOTE

You must include `<CFLOGINUSER>` in the body of the `<CFLOGIN>` tag.

Syntax:

```
<CFLOGIN
   IDLETIMOUT="seconds"
   APPLICATIONTOKEN="Application name"
   COOKIEDOMAIN="Domain of security cookie"
>
   <CFLOGINUSER>
</CFLOGIN>
```

Table B.83 `<CFLOGIN>` Attributes

ATTRIBUTE	DESCRIPTION	NOTES
APPLICATIONTOKEN	Unique application name	Optional; unique name identifying this ColdFusion application. Logins will be limited to the scope of this application.
COOKIEDOMAIN	Domain name	Optional; indicates the domain in which a security cookie is valid.
IDLETIMEOUT	Seconds	Optional; defaults to 1800. Number of seconds that a login can remain idle (no activity) before user is logged out.

Example: The following example resides within an application's `APPLICATION.CFM` file. It makes sure that a user has successfully authenticated before he or she can retrieve any ColdFusion templates within the scope of the application. It can also insure that a user is logged out after a specified amount of idle time.

Here's how it works. Assume that prior to authenticating, a user requests a ColdFusion template from an application. The `APPLICATION.CFM` file executes first, as always.

ColdFusion only executes the `<CFLOGIN>` block if the user's authentication information is not present. If the user hasn't been presented with the authentication form yet, it is presented. Note that the `ACTION` attribute of the form simply points to the originally requested URL. So when the user submits the form (after filling in a user login name and password), the form is submitted back to itself. This causes the `APPLICATION.CFM` to be called again, but as a result of the form submission, the `FORM.UserLogin` variable will be present.

The presence of the `FORM.UserLogin` variable causes the next section to execute. This section performs a database query to attempt to authenticate the user. This could be replaced by a query into an LDAP directory or some other data store used for security information for this application.

Assuming the user has authenticated properly, then `<CFLOGINUSER>` is used to log the user into the ColdFusion security framework. If the user didn't authenticate properly, he or she would be presented with a message to that effect and a link to try again. Note that the link just points to the template that the user originally requested, and this will simply force the whole process to run again.

```
<!--- The CFLOGIN block is executed if user has not
   logged in yet. --->
<CFLOGIN>
   <!--- Only execute this section if user needs to log in --->
   <CFIF NOT IsDefined("Form.UserLogin")>
      <!--- Create login form --->
      <CFOUTPUT><FORM ACTION="#CGI.SCRIPT_NAME#" METHOD="post">
      </CFOUTPUT>
      <P>User Login: <INPUT TYPE="Text" NAME="UserLogin">
      <P>Password: <INPUT TYPE="Password" NAME="PW">
      <P><INPUT TYPE="Submit">
      </FORM>
      <CFABORT>
   <CFELSE>
      <!--- If this section executes, then the user
         has filled in the login form. This section
         authenticates the user against a database
         table. --->
      <CFQUERY NAME="Authenticate" DATASOURCE="ows">
         SELECT UserLogin
         FROM Contacts
         WHERE UserLogin = '#Form.UserLogin#'
         AND UserPassword = '#Form.PW#'
      </CFQUERY>

      <!--- If user authenticated, log him/her in to
         the ColdFusion security framework. --->
      <CFIF Authenticate.RecordCount NEQ 0>
         <CFLOGINUSER NAME="#Form.UserLogin#"
          ROLES="Manager" PASSWORD="#Form.PW#">
      <CFELSE>
         <!--- User didn't authenticate. Let him/her try again --->
         You have not authenticated properly.
         <CFOUTPUT><A HREF="#CGI.SCRIPT_NAME#">Try again</A></CFOUTPUT>
         <CFABORT>
      </CFIF>
   </CFIF>
</CFLOGIN>
```

NOTE

Using `CGI.SCRIPT_NAME` to determine the requested URL is not enough. A more thorough approach would handle the presence of query strings.

NOTE

In this example, the user's roles were simply hard-coded. In an actual production system, you would probably retrieve this information from the security data repository.

NOTE

The `IsUserInRole()` function is used to on pages where either the entire page or some part of it is restricted to only users in specific roles. It works as part of the ColdFusion security framework to complete the *authorization* side of the framework.

➜ *See also* `<CFLOGINUSER>`, `<CFLOGOUT>`, `<CFFUNCTION>`, `<CFAPPLICATION>`

<CFLOGINUSER>

Description: `<CFLOGINUSER>` is part of ColdFusion's security framework. This tag must be used in a `<CFLOGIN>` block. It is used to provide login information (user name and user roles) to the ColdFusion security framework. The attributes for `<CFLOGINUSER>` are presented in Table B.84.

ColdFusion uses the `SESSION` scope to make this authentication information persist. You must have `SESSION` variables enabled in your ColdFusion Administrator and in your application's `<CFAPPLICATION>` tag.

Syntax:

```
<CFLOGINUSER
    NAME="User name or ID"
    ROLES="Array of user's security roles">
```

Table B.84 `<CFLOGINUSER>` attributes

ATTRIBUTE	DESCRIPTION	NOTES
NAME	User name	Required; this is the user name or ID by which this user will be recognized throughout the security framework.
PASSWORD	User password	Required; the user's password is required to log in.
ROLES	List of user roles	Required; this is an array of roles for the authenticated user. It can be referenced in calls to `<CFFUNCTION>` or with use of the `IsUserInRole()` function when you need to check user access to restricted functionality within your application.

Example: Please see the example in `<CFLOGIN>`.

➜ *See also* `<CFLOGIN>`, `<CFLOGOUT>`, `<CFFUNCTION>`, `<CFAPPLICATION>`

<CFLOGOUT>

Description: <CFLOGOUT> is used to log a user out of ColdFusion's security framework. It has no attributes. In the ColdFusion security framework, you log users into your system (and into the framework) with the <CFLOGIN> and <CFLOGINUSER> tags. When you want log them out, you provide a link to a page that executes the <CFLOGOUT> tag. Note that there are no attributes.

Syntax:

```
<CFLOGOUT>
```

Example: Begin by reviewing the immediately preceding example in <CFLOGIN>. Assuming you wanted to provide users with the ability to log out, you could include a link on a page that logs a user out. All that that page needs to consist of is the <CFLOGOUT> tag.

```
<!--- Log out of CF security framework --->
<CFLOGOUT>
<!--- Display link enabling user to log back in --->
<HTML>
<HEAD>
   <TITLE>Logout Page</TITLE>
</HEAD>
<BODY>
<P>You have been logged out.
<!--- Note that you can point to any CF page in
   the authenticated part of your application if
   you're using <CFLOGIN> in the APPLICATION.CFM
   page. --->
<P><A HREF="SomeAuthenticatedPage.cfm">Log back in.</A>
</BODY>
</HTML>
```

➜ *See also* <CFLOGIN>, <CFLOGINUSER>, <CFFUNCTION>, <CFAPPLICATION>

<CFLOOP>

Description: <CFLOOP> enables you to create loops within your code. *Loops* are blocks of code that are executed repeatedly until a specific condition is met. <CFBREAK> enables you to terminate a loop unconditionally. ColdFusion supports five types of loops:

- `For`—These loops repeat a specific number of times.
- `While`—These loops repeat until a set condition returns `FALSE`.
- `Query`—These loops go through the results of a <CFQUERY> once for each row returned.
- `List`—These loops go through the elements of a specified list.
- `Collection`—These loops are used to loop over collections.

Table B.85 shows attributes for this tag.

Syntax:

For loop:

```
<CFLOOP INDEX="Index"
    FROM="Loop Start"
    TO="Loop End"
    STEP="Step Value">
</CFLOOP>
```

While loop:

```
<CFLOOP CONDITION="Expression">
</CFLOOP>
```

Query loop:

```
<CFLOOP QUERY="Query Name"
    STARTROW="Start Row Value"
    ENDROW="End Row Value">
</CFLOOP>
```

List loop:

```
<CFLOOP INDEX="Index"
    LIST="List"
    DELIMITERS="Delimiters">
</CFLOOP>
```

Collection loop:

```
<CFLOOP COLLECTION="Collection"
    ITEM="Item">
</CFLOOP>
```

NOTE

The syntax and use of `<CFLOOP>` varies based on the type of loop being executed.

Table B.85 `<CFLOOP>` Attributes

ATTRIBUTE	DESCRIPTION	NOTES
COLLECTION	Collection to loop through	This attribute is required for `Collection` or structure loops.
CONDITION	`While` loop condition	This attribute is required for `While` loops and must be a valid condition.
DELIMITERS	`List` loop delimiters	This is an optional `List` loop attribute; if it is omitted, the default delimiter of a comma is used.
ENDROW	Query loop end position	This is an optional `Query` loop attribute; if it is omitted, all rows are processed.
FROM	`For` loop start position	This attribute is required for `For` loops and must be a numeric value.
INDEX	Current element	This attribute is required for `For` loops and `List` loops and holds the name of the variable that will contain the current element.

Table B.85 (continued)

ATTRIBUTE	DESCRIPTION	NOTES
ITEM	Current item	This attribute is required for Collection loops.
LIST	List loop list	This attribute is required for List loops and can be a ColdFusion list field or a static string.
QUERY	Query loop query	This attribute is required for Query loops and must be the name of a previously executed <CFQUERY>.
STARTROW	Query loop start position	This is an optional Query loop attribute; if it is omitted, the loop will start at the first row.
STEP	For loop step value	This is an optional For loop attribute; if it is omitted, the default value of 1 is used.
TO	For loop end position	This attribute is required for For loops and must be a numeric value.

Example: The following is a For loop used in a FORM to populate a select field with the years 1901and 2000. The alternative would have been to enter 100 OPTION values manually:

```
<!--- creates select field --->
<SELECT NAME="year">
<!--- loop populates select field with years sequentially --->
<CFLOOP INDEX="YearValue" FROM="1901" TO="2000">
    <OPTION><CFOUTPUT>#YearValue#</CFOUTPUT>
</CFLOOP>
</SELECT>
```

The next example does the exact same thing but presents the list in reverse order. This is done by specifying a STEP value of -1:

```
<!--- creates select field --->
<SELECT NAME="year">
<!--- loop populates select field with years in reverse --->
<CFLOOP INDEX="YearValue" FROM="2000" TO="1901" STEP="-1">
    <OPTION><CFOUTPUT>#YearValue#</CFOUTPUT>
</CFLOOP>
</SELECT>
```

This example loops until any random number between 1 and 10, excluding 5, is generated:

```
<!--- sets variable --->
<CFSET RandomNumber=0>
<!--- loop generates random number greater than or equal to
zero and not equal to 5 --->
<CFLOOP CONDITION= "(RandomNumber GTE 0) AND (RandomNumber NEQ 5)">
    <CFSET RandomNumber=RandRange(1, 10)>
</CFLOOP>
```

This example creates a `Query` loop that processes an existing `<CFQUERY>` named `Orders`, but it processes only rows `100–150`:

```
<!--- gets raw data from database --->
<CFQUERY NAME="Orders"
    DATASOURCE="OWS"
    DBTYPE="ODBC">
SELECT OrderNum, OrderDate, Total
FROM Orders
</cfquery>

<!--- loops over query from row 100 to row 150 --->
<CFLOOP QUERY="Orders" STARTROW="100" ENDROW="150">
    <!--- djsplays results --->
    <CFOUTPUT>
    #OrderNum# - #DateFormat(OrderDate)# - #DollarFormat(Total)#<BR>
    </CFOUTPUT>
</CFLOOP>
```

This example loops through a user-supplied list of titles, displaying them one at a time:

```
<!--- loops over titles passed from form --->
<CFLOOP INDEX="Title" LIST="#FORM.Titles#">
    <!--- displays results --->
    <CFOUTPUT>
    Title: #Title#<BR>
    </CFOUTPUT>
</CFLOOP>
```

This example uses `<CFBREAK>` to terminate a loop when a specific row is reached—in this case, an order number greater than `10,000`:

```
<!--- gets raw data from database --->
<CFQUERY NAME="Orders"
    DATASOURCE="OWS"
    DBTYPE="ODBC">
SELECT OrderNum, OrderDate, Total
FROM Orders
</cfquery>

<!--- loops over query --->
<CFLOOP QUERY="Orders">
    <!--- if orders number greater than 10,000, loop processing
stops --->
    <CFIF OrderNum GT 10000>
        <CFBREAK>
    </CFIF>
    <!--- displays results --->
    <CFOUTPUT>
        #OrderNum# - #DateFormat(OrderDate)# - #DollarFormat(Total)#<BR>
    </CFOUTPUT>
</CFLOOP>
```

This last example involves nesting a `COLLECTION` loop inside an `INDEX` loop.

```
<!--- creates color structure --->
<CFSCRIPT>
    Colors = StructNew();
    Colors["Red"] = 1;
```

```
    Colors["Green"] = 2;
    Colors["Blue"] = 3;
    Colors["Yellow"] = 4;
    Colors["Orange"] = 5;
    Colors["Pink"] = 6;
    Colors["Brown"] = 7;
    Colors["Black"] = 8;
    Colors["Tan"] = 9;
    Colors["White"] = 10;
</CFSCRIPT>
<!--- loops over collection loop --->
<CFLOOP FROM="1" TO="4" INDEX="ii">
    <!--- loops over color structure --->
    <CFLOOP COLLECTION="#Colors#" ITEM="Color">
    <BR><CFOUTPUT><FONT COLOR="#Color#" SIZE="#ii#">#Color# = #Colors[Color]#
      </FONT></CFOUTPUT>
   </CFLOOP>
</CFLOOP>
```

TIP

Using `<CFLOOP>` to process queries is slower than using `<CFOUTPUT>`. Whenever possible, use `<CFOUTPUT>` to loop through query results.

NOTE

The `<CFLOOP>` tag can be nested, and there is no limit placed on the number of nested loops allowed.

➜ *See also* <CFBREAK>

<CFMAIL>

Description: `<CFMAIL>` generates SMTP mail from within ColdFusion templates. `<CFMAIL>` can be used to output query results, just like `<CFOUTPUT>`, or on its own. The `<CFMAIL>` tag itself is used to set up the mail message, and all text between the `<CFMAIL>` and `</CFMAIL>` tags is sent as the message body. `<CFMAIL>` requires that you specify a sender address, recipient address, and subject. All other attributes are optional. Table B.86 shows the attributes for this tag.

Syntax:

```
<CFMAIL BCC="Blind CC Addresses"
    CC="Carbon Copy Addresses"
    FROM="Sender Address"
    GROUP="Group Name"
    GROUPCASESENSITIVE="Yes or No"
    MAILERID="ID for X-Mailer SMTP header"
    MAXROWS="Maximum Mail Messages"
    MIMEATTACH="Pathname"
    PORT="SMTP TCP/IP Port"
    QUERY="Query Name"
    SERVER="SMTP Server Address"
    SPOOLENABLE="Yes or No"
    STARTROW="Query row to start from"
    SUBJECT="Subject"
    TIMEOUT="SMTP Connection Timeout"
    TO="Recipient Address"
    TYPE="Message Type"
    MAILERID="id">
</CFMAIL>
```

Table B.86 <CFMAIL> Attributes

ATTRIBUTE	DESCRIPTION	NOTES
BCC	Blind carbon copy addresses	Optional; blind carbon copy addresses.
CC	Carbon copy addresses	Optional; one or more carbon copy addresses separated by commas.
FROM	Sender's address	Required; sender's e-mail address.
GROUP	Query column to group on	Optional; column to group on. See <CFOUTPUT> for more information on grouping dat1.
GROUPCASESENSITIVE	Enables grouping with respect to case	Optional. If the specified QUERY was generated from case-insensitive SQL, setting this to NO (it defaults to YES) will preserve order of query.
MAILERID	ID for X-Mailer SMTP header	Optional; enables you to specify an X-Mailer ID for the SMTP header. Defaults to Allaire ColdFusion Application Server.
MAXROWS	Maximum message to send	Optional attribute specifying the maximum number of e-mail messages to generate.
MIMEATTACH	Fully qualified filename	Optional; pathname to file that will be attached as a MIME encoded attachment.
PORT	TCP/IP SMTP port	Optional TCP/IP SMTP port; overrides the default value of 25 if specified.
QUERY	<CFQUERY> to draw data from	E-mail can be generated based on the results of a <CFQUERY>; to do this specify the name of the <CFQUERY> here. This is an optional attribute.
SERVER	SMTP mail server	Optional; SMTP mail server name; overrides the default setting if specified.
SPOOLENABLE	YES or NO	Optional; YES stores a copy of the message until sending is complete. NO simply places message in queue (no copy made) for sending.
SUBJECT	Message subject	Required; message subject.
TIMEOUT	Connection timeout interval	Optional; SMTP connection timeout interval overrides the default setting if specified.
TO	Recipient's address	Required; recipient's e-mail address.
TYPE	Message type	Optional message type; currently the only supported type is HTML, indicating that HTML code is embedded in the message.

Example: The following is a simple e-mail message based on a form submission. It uses form fields in both the attributes and the message body itself:

```
<!--- creates e-mail --->
<CFMAIL FROM="#FORM.EMail#"
    TO="sales@orangewhipstudios.com"
    SUBJECT="Customer inquiry">
    <!--- e-mail body --->
    The following customer inquiry was posted to our Web site:
    Name: #FORM.name#
    email: #FORM.EMail#
    Message:
    #FORM.Message#
</CFMAIL>
```

This next example sends an e-mail message based on <CFQUERY> results. The message is sent once for each row retrieved:

```
<!--- gets raw data from database --->
<CFQUERY NAME="GetInquiries" DATASOURCE="OWS">
    SELECT * FROM WebQueries
</CFQUERY>
<!--- creates e-mail --->
<CFMAIL FROM="sales@orangewhipstudios.com"
    TO="sales@orangewhipstudios.com"
    SUBJECT="Customer inquiry"
    QUERY="GetInquiries">
    <!--- e-mail body --->
    The following customer inquiry was posted to our Web site:
    Name: #GetInquiries.name#
    email: #GetInquiries.EMail#
    Message:
    #GetInquiries.Message#
</CFMAIL>
```

The next example sends an e-mail message based on <CFQUERY> results. The message is sent once for each row retrieved. Note that it also specifies a mail server other than the default SMTP server defined in the ColdFusion Administrator.

```
<!--- gets raw data from database --->
<CFQUERY NAME="GetMailingList" DATASOURCE="OWS">
    SELECT FirstName, Email
    FROM Contacts
    WHERE MailingList = 1
</CFQUERY>
<!--- creates e-mail --->
<CFMAIL QUERY="GetMailingList"
    FROM="Sales@orangewhipstudios.com"
    TO="#Email#"
    SUBJECT="Buy our stuff"
    SERVER="mail.orangewhip.com"
    MIMEATTACH="C:\OWS\Catalog\Catalog2001.pdf">
    <!--- e-mail body --->
    Dear #FirstName#,
```

```
        We sure would appreciate it if you'd visit our
        Web site and buy some of our junk.

        Please find our catalog attached.

        Thanks.
        The Management
        Orange Whip Studios
</CFMAIL>
```

NOTE

Unlike Web browsers, e-mail programs do not ignore white space. Carriage returns are displayed in the e-mail message if you embed carriage returns between the `<CFMAIL>` and `</CFMAIL>` tags.

NOTE

If you specify HTML in the `TYPE` attribute, you can send e-mail consisting of HTML code. This has become popular in recent years because it gives users much more control over the formatting, but users must still consider whether the recipients' e-mail client software supports HTML.

NOTE

To use `<CFMAIL>`, the ColdFusion SMTP interface must be set up and working. If e-mail is not being sent correctly, use the ColdFusion Administrator to verify that ColdFusion can connect to your SMTP mail server.

NOTE

The `PORT`, `SERVER`, and `TIMEOUT` attributes will never be used in normal operation. These are primarily used for debugging and troubleshooting e-mail problems.

NOTE

E-mail errors are logged to the `\CFUSION\MAIL\LOG` directory. Messages that cannot be delivered are stored in the `\CFUSION\MAIL\UNDELIVER` directory.

➜ *See also* `<CFMAILPARAM>`, `<CFPOP>`

<CFMAILPARAM>

Description: `<CFMAILPARAM>` is used inside `<CFMAIL>` `</CFMAIL>` tags and is used to specify additional headers and file attachments. Note that you can use several `<CFMAILPARAM>` tags within each `<CFMAIL>`. Table B.87 shows attributes for this tag.

Syntax:

```
<CFMAILPARAM FILE="FileName"
    NAME="Header name"
    VALUE="Header value">
```

Table B.87 `<CFMAILPARAM>` Attributes

ATTRIBUTE	DESCRIPTION	NOTES
`FILE`	Full pathname to file to be attached	Required if `NAME` is not specified.
`NAME`	Name of SMTP mail header	Required if `FILE` is not specified.
`VALUE`	Header value	Required if `NAME` is specified.

Example: This example sends an e-mail to a specific address, specifying a particular reply-to header and attaching two files:

```
<!--- creates e-mail --->
<CFMAIL FROM="MrBig@OrangeWhipStudios.com"
    TO="you@domain.org"
    SUBJECT="We need your eyes">
    <!--- e-mail body --->
    Please consider putting your eyeballs on our Web site:

    www.orangewhipstudios.com

    Thank you,
    The Management
    <!--- attaches two files and a reply-to address to e-mail --->
    <CFMAILPARAM FILE="c:\temp\tcmnote.txt">
    <CFMAILPARAM FILE="c:\temp\more.HTM">
    <CFMAILPARAM NAME="Reply-To" VALUE="John Doe <John@doe.com>">
</CFMAIL>
```

➜ *See also* <CFMAIL>

<CFMODULE>

Description: <CFMODULE> is used to call a custom tag explicitly by stating its full or relative path. This is necessary when the custom tag template is not in the current directory. Table B.88 lists the <CFMODULE> attributes. Your own tag attributes also can be added to this list.

Syntax:

```
<CFMODULE NAME="Path"
    TEMPLATE="Path"
    ATTRIBUTE_n=VALUE_n>
```

Table B.88 <CFMODULE> Attributes

ATTRIBUTE	DESCRIPTION	NOTES
NAME	Fixed path to tag file	Either TEMPLATE or NAME must be used, but not both at once; use a period for directory delimiters.
TEMPLATE	Relative path to tag file	Either TEMPLATE or NAME must be used, but not both at once.
ATTRIBUTE_n	Your attribute/value pairs	Optional; you add your custom tag's attributes to your call.
ATTRIBUTECOLLECTION	Key/value pairs stored in a structure	Optional; alternative to specifying your attributes one at a time.

NOTE

When using the NAME attribute, you place the custom tag template either in the ColdFusion custom tags directory (which by default is in C:\CFUSION\CUSTOMTAGS) or in a directory beneath ColdFusion's custom tags directory. Use periods (.) as delimiters between subdirectories.

NOTE

When using TEMPLATE, you must specify either a path relative to the current directory or a path that has been mapped in the ColdFusion Administrator.

Example: This example calls a custom tag named DUMPQUERY.CFM in the directory C:\CFUSION\CUSTOMTAGS\OUTPUT:

```
<!--- gets raw data from database --->
<CFQUERY DATASOURCE="OWS" NAME="GetContacts">
    SELECT FirstName, LastName, Address
    FROM Contacts
    WHERE State IS NOT NULL
</CFQUERY>
<!--- calls custom tag DUMPQUERY and passes attributes to it --->
<CFMODULE NAME="OUTPUT.DUMPQUERY"
    QUERY="GetContacts"
    BORDER="1"
    MAXROWS="2">
```

➜ *See also* <CFASSOCIATE>

<CFOBJECT>

Description: <CFOBJECT> enables you to use COM, Java, CORBA objects and ColdFusion components within your ColdFusion applications. You need to know an object's ID or filename to use it, as well as its methods and properties. <CFOBJECT> attributes vary depending on the type of object with which you are working. The attributes for each type are listed in the Tables B.89 through B.92.

NOTE

You should use <CFOBJECT> to instantiate a ColdFusion component on which you plan to call methods several times in the same page, rather then simply calling <CFINVOKE>. When you use <CFINVOKE>, the object is instantiated only long enough to execute the specified method and is then immediately destroyed.

To use an object with <CFOBJECT>, that object must be already installed on the server.

Syntax:

```
<CFOBJECT TYPE="COM"
    ACTION="Action"
    CLASS="Class ID"
    CONTEXT="Context"
    NAME="Name of instantiated object"
    SERVER="Server Name">

<CFOBJECT TYPE="JAVA"
    ACTION="Action"
    CLASS="Class ID"
    NAME="Name of instantiated object">

<CFOBJECT TYPE="CORBA"
    CLASS="Class ID"
    CONTEXT="Context"
    NAME="Name of instantiated object"
    LOCALE="Type/value pairs">
<CFOBJECT COMPONENT="ColdFusion component name"
    NAME="Name of instantiated object" >
```

Table B.89 <CFOBJECT> Attributes for COM

ATTRIBUTE	DESCRIPTION	NOTES
ACTION	Action	Required; must be either CREATE to instantiate an object or CONNECT to connect to a running object.
CLASS	Component ProgID	Required attribute.
CONTEXT	Operation context	Optional attribute; must be INPROC, LOCAL, or REMOTE. User's Registry setting is not specified.
NAME	Object name	Required attribute.
SERVER	Valid server name	Server name as UNC, DNS, or IP address; required only if CONTEXT = "remote".
TYPE	Object type	Required; set to COM.

Table B.90 <CFOBJECT> Attributes for CORBA

ATTRIBUTE	DESCRIPTION	NOTES
CLASS	Component ProgID	Required; if CONTEXT is IOR, this names the file containing the IOR; must be readable by ColdFusion; if CONTEXT is NAMESERVICE, specifies period-delimited class name.
CONTEXT	Operation context	Required; IOR or NAMESERVICE.
LOCALE	Type/value pair	Optional, specific arguments to VisiBroker orbs.
NAME	Object name	Required attribute.
TYPE	Object type	Required; set to CORBA.

Table B.91 <CFOBJECT> Attributes for Java

ATTRIBUTE	DESCRIPTION	NOTES
ACTION	Action	Required; set to CREATE for creating objects under WebLogic.
CLASS	Component ProgID	Required; name of Java class.
NAME	Object name	Required; name used in CFML to address object.
TYPE	Object type	Required; set to JAVA.

Table B.92 <CFOBJECT> Attributes for ColdFusion components

ATTRIBUTE	DESCRIPTION	NOTES
COMPONENT	Component name	Required; name of .CFC file.
NAME	Name for object	Required; name by which this instantiated object will be addressed.

Example: The first example instantiates a COM object named `NT.Exec` and invokes a method:

```
<!--- instantiates COM object --->
<CFOBJECT TYPE="COM"
    CLASS="NT.Exec"
    ACTION="CREATE"
    NAME="Exec">
<!--- sets variables to invoke method --->
<CFSET Exec.Command="DIR C:\">
<CFSET temp=Exec.Run()>
```

The next example instantiates an object based on a ColdFusion component:

```
<!--- Instantiates ColdFusion component object based on Films.cfc component --->
<CFOBJECT COMPONENT="FilmsObject"
    NAME="Films">
<!--- Invoke two methods in the Films object --->
<CFINVOKE COMPONENT="FIlmsObject" METHOD="GetAllFilms">
```

NOTE

Use of `<CFOBJECT>` can be disabled in the ColdFusion Administrator.

<CFOBJECTCACHE>

Description: `<CFOBJECTCACHE>` clears ColdFusion's query cache in the Application scope. The attribute is described in Table B.93.

Syntax:

```
<CFOBJECTCACHE ACTION="Clear">
```

Table B.93 `<CFOBJECTCACHE>` Attributes

ATTRIBUTE	DESCRIPTION	NOTES
ACTION	Clear	Required; must be CLEAR.

Example: The following example flushes the queries in memory:

```
<CFOBJECTCACHE ACTION="Clear">
```

<CFOUTPUT>

Description: `<CFOUTPUT>` is used to output the results of a `<CFQUERY>` or any time text includes variables that are to be expanded. If `<CFQUERY>` is used to process the results of a `<CFQUERY>` tag, any code between `<CFOUTPUT>` and `</CFOUTPUT>` is repeated once for every row. When outputting query results, an additional set of variables is available. These are documented in Table B.94. `<CFOUTPUT>` can be used with the `GROUP` attribute to specify a data group from a query. Data that is grouped together is displayed so that only the first occurrence of each value is output. The attributes for this tag are shown in Table B.95.

Syntax:

```
<CFOUTPUT QUERY="Query Name"
    MAXROWS="Maximum Rows"
    STARTROW="Start Row"
    GROUP="Group Column"
    GROUPCASESENSITIVE="Yes or No">
</CFOUTPUT>
```

Table B.94 <CFOUTPUT> Attributes

ATTRIBUTE	DESCRIPTION	NOTES
GROUP	Column to group on	This optional attribute allows you to define output groups.
GROUPCASESENSITIVE	YES or NO	Optional; indicates whether the same values but in different case should be treated as separate entries.
MAXROWS	Maximum rows to display	This optional attribute specifies the maximum number of rows to display. If omitted, all rows are displayed.
QUERY	Query name	Optional; query name refers to the query results within <CFOUTPUT> text.
STARTROW	First row to display	Optional; specifies the output start row.

Table B.95 <CFOUTPUT> Fields Available when Using the QUERY Attribute

FIELD	DESCRIPTION
#COLUMNLIST#	Comma-delimited list of columns with a query.
#CURRENTROW#	The number of the current row, starting at 1, and incremented each time a row is displayed.
#RECORDCOUNT#	The total number of records to be output.

Example: Any time you use variables or fields within your template, you must enclose them within <CFOUTPUT> tags, as shown in this example. Otherwise, the field name is sent as is and is not expanded:

```
<!--- displays client variables --->
<CFOUTPUT>
    Hi #CLIENT.Name#, thanks for dropping by again.<P>
    You have now visited us #NumberFormat(CLIENT.Visits)#
    since your first visit on #DateFormat(CLIENT.FirstVisit)#.
</CFOUTPUT>
```

This example uses <CFOUTPUT> to display the results of a query in an unordered list:

```
<!--- gets raw data from database --->
<CFQUERY NAME="GetContacts" DATASOURCE="ows">
    SELECT FirstName, LastName, Phone
    FROM Contacts
```

```
</CFQUERY>
<!--- query results is displayed in a bulleted list --->
<UL>
<CFOUTPUT QUERY="GetContacts">
    <LI>#LastName#, #FirstName# - Phone: #Phone#
</CFOUTPUT>
</UL>
```

You can use the GROUP attribute to group output results. This example groups contacts by whether they're on the mailing list:

```
<!--- gets raw data from database --->
<CFQUERY NAME="GetContacts" DATASOURCE="ows">
    SELECT FirstName, LastName, Phone, MailingList
    FROM Contacts
    ORDER BY MailingList
</CFQUERY>
<!--- displays query results by group --->
<UL>
<CFOUTPUT QUERY="GetContacts" GROUP="MailingList">
<LI><B>#Iif(MailingList EQ 1, DE("On"), DE("Not On"))# Mailing List</B>
    <UL>
    <CFOUTPUT>
        <LI>#LastName#, #FirstName# - Phone: #Phone#
    </CFOUTPUT>
    </UL>
</CFOUTPUT>
</UL>
```

NOTE

There is no limit to the number of nested groups you can use in a <CFOUTPUT>. However, every column used in a GROUP must be part of the SQL statement ORDER BY clause.

NOTE

The STARTROW and MAXROWS attributes can be used to implement a "display next n of n" type display. Even though only a subset of the retrieved data is displayed, it has all been retrieved by the <CFQUERY> statement. So, although the page might be transmitted to the browser more quickly because it contains less text, the SQL operation itself takes no less time.

➜ *See also* <CFLOOP>, <CFMAIL>, <CFQUERY>, <CFTABLE>

<CFPARAM>

Description: <CFPARAM> lets you specify default values for parameters and specify parameters that are required. <CFPARAM> requires that you specify a variable name. If a VALUE is passed as well, that value will be used as the default value if the variable is not specified. If VALUE is not specified, <CFPARAM> requires that the named variable be passed; it will generate an error message if it is not. The attributes are shown in Table B.96.

It is commonly used to ensure that variables are defined with default values. Used in this way, it replaces this conditional logic:

```
<CFIF NOT IsDefefined("MyVar")>
    <CFSET MyVar="SomeValue">
</CFIF>
```

with:

```
<CFPARAM NAME="MyVar" DEFAULT="SomeValue">
```

Syntax:

```
<CFPARAM NAME="Parameter Name"
    DEFAULT="Default"
    TYPE="Data Type">
```

Table B.96 <CFPARAM> Attributes

ATTRIBUTE	DESCRIPTION	NOTES
NAME	Name of variable	Required; name should be fully qualified with scope.
DEFAULT	Default variable value	Optional; the value is used as the default value if the variable is not already defined.
TYPE	Data type	Optional; type of data required; see the following list.

Here are the valid values for TYPE:

- Any (default)
- Array
- Binary
- Boolean
- Date
- Numeric
- Query
- String
- Struct
- UUID
- variableName (ensures the value is valid as a variable name)

Example: The following specifies a default value for a field that is to be used in a <CFQUERY> tag, making it unnecessary to write conditional code to build a dynamic SQL statement:

```
<!--- if form variable is not passed, it is set to 10 --->
<CFPARAM NAME="Form.Minimum" DEFAULT="10">
<!--- gets raw data from the database --->
<CFQUERY NAME="OverDue" DATASOURCE= "ows">
    SELECT MerchID, MerchName
    FROM Merchandise
    WHERE MerchPrice <= #Form.Minimum#
</CFQUERY>
```

This example makes the `Minimum` field required and indicates that it must be numeric; an error is generated if you request the template and the `Minimum` field is not specified or is non-numeric:

```
<!--- if form variable is not passed or not numeric,
an error is thrown --->
<CFPARAM NAME="Minimum"
    DEFAULT="10"
    TYPE="numeric">
<!--- gets raw data from the database --->
<CFQUERY NAME="OverDue" DATASOURCE= "ows">
    SELECT MerchID, MerchName
    FROM Merchandise
    WHERE MerchPrice <= #Form.Minimum#
</CFQUERY>
```

➜ *See also* `<CFSET>`

<CFPOP>

Description: `<CFPOP>` retrieves and manipulates mail in a POP3 mailbox. You must know three things to access a POP mailbox: the POP server name, the POP login name, and the account password. `<CFPOP>` has three modes of operation: It can be used to retrieve just mail headers and entire message bodies and to delete messages. POP messages are not automatically deleted when they are read and must be deleted explicitly with a `DELETE` operation. Table B.97 lists the `<CFPOP>` attributes; Table B.98 lists the columns returned when retrieving mail or mail headers.

Syntax:

```
<CFPOP ACTION="Action"
    ATTACHMENTSPATH="Path"
    MAXROWS="Number"
    MESSAGENUMBER="Messages"
    NAME="Query Name"
    PASSWORD="Password"
    PORT="Port Number"
    SERVER="Mail Server"
    STARTROW="Number"
    TIMEOUT="Timeout"
    USERNAME="User Name">
```

Table B.97 `<CFPOP>` Attributes

ATTRIBUTE	DESCRIPTION	NOTES
`ACTION`	Action	Optional; one of the values in Table B.98.
`ATTACHMENTSPATH`	Attachment path	Optional path to store mail attachments.
`MAXROWS`	Maximum messages to retrieve	Optional attribute; ignored if `MESSAGENUMBER` is used.
`MESSAGENUMBER`	Message number	Optional message number (or comma-delimited list of message numbers); required if `ACTION` is `DELETE`; specifies the messages to be deleted or retrieved.

Table B.97 (continued)

ATTRIBUTE	DESCRIPTION	NOTES
NAME	Query name	Required if ACTION is GETALL or GETHEADERONLY; name of query to be returned. Query columns are listed in Table B.99.
PASSWORD	Password	Optional POP account password; most POP servers require this.
PORT	Mail server port	Optional attribute; defaults to port 110.
SERVER	Mail server	Required; DNS name or IP address of the POP mail server.
STARTROW	Start row	Optional start row; defaults to 1; ignored if MESSAGENUMBER is used.
TIMEOUT	Timeout value	Optional timeout value.
USERNAME	Login name	Optional POP login name; most POP servers require this.

Table B.98 <CFPOP> Actions

ACTION	DESCRIPTION
DELETE	Deletes messages from a POP mailbox.
GETALL	Gets message headers and body.
GETHEADERONLY	Gets only message headers.

Table B.99 <CFPOP> Query Columns

COLUMN	DESCRIPTION
ATTACHMENTFILES	List of saved attachments; present only if ACTION is GETALL and an ATTACHMENT path was specified.
ATTACHMENTS	List of original attachment names; only present if ACTION is GETALL and an ATTACHMENT path was specified.
BODY	Body of the message.
CC	List of any carbon copy recipients.
DATE	Message date.
FROM	Sender name.
HEADER	Mail header.
MESSAGENUMBER	Message number for use in calls with future calls.
REPLYTO	E-mail address to reply to.
SUBJECT	Message subject.
TO	Recipient list.

Example: This example retrieves a list of waiting mail in a POP mailbox and then displays the message list in an HTML list:

```
<!--- retrieves e-mail headers from server --->
<CFPOP SERVER="mail.a2zbooks.com"
    USERNAME=#username#
    PASSWORD=#pwd#
    ACTION="GETHEADERONLY"
    NAME="msg">
<!--- displays e-mails in bulleted list --->
<UL>
<CFOUTPUT QUERY="msg">
    <LI>From: #from# - Subject: #subject#
</CFOUTPUT>
</UL>
```

NOTE

<CFPOP> is used to retrieve mail only. Use the <CFMAIL> tag to send mail.

➜ *See also* <CFMAIL>

<CFPROCESSINGDIRECTIVE>

Description: <CFPROCESSINGDIRECTIVE> enables you to suppress all white space between the start and end tags. If this tag is nested, the settings on the innermost tag are used. It also enables you to specify a type of character encoding to be used in the body of the tag (on just the page including the tag). It is recommended that you use this tag for only one of these two functions at a time. In other words, don't use it to suppress white space *and* to specify an alternative character encoding. Don't code a separate PROCESSINGDIRECTIVE tag when employing this tag to specify PAGEENCODING.

When ColdFusion encounters a byte order mark on the page it is processing, it uses the UTF-8 encoding scheme specified when parsing the page. If there is no byte order mark on the page, ColdFusion processes the page using the system's default page encoding scheme. If you use PAGEENCODING to specify a different page encoding scheme than is specified in a page's byte order mark, the ColdFusion will throw an error.

TIP

You should use this tag within the first 4096 bytes of a page.

NOTE

When using this to suppress white space, you must include a tag body and an ending </CFPROCESSINGDIRECTIVE> tag. When you use the PAGEENCODING attribute, you should leave off the final </CFPROCESSINGDIRECTIVE> but you can use the abbreviated closing tag: <CFPROCESSINGDIRECTIVE PAGEENCODING="xxx"/> where *xxx* is your desired canonical encoding name.

Table B.100 shows <CFPROCESSINGDIRECTIVE> attributes.

Syntax (for suppressing white space):

```
<CFPROCESSINGDIRECTIVE SUPPRESSWHITESPACE="Yes or No">
CFML code
</CFPROCESSINGDIRECTIVE>
```

Syntax (for producing encoded content):

```
<CFPROCESINGDIRECTIVE PAGEENCODING="Name of character encoding method"/>
```

Table B.100 <CFPROCESSINGDIRECTIVE> Attributes

ATTRIBUTE	DESCRIPTION	NOTES
PAGEENCODING	Character encoding to be used on this page	Optional; you can use the same canonical names for page encoding used by the Java language.
SUPPRESSWHITESPACE	YES or NO	Required; indicates whether white space is to be eliminated.

NOTE

You can find a list of Java's canonical names for page encoding here: http://java.sun.com/j2se/1.4/docs/guide/intl/encoding.doc.html

Example: The following example suppresses whitespace. To see the effects, try changing the value of the SUPPRESSWHITESPACE attribute to NO and view the source of the rendered page.

```
<!--- suppress whitespace --->
<CFPROCESSINGDIRECTIVE SUPPRESSWHITESPACE="Yes">
<!--- gets raw data from database --->
<CFQUERY NAME="GetContacts" DATASOURCE="OWS">
    SELECT LastName, Phone
    FROM CONTACTS
</CFQUERY>
<!--- sets variable --->
<CFSET MyVar="This is a variable containing whitespace">
<!--- displays variable --->
<P><CFOUTPUT>#MyVar#</CFOUTPUT>
<!--- displays query results in HTML table --->
<TABLE>
<CFOUTPUT QUERY="GetContacts">
<TR>
    <TD>#LastName#</TD>
    <TD>
        <CFIF Phone IS NOT "">
            #Phone#
        <CFELSE>
            n/a
        </CFIF>
    </TD>
</TR>
</CFOUTPUT>
</TABLE>
</CFPROCESSINGDIRECTIVE>
```

The next example demonstrates the use of the PAGEENCODING attribute to produce Japanese characters. If you try to reproduce this example, ***you must*** save the template using UTF file format rather than traditional ANSI file format or the example will not work.

```
<CFPROCESSINGDIRECTIVE PAGEENCODING="utf-8"/>
<!--- What follows is a set of Japanese characters that are
   supported by the specified encoding. --->
ìœ ë ˆì?"ë"œì--? ëŒ¤í·´
```

➜ *See also* <CFSETTING>, <CFSILENT>

<CFPROCPARAM>

Description: <CFPROCPARAM>, which must be used with <CFSTOREDPROC>, passes parameters to stored procedures on relational database management systems. <CFPROCPARAM> attributes are shown in Table B.101.

Syntax:

```
<CFPROCPARAM TYPE="In|Out|Inout"
    VARIABLE="variable"
    DBVARNAME="variable"
    VALUE="value"
    CFSQLTYPE="type"
    MAXLENGTH="length"
    NULL="Yes or No"
    SCALE="decimal places">
```

Table B.101 <CFPROCPARAM> Attributes

ATTRIBUTE	DESCRIPTION	NOTES
CFSQLTYPE	Variable type	Required. See Table B.102 for a list of supported types.
DBVARNAME	Database variable name	Required to support named notation; corresponds to name of parameter in stored procedure.
MAXLENGTH	Number	Optional; maximum parameter length.
NULL	YES or NO	Optional; indicates whether parameter passed is NULL.
SCALE	Number	Optional; number of decimal places in parameter.
TYPE	Parameter type	Optional; valid values are IN, OUT, and INOUT; defaults to IN.
VALUE	Parameter value	Required for IN and INOUT parameters.
VARIABLE	ColdFusion variable name	Required for OUT or INOUT parameters.

Table B.102 CFSQLTYPE Types

TYPE
CF_SQL_BIGINT
CF_SQL_BIT
CF_SQL_BLOB
CF_SQL_CHARCF_SQL_CLOB
CF_SQL_DATE
CF_SQL_DECIMAL
CF_SQL_DOUBLE
CF_SQL_FLOAT

Table 8.102 (continued)

TYPE
CF_SQL_IDSTAMP
CF_SQL_INTEGER
CF_SQL_LONGVARCHAR
CF_SQL_MONEY
CF_SQL_MONEY4
CF_SQL_NUMERIC
CF_SQL_REAL
CF_SQL_REFCURSOR
CF_SQL_SMALLINT
CF_SQL_TIME
CF_SQL_TIMESTAMP
CF_SQL_TINYINT
CF_SQL_VARCHAR

Example: See the example for <CFSTOREDPROC>

➜ *See also* <CFSTOREDPROC>, <CFPROCRESULT>

<CFPROCRESULT>

Description: The <CFPROCRESULT> tag, which must be used with the <CFSTOREDPROC> tag, specifies a particular resultset returned from a database stored procedure called with the <CFSTOREDPROC> tag. Table B.103 describes the available tag attributes.

Syntax:

```
<CFPROCRESULT NAME="name"
    RESULTSET="set"
    MAXROWS="rows">
```

Table B.103 <CFPROCRESULT> Attributes

ATTRIBUTE	DESCRIPTION	NOTES
MAXROWS	Maximum number of rows	Optional.
NAME	Query name	Required.
RESULTSET	Resultset number	Optional attribute; specifies the desired resultset; defaults to 1.

Example: See the example for <CFSTOREDPROC>

➜ *See also* <CFSTOREDPROC>, <CFPROCPARAM>

<CFPROPERTY>

Description: <CFPROPERTY>, which must be used within <CFCOMPONENT>, defines the component's properties. These properties can be accessed by ColdFusion templates that instantiate the component. Table B.104 shows <CFPROPERTY> attributes.

Syntax:

```
<CFPROPERTY NAME="Name of property"
     TYPE="Data type name" >
```

Table B.104 <CFPROPERTY> Attributes

ATTRIBUTE	DESCRIPTION	NOTES
NAME	Property name	Required; this is the name by which you address this property in other ColdFusion templates that employ the ColdFusion component that this property is part of.
TYPE	Data type name	Required; the data type of this property; the types are listed in Table B.105.
VALUE	Data value	Optional; the value of the property.

Table B.105 <CFPROPERTY> TYPE Attribute Values

TYPE
Any (default)
Array
Binary
Boolean
Date
Guid
Numeric
Query
String
Struct
UUID
Variable name
Component name (default if TYPE is not specified)

NOTE

<CFPROPERTY> must be positioned at the beginning of a <CFCOMPONENT>, preceding function definitions and any other code.

Example: The following example includes two files. The first is named film.cfc and it provides a definition of a ColdFusion component named *Film*. This component creates two properties: MovieTitle, and AmountBudgeted. The second file is named show_filmcomponent.cfm and it displays the contents of the component's metadata and properties:

```
<!--- This file defines the film component --->
<CFCOMPONENT OUTPUT="NO">
   <CFPROPERTY NAME="MovieTitle" TYPE="string" VALUE="Monsters, LLC">
   <CFPROPERTY NAME="AmountBudgeted" TYPE="numeric" VALUE="10000.00">
   <CFFUNCTION NAME="GetMetaDataStruct">
      <CFARGUMENT NAME="MyArgument">
      <!--- Get metadata for this function --->
      <CFSET var = GetMetaData(this)>
      <CFRETURN var>
   </CFFUNCTION>
</CFCOMPONENT>

<!--- This file displays film component
metadata and property values. --->
<CFSCRIPT>
Film = CreateObject("component", "Film_Component");
Filmcount = Film.GetMetaDataStruct("component");
</CFSCRIPT>

<CFDUMP VAR="#FilmCount#">

<CFOUTPUT>
<P>Property 1
<P>name: #Filmcount.properties[1].name#<BR>
type: #Filmcount.properties[1].type#<BR>
value: #Filmcount.properties[1].value#<BR>

<P>Property 2
<P>name: #Filmcount.properties[2].name#<BR>
value: #Filmcount.properties[2].value#<BR>
type: #Filmcount.properties[2].type#<BR>
</CFOUTPUT>
```

➜ *See also* <CFCOMPONENT>, <CFFUNCTION>

<CFQUERY>

Description: <CFQUERY> submits SQL statements to a data source that is either previously configured or dynamically generated, or to another query. SQL statements can include SELECT, INSERT, UPDATE, and DELETE, as well as calls to stored procedures. <CFQUERY> returns results in a named set if you specify a query name in the NAME attribute.

The <CFQUERY> attributes set up the query, and any text between the <CFQUERY> and </CFQUERY> tags becomes the SQL statement that is sent to the ODBC driver. ColdFusion conditional code can be used between the <CFQUERY> and </CFQUERY> tags, allowing you to create dynamic SQL statements. Table B.106 shows the attributes for this tag.

Syntax:

```
<CFQUERY
   BLOCKFACTOR="Number of rows"
   NAME="Parameter Name"
   DATASOURCE="Data Source"
   DBNAME="database name"
   USERNAME="User Name"
   PASSWORD="Password"
   TIMEOUT="timeout value"
   CACHEDAFTER="date"
   CACHEDWITHIN="time span"
   DEBUG="Yes or No">
SQL statement
</CFQUERY>
```

Table B.106 <CFQUERY> Attributes

ATTRIBUTE	DESCRIPTION	NOTES
BLOCKFACTOR	Number of rows to retrieve at once	Optional; available if using native or Oracle drivers. Valid values are 1–100; the default value is 1.
CACHEDAFTER	Cache date	Optional; specifies that query is to be cached and cached copy is to be used after specified date.
CACHEDWITHIN	Cache time span	Optional; specifies that query is to be cached and cached copy is to be used within a relative time span.
DATASOURCE	Data source	Required when data source is an existing database. Name of the datasource. Optional when DBTYPE is QUERY.
DBTYPE	Query	Optional; indicates that the data source is an earlier query result.
DEBUG	Enable query debugging	Optional attribute; turns on query debugging output.
MAXROWS	Number of rows	Optional; specifies maximum number of rows to retrieve.
NAME	Query name	Required; used to refer to the query results in <CFOUTPUT>, <CFMAIL>, or <CFTABLE> tags.
PASSWORD	Password	Optional; overrides the password specified in the ColdFusion Administrator.
TIMEOUT	Timeout value	Optional; the maximum number of seconds for the query to execute before returning an error indicating that the query timed out. ColdFusion sets this attribute for ODBC drivers and for the DB2 and Informix native drivers; it ignores this attribute for all other native drivers. This attribute is supported by the SQL Server 6.x or later ODBC drivers. Many ODBC drivers do not support this attribute; check the documentation for your ODBC driver to determine if it is supported.
USERNAME	User name	Optional; overrides the login name specified in the ColdFusion Administrator.

Example: The following example is a simple data retrieval query:

```
<!--- gets raw data from database --->
<CFQUERY DATASOURCE="OWS" NAME="Contacts">
    SELECT FirstName, LastName, Phone
    FROM Contacts
</CFQUERY>
```

The next example demonstrates the technique of querying against an existing query result. The second query uses `DBTYPE` of `QUERY`. The table it queries uses the name of the previous query resultset.

```
<!--- gets raw data from database --->
<CFQUERY DATASOURCE="OWS" NAME="GetAllContacts">
    SELECT * FROM Contacts
</CFQUERY>

<!--- queries GetAllContacts query --->
<CFQUERY NAME="GetMailingList" DBTYPE="Query">
    SELECT LastName, FirstName, MailingList
    FROM GetAllContacts
    WHERE MailingList = 1
</CFQUERY>

<H2><CFOUTPUT>#GetAllContacts.RecordCount#</CFOUTPUT> Contact Records</H2>
<!--- displays results of GetAllContacts query in HTML table --->
<CFTABLE QUERY="GetAllContacts" BORDER="Yes" HTMLTABLE="Yes">
    <CFCOL HEADER="Last Name" TEXT="#LastName#">
    <CFCOL HEADER="First Name" TEXT="#FirstName#">
    <CFCOL HEADER="On List" TEXT="#Iif( MailingList EQ 1,DE('Y'), DE(''))#">
</CFTABLE>

<H2><CFOUTPUT>#GetMailingList.RecordCount#</CFOUTPUT> Contact Records
on Mailing List</H2>
<!--- displays results of GetMailingList query in HTML table --->
<CFTABLE QUERY="GetMailingList" BORDER="Yes" HTMLTABLE="Yes">
    <CFCOL HEADER="Last Name" TEXT="#LastName#">
    <CFCOL HEADER="First Name" TEXT="#FirstName#">
    <CFCOL HEADER="On List" TEXT="#Iif( MailingList EQ 1,DE('Y'), DE(''))#">
</CFTABLE>
```

This example demonstrates how dynamic SQL statements can be constructed using the ColdFusion conditional tags.

```
<!--- gets raw data from database --->
<CFQUERY NAME="GetContacts" DATASOURCE="OWS">
    SELECT FirstName, LastName, Phone, ContactID
    FROM Contacts
    WHERE 1=1

    <!--- determines if the FirstName variable passed from
    a form is not blank and matches a pattern present in the
    FirstName database column --->
    <CFIF FORM.FirstName IS NOT "">
        AND FirstName LIKE '#FORM.FirstName#%'
    </CFIF>

    <!--- determines if the LastName variable passed from
    a form is not blank and matches a pattern present in the
```

```
        LastName database column --->
        <CFIF FORM.LastName IS NOT "">
            AND LastName LIKE '#FORM.LastName#%'
        </CFIF>

        <!--- determines if the Phone variable passed from
        a form is not blank and matches a pattern present in the
        Phone database column --->
        <CFIF FORM.Phone IS NOT "">
            AND PhoneExtension LIKE 'FORM.#Phone#%'
        </CFIF>

        <!--- if all conditions are met, query results are displayed
        last name first --->
        ORDER BY LastName, FirstName
    </CFQUERY>
```

The last example demonstrates the use of <CFQUERY> to execute a stored procedure in a SQL Server database:

```
<!--- queries database using stored procedure and URL variable --->
<CFQUERY NAME="GetContact" DATASOURCE="ContactSystem">
    <!--- calls stored procedure --->
    {Call GetContacts(#URL.ContactID#)}
</CFQUERY>
```

Note that the preferred mechanism for executing stored procedures involves using <CFSTOREDPROC> and related tags. This older technique will work but is limited to returning one recordset.

➜ *See also* <CFQUERYPARAM>, <CFOUTPUT>, <CFMAIL>, <CFTABLE>, <CFSTOREDPROC>

<CFQUERYPARAM>

Description: <CFQUERYPARAM> is embedded within the SQL of a <CFQUERY>. It enables you to define query parameters and their data types. Queries may execute more quickly when passed data-typed parameters.

<CFQUERYPARAM> attributes are listed in Table B.107.

Syntax:

```
<CFQUERYPARAM CFSQLTYPE="Param type"
    MAXLENGTH="Number"
    NULL="Yes or No"
    SCALE="Number of decimal places"
    SEPARATOR="Delimiter character"
    VALUE="Param value">
```

Table B.107 <CFQUERYPARAM> Attributes

ATTRIBUTE	DESCRIPTION	NOTES
CFSQLTYPE	Type	Optional; data type specified from list in Table B.108.
MAXLENGTH	Bytes	Optional; maximum length of parameter value.

Table B.107 (continued)

ATTRIBUTE	DESCRIPTION	NOTES
NULL	YES or NO	Optional; YES if passed parameter is null.
SCALE	Number of decimals	Optional; applicable for TYPE=CF_SQL_NUMERIC and CF_SQL_DECIMAL. Specifies number of decimals; defaults to 0.
SEPARATOR	Character	Optional; character to be used as a delimiter in lists.
VALUE	Param value	Required; the parameter's value.

Table B.108 CF SQL Types

ATTRIBUTE
CF_SQL_BIGINT
CF_SQL_BIT
CF_SQL_BLOB
CF_SQL_CHAR
CF_SQL_CLOB
CF_SQL_DATE
CF_SQL_DECIMAL
CF_SQL_DOUBLE
CF_SQL_FLOAT
CF_SQL_IDSTAMP
CF_SQL_INTEGER
CF_SQL_LONGVARCHAR
CF_SQL_MONEY
CF_SQL_MONEY4
CF_SQL_NUMERIC
CF_SQL_REAL
CF_SQL_REFCURSOR
CF_SQL_SMALLINT
CF_SQL_TIME
CF_SQL_TIMESTAMP
CF_SQL_TINYINT
CF_SQL_VARCHAR

Example: In the following example, <CFQUERYPARAM> is used to validate the data type being passed:

```
<!--- sets default value for URL variable --->
<CFPARAM NAME="URL.ContactID" DEFAULT="q">
<!--- sets trap for errors --->
<CFTRY>
<!--- gets raw data from database as interger --->
<CFQUERY NAME="GetContacts" DATASOURCE="ows">
    SELECT LastName, FirstName
    FROM Contacts
    WHERE ContactID = <CFQUERYPARAM VALUE="#URL.ContactID#"
    CFSQLTYPE="CF_SQL_INTEGER">
</CFQUERY>
<!--- catches and displays any errors --->
<CFCATCH TYPE="Any">
    <P>An error has occurred:
    <CFOUTPUT>
        <P>#CFCATCH.Detail#
        <P>#CFCATCH.Type#
    </CFOUTPUT>
</CFCATCH>
</CFTRY>
```

TIP

Use <CFQUERYPARAM> to prevent malicious database access via URL tampering.

➜ *See also* <CFQUERY>, <CFSTOREDPROC>, <CFPROCPARAM>

<CFREGISTRY>

Description: <CFREGISTRY> can be used to directly manipulate the system Registry. The <CFREGISTRY> ACTION attribute specifies the action to be performed, and depending on the action, other attributes might or might not be necessary. This tag is available on any UNIX platforms but its use is deprecated on the UNIX and related platforms.

<CFREGISTRY> attributes are listed in Table B.109. Values for the ACTION attribute are listed in Table B.110.

Syntax:

```
<CFREGISTRY ACTION="action"
    BRANCH="branch"
    ENTRY="entry"
    NAME="query"
    SORT="sort order"
    TYPE="type"
    VALUE="value"
    VARIABLE="variable">
```

Table B.109 <CFREGISTRY> Attributes

ATTRIBUTE	DESCRIPTION	NOTES
ACTION	Action	Required; one of the values in Table B.110.
BRANCH	Registry branch	Required.

Table B.109 (continued)

ATTRIBUTE	DESCRIPTION	NOTES
ENTRY	Branch entry	Required for GET, SET, and DELETE actions.
NAME	Name of record to contain keys and values	Required if ACTION is GETALL.
SORT	Sort order	Optional; can be used if ACTION is GETALL. Enables sorting on specified column(s): ENTRY, TYPE, and VALUE. You also can specify ASC for ascending sorts or DESC for descending sorts.
TYPE	Value type	Optional; can be used for all actions except DELETE; valid types are STRING, DWORD, and KEY; default is STRING.
VALUE	Value to set	Required if ACTION is SET.
VARIABLE	Variable to save	Required if ACTION value is GET.

Table B.110 <CFREGISTRY> Actions

ACTION	DESCRIPTION
DELETE	Deletes a Registry key.
GET	Gets a Registry value.
GETALL	Gets all Registry keys in a branch.
SET	Sets a Registry value.

Example: This example retrieves all the keys beneath the Liquid Audio branch.

```
<!--- queries system registry --->
<CFREGISTRY ACTION="GETALL"
    NAME="reg"
    BRANCH="HKEY_LOCAL_MACHINE\SOFTWARE\Liquid Audio Settings">

<!--- displays number of registry keys --->
<P>Number of Liquid Audio entries: <CFOUTPUT>#reg.RecordCount#</CFOUTPUT>
<!--- displays each key's details in an HTML table --->
<TABLE CELLPADDING="3">
<CFOUTPUT QUERY="reg">
<TR ALIGN="left">
    <TH>Entry</TH>
    <TH>Type</TH>
    <TH>Value</TH>
</TR>
<TR ALIGN="left">
    <TD>#Entry#</TD>
    <TD>#Type#</TD>
    <TD>#Value#</TD>
</TR>
</CFOUTPUT>
</TABLE>
```

NOTE

Only Windows platforms use the Registry concept. This tag works only on Windows platforms.

CAUTION

Take great care when using this tag, particularly when writing to the Registry. It is not hard to corrupt the integrity of the Registry. You might want to consider turning off the use of this tag in the ColdFusion Administrator, in the Tag Restrictions section under Security.

<CFREPORT>

Description: <CFREPORT> is the ColdFusion interface to reports created with the Crystal Reports. <CFREPORT> requires only a single attribute: the name of the report to be processed. The full list of supported attributes is in Table B.111.

Syntax:

```
<CFREPORT REPORT="Report File"
    ORDERBY="Sort Order"
    USERNAME="User Name"
    PASSWORD="Password"
    FORMULA="Formula">
Optional filter conditions
</CFREPORT>
```

Table B.111 <CFREPORT> Attributes

ATTRIBUTE	DESCRIPTION	NOTES
FORMULA	Crystal Reports formula	Optional; enables you to specify values for Crystal Reports formulas used in the report.
ORDERBY	Report sort order	Optional; overrides the default sort order specified when the report was created.
PASSWORD	ODBC data source password	Optional; used to override the ODBC login password specified in the ColdFusion Administrator.
REPORT	Name of RPT file to process	Required.
USERNAME	ODBC data source login name	The optional attribute is used to override the ODBC login name specified in the ColdFusion Administrator.

Example: The following example processes a report created with Crystal Reports Professional and passes it an optional filter condition:

```
<!--- retrieves report entries with ContactID of 3 --->
<CFREPORT REPORT="\ows\scripts\Contact.rpt">
    {Contacts.ContacID} = "3"
</CFREPORT>
```

This example processes a report and specifies parameters to override the ODBC data source, user login name and password, and a formula named `@Title` derived from an HTML form:

```
<!--- retrieves report entries using @Title formula
and ContractID Sales --->
<CFREPORT REPORT="\ows\scripts\ContactList.rpt"
    DATASOURCE="OWSInternal"
    USERNAME="Sales"
    PASSWORD="bigbucks"
    @Title="#FORM.title#">
    {Contacts.ContactID} = "Sales"
</CFREPORT>
```

<CFRETHROW>

Description: `<CFRETHROW>` enables you to force the current error to be invoked again within `<CFCATCH>` ... `</CFCATCH>` block. It generally is used when you have error trapping logic that traps an error that your code isn't capable of handling. In this case, you want to *rethrow the error.*

Syntax:

```
<CFRETHROW>
```

Example: In the following example, a query attempts to insert a new record using key values entered through a form. This can result in a key violation. The `<CFCATCH>` block is used to trap this type of error, but if some other type of database error occurs, you rethrow the error:

```
<!--- sets error trap --->
<CFTRY>
<!--- gets raw data from database --->
<CFQUERY NAME="InsertContactOrder" DATASOURCE="OWS">
    INSERT INTO ContactOrders (ContactID,OrderID)
    VALUES (#FORM.ContactID#,#FORM.OrderID#)
</CFQUERY>

<CFCATCH TYPE="DATABASE">
    <!--- If the database throws anything other
    than a 23000 error, the error is rethrown. --->
    <CFIF CFCATCH.sqlstate neq 23000>
    <CFRETHROW>
    </CFIF>
</CFCATCH>
</CFTRY>
```

➜ *See also* `<CFCATCH>`, `<CFTHROW>`, `<CFTRY>`

<CFRETURN>

Description: `<CFRETURN>` enables you to return a value from a `<CFFUNCTION>` in a ColdFusion component. You use it to return expressions. Note that while there are no attributes per se, you must return an expression.

Syntax:

```
<CFRETURN expression>
```

Example: Please refer to the examples in <CFFUNCTION> and <CFCARGUMENT>.

→ *See also* <CFCOMPONENT>, <CFFUNCTION>, <CFCFARGUMENT>

<CFSAVECONTENT>

Description: <CFSAVECONTENT> enables you to save the output of a page or portion of a page in a variable. It is valuable when you need to process the output in some way before it is complete. It saves the results of evaluated expressions and custom tag output in the body. The attribute is described in Table B.112.

Syntax:

```
<CFSAVECONTENT VARIABLE="variablename">
```

Table B.112 <CFSAVECONTENT> Attributes

ATTRIBUTE	DESCRIPTION	NOTES
VARIABLE	CFML variable name	Required; name of the variable in which to save content.

Example: In this example, <CFSAVECONTENT> is used to save the page output in a variable. The phrase "Profit and Loss Q1" is then replaced with the phrase "Profit and Loss Q2:"

```
<!--- saves custom tag output to a variable --->
<CFSAVECONTENT VARIABLE="ReportTitle">
    <!--- custom tag producs p&l --->
<CF_ProducePandL StartDate="4/1/2001" EndDate="6/30/2001">
</CFSAVECONTENT>
<!--- replaces text string --->
<CFOUTPUT>
#Replace(ReportTitle, "Profit and Loss Q1", "Profit And Loss Q2", "all")#
</CFOUTPUT>
```

<CFSCHEDULE>

Description: <CFSCHEDULE> enables you to create, update, delete, and execute tasks programmatically in the ColdFusion Administrator's scheduler. The scheduler enables you to run a specified page at scheduled times and intervals.

You have the option to direct page output to static HTML pages. This enables you to offer users access to pages that publish data, such as reports, without forcing them to wait while a database transaction that populates the data on the page is performed.

ColdFusion-scheduled events must be registered using the ColdFusion Administrator before they can be executed. Information supplied by the user includes the scheduled ColdFusion page to execute, the time and frequency for executing the page, and whether the output from the task should be published. A path and file are specified if the output is to be published.

<CFSCHEDULE> attributes are listed in Table B.113. The values for the `ACTION` attribute are described in Table B.114.

Syntax:

```
<CFSCHEDULE ACTION="Action"
    ENDDATE="Date"
    ENDTIME="Time"
    FILE="File Name"
    INTERVAL="Interval"
    LIMITIME="Seconds"
    OPERATION="HTTPRequest"
    PASSWORD="Password"
    PATH="Path"
    PORT="Port Number"
    PROXYSERVER="Server Name"
    PROXYPORT="port number"
    PUBLISH="Yes or No"
    RESOLVEURL="Yes or No"
    REQUESTIMEOUT="seconds"
    STARTDATE="Date"
    STARTTIME="Time"
    TASK="Task Name"
    URL="URL"
    USERNAME="User Name">
```

Table B.113 <CFSCHEDULE> Attributes

ATTRIBUTE	DESCRIPTION	NOTES
ACTION	Action (refer to Table B.114)	Required attribute.
ENDDATE	Event end date	Optional attribute; date the scheduled task should end.
ENDTIME	Event end time	Optional attribute; time the scheduled task should end; enter value in seconds.
FILE	File to create	Required if PUBLISH is Yes.
INTERVAL	Execution interval	Required if ACTION is UPDATE; can be specified as number of seconds; as daily, weekly, or monthly; or as execute.
LIMITTIME	Maximum execution time	Optional attribute; maximum number of seconds allowed for execution.
OPERATION	Operation	Required if ACTION is UPDATE. Currently only HTTPRequest is supported.
PASSWORD	Password	Optional password for protected URLs.
PATH	Path to save published files	Required if PUBLISH is YES.
PORT	Port number on server	Optional; used with RESOLVEURL set to YES to properly execute URLs that specify a port other than 80 (default).
PROXYSERVER	Proxy server name	Optional name of proxy server.
PROXYPORT	Port number on proxy server	Optional; used with RESOLVEURL set to YES to properly execute URLs that specify a port other than 80 (default).
PUBLISH	Publish static files	Optional attribute; YES if the scheduled task should publish files; default is NO.

Table B.113 (continued)

ATTRIBUTE	DESCRIPTION	NOTES
REQUESTTIMEOUT	Seconds	Before timeout Optional; used to extend the default timeout for long tasks.
RESOLVEURL	Resolve URLs	Optional attribute; resolve URLs to fully qualified URLs if YES; default is NO.
STARTDATE	Event start date	Optional attribute; date the scheduled task should start.
STARTTIME	Event start time	Optional attribute; time the scheduled task should start; enter value in seconds.
TASK	Task name	Required attribute; the registered task name.
URL	URL	Required if ACTION is UPDATE; the URL to be executed.
USERNAME	Username	Optional username for protected URLs.

Table B.114 <CFSCHEDULE> Actions

ACTION	DESCRIPTION
DELETE	Deletes a task.
UPDATE	Updates a task or creates it if it doesn't exist.
RUN	Executes a task.

Example: This example creates a recurring task that runs every 10 minutes (600 seconds). The output is saved in C:\INETPUB\WWWROOT\SAMPLE.HTML:

```
<!--- schedules update task --->
<CFSCHEDULE ACTION="UPDATE"
    TASK="TaskName"
    OPERATION="HTTPRequest"
    URL="http://127.0.0.1/testarea/test.cfm"
    STARTDATE="3/13/2001"
    STARTTIME="12:25 PM"
    INTERVAL="600"
    RESOLVEURL="Yes"
    PUBLISH="Yes"
    FILE="sample.html"
    PATH="c:\inetpub\wwwroot\"
    REQUESTTIMEOUT="600">
```

This example deletes the task created in the previous example:

```
<!--- deletes TaskName scheduled task --->
<CFSCHEDULE ACTION="delete"
    TASK="TaskName">
```

NOTE

Execution of <CFSCHEDULE> can be disabled in the ColdFusion Administrator.

<CFSCRIPT>

Description: <CFSCRIPT> and </CFSCRIPT> are used to mark blocks of ColdFusion script. ColdFusion script looks similar to JavaScript and enables you to produce certain functions of ColdFusion tags (and use many ColdFusion functions) and avoid all the wordy syntax associated with tags. Note that one major limitation of <CFSCRIPT> is that you can't execute SQL (or other) queries with it. Each line must be terminated with a semicolon.

Syntax:

```
<CFSCRIPT>
script
</CFSCRIPT>
```

Example: The following example creates a structure and then uses it in place of a <CFSWITCH> to select a value.

```
<!--- creates structure and displays results --->
<CFSCRIPT>
    Meals = StructNew();
    Meals["Breakfast"]="Bacon,Eggs,Toast,Fruit,Coffee";
    Meals["Lunch"]="Soup,Sandwich";
    Meals["Dinner"]="Pasta,Garlic bread,Red wine";
    WriteOutput("We'll be having " & Meals[Form.Meal] & " for " & Form.Meal);
</CFSCRIPT>
```

<CFSEARCH>

Description: <CFSEARCH> performs searches against Verity collections (in much the same way <CFQUERY> performs searches against ODBC data sources). To use <CFSEARCH>, you must specify the collection to be searched and the name of the query to be returned. You can search more than one collection at once, and you also can perform searches against Verity collections created with applications other than ColdFusion. Table B.115 lists the <CFSEARCH> attributes.

Syntax:

```
<CFSEARCH COLLECTION="Collection Name"
    CRITERIA="Search Criteria"
    CUSTOM1="Data"
    CUSTOM2="Data"
    LANGUAGE="language"
    MAXROWS="Number"
    NAME="Name"
    STARTROW="Number"
    TYPE="Type">
```

Table B.115 <CFSEARCH> Attributes

ATTRIBUTE	DESCRIPTION	NOTES
COLLECTION	Collection name	Required attribute; the name of the collection or collections to be searched. Multiple collections must be separated by commas; for external collections, specify the full path to the collection.
CRITERIA	Search criteria	Optional attribute; search criteria as shown in Appendix E.

Table B.115 (continued)

ATTRIBUTE	DESCRIPTION	NOTES
EXTERNAL	Deprecated	This attribute is no longer available.
LANGUAGE	Language	Optional; requires installation of International Search Page.
MAXROWS	Maximum rows to retrieve	Optional attribute; defaults to all.
NAME	Value column	Optional; column to be used for OPTION VALUE attribute.
STARTROW	Start row	Optional; default is first row.
TYPE	Search type	Optional; can be SIMPLE or EXPLICIT.

Example: This example performs a search with a user-supplied search criterion. It searches the collection built in the example for <CFCOLLECTION>.

```
<!--- schedules update task --->
<CFIF IsDefined("FORM.Searchfield")>
    <CFSEARCH COLLECTION="FilmsMerchandise"
    TYPE="SIMPLE"
    CRITERIA="#Form.SearchField#"
    NAME="GetMerch">
</CFIF>
<!--- submits search value --->
<FORM ACTION="#CGI.SCRIPT_NAME#" METHOD="post">
    <P>Find film merchandise: <INPUT NAME="searchfield" TYPE="Text">
    <p><INPUT TYPE="Submit" VALUE="Search">
</FORM>
<!--- checks for presense of form variable --->
<CFIF IsDefined("Form.searchfield")>
    <!--- if RecordCount is greater than zero, displays results --->
    <CFIF GetMerch.RecordCount GT 0>
    <UL>
        <CFOUTPUT QUERY="GetMerch">
        <LI>#Key# - #NumberFormat(Score, "__.__" )# - #Summary#
        </CFOUTPUT>
    </UL>
    <!--- if RecordCount is zero, message is displayed --->
    <CFELSE>
    <P>Nothing matching your criteria
    </CFIF>
</CFIF>
```

➔ <CFCOLLECTION>, <CFINDEX>

<CFSELECT>

Description: <CFSELECT> is used to simplify the process of creating data-driven SELECT controls. <CFSELECT> is not a Java control. <CFSELECT> requires that you pass it the name of a query for use in populating the drop-down list box. <CFSELECT> attributes are listed in Table B.116.

You can add your own options to the SELECT list by adding <OPTION> tags between the <CFSELECT> and </CFSELECT> tags.

Syntax:

```
<CFSELECT DISPLAY="Column Name"
    MESSAGE="Message Text"
    MULTIPLE="Yes or No"
    NAME="Field Name"
    ONERROR="JavaScript Error Function"
    PASSTHROUGH="attributes"
    QUERY="Query Name"
    REQUIRED="Yes or No"
    SELECTED="Value" SIZE="Size"
    VALUE="Column Name">
</CFSELECT>
```

Table B.116 <CFSELECT> Attributes

ATTRIBUTE	DESCRIPTION	NOTES
DISPLAY	Column to display	Optional query column to use as the displayed text.
MESSAGE	Validation failure message	Optional message to display upon validation failure.
MULTIPLE	Allow multiple selection	Optional attribute; defaults to NO.
NAME	Unique field name	This attribute is required.
ONERROR	JavaScript error function	Optional override to your own JavaScript error message function.
PASSTHROUGH	HTML <SELECT> attribute	Optional; <SELECT> attributes not supported by <CFSELECT>, such as TABINDEX.
QUERY	Query name	Required attribute; query to be used to populate the SELECT box.
REQUIRED	Field is required	Optional required flag; must be YES or NO if specified; defaults to NO.
SELECTED	Selected value	Value of the OPTION to be preselected.
SIZE	List size	Required attribute; number of options to display without scrolling.
VALUE	Value column	Optional attribute; column to be used for OPTION VALUE attribute.

Example: This example creates a simple data-driven SELECT control in which the user is required to make a selection:

```
<!--- gets raw data from database --->
<CFQUERY NAME="GetActors" DATASOURCE="OWS">
    SELECT ActorID, NameLast
    FROM Actors
</CFQUERY>
<!--- creates menu from query --->
```

```
<CFFORM ACTION="process.cfm">
    <CFSELECT NAME="Actors"
        QUERY="GetActors"
        VALUE="ActorID"
        DISPLAY="NameLast"
        SIZE="1"
        REQUIRED="Yes">
    </CFSELECT>
</CFFORM>
```

➜ *See also* <CFFORM>, <CFGRID>, <CFINPUT>, <CFSLIDER>, <CFTEXTINPUT>, <CFTREE>

<CFSERVLET>

This tag is deprecated and is no longer in use.

<CFSERVLETPARAM>

This tag is deprecated and is no longer in use.

<CFSET>

Description: `<CFSET>` assigns values to variables. `<CFSET>` can be used for both client variables (type `CLIENT`) and standard variables (type `VARIABLES`). `<CFSET>` takes no attributes—other than the name of the variable being assigned and its value.

Syntax:

```
<CFSET "Variable"="Value">
```

Example: The following example creates a local variable containing a constant value:

```
<!--- sets local variable --->
<CFSET MaxDisplay=25>
```

The following example creates a client variable called `#BGColor#`, which contains a user-specified value and explicitly states the variable type (`CLIENT`):

```
<!--- sets client variable --->
<CFSET CLIENT.BGColor=FORM.Color>
```

This example stores tomorrow's date in a variable called `Tomorrow`:

```
<!--- sets variable for tomorrow's date --->
<CFSET Tomorrow =Now() + 1>
```

`<CFSET>` can also be used to concatenate fields:

```
<!--- sets variable that contains two other variables --->
<CFSET VARIABLES.FullName=FORM.FirstName FORM.LastName>
```

Values of different data types also can be concatenated:

```
<!--- sets variable that contains three variables of different data types --->
<CFSET Sentence=FORM.FirstName FORM.LastName & "is" & FORM.age & "years old">
```

Note that when creating complex variables, such as arrays, structures, and queries, you must use a function to create the variables before you can set their values:

```
<!--- sets variable and creates array --->
<CFSET myBreakfast=ArrayNew(1)>
<!--- populates array with a value --->
<CFSET myBreakfast[1]="Chipped Beef on Toast">
<!--- creates structure --->
<CFSET myLunch=StructNew()>
<!--- populates structure with a value --->
<CFSET myLunch["MainCourse"]="Chili">
<!--- creates array columns --->
<CFSET myDinner=QueryNew("Monday,Tuesday,Wednesday,Thursday,Friday")>
<!--- adds row --->
<CFSET temp=QueryAddRow(myDinner)>
<!--- populates cell in myDinner --->
<CFSET temp=QuerySetCell(myDinner, "Monday", "Lasagna")>
```

TIP

If you find yourself performing a calculation or combining strings more than once in a specific template, you're better off doing it once and assigning the results to a variable with `<CFSET>`; you can then use that variable instead.

➜ *See also* `<CFAPPLICATION>`, `<CFCOOKIE>`, `<CFPARAM>`

<CFSETTING>

Description: `<CFSETTING>` is used to control various aspects of page processing, such as controlling the output of HTML code in your pages or enabling and disabling debug output. One benefit is managing whitespace that can occur in output pages that are served by ColdFusion. `<CFSETTING>` attributes are listed in Table B.117.

When using `<CFSETTING>` to disable an option, be sure you have a matching enable option later in the file.

Syntax:

```
<CFSETTING ENABLECFOUTPUTONLY="Yes or No"
    SHOWDEBUGOUTPUT="Yes|No">
```

Table B.117 `<CFSETTING>` Attributes

ATTRIBUTE	DESCRIPTION	NOTES
ENABLECFOUTPUTONLY	YES or NO	Required; forces ColdFusion to only output content in `<CFOUTPUT>` blocks.
SHOWDEBUGOUTPUT	YES or NO	Optional; when set to NO, suppresses debugging information that normally appears at bottom of page. Defaults to YES.

NOTE

For each use of `<CFSETTING>` with ENABLECFOUTPUTONLY set to YES, you must include a matching ENABLECFOUTPUTONLY set to NO. That is, if you used it twice with ENABLECFOUTPUTONLY set to YES, you must use it two more times set to NO to get ColdFusion to display regular HTML output.

Example: The following demonstrates how `<CFSETTING>` can be used to control generated whitespace:

```
<!--- text is displayed --->
This text will be displayed
<!--- suppresses all output not inside <CFOUTPUT> tags --->
<CFSETTING ENABLECFOUTPUTONLY="Yes">
<!--- text is not displayed because it lies outside of <CFOUTPUT> --->
This text will not be displayed as it is not in a CFOUTPUT block
<!--- text is displayed because it lies within <CFOUTPUT> block  --->
<CFOUTPUT>This will be displayed</CFOUTPUT>
<!--- does not suppress output outside of <CFOUTPUT> block --->
<CFSETTING ENABLECFOUTPUTONLY="No">
<!--- test is displayed --->
This text will be displayed even though it is not in a CFOUTPUT block
```

➜ *See also* `<CFSILENT>`

<CFSILENT>

Description: Similar to `<CFSETTING ENABLECFOUTPUTONLY="YES">`, `<CFSILENT>` is a mechanism for suppressing output. However, it simply suppresses all output that ColdFusion produces within the tag's scope.

Syntax:

```
<CFSILENT>
any code or text</CFSILENT>
```

Example: This example demonstrates that `<CFSILENT>` suppresses all included output in `<CFOUTPUT>` blocks. However, it does not suppress the execution of code in `<CFOUTPUT>` blocks, so the variables `#X#` and `#SENTENCE#` are still created and processed:

```
<!--- suppresses display of <CFOUTPUT> --->
<CFSILENT>
    <CFSET x="value">
    <CFSET sentence="This is a #x# to be output.">
    <P><CFOUTPUT>#sentence#</CFOUTPUT>
</CFSILENT>
<!--- variable is displayed --->
<P><CFOUTPUT>#sentence#</CFOUTPUT>
```

➜ *See also* `<CFSETTING>`

<CFSLIDER>

Description: `<CFSLIDER>` embeds a Java slider control in your HTML forms. Slider controls typically are used to select one of a range of numbers. `<CFSLIDER>` must be used between `<CFFORM>` and `</CFFORM>` tags. Table B.118 lists the entire set of `<CFSLIDER>` attributes.

Syntax:

```
<CFSLIDER ALIGN="Alignment"
    BGCOLOR="Background Color"
    BOLD="Yes or No"
    FONT="Font Face"
```

```
FONTSIZE="Font Size"
HEIGHT="Control Height"
HSPACE="Horizontal Spacing"
ITALIC="Yes or No"
LABEL="Slider Label"
LOOKANDFEEL="Motif or Windows or Metal"
MESSAGE="Error Message"
NAME="Field Name"
NOTSUPPORTED="Non Java Browser Code"
ONERROR="Error Function"
ONVALIDATE="Validation Function"
RANGE="Numeric Range"
REFRESHLABEL="Yes or No"
SCALE="Increment Value"
TEXTCOLOR="Text Color"
TICKMARKIMAGES="URL list"
TICKMARKLABELS="Yes or No or Numeric or label list"
TICKMARKMAJOR="Yes or No"
TICKMARKMINOR="Yes or No"
VALUE="Initial Value"
VERTICAL="Yes or No"
VSPACE="Vertical Spacing"
WIDTH="Control Width">
```

Table B.118 <CFSLIDER> Attributes

ATTRIBUTE	DESCRIPTION	NOTES
ALIGN	Control alignment	Optional; possible values are TOP, LEFT, BOTTOM, BASELINE, TEXTTOP, ABSBOTTOM, MIDDLE, ABSMIDDLE, and RIGHT.
BGCOLOR	Background color	Optional; possible values are BLACK, BLUE, RED, CYAN, DARKGRAY, GRAY, LIGHTGRAY, MAGENTA, ORANGE, PINK, WHITE, YELLOW, or any color specified in hex format.
BOLD	Bold face text	Optional attribute; must be YES or NO if specified; defaults to NO.
FONT	Font face	Optional font face to use.
FONTSIZE	Font size	Optional font size.
GROOVECOLOR	Deprecated	This attribute is no longer in use.
HEIGHT	Control height	Optional height in pixels.
HSPACE	Control horizontal spacing	Optional horizontal spacing in pixels.
IMG	Deprecated	This attribute is no longer in use.
IMGSTYLE	Deprecated	This attribute is no longer in use.
ITALIC	Italic face text	Optional attribute; must be YES or NO if specified; defaults to NO.
LABEL	Slider label	Optional; can contain the variable %VALUE%, in which case the current value is displayed as the slider is moved.

Table B.118 (continued)

ATTRIBUTE	DESCRIPTION	NOTES
LOOKANDFEEL	Look style name	Optional; can be MOTIF, WINDOWS, or METAL (Java Swing style). Defaults to WINDOWS.
MESSAGE	Validation failure message	Optional message to display upon validation failure.
NAME	Unique control name	Required.
NOTSUPPORTED	Text to be used for non-Java browsers	Optional text (or HTML code) to be displayed on non–Java-capable browsers.
ONERROR	JavaScript error function	Optional override to your own JavaScript error message function.
ONVALIDATE	JavaScript validation function	Optional override to your own JavaScript validation function.
RANGE	Range minimum and maximum	Optional range for numeric values only; must be specified as two numbers separated by a comma; defaults to "0,100".
REFRESHLABEL	YES or NO	Optional; if NO and slider is moved, label is not refreshed; default is YES.
SCALE	Increment scale integer	Optional; increment amount to use when slider is moved; defaults to 1.
TEXTCOLOR	Text color	Optional; possible values are BLACK, BLUE, RED, CYAN, DARKGRAY, GRAY, LIGHTGRAY, MAGENTA, ORANGE, PINK, WHITE, YELLOW, or any color specified in hex format.
TICKMARKIMAGES	URL list	Optional; comma-separated list of URLs of images to use for tick marks.
TICKMARKLABELS	YES or NO, or NUMERIC or list	Optional; YES or NUMERIC results in tick marks based on values of RANGE and SCALE attributes. NO (default) prevents the display of label tick marks. It can also provide a list of labels to be used, such as TWENTY FIVE, FIFTY, SEVENTY FIVE, ONE HUNDRED.
TICKMARKMAJOR	YES or NO	Optional; defaults to NO. Renders major tick marks based on value of SCALE attribute.
TICKMARKMINOR	YES or NO	Optional; defaults to NO. Renders major tick marks based on value of SCALE attribute.
VALUE	Initial value	Optional; initial field value; this value must be within the specified range if RANGE is used.
VSPACE	Control vertical spacing	Optional vertical spacing in pixels.
WIDTH	Control width	Optional width in pixels.

Example: The following example displays a form for searching for contacts based on last name. <CFSLIDER> enables the user to set the maximum rows that will be returned by the query.

```
<H2>Search Contacts</H2>
<!--- creates form --->
<CFFORM ACTION="ContactSearch.cfm">
<!--- creates text field --->
<P>Last name: <CFTEXTINPUT FONT="Verdana"
            BGCOLOR="white"
            TEXTCOLOR="Blue"
            NAME="LastName"
            REQUIRED="Yes">
<!--- creates slider control --->
<P><CFSLIDER NAME="volume"
    HEIGHT="100"
    WIDTH="200"
    FONT="Verdana"
    BGCOLOR="lightgray"
    TEXTCOLOR="Blue"
    GROOVECOLOR="White"
    LABEL="Maximum rows %value%"
    RANGE="0,50"
    SCALE="5">
<!--- creates submit button --->
<P><INPUT TYPE="Submit" VALUE="Search">
</CFFORM>
```

NOTE

The <CFSLIDER> control is accessible only by users with Java-enabled browsers and must be used in a <CFFORM>.

➜ *See also* <CFFORM>, <CFGRID>, <CFINPUT>, <CFSELECT>, <CFTEXTINPUT>, <CFTREE>

<CFSTOREDPROC>

Description: <CFSTOREDPROC> provides sophisticated support for database-stored procedures. Unlike <CFQUERY>, which can also call stored procedures, <CFSTOREDPROC> and its supporting tags (<CFPROCPARAM> and <CFPROCRESULT>) can pass and retrieve parameters and access multiple resultsets. <CFSTOREDPROC> attributes are listed in Table B.119.

Syntax:

```
<CFSTOREDPROC
    DATASOURCE="Data Source Name"
    USERNAME="User Name"
    PASSWORD="Password"
    PROCEDURE="Procedure"
    BLOCKFACTOR="factor"
    DEBUG="Yes or No"
    RETURNCODE="Yes or No">
```

Table B.119 <CFSTOREDPROC> Attributes

ATTRIBUTE	DESCRIPTION	NOTES
BLOCKFACTOR	Number of rows to retrieve at once	Optional; available if using ODBC or Oracle drivers; valid values are 1 to 100; default value is 1.
DATASOURCE	Data source name	Optional; used to override the data source specified when the report was created.
DEBUG	YES or NO	Optional; turns on query debugging output.
PASSWORD	Password	Optional; used to override the password provided in the ColdFusion Administrator.
PROCEDURE	Stored procedure name	Name of stored procedure to execute.
RETURNCODE	YES or NO	Optional; indicates whether to populate CFSTOREDPROC.STATUSCODE returned by stored procedure. Defaults to NO.
USERNAME	user name	Optional; used to override the login name specified in the ColdFusion Administrator.

Example: The first example executes a simple stored procedure named GETEMPLOYEES. This is just a SELECT query that builds a resultset named GETEMPLOYEES:

```
<!--- calls stored procedure --->
<CFSTOREDPROC DATASOURCE="OWS"
    PROCEDURE="GetEmployees">
    <!--- names stored procedure result --->
    <CFPROCRESULT NAME="GetEmployees">
</CFSTOREDPROC>
```

The next example invokes a stored procedure named GETNEXTNUMBER, which increments a value in a table by one and then sends the new number back to the calling routine. It takes an input parameter named TblName and generates a value named BUDGETCATEGORYID, which you can then use in your application.

```
<!--- calls stored procedure --->
<CFSTOREDPROC PROCEDURE="GetNextNumber"
    DATASOURCE="OWS"
    RETURNCODE="YES">
    <!--- passes parameter to stored procedure --->
    <CFPROCPARAM TYPE="IN"
        DBVARNAME="@TblName"
        VALUE="#KeyName#"
        CFSQLTYPE="CF_SQL_CHAR"
        MAXLENGTH="20"
        NULL="no">
    <!--- passes parameter to stored procedure --->
    <CFPROCPARAM TYPE="OUT"
        VARIABLE="BudgetCategoryID"
        DBVARNAME="@intNextNmbr"
        CFSQLTYPE="CF_SQL_INTEGER">
    <!--- names stored procedure results and selects
    partcular resultset--->
```

```
    <CFPROCRESULT NAME="Set1"
        RESULTSET="2"
</CFSTOREDPROC>
<!--- displays results from stored procedure results --->
<CFOUTPUT QUERY="Set1">
    <P>Total Actor Salary Budget=#Set1.ActorSalary#</P>
</CFOUTPUT>
```

➔ <CFPROCPARAM>, <CFPROCRESULT>, <CFQUERY>

<CFSWITCH>

Description: <CFSWITCH> is used to create case statements in ColdFusion. Every <CFSWITCH> must be terminated with a </CFSWITCH>. The individual case statements are specified using the <CFCASE> tag; a default case can be specified using the <CFDEFAULTCASE> tag.<CFSWITCH> attributes are shown in Table B.120.

Syntax:

```
<CFSWITCH EXPRESSION="expression">
    <CFCASE VALUE="value">
        HTML or CFML code
    </CFCASE>
    <CFDEFAULTCASE>
        HTML or CFML code
    </CFDEFAULTCASE>
</CFSWITCH>
```

Table B.120 <CFSWITCH> Attributes

ATTRIBUTE	DESCRIPTION	NOTES
EXPRESSION	Case expression	This attribute is required.

Example: The following example checks to see whether a state is a known state and displays an appropriate message:

```
<CFSWITCH EXPRESSION="#UCase(state)#">
  <CFCASE VALUE="CA">California</CFCASE>
  <CFCASE VALUE="FL">Florida</CFCASE>
  <CFCASE VALUE="MI">Michigan</CFCASE>
  <CFCASEDEFAULT>One of the other 47 states</CFCASEDEFAULT>
</CFSWITCH>
```

You can replace some long <CFSWITH><CFCASE...> statements with a structure. Look at this code:

```
<CFSWITCH EXPRESSION="#FORM.Meal#">
    <CFCASE VALUE="Breakfast">
        <CFSET Drink="Coffee">
    </CFCASE>
    <CFCASE VALUE="Lunch">
        <CFSET Drink="Iced Tea">
    </CFCASE>
    <CFCASE VALUE="Snack">
        <CFSET Drink="Coke">
    </CFCASE>
```

```
        <CFCASE VALUE="Dinner">
            <CFSET Drink="Wine">
        </CFCASE>
    </CFSWITCH>
```

Now, assume you have built this structure:

```
<CFSET Beverages=StructNew()>
<CFSET Beverages["Breakfast"]="Coffee">
<CFSET Beverages["Lunch"]="Iced Tea">
<CFSET Beverages["Snack"]="Coke">
<CFSET Beverages["Dinner"]="Wine">
<CFSET meal=FORM.Lunch>
```

NOTE

Given this structure, the following single line of code eliminates the need for the lengthy switch/case logic shown previously:

```
<CSET Drink=Beverages["#meal#"]>
```

➜ *See also* `<CFIF>, <CFCASE>, <CFDEFAULTCASE>`

<CFTABLE>

Description: <CFTABLE> enables you to easily create tables in which dynamically generated query data is displayed. <CFTABLE> can create HTML tables (using the <TABLE> tag) or preformatted text tables (using <PRE>, </PRE>) that display on all browsers. Using <CFTABLE> involves two tags: <CFTABLE> defines the table itself, and one or more <CFCOL> tags define the table columns. The <CFTABLE> attributes are listed in Table B.121.

Syntax:

```
<CFTABLE QUERY="Query Name"
    MAXROWS="Maximum Rows"
    COLSPACING="Column Spacing"
    BORDER="Border Size"
    HEADERLINES="Header Lines"
    HTMLTABLE
    COLHEADERS>
<CFCOL HEADER="Header Text"
    WIDTH="Width"
    ALIGN="Alignment"
    TEXT="Body Text">
</CFTABLE>
```

Table B.121 <CFTABLE> Attributes

ATTRIBUTE	DESCRIPTION	NOTES
BORDER	Adds border to HTML table	Optional; use when specifying HTMLTABLE.
COLHEADERS	Displays column headers	Optional; column headers are displayed as specified in <CFCOL>.
COLSPACING	Spaces between columns	Optional; overrides the default column spacing of 2 if present.

Table B.121 (continued)

ATTRIBUTE	DESCRIPTION	NOTES
HEADERLINES	Number of header lines	Optional; defaults to 2; one for the header and a blank row between the header and the body. You can increase this number if needed.
HTMLTABLE	Creates an HTML table	Optional; an HTML table is created if this attribute is present. If not, a preformatted text table is created.
MAXROWS	Maximum number of table rows	Optional; specifies the maximum number of rows to be displayed in the table.
QUERY	<CFQUERY> name	Required; the name of the query from which to derive the table body text.

Example: This example queries a database and then displays the output using <CFTABLE> and <CFCOL>:

```
<!--- Gets raw data from database --->
<CFQUERY NAME="GetFilms" DATASOURCE="OWS">
    SELECT FilmID, MovieTitle
    FROM Films
</CFQUERY>
<H1>Use of CFTABLE and CFCOL</H1>
<!--- creates table from query results --->
<CFTABLE QUERY="GetFilms">
    <!--- creates table column --->
    <CFCOL HEADER="Film ID"
        WIDTH="8"
        ALIGN="Right"
        TEXT="<EM>#FilmID#</EM>">
    <!--- creates table column --->
    <CFCOL HEADER="Name"
        WIDTH="30"
        ALIGN="Left"
        TEXT="#MovieTitle#">
</CFTABLE>
```

NOTE

The <CFTABLE> tag is an easy and efficient way to create tables for displaying query results. You should create HTML tables manually for greater control over table output, including cell spanning, text and background colors, borders, background images, and nested tables.

➜ *See also* <CFCOL>, <CFOUTPUT>, <CFQUERY>

<CFTEXTINPUT>

Description: <CFTEXTINPUT> embeds a highly configurable Java text input control in your HTML forms. <CFTEXTINPUT> must be used between <CFFORM> and </CFFORM> tags. Unlike the standard HTML INPUT, <CFTEXTINPUT> lets you configure the exact height and width of the edit control, as well as color, font, size, and spacing. <CFTEXTINPUT> also can automatically generate field JavaScript validation code. Table B.122 lists the <CFTEXTINPUT> attributes.

Syntax:

```
<CFTEXTINPUT ALIGN="Alignment"
    BGCOLOR="Background Color"
    BOLD="Yes or No"
    FONT="Font Face"
    FONTSIZE="Font Size"
    HEIGHT="Control Height"
    HSPACE="Horizontal Spacing"
    ITALIC="Yes or No"
    MAXLENGTH="Maximum Length"
    MESSAGE="Error Message"
    NAME="Field Name"
    NOTSUPPORTED="Non Java Browser Code"
    ONERROR="Error Function"
    ONVALIDATE="Validation Function"
    RANGE="Numeric Range"
    REQUIRED="Yes or No"
    SIZE="Field Size"
    TEXTCOLOR="Text Color"
    VALIDATE="Validation Type"
    VALUE="Initial Value"
    VSPACE="Vertical Spacing"
    WIDTH="Control Width">
```

Table B.122 <CFTEXTINPUT> Attributes

ATTRIBUTE	DESCRIPTION	NOTES
ALIGN	Control alignment	Optional. Possible values are TOP, LEFT, BOTTOM, BASELINE, TEXTTOP, ABSBOTTOM, MIDDLE, ABSMIDDLE, and RIGHT.
BGCOLOR	Background color	Optional; possible values are BLACK, BLUE, RED, CYAN, DARKGRAY, GRAY, LIGHTGRAY, MAGENTA, ORANGE, PINK, WHITE, YELLOW, or any color specified in RGB form.
BOLD	YES or NO	Optional; specifies use of boldfaced text; defaults to NO.
FONT	Font face	Optional; font face to use.
FONTSIZE	Font size number	Optional; font size.
HEIGHT	Number of pixels	Optional; controls height.
HSPACE	Number of pixels	Optional; specifies horizontal spacing in pixels.
ITALIC	YES or NO	Optional; specifies use of italic font; defaults to NO.
MAXLENGTH	Number of characters	Optional; maximum number of characters to allow.
MESSAGE	Validation failure message	Optional; message to display upon validation failure.
NAME	Unique control name	Required.
NOTSUPPORTED	Text to be used for non- Java browsers	Optional; text (or HTML code) to be displayed on non–Java-capable browsers.

Table B.122 (CONTINUED)

ATTRIBUTE	DESCRIPTION	NOTES
ONERROR	JavaScript error function	Optional; specifies your own JavaScript error message function to override ColdFusion's.
ONVALIDATE	JavaScript validation function	Optional; specifies your own JavaScript validation function to override ColdFusion's.
RANGE	Min number, Max number	Optional; range for numeric values only; specified as two numbers separated by a comm1.
REQUIRED	YES or NO	Optional; YES indicates that a value is required. Defaults to NO.
SIZE	Number of characters	Optional; field size; number of characters to display before needing horizontal scrolling.
TEXTCOLOR	Text color	Optional attribute; possible values are BLACK, BLUE, RED, CYAN, DARKGRAY, GRAY, LIGHTGRAY, MAGENTA, ORANGE, PINK, WHITE, YELLOW, or any color specified in RGB form.
VALIDATE	Field validation	Optional field validation. If specified, must be any of the validation types listed in Table B.123.
VALUE	Initial value	Optional.
VSPACE	Number of pixels	Optional; vertical spacing for control.
WIDTH	Number of pixels	Optional; controls width.

Table B.123 <CFTEXTINPUT> Validation Types

TYPE	DESCRIPTION
CREDITCARD	Correctly formatted credit card number verified using mod10 algorithm.
DATE	Date in mm/dd/yy format.
EURODATE	European date in dd/mm/yy format.
FLOAT	Number with decimal point.
INTEGER	Number with no decimal point.
SOCIAL_SECURITY_NUMBER	Social security number formatted as 999-99-9999 (using hyphens or spaces as separators).
TELEPHONE	Phone number in 999-999-9999 format (using hyphens or spaces as separators); area code and exchange must not begin with 0 or 1.
TIME	Time in hh:mm or hh:mm:ss format.
ZIPCODE	U.S. ZIP code, either 99999 or 99999-9999 format.

Example: The following example displays a form in which the user enters a credit card number and expiration date. Two <CFTEXTINPUT> controls are used—one for each field. Attributes are used to make the fields required and control their sizes and font colors. In addition, a custom validation function, CheckExpDate(), is specified to validate the expiration date.

```
<!--- creates JavaScript function --->
<SCRIPT LANGUAGE="JavaScript">
    function CheckExpDate() {
    if (blah blah blah) {return true} else {return false};
    }
</SCRIPT>
<!--- creates form --->
<CFFORM ACTION="process.cfm"
    METHOD="POST">
<!--- creates text field --->
<P>Enter your credit card number:
<CFTEXTINPUT NAME="CCnumber"
    HEIGHT="25"
    WIDTH="200"
    FONT="Verdana"
    BGCOLOR="white"
    TEXTCOLOR="Blue"
    VALIDATE="creditcard"
    REQUIRED="Yes"
    MESSAGE="Please enter a valid credit card number">
<!--- creates text field --->
<P>Enter the expiration date (mm/yy):
<CFTEXTINPUT NAME="ExpDate"
    HEIGHT="25"
    WIDTH="90"
    FONT="Verdana"
    BGCOLOR="white"
    TEXTCOLOR="Blue"
    MAXLENGTH="5"
    REQUIRED="Yes"
    ONVALIDATE="CheckExpDate()"
    MESSAGE="Please enter a valid expiration date in the form mm/yy">
<!--- creates submit button --->
<INPUT TYPE="Submit" VALUE="Buy it!">
</CFFORM>
```

NOTE

The <CFTEXTINPUT> control is accessible only by users with Java-enabled browsers.

➜ *See also* <CFFORM>, <CFGRID>, <CFINPUT>, <CFSELECT>, <CFSLIDER>, <CFTREE>

<CFTHROW>

Description: <CFTHROW> is used to force an error condition in a <CFTRY>, </CFTRY> block. Program control is then handed to a <CFCATCH> in which TYPE is set to APPLICATION, ANY, or a custom type. You can optionally use this tag to invoke a Java exception. <CFTHROW> attributes are listed in Table B.124.

Syntax for throwing a normal exception:

```
<CFTHROW
   DETAIL="Error description"
   ERRORCODE="Code"
   EXTENDEDINFO="More error information"
   MESSAGE="message"   TYPE="Error type">
```

Syntax for throwing Java exception:

```
<CFTHROW
   OBJECT="object name">
```

Table B.124 `<CFTHROW>` Attributes

ATTRIBUTE	DESCRIPTION	NOTES
DETAIL	Description of error	Optional; detailed description of error.
ERRORCODE	Custom error code	Optional; developer-specified error code.
EXTENDEDINFO	Additional info	Optional; additional information on the error.
MESSAGE	Error message	Optional; developer-specified description.
OBJECT	Name of object	Optional; mutually exclusive with all other tag attributes. This is the value of the NAME attribute from an object invoked with <CFOBJECT>.
TYPE	Type of error	Optional; must be either APPLICATION or a condition custom type. If you use APPLICATION, you do not have to specify a TYPE for <CFCATCH>.

Example: This code checks for the existence of a specified SESSION variable. If it doesn't exist, a custom, developer-specified error is thrown and trapped in the <CFCATCH> of the specified, custom type:

```
<!--- sets trap for errors --->
<CFTRY>
    <!--- if variable is not present --->
    <CFIF NOT IsDefined("SESSION.UserID")>
    <!--- creates custom error type --->
    <CFTHROW TYPE="AppSecurity"
        MESSAGE="Invalid auhthorization"
        ERRORCODE="210"
        DETAIL="Access is restricted to authenticated users">
    </CFIF>
<!--- catches app security errors --->
<CFCATCH TYPE="AppSecurity">
    <!--- displays error messages --->
    <CFOUTPUT>
        <p>(#CFCATCH.ErrorCode#) <B>#CFCATCH.Message#</B>
        <p>#CFCATCH.Detail#
    </CFOUTPUT>
</CFCATCH>
</CFTRY>
```

➜ *See also* <CFTRY>, <CFCATCH>

In this second example, a Java object is instantiated for the purpose of handling the error that you throw:

```
<CFOBJECT
   TYPE="Java"
   ACTION="Create"
   CLASS="coldfusion.tagext.InvalidTagAttributeException"
   NAME="MyObj">
<CFSET MyObj.init("SomeAttribute", "SomeValue")>

...

<CFTHROW OBJECT=#MyObj#>
```

<CFTRACE>

Description: <CFTRACE> logs and provides debugging information about the state of the application when it is called. Output is logged to the file logs\cftrace.log, in the directory in which ColdFusion was installed. It provides a variety of useful information including variable values, logic flow and execution time. This information can be displayed with the page output and in Dreamweaver 5 (or later). The <CFTRACE> attributes are list in Table B.125.

Syntax:

```
<CFTRACE ABORT="Yes or No"
    CATEGORY="Category name"
    INLINE="Yes or No"
    TEXT="String to be logged"
    TYPE="Output format type"
     VAR="Variable name">
```

Table B.125 <CFTRACE> Attributes

ATTRIBUTE	DESCRIPTION	NOTES
ABORT	YES or NO	Optional; indicates whether or not processing is to be aborted after <CFTRACE> execution.
CATEGORY	User-defined value	Optional; user-defined name of category for identifying related traces. Enables you to identify purpose of related traces in the generated log file.
INLINE	YES or NO	Optional; when set to YES, output is flushed to page as tag executes, even if used in <CFSILENT>.
TEXT	User-defined value	Optional; is output to the Text column in the log file attribute. Used for tracking related tag traces.
TYPE	Optional	Optional; indicates output format as one of the following types: Information, Warning, Error, Fatal Information. Populates CFLOG column with the same name.
VAR	Variable name	Optional; name of specific variable—either simple or complex—which is to be displayed. Complex variables are displayed in same format as using <CFDUMP>.

NOTE

Note that in order for `<CFTRACE>` to work, you must enable debugging (on the Debugging settings page) in the ColdFusion Administrator.

Example: This example logs the value of a the `OpenOrderTotal` variable and logs it with the `CATEGORY` set to the name of the current application:

```
<!--- Create structure for passing arguments and instantiate object. --->
<CFSCRIPT>
   DateRange = StructNew();
   DateRange.StartDate = "1/1/2002";
   DateRange.EndDate = "3/22/2002";
   CreateObject("Component", "Orders");
</CFSCRIPT>
<!--- Now execute the method and pass it the structure of arguments. --->
<CFINVOKE COMPONENT="Orders" METHOD="OrderTotal"
   RETURNVARIABLE="OpenOrderTotal" ARGUMENTCOLLECTION="#DateRange#">
</CFINVOKE>
<CFTRACE VAR="OpenOrderTotal" TYPE="information"
   CATEGORY="My Variables" TEXT="This is a trace operation.">
```

The resulting cftrac.log entry looks like this:

```
"Information","web-7","03/24/02","19:17:48","OWS","[{ts '2002-03-24
19:17:48'}] [0 ms] [] - [My Variables] [OpenOrderTotal = 83.99]
This is a trace operation. "
```

➜ *See also* `<CFDUMP>`

<CFTRANSACTION>

Description: `<CFTRANSACTION>` enables you to group multiple `<CFQUERY>` uses into a single transaction. Any `<CFQUERY>` tags placed between `<CFTRANSACTION>` and `</CFTRANSACTION>` tags are rolled back if an error occurs. The `<CFTRANSACTION>` attributes are listed in Table B.126.

Syntax:

```
<CFTRANSACTION ISOLATION="Lock Type"
    ACTION="Action">
Queries
</CFTRANSACTION>
```

Table B.126 `<CFTRANSACTION>` Attributes

ATTRIBUTE	DESCRIPTION	NOTES
ACTION	Type of action	Optional; BEGIN (default), COMMIT, or ROLLBACK.
ISOLATION	Type of ODBC lock	Optional lock type; possible values are READ_UNCOMMITTED, READ_COMMITTED, REPEATABLE_READ, and SERIALIZABLE.

`ACTION` of `BEGIN` signifies the start transaction. You can nest `<CFTRANSACTION>` tags and force commits or rollbacks by setting `ACTION` to `COMMIT` or `ROLLBACK` in your nested transactions.

NOTE

When <CFTRANSACTION> is used in combination with ColdFusion's error handling, you can tell when a database transaction fails. This gives you control over whether queries grouped into transactions are to be committed or rolled back.

NOTE

Not all lock types are supported by all ODBC drivers. Consult your database documentation before using the `ISOLATION` attribute.

Example: The first example demonstrates a simple use of <CFTRANSACTION> to ensure that either both queries succeed or the transaction is canceled:

```
<!--- encapsulates queries into one unit --->
<CFTRANSACTION>
    <!--- gets raw data from database --->
    <CFQUERY NAME="InsertContact" DATASOURCE="OWS">
        INSERT INTO Contacts (FirstName, LastName, Phone, UserLogin)
        VALUES ('Joe', 'Blow', '333-112-1212', 'JoeBlow')
    </CFQUERY>
    <!--- gets raw data from database --->
    <CFQUERY NAME="InsertActor" DATASOURCE="OWS">
        INSERT INTO Actors (NameFirst, NameLast, Gender)
        VALUES ('Joe', 'Blow', 'M')
    </CFQUERY>
</CFTRANSACTION>
```

The second example does the same thing but demonstrates the use of <CFTRANSACTION ACTION="Rollback"> and <CFTRANSACTION ACTION="Commit">. Note that these aren't really required in this simple example; it's just being done this way to demonstrate the technique.

```
<!--- sets variable --->
<CFSET DoCommit="Yes">
<!--- starts code execution --->
<CFTRANSACTION ACTION="BEGIN">
<!--- sets trap for errors --->
<CFTRY>
<!--- gets raw data from database --->
<CFQUERY NAME="InsertContact" DATASOURCE="OWS">
    INSERT INTO Contacts (FirstName, LastName, Phone, UserLogin)
    VALUES ('Joe', 'Blow', '333-112-1212', 'JoeBlow')
 </CFQUERY>
 <!--- gets raw data from database --->
<CFQUERY NAME="InsertActor" DATASOURCE="OWS">
    INSERT INTO Actors (NameFirst, NameLast, Gender)
    VALUES ('Joe', 'Blow', 'M')
 </CFQUERY>
<!--- catches erros --->
<CFCATCH TYPE="DATABASE">
    <!--- starts transaction over --->
    <CFTRANSACTION ACTION="ROLLBACK"/>
    <!--- sets variable --->
    <CFSET DoCommit="No">
</CFCATCH>
</CFTRY>
```

```
<!--- if variable is Yes, transaction is processed --->
<CFIF DoCommit EQ Yes>
    <CFTRANSACTION ACTION="COMMIT"/>
<!--- if variable doesn't equal Yes, message is displayed --->
<CFELSE>
    <p>Failure
</CFIF>
</CFTRANSACTION>
```

NOTE

The use of abbreviated ending tag syntax, as shown in the previous example, enables you to omit the ending tag. It's valid in this situation because there is no body between the beginning and ending tag.

➜ *See also* <CFSTOREDPROC>

<CFTREE>

Description: <CFTREE> embeds a Java tree control in your HTML forms constructed with <CFFORM>. The tree control is similar to the Explorer window used in several versions of Windows and is in fact used in the ColdFusion Administrator (when browsing for an ODBC data source). The tree is made of root entries and branches that can be expanded or closed. Branches can be nested. Each branch has a graphic displayed next to it; you can select from any of the supplied graphics or use any of your own.

<CFTREE> trees are constructed using two tags. <CFTREE> creates the tree control, and <CFTREEITEM> adds the entries into the tree. Trees can be populated one branch at a time or by using query results. <CFTREEITEM> must be used between <CFTREE> and </CFTREE> tags. <CFTREE> attributes are listed in Table B.127.

Syntax:

```
<CFTREE ALIGN="Alignment"
    APPENDKEY="Yes or No"
    BOLD="Yes or No"
    BORDER="Yes or No"
    COMPLETEPATH="Yes or No"
    DELIMITER="Delimiter Character"
    FONT="Font Face"
    FONTSIZE="Font Size"
    HEIGHT="Control Height"
    HIGHLIGHTHREF="Yes or No"
    HSPACE="Horizontal Spacing"
    HSCROLL="Yes or No"
    ITALIC="Yes or No"
    MESSAGE="Error Message"
    NAME="Field Name"
    NOTSUPPORTED="Non Java Browser Code"
    ONERROR="Error Function"
    ONVALIDATE="Validation Function"
    REQUIRED="Yes or No"
    VSPACE="Vertical Spacing"
    WIDTH="Control Width">
```

Table B.127 <CFTREE> Attributes

ATTRIBUTE	DESCRIPTION	NOTES
ALIGN	Control alignment	Optional. Possible values are TOP, LEFT, BOTTOM, BASELINE, TEXTTOP, ABSBOTTOM, MIDDLE, ABSMIDDLE, and RIGHT.
APPENDKEY	YES or NO	Optional; appends item key to URL. If YES, variable named CFTREEITEMKEY is appended to the URL containing the item selected; defaults to YES.
BOLD	YES or NO	Optional; makes text bold; defaults to NO.
BORDER	YES or NO	Optional; displays border; defaults to YES.
COMPLETEPATH	YES or NO	Optional; passes the full tree path to the selected item when set to YES; defaults to NO.
DELIMITER	Path delimiter character	Optional; defaults to \.
FONT	Font face name	Optional font face to use.
FONTSIZE	Number of pixels	Optional font size.
HEIGHT	Number of pixels	Optional height in pixels.
HIGHLIGHTHREF	YES or NO	Optional; links are highlighted and underlined if YES; defaults to YES.
HSPACE	Number of pixels	Optional; horizontal spacing in pixels.
HSCROLL	YES or NO	Optional; displays horizontal scrollbar; default is YES.
ITALIC	YES or NO	Optional; italicizes text; defaults to NO.
MESSAGE	Validation failure message	Optional; message to display upon validation failure.
NAME	Unique control name	Required.
NOTSUPPORTED	Text message	Optional; text (or HTML code) to be displayed on non-Java–capable browsers.
ONERROR	JavaScript error function	Optional override to your own JavaScript error message function.
ONVALIDATE	JavaScript function	Optional override to your own JavaScript validation function.
REQUIRED	YES OR NO	Optional; a selection will be required when set to YES; defaults to NO.
VSPACE	Number of pixels	Optional; vertical spacing in pixels.
VSCROLL	YES OR NO	Optional; displays a vertical scrollbar when set to YES; default is YES.
WIDTH	Number of pixels	Optional; width of control.

Example: This example creates a simple Java tree control with three branches:

```
<!--- creates directory structure --->
<CFTREEITEM DISPLAY="Display Text
    EXPAND="Yes or No"
    HREF="URL"
    IMG="Images"
    IMGOPEN="Images"
    QUERY="Query Name"
    QUERYASROOT="Yes or No"
    TARGET="Target Name"
    PARENT="Parent Branch"
    VALUE="Values">

<!--- creates form --->
<CFFORM ACTION="process.cfm">
<!--- populates tree branches with data --->
<CFTREE NAME="states">
    <CFTREEITEM VALUE="US">
    <CFTREEITEM VALUE="CA" DISPLAY="California" PARENT="US">
    <CFTREEITEM VALUE="MI" DISPLAY="Michigan" PARENT="US">
    <CFTREEITEM VALUE="NY" DISPLAY="New York" PARENT="US">
</CFTREE>
<!--- creates submit button --->
<INPUT TYPE="Submit" VALUE="Select a State">
</CFFORM>
```

This next example populates a tree with a query called `Users`:

```
<!--- gets raw data from database --->
<CFQUERY NAME="GetUsers" DATASOURCE="ows">
    SELECT ContactID, FirstName & ' ' & LastName as userName, UserLogin
    FROM Contacts
</CFQUERY>
<!--- creates form --->
<CFFORM ACTION="process.cfm">
<!--- creates tree --->
<CFTREE NAME="peopletree"
    HSPACE="20"
    HSCROLL="no"
    VSCROLL="Yes"
    DELIMITER="?"
    BORDER="Yes">
<!--- populates tree with query results --->
<CFTREEITEM VALUE="UserName"
    QUERYASROOT="Yes"
    QUERY="GetUsers"
    IMG="folder,document"
    HREF="EditUser.cfm">
</CFTREE>
</CFFORM>
```

The last example demonstrates the use of <CFTREE> to produce a tree with nested branches. In this case, it displays a list of movies and the actors in the movies.

```
<!--- gets raw data from database --->
<CFQUERY NAME="GetFilmActors" DATASOURCE="ows">
    SELECT F1.FilmID, 1.NameFirst, 1.NameLast, F.MovieTitle
    FROM (Actors A INNER JOIN FilmsActors FA ON 1.ActorID = F1.ActorID)
    INNER JOIN Films F ON F1.FilmID = F.FilmID
</CFQUERY>
<!--- creates form  --->
<CFFORM ACTION="process.cfm">
<!--- creates tree --->
<CFTREE NAME="FilmActors"
    HEIGHT="150"
    WIDTH="300"
    HIGHLIGHTHREF="Yes">
<!--- displays query results in table --->
<CFOUTPUT QUERY="GetFilmActors" GROUP="FilmID">
<CFTREEITEM VALUE="#MovieTitle#" EXPAND="No">
<CFOUTPUT>
<!--- creates tree branches --->
<CFTREEITEM IMG="Document"
    VALUE="#NameFirst# #NameLast#"
    HREF="ViewActor.cfm"
    PARENT="#MovieTitle#">
</CFOUTPUT>
</CFOUTPUT>
</CFTREE>
</CFFORM>
```

NOTE

The <CFTREE> control is accessible only by users with Java-enabled browsers.

➜ *See also* <CFFORM>, <CFGRID>, <CFINPUT>, <CFSELECT>, <CFSLIDER>, <CFTEXTINPUT>

<CFTREEITEM>

Description: <CFTREE> trees are constructed using two tags. <CFTREE> creates the tree control, and <CFTREEITEM> adds the entries into the tree. Trees can be populated one branch at a time or by using query results. <CFTREEITEM> must be used between <CFTREE> and </CFTREE> tags. <CFTREE> attributes are listed in Table B.128.

Syntax:

```
<CFTREEITEM DISPLAY="Display Text
    EXPAND="Yes or No"
    HREF="URL"
    IMG="Images"
    IMGOPEN="Images"
    QUERY="Query Name"
    QUERYASROOT="Yes or No"
    TARGET="Target Name"
    PARENT="Parent Branch"
    VALUE="Values">
```

Table B.128 <CFTREEITEM> Attributes

ATTRIBUTE	DESCRIPTION	NOTES
DISPLAY	Display text	Optional attribute. Defaults to value is not specified. If populating with a query resultset, this value should be a comma-delimited list of values—one for each tree item.
EXPAND	YES or NO	Optional; branch is initially expanded if YES; defaults to NO.
HREF	Item URL	Optional; URL to go to when an item is selected; if populating with a query resultset, this value can be a comma-delimited list of URLs (one for each tree item), or it can be a column name. In that case, it is populated dynamically.
IMG	Image	Optional; image to be displayed; if populating with a query resultset, this value should be a comma-delimited list of images, one for each tree level; images can be CD, COMPUTER, DOCUMENT, ELEMENT, FIXED, FOLDER, FLOPPY, REMOTE, or any image file of your own.
IMGOPEN	Open image	Optional; image to be displayed when branch is open; if populating with a query resultset, this value should be a comma-delimited list of images, one for each tree level; same selections as IMG. If omitted, the IMG image is used.
PARENT	Parent item name	Optional; name of parent item to attach this branch to.
QUERY	Query name	Optional query name to be used to populate the list.
QUERYASROOT	YES or NO	Optional; if YES, query name itself is the tree root branch; defaults to NO. Prevents having to create a parent tree item.
TARGET	Target for HREF	Optional; the window in which to open the link; this value can be a comma-delimited list of targets if populating with a query resultset, one for each tree item.
VALUE	Value to be returned	Required; value to be returned when item is selected. Value should be a comma-delimited list of values, one for each tree item, if populating with a query resultset.

Example: See example for <CFTREE>

➜ *See also* <CFTREE>

<CFTRY>

Description: <CFTRY> is used to catch exceptions thrown by ColdFusion or explicitly with <CFTHROW> or <CFRETHROW>. All code between <CFTRY> and </CFTRY> can throw exceptions, and exceptions are caught by <CFCATCH> blocks. <CFTRY> has not attribute. Explicit <CFCATCH> blocks can be created for various error types, or one block can catch all errors. <CFCATCH> has one attribute, TYPE, which is described in Table B.129. B.130 lists the acceptable values of the TYPE attribute. A special structure variable, CFCATCH, is available in your <CFCATCH> blocks. Its elements are described in Table B.131.

Syntax:

```
<CFTRY>
    <CFCATCH TYPE="type">
    </CFCATCH>
</CFTRY>
```

Table B.129 <CFCATCH> Attributes

ATTRIBUTE	DESCRIPTION	NOTES
TYPE	Exception type	Optional; values listed in Table B.130.

Table B.130 <CFCATCH> TYPE Values

TYPE
ANY
APPLICATION
Custom_Type
DATABASE
EXPRESSION
LOCK
MISSINGINCLUDE
OBJECT
SEARCHENGINE
SECURITY
TEMPLATE

Table B.131 CFCATCH Variable Elements

TYPE	ONLY FOR TYPE	DESCRIPTION
DETAIL		A detailed error message; helps determine which tag threw the exception.
ERRNUMBER	EXPRESSION	Internal expression error number.

Table B.131 (continued)

TYPE	ONLY FOR TYPE	DESCRIPTION
ERRORCODE	Custom_Type	Developer-specified error code.
EXTENDEDINFO	APPLICATION Custom Type	Developer's custom error message.
LOCKNAME	LOCK	Name of the affected lock; set to anonymous if the lock was unnamed.
LOCKOPERATION	LOCK	Operation that failed; TIMEOUT, CREATE MUTEX, or UNKNOWN.
MESSAGE		Diagnostic message; can be null.
MISSINGFILENAME	MISSINGINCLUDE	Name of file that could not be included.
NATIVEERRORCODE	DATABASE	The native error code from the database driver; -1 if no native code provided.
SQLSTATE	DATABASE	Another error code from the database driver; -1 if no native code provided.
TAGCONTEXT		Tag stack; name and position of each tag in the stack.
TYPE		Exception type, as specified in <CFCATCH>.

Example: This example traps for an error when attempting to create a new directory programmatically:

```
<!--- sets trap for errors --->
<CFTRY>
<CFDIRECTORY ACTION="CREATE" DIRECTORY="#FORM.UserDir#">
    <!--- catches any errors --->
    <CFCATCH TYPE="ANY">
    <!--- if error contains a certain phrase, message is displayed --->
    <CFIF CFCATCH.Detail CONTAINS "when that file already exists">
        <P>Cannot create directory: this directory already exists.
    <CFELSE>
    <!--- if error does not contain specified phrase, the error details
    are displayed --->
    <CFOUTPUT>#CFCATCH.Detail#</CFOUTPUT>
    </CFIF>
        <CFABORT>
</CFCATCH>
</CFTRY>
<P>Directory created.
```

You will find other useful examples in the entries for <CFRETHROW>, <CFAUTHENTICATE>, and <CFTRANSACTION>.

➜ *See also* <CFTHROW>, <CFRETHROW>

<CFUPDATE>

Description: `<CFUPDATE>` updates a single row to a database table; it requires that the database and table names be provided. All other attributes are optional. The full list of `<CFUPDATE>` attributes is explained in Table B.132.

Syntax:

```
<CFUPDATE   DATASOURCE=" Data Source"
   FORMFIELDS="List of File to Update"
   PASSWORD="Password"
   TABLENAME="Table Name"
   TABLEOWNER="owner"
   TABLEQUALIFIER="qualifier"
   USERNAME="User Name">
```

Table B.132 `<CFUPDATE>` Attributes

ATTRIBUTE	DESCRIPTION	NOTES
DATASOURCE	Name of data source	Required; data source name.
FORMFIELDS	List of fields to insert	Optional; specifies which fields are to be updated if they are present. Any fields present that are not in the list will not be updated.
PASSWORD	ODBC data source password	Optional; used to override the ODBC login password specified in the ColdFusion Administrator.
TABLENAME	Name of table to insert data into	Required; some ODBC data sources require fully qualified table names.
TABLEOWNER	Table owner name	Optional; used by databases that support table ownership.
TABLEQUALIFIER	Table qualifier	Optional; used by databases that support full qualifiers.
USERNAME	ODBC data source login name	Optional; used to override the ODBC login name specified in the ColdFusion Administrator.

NOTE

For `<CFUPDATE>` to work correctly, your form field names must match the column names in the destination table, and the primary key value of the row to be updated must be specified.

TIP

If your form contains fields that are not part of the table you are updating, use the `FORMFIELDS` attribute to instruct ColdFusion to ignore those fields.

TIP

For more control over updating rows in a database table, use the `<CFQUERY>` tag specifying `UPDATE` as the SQL statement.

Example: In the first example, a simple data entry form is used to collect data to be updated in the `Merchandise` table:

```
<!--- creates form --->
<FORM ACTION="update_act.cfm" METHOD="post">
<P>film id: <INPUT TYPE="Text" MAXLENGTH="5" NAME="filmid" value="18">
<P>merchandise name: <INPUT TYPE="Text" NAME="MerchName" MAXLENGTH="100">
<P>merchandise desc: <INPUT TYPE="Text" NAME="MerchDescription">
<P>merchandise price: <INPUT TYPE="Text" NAME="MerchPrice">
<p><INPUT TYPE="Submit">
</FORM>
```

This `<CFUPDATE>` tag updates the table from this form data:

```
<!--- updates database --->
<CFUPDATE DATASOURCE="OWS" TABLENAME="Merchandise">
```

However, if the form contains additional fields that don't correspond to the fields in the `Merchandise` table, you must use the `FORMFIELDS` attribute to identify which form fields are to be inserted:

```
<!--- updates database with only the specified variables --->
<CFUPDATE DATASOURCE="OWS"
    TABLENAME="Merchandise"
    FORMFIELDS="FilmID,MerchName,MerchDescription,MerchPrice">
```

➜ *See also* `<CFUPDATE>`, `<CFQUERY>`

<CFWDDX>

Description: `<CFWDDX>` is used to serialize and deserialize ColdFusion data structures to the XML-based WDDX format. Starting with ColdFusion MX, this tag supports different encoding formats. UTF-8 is the default. It now also preserves the case of column names in JavaScript. The attributes for this tag are shown in Table B.133. The `ACTION` attribute specifies the action to be performed. The values for the `ACTION` attribute are shown in Table B.134.

Syntax:

```
<CFWDDX ACTION="action"
    INPUT="input"
    OUTPUT="output"
    TOPLEVELVARIABLE="name"
    USETIMEZONEINFO="Yes or No">
```

Table B.133 `<CFWDDX>` Attributes

ATTRIBUTE	DESCRIPTION	NOTES
`ACTION`	Action	Required; actions are listed in Table B.134.
`INPUT`	Input value	Required.
`OUTPUT`	Output variable	Required if `ACTION` is `WDDX2CFML`.
`TOPLEVELVARIABLE`	JavaScript top-level variable	Required if `ACTION` is `WDDX2JS` or `FML2JS`.
`USETIMEZONEINFO`	`YES` or `NO`	Optional; indicates whether to include time zone information (in ISO8601 format) when data is being serialized; defaults to `YES`.

Table B.134 <CFWDDX> Actions

ACTION	DESCRIPTION
CFML2JS	Serializes CFML to JavaScript format.
CFML2WDDX	Serializes CFML to WDDX format.
WDDX2CFML	Deserializes WDDX to CFML.
WDDX2JS	Deserializes WDDX to JavaScript.

Example: The example demonstrates serializing and deserializing a ColdFusion query result.

```
<!--- gets raw data from database --->
<CFQUERY NAME="GetContacts" DATASOURCE="OWS">
   SELECT ContactID, FirstName, LastName
   FROM Contacts
</CFQUERY>
<P>The recordset data is:
<UL>
<!--- displays query results --->
<CFOUTPUT QUERY="GetContacts">
   <li>#ContactID#, #FirstName#, #LastName#
</CFOUTPUT>
</UL>
<!--- Serializes CFML to WDDX packet --->
<P>Serializing CFML data
<CFWDDX ACTION="cfml2wddx"
   INPUT="#GetContacts#"
   OUTPUT="Contacts">
<!--- displays WDDX packet --->
<P>Resulting WDDX packet is:
<XMP><CFOUTPUT>#Contacts#</CFOUTPUT></XMP>
<!--- deserializes WDDX packet --->
<P>Deserializing WDDX to CMFL <P>
<CFWDDX ACTION="WDDX2CFML" INPUT="#Contacts#" OUTPUT="NewContacts">

<P>The recordset data is:
<UL>
<!--- displays query results --->
<CFOUTPUT QUERY="GetContacts">
   <LI>#ContactID#, #FirstName#, #LastName#<BR>
</CFOUTPUT>
</UL>
```

<CFXML>

Description: <CFXML> parses an XML document and creates a ColdFusion XML document object from the tag body. The body of the tag can contain both XML content and CFML tags. If you include CFML tags in the body, they are processed first and the results are converted into a ColdFusion XML document object. A ColdFusion XML document object is a complex structure that breaks down the various parts of the XML document. The attributes for the <CFXML> tag are presented in Table B.135.

A ColdFusion XML document object is a complex structure that ColdFusion builds from a parsed XML document. All ColdFusion XML document objects are comprised of all the same elements, but the values of and number of elements will change from one object to the next (based on the underlying XML content). Once the XML document has been parsed into this format through <CFXML>, you can then do what ever your application requires using CFML.

The structure of the ColdFusion XML document object can be thought of as consisting of two main levels: a top level, the elements of which are shown in Table B.136, and all levels below the top. Table B.137 shows these elements.

Syntax:

```
<CFXML VARIABLE="Name of variable"
    CASESENSITIVE="Yes or No" >
```

Table B.135 <CFXML> Attributes

ATTRIBUTE	DESCRIPTION	NOTES
VARIABLE	Variable name	Required; the variable into which the XML document object is to be stored.
CASESENSITIVE	YES or NO	Optional; indicates whether or not the case of the original XML element names and attributes is to be preserved. Defaults to NO.

Table B.136 ColdFusion XML document object top level structure

STRUCTURE ELEMENT	TYPE	DESCRIPTION
XmlRoot	Element	The root of the entire document.
XmlComment	String	The concatenation of the XML document's prologue and epilogue comments. Note that the comments that may be contained in document elements are not included.
XmlDocType	Node	If the XML document included a doctype, it will be contained in this node. This is not displayed through <CFDUMP>.

Table B.137 ColdFusion XML document object structure for levels below top

STRUCTURE ELEMENT	TYPE	DESCRIPTION
XmlName	String	Element name.
XmlNsPrefix	String	Namespace prefix.
XmlNsURI	String	Namespace URI.
XmlText	String	All the text in the element (not including any element children). Note that any XML CData is concatenated on.

Table B.137 (continued)

STRUCTURE ELEMENT	TYPE	DESCRIPTION
`XmlComment`	String	The concatenated comments in the element (not including any element children).
`XmlAttributes`	Structure	This element's attributes, presented as name/value pairs.
`XmlChildren`	Array	The children of this element.
`XmlParent`	Node	This contains the parent DOM node of this element. It is not displayed in `<CFDUMP>` output.
`XmlNodes`	Array	Contains the XML DOM nodes of this element. Does not appear in `<CFDUMP>` output of the element.

Example: The first example demonstrates the production of an XML document object.

```
<!--- Produce a ColdFusion XML document object
      from the the 'orders' XML document --->
<CFXML VARIABLE="XMLdoc">
<orders>
   <order orderid="1"
    orderdate="3/1/2001"
    shipaddress="1 Rue Street"
    shipcity="Brussels"
    shipzip="1234"
    shipstate="">
      <orderitem orderitemid="1"
       itemid="6"
       orderqty="2"
       itemprice="30.00"/>
      <orderitem orderitemid="2"
       itemid="1"
       orderqty="1"
       itemprice="17.50"/>
      <orderitem orderitemid="3"
       itemid="9"
       orderqty="1"
       itemprice="100.00"/>
   </order>
   <order orderid="2"
    orderdate="3/1/2001"
    shipaddress="21700 Northwestern Hwy"
    shipcity="Southfield"
    shipzip="48075"
    shipstate="Michigan">
      <orderitem orderitemid="4"
       itemid="11"
       orderqty="10"
       itemprice="7.50"/>
   </order>
</orders>
</CFXML>
<!--- Display contents of XML document object --->
<CFDUMP VAR="#XMLdoc#">
```

The second example demonstrates the production of the same XML document object, but here the underlying XML document is produced dynamically based on a query result.

```
<!--- First select data to work with, linking
      order line items to orders --->
<CFQUERY NAME="GetOrders" DATABASE="OWS">
   SELECT O.OrderID, OrderDate, ShipAddress, ShipCity
     ShipZip, ShipState, OrderItemID, ItemID, OrderQty,
     ItemPrice
   FROM Orders O INNER JOIN MerchandiseOrdersItems OI
     ON O.OrderID = OI.OrderID
     ORDER BY OrderID, OrderItemID
</CFQUERY>
<!--- Produce a ColdFusion XML document object
      from the the 'orders' XML document --->
<CFXML VARIABLE="XMLdoc">
<orders>
   <!--- Outer CFOUTPUT creates order data --->
   <CFOUTPUT QUERY="GetOrders" GROUP="OrderID">
   <order orderid="#OrderID#"
    orderdate="#OrderDate#"
    shipaddress="#ShipAddress#"
    shipcity="#ShipCity#"
    shipzip="#ShipZip#"
    shipstate="#ShipState#">
      <CFOUTPUT> <!--- Line item detail --->
      <orderitem orderitemid="#OrderItemID#"
       itemid="#ItemID#"
       orderqty="#OrderQty#"
       itemprice="#ItemPrice#"/>
      </CFOUTPUT> <!--- Inner CFOUTPUT (Order lines) --->
   </order>
</CFOUTPUT> <!--- Outer CFOUTPUT (Orders) --->
</orders>
</CFXML>
<!--- Display contents of XML document object --->
<CFDUMP VAR="#XMLdoc#">
```

ColdFusion Function Reference

IN THIS APPENDIX

Macromedia ColdFusion MX provides a complete set of data-manipulation and formatting functions. Here are some things to remember when using functions:

- Function names are not case-sensitive, so `NOW()` is the same as `now()`, which is the same as `Now()`.
- When functions are used in body text rather than within a ColdFusion tag, they must be enclosed within `<CFOUTPUT>` tags.
- Functions can be nested.

In this chapter, the functions are presented in alphabetical order and are cross-referenced to any related functions wherever appropriate.

Functions by Topic

The following sections list ColdFusion by topics, meaning that the functions in each section perform related tasks.

String-Manipulation Functions

The ColdFusion string-manipulation functions can be used to perform operations on character data. Strings can be hard-coded constants, table column values, or ColdFusion fields. As with all ColdFusion functions, these string-manipulation functions can be nested.

Table C.1 contains the available functions for string manipulation–related processing.

Table C.1 String-Manipulation Functions

FUNCTION	DESCRIPTION
`Asc()`	Returns the ASCII value of the leftmost character of a string, `0` if the string is empty
`Chr()`	Converts an ASCII value into a printable character
`CJustify()`	Centers a string within a field of a specified length
`Compare()`	Performs a case-sensitive comparison on two strings
`CompareNoCase()`	Performs a case-insensitive comparison on two strings
`Decrypt()`	Decrypts a string encrypted with `Encrypt()`
`Encrypt()`	Encrypts a string using a user-specified key
`Find()`	Performs a case-sensitive substring search
`FindNoCase()`	Performs a case-insensitive substring search
`FindOneOf()`	Returns the position of the first target string character that matches any of the characters in a specified set
`GetToken()`	Extracts specific sets of data within a string by specifying its index
`Hash()`	Converts a string into a 32-byte hexadecimal string using the one-way MD5 algorithm
`InputBaseN()`	Converts a string into a number using the base specified by radix
`Insert()`	Inserts text into a string
`LCase()`	Converts a string to lowercase
`Left()`	Returns the specified leftmost characters from the beginning of a string
`Len()`	Returns the length of a specified string
`LJustify()`	Left-aligns a string within a field of a specified length
`LTrim()`	Trims white space from the beginning of a string
`Mid()`	Returns a string of characters from any location in a string
`REFind()`	Performs a case-sensitive search using regular expressions
`REFindNoCase()`	Performs a case-insensitive search using regular expressions
`RemoveChars()`	Returns a string with specified characters removed from it
`RepeatString()`	Returns a string made up of a specified string repeated multiple times
`Replace()`	Replaces text within strings with alternative text
`ReplaceList()`	Replaces all occurrences of elements in one string with corresponding elements in another
`REReplace()`	Performs a case-sensitive search and replace using regular expressions
`REReplaceNoCase()`	Performs a case-insensitive search and replace using regular expressions
`Reverse()`	Reverses the characters in a string
`Right()`	Returns the specified rightmost characters from the end of a string
`RJustify()`	Right-aligns a string within a field of a specified length

Table C.1 (continued)

FUNCTION	DESCRIPTION
`RTrim()`	Trims white space from the end of a string
`SpanExcluding()`	Extracts characters from the beginning of a string until a character that is part of a specified set is reached
`SpanIncluding()`	Extracts characters from the beginning of a string only as long as they match characters in a specified set
`StripCR()`	Removes all carriage-return characters from a string
`ToBase64()`	Returns the Base64 representation of a specified string or binary object
`ToBinary()`	Converts a Base64-encoded string to a binary object
`Trim()`	Trims white space from the beginning and end of a string
`UCase()`	Converts a string to uppercase
`Val()`	Converts the beginning of a string to a number

`Date` and `Time` Functions

The ColdFusion `Date` and `Time` functions enable you to perform date and time manipulation on table columns and user-supplied fields.

Many of these functions work with date/time objects. A date/time object is a ColdFusion internal representation of a complete date and time, with accuracy to the second. These objects are designed to facilitate the passing of date/time information between various ColdFusion functions and are not designed to be displayed as is. If you need to display a date/time object, you must use one of the date/time formatting functions.

NOTE

ColdFusion date/time objects are not the same as ODBC date/time fields. Use the `CreateODBCDateTime()` function to convert ColdFusion date/time objects to the ODBC format.

Many ColdFusion date and time functions take date and time values as parameters. These parameters must be valid and within a set range; otherwise, a ColdFusion syntax error is generated. The range of values allowed for each date and time field is listed in Table C.2.

Table C.2 Valid ColdFusion Date and Time Values

FIELD	MIN.	MAX.
Year	0	9999
Month	1	12
Day	1	31
Hour	0	23
Minute	0	59
Second	0	59

NOTE

Year values of less than `100` are treated as twentieth century values, and `1900` is added automatically to them.

Several of the ColdFusion date and time functions enable you to work with parts of the complete date/time object—to add days or weeks to a date, or to find out how many weeks apart two dates are, for example. These functions require you to pass a date/time part specifier that is passed as a string. (They must have quotation marks around them.) The complete list of specifiers is explained in Table C.3.

Table C.3 ColdFusion Date/Time Specifiers

SPECIFIER	DESCRIPTION
D	Day
H	Hour
M	Month
N	Minute
Q	Quarter
S	Second
W	Weekday (day of week)
WW	Week
Y	Day of year
YYYY	Year

Table C.4 contains the available fuctions for date- and time-related processing.

Table C.4 Date and Time Functions

FUNCTION	DESCRIPTION
`CreateDate()`	Returns a ColdFusion date/time object that can be used with other date-manipulation or formatting functions
`CreateDateTime()`	Returns a ColdFusion date/time object that can be used with other date- and time-manipulation or formatting functions
`CreateODBCDate()`	Returns a date in an ODBC date/time field that can safely be used in SQL statements
`CreateODBCDateTime()`	Returns an ODBC date/time field that can safely be used in SQL statements
`CreateODBCTime()`	Returns a time in an ODBC date/time field that can safely be used in SQL statements
`CreateTime()`	Returns a time in a ColdFusion date/time object that can be used with other time-manipulation or formatting functions

Table C.4 (continued)

FUNCTION	DESCRIPTION
`CreateTimeSpan()`	Creates a date/time object that can be used to rapidly perform date- and time-based calculations
`DateAdd()`	Adds or subtracts values to a date/time object
`DateCompare()`	Compares two dates to determine whether they are the same or whether one is greater than the other
`DateConvert()`	Converts local machine time to UTC (Universal Coordinated Time) time or vice versa
`DateDiff()`	Returns the difference between two dates
`DatePart()`	Returns the specified part of a passed date
`Day()`	Returns a date/time object's day of month as a numeric value
`DayOfWeek()`	Returns a date/time object's day of week as a numeric value
`DayOfWeekAsString()`	Returns the English weekday name for a passed day-of-week number
`DayOfYear()`	Returns a date/time object's day of year as a numeric value
`DaysInMonth()`	Returns the number of days in a specified month
`DaysInYear()`	Returns the number of days in a specified year
`FirstDayOfMonth()`	Returns the day of year on which a specified month starts
`GetHTTPTimeString()`	Formats a ColdFusion date/time object according to the HTTP standard outlined in RFC 1123
`GetTimeZoneInfo()`	Returns a structure containing relevant server time zone information
`Hour()`	Returns a date/time object's hour as a numeric value
`IsDate()`	Checks whether a string contains a valid date
`IsLeapYear()`	Checks whether a specified year is a leap year
`IsNumericDate()`	Checks whether a value passed as a date in the ColdFusion internal date format is in fact a legitimate date
`Minute()`	Returns a date/time object's minute as a numeric value
`Month()`	Returns a date/time object's month as a numeric value
`MonthAsString()`	Returns the English month name for a passed month number
`Now()`	Returns a date/time object containing the current date and time
`ParseDateTime()`	Converts a date in string form into a ColdFusion date/time object
`Quarter()`	Returns a date/time object's quarter as a numeric value
`Second()`	Returns a date/time object's second as a numeric value
`Week()`	Returns a date/time object's week in year as a numeric value
`Year()`	Returns a date/time object's year as a numeric value

Data Formatting Functions

Powerful data-manipulation functions and database-interaction capabilities are pretty useless unless you have ways to display data in a clean, readable format. ColdFusion data addresses this need by providing an array of highly capable formatting functions.

Many of these functions take optional format masks as parameters, thereby giving you an even greater level of control over the final output.

Table C.5 contains the available functions for data format–related processing.

Table C.5 Data Formatting Functions

FUNCTION	DESCRIPTION
`DateFormat()`	Displays the date portion of a date/time object in a readable format
`DecimalFormat()`	Outputs numbers with two decimal places, commas to separate the thousands, and a minus sign for negative values
`DollarFormat()`	Outputs numbers with a dollar sign at the front, two decimal places, commas to separate the thousands, and a minus sign for negative values
`FormatBaseN()`	Converts a number to a string using the base specified
`HTMLCodeFormat()`	Displays text with HTML codes using a preformatted HTML block
`HTMLEditFormat()`	Converts supplied text into a safe format, converting any HTML control characters to their appropriate entity codes
`NumberFormat()`	Displays numeric values in a readable format
`TimeFormat()`	Displays the time portion of a date/time object in a readable format
`ParagraphFormat()`	Converts text with embedded carriage returns for correct HTML display
`YesNoFormat()`	Converts `TRUE` and `FALSE` values to `Yes` and `No`

Mathematical Functions

To assist you in performing calculations, ColdFusion comes with a complete suite of mathematical functions, random number–generation functions, and arithmetic expressions. As with all ColdFusion functions, these mathematical functions can be nested.

Some of the mathematical functions take one or more numeric values as parameters. You can pass real values, integer values, and ColdFusion fields to these functions.

Table C.6 lists the supported arithmetic expressions.

Table C.6 ColdFusion Arithmetic Expressions

EXPRESSION	DESCRIPTION
+	Addition
-	Subtraction
*	Multiplication
/	Division
MOD	Modular (finds remainder)
\	Integer division (both values must be integers)
^	Power

Table C.7 contains the available functions for mathematical processing.

Table C.7 Mathematical Functions

FUNCTION	DESCRIPTION
`Abs()`	Absolute value of the passed number
`Acos()`	Arccosine of the passed number
`Asin()`	Arcsine of the passed number, in radians
`Atn()`	Arctangent of the passed number
`Ceiling()`	The closest integer greater than the passed number
`Cos()`	Cosine of the passed number
`DecrementValue()`	Number decremented by 1
`Exp()`	E to the power of the passed number
`Fix()`	The closest integer smaller than the passed number, if the passed number is greater than or equal to `0`. Otherwise, the closest integer greater than the passed number
`IncrementValue()`	Number incremented by 1
`Int()`	The closest integer smaller than the passed number
`Log()`	Natural logarithm of the passed number
`Log10()`	Base 10 log of the passed number
`Max()`	The greater of two passed numbers
`Min()`	The smaller of two passed numbers
`Pi()`	Value of pi as 3.14159265359
`Rand()`	A random number between 0 and 1

Table C.7 (continued)

FUNCTION	DESCRIPTION
`Randomize()`	The random number generator seeded with the passed number
`RandRange()`	A random integer value between two passed numbers
`Round()`	The integer closest (either greater or smaller) to the passed number
`Sgn()`	Sign—either –1, 0, or 1, depending on whether the passed number is negative, 0, or positive
`Sin()`	Sine of the passed number
`Sqr()`	Square root of the passed number
`Tan()`	Tangent of the passed number

International Functions

ColdFusion fully supports the display, formatting, and manipulation of international dates, times, numbers, and currencies. To use ColdFusion's international support, you must specify the locale. A locale is an encapsulation of the set of attributes that govern the display and formatting of international date, time, number, and currency values. The complete list of supported locales is shown in Table C.8.

NOTE

Note that because ColdFusion is now a Java-based application, you must use Java standard locales, as opposed to the locales supported by ColdFusion 5.

You will find information on standard locales here:

```
http://www.inter-locale.com/demos/locales.jsp
```

Table C.8 ColdFusion Locales

JAVA STANDARD LOCALE	COLDFUSION 5 LOCALE
nl_be	Dutch (Belgian)
nl_NL	Dutch (Standard)
en_AU	English (Australian)
en_CA	English (Canadian)
en_NZ	English (New Zealand)
en_GB	English (UK)
en_US	English (US)
fr_BE	French (Belgian)
fr_CA	French (Canadian)
fr_FR	French (Standard)
fr_CH	French (Swiss)

Table C.8 (CONTINUED)

JAVA STANDARD LOCALE	COLDFUSION 5 LOCALE
de_AT	German (Austrian)
de_DE	German (Standard)
de_CH	German (Swiss)
it_IT	Italian (Standard)
it_CH	Italian (Swiss)
ja_JP	Japanese
ko_KR	Korean
no_NO	Norwegian (Bokmal)
no_NO_nynorsk	Norwegian (Nynorsk)
pt_BR	Portuguese (Brazilian)
pt_PT	Portuguese (Standard)
Deprecated	Spanish (Mexican)
es_ES	Spanish (Modern)
es_ES	Spanish (Standard)
sv_SE	Swedish

You must use the `SetLocale()` function to set the locale. You can retrieve the name of the locale currently in use with the `GetLocale()` function.

To use ColdFusion's international support, you must use the LS functions listed later in this section. These functions behave much like the standard date, time, and formatting functions, but they honor the current locale setting.

NOTE

The ColdFusion server variable `SERVER.ColdFusion.SupportedLocales` contains a comma-delimited list of the supported locales.

Table C.9 contains the available functions for international-related processing.

Table C.9 International Functions

FUNCTION	DESCRIPTION
`GetLocale()`	Returns the name of the locale currently in use
`LSCurrencyFormat()`	Displays currency information formatted for the current locale
`LSDateFormat()`	Displays the date portion of a date/time object in a readable format
`LSEuroCurrencyFormat()`	Displays euro currency formatted correctly
`LSIsCurrency()`	Checks whether a string contains a valid currency for the current locale

Table C.9 (continued)

FUNCTION	DESCRIPTION
`LSIsDate()`	Checks whether a string contains a valid date for the current locale
`LSIsNumeric()`	Checks whether a specified value is numeric, taking into account the current locale
`LSNumberFormat()`	Displays numeric values in a locale-specific, readable format
`LSParseCurrency()`	Converts a locale-specific number in string form into a valid number
`LSParseDateTime()`	Converts a locale-specific date in string form into a ColdFusion date/time object
`LSParseEuroCurrency()`	Converts a currency string containing the euro symbol or sign to a number
`LSParseNumber()`	Converts a locale-specific number in string form into a valid number
`LSTimeFormat()`	Displays the time portion of a date/time object in a locale-specific, readable format
`SetLocale()`	Sets the name of the locale to be used by any subsequent calls to the LS functions

List-Manipulation Functions

ColdFusion lists are an efficient way to manage groups of information. Lists are made up of elements, which are values separated by delimiting characters. The default delimiter is a comma, but you can change it to any character or string if required. Lists are actually simple two-dimensional arrays. For more complex or multidimensional lists, you should use arrays instead.

This list format is well-suited for ColdFusion applications; it is both the format that HTML forms use to submit fields with multiple values and the format used by SQL to specify lists in SQL statements.

When using the list-manipulation functions, remember the following:

- List-manipulation functions that add to, delete from, or change a list do not alter the original list passed to them. Rather, they return an altered list to you for manipulation. If you do need to update the passed list itself, you must use `<CFSET>` to replace the list with the newly modified list.
- All list functions accept as an optional last parameter a string with delimiters to be used in the processing of the list. If this parameter is omitted, the default comma delimiter is used.
- The number 1 is always the starting position in any list. When referencing list functions, be sure to remember that lists always start at position 1, never 0.
- When evaluating a list, be aware that ColdFusion will ignore any empty items in a list. If you have a list defined as `"Laura, John, Sean, , ,Bryan"`, it will be evaluated as a four-element list, not a six-element list.

NOTE

All the ColdFusion list-manipulation functions have names that begin with the word `list`, making them easy to spot in your code.

TIP

Lists can be used in conjunction with the `<CFLOOP>` tag for processing.

Table C.10 contains the available functions for list manipulation–related processing.

Table C.10 List-Manipulation Functions

FUNCTION	DESCRIPTION
`ListAppend()`	Adds an element to the end of a list
`ListChangeDelims()`	Changes a list's delimiters
`ListContains()`	Performs a case-sensitive list search for an element containing specified text
`ListContainsNoCase()`	Performs a case-insensitive list search for an element containing specified text
`ListDeleteAt()`	Deletes an element from a list
`ListFind()`	Performs a case-sensitive list search for a specific element
`ListFindNoCase()`	Performs a case-insensitive list search for a specific element
`ListFirst()`	Returns the first element in a list
`ListGetAt()`	Gets a specific list element by index
`ListInsertAt()`	Inserts an element into a list
`ListLast()`	Returns the last element in a list
`ListLen()`	Returns the number of elements in a list
`ListPrepend()`	Inserts an element at the beginning of a list
`ListSort()`	Sorts a list
`ListQualify()`	Returns the contents of a specified list with qualifying characters around each list element
`ListRest()`	Returns a list containing all the elements after the first element
`ListSetAt()`	Sets a specific list element by index
`ListValueCount()`	Performs a case-sensitive search and returns the number of matching elements in a list
`ListValueCountNoCase()`	Performs a case-insensitive search and returns the number of matching elements in a list

Array-Manipulation Functions

Arrays are special variables made up of collections of data. Array elements are accessed via their indexes into the array; to access the third element of a simple array, for example, you would refer to `array[3]`.

ColdFusion supports arrays that use between one and three dimensions. A one-dimensional array is similar to a list, whereas a two-dimensional array is similar to a grid. (In fact, under the hood, ColdFusion queries are essentially two-dimensional arrays.) Three-dimensional arrays are more like cubes.

Arrays are created using the `ArrayNew()` function. To create an array, you must specify the number of dimensions needed, from one to three. You don't need to specify how many elements will be stored in the array; ColdFusion automatically expands the array as necessary.

NOTE

Array elements can be added in any order. If you add an element `10` to an array that has only five elements, ColdFusion automatically creates elements `6-9` for you.

Table C.11 contains the available functions for array manipulation–related processing.

Table C.11 Array-Manipulation Functions

FUNCTION	DESCRIPTION
`ArrayAppend()`	Appends an element to an array
`ArrayAvg()`	Returns the average numeric value in an array
`ArrayClear()`	Deletes all data from an array
`ArrayDeleteAt()`	Deletes a specific array element
`ArrayInsertAt()`	Inserts an element into an array
`ArrayIsEmpty()`	Checks whether an array has any data
`ArrayLen()`	Returns the length of an array
`ArrayMax()`	Returns the greatest numeric value in an array
`ArrayMin()`	Returns the lowest numeric value in an array
`ArrayNew()`	Creates a new array
`ArrayPrepend()`	Inserts an element at the beginning of an array
`ArrayResize()`	Resizes an array
`ArraySet()`	Sets a specific array element
`ArraySort()`	Sorts an array
`ArraySum()`	Returns the sum of numeric values in an array
`ArraySwap()`	Swaps the values in two array elements
`ArrayToList()`	Converts a one-dimensional array to a list
`IsArray()`	Checks whether a variable is a valid ColdFusion array
`ListToArray()`	Converts a list to a one-dimensional array

Structure-Manipulation Functions

ColdFusion structures are special data types that contain one or more other variables. Structures are a way to group related variables together.

Table C.12 contains the available functions for structure manipulation–related processing.

Table C.12 Structure-Manipulation Functions

FUNCTION	DESCRIPTION
`Duplicate()`	Returns a deep copy of a structure
`IsStruct()`	Checks whether a variable is a valid ColdFusion structure
`StructAppend()`	Appends an item to a structure
`StructClear()`	Deletes all data from a structure
`StructCopy()`	Returns a clone of the specified structure, with all the keys and values of the specified structure intact
`StructCount()`	Returns the number of items in a specified structure
`StructDelete()`	Deletes an item from a structure
`StructFind()`	Searches through a structure to find the key that matches the specified search text
`StructInsert()`	Inserts an item into a structure
`StructIsEmpty()`	Checks whether a structure has data
`StructKeyArray()`	Returns the keys of a specified structure in an array
`StructKeyExists()`	Checks whether a structure contains a specified key
`StructKeyList()`	Returns a list of keys in the specified ColdFusion structure
`StructFindKey()`	Finds a structure item by key
`StructFindValue()`	Finds a structure item by value
`StructGet()`	Gets a structure item
`StructNew()`	Creates a new structure
`StructSort()`	Sorts a structure
`StructUpdate()`	Updates the specified key in a given structure with a specified value

Query-Manipulation Functions

ColdFusion uses queries to return sets of data. Most queries are created with the `<CFQUERY>` tag, but other tags (`<CFPOP>` and `<CFLDAP>`) also return data in queries. Additionally, ColdFusion enables you to programmatically create your own queries using the `QueryNew` function and set query values using `QuerySetCell`.

NOTE

ColdFusion queries are essentially arrays with named columns. You therefore can use any of the array functions with queries.

Table C.13 contains the available functions for query manipulation–related processing.

Table C.13 Query-Manipulation Functions

FUNCTION	DESCRIPTION
`IsQuery()`	Checks whether a variable is a valid ColdFusion query
`QueryAddColumn()`	Adds a new column to a specified query
`QueryAddRow()`	Adds a row to an existing ColdFusion query
`QueryNew()`	Returns a new query object, optionally with specified columns
`QuerySetCell()`	Sets the values of specific cells in a query

Security Functions

ColdFusion supports advanced security contexts that let you create complete security systems to secure your applications. Security is managed and maintained using the ColdFusion Administrator. After security is established, you can make a call to the `<CFAUTHENTICATE>` tag to return security information. Use these security functions to interact with that security information.

Table C.14 contains the available functions for security-related processing.

Table C.14 Security Functions

FUNCTION	DESCRIPTION
`AuthenticatedContext()`	Deprecated (no longer in use)
`AuthenticatedUser()`	Deprecated (no longer in use)
`GetAuthUser()`	Returns the ID of the user currently logged in to the ColdFusion security framework
`IsAuthenticated()`	Deprecated (no longer in use)
`IsAuthorized()`	Deprecated (no longer in use)
`IsProtected()`	Deprecated (no longer in use)
`IsUserInRole()`	Checks to see if current user (logged in to the ColdFusion security framework) is in the specified role. Returns `True` or `False`

System Functions

The ColdFusion system functions enable you to perform manipulation of file paths, create temporary files, and verify file existence.

Table C.15 contains the available functions for system-related processing.

Table C.15 System Functions

FUNCTION	DESCRIPTION
`DirectoryExists()`	Checks for the existence of a specified directory
`ExpandPath()`	Converts a relative or absolute path into a fully qualified path
`FileExists()`	Checks for the existence of a specified file
`GetCurrentTemlatePath()`	Returns the complete path of the template calling this function
`GetDirectoryFromPath()`	Extracts the drive and directory (with a trailing backslash) from a fully specified path
`GetFileFromPath()`	Extracts the filename from a fully specified path
`GetMetaData()`	Gets metadata from an object that supports introspection
`GetMetricData()`	Deprecated (no longer in use)
`GetProfileString()`	Gets the value of a profile entry in an .ini-format initialization file
`GetTempDirectory()`	Returns the full path of the operating system temporary directory
`GetTempFile()`	Creates and returns the full path to a temporary file for use by your application
`GetTemplatePath()`	Deprecated (no longer in use)
`SetProfileString()`	Sets the value of a profile entry in an .ini-format initialization file

Client Variable-Manipulation Functions

Client variables enable you to store client information so it is available between sessions. Client variables can be accessed just like any other ColdFusion variables; standard variable access tools, such as `<CFSET>`, can therefore be used to set variables. In addition, these functions provide special variable-manipulation capabilities.

Table C.16 contains the available functions for client variable manipulation–related processing.

Table C.16 Client Variable–Manipulation Functions

FUNCTION	DESCRIPTION
`DeleteClientVariable()`	Deletes specified client variables
`GetClientVariableList()`	Returns a comma-delimited list of the read/write client variables available for use

Expression Evaluation Functions

ColdFusion enables you to perform dynamic expression evaluation. This is an advanced technique that allows you to build and evaluate expressions on the fly.

Dynamic expression evaluations are performed on string expressions. A string expression is just that—a string that contains an expression. The string `"1+2"` contains an expression that, when evaluated, returns `3`. String expressions can be as simple or as complex as necessary.

Table C.17 contains the available functions for expression evaluation–related processing.

Table C.17 Expression Evaluation Functions

FUNCTION	DESCRIPTION
`DE()`	Flags an expression for delayed evaluation
`Evaluate()`	Evaluates string expressions
`IIf()`	Performs an inline if statement
`SetVariable()`	Sets a specified variable to a passed value

Bit- and Set-Manipulation Functions

ColdFusion provides a complete set of bit-manipulation functions for use by advanced developers only. These functions enable you to manipulate the individual bits within a 32-bit integer.

NOTE

Any start, length, or position parameters passed to the bit-manipulation functions must be in the range of `0-31`.

Table C.18 contains the available functions for bit- and set-manipulation–related processing.

Table C.18 Bit-Manipulation Functions

FUNCTION	DESCRIPTION
`BitAnd(x, y)`	Returns `x` and `y`
`BitMaskClear(x, start, length)`	Returns `x` with bits of *length* cleared, beginning at the *start*ing position
`BitMaskRead(x, start, length)`	The value of x with bits of length *length*, beginning at the *start*ing position
`BitMaskSet(x, mask, start, length)`	Returns `x` with mask occupying the *length* bits beginning at the *start*ing position
`BitNot(x)`	Returns not `x`
`BitOr(x, y)`	Returns `x | y`
`BitSHLN(x, n)`	Returns `x << n`
`BitSHRN(x, n)`	Returns `x >> n`
`BitXor(x, y)`	Returns `x^y`

Conversion Functions

These functions are provided to enable you to easily convert data from one type to another. This list is not all-inclusive; some data-conversion functions are listed elsewhere throughout this appendix.

Table C.19 contains the available functions for conversion-related processing.

Table C.19 Conversion Functions

FUNCTION	DESCRIPTION
`JavaCast()`	Casts a variable for use within a Java object
`JSStringFormat()`	Formats a specified string so that it is safe to use with JavaScript
`ToString()`	Converts any value, including binary values, into a string

XML Functions

The following functions were introduced in ColdFusion MX and enable you to work with Extended Markup Language (XML) documents and ColdFusion XML objects. Table C.20 lists the functions that can be used to process XML. Also note that `ToString()` can be used on an XML document object.

Table C.20 XML Functions

FUNCTION	DESCRIPTION
`IsXMLDoc()`	Returns `TRUE` or `FALSE` indicating whether the parameter is a valid XML document object
`IsXMLElem()`	Returns `TRUE` or `FALSE` indicating whether the parameter is an XML document object element
`IsXMLRoot()`	Returns `TRUE` or `FALSE` indicating whether the function argument is the root element of an XML document object
`XMLChildPos()`	Returns the position of a child in an array of XML children
`XMLElemNew()`	Returns the XML document object (first parameter) with a new element (specified in the second parameter)
`XMLFormat()`	Returns a string formatted in which special XML characters are escaped
`XMLNew()`	Creates an XML document object
`XMLParse()`	Searches through a string of XML for a document tree object and returns that object
`XMLSearch()`	Returns an array of XML object nodes after searching for an XPath through an XML document string
`XMLTransform()`	Applies an XML style sheet (XSLT) to an XML document string and returns the XSL-formatted string

Miscellaneous Functions

The following functions are listed here to give you access to some of the lesser-known yet nonetheless important functions available to you in ColdFusion 5.

Table C.21 contains the available miscellaneous functions.

Table C.21 Miscellaneous Functions

FUNCTION	DESCRIPTION
`CreateObject()`	Instantiates COM, CORBA, Java objects, and ColdFusion components
`CreateUUID()`	Returns a 35-character string representation of a unique 128-bit number
`GetBaseTagData()`	Returns an object containing data from a specified ancestor tag
`GetBaseTagList()`	Returns a comma-delimited list of base tag names
`GetBaseTemplatePath()`	Returns the full path of the base template
`GetException()`	Retrieves a Java exception from a Java object
`GetFunctionList()`	Returns a structure containing all of the built-in functions available in ColdFusion
`GetHTTPRequestData()`	Retrieves the HTTP request headers and body and makes them available for use
`GetK2ServerCollections()`	Deprecated (no longer in use)
`GetK2ServerDocCount()`	Returns the number of documents in all Verity K2-indexed collections
`GetK2ServerDocCountLimit()`	Returns the maximum number of indexed documents allowed by the Verity K2 server
`GetTickCount()`	Returns a tick count used to perform timing tests, with millisecond accuracy
`IsBinary()`	Tests whether a specified value is binary
`IsBoolean()`	Determines whether a value can be converted to a Boolean value
`IsCustomFunction()`	Checks whether a specified function is a user-defined function
`IsDebugMode()`	Checks whether a page is being sent back to the user in debug mode
`IsDefined()`	Determines whether a specified variable exists
`IsK2ServerDocCountExceeded()`	Determines whether the maximum number of allowed documents in Verity K2 collections has been exceeded
`IsK2ServerOnline()`	Determines whether ColdFusion's Verity K2 server is up
`IsNumeric()`	Checks whether a specified value is numeric

Table C.21 (continued)

Function	Description
`IsObject()`	Determines whether the value is a specified type of object
`IsSimpleValue()`	Checks whether a value is a string, a number, a `TRUE/FALSE` value, or a date/time object
`ParameterExists()`	Deprecated (no longer in use). Use `IsDefined()` instead
`PreserveSingleQuotes()`	Instructs ColdFusion to not escape single quotation marks contained in values derived from dynamic parameters
`QuotedValueList()`	Returns a list of values in a specified query column, with all values enclosed within quotes
`URLDecode()`	Decodes a URL-encoded string
`URLEncodedFormat()`	Encodes a string in a format that can safely be used within URLs
`ValueList()`	Returns a list of values in a specified query column
`WriteOutput()`	Appends text to the page output stream

Alphabetical List of ColdFusion Functions

In the following list, note that you must insert all examples between `<CFOUTPUT>` and `</CFOUTPUT>`. In addition, all examples must be enclosed with pound signs (##).

Abs()

Description: `Abs()` returns the absolute value of a passed number. This function takes only one numeric value as a parameter. You can pass real values, integer values, and ColdFusion fields to this function.

Syntax:

```
Abs(number)
```

Example: The following example returns `5`, the absolute value of `-5`:

```
#Abs("-5")#
```

➜ *See also* `Sgn()`

Acos()

Description: `Acos()` returns the arccosine of a passed number. This function takes only one numeric value as a parameter. You can pass real values, integer values, and ColdFusion fields to this function.

Syntax:

```
Acos(number)
```

Example: The following example returns `1.53578917702`, the arccosine of .035:

```
#Acos(".035")#
```

➜ *See also* `Asin()`, `Cos()`, `Pi()`, `Sin()`, `Tan()`

ArrayAppend()

Description: `ArrayAppend()` adds an element to the end of an array. `ArrayAppend()` takes two parameters: the array to which the element is to be appended and the data to be stored in that element. `ArrayAppend()` returns `TRUE` if the operation is successful.

Syntax:

```
ArrayAppend(Array, Value)
```

Example: The following example appends an element containing the word `January` to an array:

```
#ArrayAppend(Month, "January")#
```

This next example appends an element to a three-dimensional array, setting the value of element `[10][1]`:

```
#ArrayAppend(Users[10][1], "January")#
```

NOTE

You can set the values of explicit array elements using the `<CFSET>` tag.

➜ *See also* `ArrayInsertAt()`, `ArrayPrepend()`

ArrayAvg()

Description: `ArrayAvg()` returns the average numeric value in an array. `ArrayAvg()` takes a single parameter: the array to be checked.

Syntax:

```
ArrayAvg(Array)
```

Example: The following example reports the average cost of items in an array:

```
The average cost of each item in the list is #DollarFormat(ArrayAvg(items))#
```

NOTE

`ArrayAvg()` works only with arrays containing numeric data. Do not use this function with arrays that contain text data.

➜ *See also* `ArrayMin()`, `ArrayMax()`, `ArraySum()`

ArrayClear()

Description: `ArrayClear()` deletes all data from an array. `ArrayClear()` takes a single parameter: the array to be deleted. `ArrayClear()` returns `TRUE` if the operation is successful.

Syntax:

```
ArrayClear(Array)
```

Example: The following example empties an existing array:

```
<CFSET result = #ArrayClear(Items)#>
```

NOTE

`ArrayClear()` does not delete the actual array. Rather, it removes all the contents from it. The array itself remains and can be reused.

➜ *See also* `ArrayDeleteAt()`, `ArrayIsEmpty()`

`ArrayDeleteAt()`

Description: `ArrayDeleteAt()` deletes an element from an array at a specified position, pulling all remaining elements back one place. `ArrayDeleteAt()` takes two parameters: the array from which to delete the element and the position of the element to delete. `ArrayDeleteAt()` returns `TRUE` if the operation is successful.

Syntax:

```
ArrayDeleteAt(Array, Position)
```

Example: The following example deletes the ninth element from an array:

```
#ArrayDeleteAt(Items, 9)#
```

➜ *See also* `ArrayClear()`, `ArrayInsertAt()`

`ArrayInsertAt()`

Description: `ArrayInsertAt()` inserts an element into an array at a specified position, pushing over one place all existing elements with an index greater than the index of the element inserted. `ArrayInsertAt()` takes three parameters: the array into which to insert the element, the position at which to insert the element, and the data to be stored in that element. `ArrayInsertAt()` returns `TRUE` if the operation is successful.

Syntax:

```
ArrayInsertAt(Array, Position, Value)
```

Example: The following example inserts an element containing the word `Alaska` into the second position of an existing two-dimensional array; it then sets the abbreviation `AK` into the matching second dimension:

```
<CFSET result = #ArrayInsertAt(States[1], 2, "Alaska")#>
<CFSET States[2][2] = "AK">
```

➜ *See also* `ArrayAppend()`, `ArrayDeleteAt()`, `ArrayPrepend()`

`ArrayIsEmpty()`

Description: `ArrayIsEmpty()` checks whether an array has data. `ArrayIsEmpty()` takes a single parameter: the array to be checked. `ArrayIsEmpty()` returns `TRUE` if the array is empty and `FALSE` if not.

Syntax:

```
ArrayIsEmpty(Array)
```

Example: The following example reports whether an array is empty:

```
<CFOUTPUT>Array empty: #YesNoFormat(ArrayIsEmpty(Users))#</CFOUTPUT>
```

→ *See also* `ArrayClear()`, `ArrayLen()`, `IsArray()`

ArrayLen()

Description: `ArrayLen()` returns the length of a specified array. `ArrayLen()` takes a single parameter: the array to be checked.

Syntax:

```
ArrayLen(Array)
```

Example: The following example reports the size of an array:

```
The items array has #ArrayLen(items)# elements
```

→ *See also* `ArrayIsEmpty()`, `ArrayResize()`

ArrayMax()

Description: `ArrayMax()` returns the largest numeric value in an array. `ArrayMax()` takes a single parameter: the array to be checked.

Syntax:

```
ArrayMax(Array)
```

Example: The following example reports the cost of the most expensive item in an array:

```
The most expensive item in the list costs #DollarFormat(ArrayMax(items))#
```

NOTE

`ArrayMax()` works only with arrays containing numeric data. Do not use this function with arrays that contain text data.

→ *See also* `ArrayAvg()`, `ArrayMin()`, `ArraySum()`

ArrayMin()

Description: `ArrayMin()` returns the smallest numeric value in an array. `ArrayMin()` takes a single parameter: the array to be checked.

Syntax:

```
ArrayMin(Array)
```

Example: The following example reports the cost of the least expensive item in an array:

```
The least expensive item in the list costs #DollarFormat(ArrayMin(items))#
```

NOTE

`ArrayMin()` works only with arrays containing numeric data. Do not use this function with arrays that contain text data.

→ *See also* `ArrayAvg()`, `ArrayMax()`, `ArraySum()`

ArrayNew()

Description: `ArrayNew()` is used to create an array. `ArrayNew()` takes a single parameter: the number of dimensions needed. Valid dimensions are one through three. `ArrayNew()` returns the array itself.

Syntax:

```
ArrayNew(Dimensions)
```

Example: The following example creates a one-dimensional array:

```
<CFSET Users = #ArrayNew(1)#>
```

NOTE

After an array is created, ColdFusion automatically expands it as necessary. Use the `ArrayResize()` function to resize an array manually.

➜ *See also* `IsArray()`, `ListToArray()`

ArrayPrepend()

Description: `ArrayPrepend()` adds an element to the beginning of an array. `ArrayPrepend()` takes two parameters: the array into which to insert the element and the data to be stored in that element. `ArrayPrepend()` returns `TRUE` if the operation is successful.

Syntax:

```
ArrayPrepend(Array, Value)
```

Example: The following example inserts an element containing the word `Alabama` into the beginning of an array:

```
#ArrayPrepend(States, "Alabama")#
```

NOTE

You can set the values of explicit array elements using the `<CFSET>` tag.

➜ *See also* `ArrayAppend()`, `ArrayInsertAt()`

ArrayResize()

Description: `ArrayResize()` changes the size of an array, padding it with empty elements if necessary. `ArrayResize()` takes two parameters: the array to be resized and the size at which to resize it. `ArrayResize()` returns `TRUE` if the operation is successful.

Syntax:

```
ArrayResize(Array, Size)
```

Example: The following example creates an array and immediately resizes it to hold 100 elements:

```
<CFSET Users = #ArrayNew(1)#>
<CFSET result = #ArrayResize(Users, 100)#>
```

TIP

Dynamically expanding arrays is a slow operation. You can dramatically optimize ColdFusion's array processing by resizing the array to the anticipated size immediately after creating it with `ArrayNew()`.

→ *See also* `ArrayLen()`, `ArraySet()`

`ArraySet()`

Description: `ArraySet()` initializes one or more elements in a one-dimensional array with a specified value. `ArraySet()` takes four parameters: the array itself, the element starting and ending positions, and the value to use. `ArraySet()` returns `TRUE` if the operation is successful.

Syntax:

```
ArraySet(Array, Start, End, Value)
```

Example: The following example sets elements 1–100 with the value `0`:

```
#ArraySet(OrderItems, 1, 100, 0)#
```

→ *See also* `ArrayResize()`, `ArraySort()`, `ArraySwap()`

`ArraySort()`

Description: `ArraySort()` sorts the data in an array. `ArraySort()` takes three parameters: the array to be sorted, the sort type, and an optional sort order of either ascending or descending. If the sort order is omitted, the default order of ascending is used. `ArraySort()` supports three sort types, as listed in Table C.22.

Table C.22 `ArraySort()` Sort Types

TYPE	DESCRIPTION
`Numeric`	Sorts numerically.
`Text`	Sorts text alphabetically, with uppercase before lowercase.
`TextNoCase`	Sorts text alphabetically; case is ignored.

Syntax:

```
ArraySort(Array, Type [, Order])
```

Example: The following example sorts an array alphabetically using a non–case-sensitive sort (also known as a *dictionary sort):*

```
#ArraySort(Users, "textnocase")#
```

NOTE

`ArraySort()` sorts the actual passed array, not a copy of it.

→ *See also* `ArraySet()`, `ArraySwap()`

ArraySum()

Description: `ArraySum()` returns the sum of all values in an array. `ArraySum()` takes a single parameter: the array to be checked.

Syntax:

```
ArraySum(Array)
```

Example: The following example reports the total cost of all items in an array:

```
The total cost of all item in the list is #DollarFormat(ArraySum(items))#
```

NOTE

`ArraySum()` works only with arrays containing numeric data. Do not use this function with arrays that contain text data.

→ *See also* `ArrayAvg()`, `ArrayMin()`, `ArrayMax()`

ArraySwap

Description: `ArraySwap()` is used to swap the values in two array elements. `ArraySwap()` takes three parameters: the array itself and the positions of the two elements to be swapped. `ArraySwap()` returns `TRUE` if the operation is successful.

Syntax:

```
ArraySwap(Array, Position1, Position2)
```

Example: The following example swaps elements `10` and `11` in an array:

```
#ArraySwap(Users, 10, 11)#
```

→ *See also* `ArraySet()`, `ArraySort()`

ArrayToList()

Description: `ArrayToList()` converts a one-dimensional ColdFusion array into a list. `ArrayToList()` takes two parameters: the array to be converted and an optional list delimiter. If no delimiter is specified, the default (comma) delimiter is used. `ArrayToList()` creates a new list.

Syntax:

```
ArrayToList (Array [, Delimiter])
```

Example: The following example converts an array of users into a list:

```
<CFSET UserList = #ArrayToList(UserArray)#>
```

→ *See also* `ListToArray()`

Asc()

Description: `Asc()` returns the ASCII value of the leftmost character of a string. The `Asc()` function will return `0` if the string being evaluated is empty.

Syntax:

```
Asc(character)
```

Example: The following example returns `72`, the ASCII value of the character `H`:

```
Asc("Hello")
```

TIP

The `Asc()` function processes only the leftmost character in a string. To return the ASCII characters of an entire string, you must loop through the string and process each character individually.

➜ *See also* `Chr()`, `Val()`

Asin()

Description: `Asin()` returns the arcsine of a passed number in radians. This function takes only one numeric value as a parameter. You can pass real values, integer values, and ColdFusion fields to this function.

Syntax:

```
Asin(number)
```

Example: The following example returns `0.0350071497753`, the arcsine of `.035`:

```
#Asin(".035")#
```

➜ *See also* `Cos()`, `Pi()`, `Sin()`, `Tan()`

Atn()

Description: `Atn()` returns the arctangent of a passed number. This function takes only one numeric value as a parameter. You can pass real values, integer values, and ColdFusion fields to this function.

Syntax:

```
Atn(number)
```

Example: The following example returns `0.0349857188285`, the arctangent of `.035`:

```
#Atn(".035")#
```

➜ *See also* `Cos()`, `Pi()`, `Sin()`, `Tan()`

AuthenticatedContext()

Deprecated.

AuthenticatedUser()

Deprecated.

BitAnd()

Description: `BitAnd()` returns the result of the logical addition two long integers with a bitwise `AND` operation. This function takes two 32-bit signed integer values as parameters.

Syntax:

```
BitAnd(number1, number2)
```

Example: The following example returns `1` from `5` and `255`:

```
#BitAnd(5, 255)#
```

➜ *See also* `BitNot()`, `BitOr()`, `BitXor()`

BitMaskClear()

Description: `BitMaskClear()` returns the first number with length bits from the starting number through the clear number. This function takes three numeric values as parameters. The first parameter, *number*, is a 32-bit signed integer. The second and third parameters, *start* and *clear*, must be integers between 0 and 31, inclusive.

Syntax:

```
BitMaskClear(number, start, clear)
```

Example: The following example returns `6` from `6`, `31`, and `1`:

```
#BitMaskClear(6, 31, 1)#
```

➜ *See also* `BitMaskRead()`, `BitMaskSet()`

BitMaskRead()

Description: `BitMaskRead()` returns the value of the length bits beginning with the starting number. This function takes three numeric values as parameters. The first parameter, *number*, is a 32-bit signed integer. The second and third parameters, *start* and *length*, must be integers between 0 and 31, inclusive.

Syntax:

```
BitMaskRead(number, start, length)
```

Example: The following example returns `2` from `22`, `3`, and `31`:

```
#BitMaskRead(22, 3, 31)#
```

➜ *See also* `BitMaskClear()`, `BitMaskSet()`

BitMaskSet()

Description: `BitMaskSet()` returns number with mask occupying the bits of length *length* beginning at the position indicated by the *start* parameter. This function takes four numeric parameters. The first two parameters, *number* and *mask*, are a 32-bit signed integers. The third and fourth parameters, *start* and *length*, must be integers between 0 and 31, inclusive. *Start* is the position where the mask is to start and length is the *length* of the mask.

Syntax:

```
BitMaskSet(number, mask, start, length)
```

Example: The following example returns `118` from `22`, `3`, `5`, and `31`:

```
#BitMaskSet(22, 3, 31)#
```

➜ *See also* `BitMaskClear()`, `BitMaskRead()`

BitNot()

Description: `BitNot()` returns the bitwise NOT of an integer. This function takes only one numeric value as a parameter which must be a signed 32-bit integer.

Syntax:

```
BitNot(number)
```

Example: The following example returns `-23` from `22`:

```
#BitNot(22)#
```

➜ *See also* `BitAnd()`, `BitOr()`, `BitXor()`

BitOr()

Description: `BitOr()` returns the bitwise OR of a long integer. This function takes two signed 32-bit integers as parameters. You can pass real values, integer values, and ColdFusion fields to this function.

Syntax:

```
BitMaskSet(number1, number2)
```

Example: The following example returns `39` from `35` and `7`:

```
#BitOr(35, 7)#
```

➜ *See also* `BitAnd()`, `BitNot()`, `BitXor()`

BitSHLN()

Description: `BitSHLN()` returns *number* bitwise shifted left without rotation by *count* bits. This function takes two numeric values as parameters. The *number* parameter must be a signed 32-bit integer. The *count* parameter must be an integer between 0 and 31.

Syntax:

```
BitSHLN(number, count)
```

Example: The following example returns `4480` from `35` and `7`:

```
#BitOr(35, 7)#
```

➜ *See also* `BitSHRN()`

BitSHRN()

Description: `BitSHRN()` returns *number* bitwise shifted right without rotation to by *count* bits. This function takes two numeric values as parameters. The *number* parameter must be a signed 32-bit integer. The *count* parameter must be an integer between 0 and 31.

Syntax:

```
BitSHRN(number, count)
```

Example: The following example returns `250` from `1000` and `2`:

```
#BitSHRN(1000, 2)#
```

➜ *See also* `BitSHLN()`

BitXor()

Description: `BitXor()` returns the closest integer greater than the passed number. You pass two signed 32-bit integers as parameters.

Syntax:

```
BitXor(number1, number2)
```

Example: The following example returns `1002` from `1000` and `2`:

```
#BitXor(1000, 2)#
```

➜ *See also* `BitAnd()`, `BitNot()`, `BitOr()`

Ceiling()

Description: `Ceiling()` returns the nearest integer greater than the passed number. This function takes one numeric value as a parameter. You can pass real values, integer values, and ColdFusion fields to this function.

Syntax:

```
Ceiling(number)
```

Example: The following example returns `254` from `253.42`:

```
#Ceiling(253.42)#
```

➜ *See also* `Fix()`, `Int()`, `Round()`

Chr()

Description: `Chr()` converts an ASCII value into a printable character. The `Chr()` function takes a single parameter—the ASCII value to be converted (valid ASCII values range from `0` to `255`)—and returns the specified ASCII value as a printable character.

Syntax:

```
Chr(number)
```

Example: The following example returns the letter `H`, whose ASCII value is `72`:

```
#Chr(72)#
```

➜ *See also* `Asc()`, `Val()`

Cjustify()

Description: `CJustify()` centers a string within a field of a specified length. It does this by padding spaces before and after the specified text. `CJustify()` takes two parameters: the string to process and the desired string length.

Syntax:

```
CJustify(string, length)
```

Example: The following example justifies the word `Hello` so that it is centered within a 20-character-wide field:

```
#CJustify("Hello", 20)#
```

➜ *See also* `Ljustify()`, `Ltrim()`, `Rjustify()`, `Rtrim()`, `Trim()`

Compare()

Description: The `Compare()` function compares two string values. `Compare()` performs a case-sensitive comparison. This function returns a negative number if the first string is less than the second string, a positive number if the first string is greater than the second string, and `0` if the strings are the same.

Syntax:

```
Compare(String1, String2)
```

Example: The following example returns a negative value because the first string is less than the second string:

```
#Compare("Ben", "Bill")#
```

NOTE

The two comparison functions treat white space as characters to be compared. Therefore, if you compare two strings that are identical except for extra spaces at the end of one of them, the compare will not return `0`.

TIP

You can create an alphabetical list of strings easily by sorting all the strings in increasing order with the `Compare()` function.

➜ *See also* `CompareNoCase()`, `Find()`

CompareNoCase()

Description: The `CompareNoCase()` function compares two string values. `CompareNoCase()` performs a non–case-sensitive comparison. This function returns a negative number if the first string is less than the second string, a positive number if the first string is greater than the second string, and `0` if the strings are the same.

Syntax:

```
CompareNoCase(String1, String2)
```

Example: The following example uses the non–case-sensitive comparison function and returns `0` because, aside from case, the strings are the same:

```
#CompareNoCase("Michigan", "MICHIGAN")#
```

NOTE

The two comparison functions treat white space as characters to be compared. Therefore, if you compare two strings that are identical except for extra spaces at the end of one of them, the compare will not return `0`.

➜ *See also* `Compare()`, `Find()`

`Cos()`

Description: `Cos()` returns the cosine of an angle in radians. This function takes only one numeric value as a parameter. You can pass real values, integer values, and ColdFusion fields to this function.

Syntax:

```
Cos(number)
```

Example: The following example returns `0.540302305868`, the cosine of 1:

```
#Cos("1")#
```

➜ *See also* `Abs()`, `Acos()`, `Sgn()`

`CreateDate()`

Description: The `CreateDate()` function returns a ColdFusion date/time object that can be used with other date-manipulation or formatting functions. `CreateDate()` takes three parameters: the date's year, month, and day.

Syntax:

```
#CreateDate(Year, Month, Day)#
```

Example: The following example creates a date/time object based on three user-supplied fields:

```
#CreateDate(birth_year, birth_month, birth_day)#
```

TIP

When specifying the year using the `CreateDate` function, be aware that ColdFusion will interpret the numeric values `0-29` as twenty-first century years. The numeric values `30-99` are interpreted as twentieth century years.

NOTE

Because the `CreateDate` function takes no time values as parameters, the time portion of the created date/time object is set to all `0`s.

➜ *See also* `CreateDateTime()`, `CreateODBCDate()`, `CreateTime()`

`CreateDateTime()`

Description: The `CreateDateTime()` function returns a ColdFusion date/time object that can be used with other date- and time-manipulation or formatting functions. `CreateDateTime()` takes six parameters: the date's year, month, and day, and the time's hour, minute, and second.

Syntax:

```
#CreateDateTime(Year, Month, Day, Hour, Minute, Second)#
```

Example: The following example creates a date/time object for midnight on New Year's Day, 2002:

```
#CreateDateTime(2002, 1, 1, 0, 0, 0)#
```

TIP

When specifying the year using the `CreateDateTime()` function, be aware that ColdFusion will interpret the numeric values `0-29` as twenty-first century years. The numeric values `30-99` are interpreted as twentieth century years.

→ *See also* `CreateDate()`, `CreateODBCDateTime()`, `CreateTime()`, `ParseDateTime()`

CreateODBCDate()

Description: The `CreateODBCDate()` function returns an ODBC date/time field that can safely be used in SQL statements. `CreateODBCDate()` takes a single parameter: a ColdFusion date/time object.

Syntax:

```
#CreateODBCDate(Date)#
```

Example: The following example creates an ODBC date/time field for the current day (retrieved with the `Now()` function):

```
#CreateODBCDate(Now())#
```

NOTE

`CreateODBCDate` always creates an ODBC date/time field that has the time values set to `0`s, even if the passed date/time object had valid time values.

TIP

When specifying the year using the `CreateODBCDate` function, be aware that ColdFusion will interpret the numeric values `0-29` as twenty-first century years. The numeric values `30-99` are interpreted as twentieth century years.

TIP

`CreateODBCDate()` takes a date/time object as a parameter. If you want to pass individual date values as parameters, use the `CreateDate()` as the function parameter and pass it the values.

→ *See also* `CreateDate()`, `CreateODBCDateTime()`, `CreateODBCTime()`

CreateODBCDateTime()

Description: The `CreateODBCDateTime()` function returns an ODBC date/time field that can safely be used in SQL statements. `CreateODBCDateTime()` takes a single parameter: a ColdFusion date/time object.

Syntax:

```
#CreateODBCDate(Date)#
```

Example: The following example creates an ODBC date/time field for the current day (retrieved with the `Now()` function):

```
#CreateODBCDateTime(Now())#
```

TIP

When specifying the year using the `CreateODBCDateTime()` function, be aware that ColdFusion will interpret the numeric values `0-29` as twenty-first century years. The numeric values `30-99` are interpreted as twentieth century years.

TIP

`CreateODBCDateTime()` takes a date/time object as a parameter. If you want to pass individual date and time values as parameters, use the `CreateDateTime()` as the function parameter and pass it the values.

→ *See also* `CreateDate()`, `CreateODBCDate()`, `CreateODBCTime()`

CreateODBCTime()

Description: The `CreateODBCTime()` function returns an ODBC date/time field that can safely be used in SQL statements. `CreateODBCTime()` takes a single parameter: a ColdFusion date/time object.

Syntax:

```
#CreateODBCTime(Date)#
```

Example: The following example creates an ODBC date/time field for the current day (retrieved with the `Now` function):

```
#CreateODBCTime(Now())#
```

NOTE

`CreateODBCTime()` always creates an ODBC date/time field that has the date values set to `0`s, even if the passed date/time object had valid date values.

TIP

`CreateODBCTime()` takes a date/time object as a parameter. If you want to pass individual time values as parameters, use the `CreateTime()` as the function parameter and pass it the values.

TIP

Always enclose date/time values in quotes when passing them to the `CreateODBCTime()` function as strings. Without quotes, the value passed is interpreted as a numeral representation of a date/time object.

→ *See also* `CreateODBCDate()`, `CreateODBCDateTime()`, `CreateTime()`

CreateObject()

Description: The `CreateObject()` function creates either a COM, CORBA, or Java object or a ColdFusion component. Note that the syntax varies with the type of object you're creating.

ColdFusion components are special ColdFusion templates (named with the .cfc file extension) that contain CFML code to define functions (methods) and properties. They can be invoked and use in ColdFusion applications like other objects. They can also be invoked by other applications as Web services.

These tables contain details on this function's parameters, which vary with the type of object being created: Table C.23, Table C.24, Table C.25, and Table C.26.

Syntax for COM:

```
#CreateObject("COM", class, context, servername)#
```

Syntax for CORBA:

```
#CreateObject("CORBA", class, context, locale)#
```

Syntax for Java objects:

```
#CreateObject("JAVA", class)#
```

Syntax for ColdFusion components:

```
#CreateObject("component", componentname)#
```

NOTE

You can also use the `<CFOBJECT>` tag to instantiate ColdFusion components. The `CreateObject()` function is intended for use in CFScript.

Table C.23 `CreateObject()` Parameters for COM

PARAMETER	DESCRIPTION
Type	Required; "COM".
Class	Required; ProgID of the object to be invoked.
Context	Optional; either `InProc`, `Local`, or `Remote`. Default value defined in registry.
Servername	Optional, but required when Context = "Remote". Provides server name in either DNS or UNC format. The following forms are accepted: `\\lanserver`, lanserver, `http://www.myserver.com`, `www.myserver.com`, 127.0.0.1

Table C.24 `CreateObject()` Parameters for CORBA

PARAMETER	DESCRIPTION
Type	Required; "CORBA".
Class	Required; if value of Context is "IOR", then this names the file that contains the sharing version of the Interoperable Object Reference (IOR). If value is "NameService", then this is the naming context of the naming service, delimited with forward slashes (e.g., "Macromedia/Department/object").
Context	Required; either "IOR" (to access CORBA server) or "NameService" to use a naming service to access the server. Only valid for VisiBroker.
Locale	Optional; use is specific to VisiBroker orbs. Provides initialization arguments for init_orb(). Available in C++, Version 3.2. Its value must be of the form: " -ORBagentAddr 199.99.129.33 -ORBagentPort 19000". You must use a leading hyphen for each type/value pair.

Table C.25 `CreateObject()` Parameters for Java Objects

PARAMETER	DESCRIPTION
Type	Required; "Java"
Class	Required; names a valid Java class.

Table C.26 `CreateObject()` Parameters for ColdFusion Components

PARAMETER	DESCRIPTION
Type	Required; "Component"
ComponentName	Required; names the .cfc file containing the CF component.

Example: The following example creates a ColdFusion component object and invokes one of its methods. This assumes that there is a .cfc file in the same directory (as the example), with the name Film_Component.cfc.

```
<CFSCRIPT>
Film = CreateObject("component", "Film_Component");
Filmcount = Film.CheckFilmOrderCount(1);
WriteOutput(Filmcount);
</CFSCRIPT>
```

NOTE

COM objects are not supported on UNIX platforms.

NOTE

This function may be disabled in the ColdFusion Administrator.

CreateTime()

Description: The `CreateTime()` function returns a ColdFusion date/time object that can be used with other time-manipulation or formatting functions. `CreateTime()` takes three parameters: the hour, minute, and second.

Syntax:

```
#CreateTime(Hour, Minute, Second)#
```

Example: The following example creates a date/time object based on three ColdFusion fields:

```
#CreateTime(act_hr, act_mn, act_se)#
```

NOTE

Because the `CreateTime()` function takes no date values as parameters, the date portion of the created date/time object is set to all `0`s.

➜ *See also* `CreateDate()`, `CreateDateTime()`, `CreateODBCTime()`

CreateTimeSpan()

Description: `CreateTimeSpan()` creates a date/time object that can be used to rapidly perform date- and time-based calculations. `CreateTimeSpan()` takes four parameters: days, hours, minutes, and seconds. Any of these values can be set to `0` if not needed.

Syntax:

```
#CreateTimeSpan(Days, Hours, Minutes, Seconds)#
```

Example: The following example creates a date/time object with a time exactly six hours from now:

```
<CFSET detonation# = Now() + CreateTimeSpan(0, 6, 0, 0)>
```

TIP

The `CreateTimeSpan()` function is designed to speed the process of performing date- and time-based calculations. Creating a date/time object with `30` days–and using standard addition operators to add this to an existing date/time object–is quicker than using the `DateAdd()` function.

TIP

The `CreateTimeSpan()` function can be used in conjunction with the `CACHEDWITHIN` attribute of the `<CFQUERY>` tag. You can specify a period of time, using `CreateTimeSpan()`, in which the results of a query will be cached. This use of the `CreateTimeSpan()` function is effective only if you have enabled query caching in the ColdFusion Administrator.

➜ *See also* `DateAdd()`

DateAdd()

Description: `DateAdd()` is used to add or subtract values to a date/time object—you can add a week or subtract a year, for example. `DateAdd()` takes three parameters. The first is the date specifier (see Table C.3); the second is the number of units to add or subtract; and the third is the date/time object to be processed. `DateAdd()` returns a modified date/time object.

Syntax:

```
#DateAdd(Specifier, Units, Date)#
```

Example: The following example returns tomorrow's date (it adds one day to today's date):

```
#DateAdd('D', 1, Now())#
```

The next example returns a date exactly `10` weeks earlier than today's date:

```
#DateAdd('WW', -10, Now())#
```

TIP

To subtract values from a date/time object, use the `DateAdd` function and pass a negative number of units. For example, `-5` subtracts five units of whatever specifier was passed.

TIP

You can add or subtract the modified date/time object that `DateAdd()` returns from other date/time objects and use this value in the `CACHEDWITHIN` attribute of the `<CFQUERY>` tag.

➜ *See also* `CreateTimeSpan()`

DateCompare()

Description: `DateCompare()` enables you to compare two date values to see whether they are the same or whether one is greater than the other. `DateCompare()` takes two parameters: the dates to compare, which can be specified as date/time objects or string representations of dates. `DateCompare()` returns `-1` if the first date is less than the second date, `0` if they are the same, and `1` if the first date is greater than the second date.

Syntax:

```
#DateCompare(Date1, Date2)#
```

Example: The following example verifies that a user-supplied order ship date is valid (not already passed):

```
<CFIF DateCompare(ship_date, Now()) IS -1>
 We can't ship orders yesterday!
</CFIF>
```

➜ *See also* `DateDiff()`, `DatePart()`

DateConvert()

Description: The `DateConvert()` function converts local machine time to UTC (Universal Coordinated Time) time or vice versa. The `DateConvert()` function takes two parameters. The first is the conversion type, and the second is the date/time value to be converted. Valid conversion types for the `DateConvert()` function are `"local2utc"` and `"utc2local"`. The date/time value to be converted can be constructed using any ColdFusion date/time string. If a calculation for daylight saving time is required, the function uses the settings for the machine that is executing the code.

Syntax:

```
#DateConvert(conversion_type, date)#
```

Example: The following example converts the local machine date/time to UTC:

```
<CFSET TheTime = CreateDateTime(2006, 4, 26, 12, 41, 32)>
#DateConvert("local2utc", TheTime)#
```

➜ *See also* `CreateDateTime()`, `DatePart()`

DateDiff()

Description: `DateDiff()` returns the number of units of a passed specifier by which one date is greater than a second date. Unlike `DateCompare()`, which returns the greater date, `DateDiff()` tells you how many days, weeks, or months it is greater by. `DateDiff()` takes three parameters: The first is the date specifier (refer to Table C.3), and the second and third are the dates to compare.

Syntax:

```
#DateDiff(Specifier, Date1, Date2)#
```

Example: The following example returns how many weeks are left in this year, by specifying today's date (using the `Now()` function) and the first date of next year (using the `CreateDate` function) as the two dates to compare:

```
There are #DateDiff("WW", Now(), CreateDate(Year(Now())+1, 1, 1))
➥# weeks left in this year!
```

NOTE

If the first date passed to `DateDiff()` is greater than the second date, a negative value is returned. Otherwise, a positive value is returned.

TIP

You can add or subtract the modified date/time object that `DateDiff()` returns from other date/time objects and use this value in the `CACHEDWITHIN` attribute of the `<CFQUERY>` tag.

➜ *See also* `DateCompare()`, `DatePart()`

DateFormat()

Description: `DateFormat()` displays the date portion of a date/time object in a readable format. `DateFormat()` takes two parameters: the first is the date/time object to be displayed, and the second is an optional mask value enabling you to control exactly how the data is formatted. If no mask is specified, the default mask of `DD-MMM-YY` is used. The complete set of date masks is listed in Table C.27.

Syntax:

```
#DateFormat(Date [, mask ])#
```

Table C.27 `DateFormat` Mask Characters

MASK	DESCRIPTION
D	Day of month in numeric form with no leading 0 for single-digit days.
DD	Day of month in numeric form with a leading 0 for single-digit days.
DDD	Day of week as a three-letter abbreviation (`Sun` for `Sunday`, and so on).
DDDD	Day of week as its full English name.
M	Month in numeric form with no leading 0 for single-digit months.
MM	Month in numeric form with a leading 0 for single-digit months.
MMM	Month as a three-letter abbreviation (`Jan` for `January`, and so on).
MMMM	Month as its full English name.
Y	Year as last two digits of year, with no leading 0 for years less than 10.
YY	Year as last two digits of year, with a leading 0 for years less than 10.
YYYY	Year as full four digits.
GG	Representative of a period or an era. This mask is currently ignored by ColdFusion but has been reserved for future use.

Example: The following example displays today's date with the default formatting options:

```
Today is: #DateFormat(Now())#
```

The next example displays the same date but uses the full names of both the day of week and the month:

```
It is #DateFormat(Now(), "DDDD, MMMM DD, YYYY")#
```

The final example displays today's date in the European format (day/month/year):

```
It is #DateFormat(Now(), "DD/MM/YY")#
```

NOTE

Unlike the `TimeFormat()` function mask specifiers, the `DateFormat()` function mask specifiers are not case-sensitive.

NOTE

`DateFormat()` supports U.S.-style dates only. Use the `LSDateFormat()` function for international date support.

➜ *See also* `LSDateFormat()`, `TimeFormat()`

DatePart()

Description: `DatePart()` returns the specified part of a passed date. `DatePart()` takes two parameters: The first is the date specifier (refer to Table C.3), and the second is the date/time object to process.

Syntax:

```
#DatePart(Specifier, Date)#
```

Example: The following example returns the day of the week on which a user was born (and converts it to a string date using the `DayOfWeekAsString` function):

```
You were born on a #DayOfWeekAsString(DatePart('W', dob))#
```

➜ *See also* `DateCompare()`, `DateDiff()`, `Day()`, `DayOfWeek()`, `DayOfYear()`, `Hour()`, `Minute()`, `Month()`, `Quarter()`, `Second()`, `Week()`, `Year()`

Day()

Description: `Day()` returns a date/time object's day of month as a numeric value with possible values of `1–31`. `Day()` takes a single parameter: the date/time object to be processed.

Syntax:

```
#Day(Date)#
```

Example: The following example returns today's day of month:

```
Today is day #Day(Now())# of this month
```

TIP

When specifying the year using the `Day() function`, be aware that ColdFusion will interpret the numeric values `0-29` as twenty-first century years. The numeric values `30-99` are interpreted as twentieth century years.

➜ *See also* `DayOfWeek()`, `DayOfYear()`, `Hour()`, `Minute()`, `Month()`, `Quarter()`, `Second()`, `Week()`, `Year()`

DayOfWeek()

Description: DayOfWeek() returns a date/time object's day of week as a numeric value with possible values of 1–7. DayOfWeek() takes a single parameter: the date/time object to be processed.

Syntax:

```
#DayOfWeek(Date)#
```

TIP

When specifying the year using the DayOfWeek() function, be aware that ColdFusion will interpret the numeric values 0-29 as twenty-first century years. The numeric values 30-99 are interpreted as twentieth century years.

TIP

Always enclose date/time values in quotes when passing them to the DayOfWeek() function as strings. Without quotes, the value passed is interpreted as a numeral representation of a date/time object.

Example: The following example returns today's day of week:

```
Today is day #DayOfWeek(Now())# of this week
```

➜ *See also* Day(), DayOfYear(), Hour(), Minute(), Month(), Quarter(), Second(), Week(), Year()

DayOfWeekAsString()

Description: DayOfWeekAsString() returns the English weekday name for a passed day-of-week number. DayOfWeekAsString() takes a single parameter: the day of week to be processed, with a value of 1–7.

Syntax:

```
#DayOfWeekAsString(DayNumber)#
```

Example: The following example returns today's day of week:

```
Today is day #DayOfWeekAsString(DayOfWeek(Now()))# of this week
```

TIP

When specifying the year using the DayOfWeekAsString() function, be aware that ColdFusion will interpret the numeric values 0-29 as twenty-first century years. The numeric values 30-99 are interpreted as twentieth century years.

➜ *See also* DayOfWeek(), MonthAsString()

DayOfYear()

Description: DayOfYear() returns a date/time object's day of year as a numeric value, taking into account leap years. DayOfYear() takes a single parameter: the date/time object to be processed.

Syntax:

```
#DayOfYear(Date)#
```

Example: The following example returns today's day of year:

```
Today is day #DayOfYear(Now())# of year #Year(Now())#
```

TIP

When specifying the year using the `DayOfYear()` function, be aware that ColdFusion will interpret the numeric values `0-29` as twenty-first century years. The numeric values `30-99` are interpreted as twentieth century years.

TIP

Always enclose date/time values in quotes when passing them to the `DayOfYear()` function as strings. Without quotes, the value passed is interpreted as a numeral representation of a date/time object.

➔ *See also* `Day()`, `DayOfWeek()`, `Hour()`, `Minute()`, `Month()`, `Quarter()`, `Second()`, `Week()`, `Year()`

DaysInMonth()

Description: `DaysInMonth()` returns the number of days in a specified month, taking into account leap years. `DaysInMonth()` takes a single parameter: the date/time object to be evaluated.

Syntax:

```
#DaysInMonth(Date)#
```

Example: The following example returns the number of days in the current month:

```
This month has #DaysInMonth(Now())# days
```

TIP

`DaysInMonth()` takes a date/time object as a parameter, and there is no equivalent function that takes a year and month as its parameters. Fortunately, this easily can be accomplished by combining the `DaysInMonth()` and `CreateDate()` functions. For example, to determine how many days are in February 2002, you can create a statement that looks like this: `#DaysInMonth(CreateDate(2002, 2, 1))#`.

TIP

When specifying the year using the `DaysInMonth()` function, be aware that ColdFusion will interpret the numeric values `0-29` as twenty-first century years. The numeric values `30-99` are interpreted as twentieth century years.

TIP

Always enclose date/time values in quotes when passing them to the `DaysInMonth()` function as strings. Without quotes, the value passed is interpreted as a numeral representation of a date/time object.

➔ *See also* `DaysInYear()`, `FirstDayOfMonth()`

DaysInYear()

Description: `DaysInYear()` returns the number of days in a specified year, taking into account leap years. `DaysInYear()` takes a single parameter: the date/time object to be evaluated.

Syntax:

```
#DaysInYear(Date)#
```

Example: The following example returns the number of days in the current year:

```
This year, #Year(Now())#, has #DaysInYear(Now())# days
```

TIP

`DaysInYear()` takes a date/time object as a parameter, and there is no equivalent function that takes just a year as its parameter. Fortunately, this easily can be accomplished by combining the `DaysInYear()` and `CreateDate` functions. For example, you can create a statement that looks like this to determine how many days are in the year 2002: `#DaysInYear (CreateDate(2002, 1, 1))#`.

TIP

When specifying the year using the `DaysInYear()` function, be aware that ColdFusion will interpret the numeric values `0-29` as twenty-first century years. The numeric values `30-99` are interpreted as twentieth century years.

TIP

Always enclose date/time values in quotes when passing them to the `DaysInYear()` function as strings. Without quotes, the value passed is interpreted as a numeral representation of a date/time object.

→ *See also* `DaysInMonth()`, `FirstDayOfMonth()`

DE()

Description: `DE()` stands for delay evaluation. This function is designed for use with the `IIf()` and `Evaluate()` functions, allowing you to pass strings to these functions without their being evaluated.

Syntax:

```
DE(String)
```

Example: The following example uses `DE()` to ensure that the string `"A"` is evaluated, instead of the variable `"A"`.

```
#Evaluate(DE("A"))#
```

→ *See also* `IIf()`, `Evaluate()`

DecimalFormat()

Description: `DecimalFormat()` is a simplified number formatting function that outputs numbers with two decimal places, commas to separate the thousands, and a minus sign for negative values. `DecimalFormat()` takes a single parameter: the number to be displayed. The `DecimalFormat()` function will round numbers to the nearest hundredth.

Syntax:

```
#DecimalFormat(Number)#
```

Example: The following example displays a table column in the decimal format:

```
Quantity: #DecimalFormat(quantity)#
```

TIP

For more precise numeric display, use the `NumberFormat()` function instead.

→ *See also* `NumberFormat()`

Decrypt()

Description: The `Decrypt()` function enables you to decode strings based on a user-specified key using a symmetric key–based algorithm. This means that the same key that was used to encrypt the string must be used to decrypt the string. The `Decrypt()` function takes two parameters. The first parameter is the string on which to perform encryption or decryption. The second parameter is the key with which to encrypt or decrypt the string.

Syntax:

```
Decrypt(encrypted_string, seed)
```

Example: The following example encrypts a person's name with the key `butterfly`, and subsequently decrypts that same string:

```
<CFSET x=Encrypt("John", "butterfly")>
<CFSET y=Decrypt(x, "butterfly")>
```

TIP

Remember that when encrypting a string, the string will be UUEncoded after encryption; therefore, the size of the encrypted string can be as much as three times larger than the original string.

➜ *See also* `Encrypt()`

DeleteClientVariable()

Description: `DeleteClientVariable()` deletes the client variables whose names are passed as parameters. Unlike other ColdFusion variables, client variables persist over time and must be deleted with this function. `DeleteClientVariable()` takes a single parameter: the name of the variable to be deleted. `DeleteClientVariable()` returns `TRUE` if the variable was deleted. This function deletes a variable even if it did not previously exist. To ensure that a variable actually exists before using the `DeleteClientVariable()` function, test for its existence with `IsDefined()`.

Syntax:

```
DeleteClientVariable(Variable)
```

Example: The following example deletes a variable named `login_name` and sets a local variable with the function's return value:

```
<CFSET DeleteSuccessful = #DeleteClientVariable("login_name")#>
```

➜ *See also* `GetClientVariablesList()`

DirectoryExists()

Description: `DirectoryExists()` checks for the existence of a specified directory and returns either `YES` or `NO`. `DirectoryExists()` takes a single parameter: the name of the directory for which to check. The directory name cannot be a relative path but must be specified as a fully qualified path.

Syntax:

```
DirectoryExists(Directory)
```

Example: The following example checks for the existence of a directory, creating it if it does not exist:

```
<CFIF #DirectoryExists("#directory#")# IS "No">
 <CFFILE ACTION="CREATE" DIRECTORY="#directory#">
</CFIF>
```

➜ *See also* `FileExists()`

DollarFormat()

Description: `DollarFormat()` is a simplified U.S. currency formatting function that outputs numbers with a dollar sign at the front, two decimal places, commas to separate the thousands, and a minus sign for negative values. `DollarFormat()` takes a single parameter: the number to be displayed.

Syntax:

```
DollarFormat(Number)
```

Example: The following example displays the results of an equation (quantity multiplied by item cost) in the dollar format:

```
Total cost: #DollarFormat(quantity*item_cost)#
```

TIP

For more precise currency display, use the **`NumberFormat()`** function instead.

NOTE

`DollarFormat()` supports U.S. dollars only. Use the `LSCurrencyFormat()` function for international currency support.

➜ *See also* `LSCurrencyFormat(), NumberFormat()`

Duplicate()

Description: The `Duplicate()` function returns a deep copy of complex variables (like structures). After a variable is duplicated, the duplicate copy of the variable contains no reference to the original variable. The `Duplicate()` function takes a single parameter: the name of the variable you want to duplicate.

Syntax:

```
Duplicate(variable_name)
```

Example: The following example duplicates a structure, copying it into the request scope:

```
<CFLOCK SCOPE="APPLICATION" TYPE="READONLY" TIMEOUT="10">
   <CFSET REQUEST.settings=Duplicate(APPLICATION.settings)>
</CFLOCK>
```

CAUTION

You cannot duplicate COM, CORBA, or Java objects with the **`Duplicate()`** function. An attempt to do this causes ColdFusion to throw an exception error.

➜ *See also* `StructCopy()`

Encrypt()

Description: The `Encrypt()` function enables you to encode strings based on a user-specified key using a symmetric-key–based algorithm. This means that the same key that was used to encrypt the string must be used to decrypt the string. The `Encrypt()`function takes two parameters. The first parameter is the string on which to perform encryption or decryption. The second parameter is the key with which to encrypt or decrypt the string.

Syntax:

```
Encrypt(string, seed)
```

Example: The following example encrypts a person's name with the key `butterfly`, and subsequently decrypts that same string:

```
<CFSET x=Encrypt("John", "butterfly")>
<CFSET y=Decrypt(x, "butterfly")>
```

TIP

Remember that when encrypting a string, the string will be UUEncoded after encryption; therefore, the size of the encrypted string can be as much as three times larger than the original string.

➜ *See also* `Decrypt()`

Exp()

Description: `Exp()` returns E to the power of a passed number. The constant e equals the base of the natural logarithm, that is `2.71828182845904`. This function takes only one numeric value as a parameter. You can pass real values, integer values, and ColdFusion fields to this function.

Syntax:

```
Exp(number)
```

Example: The following example returns `148.413159103`, the natural logarithm of `5`:

```
#Exp("5")#
```

➜ *See also* `Log()`, `Log10()`

ExpandPath()

Description: `ExpandPath()` converts a relative or absolute path into a fully qualified path. `ExpandPath()` takes a single parameter: the path to be converted.

Syntax:

```
ExpandPath(Path)
```

Example: The following example returns the full path of the server's default document:

```
#ExpandPath("index.cfm")#
```

Evaluate()

Description: `Evaluate()` is used to evaluate string expressions. `Evaluate()` takes one or more string expressions as parameters and evaluates them from left to right.

Syntax:

```
Evaluate(String1, ..)
```

Example: The following example evaluates the variable `A1` through `A10`:

```
<CFLOOP INDEX="i" FROM="1" TO="10">
   <CFOUTPUT>A#I#: #Evaluate("a#i#")#</CFOUTPUT>
</CFLOOP>
```

➜ *See also* `DE()`, `Iif()`

FileExists()

Description: `FileExists()` checks for the existence of a specified file and returns either `YES` or `NO`. `FileExists()` takes a single parameter: the name of the file for which to check. The filename cannot be a relative path but must be specified as a fully qualified path.

Syntax:

```
FileExists(File)
```

Example: The following example checks for the existence of an image file before using it in an `IMG` tag:

```
<CFIF #FileExists("C:\root\images\logo.gif")#>
 <IMG SRC="/images/logo.gif">
</CFIF>
```

TIP

Use the `ExpandPath()` function so you don't have to hard-code the filename passed to the `FileExists()` function; use `ExpandPath()` to convert the relative path to an actual filename.

➜ *See also* `DirectoryExists()`

Find()

Description: `Find()` performs a case-sensitive search. The first parameter is the string for which to search, and the second parameter is the target string, or string to be searched. The third, optional parameter can specify the position in the target string from which to start the search. This function returns the starting position of the first occurrence of the search string within the specified target string. If the search string is not found, `0` is returned.

Syntax:

```
Find(SearchString, TargetString [, StartPosition])
```

Example: The following example returns `18`, the starting position of the word `America`:

```
#Find("America", "United States of America")#
```

The next example returns `0` because `Find()` performs a case-sensitive search:

```
#Find("AMERICA", "United States of America")#
```

The next example searches for the word `of` in the string `The Flag of the United States of America` and specifies that the search should start from position `15`. The following example returns `31`, the position of the second `of`. Had the optional starting position parameter been omitted, the return value would have been `10`, the position of the first `of`:

```
#Find("of", "The Flag of the United States of America", 15)#
```

➜ *See also* `FindNoCase()`, `FindOneOf()`, `REFind()`, `REFindNoCase()`

FindNoCase()

Description: `FindNoCase()` performs a non–case-sensitive search. The first parameter is the string, and the second parameter is the target string, or string to be searched. The third, optional parameter can specify the position in the target string from which to start the search. This function returns the starting position of the first occurrence of the search string within the specified target string. If the search string is not found, `0` is returned.

Syntax:

```
FindNoCase(SearchString, TargetString [, StartPosition])
```

Example: The following example performs a non–case-sensitive search with the `FindNoCase()` function:

```
#FindNoCase("AMERICA", "United States of America")#
```

➜ *See also* `Find()`, `FindOneOf()`, `REFind()`, `REFindNoCase()`

FindOneOf()

Description: `FindOneOf()` returns the position of the first target string character that matches any of the characters in a specified set. `FindOneOf()` takes three parameters. The first parameter is a string containing the set of characters for which to search. The second parameter is the target string (the string to be searched). The third parameter is an optional starting position from which to begin the search. These functions return the starting position of the first occurrence of any characters in the search set within the specified target string. If no matching characters are found, `0` is returned.

Syntax:

```
FindOneOf(SearchSet, TargetString, [, StartPosition])
```

Example: The following example returns the position of the first vowel with a ColdFusion field called `LastName`:

```
The first vowel in your last name is at position #FindOneOf("aeiou", LastName)#
```

TIP

The `FindOneOf()` function is case-sensitive, and there is no non-case-sensitive equivalent function. To perform a non-case-sensitive `FindOneOf()` search, you first must convert both the search and target strings to either upper- or lowercase (using the `UCase()` or `LCase()` function).

➜ *See also* `Find()`, `FindNoCase()`

FirstDayOfMonth()

Description: `FirstDayOfMonth()` returns the day of the year on which the specified month starts. `FirstDayOfMonth()` takes a single parameter: the date/time object to be evaluated.

Syntax:

```
FirstDayOfMonth(Date)
```

Example: The following example returns the day of the year on which the current month starts:

```
#FirstDayOfMonth(Now())#
```

TIP

`FirstDayOfMonth()` takes a date/time object as a parameter, and no equivalent function exists that takes just a month and year as its parameters. Fortunately, this can easily be accomplished by combining the `FirstDayOfMonth()` and `CreateDate()` functions. For example, to determine the day of the year on which March 1999 started, you can create a statement that looks like this: `#FirstDayOfMonth(CreateDate(1999, 3, 1))#`.

TIP

When specifying the year using the `FirstDayOfMonth()` function, be aware that ColdFusion will interpret the numeric values `0-29` as twenty-first century years. The numeric values `30-99` are interpreted as twentieth century years.

TIP

Always enclose date/time values in quotes when passing them to the `FirstDayOfMonth()` function as strings. Without quotes, the value passed is interpreted as a numeral representation of a date/time object.

➜ *See also* `DaysInMonth()`, `DaysInYear()`

Fix()

Description: If the passed number is greater than or equal to `0`, `Fix()` returns the closest integer that is smaller than the passed number. If not, it returns the closest integer greater than the passed number. This function takes only one numeric value as a parameter. You can pass real values, integer values, and ColdFusion fields to this function.

Syntax:

```
Fix(number)
```

Example: The following example returns `1`, the closest integer that is smaller than `1.5`:

```
#Fix("1.5")#
```

➜ *See also* `Ceiling()`, `Int()`, `Round()`

FormatBaseN()

Description: `FormatBaseN()` converts a number to a string using the base specified. Valid radix values are `2–36`.

Syntax:

```
FormatBaseN(Number, Radix)
```

Example: The following example converts a user-supplied number into hexadecimal notation:

```
#FormatBaseN(Number, 16)#
```

To convert a number to its binary format, you can do the following:

```
#FormatBaseN(Number, 2)#
```

➜ *See also* `InputBaseN()`

GetBaseTagData()

Description: `GetBaseTagData()` is used within subtags. It returns an object containing data from a specified ancestor tag. `GetBaseTagData()` takes two parameters: the name of the tag whose data you want returned, and an optional instance number. If no instance is specified, the default value of `1` is used.

Syntax:

```
GetBaseTagData(Tag [, InstanceNumber])
```

Example: The following example retrieves the data in a caller `<CFHTTP>` tag:

```
#GetBaseTagData(CFHTTP)#
```

NOTE

Not all tags contain data (for example, the `<CFIF>` tag). Passing a tag that contains no data to the `GetBaseTagData()` function causes an exception to be thrown.

➜ *See also* `GetBaseTagList()`

GetBaseTagList()

Description: `GetBaseTagList()` is used within subtags. It returns a comma-delimited list of base tag names. The returned list is in calling order, with the parent tag listed first.

Syntax:

```
GetBaseTagList()
```

Example: The following example displays the top-level calling tag:

```
<CFOUTPUT>The top level tag is #ListFirst(GetBaseTagList())#</CFOUTPUT>
```

➜ *See also* `GetBaseTagData()`

GetBaseTemplatePath()

Description: `GetBaseTemplatePath()` returns the full path of the base template. The `GetBaseTemplatePath()` function takes no parameters.

Syntax:

```
GetBaseTemplatePath()
```

Example: The following example displays the base template path information to the user:

```
<CFOUTPUT> #GetBaseTemplatePath()#</CFOUTPUT>
```

➜ *See also* `GetCurrentTemplatePath()`, `FileExists()`

GetClientVariablesList()

Description: `GetClientVariablesList()` returns a comma-delimited list of the read/write client variables available to the template. The standard read-only system client variables, listed in Table C.28, are not returned. `GetClientVariablesList()` takes no parameters.

Syntax:

```
GetClientVariablesList()
```

Table C.28 Read-Only Client Variables

VARIABLE	DESCRIPTION
`CFID`	Unique ID assigned to this client.
`CFToken`	Unique security token used to verify the authenticity of a `CFID` value.
`URLToken`	Text to append to URLs; contains both `CFID` and `CFToken`. (Appended automatically to `<CFLOCATION>` URLs.)

Example: The following example retrieves the entire list of read/write client variables:

```
#ListLen(GetClientVariablesList())#
➥read-write client variables are currently active
```

TIP

The list of variables returned by the `GetClientVariablesList()` function is comma delimited, which makes it suitable for processing with the ColdFusion list functions.

GetCurrentTemplatePath()

Description: `GetCurrentTemplatePath()` returns the complete path of the template calling this function. The `GetCurrentTemplatePath()` function does not take any parameters.

Syntax:

```
GetCurrentTemplatePath()
```

Example: The following example, placed anywhere inside a CFML template, would output the complete path of the template running this code to the user:

```
<CFOUTPUT>#GetCurrentTemplatePath()#</CFOUTPUT>
```

➜ *See also* `GetBaseTemplatePath()`, `FileExists()`

GetDirectoryFromPath()

Description: `GetDirectoryFromPath()` extracts the drive and directory (with a trailing backslash) from a fully specified path. `GetDirectoryFromPath()` takes a single parameter: the path to be evaluated.

Syntax:

```
GetDirectoryFromPath(Path)
```

Example: The following example returns the directory portion of a current template's full file path:

```
#GetDirectoryFromPath(GetTemplatePath())#
```

➜ *See also* `GetFileFromPath()`

GetException()

Description: `GetException()` retrieves a Java exception from a Java object. `GetException()` takes a single parameter: the Java object to be used.

Syntax:

```
GetException(object)
```

Example: The following example catches a Java object's exception within a try/catch block:

```
<CFCATCH TYPE="Any">
   <CFSET exception=GetException(myObj)>
   ..
</CFCATCH>
```

GetFileFromPath()

Description: `GetFileFromPath()` extracts the filename from a fully specified path. `GetFileFromPath()` takes a single parameter: the path to be evaluated.

Syntax:

```
GetFileFromPath(Path)
```

Example: The following example returns the filename portion of a temporary file:

```
#GetFileFromPath(GetTempFile(GetTempDirectory(), "CF"))#
```

➜ *See also* `GetDirectoryFromPath()`

GetFunctionList()

Description: The `GetFunctionList()` function returns a list of all functions available in ColdFusion. The `GetFunctionList()` function takes no parameters.

Syntax:

```
GetFunctionList()
```

Example: The following returns a list of all functions available in ColdFusion:

```
<CFSET JohnsFunctions = GetFunctionList()>
<CFOUTPUT>#StructCount(JohnsFunctions)# functions<BR><BR></CFOUTPUT>
<CFLOOP COLLECTION="#JohnsFunctions#" ITEM="key">
     <CFOUTPUT>#key#<BR></CFOUTPUT>
</CFLOOP>
```

GetHttpRequestData()

Description: The `GetHttpRequestData()` function retrieves the HTTP request headers and body and makes them available for use in a CFML template. The `GetHttpRequestData()` function takes no arguments and returns a structure containing the following variables: `headers` (which returns all the HTTP request headers), `content` (which returns, in string or binary format, the form data that was submitted by the client), `method` (which returns the request method as a string), and `protocol` (which returns the server-based CGI variable `Server_Protocol` as a string).

Syntax:

```
GetHttpRequestData()
```

Example: The following example stores all information retrieved by the `GetHttpRequestData()` function in a variable:

```
<CFSET headerInfo = #GetHttpRequestData()#>
```

GetHttpTimeString()

Description: The `GetHttpTimeString` function formats a ColdFusion date/time object according to the HTTP standard outlined in RFC 1123. This function takes a single parameter: the date/time object to be formatted.

Syntax:

```
GetHttpTimeString(date_time)
```

Example: The following example converts the current system time to a date/time format compatible with RFC 1123:

```
#GetHttpTimeString(#CreateODBCDateTime(Now())#)#
```

TIP

The date/time value that is returned by the `GetHttpString()` function always is formatted as GMT (Greenwich mean time) to remain consistent with RFC 1123.

GetLocale()

Description: `GetLocale()` returns the name of the locale currently in use. The locale returned by the `GetLocale()` function is determined by the native operating system running ColdFusion Application Server.

Syntax:

```
GetLocale()
```

Example: The following example saves the current locale to a local variable:

```
<CFSET current_locale = #GetLocale()#>
```

➜ *See also* `SetLocale()`

`GetMetaData()`

Description: The `GetMetaData()` function returns key/value pairs or structured XML data depending on the type of object it is used with. `GetMetaData()` is used with objects that support introspection, such as ColdFusion components. The scope *this* is used in component bodies and function bodies at run-time to read and write variables present during the instantiation of the object.

The metadata derived from ColdFusion components is presented as a structure of structures and arrays. The initial structure returned contains the keys presented in Table C.29. Note that other keys may be present for other types of objects.

Table C.29 Metadata Derived from Components

KEY	DESCRIPTION
Name	Component name
Path	Absolute path to the component
Extends	Ancestor component metadata (Name, path and type)
Functions	Array of metadata (structures) for each component function
Type	Type of object being reported on (e.g., "component")

The metadata derived from functions contains at least the keys presented in Table C.30. Note that other keys may be present.

Table C.30 Metadata Derived from Functions

KEY	DESCRIPTION
Name	Function name
Parameters	Array of structures (argument metadata)

The metadata derived from function arguments contains at least the keys presented in Table C.31. Note that other keys may be present.

Table C.31 Metadata Derived from Function Arguments

KEY	DESCRIPTION
Name	Argument name

The metadata derived from properties contains at least the keys presented in Table C.32. Note that other keys may be present.

Table C.32 Metadata Derived from Properties

KEY	DESCRIPTION
Name	Property name

Syntax with objects:

```
GetMetaData(Object)
```

Syntax from within ColdFusion components:

```
GetMetaData(this)
```

Example: The following example returns the startup values from a passed variable:

```
<CFCOMPONENT>
   <CFFUNCTION NAME="GetMetaDataStruct">
      <CFARGUMENT NAME="MyArgument">
      <!--- Get metadata for this function --->
      <CFSET x = GetMetaData(this)>
      <CFRETURN x>
   </CFFUNCTION>
</CFCOMPONENT>
```

➜ *See also* `CreateObject()`

GetMetricData()

Deprecated.

GetProfileString()

Description: The `GetProfileString()` function retrieves the value of an entry in an initialization (*.ini) file.

Syntax:

```
GetProfileString(iniPath, section, entry)
```

Example: The following example returns the startup values from a passed variable:

```
<CFOUTPUT>GetProfileString(#FORM.inipath#, "Startup", "OnStartup")</CFOUTPUT>
```

➜ *See also* `SetProfileString()`

GetTempDirectory()

Description: The `GetTempDirectory()` function retrieves the full pathname of the temp directory on which ColdFusion Server is installed.

Syntax:

```
GetTempDirectory()
```

Example: The following example returns the temp directory pathname:

```
<CFOUTPUT>GetTempDirectory()</CFOUTPUT>
```

➜ *See also* `GetTempFile()`

GetTempFile()

Description: `GetTempFile()` returns the full path to a temporary file for use by your application. The returned filename is guaranteed to be unique. `GetTempFile()` takes two parameters: The first is the directory where you want the temporary file created, and the second is a filename prefix of up to three characters. You can't omit the prefix, but you can pass an empty string ("").

Syntax:

```
GetTempFile(Directory, Prefix)
```

Example: The following example returns the name of a temporary file beginning with the letters `CF` in the Windows temporary directory:

```
#GetTempFile(GetTempDirectory(), "CF")#
```

TIP

To create a temporary file in the Windows temporary directory, pass the **`GetTempDirectory()`** function as the directory parameter.

➜ *See also* `GetTempDirectory()`

GetTemplatePath()

Deprecated.

GetK2ServerCollections()

Deprecated.

GetK2ServerDocCount()

Description: `GetK2ServerDocCount()` returns the total number of indexed documents searchable using the Verity K2 server.

Syntax:

```
GetK2ServerDocCount()
```

Example: The following example lists the number of available searchable documents as well as the maximum number allowed:

```
<CFSET doc_max=GetK2ServerDocCountLimit()>
<CFSET doc_cur=GetK2ServerDocCount()>
<CFOUTPUT>
There are #doc_cur# indexed documents (out of an allowed #doc_max#).
</CFOUTPUT>
```

➜ *See also* `GetK2ServerDocCountExceeded()`, `IsK2ServerDocCountExceeded()`

GetK2ServerDocCountLimit()

Description: `GetK2ServerDocCountLimit()` returns the maximum number of allowed documents that may be indexed using the Verity K2 server.

Syntax:

```
GetK2ServerDocCountLimit()
```

Example: The following example lists the number of available searchable documents as well as the maximum number allowed:

```
<CFSET doc_max=GetK2ServerDocCountLimit()>
<CFSET doc_cur=GetK2ServerDocCount()>
<CFOUTPUT>
There are #doc_cur# indexed documents (out of an allowed #doc_max#).
</CFOUTPUT>
```

→ *See also* `GetK2ServerDocCount()`, `IsK2ServerDocCountExceeded()`

`GetTickCount()`

Description: `GetTickCount()` performs timing tests with millisecond accuracy. The value returned by `GetTickCount` is of no use other than to compare it with the results of another `GetTickCount()` call to check time spans.

Syntax:

```
GetTickCount()
```

Example: The following example tests how long a code block takes to execute:

```
<CFSET count1 = #GetTickCount()#>
<CFSET count2 = #GetTickCount()#>
<CFSET duration = count2-count1>
<CFOUTPUT>Code took #duration# milliseconds to execute</CFOUTPUT>
```

`GetTimeZoneInfo()`

Description: The `GetTimeZoneInfo()` function returns a structure containing relevant time zone information from the machine on which the code is run. The `GetTimeZoneInfo()` function does not take any parameters, and the structure returned contains four elements with the keys outlined in Table C.33.

Table C.33 `GetTimeZoneInfo`—Keys Returned in Structure

KEY	DESCRIPTION
`utcTotalOffset`	Returns the difference in local time (time captured from the machine executing the code) from UTC (Universal Coordinated Time). A plus sign lets you know that the time zone you are comparing is west of UTC; a minus sign lets you know that the time zone you are comparing is east of UTC.
`utcHourOffset`	Returns the difference in local time from UTC in hours.
`utcMinuteOffset`	Returns the difference in local time from UTC in minutes, after the hours offset has been figured in. For some countries, such as those in North America, the minute offset is 0 because these countries' times are offset from UTC by exactly n hours. However, the times of some countries in the world are offset from UTC by n hours and n minutes.
`isDSTOn`	Returns `TRUE` if daylight saving time is on in the machine executing the code; otherwise, if daylight saving time is off, it returns `FALSE`.

Syntax:

```
GetTimeZoneInfo()
```

Example: The following example uses `GetTimeZoneInfo()` to compare UTC offsets with the local time:

```
<CFSET myTime = GetTimeZoneInfo()>
<CFOUTPUT>
The difference in local time from UTC in seconds is #myTime.utcTotalOffset#.<BR>
The difference in local time from UTC in hours is #myTime.utcHourOffset#.<BR>
The difference in local time from UTC in minutes is #mytime.utcMinuteOffset#.<BR>
</CFOUTPUT>
```

➜ *See also* `DateConvert()`, `CreateDateTime()`, `DatePart()`

GetToken()

Description: *Tokens are delimited sets of data within a string. The* `GetToken()` function enables you to extract a particular token from a string by specifying the *token number, or index.* `GetToken()` takes three parameters. The first is the string to search. The second is the index of the token to extract; `3` will extract the third token and `5` will extract the fifth, for example. The third parameter is an optional set of delimiters `GetToken()` uses to determine where each token starts and finishes. If the delimiter's parameter is not provided, the default of spaces, tabs, and new-line characters is used. The default delimiters effectively enable this function to be used to extract specific words for a string. `GetToken()` returns the token in the specified position or any empty string if `Index` is greater than the number of tokens present.

Syntax:

```
GetToken(String, Index [, Delimiters])
```

Example: The following example uses a hyphen as a delimiter to extract just the area code from a phone number:

```
#GetToken("800-555-1212", 1, "-")#
```

TIP

Use the ColdFusion list functions instead of `GetToken()` when working with strings that contain lists of data.

➜ *See also* `Left()`, `Right()`, `Mid()`, `SpanExcluding()`, `SpanIncluding()`

Hash()

Description: The `Hash()` function converts a string into a 32-byte hexadecimal string using the one-way MD5 algorithm. Because this conversion is one-way, a string that has been converted to hexadecimal using the `Hash()` function can't be converted back to its original form. The `Hash()` function takes a single parameter: the string to be converted using `Hash()`.

Syntax:

```
Hash(string)
```

Example: The following example hashes a user-defined password value:

```
#Hash("#form.password#")#
```

TIP

The `Hash()` function is useful for converting sensitive data (such as user passwords) into a hexadecimal string for storage in the database. If you store the converted value in the database, you can then have users reenter their passwords, hash the value they enter, and compare the hexadecimal string returned with the hexadecimal value stored in the database.

Hour()

Description: `Hour()` returns a date/time object's hour as a numeric value with possible values of `0–23`. `Hour()` takes a single parameter: the date/time object to be processed.

Syntax:

```
Hour(Date)
```

Example: The following example returns the current hour of the day:

```
This is hour #Hour(Now())# of the day
```

TIP

When specifying the year using the `Hour()` function, be aware that ColdFusion will interpret the numeric values `0-29` as twenty-first century years. The numeric values `30-99` are interpreted as twentieth century years.

TIP

Always enclose date/time values in quotes when passing them to the `Hour()` function as strings. Without quotes, the value passed is interpreted as a numeral representation of a date/time object.

➜ *See also* `Day()`, `DayOfWeek()`, `DayOfYear()`, `Minute()`, `Month()`, `Quarter()`, `Second()`, `Week()`, `Year()`

HTMLCodeFormat()

Description: `HTMLCodeFormat()` displays text with HTML codes with a preformatted HTML block (using the `<PRE>` and `</PRE>` tags). `HTMLCodeFormat()` takes a single parameter: the text to be processed. When you evaluate a string with the `HTMLCodeFormat()` function, all carriage returns are removed from the string and all special characters contained within the string are escaped.

Syntax:

```
HTMLCodeFormat(Text)
```

Example: The following example uses preformatted text to display the code used to generate a dynamic Web page:

```
#HTMLCodeFormat(page)#
```

TIP

`HTMLCodeFormat()` is useful for displaying data in `FORM TEXTAREA` fields.

➜ *See also* `HTMLEditFormat()`, `ParagraphFormat()`

HTMLEditFormat()

Description: `HTMLEditFormat()` converts supplied text into a safe format, with any HTML control characters converted to their appropriate entity codes. `HTMLEditFormat()` takes a single parameter: the text to be converted.

Syntax:

```
HTMLEditFormat(Text)
```

Example: The following example displays the HTML code used to render a dynamic Web page inside a bordered box:

```
<TABLE BORDER>
 <TR>
  <TD>#HTMLEditFormat(page)#</TD>
 </TR>
</TABLE>
```

TIP

Use `HTMLEditFormat()` to display HTML code and tags within your page.

➜ *See also* `HTMLCodeFormat()`, `ParagraphFormat()`

`IIf()`

Description: `IIf()` evaluates a Boolean condition and evaluates one of two expressions depending on the results of that evaluation. If the Boolean condition returns `TRUE`, the first expression is evaluated; if the condition returns `FALSE`, the second expression is evaluated.

Syntax:

```
IIF(Boolean condition, Expression if TRUE, Expression if FALSE)
```

Example: The following example determines whether `#cnt#` has a value of `1`; it evaluates `"A"` if it does and `"B"` if it does not:

```
#IIf("#cnt# IS 1", "A", "B")#
```

➜ *See also* `DE()`, `Evaluate()`

`IncrementValue()`

Description: The `IncrementValue()` function increments the passed number by 1. This function takes only one numeric value as a parameter. You can pass real values, integer values, and ColdFusion fields to this function.

Syntax:

```
IncrementValue(number)
```

Example: The following example returns `100`, which is `99` incremented by `1`:

```
#IncrementValue("99")#
```

➜ *See also* `Ceiling()`, `Int()`, `Round()`

`InputBaseN()`

Description: `InputBaseN()` converts a string into a number using the base specified. Valid radix values are 2–36.

Syntax:

```
InputBaseN(String, Radix)
```

Example: The following example converts the string containing the binary number `10100010` into its base 10 equivalent of `162`:

```
#InputBaseN("10100010", 2)#
```

TIP

The code `InputBaseN(String, 10)` is functionally equivalent to the code `Val(String)`. If you are converting a number that is base 10, the `Val()` function is simpler to use.

➜ *See also* `FormatBaseN()`, `Val()`

Insert()

Description: `Insert()` is used to insert text into a string and takes three parameters. The first parameter, `SourceString`, is the string you want to insert. The second parameter, `TargetString`, is the string into which you will insert `SourceString`. The third parameter, `Position`, is a numeric value that specifies the location in the `TargetString` at which to insert the `SourceString`. `Insert()` returns the modified string.

Syntax:

```
Insert(SourceString, TargetString, Position)
```

Example: The following example inserts a field called area code in front of a phone number:

```
#Insert(area_code, phone, 0)#
```

TIP

To insert a string at the very beginning of another, use the `Insert()` function specifying a `Position` of `0`.

➜ *See also* `RemoveChars()`, `SpanExcluding()`, `SpanIncluding()`

Int()

Description: `Int()` decrements the passed number by 1. This function takes only one numeric value as a parameter. You can pass real values, integer values, and ColdFusion fields to this function.

Syntax:

```
IncrementValue(number)
```

Example: The following example returns `99`, which is 100 incremented by 1:

```
#Int("100")#
```

➜ *See also* `Ceiling()`, `Fix()`, `Round()`

IsArray()

Description: `IsArray()` checks whether a variable is a valid ColdFusion array; it also determines whether an array has a specific number of dimensions. `IsArray()` takes two parameters: the variable to be checked and an optional number of dimensions to check for. `IsArray()` returns `TRUE` if the variable is an array and `FALSE` if not.

Syntax:

```
IsArray (Array [, Dimension])
```

Example: The following example checks whether a variable named `Users` is an array:

```
#IsArray(Users)#
```

The following example checks whether `Users` is a three-dimensional array:

```
#IsArray(Users, 3)#
```

➜ *See also* `ArrayIsEmpty()`

`IsAuthenticated()`

Deprecated.

`IsAuthorized()`

Deprecated.

`IsBinary()`

Description: `IsBinary()` tests whether a specified value is a binary value. Returns `TRUE` if the specified value is binary and `FALSE` if it is not. The `IsBinary()` function takes a single parameter: the value to be evaluated.

Syntax:

```
IsBinary(value)
```

Example: The following example checks whether a specified value is a binary value:

```
#IsBinary(myValue)#
```

➜ *See also* `ToBinary()`, `ToBase64()`, `IsNumeric()`

`IsBoolean()`

Description: `IsBoolean()` determines whether a value can be converted to a Boolean value. (Boolean values have two states only, `ON` and `OFF` or `TRUE` and `FALSE`.) `IsBoolean()` takes a single parameter: the number, string, or expression to be evaluated. When evaluating numbers, `IsBoolean()` treats `0` as `FALSE` and any nonzero value as `TRUE`.

Syntax:

```
IsBoolean(Value)
```

Example: The following example checks to see whether a value can be safely converted into a Boolean value before passing it to a formatting function:

```
<CFIF IsBoolean(status) >
 #YesNoFormat(status)#
</CFIF>
```

➜ *See also* `YesNoFormat()`

IsCustomFunction()

Description: `IsCustomFunction()` is used to verify that a function being used is a user-defined function. `IsCustomFunction()` takes a single parameter: the function to be verified. It returns `Yes` if the function being evaluated is a user-defined function and `No` if it is not.

Syntax:

```
IsCustomFunction(function)
```

Example: The following example checks the function `UDF` to determine whether it is in fact a user-defined function:

```
#IsCustomFunction(UDF)#
```

IsDebugMode()

Description: `IsDebugMode()` checks whether a page is being sent back to the user in debug mode. `IsDebugMode()` returns `TRUE` if debug mode is on and `FALSE` if not. `IsDebugMode()` takes no parameters.

Syntax:

```
IsDebugMode()
```

Example: The following example writes debug data to a log file if debug mode is on:

```
<CFIF IsDebugMode()>
 <CFFILE ACTION= APPEND" FILE="log.txt" OUTPUT="#debug_info#">
</CFIF>
```

IsDefined()

Description: `IsDefined()` determines whether a specified variable exists. `IsDefined()` returns `TRUE` if the specified variable exists and `FALSE` if not. `IsDefined()` takes a single parameter: the variable for which to check. This parameter can be passed as a fully qualified variable, with a preceding variable type designator. The variable name must be enclosed in quotation marks; otherwise, ColdFusion checks for the existence of the variable's contents rather than of the variable itself.

Syntax:

```
IsDefined(Parameter)
```

Example: The following example checks whether a variable of any type named `USER_ID` exists:

```
<CFIF IsDefined("USER_ID")>
```

The next example checks to see whether a CGI variable named `USER_ID` exists and ignores variables of other types:

```
<CFIF IsDefined("CGI.USER_ID")>
```

NOTE

`IsDefined()` is a little more complicated than `ParameterExists()`, but it does enable you to dynamically evaluate and redirect expressions. Because `ParameterExists()` is a deprecated function, you should always use `IsDefined()` in its place.

→ *See also* `Evaluate()`, `IsSimpleValue()`

IsDate

Description: `IsDate()` checks whether a string contains a valid date; it returns `TRUE` if it does and `FALSE` if it does not. `IsDate()` takes a single parameter: the string to be evaluated.

Syntax:

```
IsDate(String)
```

Example: The following example checks whether a user-supplied date string contains a valid date:

```
<CFIF IsDate(ship_date) IS "No">
 You entered an invalid date!
</CFIF>
```

NOTE

`IsDate()` checks U.S.-style dates only. Use the `LSIsDate()` function for international date support.

TIP

When specifying the year using the `IsDate()` function, be aware that ColdFusion will interpret the numeric values `0-29` as twenty-first century years. The numeric values `30-99` are interpreted as twentieth century years.

➜ *See also* `IsLeapYear()`, `LSIsDate()`, `ParseDateTime()`

IsK2ServerDocCountExceeded()

Description: `IsK2ServerDocCountExceeded()` checks whether the maximum number of documents that may be indexed by Verity K2 server has been reached. It returns `TRUE` if the limit has been exceeded and `FALSE` if not.

Syntax:

```
IsK2ServerDocCountExceeded()
```

Example: The following example reports whether the K2 server document count has been exceeded:

```
<CFOUTPUT>
Verity K2 Server full: #YesNoFormat(IsK2ServerDocCountExceeded())#
</CFOUTPUT>
```

➜ *See also* `GetK2ServerDocCount()`, `GetK2ServerDocCountExceeded()`

IsK2ServerOnline()

Description: `IsK2ServerOnline()` returns `TRUE` if the Verity K2 server that is part of ColdFusion is up and running.

Syntax:

```
IsK2ServerOnline()
```

Example: The following example demonstrates a test of the K2 server's status before a search is attempted:

```
<CFIF NOT IsK2ServerOnline()>
   <P>The K2 Server is not on-line at this time. Please contact your
   system administrator.
<CFELSE>
   <!--- Do search against K2 Server index.  --->
</CFIF>
```

➜ *See also* `GetK2ServerDocCountExceeded()`, `IsK2ServerDocCountExceeded()`

IsLeapYear()

Description: `IsLeapYear()` checks whether a specified year is a leap year. `IsLeapYear()` takes a single parameter: the year to be checked. It returns `TRUE` if it is a leap year and `FALSE` if not.

Syntax:

```
IsLeapYear(Year)
```

Example: The following example checks whether this year is a leap year:

```
<CFIF IsLeapYear(Year(Now()))>
 #Year(Now())# is a leap year
<CFELSE>
#Year(Now())# is not a leap year
</CFIF>
```

TIP

`IsLeapYear()` takes a year, not a date/time object, as a parameter. To check whether a date stored in a date/time object is a leap year, use the `-Year()` function to extract the year and pass that as the parameter to `IsLeapYear()`.

➜ *See also* `IsDate()`

IsNumeric()

Description: `IsNumeric()` checks whether a specified value is numeric. `IsNumeric()` takes a single parameter: the value to be evaluated. `IsNumeric()` returns `TRUE` if the specified string can be converted to a number and `FALSE` if it can't.

Syntax:

```
IsNumeric(Value)
```

Example: The following example checks to ensure that a user has entered a valid age (numeric characters only):

```
<CFIF IsNumeric(age) IS "No">
 You entered an invalid age!
</CFIF>
```

NOTE

Use the `LSIsNumeric()` function for international number support.

➜ *See also* `InputBaseN()`, `LSIsNumeric()`, `Val()`

IsNumericDate()

Description: `IsNumericDate()` checks whether a value passed as a date in the ColdFusion internal date format is in fact a legitimate date. `IsNumericDate()` takes a single parameter: the date to be checked. This date is a floating-point value with precision until the year 9999. `IsNumericDate()` returns `TRUE` if the passed date value is valid and `FALSE` if it is not.

Syntax:

```
IsNumericDate(Real)
```

Example: The following example checks whether a local variable contains a valid date:

```
<CFIF IsNumericDate(var.target_date) IS "Yes">
```

➜ *See also* `IsDate()`

IsObject()

Description: The `IsObject()` function returns `True` if the specified variable is an object. If it is a basic ColdFusion variable type, the function returns `False`. Basic ColdFusion variable types include string, integer, float, date, structure, array, query, XML object, and user-defined funciton. The various object types you can test for are listed in Table C.34. This function can also optionally take component-specific arguments—arguments that differ depending on the type of object you're testing for.

Syntax:

```
IsObject(variable, type, component-specific-param)
```

Table C.34 Object Types Used in `IsObject`

OBJECT TYPES
Component
Java
Corba
Com
Template
Webservice

Example: The following example returns a value indicating whether or not it is running inside a component:

```
<CFCOMPONENT>
<CFFUNCTION NAME="tester">
   <CFRETURN IsObject(this)>
</CFFUNCTION>
</CFCOMPONENT>
```

➜ *See also* `CreateObject()`

`IsProtected()`

Deprecated.

`IsSimpleValue()`

Description: `IsSimpleValue()` checks whether a value is a string, a number, a `TRUE/FALSE` value, or a `DATE/TIME` value. `IsSimpleValue()` takes a single parameter: the value to be checked. `IsSimpleValue()` returns `TRUE` if the value is a simple value and `FALSE` if not.

Syntax:

```
IsSimpleValue(Value)
```

Example: The following example checks to see that a description field is a simple value:

```
<CFIF IsSimpleValue(Description)>
```

➜ *See also* `Evaluate()`, `IsDefined()`

`IsStruct()`

Description: The `IsStruct()` function returns `TRUE` if the variable being evaluated is a structure. The `IsStruct()` function takes a single parameter: the variable to be evaluated.

Syntax:

```
IsStruct(variable)
```

Example: The following example checks to see whether the variable `People` is a structure:

```
#IsStruct(People)#
```

`IsQuery()`

Description: `IsQuery()` checks whether a variable is a valid ColdFusion query. `IsQuery()` takes a single parameter: the variable to be checked. `IsQuery()` returns `TRUE` if the variable is a query and `FALSE` if not.

Syntax:

```
IsQuery(Query)
```

Example: The following example checks whether a variable named `Users` is a query:

```
<CFIF IsQuery(Users)>
```

TIP

> `IsQuery()` is particularly useful within custom tags that expect queries as parameters. `IsQuery()` can be used to check that a valid value was passed before any processing occurs.

➜ *See also* `QueryAddRow()`

IsUserInRole()

Description: `IsUserInRole()` is part of ColdFusion's security framework and works in conjunction with the use of other parts of the framework. `IsUserInRole()` checks the current authenticated user's roles, looking for the role specifed in the parameter, role.

NOTE

Note that the user must have been authenticated through use of the `<CFLOGINUSER>` tag, which along with `<CFLOGIN>` and `<CFLOGOUT>` is part of the ColdFusion security framework. `<CFLOGINUSER>` enables you to indicate that the user is part of a role (which you define: Managers, Staff, Admin, and so on).

Syntax:

```
IsUserInRole(role)
```

Example: The following example checks the current authenticated user to see if he or she is in the Managers role and provides different content based on return value.

```
<CFIF IsUserInRole("Managers")>
   <CFINCLUDE TEMPLATE="FinancialReport.cfm">
<CFELSE>
   <P>Access denied.
</CFIF>
```

➜ *See also* `QueryAddRow()`

IsWDDX()

Description: `IsWDDX()` checks whether a variable contains a valid WDDX packet. `IsWDDX()` takes a single parameter: the variable to be checked. `IsWDDX()` returns `TRUE` if the variable contains a valid packet and `FALSE` if not.

Syntax:

```
IsWDDX(Query)
```

Example: The following example checks whether a variable named stream is a valid WDDX packet:

```
<CFIF IsWDDX(stream)>
```

TIP

`IsWDDX()` should be used to verify a WDDX packet before passing it to `<CFWDDX>`.

IsXMLDoc()

Description: `IsXMLDoc()` indicates whether the parameter value is a valid ColdFusion XML document object. Returns `TRUE` if it is and `FALSE` if it is not.

NOTE

Note that the ColdFusion XML document object was introduced starting with ColdFusion MX.

Syntax:

```
IsXMLDoc(document)
```

Example: The following example checks whether a variable named `XMLstream` is a valid XML document object:

```
<!--- Create an ColdFusion XML doc object --->
<CFXML VARIABLE="myXMLdoc">
<orders>
   <order orderid="1"
    orderdate="3/1/2001"
    shipaddress="1 Rue Street"
    shipcity="Brussels"
    shipzip="1234"
    shipstate="">
      <orderitem orderitemid="1"
       itemid="6"
       orderqty="2"
       itemprice="30.00"/>
      <orderitem orderitemid="2"
       itemid="1"
       orderqty="1"
       itemprice="17.50"/>
      <orderitem orderitemid="3"
       itemid="9"
       orderqty="1"
       itemprice="100.00"/>
   </order>
   <order orderid="2"
    orderdate="3/1/2001"
    shipaddress="21700 Northwestern Hwy"
    shipcity="Southfield"
    shipzip="48075"
    shipstate="Michigan">
      <orderitem orderitemid="4"
       itemid="11"
       orderqty="10"
       itemprice="7.50"/>
   </order>
</orders>
</CFXML>
<!--- Test to make sure it worked --->
<CFIF IsXMLDoc(myXMLdoc)>
   <P/><CFOUTPUT>#IsXMLRoot("orderitem")#</CFOUTPUT>
<CFELSE>
   <CFABORT SHOWERROR="This is not a vaild XML document object">
</CFIF>
```

IsXMLElem()

Description: `IsXMLElem()` returns `TRUE` or `FALSE` to indicate whether the parameter is an XML document object element.

Syntax:

```
IsXMLElem(XML_element)
```

Example: The following example reads an XML document file into a text vairable. This is then parsed into an XML document object. The elements of this document object are split into an array using `XMLSearch()`. Then the array is looped through, to verify that each element is valid.

```
<!--- Read XML file into a text variable --->
<CFFILE ACTION="READ" FILE="c:\neo\wwwroot\ows\c\orders.xml" VARIABLE="myXMLfile">
<!--- Transform it to an XML document object --->
<CFSET myXMLdoc = XMLParse(myXMLfile)>
<!--- Test to make sure it worked --->
<CFIF IsXMLDoc(myXMLdoc)>
   <CFSCRIPT>
   // Create an array of XML document elements
   myXMLarray = XMLSearch(myXMLDoc, "/orders/order/orderitem");
   // Loop through array
   for (i=1;i LTE ArrayLen(myXMLarray); i=i+1) {
      // Verify that each is an element
      WriteOutput(IsXMLElem(myXMLarray[i]) & "<BR/>");
   }
   </CFSCRIPT>
<CFELSE>
   <!--- Not a valid XML document object, warn user --->
   <CFABORT SHOWERROR="This is not a vaild XML document object">
</CFIF>
```

IsXMLRoot()

Description: `IsXMLRoot()` returns `TRUE` or `FALSE` indicating whether the parameter is the root element of an XML document object.

Syntax:

```
IsXMLRoot(XML_element_name)
```

Example: See the example for `IsXMLDoc()` above.

➜ *See also* `IsXMLDoc()`

JavaCast()

Description: The `JavaCast()` function is used to indicate that a ColdFusion variable should be converted to be passed as an argument to an overloaded method of a Java object. The `JavaCast()` function should be used only to pass scalar and string arguments. This function takes two parameters. The first is the data type the variable should be converted to prior to being passed. Possible valid data types are Boolean, `int`, `long`, `double`, and `String`. The second parameter is the variable to be converted.

Syntax:

```
JavaCast(type, variable)
```

Example: The following example converts the specified variable to the `int` data type:

```
#JavaCast("int", myNum)#
```

➜ *See also* `CreateObject()`, `CFOBJECT()`

JSStringFormat()

Description: The `JSStringFormat()` function formats a specified string so that it is safe to use with JavaScript. The `JSStringFormat()` function takes a single parameter: the string to be formatted. The function escapes any special JavaScript characters, so you can put these characters in strings that you pass as JavaScript. The characters that are escaped by the `JSStringFormat()` function include the `'` (single quotation mark), `"` (double quotation mark), and new-line characters.

Syntax:

```
JSStringFormat(string)
```

Example: The following example converts the specified string to a format that is safe to use with JavaScript:

```
#JSStringFormat("mystring")#
```

LCase()

Description: `LCase()` converts a string to lowercase. `LCase()` takes a single parameter—the string to be converted—and returns the converted string.

Syntax:

```
LCase(String)
```

Example: The following example converts a user-supplied string to lowercase:

```
#LCase(string_field)#
```

➜ *See also* `UCase()`

Left()

Description: `Left()` returns the specified leftmost characters from the beginning of a string. `Left()` takes two parameters: the string from which to extract the characters and the number of characters to extract.

Syntax:

```
Left(String, Count)
```

Example: The following example returns the first three characters of a phone number column:

```
#Left(phone_number, 3)#
```

➜ *See also* `Find()`, `Mid()`, `RemoveChars()`, `Right()`

Len()

Description: `Len()` returns the length of a specified string. `Len()` takes a single parameter: the string whose length you want to determine.

Syntax:

```
Len(String)
```

Example: The following example returns the length of a user-supplied address field after it has been trimmed:

```
#Len(Trim(address))#
```

➜ *See also* `ToBinary()`, `Left()`, `Mid()`, `Right()`

ListAppend()

Description: `ListAppend()` adds an element to the end of a list and returns the new list with the appended element. `ListAppend()` takes two parameters: the first is the current list, and the second is the element to be appended.

Syntax:

```
ListAppend(List, Element)
```

Example: The following example appends `John` to an existing list of users and replaces the old list with the new one:

```
<CFSET Users = ListAppend(Users, "John")>
```

➜ *See also* `ListInsertAt()`, `ListPrepend()`, `ListSetAt()`

ListChangeDelims()

Description: `ListChangeDelims()` returns a passed list reformatted to use a different delimiter. `ListChangeDelims()` takes two parameters: the first is the list to be reformatted, and the second is the new delimiter character.

Syntax:

```
ListChangeDelims(List, Delimiter)
```

Example: The following example creates a new list containing the same elements as the original list but separated by plus signs:

```
<CFSET URLUsers = ListChangeDelims(Users, "+")>
```

TIP

The default list delimiter, a comma, is the delimiter that SQL lists use. If you are going to pass ColdFusion lists to SQL statements, you should use the default delimiter.

➜ *See also* `ListFirst()`, `ListQualify()`

ListContains()

Description: The `ListContains()` function performs a case-sensitive search through a list to find the first element that contains the specified search text. If the search text is found, the position of the element containing the text is returned. If no match is found, `0` is returned. It takes two parameters: the first parameter is the list to be searched, and the second parameter is the value for which to search.

Syntax:

```
ListContains(List, Value)
```

Example: The following example returns the position of the first element that contains the text `cash`:

```
Element #ListContains(Payments, "cash")# contains the word "cash"
```

NOTE

`ListContains()` finds substrings within elements that match the specified search text. To perform a search for a matching element, use the `ListFind()` function instead.

➜ *See also* `ListContainsNoCase()`, `ListFind()`, `ListFindNoCase()`

ListContainsNoCase()

Description: The `ListContainsNoCase()` function performs a non–case-sensitive search through a list to find the first element that contains the specified search text. If the search text is found, the position of the element containing the text is returned. If no match is found, `0` is returned. It takes two parameters: the first parameter is the list to be searched, and the second parameter is the value for which to search.

Syntax:

```
ListContainsNoCase(List, Value)
```

Example: The following example returns the position of the first element that contains the text `cash` (regardless of case):

```
Element #ListContainsNoCase(Payments, "cash")# contains the word "cash"
```

NOTE

`ListContainsNoCase()` finds substrings within elements that match the specified search text. To perform a search for a matching element, use the `ListFindNoCase()` function instead.

➜ *See also* `ListContains()`, `ListFind()`, `ListFindNoCase()`

ListDeleteAt()

Description: `ListDeleteAt()` deletes a specified element from a list. `ListDeleteAt()` takes two parameters: the first is the list to be processed, and the second is the position of the element to be deleted. `ListDeleteAt()` returns a modified list with the specified element deleted. The specified element position must exist; an error message is generated if you specify an element beyond the range of the list.

Syntax:

```
ListDeleteAt(List, Position)
```

Example: The following example deletes the second element in a list, but it first verifies that it exists:

```
<CFIF #ListLen(Users)# GTE 2>
 <CFSET Users = ListDeleteAt(Users, 2)>
</CFIF>
```

➜ *See also* `ListRest()`

`ListFind()`

Description: The `ListFind()` function performs a case-sensitive search through a list to find the first element that matches the specified search text. If a matching element is found, the position of that element is returned; if no match is found, `0` is returned. It takes two parameters: the first parameter is the list to be searched, and the second parameter is the element text fo which to search.

Syntax:

```
ListFind(List, Value)
```

Example: The following example returns the position of the first element whose value is `MI`:

```
MI is element #ListFind(States, "MI")#
```

NOTE

`ListFind()` finds only elements that exactly match the specified search text. To perform a search for substrings within elements, use the `ListContains()` function.

➜ *See also* `ListContains()`, `ListContainsNoCase()`, `LindFindNoCase()`

`ListFindNoCase()`

Description: The `ListFindNoCase()` function performs a non–case-sensitive search through a list to find the first element that matches the specified search text. If a matching element is found, the position of that element is returned; if no match is found, `0` is returned. It takes two parameters: the first parameter is the list to be searched, and the second parameter is the element text for which to search.

Syntax:

```
ListFindNoCase(List, Value)
```

Example: The following example returns the position of the first element whose value is `MI`, regardless of case:

```
MI is element #ListFindNoCase(States, "MI")#
```

NOTE

`ListFindNoCase()` finds only elements that exactly match the specified search text. To perform a search for substrings within elements, use the `ListContainsNoCase()` function.

➜ *See also* `ListContains()`, `ListContainsNoCase()`, `ListFind()`

ListFirst()

Description: `ListFirst()` returns the first element in a list. `ListFirst()` takes a single parameter: the list to be processed.

Syntax:

```
ListFirst(List)
```

Example: The following example returns the first selection from a field of book titles submitted by a user:

```
The first title you selected is #ListFirst(titles)#
```

➜ *See also* `ListGetAt()`, `ListLast()`, `ListRest()`

ListGetAt()

Description: `ListGetAt()` returns the list element at a specified position. `ListGetAt()` takes two parameters: The first is the list to process, and the second is the position of the desired element. The value passed as the position parameter must not be greater than the length of the list; otherwise, a ColdFusion error message is generated.

Syntax:

```
ListGetAt(List, Position)
```

Example: The following example returns the name of the fourth selection from a field of book titles submitted by a user:

```
The fourth title you selected is #ListGetAt(titles, 4)#
```

➜ *See also* `ListFirst()`, `ListLast()`, `ListRest()`

ListInsertAt()

Description: `ListInsertAt()` inserts a specified element into a list, shifting all elements after it one position to the right. `ListInsertAt()` takes three parameters: The first is the list to be processed; the second is the desired position for the new element; and the third is the value of the new element. The position parameter must be no greater than the number of elements in the list. A ColdFusion error message is generated if a greater value is provided.

Syntax:

```
ListInsertAt(List, Position, Value)
```

Example: The following example inserts `John` into the third position of an existing list of users and replaces the old list with the new one:

```
<CFSET Users = #ListInsertAt(Users, 3, "John")#>
```

➜ *See also* `ListAppend()`, `ListPrepend()`, `ListSetAt()`

ListLast()

Description: `ListLast()` returns the last element in a list. `ListLast()` takes a single parameter: the list to be processed.

Syntax:

```
ListLast(List)
```

Example: The following example returns the last selection from a field of book titles submitted by a user:

```
The last title you selected is #ListLast(titles)#
```

➜ *See also* `ListFirst()`, `ListGetAt()`, `ListRest()`

ListLen()

Description: `ListLen()` returns the number of elements present in a list. `ListLen()` takes a single parameter: the list to be processed.

Syntax:

```
ListLen(List)
```

Example: The following example returns the number of books selected by a user:

```
You selected #ListLen(titles)# titles
```

➜ *See also* `ListAppend()`, `ListDeleteAt()`, `ListInsertAt()`, `ListPrepend()`

ListPrepend()

Description: `ListPrepend()` inserts an element at the beginning of a list, pushing any other elements to the right. `ListPrepend()` returns the new list with the prepended element. `ListPrepend()` takes two parameters: The first is the current list, and the second is the element to be prepended.

Syntax:

```
ListPrepend(List, Element)
```

Example: The following example prepends `John` to an existing list of users and replaces the old list with the new one:

```
<CFSET Users = ListPrepend(Users, "John")>
```

➜ *See also* `ListAppend()`, `ListInsertAt()`, `ListSetAt()`

ListSort()

Description: `ListSort()` sorts the items in a list according to the specified sort type and order. The `ListSort()` function takes four parameters. The first, `list`, specifies the list you want to sort. The second, `sort_type`, specifies the type of sort you want to perform. Valid sort types are `Numeric` (which sorts numerically), `Text` (which sorts alphabetically), and `TextNoCase` (which sorts alphabetically without regard to case). The third parameter, `sort_order`, is optional. You can specify either `ASC` (ascending) or `DESC` (descending). When no sort order is chosen, ascending order is used. The fourth parameter, `delimiter`, specifies the character to use to delimit items in the list. This parameter is also optional. If no delimiter is provided, a comma is used by default.

Syntax:

```
ListSort(list, sort_type [, sort_order] [, delimiter ])
```

Example: The following example sorts a list with the `TextNoCase` sort type. By default, the list items are returned in ascending order, with a comma delimiting items in the list:

```
#ListSort(JohnList, "TextNoCase")#
```

ListToArray()

Description: `ListToArray()` converts a ColdFusion list to a one-dimensional array. `ListToArray()` takes two parameters: the list to be converted and an optional list delimiter. If no delimiter is specified, the default (comma) delimiter is used. `ListToArray()` creates a new array.

Syntax:

```
ListToArray(List [, Delimiter])
```

Example: The following example converts a list of users into an array:

```
<CFSET UserArray = #ListToArray(UserList)#>
```

CAUTION

When evaluating a list, be aware that ColdFusion will ignore any empty items in a list. If you have a list defined as `"Laura, John, Sean, , ,Bryan"`, it will be evaluated as a four-element list, not a six-element list.

➜ *See also* `ArrayToList()`

ListQualify()

Description: The `ListQualify()` function returns the contents of a specified list with qualifying characters around each list item. The `ListQualify()` function takes four parameters. The first parameter is the list through which you want to parse. The second parameter is the qualifying character you want to have placed around each list item. The third parameter is the delimiter used in the list you are evaluating, and the fourth is whether you want to evaluate every list item or only the list items composed of alphabetic characters. You specify this by defining the elements parameter as either `ALL` or `CHAR`.

Syntax:

```
ListQualify(list, qualifier [, delimiters ] [, elements ])
```

Example: The following example looks through the elements of a list that is delimited with a comma, placing double quotation marks around all list items, regardless of whether the list item is numeric or composed of alphabetic characters:

```
#ListQualify(JohnList,"""",",","ALL")#
```

ListRest()

Description: `ListRest()` returns a list containing all the elements after the first element. If the list contains only one element, an empty list (an empty string) is returned. `ListRest()` takes a single parameter: the list to be processed.

Syntax:

```
ListRest(List)
```

Example: The following example replaces a list with the list minus the first element:

```
<CFSET Users = ListRest(Users)>
```

→ *See also* `ListDeleteAt()`

ListSetAt()

Description: `ListSetAt()` replaces the value of a specific element in a list with a new value. `ListSetAt()` takes four parameters: The first is the list to be processed; the second is the position of the element to be replaced; the third is the new value; and the fourth is the delimiter or set of delimiters to use. If more than one delimiter is specified, ColdFusion defaults to the first delimiter in the list. If no delimiter is specified, the delimiter defaults to a comma. The value passed to the position parameter must be no greater than the number of elements in the list; otherwise, a ColdFusion error message is generated.

Syntax:

```
ListSetAt(List, Position, Value [, delimiters])
```

Example: The following example searches for an element with the value of `"Honda"` and replaces it with the value `"Harley"`:

```
<CFIF ListFindNoCase(Users, "Honda") GT 0>
 <CFSET Users = ListSetAt(Users, ListFindNoCase(Users, "Honda"), "Harley")>
</CFIF>
```

→ *See also* `ListAppend()`, `ListInsertAt()`, `ListPrepend()`

ListValueCount()

Description: `ListValueCount()` searches a list for a specific value and returns the number of occurrences it finds of the specified value. The `ListValueCount()` function is case-sensitive. It takes three parameters. The first parameter is the list to search; the second parameter is the value for which to search the list. The third, optional parameter is the character used to delimit elements in the specified list. If the delimiter parameter is omitted, the default comma is used.

Syntax:

```
ListValueCount(list, value [, delimiters ])
```

Example: The following example searches through a list of users to see how many have the first name Laura:

```
#ListValueCount(usersList, "Laura")#
```

→ *See also* `ListValueCountNoCase()`

ListValueCountNoCase()

Description: `ListValueCountNoCount()` performs a non–case-sensitive search of a list for a specific value and returns the number of occurrences it finds of the specified value. It takes three parameters. The first parameter is the list to search; the second parameter is the value for which to search the list. The third, optional parameter is the character used to delimit elements in the specified list. If the delimiter parameter is omitted, the default comma is used.

Syntax:

```
ListValueCountNoCase(list, value [, delimiters ])
```

Example: The following example searches through a list of users to see how many have the first name Laura:

```
#ListValueCountNoCase(usersList, "laura")#
```

➜ *See also* `ListValueCount()`

LJustify()

Description: `LJustify()` left-aligns a string within a field of a specified length. It does this by padding spaces after the specified text. `LJustify()` takes two parameters: the string to process and the desired string length.

Syntax:

```
#LJustify(String, Length)#
```

Example: The following example left-justifies the string `"First Name:"` so that it is left-aligned within a 25-character-wide field:

```
#LJustify("First Name:", 25)#
```

➜ *See also* `CJustify()`, `LTrim()`, `RJustify()`, `RTrim()`, `Trim()`

Log()

Description: `Log()` returns the natural logarithm of a passed number. This function takes only one numeric value as a parameter. You can pass real values, integer values, and ColdFusion fields to this function.

Syntax:

```
Log(number)
```

Example: The following example returns `1.60943791243`, the natural logarithm of `5`:

```
#Log(5)#
```

➜ *See also* `Log10()`, `Exp()`

Log10()

Description: `Log10()` returns the base 10 log of a passed number. This function takes only one numeric value as a parameter. You can pass real values, integer values, and ColdFusion fields to this function.

Syntax:

```
Log10(number)
```

Example: The following example returns `0.698970004336`, the natural logarithm of `5`:

```
#Log10(5)#
```

➜ *See also* `Log()`, `Exp()`

`LSCurrencyFormat()`

Description: `LSCurrencyFormat()` displays currency information formatted for the current locale. `LSCurrencyFormat()` takes two parameters: the number to display and an optional format type. If a type is specified, its value must be `none`, `local`, or `international`. `Type` defaults to `none`.

Syntax:

```
LSCurrencyFormat(Number [, Type])
```

Example: The following example displays the results of an equation (quantity multiplied by item cost) in formatting appropriate for the French locale:

```
<CFSET previous_locale = SetLocale("French (Standard)")>
Total cost: #LSCurrencyFormat(quantity*item_cost)#
```

NOTE

Unlike versions of ColdFusion prior to ColdFusion MX, the locales used for formatting are now defined by Java standard locale formatting rules on all platforms.

TIP

For more precise currency display, use the `NumberFormat()` function instead.

NOTE

You can use the simpler `DollarFormat()` function for U.S. currency formatting.

➜ *See also* `DollarFormat()`, `NumberFormat()`

`LSDateFormat()`

Description: `LSDateFormat()` displays the date portion of a date/time object in a readable format. `LSDateFormat()` is the locale-specific version of the `DateFormat()` function. Similar to `DateFormat()`, `LSDateFormat()` takes two parameters: the first is the date/time object to be displayed, and the second is an optional mask value enabling you to control exactly how the data is formatted. If no mask is specified, a format suitable for the current locale is used. The complete set of date masks is listed in the `DateFormat()` section.

Syntax:

```
LSDateFormat(Date [, mask ])
```

Example: The following example displays today's date with the default formatting options for the current locale:

```
Today is: #LSDateFormat(Now())#
```

The next example displays the same date but uses the current locale's full names of both the day of week and the month:

```
It is #LSDateFormat(Now(), "DDDD, MMMM DD, YYYY")#
```

NOTE

Unlike versions of ColdFusion prior to ColdFusion MX, the locales used for formatting are now defined by Java standard locale formatting rules on all platforms.

NOTE

You can use the simpler `DateFormat()` function for U.S. dates.

➜ *See also* `DateFormat()`, `LSNumberFormat()`, `LSTimeFormat()`

LSEuroCurrencyFormat()

Description: `LSEuroCurrencyFormat()` returns a currency value formatted in the convention of the locale enabled on the executing machine, using the euro currency symbol. The `LSEuroCurrencyFormat` function takes two parameters. The first, `currency-value`, is the actual amount or value of the currency you want to format. The second parameter, `type`, is an optional parameter that enables you to specify a currency type of `none`, `local`, or `international`. If no currency type is specified, the default of `local` is used. Depending on which type you choose, ColdFusion will display the value with differing currency symbols. If `none` is chosen, the value is displayed as a simple numeric value. If `local` is chosen, the value is displayed in the convention of the locale that is set on the executing machine, displaying the symbol for the euro if an accommodating character set is installed. If `international` is chosen, then the value is displayed with `EUR`, the international symbol for the euro.

Syntax:

```
LSEuroCurrencyFormat(currency-value [,type])
```

NOTE

Unlike versions of ColdFusion prior to ColdFusion MX, the locales used for formatting are now defined by Java standard locale formatting rules on all platforms.

Example: The following formats the value `70,000` to display as `EUR70,000.00`:

```
#LSEuroCurrencyFormat(70000, "international")#
```

➜ *See also* `LSParseEuroCurrency()`, `SetLocale()`

LSIsCurrency()

Description: `LSIsCurrency()` checks whether a string contains a valid currency for the current locale; it returns `TRUE` if it does and `FALSE` if it does not. `LSIsCurrency()` takes a single parameter: the string to be evaluated.

Syntax:

```
LSIsCurrency(String)
```

NOTE

Unlike versions of ColdFusion prior to ColdFusion MX, the locales used for formatting are now defined by Java standard locale formatting rules on all platforms.

Example: The following example checks whether a user-supplied date string contains a valid German currency value:

```
<CFSET previous_locale = SetLocale("German (Standard)")>
<CFIF LSIsCurrency(total) IS "No">
 You entered an invalid currency amount!
</CFIF>
```

➜ *See also* `IsNumber()`, `LSIsNumeric()`

LSIsDate()

Description: `LSIsDate()` checks whether a string contains a valid date for the current locale; it returns `TRUE` if it does and `FALSE` if it does not. `LSIsDate()` takes a single parameter: the string to be evaluated.

Syntax:

```
LSIsDate(String)
```

NOTE

Unlike versions of ColdFusion prior to ColdFusion MX, the locales used for formatting are now defined by Java standard locale formatting rules on all platforms.

Example: The following example checks whether a user-supplied date string contains a valid German date:

```
<CFSET previous_locale = SetLocale("German (Standard)")>
<CFIF LSIsDate(ship_date) IS "No">
 You entered an invalid date!
</CFIF>
```

NOTE

To check U.S. dates, you can use the `IsDate()` function.

➜ *See also* `IsDate()`, `IsLeapYear()`, `LSParseDateTime()`, `ParseDateTime()`

LSIsNumeric()

Description: `LSIsNumeric()` checks whether a specified value is numeric. `LSIsNumeric()` is the locale-specific version of the `IsNumeric()` function. `LSIsNumeric()` takes a single parameter: the value to be evaluated.

Syntax:

```
LSIsNumeric(Value)
```

NOTE

Unlike versions of ColdFusion prior to ColdFusion MX, the locales used for formatting are now defined by Java standard locale formatting rules on all platforms.

Example: The following example checks to ensure that a user has entered a valid locale-specific age (numeric characters only):

```
<CFIF LSIsNumeric(age) IS "No">
 You entered an invalid age!
</CFIF>
```

NOTE

You can use the simpler `IsNumeric()` function for U.S. number support.

→ *See also* `InputBaseN()`, `IsNumeric()`, `Val()`

LSNumberFormat()

Description: `LSNumberFormat()` enables you to display numeric values in a locale-specific, readable format. `LSNumberFormat()` is the locale-specific version of the `NumberFormat` function. `LSNumberFormat()` takes two parameters: the number to be displayed and an optional mask value. If the mask is not specified, the default mask of `,99999999999999` is used. The complete set of number masks is listed in Table C.35 in the description of the `NumberFormat()` function.

If the mask you use cannot format the specified number, this function returns the number unformatted.

Syntax:

```
LSNumberFormat(Number [, mask ])
```

NOTE

Unlike versions prior to ColdFusion MX, the locales used for formatting are now defined by Java standard locale formatting rules on all platforms.

NOTE

To display numbers in any of the U.S. formats, you can use the `NumberFormat()` function.

Example: The following example displays a submitted form field in the default format for the current locale:

```
#LSNumberFormat(FORM.quantity)#
```

→ *See also* `DecimalFormat()`, `DollarFormat()`, `LSCurrencyFormat()`, `LSParseNumber()`, `NumberFormat()`

LSParseCurrency()

Description: `LSParseCurrency()` converts a locale-specific number in string form into a valid number. `LSParseCurrency()` takes two parameters: the string to be converted and an optional type. If a type is specified, its value must be `none`, `local`, or `international`. `Type` defaults to all types if not provided.

Syntax:

```
LSParseCurrency(String [, Type])
```

NOTE

Unlike versions of ColdFusion prior to ColdFusion MX, the locales used for formatting are now defined by Java standard locale formatting rules on all platforms.

Example: The following example converts a user-supplied currency string into a number:

```
<CFSET sale_price = LSParseCurrency(FORM.sale_price)>
```

➜ *See also* `LSCurrencyFormat()`, `LSParseNumber()`

`LSParseDateTime()`

Description: `LSParseDateTime()` converts a locale-specific date in string form into a ColdFusion date/time object. `LSParseDateTime()` is the locale-specific version of the `ParseDateTime()` function. `LSParseDateTime()` takes a single parameter: the string to be converted.

Syntax:

```
LSParseDateTime(String)
```

NOTE

Unlike versions of ColdFusion prior to ColdFusion MX, the locales used for formatting are now defined by Java standard locale formatting rules on all platforms.

Example: The following example converts a user-supplied string containing a date into a ColdFusion date/time object:

```
<CFSET ship_date = LSParseDateTime(FORM.ship_date)>
```

NOTE

For U.S. dates and times, you can use the simpler `ParseDateTime()` function.

CAUTION

Unlike the `ParseDateTime()` function, the `LSParseDateTime()` function does not support POP date/time fields. Passing a POP date/time field to `LSParseDateTime()` generates an error.

➜ *See also* `CreateDateTime()`, `ParseDateTime()`

`LSParseEuroCurrency()`

Description: The `LSParseEuroCurrency()` function converts a currency string that contains the euro symbol or sign to a number. This function attempts conversion of the string based on all three default currency formats (`none`, `local`, and `international`). This function takes a single parameter: the string to be converted.

Syntax:

```
LSParseEuroCurrency(currency-string)
```

NOTE

Unlike versions of ColdFusion prior to ColdFusion MX, the locales used for formatting are now defined by Java standard locale formatting rules on all platforms.

Example: The following example converts a currency string in the euro currency format into a simple number:

```
#LSParseEuroCurrency("EUR1974")#
```

➜ *See also* `LSEuroCurrencyFormat()`, `LSParseCurrency()`

CAUTION

For the `LSParseEuroCurrency()` function to be able to read the euro currency symbol, the machine running the code must have euro-enabled fonts installed.

`LSParseNumber()`

Description: `LSParseNumber()` converts a locale-specific number in string form into a valid number. `LSParseNumber()` takes a single parameter: the string to be converted.

Syntax:

```
LSParseNumber(String)
```

NOTE

Unlike versions of ColdFusion prior to ColdFusion MX, the locales used for formatting are now defined by Java standard locale formatting rules on all platforms.

Example: The following example converts a user-supplied numeric string into a number:

```
<CFSET quantity = LSParseNumber(FORM.quantity)>
```

➜ *See also* `LSCurrencyFormat()`, `LSParseCurrency()`, `Val()`

`LSTimeFormat()`

Description: `LSTimeFormat()` displays the time portion of a date/time object in a locale-specific, readable format. `LSTimeFormat()` is the locale-specific version of the `TimeFormat()` function. `LSTimeFormat()` takes two parameters: The first is the date/time object to be displayed, and the second is an optional mask value that enables you to control exactly how the data is formatted. If no mask is specified, a mask appropriate for the current locale is used. The complete set of date masks is listed in Table C.37, in the description of the `TimeFormat()` function.

Syntax:

```
LSTimeFormat(Date [, mask ])
```

NOTE

Unlike versions of ColdFusion prior to ColdFusion MX, the locales used for formatting are now defined by Java standard locale formatting rules on all platforms.

Example: The following example displays the current time with the default formatting options for the current locale:

```
The time is: #LSTimeFormat(Now())#
```

NOTE

You can use the simpler `TimeFormat()` function for U.S. times.

→ *See also* `LSDateFormat()`, `LSNumberFormat()`, `TimeFormat()`

`LTrim()`

Description: `LTrim()` trims white space (spaces, tabs, and new-line characters) from the beginning of a string. `LTrim()` takes a single parameter: the string to be trimmed.

Syntax:

```
LTrim(String)
```

Example: The following example trims spaces from the beginning of a table note field:

```
#LTrim(notes)#
```

→ *See also* `CJustify()`, `LJustify()`, `RJustify()`, `RTrim()`, `Trim()`, `StripCR()`

`Max()`

Description: `Max()` returns the greater of two passed numbers. This function takes two numeric values as parameters. You can pass real values, integer values, and ColdFusion fields to this function.

Syntax:

```
Max(number1, number2)
```

Example: The following example returns `2`, the greater value of `2` and `1`:

```
#Max(1, 2)#
```

→ *See also* `Min()`

`Mid()`

Description: `Mid()` returns a string of characters from any location in a string. `Mid()` takes three parameters. The first is the string from which to extract the characters; the second is the desired characters' starting position; and the third is the number of characters required.

Syntax:

```
Mid(String, StartPosition, Count)
```

Example: The following example extracts eight characters from the middle of a table column, starting at position 3:

```
#Mid(order_number, 3, 8)#
```

→ *See also* `Find()`, `Left()`, `RemoveChars()`, `Right()`

Min()

Description: `Min()` returns the smaller of two passed numbers. This function takes two numeric values as parameters. You can pass real values, integer values, and ColdFusion fields to this function.

Syntax:

```
Min(number1, number2)
```

Example: The following example returns `1`, the smaller value of `2` and `1`:

```
#Min(1, 2)#
```

➜ *See also* `Max()`

Minute()

Description: `Minute()` returns a date/time object's minute as a numeric value with possible values of `0`–`59`. `Minute()` takes a single parameter: the date/time object to be processed.

Syntax:

```
Minute(Date)
```

Example: The following example returns the current time's minutes:

```
#Minute(Now())# minutes have elapsed since #Hour(Now())# o'clock
```

TIP

When specifying the year using the `Minute()` function, be aware that ColdFusion will interpret the numeric values `0-29` as twenty-first century years. The numeric values `30-99` are interpreted as twentieth century years.

TIP

Always enclose date/time values in quotes when passing them to the `Minute()` function as strings. Without quotes, the value passed is interpreted as a numeral representation of a date/time object.

➜ *See also* `Day()`, `DayOfWeek()`, `DayOfYear()`, `Hour()`, `Month()`, `Quarter()`, `Second()`, `Week()`, `Year()`

Month()

Description: `Month()` returns a date/time object's month as a numeric value with possible values of `1`–`12`. `Month()` takes a single parameter: the date/time object to be processed.

Syntax:

```
Month(Date)
```

Example: The following example returns the current month:

```
It is month #Month(Now())# of year #Year(Now())#
```

➜ *See also* `Day()`, `DayOfWeek()`, `DayOfYear()`, `Hour()`, `Minute()`, `Quarter()`, `Second()`, `Week()`, `Year()`

MonthAsString()

Description: `MonthAsString()` returns the English month name for a passed month number. `MonthAsString()` takes a single parameter: the number of the month to be processed, with a value of `1–12`.

Syntax:

```
MonthAsString(MonthNumber)
```

Example: The following example returns the English name of the current month:

```
It is #MonthAsString(Month(Now()))#".
```

➜ *See also* `DayOfWeek()`, `Month()`

Now()

Description: `Now()` returns a date/time object containing the current date and time precisely to the second. `Now()` takes no parameters.

Syntax:

```
Now()
```

Example: The following example returns the current date and time formatted for correct display:

```
It is now #DateFormat(Now())# #TimeFormat(Now())#
```

NOTE

The `Now()` function returns the system date and time of the computer running the ColdFusion service, not of the system running the Web browser. The date/time object that the `Now()` function returns can be passed to many other date/time functions.

➜ *See also* `CreateDateTime()`, `DatePart()`

NumberFormat()

Description: `NumberFormat()` enables you to display numeric values in a readable format. `NumberFormat()` takes two parameters: the number to be displayed and an optional mask value. If the mask is not specified, the default mask of `",99999999999999"` is used. The complete set of number masks is listed in Table C.35.

Syntax:

```
NumberFormat(Number [, mask ])
```

Table C.35 `NumberFormat()` Mask Characters

MASK	DESCRIPTION
`_`	Optional digit placeholder
`9`	Optional digit placeholder (same as _ but shows decimal place more clearly)
`.`	Specifies the location of the decimal point
`0`	Forces padding with `0`s

Table C.35 (continued)

MASK	DESCRIPTION
`()`	Displays parentheses around the number if it is less than `0`
`+`	Displays a plus sign in front of positive numbers and a minus sign in front of negative numbers
`-`	Displays a minus sign in front of negative numbers and leaves a space in front of positive numbers
`,`	Separates thousands with commas
`C`	Centers the number within mask width
`L`	Left-justifies the number within mask width
`$`	Places a dollar sign in front of the number
`^`	Specifies the location for separating left and right formatting

Example: To demonstrate how the number masks can be used, Table C.36 lists examples of various masks being used to format the numbers 1453.876 and –1453.876.

Table C.36 Number Formatting Examples

MASK	RESULT	NOTES
`NumberFormat(1453.876,`	`1454`	No decimal point is specified in the `"9999")` mask, so the number is rounded to the nearest integer value.
`NumberFormat(-1453.876,`	`–1454`	No decimal point is specified in the `"9999")` mask, so the number is rounded to the nearest integer value.
`NumberFormat(1453.876,`	`1453.88`	Even though a decimal point is `"9999.99")` provided, the number of decimal places specified is less than needed; the decimal portion must be rounded to the nearest integer value.
`NumberFormat(1453.876,`	`1453.88`	The number is positive, so the `"(9999.99)")` parentheses are ignored.
`NumberFormat(-1453.876,`	`(1453.88)`	The number is negative, so `"(9999.99)")` parentheses are displayed around the number.
`NumberFormat(1453.876,`	`1453.88`	The number is positive, so the `"-9999.99")` minus sign is ignored.
`NumberFormat(-1453.876,`	`-1453.88`	The number is negative, so `"-9999.99")` a minus sign is displayed.
`NumberFormat(1453.876,`	`+1453.88`	The number is positive, so a `"+9999.99")` plus sign is displayed.
`NumberFormat(-1453.876,`	`-1453.88`	The number is negative, so a `"+9999.99")` minus sign is displayed.

Table C.36 (continued)

MASK	RESULT	NOTES
`NumberFormat(1453.876,`	`$1453.88`	Using the dollar sign as the first `"$9999.99")` character of the mask places a dollar sign at the beginning of the output.
`NumberFormat(1453.876,`	`1453.876`	Position six of the mask is a carat `"C99999^9999")` character, so the decimal point is positioned there even though fewer than six digits appear before the decimal point. This enables you to align columns of numbers at the decimal point.

NOTE

Use the `LSNumberFormat()` function for international number support.

→ *See also* `DecimalFormat()`, `DollarFormat()`, `LSNumberFormat()`

`ParagraphFormat()`

Description: `ParagraphFormat()` converts text with embedded carriage returns for correct HTML display. HTML ignores carriage returns in text, so they must be converted to HTML paragraph markers (the `<P>` tag) to be displayed correctly. `ParagraphFormat()` takes a single parameter: the text to be processed.

Syntax:

```
ParagraphFormat(Text)
```

Example: The following example displays a converted text file inside a `FORM TEXTAREA` field:

```
<TEXTAREA NAME="comments">#ParagraphFormat(comments)#</TEXTAREA>
```

TIP

`ParagraphFormat()` is useful for displaying data in `FORM TEXTAREA` fields.

→ *See also* `HTMLCodeFormat()`, `HTMLEditFormat()`

`ParameterExists()`

Deprecated.

`ParseDateTime()`

Description: `ParseDateTime()` converts a date in string form into a ColdFusion date/time object. `ParseDateTime()` takes two parameters: the string to be converted and, if specified, the POP conversion method. When a POP conversion method (POP or STANDARD) is specified, this function parses the date/time string passed from a POP mail server.

Syntax:

```
ParseDateTime(String)# or #ParseDateTime(String [,pop-conversion method])
```

NOTE

When using the `ParseDateTime()` function with a POP conversion method, one of two POP conversion methods can be specified. The first of these methods, POP, converts the date/time string passed from a POP mail server to GMT for the U.S. locale. The second POP conversion method available, STANDARD, provides no conversion on the date/time string passed and simply returns the time string as it was retrieved from the POP mail server.

Example: The following example converts a user-supplied string containing a date into a ColdFusion date/time object:

```
<CFSET ship_date = ParseDateTime(FORM.ship_date) >
```

NOTE

`ParseDateTime()` supports U.S.-style dates and times only. Use the `LSParseDateTime()` function for international date and time support.

➜ *See also* `CreateDateTime()`, `LSParseDateTime()`

`Pi()`

Description: `Pi()` returns the value of Pi as `3.14159265359`. It takes no parameters.

Syntax:

```
Pi()
```

Example: The following example displays the value of pi:

```
Pi equals #Pi()#.
```

➜ *See also* `Asin()`, `Cos()`, `Sin()`, `Tan()`

`PreserveSingleQuotes()`

Description: `PreserveSingleQuotes()` instructs ColdFusion to not escape single quotation marks contained in values derived from dynamic parameters. `PreserveSingleQuotes()` takes a single parameter: the string to be preserved. This function is particularly useful when you are constructing SQL statements that will contain ColdFusion variables.

Syntax:

```
PreserveSingleQuotes(String)
```

Example: The following example uses `PreserveSingleQuotes()` to ensure that a dynamic parameter in a SQL statement is included correctly:

```
SELECT * FROM Customers
WHERE CustomerName IN ( #PreserveSingleQuotes(CustNames)#)
```

`Quarter()`

Description: `Quarter()` returns a date/time object's quarter as a numeric value with possible values of `1–4`. `Quarter()` takes a single parameter: the date/time object to be processed.

Syntax:

```
Quarter(Date)
```

Example: The following example returns the current quarter:

```
We are in quarter #Quarter(Now())# of year #Year(Now())#
```

TIP

When specifying the year using the `Quarter()` function, be aware that ColdFusion will interpret the numeric values `0-29` as twenty-first century years. The numeric values `30-99` are interpreted as twentieth century years.

TIP

Always enclose date/time values in quotes when passing them to the `Quarter()` function as strings. Without quotes, the value passed is interpreted as a numeral representation of a date/time object.

➜ *See also* `Day()`, `DayOfWeek()`, `DayOfYear()`, `Hour()`, `Minute()`, `Month()`, `Second()`, `Week()`, `Year()`

`QueryAddColumn()`

Description: `QueryAddColumn()` adds a new column to a specified query and populates that column with data from a one-dimensional array. The number of the column that was added is returned. If necessary, the contents of other query columns are padded to ensure that all columns retain the same number of rows. The `QueryAddColumn()` function takes three parameters. The first is the name of the query to which you want to add a column. The second is the name of the new column you are about to create, and the third is the name of the array that will be used to populate the query column.

Syntax:

```
QueryAddColumn(query, column-name, array-name)
```

Example: The following example creates a new column called `UserName` in the query `GetUsers` and updates that column with the data contained in the `UserNameArray` array:

```
#QueryAddColumn(qGetUsers, "UserName", UserNameArray)#>
```

TIP

When using the `QueryAddColumn()` function, remember that you cannot add columns to cached queries.

➜ *See also* `QueryNew()`, `<CFQUERY>`, `QueryAddRow()`

`QueryAddRow()`

Description: `QueryAddRow()` adds a row to an existing ColdFusion query. `QueryAddRow()` takes two parameters: the query to which to add a row and an optional number of rows to add. If the number of rows is omitted, the default number of `1` is used.

Syntax:

```
QueryAddRow(Query [, Number])
```

Example: The following example creates a new query called `Users` and adds 10 rows to it:

```
<CFSET Users = QueryNew("FirstName, LastName")>
<CFSET temp = QueryAddRow(Users, 10)>
```

➜ *See also* `QueryNew()`, `QuerySetCell()`

QueryNew()

Description: QueryNew() either returns an empty query with a user-defined set of columns, as specified with the columnlist argument, or—if an empty string is specified in the columnlist argument—returns an empty query with no columns.

Syntax:

```
QueryNew( columnlist)
```

Example: The following example creates a new query called Users with columns for FirstName and LastName:

```
<CFSET Users = QueryNew("FirstName, LastName")>
<CFSET temp = QueryAddRow(Users, 10)>
```

➜ *See also* QueryAddRow(), QuerySetCell()

QuerySetCell()

Description: QuerySetCell() is used to set the values of specific cells in a table. QuerySetCell() takes four parameters: the query name, the column name, the value, and an optional row number. If the row number is omitted, the cell in the last query row is set.

Syntax:

```
QuerySetCell(Query, Column, Value [, Row])
```

Example: The following example sets the FirstName column in the third row to the value Ben:

```
<CFSET temp = QuerySetCell(Users, "FirstName", "John", 3)>
```

NOTE

Query cells can also be set using the <CFSET> tag, treating the query as a two-dimensional array.

➜ *See also* QueryAddRow(), QueryNew()

QuotedValueList()

Description: QuotedValueList() drives one query with the results of another. It takes a single parameter—the name of a query column—and return a list of all the values in that column. QuotedValueList() returns a list of values that are each enclosed within quotation marks and separated by commas.

Syntax:

```
QuotesValueList(Column)
```

Example: The following example passes the results from one query to a second query:

```
SELECT * FROM Customers
WHERE CustomerType IN (#QuotedValueList(CustType.type)#)
```

NOTE

The QuotedValueList() function is typically used only when constructing dynamic SQL statements.

TIP

The values returned by `QuotedValueList()` is in the standard ColdFusion list format and can therefore be manipulated by the list functions.

TIP

As a general rule, you should always try to combine both of the queries into a single SQL statement, unless you need to manipulate the values in the list. The time it takes to process one combined SQL statement is far less than the time it takes to process two simpler statements.

→ *See also* `ValueList()`

Rand()

Description: `Rand()` returns a random number between `0` and `1`. This function does not accept any parameters.

Syntax:

```
Rand()
```

Example: The following example returns a random number:

```
#Rand()#
```

→ *See also* `Randomize()`, `RandRange()`

Randomize()

Description: `Randomize()` seeds the random number generator with the passed number. This function takes only one numeric value as a parameter. You can pass real values, integer values, and ColdFusion fields to this function.

Syntax:

```
Randomize(number)
```

Example: The following example returns `0.57079106`, a random number that was seeded with `5`:

```
#Randomize(5)#
```

→ *See also* `Rand()`, `RandRange()`

RandRange()

Description: `RandRange()` returns a random integer value between the two passed numbers. This function takes two numeric values as a parameter. You can pass real values, integer values, and ColdFusion fields to this function.

Syntax:

```
RandRange(number1, number2)
```

Example: The following example returns a random integer value between `5` and `10`:

```
#RandRange(5, 10)#
```

→ *See also* `Randomize()`, `Rand()`

REFind()

Description: `REFind()` performs a case-sensitive search using regular expressions. The first parameter is the string (or regular expression) for which to search, and the second parameter is the target string, or string to be searched. The third, optional parameter can specify the position in the target string from which to start the search. All of these functions return the starting position of the first occurrence of the search string within the specified target string. If the search string is not found, `0` is returned.

Syntax:

```
REFind(RegularExpression, TargetString [, StartPosition])
```

Example: The following example returns `2`, the position of the first vowel:

```
#REFind("[aeiou]", "somestring", "1")#
```

TIP

Regular expressions enable you to perform complex searches through text strings with relative ease. Rather than forcing you to provide the exact text for which you are searching, using the **`REFind`** and **`REFindNoCase`** functions gives you the flexibility of searching for dynamic data. Suppose you wanted to search a string for the first occurrence of any character except vowels. In this case, using **`REFindNoCase`** would make your job much easier.

➜ *See also* `REFindNoCase()`, `FindOneOf()`, `GetToken()`, `Left()`, `Mid()`, `Right()`

REFindNoCase()

Description: `REFindNoCase()` performs a non–case-sensitive search using regular expressions. The first parameter is the string (or regular expression) for which to search, and the second parameter is the target string, or string to be searched. The third, optional parameter can specify the position in the target string from which to start the search. All these functions return the starting position of the first occurrence of the search string within the specified target string. If the search string is not found, `0` is returned.

Syntax:

```
REFindNoCase(RegularExpression, TargetString [, StartPosition])
```

Example: The following example returns `2`, the position of the first `o`:

```
#REFindNoCase("[O]", "somestring", "1")#
```

TIP

Regular expressions enable you to perform complex searches through text strings with relative ease. Rather than forcing you to provide the exact text for which you are searching, using the **`REFindNoCase()`** function gives you the flexibility of searching for dynamic data. Suppose you wanted to search a string for the first occurrence of any character except vowels.

➜ *See also* `REFind()`, `FindOneOf()`, `GetToken()`, `Left()`, `Mid()`, `Right()`

RemoveChars()

Description: `RemoveChars()` returns a string with specified characters removed from it. This function is the exact opposite of the `Mid()` function. `RemoveChars()` takes three parameters: The first is the string from which to remove the characters; the second is the starting position of the characters to be removed; and the third is the number of characters to be removed. If no characters are found in the string being evaluated, the `RemoveChars` function returns `0`.

Syntax:

```
RemoveChars(String, StartPosition, Length)
```

Example: The following example returns a field with characters `10` through `14` removed:

```
#RemoveChars(product_code, 10, 5)#
```

→ *See also* `Left()`, `Mid()`, `Right()`

RepeatString()

Description: `RepeatString()` returns a string made up of a specified string multiple times. `RepeatString()` takes two parameters: The first is the string to repeat, and the second is the number of occurrences.

Syntax:

```
RepeatString(String, Count)
```

Example: The following example creates a horizontal line made up of equals signs:

```
#RepeatString("=", 80)#
```

Replace()

Description: `Replace()` enables you to replace text within strings with alternative text. `Replace()` does a simple text comparison to locate the text to be replaced. It takes four parameters. The first parameter is the string to be processed; the second is the text to be replaced; and the third is the text to replace it with. The fourth parameter is optional and specifies the scope of the replacements. Possible scope values are `"ONE"` to replace the first occurrence only, `"ALL"` to replace all occurrences, and `"RECURSIVE"` to replace all occurrences recursively.

Syntax:

```
Replace(String, WhatString, WithString [, Scope])
```

Example: The following example replaces all occurrences of the text `"US"` in an address field with the text `"USA"`:

```
#Replace(address, "US", "USA", "ALL")#
```

This next example replaces the area code `"(313)"` with the area code `"(810)"`, and because no scope is specified, only the first occurrence of `"(313)"` is replaced:

```
#Replace(phone, "(313)", "(810)")#
```

TIP

The `Replace()` function is case-sensitive, and there is no non-case-sensitive equivalent function. To perform a non-case-sensitive replacement, you first must convert both the search and target strings to either upper- or lowercase (using the `UCase()` or `LCase()` function).

→ *See also* `REReplace()`, `REReplaceNoCase()`, `ReplaceList()`

REReplace()

Description: `REReplace()` enables you to perform case-sensitive searches and replace text within strings with alternative text using regular expressions. It takes four parameters. The first parameter is the string to be processed; the second is the text to be replaced; and the third is the text to replace it with. The fourth parameter is optional and specifies the scope of the replacements. Possible scope values are `"ONE"` to replace the first occurrence only, `"ALL"` to replace all occurrences, and `"RECURSIVE"` to replace all occurrences recursively.

Syntax:

```
REReplace(String, WhatString, WithString [, Scope])
```

Example: The following example returns `Cohn`, by replacing the capital letter `J` with the capital letter `C`. The lowercase `n` was ignored because `REReplace()` is case-sensitive.

```
#REReplace("John","J|N","C","ALL")#
```

➜ *See also* `Replace()`, `REReplace()`, `ReplaceList()`

REReplaceNoCase()

Description: `REReplaceNoCase()` enables you to perform non–case-sensitive searches and replace text within strings with alternative text using regular expressions. It takes four parameters. The first parameter is the string to be processed; the second is the text to be replaced; and the third is the text to replace it with. The fourth parameter is optional and specifies the scope of the replacements. Possible scope values are `"ONE"` to replace the first occurrence only, `"ALL"` to replace all occurrences, and `"RECURSIVE"` to replace all occurrences recursively.

Syntax:

```
REReplaceNoCase(String, WhatString, WithString [, Scope])
```

Example: The following example returns `CohC`, by replacing the capital letter `J` and `n` with the capital letter `C`.

```
#REReplaceNoCase("John","J|N","C","ALL")#
<P>REReplaceNoCase("John","J|N","C","ALL"):
<CFOUTPUT>#REReplaceNoCase("John","J|N","C","ALL")#</CFOUTPUT>
<P>REReplaceNoCase("John","[A-Z]","C","ALL")
<CFOUTPUT>#REReplaceNoCase("John","[A-Z]","C","ALL")#</CFOUTPUT>
```

➜ *See also* `Replace()`, `REReplace()`, `ReplaceList()`

ReplaceList()

Description: `ReplaceList()` replaces all occurrences of elements in one string with corresponding elements in another. Both sets of elements must be specified as comma-delimited values, and an equal number of values must exist in each set. `ReplaceList` takes three parameters. The first is the string to be processed; the second is the set of values to be replaced; and the third is the set of values with which to replace them.

Syntax:

```
ReplaceList(String, FindWhatList, ReplaceWithList)
```

Example: The following example replaces all occurrences of state names with their appropriate abbreviations:

```
#ReplaceList(address, "CA, IN, MI", "California, Indiana, Michigan")#
```

TIP

The `ReplaceList()` function is case-sensitive, and there is no non-case-sensitive equivalent function. To perform a non-case-sensitive replacement, you first must convert both the search and target strings to either upper- or lowercase (using the `UCase()` or `LCase()` function).

NOTE

Unlike other replacement functions, the `ReplaceList()` function takes no scope parameter. `ReplaceList()` replaces all occurrences of matching elements.

➜ *See also* `Replace()`

`Reverse()`

Description: `Reverse()` reverses the characters in a string. `Reverse()` takes a single parameter: the string to be reversed.

Syntax:

```
Reverse(String)
```

Example: The following example reverses the contents of a user-supplied field:

```
#Reverse(sequence_id)#
```

`Right()`

Description: `Right()` returns the specified rightmost characters from the end of a string. `Right()` takes two parameters: the string from which to extract the characters and the number of characters to extract.

Syntax:

```
Right(String, Count)
```

Example: The following example returns the last seven characters of a phone number column:

```
#Right(phone_number, 7)#
```

TIP

`Right()` does not trim trailing spaces before extracting the specific characters. To ignore white space when using `Right()`, you should nest the `RTrim()` within `Right()`, as in `#Right(RTrim(String), Count)#`.

➜ *See also* `Find()`, `Left()`, `Mid()`, `RemoveChars()`

`RJustify()`

Description: `RJustify()` right-aligns a string within a field of a specified length. It does this by padding spaces before the specified text. `RJustify()` takes two parameters: the string to process and the desired string length.

Syntax:

```
RJustify(string, length)
```

Example: The following example right-justifies the contents of a field named Zip so that it is right-aligned within a 10-character-wide field:

```
#RJustify(Zip, 10)#
```

➜ *See also* `CJustify()`, `LJustify()`, `LTrim()`, `RTrim()`, `Trim()`

`Round()`

Description: `Round()` returns the integer (either greater or smaller) closest to the passed number. This function takes only one numeric value as a parameter. You can pass real values, integer values, and ColdFusion fields to this function.

Syntax:

```
Round(number)
```

Example: The following example returns `2`, the closest integer to `1.7`:

```
#Round("1.7")#
```

➜ *See also* `Ceiling()`, `Fix()`, `Int()`

`RTrim()`

Description: `RTrim()` trims white space (spaces, tabs, and new-line characters) from the end of a string. `RTrim()` takes a single parameter: the string to be trimmed.

Syntax:

```
RTrim(String)
```

Example: The following example trims spaces from the end of a user-supplied field:

```
#RTrim(first_name)#
```

➜ *See also* `CJustify()`, `LJustify()`, `LTrim()`, `RJustify()`, `Trim()`, `StripCR()`

`Second()`

Description: `Second()` returns a date/time object's second as a numeric value with possible values of `0`–`59`. `Second()` takes a single parameter: the date/time object to be processed.

Syntax:

```
Second(Date)
```

Example: The following example returns the current minute's seconds:

```
We are now #Second(Now())# seconds into the current minute
```

TIP

Always enclose date/time values in quotes when passing them to the `Second()` function as strings. Without quotes, the value passed is interpreted as a numeral representation of a date/time object.

➜ *See also* `Day()`, `DayOfWeek()`, `DayOfYear()`, `Hour()`, `Minute()`, `Month()`, `Quarter()`, `Week()`, `Year()`

SetLocale()

Description: `SetLocale()` sets the name of the locale to be used by any subsequent calls to the LS functions. `SetLocale()` also returns the name of the currently active locale so that it can be saved if necessary.

Syntax:

```
SetLocale(locale)
```

Example: The following example sets the locale to British English and saves the current locale to a local variable:

```
<CFSET previous_locale = #SetLocale("English (UK)")#>
```

➜ *See also* `GetLocale()`

SetProfileString()

Description: The `SetProfileString()` function sets the value of an entry in an initialization (*.ini) file.

Syntax:

```
SetProfileString(iniPath, section, entry, value)
```

Example: The following example sets the startup values to a passed value:

```
#SetProfileString("app.ini", "Startup", "OnStartup", "#FORM.value#")#
```

➜ *See also* `GetProfileString()`

SetVariable()

Description: `SetVariable()` sets a specified variable to a passed value.

Syntax:

```
SetVariable(Variable, Value)
```

Example: The following example sets variable `#cnt#` to the value returned by the passed expression:

```
#SetVariable(#cnt#, "A")#
```

Sgn()

Description: `Sgn()` returns the sign: either `-1`, `0`, or `1`, depending on whether the passed number is negative, `0`, or positive. This function takes only one numeric value as a parameter. You can pass real values, integer values, and ColdFusion fields to this function.

Syntax:

```
Sgn(number)
```

Example: The following example returns `1`, the sign of `4`:

```
#Sgn("4")#
```

➜ *See also* `Abs()`

Sin()

Description: `Sin()` returns the sine of a passed number. This function takes only one numeric value as a parameter. You can pass real values, integer values, and ColdFusion fields to this function.

Syntax:

```
Sin(number)
```

Example: The following example returns `-0.756802495308`, the sine of `4`:

```
#Sin("4")#
```

➜ *See also* `Asin()`, `Atn()`, `Cos()`, `Pi()`, `Tan()`

SpanExcluding()

Description: `SpanExcluding()` extracts characters from the beginning of a string until a character that is part of a specified set is reached. `SpanExcluding()` takes two parameters: the string to process and a comma-delimited set of values to compare against.

Syntax:

```
SpanExcluding(String,  Set)
```

Example: The following example extracts the first word of a sentence by specifying a space as the character to compare against:

```
#SpanExcluding(sentence, " ")#
```

TIP

The `SpanExcluding()` function is case-sensitive, and there is no non-case-sensitive equivalent function. To perform a non-case-sensitive extraction, you first must convert both the search and target strings to either upper- or lowercase (using the `UCase()` or `LCase()` function).

➜ *See also* `SpanIncluding()`

SpanIncluding()

Description: `SpanIncluding()` extracts characters from the beginning of a string only as long as they match characters in a specified set. `SpanIncluding()` takes two parameters: the string to process and a comma-delimited set of values to compare against.

Syntax:

```
SpanIncluding(String,  Set)
```

Example: The following example extracts the house number from a street address by specifying a set of values that are digits only:

```
#SpanIncluding(address, "1234567890")#
```

TIP

The `SpanIncluding()` function is case-sensitive, and there is no non-case-sensitive equivalent function. To perform a non-case-sensitive extraction, you first must convert both the search and target strings to either upper- or lowercase (using the `UCase()` or `LCase()` function).

➜ *See also* `SpanExcluding()`

Sqr()

Description: `Sqr()` returns the square root of a passed number. This function takes only one numeric value as a parameter. You can pass real values, integer values, and ColdFusion fields to this function.

Syntax:

```
Sqr(number)
```

Example: The following example returns 2, the square root of 4:

```
#Sqr("4")#
```

➜ *See also* `Abs()`

StripCR()

Description: `StripCR()` removes all carriage return characters from a string. `StripCR()` takes a single parameter: the string to be processed.

Syntax:

```
StripCR(String)
```

Example: The following example removes carriage returns for a field to be displayed in a preformatted text block:

```
<PRE>#StripCR(comments)#</PRE>
```

TIP

The `StripCR()` function is particularly useful when displaying a string within HTML preformatted text tags (`<PRE>` and `</PRE>`) where carriage returns are not ignored.

➜ *See also* `CJustify()`, `LJustify()`, `LTrim()`, `RJustify()`, `RTrim()`, `Trim()`

StructAppend()

Description: `StructAppend()` appends one structure to another. `StructAppend()` takes three parameters: the two structures (the second is appended to the first), and an overwrite flag specifying whether to overwrite existing items. `StructAppend()` always returns `YES`.

Syntax:

```
StructAppend(struct1, struct2, flag)
```

Example: The following example appends a structure overwriting any existing items:

```
#StructAppend(keys, newkeys, TRUE)#
```

➜ *See also* `Duplicate()`, `StructNew()`, `StructCopy()`

StructClear()

Description: `StructClear()` deletes all data from a structure. `StructClear()` takes a single parameter: the structure to be cleared. `StructClear()` always returns `YES` if the operation is successful.

Syntax:

```
StructClear(Structure)
```

Example: The following example empties an existing structure:

```
<CFSET result = StructClear(Items)>
```

NOTE

`StructClear()` does not delete the actual structure. Rather, it removes all of its contents. The structure itself remains and can be reused.

➜ *See also* `StructDelete()`, `StructIsEmpty()`

StructCopy()

Description: `StructCopy()` returns a clone of the specified structure, with all the keys and values of the specified structure intact. The `StructCopy()` function takes a single parameter: the structure to be copied.

Syntax:

```
StructCopy(structure)
```

Example: The following example produces a clone of the structure `People`:

```
StructCopy(People)
```

NOTE

On the surface, `StructCopy()` appears similar to the `Duplicate()` function. The main difference is that when using the `Duplicate()` function to copy a structure, you are creating a completely new copy of the specified structure, with no reference to the original. `StructCopy()` assigns any nested structures, objects, or query values to the new structure by making reference to the original.

➜ *See also* `Duplicate()`, `StructClear()`

StructCount()

Description: `StructCount()` returns the number of items in a specified structure. `StructCount()` takes a single parameter: the structure to be checked. ColdFusion will throw an error if the structure you are attempting to evaluate with `StructCount()` does not exist.

Syntax:

```
StructCount(Structure)
```

Example: The following example reports the number of elements in a structure:

```
The items structure has #StructCount(items)# elements
```

➜ *See also* `StructIsEmpty()`

StructDelete()

Description: `StructDelete()` deletes an item from a structure. `StructDelete()` takes three parameters: the structure, the name of the key to be deleted, and an optional flag that specifies how to handle requests to delete a key that does not exist. `StructDelete()` returns `YES` if the operation is successful and `NO` if not. If an attempt is made to delete a key that does not exist, and the `IndicateNotExisting` flag is not set to `TRUE`, the `StructDelete()` returns `YES`.

Syntax:

```
StructDelete(Structure, Key [, IndicateNotExisting])
```

Example: The following example deletes the `name` key from a `user` structure:

```
#StructDelete(user, name)#
```

➜ *See also* `StructClear()`, `StructKeyExists()`, `StructIsEmpty()`

StructFind()

Description: The `StructFind()` function searches through a structure to find the key that matches the specified search text. If a matching key is found, the value in that key is returned; if no match is found, an empty value is returned. This function takes two parameters: the first is the structure to be searched, and the second is the key for which to search.

Syntax:

```
StructFind(Structure, Key)
```

Example: The following example returns the user name stored in a `user` structure:

```
Username is #StructFind(user, first_name)#
```

➜ *See also* `StructFindKey()`, `StructFindValue()`

StructFindKey()

Description: The `StructFindKey()` function searches recursively through a structure to find any keys that match the specified search text. If matching keys are found, they are returned in an array. This function takes three parameters: the first is the structure (or array) to be searched, the second is the key for which to search, the third is a scope flag specifying `ONE` to find the first match or `ALL` to find all matches.

Syntax:

```
StructFindKey(Structure, Key, Scope)
```

Example: The following example returns all keys that match a user specified string:

```
<CFSET results=StructFindKey(prods, FORM.search, "ALL")>
```

➜ *See also* `StructFind()`, `StructFindValue()`

StructFindValue()

Description: The `StructFindValue()` function searches recursively through a structure to find any items with values that match the specified search text. If matching items are found, they are returned in an array. This function takes three parameters: The first is the structure (or array) to be searched; the second is the key for which to search; and the third is a scope flag specifying `ONE` to find the first match or `ALL` to find all matches.

Syntax:

```
StructFindValue(Structure, Key, Scope)
```

Example: The following example returns all items with values that match a user-specified string:

```
<CFSET results=StructFindValue(prods, FORM.search, "ALL")>
```

→ *See also* `StructFind()`, `StructFindKey()`

`StructGet()`

Description: `StructGet()` gets an array of structures from a specified path. `StructGet()` takes a single parameter: the path to be used.

Syntax:

```
StructGet(Path)
```

Example: The following example gets a structure from a specified path:

```
<CFSET struct=StructGet("catalog.product.widgets")>
```

→ *See also* `StructNew()`

`StructInsert()`

Description: `StructInsert()` inserts an item into a structure. `StructInsert()` takes four parameters: the structure, the name of the key to be inserted, the value, and an optional flag that specifies whether a key can be overwritten. `StructInsert()` returns `YES` if the operation is successful and `NO` if not. Values can be overwritten unless `AllowOverwrite` is set to `FALSE`.

Syntax:

```
StructInsert(Structure, Key, Value [, AllowOverwrite])
```

Example: The following example inserts a key named `first_name` into a `user` structure:

```
#StructInsert(user, "first_name", "Ben")#
```

→ *See also* `StructDelete()`

`StructIsEmpty()`

Description: `StructIsEmpty()` checks whether a structure has data. `StructIsEmpty()` takes a single parameter: the structure to be checked. `StructIsEmpty()` returns `TRUE` if the array is empty and `FALSE` if not.

Syntax:

```
StructIsEmpty(Structure)
```

Example: The following example reports whether a structure is empty:

```
<CFOUTPUT>Strucure empty: YesNoFormat(StructIsEmpty(Users))</CFOUTPUT>
```

→ *See also* `StructClear()`, `StructCount()`, `StructKeyExists()`

StructKeyArray()

Description: The `StructKeyArray()` function returns the keys of a specified structure in an array. The `StructKeyArray()` function takes a single parameter: the structure to be evaluated.

Syntax:

```
StructKeyArray(structure)
```

Example: The following example returns, as an array, the keys of the specified structure:

```
#StructKeyArray(family)#
```

NOTE

The array the `StructKeyArray()` function returns is in no particular order. To sort the array, use the `ArraySort()` function. Also, remember that if the structure you are attempting to evaluate with the `StructKeyArray()` function does not exist, ColdFusion throws an error.

➜ *See also* `StructClear()`, `StructDelete()`, `StructFind()`, `StructUpdate()`

StructKeyExists()

Description: `StructKeyExists()` checks whether a structure contains a specific key. `StructKeyExists()` takes two parameters: the structure to be checked and the key for which to look. `StructKeyExists()` returns `TRUE` if the key exists and `FALSE` if not.

Syntax:

```
StructKeyExists(Structure, Key)
```

Example: The following example checks whether a key named `first_name` exists:

```
<CFIF StructKeyExists(user, "first_name")>
```

➜ *See also* `StructCount()`, `StructIsEmpty()`

StructKeyList()

Description: `StructKeyList()` returns a list of keys in the specified ColdFusion structure. The `StructKeyList()` function takes two parameters. The first parameter is the structure to be evaluated. The second, optional parameter is the delimiter to separate each list item that is returned.

Syntax:

```
StructKeyList(structure [,delimiter])
```

Example: The following example retrieves a list of keys, delimited by a comma, from the specified structure:

```
#StructKeyList(MyStructure ,",")#
```

➜ *See also* `StructKeyArray()`, `StructClear()`

StructNew()

Description: `StructNew()` creates a new structure. `StructNew()` takes no parameters and returns the structure itself.

Syntax:

```
StructNew()
```

Example: The following example creates a simple structure:

```
<CFSET Orders = StructNew()>
```

StructSort()

Description: The `StructSort()` function returns an array of structure keys sorted as needed. The `StructSort()` function takes four parameters. The first is the structure to sort. The second is an optional path to append to keys to reach the element to sort by. The third is the sort type, either `NUMERIC`, `TEXT` (the default), or `TEXTNOCASE`. The fourth is the sort order (`ASC` or `DESC`).

Syntax:

```
StructSort(structure, path, sort, order)
```

Example: The following example displays a list of keys sorted using defaults:

```
<CFOUTPUT>#ArrayToList(StructSort(products))##</CFOUTPUT>
```

StructUpdate()

Description: The `StructUpdate()` function updates the specified key in a given structure with a specified value. The function returns `YES` if the update is successful, and throws an exception if an error is encountered. The `StructUpdate()` function takes three parameters. The first is the structure you are attempting to update; the second is the key within the structure you are attempting to update; and the third is the value with which you want to update the specified key.

Syntax:

```
StructUpdate(structure, key, value)
```

Example: The following example updates the specified structure:

```
#StructUpdate(stFamily, "wife", "Laura")#
```

➜ *See also* `StructClear()`, `StructDelete()`, `StructFind()`

Tan()

Description: `Tan()` returns the tangent of a passed number. This function takes only one numeric value as a parameter. You can pass real values, integer values, and ColdFusion fields to this function.

Syntax:

```
Tan(number)
```

Example: The following example returns `1.15782128235`, the tangent of `4`:

```
#Tan("4")#
```

➜ *See also* `Atn()`, `Asin()`, `Cos()`, `Sin()`, `Pi()`

TimeFormat()

Description: `TimeFormat()` displays the time portion of a date/time object in a readable format. `TimeFormat()` takes two parameters. The first is the date/time object to be displayed, and the second is an optional mask value enabling you to control exactly how the data is formatted. If no mask is specified, the default mask of `hh:mm:tt` is used. The complete set of date masks is listed in Table C.37.

Syntax:

```
TimeFormat(Date [, mask ])
```

Table C.37 `TimeFormat()` Mask Characters

MASK	DESCRIPTION
h	Hours in 12-hour clock format with no leading 0 for single-digit hours
hh	Hours in 12-hour clock format with a leading 0 for single-digit hours
H	Hours in 24-hour clock format with no leading 0 for single-digit hours
HH	Hours in 24-hour clock format with a leading 0 for single-digit hours
m	Minutes with no leading 0 for single-digit minutes
mm	Minutes with a leading 0 for single-digit minutes
s	Seconds with no leading 0 for single-digit seconds
ss	Seconds with a leading 0 for single-digit seconds
t	Single-character meridian specifier, either A or P
tt	Two-character meridian specifier, either AM or PM

Example: The following example displays the current time with the default formatting options:

```
The time is: #TimeFormat(Now())#
```

The next example displays the current time with seconds in 24-hour clock format:

```
The time is: #TimeFormat(Now(), "HH:mm:ss")#
```

NOTE

Unlike the `DateFormat()` function mask specifiers, the `TimeFormat()` function mask specifiers are case-sensitive on the hour mask.

NOTE

`TimeFormat()` supports U.S.-style times only. Use the `LSTimeFormat()` function for international time support.

➜ *See also* `DateFormat()`, `LSTimeFormat()`

ToBase64()

Description: The `ToBase64()` function returns the Base64 representation of a specified string or binary object. Base64 format converts a string or an object to printable characters that can then be sent as text in e-mail or stored in a database. The `ToBase64()` function can take two parameters.

The first is the string or binary value to be encoded. The second parameter, *encoding*, is optional and is used when working with binary data. It indicates how string data is to be encoded and can be set to US-ASCII, ISO-8859-1, UTF-8, or UTF-16.

Syntax:

```
ToBase64(string or binary_value, encoding)
```

Example: The following example converts a simple text string to Base64-encoded format:

```
#ToBase64("Laura is a pretty girl")#
```

NOTE

When converting a Base64-encoded string back to its original state, you first must convert this string to a binary object. After you've done that, you can use the `ToString()` function to convert the resulting binary object back into a string.

→ *See also* `ToBinary()`, `IsBinary()`, `ToString()`

ToBinary()

Description: The `ToBinary()` function either converts a Base64-encoded string to a binary representation. The `ToBinary()` function also takes a single parameter: the Base64-encoded string to be converted.

Syntax:

```
ToBinary(encoded_string or binary_value)
```

Example: The following example reads the contents of an image file into memory, converts the image file to a Base64-encoded string, and then converts the file from a Base64-encoded string back to a binary value:

```
<CFFILE ACTION="READ"
        FILE="FULL PATH OF THE IMAGE FILE"
        VARIABLE="ImgFile">
<CFSET EncodedImage = ToBase64(ImgFile)>
<CFSET BinaryImage = ToBinary(EncodedImage)>
```

TIP

If you receive data in Base64-encoded format, the `ToBinary` function is useful for re-creating, out of the Base64-encoded string, the original binary object (.gif, .jpg, and so on).

NOTE

When converting a Base64-encoded string back to its original state, you first must convert this string to a binary object. After you've done that, you can use the `ToString()` function to convert the resulting binary object back into a string.

→ *See also* `ToBase64()`, `IsBinary()`, `ToString()`

ToString()

Description: The `ToString()` function attempts to convert any value, including binary values, into a string. If the value specified cannot be converted into a string, the `ToString()` function throws an exception error. The `ToString()` function takes two parameters. The first is the value to be converted to a string. The second is the name of the encoding scheme. This can be used when working with binary data and can be set to US-ASCII, ISO-8859-1, UTF-8 or UTF-16.

Syntax:

```
ToString(any_value, encoding)
```

Example: The following example converts the specified value into a string:

```
#ToString(BinaryData, "ISO-8859-1")#
```

Trim()

Description: `Trim()` trims white space (spaces, tabs, and new-line characters) from both the beginning and the end of a string. `Trim()` takes a single parameter: the string to be trimmed.

Syntax:

```
Trim(String)
```

Example: The following example trims spaces from both the beginning and the end of a user-supplied field:

```
#Trim(notes)#
```

➜ *See also* `CJustify()`, `LJustify()`, `LTrim()`, `RJustify()`, `RTrim()`, `StripCR()`

UCase()

Description: `UCase()` converts a string to uppercase. `UCase()` takes a single parameter—the string to be converted—and returns the converted string.

Syntax:

```
UCase(String)
```

Example: The following example converts the contents of a table column called States to uppercase:

```
#UCase(State)#
```

➜ *See also* `LCase()`

URLDecode()

Description: The `URLDecode()` function decodes a specified `URLEncoded` string. The `URLDecode()` function takes a single parameter: the `URLEncoded` string to be decoded.

Syntax:

```
URLDecode(urlEncodedString)
```

Example: The following example decodes a `URLEncoded` string:

```
#URLDecode(myEncodedString)#
```

➜ *See also* `URLEncodedFormat()`

URLEncodedFormat()

Description: `URLEncodedFormat()` encodes a string in a format that can safely be used within URLs. URLs can't contain spaces or any nonalphanumeric characters. The `URLEncodedFormat()` function replaces spaces with a plus sign; nonalphanumeric characters are replaced with equivalent hexadecimal escape sequences. `URLEncodedFormat()` takes a single parameter—the string to be encoded—and returns the encoded string.

Syntax:

```
URLEncodedValue(String)
```

NOTE

ColdFusion automatically decodes all URL parameters that are passed to a template.

Example: The following example creates a URL with a name parameter that can safely include any characters:

```
<A HREF="details.cfm?name=#URLEncodedFormat(name)#">Details</A>
```

➜ *See also* `URLDecode()`

Val()

Description: `Val()` converts the beginning of a string to a number. `Val()` takes a single parameter: the string to be processed. Conversion is possible only if the string begins with numeric characters. If conversion is impossible, `0` is returned.

Syntax:

```
Val(String)
```

Example: The following example extracts the hour portion from a time field:

```
Hour: #Val(time)#
```

TIP

`Val()` converts characters to numbers using a base of `10` only. To convert the string to numbers with a base other than `10`, use the `InputBaseN()` function.

➜ *See also* `Asc()`, `Chr()`, `InputBaseN()`, `IsNumeric()`

WriteOutput()

Description: The `WriteOutput()` function appends text to the page output stream, regardless of the setting specified in a given `CFSETTING` block. The `WriteOutput()` function takes a single parameter: the string to be output to the page.

Syntax:

```
WriteOutput(string)
```

Example: The following example writes the specified output to the page output stream:

```
#WriteOutput("Users Processed: Sean, Misty, Parker, Laura, Peggy, Delane")#
```

ValueList()

Description: `ValueList()` drives one query with the results of another. It takes a single parameter—the name of a query column—and return a list of all the values in that column. `ValueList()` returns a list of values that are separated by commas.

Syntax:

```
ValueList(Column)
```

Example: The following example passes the results from one query to a second query:

```
SELECT * FROM Customers
WHERE CustomerType IN (#ValueList(CustType.type)#)
```

NOTE

The `ValueList()` function is typically used only when constructing dynamic SQL statements.

TIP

The values returned by `ValueList()` is in the standard ColdFusion list format and can therefore be manipulated by the list functions.

TIP

As a general rule, you always should try to combine both of the queries into a single SQL statement, unless you need to manipulate the values in the list. The time it takes to process one combined SQL statement is far less than the time it takes to process two simpler statements.

➜ *See also* `ValueList()`

Week()

Description: `Week()` returns a date/time object's week in year as a numeric value with possible values of 1–52. `Week()` takes a single parameter: the date/time object to be processed.

Syntax:

```
Week(Date)
```

Example: The following example returns the current week in the year:

```
This is week #Week(Now())# of year #Year(Now())#
```

TIP

When specifying the year using the `Week()` function, be aware that ColdFusion will interpret the numeric values **0-29** as twenty-first century years. The numeric values **30-99** are interpreted as twentieth century years.

TIP

Always enclose date/time values in quotes when passing them to the `Week()` function as strings. Without quotes, the value passed is interpreted as a numeral representation of a date/time object.

➜ *See also* `Day()`, `DayOfWeek()`, `DayOfYear()`, `Hour()`, `Minute()`, `Month()`, `Quarter()`, `Second()`, `Year()`

XMLChildPos()

Description: The `XMLChildPos()` function returns the position (within the children array) of a specified child, within an element.

Syntax:

```
XMLChildPos(element, ChildName, StartingPos)
```

Example: The following example converts the specified string to a format that is safe to use with XML:

```
<CFSCRIPT>
PhoneNbrPos = XmlChildPos( Employees.Employee, PhoneNbr, 1);
if ( if PhoneNbrPos GT 0) {
   // Employee has phone, delete it
   ArrayDeleteAt( EmpPhone, PhoneNbrPos );
} else {
   // Employee doesn't have phone, insert it
   ArrayInsertAt( EmpPhone, PhoneNbrPos, Form.PhoneNbr );
}
</CFSCRIPT>
```

XMLElemNew()

Description: Returns the XML document object (first parameter) with a new child element created(specified in the second parameter).

Syntax:

```
XMLElemNew(XML_doc_obj, child_name)
```

Example: The following example adds the element named "order" to the Orders XML document object:

```
<CFFILE ACTION="READ" FILE="c:\neo\wwwroot\ows\c\orders.xml" VARIABLE="myXMLfile">
<!--- Create XML document object --->
<CFSET MyXMLdoc = XMLParse(myXMLfile)>
<CFSCRIPT>
MyXMLdoc = XMLElemNew( MyXMLdoc, "order");
</CFSCRIPT>
```

XMLFormat()

Description: The `XMLFormat()` function formats a specified string so that it is safe to use with XML. The `XMLFormat()` function takes a single parameter: the string to be formatted. The function escapes any special XML characters so you can put these characters in strings that you pass as XML. The characters that are escaped by the `XMLFormat()` function include `>` (greater than sign), `<` (less than sign), `'` (single quotation mark), `"` (double quotation mark), and `&` (ampersand).

Syntax:

```
XMLFormat("Text to be formatted")
```

Example: The following example converts the specified string to a format that is safe to use with XML:

```
<XMP>
<?xml version = "1.0"?>
<CFOUTPUT>
<BizRules>
   <rule body="#xmlFormat('Value >= 1')#" action="#xmlFormat('Set value to
"Bob"')#">
   <rule body="#xmlFormat('Value < 1')#" action='#xmlFormat("Set value to
'Jane'")#'>
</BizRules>
</CFOUTPUT>
</XMP>
```

XMLNew()

Description: The `XMLNew()` function returns a new, empty XML document object. It takes one parameter, which indicates whether case sensitivity is to be used. This should be set to either `YES` or `NO`.

Syntax:

```
XMLNew(CaseSensitive)
```

Example: The following example converts the specified string to a format that is safe to use with XML:

```
<!--- Create new XML document object --->
<CFSET NewDoc = XMLNew("No")>
<!--- Display the new object --->
<CFDUMP VAR="#NewDoc#">
```

XMLParse()

Description: The `XMLParse()` function converts a string of XML into an XML document object. It takes two parameters: the string value and a value of `YES` or `NO`, indicating case sensitivity.

Syntax:

```
XMLParse(string, CaseSensitive)
```

Example: The following example converts the specified string to a format that is safe to use with XML:

```
<!--- Read XML document into a variable. --->
<CFFILE ACTION="READ"
   FILE="c:\neo\wwwroot\ows\c\Orders.xml"
   VARIABLE="myXMLfile">
<!--- Create new CF XML document object --->
<CFSET x=XMLParse(myXMLfile, "no")>
<!--- Display new CF XML document object --->
<CFDUMP VAR="#x#">
```

XMLSearch()

Description: The `XMLSearch()` function uses an XPath expression to search an XML document object. It returns an array of matching object nodes that match the search criteria.

Syntax:

```
XMLSearch(XMLDocObj, XPath_exp)
```

Example: The following example reads an XML file into a string and converts it to an XML document object. It then searches for the “order” elements in the “orders” node. It then outputs the name for each order that it found:

```
<CFFILE ACTION="READ" FILE="c:\neo\wwwroot\ows\c\Orders.xml" VARIABLE="myXMLfile">
<CFSCRIPT>
myXMLdoc = XMLParse(myXMLfile);
someElements = XMLSearch(myXMLdoc, "/orders/order");
for (i = 1; i LTE ArrayLen(someElements); i = i + 1) {
   WriteOutput( "Child " & i & " = " & someElements[i].XMLName & "<br>");
}
</CFSCRIPT>
```

XMLTransform()

Description: `XMLTransform()` transforms an XML document object to a string, formatted via a specified XSLT (an XML transformation style sheet). It takes two parameters: the XML string and the XML style sheet string.

Syntax:

```
XMLTransform(XMLDoc, XSLTdoc)
```

Example: The following example reads an XML file into a string and reads an XSLT transformation template into another vairable. These are used by XMLTransform() to genearate nicely formatted HTML output:

```
<!--- Read XML file into xmlsource variable --->
<CFFILE action="READ"
   file="c:\neo\wwwroot\ows\c\Orders.xml" variable="xmlsource">
<!--- Read XSLT template into xslsource variable --->
<CFFILE action="READ"
   file="c:\neo\wwwroot\ows\c\Orders.xsl" variable="xslsource">
<!--- Transform xmlsource into nicely formatted HTML --->
<CFSET Result = XmlTransform(xmlsource, xslsource)>

<!--- Display output --->
<CFCONTENT TYPE="text/html">
<CFOUTPUT>#Result#</CFOUTPUT>
```

Year()

Description: `Year()` returns a date/time object's year as a numeric value with possible values of `100–9999`. `Year()` takes a single parameter: the date/time object to be processed.

Syntax:

```
Year(Date)
```

Example: The following example returns the current year value:

```
It is year #Year(Now())#
```

➜ *See also* `Day()`, `DayOfWeek()`, `DayOfYear()`, `Hour()`, `Minute()`, `Month()`, `Quarter()`, `Second()`, `Week()`

`YesNoFormat()`

Description: `YesNoFormat()` converts `TRUE` and `FALSE` values to `Yes` and `No`. `YesNoFormat()` takes a single parameter—the number, string, or expression to evaluate. When evaluating numbers, `YesNoFormat()` treats `0` as `NO` and any nonzero value as `YES`.

Syntax:

```
YesNoFormat(Value)
```

Example: The following example converts a table Boolean value to a `Yes` or `No` string:

```
Member: #YesNoFormat(member)#
```

➜ *See also* `IsBoolean()`

APPENDIX D

Special ColdFusion Variables and Result Codes

Special ColdFusion Variables and Result Codes

Macromedia ColdFusion MX provides access to many special variables that can be used within your applications. These variables generally fall into one of several categories:

- System variables
- Scope-related variables
- Tag-specific variables
- Query-related variables

All of these variables can be used like any variables, by simply referencing them. Some have a specific prefix; others use a designated name (for example, a query name) as their prefix.

The following is a list of all special ColdFusion variables. Descriptions are provided for those that are not tag related (tag-related variables are described along with the appropriate tags in Appendix B, "ColdFusion Tag Reference"). For your convenience, cross-references to appropriate chapters in this book are provided as well.

`APPLICATION` Variables

`APPLICATION` is a special scope whose contents are available to all requests within an application. `APPLICATION` is used primarily for the storage of custom information, but one predefined variable exists within it, as listed in Table D.1.

Table D.1 APPLICATION **Variables**

VARIABLE	DESCRIPTION
APPLICATION.ApplicationName	Application name, as specified in the <CFAPPLICATION> tag

NOTE

APPLICATION variables must be locked (using <CFLOCK>) before they are accessed.

→ APPLICATION variables and the <CFAPPLICATION> tag are covered in detail in Chapter 16, "Introducing the Web Application Framework."

ATTRIBUTE Variables

ATTRIBUTE is a special scope within ColdFusion, but it does not contain any predefined variables. This scope is used in ColdFusion custom tags to reference the tag's attribute values.

CALLER Variables

CALLER is a special scope that contains no predefined variables. Valid only for use within custom tags, CALLER provides access to variables in the calling page's scope as a structure.

→ The CALLER scope is explained in Chapter 20, "Building Reusable Components."

CGI Variables

CGI variables are read-only variables that are prepopulated by ColdFusion for your use. They contain information about the server, request, and client. Some of the more common CGI variables are listed in Table D.2.

NOTE

Not all servers and clients set all these variables; check for their existence before use.

Table D.2 CGI Variables

VARIABLE	DESCRIPTION
CGI.ALL_HTTP	All HTTP headers in header:value sets
CGI.ALL_RAW	All HTTP headers in raw form (as submitted by the client)
CGI.APPL_MD_PATH	Metabase path for the application when using ISAPI
CGI.APPL_PHYSICAL_PATH	Physical metabase path for the application when using ISAPI
CGI.AUTH_GROUP	Authentication group
CGI.AUTH_PASSWORD	Authentication password as specified by the client (if AUTH_TYPE is Basic)
CGI.AUTH_REALM	Authentication realm
CGI.AUTH_REALM_DESCRIPTION	Authentication realm browser string
CGI.AUTH_TYPE	Authentication method if authentication is supported and used, usually null or Basic

Table D.2 (continued)

VARIABLE	DESCRIPTION
CGI.AUTH_USER	Authenticated username if authenticated by the operating system
CGI.CERT_COOKIE	Unique ID of client certificate
CGI.CERT_FLAGS	Certification flags; first bit will be on if client certificate is present; second bit will be on if the client certificate certifying authority (CA) is unknown
CGI.CERT_ISSUER	Client certificate issuer
CGI.CERT_KEYSIZE	Number of bits in SSL connection key size
CGI.CERT_SECRETKEYSIZE	Number of bits in server certificate private key
CGI.CERT_SERIALNUMBER	Client certificate serial number
CGI.CERT_SERVER_ISSUER	Server certificate issuer field
CGI.CERT_SERVER_SUBJECT	Server certificate subject field
CGI.CERT_SUBJECT	Server certificate subject field
CGI.CF_TEMPLATE_PATH	Path of ColdFusion file being executed
CGI.CLIENT_CERT_ENCODED	The binary, base-64 encoded certificate; used for integrating with client certificates
CGI.CONTENT_LENGTH	Length of submitted content (as reported by the client)
CGI.CONTENT_TYPE	Content type of submitted data
CGI.DATE_GMT	Current GMT date and time
CGI.DATE_LOCAL	Current local date and time
CGI.DOCUMENT_NAME	The complete local directory path of the current document
CGI.DOCUMENT_URI	Local path of the current document relative to the Web site base directory
CGI.GATEWAY_INTERFACE	CGI interface revision number (if CGI interface is used)
CGI.HTTP_ACCEPT	List of content types that the client browser will accept
CGI.HTTP_ACCEPT_CHARSET	ID of the client browser ISO character set in use
CGI.HTTP_ACCEPT_ENCODING	List of types of encoded data that the browser will accept
CGI.HTTP_ACCEPT_LANGUAGE	The human languages that the client can accept
CGI.HTTP_AUTHORIZATION	Authorization string within the Web server (used by IIS)
CGI.HTTP_CONNECTION	HTTP connection type; usually `Keep-Alive`
CGI.HTTP_COOKIE	The cookie sent by the client
CGI.HTTP_FORWARDED	Any proxies or gateways that forwarded the request
CGI.HTTP_HOST	HTTP host name, as sent by the client
CGI.HTTP_IF_MODIFIED_SINCE	Cache request value as submitted by the client
CGI.HTTP_PRAGMA	Any pragma directives

Table D.2 (continued)

VARIABLE	DESCRIPTION
`CGI.HTTP_REFERER`	URL of the referring document (if referred)
`CGI.HTTP_UA_CPU`	Client computer CPU (processor) identifier (as provided by the client browser)
`CGI.HTTP_UA_COLOR`	Client computer color capabilities (as provided by the client browser)
`CGI.HTTP_UA_OS`	Client computer operating system (as provided by the client browser)
`CGI.HTTP_UA_PIXELS`	Client computer display resolution
`CGI.HTTP_USER_AGENT`	Client browser identifier (as provided by the client itself)
`CGI.HTTPS`	Flag indicating whether the request was via a secure HTTPS connection
`CGI.HTTPS_KEYSIZE`	Number of bits in SSL connection key size
`CGI.HTTPS_SECRETKEYSIZE`	Number of bits in server certificate private key
`CGI.HTTPS_SERIALNUMBER`	Server certificate serial number
`CGI.HTTPS_SERVER_ISSUER`	Server certificate issuer field
`CGI.HTTPS_SERVER_SUBJECT`	Server certificate subject field
`CGI.INSTANCE_ID`	ID of IIS instance
`CGI.INSTANCE_META_PATH`	Metabase path for the instance of IIS responding to a request
`CGI.LAST_MODIFIED`	Date and time of the last modification to the document
`CGI.LOCAL_ADDRESS`	IP address of server on which the request came in (used primarily in multihomed hosts)
`CGI.LOGON_USER`	Windows account the user is logged in to
`CGI.PATH_INFO`	Requested file path information (as provided by the client)
`CGI.PATH_TRANSLATED`	Server translation of `CGI.PATH_INFO` (can be set even if `CGI.PATH_INFO` is empty)
`CGI.QUERY_STRING`	Contents of the URL after the `?`
`CGI.QUERY_STRING_UNESCAPED`	Unescaped version of `CGI.QUERY_STRING`
`CGI.REMOTE_ADDR`	Client IP address
`CGI.REMOTE_HOST`	Client host name (if available)
`CGI.REMOTE_IDENT`	Remote user identification (if server supports RFC 931)
`CGI.REMOTE_USER`	Authentication method if authentication is supported and used
`CGI.REQUEST_BODY`	Request body text (used by Apache)
`CGI.REQUEST_METHOD`	Request method (for example, `GET`, `HEAD`, or `POST`)
`CGI.REQUEST_URI`	Requested URL; useful when multiple hosts share a single IP address (used by Apache)

Table D.2 (continued)

VARIABLE	DESCRIPTION
CGI.SCRIPT_FILENAME	Logical path of script being executed (used by Apache)
CGI.SCRIPT_NAME	Logical path of script being executed
CGI.SERVER_ADMIN	Email address of server administrator (used by Apache)
CGI.SERVER_CHARSET	Server default character set
CGI.SERVER_NAME	Server name
CGI.SERVER_PORT	Server port on which the request was received
CGI.SERVER_PORT_SECURE	Server port on which the secure request was received (usually 0 if not secure)
CGI.SERVER_PROTOCOL	Name and version of the server protocol with which the request was received
CGI.SERVER_SIGNATURE	Server ID, host, and port (used by Apache)
CGI.SERVER_SOFTWARE	HTTP server software name and version
CGI.URL	URL base
CGI.WEB_SERVER_API	Web server API used (if not CGI)

TIP

CGI variable support varies from server to server and from browser to browser. Not all the CGI variables listed in Table D.2 will always be available, so check for their existence before using them.

NOTE

The ColdFusion function GetHTTPRequestData() returns a structure containing all browser-specified information, potentially including information not available via CGI variables.

<CFCATCH> Variables

<CFCATCH> is part of ColdFusion's error-handling system; when errors occur, details are made available via these variables:

- CFCATCH.Detail
- CFCATCH.ErrNumber
- CFCATCH.ErrorCode
- CFCATCH.ExtendedInfo
- CFCATCH.LockName
- CFCATCH.LockOperation
- CFCATCH.Message

- `CFCATCH.MissingFileName`
- `CFCATCH.NativeErrorCode`
- `CFCATCH.SQLState`
- `CFCATCH.TagContext`
- `CFCATCH.Type`

These variables are described in Appendix B.

→ `CFCATCH` variables and the `<CFCATCH>` tag are covered in detail in Chapter 31, "Error Handling."

`<CFCOLLECTION ACTION="list">` Query Columns

`<CFCOLLECTION>` is used to administer ColdFusion's internal Verity collections. It cannot be used to administer Verity K2 collections. When `ACTION="list"` a query object is produced. There will be one row for each collection. The query object will contain the following columns:

- `query.External`
- `query.Language`
- `query.Mapped`
- `query.Name`
- `query.Online`
- `query.Path`
- `query.Registered`

These columns are described in Appendix B.

`<CFDIRECTORY ACTION="list">` Query Columns

`<CFDIRECTORY>` is used to perform operations on file system directories. When `ACTION="list"` is used to retrieve directory contents, a query is returned containing the following columns:

- `query.Attributes`
- `query.DateLastModified`
- `query.Mode`
- `query.Name`
- `query.Size`
- `query.Type`

These columns are described in Appendix B.

NOTE

As with all queries, the standard query variables can also be used with the result set. The standard query variables are listed in the section "`Query` Variables," later in this appendix.

➜ The `<CFDIRECTORY>` tag is covered in detail in Chapter 33, "Interacting with the Operating System," on the accompanying CD-ROM.

`<CFFILE ACTION="upload">` Variables

`<CFFILE>` is used to perform file system operations. When `ACTION="upload"` is used to process uploaded files, process details are made available with the following variables:

- `CFFILE.AttemptedServerFile`
- `CFFILE.ClientDirectory`
- `CFFILE.ClientFile`
- `CFFILE.ClientFileExt`
- `CFFILE.ClientFileName`
- `CFFILE.ContentSubType`
- `CFFILE.ContentType`
- `CFFILE.DateLastAccessed`
- `CFFILE.FileExisted`
- `CFFILE.FileSize`
- `CFFILE.FileWasAppended`
- `CFFILE.FileWasOverwritten`
- `CFFILE.FileWasRenamed`
- `CFFILE.FileWasSaved`
- `CFFILE.OldFileSize`
- `CFFILE.ServerDirectory`
- `CFFILE.ServerFile`
- `CFFILE.ServerFileExt`
- `CFFILE.ServerFileName`
- `CFFILE.TimeCreated`
- `CFFILE.TimeLastModified`

These variables are described in Appendix B.

➜ `CFFILE` variables and the `<CFFILE>` tag are covered in detail in Chapter 33 on the accompanying CD-ROM.

`<CFFTP>` Variables

`<CFFTP>` is used to perform server-side FTP operations. Upon the completion of an operation, the following variables will contain status information:

- `CFFTP.ErrorCode`
- `CFFTP.ErrorText`
- `CFFTP.ReturnValue`
- `CFFTP.Succeeded`

These variables are described in Appendix B.

➜ `CFFTP` variables and the `<CFFTP>` tag are covered in the sequel to this book, *Advanced ColdFusion MX Application Development* (Macromedia Press, ISBN: 0-321-12710-2).

`<CFFTP ACTION="ListDir">` Query Columns

`<CFFTP>` is used to perform server-side FTP operations. When `ACTION="listdir"` is used to retrieve directory contents, a query is returned containing the following columns:

- `query.Attributes`
- `query.IsDirectory`
- `query.LastModified`
- `query.Length`
- `query.Mode`
- `query.Name`
- `query.Path`
- `query.URL`

These columns are described in Appendix B.

NOTE

As with all queries, the standard query variables can also be used with a result set. The standard query variables are listed in the section "`Query` Variables," later in this appendix.

➜ `<CFFTP>` results and the `<CFFTP>` tag are covered in the sequel to this book, *Advanced ColdFusion MX Application Development* (Macromedia Press, ISBN: 0-321-12710-2).

<CFHTTP> Variables

<CFHTTP> is used to perform server-side HTTP operations. Upon the completion of an operation, the following variables will contain status information:

- CFHTTP.FileContent
- CFHTTP.Header
- CFHTTP.MimeType
- CFHTTP.Response
- CFHTTP.ResponseHeader
- CFHTTP.StatusCode

These variables are described in Appendix B.

NOTE

Not all available variables are returned when METHOD="post".

→ CFHTTP variables and the <CFHTTP> tag are covered in the sequel to this book, *Advanced ColdFusion MX Application Development* (Peachpit Press, ISBN: 0-321-12710-2).

<CFLDAP ACTION="query"> Query Columns

<CFLDAP> is used to interact with LDAP servers. When ACTION="query" is used to retrieve directory information, a query is returned containing the requested data. There are no predefined query columns; the query will contain a column for each value specified in ATTRIBUTES.

NOTE

As with all queries, the standard query variables can also be used with a result set. The standard query variables are listed in the section "Query Variables," later in this appendix.

→ The <CFLDAP> tag is covered in the sequel to this book, *Advanced ColdFusion MX Application Development* (Macromedia Press, ISBN: 0-321-12710-2).

<CFPOP ACTION="GetHeaderOnly|GetAll"> Query Columns

<CFPOP> is used to access POP3 mailboxes. When either ACTION="GetHeaderOnly" or ACTION="GetAll" is used to retrieve mailbox contents, a query is returned containing the following columns:

- query.AttachmentFiles (returned only when ACTION = "GetAll")
- query.Attachments (returned only when ACTION = "GetAll")
- query.Body (returned only when ACTION = "GetAll")
- query.CC
- query.Date

- `query.From`
- `query.Header (returned only when ACTION = "GetAll")`
- `query.MessageNumber`
- `query.ReplyTo`
- `query.Subject`
- `query.To`

These columns are described in Appendix B.

NOTE

As with all queries, the standard query variables can also be used with a result set. The standard query variables are listed in the section "`Query` Variables," later in this appendix.

Not all query columns are returned when `ACTION="GetHeaderOnly"`.

→ `<CFPOP>` results and the `<CFPOP>` tag are covered in detail in Chapter 26, "Interacting with Email."

`<CFQUERY>` Variables

`<CFQUERY>` is used to execute SQL statements. In addition to returning a query (named in the `NAME` attribute), one predefined variable exists, as listed in Table D.3.

Table D.3 `<CFQUERY>` Variables

VARIABLE	DESCRIPTION
`CFQUERY.ExecutionTime`	Query execution time (in milliseconds)

NOTE

As with all queries, the standard query variables can also be used with a result set. The standard query variables are listed in the section "`Query` Variables," later in this appendix.

→ The `<CFQUERY>` tag is introduced in Chapter 10, "Creating Data-Driven Pages."

`<CFREGISTRY>` Query Variables

`<CFREGISTRY>` is used to access the Windows Registry. When `ACTION="GetAll"` is used to retrieve Registry data, a query is returned containing the following columns:

- `query.Entry`
- `query.Type`
- `query.Value`

These columns are described in Appendix B.

NOTE

As with all queries, the standard query variables can also be used with a result set. The standard query variables are listed in the section "Query Variables," later in this appendix.

➔ The <CFREGISTRY> tag and returned query columns are covered in detail in Chapter 33 on the accompanying CD-ROM.

<CFSEARCH> Results Variables

<CFSEARCH> is used to perform full-text searches using the integrated Verity search engine. When a search is performed, a query is returned containing the following columns:

- query.Custom1
- query.Custom2
- query.Key
- query.RecordsSearched
- query.Score
- query.Summary
- query.Title
- query.URL

These columns are described in Appendix B.

NOTE

As with all queries, the standard query variables can also be used with a result set. The standard query variables are listed in the section "Query Variables," later in this appendix.

➔ The <CFSEARCH> tag and returned query columns are covered in detail in Chapter 34, "Full-Text Searching."

<CFSERVLET> Variables

No<CFSERVLET> has been deprecated and is no longer in use as of the release of ColdFusion MX.

<CFSTOREDPROC> Variables

<CFSTOREDPROC> is used to execute SQL stored procedures. In addition to returning one or more queries, two predefined variables exist, as listed in Table D.4.

Table D.4 <CFSTOREDPROC> Variables

VARIABLE	DESCRIPTION
CFSTOREDPROC.ExecutionTime	Stored procedure execution time (in milliseconds)
CFSTOREDPROC.StatusCode	Stored procedure returned status code

NOTE

Query-related tags are listed in the section "Query Variables," later in this appendix.

➜ The <CFSTOREDPROC> tag is covered in Chapter 30, "Working with Stored Procedures" on the accompanying CD-ROM.

CLIENT Variables

CLIENT is a special scope whose contents are client-specific and persistent. CLIENT is used primarily for the storage of custom information, but several predefined variables exist within it, as listed in Table D.5.

Table D.5 CLIENT Variables

VARIABLE	DESCRIPTION
CLIENT.CFID	Client ID, used as part of the client identification mechanism
CLIENT.CFToken	Client token, used as part of the client identification mechanism
CLIENT.HitCount	Request counter
CLIENT.LastVisit	Date and time of last client visit
CLIENT.TimeCreated	Date and time of first client visit
CLIENT.URLToken	String containing complete CFID and CFToken values (for URL embedding)

➜ CLIENT variables and the <CFAPPLICATION> tag are covered in detail in Chapter 17, "Working with Sessions."

COOKIE Variables

COOKIE is a special scope within ColdFusion, but it does not contain any predefined variables.

➜ The COOKIE scope is explained in Chapter 17.

<CFERROR> is used to create alternate error pages to be displayed when errors occur. Within those pages, the following ERROR variables are available for use:

- ERROR.Browser
- ERROR.DateTime
- ERROR.Detail
- ERROR.Diagnostics
- ERROR.ErrNumber
- ERROR.ErrorCode
- ERROR.ExtendedInfo
- ERROR.GeneratedContent

- `ERROR.HTTPReferer`
- `ERROR.InvalidFields` (only on validation errors)
- `ERROR.LockName`
- `ERROR.LockOperation`
- `ERROR.MailTo`
- `ERROR.Message`
- `ERROR.MissingFileName`
- `ERROR.NativeErrorCode`
- `ERROR.QueryString`
- `ERROR.RemoteAddress`
- `ERROR.RootCause`
- `ERROR.SQLState`
- `ERROR.TagContext`
- `ERROR.Template`
- `ERROR.Type`
- `ERROR.ValidationHeader` (only on validation errors)
- `ERROR.ValidationFooter` (only on validation errors)

These variables are described in Appendix B.

NOTE

Not all `ERROR` variables are always available; this varies based on the type of error and error page.

→ `ERROR` variables and the `<CFERROR>` tag are covered in detail in Chapter 16.

`FORM` Variables

`FORM` is a special scope that contains form submissions. `FORM` also contains one predefined variable within it, as listed in Table D.6.

Table D.6 `FORM` Variables

VARIABLE	DESCRIPTION
`FORM.FieldNames`	Comma-delimited list of all submitted form field names

→ Form use within ColdFusion is introduced in Chapter 11, "ColdFusion Forms."

Query Variables

Queries are result sets returned by many ColdFusion tags (or created with the `QueryNew()` function). Queries primarily contain columns of data, but three predefined variables also exist, as listed in Table D.7.

Table D.7 Query Variables

VARIABLE	DESCRIPTION
`ColumnList`	Comma-delimited list of query column names
`CurrentRow`	Current row (when being looped within `<CFOUTPUT>`)
`RecordCount`	Number of rows in a query

NOTE

ColdFusion queries are introduced in Chapter 10.

REQUEST Variables

`REQUEST` is a special scope within ColdFusion, but it does not contain any predefined variables.

➜ The `REQUEST` scope is explained in Chapter 20.

SERVER Variables

`SERVER` is a special scope whose contents are available to all requests within all applications. `SERVER` should generally not be used for the storage of custom information. Several predefined variables exist within it, as listed in Table D.8.

Table D.8 `SERVER` Variables

VARIABLE	DESCRIPTION
`SERVER.ColdFusion.ProductName`	ColdFusion product name
`SERVER.ColdFusion.ProductVersion`	ColdFusion product version
`SERVER.ColdFusion.ProductLevel`	ColdFusion product level
`SERVER.ColdFusion.SerialNumber`	ColdFusion serial number
`SERVER.ColdFusion.SupportedLocales`	List of supported ColdFusion locales
`SERVER.OS.Name`	Operating system name
`SERVER.OS.AdditionalInformation`	Operating system additional information
`SERVER.OS.Version`	Operating system version
`SERVER.OS.BuildNumber`	Operating system build number

NOTE

SERVER variables must be locked (using <CFLOCK>) before they are accessed.

SESSION Variables

SESSION is a special scope, the contents of which are client-specific and persistent for a specified duration. SESSION is used primarily for the storage of custom information, but several predefined variables exist within it, as listed in Table D.9.

Table D.9 SESSION Variables

VARIABLE	DESCRIPTION
SESSION.CFID	Client ID, used as part of the client identification mechanism
SESSION.CFToken	Client token, used as part of the client identification mechanism
SESSION.URLToken	String containing complete CFID and CFToken values (for URL embedding)

➜ SESSION variables and the <CFAPPLICATION> tag are covered in detail in Chapter 16.

TIP

SESSION variables must be locked (using <CFLOCK>) before they are accessed.

ThisTag Variables

ThisTag is a special scope that exists only within ColdFusion custom tags. It can be used for the storage of data and also includes several predefined variables within it, as listed in Table D.10.

Table D.10 ThisTag Variables

VARIABLE	DESCRIPTION
ThisTag.AssocAttribs	Associated attributes (if an associated tag is used)
ThisTag.ExecutionMode	Tag execution mode
ThisTag.GeneratedContent	Content between the tag pairs in the caller page
ThisTag.HasEndTag	Flag indicating calling convention (as a single tag, or as part of a tag pair)

➜ The ThisTag scope and custom tags in general are covered in detail in Chapter 20.

URL Variables

URL is a special scope within ColdFusion, but it does not contain any predefined variables.

➜ URL use within ColdFusion is introduced in Chapter 10.

APPENDIX E

Verity Search Language

IN THIS APPENDIX

This appendix describes each of the search operators that can be passed to Verity in the `CRITERIA` parameter of a `<CFSEARCH>` tag. See Chapter 34, "Full-Text Searching," for details on incorporating Verity into your Macromedia ColdFusion MX applications.

This is not meant as an exhaustive reference. You should consult your ColdFusion documentation for each operator's precise definition and syntax. Verity's Web site (`www.verity.com`) is also a good resource for information regarding the syntax and impact of the search operators discussed here. The site offers many FAQs and examples of search syntax in action. Just keep in mind that Verity's search functionality does not only pertain to ColdFusion. You will find references to features that you won't encounter as a ColdFusion developer.

Using Angle Brackets Around Operators

With the exception of `AND`, `OR`, and `NOT`, all Verity operators require that you use angle brackets around them. This tells Verity that you're interested in actually using the `NEAR` operator, for example, rather than just trying to search for the word *near* in your document. The following line is not searching for the word *near*, but making use of `NEAR`:

```
CRITERIA="Sick <NEAR> Days"
```

`AND`, `OR`, and `NOT`, on the other hand, do not need the angle brackets—they get used very often, and people only infrequently need to search for the actual words *and*, *or*, or *not* in their documents. The following two lines are equivalent:

```
CRITERIA="Sick AND Days"
CRITERIA="Sick <AND> Days"
```

Operators Are Not Case Sensitive

Verity search operators are not case sensitive, though the search itself might be case sensitive. Therefore, these two statements are also equivalent:

```
CRITERIA="Sick <NEAR> Days"
CRITERIA="Sick <near> Days"
```

Using Prefix Instead of Infix Notation

You can specify all Verity operators except for the evidence operators (`STEM`, `WILDCARD`, and `WORD`) using *prefix notation.*

For instance, suppose you have several search words on which you want to use the `NEAR` operator. Instead of sticking `<NEAR>` between each word, you can just specify `NEAR` once and then put the list of words in parentheses. The following two lines are equivalent:

```
CRITERIA="sick <NEAR> days <NEAR> illness"
CRITERIA="<NEAR>(sick,days,illness)"
```

Searching for Special Characters as Literals

Special characters—most obviously, the greater-than and less-than signs (< and >)—have special meaning for Verity. If you want to actually search for these characters, you must use a backslash (\) to "escape" each special character. For example, if you want to search for documents that contain `<TABLE>`, you must do it like this:

```
CRITERIA="\<TABLE\>"
```

Understanding Concept Operators

You use Verity's *concept operators* to specify more than one search word or search element. The concept operator tells Verity whether you mean that all the search words or elements must be present in the document for it to count as a match, or if any one word or element makes the document count as a match. The concept operators include `AND` and `OR`.

The `AND` operator indicates that all the search words or elements must be present in a document to make it count as a match. Here are some examples:

```
CRITERIA="sick AND days AND illness"
CRITERIA="sick <AND> days <AND> illness"
CRITERIA="AND (sick,days,illness)"
```

The `OR` operator indicates that a document counts as a match if any of the search words or elements are present in it. Here are some examples:

```
CRITERIA="sick OR days OR illness"
CRITERIA="sick <OR> days <OR> illness"
CRITERIA="OR (sick,days,illness)"
```

Understanding Evidence Operators

Verity's *evidence operators* control whether Verity steps in and searches for words that are slightly different from the search words you actually specify.

Remember that you cannot use prefix notation with evidence operators, unlike other operators. Instead, you must specify them with *infix notation*—that is, insert them between each word of a set. Evidence operators include `STEM`, `WILDCARD`, and `WORD`.

The `STEM` operator tells Verity to expand the search to include grammatical variations of the search words you specify. You specify something other than the root word and Verity finds the root of each word and then searches for all the common variations of that root. If you used *permitting* as the search criterion, Verity would take it upon itself to search for *permit* and *permitted* as well. Here are some examples:

```
CRITERIA="<STEM> permitting"
CRITERIA="AND (<STEM> permitting, <STEM> smoke)"
```

NOTE

The ***STEM*** operator is implied in simple Verity searches. To prevent this behavior, specify explicit searches with the ***TYPE*** attribute in the `<CFSEARCH>` tag.

The `WILDCARD` operator tells Verity that the search words contain wildcards it should consider during the search. Note that Verity assumes two of the wildcard characters—the question mark (`?`) and asterisk (`*`)—to be wildcards, even if you don't specify the `WILDCARD` operator. The other wildcard characters will behave as such only if you use the `WILDCARD` operator. The following statements are examples:

```
CRITERIA="smok*"
CRITERIA="smok?"
CRITERIA="<WILDCARD>smok*"
CRITERIA="<WILDCARD>'smok{ed,ing}'"
```

Table E.1 summarizes the possible operators for a wildcard value.

Table E.1 Verity Wildcards

WILDCARD	PURPOSE
`*`	Like the percent (`%`) wildcard in SQL, `*` stands in for any number of characters (including 0). A search for `Fu*` would find Fusion, Fugazi, *and* Fuchsia.
`?`	Just as in SQL, `?` stands in for any single character. It's more precise—and thus generally less helpful—than the `*` wildcard. A search for `?ar?et` would find both carpet and target, *but not* Learjet.
`{ }`	The curly brackets enable you to specify a number of possible word fragments, separated by commas. A search for `{gr,frag,deodor}rant` would find documents that contained grant, fragrant, *or* deodorant.
`[ ]`	The square brackets work like `{ }`, except that they stand in for only one character at a time. A search for `f[eao]ster` would find documents that contained fester, faster, *or* foster.
`-`	The minus sign allows you to place a range of characters within square brackets. Searching for `A[C-H]50993` is the same as searching for `A[DEFGH]50993`.

If you use any wildcard other than `?` or `*`, you must use either single or double quotation marks around the actual wildcard pattern. I recommend that you use single quotation marks because you should contain the criterion parameter as a whole within double quotation marks.

The `WORD` operator tells Verity to perform a simple word search, without any use of wildcards or the `STEM` operator. Including a `WORD` operator is a good way to suppress Verity's default use of the `STEM` operator; it is also effective if you don't want the `?` in a search for `Hello?` to be treated as a wildcard character. Here are some examples:

```
CRITERIA="<WORD>smoke"
CRITERIA="<WORD>Hello?"
```

The `SOUNDEX` operator enables you to search for documents containing words that sound like or have a similar spelling to the word in your search criteria; for example:

```
CRITERIA="<SOUNDEX>hire"
```

This would find documents containing *higher* and *hear*. The use of the `<SOUNDEX>` operator is not supported by ColdFusion MX as installed, but with a little coaxing, you can add support for soundex Verity searches. Adding this functionality involves editing a couple of simple text files that Verity uses for configuration information. Both files are named `style.prm` but they're located in two different directories. One affects searches against collections built using files or paths; the other affects searches against other custom collections (in other words, collections built on query result sets).

To enable the use of `<SOUNDEX>` in searches against collections of type *file* or *path*, edit the `style.prm` file in the folder:

```
c:\CFusionMX\lib\common\style\file
```

To enable the use of `<SOUNDEX>` in searches against collections of type *custom*, edit the `style.prm` file in the folder:

```
c:\CFusionMX\lib\common\style\custom
```

NOTE

If you did not install ColdFusion in the default path (i.e., something other than c:\CfusionMX\), then you must replace c:\CfusionMX\ above with the path in which you installed ColdFusion.

Look for this text:

```
$define     WORD-IDXOPTS     "Stemdex Casedex"
```

Replace it with this text:

```
$define     WORD-IDXOPTS     "Stemdex Casedex Soundex"
```

You are not giving anything up by defining this value differently. Once you've made this change, you'll be able to use the `<SOUNDEX>` operator in your search criteria.

The `THESAURUS` operator tells Verity to search for the word specified in your criteria and any synonyms. Here are some examples:

```
CRITERIA="<THESAURUS>weak"
```

This could be used to find documents containing *frail*, *feeble*, and so forth.

The Thesaurus operator is supported in ColdFusion MX but only for the following languages:

- Danish
- Dutch
- English
- Finnish
- French
- German
- Italian
- Norwegian
- Norwegian (Bokmal)
- Norwegian (Nynork)
- Portuguese
- Spanish
- Swedish

The `TYPO/n` operator lets you search for words similar in spelling to, but not the same as, the search criteria. The `n` represents the number of letters that can be different and still result in a match, as in this search:

```
CRITERIA="<TYPO/1>receipt"
```

This would find documents containing *recieve* but not *receive*.

The default value of *n* in ColdFusion is 2.

Here are some notes about using these advanced operators. `<SOUNDEX>` cannot be used together `<THESAURUS>`. It is recommended that you not use `<TYPO/n>` on collections containing more than 100,000 documents. You must use `TYPE="Explicit"` in your `<CFSEARCH>` tag when using the `<THESAURUS>`, `<SOUNDEX>` and `<TYPO/n>` operators in your search criteria. You won't get an error if you don't, but you may not get the expected results.

Understanding Proximity Operators

Verity's *proximity operators* specify how close together search words must be within a document for it to count as a match. For example, if you are looking for rules about where smoking is permitted, you might want only documents that have the words *smoking* and *permitted* sitting pretty close to one another within the actual text. A document that has the word *smoking* at the beginning and the word *permitted* way at the end probably won't interest you. The proximity operators include `NEAR`, `NEAR/N`, `PARAGRAPH`, and `SENTENCE`.

The NEAR operator specifies that you are most interested in those documents in which the search words are closest together. Verity considers all documents in which the words are within 1,000 words of each other to be "found," but the closer together the words are, the higher the document's score is, which means it will be up at the top of the list. The following is an example:

```
CRITERIA="smoking <NEAR> permitted"
```

The NEAR/N operator is just like NEAR, except that you get to specify how close together the words must be to qualify as a match. This operator still ranks documents based on the closeness of the words. In reality, NEAR is just shorthand for NEAR/1000. Some examples of the NEAR/N operator are as follows:

```
CRITERIA="smoking <NEAR/3> permitted"
CRITERIA="<NEAR/3>(smoking,permitted)"
```

The PARAGRAPH and SENTENCE operators specify that the words need to be in the same paragraph or sentence, respectively. Sometimes these work better than NEAR or NEAR/N because you know that the words are related in some way having to do with their actual linguistic contexts, rather than their proximity in the text. Some examples follow:

```
CRITERIA="smoking <PARAGRAPH> permitted"
CRITERIA="<SENTENCE> (smoking permitted)"
```

The PHRASE operator enables you to search for a phrase. A phrase consists of two or more words in a specific order, as in this example:

```
CRITERIA="<PHRASE>(not permitted) <OR> (not allowed)"
```

Another proximity operator, IN, enables you to search HTML, XML, and SGML documents and limit your search to certain tag bodies or *zones*. For example, suppose you want to search for specific film descriptions in the following XML file:

```
<?xml version="1.0" encoding="ISO-8859-1" ?>
<films>
   <film>
      <filmtitle id="1">Horror From the Deep</filmtitle>
      <filmgenre>Horror</filmgenre>
      <filmdesc>Grade B monster-flick rip-off of Creature the
        Depths</filmdesc>
   </film>
   <film>
      <filmtitle id="2">Dracula Sucks</filmtitle>
      <filmgenre>Horror</filmgenre>
      <filmdesc>Cheesy horror flick/black comedy about a
        disrespected vampire.</filmdesc>
   </film>
   <film>
      <filmtitle id="3">Little Ship of Horror</filmtitle>
      <filmgenre>Comedy</filmgenre>
      <filmdesc>Schlocky takeoff on the classic from the '50s
        featuring Seymour Krelboing.</filmdesc>
   </film>
</films>
```

If you wanted to search only the <filmgenre> tag body for the word *Horror*, the following search would do it:

```
CRITERIA="Horror <IN> filmgenre"
```

Understanding Relational Operators

Verity's *relational operators* enable you to search for words within specific document fields, such as the title of the document or a custom field. These operators do not rank searches by relevance. The relational operators include the following:

- CONTAINS
- MATCHES
- STARTS
- ENDS
- SUBSTRING
- =, <, >, <=, and >=

Table E.2 summarizes the document fields available for use with relational operators.

Table E.2 Document Fields Available for Use with Relational Operators

FIELD	EXPLANATION
CF_TITLE	The filename of the document if the collection is based on normal documents, or whatever table column you specified for TITLE if the collection is based on database data.
CF_CUSTOM1	Whatever table column you specified for CUSTOM1, if any, if your collection is based on database data.
CF_CUSTOM2	Whatever table column you specified for CUSTOM2, if any, if your collection is based on database data.
CF_KEY	The filename of the document if the collection is based on normal documents, or whatever table column you specified for KEY if the collection is based on database data. You use relational operators with this field if the user already knows the unique ID for the record he or she wanted, such as a knowledge-base article number.
CF_URL	The URL path to the document, as defined when you indexed the collection.

The CONTAINS operator finds documents in which a specific field contains the exact word(s) you specify; it's similar to using the WORD operator on a specific field. If you specify more than one word, the words must appear in the correct order for the document to be considered a match. Here are some examples:

```
CRITERIA="CF_TITLE <CONTAINS> smoking"
CRITERIA="CF_TITLE <CONTAINS>'smoking,policy'"
```

The MATCHES operator finds documents in which the entirety of a specific field is exactly what you specify. This operator looks at the field as a whole, not as individual words. A search for the words *Smoking Policy* in the CF_TITLE field would match only documents in which the title was literally "Smoking Policy," verbatim. This feature is probably most useful with custom fields, if the custom field holds nothing more than some type of rating, category code, or the like. Here are some examples:

```
CRITERIA="CF_TITLE <MATCHES>'Smoking Policy'"
CRITERIA="CF_CUSTOM1 <MATCHES> Policies"
```

The STARTS operator finds documents in which a specific field starts with the characters you specify, such as this:

```
CRITERIA="CF_TITLE <STARTS> smok"
```

The ENDS operator finds documents in which a specific field ends with the characters you specify, such as the following:

```
CRITERIA="CF_TITLE <ENDS> olicy"
```

The SUBSTRING operator finds documents in which a specific field contains any portion of what you specify. Unlike CONTAINS, this operator matches incomplete words. Here is an example:

```
CRITERIA="CF_TITLE <SUBSTRING> smok"
```

The =, <, >, <=, and >= operators perform arithmetic comparisons on numeric and date values stored in specific fields. These are probably useful only with custom fields, if the table columns you specify for the custom fields hold only numeric or date values.

NOTE

These operators don't need angle brackets around them.

The following are some examples:

```
CRITERIA="CF_CUSTOM1 = 5"
CRITERIA="CF_CUSTOM2 >= 1990"
CRITERIA="CF_CUSTOM2 < #DateFormat(Form.SearchDate, 'yyyy-mm-dd')
```

Understanding Search Modifiers

Verity's search modifiers cause the search engine to behave slightly differently from how it would otherwise. The search modifiers include the following:

- CASE
- MANY
- NOT
- ORDER

The CASE modifier forces Verity to perform a case-sensitive search, even if the search words are all lowercase or all uppercase. Here are some examples:

```
CRITERIA="<CASE>smoking"
CRITERIA="AND(<CASE>smoking,<CASE>policy)"
```

Verity often runs searches that are case-sensitive even when it doesn't use the CASE operator.

The MANY operator ranks documents based on the density of search words or search elements found in a document. It is automatically in effect whenever the search type is SIMPLE, and it cannot be used with the concept operators AND, OR, and ACCRUE. Here are some examples:

```
CRITERIA="<MANY>(smoking,policy)"
CRITERIA="<MANY> smoking"
```

The NOT modifier causes Verity to eliminate documents found by the search word(s), such as

```
CRITERIA="NOT smoking"
CRITERIA="smoking NOT policy"
CRITERIA="NOT(smoking,days)"
CRITERIA="<NOT>(smoking,days)"
```

Note that if you want to find documents that contain *not smoking*, you must indicate this to Verity by using quotation marks:

```
CRITERIA="'not smoking'"
CRITERIA="AND('not',smoking)"
CRITERIA="AND(""not"",smoking)"
```

When used with a PARAGRAPH, SENTENCE, or NEAR/N operator, the ORDER modifier indicates that your search words must be found *in the specified order* for the document to be considered a match. The following is an example:

```
CRITERIA="<ORDER><PARAGRAPH>(smoking,policy)"
```

Understanding Score Operators

Every time Verity finds a document, it assigns the document a score that represents how closely the document matches the search criteria. The score is always somewhere from 0 to 1, where 1 is a perfect match and 0 is a perfectly miserable match. In most cases, Verity orders the search results in score order, with the highest scores at the top.

Score operators tell Verity to compute this score differently from what it would do normally. To a certain extent, this allows you to control the order of the documents in the result set. The score operators include the following:

- YESNO
- COMPLEMENT
- PRODUCT
- SUM

The YESNO operator forces the score for any match to be 1, no matter what. In other words, all documents that are relevant at all are equally relevant. The records will not appear in any particular order—even though Verity is trying to rank the search results by relevance—because sorting by a bunch of 1s doesn't really do anything. Here is an example:

```
CRITERIA="YESNO(policy)"
```

The COMPLEMENT operator is kind of strange. This operator subtracts the score from 1 before returning it to you. A closely matching document that would ordinarily get a score of .97 would therefore get a score of only .03. If Verity is ranking records by relevance, using `COMPLEMENT` makes the search results appear in reverse order (best matches last instead of first). Unfortunately, this also means a score of 0 now has a score of 1, which means that all documents that didn't match at all will be returned—and returned first.

If for some bizarre reason you wanted only documents completely unrelated to smoking—ranked by irrelevance—you could use this:

```
CRITERIA="<COMPLEMENT>smoking"
```

The `PRODUCT` operator causes Verity to calculate the score for the document by multiplying the scores for each search word found. The net effect is that relevant documents appear even more relevant, and less relevant documents are even less relevant. This operator can cause fewer documents to be found. The following is an example:

```
CRITERIA="<PRODUCT>smoking"
```

The `SUM` operator causes Verity to calculate the score for the document by adding the scores for each search word found, up to a maximum document score of 1. The net effect is that more documents appear to get perfect scores. Here is an example:

```
CRITERIA="<SUM>smoking">
```

ColdFusion MX Directory Structure

Macromedia ColdFusion MX and its supporting files and systems are installed in a directory structure on your server. The default is a directory named `c:\cfusionmx`, but you may specify an alternate directory during the installation process.

The following is a list of the directories in ColdFusion MX, with a description of what they contain and do. Special files and other points of interest are noted as well.

NOTE

The format of the ColdFusion MX directory structure is that of a Java EAR file, since ColdFusion is deployed as a J2EE application.

NOTE

If you are using ColdFusion deployed on an external J2EE Server (such as IBM WebSphere), the directory structure will be slightly different from what is listed below, since ColdFusion is deployed as a WAR file beneath the Web root in a directory named `cfusion`. All files and directories will be there except the `wwwroot` itself.

CAUTION

While you may tweak and modify many of the contents of the directories listed here, realize that you do so at your own risk. Make sure to first make backups of any files that you want to play with.

bin

Contains supporting ColdFusion files. Table F.1 lists files of special interest.

Table F.1 bin Files

FILE	DESCRIPTION
`cfencode.exe`	CFML source encoding utility
`cfstart.bat`	Batch file to start ColdFusion MX
`cfstat.bat`	Batch file to launch the cfstat utility
`cfstop.bat`	Batch file to stop ColdFusion MX
`ColdFusionMXServer.pmc`	Windows PerfMon profile (launch this to run PerfMon)

In Windows installations, this directory will also contain the Crystal Reports runtime (used by the `<CFREPORT>` tag).

bin/connectors

Contains batch scripts to installed Web Server connectors.

cache

Used by ColdFusion MX internally.

CFX

This directory structure contains files used to create ColdFusion CFX tags, as well as example tags. (There are no files in this directory, just subdirectories.)

CFX/examples

Contains example CFX tags.

CFX/include

Contains the C header file that must be included in any C-based CFX tags.

CFX/java/distrib/examples

Java-based CFX examples. The file `examples.html` lists the example `.java` source files along with explanations of each.

NOTE

The files within this directory are Java source, not compiled code. They must be compiled before they can be executed.

charting

This directory structure contains files used by the ColdFusion MX charting engine. (There are no files in this directory, just subdirectories.)

charting/cache

Generated charts are cached in this directory in numeric sequence. Cached charts are deleted automatically when they time out; this cleanup occurs each time `<CFCHART>` is used, as well as on server shutdown.

TIP

To force an immediate time-out of cached charts, the files in this directory may be deleted manually.

charting/fonts

Fonts used in charts generated using `<CFCHART>`.

CustomTags

This is the default location for ColdFusion Custom Tags (in this directory and any directory beneath it).

➜ See Chapter 20, "Building Reusable Components," for an explanation of Custom Tags and the use of this directory.

db

This directory contains databases used by the sample ColdFusion applications.

db/slserver52

This directory structure contains the Merant DataDirect SequeLink engine used by ColdFusion MX when ODBC (as opposed to JDBC) data drivers are used.

A subdirectory of interest is `cfg`, which contains ODBC registration and configuration information in a file named `swandm.ini`.

The `books` subdirectory contains DataDirect SequeLink documentation in PDF format.

jintegra/bin

This directory contains the J-Integra engine used to provide COM support in ColdFusion MX (via the `<CFOBJECT>` tag and the `CreateObject()` function). Table F.2 lists some files of particular interest.

Table F.2 jintegra/bin Files

FILE	DESCRIPTION
`CheckConfig.exe`	Checks J-Integra configuration settings, execute `CheckConfig /?` for exact syntax
`com2java.exe`	Produces Java files that can access specified COM objects
`com2javacmd.exe`	Command-line version of `com2java.exe`
`java2com.bat`	Batch file that produces COM IDL files for specified Java classes

Table F.2 (CONTINUED)

FILE	DESCRIPTION
`regjvm.exe`	Registers and unregisters JVMs, which may be accessed via COM
`regjvmcmd.exe`	Command-line version of `regjvm.exe`
`regtlb.exe`	Registers and unregisters IDL files generated using `java2com.bat`

NOTE

J-Integra is used only in the Windows version of ColdFusion MX.

lib

This directory contains the ColdFusion MX run time (basically, ColdFusion MX itself). Table F.3 lists some files of particular interest.

Table F.3 lib Files

FILE	DESCRIPTION
`client.properties`	Next client ID (sequential ID for `CLIENT` variables). This is a text file; the value `LastID` contains the most recently used client ID.
`coldfusion.policy`	Specifies ColdFusion security policies. This is a Java policy file; see documentation on Java policies for details on the format and contents.
`k2server.exe`	Verity K2 server
`k2server.ini`	Verity K2 server configuration file; this file must be edited if the K2 engine is to be used
`neo-query.xml`	Contains all datasources defined in the ColdFusion MX Administrator
`password.properties`	Password and settings for ColdFusion Administrator and RDS. This is a text file and may be edited if a password needs to be reset. The ColdFusion Administrator password is stored in the `password` field, and the RDS password is in the `rdspassword` field. All passwords are encrypted if the `encrypted` field is set to `true`.
`startk2server.bat`	Batch file used to start the Verity K2 server

NOTE

Datasource information is also stored in `jrun-resources.xml` (in `runtime/servers/default/server-INF`). See JRun documentation for the format of this file.

This directory contains XML files that store ColdFusion Administrator settings. These files are in WDDX format and generally should be edited only through the ColdFusion Administrator, not directly.

TIP

If you have forgotten your ColdFusion Administrator or RDS passwords, do the following:

1. Edit the `password.properties` files.
2. Set `encrypted` to `false`.
3. Delete the password values.
4. Save the file.
5. Go into ColdFusion Administrator (you won't be prompted for a password) and specify new passwords.

The subdirectories here contain the Verity engine (but not collections; those are in a separate directory). The exact directory names will vary depending on the operating system, but beneath the OS-specific directory is a subdirectory named `bin` that contains several useful files, as listed in Table F.4.

Table F.4 Verity bin Files

FILE	DESCRIPTION
`browse`	Browses raw collection contents
`merge`	Merges two Verity collections
`mkvdk`	Performs maintenance on Verity collections
`rck2`	A search utility for K2-based Verity collections
`rcvdk`	A search utility for VDK-based Verity collections
`vspider`	A spider utility for indexing content on the ColdFusion server

➜ See Chapter 34, "Full-Text Searching," for coverage of the Verity search engine.

logs

Contains ColdFusion MX log files, as listed in Table F.5.

Table F.5 logs Files

FILE	DESCRIPTION
`application.log`	ColdFusion MX application errors
`car.log`	Errors associated with archive and restore operations
`customtag.log`	Errors generated when processing Custom Tags
`exception.log`	Stack traces for generated by server errors
`mail.log`	SMTP errors generated when processing `<CFMAIL>` messages
`mailsent.log`	Log of all sent mail (if enabled in ColdFusion Administrator)
`migration.log`	Log of ColdFusion settings migration (optionally occurs after ColdFusion MX is installed if a prior version of ColdFusion is present)
`rdsservice.log`	Errors reported by the RDS engine

Table F.5 (continued)

FILE	DESCRIPTION
`scheduler.log`	Errors occurring in scheduled events
`server.log`	Server startup and shutdown log.
`webserver.log`	Errors occurring in communications between ColdFusion and the HTTP server

NOTE

Not all of the files listed in Table F.5 will be present in this directory. Log files are created the first time they are needed.

Additional logging occurs at the JRun level; those log files are in the `runtime/logs` directory.

Mail

This directory structure is used by the mail engine when processing `<CFMAIL>` tags. (There are no files in this directory, just subdirectories.)

Mail/Spool

Contains spooled messages created by `<CFMAIL>`; ColdFusion MX delivers these files as soon as it can.

Mail/Undelivr

Mail that cannot be delivered (usually because of a server error or a message formatting problem) is moved into this directory.

TIP

It is a good idea to check this directory regularly so that it does not grow too large and waste disk space, and so you can be sure that mail is being delivered properly.

META-INF

Contains the files that register the ColdFusion MX application with the J2EE server.

`application.xml` can be edited to register EJBs.

TIP

There should be no need to register EJBs manually. Instead, just drop them in `runtime/servers/default`, and JRun should find and register them automatically.

runtime

This directory is the JRun directory structure. (There are no files in this directory, just subdirectories.)

NOTE

For full documentation of this directory structure, refer to the JRun documentation.

runtime/bin

This directory contains JRun utilities and executables.

One extremely useful program in this directory is `sniffer.exe`, an HTTP sniffer that can be used to look at raw HTTP response data.

runtime/jre

This directory (and its subdirectories) contains the Java Virtual Machine (JVM) installed with JRun (and ColdFusion MX).

runtime/lib

This directory contains JRun itself.

runtime/logs

Contains JRun log files. These do not log ColdFusion events or errors, but may contain information that is useful if you are trying to diagnose why ColdFusion does not start (or shuts down prematurely).

runtime/servers/default/SERVER-INF

JRun server configuration files.

`jrun.xml` contains JRun configuration options, including settings used by all services (including the internal HTTP server).

TIP

> To change the HTTP port used by the internal HTTP server, modify `jrun.xml` and change the `port` attribute in the `run.servlet.http.WebService` section.

`jrun-resources.xml` contains datasource definitions.

stubs

Stores Web Service access code generated by ColdFusion MX. This occurs when a Web Service is registered in ColdFusion Administrator, or when `<CFINVOKE>` is used.

verity

Storage location of Verity collections (in a `collections` subdirectory). Each collection has its own directory structure that uses the collection name.

➜ See Chapter 34, "Full-Text Searching,", for coverage of Verity collections and their use in ColdFusion.

wwwroot

This is the Web root, which contains all Web applications if the integrated HTTP server is used. In addition to containing Web content, it contains some special directories.

wwwroot/cfdocs

ColdFusion's documentation directory structure. The `dochome.htm` file provides access to all documentation.

wwwroot/CFIDE

Code and applications used by ColdFusion and supporting utilities including:

- ColdFusion Administrator
- CFC introspection
- Client-side JavaScript code used by <CFFORM>
- Client-side JavaScript code used by <CFWDDX>

wwwroot/WEB-INF

Contains Web application resources used by the application server.

`web.xml` configures the JRun server. Some of the attributes that may be configured here are the default page names (`welcome-file-list`), Servlet mapping (which defines the extensions processed), and error pages (which map `CFM` files to HTTP errors).

TIP

If you'd like ColdFusion MX to process files with other extensions—for example, `HTM` and `HTML` files—add a mapping that binds the extension to the `CfmServlet` Servlet.

`jrun-web.xml` configures the JRun HTTP server. Use it to define virtual mappings (virtual hosts).

NOTE

For security reasons, this directory is not Web accessible. An error will be thrown if Web access is attempted.

wwwroot/WEB-INF/cfc-skeletons

Stores the Java versions of Web Services created as CFCs (ColdFusion Components).

➜ Chapter 20, "Building Reusable Components," introduced CFCs.

wwwroot/WEB-INF/cfclasses

ColdFusion MX compiles CFM pages into Java bytecode (`.class` files). These compiled class files are stored in this directory. Files may be deleted manually to force a recompile.

TIP

If files are recompiled because of manual deletion, it may be necessary to restart ColdFusion for the changes to be recognized, since files may have been cached.

wwwroot/WEB-INF/cftags

Some CFML tags (like `<CFDUMP>` and `<CFSAVECONTENT>`) are actually written in CFML, and the CFM files are stored in this directory.

NOTE

The CFM files in this directory are not encoded, but this is likely to change in future versions of ColdFusion.

TIP

It is possible to *add* your own tags to CFML; just drop them in this directory.

wwwroot/WEB-INF/classes

The location for any Servlets to be loaded automatically by ColdFusion MX.

wwwroot/WEB-INF/debug

In ColdFusion MX, all debug output is generated programmatically by CFM files. There are three default files in this directory, as listed in Table F.6.

Table F.6 wwwroot/WEB-INF/debug Files

FILE	DESCRIPTION
`classic.cfm`	Debug output that mimics the behavior of debugging in ColdFusion 5 and earlier
`dockable.cfm`	DHTML tree-control debug window
`dreamweaver.cfm`	Dreamweaver debug output, used by Dreamweaver MX exclusively

`classic.cfm` and `dockable.cfm` may be selected using the ColdFusion Administrator (`dreamweaver.cfm` will not be a selectable option, as it is used only by Dreamweaver MX). You may create your own debugging templates too (containing any CFML code); simply drop them in this directory, and they'll be available options in the ColdFusion Administrator.

TIP

If you want to create your own debugging templates, use `classic.cfm` as the model. Some basic steps are required to be able to access the debug data (all are available as queries), and `classic.cfm` is the simplest and cleanest demonstration of this process.

wwwroot/WEB-INF/exception

This directory structure contains the CFM files that are displayed when an error occurs. The `Java` subdirectory contains error files used for Java errors, and the `coldfusion` directory contains those used for ColdFusion and CFML errors. Each directory contains subdirectories named for their appropriate Java classes.

The CFM files in these directories may be modified. In addition, custom error handling may be specified by providing CFM files named for the appropriate class of exception.

wwwroot/WEB-INF/jsp

Code generated by JRun when processing JSP pages is stored in this directory.

wwwroot/WEB-INF/lib

To autoload any Java JAR files, place them in this directory.

wwwroot/WEB-INF/sessions

Persistent session data is stored in this directory. Files may be deleted to manually kill sessions.

APPENDIX G

Sample Application Data Files

IN THIS APPENDIX

Sample Application Data Files

"Orange Whip Studios" is a fictitious company used in the examples throughout this book. The various examples and applications use a total of 12 database tables, as described in the following sections.

The `Actors` Table

The `Actors` table contains a list of all the actors along with name, address, and other personal information. `Actors` contains the columns listed in Table G.1.

Table G.1 The `Actors` Table

COLUMN	DATATYPE	DESCRIPTION
`ActorID`	Numeric (Auto Number)	Unique actor ID
`NameFirst`	Text (50 chars)	Actor's (stage) first name
`NameLast`	Text (50 chars)	Actor's (stage) last name
`Age`	Numeric	Actor's (stage) age
`NameFirstReal`	Text (50 chars)	Actor's real first name
`NameLastReal`	Text (50 chars)	Actor's real last name
`AgeReal`	Numeric	Actor's real age
`IsEgomaniac`	Bit (Yes/No)	Egomaniac flag
`IsTotalBabe`	Bit (Yes/No)	Total babe flag
`Gender`	Text (1 char)	Gender (`M` or `F`)

Primary Key

- `ActorID`

Foreign Keys

- None

The `Contacts` Table

The `Contacts` table stores all contacts, including mailing list members and online store customers. `Contacts` contains the columns listed in Table G.2.

Table G.2 The `Contacts` Table

COLUMN	DATATYPE	DESCRIPTION
`ContactID`	Numeric (Auto Number)	Unique contact ID
`FirstName`	Text (50 chars)	Contact first name
`LastName`	Text (50 chars)	Contact last name
`Address`	Text (100 chars)	Contact address
`City`	Text (50 chars)	Contact city
`State`	Text (5 chars)	Contact state
`Zip`	Text (10 chars)	Contact ZIP
`Country`	Text (50 chars)	Contact country
`Email`	Text (100 chars)	Contact email address
`Phone`	Text (50 chars)	Contact phone number
`UserLogin`	Text (50 chars)	Contact user login
`UserPassword`	Text (50 chars)	Contact login password
`MailingList`	Bit (Yes/No)	Mailing list flag
`UserRoleID`	Numeric	ID of the associated role

Primary Key

- `ContactID`

Foreign Keys

- The `UserRoleID` column is related to the primary key of the `UserRoles` table.

The `Directors` Table

The `Directors` table stores all movie directors. `Directors` contains the columns listed in Table G.3.

Table G.3 The `Directors` Table

COLUMN	DATATYPE	DESCRIPTION
`DirectorID`	Numeric (Auto Number)	Unique director ID
`FirstName`	Text (50 chars)	Director first name
`LastName`	Text (50 chars)	Director last name

Primary Key

- `DirectorID`

Foreign Keys

- None

The `Expenses` Table

The `Expenses` table lists the expenses associated with listed movies. `Expenses` contains the columns in Table G.4.

Table G.4 The `Expenses` Table

COLUMN	DATATYPE	DESCRIPTION
`ExpenseID`	Numeric (Auto Number)	Unique expense ID
`FilmID`	Numeric	Movie ID
`ExpenseAmount`	Currency (or numeric)	Expense amount
`Description`	Text (100 chars)	Expense description
`Expense` Date	Date Time	Expense date

Primary Key

- `ExpenseID`

Foreign Keys

- `FilmID` related to primary key in `Films` table

The `Films` Table

The `Films` table lists all movies and related information. `Films` contains the columns in Table G.5.

Table G.5 The `Films` Table

COLUMN	DATATYPE	DESCRIPTION
`FilmID`	Numeric (Auto Number)	Unique movie ID
`MovieTitle`	Text (255 chars)	Movie title
`PitchText`	Text (100 chars)	Movie one-liner
`AmountBudgeted`	Currency (or numeric)	Movie budget (planned)
`RatingID`	Numeric	Movie rating ID
`Summary`	Memo (or text)	Movie plot summary
`ImageName`	Text (50 chars)	Movie poster image filename
`DateInTheaters`	Date Time	Date movie is in theaters

Primary Key

- `FilmID`

Foreign Keys

- `RatingID` related to primary key in `FilmsRatings` table

The `FilmsActors` Table

The `FilmsActors` table associates actors with the movies they are in. `FilmsActors` contains the columns in Table G.6. Retrieving actors with their movies requires a three-way join (`Films`, `Actors`, and `FilmsActors`).

Table G.6 The `FilmsActors` Table

COLUMN	DATATYPE	DESCRIPTION
`FARecID`	Numeric (Auto Number)	Unique film actor ID
`FilmID`	Numeric	Movie ID
`ActorID`	Numeric	Actor ID
`IsStarringRole`	Bit (Yes/No)	Is star flag
`Salary`	Currency (or numeric)	Actor salary

Primary Key

- `FARecID`

Foreign Keys

- `FilmID` related to primary key in `Films` table
- `ActorID` related to primary key in `Actors` table

The `FilmsDirectors` Table

The `FilmsDirectors` table associates directors with their movies. `FilmsDirectors` contains the columns in Table G.7. Retrieving actors with their movies requires a three-way join (`Films`, `Directors`, and `FilmsDirectors`).

Table G.7 The `FilmsDirectors` Table

COLUMN	DATATYPE	DESCRIPTION
`FDRecID`	Numeric (Auto Number)	Unique films director ID
`FilmID`	Numeric	Movie ID
`DirectorID`	Numeric	Director ID
`Salary`	Currency (or numeric)	Director salary

Primary Key

- `FDRecID`

Foreign Keys

- `FilmsID` related to primary key in `Films` table
- `DirectorID` related to primary key in `Directors` table

The `FilmsRatings` Table

The `FilmsRatings` table lists all movie ratings. `FilmsRatings` contains the columns in Table G.8.

Table G.8 The `FilmsRatings` Table

COLUMN	DATATYPE	DESCRIPTION
`RatingID`	Numeric (Auto Number)	Unique rating ID
`Rating`	Text (50 chars)	Rating description

Primary Key

- `RatingID`

Foreign Keys

- None

The `Merchandise` Table

The `Merchandise` table lists the movie-related merchandise for sale in the online store. `Merchandise` contains the columns in Table G.9.

Table G.9 The `Merchandise` **Table**

COLUMN	DATATYPE	DESCRIPTION
`MerchID`	Numeric (Auto Number)	Unique merchandise ID
`FilmID`	Numeric	Movie ID
`MerchName`	Text (50 chars)	Merchandise name
`MerchDescription`	Text (100 chars)	Merchandise description
`MerchPrice`	Currency (or numeric)	Merchandise price
`ImageNameSmall`	Text (50 chars)	Item's small image filename
`ImageNameLarge`	Text (50 chars)	Item's large image filename

Primary Key

- `MerchID`

Foreign Keys

- `FilmID` related to primary key in `Films` table

The `MerchandiseOrders` Table

The `MerchandiseOrders` table stores online merchandise order information. `MerchandiseOrders` contains the columns in Table G.10.

Table G.10 The `MerchandiseOrders` Table

COLUMN	DATATYPE	DESCRIPTION
`OrderID`	Numeric (Auto Number)	Unique order ID
`ContactID`	Numeric	Buyer contact ID
`OrderDate`	Date Time	Order date

Table G.10 (continued)

COLUMN	DATATYPE	DESCRIPTION
`ShipAddress`	Text (100 chars)	Ship to address
`ShipCity`	Text (50 chars)	Ship to city
`ShipState`	Text (5 chars)	Ship to state
`ShipZip`	Text (10 chars)	Ship to ZIP
`ShipCountry`	Text (50 chars)	Ship to country
`ShipDate`	Date Time	Ship date

Primary Key

- `OrderID`

Foreign Keys

- `ContactID` related to primary key in `Contacts` table

The `MerchandiseOrdersItems` Table

The `MerchandiseOrdersItems` table contains the items in each order. `MerchandiseOrdersItems` contains the columns in Table G.11.

Table G.11 The `MerchandiseOrdersItems` Table

COLUMN	DATATYPE	DESCRIPTION
`OrderItemID`	Numeric (Auto Number)	Unique order item ID
`OrderID`	Numeric	Order ID
`ItemID`	Numeric	Ordered item ID
`OrderQty`	Numeric	Number of items ordered
`ItemPrice`	Currency (or numeric)	Item sale price

Primary Key

- `OrderItemID`

Foreign Keys

- `OrderID` related to primary key in `MerchandiseOrders` table
- `ItemID` related to primary key in `Merchandise` table

The `UserRoles` Table

The `UserRoles` table defines user security roles used by secured applications. `UserRoles` contains the columns in Table G.12.

Table G.12 The `UserRoles` Table

COLUMN	DATATYPE	DESCRIPTION
`UserRoleID`	Numeric (Auto Number)	Unique user role ID
`UserRoleName`	Text (20 chars)	Role name
`UserRoleFunction`	Text (75 chars)	Role purpose

Primary Key

- `UserRoleID`

Foreign Keys

- None

INDEX

B

C

F

G

H

J

M

P

Q

R

S

W

X

Y

Z